PRINCIPLES OF ACCOUNTING

PRINCIPLES OF ACCOUNTING

FOURTH EDITION

Belverd E. Needles, Jr.
Ph.D., C.P.A., C.M.A.
Arthur Andersen & Co. Alumni
Distinguished Professor of Accounting
DePaul University

Henry R. Anderson
Ph.D., C.P.A., C.M.A.
Professor of Accounting
Director, School of Accounting
University of Central Florida

James C. Caldwell
Ph.D., C.P.A.
Partner, Change Management Services
Andersen Consulting
Dallas/Fort Worth

Houghton Mifflin Company   **Boston**

Dallas   Geneva, Illinois   Palo Alto   Princeton, New Jersey

To Marian Needles, and to Jennifer, Jeff, and Annabelle

To Sue Anderson, and to Deborah and Gregor Shewman, and to Howard, Christine, and Nichole Anderson, and to Randy Anderson and Hugh Anderson

To Bonnie Caldwell, and to Stephanie, Susan, and Sharon

This book is written to provide accurate and authoritative information concerning the covered topics. It is not meant to take the place of professional advice.

Cover photograph by Ralph Mercer.

Printed in the U.S.A.

Library of Congress Catalog Card Number: 89-80950

ISBN: 0-395-43350-9

DEFGHIJ-VH-965432

TO THE STUDENT: HOW TO STUDY ACCOUNTING SUCCESSFULLY

Success in your accounting class depends first on your desire to learn and your willingness to work hard. But it also depends on your understanding of how the text complements the way your instructor teaches and the way you learn. An understanding of how this text is structured will help you to study more efficiently, make better use of classroom time, and improve your performance on exams.

The Teaching/Learning Cycle™

Both teaching and learning have natural, parallel, and mutually compatible cycles. This teaching/learning cycle, as shown in Figure 1 on the following page, interacts with the basic structure of learning objectives in this text.

The Teaching Cycle. Refer to the inner (green) circle in Figure 1, which shows the steps an instructor takes in teaching a chapter. Your teacher *assigns* material, *presents* the subject in lecture, *explains* by going over assignments and answering questions, *reviews* the subject prior to an exam, and *tests* your knowledge and understanding on the exam.

The Learning Cycle. Now refer in Figure 1 to the next circle (blue), which shows the steps you should take in studying a chapter. You should *preview* the material, *read* the chapter, *apply* your understanding by working the assignments, *review* the chapter prior to the examination, and *recall* and *demonstrate* your knowledge and understanding of the material on the exam. Your textbook supports these cycles through the use of integrated learning objectives. **Learning objectives** are simply statements of what you should be able to do after you have completed a chapter.

Integrated Learning Objectives. In Figure 1, the outside (red) circle shows how learning objectives are integrated into your text and other study aids and how they interact with the teaching/learning cycle.

1. Learning objectives appear at the beginning of the chapter, as an aid to your teacher in making assignments and as a preview of the chapter for you.
2. Each learning objective is repeated in the text at the point where that subject is covered to assist your teacher in presenting the material and to help you in reading the material.
3. Every exercise, problem, and case in the chapter assignments shows the applicable learning objective(s) so that you can refer to the text if you need help.
4. A summary of the key points for each learning objective, a list of new concepts and terms referenced by learning objectives, and a review

Figure 1. Teaching/Learning Cycles with Learning Objectives

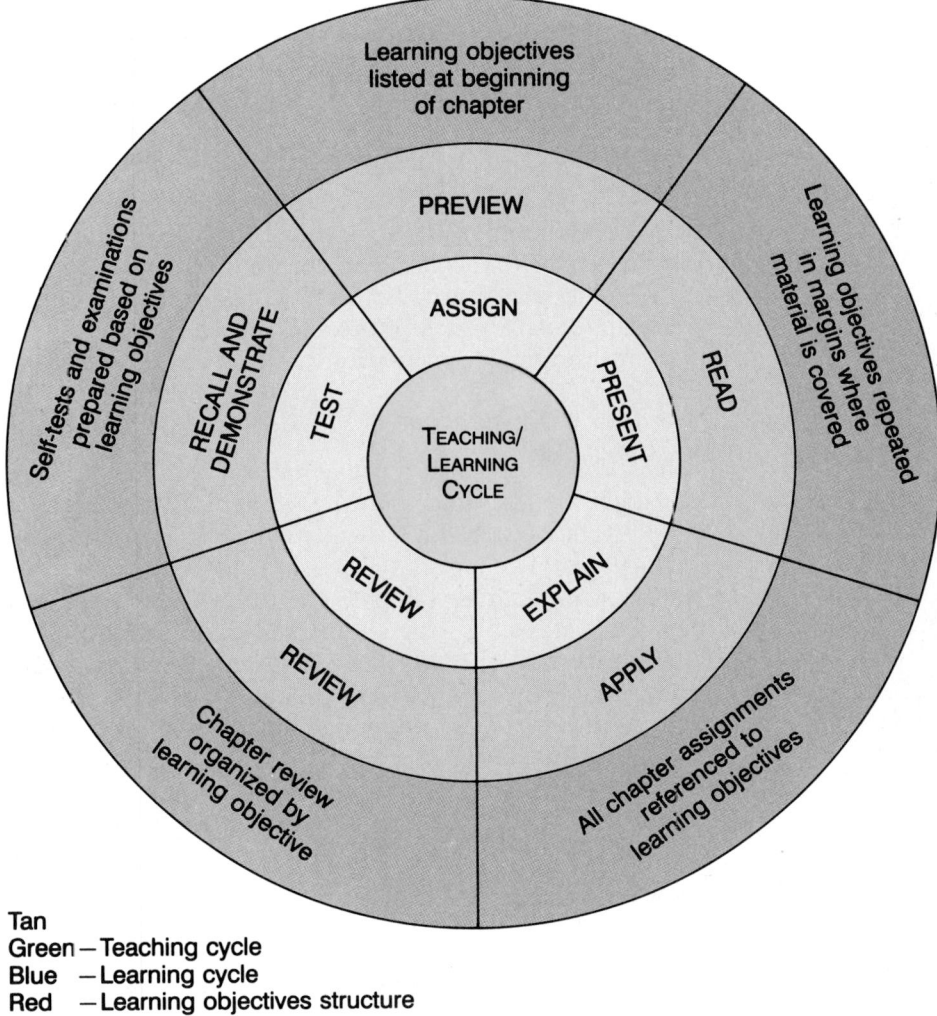

Tan
Green — Teaching cycle
Blue — Learning cycle
Red — Learning objectives structure

problem covering key learning objectives assist you in reviewing each
chapter. Your Study Guide, also organized by learning objectives,
provides for additional review.

5. Finally, a self-test in each chapter review helps you prepare for the
examination that your teacher will give based on the learning objectives
assigned and covered in class. The questions, exercises, and problems
in the Study Guide also help you prepare for examinations.

Why Students Succeed. Students succeed in their accounting course
when their personal learning cycle is in phase with their instructor's
cycle. Students who do a good job of previewing their assignments,
reading the chapters before the instructor is ready to present them,
preparing homework assignments before they are to be gone over in

class, and reviewing carefully will ultimately achieve their potential on exams. Those who get out of phase with their instructor, for whatever reason, will do poorly or fail. To ensure that you are in phase with your instructor, check your study habits against these suggestions.

Previewing The Chapter

1. Read the learning objectives at the beginning of the chapter. These learning objectives are specific action statements of what you should be able to do after completing the chapter.
2. Study your syllabus. Know where you are in the course and where you are going. Know the rules of the course.
3. Studying accounting is not like studying history or political science. Each assignment builds on previous ones. If you do poorly in Chapter 1, you may have difficulty in Chapter 2, and be lost in Chapter 3.

Reading The Chapter

1. As you read each chapter, be aware of the learning objectives in the margins. They will tell you why the material is relevant.
2. Allow yourself plenty of time to read the text. Accounting is a technical subject. Accounting books are condensed and almost every sentence is important.
3. Strive to be able to say "I understand why they do that." Accounting is logical and requires reasoning. If you understand why something is done in accounting, there is little need to memorize.
4. Relate each new topic to its learning objective and be able to explain it in your own words.
5. Be aware of colors as you read. They are designed to help you understand the text. (See the chart on page xxxiv of the preface.)

   Red All learning objectives and references to them are in red, as well as all key terms. Make sure you know their meanings. Remember, they are listed with definitions in the chapter reviews and a comprehensive glossary is located at the end of the book. In addition to learning objectives and key terms, source documents are shown in red.

   Green All accounting forms and working papers are shown in green.

   Blue All financial statements, the final product of the accounting process, are shown in blue. In addition, blue is used to emphasize the major headings in each chapter.

   Beige Selected tables and illustrations use beige to heighten contrasts and aid student understanding. This color is also used in the part openers and comprehensive problems.

6. If there is something you do not understand, prepare specific questions for your instructor. Pinpoint the topic or concept that confuses you. Some students keep a notebook of points with which they have difficulty.

Applying The Chapter

1. In addition to understanding "why they do that," you must also be able to do it yourself by working exercises, problems, and cases. Accounting is a "do-it-yourself" course.
2. Read assignments and the instructions carefully. The wording is precise, and a clear understanding of it will save time and improve your performance.
3. Try to work exercises, problems, and cases without flipping back to the chapter. If you cannot work the assignment without looking in the chapter, you will not be able to work a similar problem on an exam. After you have tried on your own, refer to the chapter (based on the learning objective reference) and check your answer. Try to understand any mistakes you may have made.
4. Be neat and orderly. Sloppy calculations, messy papers, and general carelessness cause most errors on accounting assignments.
5. Allow plenty of time to work the chapter assignments. Assignments are harder to work and more errors occur when prepared under time pressure.
6. Keep up with your class. Check your answer against the solution presented in class. Find your mistakes. Be sure you understand the correct solution.
7. Note the part of an exercise, problem, or case with which you have difficulty so that you can ask for help.
8. Attend class. Most instructors design class to help you and to answer your questions. Absence from even one class can have a negative effect on your performance.

Reviewing The Chapter

1. Read the summary of learning objectives in the chapter review. Be sure you know all the words in the review of concepts and terminology.
2. Take the chapter self-test and review the learning objective for any question you answered incorrectly.
3. Review all assigned exercises, problems, and cases. Know them "cold!" Be sure you can work these assignments without the aid of the book.
4. Determine the learning objectives for which most of the problems were assigned. These are the topics that your instructor is most likely to emphasize on an exam. Scan the text for these learning objectives and pay particular attention to the examples and illustrations.
5. Look for and scan other similar assignments that cover the same learning objectives. These may be helpful on an exam.
6. Review quizzes. These questions are often similar to longer exams.
7. Attend any labs or visit any tutors your school provides, or see your instructor during office hours to get assistance. Be sure to have specific questions ready.

Taking The Exam

1. Arrive to class early so you can get the feel of the room and make a last minute review of your notes.

2. Have plenty of sharp pencils and your calculator (if allowed) ready.
3. Review the exam quickly when it is handed out to get an overview of your task. Start with a part you know. It will give you confidence and save time.
4. Allocate your time to the various parts of the exam, and stick to your schedule. Every exam has an element of speed. You need to move ahead and make sure you attempt all parts of the exam.
5. Read the questions carefully. Some may not be exactly like a homework assignment. They may approach the material from a slightly different angle to test your understanding and ability to reason, rather than your ability to memorize.
6. Be neat, use good form, and show calculations. These techniques prevent errors.
7. Relax. If you have followed the above guidelines, your effort will be rewarded.

CONTENTS

Note: The topic of income tax is integrated throughout the book. It is covered at those points where it is relevant to the discussion.

PART
THREE
Measuring
and
Reporting
Assets and
Current
Liabilities

PREFACE

PRINCIPLES OF ACCOUNTING, Fourth Edition, is a comprehensive first course in accounting for students with no previous training in accounting or business. It is intended for use in the traditional two-semester or two- and three-quarter sequence. Designed for both majors and nonmajors, the textbook is part of a well-integrated package for students and instructors that includes many manual and computer ancillaries not found in previous editions.

Goals of the Fourth Edition

We wrote this book believing that integrated learning objectives can significantly improve the teaching and learning of accounting. This system of learning by objective enhances the role of the overall package, and particularly that of the textbook, in achieving good communication between the instructor and the student.

The success of the first three editions of this book has justified our confidence in the principle of learning by integrated objectives. At the same time, several goals guided us in developing and writing PRINCIPLES OF ACCOUNTING, Fourth Edition. Those goals were: (1) to write for the student's first exposure to accounting; (2) to extend learning by objectives to the entire package; (3) to make the content authoritative, practical, and contemporary; (4) to emphasize the role of accounting in decision making; (5) to adhere to a strict system of quality control; and (6) to develop the most complete and flexible package available.

The Student's First Exposure to Accounting

When organizing the text, we specifically focused on the needs of the intended audience, the freshman and sophomore student. First, we carefully paced new concepts and techniques to ensure that students would grasp and retain the material. Second, we limited the number of difficult concepts or practices in each chapter, particularly in the early part of the book. Third, we rigorously provided a clear presentation, a consistent reading level, and a uniform use of terminology throughout the text. Fourth, we focused on understanding, not memorization, believing that concepts acquire meaning when applied and practices become most easily understood when related to those concepts. Fifth, we emphasized concepts and practices useful to students throughout their careers, whether in accounting or not.

Integrated Learning by Objectives

We took a definite pedagogical approach to writing PRINCIPLES OF ACCOUNTING, Fourth Edition. We extensively used learning objectives and learning theory. Learning objectives were integrated throughout the text and package from the chapter previews and presentations to the chapter reviews, assignments, study aids, and testing and evaluation material.

Authoritative, Practical, and Contemporary

This book presents accounting as it is practiced and carefully explains the theory underlying those practices. Accounting terms and concepts are defined according to pronouncements of the AICPA, APB, FASB, and CASB. The Statements of Financial Accounting Concepts of the FASB's Conceptual Framework Study form the theoretical underpinning of the book and are used to assess various accounting situations and controversies. In addition, steps were taken to ensure that, to the extent possible within the framework of introductory accounting, the material realistically reflects the way accounting is practiced today.

The topics covered are up to date and correspond with current trends in business and accounting. Ethical considerations in accounting are integrated at appropriate points throughout the book. They are included in the discussions of the auditor's professional responsibilities, financial reporting, managerial accounting, and in a general business context. New appendices have been added on not-for-profit accounting and the just-in-time philosophy in managerial accounting. Complete coverage of the new statement of cash flows is contained in Chapter 18. International accounting is now the primary focus of Chapter 21.

Decision-Making Emphasis

Another of our goals was to present the contemporary business world and the real-life complexities of accounting in a clear, concise, easy-to-understand manner. Accounting is treated as an information system that helps managers, investors, and creditors make economic decisions. In addition to questions, exercises, and problems, the chapter assignments include two decision-oriented features: an "Interpreting Accounting Information" exercise and either a "Financial Decision Case" or a "Management Decision Case." In each situation, the student must extract quantitative information from the exercise or case and make an interpretation or a decision.

Quality Control

Together with our publisher, we developed a system of quality control for all parts of the package to ensure the most technically and conceptually accurate program possible. This system, which utilizes an innovative computer database technology, involved many steps, including thorough reviews by users, visits to and discussions with users by the authors, extensive in-house editorial review, accuracy checking by over forty introductory accounting teachers, class testing, and finally an audit for technical and conceptual accuracy by the international accounting firm, Ernst & Young.

Complete and Flexible Learning System

We believe that PRINCIPLES OF ACCOUNTING, Fourth Edition, represents the most complete and flexible package available for a first course in accounting. All parts of the package fit within the exclusive pedagogical system of integrated learning by objectives established by the authors. This system fits within the framework of the Teaching/Learning Cycle, which is described in detail in the To the Student section at the beginning of this text and in the following sections.

Organization of the Fourth Edition

The book is organized into seven parts so it may be used by schools on either a semester or quarter sequence. Those using the two-semester or two-quarter sequence may cover three parts during the first term and four parts during the second. Those using the three-quarter sequence may cover two parts in each of the first two quarters and three parts in the last quarter. If a shorter course is required, all or parts of chapters 4, 6, 13, 19, 20, 21, and 24 may be omitted or covered briefly without hindering comprehension of the later chapters. For instructors wanting to introduce students to the present and future value of money, individual income taxes, not-for-profit accounting, or the just-in-time philosophy, appendices on these subjects along with examples and assignments are provided at the end of the text.

Focus on Ethics and Communication Skills

There is a recognized need in our society for accounting and business students to be exposed in all their courses to ethical considerations and to be better prepared in writing and communication skills. As authors, we feel an obligation to help students achieve these goals. First, we introduce ethical concerns, throughout the text, not only as they apply to auditors but also as they apply to financial and managerial accountants and to business professionals. Second, we have provided ample assignments to enhance student communication skills. All sections of the end-of-chapter material now contain written assignments. The Discussion Questions and Writing Assignments focus on this objective as do the Interpreting Accounting Information and Financial and Management Decision Cases. In addition, selected classroom exercises and A and B problems in each chapter contain writing components. We have found the Interpreting Accounting Information and Financial and Management Decision Cases to be excellent vehicles for the improvement of communication skills through small group discussion and oral reports. Appropriately structured, these activities take far less time than might be thought and are valuable to the students.

Textbook Features

Pedagogical Use of Color

The text uses a five-color design consistently throughout the illustrations to enhance students' understanding of the accounting process. The chart below displays the value of this pedagogical approach to color. First, pedagogical features such as learning objectives, key terms, and emphasized material in the text are printed in red, as are all source documents. Second, green is used to represent accounting forms and working papers, which are part of the ongoing process of accounting. Third, blue is used to emphasize the major headings in the chapter and to highlight the actual financial statements, the final product of the accounting process. Blue is also used to indicate alternative methods that are presented in the text. Beige is used in selected tables and illustrations to heighten the contrasts and aid student understanding. In addition, it helps students locate the three new comprehensive problems.

Integrated Learning Objectives

Action-oriented objectives at the beginning of each chapter indicate in precise terms what students should be able to do when they complete the chapter. The learning objective is restated in the margin beside pertinent text. All end-of-chapter components—Review of Learning Objectives, Review of Concepts and Terminology, Self-Test, and Review Problem—are clearly referenced to learning objectives, and end-of-chapter assignments are keyed to specific objectives.

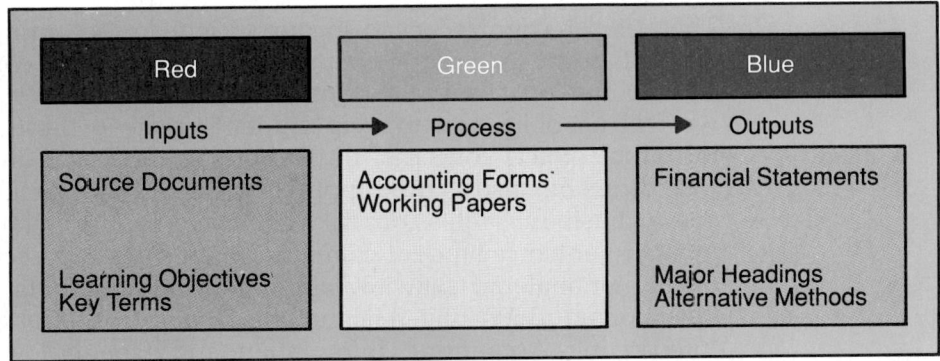

Real-World Applications

Many chapters include graphs or tables illustrating how the actual business practices relate to chapter topics. Most Interpreting Accounting Information exercises are based on the published financial reports of real companies.

Key Terms and Glossary

Throughout the book, key accounting terms are emphasized in bold, red type and are clearly defined in context. These terms are listed alphabetically with definitions and learning objective references in each Chapter Review; they are also assembled in a comprehensive glossary at the end of the book.

Transaction Index

A new feature of the Fourth Edition, the index of transactions, appears inside the front cover of the text. This unique index allows students to look up any transaction and find the page number on which it is discussed and illustrated. The transaction index is especially useful to students when solving homework assignments.

Guide to Accounting Formats and Financial Statements

Inside the back cover of the text, another new student aid is provided. This guide illustrates the proper formats for financial statements and references pages on which common accounting forms and financial statements can be found.

Chapter Review

A unique feature of each chapter is a special review section. The Review of Learning Objectives summarizes the chapter's main points in relation to the objectives. The Review of Concepts and Terminology presents all key terms from the chapter with definitions and learning objective references. The Review Problem with a complete solution demonstrates the chapter's major procedures before students work the exercises and problems. Self-Tests, now in every chapter, review the basic concepts and are referenced to learning objectives. The Answers to Self-Test section provides immediate feedback to students and is located after each chapter's assignments.

Discussion Questions and Writing Assignments

Review questions at the end of each chapter focus on major concepts and terms and provide thought-provoking questions for writing assignments.

Classroom Exercises

Classroom exercises provide practice in applying concepts and procedures taught in the chapter and are effective in illustrating lecture points. Each exercise is keyed to one or more learning objectives. There are 25 percent new exercises in this edition. In addition, solution transparencies are available for all exercise solutions.

Interpreting Accounting Information

This feature asks the student to interpret published financial information in Chapters 1–21 and internal management reports in Chapters 22–28. Such reports and information are based on excerpts from actual reports or on published articles about well-known corporations and organizations. Among the companies included are K mart, Sears, U.S. Steel, Marathon Oil, Chrysler, and Lockheed. Each exercise requires students to analyze published information by extracting data and making computations and interpretations.

A and B Problems

We have included two sets of problems to provide maximum flexibility in homework assignments. Generally, the problems are arranged in order of difficulty, with problems A-1 and B-1 for each chapter being the simplest. A and B problems have been matched by topic, thus A-1 and B-1 are equivalent in content and level of difficulty. In addition, all problems are keyed to the learning objectives. For each problem, ratings of difficulty, time estimates, and solutions are available to the instructor as are transparencies of all solutions. Additional assignment material is provided in the Demonstration Problems Book.

Financial and Management Decision Cases

Each chapter contains a case emphasizing the usefulness of accounting information in decision making. The business background and financial information for each case are presented in the context of the decision. The decision maker may be a manager, an investor, an analyst, or a creditor. In the role of decision maker, the student is asked to extract relevant data from the case, make computations as necessary, and arrive at a decision.

Comprehensive Problems

Comprehensive Problems covering several chapters have been added to the Fourth Edition. After Chapter 4, the first Comprehensive Problem covers the accounting cycle for a service company. The cycle is the second month of operations for Joan Miller Advertising Agency, the same company which was used to introduce the accounting cycle in Chapters 2 through 4. After Chapter 6, the accounting cycle for a merchandising concern using special journals is the subject of the Comprehensive Problem. The company, Fenwick Fashions, is the same company as used to introduce merchandising in Chapter 5. After Chapter 16, comprehensive stockholders' equity transactions for Sundial Corporation are recorded and a statement of stockholders' equity is prepared.

Supplementary Learning Ancillaries

The supplementary learning aids provide a variety of useful items for students and instructors. A complete description is contained in the Instructor's Handbook. Briefly, they consist of the following:

Study Guide with Selected Readings, also available in a Spanish edition
Working Papers, four sets, plus a set of Blank Working Papers
Demonstration Problems Book
Traditional Practice Sets, including
  Micro-Tec, Third Edition
    A Merchandising Sole Proprietorship Practice Set, in narrative and working-papers formats
  College Words and Sounds Store, Third Edition
    A Sole Proprietorship Merchandising Business with Payroll Practice Set
  The Windham Company, Second Edition
    A Managerial Accounting Practice Set
Practice Analysis Cases, including
  Richland Home Centers, Inc. Annual Report, Second Edition
    A Practice Case in Financial Analysis
  Heartland Airways, Inc. Annual Report, Second Edition
    A Practice Case in Financial Analysis
  McHenry Hotels, Inc.
    A Practice Case in Managerial Accounting
Computer-Assisted Practice Sets
  Parks Computer Company
  Matthew Sports Company
  Cooks Solar Energy Systems, Second Edition
  Sounds Abound
Other Computerized Study Materials
  Lotus® Problems for Accounting: A Working Papers Approach
  Correlation Chart to Accompany PRINCIPLES OF ACCOUNTING, Fourth Edition
  Rags to Riches®: General Ledger Software and Workbook
  The Accounting Transaction Tutor
  Computerized Diagnostic Tests
Check List of Key Figures
Student Resource Videos

Instructor's Aids

Print-Based Materials

Instructor's Handbook
Instructor's Solutions Manual, Volume 1: Chapters 1–14
Instructor's Solutions Manual, Volume 2: Chapters 15–28 and Appendices

Test Bank with Answers
Four Sets of Achievement Tests: Chapters 1–14; A and B Versions
                                               Chapters 15–28; A and B Versions
Teaching Transparencies
Solutions Transparencies and Lecture Outlines

Microcomputer-Based Materials

Computerized Testing Program and Gradebook
Presentation Software: A.S.S.E.T.: Accounting Software System for Enhanced Teaching

Changes in the Fourth Edition

This new edition benefited from suggestions by the many users and reviewers who corresponded with us. Since satisfaction with the approach and organization of the Third Edition was broad, changes in this Fourth Edition were primarily designed to enhance the content and pedagogical quality of the previous edition.

All learning objectives have been reviewed and modified as necessary. Many small changes to increase clarity have been made in every chapter as a result of reviewers' comments.

Alternative methods and procedures are clearly identified in the text so that students can focus on the method preferred by their instructor.

Part openers were added to guide the student through the text.

The insides of the front and back covers of the book are utilized for student reference aids. Inside the front of the book, the Transaction Index allows students to look up any transaction and find the page on which it is presented. Inside the back of the book, the Guide to Accounting Formats and Financial Statements provides model formats for and page references to essential accounting forms and financial statements.

The chapter reviews have been expanded by adding a Review of Concepts and Terminology with definitions and learning objective references, by including a Review Problem in every chapter, and by including a learning objective referenced Self-Test with every chapter.

The text was updated to reflect recent data and changes in authoritative pronouncements including the statement of cash flows and the latest concepts of internal control structure.

All retained exercises, problems, and cases were revised with special attention paid to the wording of transactions and of "Required" statements. The number of classroom exercises has been expanded by 25 percent.

Comprehensive Problems covering several chapters were added after Chapters 4, 6, and 16.

Quality control procedures were applied to the text, assignment material, and solutions.

Changes in the content of specific chapters are described below.

Chapter 1 Accounting as an Information System. A section on ethical considerations in accounting has been added with appropriate coverage in the chapter assignments.

Chapter 3 Business Income and Adjusting Entries. The preparation of the adjusted trial balance using the initial columns of the work sheet at the end of the chapter has been deleted so that the entire coverage of the work sheet can be found in Chapter 4.

Chapter 4 Completing the Accounting Cycle. A new Comprehensive Problem, month two of the accounting cycle for Joan Miller Advertising Agency, a service company, has been added after the end of this chapter.

Chapter 5 Accounting for Merchandising Operations. A new illustration comparing the income statements for service and merchandising companies has been introduced. The section on inventory losses has been moved for a more linear presentation. The alternative methods of preparing the work sheet are clearly distinguished to avoid student confusion.

Chapter 6 Accounting Systems and Special-Purpose Journals. A new Comprehensive Problem covering the accounting cycle with special journals for Fenwick Fashions, a merchandising company, has been added after the end of this chapter.

Chapter 7 Internal Control and Merchandising Transactions. The first two objectives of this chapter have been combined and extensively revised to represent current theory of the internal control structure.

Chapter 8 Accounting Concepts and Classified Financial Statements. A section on ethics and financial reporting has been added to this chapter. A new illustration of the operating cycle is included. The discussion of qualitative characteristics at the beginning of the chapter has been greatly simplified. An illustration of the financial accounting concepts presented thus far in the text assists the student in seeing the interrelationships of these concepts. The topic of comprehensive income has been deleted and the profitability ratio asset turnover has been added. The financial statements of Toys "R" Us are used in illustrations because Toys "R" Us is a well-known and successful merchandising company. The statements are simple and relatively easy for the beginning student to understand.

Chapter 9 Short-Term Liquid Assets. An annotated illustration of a note receivable has been added. Many new illustrative journal entries provide further clarity.

Chapter 10 Inventories. The first objective and the concept of nonmonetary assets have been deleted. The section on the effect of income taxes on inventory methods has been revised in accordance with tax law changes.

Chapter 11 Current Liabilities and Payroll Accounting. A short section on disclosure of liabilities has been inserted. A new illustration of contingent liabilities has been provided. The discussion of payroll tax rates has been updated.

Chapter 12 Long-Term Assets: Acquisition and Depreciation.   The section on cost recovery for federal tax purposes was revised.

Chapter 13 Long-Term Assets: Other Issues and Types.   A new learning objective concerning accounting for disposals of depreciable assets involving exchanges has been inserted, and the material under this objective was extensively revised. A short section on accounting for software costs has been added under intangible assets.

Chapter 14 Accounting for Partnerships.   Learning objectives 1 and 2 have been combined. The admission and withdrawal of partners from partnerships was split into two objectives.

Chapter 16 Retained Earnings and Corporate Income Statements.   The section on appropriation of retained earnings has been shortened and rewritten to focus on the disclosure of restrictions on retained earnings instead of on journal entries. An objective to prepare a corporate income statement was added.

Chapter 17 Long-Term Liabilities.   This chapter has been completely reorganized and extensively revised. The issuance of bonds at a premium and the issuance of bonds at a discount are now explained together. Both the straight-line and effective interest methods of amortization are presented as alternative methods. New illustrations show the relationships of carrying value and interest expense for bonds issued at a discount and at a premium. The section on bond sinking funds has been deleted. The discussion of pensions has been shortened and simplified. A new summary table of bonds issued at a discount and at a premium is presented in the Chapter Review.

Chapter 18 Statement of Cash Flows.   This entirely new chapter, widely class-tested as a supplement (and appendix) to the Third Edition, provides the finest guidance to the FASB's statement of cash flows of any text. It also provides great flexibility for the instructor, allowing the coverage of the direct method or the indirect method as well as optional coverage of the work sheet method.

Chapter 19 Financial Statement Analysis.   The illustrated analysis of Eastman Kodak Company has been updated, and new pie charts illustrate common-size financial statements.

Chapter 20 Intercompany Investments.   This chapter has been revised to reflect the FASB Statement No. 94 on consolidation of all majority-owned subsidiaries.

Chapter 21 International Accounting and Inflation Accounting.   International accounting has been moved to the beginning of this chapter and inflation accounting has been reduced to reflect the growing importance of the international sphere on society and business. A new graphic shows the market capitalization of the world's stock markets. The section on the search for comparability of international accounting standards reflects new developments in the establishment of such standards.

Chapter 22 Introduction to Management Accounting. This chapter has been reorganized so that management accounting is defined earlier. In addition, a section on ethics in management accounting, with an accompanying exercise, has been added.

Chapter 24 Product Costing: The Process Cost System. New assignment material has been added to this chapter.

Chapter 25 Cost Planning and Control Tools. The introductory section on cost behavior has been revised significantly and the chapter has been reorganized.

Chapter 26 The Budgeting Process. This chapter has been revised to include a new introduction and illustrations of all types of budgets discussed. Each exhibited budget is clearly explained and linked to the master budget. New exercises have also been added.

Chapter 27 Cost Control Using Standard Costing and Variance Analysis. A new exhibit illustrating labor variance analysis computations has been added to match those for materials and overhead variance analyses.

Chapter 28 Management Decision Analysis Including Capital Budgeting. This chapter has been completely restructured so that the day-to-day decisions, such as special order and sales mix decisions, are discussed first. Capital budgeting is then analyzed and illustrated.

Appendix D Overview of Governmental and Not-for-Profit Accounting. This new appendix is a mini-chapter on accounting for an important segment of society. Emphasis is placed on both the financial and management aspects of the discipline. This appendix assists instructors in schools that need to cover public sector accounting for AACSB accreditation purposes.

Appendix E The Just-in-Time Philosophy. This new approach to operating a business affects service and merchandising organizations as well as manufacturing companies. The JIT philosophy is described and explained, and examples of current practice are provided. This appendix is also in mini-chapter format.

Acknowledgments

Developing the Fourth Edition of PRINCIPLES OF ACCOUNTING was a long and demanding project that could not succeed without the help of one's colleagues. We would like to thank the following individuals for their contributions to the ancillary program.

Deanna O. Burgess *University of Central Florida* Debra Goorbin *Westchester Community College* William Grollman *Fordham University* Anita Hope *Tarrant County Junior College—Northeast Campus* Carol Johnson *California Lutheran University* Edward Julius *California Lutheran University* John Lacey *California State University—Long Beach* Glenn Owen *University of*

California—Santa Barbara James Seivwright *Hillsborough Community College—Dale Mabry Campus* S. Murray Simons *Northeastern University*

We are also grateful to a large number of professors and other professional colleagues as well as students for constructive comments that have led to improvements in the text. Unfortunately, space does not permit us to mention all those who have contributed to this volume.

Some of those who have been supportive and have had an impact on the textbook and ancillaries as reviewers are:

Melody Ashenfelter
Southwestern Oklahoma State University

Peter Barton
University of Wisconsin—Whitewater

Mohamed E. Bayou
University of Detroit

Rick Behr
Broome Community College

Ann Benoit
*Clermont General & Technical College
University of Cincinnati*

Linda Benz
*Jefferson Community College—
Downtown Campus*

Teri Bernstein
Santa Monica College

Janice Black
Heald Business College

Wayne G. Bremser
Villanova University

Deanna O. Burgess
University of Central Florida

John Caspari
Grand Valley State University

Brian Cornwall

Sharon Cotton
Schoolcraft College

Lamar Crall
Southwestern Oklahoma State University

Lynn Dale
Spartanburg Technical College

W. Terry Dancer
Arkansas State University

Alan E. Davis
Community College of Philadelphia

Freddy G. Dial
Stephen F. Austin State University

Hazel Dickey
Arkansas State University—Beebe

Walter Doehring
Genesee Community College

Joan A. Donen
Spokane Falls Community College

Joseph G. Doser
Truckee Meadows Community College

Charles G. Ericksen
Kearney State College

Estelle Faier
Metropolitan Community College

Carl Fisher
Foothill College

Thomas Flannagan

Kathleen Forestieri
LaGuardia Community College

Roy S. Fox
Palm Beach Community College

Robert A. Garcia
Fayetteville Technical Community College

Roger Gee
San Diego Mesa College

Mary E. Govan
Sinclair Community College

Parker Granger
Jacksonville State University

Ann Gregory
South Plains College

Philip Grove
Illinois Institute of Technology—ITT Center

Nabil Hassan
Wright State University

Roger Hehman
*Raymond Walters College—
University of Cincinnati*

Alice James
Meridian Jr. College

Richard C. Jarvies
Fayetteville Technical Community College

Stanley Johnson
University of Wisconsin—Stout

Christopher Jones
Utah Valley Community College

Gudmund Julseth
North Hennepin Community College

Wallace Kartsen
New Hampshire College

Jack Kockentiet
Columbus State Community College

Gerard Lange
St. John's University

Patrick Levantino
Sam Houston State University

Ellen Lippman
University of Portland

Dorothy Masterson
Quinsigamond Community College

Harry McAlum
Lander College

Sylvia Meyer
Scottsdale Community College

Joseph W. Milligan
College of DuPage

Michael F. Monahan

Andre Montero
Kingsborough Community College

John Morgan
St. Mary's College of Minnesota

Paul Nieball
El Paso Community College

Connie Nieser
Oklahoma City Community College

Terry J. Nunley
University of North Carolina

Aileen Ormiston
Mesa Community College

Charles Page
Southwestern Oklahoma State University

Sarah Palmer
Rio Grande College

Diane Pattison
University of San Diego

Leslie Paul
Collin County Community College

Tom Pinckney
Trident Tech University

Kenneth J. Plucinski
State University of New York—College at Fredonia

Michael C. Raff
Prince George's Community College

Alan F. Rainford
Greenfield Community College

Jean Redfern
Golden West College

David E. Rogers
Mesa State College

Leo A. Ruggle
Mankato State University

Marilyn Salter
University of Central Florida

James Schnell
Monroe Community College

Robbie Sheffy
Tarrant County Junior College

S. Murray Simons
Northeastern University

Elaine Simpson
St. Louis Community College—Florissant Valley

Jim Sloan
Austin Community College

G. R. Smith, Jr.
Texas Tech University

Patricia Sommerville
St. Mary's College

Marie Stone
Skidmore College

V. F. Stone
Texas A & I University

Pierre L. Titard
West Virginia University

Tom Vannaman
Midland College

Sandra VanTrease
Price Waterhouse

Vicki Vorell
Cuyahoga Community College—West

Ronald Ward
Robert Morris College

Bob Wennagel
College of the Mainland

Don Whisler
Falls Community College—Spokane

Charles P. Zlatkovich
University of Texas—El Paso

A special note of thanks to the individuals who contributed greatly by reviewing and checking the end-of-chapter assignment material.

Rebecca A. Andrews
Roane State Community College—Oak Ridge Campus

Gerald Ashley
Grossmont Community College

Wilfred H. Beaupre*
San Juan College

Quinton Booker
Jackson State University

Kenneth Boyce*
Seattle Central Community College

Sallie D. Branscom
Virginia Western Community College

Ronald P. Brooker
Phoenix College

William S. Brooks
Southwestern Oklahoma State University

Sarah R. Brown
University of North Alabama

Lois D. Bryan*
Robert Morris College

Tollie L. Carter
Chicago State University

Judith Cook
Grossmont College

Carolyn Cunningham
Missouri Southern State College

Donald Daggett
Mankato State University

Jarvis Dean*
Chattanooga State Technical Community College

John H. Espey
Cecil Community College

Carolyn Fitzmorris
Hutchinson Community College

Dan Galvin
Diablo Valley College

Shirley Glass
Macomb Community College

Dennis A. Gutting
Orange County Community College

Austin L. Hamilton
Southeastern Oklahoma State University

Margaret Hicks
Howard University

Thomas L. Hofmeister
Northwestern Business College

Anita V. Hope*
Tarrant County Junior College—Northeast Campus

George Ihorn
El Paso Community College

Eugene Janner*
Blinn College

George F. Johnson
Norfolk State University

Vicky Arnold King
University of Arkansas at Little Rock

Marjorie Lapham
Quinsigamond Community College

Michael Layne
Nassau Community College

Robert Littlejohn*
State University of New York, College of Agricultural and Technology—Cobleskill

John A. Miller, Jr.
St. Louis Community College at Florissant Valley

Marguerite Nagy
Cuyahoga Community College—West

Charles J. Pineno*
Clarion University of Pennsylvania

James Seivwright*
Hillsborough Community College—Dale Mabry Campus

Lou Squyres
DeKalb College—Central Campus

Ellen L. Sweatt
DeKalb College—North Campus

Churchill Ward   Stan Weikert
Austin Community College   *College of the Canyons*

*These individuals also served as academic reviewers for the text and/or ancillaries.

We would also like to acknowledge the assistance of Ernst & Young, Boston, who reviewed the entire text and solutions manual to ascertain that the presentation is up-to-date and accurate. We are especially indebted to Robert H. Temkin, C.P.A., Patricia G. Smith, C.P.A., Susan G. Katcher, C.P.A., Jocelyn Dudack, Michael Nyhan, Olga Volfson, Arthur Pearce, and Howard Wagner.

We wish to thank Fred Shafer and Tari Szatkowski for their assistance with the preparation of the manuscript.

Without the help of these and others, this book would not be possible.

B.E.N.   H.R.A.   J.C.C.

Ernst & Young

One Boston Place
Boston, Massachusetts 02108-4494

Telephone: (617) 725-1100
Fax: (617) 227-5591
Telex: 940800

Houghton Mifflin Company
College Division
One Beacon Street
Boston, MA 02108

We have examined the text of PRINCIPLES OF ACCOUNTING, Fourth Edition, by Needles, Anderson and Caldwell, together with its accompanying Instructor's Solutions Manual. Our examination, which was directed at this work's technical and mathematical accuracy, internal consistency, and the appropriateness and accuracy of references to professional and other pronouncements, was made in accordance with standards established by the American Institute of Certified Public Accountants and, accordingly, included such procedures as we considered necessary in the circumstances. Our examination was carried out during the composition process and before final page proof. In our opinion, the material in this book is technically and mathematically accurate, internally consistent, and references to professional and other pronouncements are accurate and appropriate.

Ernst & Young

ERNST & YOUNG

November 9, 1989

PRINCIPLES OF ACCOUNTING

FINANCIAL ACCOUNTING

PART ONE
The Basic Accounting Model

Chapter 1
Accounting as an Information System

Chapter 2
The Double-Entry System

Chapter 3
Business Income and Adjusting Entries

Chapter 4
Completing the Accounting Cycle

PART TWO
Extensions of the Basic Accounting Model

PART THREE
Measuring and Reporting Assets and Current Liabilities

PART FOUR
Accounting for Partnerships and Corporations

PART FIVE
Special Reports and Analyses of Accounting Information

MANAGERIAL ACCOUNTING

PART SIX
Basic Concepts of Management Accounting

PART SEVEN
Accounting for Management Decision Making

Accounting is an information system for measuring, processing, and communicating information that is useful in making economic decisions. Part One presents the fundamental concepts and techniques of the basic accounting system, including accounting for a complete cycle of business activities for a service enterprise.

PART ONE

The Basic
Accounting Model

Chapter 1 explores the nature and environment of accounting, with special emphasis on the users of accounting information, the roles of accountants in society, and the organizations that influence accounting practice. It introduces the four basic financial statements, the concept of accounting measurement, and the effects of business transactions on financial position. Chapter 1 concludes with a discussion of the ethical responsibilities in the accounting profession.

Chapter 2 continues with accounting measurement by focusing on the issues of recognition, valuation, and classification and how they are solved in the recording of business transactions.

Chapter 3 defines the accounting concept of business income, discusses the role of adjusting entries in its measurement, and demonstrates the preparation of financial statements.

Chapter 4 completes the accounting system with a presentation of the work sheet and closing entries.

LEARNING OBJECTIVES

1. Define accounting and describe its role in making informed decisions.
2. Identify the many users of accounting information in society.
3. Distinguish between financial and management accounting, define generally accepted accounting principles (GAAP), and identify the organizations that influence GAAP.
4. Explain the importance of business transactions, money measure, and separate entity to accounting measurement.
5. Identify the three basic forms of business organization.
6. Define financial position and show how it is affected by simple transactions.
7. Identify the four basic financial statements.
8. Describe accounting as a profession with ethical responsibilities and a wide career choice.

CHAPTER 1

Accounting as an Information System

Your first accounting course begins with a general view of the accounting discipline and profession. In this chapter, you will begin the study of accounting measurement of business transactions and communication through financial statements. You will also learn about the important roles that accountants play in society and about the organizations where accountants work. After studying this chapter, you should be able to meet the learning objectives listed on the left.

Every individual or group in society must make economic decisions about the future. For example, the manager of a company needs to know which products have been unsuccessful. With this information, the manager can decide whether to stop selling them or to do something that will increase their appeal to customers. Other persons will want to find out if a firm is financially sound before accepting a job or investing money in the company. Similarly, not-for-profit organizations need financial information. Federal, state, and local governments, for example, need financial information to levy taxes. Other not-for-profit institutions such as churches and charities need meaningful and easily understood economic information before planning their programs. Because of their financial knowledge, accountants are often asked to analyze the available financial data for clues that will serve as guides to the future.

Accounting Defined

Early definitions of accounting generally focused on the traditional recordkeeping functions of the accountant. In 1941, the American Institute of Certified Public Accountants (AICPA) defined accounting as "the art of recording, classifying, and summarizing in a significant manner and in terms of money, transactions and events which are, in part at least, of a financial character, and interpreting the results thereof."[1] The modern definition of accounting, however, is much broader.

In 1970, the AICPA stated that the function of accounting is "to provide quantitative information, primarily financial in nature, about economic entities that is intended to be useful in

1. Committee on Accounting Terminology, *Accounting Terminology Bulletin No. 1* (New York: American Institute of Certified Public Accountants, 1953), par. 9.

OBJECTIVE 1
*Define accounting
and describe its
role in making
informed decisions*

making economic decisions."[2] (An economic entity is a unit such as a business that has an independent existence.)

The modern accountant, therefore, is concerned not only with record-keeping but also with a whole range of activities involving planning and problem solving; control and attention directing; and evaluation, review, and auditing. Today's accountant focuses on the ultimate needs of those who use accounting information, whether these users are inside or outside the business itself. So accounting "is not an end in itself."[3] Instead it is defined as **an information system that measures, processes, and communicates financial information about an identifiable economic entity.** This information allows users to make "reasoned choices among alternative uses of scarce resources in the conduct of business and economic activities."[4]

This modern view of accounting is shown in Figure 1-1. In this view, accounting is seen as a service activity. It is a link between business activities and decision makers. First, accounting measures business activities by recording data about them for future use. Second, through data processing, the data are stored until needed, then processed in such a way as to become useful information. Third, the information is communicated, through reports, to those who can use it in making decisions. One might say that data about business activities are the input to the accounting system, and useful information for decision makers is the output.

Figure 1-1. Accounting as an Information System for Business Decisions

2. *Statement of the Accounting Principles Board No. 4*, "Basic Concepts and Accounting Principles Underlying Financial Statements of Business Enterprises" (New York: American Institute of Certified Public Accountants, 1970), par. 40.

3. *Statement of Financial Accounting Concepts No. 1*, "Objectives of Financial Reporting by Business Enterprises" (Stamford, Conn.: Financial Accounting Standards Board, 1978), par. 9.

4. Ibid.

To avoid certain misunderstandings about accounting, it is important to clarify its relationship with bookkeeping, the computer, and management information systems.

People often fail to understand the difference between accounting and bookkeeping. **Bookkeeping**, which is a process of accounting, is the means of recording transactions and keeping records. Mechanical and repetitive, bookkeeping is only a small, simple but important part of accounting. Accounting, on the other hand, includes the design of an information system that meets user needs. The major goal of accounting is the analysis, interpretation, and use of information. Accountants look for important relationships in the information they produce. They are interested in finding trends and studying the effects of different alternatives. Accounting includes systems design, budgeting, cost analysis, auditing, and income tax preparation or planning.

The **computer** is an electronic tool that is used to collect, organize, and communicate vast amounts of information with great speed. Accountants were among the earliest and most enthusiastic users of computers, and today they use microcomputers in all aspects of their work. It may appear that the computer is doing the accountant's job, but it is in fact only a tool that is instructed to do the routine bookkeeping and to perform complex calculations for decision-making purposes in a more time-efficient way. It is important that the user of accounting information and the new accountant understand the processes underlying accounting. For this reason, most examples in this book are treated from the standpoint of manual accounting. You should remember, however, that most accounting operations are now computerized.

Most businesses also use a large amount of nonfinancial information. Their marketing departments, for example, are interested in the style or packaging of competitors' products. Personnel departments keep health and employment records of employees. Manufacturing departments must operate in the new environment of automation. With the widespread use of the computer today, many of these varied information needs are being organized into what might be called a **management information system (MIS)**. The management information system consists of the interconnected subsystems that provide the information needed to run a business. The accounting information system is the most important subsystem because it plays the primary role of managing the flow of economic data to all parts of a business and to interested parties outside the business. Accounting is the financial hub of the management information system. It gives both management and outsiders a complete view of the business organization.

Accounting Information and Decision Making

The major reason for studying accounting is to acquire the knowledge and skills to participate in important economic decisions. The information that accounting provides is the basis for such decisions both inside and outside the business enterprise.

Thus accounting information
is a tool and, like most tools, cannot be of much direct help to those who are
unable or unwilling to use it or who misuse it. Its use can be learned, however,
and [accounting] should provide information that can be used by all—nonpro-
fessionals as well as professionals—who are willing to use it properly.[5]

The first step in this learning process is to understand how decisions
are made and how accountants can contribute to the process.

To make a wise decision and carry it out effectively, the decision
maker must answer the following questions:

What is the goal to be achieved? (Step 1)

What different means are available to reach the goal? (Step 2)

Which alternative provides the best way to achieve the goal? (Step 3)

What action should be taken? (Step 4)

Was the goal achieved? (Step 5)

Figure 1-2 shows the steps that an individual or an institution follows
in making a decision.

When the decision involves business and economic questions, accounting information is essential to the decision-making system. It provides quantitative information for three functions: planning, control,
and evaluation.

Planning is the process of formulating a course of action. It includes
setting a goal, finding alternative ways of accomplishing the goal, and
deciding which alternative is the best. In this stage, the accountant
should be able to present a clear statement of financial alternatives. Accounting information dealing with projections of income and budgets
of cash requirements are also important in planning for the future.

Control is the process of seeing that plans are, in fact, carried out. In
other words, do actions agree with plans? At this point, the accountant

Figure 1-2. A Decision System

5. Ibid., par. 36.

might be expected to present information that compares actual costs and revenues with those planned earlier.

Evaluation, which involves the whole decision system, is the process of studying the system to improve it. It asks the question: Was the original goal satisfactorily met (feedback)? If not, the reason could have been poor planning or control, or perhaps the wrong goal was chosen. An evaluation may be given in annual reports and other financial statements based on accounting information.

Decision Makers: The Users of Accounting Information

OBJECTIVE 2
Identify the many users of accounting information in society

Accounting and accounting information are used more than commonly realized. The users of accounting information can be divided roughly into three groups: (1) those who manage a business; (2) those outside a business enterprise who have a direct financial interest in the business; and (3) those persons, groups, or agencies that have an indirect financial interest in the business. These groups are shown in Figure 1-3.

Management

Management is the group of people in a business who have overall responsibility for operating the business and for achieving the company's goals. In a small business, management may include the owners of the business. In a large business, management more often consists of hired managers. Business enterprises have numerous, varied, and often complex objectives. These goals include achieving an acceptable level of earnings, providing quality goods and services at low cost, creating new and improved products, increasing the number of jobs available, improving the environment, and accomplishing many other tasks. To achieve these general goals, of course, the company must be successful. Success and survival in a competitive business environment require that management concentrate much of its effort on two important goals: profitability and liquidity. **Profitability** is the ability to earn enough income to attract and hold investment capital. **Liquidity** means having enough funds on hand to pay debts when they fall due.

Managers must constantly decide what to do, how to do it, and whether the results match the original plans. Successful managers consistently make the right decisions on the basis of timely and valid information. Many of these decisions are based on the flow of accounting data and their analysis. For this reason, management is one of the most important users of accounting information, and a major function of accounting is to provide management with relevant and useful information. For example, some typical questions that a manager might ask include: What was the company's net income during the past quarter? Is the rate of return to the owners adequate? Does the company have enough cash? What products are most profitable? What is the cost of manufacturing each product?

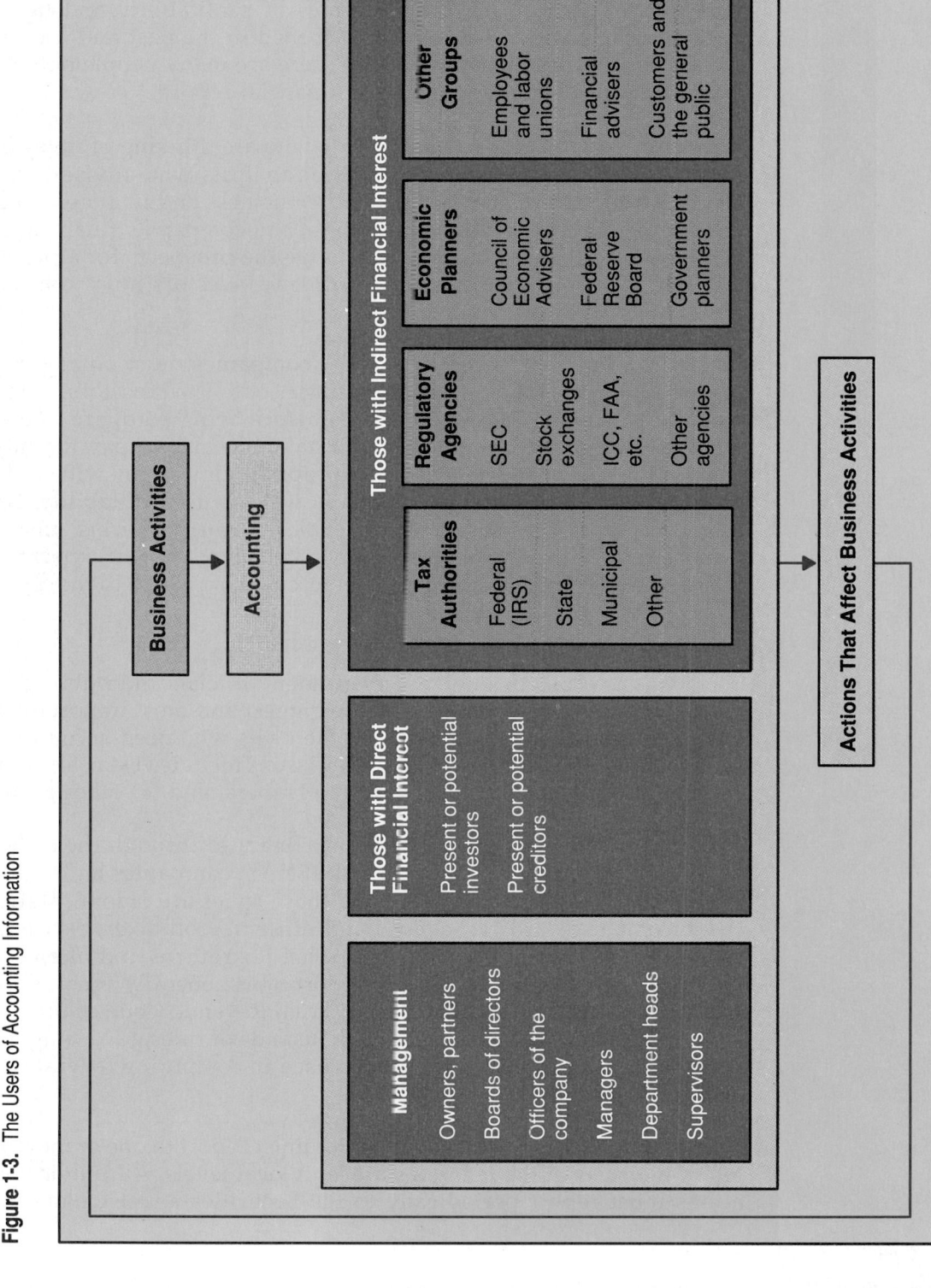

Figure 1-3. The Users of Accounting Information

Users with a Direct Financial Interest

Another major function of accounting is to measure and report information about how a business has performed. Most businesses periodically publish a set of general-purpose financial statements that report on their success in meeting the objectives of profitability and liquidity. These statements show what has happened in the past and are important guides to future success. Today there are many people outside the company who carefully study these financial reports.

Present or Potential Investors. Those who are thinking of investing in a company and those such as financial analysts who advise investors are interested in the past success of the business and its potential earnings in the future. A thorough study of the company's financial statements will help potential investors judge the prospects for a profitable investment. After investing in a company, investors must continually review their commitment.

Present or Potential Creditors. Most companies must borrow money for both long- and short-term operating needs. The creditors, who lend money or deliver goods and services before being paid, are interested mainly in whether the company will have the cash to pay the interest charges and repay the debt at the appropriate time. They will study the company's liquidity and cash flow as well as its profitability. Banks, finance companies, mortgage companies, securities firms, insurance firms, suppliers, individuals, and others who lend money expect to analyze a company's financial position before making a loan to the company.

Users with an Indirect Financial Interest

Society as a whole, through its government officials and public groups, has in recent years become one of the biggest and most important users of accounting information. Some of the users who need accounting information to make decisions on public issues include (1) tax authorities, (2) regulatory agencies, (3) economic planners, and (4) other groups.

Tax Authorities. Our governments are financed through the collection of taxes. Under federal, state, and local laws, companies and individuals pay many kinds of taxes. Among these levies are federal, state, and city income taxes, social security and other payroll taxes, excise taxes, and sales taxes. Each tax requires special tax returns and often a complex set of records as well. Proper reporting is generally a matter of law and can be very complicated. The Internal Revenue Code of the federal government, for instance, contains thousands of rules governing preparation of the accounting information used in computing federal income taxes.

Regulatory Agencies. Most companies must report to one or more regulatory agencies at the federal, state, and local levels. All public corporations must report periodically to the Securities and Exchange Commission. This body was set up by Congress to protect the public and regulates the issuing, buying, and selling of stocks in the United States. Companies that are listed on stock exchanges, such as the New York Stock Exchange, must also meet the special reporting requirements of their exchange. The Interstate Commerce Commission (ICC) regulates industries such as trucking and railroads, and the Federal Aviation Administration (FAA) regulates airlines. Most public utilities, such as electric and gas companies, are regulated and must defend their rates with accounting reports. Accounting is also involved in new and broader regulations like those of the Environmental Protection Agency, which is concerned, among other things, with the cost and speed of reducing environmental pollution.

Economic Planners. Since the 1930s, the federal government's wish to take a more active part in planning and forecasting economic activity has led to greater use of accounting and accounting information. A system of accounting called national income accounting has been developed for the whole economy. It deals with the total production, inventories, income, dividends, taxes, and so forth of our economy. Planners who are members of the President's Council of Economic Advisers or are connected with the Federal Reserve System use this information to set economic policies and judge economic programs.

Other Groups. Labor unions study the financial statements of corporations as part of their task of preparing for important contract negotiations. The amount and computation of income and costs are often important in these negotiations. Those who advise investors and creditors also have an indirect interest in the financial performance and prospects of a business. In this group are financial analysts and advisers, brokers, underwriters, lawyers, economists, and the financial press. Consumers' groups, customers, and the general public have become more concerned about the financing and earnings of corporations as well as with the effects that corporations have on inflation, the environment, social problems, and the quality of life.

Financial and Management Accounting

OBJECTIVE 3
Distinguish between financial and management accounting, define generally accepted accounting principles (GAAP), and identify the organizations that influence GAAP

Accounting was defined earlier as an information system that measures, processes, and communicates information that is useful for decision making. A distinction is commonly made between the concepts of management accounting and financial accounting. **Management accounting** refers to all types of accounting information that are measured, processed, and communicated for the internal use of management. **Financial accounting** refers to accounting information that, in addition to being used internally by management, is communicated to those outside the organization. Chapters 1–21 of this book focus on financial accounting. Chapters 22–28 are primarily concerned with management accounting.

Generally Accepted Accounting Principles

Because it is important that all who receive accounting reports be able to interpret them, a set of practices has developed that provides guidelines for financial accounting. The term used to describe these practices is **generally accepted accounting principles (GAAP)**. Although the term has several meanings in the literature, perhaps the best definition is the following: "Generally accepted accounting principles encompass the conventions, rules, and procedures necessary to define accepted accounting practice at a particular time."[6] In other words, GAAP arise from wide agreement on the theory and practice of accounting at a particular time. These "principles" are not like the unchangeable laws of nature found in chemistry or physics. They are developed by accountants and businesses to serve the needs of decision makers, and they can be altered as better methods are developed or as circumstances change.

In this book, we present accounting practice, or GAAP, as it is today. We also try to explain the reasons or theory on which the practice is based. The two—theory and practice—are part and parcel of the study of accounting. However, you should realize that accounting is a discipline that is always growing, changing, and improving. Just as years of research may be necessary before a new surgical method or lifesaving drug can be introduced into medical practice, research and new discoveries in accounting frequently take years to become common practice. As a result, you may sometimes hear of practices that seem inconsistent. In some cases, we have pointed toward new directions in accounting. Your instructor may also mention certain weaknesses in current theory or practice.

Organizations That Influence Current Practice

Many organizations directly or indirectly influence GAAP and thus influence much of what is in this book. The most important of these organizations are the Financial Accounting Standards Board, the American Institute of Certified Public Accountants, the Securities and Exchange Commission, the Internal Revenue Service, and the Government Accounting Standards Board. There are international and other groups as well.

Financial Accounting Standards Board. Founded in 1973, the **Financial Accounting Standards Board (FASB)** has the primary responsibility for developing and issuing rules on accounting practice. This independent body issues Statements of Financial Accounting Standards. Departures from these statements must be justified and reported in a company's financial statements. The FASB is governed by the Financial Accounting Foundation.

American Institute of Certified Public Accountants. The **American Institute of Certified Public Accountants (AICPA)** has been concerned

6. *Statement of the Accounting Principles Board No. 4,* par. 138.

with accounting practice longer than most other groups. From 1938 to 1958 the AICPA's Committee on Accounting Procedures issued a series of pronouncements dealing with accounting principles, procedures, and terms. In 1959 the AICPA organized the Accounting Principles Board (APB) to replace the Committee on Accounting Procedures. The board published a number of APB Opinions on accounting practice, many of which are still in effect even though the APB was ended in 1973 when the FASB took over the standard-setting authority. The AICPA still influences accounting practice through the activities of its senior technical committees.

Securities and Exchange Commission. The **Securities and Exchange Commission (SEC)** is an agency of the U.S. government that has the legal power to set and enforce accounting practices for companies whose securities are offered for sale to the general public. As such, it has great influence on accounting practice. Because the APB failed to solve some of the major problems and abuses in accounting practice, the SEC began to play a larger and more aggressive part in deciding rules of accounting. The FASB represents a major effort on the part of accountants to keep control over their profession and to limit the SEC to its traditional role of allowing the accounting profession to regulate itself. It appears certain that during the coming years the SEC will keep putting pressure on the accounting profession to regulate itself. The success or failure of the FASB will be important in determining how much future influence the SEC will have on accounting.

Internal Revenue Service. The U.S. tax laws govern the assessment and collection of revenue for operating the government. Because a major source of the government's revenue is the income tax, the law specifies the rules for determining taxable income. These rules are interpreted and enforced by the **Internal Revenue Service (IRS)**. In some cases, these rules may be in conflict with good accounting practice, but they are an important influence on practice. Businesses must use certain accounting practices simply because they are required by the tax law. Sometimes companies follow an accounting practice specified in the tax law to take advantage of rules that will help them financially. Cases where the tax law may affect accounting practice are noted throughout this book.

Government Accounting Standards Board. Concern over the financial reporting of government units has resulted in increased attention to the development of accounting principles for these units. The **Government Accounting Standards Board (GASB)**, which was established in 1984 under the same governing body as the Financial Accounting Standards Board, is responsible for issuing accounting standards for state and local governments. The GASB will undoubtedly have a great influence on financial reporting by these units.

International Organizations. Worldwide cooperation in the development of accounting principles has made great strides in recent years.

The International Accounting Standards Committee (IASC) has approved more than twenty international standards; these have been translated into six languages. In 1977, the International Federation of Accountants (IFAC), made up of professional accounting bodies from more than sixty countries, was founded to promote international agreement on accounting questions.

Other Organizations Concerned with Accounting. The National Association of Accountants (NAA) is composed mainly of management accountants. This organization is engaged in education and research, with an emphasis on management accounting and accounting for management decisions. The Financial Executives Institute (FEI) is made up of persons who hold the highest financial positions in large businesses. It is most interested in standards and research in financial accounting.

The American Accounting Association (AAA) was founded in 1935, succeeding the American Association of University Instructors in Accounting, which was started in 1916. This group has an academic and theoretical point of view. Its members have contributed greatly to the development of accounting theory.

Accounting Measurement

OBJECTIVE 4
Explain the importance of business transactions, money measure, and separate entity to accounting measurement

Accounting has been defined thus far as an information system that measures, processes, and communicates financial information. This section begins the study of the measurement aspects of accounting. You will learn what accounting actually measures and study the effects of certain transactions on a company's financial position.

The accountant must answer four basic questions to make an accounting measurement:

1. What is to be measured?
2. When should the measurement occur?
3. What value should be placed on what is measured?
4. How is what is measured to be classified?

All the questions deal with basic underlying assumptions and generally accepted accounting principles, and their answers establish what accounting is and what it is not. Accountants in industry, professional associations, public accounting, government, and academic circles debate the answers to these questions constantly. As explained earlier, the answers change as new knowledge and practice require, but the basis of today's accounting practice rests on a number of widely accepted concepts and conventions, which are described in this book. The answers to questions 2, 3, and 4 are reserved for Chapter 2.

What Is to Be Measured?

The world contains an unlimited number of things to measure. For example, consider a machine that makes bottle caps. How many measurements of this machine could be made? They might include size, location, weight, cost, and many others. Some attributes of this machine are relevant to accounting; some are not. Every system must define what it measures, and accounting is no exception. Basically, **financial accounting is concerned with measuring the impact of business transactions on specific business entities in terms of money measures.** The concepts of business transactions, money measure, and separate entity are discussed below and on the next page.

Business Transactions as the Object of Measurement

Business transactions are economic events that affect the financial position of a business entity. Business entities may have hundreds or even thousands of transactions every day. These transactions are the raw material of accounting reports.

A transaction may involve an exchange of value (such as a purchase, sale, payment, collection, or borrowing) between two or more independent parties. A transaction may also involve a nonexchange economic event that has the same effect as an exchange transaction. Some examples of nonexchange transactions are losses from fire, flood, explosion, and theft; physical wear and tear on machinery and equipment; and the day-by-day accumulation of interest.

In any case, to be recorded the transaction must relate directly to the business entity. For example, a customer buys a shovel from Ace Hardware but must buy a hoe from a competing store because Ace is sold out of hoes. The transaction for selling the shovel is recorded in Ace's records. However, the purchase of a hoe from a competitor is not recorded in Ace's records because, even though it indirectly affects Ace economically, it does not directly involve an exchange of value between Ace and the customer.

Money Measure

All business transactions are recorded in terms of money. This concept is termed the **money measure.** Of course, information of a nonfinancial nature may be recorded, but it is only through the recording of dollar amounts that the diverse transactions and activities of a business are measured. Money is the only factor common to all business transactions, and thus it is the only practical unit of measure that can produce financial data that are alike and can be compared.

The monetary unit used by a business depends on the country in which it resides. For example, in the United States, the basic unit of money is the dollar. In Japan, it is the yen; in France, the franc; in Germany, the mark; and in the United Kingdom, the pound. If there are transactions between countries, the units must be translated from one currency to another. Our discussion in this book focuses on dollars.

The Concept of Separate Entity

For accounting purposes, a business is treated as a **separate entity** that is distinct not only from its creditors and customers but also from its owner or owners. It should have a completely separate set of records. Its financial records and reports refer only to its own financial affairs. The business owns assets and owes creditors and owners in the amount of their claims.

For example, the Jones Florist Company should have a bank account that is separate from the account of Kay Jones, the owner. Kay Jones may own a home, a car, and other property, and she may have personal debts, but these are not the Jones Florist Company's assets or debts. Kay Jones may also own another business such as a stationery shop. If she does own another business, she should have a completely separate set of records for each business.

Forms of Business Organization

OBJECTIVE 5
Identify the three basic forms of business organization

Accountants need to understand the three basic forms of business organization: sole proprietorships, partnerships, and corporations. Accountants recognize each form as an economic unit separate from its owners, although legally only the corporation is considered separate from its owners. Other legal differences among the three forms are summarized in Table 1-1 and discussed briefly below. In this book, we first show accounting for the sole proprietorship because it is the simplest form of accounting. At critical points, however, we call attention to its essential differences from accounting for corporations and partnerships. Later, in Part Four, we deal specifically with partnership and corporation accounting.

Table 1-1. Comparative Features of the Forms of Business Organization			
	Sole Proprietorship	**Partnership**	**Corporation**
1. Legal status	Not a separate legal entity	Not a separate legal entity	Separate legal entity
2. Risk of ownership	Owner's personal resources at stake	Partners' resources at stake	Limited to investment in corporation
3. Duration or life	Limited by desire or death of owner	Limited by desire or death of each partner	Indefinite, possibly unlimited
4. Transferability of ownership	Sale by owner establishes new company	Changes in any partner's percentage of interest requires new partnership	Transferable by sale of stock
5. Accounting treatment	Separate economic unit	Separate economic unit	Separate economic unit

Sole Proprietorships

A **sole proprietorship** is a business owned by one person. This form of business gives the individual a means of controlling the business apart from his or her personal interests. Legally, however, the proprietorship is the same economic unit as the individual. The individual receives all profits or losses and is liable for all obligations of the business. Proprietorships represent the largest number of businesses in the United States, but typically they are the smallest in size. The life of a sole proprietorship ends when the owner wishes it to, or at the owner's death or incapacity.

Partnerships

A **partnership** is like a proprietorship in most ways except that it has more than one owner. A partnership is not a legal economic unit separate from the owners but an unincorporated association that brings together the talents and resources of two or more people. The partners share profits and losses of the partnership according to an agreed-upon formula. Generally, any partner can bind the partnership to another party and, if necessary, the personal resources of each partner can be called on to pay obligations of the partnership. In some cases, one or more partners may limit their liability, but at least one partner must have unlimited liability. A partnership must be dissolved if the ownership changes, as when a partner leaves or dies. If the business is to continue as a partnership, a new partnership must be formed.

Corporations

A **corporation** is a business unit that is legally separate from its owners (the stockholders). The owners, whose ownership is represented by shares of stock in the corporation, do not directly control the operations of the corporation. Instead they elect a board of directors who run the corporation for the benefit of the stockholders. In exchange for limited involvement in the corporation's actual operations, stockholders enjoy limited liability. That is, their risk of loss is limited to the amount paid for their shares. If they wish, stockholders can sell their shares to other persons without affecting corporate operations. Because of this limited liability, stockholders are often willing to invest in riskier, but potentially more profitable, activities. Also, because ownership can be transferred without dissolving the corporation, the life of the corporation is unlimited and not subject to the whims or health of a proprietor or of a partner.

Corporations have several important advantages over proprietorships and partnerships (see Chapter 15) that make them very efficient in amassing capital for the formation and growth of very large companies. Even though corporations are fewer in number than proprietorships and partnerships, they contribute much more to the U.S. economy in monetary terms. For example, in 1989, General Motors generated more revenues than all but thirteen of the world's countries.

Financial Position and the Accounting Equation

OBJECTIVE 6
Define financial position and show how it is affected by simple transactions

Financial position refers to the economic resources belonging to a company and the claims against those resources at a point in time. Another term for claims is equities. Thus, a company can be viewed as economic resources and equities:

Economic resources = equities

Every company has two types of equities, creditors' equity and owner's equity. Thus,

Economic resources = creditors' equity + owner's equity

Since in accounting terminology, economic resources are referred to as assets and creditors' equities are referred to as liabilities, this equation may be presented as follows:

Assets = liabilities + owner's equity

This equation is known as the **accounting equation**. The two sides of the equation must always be equal or "in balance." The components of this equation will now be defined.

Assets

Assets are "probable future economic benefits obtained or controlled by a particular entity as a result of past transactions or events."[7] In other words, they are economic resources owned by a business that are expected to benefit future operations. Certain kinds of assets are monetary items such as cash and money owed to the company from customers (called *Accounts Receivable*). Other assets are nonmonetary physical things such as inventories (goods held for sale), land, buildings, and equipment. Still other assets are nonphysical rights such as those granted by patent, trademark, or copyright.

Liabilities

Liabilities are "probable future sacrifices of economic benefits arising from present obligations of a particular entity to transfer assets or provide services to other entities in the future as a result of past transactions or events."[8] Among these are debts of the business, amounts owed to creditors for goods or services bought on credit (called *Accounts Payable*), borrowed money such as owed on loans payable to banks, salaries and wages owed to employees, taxes owed to the government, and services to be performed.

As debts, liabilities are a claim recognized by law. That is, the law gives creditors the right to force the sale of a company's assets if the

---

7. *Statement of Financial Accounting Concepts No. 6*, "Elements of Financial Statements" (Stamford, Conn.: Financial Accounting Standards Board, December, 1985), par. 25.
8. Ibid., par. 35.

company fails to pay the debt. Creditors have rights over owners and must be paid in full before the owners may receive anything, even if payment of the debt uses up all assets of the business.

Owner's Equity

Equity is "the residual interest in the assets of an entity that remains after deducting its liabilities."[9] In a business, the equity is called the ownership interest or **owner's equity**. Owner's equity represents the claims by the owner on the assets of the business. Owner's equity is also known as the residual equity because, theoretically, it is what would be left over if all the liabilities were paid. Transposing the accounting equation, we can state owner's equity as follows:

$$\text{Owner's equity} = \text{assets} - \text{liabilities}$$

Because it equals the assets after deducting the liabilities, owner's equity is sometimes said to equal **net assets**.

The four types of transactions that affect owner's equity are shown in Figure 1-4. Two of these transactions, **owner's investments** and **owner's withdrawals**, designate assets that the owner either puts into the business or takes out of the business. For instance, if the owner of Shannon Realty, John Shannon, takes cash out of his personal bank account and places it in the business bank account, it is an owner's investment. The assets (cash) of the business increased, and John Shannon's equity in those assets also increased. Conversely, if John Shannon takes cash out of the business bank account and places it in his personal bank account, he has made a withdrawal from the business. The assets of the business have decreased, and John Shannon's equity in the business has also decreased.

The other two types of transactions that affect owner's equity are **revenues** and **expenses**. Simply stated, **revenues** and **expenses** are the increases and decreases in owner's equity that result from operating the

Figure 1-4. Four Types of Transactions That Affect Owner's Equity

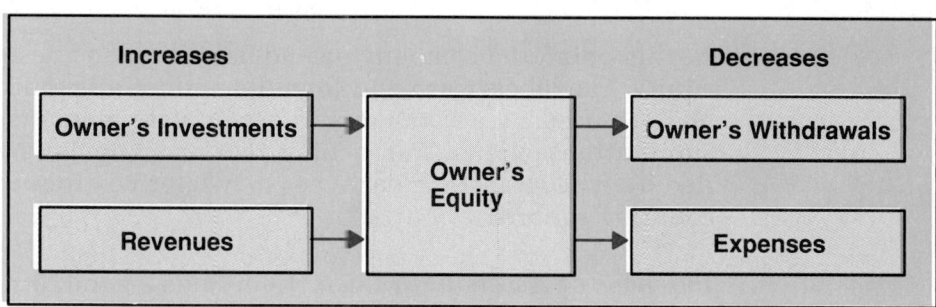

9. Ibid., par. 49.

business. For example, if a customer pays cash (or agrees to pay cash in the future) to Shannon Realty in return for a service provided by the company, a revenue results. Assets (cash or accounts receivable) of Shannon Realty have increased, and the owner's equity in those assets has also increased. On the other hand, if Shannon Realty pays out cash (or agrees to pay cash in the future) in the process of providing a service, an expense results and is represented by a decrease in assets (cash) or an increase in liabilities (accounts payable) and a decrease in the owner's equity in those assets. Generally speaking, a company is successful if its revenues exceed its expenses. When revenues exceed expenses, the difference is called **net income**, and when expenses exceed revenues, the difference is called **net loss**.

Some Illustrative Transactions

Let us now examine the effect of some of the most common business transactions on the accounting equation. Suppose that John Shannon opens a real estate agency called Shannon Realty on December 1. During December, his business engages in the transactions described in the following paragraphs.

Owner's Investment. John begins his business by depositing $50,000 in a bank account in the name of Shannon Realty. The transfer of cash from his personal account to the business account is an owner's investment and increases the assets (Cash) and the owner's equity (John Shannon, Capital) of Shannon Realty:

	Assets	=	Owner's Equity	
	Cash		John Shannon, Capital	Type of OE Transaction
1.	$50,000		$50,000	Owner's Investment

At this point, the company has no liabilities, and assets equal owner's equity. The labels Cash and John Shannon, Capital are called **accounts** and are used by accountants to accumulate amounts that result from similar transactions. Transactions that affect owner's equity are identified by type so that similar types may later be grouped together on accounting reports.

Purchase of Assets with Cash. John finds a good location for his business and purchases with cash a lot for $10,000 and a small building on the lot for $25,000. This transaction does not change the total assets, liabilities, or owner's equity of Shannon Realty, but it does change the composition of the assets—decreasing Cash and increasing Land and Building:

		Assets		=	Owner's Equity	
	Cash	Land	Building		John Shannon, Capital	Type of OE Transaction
bal.	$50,000				$50,000	
2.	−35,000	+$10,000	+$25,000			
bal.	$15,000	$10,000	$25,000		$50,000	

$50,000

Purchase of Assets by Incurring a Liability. Assets do not always have to be purchased with cash. They may also be purchased on credit, that is, on the basis of an agreement to pay for them later. Suppose John buys some office supplies for $500 on credit. This transaction increases the assets (Supplies) and increases the liabilities of Shannon Realty. This liability is designated by an account called Accounts Payable:

		Assets			= Liabilities +	Owner's Equity	
	Cash	Supplies	Land	Building	Accounts Payable	John Shannon, Capital	Type of OE Transaction
bal.	$15,000		$10,000	$25,000		$50,000	
3.		+$500			+$500		
bal.	$15,000	$500	$10,000	$25,000	$500	$50,000	

$50,500 $50,500

Note that this transaction increases both sides of the accounting equation to $50,500.

Payment of a Liability. If John later pays $200 of the $500 owed for the supplies, both assets (Cash) and liabilities (Accounts Payable) will decrease, but Supplies will be unaffected:

		Assets			= Liabilities +	Owner's Equity	
	Cash	Supplies	Land	Building	Accounts Payable	John Shannon, Capital	Type of OE Transaction
bal.	$15,000	$500	$10,000	$25,000	$500	$50,000	
4.	−200				−200		
bal.	$14,800	$500	$10,000	$25,000	$300	$50,000	

$50,300 $50,300

Note that the accounting equation is still equal on both sides of the equation, although now at a total of $50,300.

Revenues. Shannon Realty earns revenues in the form of commissions received from selling houses for clients. Sometimes these commissions are paid to Shannon Realty immediately in the form of cash, and sometimes the client agrees to pay the commission later. In either case, the commission is recorded when it is earned, and Shannon Realty has a right to a current or future receipt of cash. First, assume that Shannon Realty sells a house and receives a commission in cash of $1,500. This transaction increases assets (Cash) and owner's equity (John Shannon, Capital):

	Assets				= Liabilities +	Owner's Equity	
	Cash	Supplies	Land	Building	Accounts Payable	John Shannon, Capital	Type of OE Transaction
bal.	$14,800	$500	$10,000	$25,000	$300	$50,000	
5.	+1,500					+1,500	Commissions Earned
bal.	$16,300	$500	$10,000	$25,000	$300	$51,500	
			$51,800			$51,800	

Now assume that John sells a house calling for a commission of $2,000, but John agrees to wait for the payment. Since the commission is earned now, a bill or invoice is sent to the client and the transaction is recorded now. This revenue transaction increases both assets and owner's equity as before, but a new asset account, Accounts Receivable, shows that Shannon Realty is awaiting receipt of the commission:

	Assets					= Liabilities +	Owner's Equity	
	Cash	Accounts Receivable	Supplies	Land	Building	Accounts Payable	John Shannon, Capital	Type of OE Transaction
bal.	$16,300		$500	$10,000	$25,000	$300	$51,500	
6.		+$2,000					+2,000	Commissions Earned
bal.	$16,300	$2,000	$500	$10,000	$25,000	$300	$53,500	
			$53,800				$53,800	

The use of separate accounts for revenue accounts, like Commissions Earned, will be introduced in Chapter 2.

Collection of Accounts Receivable. If it is assumed that a few days later Shannon receives $1,000 from the client in transaction **6**, the asset Cash is increased and the asset Accounts Receivable is decreased:

	Assets					=	Liabilities	+	Owner's Equity	
	Cash	Accounts Receiv- able	Supplies	Land	Building		Accounts Payable		John Shannon, Capital	Type of OE Transaction
bal.	$16,300	$2,000	$500	$10,000	$25,000		$300		$53,500	
7.	+1,000	−1,000								
bal.	$17,300	$1,000	$500	$10,000	$25,000		$300		$53,500	

$53,800 $53,800

Note that this transaction does not affect owner's equity because the commission revenue has already been recorded in transaction **6**. Also, note that the balance of Accounts Receivable is $1,000, indicating that $1,000 is still to be collected.

Expenses. Just as revenues are recorded when they are earned, expenses are recorded when they are incurred. Expenses may be paid in cash when they occur; or if payment is to be made later, a liability such as Accounts Payable or Wages Payable is increased. In both cases, owner's equity is decreased. Assume that John Shannon pays $1,000 to rent some equipment for the office and $400 in wages to a part-time helper. These transactions reduce assets (Cash) and owner's equity (John Shannon, Capital):

	Assets					=	Liabilities	+	Owner's Equity	
	Cash	Accounts Receiv- able	Supplies	Land	Building		Accounts Payable		John Shannon, Capital	Type of OE Transaction
bal.	$17,300	$1,000	$500	$10,000	$25,000		$300		$53,500	
8.	−1,000								−1,000	Equip. Rental Expense
9.	− 400								− 400	Wages Expense
bal.	$15,900	$1,000	$500	$10,000	$25,000		$300		$52,100	

$52,400 $52,400

Also, John has not paid the bill for utility expense of $300 that was incurred by Shannon Realty for December. In this case, the effect on owner's equity is the same as when the expense is paid in cash, but instead of a reduction in assets, there is an increase in liabilities (Accounts Payable), as follows:

	Assets				=	Liabilities	+	Owner's Equity	
Cash	Accounts Receiv- able	Supplies	Land	Building		Accounts Payable		John Shannon, Capital	Type of OE Transaction
bal. $15,900	$1,000	$500	$10,000	$25,000		$300		$52,100	
10.						+300		−300	Utility Expense
bal. $15,900	$1,000	$500	$10,000	$25,000		$600		$51,800	
		$52,400					$52,400		

The use of separate accounts for expenses will be introduced in Chapter 2.

Owner's Withdrawals. John now withdraws $600 in cash from Shannon Realty and deposits it in his personal account. The effect of this transaction is to reduce assets (Cash) and owner's equity (John Shannon, Capital). Although, as can be seen below, withdrawals have the same effect on the accounting equation as expenses (see transactions **8** and **9**), it is important not to confuse them. Withdrawals are not expenses, but personal distributions of assets to the owner whereas expenses are incurred by the business in its operation.

	Assets				=	Liabilities	+	Owner's Equity	
Cash	Accounts Receiv- able	Supplies	Land	Building		Accounts Payable		John Shannon, Capital	Type of OE Transaction
bal. $15,900	$1,000	$500	$10,000	$25,000		$600		$51,800	
11. −600								−600	Withdrawal
bal. $15,300	$1,000	$500	$10,000	$25,000		$600		$51,200	
		$51,800					$51,800		

Summary. A summary of these eleven illustrative transactions is presented in Exhibit 1-1.

Accounting Communication Through Financial Statements

Financial statements are a central feature of accounting because they are the primary means of communicating important accounting infor-

Exhibit 1-1. Summary of Effects of Illustrative Transactions on the Accounting Equation

	Assets					= Liabilities +	Owner's Equity	
	Cash	Accounts Receivable	Supplies	Land	Building	Accounts Payable	John Shannon, Capital	Type of OE Transaction
1.	$50,000						$50,000	Owner's Investment
2.	−35,000			+$10,000	+$25,000			
bal.	$15,000			$10,000	$25,000		$50,000	
3.			+$500			+$500		
bal.	$15,000		$500	$10,000	$25,000	$500	$50,000	
4.	−200					−200		
bal.	$14,800		$500	$10,000	$25,000	$300	$50,000	
5.	+1,500						+1,500	Commissions Earned
bal.	$16,300		$500	$10,000	$25,000	$300	$51,500	
6.		+$2,000					+2,000	Commissions Earned
bal.	$16,300	$2,000	$500	$10,000	$25,000	$300	$53,500	
7.	+1,000	−1,000						
bal.	$17,300	$1,000	$500	$10,000	$25,000	$300	$53,500	
8.	−1,000						−1,000	Equip. Rental Expense
9.	−400						−400	Wages Expense
bal.	$15,900	$1,000	$500	$10,000	$25,000	$300	$52,100	
10.						+300	−300	Utility Expense
bal.	$15,900	$1,000	$500	$10,000	$25,000	$600	$51,800	
11.	−600						−600	Withdrawal
bal.	$15,300	$1,000	$500	$10,000	$25,000	$600	$51,200	

$51,800 = $51,800

mation to users. It is helpful to think of these statements as models of the business enterprise, because they are attempts to show the business in financial terms. As is true of all models, however, financial statements are not perfect pictures of the real thing but rather the accountant's best effort to represent what is real.

Four major financial statements are used to communicate the required accounting information about a business. One is the income statement, which reports income-generating activities or earnings of a business during the period. A second statement, called the statement of owner's equity, shows the changes in the owner's interest in the business. These statements are prepared from the four types of transactions that affect owner's equity. This is why in Exhibit 1-1 and prior examples, these transactions were identified by type.

A third financial statement is the balance sheet. The balance sheet shows the financial position of the business at a particular date, such as at the end of the accounting period. A fourth statement, called the statement of cash flows, is used to summarize all the changes in cash that result from operating activities, investing activities, and financing activities. Exhibit 1-2 illustrates the relationships of the first three statements by showing how they would appear for Shannon Realty after the eleven illustrative transactions shown in Exhibit 1-1. It is assumed that these transactions took place during the month of December 19xx.

Note that each statement is headed in a similar way. Each heading identifies the company and the kind of statement. The balance sheet gives the specific date to which it applies, and the income statement and statement of owner's equity give the time period to which they apply. These statements are typical ones for proprietorships. Statements for partnerships and corporations, which are similar to those of a proprietorship, are discussed in Chapter 14 and later chapters.

The Income Statement

The **income statement** is a financial statement that summarizes the amount of revenues earned and expenses incurred by a business over a period of time. Many people consider it the most important financial report because its purpose is to measure whether or not the business achieved or failed to achieve its primary objective of earning an acceptable income. In Exhibit 1-2, Shannon Realty had revenues in the form of commissions earned of $3,500. From this amount total expenses of $1,700 were deducted, consisting of equipment rental expense of $1,000, wages expense of $400, and utility expense of $300, to arrive at a net income of $1,800. To show that it applies to a period of time, the statement is dated, "For the Month Ended December 31, 19xx."

The Statement of Owner's Equity

The **statement of owner's equity** shows the changes in the owner's capital account over a period of time. In Exhibit 1-2, the beginning capital is zero because the company was started in this accounting period. During the month John Shannon made an investment in the business of

Exhibit 1-2. Income Statement, Statement of Owner's Equity, and Balance Sheet for Shannon Realty

Shannon Realty
Income Statement
For the Month Ended December 31, 19xx

Revenues		
Commissions Earned		$3,500
Expenses		
Equipment Rental Expense	$1,000	
Wages Expense	400	
Utility Expense	300	
Total Expenses		1,700
Net Income		$1,800

Shannon Realty
Statement of Owner's Equity
For the Month Ended December 31, 19xx

John Shannon, Capital, December 1, 19xx		$ 0
Add: Investments by John Shannon	$50,000	
Net Income for the Month	1,800	51,800
Subtotal		$51,800
Less: Withdrawals by John Shannon		600
John Shannon, Capital, December 31, 19xx		$51,200

Shannon Realty
Balance Sheet
December 31, 19xx

Assets		Liabilities	
Cash	$15,300	Accounts Payable	$ 600
Accounts Receivable	1,000	**Owner's Equity**	
Supplies	500		
Land	10,000	John Shannon, Capital	51,200
Building	25,000	Total Liabilities and	
Total Assets	$51,800	Owner's Equity	$51,800

$50,000, and the company earned an income (as shown in the income statement) of $1,800, for a total increase of $51,800. Deducted from this amount are the withdrawals for the month of $600, leaving an ending balance of $51,200 in the capital account.

The Balance Sheet

The purpose of the **balance sheet** is to show the financial position of a business on a certain date. For this reason, it is often called the statement of financial position and is dated as of a certain date. The balance sheet presents a view of the business as the holder of resources or assets that are equal to the sources of or claims against those assets. The sources or claims consist of the company's liabilities and the owner's equity in the company. In Exhibit 1-2, Shannon Realty has several categories of assets, which total $51,800. These assets equal the total liabilities of $600 (Accounts Payable) plus the ending balance of owner's equity of $51,200 (John Shannon, Capital). Note that the capital account on the balance sheet comes from the ending balance shown on the statement of owner's equity.

The Statement of Cash Flows

During the past three decades it has become clear that the income statement has a major deficiency. It only shows the changes in financial position caused by those operations that produced a net income or loss. Many important events, especially those relating to investing and financing activities, can take place during an accounting period and not appear on the income statement. For example, the owner may put more money into the business or take it out. Buildings, equipment, or other assets may be bought or sold. New liabilities can be incurred or old ones paid off. For this reason, the **statement of cash flows** is now widely used to show the cash produced by operating the business as well as important investing and financing transactions that take place during an accounting period.

Exhibit 1-3 is an example of the statement of cash flows for Shannon Realty. Note that the name of the company, the title of the statement, and the period covered by the statement are identified. Also note that the statement explains how the Cash account changed during the period. Cash increased by $15,300. Operating activities produced net cash flows of $900, and financing activities produced net cash flows of $49,400. Investment activities used cash flows of $35,000.

This statement is directly related to the other three statements. Notice that net income comes from the income statement and that investments and withdrawals by John Shannon come from the statement of owner's equity. The other items in the statement represent changes in the balance sheet accounts of Accounts Receivable, Supplies, Accounts Payable, Land, and Buildings. The construction and use of the statement of cash flows is discussed in detail in Chapter 18.

Relationships Among the Four Statements

At this stage, you are not expected to understand all the fine points and terminology of these four statements. They are presented to show that accounting tries to sum up in a meaningful and useful way the financial history of a business, no matter how large and complex, in four relatively simple financial statements—an amazing feat. Two of the state-

Exhibit 1-3. Statement of Cash Flows for Shannon Realty

Shannon Realty
Statement of Cash Flows
For the Month Ended December 31, 19xx

Cash Flows from Operating Activities		
Net Income		$ 1,800
Noncash Expenses and Revenues		
Included in Income		
Increase in Accounts Receivable	$ (1,000)	
Increase in Supplies	(500)	
Increase in Accounts Payable	600	(900)
Net Cash Flows from Operating Activities		$ 900
Cash Flows from Investing Activities		
Purchase of Land	$(10,000)	
Purchase of Building	(25,000)	
Net Cash Flows from Investing Activities		(35,000)
Cash Flows from Financing Activities		
Investment by John Shannon	$ 50,000	
Withdrawals by John Shannon	(600)	
Net Cash Flows from Financing		
Activities		49,400
Net Increase (Decrease) in Cash		**$15,300**
Cash at Beginning of Year		0
Cash at End of Year		$15,300

ments—the income statement and the statement of cash flows—deal with the activities of the business over time. One statement—the balance sheet—shows the financial position of the business at a particular point in time. Another statement—the statement of owner's equity—ties the balance sheet and income statement together over a period of time. Much of the rest of this book deals with how to develop, use, and interpret these four statements.

Professional Ethics and the Accounting Profession

OBJECTIVE 8
Describe accounting as a profession with ethical responsibilities and a wide career choice

Ethics is the application of a code of conduct to everyday life. It addresses the question of whether actions are good or bad, right or wrong. Ethical actions are the results of individual decisions, and you are faced with many ethical situations every day. Some may be potentially illegal, such as the temptation to take office supplies from your employer to use when you do homework. Others are not illegal, but are equally unethical, such as knowingly failing to tell a fellow student who missed class that a test has been announced for the next class period. When an organization is said to act ethically or unethically, it means individuals within the organization have made a decision to act ethically or unethically. When a company uses false advertising, cheats a customer, pollutes the environment, treats employees poorly, or misleads investors by presenting false financial statements, members of management and other employees of the company have consciously made decisions to lead the company in these directions. Likewise, in a company that subscribes to ethical practices, that ethical behavior is a direct result of the actions and decisions of employees in the company.

Professional ethics is the application of a code of conduct to the practice of a profession. Like the ethical conduct of a company, the ethical actions of a profession are a collection of individual actions. As members of a profession, accountants have a responsibility, not only to their employers and clients but to society as a whole, to uphold the highest ethical standards. A recent survey of over 1,000 prominent people in business, education, and government ranked the accounting profession second only to the clergy as having the highest ethical standards.[10]

The accounting function is as old as the need to exchange things of value and keep track of the wealth. The commercial and trading revolution of the Renaissance was a great impetus to accounting, as was the Industrial Revolution. The enormous growth of industry and government in the twentieth century has expanded the need for accountants even further. Today, the accounting profession offers interesting, challenging, well-paying, and satisfying careers. It is the responsibility of every person who becomes an accountant to uphold the high standards of the profession regardless of the field of accounting in which the individual engages.

Management Accounting

An accountant who is employed by a business is said to be in **management accounting**. A small business may have only one person doing this work, though a medium-size or large company may have hundreds of accountants working under a chief accounting officer called a controller, treasurer, or financial vice president. Other positions that may be held by accountants at lower managerial levels are assistant controller, chief accountant, accounting manager, internal auditor, plant accountant, systems analyst, financial accountant, and cost accountant.

Because of their broad and intimate view of all aspects of a company's operations, management accountants often have an important effect on management decision making. According to most recent surveys, more top-level business executives have backgrounds in accounting and finance than in any other field. Just a few of the well-known companies whose presidents or chairmen of the board are (or have been) accountants are American Airlines, General Foods, International Business Machines, Caterpillar Tractor, General Motors, Kennecott Copper, Ford,

---

10. Touche Ross & Co., "Ethics in American Business" (New York: Touche Ross & Co., 1988), p. 7.

General Electric, General Telephone and Electronics, Consolidated Edison, International Telephone and Telegraph, and 3M.

The main task of management accountants is to give management the information it needs to make wise decisions. Management accountants also set up a system of internal control to increase efficiency and prevent fraud. They aid in profit planning, budgeting, and cost control. It is their duty to see that a company has good records, prepares proper financial reports, and complies with tax laws and government regulations. Management accountants also need to keep up with the latest developments in the uses of computers and in computer systems design.

Management accountants may certify their professional competence and training by qualifying for the status of **Certified Management Accountant (CMA)**, which is awarded to qualified accountants by the Institute of Certified Management Accountants of the National Association of Accountants. Under the CMA program, candidates must pass an examination consisting of several parts and meet educational and professional standards.

The National Association of Accountants has adopted a Code of Professional Conduct for Management Accountants. This ethical code emphasizes that management accountants have a responsibility to achieve the competence necessary to do their jobs, to keep information confidential except when authorized or legally required to disclose it, to maintain integrity and avoid conflicts of interest, and to communicate information objectively and without bias.[11]

Public Accounting

The field of **public accounting** offers services in auditing, taxes, and management consulting to the public for a fee. In the short time since about 1900, public accounting in this country has gained a stature similar to that of the older professions of law and medicine. **Certified Public Accountants (CPAs)** are licensed by all states for the same reason that lawyers and doctors are—to protect the public by ensuring a high quality of professional service.

Requirements. To become a CPA, the applicant must meet rigorous requirements. These requirements vary from state to state but have certain characteristics in common. An applicant must be a person of integrity and have at least a high school education. Most states require four years of college (a few require five years) with a major in accounting, and the AICPA has voted to make 150 college-level semester hours of education (i.e., five years) a requirement for membership after the year 2000. Further, the applicant must pass a difficult and comprehensive two-and-one-half-day examination in accounting practice, accounting theory, auditing, and business law. Although the examination is uniform in all states, some states also require an examination in such areas as economics or professional ethics. The examination is prepared by the American Institute of Certified Public Accountants and is given

11. *Statement Number 1C*, "Standards of Ethical Conduct for Management Accountants" (Montvale, N. J.: National Association of Accountants, June 1, 1983).

twice a year. Most states also require from one to five years' experience in the office of a certified public accountant or acceptable equivalent experience. In some cases, additional education can be substituted for one or more years of accounting experience.

Professional Ethics. The profession can be divided into four broad fields: (1) management accounting, (2) public accounting, (3) government and not-for-profit accounting, and (4) accounting education. To ensure that its members understand the responsibilities of being professional accountants, the AICPA and each state have adopted Codes of Professional Conduct as guides to action. Fundamental to these codes is responsibility to the public, including clients, creditors, investors, and anyone else who relies on the work of the accountant. In resolving conflicts among these various groups, the accountant must act with integrity even to the sacrifice of personal benefit. **Integrity** means that the accountant is honest and candid and subordinates personal gain to service and the public trust. The accountant must also be objective. **Objectivity** means that he or she is impartial and intellectually honest. Furthermore, the accountant must be independent. **Independence** is the avoidance of all relationships that impair or appear to impair the objectivity of the accountant. One way in which an auditor of a company upholds independence is by having no direct financial interest in that company and not being an employee of the company. The accountant must exercise **due care** in all activities, carrying out professional responsibilities with competence and diligence. For example, an accountant must not accept a job for which he or she is not qualified, even at the risk of losing a client to another firm; and careless work is not acceptable. These broad principles are supported by more specific rules that accountants must follow (for instance, with certain exceptions, client information must be kept confidential). Accountants who violate the rules may be disciplined or suspended from the practice of accounting.

Accounting Firms. Certified public accountants offer their services to the public for a fee, just as doctors or lawyers do. Accounting firms are made up of partners, who must be CPAs, and staff accountants, many of whom are CPAs and hope to become partners someday. Accounting firms vary in size from large international firms with hundreds of partners and thousands of employees (see Table 1-2) to small one- or two-person firms.

The work of the public accountant is varied, complex, and interesting. Most accounting firms organize themselves into several principal areas of specialization, which may include (1) auditing, (2) tax services, (3) management advisory services, and (4) small business services.

Auditing. The most important and distinctive function of a certified public accountant is **auditing** (also called the **attest function**), which is the examination and testing of financial statements. Society relies heavily on the auditing function for credible financial reports. All public corporations and many companies that apply for sizable loans must

	Home	
Firm	**Office**	**Some Major Clients**
Arthur Andersen & Co.	Chicago	ITT, Texaco, United Airlines
Coopers & Lybrand	New York	AT&T, Ford
Deloitte, Haskins & Sells*	New York	General Motors, Procter & Gamble
Ernst & Young	New York	Mobil, McDonald's, Coca-Cola
KPMG Peat Marwick Mair	New York	General Electric, Xerox
Price Waterhouse	New York	IBM, Exxon, DuPont
Touche Ross & Co.*	New York	Chrysler, Boeing, Sears
Lavanthol & Horwath	Philadelphia	Lorimar, Giant Food, Reebok
Grant Thornton	Chicago	Fretter, Grainger Home Shopping Network

Table 1-2. Accounting's Large International Certified Public Accounting Firms

* Merger discussions in progress at time of publication

have their financial statements and records audited by an independent certified public accountant.

An audit's purpose is to give the auditor's professional opinion as to whether the company's financial reports fairly present its financial position, operating results and cash flows. **Auditors** check and test the accounting records and controls as necessary to satisfy themselves about the quality of the financial statements. Auditors must prove cash balances, confirm physical inventories, and verify the amounts owed by customers. They must also decide if there are adequate controls and if the company's records are kept in accordance with accepted accounting practices. In the end, auditors must depend on their own judgment to reach an opinion about a company's financial reports. Their professional reputation is at stake because banks, investors, and creditors depend on the financial statements bearing the auditor's opinions in buying and selling the company's stocks, making loans, and extending credit.

Tax Services. In the area of **tax services,** public accountants assist businesses and individuals in preparing tax returns and complying with tax laws. They also help plan business decisions to reduce taxes in the future. Tax accounting work calls for specific knowledge and skill regardless of the size of a business. Few business decisions are without tax effects.

Management Advisory Services. An increasingly important part of most public accounting firms' practice is **management advisory services,** or consulting. With their intimate knowledge of a business's operations, auditors can make important suggestions for improvements and, as a matter of course, usually do. In the past, these recommendations have dealt mainly with accounting records, budgeting, and cost accounting. But in the last few years they have expanded into marketing, organizational planning, personnel and recruiting, production, and many other business areas. The wide use of computers has led to services in systems design and control and to the use of mathematical and statistical decision models. All these different services combined make up management advisory services.

Small Business Services. Many small businesses look to their CPAs for advice on operating their businesses and keeping their accounting records. Although small CPA firms have traditionally performed these functions, large firms are also establishing small business practice units. Among the types of services a CPA might provide are setting up or revising an accounting system, compiling monthly financial statements, preparing a budget of cash needs over the coming year, and assisting the client in obtaining a bank loan.

Government and Other Not-for-Profit Accounting

Agencies and departments at all levels of government hire accountants to prepare reports so that officials can responsibly carry out their duties. Millions of income, payroll, and sales tax returns must be checked and audited. The Federal Bureau of Investigation and the Internal Revenue Service use thousands of accountants. The General Accounting Office audits government activities for Congress, using many auditors and other accounting specialists all over the world. Federal agencies such as the Securities and Exchange Commission, Interstate Commerce Commission, and Federal Communications Commission hire accountants. State agencies such as those dealing with public utilities regulation or tax collection also use the services of accountants.

Many other not-for-profit enterprises employ accountants. Some of these organizations are hospitals, colleges, universities, and foundations. These institutions, like the government, are interested in compliance with the law and efficient use of public resources. They account for over 25 percent of the gross output of our economy. Clearly, the role of accountants in helping these organizations use their resources wisely is important to our society.

Accounting Education

Training new accountants is a challenging and rewarding career, and today instructors of accounting are in great demand. Accounting instructors at the secondary level must have a college degree with a major in accounting and must meet state teacher certification requirements. One entry-level requirement for teaching at the smaller and two-year college level is the master's degree. Faculty members at most larger universities must have a Ph.D. degree and engage in research. In many schools, holding the CPA, CMA, or **CIA (Certified Internal Auditor)** certificate will help an instructor to advance professionally.

Chapter Review

Review of Learning Objectives

1. **Define accounting and describe its role in making informed decisions.**
   Accounting is an information system that measures, processes, and communicates information, primarily financial in nature, about an identifiable entity for the purpose of making economic decisions. It is not an end in itself but is a tool to be used in providing information that is useful in making reasoned choices among alternative uses of scarce resources in the conduct of business and economic activities.

2. **Identify the many users of accounting information in society.**
   Accounting plays a significant role in society by providing information to managers of all institutions and to individuals with direct financial interest in those institutions, such as present or potential investors or creditors. Accounting information is also important to those with an indirect financial interest in the business, such as tax authorities, regulatory agencies, economic planners, and other groups.

3. **Distinguish between financial and management accounting, define generally accepted accounting principles (GAAP), and identify the organizations that influence GAAP.**
   Financial accounting refers to the development and use of accounting reports that are communicated to those external to the business organization as well as to management, whereas management accounting refers to the preparation of information primarily for internal use by management. Acceptable accounting practice at a particular time consists of those conventions, rules, and procedures that make up generally accepted accounting principles. GAAP are essential to the preparation and interpretation of financial accounting reports. Among the organizations that influence the formulation of GAAP are the American Institute of Certified Public Accountants, the Financial Accounting Standards Board, the Securities and Exchange Commission, and the Internal Revenue Service. Other organizations with an interest in accounting are the National Association of Accountants, the Financial Executives Institute, and the American Accounting Association.

4. **Explain the importance of business transactions, money measure, and separate entity to accounting measurement.**
   To make an accounting measurement, the accountant must determine what is to be measured, when the measurement should occur, what value should be placed on what is measured, and how what is measured should be classified. Generally accepted accounting principles define the objects of accounting measurement as business transactions, money measures, and separate entities. Relating these three concepts, financial accounting measures the business transactions of separate entities in terms of money measures.

5. **Identify the three basic forms of business organization.**
   The three basic forms of business organization are sole proprietorships, partnerships, and corporations. Sole proprietorships, which are formed

by one individual, and partnerships, which are formed by more than one individual, are not separate economic units from the legal standpoint. In accounting, however, they are treated separately. Corporations, whose ownership is represented by shares of stock, are separate entities for both legal and accounting purposes.

6. **Define financial position and show how it is affected by simple transactions.**
   Financial position is the economic resources belonging to a company and the claims against those resources at a point in time. Business transactions affect financial position by decreasing or increasing assets, liabilities, and/or owner's equity in such a way that the basic accounting equation (assets = liabilities + owner's equity) is always in balance.

7. **Identify the four basic financial statements.**
   Financial statements are the means by which accountants communicate the financial condition and activities of a business to those who have an interest in the business. The four basic financial statements are the balance sheet, the income statement, the statement of owner's equity, and the statement of cash flows.

8. **Describe accounting as a profession with ethical responsibilities and a wide career choice.**
   The people who provide accounting information to users make up the accounting profession. They may be management accountants, public accountants, or government or other not-for-profit accountants. All accountants are required to follow a code of professional ethics, the foundation of which is responsibility to the public. Accountants must act with integrity, objectivity, and independence, and they must exercise due care in all activities. Another career choice open to accountants is that of being accounting educators. Each type of accounting work is an important specialization and represents a challenging career.

Review of Concepts and Terminology

The following concepts and terms were introduced in this chapter:

(L.O. 6)   **Accounts:**   Labels used by accountants to accumulate amounts from similar transactions.

(L.O. 1)   **Accounting:**   An information system that measures, processes, and communicates financial information about an identifiable economic entity.

(L.O. 6)   **Accounting equation:**   Assets = liabilities + owner's equity, or, Owner's equity = assets − liabilities.

(L.C. 3)   **American Institute of Certified Public Accountants (AICPA):**   The professional association of CPAs.

(L.O. 6)   **Assets:**   Probable future economic benefits obtained or controlled by a particular entity as a result of past transactions or events.

(L.O. 8)   **Attest function:**   The examination and testing of financial statements by a certified public accountant. (Also called auditing.)

(L.O. 8)   **Auditing:**   The process of examining and testing the financial statements of a company in order to render an independent professional opinion as to

the fairness of their presentation. (Also described as attest function.)

(L.O. 8) **Auditors:** Independent certified public accountants who check and test the accounting records and controls of a business as necessary in determining the quality of the financial statements of the business.

(L.O. 7) **Balance sheet:** The financial statement that shows the assets, liabilities, and owner's equity of a business at a point in time.

(L.O. 1) **Bookkeeping:** The means by which transactions are recorded and records are kept.

(L.O. 4) **Business transactions:** Economic events that affect the financial position of the business entity.

(L.O. 8) **Certified internal auditor (CIA):** Professional certification for auditors who carry out their work from within a company.

(L.O. 8) **Certified management accountant (CMA):** Professional certification awarded qualified management accountants by the Institute of Certified Management Accountants.

(L.O. 8) **Certified public accountant (CPA):** Public accountant who has met stringent licensing requirements as set by the individual states.

(L.O. 1) **Computer:** An electronic tool for the rapid collection, organization, and communication of large amounts of information.

(L.O. 1) **Control:** The process of seeing that plans are carried out.

(L.O. 5) **Corporation:** A body of persons granted a charter legally recognizing it as a separate entity having its own rights, privileges, and liabilities distinct from those of its owners.

(L.O. 8) **Due care:** The act of carrying out professional responsibilities with competence and diligence.

(L.O. 6) **Equity:** The residual interest in the assets of an entity that remains after deducting its liabilities.

(L.O. 8) **Ethics:** The application of a code of conduct, addressing whether actions are good or bad, right or wrong, to everyday life.

(L.O. 1) **Evaluation:** The examination of the entire decision system with a view to improving it.

(L.O. 6) **Expenses:** Decreases in owner's equity that result from operating the business.

(L.O. 3) **Financial accounting:** Accounting information that is communicated to those outside the organization for their use in evaluating the entity as well as being used internally.

(L.O. 3) **Financial Accounting Standards Board (FASB):** Body that has responsibility for developing and issuing rules on accounting practice; issues Statements of Financial Accounting Standards.

(L.O. 6) **Financial position:** The economic resources belonging to a company and the claims against those resources at a point in time.

(L.O. 7) **Financial statements:** The primary means of communicating important accounting information to users.

(L.O. 3) **Generally accepted accounting principles (GAAP):** The conventions, rules, and procedures necessary to define accepted accounting practice at a particular time.

(L.O. 3)   **Government Accounting Standards Board (GASB):**   Board established in 1984 under the same governing body as FASB with responsibility for issuing accounting standards for state and local governments.

(L.O. 7)   **Income statement:**   The financial statement that summarizes the amount of revenues earned and expenses incurred by a business entity over a period of time.

(L.O. 8)   **Independence:**   The avoidance of all relationships that impair or appear to impair the objectivity of the accountant.

(L.O. 8)   **Integrity:**   An accountant exhibits integrity when he or she is honest and candid and subordinates personal gain to service and the public trust.

(L.O. 3)   **Internal Revenue Service (IRS):**   Federal agency that interprets and enforces the U.S. tax laws governing the assessment and collection of revenue for operating the government.

(L.O. 6)   **Liabilities:**   Probable future sacrifices of economic benefits arising from present obligations of a particular entity to transfer assets or provide services to other entities in the future as a result of past transactions or events.

(L.O. 2)   **Liquidity:**   Having enough funds on hand to pay debts when they are due.

(L.O. 2)   **Management:**   The group of people in a business who have overall responsibility for operating the business and for achieving the company's goals.

(L.O. 3, 8)   **Management accounting:**   Accounting information for the internal use of a company's management.

(L.O. 8)   **Management advisory services:**   Consulting services, offered by public accountants.

(L.O. 1)   **Management information system:**   The interconnected subsystems that provide the information necessary to operate a business.

(L.O. 4)   **Money measure:**   The recording of all business transactions in the form of money.

(L.O. 6)   **Net assets:**   Owner's equity, or assets minus liabilities.

(L.O. 6)   **Net income (loss):**   Revenues minus expenses.

(L.O. 8)   **Objectivity:**   The act of being impartial and intellectually honest.

(L.O. 6)   **Owner's equity:**   The claims by the owner against the assets of the business.

(L.O. 6)   **Owner's investments:**   The assets that the owner puts into a business.

(L.O. 6)   **Owner's withdrawals:**   The assets that the owner takes out of a business.

(L.O. 5)   **Partnership:**   An association of two or more persons to carry on as co-owners of a business for profit.

(L.O. 1)   **Planning:**   The process of formulating a course of action.

(L.O. 8)   **Professional ethics:**   The application of a code of conduct to the practice of a profession.

(L.O. 2)   **Profitability:**   The ability to earn enough income to attract and hold investment capital.

(L.O. 8)   **Public accounting:**   The field of accounting that offers services in auditing, taxes, and management advising to the public for a fee.

(L.O. 6)   **Revenues:**   Increases in owner's equity that result from operating the business.

(L.O. 3)   **Securities and Exchange Commission (SEC):**   An agency of the federal government that has the legal power to set and enforce accounting practices for firms reporting to it.

(L.O. 4)   **Separate entity:**   The concept that treats a business as distinct and apart from its creditors, customers, and owners.

(L.O. 5)   **Sole proprietorship:**   A business owned by one person.

(L.O. 7)   **Statement of cash flows:**   The financial statement that shows the inflows and outflows of cash from operating activities, investing activities, and financing activities over a period of time.

(L.O. 7)   **Statement of owner's equity:**   The financial statement that shows the changes in the owner's capital account over a period of time.

(L.O. 8)   **Tax services:**   Services offered by public accountants in tax planning, compliance, and reporting.

Self-Test

Test your knowledge of the chapter by choosing the best answer for each item below.

1. Which of the following is an important reason for studying accounting?
   a. The information provided by accounting and accountants is useful in making many economic decisions.
   b. Accounting plays an important role in society.
   c. The study of accounting could lead to a challenging career.
   d. All of the above are important reasons.   *(L.O. 1)*

2. Which of the following groups uses accounting information for planning a company's profitability and liquidity?
   a. Management   c. Creditors
   b. Investors   d. Economic planners   *(L.O. 2)*

3. Generally accepted accounting principles
   a. define accounting practice at a point in time.
   b. are similar in nature to the principles of chemistry or physics.
   c. are rarely changed.
   d. are not affected by changes in the ways businesses operate.   *(L.O. 3)*

4. Economic events that affect the financial position of a business are called
   a. separate entities.   c. money measures.
   b. business transactions.   d. financial actions.   *(L.O. 4)*

5. Which of the following forms of organization is not treated as a separate economic unit in accounting?
   a. Sole proprietorship   c. Partnership
   b. Committee   d. Corporation   *(L.O. 5)*

6. If a company has liabilities of $19,000 and owner's equity of $57,000, the assets of the company are
   a. $38,000.   c. $57,000.
   b. $76,000.   d. $19,000.   *(L.O. 6)*

7. The payment of a liability will
    a. increase both assets and liabilities.
    b. increase assets and decrease liabilities.
    c. decrease assets and increase liabilities.
    d. decrease assets and decrease liabilities.   *(L.O. 6)*

8. The balance sheet is related to the income statement in the same way that
    a. a point in time is related to a period of time.
    b. a period of time is related to a point in time.
    c. a point in time is related to another point in time.
    d. a period of time is related to another period of time.   *(L.O. 7)*

9. Expenses and withdrawals appear, respectively, on which of the following financial statements?
    a. Balance sheet and income statement
    b. Income statement and balance sheet
    c. Statement of owner's equity and balance sheet
    d. Income statement and statement of owner's equity   *(L.O. 7)*

10. Auditing, tax services, and management consulting are services provided by
    a. government accountants.
    b. Certified Management Accountants.
    c. Certified Public Accountants.
    d. accounting educators.   *(L.O. 8)*

Answers to Self-Test are at the end of this chapter.

Review Problem
Effect of Transactions on the Accounting Equation

(L.O. 6)   Charlene Rudek finished law school in June and immediately set up her own law practice. During the first month of operation she completed the following transactions:

a. Began the law practice by placing $2,000 in a bank account established for the business.
b. Purchased a law library for $900 cash.
c. Purchased office supplies for $400 on credit.
d. Accepted $500 in cash for completing a contract.
e. Billed clients $1,950 for services rendered during the month.
f. Paid $200 of the amount owed for office supplies.
g. Received $1,250 in cash from one client who had been previously billed for services rendered.
h. Paid rent expense for the month in the amount of $1,200.
i. Withdrew $400 from the practice for personal use.

Required   Show the effect of each of these transactions on the balance sheet equation by completing a table similar to Exhibit 1-1 (page 23). Identify each owner's equity transaction.

Answer to Review Problem

	Cash	Accounts Receivable	Office Supplies	Law Library	Accounts Payable	Rudek, Capital	Type of OE Transaction
		Assets			= Liabilities +	Owner's Equity	
a.	$2,000					$2,000	Owner's Investment
b.	−900			+$900			
bal.	$1,100			$900		$2,000	
c.			+$400		+$400		
bal.	$1,100		$400	$900	$400	$2,000	
d.	+500					+500	Service Revenue
bal.	$1,600		$400	$900	$400	$2,500	
e.		+$1,950				+1,950	Service Revenue
bal.	$1,600	$1,950	$400	$900	$400	$4,450	
f.	−200				−200		
bal.	$1,400	$1,950	$400	$900	$200	$4,450	
g.	+1,250	−1,250					
bal.	$2,650	$ 700	$400	$900	$200	$4,450	
h.	−1,200					−1,200	Rent Expense
bal.	$1,450	$ 700	$400	$900	$200	$3,250	
i.	−400					−400	Owner's Withdrawal
bal.	$1,050	$ 700	$400	$900	$200	$2,850	

$3,050 $3,050

Chapter Assignments

Discussion Questions and Writing Assignments

1. Why is accounting considered an information system?
2. Distinguish among these terms: accounting, bookkeeping, and management information systems.
3. How are decisions made, and what is the role of accounting in the decision system?
4. What decision makers use accounting information?
5. What broad management objectives are facilitated by using accounting information?
6. Why are investors and creditors interested in the financial statements of a company?
7. Why has society as a whole become one of the biggest users of accounting information? What groups besides business managers, investors, and creditors use accounting information?
8. Define assets, liabilities, and owner's equity.
9. What four items affect owner's equity, and how?
10. Arnold Smith's company has assets of $22,000 and liabilities of $10,000. What is the amount of his owner's equity?
11. Give examples of the types of transactions that will (a) increase assets, and (b) increase liabilities.

12. Why is the balance sheet sometimes called the statement of financial position?
13. Contrast balance sheet purposes with those of the income statement.
14. How does the income statement differ from the statement of cash flows?
15. A statement for an accounting period that ends in June may have either (1) June 30, 19xx, or (2) For the Year Ended June 30, 19xx, as part of its identification. State which heading would be appropriate with (a) a balance sheet, and (b) an income statement.
16. What are some of the fields encompassed by the accounting profession?
17. What are some activities in which the management accountant might participate?
18. How is a public accountant different from a management accountant?
19. Describe in general terms the requirements that an individual must meet to become a CPA and the four major activities of CPAs.
20. How do sole proprietorships, partnerships, and corporations differ?
21. Accounting can be viewed as (a) an intellectual discipline, (b) a profession, or (c) a social force. In what sense is it each of these?
22. Compare and contrast the professional ethics of public accountants and management accountants as reflected by their respective codes of professional conduct.

Classroom Exercises

Exercise 1-1.
Role of Computer, Bookkeeper, and Accountant
(L.O. 1)

Jane, Judy, and Jud opened a clothing store earlier this year called The 3 Js. They began by opening a checking account in the name of the business, renting a store, and buying some clothes to sell. They paid for the purchases and expenses out of the checking account and deposited cash in the account when they sold the clothes. At this point, they are arguing over how their business is doing and how much each of them should be paid. They also realize that they are supposed to make certain tax reports and payments, but they know very little about them. The following statements are excerpts from their conversation:

Jane: If we just had a computer, we wouldn't have had this argument.
Judy: No, what we need is a bookkeeper.
Jud: I don't know, but maybe we need an accountant.

Distinguish among a computer, a bookkeeper, and an accountant, and comment on how each might help the operations of The 3 Js.

Exercise 1-2.
Users of Accounting Information
(L.O. 2)

Public companies report annually on their success or failure in making a net income or net loss. Suppose that the following item appeared in the newspaper:

New York. Commonwealth Power Company, a major electric utility, reported yesterday that its net income for the year just ended represented a 50 percent increase over the previous year. . . .

Explain why each of the following individuals or groups may be interested in seeing the accounting reports that support the above statement.

1. The management of Commonwealth Power
2. The stockholders of Commonwealth Power
3. The creditors of Commonwealth Power

4. Potential stockholders of Commonwealth Power
5. The Internal Revenue Service
6. The Securities and Exchange Commission
7. The electrical workers' union
8. A consumers' group called the Public Cause
9. An economic adviser to the president

Exercise 1-3.
The Accounting Equation
(L.O. 6)

Use the accounting equation to answer each question below. Show any calculations you make.

1. The assets of Newport Company are $650,000, and the owner's equity is $360,000. What is the amount of the liabilities?
2. The liabilities and owner's equity of Fitzgerald Company are $95,000 and $32,000, respectively. What is the amount of the assets?
3. The liabilities of Emerald Co. equal one-third of the total assets, and owner's equity is $120,000. What is the amount of the liabilities?
4. At the beginning of the year, Sherman Company's assets were $220,000, and its owner's equity was $100,000. During the year, assets increased $60,000, and liabilities decreased $10,000. What was the owner's equity at the end of the year?

Exercise 1-4.
Owner's Equity Transactions
(L.O. 6)

Identify the following transactions by type of owner's equity transaction by marking each as either an owner's investment (I), owner's withdrawal (W), revenue (R), expense (E), or not an owner's equity transaction (NOE).

a. Received cash for providing a service.
b. Took assets out of business for personal use.
c. Received cash from a customer previously billed for a service.
d. Transferred assets to the business from a personal account.
e. Paid service station for gasoline.
f. Performed a service and received a promise of payment.
g. Paid cash to purchase equipment.
h. Paid cash to employee for services performed.

Exercise 1-5.
Effect of Transactions on Accounting Equation
(L.O. 6)

During the month of April, Grissom Co. had the following transactions:

a. Paid salaries for April, $1,800.
b. Purchased equipment on credit, $3,000.
c. Purchased supplies with cash, $100.
d. Additional investment by owner, $4,000.
e. Received payment for services performed, $600.
f. Paid for part of equipment previously purchased on credit, $1,000.
g. Billed customers for services performed, $1,600.
h. Withdrew cash, $1,500.
i. Received payment from customers billed previously, $300.
j. Received utility bill, $70.

On a sheet of paper, list the letters a through j, with columns for Assets, Liabilities, and Owner's Equity. In the columns, indicate whether each transaction caused an increase (+), a decrease (−), or no change (NC) in assets, liabilities, and owner's equity.

Exercise 1-6.
Examples of
Transactions
(L.O. 6)

For each of the following categories, describe a transaction that will have the required effect on the elements of the accounting equation.

1. Increase one asset and decrease another asset.
2. Decrease an asset and decrease a liability.
3. Increase an asset and increase a liability.
4. Increase an asset and increase owner's equity.
5. Decrease an asset and decrease owner's equity.

Exercise 1-7.
Effect of
Transactions on
Accounting
Equation
(L.O. 6)

The total assets and liabilities at the beginning and end of the year for Pizarro Company are listed below.

	Assets	Liabilities
Beginning of the year	$110,000	$ 45,000
End of the year	200,000	120,000

Determine Pizarro Company's net income for the year under each of the following alternatives:

1. The owner made no investments in the business or withdrawals from the business during the year.
2. The owner made no investments in the business, but the owner withdrew $22,000 during the year.
3. The owner made an investment of $13,000, but made no withdrawals during the year.
4. The owner made an investment of $10,000, and withdrew $22,000 during the year.

Exercise 1-8.
Identification of
Accounts
(L.O. 6, 7)

Indicate below whether each account is an asset (A), a liability (L), or a part of owner's equity (OE):

_____ a. Cash
_____ b. Salaries Payable
_____ c. Accounts Receivable
_____ d. J. Johnson, Capital

_____ e. Land
_____ f. Accounts Payable
_____ g. Supplies

Indicate below whether each account would be shown on the income statement (IS), the Statement of Owner's Equity (OE), or the Balance Sheet (BS):

_____ h. Repair Revenue
_____ i. Automobile
_____ j. Fuel Expense
_____ k. Cash

_____ l. Rent Expense
_____ m. Accounts Payable
_____ n. J. Johnson, Withdrawals

Exercise 1-9.
Preparation of
Balance Sheet
(L.O. 7)

Appearing in random order below are the balances for balance sheet items for Herron Company as of December 31, 19xx.

Accounts Payable	$ 40,000	Accounts Receivable	$50,000
Building	90,000	Cash	20,000
T. Herron, Capital	170,000	Equipment	40,000
Supplies	10,000		

Sort the balances and prepare a balance sheet similar to the one in Exhibit 1-2.

Exercise 1-10.
Accounting
Abbreviations
(L.O. 3, 8)

Identify the accounting meaning of each of the following abbreviations: AICPA, SEC, GAAP, FASB, IRS, GASB, IASC, IFAC, NAA, FEI, AAA, CMA, CPA, and CIA.

Exercise 1-11.
Completion of
Financial
Statements
(L.O. 7)

Determine the amounts corresponding to the letters by completing the following independent sets of financial statements:

Income Statement	Set A	Set B	Set C
Revenues	$ 550	$ g	$120
Expenses	a	2,600	m
Net Income	$ b	$ h	$ 40
Statement of Owner's Equity			
Beginning Balance	$1,450	$ 7,700	$100
Net Income	c	800	n
Investments (Withdrawals)	(100)	i	o
Ending Balance	$1,500	$ j	$ p
Balance Sheet			
Total Assets	$ d	$10,500	$ q
Liabilities	$ 800	$ 2,500	$ r
Owner's Equity	e	k	140
Total Liabilities and Owner's Equity	$ f	$ l	$240

Exercise 1-12.
Preparation of
Financial
Statements
(L.O. 7)

Kingsley Company engaged in the following activities during 19x1: Service Revenues, $26,400; Rent Expense, $2,400; Wages Expense, $16,540; Advertising Expense, $2,700; Utility Expense, $1,800; and Walter Kingsley, Withdrawals, $1,400. In addition, the year-end balances of selected accounts were as follows: Cash, $3,100; Accounts Receivable, $1,500; Supplies, $200; Land, $2,000; Accounts Payable, $900; and Walter Kingsley, Capital, $4,340.

Prepare in good form the Income Statement, Statement of Owner's Equity, and Balance Sheet for Kingsley Company for 19x1 (assume December 31 year end). **Hint:** The amount given for Walter Kingsley, Capital is the beginning balance.

Exercise 1-13.
Professional
Ethics
(L.O. 8)

Discuss the ethical choices you would face in the situations below. In each case, determine the alternative courses of action, describe the ethical dilemmas, and tell what you would do.

a. You are the payroll accountant for a small business. A friend asks you how much the hourly pay of another employee in the business is.

b. As an accountant for the branch office of a wholesale supplier, you become aware of several instances when the branch manager has submitted the receipts from "nights out" with his spouse for reimbursement as selling expense by the home office.

c. You are an accountant in the purchasing department of a construction company. Upon arriving home from work on December 22, you find a large ham in a box marked "Happy Holidays—It's a pleasure to work with you." You note the gift is from a supplier who has bid on a contract to be awarded by your employer next week.

d. As an auditor with one year's experience at a local CPA firm, you are expected to complete a certain part of an audit in 20 hours. Due to your lack of experience, you cannot finish the job within this timeframe. Rather than admit this, you are thinking of working late to finish the job, but not telling anyone about it.

e. You are a tax accountant at a local CPA firm. You assist your neighbor in filling out her tax return. She pays you $200 in cash. Since there is no record of this transaction, you are considering not reporting it on your tax return.

f. The accounting firm for which you work as a CPA has just gained a new client in which you own 200 shares of stock that you received as an inheritance from your grandmother. Since it is only a small number of shares and you think the company will be very successful, you are thinking of not disclosing the investment.

Interpreting Accounting Information

Merrill Lynch & Co.*
(L.O. 6)

Merrill Lynch & Co. is a United States-based global financial services firm. Condensed and adapted balance sheets for 1986 and 1987 from the company's annual report are presented on the following page. (All numbers are in thousands.) The owner's equity section has been adapted for use in this case.

Three students who were looking at Merrill Lynch's annual report were overheard to make the following comments:

Student A: What a superb year Merrill Lynch & Co. had in 1987! The company earned a net income of $1,810,198, because total assets increased by that amount ($55,192,646 − $53,382,448).

Student B: But the change in total assets is not the same as net income! The company had a net income of $546,636, because cash increased by that amount ($2,838,642 − $2,292,006).

Student C: I see from the annual report that Merrill Lynch paid cash dividends of $105,097 in 1987. Don't you have to take this fact into consideration when analyzing the company's performance? (**Note:** For a corporation, cash dividends are similar to withdrawals in a sole proprietorship.)

Required

1. Comment on the interpretation of students A and B and answer student C's question.
2. Calculate the 1987 net income for Merrill Lynch & Co. from the information given.

* Excerpts from the 1986 and 1987 annual reports used by permission of Merrill Lynch & Co. Copyright © 1986 and 1987.

Merrill Lynch & Co.
Condensed Balance Sheets
December 31, 1987 and 1986

	1987	1986
Assets		
Cash	$ 2,838,642	$ 2,292,006
Marketable Securities	14,521,263	15,094,492
Accounts Receivable	32,528,726	32,254,252
Property and Equipment	1,702,878	1,359,105
Other Assets	3,601,137	2,382,593
Total Assets	$55,192,646	$53,382,448
Liabilities		
Short-Term Liabilities	$29,400,904	$28,675,057
Long-Term Liabilities	5,261,207	4,786,874
Other Liabilities	17,199,664	17,045,003
Total Liabilities	$51,861,775	$50,506,934
Owner's Equity		
Merrill Lynch, Capital	3,330,871	2,875,514
Total Liabilities and Owner's Equity	$55,192,646	$53,382,448

Problem Set A

Problem 1A-1.
Effect of Transactions on the Balance Sheet Equation
(L.O. 6)

Selected transactions for the Redmond Transport Company, begun on June 1 by Henry Redmond, are as follows:

a. Henry Redmond invests $66,000 in a new business called Redmond Transport Company.
b. A truck is purchased by the business for $43,000.
c. Equipment is purchased on credit for $9,000.
d. A fee of $1,200 for hauling goods is billed to a customer.
e. A fee of $2,300 for hauling goods is received in cash.
f. Cash of $600 is received from the customer who was billed in d.
g. A payment of $5,000 is made on the equipment purchased in c.
h. Expenses of $1,700 are paid in cash.
i. Cash of $1,200 is withdrawn from the business for Henry Redmond's personal use.

Required

1. Arrange the asset, liability, and owner's equity accounts in an equation similar to Exhibit 1-1, using the following account titles: Cash; Accounts Receivable; Truck; Equipment; Accounts Payable; and Henry Redmond, Capital.

2. Show by addition and subtraction, as in Exhibit 1-1, the effects of the transactions on the balance sheet equation. Show new balances after each transaction, and identify each owner's equity transaction by type.

Problem 1A-2.
Effect of
Transactions on
the Balance Sheet
Equation
(L.O. 6)

Carmen Vega, after receiving her degree in computer science, began her own business called Custom Systems Company. She completed the following transactions soon after starting the business:

a. Carmen began her business with a $9,000 cash investment, which she deposited in the bank, and a systems library, which cost $920.
b. Paid one month's rent on an office for her business. Rent is $360 per month.
c. Purchased a minicomputer for $7,000 cash.
d. Purchased computer supplies on credit, $600.
e. Collected revenue from a client, $800.
f. Billed a client $710 upon completion of a short project.
g. Paid expenses of $400.
h. Received $80 from the client billed previously.
i. Withdrew $250 in cash for personal expenses.
j. Paid $200 of amount owed on computer supplies purchased in **d**.

Required

1. Arrange the asset, liability, and owner's equity accounts in an equation similar to Exhibit 1-1, using the following account titles: Cash; Accounts Receivable; Supplies; Equipment; Systems Library; Accounts Payable; and Carmen Vega, Capital.
2. Show by addition and subtraction, as in Exhibit 1-1, the effects of the transactions on the balance sheet equation. Show new totals after each transaction, and identify each owner's equity transaction by type.

Problem 1A-3.
Effect of
Transactions on
the Balance Sheet
Equation
(L.O. 6)

Dr. Paul Rosello, psychologist, moved from his home town to set up an office in Cincinnati. After one month, the business had the following assets: Cash, $2,800; Accounts Receivable, $680; Office Supplies, $300; and Office Equipment, $7,500. Owner's Equity consisted of $8,680 of Capital. The Accounts Payable were $2,600 for purchases of office equipment on credit. During a short period of time, the following transactions were completed:

a. Paid one month's rent, $350.
b. Billed patient $60 for services rendered.
c. Paid $300 on office equipment previously purchased.
d. Paid for office supplies, $100.
e. Paid secretary's salary, $300.
f. Received $800 from patients not previously billed.
g. Made payment on accounts owed, $360.
h. Withdrew $500 for living expenses.
i. Paid telephone bill for current month, $70.
j. Received $290 from patients previously billed.
k. Purchased additional office equipment on credit, $300.

Required

1. Arrange the asset, liability, and owner's equity accounts in an equation similar to Exhibit 1-1, using the following account titles: Cash; Accounts Receivable; Office Supplies; Office Equipment; Accounts Payable; and Paul Rosello, Capital.

2. Enter the beginning balances of the assets, liabilities, and owner's equity into your equation.
3. Show by addition and subtraction, as in Exhibit 1-1, the effects of the transactions on the balance sheet equation. Show new totals after each transaction and identify each owner's equity transaction by type.

Problem 1A-4.
Preparation of
Financial
Statements
(L.O. 7)

At the end of October 19xx, the Cliff Young, Capital account had a balance of $37,300. After operating during November, his Sunnydale Riding Club had the following account balances:

Cash	S 8,700	Building	$30,000
Accounts Receivable	1,200	Horses	10,000
Supplies	1,000	Accounts Payable	17,800
Land	21,000		

In addition, the following transactions affected owner's equity:

Withdrawal by Cliff Young	$ 3,200	Salaries Expense	$2,300
Investment by Cliff Young	16,000	Feed Expense	1,000
Riding Lesson Revenue	6,200	Utility Expense	600
Locker Rental Revenue	1,700		

Required

Using Exhibit 1-2 as a model, prepare an income statement, a statement of owner's equity, and a balance sheet for Sunnydale Riding Club. (**Hint:** The final balance of Cliff Young, Capital is $54,100.)

Problem 1A-5.
Effect of
Transactions on
the Balance Sheet
Equation and
Preparation of
Financial
Statements
(L.O. 6, 7)

On April 1, 19xx, Dependable Taxi Service began operation and engaged in the following transactions during April:

a. Investment by owner, Madeline Curry, $42,000.
b. Purchase of taxi for cash, $19,000.
c. Purchase of uniforms on credit, $400.
d. Taxi fares received in cash, $3,200.
e. Paid wages to part-time drivers, $500.
f. Purchased gasoline during month for cash, $800.
g. Purchased car washes during month on credit, $120.
h. Further investment by owner, $5,000.
i. Paid part of the amount owed for the uniforms purchased on credit in c, $200.
j. Billed major client for fares, $900.
k. Paid for automobile repairs, $250.
l. Withdrew cash from business for personal use, $1,000.

Required

1. Arrange the asset, liability, and owner's equity accounts in an equation similar to Exhibit 1-1, using these account titles: Cash; Accounts Receivable; Uniforms; Taxi; Accounts Payable; and Madeline Curry, Capital.
2. Show by addition and subtraction, as in Exhibit 1-1, the effects of the transactions on the balance sheet equation. Show new balances after each transaction, and identify each owner's equity transaction by type.
3. Using Exhibit 1-2 as a guide, prepare an income statement, a statement of owner's equity, and a balance sheet for Dependable Taxi Service.

Problem Set B

Problem 1B-1.
Effect of
Transactions on
the Balance Sheet
Equation
(L.O. 6)

The Jiffy Messenger Company was founded by Hector Moreno on December 1 and engaged in the following transactions:

a. Hector Moreno began the business by placing $9,000 cash in a bank account established in the name of Jiffy Messenger Company.
b. Purchased a motor bike on credit, $3,100.
c. Purchased delivery supplies for cash, $200.
d. Billed customer for delivery fee, $100.
e. Received delivery fees in cash, $300.
f. Made payment on motor bike, $700.
g. Paid expenses, $120.
h. Received payment from customer billed in **d**, $50.
i. Withdrew cash for personal expenses, $150.

Required

1. Arrange the following asset, liability, and owner's equity accounts in an equation similar to Exhibit 1-1: Cash; Accounts Receivable; Delivery Supplies; Motor Bike; Accounts Payable; and Hector Moreno, Capital.
2. Show by addition and subtraction, as in Exhibit 1-1, the effects of the transactions on the balance sheet equation. Show new balances after each transaction and identify each owner's equity transaction by type.

Problem 1B-2.
Effect of
Transactions on
the Balance Sheet
Equation
(L.O. 6)

Frame-It Center was started by Brenda Kuzma in a small shopping center. In the first weeks, she completed the following transactions:

a. Deposited $7,000 in a bank account in the name of the company to start a business.
b. Paid current month's rent, $500.
c. Purchased store equipment on credit, $3,600.
d. Purchased framing supplies for cash, $1,700.
e. Received framing revenues, $800.
f. Billed customers for framing services, $700.
g. Paid utility expenses, $250.
h. Received payment from customers in **f**, $200.
i. Made payment on store equipment purchased in transaction **c**, $1,800.
j. Withdrew cash for personal expenses, $400.

Required

1. Arrange the following asset, liability, and owner's equity accounts in an equation similar to Exhibit 1-1: Cash; Accounts Receivable; Framing Supplies; Store Equipment; Accounts Payable; and Brenda Kuzma, Capital.
2. Show by addition and subtraction, as in Exhibit 1-1, the effects of the transactions on the balance sheet equation. Show new balances after each transaction, and identify each owner's equity transaction by type.

Problem 1B-3.
Effect of
Transactions on
the Balance Sheet
Equation
(L.O. 6)

After completing her Ph.D. in management, Delia Chan set up a consulting practice. At the end of her first month of operation, Dr. Chan had the following account balances: Cash, $2,930; Accounts Receivable, $1,400; Office Supplies, $270; Office Equipment, $4,200; Accounts Payable, $1,900; and Delia Chan, Capital, $6,900. Soon thereafter the transactions below and on the following page were completed:

a. Paid current month's rent, $400.
b. Made payment toward accounts payable, $450.

c. Billed clients for services performed, $800.
d. Received amount from clients billed last month, $1,000.
e. Purchased office supplies, $80.
f. Paid secretary's salary, $850.
g. Paid utility expense, $50.
h. Paid telephone expense, $50.
i. Purchased additional office equipment for cash, $400.
j. Received cash from clients for services performed, $1,200.
k. Withdrew cash for personal use, $500.

Required

1. Arrange the following asset, liability, and owner's equity accounts in an equation similar to Exhibit 1-1: Cash; Accounts Receivable; Office Supplies; Office Equipment; Accounts Payable; and Delia Chan, Capital.
2. Enter the beginning balances of the assets, liabilities, and owner's equity.
3. Show by addition and subtraction, as in Exhibit 1-1, the effects of the transactions on the balance sheet equation. Show new balances after each transaction, and identify each owner's equity transaction by type.

Problem 1B-4.
Preparation of Financial Statements
(L.O. 7)

At the end of its first month of operation, June 19xx, Lerner Plumbing Company had the following account balances:

Cash	$29,300	Tools	$3,800
Accounts Receivable	5,400	Accounts Payable	4,300
Delivery Truck	19,000		

In addition, during the month of June the following transactions affected owner's equity:

Investment by M. Lerner	$20,000	Repair Revenue	$2,800
Withdrawal by M. Lerner	2,000	Salaries Expense	8,300
Further investment by M. Lerner	30,000	Rent Expense	700
Contract Revenue	11,600	Fuel Expense	200

Required

Using Exhibit 1-2 as a model, prepare an income statement, a statement of owner's equity, and a balance sheet for Lerner Plumbing Company. (**Hint:** The final balance of M. Lerner, Capital is $53,200.)

Problem 1B-5.
Effect of Transactions on the Balance Sheet Equation and Preparation of Financial Statements
(L.O. 6, 7)

Royal Copying Service began operation and engaged in the following transactions during July 19xx:

a. Investment by owner, Linda Friedman, $5,000.
b. Paid current month's rent, $450.
c. Purchased copier, $2,500.
d. Copying jobs payments received in cash, $890.
e. Copying job billed to major customer, $680.
f. Paid cash for paper and other copier supplies, $190.
g. Paid wages to part-time employees, $280.
h. Purchased additional copier supplies on credit, $140.
i. Received partial payment from customer in **e**, $300.
j. Paid current month's utility bill, $90.

k. Made partial payment on supplies purchased in **h**, $70.

l. Withdrew cash for personal use, $700.

Required

1. Arrange the asset, liability, and owner's equity accounts in an equation similar to Exhibit 1-1, using these account titles: Cash; Accounts Receivable; Supplies; Copier; Accounts Payable; and L. Friedman, Capital.
2. Show by addition and subtraction, as in Exhibit 1-1, the effects of the transactions on the balance sheet equation. Show new balances after each transaction, and identify each owner's equity transaction by type.
3. Using Exhibit 1-2 as a guide, prepare an income statement, a statement of owner's equity, and a balance sheet for Royal Copying Service.

Financial Decision Case

Murphy Lawn Services Company (L.O. 6, 7)

Instead of hunting for a summer job after finishing her junior year in college, Beth Murphy organized a lawn service company in her neighborhood. To start her business on June 1, she deposited $2,700 in a new bank account in the name of her company. The $2,700 consisted of a $1,000 loan from her father and $1,700 of her own money.

Using the money in this checking account, she rented lawn equipment, purchased supplies, and hired neighborhood high school students to mow and trim the lawns of neighbors who had agreed to pay her for the service.

At the end of each month, she mailed bills to her customers. On September 30, Beth was ready to dissolve her business and go back to school for the fall quarter. Because she had been so busy, she had not kept any records other than her checkbook and a list of amounts owed to her by customers.

Her checkbook had a balance of $3,520, and the amount owed to her by the customers totaled $875. She expected these customers to pay her during October. She remembered that she could return unused supplies to the Lawn Care Center for a full credit of $50. When she brought back the rented lawn equipment, the Lawn Care Center would also return a deposit of $200 she had made in June. She owed the Lawn Care Center $525 for equipment rentals and supplies. In addition, she owed the students who had worked for her $100, and she still owed her father $700. Though Beth feels she did quite well, she is not sure just how successful she was.

Required

1. Prepare a balance sheet dated June 1 and one dated September 30 for Murphy Lawn Services Company.
2. Comment on the performance of Murphy Lawn Services Company by comparing the two balance sheets. Did the company have a profit or loss? (Assume Beth used none of the company's assets for personal purposes.)
3. If Beth is to continue her business next summer, what kind of information from her recordkeeping system would help make it easier to tell whether she is earning a profit or losing money?

Answers to Self-Test

1. d	3. a	5. b	7. d	9. d
2. a	4. b	6. b	8. a	10. c

LEARNING OBJECTIVES

1. Explain in simple terms the generally accepted ways of solving the measurement issues of recognition, valuation, and classification.
2. Define and use the terms account and general ledger.
3. Recognize commonly used asset, liability, and owner's equity accounts.
4. Define double-entry system and state the rules for debit and credit.
5. Apply the procedure for transaction analysis to simple transactions.
6. Record transactions in the general journal.
7. Explain the relationship of the general journal to the general ledger.
8. Prepare a trial balance and recognize its value and limitations.

CHAPTER 2

The Double-Entry System

In the last chapter you learned the answer to the question: What is to be measured? Chapter 2 opens with a discussion of these questions: When should the measurement occur? What value should be placed on the measurement? and How is the measurement to be classified? Then, as the focus shifts from accounting concepts to actual practice, you begin working with the double-entry system and applying it to the analysis and recording of business transactions. After studying this chapter, you should be able to meet the learning objectives listed on the left.

Measurement Issues

Business transactions were defined earlier as economic events that affect the financial position of a business entity. To measure a business transaction, the accountant must decide when the transaction occurred (the recognition issue), what value should be placed on the transaction (the valuation issue), and how the components of the transaction should be categorized (the classification issue).

These three issues—recognition, valuation, and classification—are the basis of almost every major issue in financial accounting today. They lie at the heart of such complex issues as accounting for pension plans, mergers of giant companies, international transactions, and the effects of inflation. In discussing the three basic issues, we follow generally accepted accounting principles and use an approach that promotes the understanding of the basic ideas of accounting. Keep in mind, however, that controversy does exist; and some solutions to the problems are not as cut and dried as they may appear.

The Recognition Issue

The **recognition** issue refers to the difficulty of deciding when a business transaction should be recorded. Often the facts of a situation are known, but there is disagreement as to *when* the events should be recorded. For instance, consider when to recognize or first record a simple purchase. A company orders, receives, and pays for an office desk. Which of the following actions constitutes a recordable event?

1. An employee sends a purchase requisition to the purchasing department.
2. The purchasing department sends a purchase order to the supplier.
3. The supplier ships the desk.
4. The company receives the desk.
5. The company receives the bill from the supplier.
6. The company pays the bill.

OBJECTIVE 1
Explain in simple terms the generally accepted ways of solving the measurement issues of recognition, valuation, and classification

The answer to this question is important because amounts in the financial statements are affected by the date on which the purchase is recorded. Accounting tradition provides for the transaction to be recorded when the title to the desk passes from supplier to purchaser and an obligation to pay results. Thus, depending on the details of the shipping agreement, the transaction is recognized at the time of either action 3 or action 4. This is the guideline that we will generally use in this book. However, in many small businesses that have simple accounting systems, the initial recording of the transaction occurs when the bill is received (action 5) or when the transfer of cash occurs (action 6) because these are the implied points of title transfer. The predetermined time at which a transaction is to be recorded is the **recognition point**.

The recognition problem is not always solved easily. Consider the case of an advertising agency that is asked by a client to prepare a major advertising campaign. People may work on the campaign several hours per day for a number of weeks. Value is added to the plan as the employees develop it. Should the amount of value added be recognized as the campaign is being produced or at the time it is completed? Normally, the increase in value is recorded at the time the plan is finished and the client is billed for it. However, if the plan will take a long period to develop, the agency and the client may agree that the client will be billed at key points during its development.

The Valuation Issue

The **valuation** issue is perhaps the most controversial issue in accounting. It concerns the difficulty of assigning a monetary value to a business transaction. Generally accepted accounting principles state that the appropriate valuation to assign to all business transactions, and therefore to all assets, liabilities, owner's equity, revenues, and expenses acquired by a business, is the original cost (often called historical cost). **Cost** is defined here as the exchange price associated with a business transaction at the point of recognition. According to this guideline, the purpose of accounting is not to account for "value," which may change after a transaction occurs, but to account for the cost or value at the time of the transaction. For example, the cost of assets is recorded when they are acquired, and their "value" is also held at that level until they are sold, expire, or are consumed. In this context, value in accounting means the cost at the time of the transaction. This practice is referred to by accountants as the **cost principle**.

Suppose that a person offers a building for sale at $120,000. It may be valued for real estate taxes at $75,000, and it may be insured for $90,000. One prospective buyer may offer $100,000 for the building, and another may offer $105,000. At this point, several different, unverifiable opinions of value have been expressed. Finally, the seller and a buyer may settle on a price and complete a sale for $110,000. All these figures are values of one kind or another, but only the last figure is sufficiently reliable to be used in the records. The market value of this building may vary over the years, but it will remain on the new buyer's records at $110,000 until it is sold again. At that point, the accountant would record the new transaction at the new exchange price, and a profit or loss would be recognized.

The cost principle is used because it meets the standard of verifiability. Cost is verifiable because it results from the actions of independent buyers and sellers who come to an agreement about price. This exchange price is an objective price that can be verified by evidence created at the time of the transaction. Both the buyer and the seller may have thought they got the better deal, but their opinions are irrelevant in recording cost. The final price of $110,000, verified by agreement of the two parties, is the price at which the transaction is recorded.

The Classification Issue

The **classification** issue is that of assigning all the transactions in which a business engages to the appropriate accounts. For example, a company's ability to borrow money may be affected by the way in which some of its debts are categorized. Or a company's income may be affected by whether purchases of small items such as tools are considered repair expenses or equipment (assets). Proper classification depends not only on the correct analysis of the effect of each transaction on the business enterprise but also on the maintenance of a system of accounts that will reflect that effect. The rest of this chapter explains the classification of accounts and the analysis and recording of transactions.

Accounts

OBJECTIVE 2
Define and use the terms account *and* general ledger

When large amounts of data are gathered in the measurement of business transactions, a method of storage is required. Business people should be able to retrieve transaction data quickly and in the form desired. In other words, there should be a filing system to sort out or classify all the transactions that occur in a business. Only in this way can financial statements and other reports be prepared quickly and easily. This filing system consists of accounts. An **account** is the basic storage unit for accounting data. An accounting system has separate accounts for each asset, each liability, and each component of owner's equity, including revenues and expenses. Whether a company keeps records by hand or by computer, management must be able to refer to these accounts so that it can study the company's financial history and plan for the future. A very small company may need only a few dozen accounts, whereas a multinational corporation will have thousands.

In a manual accounting system, each account is kept on a separate page or card. These pages or cards are placed together in a book or file.

This book or file, which contains the company's accounts, is called the **general ledger**. In a computer system, which most companies have today, the accounts are maintained on magnetic tapes or disks. However, as a matter of convenience, the accountant still refers to the group of company accounts as the general ledger, or simply, the **ledger**.

To be able to find an account in the ledger easily and to identify accounts, an accountant often numbers them. A list of these numbers with the corresponding account names is called a **chart of accounts**. A very simple chart of accounts appears in Exhibit 2-1. Note that the first digit refers to the major financial statement classifications. An account number beginning with the digit 1 is an asset, an account number beginning with a 2 is a liability, and so forth.

You will be introduced to these accounts in the following section and over the next two-and-a-half chapters through the illustrative case of the Joan Miller Advertising Agency. At this time, notice the gaps in the sequence of numbers. These gaps allow for expansion in the number of accounts. Of course, every company develops a chart of accounts for its own needs. Seldom will two companies have exactly the same chart of

Exhibit 2-1. Chart of Accounts for a Small Business

Assets		Liabilities	
Cash	111	Notes Payable	211
Notes Receivable	112	Accounts Payable	212
Accounts Receivable	113	Unearned Art Fees	213
Fees Receivable	114	Wages Payable	214
Art Supplies	115	Mortgage Payable	221
Office Supplies	116		
Prepaid Rent	117	**Owner's Equity**	
Prepaid Insurance	118	Joan Miller, Capital	311
Land	141	Joan Miller, Withdrawals	312
Buildings	142	Income Summary	313
Accumulated Depreciation,			
Buildings	143	**Revenues**	
Art Equipment	144	Advertising Fees Earned	411
Accumulated Depreciation,		Art Fees Earned	412
Art Equipment	145		
Office Equipment	146	**Expenses**	
Accumulated Depreciation,		Office Wages Expense	511
Office Equipment	147	Utility Expense	512
		Telephone Expense	513
		Rent Expense	514
		Insurance Expense	515
		Art Supplies Expense	516
		Office Supplies Expense	517
		Depreciation Expense,	
		Buildings	518
		Depreciation Expense,	
		Art Equipment	519
		Depreciation Expense,	
		Office Equipment	520

accounts, and larger companies will require more digits to accommodate all of their accounts. In keeping its records, each company should follow a consistent framework for its own chart of accounts.

Types of Commonly Used Accounts

OBJECTIVE 3
*Recognize
commonly used
asset, liability, and
owner's equity
accounts*

The specific accounts used by a company depend on the nature of the company's business. A steel company will have many equipment and inventory accounts, whereas an advertising agency may have only a few. Each company must design its accounts in a way that reflects the nature of its business and the needs of its management. There are, however, accounts that are common to most businesses. Some important ones are described in the following paragraphs.

Asset Accounts. A company must keep records of the increases and decreases in each asset that it owns. Some of the more common asset accounts are as follows:

Cash "Cash" is the title of the account used to record increases and decreases in cash. Cash consists of money or any medium of exchange that a bank will accept at face value for deposit. Included are coins, currency, checks, postal and express money orders, and money deposited in a bank or banks. The Cash account also includes cash on hand such as that in a cash register or a safe.

Notes Receivable A promissory note is a written promise to pay a definite sum of money at a fixed future date. Amounts due from others in the form of promissory notes are recorded in an account called Notes Receivable.

Accounts Receivable Companies often sell goods and services to customers on the basis of the customers' oral or implied promises to pay in the future, such as in thirty days or at the first of the month. These sales are called Credit Sales, or Sales on Account, and the promises to pay are known as Accounts Receivable. Credit sales increase Accounts Receivable, and collections from customers decrease Accounts Receivable. Of course, it is necessary to keep a record of how much each customer owes the company. How these records are kept is explained in Chapter 6.

Prepaid Expenses Companies often pay for goods and services before they receive or use them. These prepaid expenses are considered assets until they are used, or expire, at which time they become expenses. There should be a separate account for each prepaid expense. An example of a prepaid expense is Prepaid Insurance (or Unexpired Insurance). Insurance protection against fire, theft, and other hazards is usually paid in advance for a period of one to five years. When the premiums are paid, the Prepaid Insurance account is increased. These premiums expire day by day and month by month. Therefore, at intervals, usually at the end of the accounting period, Prepaid Insurance must be reduced by the amount of insurance that has expired. Another common type of prepaid expense is Office Supplies. Stamps, stationery, pencils, pens, paper, and other office supplies are assets when they are purchased and are recorded as an increase in Office Supplies. As the office supplies are used, the account is reduced. Other typical prepaid expenses that are assets when they are purchased and become expenses through use or the passage of time are prepaid rent (rent paid for more than one month in advance), store supplies, and prepaid taxes.

Land An account called Land is used to record purchases of property to be used in the ordinary operations of the business.

Buildings Purchases of structures to be used in the business are recorded in an account called Buildings. Although a building cannot be separated from the land it occupies, it is important to maintain separate accounts for the land and the building. The reason for doing so is that the building is subject to wear and tear, but the land is not. Later in the book the subject of depreciation will be introduced. Wear and tear is an important aspect of depreciation.

Equipment A company may own many different types of equipment. Usually there is a separate account for each type. Transactions involving desks, chairs, office machines, filing cabinets, and typewriters are recorded in an account called Office Equipment. Increases and decreases in cash registers, counters, showcases, shelves, and similar items are recorded in the Store Equipment account. When a company has a factory, it may own lathes, drill presses, and other equipment and would record changes in such items in an account titled Machinery and Equipment. Some companies may have use for a Trucks and Automobiles account.

Liability Accounts. Another word for *liability* is *debt*. Most companies have fewer liability accounts than asset accounts. But it is just as important to keep records of what the company owes as what it owns (assets). There are two types of liabilities: short-term and long-term. The distinction between them is introduced in Chapter 8. The following accounts are classified as liabilities:

Notes Payable The account called Notes Payable is the opposite of Notes Receivable. It is used to record increases and decreases in promissory note amounts owed to creditors within the next year or operating cycle.

Accounts Payable Similarly, Accounts Payable is the opposite of Accounts Receivable. It represents amounts owed to creditors on the basis of an oral or implied promise to pay. Accounts payable usually arise as the result of the purchase of merchandise, services, supplies, or equipment on credit. When Company A buys an item from Company B and promises to pay at the beginning of the month, the amount of the transaction is an Account Payable on Company A's books and an Account Receivable on Company B's books. As with Accounts Receivable, records of amounts owed to individual creditors must be known. Chapter 6 covers the method of accomplishing this task.

Other Short-Term Liabilities A few other liability accounts are Wages Payable, Taxes Payable, Rent Payable, and Interest Payable. Often customers make deposits on, or pay in advance for, goods and services to be delivered in the future. Such customers' deposits are also recorded as liabilities. They are liabilities because they represent claims by the customers for goods to be delivered or services to be performed. These kinds of liability accounts are often called Unearned Fees, Customer Deposits, Advances from Customers, or more commonly, Unearned Revenues.

Long-Term Liabilities The most common types of long-term liabilities are notes due in more than one year, bonds, and property mortgages. Because a wide variety of bonds and mortgages have been developed for special financing needs, it is difficult to classify them. They may or may not require the backing of certain of the company's assets for security. For example, a mortgage holder may have the right to force the sale of certain assets if the mortgage debt is not paid when due.

Owner's Equity Accounts. In Chapter 1, several transactions affected owner's equity. The effects of all these transactions were shown by the increases or decreases in the single column representing owner's equity (see Exhibit 1-1, page 23) with an indication of the type of each transaction. For legal and managerial reasons, it is important to sort these transactions into separate owner's equity accounts. Among the most important information that management receives for business planning is a detailed breakdown of revenues and expenses. For income tax reporting, financial reporting, and other reasons, the law requires that capital contributions and withdrawals be separated from revenues and expenses. Ownership and equity accounts, especially those for partnerships and corporations, are covered in much more detail in Part Four. For now, the following accounts, whose relationships are shown in Figure 2-1, are important to the study of sole proprietorships.

Capital Account When someone invests in his or her own company, the amount of the investment is recorded in a capital account. For instance, in Chapter 1 when John Shannon invested his personal resources in his firm, he recorded the amount in the owner's equity account titled John Shannon, Capital. Any additional investments by John Shannon in his firm would be recorded in this account.

Withdrawals Account A person who invests in a business usually expects to earn an income and to use at least part of the assets earned from profitable operations to pay personal living expenses. Since the income for a business is determined at the end of the accounting period, the owner often finds it necessary to withdraw assets from the business for living expenses long before income has been determined. We do not describe these withdrawals as salary, although the owner might think of them as such, because there is no change in the ownership of the money withdrawn. We say, simply, that the owner has withdrawn assets for personal use. As a result, it has become common practice to set up a withdrawals account to record these payments, which are made with the expectation of earning an income. For example, an account called John Shannon, Withdrawals, would be used to record John Shannon's withdrawals from his firm. In practice, the withdrawals account often

Figure 2-1. Relationships of Owner's Equity Accounts

goes by several other names. Among these other titles are Personal and Drawing. This account is not used by corporations.

Revenue and Expense Accounts Revenues increase owner's equity, and expenses decrease owner's equity. The greater the revenues, the more the owner's equity is increased. The greater the expenses, the more the owner's equity is decreased. Of course, when revenues are greater than expenses, the company has earned a profit or net income. When expenses are more than revenues, the company has suffered a loss or net loss. Management's major goal is to earn net income, and an important function of accounting is to give management the information that will help it meet this goal. One way of doing this is to have a ledger account for every revenue and expense item. From these accounts, which are included on the income statement, management can identify exactly the source of all revenues and the nature of all expenses. A particular company's revenue and expense accounts will depend on its kind of business and the nature of its operations. A few of the revenue accounts used in this book are Commissions Earned, Advertising Fees Earned, and Sales. Some of the expense accounts are Wages Expense, Supplies Expense, Rent Expense, and Advertising Expense.

Titles of Accounts

The names of accounts are often confusing to beginning accounting students because some of the words are new or have technical meanings. It is also true that the same asset, liability, or owner's equity account may have different names in different companies. This fact is not so strange. People too are often called different names by their friends, families, and associates.

Similarly, long-term assets may be known in various contexts as Fixed Assets, Plant and Equipment, Capital Assets, Long-Lived Assets, and so forth. Even the most acceptable names change over a period of time in accounting, and by habit some companies may use names that are out of date. In general, the account title should describe what is recorded in the account. When you encounter an account title that you do not recognize, you should examine the context of the name—whether it is classified as asset, liability, owner's equity, revenue, or expense on the financial statements—and look for the kind of transaction that gave rise to the account.

The Double-Entry System: The Basic Method of Accounting

OBJECTIVE 4
Define double-entry system *and state the rules for debit and credit*

The double-entry system, the backbone of accounting, evolved during the Renaissance. The first systematic presentation of double-entry bookkeeping appeared in 1494, two years after Columbus discovered America. It was described in a mathematics book written by Fra Luca Pacioli, a Franciscan monk who was a friend of Leonardo da Vinci. Goethe, the famous German poet and dramatist, referred to double-entry bookkeeping as "one of the finest discoveries of the human intellect." Werner Sombart, an eminent economist-sociologist, expressed the belief that "double-entry bookkeeping is born of the same spirit as the system of Galileo and Newton."

What is the significance of the double-entry system for accounting? The double-entry system is based on the principle of duality, which means that all events of economic importance have two aspects—effort and reward, sacrifice and benefit, sources and uses—that offset or balance each other. In the **double-entry system** each transaction must be recorded with at least one debit and one credit, in such a way that the total dollar amount of debits and the total dollar amount of credits equal each other. Because of the way it is designed, the whole system is always in balance. All accounting systems, no matter how sophisticated, are based on this principle of duality. The T account is a helpful place to begin the study of the double-entry system.

The T Account

In its simplest form, an account has three parts: (1) a title, which describes the asset, liability, or owner's equity account; (2) a left side, which is called the **debit** side; and (3) a right side, which is called the **credit** side. This form of the account, called a **T account** because it resembles the letter *T*, is used to analyze transactions. It appears as follows:

Title of Account

Left or Debit Side	Right or Credit Side

Thus any entry made on the left side of the account is a debit, or debit entry, and any entry made on the right side of the account is a credit, or credit entry. The terms *debit* (abbreviated Dr., from the Latin *debere*) and *credit* (abbreviated Cr., from the Latin *credere*) are simply the accountant's words for "left" and "right" (not for "increase" or "decrease"). A more formal version of the T account will be presented later in this chapter.

The T Account Illustrated

In Chapter 1, Shannon Realty had several transactions that involved the receipt or payment of cash. (See Exhibit 1-1, page 23, for a summary of the numbered transactions given below.) These transactions can be summarized in the Cash account by recording receipts on the left or debit side of the account and payments on the right or credit side of the account as follows:

	Cash		
(1)	50,000	(2)	35,000
(5)	1,500	(4)	200
(7)	1,000	(8)	1,000
		(9)	400
		(11)	600
	52,500		37,200
Bal.	15,300		

The cash receipts on the left have been totaled as $52,500, and this total is written in small-size figures so that it will not be confused with an actual debit entry. The cash payments are totaled in a similar way on the right side. These figures are simply working totals called **footings**. Footings are calculated at the end of the month as an easy way to determine cash on hand. The difference in dollars between the total debit footings and the total credit footings is called the **balance** or **account balance**. If the balance is a debit, it is written on the left side. If it is a credit, it is written on the right. Notice that Shannon Realty's Cash account has a debit balance of $15,300 ($52,500 − $37,200). This amount represents Shannon's cash on hand at the end of the month.

Analysis of Transactions

The rules of double-entry bookkeeping are that every transaction affects at least two accounts. In other words, there must be one or more accounts debited and one or more accounts credited, and the total dollar amount of the debits must equal the total dollar amount of the credits.

When we look at the accounting equation

$$\text{Assets} = \text{liabilities} + \text{owner's equity}$$

we can see that if a debit increases assets, then a credit must be used to increase liabilities or owner's equity. On the other hand, if a credit decreases assets, then a debit must be used to show a decrease in liabilities or owner's equity. These rules are opposite because assets are on the opposite side of the equation from liabilities and owner's equity. These rules can be shown as follows:

Assets		=	Liabilities		+	Owner's Equity	
Debit for Increases	Credit for Decreases		Debit for Decreases	Credit for Increases		Debit for Decreases	Credit for Increases

1. Increases in assets are debited to asset accounts. Decreases in assets are credited to asset accounts.
2. Increases in liabilities and owner's equity are credited to liability and owner's equity accounts. Decreases in liabilities and owner's equity are debited to liability and owner's equity accounts.

One of the more difficult points to understand is the application of these rules to the owner's equity components of revenues, expenses, and withdrawals. Since revenues increase owner's equity and expenses and withdrawals decrease it, the following relationships hold:

Owner's Equity

Decrease (Debits)	Increases (Credits)

Expenses		**Revenues**	
Increases (Debits)	Decreases (Credits)	Decreases (Debits)	Increases (Credits)

Withdrawals	
Increases (Debits)	Decreases (Credits)

Thus, a transaction that increases revenues by a credit also increases owner's equity by a credit. However, expenses and withdrawals, which are *increased* by debits, *decrease* owner's equity. In other words, the more expenses and withdrawals are *increased* by debits, the more these debits *decrease* owner's equity; and the more expenses and withdrawals are *decreased* by credits, the more these credits *increase* owner's equity. The reason for these effects is that expenses and withdrawals are a component of owner's equity, which is on the right hand side of the accounting equation.

At this point we can explain how to analyze transactions. Transactions are usually supported by some kind of document, such as an invoice, a receipt, a check, or a contract. These source documents provide the basis for analyzing each transaction. As an example, let us suppose that Jones Company borrows $1,000 from its bank on a promissory note. The procedure is as follows:

1. Analyze the effect of the transaction on assets, liabilities, and owner's equity. In this case, both an asset (Cash) and a liability (Notes Payable) were increased.
2. Apply the correct double-entry rule. Increases in assets are recorded by debits. Increases in liabilities are recorded by credits.
3. Make the entry. The increase in assets is recorded by a debit to the Cash account, and the increase in liabilities is recorded by a credit to the Notes Payable account.

Cash		Notes Payable	
1,000			1,000

The debit to Cash of $1,000 equals the credit to Notes Payable of $1,000.

Another form of this entry, which will be explained later in this chapter, is as follows:

	Dr.	Cr.
Cash	1,000	
Notes Payable		1,000

Transaction Analysis Illustrated

OBJECTIVE 5
Apply the procedure for transaction analysis to simple transactions

The next few pages consist of the transactions for the Joan Miller Advertising Agency during the month of January. We will use the following transactions to illustrate the principle of duality and to show how transactions are recorded in the accounts.

January 1: Joan Miller invested $10,000 to start her own advertising agency.

Cash	
Jan. 1 10,000	

Joan Miller, Capital	
	Jan. 1 10,000

Transaction: Investment in business.
Analysis: Assets increased. Owner's equity increased.
Rules: Increases in assets are recorded by debits. Increases in owner's equity are recorded by credits.
Entry: Increase in assets is recorded by a debit to Cash. Increase in owner's equity is recorded by a credit to Joan Miller, Capital.

	Dr.	Cr.
Cash	10,000	
Joan Miller, Capital		10,000

If Joan Miller had invested assets other than cash in the business, the appropriate asset accounts would be debited.

January 2: Rented an office, paying two months' rent in advance, $800.

Cash

| Jan. 1 | 10,000 | Jan. 2 | 800 |

Prepaid Rent

| Jan. 2 | 800 | |

Transaction: Expense paid in advance.
Analysis: Assets increased. Assets decreased.
Rules: Increases in assets are recorded by debits. Decreases in assets are recorded by credits.
Entry: Increase in assets is recorded by a debit to Prepaid Rent. Decrease in assets is recorded by a credit to Cash.

	Dr.	Cr.
Prepaid Rent	800	
Cash		800

January 3: Ordered art supplies, $1,800, and office supplies, $800.

Analysis: No entry is made because no transaction has occurred. According to the recognition issue, there is no liability until the supplies are shipped or received and there is an obligation to pay for them.

January 4: Purchased art equipment for $4,200 cash.

Cash

| Jan. 1 | 10,000 | Jan. 2 | 800 |
| | | 4 | 4,200 |

Art Equipment

| Jan. 4 | 4,200 | |

Transaction: Purchase of equipment.
Analysis: Assets increased. Assets decreased.
Rules: Increases in assets are recorded by debits. Decreases in assets are recorded by credits.
Entry: Increase in assets is recorded by a debit to Art Equipment. Decrease in assets is recorded by a credit to Cash.

	Dr.	Cr.
Art Equipment	4,200	
Cash		4,200

January 5: Purchased office equipment from Morgan Equipment for $3,000, paying $1,500 in cash and agreeing to pay the rest next month.

Cash

Jan. 1	10,000	Jan. 2	800
		4	4,200
		5	1,500

Office Equipment

| Jan. 5 | 3,000 | |

Accounts Payable

| | | Jan. 5 | 1,500 |

Transaction: Purchase of equipment, partial payment.
Analysis: Assets increased. Assets decreased. Liabilities increased.
Rules: Increases in assets are recorded by debits. Decreases in assets are recorded by credits. Increases in liabilities are recorded by credits.
Entry: Increase in assets is recorded by a debit to Office Equipment. Decrease in assets is recorded by a credit to Cash. Increase in liabilities is recorded by a credit to Accounts Payable.

	Dr.	Cr.
Office Equipment	3,000	
Cash		1,500
Accounts Payable		1,500

January 6: Purchased on credit art supplies for $1,800 and office supplies for $800 from Taylor Supply Company.

Art Supplies		
Jan. 6	1,800	

Office Supplies		
Jan. 6	800	

Accounts Payable			
		Jan. 5	1,500
		6	2,600

Transaction: Purchase of supplies on credit.
Analysis: Assets increased. Liabilities increased.
Rules: Increases in assets are recorded by debits. Increases in liabilities are recorded by credits.
Entry: Increase in assets is recorded by debits to Art Supplies and Office Supplies. Increase in liabilities is recorded by a credit to Accounts Payable.

	Dr.	Cr.
Art Supplies	1,800	
Office Supplies	800	
Accounts Payable		2,600

January 8: Paid $480 for a one-year insurance policy with coverage effective January 1.

Cash			
Jan. 1	10,000	Jan. 2	800
		4	4,200
		5	1,500
		8	480

Prepaid Insurance		
Jan. 8	480	

Transaction: Paid for insurance coverage in advance.
Analysis: Assets increased. Assets decreased.
Rules: Increases in assets are recorded by debits. Decreases in assets are recorded by credits.
Entry: Increase in assets is recorded by a debit to Prepaid Insurance. Decrease in assets is recorded by a credit to Cash.

	Dr.	Cr.
Prepaid Insurance	480	
Cash		480

January 9: Paid Taylor Supply Company $1,000 of the amount owed.

Cash			
Jan. 1	10,000	Jan. 2	800
		4	4,200
		5	1,500
		8	480
		9	1,000

Accounts Payable			
Jan. 9	1,000	Jan. 5	1,500
		6	2,600

Transaction: Partial payment on a liability.
Analysis: Assets decreased. Liabilities decreased.
Rules: Decreases in assets are recorded by credits. Decreases in liabilities are recorded by debits.
Entry: Decrease in liabilities is recorded by a debit to Accounts Payable. Decrease in assets is recorded by a credit to Cash.

	Dr.	Cr.
Accounts Payable	1,000	
Cash		1,000

January 10: Performed a service by placing advertisements for an automobile dealer in the newspaper and collected a fee of $1,400.

Cash

Jan. 1	10,000	Jan. 2	800
10	1,400	4	4,200
		5	1,500
		8	480
		9	1,000

Advertising Fees Earned

		Jan. 10	1,400

Transaction: Revenue earned and cash collected.
Analysis: Assets increased. Owner's equity increased.
Rules: Increases in assets are recorded by debits. Increases in owner's equity are recorded by credits.
Entry: Increase in assets is recorded by a debit to Cash. Increase in owner's equity is recorded by a credit to Advertising Fees Earned.

	Dr.	Cr.
Cash	1,400	
Advertising Fees Earned		1,400

January 12: Paid the secretary two weeks' wages, $600.

Cash

Jan. 1	10,000	Jan. 2	800
10	1,400	4	4,200
		5	1,500
		8	480
		9	1,000
		12	600

Office Wages Expense

Jan. 12	600	

Transaction: Payment of wages expense.
Analysis: Assets decreased. Owner's equity decreased.
Rules: Decreases in assets are recorded by credits. Decreases in owner's equity are recorded by debits.
Entry: Decrease in owner's equity is recorded by a debit to Office Wages Expense. Decrease in assets is recorded by a credit to Cash.

	Dr.	Cr.
Office Wages Expense	600	
Cash		600

January 15: Accepted $1,000 as an advance fee for art work to be done for another agency.

Cash

Jan. 1	10,000	Jan. 2	800
10	1,400	4	4,200
15	1,000	5	1,500
		8	480
		9	1,000
		12	600

Unearned Art Fees

		Jan. 15	1,000

Transaction: Accepted payment for services to be performed.
Analysis: Assets increased. Liabilities increased.
Rules: Increases in assets are recorded by debits. Increases in liabilities are recorded by credits.
Entry: Increase in assets is recorded by a debit to Cash. Increase in liabilities is recorded by a credit to Unearned Art Fees.

	Dr.	Cr.
Cash	1,000	
Unearned Art Fees		1,000

January 19: Performed a service by placing several major advertisements for Ward Department Stores. The fee of $2,800 is billed now but will be collected next month.

Accounts Receivable	
Jan. 19 2,800	

Advertising Fees Earned	
	Jan. 10 1,400
	19 2,800

Transaction: Revenue earned, to be received later.
Analysis: Assets increased. Owner's equity increased.
Rules: Increases in assets are recorded by debits. Increases in owner's equity are recorded by credits.
Entry: Increase in assets is recorded by a debit to Accounts Receivable. Increase in owner's equity is recorded by a credit to Advertising Fees Earned.

	Dr.	Cr.
Accounts Receivable	2,800	
Advertising Fees Earned		2,800

January 25: Joan Miller withdrew $1,400 from the business for personal living expenses.

Cash			
Jan. 1 10,000	Jan. 2	800
10 1,400	4	4,200
15 1,000	5	1,500
	8	480
	9	1,000
	12	600
	25	1,400

Joan Miller, Withdrawals	
Jan. 25 1,400	

Transaction: Withdrawal of assets for personal use.
Analysis: Assets decreased. Owner's equity decreased.
Rules: Decreases in assets are recorded by credits. Decreases in owner's equity are recorded by debits.
Entry: Decrease in owner's equity is recorded by a debit to Joan Miller, Withdrawals. Decrease in assets is recorded by a credit to Cash.

	Dr.	Cr.
Joan Miller, Withdrawals	1,400	
Cash		1,400

January 26: Paid the secretary two more weeks' wages, $600.

Cash			
Jan. 1 10,000	Jan. 2	800
10 1,400	4	4,200
15 1,000	5	1,500
	8	480
	9	1,000
	12	600
	25	1,400
	26	600

Office Wages Expense	
Jan. 12 600	
26 600	

Transaction: Payment of wages expense.
Analysis: Assets decreased. Owner's equity decreased.
Rules: Decreases in assets are recorded by credits. Decreases in owner's equity are recorded by debits.
Entry: Decrease in owner's equity is recorded by a debit to Office Wages Expense. Decrease in assets is recorded by a credit to Cash.

	Dr.	Cr.
Office Wages Expense	600	
Cash		600

January 29: Received and paid the utility bill of $100.

Cash

Jan. 1	10,000	Jan. 2	800
10	1,400	4	4,200
15	1,000	5	1,500
		8	430
		9	1,000
		12	600
		25	1,400
		26	600
		29	100

Utility Expense

Jan. 29	100	

Transaction: Payment of expenses.

Analysis: Assets decreased. Owner's equity decreased.

Rules: Decreases in assets are recorded by credits. Decreases in owner's equity are recorded by debits.

Entry: Decrease in owner's equity is recorded by a debit to Utility Expense. Decrease in assets is recorded by a credit to Cash.

	Dr.	Cr.
Utility Expense	100	
Cash		100

January 30: Received (but did not pay) a telephone bill, $70.

Accounts Payable

Jan. 9	1,000	Jan. 5	1,500
		6	2,600
		30	70

Telephone Expense

Jan. 30	70	

Transaction: Expense incurred, payment deferred.

Analysis: Liabilities increased. Owner's equity decreased.

Rules: Increases in liabilities are recorded by credits. Decreases in owner's equity are recorded by debits.

Entry: Decrease in owner's equity is recorded by a debit to Telephone Expense. Increase in liabilities is recorded by a credit to Accounts Payable.

	Dr.	Cr.
Telephone Expense	70	
Accounts Payable		70

Summary of Transactions

As you may have discovered from the examples, there are only a few ways in which transactions can affect the accounting equation. The following table summarizes them:

Effect	Example Transactions
1. Increase both assets and liabilities	Jan. 6, 15
2. Increase both assets and owner's equity	Jan. 1, 10, 19
3. Decrease both assets and liabilities	Jan. 9
4. Decrease both assets and owner's equity	Jan. 12, 25, 26, 29
5. Increase one asset and decrease another	Jan. 2, 4, 8
6. Increase one liability or owner's equity and decrease another liability or owner's equity	Jan. 30
7. No effect	Jan. 3

The January 5 transaction is a slightly more complex transaction; it increases one asset (Office Equipment), decreases another asset (Cash), and increases a liability (Accounts Payable). All the previous transactions are presented in Exhibit 2-2 in their correct accounts. Their relation to the accounting equation is also shown.

Recording Transactions

OBJECTIVE 6
Record transactions in the general journal

So far, the analysis of transactions has been illustrated by entering the transactions directly into the T accounts. This method was used because it is a very simple and useful way of analyzing the effects. Advanced accounting students and professional accountants often use T accounts to analyze very complicated transactions. However, there are three steps to be followed in the recording process.

1. Analyze the transactions from the source documents.
2. Enter the transactions into the journal (a procedure usually called journalizing).
3. Post the entries to the ledger (a procedure usually called posting).

The Journal

As illustrated in this chapter, transactions can be recorded directly into the accounts. When this method is used, however, it is very difficult to identify individual transactions with the debit recorded in one account and the credit in another. When a large number of transactions is involved, errors in analyzing or recording transactions are very difficult to find. The solution to this problem is to chronologically record all transactions in a **journal**. The journal is sometimes called the book of original entry, because this is where transactions are first recorded. The journal shows the transactions for each day and may contain explanatory information. The debit and credit portion of each transaction can then be transferred to the appropriate accounts.

A separate **journal entry** is used to record each transaction, and the process of recording transactions is called **journalizing**.

The General Journal

It is common for a business to have more than one kind of journal. Several types of journals are discussed in Chapter 6. The simplest and most flexible type is the **general journal**, which is used in the rest of this chapter. The general journal provides for recording the following information about each transaction:

1. The date
2. The names of the accounts debited and the dollar amounts in the debit columns on the same lines
3. The names of the accounts credited and the dollar amounts in the credit columns on the same lines
4. An explanation of the transaction
5. The account identification numbers, if appropriate

Exhibit 2-2. Summary of Illustrative Accounts and Transactions for Joan Miller Advertising Agency

Assets	=	Liabilities	+	Owner's Equity

Cash

Jan.	1	10,000	Jan.	2	800
	10	1,400		4	4,200
	15	1,000		5	1,500
				8	480
				9	1,000
				12	600
				25	1,400
				26	600
				29	100
		12,400			10,680
Bal.		1,720			

Accounts Payable

Jan. 9	1,000	Jan.	5	1,500
			6	2,600
			30	70
	1,000			4,170
		Bal.		3,170

Joan Miller, Capital

	Jan.	1	10,000

Joan Miller, Withdrawals

Jan. 25	1,400	

Unearned Art Fees

	Jan. 15	1,000

Advertising Fees Earned

	Jan.	10	1,400
		19	2,800
	Bal.		4,200

Accounts Receivable

Jan. 19	2,800	

Office Wages Expense

Jan.	12	600	
	26	600	
Bal.		1,200	

Art Supplies

Jan. 6	1,800	

Utility Expense

Jan. 29	100	

Office Supplies

Jan. 6	800	

Telephone Expense

Jan. 30	70	

Prepaid Rent

Jan. 2	800	

Prepaid Insurance

Jan. 8	480	

Art Equipment

Jan. 4	4,200	

Office Equipment

Jan. 5	3,000	

Two transactions for the Joan Miller Advertising Agency are recorded in Exhibit 2-3.

The procedure for recording transactions in the general journal is summarized as follows:

1. Record the date by writing the year in small figures on the first line at the top of the first column, the month on the next line of the first column, and the day in the second column opposite the month. For

Exhibit 2-3. The General Journal

			Post. Ref.	Debit	Credit
		General Journal			**Page 1**
Date		**Description**			
19xx Jan.	6	Art Supplies		1,800	
		Office Supplies		800	
		Accounts Payable			2,600
		Purchase of art and office supplies on credit			
	8	Prepaid Insurance		480	
		Cash			480
		Paid one-year life insurance premium			

subsequent entries on the same page for the same month and year, the month and year can be omitted.

2. Write the exact names of the accounts debited and credited under the heading "Description." Write the name of the account debited next to the left margin of the second line, and indent the name of the account credited. The explanation is placed on the next line and further indented. It should be brief but sufficient to explain and identify the transaction. A transaction can have more than one debit and/or credit entry; in such a case it is called a **compound entry**. In a compound entry, all debit accounts involved are listed before any credit accounts. (The January 6 transaction of Joan Miller Advertising Agency is an example of a compound entry; see above.)

3. Write the debit amounts in the appropriate column opposite the accounts to be debited, and write the credit amounts in the appropriate column opposite the accounts to be credited.

4. At the time of recording the transactions, nothing is placed in the Post. Ref. (posting reference) column. (This column is sometimes called LP or Folio.) Later, if the company uses account numbers to identify accounts in the ledger, fill in the account numbers to provide a convenient cross-reference from general journal to ledger and to indicate that posting to the ledger has been completed. If account numbers are not appropriate, a check (✔) is used.

5. It is customary to skip a line after each journal entry.

The Ledger Account Form

So far, the T form of account has been used as a simple and direct means of recording transactions. In practice, a somewhat more complicated form of the account is needed to record more information. The **ledger account form**, with four columns for dollar amounts, is illustrated in Exhibit 2-4.

Exhibit 2-4. Accounts Payable in the General Ledger

General Ledger

Accounts Payable — Account No. *212*

Date		Item	Post. Ref.	Debit	Credit	Balance Debit	Balance Credit
19xx Jan.	5		J1		1,500		1,500
	6		J1		2,600		4,100
	9		J1	1,000			3,100
	30		J2		70		3,170

The *account title* and *number* appear at the top of the account form. The *date* of the transaction appears in the first two columns as it does in the journal. The Item column is used only rarely to identify transactions, because an explanation already appears in the journal. The Post. Ref. column is used to note the journal page where the original entry for the transaction can be found. The dollar amount of the entry is entered in the appropriate Debit or Credit column, and a new account balance is computed in the final two columns after each entry. The advantage of this form of account over the T account is that the current balance of the account is readily available.

Relationship Between the Journal and the Ledger

OBJECTIVE 7
Explain the relationship of the general journal to the general ledger

After the transactions have been entered in the journal, they must be transferred to the general ledger. This process of transferring journal entry information from the journal to the ledger is called **posting**. Posting is usually done, not after each journal entry, but after several entries have been made—for example, at the end of each day or less frequently, depending on the number of transactions.

Through posting, each amount in the Debit column of the journal is transferred into the Debit column of the appropriate account in the ledger and each amount in the Credit column of the journal is transferred into the Credit column of the appropriate account in the ledger. This procedure is illustrated in Exhibit 2-5. The steps in posting are as follows:

1. Locate in the ledger the debit account named in the journal entry.
2. Enter the date of the transaction and, in the Post. Ref. column of the ledger, the journal page number from which the entry comes.
3. Enter in the Debit column of the ledger account the amount of the debit as it appears in the journal.
4. Enter in the Post. Ref. column of the journal the account number to which the amount was posted.
5. Repeat the preceding four steps for the credit side of the journal entry.

Exhibit 2-5. Posting from the General Journal to the Ledger

General Journal
②Page 2

Date		Description	Post. Ref.	Debit	Credit
19xx Jan.	② 30	① Telephone Expense	④ 513	③ 70	
		Accounts Payable	212		70
		Received bill for			
		telephone expense			

General Ledger

Accounts Payable · Account No. 212

Date		Item	Post. Ref.	Debit	Credit	Balance Debit	Balance Credit
19xx Jan.	5		J1		1,500		1,500
	6		J1		2,600		4,100
	9		J1	1,000			3,100
	30		J2		70		3,170

General Ledger

Telephone Expense · Account No. 513

Date		Item	Post. Ref.	Debit	Credit	Balance Debit	Balance Credit
19xx Jan.	30		J2	70		70	

Note that Step 4 is the last step in the posting process for each debit and credit. In addition to serving as an easy reference between journal entry and ledger account, this entry in the Post. Ref. column of the journal serves as a check, indicating that all steps for the item are completed. For example, when accountants are called away from their work by telephone calls or other interruptions, they can easily find where they were before the interruption.

In a microcomputer accounting system such as many small businesses have today, the posting is done automatically by the computer after the transactions have been entered. The computer will also do the next step in the account:ng cycle, which is to prepare a trial balance.

The Trial Balance

OBJECTIVE 8
Prepare a trial balance and recognize its value and limitations

The equality of debit and credit balances in the ledger should be tested periodically by preparing a **trial balance**. Exhibit 2-6 shows a trial balance for the Joan Miller Advertising Agency. It was prepared from the accounts in Exhibit 2-2, on page 69. The steps in preparing a trial balance follow.

1. Determine the balance of each account in the ledger.
2. List each ledger account that has a balance, with the debit balances in the left column and the credit balances in the right column. Accounts are listed in the order they appear in the ledger.
3. Add each column.
4. Compare the totals of each column.

In performing steps **1** and **2**, recall that the account form in the ledger has two balance columns, one for debit balances and one for credit balances. The usual balance for an account is known as the **normal balance**.

Exhibit 2-6. Trial Balance

Joan Miller Advertising Agency
Trial Balance
January 31, 19xx

Cash	$ 1,720	
Accounts Receivable	2,800	
Art Supplies	1,800	
Office Supplies	800	
Prepaid Rent	800	
Prepaid Insurance	480	
Art Equipment	4,200	
Office Equipment	3,000	
Accounts Payable		$ 3,170
Unearned Art Fees		1,000
Joan Miller, Capital		10,000
Joan Miller, Withdrawals	1,400	
Advertising Fees Earned		4,200
Office Wages Expense	1,200	
Utility Expense	100	
Telephone Expense	70	
	$18,370	$18,370

Consequently, if increases are recorded by debits, the normal balance is a debit balance; if increases are recorded by credits, the normal balance is a credit balance. The table below summarizes the normal account balances of the major account categories. According to the table, the ledger account for Accounts Payable will typically have a credit balance and can be copied into the Trial Balance columns as a credit balance.

Account Category	Increases Recorded by		Normal Balance	
	Debit	Credit	Debit	Credit
Asset	x		x	
Liability		x		x
Owner's Equity:				
Capital		x		x
Withdrawals	x		x	
Revenues		x		x
Expenses	x		x	

Once in a while, a transaction will cause an account to have a balance opposite from its normal balance. Examples are when a customer overpays a bill or when a company overdraws its account at the bank. If this happens, the abnormal balance should be copied into the Trial Balance columns as it stands as a debit or credit.

The significance of the trial balance is that it proves whether or not the ledger is in balance. "In balance" means that equal debits and credits have been recorded for all transactions so total debits equals total credits. The trial balance proof does not mean, however, that transactions were analyzed correctly or recorded in the proper accounts. For example, there would be no way of determining from the trial balance that a debit should have been made in the Art Equipment account rather than the Office Equipment account. Further, if a transaction that should be recorded is omitted, it will not be detected because equal debits and credits will have been omitted. Also, if an error of the same amount is made both as a debit and as a credit, it will not be discovered by the trial balance. The trial balance proves only the equality of the debits and credits in the accounts.

If the debit and credit columns of the trial balance do not equal each other, it may be the result of one or more of the following errors: (1) a debit was entered in an account as a credit, or vice versa, (2) the balance of an account was incorrectly computed, (3) an error was made in carrying the account balance to the trial balance, or (4) the trial balance was incorrectly summed.

Other than simply adding the columns wrong, the two most common mistakes in preparing a trial balance are (1) recording an account with a debit balance as a credit, or vice versa, and (2) transposing two numbers in an amount when transferring it to the trial balance (for example, transferring $23,459 as $23,549). The first of these mistakes will cause the trial balance to be out of balance by an amount divisible by 2. The second will cause the trial balance to be out of balance by a number divisible by 9. Thus if a trial balance is out of balance and the addition has been verified, determine the amount by which the trial balance is out of balance and divide it first by 2 and then by 9. If the amount is divisible by 2, look in the trial balance for an amount equal to the quotient. If such a number exists, it is likely that this amount is in the wrong column. If the amount is divisible by 9, trace each amount to the ledger account balance, checking carefully for a transposition error. If neither of these techniques identifies the error, it is necessary first to recompute the balance of each account in the ledger and, if the error still has not been found, then retrace each posting from the journal to the ledger.

Some Notes on Presentation Techniques

Ruled lines appear in financial reports before each subtotal or total to indicate that the amounts above are to be added or subtracted. It is common practice to use a double line under a final total to show that it has been cross checked or verified.

Dollars signs ($) are required in all financial statements including the balance sheet and income statement and in schedules such as the trial balance. On these statements, a dollar sign should be placed before the first amount in each column and before the first amount in a column following a ruled line. Dollar signs are *not* used in journals or ledgers.

On unruled paper, commas and decimal points are used in representing dollar amounts, but when paper with ruled columns is used in journals and ledgers, commas and periods are not needed. In this book, because most problems and illustrations are in whole dollar amounts, the cents column is usually omitted. When professional accountants deal with whole dollars, they will often use a dash in the cents column to indicate whole dollars rather than take the time to write zeros.

Chapter Review

Review of Learning Objectives

1. **Explain in simple terms the generally accepted ways of solving the measurement issues of recognition, valuation, and classification.**
   To measure a business transaction, the accountant must determine when the transaction occurred (the recognition issue), what value should be placed on the transaction (the valuation issue), and how the components

of the transaction should be categorized (the classification issue). In general, recognition occurs when title passes, and a transaction is valued at the cost or exchange price when the transaction is recognized. Classification refers to the categorizing of transactions according to a system of accounts.

2. **Define and use the terms** *account* **and** *general ledger.*
   An account is a device for storing data from transactions. There is one account for each asset, liability, and component of owner's equity, including revenues and expenses. The general ledger is a book or file consisting of all of a company's accounts arranged according to a chart of accounts.

3. **Recognize commonly used asset, liability, and owner's equity accounts.**
   Commonly used asset accounts are Cash, Notes Receivable, Accounts Receivable, Prepaid Expenses, Land, Buildings, and Equipment. Common liability accounts are Notes Payable, Accounts Payable, and Mortgages Payable. Common owner's equity accounts are Capital, Withdrawals, Revenues, and Expenses.

4. **Define** *double-entry system* **and state the rules for debit and credit.**
   In the double-entry system, each transaction must be recorded with at least one debit and one credit, in such a way that the total dollar amount of the debits equals the total dollar amount of the credits. The rules for debit and credit are (1) increases in assets are debited to asset accounts; decreases in assets are credited to asset accounts; (2) increases in liabilities and owner's equity are credited to those accounts; decreases in liabilities and owner's equity are debited to those accounts.

5. **Apply the procedure for transaction analysis to simple transactions.**
   The procedures for analyzing transactions are to (1) analyze the effect of the transaction on assets, liabilities, and owner's equity; (2) apply the appropriate double-entry rule; and (3) make the entry.

6. **Record transactions in the general journal.**
   The general journal is a chronological record of all transactions. The record of a transaction in the general journal contains the date of the transaction, the names of the accounts and dollar amounts debited and credited, an explanation of the journal entries, and the account numbers to which postings have been made.

7. **Explain the relationship of the general journal to the general ledger.**
   After the transactions have been entered in the general journal, they must be posted to the general ledger. Posting is done by transferring each amount in the debit column of the general journal to the debit column of the appropriate account in the general ledger and transferring each amount in the credit column of the general journal to the credit column of the appropriate account in the general ledger.

8. **Prepare a trial balance and recognize its value and limitations.**
   A trial balance is used to test the equality of the debit and credit balances in the ledger. It is prepared by listing each account with its balance in the appropriate debit or credit column. The two columns are added and compared to test their balances. The major limitation of the trial balance is that the equality of debit and credit balances does not mean that transactions were analyzed correctly or recorded in the proper accounts.

Review of Concepts and Terminology

The following concepts and terms were introduced in this chapter:

(L.O. 2) **Account:** The basic storage unit of accounting. There is a separate account for each asset, liability, and component of owner's equity, including revenues and expenses.

(L.O. 4) **Balance (or account balance):** The difference in total dollars between the total debit footing and the total credit footing of an account.

(L.O. 2) **Chart of accounts:** A numbering scheme that assigns a unique number to each account to facilitate finding the account in the ledger; also the list of account numbers and titles.

(L.O. 1) **Classification:** The process of assigning all transactions to the appropriate accounts.

(L.O. 6) **Compound entry:** A journal entry that has more than one debit and/or credit entry.

(L.O. 1) **Cost:** The exchange price associated with a business transaction at the point of recognition. Often referred to as the cost principle.

(L.O. 4) **Credit:** The right side of an account.

(L.O. 4) **Debit:** The left side of an account.

(L.O. 4) **Double-entry system:** Accounting system in which each transaction must be recorded with at least one debit and one credit, in such a way that the total dollar amount of debits and total dollar amount of credits equal each other.

(L.O. 4) **Footing:** A memorandum total of a column of numbers; to foot, total a column of numbers.

(L.O. 6) **General journal:** The simplest and most flexible type of journal.

(L.O. 2) **General ledger:** The book or file that contains all or groups of the company's accounts.

(L.O. 6) **Journal:** A chronological record of all transactions; place where transactions are first recorded.

(L.O. 6) **Journal entry:** A separate entry in the journal, used to record a single transaction.

(L.O. 6) **Journalizing:** The process of recording transactions in a journal.

(L.O. 2) **Ledger:** A book or file of all of a company's accounts, arranged as in the chart of accounts.

(L.O. 6) **Ledger account form:** A form of the account that has four columns, one for debit entries, one for credit entries, and two columns (debit and credit) for showing the balance of the account.

(L.O. 8) **Normal balance:** The balance that one would expect an account to have; the usual balance of an account; also the side (debit or credit) that increases the account.

(L.O. 7) **Posting:** The process of transferring journal entry information from the journal to the ledger.

(L.O. 1) **Recognition:** The determination of when a business transaction is to be recorded.

(L.O. 1) **Recognition point**: The predetermined time at which a transaction is to be recorded. Usually the point at which title passes.

(L.O. 4) **T account**: A form of an account that has a physical resemblance to the letter *T*; used to analyze transactions.

(L.O. 8) **Trial balance**: A listing of accounts in the general ledger with their debit or credit balances in respective columns and a totaling of the columns; used to test the equality of debit and credit balances in the ledger.

(L.O. 1) **Valuation**: The process of assigning a value to all business transactions.

Self-Test

Test your knowledge of the chapter by choosing the best answer for each item below.

1. Deciding whether to record a sale when the order for services is received or when the services are performed is an example of
   a. a recognition issue.   c. a classification issue.
   b. a valuation issue.   d. a communication issue.   *(L.O. 1)*

2. Which of the following statements is true?
   a. The chart of accounts is most often presented in alphabetical order.
   b. The general ledger contains all the accounts found in the chart of accounts.
   c. The general journal contains a list of the chart of accounts.
   d. Most companies use the same chart of accounts.   *(L.O. 2)*

3. Which of the following is a liability account?
   a. Accounts Receivable   c. Rent Expense
   b. Withdrawals   d. Accounts Payable   *(L.O. 3)*

4. The left side of an account is referred to as
   a. the balance.   c. a credit.
   b. a debit.   d. a footing.   *(L.O. 4)*

5. Although debits may be used to increase assets, they may also be used to
   a. decrease assets.   c. increase expenses.
   b. increase owner's equity.   d. increase liabilities.   *(L.O. 4)*

6. Payment for a two-year insurance policy requires a debit to
   a. Prepaid Insurance.   c. Cash.
   b. Insurance Expense.   d. Accounts Payable.   *(L.O. 5)*

7. An agreement to spend $100 a month on advertising beginning next month requires
   a. a debit to Advertising Expense.   c. no entry.
   b. a debit to Prepaid Advertising.   d. a credit to Cash.   *(L.O. 5)*

8. Transactions are initially recorded in the
   a. trial balance.   c. journal.
   b. T account.   d. ledger.   *(L.O. 6)*

9. In posting from the general journal to the general ledger, the page number on which the transaction is recorded will appear in the
   a. Post. Ref. column of the general ledger.
   b. Item column of the general ledger.
   c. Post. Ref. column of the general journal.
   d. Description column of the general journal.   *(L.O. 7)*

10. The equality of debits and credits is tested periodically by preparing a
 a. trial balance.
 b. T account.
 c. general journal.
 d. ledger.
 (L.O. 8)

Answers to Self-Test are at the end of this chapter.

Review Problem
Transaction Analysis, General
Journal, Ledger Accounts, and Trial Balance

(L.O. 5, 6, 8) After graduation from veterinary school, Laura Cox entered private practice. The transactions of the business through May 27 are as follows:

19xx
May 1 Laura Cox deposited $2,000 in her business bank account.
 3 Paid $300 for two months' rent in advance for an office.
 9 Purchased medical supplies for $200 in cash.
 12 Purchased $400 of equipment on credit, making a one-fourth down payment.
 15 Delivered a calf for a fee of $35.
 18 Made a partial payment of $50 on the equipment purchased May 12.
 27 Paid a utility bill for $40.

Required
1. Record the above entries in the general journal.
2. Post the entries from the journal to the following accounts in the ledger: Cash (111), Medical Supplies (115), Prepaid Rent (116), Equipment (141), Accounts Payable (211), Laura Cox, Capital (311), Veterinary Fees Earned (411), Utility Expense (511).
3. Prepare a trial balance.

Answer to Review Problem

1. Recording journal entries

General Journal					Page 1
Date		Description	Post. Ref.	Debit	Credit
19xx May	1	Cash	111	2,000	
		Laura Cox, Capital	311		2,000
		Deposited $2,000 in her business bank account			
	3	Prepaid Rent	116	300	
		Cash	111		300
		Paid two months' rent in advance for an office			

(continued)

General Journal				Page 1
Date	**Description**	**Post. Ref.**	**Debit**	**Credit**
19xx May 9	Medical Supplies	115	200	
	Cash	111		200
	Purchased medical supplies for cash			
12	Equipment	141	400	
	Accounts Payable	211		300
	Cash	111		100
	Purchased equipment on credit, paying 25 percent down			
15	Cash	111	35	
	Veterinary Fees Earned	411		35
	Collected fee for delivery of a calf			
18	Accounts Payable	211	50	
	Cash	111		50
	Partial payment for equipment purchased on May 12			
27	Utility Expense	511	40	
	Cash	111		40
	Paid utility bill			

2. Posting transactions to the ledger accounts

General Ledger						Page 1
Cash					Account No. 111	
					Balance	
Date	**Item**	**Post. Ref.**	**Debit**	**Credit**	**Debit**	**Credit**
19xx May 1		J1	2,000		2,000	
3		J1		300	1,700	
9		J1		200	1,500	
12		J1		100	1,400	
15		J1	35		1,435	
18		J1		50	1,385	
27		J1		40	1,345	

(continued)

Medical Supplies **Account No. *115***

Date		Item	Post. Ref.	Debit	Credit	Balance Debit	Balance Credit
19xx May	9		J1	200		200	

Prepaid Rent **Account No. *116***

Date		Item	Post. Ref.	Debit	Credit	Balance Debit	Balance Credit
19xx May	3		J1	300		300	

Equipment **Account No. *141***

Date		Item	Post. Ref.	Debit	Credit	Balance Debit	Balance Credit
19xx May	12		J1	400		400	

Accounts Payable **Account No. *211***

Date		Item	Post. Ref.	Debit	Credit	Balance Debit	Balance Credit
19xx May	12		J1		300		300
	18		J1	50			250

Laura Cox, Capital **Account No. *311***

Date		Item	Post. Ref.	Debit	Credit	Balance Debit	Balance Credit
19xx May	1		J1		2,000		2,000

Veterinary Fees Earned **Account No. *411***

Date		Item	Post. Ref.	Debit	Credit	Balance Debit	Balance Credit
19xx May	15		J1		35		35

(continued)

Utility Expense　　　　　　　　　　　　　　　　　　　**Account No.** *511*

Date	Item	Post. Ref.	Debit	Credit	Balance Debit	Balance Credit
19xx *May* *27*		*J1*	*40*		*40*	

3. Completing trial balance

Laura Cox, Veterinarian
Trial Balance
May 31, 19xx

Cash	*$1,345*	
Medical Supplies	*200*	
Prepaid Rent	*300*	
Equipment	*400*	
Accounts Payable		*$ 250*
Laura Cox, Capital		*2,000*
Veterinary Fees Earned		*35*
Utility Expense	*40*	
	$2,285	*$2,285*

Chapter Assignments

Discussion Questions and Writing Assignments

1. What three problems underlie most accounting issues?
2. Why is recognition a problem to accountants?
3. A customer asks the owner of a store to save an item for him and says that he will pick it up and pay for it next week. The owner agrees to hold it. Should this transaction be recorded as a sale? Explain.
4. Why is it practical for the accountant to rely on original cost for valuation purposes?
5. Comment on the basic limitation of using original cost in accounting measurements.
6. What is an account, and how is it related to the ledger?
7. "Debits are bad; credits are good." Comment on this statement.
8. Why is the system of recording entries called the double-entry system? What is so special about it?

9. Give the rules of debits and credits for (a) assets, (b) liabilities, and (c) owner's equity.
10. Why are the rules the same for liabilities and owner's equity?
11. Explain why debits, which decrease owner's equity, also increase expenses, which are a component of owner's equity.
12. What is the meaning of the statement, "The Cash account has a debit balance of $500"?
13. What are the three steps in transaction analysis?
14. Tell whether each of the following accounts is an asset account, a liability account, or an owner's equity account:
    a. Notes Receivable   d. Bonds Payable   f. Insurance Expense
    b. Land   e. Prepaid Rent   g. Service Revenue
    c. Withdrawals
15. List the following six items in a logical sequence to illustrate the flow of events through the accounting system:
    a. Analysis of transaction
    b. Debits and credits posted from the journal to the ledger
    c. Occurrence of business transaction
    d. Preparation of financial statements
    e. Entry made in a journal
    f. Preparation of trial balance
16. What purposes are served by a trial balance?
17. Can errors be present even though the trial balance balances? Comment.
18. In recording entries in a journal, which is written first, the debit or the credit? How is indentation used in the general journal?
19. What is the relationship between the journal and the ledger?
20. Describe each of the following:
    a. Account   d. Book of original entry   g. Posting
    b. Journal   e. Post. Ref. column   h. Footings
    c. Ledger   f. Journalizing   i. Compound entry
21. Does double-entry accounting refer to entering a transaction in both the journal and the ledger? Comment.
22. Is it possible or desirable to forgo the journal and enter the transaction directly into the ledger? Comment.
23. What is the normal balance of Accounts Payable? Under what conditions could Accounts Payable have a debit balance?

Classroom Exercises

Exercise 2-1.
Recognition
(L.O. 1)

Which of the following events would be recognized and recorded in the accounting records of the Gugiri Company on the date indicated?

Jan. 15   Gugini Company offers to purchase a tract of land for $140,000. There is a high likelihood the offer will be accepted.

Feb. 2   Gugini Company receives notice that its rent will be increased from $500 per month to $600 per month effective March 1.

Mar. 29   Gugini Company receives its utility bill for the month of March. The bill is not due until April 9.

June 10   Gugini Company places a firm order for new office equipment costing $21,000.

July 6   The office equipment ordered on June 10 arrives. Payment is not due until August 1.

Exercise 2-2.
Classification of
Accounts
(L.O. 3)

Listed below are the ledger accounts of the Wonder Service Company:

a. Cash
b. Accounts Receivable
c. Reg Wonder, Capital
d. Reg Wonder, Withdrawals
e. Service Revenue
f. Prepaid Rent
g. Accounts Payable
h. Investments in Stocks and Bonds
i. Bonds Payable
j. Land
k. Supplies Expense

l. Prepaid Insurance
m. Utility Expense
n. Fees Earned
o. Unearned Revenue
p. Office Equipment
q. Rent Payable
r. Notes Receivable
s. Interest Expense
t. Notes Payable
u. Supplies
v. Interest Receivable

Complete the following table indicating with two Xs for each account its classification and its normal balance (whether a debit or credit increases the account):

Type of Account

| | | | Owner's Equity | | | | Normal Balance (increases balance) | |
Item	Asset	Liability	Owner's Capital	Owner's Withdrawals	Revenue	Expense	Debit	Credit
a.	x						x	

Exercise 2-3.
Application of
Recognition Point
(L.O. 1)

Skowron's Body Shop uses a large amount of supplies in its business. The following table summarizes selected transaction data for orders of supplies purchased.

Order	Date Shipped	Date Received	Amount
a	June 26	July 5	$ 600
b	July 10	15	1,500
c	16	22	800
d	23	30	1,200
e	27	August 2	1,500
f	August 1	5	1,000

Determine the total purchases of supplies for July alone under each of the following assumptions:

1. Skowron's Body Shop recognizes purchases when orders are shipped.
2. Skowron's Body Shop recognizes purchases when orders are received.

Exercise 2-4.
Transaction
Analysis
(L.O. 5)

Analyze each of the following transactions, using the form shown in the example below the list.

a. Clarence Davis established Royal Barber Shop by placing $1,200 in a bank account.

b. Paid two months' rent in advance, $420.
c. Purchased supplies on credit, $60.
d. Received cash for barbering services, $50.
e. Paid for supplies purchased in c.
f. Paid utility bill, $36.
g. Took cash out of business for personal expenses, $50.

Example

a. The asset Cash was increased. Increases in assets are recorded by debits. Debit Cash, $1,200. The owner's equity Clarence Davis, Capital, was increased. Increases in owner's equity are recorded by credits. Credit Clarence Davis, Capital, $1,200.

Exercise 2-5.
Recording
Transactions in
T Accounts
(L.O. 5)

Open the following T accounts: Cash; Repair Supplies; Repair Equipment; Accounts Payable; Michelle Donato, Capital; Michelle Donato, Withdrawals; Repair Fees Earned; Salary Expense; and Rent Expense. Record the following transactions for the month of June directly in the T accounts; use the letters to identify the transactions in your T accounts. Determine the balance in each account.

a. Michelle Donato opened the Eastmoor Repair Service by investing $4,300 in cash and $1,600 in repair equipment.
b. Paid $400 for current month's rent.
c. Purchased repair supplies on credit, $500.
d. Purchased additional repair equipment for cash, $300.
e. Paid salary to a helper, $450.
f. Paid $200 of amount purchased on credit in c.
g. Withdrew $600 from business for living expenses.
h. Accepted cash for repairs completed, $860.

Exercise 2-6.
Trial Balance
(L.O. 8)

After recording the transactions in Exercise 2-5, prepare a trial balance in proper sequence for Eastmoor Repair Service, June 30, 19xx.

Exercise 2-7.
Preparation of
Ledger Account
(L.O. 7)

A T account showing the cash transactions for a month follows:

		Cash			
Mar.	1	9,400	Mar.	2	900
	7	1,200		4	200
	14	4,000		8	1,700
	21	200		9	5,000
	28	6,400		23	600

Prepare the account in ledger form for Cash (Account 111) in a manner similar to the example in Exhibit 2-4.

Exercise 2-8.
Recording
Transactions in
General Journal
and Posting to
Ledger Accounts
(L.O. 6, 7)

Open a general journal form like the one in Exhibit 2-3, and label it Page 10. After completing the form, record the following transactions in the journal.

Dec. 14   Purchased an item of equipment for $6,000, paying $2,000 as a cash down payment.
     28   Paid $3,000 of the amount owed on the equipment.

Prepare three ledger account forms like those shown in Exhibit 2-4. Use the following account numbers: Cash, 111; Equipment, 143; and Accounts Payable, 212. Then post the two transactions from the general journal to the ledger accounts, at the same time making proper posting references.

Assume that the Cash account has a debit balance of $8,000 a day prior to these transactions.

Exercise 2-9.
Preparation of Trial
Balance
(L.O. 8)

The following accounts of the Emory Service Company as of March 31, 19xx are listed in alphabetical order. The amount of Accounts Payable is omitted.

Accounts Payable	?	Mark Emory, Capital	$31,450
Accounts Receivable	$ 3,000	Land	5,200
Building	34,000	Notes Payable	20,000
Cash	9,000	Prepaid Insurance	1,100
Equipment	12,000		

Prepare a trial balance with the proper heading and with the accounts listed in the balance sheet sequence (see Exhibit 2-6). Compute the balance of Accounts Payable.

Exercise 2-10.
Effect of Errors on
Trial Balance
(L.O. 8)

Which of the following errors would cause a trial balance to have unequal totals? Explain your answers.

a. A payment to a creditor was recorded as a debit to Accounts Payable for $86 and a credit to Cash for $68.
b. A payment of $100 to a creditor for an account payable was debited to Accounts Receivable and credited to Cash.
c. A purchase of office supplies of $280 was recorded as a debit to Office Supplies for $28 and a credit to Cash for $28.
d. A purchase of equipment of $300 was recorded as a debit to Supplies for $300 and a credit to Cash for $300.

Exercise 2-11.
Correcting Errors
in Trial Balance
(L.O. 8)

The following trial balance for Engelman Services at the end of July does not balance because of a number of errors. The accountant for Engelman has compared the amounts in the trial balance with the ledger, recomputed the account balances, and compared the postings. He found the following errors:

a. The balance of Cash was understated by $200.
b. A cash payment of $210 was credited to Cash for $120.
c. A debit of $60 to Accounts Receivable was not posted.
d. Supplies purchased for $30 were posted as a credit to Supplies.
e. A debit of $90 to Prepaid Insurance was overlooked and not posted.

f. The Accounts Payable account had debits of $2,660 and credits of $4,590.
g. A Notes Payable account with a credit balance of $1,200 was not included in the trial balance.
h. The debit balance of S. Engelman, Withdrawals, was listed in the trial balance as a credit.
i. A $100 debit to S. Engelman, Withdrawals, was posted as a credit.
j. The Utility Expense of $130 was listed as $13 in the trial balance.

Prepare a correct trial balance.

Engelman Services
Trial Balance
July 31, 19xx

Cash	$ 1,920	
Accounts Receivable	2,830	
Supplies	60	
Prepaid Insurance	90	
Equipment	4,200	
Accounts Payable		$ 2,270
S. Engelman, Capital		5,780
S. Engelman, Withdrawals		350
Revenues		2,960
Salaries Expense	1,300	
Rent Expense	300	
Advertising Expense	170	
Utility Expense	13	
	$10,883	$11,360

Exercise 2-12.
Preparation of Trial Balance
(L.O. 8)

The Viola Construction Company builds foundations for buildings and parking lots. The following alphabetical list shows the account balances as of April 30, 19xx.

Accounts Payable	$ 3,900		Prepaid Insurance	$ 4,600
Accounts Receivable	10,120		Revenue Earned	17,400
Cash	?		Supplies Expense	7,200
Construction Supplies	1,900		Utility Expense	420
Equipment	24,500		Eric Viola, Capital	40,000
Notes Payable	20,000		Eric Viola, Withdrawals	7,800
Office Trailer	2,200		Wages Expense	8,800

Prepare a trial balance for the company with the proper heading and with the accounts in balance sheet sequence. Determine the correct balance for the Cash account on April 30, 19xx.

Interpreting Accounting Information

First Chicago Corporation is the largest bank in Illinois. Selected accounts from the company's 1988 annual report are as follows (in millions):

Cash and Due from Banks	$ 2,600
Loans[†]	27,874
Investment Securities	2,093
Deposits[††]	32,018

[†]To customers   [††]By customers

Required

1. Indicate whether each of the above accounts would be an asset, liability, or owner's equity on First Chicago's balance sheet.
2. Assume that you were in a position to do business with First Chicago. Prepare the general journal entry (in First Chicago's records) to record each of the following transactions:

   a. You sell securities in the amount of $2,000 to the bank.
   b. You deposit the $2,000 received in step **a** in the bank.
   c. You borrow $5,000 from the bank.

Problem Set A

**Problem 2A-1.
Transaction
Analysis, T
Accounts, and
Trial Balance**
(L.O. 5, 8)

Pat McNally opened a secretarial school called VIP Secretarial Training.

a. As an individual, he contributed the following assets to the business:

Cash	$5,700
Word Processors	4,300
Office Equipment	3,600

b. Found a location for his business and paid the first month's rent, $260.
c. Paid $190 for advertisement announcing the opening of the school.
d. Received applications from three students in a four-week secretarial program and two students in a ten-day keyboarding course. The students will be billed later a total of $1,300.
e. Purchased supplies on credit, $330.
f. Billed enrolled students, $1,300.
g. Paid assistant one week's salary, $220.
h. Purchased a word processor, $480, and office equipment, $380, on credit.
i. Paid for supplies purchased on credit in **e** above.
j. Repaired broken word processor, paid cash, $40.
k. Billed new students who enrolled late in the course, $440.
l. Transferred $300 in cash to personal checking account.
m. Received payment from students previously billed, $1,080.
n. Paid utility bill for current month, $90.

* Excerpts from the 1988 annual report used by permission of First Chicago Corporation. Copyright © 1988.

o. Paid assistant one week's salary, $220.
p. Received cash revenue from another new student, $250.

Required

1. Set up the following T accounts: Cash; Accounts Receivable; Supplies; Word Processors: Office Equipment; Accounts Payable; Pat McNally, Capital; Pat McNally, Withdrawals; Revenue from Business; Rent Expense; Advertising Expense; Salary Expense; Repair Expense; Utility Expense.
2. Record transactions by entering debits and credits directly in the T accounts, using the transaction letter to identify each debit and credit.
3. Prepare a trial balance using the current date.

Problem 2A-2.
Transaction
Analysis, General
Journal, T
Accounts, and
Trial Balance
(L.O. 5, 6, 8)

John Powers is a house painter. During the month of April, he completed the following transactions:

Apr. 2 Began his business with equipment valued at $1,230 and placed $7,100 in a business checking account.
3 Purchased a used truck costing $1,900. Paid $500 cash and signed a note for the balance.
4 Purchased supplies on account, $320.
5 Completed painting a two-story house and billed the customer, $480.
7 Received cash for painting two rooms, $150.
8 Hired assistant to work with him, to be paid $6 per hour.
10 Purchased supplies for cash, $160.
11 Received check from customer previously billed, $480.
12 Paid $400 on insurance policy for eighteen months' coverage.
13 Billed customer for painting job, $620.
14 Paid assistant for twenty-five hours' work, $150.
15 Purchased a tune-up for truck, $40.
18 Paid for supplies purchased on April 4.
20 Purchased new ladder (equipment) for $60 and supplies for $290, on account.
22 Received telephone bill to be paid next month, $60.
23 Received cash from customer previously billed, $330.
24 Transferred $300 to personal checking account.
25 Received cash for painting five-room apartment, $360.
27 Paid $200 on note signed for truck.
29 Paid assistant for thirty hours' work, $180.

Required

1. Prepare journal entries to record the above transactions in the general journal. Use the accounts listed below.
2. Set up the following T accounts and post all the journal entries: Cash; Accounts Receivable; Supplies; Prepaid Insurance; Equipment; Truck; Notes Payable; Accounts Payable; John Powers, Capital; John Powers, Withdrawals; Painting Fees Earned; Wages Expense; Telephone Expense; Truck Expense.
3. Prepare a trial balance for Powers Painting Service as of April 30, 19xx.
4. Compare how recognition applies to the transactions of April 5 and 7 and how classification applies to the transactions of April 12 and 14.

Problem 2A-3.
Transaction
Analysis, General
Journal, Ledger
Accounts, and
Trial Balance
(L.O. 5, 6, 8)

Kwan Lee began a rug cleaning business on October 1 and engaged in the following transactions during the month:

Oct. 1   Began business by transferring $6,000 from his personal bank account to the business bank account.
    2   Ordered cleaning supplies, $500.
    3   Purchased cleaning equipment for cash, $1,400.
    4   Leased a van by making two months' lease payment in advance, $600.
    7   Received the cleaning supplies ordered on October 2 and agreed to pay half the amount in ten days and the rest in thirty days.
    9   Paid for repairs on the van with cash, $40.
   12   Received cash for cleaning carpets, $480.
   17   Paid half of the amount owed on supplies purchased on October 7, $250.
   21   Billed customers for cleaning carpets, $670.
   24   Paid for additional repairs on the van with cash, $40.
   27   Received $300 from the customers billed on October 21.
   31   Withdrew $350 from the business for personal use.

Required

1. Prepare journal entries to record the above transactions in the general journal (Pages 1 and 2). Use the accounts listed below.
2. Set up the following ledger accounts and post the journal entries: Cash (111); Accounts Receivable (113); Cleaning Supplies (115); Prepaid Lease (116); Cleaning Equipment (141); Accounts Payable (211); Kwan Lee, Capital (311); Kwan Lee, Withdrawals (312); Cleaning Revenues (411); Repair Expense (511).
3. Prepare a trial balance for Lee Carpet Cleaning Service as of October 31, 19xx.

Problem 2A-4.
Transaction
Analysis, General
Journal, Ledger
Accounts, and
Trial Balance
(L.O. 5, 6, 8)

The account balances for Lou's Landscaping Service at the end of July are presented in the trial balance shown on the next page. During August, Mr. Jacobson completed the following transactions:

Aug. 1   Paid for supplies purchased on credit last month, $140.
    2   Billed customers for services, $410.
    3   Paid lease on pickup for August, $290.
    5   Purchased supplies on credit, $150.
    7   Received cash from customers not previously billed, $290.
    8   Purchased new equipment from Pendleton Manufacturing Company on account, $1,300.
    9   Received bill for oil change on pickup, $40.
   12   Returned a portion of equipment that was defective, $320. Purchase was made August 8. Reduce equipment and accounts payable.
   13   Received payment from customers previously billed, $190.
   14   Paid bill received on August 9.
   16   Took $110 in cash from business for personal use.
   19   Paid for supplies purchased on August 5.
   20   Billed customers for services, $270.

Aug. 23 Purchased equipment from a friend who is retiring, $280. Payment was made from personal checking account but equipment will be used in the business. (**Hint:** Treat as owner's investment.)
   25 Received payment from customers previously billed, $390.
   27 Purchased gasoline for pickup with cash, $30.
   29 Paid $600 to reduce principal of note payable.

Lou's Landscaping Service Trial Balance July 31, 19xx		
Cash (111)	$3,100	
Accounts Receivable (113)	220	
Supplies (115)	460	
Prepaid Insurance (116)	400	
Equipment (141)	4,400	
Notes Payable (211)		$3,000
Accounts Payable (212)		700
Lou Jacobson, Capital (311)		4,200
Lou Jacobson, Withdrawals (312)	420	
Service Revenue (411)		1,490
Lease Expense (412)	290	
Pickup Expense (413)	100	
	$9,390	$9,390

Required

1. Prepare journal entries to record the August transactions in the general journal (Pages 11 and 12).
2. Open ledger accounts for the accounts shown in the trial balance. Enter the July 31 trial balance amounts in the ledger accounts.
3. Post the entries to the ledger accounts.
4. Prepare a trial balance as of August 31, 19xx.

**Problem 2A-5.
Relationship of
General Journal,
Ledger Accounts,
and Trial Balance
(L.O. 6, 7, 8)**

The Other Mother Child Care Company provides babysitting and child-care programs. On January 31, 19xx, the company had a trial balance as shown on page 92. During the month of February, the company completed the following transactions:

Feb. 2 Paid this month's rent, $270.
   3 Received fees for this month's services, $650.
   4 Purchased supplies on account, $85.
   5 Reimbursed bus driver for gas expenses, $40.
   6 Ordered playground equipment, $1,000.
   7 Paid part-time assistants for two weeks' services, $230.
   8 Paid $170 on account.
   9 Received $1,200 from customers on account.
   10 Billed customers who had not yet paid for this month's services, $700.

Feb. 11 Paid for supplies purchased on February 4.
    13 Purchased playground equipment for cash, $1,000.
    14 Withdrew $110 in cash for personal expenses.
    17 Equipment invested in business by owner, $290.
    19 Paid this month's utility bill, $145.
    21 Paid part-time assistants for two weeks' services, $230.
    22 Received $500 for one month's services from customers previously billed.
    27 Purchased gas and oil for bus on account, $35.
    28 Paid $290 for a one-year insurance policy.

Other Mother Child Care Company
Trial Balance
January 31, 19xx

Cash (111)	$ 1,870	
Accounts Receivable (113)	1,700	
Equipment (141)	1,040	
Buses (143)	17,400	
Notes Payable (211)		$15,000
Accounts Payable (212)		1,640
Esther Clay, Capital (311)		5,370
	$22,010	$22,010

Required

1. Enter the above transactions in the general journal (Pages 17 and 18).
2. Open accounts in the ledger for the accounts in the trial balance plus the following ones: Supplies (115); Prepaid Insurance (116); Esther Clay, Withdrawals (312); Service Revenue (411); Rent Expense (511); Bus Expense (512); Wages Expense (513); Utility Expense (514).
3. Enter the January 31, 19xx account balances from the trial balance.
4. Post the entries to the ledger accounts. Be sure to make the appropriate posting references in the journal and ledger as you post.
5. Prepare a trial balance as of February 29, 19xx.

Problem Set B

Problem 2B-1.
Transaction
Analysis, T
Accounts, and
Trial Balance
(L.O. 5, 8)

Diane Pastore established a small business, Pastore Training Center, to teach individuals how to use spreadsheet analysis, word processing, and other techniques on microcomputers.

a. Pastore began by transferring the following assets to the business:

Cash	$9,200
Furniture	3,100
Microcomputer	7,300

b. Paid the first month's rent on a small storefront, $280.
c. Purchased computer software on credit, $750.

d. Paid for an advertisement in the school newspaper, $100.
e. Received enrollment applications from five students for a five-day course to start next week. Each student will pay $200 if he or she actually begins the course.
f. Paid wages to a part-time helper, $150.
g. Received cash payment from three of the students enrolled in **e**, $600.
h. Billed the two other students in **e** who attended but did not pay in cash, $400.
i. Paid utility bill for the current month, $110.
j. Made payment toward software purchased in **c**, $250.
k. Received payment from one student billed in **h**, $200.
l. Purchased a second microcomputer for cash, $4,700.
m. Transferred cash to personal checking account, $300.

Required

1. Set up the following T accounts: Cash; Accounts Receivable; Software; Furniture; Microcomputer; Accounts Payable; Diane Pastore, Capital; Diane Pastore, Withdrawals; Tuition Revenue; Rent Expense; Wages Expense; Advertising Expense; Utility Expense.
2. Record transactions by entering debits and credits directly in the T accounts, using the transaction letter to identify each debit and credit.
3. Prepare a trial balance using the proper heading and the current date.

Problem 2B-2.
Transaction
Analysis, General
Journal, T
Accounts, and
Trial Balance
(L.O. 5, 6, 8)

Hassan Rahim won a concession to rent bicycles in the local park during the summer. During the month of June, Hassan completed the following transactions for his bicycle rental business:

June 2 Began business by placing $7,200 in a business checking account.
3 Purchased supplies on account, $150.
4 Purchased 10 bicycles for $2,500, paying $1,200 down and agreeing to pay the rest in thirty days.
5 Purchased for cash a small shed to hold the bicycles and to use for other operations, $2,900.
6 Paid cash for shipping and installation costs (considered as an addition to the cost of the shed) to place the shed at the park entrance, $400.
8 Received cash of $470 for rentals during the first week of operation.
13 Hired a part-time assistant to help out on weekends at $4 per hour.
14 Paid a maintenance person to clean the grounds, $75.
15 Received cash, $500, for rentals during the second week of operation.
16 Paid the assistant for a weekend's work, $80.
20 Paid for the supplies purchased on June 3, $150.
21 Paid repair bill on bicycles, $55.
22 Received cash for rentals during the third week of operation, $550.
23 Paid the assistant for a weekend's work, $80.
26 Billed a company for bicycle rentals for an employee outing, $110.
27 Paid the fee for June to the Park District for the right to the bicycle concession, $100.
28 Received cash for rentals during the week, $410.
29 Paid the assistant for a weekend's work, $80.
30 Transferred $500 to personal checking account.

Required

1. Prepare journal entries to record the above transactions in the general journal.
2. Set up the following T accounts and post all the journal entries: Cash; Accounts Receivable; Supplies; Shed; Bicycles; Accounts Payable; Hassan Rahim, Capital; Hassan Rahim, Withdrawals; Rental Income; Wages Expense; Maintenance Expense; Repair Expense; Concession Fee Expense.
3. Prepare a trial balance for Rahim Rentals as of June 30, 19xx.
4. Compare how recognition applies to the transactions of June 26 and 28 and how classification applies to the transactions of June 6 and 14.

**Problem 2B-3.
Transaction
Analysis, General
Journal, Ledger
Accounts, and
Trial Balance**
(L.O. 5, 6, 8)

Vic Kostro opened a photography and portrait studio on March 1 and completed the following transactions during the month:

Mar. 1 Began business by depositing $17,000 in the business checking account.
2 Paid two months' rent in advance for a studio, $900.
3 Transferred to the business personal photography equipment valued at $4,300.
4 Ordered additional photography equipment, $2,500.
5 Purchased office equipment for cash, $1,800.
8 Received and paid for the photography equipment ordered on March 4, $2,500.
10 Purchased photography supplies on credit, $700.
15 Received cash for portraits, $380.
16 Billed customers for portraits, $750.
21 Paid for one-half the supplies purchased on March 10, $350.
24 Paid utility bill for March, $120.
25 Paid telephone bill for March, $70.
29 Received payment from customers billed on March 16, $250.
30 Paid wages to assistant, $400.
31 Withdrew cash for personal expenses, $1,200.

Required

1. Prepare journal entries to record the above transactions in the general journal (Pages 1 and 2).
2. Set up the following ledger accounts and post the journal entries: Cash (111); Accounts Receivable (113); Photography Supplies (115); Prepaid Rent (116); Photography Equipment (141); Office Equipment (143); Accounts Payable (211); Vic Kostro, Capital (311); Vic Kostro, Withdrawals (312); Portrait Revenue (411); Wages Expense (511); Utility Expense (512); and Telephone Expense (513).
3. Prepare a trial balance for Kostro Portrait Studio as of March 31, 19xx.

**Problem 2B-4.
Transaction
Analysis, General
Journal, Ledger
Accounts, and
Trial Balance**
(L.O. 5, 6, 8)

Delta Security Service provides ushers and security personnel for athletic events and other functions. Delta's trial balance at the end of April was as shown on page 95. During May, Delta engaged in the following transactions:

May 1 Received cash from customers billed last month, $4,200.
2 Made payment on accounts payable, $3,100.
3 Purchased new one-year insurance policy in advance, $3,600.
5 Purchased supplies on credit, $430.

May   6   Billed client for security services, $2,200.
      7   Made rent payment for May, $800.
      9   Received cash from customers for security services, $1,600.
     14   Paid wages for services provided, $1,400.
     16   Ordered equipment, $800.
     17   Paid current month's utility bill, $400.
     18   Received and paid for equipment ordered on May 16, $800.
     19   Returned for full credit some of the supplies purchased on May 5
          because they were defective, $120.
     24   Withdrew cash for personal expenses, $1,000.
     28   Paid for supplies purchased on May 5, less return on May 19, $310.
     30   Billed customer for security services performed, $1,800.
     31   Paid wages in connection with security services, $1,050.

Delta Security Service
Trial Balance
April 30, 19xx

Cash (111)	$13,300	
Accounts Receivable (113)	9,400	
Supplies (115)	560	
Prepaid Insurance (116)	600	
Equipment (141)	7,800	
Accounts Payable (211)		$ 5,300
Dennis Kinsella, Capital (311)		21,160
Dennis Kinsella, Withdrawals (312)	2,000	
Security Services Revenue (411)		28,000
Wages Expense (512)	16,000	
Rent Expense (513)	3,200	
Utility Expense (514)	1,600	
	$54,460	$54,460

Required

1. Prepare journal entries to record the above transactions in the general journal (Pages 26 and 27).
2. Open ledger accounts for the accounts shown in the trial balance. Enter the April 30 trial balance amounts in the ledger.
3. Post the journal entries to the ledger.
4. Prepare a trial balance as of May 31, 19xx.

Problem 2B-5.
Relationship of
General Journal,
Ledger Accounts,
and Trial Balance
(L.O. 6, 7, 8)

Embassy Communications Company is a public relations firm. On July 31, 19xx, the company's trial balance was as shown on page 96. During the month of August, the company completed the following transactions:

Aug. 2   Paid rent for August, $650.
      3   Received cash from customers on account, $2,300.
      7   Ordered supplies, $380.

Aug. 10   Billed customers for services provided, $2,800.
       12   Made payment on accounts payable, $1,100.
       15   Paid salaries for first half of August, $1,900.
       16   Received the supplies ordered on August 7 and agreed to pay for them in thirty days, $380.
       17   Discovered some of the supplies were not as ordered and returned them for full credit, $80.
       19   Received cash from a customer for services provided, $4,800.
       24   Paid utility bill for August, $160.
       25   Paid telephone bill for August, $120.
       26   Received a bill, to be paid in September, for advertisements placed during the month of August in the local newspaper to promote Embassy Communications, $700.
       29   Billed customer for services provided, $2,700.
       30   Paid salaries for last half of August, $1,900.
       31   Withdrew cash for personal use, $1,200.

Embassy Communications Company
Trial Balance
July 31, 19xx

Cash (111)	$10,200	
Accounts Receivable (113)	5,500	
Supplies (115)	610	
Office Equipment (141)	4,200	
Accounts Payable (211)		$ 2,600
Beth Logan, Capital (311)		17,910
	$20,510	$20,510

Required

1. Enter the above transactions in the general journal (Pages 22 and 23).
2. Open accounts in the ledger for the accounts in the trial balance plus the following accounts: Beth Logan, Withdrawals (312); Public Relations Fees (411); Salaries Expense (511); Rent Expense (512); Utility Expense (513); Telephone Expense (514); Advertising Expense (515).
3. Enter the July 31 account balances from the trial balance to the appropriate ledger account forms.
4. Post the entries to the ledger accounts. Be sure to make the appropriate posting references in the journal and ledger as you post.
5. Prepare a trial balance as of August 31, 19xx.

Financial Decision Case

Ruiz Repair Service Company
(L.O. 1, 3, 5, 8)

Luis Ruiz engaged an attorney to help him start Ruiz Repair Service Company. On March 1, Luis invested $11,500 cash in the business. When he paid the attorney's bill of $700, the attorney advised him to hire an accountant to keep his records. However, Luis was so busy that it was March 31 before he asked you to straighten out his records. Your first task is to develop a trial balance based on the March transactions. You discover the following information.

After the investment and payment to the attorney, Mr. Ruiz borrowed $5,000 from the bank. He later paid $260, including interest of $60, on this loan. He also purchased a pickup truck in the company name, paying $2,500 down and financing $7,400. The first payment on the truck is due April 15. Luis then rented an office and paid three months' rent of $900 in advance. Credit purchases of office equipment of $700 and repair tools of $500 must be paid by April 10.

In March, Ruiz Repair Service completed repairs of $1,300—$400 were cash transactions. Of the credit transactions, $300 was collected during March, and $600 remained to be collected at the end of March. Wages of $400 were paid to employees. On March 31, the company received a $75 bill for March utility expense and a $50 check from a customer for work to be completed in April.

Required

1. Prepare a March 31 trial balance for Ruiz Repair Service Company. First you must record the March transactions and determine the balance of each T account.
2. Luis Ruiz is unsure how to evaluate the trial balance. His Cash account balance is $12,490, which exceeds his original investment of $11,500 by $990. Did he make a profit of $990? Explain why the Cash account is not an indicator of business earnings. Cite specific examples to show why it is difficult to determine net income by looking solely at figures in the trial balance.

Answers to Self-Test

1. a	3. d	5. c	7. c	9. a
2. b	4. b	6. a	8. c	10. a

LEARNING OBJECTIVES

1. *Define* net income *and its two major components, revenues and expenses.*
2. *Explain the difficulties of income measurement caused by (a) the accounting period issue, (b) the continuity issue, and (c) the matching issue.*
3. *Define accrual accounting and explain two broad ways of accomplishing it.*
4. *State the four principal situations that require adjusting entries.*
5. *Prepare typical adjusting entries.*
6. *Prepare financial statements from an adjusted trial balance.*
7. *Relate the need for adjusting entries to the usefulness of accounting information.*
8. *Prepare correcting entries.*

CHAPTER 3

Business Income and Adjusting Entries

In this chapter you will learn how accountants define business income. The chapter should also help you recognize the problems of assigning income to specific time periods. Then, through a realistic example, you can gain an understanding of the adjustment process necessary for measuring periodic business income. Finally, you will prepare financial statements from the adjusted trial balance. After studying this chapter, you should be able to meet the learning objectives listed on the left.

Profitable operation is essential for a business to succeed or even to survive, so earning a profit is an important goal of most businesses. A major function of accounting, of course, is to measure and report the success or failure of a company in achieving this goal.

Profit has many meanings. One definition is the increase in owner's equity resulting from business operations. However, even this definition can be interpreted differently by economists, lawyers, business people, and the public. Because the word *profit* has more than one meaning, accountants prefer to use the term *net income*, which has a precise definition from an accounting point of view. To the accountant, net income equals revenues minus expenses, provided revenues exceed expenses.

The Measurement of Business Income

Business enterprises engage in continuous activities aimed at earning income. These activities do not naturally coincide with standard periods of time, but the business environment requires a firm to report income or loss regularly. For example, owners must receive income reports every year, and the government requires corporations to pay taxes on annual income. Within the business, management often wants financial statements prepared every month or more often to monitor performance.

Faced with these demands, a primary objective of accounting is measuring net income in accordance with generally accepted accounting principles. Readers of financial reports who are familiar with these principles understand how the accountant is defining net income and are aware of its strengths and weaknesses as a measurement of company performance. The following sections present the accounting definition of net income and explain the problems in implementing it.

Net Income

OBJECTIVE 1
Define net income *and its two major components,* revenues *and* expenses

Net income is the net increase in owner's equity resulting from the operations of the company. Net income, in its simplest form, is measured by the difference between revenues and expenses:

$$\text{Net income} = \text{revenues} - \text{expenses}$$

If expenses exceed revenues, a **net loss** occurs.

Revenues. **Revenues** "are inflows or other enhancements of assets of an entity or settlement of its liabilities (or a combination of both) from delivering or producing goods, rendering services, or other activities that constitute the entity's ongoing major or central operations."[1] In the simplest case, they equal the price of goods sold and services rendered during a period of time. When a business provides a service or delivers a product to a customer, it usually receives either cash or a promise to pay cash in the near future. The promise to pay is recorded in either Accounts Receivable or Notes Receivable. The revenue for a given period of time equals the total of cash and receivables from goods and services provided to customers during that period.

As shown in Chapter 1, revenues increase owner's equity. Note that liabilities are not generally affected by revenues and that some transactions increase cash and other assets but are not revenues. For example, borrowing money from a bank increases cash and liabilities but does not result in revenue. The collection of accounts receivable, which increases cash and decreases accounts receivable, does not result in revenue either. Remember that when a sale on credit took place, the asset Accounts Receivable was increased, and at the same time an owner's equity revenue account was increased. So counting the collection of the receivable as revenue later would be counting the same sale twice.

Not all increases in owner's equity arise from revenues. The investment in the company by an owner increases owner's equity, but it is not revenue.

Expenses. **Expenses** are "outflows or other using up of assets or incurrences of liabilities (or a combination of both) from delivering or producing goods, rendering services, or carrying out other activities that constitute the entity's ongoing major or central operations."[2] In other words, expenses are the costs of the goods and services used up in the course of gaining revenues. Often called the cost of doing business, expenses include the costs of goods sold, the costs of activities necessary

1. *Statement of Financial Accounting Concepts No. 6,* "Elements of Financial Statements" (Stamford, Conn.: Financial Accounting Standards Board, December 1985), par. 78.
2. Ibid., par. 80.

to carry on the business, and the costs of attracting and serving customers. Examples are salaries, rent, advertising, telephone service, and the depreciation (allocation of the cost) of a building or office equipment.

Expenses are the opposite of revenues in that they cause a decrease in owner's equity. They also result in a decrease in assets or an increase in liabilities. Just as not all cash receipts are revenues, not all cash payments are expenses. A cash payment to reduce a liability does not result in an expense. The liability, however, may have come from incurring a previous expense, such as for advertising, that is to be paid later. There may also be two steps before an expenditure of cash becomes an expense. For example, prepaid expenses or plant assets (such as machinery and equipment) are recorded as assets when they are acquired. Later, as their usefulness expires in the operation of the business, their cost is allocated to expenses. In fact, expenses are sometimes called expired costs. We shall explain these terms and processes further.

Not all decreases in owner's equity arise from expenses. Withdrawals from the company by the owner decrease owner's equity, but they are not expenses.

Temporary and Permanent Accounts. As you saw in Chapter 1, revenues and expenses can be recorded directly in owner's equity as increases and decreases. In practice, management and others want to know the details of the increases and decreases in owner's equity caused by revenues and expenses. For this reason, separate accounts for each revenue and expense are needed to accumulate the amounts. Because these account balances apply only to the current accounting period, they are sometimes called **temporary** or **nominal accounts**. Temporary accounts show the accumulation of revenues and expenses during the accounting period. At the end of the accounting period, their account balances are transferred to owner's equity. Thus these nominal accounts start each accounting period with zero balances and then accumulate the specific revenues and expenses of that period. On the other hand, the balance sheet accounts, such as assets, liabilities, and the owner's capital account, are called **permanent** or **real accounts** because their balances extend past the end of an accounting period. The process of transferring the totals from the temporary revenue and expense accounts to the permanent owner's equity accounts is found in Chapter 4.

The Accounting Period Issue

OBJECTIVE 2a
Explain the difficulties of income measurement caused by the accounting period issue

The **accounting period issue** addresses the difficulty of assigning revenues and expenses to a short period of time such as a month or a year. Not all transactions can be easily assigned to specific time periods. Purchases of buildings and equipment, for example, have an effect that extends over many years of a company's life. How many years the buildings or equipment will be in use and how much of the cost should be assigned to each year must of course be an estimate. Accountants solve this problem with an assumption about **periodicity**. The assumption is that the net income for any period of time less than the life of the business must be regarded as tentative but still is a useful estimate of the net income for the period. Generally the time periods are of equal length to make comparisons easier. The time period should be noted in the financial statements.

Any twelve-month accounting period used by a company is called its **fiscal year**. Many companies use the calendar year, January 1 to December 31, for their fiscal year. Many other companies find it convenient to choose a fiscal year that ends during a slack season rather than a peak season. In this case, the fiscal year would correspond to the natural yearly cycle of business activity for the company. The list below shows the diverse fiscal years used by some well-known companies:

Company	Last Month of Fiscal Year
American Greetings	February
Caesar's World	July
Coleco Industries	December
Walt Disney Productions	September
Eastman Kodak	December
Fleetwood Enterprises	April
Lorimar	July
MGM/UA Entertainment	August
Mattel	January
Polaroid	December

Many government and educational units use fiscal years that end September 30 or June 30.

The Continuity Issue

OBJECTIVE 2b
Explain the difficulties of income measurement caused by the continuity issue

Income measurement, as noted above, requires that certain expense and revenue transactions be allocated over several accounting periods. Another problem confronts the accountant, who does not know how long the business entity will last. Many businesses last less than five years, and in any given year, thousands will go bankrupt. This dilemma is called the **continuity issue**. To prepare financial statements for an accounting period, the accountant must make an assumption about the ability of the business to continue. Specifically, the accountant assumes that unless there is evidence to the contrary, the business entity will continue to operate for an indefinite period. This method of dealing with the issue is sometimes called the **going concern** or **continuity** assumption. The justification for all the techniques of income measurement rests on this assumption of continuity.

In measuring net income, the accountant must also make assumptions regarding the life expectancy of assets. The value of assets often is much less if the company is not expected to continue than if it is a going concern. However, we have already pointed out in Chapter 2 that the accountant records assets at cost and does not record subsequent changes in their value. Assets become expenses as they are used up. If accountants have evidence that a company will not continue, of course, then their procedures must change. Sometimes accountants are asked, in bankruptcy cases, to drop the continuity assumption and prepare statements based on the assumption that the firm will go out of business and sell all its assets at liquidation values—that is, for what they will bring in cash.

The Matching Issue

Revenues and expenses may be accounted for on a cash received and cash paid basis. This practice is known as the **cash basis of accounting**. In certain cases, an individual or business may use the cash basis of accounting for income tax purposes. Under this method, revenues are reported as earned in the period in which cash is received; expenses are reported in the period in which cash is paid. Taxable income is therefore calculated as the difference between cash receipts from revenues and cash payments for expenses.

Even though the cash basis of accounting works well for some small businesses and many individuals, it does not meet the needs of most businesses. As explained above, revenues can be earned in a period other than when cash is received, and expenses can be incurred in a period other than when cash is paid. If net income is to be measured adequately, revenues and expenses must be assigned to the appropriate accounting period. The accountant solves this problem by applying the **matching rule**:

Revenues must be assigned to the accounting period in which the goods were sold or the services performed, and expenses must be assigned to the accounting period in which they were used to produce revenue.

Though direct cause-and-effect relationships can seldom be demonstrated for certain, many costs appear to be related to particular revenue. The accountant will recognize such expenses and related revenues in the same accounting period. Examples are the costs of goods sold and sales commissions. When there is no direct means of connecting cause and effect, the accountant tries to allocate costs in a systematic and rational way among the accounting periods that benefit from the cost. For example, a building is converted from an asset to an expense by allocating its cost over the years that benefit from its use.

Accrual Accounting

To apply the matching rule stated above, accountants have developed accrual accounting. **Accrual accounting** "attempts to record the financial effects on an enterprise of transactions and other events and circumstances . . . in the periods in which those transactions, events, and circumstances occur rather than only in the periods in which cash is received or paid by the enterprise."[3] In other words, accrual accounting consists of all the techniques developed by accountants to apply the

---

3. *Statement of Financial Accounting Concepts No. 1,* "Objectives of Financial Reporting by Business Enterprises" (Stamford, Conn.: Financial Accounting Standards Board, 1978), par. 44.

matching rule. It is done in two general ways: (1) by recognizing revenues when earned and expenses when incurred and (2) by adjusting the accounts.

Recognizing Revenues When Earned and Expenses When Incurred. The first method of accrual accounting has been illustrated several times in Chapter 2. For example, when the Joan Miller Advertising Agency made sales on credit by placing advertisements for clients (in the January 19 transaction), revenue was recorded at the time of the sale by debiting Accounts Receivable and crediting Advertising Fees Earned. In this way, the revenue from a credit sale is recognized before the cash is collected. Accounts Receivable serves as a holding account until the payment is received. This process of determining when a sale takes place is known as **revenue recognition.**

When the Joan Miller Advertising Agency received the telephone bill on January 30, the expense was recognized both as having been incurred and as helping to produce revenue in the current month. The transaction was recorded by debiting Telephone Expense and crediting Accounts Payable. Until the bill is paid, Accounts Payable serves as a holding account. It is important to note that recognition of the expense does *not* depend on payment of cash.

Adjusting the Accounts. An accounting period by definition must end on a particular day. The balance sheet must contain all assets and liabilities as of the end of that day. The income statement must contain all revenues and expenses applicable to the period ending on that day. Although a business is recognized as a continuous process, there must be a cutoff point for the periodic reports. Some transactions invariably span the cutoff point; as a result some of the accounts need adjustment.

For example, some of the accounts in the end-of-the-period trial balance for the Joan Miller Advertising Agency from Chapter 2 (also shown in Exhibit 3-1) do not show the proper balances for preparing financial statements. On January 31, the trial balance contains prepaid rent of $800. At $400 per month, this represented rent for the months of January and February. So on January 31, one-half of the $800, or $400, represents rent expense for January, and the remaining $400 represents an asset to be used in February. An adjustment is needed to reflect the $400 balance of the Prepaid Rent account on the balance sheet and the $400 rent expense on the income statement. As you will see in the following section, several other accounts of the Joan Miller Advertising Agency do not reflect their proper balances. Like the Prepaid Rent account, they also need adjusting entries.

The Adjustment Process

Accountants use **adjusting entries** to apply accrual accounting to transactions that span more than one accounting period. Adjusting entries have at least one balance sheet (or permanent) account entry and at least one income statement (or temporary) account entry. Adjusting entries

Exhibit 3-1. Trial Balance for the Joan Miller Advertising Agency

Joan Miller Advertising Agency
Trial Balance
January 31, 19xx

Cash	$ 1,720	
Accounts Receivable	2,800	
Art Supplies	1,800	
Office Supplies	800	
Prepaid Rent	800	
Prepaid Insurance	480	
Art Equipment	4,200	
Office Equipment	3,000	
Accounts Payable		$ 3,170
Unearned Art Fees		1,000
Joan Miller, Capital		10,000
Joan Miller, Withdrawals	1,400	
Advertising Fees Earned		4,200
Office Wages Expense	1,200	
Utility Expense	100	
Telephone Expense	70	
	$18,370	$18,370

OBJECTIVE 4
State the four principal situations that require adjusting entries

will never involve the Cash account. They are needed when deferrals or accruals exist. A **deferral** is the postponement of the recognition of an expense already paid or incurred or of a revenue already received. Deferrals would be needed in the following two cases:

1. There are costs recorded that must be apportioned between two or more accounting periods. Examples are the cost of a building, prepaid insurance, and supplies. The adjusting entry will involve an asset account and an expense account.

2. There are revenues recorded that must be apportioned between two or more accounting periods. An example is commissions collected in advance for services to be rendered in later periods. The adjusting entry will involve a liability account and a revenue account.

An **accrual** is the recognition of an expense or revenue that has arisen but has not yet been recorded. Accruals would be required in the following two cases:

1. There are unrecorded revenues. An example is commissions earned but not yet collected or billed to customers. The adjusting entry will involve an asset account and a revenue account.

2. There are unrecorded expenses. Examples are the wages earned by employees in the current accounting period but after the last pay pe-

riod. The adjusting entry will involve an expense account and a liability account.

Once again the Joan Miller Advertising Agency will be used to illustrate the kinds of adjusting entries that most businesses will have.

Apportioning Recorded Expenses Between Two or More Accounting Periods (Deferrals)

OBJECTIVE 5
Prepare typical adjusting entries

Companies often make expenditures that benefit more than one period. These expenditures are generally debited to an asset account. At the end of the accounting period, the amount that has been used is transferred from the asset account to an expense account. Two of the more important kinds of adjustments are for prepaid expenses and depreciation of plant and equipment.

Prepaid Expenses. Some expenses are customarily paid in advance. These expenditures are called **prepaid expenses.** Among these items are rent, insurance, and supplies. At the end of an accounting period, a portion (or all) of these goods or services most likely will have been used up or will have expired. The part of the expenditure that has benefited current operations is treated as an expense of the period. On the other hand, the part not consumed or expired is treated as an asset applicable to future operations of the company. If adjusting entries for prepaid expenses are not made at the end of the period, both the balance sheet and income statement will be stated wrong. First, the assets of the company will be overstated. Second, the expenses of the company will be understated. For this reason, owner's equity on the balance sheet and net income on the income statement will be overstated.

At the beginning of the month, the Joan Miller Advertising Agency paid two months' rent in advance. This expenditure resulted in an asset consisting of the right to occupy the office for two months. As each day in the month passed, part of the asset's costs expired and became an expense. By January 31, one-half had expired and should be treated as an expense. The analysis of this economic event is shown below:

Prepaid Rent (Adjustment a)

Prepaid Rent			
Jan. 2	800	Jan. 31	400

Rent Expense	
Jan. 31	400

Transaction: Expiration of one month's rent.
Analysis: Assets decreased. Owner's equity decreased.
Rules: Decreases in assets are recorded by credits. Decreases in owner's equity are recorded by debits.
Entries: Decrease in owner's equity is recorded by a debit to Rent Expense. Decrease in assets is recorded by a credit to Prepaid Rent.

	Dr.	Cr.
Rent Expense	400	
Prepaid Rent		400

The Prepaid Rent account now has a balance of $400, which represents one month's rent paid in advance. The Rent Expense account reflects the $400 expense for the month.

Besides rent, the Joan Miller Advertising Agency has prepaid expenses for insurance, art supplies, and office supplies, all of which call for adjusting entries.

On January 8, the Joan Miller Advertising Agency purchased a one-year insurance policy, paying for it in advance. In a manner similar to prepaid rent, prepaid insurance offers protection that expires day by day. By the end of the month, one-twelfth of the protection had expired. The adjustment is analyzed and recorded as shown below:

Prepaid Insurance (Adjustment b)

Prepaid Insurance		
Jan. 8	480	Jan. 31	40

Insurance Expense	
Jan. 31	40

Transaction: Expiration of one month's insurance.

Analysis: Assets decreased. Owner's equity decreased.

Rules: Decreases in assets are recorded by credits. Decreases in owner's equity are recorded by debits.

Entries: Decrease in owner's equity is recorded by a debit to Insurance Expense. Decrease in assets is recorded by a credit to Prepaid Insurance.

	Dr.	Cr.
Insurance Expense	40	
Prepaid Insurance		40

The Prepaid Insurance account now has the proper balance of $440, and Insurance Expense reflects the expired cost of $40 for the month.

Early in the month, the Joan Miller Advertising Agency purchased art supplies and office supplies. As Joan Miller did art work for various clients during the month, art supplies were consumed. Her secretary also used office supplies. There is no need to account for these supplies every day because the financial statements are not prepared until the end of the month and the recordkeeping would involve too much work.

Instead, Joan Miller makes a careful inventory of the art and office supplies at the end of the month. This inventory records the number and cost of those supplies that are still assets of the company—yet to be consumed. The inventory shows that art supplies costing $1,300 and office supplies costing $600 are still on hand. This means that of the $1,800 of art supplies originally purchased, $500 worth were used up or became an expense. Of the original $800 of office supplies, $200 worth were consumed. These transactions are analyzed and recorded as follows:

Art Supplies and Office Supplies (Adjustments c and d)

Art Supplies		
Jan. 6	1,800	Jan. 31	500

Art Supplies Expense	
Jan. 31	500	

Office Supplies		
Jan. 6	800	Jan. 31	200

Office Supplies Expense	
Jan. 31	200	

Transaction: Consumption of supplies.

Analysis: Assets decreased. Owner's equity decreased.

Rules: Decreases in assets are recorded by credits. Decreases in owner's equity are recorded by debits.

Entries: Decreases in owner's equity are recorded by debits to Art Supplies Expense and Office Supplies Expense. Decreases in assets are recorded by credits to Art Supplies and Office Supplies.

	Dr.	Cr.
Art Supplies Expense	500	
Art Supplies		500
Office Supplies Expense	200	
Office Supplies		200

The asset accounts of Art Supplies and Office Supplies now reflect the proper amounts of $1,300 and $600, respectively, yet to be consumed. In addition, the amount of art supplies used up during the accounting period is reflected as $500 and the amount of office supplies used up is reflected as $200.

Depreciation of Plant and Equipment. When a company buys a long-lived asset such as a building, equipment, trucks, automobiles, a computer, store fixtures, or office furniture, it is basically prepaying for the usefulness of that asset for as long as it benefits the company. In other words, the asset is a deferral of an expense. Proper accounting therefore requires allocating the cost of the asset over its estimated useful life. The amount allocated to any one accounting period is called **depreciation** or **depreciation expense**. Depreciation is an expense like others incurred during an accounting period to obtain revenue.

It is often impossible to tell how long an asset will last or how much of the asset is used in any one period. For this reason, depreciation must be estimated. Accountants have developed a number of methods for estimating depreciation and for dealing with other complex problems concerning it. Only the simplest case is presented in this discussion as an illustration.

Suppose that the Joan Miller Advertising Agency estimates that the art equipment and office equipment will last five years (sixty months) and will be worthless at the end of that time. The depreciation of art equipment and office equipment for the month is computed as $70 ($4,200 ÷ 60 months) and $50 ($3,000 ÷ 60 months), respectively. These amounts represent the cost allocated to the month, thus reducing the asset accounts and increasing the expense accounts (reducing owner's equity). These transactions can be analyzed as shown on the next page.

The use of the contra-asset account called Accumulated Depreciation is described in the next section.

Art Equipment and Office Equipment (Adjustments e and f)

Art Equipment

Jan. 4 4,200	

Accumulated Depreciation, Art Equipment

	Jan. 31 70

Office Equipment

Jan. 5 3,000	

Accumulated Depreciation, Office Equipment

	Jan. 31 50

Depreciation Expense, Art Equipment

Jan. 31 70	

Depreciation Expense, Office Equipment

Jan. 31 50	

Transaction: Recording depreciation expense.

Analysis: Assets decreased. Owner's equity decreased.

Rules: Decreases in assets are recorded by credits. Decreases in owner's equity are recorded by debits.

Entries: Owner's equity is decreased by debits to Depreciation Expense, Art Equipment, and Depreciation Expense, Office Equipment. Assets are decreased by credits to contra-asset accounts Accumulated Depreciation, Art Equipment, and Accumulated Depreciation, Office Equipment.

	Dr.	Cr.
Depreciation Expense, Art Equipment	70	
Accumulated Depreciation, Art Equipment		70
Depreciation Expense, Office Equipment	50	
Accumulated Depreciation, Office Equipment		50

Accumulated Depreciation—A Contra Account. Note that in the analysis of the case above, the asset accounts were not credited directly. Instead, new accounts—Accumulated Depreciation, Art Equipment, and Accumulated Depreciation, Office Equipment—were credited. These **accumulated depreciation** accounts are contra-asset accounts used to total the past depreciation expense on a specific long-lived asset. A **contra account** is one that is paired with and deducted from another related account in the financial statements. There are several types of contra accounts. In this case, the balance of Accumulated Depreciation, Art Equipment, is a deduction from the associated account Art Equipment. Likewise, Accumulated Depreciation, Office Equipment, is a deduction from Office Equipment. After these adjusting entries have been made, the plant and equipment section of the balance sheet for the Joan Miller Advertising Agency appears as in Exhibit 3-2.

The contra account is used for two very good reasons. First, it recognizes that depreciation is an estimate. Second, the use of the contra account preserves the original cost of the asset and shows how much of

Exhibit 3-2. Plant and Equipment Section of Balance Sheet		
Joar Miller Advertising Agency **Partial Balance Sheet** **January 31, 19xx**		
Plant and Equipment		
Art Equipment	$4,200	
Less Accumulated Depreciation	70	$4,130
Office Equipment	$3,000	
Less Accumulated Depreciation	50	2,950
Total Plant and Equipment		$7,080

the asset has been allocated as an expense as well as the balance left to be depreciated. As the months pass, the amount of the accumulated depreciation will grow, and the net amount shown as an asset will decline. In six months, for instance, Accumulated Depreciation, Art Equipment, will have a total of $420; when this amount is subtracted from Art Equipment, a net amount of $3,780 will remain. This net amount is referred to as the **carrying value** or book value.

Other names are sometimes used for accumulated depreciation, such as "allowance for depreciation." Accumulated depreciation is the newer, better term.

Apportioning Recorded Revenues
Between Two or More Accounting Periods (Deferrals)

Just as expenses may be paid before they are used, revenues may be received before they are earned. When such revenues are received in advance, the company has an obligation to deliver goods or perform services. Therefore, **unearned revenues** would be a liability account. For example, publishing companies usually receive payment in advance for magazine subscriptions. These receipts are recorded in a liability account. If the company fails to deliver the magazines, subscribers are entitled to their money back. As the company delivers each issue of the magazine, it earns a part of the advance payments. This earned portion must be transferred from the Unearned Subscription account to the Subscription Revenue account.

During the month, the Joar Miller Advertising Agency received $1,000 as an advance payment for art work to be done for another agency. Assume that by the end of the month, $400 of the art work was done and accepted by the other agency. This transaction is analyzed as shown on the top of the following page

Unearned Art Fees (Adjustment g)

Unearned Art Fees			
Jan. 31	400	Jan. 15	1,000

Art Fees Earned			
		Jan. 31	400

Transaction: Performance of services paid for in advance.

Analysis: Liabilities decreased. Owner's equity increased.

Rules: Decreases in liabilities are recorded by debits. Increases in owner's equity are recorded by credits.

Entries: Decrease in liabilities is recorded by a debit to Unearned Art Fees. Increase in owner's equity is recorded by a credit to Art Fees Earned.

	Dr.	Cr.
Unearned Art Fees	400	
Art Fees Earned		400

The liability account Unearned Art Fees now reflects the amount of work still to be performed, or $600. The revenue account Art Fees Earned reflects the amount of services performed and earned during the month, or $400.

Unrecorded or Accrued Revenues

Unrecorded or **accrued revenues** are revenues for which the service has been performed or the goods delivered but for which no entry has been recorded. Any revenues that have been earned but not recorded during the accounting period call for an adjusting entry that debits an asset account and credits a revenue account. For example, the interest on a note receivable is earned day by day but may not in fact be received until another accounting period. Interest Income should be credited and Interest Receivable debited for the interest accrued at the end of the current period.

Suppose that the Joan Miller Advertising Agency has agreed to place a series of advertisements for Marsh Tire Company and that the first appears on January 31, the last day of the month. The fee of $200 for this advertisement, which has now been earned but not recorded, should be recorded as shown below:

Unrecorded or Accrued Advertising Fees (Adjustment h)

Fees Receivable			
Jan. 31	200		

Advertising Fees Earned			
		Jan. 10	1,400
		19	2,800
		31	**200**

Transaction: Accrual of unrecorded revenue.

Analysis: Assets increased. Owner's equity increased.

Rules: Increases in assets are recorded by debits. Increases in owner's equity are recorded by credits.

Entries: Increase in assets is recorded by a debit to Fees Receivable. Increase in owner's equity is recorded by a credit to Advertising Fees Earned.

	Dr.	Cr.
Fees Receivable	200	
Advertising Fees Earned		200

Asset and revenue accounts now both show the proper balance: $200 in Fees Receivable is owed to the company, and $4,400 in Advertising Fees has been earned by the company during the month. Marsh will be billed for the series of advertisements when they are completed. At that time, Accounts Receivable will be debited and Fees Receivable will be credited.

Unrecorded or Accrued Expenses

At the end of an accounting period, there are usually expenses that have been incurred but not recorded in the accounts. These expenses require adjusting entries. One such case is borrowed money. Each day interest accumulates on the debt. An adjusting entry at the end of each accounting period records this accumulated interest, which is an expense of the period, and the corresponding liability to pay the interest. Other comparable expenses are taxes, wages, and salaries. As the expense and the corresponding liability accumulate, they are said to accrue—hence the term **accrued expenses**.

Suppose that the calendar for January appears as follows:

January

Su	M	T	W	Th	F	Sa
	1	2	3	4	5	6
7	8	9	10	11	12	13
14	15	16	17	18	19	20
21	22	23	24	25	26	27
28	29	30	31			

By the end of business on January 31, the Joan Miller Advertising Agency's secretary will have worked three days (Monday, Tuesday, and Wednesday) beyond the last biweekly pay period, which ended on January 26. The employee has earned the wages for these days, but they are not due to be paid until the regular payday in February. The wages for these three days are rightfully an expense for January, and the liabilities should reflect the fact that the company does owe the secretary for those days. Because the secretary's wage rate is $600 every two weeks or $60 per day ($600 ÷ 10 working days), the expense is $180 ($60 × 3 days). This unrecorded or accrued expense can be analyzed as shown on the next page.

Unrecorded or Accrued Wages (Adjustment i)

Wages Payable

| | Jan. 31 | 180 |

Office Wages Expense

Jan. 12	600
26	600
31	**180**

Transaction: Accrual of unrecorded expense.
Analysis: Liabilities increased. Owner's equity decreased.
Rules: Increases in liabilities are recorded by credits. Decreases in owner's equity are recorded by debits.
Entries: Decrease in owner's equity is recorded by a debit to Office Wages Expense. Increase in liabilities is recorded by a credit to Wages Payable.

	Dr.	Cr.
Office Wages Expense	180	
Wages Payable		180

The liability of $180 is now correctly reflected in the Wages Payable account. The actual expense incurred for office wages during the month is also correct at $1,380.

Using the Adjusted Trial Balance to Prepare Financial Statements

OBJECTIVE 6
Prepare financial statements from an adjusted trial balance

In Chapter 2, a trial balance was prepared before any adjusting entries were recorded. It is also desirable to prepare an **adjusted trial balance**, which is a list of the accounts and balances after the recording and posting of the adjusting entries. The adjusted trial balance for the Joan Miller Advertising Agency is shown on the left side of Exhibit 3-3. Note that some accounts, such as Cash and Accounts Receivable, have the same balances as they did in the trial balance (see Exhibit 3-1 on page 104) because no adjusting entries affected these accounts. Other accounts, such as Art Supplies, Office Supplies, Prepaid Rent, and Prepaid Insurance, have different balances from those in the trial balance because adjusting entries affected these accounts. If the adjusting entries have been posted correctly to the accounts, the adjusted trial balance will have equal debit and credit totals.

From the adjusted trial balance, the financial statements can be easily prepared. The income statement is prepared from the revenue and expense accounts, as shown in Exhibit 3-3. Then, in Exhibit 3-4, the balance sheet has been prepared from the asset and liability accounts and Joan Miller, Capital, which must come from the statement of owner's equity. Notice that the net income from the income statement is combined with investments and withdrawals on the statement of owner's equity to give the net change in Joan Miller's capital account of $10,590. In more complex situations, accountants use a device called a work sheet to prepare financial statements. The preparation of a work sheet is covered in Chapter 4.

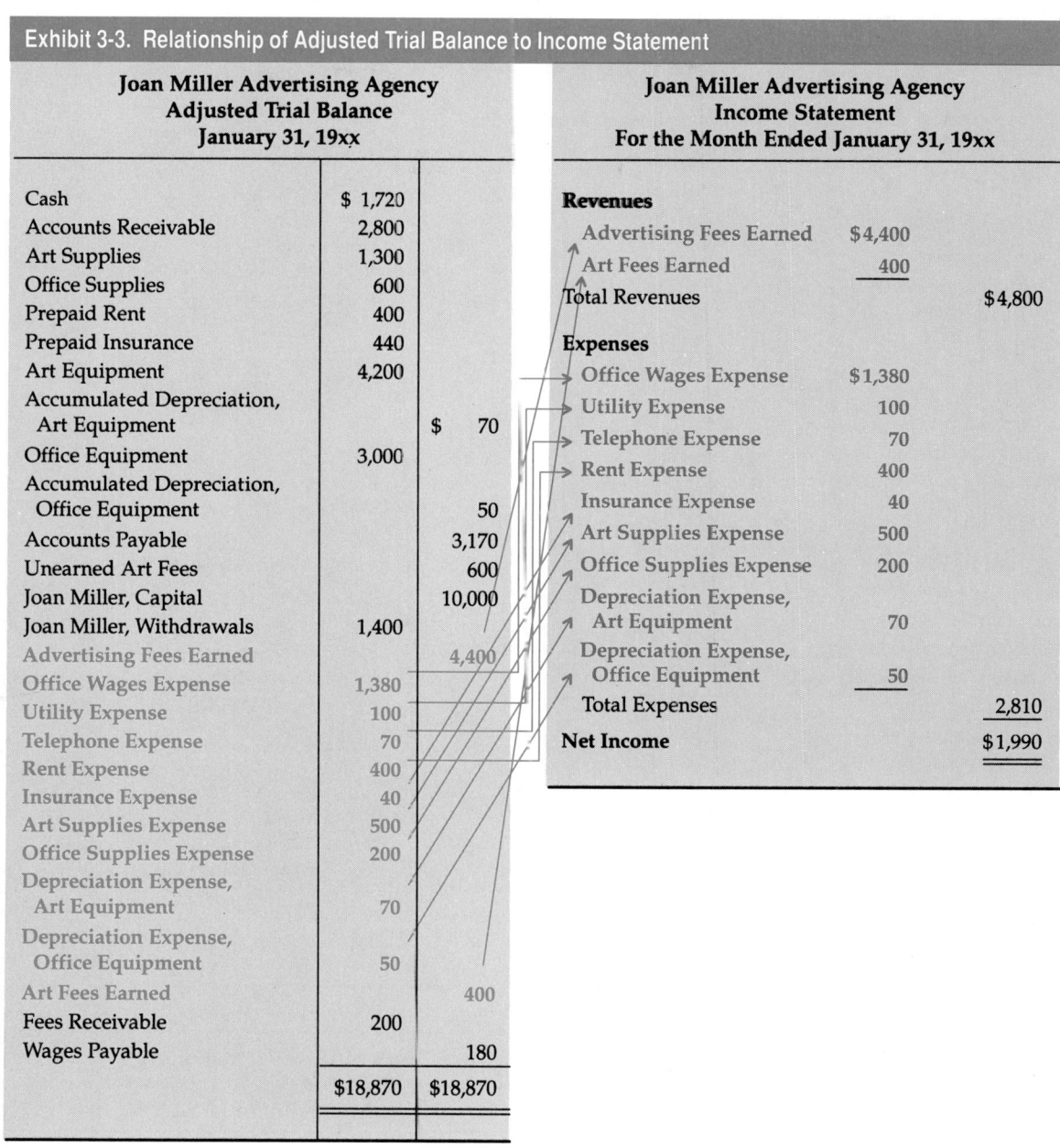

Exhibit 3-3. Relationship of Adjusted Trial Balance to Income Statement

Joan Miller Advertising Agency
Adjusted Trial Balance
January 31, 19xx

Cash	$ 1,720	
Accounts Receivable	2,800	
Art Supplies	1,300	
Office Supplies	600	
Prepaid Rent	400	
Prepaid Insurance	440	
Art Equipment	4,200	
Accumulated Depreciation, Art Equipment		$ 70
Office Equipment	3,000	
Accumulated Depreciation, Office Equipment		50
Accounts Payable		3,170
Unearned Art Fees		600
Joan Miller, Capital		10,000
Joan Miller, Withdrawals	1,400	
Advertising Fees Earned		4,400
Office Wages Expense	1,380	
Utility Expense	100	
Telephone Expense	70	
Rent Expense	400	
Insurance Expense	40	
Art Supplies Expense	500	
Office Supplies Expense	200	
Depreciation Expense, Art Equipment	70	
Depreciation Expense, Office Equipment	50	
Art Fees Earned		400
Fees Receivable	200	
Wages Payable		180
	$18,870	$18,870

Joan Miller Advertising Agency
Income Statement
For the Month Ended January 31, 19xx

Revenues		
Advertising Fees Earned	$4,400	
Art Fees Earned	400	
Total Revenues		$4,800
Expenses		
Office Wages Expense	$1,380	
Utility Expense	100	
Telephone Expense	70	
Rent Expense	400	
Insurance Expense	40	
Art Supplies Expense	500	
Office Supplies Expense	200	
Depreciation Expense, Art Equipment	70	
Depreciation Expense, Office Equipment	50	
Total Expenses		2,810
Net Income		$1,990

The Importance of Adjustments in Accounting

OBJECTIVE 7
Relate the need for adjusting entries to the usefulness of accounting information

One might ask, Why worry about adjustments? Doesn't everything come out all right in the end? The main reason for making adjustments is that they help accountants compile information that will be useful to decision makers. For example, adjusting entries are necessary to measure income and financial position in a relevant and a useful way. The management of a company might want to know how much it has earned

Exhibit 3-4. Relationship of Adjusted Trial Balance to Balance Sheet

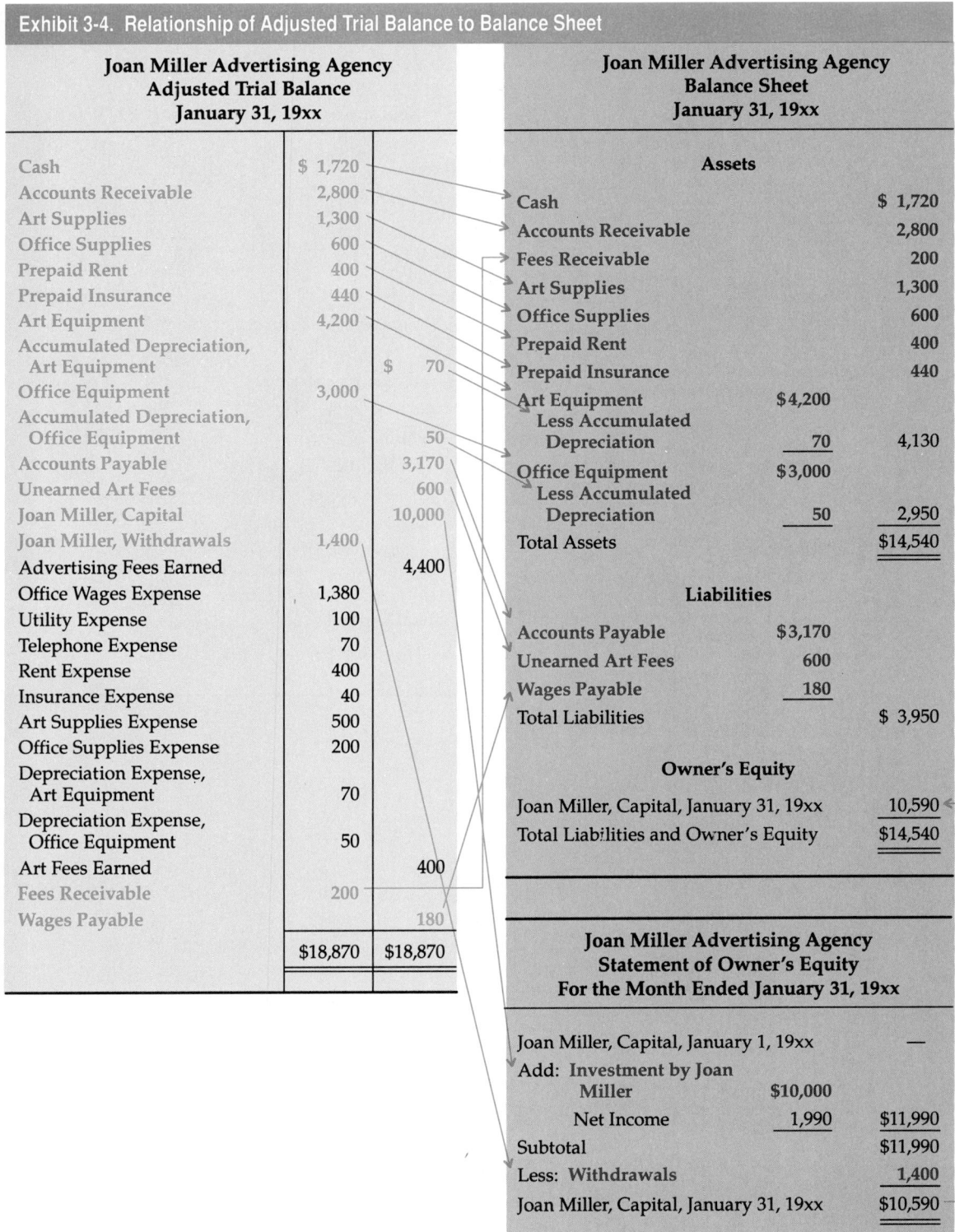

Joan Miller Advertising Agency
Adjusted Trial Balance
January 31, 19xx

Cash	$ 1,720	
Accounts Receivable	2,800	
Art Supplies	1,300	
Office Supplies	600	
Prepaid Rent	400	
Prepaid Insurance	440	
Art Equipment	4,200	
Accumulated Depreciation, Art Equipment		$ 70
Office Equipment	3,000	
Accumulated Depreciation, Office Equipment		50
Accounts Payable		3,170
Unearned Art Fees		600
Joan Miller, Capital		10,000
Joan Miller, Withdrawals	1,400	
Advertising Fees Earned		4,400
Office Wages Expense	1,380	
Utility Expense	100	
Telephone Expense	70	
Rent Expense	400	
Insurance Expense	40	
Art Supplies Expense	500	
Office Supplies Expense	200	
Depreciation Expense, Art Equipment	70	
Depreciation Expense, Office Equipment	50	
Art Fees Earned		400
Fees Receivable	200	
Wages Payable		180
	$18,870	$18,870

Joan Miller Advertising Agency
Balance Sheet
January 31, 19xx

Assets

Cash		$ 1,720
Accounts Receivable		2,800
Fees Receivable		200
Art Supplies		1,300
Office Supplies		600
Prepaid Rent		400
Prepaid Insurance		440
Art Equipment	$4,200	
Less Accumulated Depreciation	70	4,130
Office Equipment	$3,000	
Less Accumulated Depreciation	50	2,950
Total Assets		$14,540

Liabilities

Accounts Payable	$3,170	
Unearned Art Fees	600	
Wages Payable	180	
Total Liabilities		$ 3,950

Owner's Equity

Joan Miller, Capital, January 31, 19xx		10,590
Total Liabilities and Owner's Equity		$14,540

Joan Miller Advertising Agency
Statement of Owner's Equity
For the Month Ended January 31, 19xx

Joan Miller, Capital, January 1, 19xx		—
Add: Investment by Joan Miller	$10,000	
Net Income	1,990	$11,990
Subtotal		$11,990
Less: Withdrawals		1,400
Joan Miller, Capital, January 31, 19xx		$10,590

during the last month, quarter, or year and what its liabilities and assets are on a certain date. This need is an important reason for making the adjusting entries. For instance, if the three days' accrued salary for Joan Miller's secretary is not recorded, the income of the agency will be overstated by $180 and the liabilities understated by $180.

Another important reason for the use of adjusting entries is that they allow financial statements to be compared from one period to the next. Management can see if the company is making progress toward earning a profit or if the company has improved its financial position. To return to our example, if the three days' accrued wages for Joan Miller's secretary are not recorded, not only will the income for January be overstated by $180, but the net income for February (the month when payment is made) will be understated by $180. This error will make the February earnings, whatever they may be, appear worse than they actually are. Look back over all the adjustments for the Joan Miller Advertising Agency for prepaid rent and insurance, art and office supplies, depreciation of office and art equipment, unearned art fees, accrued wages and expenses, and accrued advertising fees. These are normal and usual adjustments; their combined effect on net income is significant.

Accountants also insist that adjusting procedures and entries be complete and consistent at the end of every accounting period because there is often more than one acceptable way to apply the matching rule in a given case. For example, there are several methods of determining depreciation expense. Consequently, there is a need for the consistent application of accounting practice from one period to the next so that the financial statements of successive periods can be compared and understood. Accounting methods can be changed if new circumstances require that they be changed. Since a change would make it hard to compare the financial statements of different periods, however, the company must explain in the financial statements the nature and effect of the change. Without such a disclosure, the statement reader can assume that accounting methods have been consistently applied from one period to the next.

The adjustment process can also be related to the characteristic of verifiability. To the fullest extent possible, accounting practice should be based on objective, verifiable evidence. For example, transactions are recorded at cost because two independent parties have produced objective and verifiable evidence as to the value of the transactions. Accounting transactions should be supported by verifiable business documents. In making adjustments, a problem arises because estimates often must be used. Estimates, however, can be supported by objective evidence. For example, in estimating how long buildings or equipment may last, the accountant can rely on studies of past experience.

Correcting Errors

OBJECTIVE 8
Prepare correcting entries

When an error is discovered in either the journal or the ledger, it must be corrected. The method of correction will depend on the kind of error. However, the error must *never* be erased because this action would seem to indicate an effort to hide something. If an error is discovered in a journal entry before it is posted to the ledger, a line drawn through the incorrect item and the correct item written above will suffice. Similarly, when a posting error involves entering an incorrect amount in the ledger, it is acceptable to draw a line through the wrong amount and write in the correct amount.

If a journal entry has been posted to the wrong account in the ledger, however, then it is necessary to prepare another journal entry to correct the error. For example, suppose that a purchase of art equipment was recorded as follows:

Feb. 20	Art Supplies	100	
	Cash		100
	To record purchase of art equipment		

It is clear that the debit should be to Art Equipment, not to Art Supplies. Therefore, the following entry is needed to correct the error:

Feb. 24	Art Equipment	100	
	Art Supplies		100
	To correct error of Feb. 20, when Art Supplies was debited in error for the purchase of art equipment		

The full explanation provides a record for those who might later question the entry. The Cash account is not involved in the correction, because it was correct originally. The effect of the correction is to reduce Art Supplies by $100 and increase Art Equipment by $100.

A Note About Journal Entries

Throughout Chapters 2 and 3, except in the above section, journal entries have been presented with a full analysis of the transaction. This complete analysis showed you the thought process behind each entry. By now, you should be fully aware of the effects of transactions on the accounting equation and the rules of debit and credit. For this reason, journal entries will be presented in the rest of the book without the full analysis and rules.

Chapter Review

Review of Learning Objectives

1. Define *net income* and its two major components, revenues and expenses.

Net income is the net increase in owner's equity resulting from the profit-seeking operations of a company. Net income equals revenues minus expenses, unless expenses exceed revenues, in which case a net loss results. Revenues are a measure of the asset values received from customers as a result of income-earning activity during a specific period of time. Expenses are the costs of goods and services used up in the process of obtaining revenues.

2. **Explain the difficulties of income measurement caused by (a) the accounting period issue, (b) the continuity issue, and (c) the matching issue.**

   The accounting period issue recognizes that net income measurements for short periods of time are necessarily tentative. The continuity issue recognizes that even though businesses face an uncertain future, accountants must assume that without evidence to the contrary, a business will continue indefinitely. The matching issue results from the difficulty of assigning revenues and expenses to a period of time and is solved by application of the matching rule. The matching rule states that revenues must be assigned to the accounting period in which the goods are sold or the services performed, and expenses must be assigned to the accounting period in which they were used to produce revenue.

3. **Define accrual accounting and explain two broad ways of accomplishing it.**

   Accrual accounting consists of all the techniques developed by accountants to apply the matching rule. The two general ways of accomplishing it are (1) by recognizing revenue when earned and expenses when incurred and (2) by adjusting the accounts.

4. **State the four principal situations that require adjusting entries.**

   Adjusting entries are required (1) when recorded expenses are to be apportioned between two or more accounting periods, (2) when recorded revenues are to be apportioned between two or more accounting periods, (3) when unrecorded expenses exist, and (4) when unrecorded revenues exist.

5. **Prepare typical adjusting entries.**

   The preparation of adjusting entries is summarized in the following table:

Type of Adjusting Entry	Type of Account		Examples
	Debited	Credited	
Deferrals			
1. Apportioning Recorded Expenses (Recorded, not incurred)	Expense	Asset (or contra asset)	Prepaid Rent Prepaid Insurance Supplies Buildings Equipment
2. Apportioning Recorded Revenues (Recorded, not earned)	Liability	Revenue	Commissions Received in Advance

(continued)

Type of Adjusting Entry	Type of Account		Examples
	Debited	**Credited**	
Accruals			
1. Unrecorded Revenues (Earned, not received)	Asset	Revenue	Commissions Receivable Interest Receivable
2. Unrecorded Expenses (Incurred, not paid)	Expense	Liability	Wages Payable Interest Payable

6. **Prepare financial statements from an adjusted trial balance.**

   An adjusted trial balance is prepared after adjusting entries have been posted to the ledger accounts. Its purpose is to test the balance of the ledger after the adjusting entries are made and before financial statements are prepared. The income statement is then prepared from the revenue and expense accounts. The balance sheet is prepared from the balance sheet accounts and from the statement of owner's equity.

7. **Relate the need for adjusting entries to the usefulness of accounting information.**

   Adjusting entries are a means of implementing accrual accounting and thereby aid in producing financial statements that are comparable from period to period and relevant to the needs of users. Although adjusting entries often require estimates, the estimates should be based on verifiable information.

8. **Prepare correcting entries.**

   When a correcting entry is required, it should be made in such a way as to adjust the appropriate accounts to the correct balances. A full explanation should accompany each correcting entry.

Review of Concepts and Terminology

The following concepts and terms were introduced in this chapter:

(L.O. 2) **Accounting period issue:** The difficulty of assigning revenues and expenses to a short period of time such as a month or a year; net income must be regarded as tentative but useful.

(L.O. 4) **Accrual:** The recognition of an expense that has been incurred or a revenue that has been earned but that has not yet been recorded.

(L.O. 3) **Accrual accounting:** The attempt to record the financial effects on an enterprise of transactions and other events in the periods in which those transactions or events occur rather than only in the periods in which cash is received or paid by the enterprise.

(L.O. 5) **Accrued expenses:** Expenses that have been incurred but are not recognized in the accounts, necessitating an adjusting entry; unrecorded expenses.

(L.O. 5) **Accumulated depreciation:** A contra-asset account used to accumulate the total past depreciation of a specific long-lived asset.

(L.O. 6) **Adjusted trial balance:** A trial balance prepared after all adjusting entries have been posted to the accounts.

(L.O. 4) **Adjusting entries:** Entries made to apply accrual accounting to transactions that span more than one accounting period.

(L.O. 5) **Carrying value:** The unexpired portion of the cost of an asset; sometimes called book value.

(L.O. 2) **Cash basis of accounting:** A basis of accounting under which revenues and expenses are accounted for on a cash received and cash paid basis.

(L.O. 2) **Continuity issue:** The difficulty associated with not knowing how long the business entity will last.

(L.O. 5) **Contra account:** An account whose balance is subtracted from an associated account in the financial statements.

(L.O. 4) **Deferral:** The postponement of the recognition of an expense already paid or incurred or of a revenue already received.

(L.O. 5) **Depreciation (depreciation expense):** The periodic allocation of the cost of a tangible long-lived asset over its estimated useful life.

(L.O. 1) **Expenses:** Outflows or other using up of assets or incurrences of liabilities from delivering or producing goods, rendering services, or carrying out other activities that constitute the entity's ongoing major or central operations.

(L.O. 2) **Fiscal year:** Any twelve-month accounting period used by an economic entity.

(L.O. 2) **Going concern (continuity)** Assumption that unless there is evidence to the contrary, the business entity will continue to operate for an indefinite period.

(L.O. 2) **Matching rule:** Revenues must be assigned to the accounting period in which the goods were sold or the services rendered, and expenses must be assigned to the accounting period in which they were used to produce revenue.

(L.O. 1) **Net income:** The net increase in owner's equity resulting from the operations of the company.

(L.O. 1) **Net loss:** Net decrease in owner's equity that develops when expenses exceed revenues.

(L.O. 2) **Periodicity:** The recognition that net income for any period less than the life of the business must be regarded as tentative but is still a useful estimate of the net income for that period.

(L.O. 1) **Permanent (real) accounts:** Balance sheet accounts; accounts whose balances can extend past the end of an accounting period.

(L.O. 5) **Prepaid expenses:** Expenses paid in advance that do not expire during the current accounting period; an asset account.

(L.O. 1) **Profit:** Imprecise term for the earnings of a business enterprise.

(L.O. 3) **Revenue recognition:** The process in accrual accounting of determining when a sale takes place.

(L.O. 1)   **Revenues:**   Inflows or other enhancements of assets of an entity or settlements of its liabilities from delivering or producing goods, rendering services, or other activities that constitute the entity's ongoing major or central operations.

(L.O. 1)   **Temporary (nominal) accounts:**   Accounts showing the accumulation of revenue and expenses for only one accounting period; at the end of the accounting period, these account balances are transferred to owner's equity.

(L.O. 5)   **Unearned revenues:**   A revenue received in advance for which the goods will not be delivered or the services performed during the current accounting period; a liability account.

(L.O. 5)   **Unrecorded (accrued) revenues:**   Revenues for which the service has been performed or the goods have been delivered but have not been recorded.

Self-Test

Test your knowledge of the chapter by choosing the best answer for each item below.

1. The net increase in owner's equity resulting from business operations is called
   a. net income.   c. expense.
   b. revenue.   d. asset.   *(L.O. 1)*

2. In general, the accounts in the income statement are known as
   a. permanent accounts.   c. unearned revenue accounts.
   b. temporary accounts.   d. contra-asset accounts.   *(L.O. 1)*

3. A business may choose a fiscal year that corresponds to
   a. the calendar year.   c. any twelve-month period.
   b. the natural business year.   d. any of the above.   *(L.O. 2)*

4. Assigning revenues to the accounting period in which the goods were delivered or the services performed and expenses to the accounting period in which they were used to produce revenues is known as the
   a. accounting period.   c. matching rule.
   b. continuity assumption.   d. recognition rule.   *(L.O. 2)*

5. The objective of accrual accounting would not necessarily be met by
   a. recording all revenues when cash was received.
   b. applying the matching rule.
   c. recognizing expenses when incurred.
   d. adjusting the accounts.   *(L.O. 3)*

6. Which of the following is an example of a deferral?
   a. Apportioning costs between two or more periods
   b. Recognizing an accrued expense
   c. Recognizing an unrecorded revenue
   d. Recognizing an accrued revenue   *(L.O. 4)*

7. Prepaid Insurance has an ending balance of $2,300. During the period, insurance in the amount of $1,200 expired. The adjusting entry would contain a debit to
   a. Prepaid Insurance for $1,200. c. Unexpired Insurance for $1,100.
   b. Insurance Expense for $1,200. d. Insurance Expense for $1,100.
                                                                       (L.O. 5)

8. The adjusted trial balance is a list of accounts and their balances
   a. at the beginning of the accounting period.
   b. at the end of the accounting period.
   c. at the end of the accounting period immediately following the posting of adjusting entries.
   d. at any point during the accounting period when desired.   *(L.O. 6)*

9. An important reason for preparing adjusting entries is
   a. to make financial statements from one period to the next period more comparable.
   b. to make net income more readily reflect cash flow.
   c. to correct errors in the recording of earlier transactions.
   d. to record transactions initially.   *(L.O. 7)*

10. A purchase of office supplies that was incorrectly recorded as office equipment would require a correcting entry that
    a. credits office supplies.   c. debits office equipment.
    b. credits cash.   d. credits office equipment. *(L.O. 8)*

Answers to Self-Test are at the end of this chapter.

Review Problem
Adjusting Entries, T Accounts, and Adjusted Trial Balance

(L.O. 5, 6)   The unadjusted trial balance for Certified Answering Service appears as follows on December 31, 19x2:

Certified Answering Service Trial Balance December 31, 19x2		
Cash	$2,160	
Accounts Receivable	1,250	
Office Supplies	180	
Prepaid Insurance	240	
Office Equipment	3,400	
Accumulated Depreciation, Office Equipment		$ 600
Accounts Payable		700
Unearned Revenue		460
James Neal, Capital		4,870
James Neal, Withdrawals	400	
Answering Service Revenue		2,900
Wages Expense	1,500	
Rent Expense	400	
	$9,530	$9,530

The following information is also available:

a. Insurance that expired during December amounted to $40.
b. Office supplies on hand at the end of December totaled $75.
c. Depreciation for the month of December totaled $100.
d. Accrued wages at the end of December totaled $120.
e. Revenues earned for services performed but not yet billed on December 31 totaled $300.
f. Revenues earned for services performed that were paid in advance totaled $160.

Required

1. Prepare T accounts for the accounts in the trial balance and enter the balances.
2. Determine the required adjusting entries and record them directly to the T accounts. Open new T accounts as needed.
3. Prepare an adjusted trial balance.
4. Prepare an income statement, statement of owner's equity, and a balance sheet for the month ended December 31, 19x2.

Answer to Review Problem

1. T accounts set up and amounts from trial balance entered
2. Adjusting entries recorded

Cash			Accounts Receivable		
Bal.	2,160		Bal.	1,250	

Service Revenue Receivable			Office Supplies		
(e)	300		Bal.	180	(b) 105
			Bal.	**75**	

Prepaid Insurance			Office Equipment		
Bal.	240	(a) 40	Bal.	3,400	
Bal.	**200**				

Accumulated Depreciation, Office Equipment			Accounts Payable		
		Bal. 600			Bal. 700
		(c) 100			
		Bal. 700			

Unearned Revenue			Wages Payable		
(f)	160	Bal. 460			(d) 120
		Bal. 300			

James Neal, Capital		
	Bal.	4,870

James Neal, Withdrawals		
Bal.	400	

Answering Service Revenue		
	Bal.	2,900
	(e)	300
	(f)	160
	Bal.	**3,360**

Wages Expense		
Bal.	1,500	
(d)	120	
Bal.	**1,620**	

Rent Expense		
Bal.	400	

Insurance Expense		
(a)	40	

Office Supplies Expense		
(b)	105	

Depreciation Expense, Office Equipment		
(c)	100	

3. Adjusted trial balance prepared

Certified Answering Service Adjusted Trial Balance December 31, 19x2		
Cash	$ 2,160	
Accounts Receivable	1,250	
Service Revenue Receivable	300	
Office Supplies	75	
Prepaid Insurance	200	
Office Equipment	3,400	
Accumulated Depreciation, Office Equipment		$ 700
Accounts Payable		700
Unearned Revenue		300
Wages Payable		120
James Neal, Capital		4,870
James Neal, Withdrawals	400	
Answering Service Revenue		3,360
Wages Expense	1,620	
Rent Expense	400	
Insurance Expense	40	
Office Supplies Expense	105	
Depreciation Expense, Office Equipment	100	
	$10,050	$10,050

4. Financial statements prepared

Certified Answering Service Income Statement For the Month Ended December 31, 19x2		
Revenues		
Answering Service Revenue		$3,360
Expenses		
Wages Expense	$1,620	
Rent Expense	400	
Insurance Expense	40	
Office Supplies Expense	105	
Depreciation Expense, Office Equipment	100	
Total Expenses		2,265
Net Income		$1,095

Certified Answering Service Statement of Owner's Equity For the Month Ended December 31, 19x2	
James Neal, Capital, November 30, 19x2	$4,870
Net Income	1,095
Subtotal	$5,965
Less Withdrawals	400
James Neal, Capital, December 31, 19x2	$5,565

Certified Answering Service Balance Sheet December 31, 19x2		
Assets		
Cash		$2,160
Accounts Receivable		1,250
Service Revenue Receivable		300
Office Supplies		75
Prepaid Insurance		200
Office Equipment	$3,400	
Less Accumulated Depreciation	700	2,700
Total Assets		$6,685
Liabilities		
Accounts Payable		$ 700
Unearned Revenue		300
Wages Payable		120
Total Liabilities		$1,120
Owner's Equity		
James Neal, Capital		5,565
Total Liabilities and Owner's Equity		$6,685

Chapter Assignments

Discussion Questions and Writing Assignments

1. Why does the accountant use the term *net income* instead of *profit*?
2. Define the terms *revenues* and *expenses*.
3. Why are income statement accounts called nominal accounts?
4. Why does the need for an accounting period cause problems?
5. What is the significance of the continuity assumption?
6. "The matching rule is the most significant concept in accounting." Do you agree with this statement? Explain.
7. What is the difference between the cash basis and the accrual basis of accounting?
8. In what two ways is accrual accounting accomplished?
9. Why do adjusting entries need to be made?
10. What are the four situations that require adjusting entries? Give an example of each.
11. Explain the statement, "Some assets are expenses that have not expired."
12. What is a contra account? Give an example.
13. What do plant and equipment, office supplies, and prepaid insurance have in common?
14. What is the difference between accumulated depreciation and depreciation expense?
15. Why are contra accounts used in recording depreciation?
16. How does unearned revenue arise? Give an example.
17. Where does unearned revenue appear on the balance sheet?
18. What accounting problem does a magazine publisher who sells three-year subscriptions have?
19. What is an accrued expense? Give three examples.
20. Under what circumstances might a company have unrecorded revenue? Give an example.
21. Why is the income statement usually the first statement prepared from the trial balance?
22. "Why worry about adjustments? Doesn't it all come out in the wash?" Discuss these questions.
23. What is the difference between an adjusting entry and a correcting entry?

Classroom Exercises

**Exercise 3-1.
Applications of
Accounting
Concepts
Related to
Accrual
Accounting**
(L.O. 2, 3, 4)

The accountant for Boulder Company makes the following assumptions or performs the following activities:

a. In estimating the life of a building, assumes that the business will last indefinitely.
b. Records a sale at the point in time when the customer is billed.
c. Postpones the recognition as an expense of a one-year insurance policy by initially recording the expenditure as an asset.
d. Recognizes the usefulness of financial statements prepared on a monthly basis even though it is recognized that they are tentative and based on estimates.

e. Recognizes, by making an adjusting entry, wages expense that has been incurred but not yet recorded.

f. Prepares an income statement that shows the revenues earned and the expenses incurred during the accounting period.

Tell which of the following concepts of accrual accounting most directly relates to each of the above actions: (1) periodicity, (2) going concern, (3) matching rule, (4) revenue recognition, (5) deferral, (6) accrual.

Exercise 3-2.
Adjusting
Entries for
Prepaid
Insurance
(L.O. 5)

An examination of the Prepaid Insurance account shows a balance of $2,056 at the end of an accounting period before adjustments.

Prepare journal entries to record the insurance expense for the period under each of the following independent assumptions:

1. An examination of insurance policies shows unexpired insurance that cost $987 at the end of the period.
2. An examination of insurance policies shows insurance that cost $347 has expired during the period.

Exercise 3-3.
Supplies
Account:
Missing Data
(L.O. 5)

Determine the amounts indicated by question marks in the columns below. Consider each column a separate problem. Make the adjusting entry for column **a**, assuming supplies purchased are debited to an asset account.

	a	b	c	d
Supplies on hand July 1	$132	$217	$98	$?
Supplies purchased during month	26	?	87	964
Supplies consumed during month	97	486	?	816
Supplies remaining on July 31	?	218	28	594

Exercise 3-4.
Adjusting Entry
for Accrued
Salaries
(L.O. 5)

Photex, which has a five-day workweek, pays salaries of $35,000 each Friday.

a. Make the adjusting entry required on May 31, assuming that June 1 falls on a Wednesday.
b. Make the entry to pay the salaries on June 3.

Exercise 3-5.
Adjusting
Entries
(L.O. 5)

Prepare year-end adjusting entries for each of the following:

a. Office supplies had a balance of $84 on January 1. Purchases debited to Office Supplies during the year amount to $415. A year-end inventory reveals supplies of $285 on hand.
b. Depreciation of office equipment is estimated to be $2,130 for the year.
c. Property taxes for six months, estimated to total $875, have accrued but are unrecorded.
d. Unrecorded interest receivable on U.S. government bonds is $850.
e. Unearned Revenue has a balance of $900. The services for $300 received in advance have now been performed.
f. Services totaling $200 have been performed for which the customer has not yet been billed.

Exercise 3-6.
Relationship of
Cash to
Expenses Paid
(L.O. 5)

The 19x1 and 19x2 balance sheets of Target Company showed the following asset and liability amounts at the end of each year after adjusting entries:

	19x1	19x2
Prepaid Insurance	$2,900	$2,400
Wages Payable	2,200	1,200
Unearned Fees	1,900	4,200

From the accounting records the following amounts of cash disbursements and cash receipts for 19x2 were determined:

Cash disbursed to pay insurance premiums	$ 3,800
Cash disbursed to pay wages	19,500
Cash received for fees	8,900

Calculate the amount of insurance expense, wages expense, and fees earned to be reported on the 19x2 income statement.

Exercise 3-7.
Relationship of
Expenses to
Cash Paid
(L.O. 5)

The income statement for Gemini Company included the following expenses for 19xx:

Rent Expense	$ 2,600
Interest Expense	3,900
Salaries Expense	41,500

Listed below are the related balance sheet account balances at year end for last year and this year.

	Last Year	This Year
Prepaid Rent	—	$ 450
Interest Payable	$ 600	—
Salaries Payable	2,500	4,800

1. Compute cash paid for rent during the year.
2. Compute cash paid for interest during the year.
3. Compute cash paid for salaries during the year.

Exercise 3-8.
Accounting for
Revenue
Received in
Advance
(L.O. 5, 7)

Michelle Demetri, a lawyer, was paid $24,000 on September 1 to represent a client in certain real estate negotiations during the next twelve months. Give the entries required on September 1 and at the end of the year, December 31. How would this transaction be reflected in the balance sheet and income statement on December 31?

Exercise 3-9.
Determining
Cash Flows
(L.O. 5)

Suburban East News Service provides home delivery of day, evening, and Sunday city newspapers to subscribers who live in the suburbs. Customers may pay a yearly subscription fee in advance (at a savings) or pay monthly after delivery of their newspapers. The following data are available for subscriptions receivable and unearned subscriptions at the beginning and end of May, 19xx:

	May 1	May 31
Subscriptions Receivable	$ 3,800	$4,600
Unearned Subscriptions	11,400	9,800

The income statement shows subscriptions revenue for May of $22,400. Determine the amount of cash received from customers for subscriptions during May.

Exercise 3-10.
Preparation of
Financial
Statements
(L.O. 6)

Prepare the monthly income statement, statement of owner's equity, and balance sheet for Miracle Janitorial Service from the data provided in the following adjusted trial balance:

Miracle Janitorial Service
Adjusted Trial Balance
June 30, 19xx

Cash	$ 2,295	
Accounts Receivable	1,296	
Prepaid Insurance	190	
Prepaid Rent	100	
Cleaning Supplies	76	
Cleaning Equipment	1,600	
Accumulated Depreciation, Cleaning Equipment		$ 160
Truck	3,600	
Accumulated Depreciation, Truck		360
Accounts Payable		210
Wages Payable		40
Unearned Janitorial Revenue		460
Mae Farber, Capital		7,517
Mae Farber, Withdrawals	1,000	
Janitorial Revenue		7,310
Wages Expense	2,840	
Rent Expense	600	
Gas, Oil, and Other Truck Expense	290	
Insurance Expense	190	
Supplies Expense	1,460	
Depreciation Expense, Cleaning Equipment	160	
Depreciation Expense, Truck	360	
	$16,057	$16,057

Exercise 3-11.
Correction of
Errors
(L.O. 8)

A number of errors in journalizing and posting transactions are described below. Prepare the journal entries to correct the errors.

1. Rent payment of $450 for the current month was recorded as a debit to Prepaid Rent and a credit to Cash.
2. Payment of $450 to a creditor was recorded in the amount of $540 as a debit to Accounts Payable and a credit to Cash.
3. A $380 cash payment for equipment repair expense was recorded as a debit to Equipment.
4. Payment of the gas and oil bill of $90 for the owner's personal car was recorded as a debit to Delivery Truck Expense and a credit to Cash.
5. A cash receipt of $150 for services yet to be performed was debited to Cash and credited to Service Revenue.

Interpreting Accounting Information

Walt Disney
Productions
(L.O. 2, 5)

In addition to owning and operating theme parks like Disneyland and Disney World, Walt Disney Productions makes films for motion pictures and for television. In Walt Disney's 1986 annual report the balance sheet contains an asset called Film Production Costs. The amount of this asset was $182.1 million in 1985 and $214.0 million in 1986. In management's analysis of the Statement of Cash Flows, it is revealed that the company spent $203.7 million for new film productions in 1986.

Required

1. What is the nature of the asset Film Production Costs?
2. Prepare an entry to record the amount spent on new film production during 1986 (assume all expenditures are paid for in cash).
3. How much was the film production expense in 1986 that would appear on the income statement? Prepare the adjusting entry that would be made to record the expense.
4. Can you suggest a method by which Walt Disney Productions might have determined the expense in 3 in accordance with the matching rule?

Problem Set A

Problem 3A-1.
Preparation of
Adjusting
Entries
(L.O. 5)

On June 30, the end of the current fiscal year, the following information was available to aid the Sterling Company accountants in making adjusting entries.

a. Among the liabilities of the company is a mortgage payable in the amount of $240,000. On June 30, the accrued interest on this mortgage amounted to $12,000.
b. On Friday, July 2, the company, which is on a five-day workweek and pays employees weekly, will pay its regular salaried employees $19,200.
c. On June 29, the company completed negotiations and signed a contract to provide services to a new client at an annual rate of $3,600.
d. The Supplies account showed a beginning balance of $1,615 and purchases during the year of $3,766. The end-of-year inventory revealed supplies on hand that cost $1,186.

e. The Prepaid Insurance account showed the following entries on June 30:

Beginning Balance	$1,530
January 1	2,900
May 1	3,366

The beginning balance represents the unexpired portion of a one-year policy purchased the previous year. The January 1 entry represents a new one-year policy, and the May 1 entry represents additional coverage in the form of a three-year policy.

f. The table below contains the cost and annual depreciation for buildings and equipment, all of which were purchased before the current year:

Account	Cost	Annual Depreciation
Buildings	$185,000	$ 7,300
Equipment	218,000	21,800

g. On June 1, the company completed negotiations with another client and accepted a payment of $21,000, representing one year's services paid in advance. The $21,000 was credited to Services Collected in Advance.

h. The company calculated that as of June 30 it had earned $3,500 on a $7,500 contract that would be completed and billed in August.

Required

Prepare adjusting entries for each item listed above.

**Problem 3A-2.
Determining
Adjusting
Entries, Posting
to T Accounts,
and Preparing
Adjusted Trial
Balance
(L.O. 5)**

The schedule below presents the trial balance for the Sigma Consultants Company on December 31, 19x2.

Sigma Consultants Company Trial Balance December 31, 19x2		
Cash	$ 12,786	
Accounts Receivable	24,840	
Office Supplies	991	
Prepaid Rent	1,400	
Office Equipment	6,700	
Accumulated Depreciation, Office Equipment		$ 1,600
Accounts Payable		1,820
Notes Payable		10,000
Unearned Fees		2,860
Kevin Moriarty, Capital		29,387
Kevin Moriarty, Withdrawals	15,000	
Fees Revenue		58,500
Salaries Expense	33,000	
Utility Expense	1,750	
Rent Expense	7,700	
	$104,167	$104,167

The following information is also available:

a. Ending inventory of office supplies, $86.
b. Prepaid rent expired, $700.
c. Depreciation of office equipment for period, $600.
d. Interest accrued on note payable, $600.
e. Salaries accrued at end of period, $200.
f. Fees still unearned at end of period, $1,410.
g. Fees earned but not billed, $600.

Required

1. Open T accounts for the accounts in the trial balance plus the following: Fees Receivable; Interest Payable; Salaries Payable; Office Supplies Expense; Depreciation Expense, Office Equipment; and Interest Expense.
2. Determine adjusting entries and post them directly to the T accounts.
3. Prepare an adjusted trial balance.

**Problem 3A-3.
Determining
Adjusting
Entries and
Tracing Their
Effects to
Financial
Statements
(L.O. 5, 6)**

Having graduated from college with a degree in accounting, Joyce Ozaki opened a small tax preparation service. At the end of its second year of operation, the Ozaki Tax Service has the following trial balance:

**Ozaki Tax Service
Trial Balance
December 31, 19xx**

Cash	$ 2,268	
Accounts Receivable	1,031	
Prepaid Insurance	240	
Office Supplies	782	
Office Equipment	4,100	
Accumulated Depreciation, Office Equipment		$ 410
Copier	3,000	
Accumulated Depreciation, Copier		360
Accounts Payable		635
Unearned Tax Fees		219
Joyce Ozaki, Capital		5,439
Joyce Ozaki, Withdrawals	6,000	
Fees Revenue		21,926
Office Salaries Expense	8,300	
Advertising Expense	650	
Rent Expense	2,400	
Telephone Expense	218	
	$28,989	$28,989

Joyce Ozaki made no investments in her business during the year. The following information was also available:

a. Supplies on hand, December 31, 19xx, were $227.
b. Insurance still unexpired amounted to $120.
c. Estimated depreciation of office equipment was $410.
d. Estimated depreciation of copier was $360.
e. The telephone expense for December was $19. This bill has been received but not recorded.
f. The services for all unearned tax fees had been performed by the end of the year.

Required

1. Open T accounts for the accounts of the trial balance plus the following: Insurance Expense; Office Supplies Expense; Depreciation Expense, Office Equipment; Depreciation Expense, Copier. Record the balances as shown in the trial balance.
2. Determine adjusting entries and post them directly to the T accounts.
3. Prepare an adjusted trial balance, an income statement, a statement of owner's equity, and a balance sheet.

**Problem 3A-4.
Determining
Adjusting
Entries and
Tracing Their
Effects to
Financial
Statements**
(L.O. 5, 6)

The Elite Livery Service was organized to provide limousine service between the airport and various suburban locations. It has just completed its second year of business. Its trial balance appears as follows (account numbers are included):

	Elite Livery Service Trial Balance June 30, 19x2	
Cash (111)	$ 9,812	
Accounts Receivable (112)	14,227	
Prepaid Rent (117)	12,000	
Prepaid Insurance (118)	4,900	
Prepaid Maintenance (119)	12,000	
Spare Parts (141)	11,310	
Limousines (142)	200,000	
Accumulated Depreciation, Limousines (143)		$ 25,000
Notes Payable (211)		45,000
Unearned Passenger Service Revenue (212)		30,000
Raymond Lewis, Capital (311)		78,211
Raymond Lewis, Withdrawals (312)	20,000	
Passenger Service Revenue (411)		428,498
Gas and Oil Expense (511)	89,300	
Salaries Expense (512)	206,360	
Advertising Expense (513)	26,800	
	$606,709	$606,709

Raymond Lewis made no investments during the year. The following information is also available:

a. To obtain space at the airport, Elite paid two years' rent in advance when it began business.
b. An examination of insurance policies reveals that $2,800 expired during the year.
c. To provide regular maintenance for the vehicles, a deposit of $12,000 was made with a local garage. Examination of maintenance invoices reveals that there are $10,944 in charges against the deposit.
d. An inventory of spare parts shows $1,902 on hand.
e. All of the Elite Livery Service's limousines are to be depreciated at the rate of 12.5 percent a year. There were no limousines purchased during the year.
f. A payment of $10,500 for one full year's interest on notes payable is now due.
g. Unearned Passenger Service Revenue on June 30 includes $17,815 in tickets that were purchased by employers for use by their executives and have not been redeemed.

Required

1. Open ledger accounts for the accounts in the trial balance plus the following: Interest Payable (213); Rent Expense (514); Insurance Expense (515); Spare Parts Expense (516); Depreciation Expense, Limousines (517); Maintenance Expense (518); Interest Expense (519). Record the balances as shown in the trial balance.
2. Record the adjusting entries in the general journal (record them on journal Page 14).
3. Post the adjusting entries from the general journal to the ledger accounts, showing proper references.
4. Prepare an adjusted trial balance, an income statement, a statement of owner's equity, and a balance sheet.

**Problem 3A-5.
Determining
Adjusting
Entries and
Tracing Their
Effects to
Financial
Statements**
(L.O. 3, 5, 6)

At the end of its accounting period, the trial balance for Apollo Cleaners appears as shown on the top of page 134. Gregory Katz, the owner, made no investments during the year. The following information is also available:

a. A study of insurance policies shows that $340 is unexpired at the end of the year.
b. An inventory of cleaning supplies shows $622 on hand.
c. Estimated depreciation for the year was $4,300 on the building and $2,100 on the delivery truck.
d. Accrued interest on the mortgage payable amounted to $500.
e. On August 1, the company signed a contract effective immediately with Stark County Hospital to dry clean, for a fixed monthly charge of $200, the uniforms used by doctors in surgery. The hospital paid for four months of service in advance.
f. Unrecorded plant wages totaled $982.
g. Sales and delivery wages are paid on Saturday. The weekly payroll is $480. September 30 falls on a Thursday and the company has a six-day pay week.

Apollo Cleaners
Trial Balance
September 30, 19x2

Cash (111)	$ 5,894	
Accounts Receivable (112)	13,247	
Prepaid Insurance (115)	1,700	
Cleaning Supplies (116)	3,687	
Land (141)	9,000	
Building (142)	81,000	
Accumulated Depreciation, Building (143)		$ 20,200
Delivery Truck (144)	11,500	
Accumulated Depreciation, Delivery Truck (145)		2,600
Accounts Payable (212)		10,200
Unearned Dry Cleaning Revenue (215)		800
Mortgage Payable (221)		60,000
Gregory Katz, Capital (311)		28,280
Gregory Katz, Withdrawals (312)	10,000	
Dry Cleaning Revenue (411)		60,167
Laundry Revenue (412)		18,650
Plant Wages Expense (511)	32,560	
Sales and Delivery Wages Expense (512)	18,105	
Cleaning Equipment Rent Expense (513)	3,000	
Delivery Truck Expense (514)	2,187	
Interest Expense (519)	5,500	
Other Expenses (520)	3,517	
	$200,897	$200,897

Required

1. Open ledger accounts for each account in the trial balance plus the following: Wages Payable (213); Interest Payable (214); Insurance Expense (515); Cleaning Supplies Expense (516); Depreciation Expense, Building (517); Depreciation Expense, Delivery Truck (518). Record the balances as shown in the trial balance.
2. Determine adjusting entries, and enter them in the general journal (Page 42).
3. Post the adjusting entries to the ledger accounts, showing all the proper references.
4. Prepare an adjusted trial balance.
5. Prepare an income statement, a statement of owner's equity, and a balance sheet for the year ended September 30, 19x2.
6. Give examples of how the techniques of accrual accounting affect the income statement in **5**.

Problem Set B

**Problem 3B-1.
Preparation of
Adjusting
Entries
(L.O. 5)**

On November 30, the end of the current fiscal year, the following information was available to assist Pinder Company's accountants in making adjusting entries:

a. The Supplies account showed a beginning balance of $2,174. Purchases during the year were $4,526. The end-of-year inventory revealed supplies on hand that cost $1,397.

b. The Prepaid Insurance account showed the following on November 30:

Beginning Balance	$3,580
July 1	4,200
October 1	7,272

The beginning balance represents the unexpired portion of a one-year policy purchased the previous year. The July 1 entry represents a new one-year policy, and the October 1 entry represents additional coverage in the form of a three-year policy.

c. The table below contains the cost and annual depreciation for buildings and equipment, all of which were purchased before the current year.

Account	Cost	Annual Depreciation
Buildings	$286,000	$14,500
Equipment	374,000	35,400

d. On September 1, the company completed negotiations with a client and accepted a payment of $16,800, which represented one year's services paid in advance. The $16,800 was credited to Unearned Services Revenue.

e. The company calculated that as of November 30 it had earned $4,000 on an $11,000 contract that would be completed and billed in January.

f. Among the liabilities of the company is a note payable in the amount of $300,000. On November 30, the accrued interest on this note amounted to $15,000.

g. On Saturday, December 2, the company, which is on a six-day workweek, will pay its regular salaried employees $12,300.

h. On November 29, the company completed negotiations and signed a contract to provide services to a new client at an annual rate of $17,500.

Required

Prepare adjusting entries for each item listed above.

**Problem 3B-2.
Determining
Adjusting
Entries, Posting
to T Accounts,
and Preparing
Adjusted Trial
Balance
(L.O. 5)**

The schedule on page 136 presents the trial balance for Financial Strategies Service on December 31. The following information is also available:

a. Ending inventory of office supplies, $264.

b. Prepaid rent expired, $440.

c. Depreciation of office equipment for period, $660.

d. Accrued interest expense at end of period, $550.

e. Accrued salaries at end of month, $330.

f. Fees still unearned at end of period, $1,166.

g. Fees earned but unrecorded, $2,200.

Financial Strategies Service
Trial Balance
December 31, 19xx

Cash	$ 16,500	
Accounts Receivable	8,250	
Office Supplies	2,662	
Prepaid Rent	1,320	
Office Equipment	9,240	
Accumulated Depreciation, Office Equipment		$ 1,540
Accounts Payable		5,940
Notes Payable		11,000
Unearned Fees		2,970
Karen Howard, Capital		24,002
Karen Howard, Withdrawals	22,000	
Fees Revenue		72,600
Salaries Expense	49,400	
Rent Expense	4,400	
Utility Expense	4,280	
	$118,052	$118,052

Required

1. Open T accounts for the accounts in the trial balance plus the following: Fees Receivable; Interest Payable; Salaries Payable; Office Supplies Expense; Depreciation Expense, Office Equipment; and Interest Expense. Enter balances.
2. Determine adjusting entries and post them directly to the T accounts.
3. Prepare an adjusted trial balance.

Problem 3B-3.
Determining
Adjusting
Entries and
Tracing Their
Effects to
Financial
Statements
(L.O. 5, 6)

The Crescent Custodial Service is owned by Mike Podgorney. After six months of operation, the June 30, 19xx trial balance for the company, presented on the next page, was prepared. The following information is also available:

a. Cleaning supplies on hand, $117.
b. Prepaid insurance is the cost of a one-year policy purchased on January 1.
c. Prepaid rent represents a $100 payment made on January 1 toward the last month's rent of a three-year lease plus $100 rent per month for each of the six past months.
d. The cleaning equipment and trucks are depreciated at the rate of 20 percent per year (10 percent for each six months).
e. The unearned revenue represents a six-month payment in advance made by a customer on May 1.
f. During the last week of June, Mike completed the first stage of work on a contract that will not be billed until the contract is completed. The price of this stage is $400.
g. On Saturday, July 3, Mike will owe his employees $540 for one week's work (six-day workweek).

The balance of the capital account represents the investments made by Mike Podgorney.

Crescent Custodial Service Trial Balance June 30, 19xx		
Cash	$ 762	
Accounts Receivable	914	
Prepaid Insurance	380	
Prepaid Rent	700	
Cleaning Supplies	1,396	
Cleaning Equipment	1,740	
Truck	3,600	
Accounts Payable		$ 170
Unearned Janitorial Fees		480
Mike Podgorney, Capital		7,095
Mike Podgorney, Withdrawals	3,000	
Janitorial Fees		7,487
Wages Expense	2,400	
Gas, Oil, and Other Truck Expenses	340	
	$15,232	$15,232

Required

1. Open T accounts for the accounts in the trial balance plus the following: Fees Receivable; Accumulated Depreciation, Cleaning Equipment; Accumulated Depreciation, Truck; Wages Payable; Rent Expense; Insurance Expense; Cleaning Supplies Expense; Depreciation Expense, Cleaning Equipment; Depreciation Expense, Truck.
2. Determine adjusting entries and post them directly to the T accounts.
3. Prepare an adjusted trial balance, an income statement, a statement of owner's equity, and a balance sheet.

**Problem 3B-4.
Determining
Adjusting
Entries and
Tracing Their
Effects to
Financial
Statements
(L.O. 5, 6)**

The trial balance for New Wave Dance Studio at the end of the current fiscal year appears as shown on page 138. Midge Bronson made no investments in the business during the year. The following information is available to assist in the preparation of adjusting entries:

a. An inventory of supplies reveals $92 still on hand.
b. The prepaid rent reflects the rent for October plus the rent for the last month of the lease.
c. Prepaid insurance consists of a two-year policy purchased on May 1, 19x2.
d. Depreciation on equipment is estimated to be $800.
e. Accrued wages are $65 on October 31.
f. Two thirds of the unearned dance fees have been earned by October 31.

New Wave Dance Studio
Trial Balance
October 31, 19x2

Cash (111)	$ 1,028	
Accounts Receivable (112)	517	
Supplies (115)	170	
Prepaid Rent (116)	400	
Prepaid Insurance (117)	360	
Equipment (141)	4,100	
Accumulated Depreciation, Equipment (142)		$ 400
Accounts Payable (211)		380
Unearned Dance Fees (213)		900
Midge Bronson, Capital (311)		2,500
Midge Bronson, Withdrawals (312)	12,000	
Dance Fees (411)		20,995
Wages Expense (511)	3,200	
Rent Expense (512)	2,200	
Utility Expense (515)	1,200	
	$25,175	$25,175

Required

1. Open ledger accounts for the accounts in the trial balance plus the following: Wages Payable (212); Supplies Expense (513); Insurance Expense (514); Depreciation Expense, Equipment (516).
2. Record the adjusting entries in the general journal (use journal Page 53).
3. Post the adjusting entries from the general journal to the ledger accounts, showing proper references.
4. Prepare an adjusted trial balance, an income statement, a statement of owner's equity, and a balance sheet.

Problem 3B-5.
Determining
Adjusting
Entries and
Tracing Their
Effects to
Financial
Statements
(L.O. 3, 5, 6)

At the end of the first three months of operations, the trial balance of the Metropolitan Answering Service appeared as shown on the next page. Ben Stuckey, the owner, engaged an accountant to prepare financial statements for the company in order to determine how well the company was doing after three months. Upon examining the accounting records, the accountant found the following items of interest:

a. An inventory of office supplies reveals supplies on hand of $133.
b. The Prepaid Rent account includes the rent for the first three months plus a deposit for the last month's rent.
c. Prepaid Insurance reflects a one-year policy purchased on January 4.
d. Depreciation is computed to be $102 on the office equipment and $106 on the communications equipment for the first three months.
e. The balance of the Unearned Answering Service Revenue account represents a 12-month service contract paid in advance on February 1.
f. On March 31, accrued wages totaled $80.

The balance of the capital account represents investments by Ben Stuckey.

Metropolitan Answering Service
Trial Balance
March 31, 19x2

Cash (111)	$ 2,762	
Accounts Receivable (112)	4,236	
Office Supplies (115)	903	
Prepaid Rent (116)	800	
Prepaid Insurance (117)	720	
Office Equipment (141)	2,300	
Communications Equipment (143)	2,400	
Accounts Payable (211)		$ 2,673
Unearned Answering Service Revenue (213)		888
Ben Stuckey, Capital (311)		5,933
Ben Stuckey, Withdrawals (312)	2,130	
Answering Service Revenue (411)		9,002
Wages Expense (511)	1,900	
Office Cleaning Expense (513)	345	
	$18,496	$18,496

Required

1. Open ledger accounts for the accounts in the trial balance plus the following: Accumulated Depreciation, Office Equipment (142); Accumulated Depreciation, Communications Equipment (144); Wages Payable (212); Rent Expense (512); Insurance Expense (514); Office Supplies Expense (515); Depreciation Expense, Office Equipment (516); Depreciation Expense, Communications Equipment (517).
2. Record the adjusting entries in the general journal (use journal Page 12).
3. Post the adjusting entries from the general journal to the ledger accounts, showing proper references.
4. Prepare an adjusted trial balance.
5. Prepare an income statement, a statement of owner's equity, and a balance sheet.
6. Give examples of how the techniques of accrual accounting affect the income statement in **5**.

Financial Decision Case

Lockyer Systems Company
(L.O. 5, 6, 7)

Tim Lockyer began his new business, called Lockyer Systems Company, on July 1, 19xx. The Company is engaged in writing computer programs with special applications for businesses that own small computers. During the first six months of operation, the business was so successful that Tim had to hire new employees on several occasions. Yet he continually had to put off creditors because he lacked the funds to pay them. He wants to apply for a bank loan, but after preparing a statement showing the totals of receipts of cash and payments of cash, he wonders whether a bank will make a loan to him on the basis of such apparently poor results. Deciding that he needs some accounting help, Tim asks you to review the statement and the company's operating results.

Lockyer Systems Company
Statement of Cash Receipts and Payments
For the Six Months Ended December 31, 19xx

Receipts from

Investment by Tim Lockyer		$15,000
Customers for Programming Services Provided		25,200
Total Cash Receipts		$40,200

Payments for

Wages	$9,780	
Insurance	2,400	
Rent	4,200	
Supplies	1,980	
Office Equipment	6,200	
Computer Rental	8,000	
Maintenance	900	
Service Van	5,000	
Oil and Gas Reimbursements	690	
Utility	540	
Telephone	300	
Total Cash Payments		39,990
Bank Balance		$ 210

After verifying the information in Tim's statement, you assemble the following additional facts about Lockyer Systems Company:

a. In addition to the amount received from customers, programming services totaling $9,700 had been performed but were not yet paid for.
b. Employees have been paid all the wages owed to them except for $350 earned since the last payday. The next regular payday is January 3.
c. The insurance account represents a two-year policy purchased on July 1.
d. The rent account represents rent of $600 per month, including the rent for January.
e. In examining the expenditures for supplies, you find invoices for $650 that have not been paid, and an inventory reveals $875 of unused supplies still on hand.
f. The office equipment is fully paid for, and it is estimated it will last five years and be worthless at the end of that time.
g. The computer rental agreement provides for a security deposit of $2,000 plus monthly payments of $1,000.
h. The maintenance account represents a one-year maintenance agreement, paid in advance on July 1.
i. The service van account represents the down payment on a van purchased on December 30 for $15,000. Prior to this purchase, the company

had reimbursed employees for oil and gas when using their own cars for business. A study of the documents shows that $120 in employee oil and gas receipts must still be reimbursed.

Required

1. From the information given, open T accounts and record the transactions and any adjustments.
2. Then prepare an adjusted trial balance, an income statement, and a balance sheet for Lockyer Systems Company.
3. What is your assessment of the company's performance? If you were a bank loan officer, would you look favorably on a loan application from Lockyer Systems Company?

Answers to Self-Test

1. a	3. d	5. a	7. b	9. a
2. b	4. c	6. a	8. c	10. d

LEARNING OBJECTIVES

1. State all the steps in the accounting cycle.
2. Prepare a work sheet.
3. Identify the three principal uses of a work sheet.
4. Prepare financial statements from a work sheet.
5. Record the adjusting entries from a work sheet.
6. Explain the purposes of closing entries.
7. Prepare the required closing entries.
8. Prepare the post-closing trial balance.
9. Prepare reversing entries as appropriate.

CHAPTER 4

Completing the Accounting Cycle

You will see the accounting cycle completed in this chapter. First you study the uses and preparation of the work sheet, an important tool for accountants. Then, as the final step in the accounting cycle, you learn how to prepare closing entries.

In previous chapters, the main focus was on the measurement process in accounting. In this chapter, the emphasis is on the accounting system itself and the sequence of steps used by the accountant in completing the accounting cycle. An important part of the accounting system involves the preparation of a work sheet, so we present in detail each step in its preparation. This chapter also explains the uses of the work sheet in accomplishing the end-of-period procedures of recording the adjusting entries, preparing financial statements, and closing the accounts. The optional first step of the next accounting period, preparation of reversing entries, is also discussed. After studying this chapter, you should be able to meet the learning objectives listed on the left.

Overview of the Accounting System

The **accounting system** encompasses the sequence of steps followed in the accounting process, from analyzing transactions to preparing financial statements and closing the accounts. This system is sometimes called the **accounting cycle**. The purpose of the system, as illustrated in Figure 4-1, is to treat the business transactions as raw material and develop the finished product of accounting—the financial statements—in a systematic way. The steps in this system are as follows:

1. The transactions are *analyzed* from the *source documents*.
2. The transactions are *recorded* in the *journal*.
3. The entries are *posted* to the *ledger*.
4. The accounts are *adjusted* at the end of the period with the aid of a *work sheet*.
5. *Financial statements* are *prepared* from the work sheet.
6. The accounts are *closed* to conclude the current accounting period and prepare for the beginning of the new accounting period.

Figure 4-1. An Overview of the Accounting System

OBJECTIVE 1
State all the steps
in the accounting
cycle

The first four steps were introduced in Chapters 2 and 3. In this chapter, they are reviewed in conjunction with the use of the work sheet. The use of the work sheet and the final two steps are the major topics of this chapter.

The Work Sheet: A Tool of Accountants

OBJECTIVE 2
Prepare a work
sheet

As seen in Chapter 3, the flow of information affecting a business does not arbitrarily stop at the end of an accounting period. In order to prepare the financial reports, accountants must collect relevant data to determine what should be included. For example, accountants must examine insurance policies to see how much prepaid insurance has expired, examine plant and equipment records to determine depreciation, take an inventory of supplies on hand, and calculate the amount of accrued wages. These calculations, together with the other computations, analyses, and preliminary drafts of statements, make up the accountants' **working papers**. Working papers are important for two reasons. First, they aid accountants in organizing their work so that they do not omit important data or steps that affect the accounting statements. Second, they provide evidence of what has been done so that accountants or auditors can retrace their steps and support the basis of the financial statements.

A special kind of working paper is the **work sheet**. The work sheet is used frequently as a preliminary step in the preparation of financial statements. Using a work sheet lessens the possibility of ignoring an adjustment, aids in checking the arithmetical accuracy of the accounts, and facilitates the preparation of financial statements. The work sheet is never published and is rarely seen by management. Nevertheless, it is a useful tool for the accountant. Because preparation of the work sheet is a very mechanical process, accountants often use a microcomputer to assist in its preparation.

Steps in Preparing the Work Sheet

In Chapter 3, the adjustments were entered directly in the journal and posted to the ledger, and the financial statements were prepared from the adjusted trial balance. These steps were done rather easily for the Joan Miller Advertising Agency because it is a small company. For larger companies, which may require many adjusting entries, a work sheet is essential. To illustrate the preparation of the work sheet, the Joan Miller Advertising Agency case will be continued.

A commonly used form of work sheet has one column for account names and/or numbers and ten more columns with headings as shown in Exhibit 4-1. Note that the work sheet is identified by a heading that consists of (1) the name of the company, (2) the title "Work Sheet," and (3) the period of time covered (as on the income statement).

There are five steps in the preparation of a work sheet, as follows:

1. Enter and total the account balances in the Trial Balance columns.
2. Enter and total the adjustments in the Adjustments columns.
3. Enter and total the account balances as adjusted in the Adjusted Trial Balance columns.
4. Extend the account balances from the Adjusted Trial Balance columns to the Income Statement columns or the Balance Sheet columns.
5. Total the Income Statement columns and the Balance Sheet columns. Enter the net income or net loss in both pairs of columns as a balancing figure, and recompute column totals.

1. Enter and total the account balances in the Trial Balance columns. The titles and balances of the accounts as of January 31 are copied directly from the ledger into the Trial Balance columns, as shown in Exhibit 4-1. This trial balance is the same as illustrated in Exhibit 3-1 in Chapter 3 (page 104). When a work sheet is prepared, a separate trial balance is not required.

2. Enter and total the adjustments in the Adjustments columns. The required adjustments for the Joan Miller Advertising Agency were explained in Chapter 3. The same adjustments are entered in the Adjustments columns of the work sheet in Exhibit 4-2. As each adjustment is entered, a letter is used to identify the debit and credit parts of the same entry. The first adjustment, identified by the letter **a**, is for recognition of rent expense, which results in a debit to Rent Expense and a credit to Prepaid Rent. In practice, this letter may be used to reference supporting computations or documentation underlying the adjusting entry.

Exhibit 4-1. Entering the Account Balances in the Trial Balance Columns

Joan Miller Advertising Agency
Work Sheet
For the Month Ended January 31, 19xx

Account Name	Trial Balance		Adjustments		Adjusted Trial Balance		Income Statement		Balance Sheet	
	Debit	Credit	Debit	Credit	Debit	Credit	Debit	Credit	Debit	Credit
Cash	1,720									
Accounts Receivable	2,800									
Art Supplies	1,800									
Office Supplies	800									
Prepaid Rent	800									
Prepaid Insurance	480									
Art Equipment	4,200									
Accumulated Depreciation, Art Equipment										
Office Equipment	3,000									
Accumulated Depreciation, Office Equipment										
Accounts Payable		3,170								
Unearned Art Fees		1,000								
Joan Miller, Capital		10,000								
Joan Miller, Withdrawals	1,400									
Advertising Fees Earned		4,200								
Office Wages Expense	1,200									
Utility Expense	100									
Telephone Expense	70									
	18,370	18,370								

If the adjustment calls for an account that has not already been used in the trial balance, the new account is added below the accounts listed for the trial balance. The trial balance only includes those accounts that have balances. For example, Rent Expense has been added in Exhibit 4-2. The only exception to this rule is the Accumulated Depreciation accounts, which will have a zero balance only in the initial period of operation. Accumulated Depreciation accounts are listed immediately after their associated asset account.

When all the adjustments have been made, the two Adjustments columns must be totaled. This step proves that the debits and credits of the adjustments are equal and generally reduces errors in the preparation of the work sheet.

3. Enter and total the account balances as adjusted in the Adjusted Trial Balance columns. Exhibit 4-3 (page 147) shows the adjusted trial balance. It is prepared by combining the amount of each account in the

Exhibit 4-2. Entries in the Adjustments Columns

Joan Miller Advertising Agency
Work Sheet
For the Month Ended January 31, 19xx

Account Name	Trial Balance Debit	Trial Balance Credit	Adjustments Debit	Adjustments Credit	Adjusted Trial Balance Debit	Adjusted Trial Balance Credit	Income Statement Debit	Income Statement Credit	Balance Sheet Debit	Balance Sheet Credit
Cash	1,720									
Accounts Receivable	2,800									
Art Supplies	1,800			(c) 500						
Office Supplies	800			(d) 200						
Prepaid Rent	800			(a) 400						
Prepaid Insurance	480			(b) 40						
Art Equipment	4,200									
Accumulated Depreciation, Art Equipment				(e) 70						
Office Equipment	3,000									
Accumulated Depreciation, Office Equipment				(f) 50						
Accounts Payable		3,170								
Unearned Art Fees		1,000	(g) 400							
Joan Miller, Capital		10,000								
Joan Miller, Withdrawals	1,400									
Advertising Fees Earned		4,200		(h) 200						
Office Wages Expense	1,200		(i) 180							
Utility Expense	100									
Telephone Expense	70									
	18,370	18,370								
Rent Expense			(a) 400							
Insurance Expense			(b) 40							
Art Supplies Expense			(c) 500							
Office Supplies Expense			(d) 200							
Depreciation Expense, Art Equipment			(e) 70							
Depreciation Expense, Office Equipment			(f) 50							
Art Fees Earned				(g) 400						
Fees Receivable			(h) 200							
Wages Payable				(i) 180						
			2,040	2,040						

original Trial Balance columns with the corresponding amounts in the Adjustments columns and entering the combined amounts on a line-by-line basis in the Adjusted Trial Balance columns.

Some examples from Exhibit 4-3 will illustrate **crossfooting**, or adding and subtracting a group of numbers horizontally. The first line shows Cash with a debit balance of $1,720. Because there are no adjustments to

Exhibit 4-3. Entries in the Adjusted Trial Balance Columns

Joan Miller Advertising Agency
Work Sheet
For the Month Ended January 31, 19xx

Account Name	Trial Balance Debit	Trial Balance Credit	Adjustments Debit	Adjustments Credit	Adjusted Trial Balance Debit	Adjusted Trial Balance Credit	Income Statement Debit	Income Statement Credit	Balance Sheet Debit	Balance Sheet Credit
Cash	1,720				1,720					
Accounts Receivable	2,800				2,800					
Art Supplies	1,800			(c) 500	1,300					
Office Supplies	800			(d) 200	600					
Prepaid Rent	800			(a) 400	400					
Prepaid Insurance	480			(b) 40	440					
Art Equipment	4,200				4,200					
Accumulated Deprecia-tion, Art Equipment				(e) 70		70				
Office Equipment	3,000				3,000					
Accumulated Deprecia-tion, Office Equipment				(f) 50		50				
Accounts Payable		3,170				3,170				
Unearned Art Fees		1,000	(g) 400			600				
Joan Miller, Capital		10,000				10,000				
Joan Miller, Withdrawals	1,400				1,400					
Advertising Fees Earned		4,200		(h) 200		4,400				
Office Wages Expense	1,200		(i) 180		1,380					
Utility Expense	100				100					
Telephone Expense	70				70					
	18,370	18,370								
Rent Expense			(a) 400		400					
Insurance Expense			(b) 40		40					
Art Supplies Expense			(c) 500		500					
Office Supplies Expense			(d) 200		200					
Depreciation Expense, Art Equipment			(e) 70		70					
Depreciation Expense, Office Equipment			(f) 50		50					
Art Fees Earned				(g) 400		400				
Fees Receivable			(h) 200		200					
Wages Payable				(i) 180		180				
			2,040	2,040	18,870	18,870				

the Cash account, $1,720 is entered in the debit column of the Adjusted Trial Balance. The second line is Accounts Receivable, which shows a debit of $2,800 in the Trial Balance columns. Because there are no adjustments to Accounts Receivable, the $2,800 balance is carried over to the debit column of the Adjusted Trial Balance. The next line is Art Supplies, which shows a debit of $1,800 in the Trial Balance columns and a credit of $500 from adjustment **c** in the Adjustments columns. Subtracting $500 from $1,800 results in a $1,300 debit balance in the Adjusted Trial Balance. This process is followed for all the accounts, including those added below the trial balance. The Adjusted Trial Balance columns are then footed (totaled) to check the accuracy of the crossfooting.

4. Extend the account balances from the Adjusted Trial Balance columns to the Income Statement columns or the Balance Sheet columns. Every account in the adjusted trial balance is either a balance sheet account or an income statement account. Each account is extended to its proper place as a debit or credit in either the Income Statement columns or the Balance Sheet columns. The result of extending the accounts is shown in Exhibit 4-4. Revenue and expense accounts are copied to the Income Statement columns. Assets and liabilities as well as the capital and withdrawals accounts are extended to the Balance Sheet columns. To avoid overlooking an account, extend the accounts line by line, beginning with the first line (which is Cash) and not omitting any subsequent lines. For instance, the Cash debit balance of $1,720 is extended to the debit column of the balance sheet; the Accounts Receivable debit balance of $2,800 is extended to the same debit column, and so forth. Each amount is carried forward to only one column.

5. Total the Income Statement columns and the Balance Sheet columns. Enter the net income or net loss in both pairs of columns as a balancing figure, and recompute column totals. This last step, as shown in Exhibit 4-5 (page 150), is necessary to compute net income or net loss and to prove the arithmetical accuracy of the work sheet.

Net income (or net loss) is equal to the difference between the debit and credit columns of the income statement. It is also equal to the difference between the debit and credit columns of the balance sheet.

Revenue (Income Statement credit column total)	$4,800
Expenses (Income Statement debit column total)	(2,810)
Net Income	$1,990

In this case, the revenue (credit column) has exceeded the expenses (debit column). Consequently, the company has a net income of $1,990. The same difference is shown between the debit and credit columns of the balance sheet.

The $1,990 is entered in the debit side of the Income Statement columns to balance the columns, and it is entered on the credit side of the Balance Sheet columns. This is done because excess revenue (net income) increases owner's equity, and increases in owner's equity are recorded by credits.

If a net loss had occurred, the opposite rule would apply. The excess of expenses (net loss) would be placed in the credit side of the Income Statement columns as a balancing figure. It would then be extended to the debit side of the Balance Sheet columns because a net loss causes a decrease in owner's equity, which would be shown by a debit.

As a final check, the four columns are totaled again. If the Income Statement columns and the Balance Sheet columns do not balance, there

Exhibit 4-4. Entries in the Income Statement and Balance Sheet Columns

Joan Miller Advertising Agency
Work Sheet
For the Month Ended January 31, 19xx

Account Name	Trial Balance Debit	Trial Balance Credit	Adjustments Debit	Adjustments Credit	Adjusted Trial Balance Debit	Adjusted Trial Balance Credit	Income Statement Debit	Income Statement Credit	Balance Sheet Debit	Balance Sheet Credit
Cash	1,720				1,720				1,720	
Accounts Receivable	2,800				2,800				2,800	
Art Supplies	1,800			(c) 500	1,300				1,300	
Office Supplies	800			(d) 200	600				600	
Prepaid Rent	800			(a) 400	400				400	
Prepaid Insurance	480			(b) 40	440				440	
Art Equipment	4,200				4,200				4,200	
Accumulated Depreciation, Art Equipment				(e) 70		70				70
Office Equipment	3,000				3,000				3,000	
Accumulated Depreciation, Office Equipment				(f) 50		50				50
Accounts Payable		3,170				3,170				3,170
Unearned Art Fees		1,000	(g) 400			600				600
Joan Miller, Capital		10,000				10,000				10,000
Joan Miller, Withdrawals	1,400				1,400				1,400	
Advertising Fees Earned		4,200		(h) 200		4,400		4,400		
Office Wages Expense	1,200		(i) 180		1,380		1,380			
Utility Expense	100				100		100			
Telephone Expense	70				70		70			
	18,370	18,370								
Rent Expense			(a) 400		400		400			
Insurance Expense			(b) 40		40		40			
Art Supplies Expense			(c) 500		500		500			
Office Supplies Expense			(d) 200		200		200			
Depreciation Expense, Art Equipment			(e) 70		70		70			
Depreciation Expense, Office Equipment			(f) 50		50		50			
Art Fees Earned				(g) 400		400		400		
Fees Receivable			(h) 200		200				200	
Wages Payable				(i) 180		180				180
			2,040	2,040	18,870	18,870				

may be an account extended or sorted to the wrong column, or an error may have been made in adding the columns. Equal totals in the two pairs of columns, however, are not absolute proof of accuracy. If an asset has been carried to the debit Income Statement column and if a similar error involving revenues or liabilities has been made, the work sheet will still balance, but the net income figure will be wrong.

Exhibit 4-5. Entries in the Income Statement and Balance Sheet Columns and Totals

Joan Miller Advertising Agency
Work Sheet
For the Month Ended January 31, 19xx

Account Name	Trial Balance Debit	Trial Balance Credit	Adjustments Debit	Adjustments Credit	Adjusted Trial Balance Debit	Adjusted Trial Balance Credit	Income Statement Debit	Income Statement Credit	Balance Sheet Debit	Balance Sheet Credit
Cash	1,720				1,720				1,720	
Accounts Receivable	2,800				2,800				2,800	
Art Supplies	1,800			(c) 500	1,300				1,300	
Office Supplies	800			(d) 200	600				600	
Prepaid Rent	800			(a) 400	400				400	
Prepaid Insurance	480			(b) 40	440				440	
Art Equipment	4,200				4,200				4,200	
Accumulated Depreciation, Art Equipment				(e) 70		70				70
Office Equipment	3,000				3,000				3,000	
Accumulated Depreciation, Office Equipment				(f) 50		50				50
Accounts Payable		3,170				3,170				3,170
Unearned Art Fees		1,000	(g) 400			600				600
Joan Miller, Capital		10,000				10,000				10,000
Joan Miller, Withdrawals	1,400				1,400				1,400	
Advertising Fees Earned		4,200		(h) 200		4,400		4,400		
Office Wages Expense	1,200		(i) 180		1,380		1,380			
Utility Expense	100				100		100			
Telephone Expense	70				70		70			
	18,370	18,370								
Rent Expense			(a) 400		400		400			
Insurance Expense			(b) 40		40		40			
Art Supplies Expense			(c) 500		500		500			
Office Supplies Expense			(d) 200		200		200			
Depreciation Expense, Art Equipment			(e) 70		70		70			
Depreciation Expense, Office Equipment			(f) 50		50		50			
Art Fees Earned				(g) 400		400		400		
Fees Receivable			(h) 200		200				200	
Wages Payable				(i) 180		180				180
			2,040	2,040	18,870	18,870	2,810	4,800	16,060	14,070
Net Income							1,990			1,990
							4,800	4,800	16,060	16,060

Uses of the Work Sheet

OBJECTIVE 3
Identify the three principal uses of a work sheet

After all the columns of the work sheet are completed, the work sheet assists the accountant in three principal ways: (1) preparing the financial statements, (2) recording the adjusting entries, and (3) recording the closing entries in the general journal in order to prepare the records for the beginning of the next period.

Preparing the Financial Statements

OBJECTIVE 4
Prepare financial statements from a work sheet

After completion of the work sheet, it is simple to prepare the financial statements because the account balances have been sorted into Income Statement and Balance Sheet columns. The income statement shown in Exhibit 4-6 is prepared from the accounts in the Income Statement columns of Exhibit 4-5.

The statement of owner's equity and the balance sheet of the Joan Miller Advertising Agency are presented in Exhibits 4-7 and 4-8. The account balances for these statements are drawn from the Balance Sheet columns of the work sheet shown in Exhibit 4-5. Notice that the totals of the assets and of the liabilities and owner's equity in the balance sheet do not agree with the totals of the Balance Sheet columns of the work

---

Exhibit 4-6. Income Statement for the Joan Miller Advertising Agency

Joan Miller Advertising Agency
Income Statement
For the Month Ended January 31, 19xx

Revenues		
Advertising Fees Earned	$4,400	
Art Fees Earned	400	
Total Revenues		$4,800
Expenses		
Office Wages Expense	$1,380	
Utility Expense	100	
Telephone Expense	70	
Rent Expense	400	
Insurance Expense	40	
Art Supplies Expense	500	
Office Supplies Expense	200	
Depreciation Expense, Art Equipment	70	
Depreciation Expense, Office Equipment	50	
Total Expenses		2,810
Net Income		**$1,990**

Exhibit 4-7. Statement of Owner's Equity for the Joan Miller Advertising Agency

Joan Miller Advertising Agency
Statement of Owner's Equity
For the Month Ended January 31, 19xx

Joan Miller, Capital, January 1, 19xx		—
Add: Investment by Joan Miller	$10,000	
Net Income	1,990	$11,990
Subtotal		$11,990
Less: Withdrawals		1,400
Joan Miller, Capital, January 31, 19xx		$10,590

Exhibit 4-8. Balance Sheet for the Joan Miller Advertising Agency

Joan Miller Advertising Agency
Balance Sheet
January 31, 19xx

Assets

Cash		$ 1,720
Accounts Receivable		2,800
Fees Receivable		200
Art Supplies		1,300
Office Supplies		600
Prepaid Rent		400
Prepaid Insurance		440
Art Equipment	$4,200	
Less: Accumulated Depreciation	70	4,130
Office Equipment	$3,000	
Less: Accumulated Depreciation	50	2,950
Total Assets		$14,540

Liabilities

Accounts Payable	$3,170	
Unearned Art Fees	600	
Wages Payable	180	
Total Liabilities		$ 3,950

Owner's Equity

Joan Miller, Capital, January 31, 19xx		10,590
Total Liabilities and Owner's Equity		$14,540

sheet. Accounts such as Accumulated Depreciation and Withdrawals have different normal balances than their associated accounts on the balance sheet. In addition, the capital account on the balance sheet is the amount determined on the statement of owner's equity. At this point, the financial statements have been prepared from the work sheet, not from the ledger accounts. For the ledger accounts to show the correct balances, the adjusting entries have to be journalized and posted to the ledger.

Recording the Adjusting Entries

OBJECTIVE 5
Record the adjusting entries from a work sheet

For the Joan Miller Advertising Agency, the adjustments were determined during completion of the work sheet because they are essential to the preparation of the financial statements. The adjusting entries could have been recorded in the general journal at that point. However, it is usually convenient to delay recording them until after the work sheet and the financial statements have been prepared because this task can be done at the same time as the recording of the closing entries, which is described in the next section. Recording the adjusting entries with appropriate explanations in the general journal, as shown in Exhibit 4-9, is an easy step. The information may simply be copied from the work sheet. Adjusting entries are then posted to the general ledger.

Recording the Closing Entries

OBJECTIVE 6
Explain the purposes of closing entries

Closing entries, which are journal entries made at the end of the accounting period, accomplish two purposes. First, closing entries set the stage for the next accounting period by closing or clearing the expense and revenue accounts of their balances. This step must be carried out because an income statement reports the net income for a single accounting period and shows the expenses and revenues only for that period. For this reason, the expense and revenue accounts must be closed or cleared of their balances at the end of the period so that the next period begins with a zero balance in those accounts. The Withdrawals account is closed in a similar manner.

The second aim of closing entries is to summarize a period's revenues and expenses. This is done by transferring the balances of revenues and expenses to the Income Summary account to record the net profit or loss in that account. **Income Summary,** a new temporary account, appears in the chart of accounts between the withdrawals account and the first revenue account. This account provides a place to summarize all revenues and expenses in a single net figure before transferring the result to the capital account. It is used only in the closing process and never appears in the financial statements.

The balance of Income Summary equals the net income or loss reported on the income statement. The net income or loss is then transferred to the owner's Capital account. This step is needed because, even though expenses and revenues are recorded in expense and revenue accounts, they actually represent decreases and increases in owner's equity. Thus closing entries must transfer the net effect of increases (revenues) and decreases (expenses) to the owner's Capital account.

Exhibit 4-9. Adjustments on Work Sheet Entered in the General Journal				
General Journal				**Page 3**
Date	**Description**	**Post. Ref.**	**Debit**	**Credit**
19xx				
Jan. 31	Rent Expense	514	400	
	Prepaid Rent	117		400
	To recognize expiration of one month's rent			
31	Insurance Expense	515	40	
	Prepaid Insurance	118		40
	To recognize expiration of one month's insurance			
31	Art Supplies Expense	516	500	
	Art Supplies	115		500
	To recognize art supplies used during the month			
31	Office Supplies Expense	517	200	
	Office Supplies	116		200
	To recognize office supplies used during the month			
31	Depreciation Expense, Art Equipment	519	70	
	Accumulated Depreciation, Art Equipment	145		70
	To record depreciation of art equipment for a month			
31	Depreciation Expense, Office Equipment	520	50	
	Accumulated Depreciation, Office Equipment	147		50
	To record depreciation of office equipment for a month			
31	Unearned Art Fees	213	400	
	Art Fees Earned	412		400
	To recognize performance of services paid for in advance			
31	Fees Receivable	114	200	
	Advertising Fees Earned	411		200
	To accrue advertising fees earned but unrecorded			
31	Office Wages Expense	511	180	
	Wages Payable	214		180
	To accrue unrecorded wages			

As stated in Chapter 3, revenue and expense accounts are called temporary or nominal accounts. Nominal accounts begin each period at zero, accumulate a balance during the period, and return to zero by means of closing entries when the balance is transferred to the owner's Capital account. The accountant uses these accounts to keep track of the increases and decreases in owner's equity in a way that is helpful to management and others interested in the success or progress of the company. Temporary accounts are different from balance sheet accounts. Balance sheet, or permanent, accounts often begin with a balance, increase or decrease during the period, and carry the end-of-period balance into the next accounting period.

Required Closing Entries

OBJECTIVE 7
Prepare the required closing entries

Closing entries consist of four important steps:

1. Transferring the credit balances from income statement accounts to Income Summary
2. Transferring the debit balances from income statement accounts to Income Summary
3. Transferring the Income Summary balance to the Capital account
4. Transferring the Withdrawals account balance to the Capital account

With the exception of the Withdrawals account balance, all the data needed to perform these closing steps are found in the Income Statement columns of the work sheet.

Closing the Credit Balances from Income Statement Accounts to the Income Summary

From the credit side of the Income Statement columns of the work sheet in Exhibit 4-5, two revenue accounts have balances. An entry debiting each of these revenue accounts in the amount of its balance is needed to close the account. The Income Summary account is credited for the total (which can be found in the credit side of the Income Statement columns of the work sheet). The compound entry that closes the two revenue accounts for the Joan Miller Advertising Agency is as follows:

Jan. 31	Advertising Fees Earned	411	4,400	
	Art Fees Earned	412	400	
	Income Summary	313		4,800
	To close revenue accounts			

The effect of posting the entry is shown in Exhibit 4-10. Note that the dual effect of the entry is to (1) set the balances of the revenue accounts equal to zero, and (2) transfer the total revenues to the credit side of the Income Summary account. If a work sheet is not used, this data may also be found in the appropriate general ledger accounts after the adjusting entries have been posted.

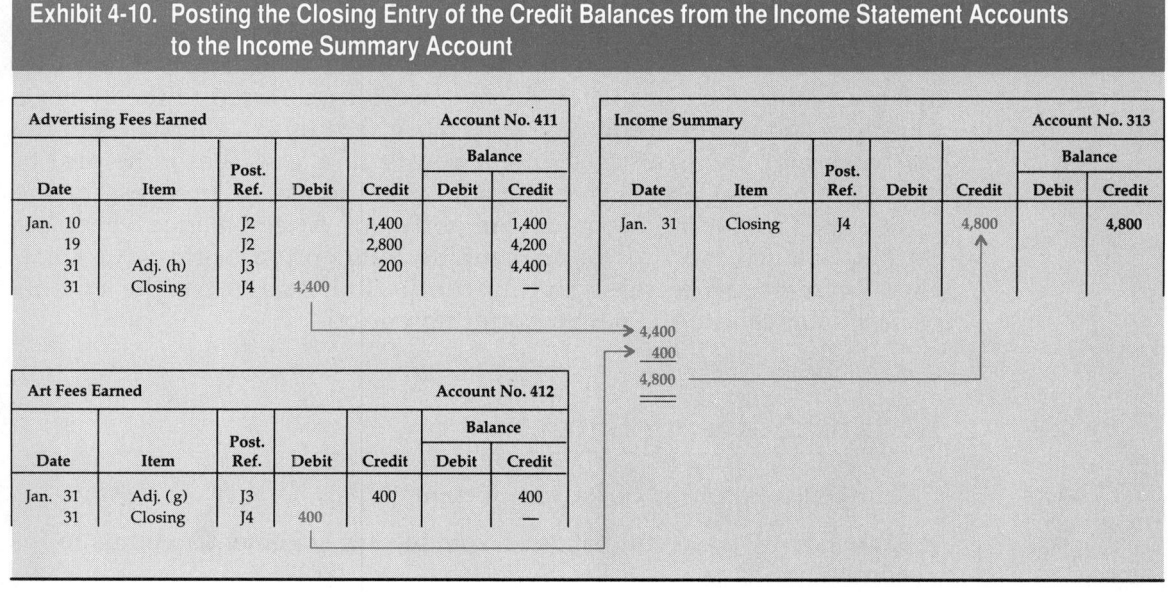

Exhibit 4-10. Posting the Closing Entry of the Credit Balances from the Income Statement Accounts to the Income Summary Account

Advertising Fees Earned — Account No. 411

Date	Item	Post. Ref.	Debit	Credit	Balance Debit	Balance Credit
Jan. 10		J2		1,400		1,400
19		J2		2,800		4,200
31	Adj. (h)	J3		200		4,400
31	Closing	J4	4,400			—

Income Summary — Account No. 313

Date	Item	Post. Ref.	Debit	Credit	Balance Debit	Balance Credit
Jan. 31	Closing	J4		4,800		4,800

Art Fees Earned — Account No. 412

Date	Item	Post. Ref.	Debit	Credit	Balance Debit	Balance Credit
Jan. 31	Adj. (g)	J3		400		400
31	Closing	J4	400			—

4,400
  400
4,800

Closing the Debit Balances from Income Statement Accounts to the Income Summary

From the debit side of the Income Statement columns of the work sheet in Exhibit 4-5, several expense accounts have balances. A compound entry is needed crediting each of these expense accounts for its balance and debiting the Income Summary for the total (which can be found in the debit side of the Income Statement columns):

Jan. 31	Income Summary	313	2,810	
	Office Wages Expense	511		1,380
	Utility Expense	512		100
	Telephone Expense	513		70
	Rent Expense	514		400
	Insurance Expense	515		40
	Art Supplies Expense	516		500
	Office Supplies Expense	517		200
	Depreciation Expense, Art Equipment	519		70
	Depreciation Expense, Office Equipment	520		50
	To close the expense accounts			

The effect of posting the closing entries to the ledger accounts is shown in Exhibit 4-11. Note again the double effect of (1) reducing expense account balances to zero and (2) transferring the total of the account balances to the debit side of the Income Summary account.

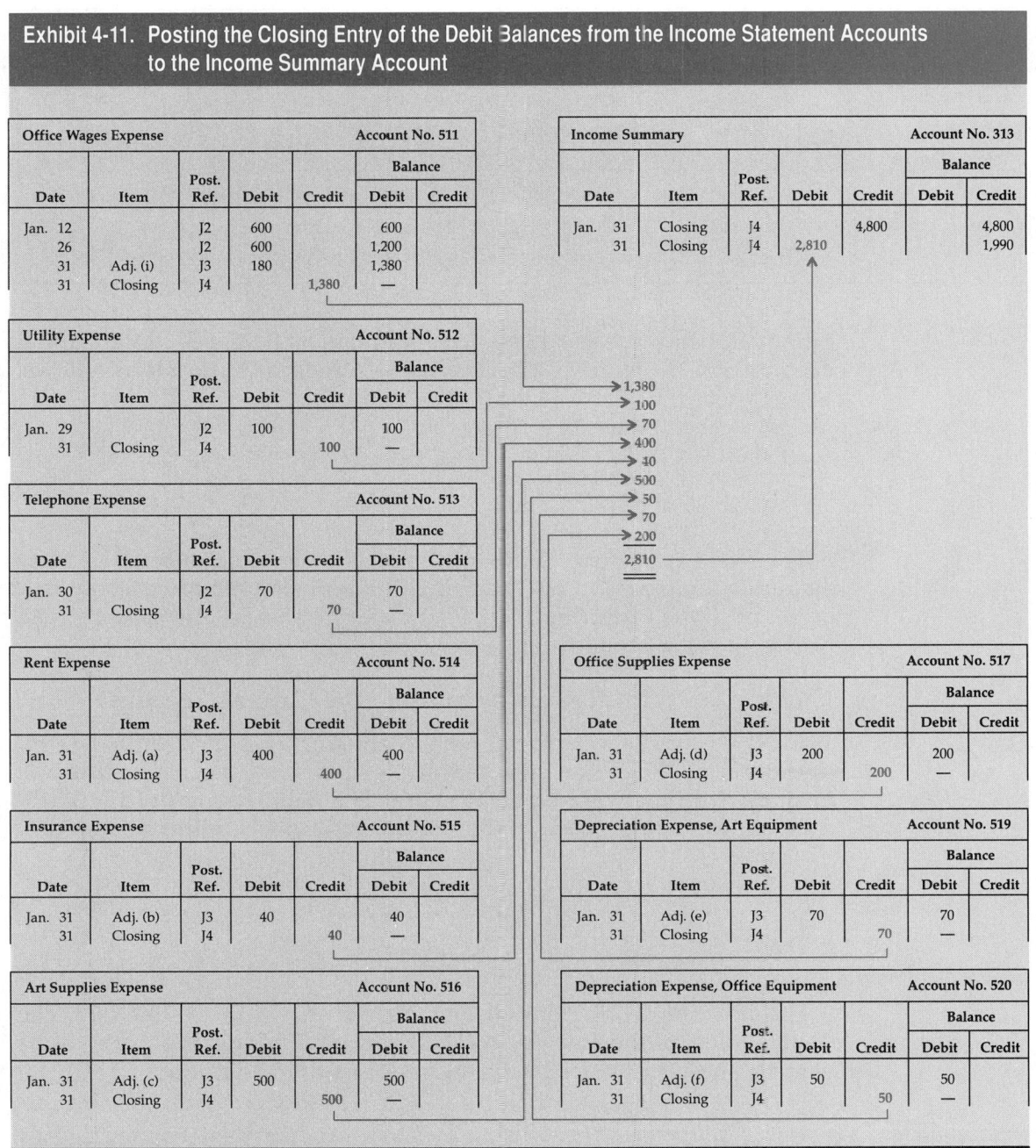

Exhibit 4-11. Posting the Closing Entry of the Debit Balances from the Income Statement Accounts to the Income Summary Account

Office Wages Expense — Account No. 511

Date	Item	Post. Ref.	Debit	Credit	Balance Debit	Balance Credit
Jan. 12		J2	600		600	
26		J2	600		1,200	
31	Adj. (i)	J3	180		1,380	
31	Closing	J4		1,380	—	

Utility Expense — Account No. 512

Date	Item	Post. Ref.	Debit	Credit	Balance Debit	Balance Credit
Jan. 29		J2	100		100	
31	Closing	J4		100	—	

Telephone Expense — Account No. 513

Date	Item	Post. Ref.	Debit	Credit	Balance Debit	Balance Credit
Jan. 30		J2	70		70	
31	Closing	J4		70	—	

Rent Expense — Account No. 514

Date	Item	Post. Ref.	Debit	Credit	Balance Debit	Balance Credit
Jan. 31	Adj. (a)	J3	400		400	
31	Closing	J4		400	—	

Insurance Expense — Account No. 515

Date	Item	Post. Ref.	Debit	Credit	Balance Debit	Balance Credit
Jan. 31	Adj. (b)	J3	40		40	
31	Closing	J4		40	—	

Art Supplies Expense — Account No. 516

Date	Item	Post. Ref.	Debit	Credit	Balance Debit	Balance Credit
Jan. 31	Adj. (c)	J3	500		500	
31	Closing	J4		500	—	

Income Summary — Account No. 313

Date	Item	Post. Ref.	Debit	Credit	Balance Debit	Balance Credit
Jan. 31	Closing	J4		4,800		4,800
31	Closing	J4	2,810			1,990

1,380
100
70
400
40
500
50
70
200
2,810

Office Supplies Expense — Account No. 517

Date	Item	Post. Ref.	Debit	Credit	Balance Debit	Balance Credit
Jan. 31	Adj. (d)	J3	200		200	
31	Closing	J4		200	—	

Depreciation Expense, Art Equipment — Account No. 519

Date	Item	Post. Ref.	Debit	Credit	Balance Debit	Balance Credit
Jan. 31	Adj. (e)	J3	70		70	
31	Closing	J4		70	—	

Depreciation Expense, Office Equipment — Account No. 520

Date	Item	Post. Ref.	Debit	Credit	Balance Debit	Balance Credit
Jan. 31	Adj. (f)	J3	50		50	
31	Closing	J4		50	—	

Closing the Income Summary Account to the Capital Account

After the entries closing the revenue and expense accounts have been posted, the balance of the Income Summary account is equal to the net income or loss for the period. A net income will be indicated by a credit balance and a net loss by a debit balance. At this point, the Income

Exhibit 4-12. Posting the Closing Entry of the Income Summary Account to the Capital Account

Income Summary						Account No. 313		Joan Miller, Capital						Account No. 311
					Balance								Balance	
Date	Item	Post. Ref.	Debit	Credit	Debit	Credit		Date	Item	Post. Ref.	Debit	Credit	Debit	Credit
Jan. 31	Closing	J4		4,800		4,800		Jan. 1		J1		10,000		10,000
31	Closing	J4	2,810			1,990		31	Closing	J4		1,990		11,990
31	Closing	J4	1,990			—								

Summary balance, regardless of its nature, must be closed to the Capital account. For the Joan Miller Advertising Agency the entry is as follows:

Jan. 31   Income Summary   313   1,990
                Joan Miller, Capital   311   1,990
                    To close the Income
                    Summary account

The effect of posting the closing entry is shown in Exhibit 4-12. Note again the double effect of (1) closing the Income Summary account balance and (2) transferring the balance, net income in this case, to Joan Miller's capital account.

Closing the Withdrawals Account to the Capital Account

The Withdrawals account shows the amount by which capital is reduced during the period by withdrawals of cash or other assets from the business for the owner's personal use. The debit balance of the Withdrawals account is closed to the Capital account, as follows:

Jan. 31   Joan Miller, Capital   311   1,400
                Joan Miller, Withdrawals   312   1,400
                    To close the Withdrawals
                    account

The effect of posting this closing entry is shown in Exhibit 4-13. The double effect of the entry is to (1) close the Withdrawals account of its balance and (2) transfer the balance to the Capital account.

Exhibit 4-13. Posting the Closing Entry of the Withdrawals Account to the Capital Account

Joan Miller, Withdrawals						Account No. 312		Joan Miller, Capital						Account No. 311
					Balance								Balance	
Date	Item	Post. Ref.	Debit	Credit	Debit	Credit		Date	Item	Post. Ref.	Debit	Credit	Debit	Credit
Jan. 25		J2	1,400		1,400			Jan. 1		J1		10,000		10,000
31	Closing	J4		1,400	—			31	Closing	J4		1,990		11,990
								31	Closing	J4	1,400			10,590

The Accounts After Closing

After all the steps in the closing process have been completed and all of the adjusting and closing entries have been posted to the accounts, the stage is set for the next accounting period. The ledger accounts of the Joan Miller Advertising Agency as they appear at this point are shown in Exhibit 4-14. The revenue, expense, and withdrawals accounts (temporary accounts) have zero balances. The Capital account has been increased or decreased depending on net income or loss and withdrawals. The balance sheet accounts (permanent accounts) have the appropriate balances, which are carried forward to the next period.

The Post-Closing Trial Balance

OBJECTIVE 8
Prepare the post-closing trial balance

Because it is possible to make an error in posting the adjustments and closing entries to the ledger accounts, it is necessary to determine that all temporary (nominal) accounts have zero balances and to retest the equality of total debits and credits by preparing a new trial balance. This final trial balance, called a post-closing trial balance, is shown in Exhibit 4-15 for the Joan Miller Advertising Agency (see page 162). Notice that only balance sheet (permanent) accounts have balances since the income statement accounts have all been closed.

Reversing Entries: Optional First Step of the Next Accounting Period

OBJECTIVE 9
Prepare reversing entries as appropriate

At the end of each accounting period, adjusting entries are made to bring revenues and expenses into conformity with the matching rule. A reversing entry is a general journal entry made on the first day of the new accounting period that is the exact reverse of an adjusting entry made in the previous period. Reversing entries are optional journal entries that are intended to simplify the bookkeeping process for transactions involving certain types of adjustments. Not all adjusting entries are reversed. For the system of recording used in this book, only adjustments for accruals (accrued revenues and accrued expenses) need to be reversed. Deferrals do not need to be reversed, as reversing adjustments for deferrals would not simplify the bookkeeping process in future accounting periods.

To show how reversing entries can be helpful, consider the adjusting entry made in the records of the Joan Miller Advertising Agency to accrue office wages expense:

Jan. 31	Office Wages Expense	180	
	Wages Payable		180
	To accrue unrecorded wages		

When the secretary is paid on the next regular payday, the accountant would make the entry on page 162, using the accounting procedure that you know to this point.

Exhibit 4-14. The Accounts After Closing Entries Are Posted

Cash   Account No. 111

Date	Item	Post. Ref.	Debit	Credit	Balance Debit	Balance Credit
Jan. 1		J1	10,000		10,000	
2		J1		800	9,200	
4		J1		4,200	5,000	
5		J1		1,500	3,500	
8		J1		480	3,020	
9		J1		1,000	2,020	
10		J2	1,400		3,420	
12		J2		600	2,820	
15		J2	1,000		3,820	
25		J2		1,400	2,420	
26		J2		600	1,820	
29		J2		100	1,720	

Accounts Receivable   Account No. 113

Date	Item	Post. Ref.	Debit	Credit	Balance Debit	Balance Credit
Jan. 19		J2	2,800		2,800	

Fees Receivable   Account No. 114

Date	Item	Post. Ref.	Debit	Credit	Balance Debit	Balance Credit
Jan. 31	Adj. (h)	J3	200		200	

Art Supplies   Account No. 115

Date	Item	Post. Ref.	Debit	Credit	Balance Debit	Balance Credit
Jan. 6		J1	1,800		1,800	
31	Adj. (c)	J3		500	1,300	

Office Supplies   Account No. 116

Date	Item	Post. Ref.	Debit	Credit	Balance Debit	Balance Credit
Jan. 6		J1	800		800	
31	Adj. (d)	J3		200	600	

Prepaid Rent   Account No. 117

Date	Item	Post. Ref.	Debit	Credit	Balance Debit	Balance Credit
Jan. 2		J1	800		800	
31	Adj. (a)	J3		400	400	

Prepaid Insurance   Account No. 118

Date	Item	Post. Ref.	Debit	Credit	Balance Debit	Balance Credit
Jan. 8		J1	480		480	
31	Adj. (b)	J3		40	440	

Art Equipment   Account No. 144

Date	Item	Post. Ref.	Debit	Credit	Balance Debit	Balance Credit
Jan. 4		J1	4,200		4,200	

Accumulated Depreciation, Art Equipment   Account No. 145

Date	Item	Post. Ref.	Debit	Credit	Balance Debit	Balance Credit
Jan. 31	Adj. (e)	J3		70		70

Office Equipment   Account No. 146

Date	Item	Post. Ref.	Debit	Credit	Balance Debit	Balance Credit
Jan. 5		J1	3,000		3,000	

Accumulated Depreciation, Office Equipment   Account No. 147

Date	Item	Post. Ref.	Debit	Credit	Balance Debit	Balance Credit
Jan. 31	Adj. (f)	J3		50		50

Accounts Payable   Account No. 212

Date	Item	Post. Ref.	Debit	Credit	Balance Debit	Balance Credit
Jan. 5		J1		1,500		1,500
6		J1		2,600		4,100
9		J1	1,000			3,100
30		J2		70		3,170

Unearned Art Fees   Account No. 213

Date	Item	Post. Ref.	Debit	Credit	Balance Debit	Balance Credit
Jan. 15		J2		1,000		1,000
31	Adj. (g)	J3	400			600

Wages Payable   Account No. 214

Date	Item	Post. Ref.	Debit	Credit	Balance Debit	Balance Credit
Jan. 31	Adj. (i)	J3		180		180

Exhibit 4-14. *(continued)*

Joan Miller, Capital — Account No. 311

Date	Item	Post. Ref.	Debit	Credit	Balance Debit	Balance Credit
Jan. 1		J1		10,000		10,000
31	Closing	J4		1,990		11,990
31	Closing	J4	1,400			10,590

Joan Miller, Withdrawals — Account No. 312

Date	Item	Post. Ref.	Debit	Credit	Balance Debit	Balance Credit
Jan. 25		J2	1,400		1,400	
31	Closing	J4		1,400	—	

Income Summary — Account No. 313

Date	Item	Post. Ref.	Debit	Credit	Balance Debit	Balance Credit
Jan. 31	Closing	J4		4,800		4,800
31	Closing	J4	2,810			1,990
31	Closing	J4	1,990			—

Advertising Fees Earned — Account No. 411

Date	Item	Post. Ref.	Debit	Credit	Balance Debit	Balance Credit
Jan. 10		J2		1,400		1,400
19		J2		2,800		4,200
31	Adj. (h)	J3		200		4,400
31	Closing	J4	4,400			—

Art Fees Earned — Account No. 412

Date	Item	Post. Ref.	Debit	Credit	Balance Debit	Balance Credit
Jan. 31	Adj. (g)	J3		400		400
31	Closing	J4	400			—

Office Wages Expense — Account No. 511

Date	Item	Post. Ref.	Debit	Credit	Balance Debit	Balance Credit
Jan. 12		J2	600		600	
26		J2	600		1,200	
31	Adj. (i)	J3	180		1,380	
31	Closing	J4		1,380	—	

Utility Expense — Account No. 512

Date	Item	Post. Ref.	Debit	Credit	Balance Debit	Balance Credit
Jan. 29		J2	100		100	
31	Closing	J4		100	—	

Telephone Expense — Account No. 513

Date	Item	Post. Ref.	Debit	Credit	Balance Debit	Balance Credit
Jan. 30		J2	70		70	
31	Closing	J4		70	—	

Rent Expense — Account No. 514

Date	Item	Post. Ref.	Debit	Credit	Balance Debit	Balance Credit
Jan. 31	Adj. (a)	J3	400		400	
31	Closing	J4		400	—	

Insurance Expense — Account No. 515

Date	Item	Post. Ref.	Debit	Credit	Balance Debit	Balance Credit
Jan. 31	Adj. (b)	J3	40		40	
31	Closing	J4		40	—	

Art Supplies Expense — Account No. 516

Date	Item	Post. Ref.	Debit	Credit	Balance Debit	Balance Credit
Jan. 31	Adj. (c)	J3	500		500	
31	Closing	J4		500	—	

Office Supplies Expense — Account No. 517

Date	Item	Post. Ref.	Debit	Credit	Balance Debit	Balance Credit
Jan. 31	Adj. (d)	J3	200		200	
31	Closing	J4		200	—	

Depreciation Expense, Art Equipment — Account No. 519

Date	Item	Post. Ref.	Debit	Credit	Balance Debit	Balance Credit
Jan. 31	Adj. (e)	J3	70		70	
31	Closing	J4		70	—	

Depreciation Expense, Office Equipment — Account No. 520

Date	Item	Post. Ref.	Debit	Credit	Balance Debit	Balance Credit
Jan. 31	Adj. (f)	J3	50		50	
31	Closing	J4		50	—	

Exhibit 4-15. Post-Closing Trial Balance		
Joan Miller Advertising Agency **Post-Closing Trial Balance** **January 31, 19xx**		
Cash	$ 1,720	
Accounts Receivable	2,800	
Fees Receivable	200	
Art Supplies	1,300	
Office Supplies	600	
Prepaid Rent	400	
Prepaid Insurance	440	
Art Equipment	4,200	
Accumulated Depreciation, Art Equipment		$ 70
Office Equipment	3,000	
Accumulated Depreciation, Office Equipment		50
Accounts Payable		3,170
Unearned Art Fees		600
Wages Payable		180
Joan Miller, Capital		10,590
	$14,660	$14,660

Feb. 9	Wages Payable	180	
	Office Wages Expense	420	
	Cash		600
	To record payment of two weeks' wages to secretary, $180 of which accrued in the previous period		

Note that when the payment is made, without a prior reversing entry, the accountant must look in the records to find out how much of the $600 applied to the current accounting period and how much was applicable to the previous period. This step may appear easy in this simple case, but think of how difficult and time consuming it would be if the company had many employees, especially if some of them are paid on different time schedules such as weekly or monthly. A reversing entry is an accounting procedure that helps to solve this problem of applying revenues and expenses to the correct accounting period. As noted above, a reversing entry is exactly what its name implies. It is a reversal of the adjusting entry made by debiting the credits and crediting the debits of the adjusting entry. For example, note the sequence of transactions and their effects on the ledger account for Office Wages Expense presented at the top of the following page.

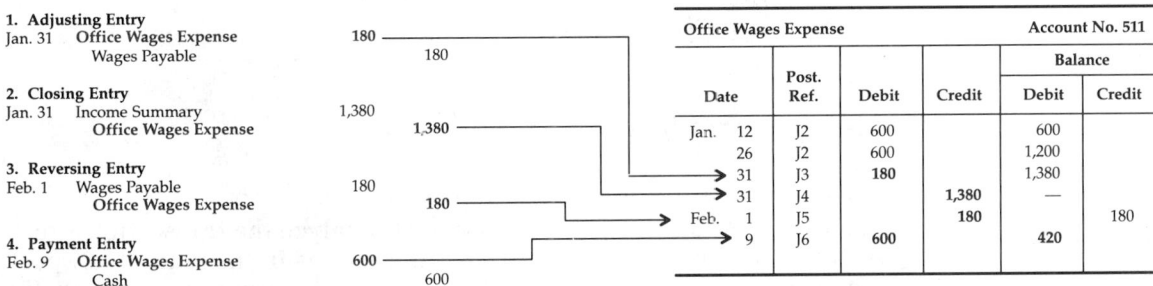

1. Adjusting Entry					Office Wages Expense				Account No. 511	
Jan. 31 Office Wages Expense	180		180							
Wages Payable									Balance	
					Date	Post. Ref.	Debit	Credit	Debit	Credit
2. Closing Entry										
Jan. 31 Income Summary	1,380				Jan. 12	J2	600		600	
Office Wages Expense			1,380		26	J2	600		1,200	
					31	J3	180		1,380	
3. Reversing Entry					31	J4		1,380	—	
Feb. 1 Wages Payable	180				Feb. 1	J5			180	180
Office Wages Expense			180		9	J6	600		420	
4. Payment Entry										
Feb. 9 Office Wages Expense	600									
Cash			600							

These transactions had the following effects on Office Wages Expense:

1. Adjusted Office Wages Expense to accrue $180 in the January accounting period.
2. Closed the $1,380 in total Office Wages Expense for January to Income Summary, leaving a zero balance.
3. Set up a credit balance of $180 on February 1 in Office Wages Expense equal to the expense recognized through the adjusting entry in January (and also reduced the liability account Wages Payable to a zero balance). Note that the reversing entry always sets up a non-normal balance in the income statement account and a zero balance in the balance sheet account.
4. Recorded the $600 payment of two weeks' wages, as a debit to Office Wages Expense, automatically leaving a balance of $420, which represents the correct wages expense so far for February.

Making the February 9 payment entry was simplified by the reversing entry. Reversing entries apply to any accrued expenses or revenues. In the case of the Joan Miller Advertising Agency, Office Wages Expense was the only accrued expense. However, the asset Fees Receivable was created as a result of the adjusting entry made to accrue fees earned but not yet billed. The adjusting entry for this accrued revenue would therefore require a reversing entry, as follows:

Feb. 1 Advertising Fees Earned   200
     Fees Receivable   200
        To reverse adjusting entry for
        accrued fees receivable

When the series of advertisements is finished, the company can credit the entire proceeds to Advertising Fees Earned without regard to the amount accrued in the previous period. The credit will automatically be reduced to the amount earned during February by the $200 debit in the account.

As noted above, under the system of recording used in this book, reversing entries apply only to accruals. For this reason, reversing entries do not apply to deferrals such as those that involve supplies, prepaid rent, prepaid insurance, depreciation, and unearned art fees.

Chapter Review

Review of Learning Objectives

1. **State all the steps in the accounting cycle.**
   The steps in the accounting cycle are to (1) analyze the transactions from the source documents, (2) record the transactions in the journal, (3) post the entries to the ledger, (4) adjust the accounts at the end of the period, (5) prepare the financial statements, and (6) close the accounts.

2. **Prepare a work sheet.**
   A work sheet is prepared by first entering the account balances in the Trial Balance columns, the adjustments in the Adjustments columns, and the adjusted account balances in the Adjusted Trial Balance columns. Then the amounts from the Adjusted Trial Balance columns are extended to the Income Statement or Balance Sheet columns as appropriate. Next, the Income Statement and Balance Sheet columns are totaled. Net income or net loss is determined from the Income Statement columns and extended to the Balance Sheet columns. The statement columns are now added to determine that they are in balance.

3. **Identify the three principal uses of a work sheet.**
   A work sheet is useful in (1) preparing the financial statements, (2) recording the adjusting entries, and (3) recording the closing entries.

4. **Prepare financial statements from a work sheet.**
   The balance sheet and income statements can be prepared directly from the Balance Sheet and Income Statement columns of a completed work sheet. The statement of owner's equity is also prepared using withdrawals, net income, additional investments, and the beginning balance of owner's capital. Note that the ending balance of owner's equity does not appear on the work sheet but is a result of it.

5. **Record the adjusting entries from a work sheet.**
   Adjusting entries can be recorded in the general journal directly from the Adjustments columns of the work sheet.

6. **Explain the purposes of closing entries.**
   Closing entries have two objectives. First, they transfer the balances of all temporary accounts, including the revenue and expense accounts, and withdrawals, so that they will have zero balances for the next accounting period. Second, they summarize a period's revenues and expenses in the Income Summary so that the net income or loss for the period may be transferred as a total to owner's equity.

7. **Prepare the required closing entries.**
   Closing entries are prepared by first transferring the revenue and expense account balances (credit and debit entries in the Income Statement columns of the work sheet) to the Income Summary account. Then the balance of the Income Summary account is transferred to the Capital account. And finally, the balance of the Withdrawals account is transferred to the Capital account.

8. **Prepare the post-closing trial balance.**
   As a final check on the balance of the ledger and to ensure that all temporary (nominal) accounts have been closed, a post-closing trial balance is prepared after the closing entries are posted to the ledger accounts.

9. **Prepare reversing entries as appropriate.**
   Reversing entries are optional general journal entries made on the first day of a new accounting period. They exactly reverse certain adjusting entries made in the prior period. Under the system used in this text, they apply only to accruals and facilitate routine bookkeeping procedures.

Review of Concepts and Terminology

The following concepts and terms were introduced in this chapter:

(L.O. 1) **Accounting system** or **accounting cycle**: Sequence of steps followed in the accounting process, from analyzing transactions to preparing financial statements and closing the accounts.

(L.O. 6) **Closing entries**: Journal entries made at the end of the accounting period that set the stage for the next accounting period by clearing the temporary accounts of their balances.

(L.O. 2) **Crossfooting**: Horizontal addition and subtraction of adjacent columns on the same row.

(L.O. 6) **Income Summary**: A temporary account used during the closing process in which all revenues and expenses are summarized before the net income or loss is transferred to the capital account.

(L.O. 8) **Post-closing trial balance**: A trial balance prepared at the end of the accounting period after all adjusting and closing entries have been posted. It serves as a final check on the balance of the ledger.

(L.O. 9) **Reversing entry**: Entry made at the beginning of the accounting period after the closing of records for the prior accounting period; it reverses certain adjusting entries and is designed to aid in routine bookkeeping for the next accounting period.

(L.O. 2) **Working papers**: Documents prepared and used by the accountant that aid in organizing the accountant's work and provide evidence to support the financial statements.

(L.O. 2) **Work sheet**: A type of working paper that is used as a preliminary step in and aid to the preparation of financial statements.

Self-Test

Test your knowledge of the chapter by choosing the best answer for each item below and on page 166.

1. Which of the following sequences of actions describes the proper sequence in the accounting cycle?
   a. Post, record, analyze, prepare, close, adjust
   b. Analyze, record, post, adjust, prepare, close
   c. Prepare, record, post, adjust, analyze, close
   d. Enter, record, close, prepare, adjust, analyze   *(L.O. 1)*

2. The work sheet is a type of
   a. ledger.
   b. journal.
   c. working paper.
   d. financial statement.   *(L.O. 2)*

3. When preparing a work sheet, the amount of which of the following is shown directly on the work sheet?
   a. Ending owner's capital
   b. Total assets
   c. Net income
   d. Total liabilities   *(L.O. 2)*

4. The work sheet is useful in
   a. preparing financial statements.
   b. recording adjusting entries.
   c. recording closing entries.
   d. All of the above.   *(L.O. 3)*

5. An important purpose of closing entries is
   a. to adjust the accounts in the ledger.
   b. to set balance sheet accounts to zero in order to begin the next period.
   c. to set income statement accounts to zero in order to begin the next accounting period.
   d. None of the above.   *(L.O. 6)*

6. In preparing closing entries, it is helpful to refer first to
   a. the Adjustments columns of the work sheet.
   b. the Adjusted Trial Balance columns of the work sheet.
   c. the Income Statement columns of the work sheet.
   d. the general journal.   *(L.O. 7)*

7. After all closing entries have been posted, the balance of the Income Summary account will be
   a. a debit if a net income has been earned.
   b. a debit if a net loss has been incurred.
   c. a credit if a net loss has been incurred.
   d. zero.   *(L.O. 7)*

8. After closing entries have been posted, which of the following accounts would have a nonzero balance?
   a. Service Revenue Earned
   b. Depreciation Expense
   c. Unearned Service Revenue
   d. Service Wages Expense   *(L.O. 7)*

9. The post-closing trial balance will
   a. contain only income statement accounts.
   b. contain only balance sheet accounts.
   c. contain both income statement and balance sheet accounts.
   d. be prepared before closing entries are posted to the ledger.   *(L.O. 8)*

10. For which of the following adjustments would a reversing entry facilitate bookkeeping procedures?
    a. Adjustment for depreciation expense
    b. Adjustment to allocate prepaid insurance to the current period
    c. Adjustment made as a result of inventory of supplies
    d. Adjustment for wages earned by employees but not yet paid to the employees   *(L.O. 9)*

Answers to Self-Test are at the end of this chapter.

Review Problem
Completion of Work Sheet; Preparation of Financial Statements, Adjusting Entries, and Closing Entries

(L.O. 2, 4, 5, 7, 8) This chapter contains an extended example of the preparation of a work sheet and the last two steps of the accounting cycle for the Joan Miller Advertising Agency. Instead of studying a demonstration problem, carefully review and retrace the steps through the illustrations in the chapter.

Required
1. In Exhibit 4-5, what is the source of the trial balance figures?
2. Trace the entries in the Adjustments columns of Exhibit 4-5 to the journal entries in Exhibit 4-9.
3. Trace the journal entries in Exhibit 4-9 to the ledger accounts in Exhibit 4-14.
4. Trace the amounts in the Income Statement and Balance Sheet columns of Exhibit 4-5 to the income statement in Exhibit 4-6, the statement of owner's equity in Exhibit 4-7, and the balance sheet in Exhibit 4-8.
5. Trace the amounts in the Income Statement columns and the Withdrawals account balance of Exhibit 4-5 to the closing entries on pages 155–158.
6. Trace the closing entries on pages 155–158 to the ledger accounts in Exhibit 4-14.
7. Trace the balances of the ledger accounts in Exhibit 4-14 to the post-closing trial balance in Exhibit 4-15.

Chapter Assignments

Discussion Questions and Writing Assignments

1. Arrange the following activities in proper order by placing the numbers 1 through 6 in the blanks:

   _____ a. The transactions are entered in the journal.
   _____ b. Financial statements are prepared.
   _____ c. The transactions are analyzed from the source documents.
   _____ d. The accounts are adjusted with the aid of a work sheet.
   _____ e. Closing entries are prepared.
   _____ f. The transactions are posted to the ledger.

2. Why are working papers important to the accountant?
3. Why are work sheets never published and rarely seen by management?
4. Is the work sheet a substitute for the financial statements? Discuss.
5. At the end of the accounting period, does the posting of adjusting entries to the ledger precede or follow the preparation of the work sheet?
6. What is the normal balance of the following accounts, in terms of debit and credit? Cash; Accounts Payable; Prepaid Rent; Sam Jones, Capital; Commission Revenue; Sam Jones, Withdrawals; Rent Expense; Accumulated Depreciation, Office Equipment; Office Equipment.
7. What is the probable cause of a credit balance in the Cash account?

8. Should the Adjusted Trial Balance columns of the work sheet be totaled before or after the adjusted amounts are carried to the Income Statement and Balance Sheet columns? Discuss.

9. What sequence should be followed in extending the Adjusted Trial Balance columns to the Income Statement and Balance Sheet columns? Discuss your answers.

10. Do the totals of the Balance Sheet columns of the work sheet agree with the totals on the balance sheet? Explain.

11. Do the Income Statement columns and Balance Sheet columns of the work sheet balance after the amounts from the Adjusted Trial Balance columns are extended?

12. What is the purpose of the Income Summary account?

13. Should adjusting entries be posted to the ledger accounts before or after the closing entries? Explain.

14. What is the difference between adjusting and closing entries?

15. What are the four basic tasks of closing entries?

16. Which of the following accounts will not have a balance after closing entries are prepared and posted? Insurance Expense; Accounts Receivable; Commission Revenue; Prepaid Insurance; Withdrawals; Supplies; Supplies Expense.

17. What is the significance of the post-closing trial balance?

18. Which of the following accounts would you expect to find on the post-closing trial balance? Insurance Expense; Accounts Receivable; Commission Revenue; Prepaid Insurance; Withdrawals; Supplies; Supplies Expense; Capital.

19. How can reversing entries aid in the bookkeeping process?

20. To what types of adjustments do reversing entries apply? To what types do they not apply?

Classroom Exercises

**Exercise 4-1.
Preparation of
Trial Balance
(L.O. 2)**

The following alphabetical list represents the accounts and balances for Sklar Realty on December 31, 19xx. All accounts have normal balances.

Accounts Payable	$ 5,140
Accounts Receivable	2,550
Accumulated Depreciation, Office Equipment	450
Advertising Expense	600
Cash	2,545
Office Equipment	5,170
Prepaid Insurance	560
Rent Expense	2,400
Revenue from Commissions	19,300
Sklar, Capital	10,210
Sklar, Withdrawals	9,000
Supplies	275
Wages Expense	12,000

Prepare a trial balance by listing the accounts in proper order, with the balances in the appropriate debit or credit column.

Exercise 4-2.
Preparation of Statement of Owner's Equity
(L.O. 4)

The Capital, Withdrawal, and Income Summary accounts for Ruben's Barber Shop are presented in T account form below. The closing entries have been recorded for the year ended December 31, 19xx.

Ruben Ortega, Capital		Ruben Ortega, Withdrawals		Income Summary	
12/31 9,000	1/1 26,000	4/1 3,000	12/31 9,000	12/31 43,000	12/31 62,000
	12/31 19,000	7/1 3,000		12/31 19,000	
	Bal. 36,000	10/1 3,000		Bal. —	
		Bal. —			

Prepare a statement of owner's equity for Ruben's Barber Shop.

Exercise 4-3.
Preparation of Adjusting and Reversing Entries from Work Sheet Columns
(L.O. 5, 9)

The items listed below are from the Adjustments columns of a work sheet as of December 31.

	Adjustments	
Account Name	Debit	Credit
Prepaid Insurance		(a) 120
Office Supplies		(b) 315
Accumulated Depreciation, Office Equipment		(c) 700
Accumulated Depreciation, Store Equipment		(d) 1,100
Office Salaries Expense	(e) 120	
Store Salaries Expense	(e) 240	
Insurance Expense	(a) 120	
Office Supplies Expense	(b) 315	
Depreciation Expense, Office Equipment	(c) 700	
Depreciation Expense, Store Equipment	(d) 1,100	
Salaries Payable		(e) 360
	2,595	2,595

1. Prepare the adjusting entries from the information.
2. If required, prepare appropriate reversing entries.

Exercise 4-4.
Preparation of Closing Entries from Work Sheet
(L.O. 7)

The items at the top of page 170 are from the Income Statement columns of the work sheet of the DiPietro Repair Shop for the year ended December 31, 19xx.

Account Name	Income Statement	
	Debit	**Credit**
Repair Revenue		25,620
Wages Expense	8,110	
Rent Expense	1,200	
Supplies Expense	4,260	
Insurance Expense	915	
Depreciation Expense, Repair Equipment	1,345	
	15,830	25,620
Net Income	9,790	
	25,620	25,620

Prepare entries to close the revenue, expense, Income Summary, and Withdrawals accounts. Mr. DiPietro withdrew $5,000 during the year.

Exercise 4-5.
Completion of
Work Sheet
(L.O. 2)

The following is a list of alphabetically arranged accounts and balances, in highly simplified form. This information is for the month ended October 31, 19xx.

Trial Balance Accounts and Balances

Accounts Payable	$4	Office Equipment	$ 8
Accounts Receivable	7	Prepaid Insurance	2
Accumulated Depreciation,		Rita Wilkins, Capital	12
Office Equipment	1	Rita Wilkins, Withdrawals	6
Cash	4	Service Revenue	23
		Supplies	4
		Unearned Revenue	3
		Utility Expense	2
		Wages Expense	10

1. Prepare a work sheet, entering the trial balance accounts in the order in which they would normally appear, and arranging the balances in the correct debit or credit column.
2. Complete the work sheet using the following information:
   a. Expired insurance, $1.
   b. Of the unearned revenue balance, $2 has been earned by the end of the month.
   c. Estimated depreciation on office equipment, $1.
   d. Accrued wages, $1.
   e. Unused supplies on hand, $1.

**Exercise 4-6.
Derivation of
Adjusting Entries
from Trial Balance
and Income
Statement
Columns**
(L.O. 4, 5)

Presented below is a partial work sheet in which the Trial Balance and Income Statement columns have been completed. All amounts shown are in dollars.

Account Name	Trial Balance Debit	Trial Balance Credit	Income Statement Debit	Income Statement Credit
Cash	7			
Accounts Receivable	12			
Supplies	11			
Prepaid Insurance	8			
Building	25			
Accumulated Depreciation, Building		8		
Accounts Payable		4		
Unearned Revenue		2		
M. B., Capital		32		
Revenue		44		46
Wages Expense	27		30	
	90	90		
Insurance Expense			4	
Supplies Expense			8	
Depreciation Expense, Building			2	
			44	46
Net Income			2	
			46	46

1. Determine the adjustments that have been made. Assume that no adjustments are made to Accounts Receivable or Accounts Payable.
2. Prepare a balance sheet.

**Exercise 4-7.
Reversing Entries**
(L.O. 9)

Selected December T accounts for Jefferson Company are presented below and on the following page:

Supplies			
12/1 Bal.	430	12/31 Adjust.	640
Dec. purchases	470		
Bal.	260		

Supplies Expense			
12/31 Adjust.	640	12/31 Closing	640
Bal.	—		

Wages Payable		
	12/31 Adjust.	320
	Bal.	320

Wages Expense			
Dec. wages	1,970	12/31 Closing	2,290
12/31 Adjust.	320		
Bal.	—		

1. In which case is a reversing entry helpful? Why?
2. Prepare the appropriate reversing entry.
3. Prepare the entry to record payments on January 5 for wages totaling $1,570. How much is Wages Expense for January?

Interpreting Accounting Information

City of Chicago
(L.O. 5)

In 1979, Mayor Jane Byrne won the election in the city of Chicago partly on the basis of her charge that Michael Bilandic, the former mayor, had caused a budget deficit. Taking office in 1980, she hired a major international accounting firm, Peat, Marwick, Mitchell & Co., to straighten things out. The following excerpt appeared in an article from a leading Chicago business publication:

> [A riddle]
> Q: When is a budget deficit not a deficit?
> A: When it is a surplus, of course.

Chicago Mayor Jane Byrne was once again caught with egg on her face last week as she and her financial advisers tried to defend that riddle. On one hand, Comptroller Daniel J. Grim [Byrne appointee], explaining $75 million in assets the mayor [Byrne] hopes to hold in reserve in the 1981 Chicago city budget, testified in hearings that the city had actually ended 1979 with a $6 million surplus, not the much-reported deficit. He said further that the modest surplus grew to $54 million as a result of tax-enrichment supplements to the 1979 balance sheet. On the other hand, the mayor stuck by the same guns she used last year on her predecessor: The city had ended 1979, under the Michael Bilandic Administration, not merely without a surplus, but with a deficit. The apparent discrepancy can be explained.[1]

Like most U.S. cities, Chicago operates under the modified accrual accounting basis. This is a combination of the straight cash basis and the accrual basis. The modified accrual basis differs from the accrual method in that an account receivable is recorded only when it is collected in the next accounting period. The collection of Chicago's parking tax, which is assessed on all city parking lots and garages, is an example:

The tax is assessed and collected on a quarterly basis but the city doesn't collect the amount due for the last quarter of 1980 until the first quarter of 1981. Under ideal accrual methods, the parking revenues should be recorded in the 1980 financial statement. Under a cash approach, the revenues would be recorded in the 1981 budget. What the city did before was to record the money whenever it was advantageous politically. That, combined with the infamous revolving funds, allowed the city to hide the fact it was running large deficits under [former] Mayor Bilandic. That also means that no one really knew where the city stood.[2]

---

1. Reprinted with permission from the December 8, 1980 issue of *Crain's Chicago Business.* Copyright 1980 by Crain Communications, Inc.
2. Ibid.

The auditors are now reallocating the parking revenues to the 1981 budget but are accruing other revenues by shifting the period of collection from a year in the past. Overall, more revenues were moved into earlier fiscal years than into later years, inflating those budgets. Thus, the 1979 deficit is considered a surplus.

The upshot is that both Mayor Byrne and Mr. Grim [the comptroller] were correct. There was a deficit in the 1979 corporate or checkbook fund, but because of corrections taking place now, a surplus exists.[3]

Required

1. Do you agree with how the auditors handled parking revenues? Support your answer by explaining which method of accounting you think a city should use.
2. Comment on the statement, "Systematically applied accounting principles will allow all to know exactly where the city stands," made by the author in another part of the same article that was quoted above.

Problem Set A

**Problem 4A-1.
Preparation of
Financial
Statements and
End-of-Period
Entries
(L.O. 4, 7, 9)**

Hillcrest Campgrounds rents one hundred campsites in a wooded park to campers. The adjusted trial balance for Hillcrest Campgrounds on May 31, 19x2, the end of the current fiscal year, is presented below.

Hillcrest Campgrounds
Adjusted Trial Balance
May 31, 19x2

Cash	$ 2,040	
Accounts Receivable	3,660	
Supplies	114	
Prepaid Insurance	594	
Land	15,000	
Building	45,900	
Accumulated Depreciation, Building		$ 10,500
Accounts Payable		1,725
Wages Payable		825
Cynthia Tobin, Capital		46,535
Cynthia Tobin, Withdrawals	18,000	
Campsite Rentals		44,100
Wages Expense	11,925	
Insurance Expense	1,892	
Utility Expense	900	
Supplies Expense	660	
Depreciation Expense, Building	3,000	
	$103,685	$103,685

3. Ibid.

Required

1. From the information given, prepare an income statement, a statement of owner's equity, and a balance sheet. Assume no additional investments by Cynthia Tobin.
2. Record the closing entries in the general journal.
3. Assuming Wages Payable represents wages accrued at the end of the accounting period, record the reversing entry required on June 1.

Problem 4A-2.
Preparation of
Work Sheet,
Adjusting, Closing,
and Reversing
Entries
(L.O. 2, 4, 5, 7, 9)

Jose Vargas opened his executive search service on July 1, 19xx. Some customers paid for his services after they were rendered, and others paid in advance for one year of service. After six months of operation, Jose wanted to know how his business stood. The trial balance on December 31 appears below:

Vargas Executive Search Service
Trial Balance
December 31, 19xx

Cash	$ 1,713	
Prepaid Rent	1,800	
Office Supplies	413	
Office Equipment	3,750	
Accounts Payable		$ 3,173
Unearned Revenue		1,823
Jose Vargas, Capital		10,000
Jose Vargas, Withdrawals	7,200	
Search Revenue		10,140
Telephone and Utility Expense	1,260	
Wages Expense	9,000	
	$25,136	$25,136

Required

1. Enter the trial balance amounts in the Trial Balance columns of the work sheet. Remember that accumulated depreciation is listed with its asset account. Complete the work sheet using the following information:
   a. One year's rent had been paid in advance when Jose began business.
   b. Inventory of unused office supplies, $75.
   c. One-half year's depreciation on office equipment, $300.
   d. Service rendered that had been paid for in advance, $863.
   e. Executive search services rendered during the month but not yet billed, $270.
   f. Wages earned by employees but not yet paid, $188.
2. From the work sheet, prepare an income statement, a statement of owner's equity, and a balance sheet.
3. From the work sheet, prepare adjusting and closing entries and, if required, reversing entries.
4. What is your evaluation of Jose's first six months in business?

Problem 4A-3.
Completion of Work Sheet, Preparation of Financial Statements, Adjusting, Closing, and Reversing Entries
(L.O. 2, 4, 5, 7, 9)

The trial balance below was taken from the ledger of Zolnay Package Delivery Company on August 31, 19x2, the end of the company's fiscal year.

Zolnay Package Delivery Company
Trial Balance
August 31, 19x2

Cash	$ 5,036	
Accounts Receivable	14,657	
Prepaid Insurance	2,670	
Delivery Supplies	7,350	
Office Supplies	1,230	
Land	7,500	
Building	98,000	
Accumulated Depreciation, Building		$ 26,700
Trucks	51,900	
Accumulated Depreciation, Trucks		15,450
Office Equipment	7,950	
Accumulated Depreciation, Office Equipment		5,400
Accounts Payable		4,698
Unearned Lockbox Fees		4,170
Mortgage Payable		36,000
Ruth Zolnay, Capital		64,365
Ruth Zolnay, Withdrawals	15,000	
Delivery Services Revenue		141,735
Lockbox Fees Earned		14,400
Truck Drivers' Wages Expense	63,900	
Office Salaries Expense	22,200	
Gas, Oil, and Truck Repairs Expense	15,525	
	$312,918	$312,918

Required

1. Enter the trial balance amounts in the Trial Balance columns of a work sheet and complete the work sheet using the following information:
   a. Expired insurance, $1,530.
   b. Inventory of unused delivery supplies, $715.
   c. Inventory of unused office supplies, $93.
   d. Estimated depreciation, building, $7,200.
   e. Estimated depreciation, trucks, $7,725.
   f. Estimated depreciation, office equipment, $1,350.
   g. The company credits the lockbox fees of customers who pay in advance to the Unearned Lockbox Fees account. Of the amount credited to this account during the year, $2,815 has been earned by August 31.
   h. There are $408 worth of lockbox fees earned but unrecorded and uncollected at the end of the accounting period.
   i. There are $960 worth of accrued but unpaid truck drivers' wages at the end of the year.

2. Prepare an income statement, a statement of owner's equity, and a balance sheet. Assume no additional investments by Ruth Zolnay.
3. Prepare adjusting, closing, and, if required, reversing entries from the work sheet.

Problem 4A-4.
The Complete
Accounting Cycle:
Two Months
(L.O. 1, 2, 4, 5, 7, 8)

On October 1, 19xx, Jeff Romanoff opened Romanoff Appliance Service and during the month completed the following transactions for the company:

Oct. 1 Deposited $5,000 of his savings in a bank account for the company.
      1 Paid the rent for a store for one month, $425.
      1 Paid the premium on a one-year insurance policy, $480.
      2 Purchased repair equipment from Perry Company for $4,200 on the basis of $600 down payment and $300 per month for one year. The first payment is due November 1.
      5 Purchased repair supplies from Bridger Company for $468 on credit.
      8 Purchased for cash an advertisement in a local newspaper for $60.
     15 Received cash repair revenue for the first half of the month, $400.
     21 Paid $225 of the amount owed to Bridger Company.
     25 Jeff withdrew cash of $450 from the company bank account to pay living expenses.
     31 Received cash repair revenue for the second half of October, $975.

Required for
October

1. Prepare journal entries to record the October transactions.
2. Open the following accounts: Cash (111); Prepaid Insurance (117); Repair Supplies (119); Repair Equipment (144); Accumulated Depreciation, Repair Equipment (145); Accounts Payable (212); Jeff Romanoff, Capital (311); Jeff Romanoff, Withdrawals (312); Income Summary (313); Repair Revenue (411); Store Rent Expense (511); Advertising Expense (512); Insurance Expense (513); Repair Supplies Expense (514); Depreciation Expense, Repair Equipment (515). Post the October journal entries to the ledger accounts.
3. Prepare a trial balance in the Trial Balance columns of a work sheet, and complete the work sheet using the following information:
   a. One month's insurance has expired.
   b. Remaining inventory of unused repair supplies, $169.
   c. Estimated depreciation on repair equipment, $70.
4. From the work sheet, prepare an income statement, a statement of owner's equity, and a balance sheet for October.
5. From the work sheet, prepare and post adjusting and closing entries.
6. Prepare a post-closing trial balance.

During November Jeff Romanoff completed the following transactions for the Romanoff Appliance Service:

Nov. 1 Paid the monthly rent, $425.
      1 Made monthly payment to Perry Company, $300.
      6 Purchased additional repair supplies on credit from Bridger Company, $863.
     15 Received cash repair revenue for the first half of the month, $914.
     20 Purchased for cash an additional advertisement in local newspaper, $60.
     23 Paid Bridger Company on account, $600.

Nov. 25 Jeff withdrew cash of $450 from the company for living expenses.
   30 Cash repair revenue for the last half of the month, $817.

Required for November

7. Prepare and post journal entries to record November transactions.
8. Prepare a trial balance in the Trial Balance columns of a work sheet and complete the work sheet based on the following information:
   a. One month's insurance has expired.
   b. Inventory of unused repair supplies, $413.
   c. Estimated depreciation on repair equipment, $70.
9. From the work sheet, prepare the November income statement, statement of owner's equity, and balance sheet.
10. From the work sheet, prepare and post adjusting and closing entries.
11. Prepare a post-closing trial balance.

Problem 4A-5.
Preparation of
Work Sheet from
Limited Data
(L.O. 2, 4, 5)

Douglas Noh started work as an accountant with the East Bend Tennis Club on April 30, the end of the fiscal year. His boss tells him that he must have an income statement and a balance sheet by 9:00 A.M. the next day in order to obtain a renewal of the bank loan. Douglas takes home the general ledger and supporting data for adjusting entries. At 3:00 A.M., after completing the statements, he lights a cigarette and falls asleep. A few minutes later he awakes to find the papers on fire. He quickly puts out the fire but is horrified to discover that except for the general ledger and the income statement, everything else, including the work sheet, supporting data, and balance sheet, is destroyed. He decides that he should be able to reconstruct the balance sheet and adjusting entries from the general ledger and the income statement, even though he had not yet recorded and posted the adjusting and closing entries. The information available is as follows:

General Ledger

Cash	Accounts Payable	Maintenance Expense
Bal. 13,100	Bal. 151,500	Bal. 25,800

Supplies	Unearned Revenue, Locker Fees	Water and Utility Expense
Bal. 3,600	Bal. 6,300	Bal. 32,400

Prepaid Advertising	Lucille Davis, Capital	Land
Bal. 7,050	Bal. 235,575	Bal. 372,600

Equipment	Lucille Davis, Withdrawals	Wages Expense
Bal. 78,000	Bal. 27,000	Bal. 171,000

Accumulated Depreciation, Equipment	Revenue from Court Fees	Advertising Expense
Bal. 19,200	Bal. 339,050	Bal. 17,625

		Miscellaneous Expense
		Bal. 3,450

East Bend Tennis Club
Income Statement
For the Year Ended April 30, 19x2

Revenues

Revenue from Court Fees	$339,050	
Revenue from Locker Fees	4,800	
Total Revenues		$343,850

Expenses

Wages Expense	$175,500	
Maintenance Expense	25,800	
Advertising Expense	19,875	
Water and Utility Expense	32,400	
Miscellaneous Expense	3,450	
Property Taxes Expense	11,250	
Supplies Expense	3,000	
Depreciation Expense, Equipment	6,000	
Total Expenses		277,275
Net Income		**$ 66,575**

Required

1. Using the information provided above for the East Bend Tennis Club, fill in the Trial Balance and Income Statement columns of a work sheet.
2. Reconstruct the adjusting entries and complete the work sheet. Then record the adjusting entries (be certain to provide explanations) in the general journal.
3. Prepare the statement of owner's equity and the balance sheet for April 30, 19x2.

Problem Set B

**Problem 4B-1.
Preparation of
Financial
Statements and
End-of-Period
Entries
(L.O. 4, 7, 9)**

Quality Trailer Rental owns thirty small trailers that are rented by the day for local moving jobs. The Adjusted Trial Balance for Quality Trailer Rental for the year ended June 30, 19x2, which is the end of the current fiscal year, is shown at the top of page 179.

Required

1. Prepare an income statement, a statement of owner's equity, and a balance sheet. Assume no additional investments by Elena Mota.
2. From the information given, record closing entries.
3. Assuming Wages Payable represents wages accrued at the end of the period, record the required reversing entry.

Quality Trailer Rental
Adjusted Trial Balance
For the Year Ended June 30, 19x2

Cash	$ 692	
Accounts Receivable	972	
Supplies	119	
Prepaid Insurance	360	
Trailers	12,000	
Accumulated Depreciation, Trailers		$ 7,200
Accounts Payable		271
Wages Payable		200
Elena Mota, Capital		5,694
Elena Mota, Withdrawals	7,200	
Trailer Rentals		45,546
Wages Expense	23,400	
Insurance Expense	720	
Supplies Expense	266	
Depreciation Expense, Trailers	2,400	
Other Expenses	10,782	
	$58,911	$58,911

**Problem 4B-2.
Preparation of
Work Sheet,
Adjusting Entries,
and Closing
Entries**
(L.O. 2, 4, 5, 7, 9)

Roman Patel began his consulting practice immediately after graduating with his M.B.A. To help him get started, several clients paid him retainers (payment in advance) for future services. Other clients paid when service was provided. After one year, the firm had the trial balance that follows.

Roman Patel, Consultant
Trial Balance
December 31, 19xx

Cash	$ 3,250	
Accounts Receivable	2,709	
Office Supplies	382	
Office Equipment	3,755	
Accounts Payable		$ 1,296
Unearned Retainers		5,000
Roman Patel, Capital		4,000
Roman Patel, Withdrawals	6,000	
Consulting Fees		18,175
Rent Expense	1,800	
Utility Expense	717	
Wages Expense	9,858	
	$28,471	$28,471

Required

1. Enter the trial balance amounts in the Trial Balance columns of a work sheet, and complete the work sheet using the following information:
   a. Inventory of unused supplies, $58.
   b. Estimated depreciation on equipment, $600.
   c. Services rendered during the month but not yet billed, $725.
   d. Services rendered to clients who paid in advance that should be applied against unearned retainers, $3,150.
   e. Wages earned by employees, but not yet paid, $120.
2. Prepare an income statement, statement of owner's equity, and balance sheet.
3. Prepare adjusting, closing, and, if required, reversing entries.
4. How would you evaluate the first year of Mr. Patel's consulting practice?

Problem 4B-3.
Completion of
Work Sheet,
Preparation of
Financial
Statements,
Adjusting, Closing,
and Reversing
Entries
(L.O. 2, 4, 5, 7, 9)

At the end of the current fiscal year, the trial balance of the Esquire Theater appeared as follows:

Esquire Theater
Trial Balance
December 31, 19x2

Cash	$ 15,900	
Accounts Receivable	9,272	
Prepaid Insurance	9,800	
Office Supplies	390	
Cleaning Supplies	1,795	
Land	10,000	
Building	200,000	
Accumulated Depreciation, Building		$ 19,700
Theater Furnishings	185,000	
Accumulated Depreciation, Theater Furnishings		32,500
Office Equipment	15,800	
Accumulated Depreciation, Office Equipment		7,780
Accounts Payable		22,753
Gift Books Liability		20,950
Mortgage Payable		150,000
Mildred Brown, Capital		156,324
Mildred Brown, Withdrawals	30,000	
Ticket Sales		205,700
Theater Rental		22,600
Usher Wages Expense	92,000	
Office Wages Expense	12,000	
Utility Expense	56,350	
	$638,307	$638,307

Required

1. Enter the trial balance amounts in the Trial Balance columns of a work sheet and complete the work sheet using the following information:
   a. Expired insurance, $8,700.
   b. Inventory of unused office supplies, $122.
   c. Inventory of unused cleaning supplies, $234.
   d. Estimated depreciation, building, $7,000.
   e. Estimated depreciation on theater furnishings, $18,000.
   f. Estimated depreciation, office equipment, $1,580.
   g. The company credits all gift books sold during the year to a Gift Books Liability account. Gift books are booklets of ticket coupons that are purchased in advance to give to someone. The recipient may then use the coupons to attend future movies. On December 31 it was estimated that $18,900 worth of the gift books had been redeemed.
   h. There are $430 worth of accrued but unpaid usher wages at the end of the accounting period.
2. Prepare an income statement, a statement of owner's equity, and a balance sheet. Assume no additional investments by Mildred Brown.
3. Prepare adjusting, closing, and, if required, reversing entries.

Problem 4B-4.
The Complete
Accounting Cycle:
Two Months
(L.O. 1, 2, 4, 5, 7, 8)

During the two months of operation, the Springer Repair Store completed the following transactions:

May 1 Began business by depositing $6,000 in a company bank account.
    1 Paid the premium on a one-year insurance policy, $600.
    1 Paid current month's rent, $520.
    2 Purchased repair equipment from Fisk Company for $2,200. The terms were $300 down payment and $100 per month for nineteen months. The first payment is due June 1.
    5 Purchased repair supplies from Cordero Company for $195 on credit.
   14 Paid utility expense for the month of May, $77.
   15 Cash bicycle repair revenue for the first half of May, $681.
   20 Paid $100 of the amount owed to Cordero Company.
   29 Owner withdrew $400 from the company for personal living expenses.
   31 Cash bicycle repair revenue for the last half of May, $655.

June 1 Paid the monthly rent, $520.
     1 Made the monthly payment to Fisk Company, $100.
     9 Purchased repair supplies on credit from Cordero Company, $447.
    15 Cash bicycle repair revenue for the first half of June, $525.
    18 Paid utility expense for June, $83.
    19 Paid Cordero Company on account, $200.
    28 Withdrew $400 from the company for personal living expenses.
    30 Cash bicycle repair revenue for the last half of June, $687.

Required

1. Prepare journal entries to record the May transactions.
2. Open the following accounts: Cash (111); Prepaid Insurance (117); Repair Supplies (119); Repair Equipment (144); Accumulated Depreciation, Repair Equipment (145); Accounts Payable (212); Will Springer, Capital (311); Will Springer, Withdrawals (312); Income Summary (313); Bicycle Repair Revenue (411) Store Rent Expense (511); Utility Expense (512); Insurance Expense (513); Repair Supplies Expense (514); Depreciation

Expense, Repair Equipment (515). Post the May journal entries to ledger accounts.

3. Prepare a trial balance in the Trial Balance columns of a work sheet, and complete the work sheet using the following information:
    a. One month's insurance has expired.
    b. Remaining inventory of unused repair supplies, $97.
    c. Estimated depreciation on repair equipment, $35.

4. From the work sheet, prepare an income statement, a statement of owner's equity, and a balance sheet for May.

5. From the work sheet, prepare and post adjusting and closing entries for May.

6. Prepare a post-closing trial balance.

7. Prepare and post journal entries to record June transactions.

8. Prepare a trial balance for June in the Trial Balance columns of a work sheet, and complete the work sheet based on the following information:
    a. One month's insurance has expired.
    b. Inventory of unused repair supplies, $209.
    c. Estimated depreciation on repair equipment, $35.

9. From the work sheet, prepare an income statement, a statement of owner's equity, and a balance sheet for June.

10. From the work sheet, prepare and post adjusting and closing entries for June.

11. Prepare a post-closing trial balance.

**Problem 4B-5.
Preparation of
Work Sheet from
Limited Data
(L.O. 2, 4, 5)**

Presented below and on page 183 are the income statement and trial balance for Whitehead Bowling Lanes for the year ended December 31, 19x2.

**Whitehead Bowling Lanes
Income Statement
For the Year Ended December 31, 19x2**

Revenues		$618,263
Expenses		
Wages Expense	$381,076	
Advertising Expense	15,200	
Utility Expense	42,200	
Maintenance Expense	84,100	
Miscellaneous Expense	9,500	
Supplies Expense	1,148	
Insurance Expense	1,500	
Depreciation Expense, Building	4,800	
Depreciation Expense, Equipment	11,000	
Property Taxes Expense	10,000	
Total Expenses		560,524
Net Income		$ 57,739

Whitehead Bowling Lanes
Trial Balance
December 31, 19x2

Cash	$ 16,214	
Accounts Receivable	7,388	
Supplies	1,304	
Prepaid Insurance	1,800	
Prepaid Advertising	900	
Land	5,000	
Building	100,000	
Accumulated Depreciation, Building		$ 22,400
Equipment	125,000	
Accumulated Depreciation, Equipment		22,000
Accounts Payable		15,044
Notes Payable		70,000
Unearned Revenues		2,300
Donna Webb, Capital		60,813
Donna Webb, Withdrawals	24,000	
Revenues		616,263
Wages Expense	377,114	
Advertising Expense	14,300	
Utility Expense	42,200	
Maintenance Expense	84,100	
Miscellaneous Expense	9,500	
	$808,820	$808,820

Required

1. Fill in the Trial Balance and Income Statement columns of a work sheet.
2. Reconstruct the adjustments and complete the work sheet. Assume that there is no adjustment to Accounts Receivable. Then record the adjusting entries with explanations in the general journal.
3. Prepare the statement of owner's equity and the balance sheet as of December 31, 19x2.

Financial Decision Case

Donna's Quik-Type
(L.O. 4)

Donna's Quik-Type is a very simple business. Donna provides typing services for students at the local university. Her accountant prepared the income statement on page 184 for the year ended August 31, 19x2.

In reviewing this statement, Donna is puzzled. She knows she withdrew $7,800 in cash for personal expenses, and yet the cash balance in the company's bank account increased from $230 to $1,550 from last August 31 to this August 31. She wants to know how her net income could be less than the cash she took out of the business if there is an increase in the cash balance.

Her accountant shows her the balance sheet for August 31, 19x2 and compares it to the one for August 31, 19x1. She explains that besides the change in the cash balance, accounts receivable from customers decreased by $740 and accounts payable increased by $190 (supplies are the only items Donna buys on credit). The only other asset or liability account that changed during the year was accumulated depreciation on office equipment, which increased by $1,100.

Donna's Quik-Type
Income Statement
For the Year Ended August 31, 19x2

Revenues		
Typing Services		$10,490
Expenses		
Rent Expense	$1,200	
Depreciation Expense, Office Equipment	1,100	
Supplies Expense	480	
Other Expenses	620	
Total Expenses		3,400
Net Income		$ 7,090

Required   Explain to Donna why the accountant is answering Donna's question by pointing out year-to-year changes in the balance sheet. Verify the cash balance increase by preparing a statement that lists the receipts of cash and the expenditures of cash during the year. How did you treat depreciation expense? Why?

Answers to Self-Test

1. b	3. c	5. c	7. d	9. b
2. c	4. d	6. c	8. c	10. d

Comprehensive Problem:
Joan Miller Advertising Agency

This problem is a continuation of the Joan Miller Advertising Agency, which illustrated the accounting cycle in Chapters 2 through 4. It will be necessary in some instances to refer to these chapters in completing this problem. The January 31, 19xx, post-closing trial balance for Joan Miller Advertising Agency is as follows:

Cash	$ 1,720	
Accounts Receivable	2,800	
Fees Receivable	200	
Art Supplies	1,300	
Office Supplies	600	
Prepaid Rent	400	
Prepaid Insurance	440	
Art Equipment	4,200	
Accumulated Depreciation, Art Equipment		$ 70
Office Equipment	3,000	
Accumulated Depreciation, Office Equipment		50
Accounts Payable		3,170
Unearned Art Fees		600
Wages Payable		180
Joan Miller, Capital		10,590
	$14,660	$14,660

During February, the agency engaged in the following transactions:

Feb. 1 Received an additional investment of cash from Joan Miller in the business of $5,000.

2 Received art equipment transferred to the business from Joan Miller $1,200.

5 Purchased additional office equipment, $900 cash.

6 Purchased additional art supplies on credit from Taylor Supply Company, $450.

7 Purchased additional office supplies with cash, $90.

8 Completed the series of Marsh Tire Company advertisements that had begun on January 31, Fees Receivable of $200 (see page 110).

8 Billed Marsh Tire Company for the total services performed including the accrued revenues (Fees Receivable) that had been recognized in an adjusting entry in January, $800.

9 Paid the secretary for two weeks' wages, $600.

12 Accepted an advance fee in cash for art work to be done for another agency, $1,600.

13 Paid the amount due to Morgan Equipment for the office equipment purchased last month, $1,500 (see page 63).

14 Purchased a copier (office equipment) from Morgan Equipment for $2,100, paying $350 in cash and agreeing to pay the rest in equal payments over the next five months.

Feb. 15   Performed advertising services and accepted a cash fee, $950.
16   Received payment on account from Ward Department Stores for services performed last month, $2,800 (see page 66).
19   Paid amount due for the telephone bill that had been received and recorded at the end of January, $70 (see page 67).
20   Performed advertising services for Ward Department Stores and agreed to accept payment next month, $3,200.
21   Performed art services for a cash fee, $580.
22   Received and paid the utility bill for February, $110.
23   Paid the secretary for two weeks' wages, $600.
26   Paid the rent for March in advance, $400.
27   Received the telephone bill for February, which is to be paid next month, $80.
28   Paid out cash to Joan Miller as a withdrawal for personal living expenses, $1,400.

Required

1. Record in the general journal and post to the general ledger the reversing entries necessary on February 1 for Wages Payable and Advertising Fees Earned (see pages 110–112). (Begin the general journal on page 5.)
2. Record transactions for February in the general journal.

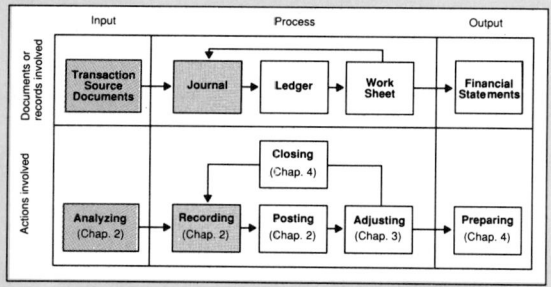

3. Post the February entries to the ledger accounts.

4. Prepare a trial balance in the Trial Balance columns of a work sheet.
5. Prepare adjusting entries and complete the work sheet using the following information:
   a. One month's prepaid rent has expired, $400.
   b. One month's prepaid insurance has expired, $40.
   c. An inventory of art supplies reveals $660 still on hand on February 28.

d. An inventory of office supplies reveals $410 still on hand on February 28.

e. Depreciation on Art Equipment for February is calculated to be $90.

f. Depreciation on Office Equipment for February is calculated to be $100.

g. Art services performed for which payment had been received in advance totalled $1,300.

h. Advertising services performed that will not be billed until March totalled $290.

i. Three days' wages had accrued by the end of February.

6. From the work sheet prepare an income statement, a statement of owner's equity, and a balance sheet.

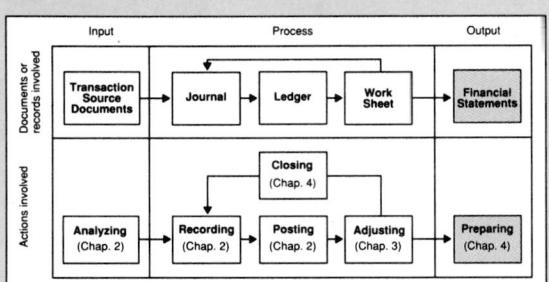

7. Record the adjusting entries in the general journal, and post them to the general ledger.

8. Record the closing entries in the general journal, and post them to the general ledger.

9. Prepare a post-closing trial balance.

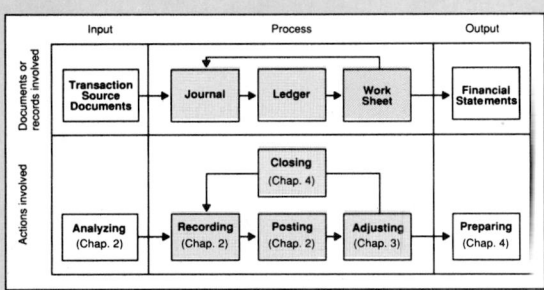

This Comprehensive Problem covers all of the Learning Objectives in Chapters 2, 3, and 4.

PRINCIPLES OF ACCOUNTING

FINANCIAL ACCOUNTING

PART ONE
The Basic Accounting Model

PART THREE
Measuring and Reporting Assets and Current Liabilities

PART TWO
Extensions of the Basic Accounting Model

Chapter 5
Accounting for Merchandising Operations

Chapter 6
Accounting Systems and Special-Purpose Journals

Chapter 7
Internal Control and Merchandising Transactions

Chapter 8
Accounting Concepts and Classified Financial Statements

PART FOUR
Accounting for Partnerships and Corporations

PART FIVE
Special Reports and Analyses of Accounting Information

MANAGERIAL ACCOUNTING

PART SIX
Basic Concepts of Management Accounting

PART SEVEN
Accounting for Management Decision Making

Accounting, as you have seen, is an information system that measures, processes, and communicates information, primarily financial in nature, for decision making. Part One presented the principles and practices of the basic accounting system. In Part Two, the basic accounting system is extended to more complex applications.

PART TWO

Extensions of the Basic Accounting Model

Chapter 5 deals with accounting for merchandising companies, which are companies that sell products, as opposed to the companies you studied earlier, which sell services.

Chapter 6 addresses the goals of organizing accounting systems in order to process a large number of transactions in an efficient and time-saving way.

Chapter 7 first describes the basic principles of internal control and then applies these principles to merchandising transactions.

Chapter 8 presents the objectives and conventions underlying the use of financial statements and relates financial accounting concepts to ethical reporting practices. It also shows how classified and general-purpose external financial statements are constructed and how they are analyzed using simple ratios.

LEARNING OBJECTIVES

1. Compare the income statements for service and merchandising concerns.
2. Record transactions involving revenues for merchandising concerns.
3. Calculate cost of goods sold.
4. Record transactions involving purchases of merchandise.
5. Differentiate the perpetual inventory method from the periodic inventory method.
6. Explain the objectives of handling merchandise inventory at the end of the accounting period and two approaches to achieving them.
7. Prepare a work sheet for a merchandising concern under one of two alternative methods.
8. Prepare adjusting and closing entries for a merchandising concern.
9. Prepare an income statement for a merchandising concern.

CHAPTER 5

Accounting for Merchandising Operations

Up to this point, you have studied the accounting records and reports for the simplest type of business—the service company. In this chapter, you will study a more complex type of business—the merchandising company. This chapter focuses on the merchandising company's special buying and selling transactions and their effects on the income statement. After studying this chapter, you should be able to meet the learning objectives listed on the left.

Income Statement for a Merchandising Concern

Service companies such as advertising agencies or law firms perform a service for a fee or commission. In determining net income, a simple income statement is often all that is needed. As shown in Figure 5-1, net income is measured as the difference between revenues and expenses.

In contrast, many other companies attempt to earn an income by buying and selling products or merchandise. Merchandising companies, whether wholesale or retail, use the same basic accounting methods as service companies, but the process of buying and selling merchandise requires some additional accounts and concepts. This process results in a more complicated income statement than is needed by a service business. As illustrated in Figure 5-1, the income statement for a merchandising concern has three major parts: (1) revenues from sales, (2) cost of goods sold, and (3) operating expenses. Such an income statement differs from the income statement for a service firm in that gross margin from sales must be computed before operating expenses are deducted in order to arrive at net income.

Revenues from sales arise from sales of goods by the merchandising company, and the **cost of goods sold** tells how much the merchant paid for the goods that were sold. The difference between revenues from sales and cost of goods sold is known as **gross margin from sales**, or simply **gross margin** (also referred to as gross profit). To be successful, the merchant must sell the goods for an amount greater than cost—that is, gross margin from sales must be large enough—to pay operating expenses and have an adequate income left over. **Operating expenses** are

Figure 5-1. Components of Income Statements for Service and Merchandising Companies

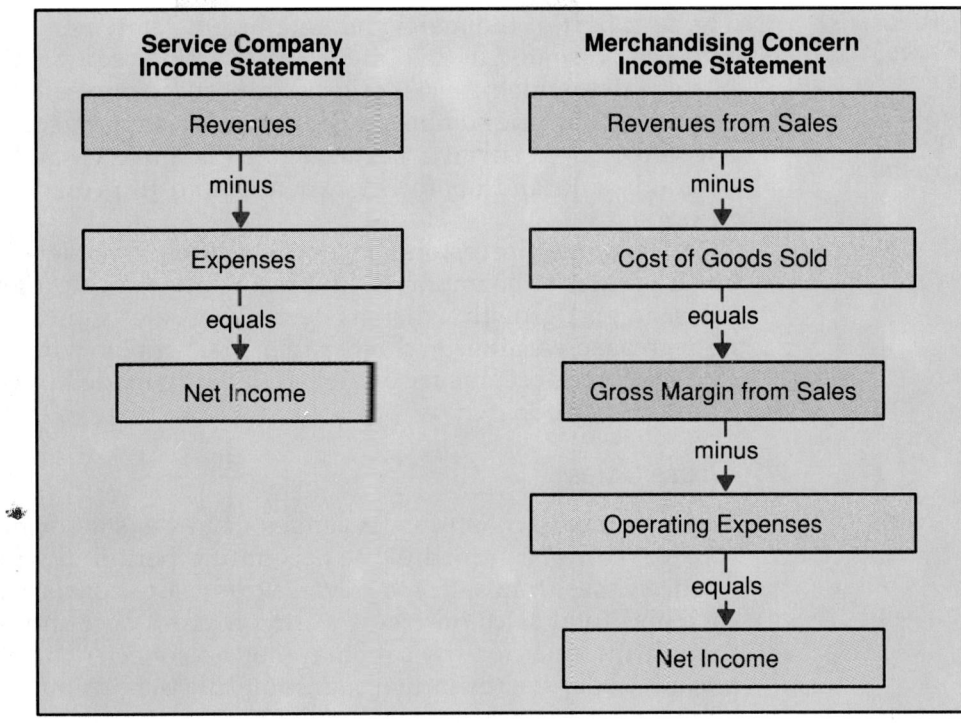

those expenses, other than cost of goods sold, that are incurred in running the business. In a merchandising company, operating expenses are similar to the expenses you have seen in a service company. **Net income** for merchandising companies is what is left after deducting operating expenses from gross margin.

OBJECTIVE 1
Compare the income statements for service and merchandising concerns

All three parts of the merchandising income statement are important to a company's management. Management is interested both in the percentage of gross margin from sales and in the amount of gross margin. This information is helpful in planning business operations. For instance, management may try to increase total sales dollars by reducing the selling price. This strategy results in a reduction in the percentage of gross margin. It will work if total items sold increase enough to raise gross margin (which raises income from operations). On the other hand, management may increase operating expenses (such as advertising expense) in an effort to increase sales dollars and the amount of gross margin. If the increase in gross margin is greater than the increase in advertising, net income will improve. Other strategies, such as reducing cost of goods sold or operating expenses, may also be examined.

In this chapter, we discuss the three parts of the merchandising income statement and the transactions that give rise to the amounts in each part. Then we present two alternative methods for preparing the work sheet for a merchandising company. The chapter ends with a comprehensive illustration of the merchandising income statement.

Revenues from Sales

OBJECTIVE 2
Record
transactions
involving revenues
for merchandising
concerns

The first part of the merchandising income statement is revenues from sales, as presented in Exhibit 5-1. This section requires the computation of **net sales,** which consist of gross proceeds from sales of merchandise less sales returns and allowances and sales discounts. If a business is to succeed or even survive, net sales must be great enough to pay for cost of goods sold and operating expenses and to provide a sufficient net income.

Management, investors, and others often consider the amount and trend of sales to be important indicators of a firm's progress. Increasing sales suggest growth, whereas decreasing sales indicate the possibility of decreased earnings and other financial problems in the future. Thus, to detect trends, comparisons are frequently made between net sales of different periods.

Gross Sales

Under accrual accounting, revenues from the sale of merchandise are considered to be earned in the accounting period in which title for the goods passes from seller to buyer. **Gross sales** consist of total sales for cash and total sales on credit during a given accounting period. Even though the cash for the sale may not be collected until the following period, under the revenue recognition rule the revenue is recognized as being earned at the time of the sale. For this reason, there is likely to be a difference between revenues from sales and cash collected from those sales in a given period.

The Sales account is used only for recording sales of merchandise, whether the sale is made for cash or for credit. The journal entry to record a sale of merchandise for cash is as follows:

Sept. 16	Cash	1,286	
	Sales		1,286
	To record the sale of		
	merchandise for cash		

Exhibit 5-1. Partial Income Statement: Revenues from Sales		
Fenwick Fashions Company **Partial Income Statement** **For the Year Ended December 31, 19xx**		
Revenues from Sales		
Gross Sales		$246,350
Less: Sales Returns and Allowances	$2,750	
Sales Discounts	4,275	7,025
Net Sales		$239,325

If the sale of merchandise is made on credit, the entry is as follows:

Sept. 16 Accounts Receivable   746
          Sales   746
              To record the sale of
              merchandise on credit

Trade Discounts

In order to avoid reprinting wholesale and retail catalogues and price lists every time there is a price change, some manufacturers and wholesalers quote prices of merchandise at a discount (usually 30 percent or more) off the list or catalogue price (retail). Such discounts are called **trade discounts**. For example, the seller of an article listed at $1,000 with a trade discount of 40 percent, or $400, would record the sale at $600. The buyer would also record the transaction as a purchase of $600. The list price and related trade discounts are used only for the convenience of arriving at the agreed upon price and do not appear in the accounting records.

Sales Returns and Allowances

If a customer receives a defective or otherwise unsatisfactory product, the seller will usually try to accommodate the customer. The business may allow the customer to return the item for a cash refund or credit on account, or it may give the customer an allowance off the sales price. A good accounting system will provide management with information for determining the reason for sales returns and allowances because such transactions reveal dissatisfied customers. Each return or allowance is recorded as a debit to an account called **Sales Returns and Allowances**. An example of such a transaction follows:

Sept. 17 Sales Returns and Allowances   76
          Accounts Receivable (or Cash)   76
              To record return or
              allowance on unsatisfactory
              merchandise

If Sales were debited instead of Sales Returns and Allowances, management would not know the extent of customer dissatisfaction. Sales Returns and Allowances is a contra revenue account with a normal debit balance. Accordingly, it is deducted from gross sales in the income statement (see Exhibit 5-1).

Sales Discounts

When goods are sold on credit, both parties should have an understanding as to the amount and time of payment. These terms are usually printed on the sales invoice and constitute part of the sales agreement. Customary terms differ from industry to industry. In some industries payment is expected in a short period of time such as ten days or thirty days. In these cases, the invoice may be marked "n/10" or "n/30" (read as "net 10" or "net 30") meaning that the amount of the invoice is due ten days or thirty days, respectively, after the invoice date. If the invoice is due ten days after the end of the month, it may be marked "n/10 eom."

Some industries give discounts for early payment, called **sales discounts**. This practice increases the seller's liquidity by reducing the amount of money tied up in accounts receivable. Examples of these invoice terms are 2/10, n/30 or 2/10, n/60. Terms of **2/10, n/30** mean the debtor may take a 2 percent discount if the invoice is paid within ten days of the invoice date. Otherwise, the debtor may wait thirty days and then pay the full amount of the invoice without the discount.

Because it is not usually possible to know at the time of sale whether the customer will take advantage of the discount by paying within the discount period, sales discounts are recorded only at the time the customer pays. For example, assume that Fenwick Fashions Company sells merchandise to a customer on September 20 for $300, on terms of 2/10, n/60. At the time of sale the entry would be:

Sept. 20	Accounts Receivable	300	
	Sales		300
	To record sale of merchandise on credit, terms 2/10, n/60		

The customer may take advantage of the sales discount any time on or before September 30, which is ten days after the date of the invoice. If he or she pays on September 29, the entry in Fenwick's records is:

Sept. 29	Cash	294	
	Sales Discounts	6	
	Accounts Receivable		300
	To record payment for Sept. 20 sale; discount taken		

If the customer does not take advantage of the sales discount but waits until November 19 to pay for the merchandise, the entry would be as follows:

Nov. 19	Cash	300	
	Accounts Receivable		300
	To record payment for Sept. 20 sale; no discount taken		

At the end of the accounting period, the Sales Discounts account has accumulated all the sales discounts taken during the period. Because sales discounts reduce revenues from sales, they are considered a contra revenue account with a normal debit balance and are deducted from gross sales in the income statement (see Exhibit 5-1).

Cost of Goods Sold

OBJECTIVE 3
Calculate cost of goods sold

Every merchandising business has goods on hand that it holds for sale to customers. The amount of goods on hand at any one time is known as **merchandise inventory**. The cost of **goods available for sale** during the year is the sum of two factors—merchandise inventory at the beginning of the year plus net purchases during the year.

If a company were to sell all the goods available for sale during a given accounting period or year, the cost of goods sold would then equal goods that had been available for sale. In most cases, however, the business will have goods still unsold and on hand at the end of the year. To find out how much the merchant paid for the goods that were actually sold (the cost of goods sold), the merchandise inventory at the end of the year must be subtracted from the goods available for sale.

The partial income statement in Exhibit 5-2 shows the cost of goods sold section for Fenwick Fashions Company. In this case, goods costing $179,660 were available and could have been sold; Fenwick started with $52,800 in merchandise inventory at the beginning of the year and purchased a net of $126,860 in goods during the year. At the end of the year, $48,300 in goods were left unsold and should appear as merchandise inventory on the balance sheet. When this unsold merchandise inventory is subtracted from the total available goods that could have been

---

Exhibit 5-2. Partial Income Statement: Cost of Goods Sold

Fenwick Fashions Company
Partial Income Statement
For the Year Ended December 31, 19xx

Cost of Goods Sold			
Merchandise Inventory, January 1, 19xx			$ 52,800
Purchases		$126,400	
Less: Purchases Returns and Allowances	$5,640		
Purchases Discounts	2,136	7,776	
		$118,624	
Freight In		8,236	
Net Purchases			126,860
Goods Available for Sale			$179,660
Less Merchandise Inventory, December 31, 19xx			48,300
Cost of Goods Sold			$131,360

sold, the resulting cost of goods sold is $131,360, which should appear on the income statement.

To understand fully the concept of the cost of goods sold, it is necessary to examine net purchases and merchandise inventory.

Net Purchases

OBJECTIVE 4
Record
transactions
involving purchases
of merchandise

Net purchases consist of gross purchases less purchases returns and allowances and purchases discounts plus any freight charges on the purchases.

Purchases. Merchandise bought for resale is debited to the Purchases account at the gross purchase price, as shown below.

```
Nov. 12   Purchases                                    1,500
              Accounts Payable                                  1,500
                  To record purchases of
                  merchandise, terms 2/10, n/30
```

The **Purchases** account, a temporary or nominal account, is used only for merchandise purchased for resale. Its sole purpose is to accumulate the total cost of merchandise purchased during an accounting period. Inspection of the Purchases account alone does not indicate whether the merchandise has been sold or is still on hand. Purchases of other assets such as equipment should be recorded in the appropriate asset account, not the Purchases account.

Purchases Returns and Allowances. For various reasons, a company may need to return merchandise acquired for resale. The firm may not have been able to sell the merchandise and returns it to the original supplier. Or the merchandise may be defective or damaged in some way and have to be returned. In some cases, the supplier may suggest that an allowance be given as an alternative to returning the goods for full credit. In any event, **purchases returns and allowances** form a separate account and should be recorded in the journal as follows:

```
Nov. 14   Accounts Payable                             200
              Purchases Returns and Allowances                    200
                  Return of damaged merchandise
                  purchased on November 12
```

Here, the purchaser receives "credit" (in the seller's accounts receivable) for the returned merchandise. The Purchases Returns and Allowances account is used only for returns and allowances of merchandise purchased for resale. Other returns, such as office supplies or equipment are credited directly to the related asset account, not to a contra account.

Purchases Returns and Allowances is a contra purchases account with a normal credit balance and is accordingly deducted from purchases in the income statement (see Exhibit 5-2). It is important that a separate account be used to record purchases returns and allowances because management needs the information for making decisions. It can be very costly to return merchandise for credit. There are many costs that cannot be recovered, such as ordering costs, accounting costs, sometimes freight costs and interest on the money invested in the goods. Sometimes there are lost sales resulting from poor ordering or unusable goods. Excessive returns may indicate a need for new purchasing procedures or new suppliers.

Purchases Discounts. Merchandise purchases are usually made on credit and commonly involve **purchases discounts** for early payment. It is almost always worthwhile for the company to take a discount if offered. For example, the terms 2/10, n/30 offer a 2 percent discount for paying only twenty days early (before the period including the eleventh and the thirtieth days). This is an effective interest rate of 36 percent on a yearly basis.[1] Most companies can borrow money for less than this rate. For this reason, management wants to know the amount of discounts taken, which form a separate account and are recorded as follows when the payment is made:

Nov. 22	Accounts Payable		1,300	
	Purchases Discounts			26
	Cash			1,274
	Paid the invoice of Nov. 12			
	Purchase Nov. 12	$1,500		
	Less return	200		
	Net purchase	$1,300		
	Discount: 2%	26		
	Cash	$1,274		

If the purchase is not paid for within the discount period, the entry is as follows:

Dec. 12	Accounts Payable		1,300	
	Cash			1,300
	Paid the invoice of Nov. 12			
	on due date; no discount taken			

Like Purchases Returns and Allowances, Purchases Discounts is a contra purchases account with a normal credit balance that is deducted from Purchases on the income statement (see Exhibit 5-2). If a company is able to make only a partial payment on an invoice, most creditors will allow the company to take the discount applicable to the partial payment. The discount usually does not apply to freight, postage, taxes, or other charges that might appear on the invoice.

1. (360 days/20 days) × 2 = 36

Good management of cash resources calls for both taking the discount and waiting as long as possible to pay. To accomplish these two objectives, some companies file invoices according to their due dates as they get them. Each day, the invoices due on that day are pulled from the file and paid. In this manner, the company uses cash as long as possible and also takes advantage of the discounts. A method commonly used to control these discounts (the net method) is illustrated on pages 195–196.

Freight In. In some industries, it is customary for the supplier (seller) to pay transportation costs, charging a higher price to include them. In other industries, it is customary for the purchaser to pay transportation charges on merchandise. These charges, called **freight in** or **transportation in**, should logically be included as an addition to purchases, but as in the case of purchases discounts, they should be accumulated in the Freight In account so that management can monitor this cost. The entry for the purchaser is as follows:

Nov. 12	Freight In	134	
	Cash (or Accounts Payable)		134
	Incurred freight charges		
	on merchandise purchased		

Special terms designate whether the supplier or the purchaser is to pay the freight charges. **FOB shipping point** means that the supplier will place the merchandise "free on board" at the point of origin, and the buyer bears the shipping costs from that point. In addition, the title to the merchandise passes to the buyer at that point. When purchasing a car, you know that if the sales agreement says "FOB Detroit," you must pay the freight from Detroit to where you are.

On the other hand, **FOB destination** means that the supplier is bearing the transportation costs to the destination. In this case, title remains with the supplier until the merchandise reaches its destination. The supplier normally prepays the amount, in which case the buyer makes no entry for freight. In rare cases, the buyer may pay the charges and then deduct them from the invoice.

The effects of these special shipping terms are summarized below:

Shipping Term	Where Title Passes	Who Bears Cost of Transportation
FOB shipping point	At origin	Buyer
FOB destination	At destination	Seller

In some cases, the supplier pays the freight charges but bills the buyer by including them as a separate item on the sales invoice. When this occurs the buyer should still record the purchase and the freight in separate accounts. For example, assume that an invoice for purchase of merchandise totaling $1,890 included the cost of merchandise of $1,600, freight charges of $290, and terms of 2/10, n/30. The entry to record this transaction would be:

Nov. 25	Purchases	1,600	
	Freight In	290	
	Accounts Payable		1,890
	Purchased merchandise for $1,600;		
	included in the invoice were		
	freight charges of $290 and terms		
	of 2/10, n/30		

If this invoice is paid within ten days, the discount will be $32 ($1,600 × .02), because it would not apply to the freight charges.

It is important not to confuse freight-in costs with freight-out or delivery costs. If you, as seller, agree to pay transportation charges on goods you have sold, this expense is a cost of *selling* merchandise, not a cost of *purchasing* merchandise. Freight Out is shown as an operating expense on the income statement.

Control of Purchases Discounts Using the Net Method

Alternative Method

As noted earlier, it is usually worthwhile to pay invoices promptly to qualify for the purchase discount. In fact, it is bad management not to take advantage of such discounts. The system of recording purchases initially at the gross purchase price, called the **gross method** and described on pages 192–194, has the disadvantage of telling management only about what discounts were taken. It records no information about the discounts that were not taken, or in other words, were "lost."

A procedure called the **net method** of recording purchases, which will identify the discounts that are lost, requires that purchases be recorded initially at the net price. Then, if the discount is not taken, a special account is debited for the amount of the lost discount. For example, suppose that a company purchases goods on November 12 for $1,500, with terms of 2/10, n/30, and that it returns $200 worth of merchandise on November 14. Suppose also that payment is not made until December 12, so the company is not eligible for the 2 percent discount. The entries to record these three transactions are as follows:

Nov. 12	Purchases	1,470	
	Accounts Payable		1,470
	To record purchases of		
	merchandise at net price,		
	terms 2/10, n/30;		
	$1,500 − (.02 × $1,500) = $1,470		

Nov. 14	Accounts Payable	196	
	Purchases Returns and Allowances		196
	Return of damaged merchandise		
	purchased on November 12;		
	recorded at net price:		
	$200 − (.02 × $200) = $196		

Dec. 12	Accounts Payable		1,274	
	Purchases Discounts Lost		26	
	Cash			1,300
	Paid invoice of Nov. 12			
	Purchase Nov. 12	$1,500		
	Less return Nov. 14	200		
	Net purchase	$1,300		

Discount lost: $.02 \times \$1,300 = \$26$

If the company pays the invoice by November 22 and uses the net method of recording purchases, it will make a payment of $1,274. Since purchases were recorded at net prices, no Purchases Discounts Lost account would be required, and the entry would be recorded as follows:

Nov. 22	Accounts Payable	1,274	
	Cash		1,274
	Payment of Nov. 12 invoice		
	within discount period		

However, if the company makes the payment after the discount period, management learns of the failure to take the discount by examining the Purchases Discounts Lost account. The amount of Purchases Discounts Lost is shown as an operating expense on the income statement.

Merchandise Inventory

OBJECTIVE 5
Differentiate the perpetual inventory method from the periodic inventory method

The inventory of a merchandising concern consists of the goods on hand and available for sale to customers. For a grocery store, inventory would be the meats, vegetables, canned goods, and other items for sale. For a service station, it would be gasoline, oil, and automobile parts. Merchandising concerns purchase their inventories from wholesalers, manufacturers, and other suppliers.

The merchandise inventory on hand at the beginning of the accounting period is called the **beginning inventory**. Conversely, the merchandise inventory on hand at the end of the accounting period is called the **ending inventory**. As we have seen, beginning and ending inventories are used in calculating the cost of goods sold on the income statement. Ending inventory also appears on the balance sheet as an asset. It will become a part of cost of goods sold in a later period when it is sold. This year's beginning inventory was last year's ending inventory.

Measuring Merchandise Inventory. Merchandise inventory is a key factor in determining cost of goods sold. Because merchandise inventory represents goods available for sale that are still unsold, there must be a method for determining both the quantity and the cost of these goods on hand. The two basic methods of accounting for the number of items in the merchandise inventory are the periodic inventory method and the perpetual inventory method.

Under the **periodic inventory method**, the count of the physical inventory takes place periodically, usually at the end of the accounting period, and no detailed records of the physical inventory on hand are maintained during the period. Under the **perpetual inventory method**, records are kept of the quantity and, usually, the cost of individual items of inventory as they are bought and sold.

Cost of goods sold under the periodic inventory method is determined at the end of the accounting period in a manner similar to the method of accounting for supplies expense, with which you are already familiar. In the simplest case, the cost of inventory purchased is accumulated in a Purchases account. Then, at the end of the accounting period, the actual count of the physical inventory is deducted from the total of purchases plus beginning merchandise inventory to determine cost of goods sold.

Under the perpetual inventory method, on the other hand, the cost of each item is debited to the Merchandise Inventory account as it is purchased. As items are sold, the Merchandise Inventory account is credited and the Cost of Goods Sold account is debited for the cost of the items sold. In this way the balance of the Merchandise Inventory account always equals the cost of goods on hand at a point in time, and the Cost of Goods Sold account equals total cost associated with items sold to that point in time.

Traditionally, the periodic inventory method has been used by companies that sell items of low value and high volume because of the difficulty and expense of accounting for the purchase and sale of each item. Examples of such companies are drugstores, automobile parts stores, department stores, discount companies, and grain companies. In contrast, companies that sell items of high unit value, such as appliances or automobiles, have tended to use the perpetual inventory method. This distinction between high and low unit value for inventory methods has blurred considerably in recent years because of the widespread use of the computer. Although the periodic inventory method is still widely used, use of the perpetual inventory method has increased greatly. For example, many grocery stores, which traditionally used the periodic inventory method, can now, through the use of electronic markings on each product, update the physical inventory as items are sold by linking their cash registers to a computer. It has become common for some retail businesses to use the perpetual method for keeping track of the physical flow of inventory and the periodic method for preparing the financial statements.

The periodic inventory method for determining cost of goods sold is described in this chapter. The perpetual inventory method is discussed further in Chapters 10 and 23.

The Periodic Inventory Method. Most companies rely on an actual count of goods on hand at the end of an accounting period to determine ending inventory and, indirectly, the cost of goods sold. The procedure for determining the merchandise inventory under the periodic inventory method can be summarized as follows:

1. Make a physical count of merchandise on hand at the end of the accounting period.

2. Multiply the quantity of each type of merchandise by its unit cost.
3. Add the resulting costs of each type of merchandise to obtain a total. This amount is the ending merchandise inventory.

The cost of the ending merchandise inventory is deducted from goods available for sale to determine cost of goods sold. The ending inventory of one period is the beginning inventory of the next period. Entries are made at the end of the accounting period to remove the beginning inventory (the last period's ending inventory) and to enter the ending inventory of the current period. These entries are the only ones made to the Merchandise Inventory account during the period. Consequently, only on the balance sheet date and after the closing entries does the Inventory account represent the actual inventory on hand. As soon as purchases or sales are made, the figure becomes a historical amount and remains so until the new inventory is entered at the end of the accounting period.

Taking the Physical Inventory. Making a physical count of all merchandise on hand is referred to as **taking a physical inventory**. It can be a difficult task, since it is easy to omit items or to count them twice.

Merchandise inventory includes all salable goods owned by the concern regardless of where they are located. It includes all goods on shelves, in storerooms, in warehouses, and in trucks en route between warehouses and stores. It includes goods in transit from suppliers if title to the goods has passed to the merchant. Ending inventory does not include merchandise sold to customers but not delivered or goods that cannot be sold because they are damaged or obsolete. If the damaged or obsolete goods can be sold at a reduced price, however, they should be included in ending inventory at the reduced value.

The actual count is usually taken after the close of business on the last day of the fiscal year. Many companies end their fiscal year in a slow season to facilitate taking the physical inventory. Retail department stores often end their fiscal year in January or February, for example. After hours, at night or on the weekend, employees count and record all items on numbered inventory tickets or sheets. Sometimes a store will close for all or part of a day for inventory taking. They follow established procedures to make sure that no items are missed. When the inventory tickets or sheets are completed, they are forwarded to the accounting office.

The accounting office checks to see that all numbered tickets and sheets are accounted for, and copies the information onto inventory ledgers. The appropriate unit costs are then entered and the computations made to determine ending merchandise inventory.

Inventory Losses

Many companies have substantial losses in merchandise inventory from spoilage, shoplifting, and employee pilferage. Management will, of course, want to take steps to prevent such losses from occurring. But if they do occur, the periodic inventory method provides no means to determine such losses because these costs are automatically included in the cost of goods sold. For example, assume that a company lost $1,250 during an accounting period because merchandise had been stolen or spoiled. Thus, when the physical inventory is taken, the missing items will not be in stock and cannot be counted. Because the ending inventory will not contain these items, the amount subtracted from goods available for sale is less than it would be if the goods were in stock. Cost of goods sold, therefore, is greater by $1,250. In a sense, cost of goods sold is inflated by the amount of merchandise that has been lost. If the perpetual inventory method is used, it is easier to identify these types of losses. Since the merchandise inventory account is continuously updated for sales, purchases, and returns, the loss will show up as the difference between the inventory records and the physical inventory at the end of the accounting period.

Operating Expenses

Operating expenses make up the third major part of the income statement for a merchandising concern. As noted earlier, they are the expenses, other than the cost of goods sold, that are necessary to run the business. It is customary to group operating expenses into useful categories. Selling expenses and general and administrative expenses are common categories. Selling expenses include all expenses of storing and preparing goods for sale; displaying, advertising, and otherwise promoting sales; making the sales; and delivering the goods to the buyer if the seller bears the cost of delivery. Among the general and administrative expenses are general office expenses, those for accounting, personnel, and credit and collections, and any other expenses that apply to the overall operation of the company. Although general occupancy expenses, such as rent expense and utility expenses, are often classified as general and administrative, they are sometimes allocated or divided between the selling and the general and administrative categories on a basis determined by management.

Handling Merchandise Inventory at the End of the Accounting Period

OBJECTIVE 6
Explain the objectives of handling merchandise inventory at the end of the accounting period and two approaches to achieving them

Recall that under the periodic inventory system, purchases of merchandise are accumulated in the Purchases account. During the accounting period, no entries are made to the Merchandise Inventory account. Its balance at the end of the period, before adjusting and closing entries, is the same as it was at the beginning of the period. Thus its balance at this point represents beginning merchandise inventory. Recall also that the cost of goods sold is determined by adding beginning merchandise inventory to net purchases and then subtracting ending merchandising inventory. The objectives of handling merchandise inventory at the end of the period are to (1) remove the beginning balance from the Merchandise Inventory account, (2) enter the ending balance into the Merchandise Inventory account, and (3) enter the beginning inventory as a debit and the ending inventory as a credit to the Income Summary account to properly calculate net income. Using the figures for Fenwick Fashions, these objectives can be accomplished if the following effects on the Merchandise Inventory and Income Summary accounts are achieved:

		Merchandise Inventory		
Jan. 1	Beginning Balance	52,800	Dec. 31	52,800
Dec. 31	Ending Balance	48,300		

Effect A   Effect B

	Income Summary		
Dec. 31	52,800	Dec. 31	48,300

In this example, merchandise inventory was $52,800 at the beginning of the year and $48,300 at the end of the year. Effect A removes the $52,800 from Merchandise Inventory, leaving a zero balance, and transfers it to Income Summary. In Income Summary, the $52,800 is in effect added to net purchases because, like expenses, the balance of the Purchases account is debited to Income Summary by a closing entry. Effect B establishes the ending balance of Merchandise Inventory of $48,300 and enters it as a credit in the Income Summary account. The credit entry in Income Summary has the effect of deducting the ending inventory from goods available for sale because both purchases and beginning inventory were entered on the debit side. In other words, beginning merchandise inventory and purchases are debits to Income Summary, and ending merchandise inventory is a credit to Income Summary.

Thus the three objectives stated above are accomplished if effects A and B both occur. The question then arises as to how to achieve the effects. Two acceptable methods are available. They are the adjusting entry method and the closing entry method. Each method produces exactly the same result, so only one of them would be used by a company. However, since practice varies in different regions of the country as to which method is most used, both are described here. Each method is simply a bookkeeping technique designed to deal with the Merchandise Inventory account under the periodic inventory system.

Using the adjusting entry method, the two entries indicated by effects A and B are prepared at the same time the other adjusting entries are made, as follows:

Adjusting Entries

Dec. 31	Income Summary	52,800	
	Merchandise Inventory		**52,800**
	To remove beginning balance of Merchandise Inventory and transfer it to Income Summary		

Dec. 31 **Merchandise Inventory**   **48,300**
         Income Summary   48,300
             To establish ending balance
             of Merchandise Inventory and
             deduct it from goods available
             for sale in Income Summary

The closing entry method makes the debit and the credit to Merchandise Inventory by including them among the closing entries, as follows:

Closing Entries

			Total of credits
Dec. 31	Income Summary		
	Merchandise Inventory		**52,800**
	Expenses and Other Income Statement		Various
	Accounts with Debit Balances		amounts
	To close temporary expense and revenue		
	accounts having debit balances and		
	to remove beginning inventory		

Dec. 31 **Merchandise Inventory**   **48,300**
         Revenues and Other Income Statement   Various
             Accounts with Credit Balances   amounts
             Income Summary   Total
                 To close temporary expense and revenue   of debits
                 accounts having credit balances
                 and to establish the ending
                 merchandise inventory

Notice that under both methods, Merchandise Inventory is credited for the beginning balance and debited for the ending balance and that the opposite entries are made to Income Summary.

Work Sheet for a Merchandising Concern

OBJECTIVE 7
Prepare a work sheet for a merchandising concern under one of two alternative methods

In Chapter 4, the work sheet was presented as a useful tool in preparing adjusting entries, closing entries, and financial statements. The work sheet of a merchandising business is basically the same as that of a service business except that it has to deal with the new accounts that are needed to handle merchandising transactions. These accounts include Sales, Sales Returns and Allowances, Sales Discounts, Purchases, Purchases Returns and Allowances, Purchases Discounts, Freight In, and Merchandise Inventory. Except for Merchandise Inventory, these accounts are treated much as revenue and expense accounts are for a service company. They are transferred to the Income Summary account in the closing process. On the work sheet, they are extended to the Income Statement columns.

The way in which merchandise inventory is handled, however, depends on whether the adjusting entry method or the closing entry method is to be used. The student needs to learn only one of these methods because, as already noted, they are both acceptable and they accomplish the same objectives. You should ask your instructor which method is to be used in your course.

The Adjusting Entry Method

The work sheet for Fenwick Fashions Company using the adjusting entry method is presented in Exhibit 5-3. Each pair of columns in the work sheet and the adjusting and closing entries are discussed below.

Trial Balance Columns. The first step in the preparation of the work sheet is to enter the balances from the ledger accounts into the Trial Balance columns. You are already familiar with this procedure. Total the Trial Balance columns to prove the equality of debits and credits.

Adjustments Columns. Under the adjusting entry method of handling merchandise inventory, the first two adjusting entries to be entered in the work sheet were explained in the previous section. The first entry transfers beginning merchandise inventory to the Income Summary account by crediting Merchandise Inventory and debiting Income Summary for $52,800 (adjustment **a**). The second entry establishes the ending merchandise inventory by debiting Merchandise Inventory and crediting Income Summary for $48,300 (adjustment **b**). Note that the Income Summary account is listed immediately below the trial balance totals. The remaining adjustments for Fenwick Fashions are familiar to you. They involve insurance expired during the period (adjustment **c**), store and office supplies used (adjustments **d** and **e**), and depreciation of building and office equipment (adjustments **f** and **g**). After the adjusting entries are entered on the work sheet, the Adjustments columns are totaled to prove the equality of the debits and credits.

Omission of Adjusted Trial Balance Columns. These two columns, which appeared in the work sheet for a service company in Chapter 4, may be omitted. These columns are optional and are used when there are many adjusting entries to record. When only a few adjusting entries are required, as is the case for Fenwick Fashions Company, these columns are not necessary and may be omitted to save time.

Income Statement and Balance Sheet Columns. After the Trial Balance columns have been totaled, the adjustments entered, and the equality of the columns proved, the balances are extended to the statement columns. This process is accomplished most efficiently by beginning with the Cash account at the top of the work sheet and moving sequentially down the work sheet one account at a time. Each account balance is entered in the proper column of the income statement or balance sheet. The only exception to this rule is that both the debit (beginning merchandise inventory of $52,800) and the credit (ending merchandise inventory of $48,300) to Income Summary are extended to the corresponding Income Statement columns. The reason for this is that both

Exhibit 5-3. Work Sheet for Fenwick Fashions Company: Adjusting Entry Method

Fenwick Fashions Company
Work Sheet
For the Year Ended December 31, 19xx

Account Name	Trial Balance Debit	Trial Balance Credit	Adjustments Debit	Adjustments Credit	Income Statement Debit	Income Statement Credit	Balance Sheet Debit	Balance Sheet Credit
Cash	29,410						29,410	
Accounts Receivable	42,400						42,400	
Merchandise Inventory	52,800		(b) 48,300	(a) 52,800			48,300	
Prepaid Insurance	17,400			(c) 5,800			11,600	
Store Supplies	2,600			(d) 1,540			1,060	
Office Supplies	1,840			(e) 1,204			636	
Land	4,500						4,500	
Building	20,260						20,260	
Accumulated Depreciation, Building		5,650		(f) 2,600				8,250
Office Equipment	8,600						8,600	
Accumulated Depreciation, Office Equipment		2,800		(g) 2,200				5,000
Accounts Payable		25,683						25,683
Joseph Fenwick, Capital		118,352						118,352
Joseph Fenwick, Withdrawals	20,000						20,000	
Sales		246,350				246,350		
Sales Returns and Allowances	2,750				2,750			
Sales Discounts	4,275				4,275			
Purchases	126,400				126,400			
Purchases Returns and Allowances		5,640				5,640		
Purchases Discounts		2,136				2,136		
Freight In	8,236				8,236			
Sales Salaries Expense	22,500				22,500			
Freight Out Expense	5,740				5,740			
Advertising Expense	10,000				10,000			
Office Salaries Expense	26,900				26,900			
	406,611	406,611						
Income Summary			(a) 52,800	(b) 48,300	52,800	48,300		
Insurance Expense, Selling			(c) 1,600		1,600			
Insurance Expense, General			(c) 4,200		4,200			
Store Supplies Expense			(c) 1,540		1,540			
Office Supplies Expense			(e) 1,204		1,204			
Depreciation Expense, Building			(f) 2,600		2,600			
Depreciation Expense, Office Equipment			(g) 2,200		2,200			
			114,444	114,444	272,945	302,426	186,766	157,285
Net Income					29,481			29,481
					302,426	302,426	186,766	186,766

the beginning and ending inventory figures are needed to prepare the cost of goods sold section of the income statement.

After all the items have been extended to the proper statement columns, the four columns are totaled. The net income or net loss is determined as the difference in the debit and credit columns of the income statement. In this case, Fenwick Fashions Company has earned a net income of $29,481, which is extended to the credit column of the balance sheet. The four columns are then added to prove the equality of the debits and credits.

OBJECTIVE 8
Prepare adjusting and closing entries for a merchandising concern

Adjusting Entries. The adjusting entries are now entered from the work sheet into the general journal and posted to the ledger, as they would be in a service company. The only difference is that under the adjusting entry method, the two adjustments involving Merchandise Inventory and Income Summary, already illustrated on pages 200–201, appear among the adjusting entries.

Closing Entries. The closing entries for Fenwick Fashions Company under the adjusting entry method appear in Exhibit 5-4. These closing entries are very similar to those for a service company except that the new accounts for merchandising companies must also be closed to Income Summary. All income statement accounts with debit balances, including Sales Returns and Allowances, Sales Discounts, Purchases, and Freight In, are credited in the first entry. All income statement accounts with credit balances, including Sales, Purchases Returns and Allowances, and Purchases Discounts, are debited in the second entry. When copying the accounts and their balances out of the Income Statement columns of the work sheet, do not include the debit and credit merchandise inventory amounts already in the Income Summary account. The third and fourth entries are used to close the Income Summary account and transfer net income to the Capital account, and to close the Withdrawals account to the Capital account.

The Closing Entry Method

Alternative Method

The work sheet for Fenwick Fashions Company using the closing entry method is presented in Exhibit 5-5. Each pair of columns in the work sheet and the adjusting and closing entries are discussed on the following pages.

Trial Balance Columns. The first step in the preparation of the work sheet is to enter the balances from the ledger accounts into the Trial Balance columns. You are already familiar with this procedure.

Adjustments Columns. Under the closing entry method of handling merchandise inventory, the adjusting entries for Fenwick Fashions Company are entered in the adjustments columns in the same way that they were for service companies. They involve insurance expired during the period (adjustment **a**), store and office supplies used during the period (adjustments **b** and **c**), and depreciation of building and office

	Exhibit 5-4. Closing Entries for a Merchandising Concern: Adjusting Entry Method

	General Journal		**Page 1**

	Date	**Description**	**Post. Ref.**	**Debit**	**Credit**
19xx		*Closing entries:*			
Dec.	31	Income Summary		220,145	
		Sales Returns and Allowances			2,750
		Sales Discounts			4,275
		Purchases			126,400
		Freight In			8,236
		Sales Salaries Expense			22,500
		Freight Out Expense			5,740
		Advertising Expense			10,000
		Office Salaries Expense			26,900
		Insurance Expense, Selling			1,600
		Insurance Expense, General			4,200
		Store Supplies Expense			1,540
		Office Supplies Expense			1,204
		Depreciation Expense, Building			2,600
		Depreciation Expense, Office Equipment			2,200
		To close temporary expense and revenue accounts having debit balances			
	31	Sales		246,350	
		Purchases Returns and Allowances		5,640	
		Purchases Discounts		2,136	
		Income Summary			254,126
		To close temporary expense and revenue accounts having credit balances			
	31	Income Summary		29,481	
		Joseph Fenwick, Capital			29,481
		To close the Income Summary account			
	31	Joseph Fenwick, Capital		20,000	
		Joseph Fenwick, Withdrawals			20,000
		To close the Withdrawals account			

Exhibit 5-5. Work Sheet for Fenwick Fashions Company: Closing Entry Method

Fenwick Fashions Company
Work Sheet
For the Year Ended December 31, 19xx

Account Name	Trial Balance Debit	Trial Balance Credit	Adjustments Debit	Adjustments Credit	Income Statement Debit	Income Statement Credit	Balance Sheet Debit	Balance Sheet Credit
Cash	29,410						29,410	
Accounts Receivable	42,400						42,400	
Merchandise Inventory	52,800				52,800	48,300	48,300	
Prepaid Insurance	17,400			(a) 5,800			11,600	
Store Supplies	2,600			(b) 1,540			1,060	
Office Supplies	1,840			(c) 1,204			636	
Land	4,500						4,500	
Building	20,260						20,260	
Accumulated Depreciation, Building		5,650		(d) 2,600				8,250
Office Equipment	8,600						8,600	
Accumulated Depreciation, Office Equipment		2,800		(e) 2,200				5,000
Accounts Payable		25,683						25,683
Joseph Fenwick, Capital		118,352						118,352
Joseph Fenwick, Withdrawals	20,000						20,000	
Sales		246,350				246,350		
Sales Returns and Allowances	2,750				2,750			
Sales Discounts	4,275				4,275			
Purchases	126,400				126,400			
Purchases Returns and Allowances		5,640				5,640		
Purchases Discounts		2,136				2,136		
Freight In	8,236				8,236			
Sales Salaries Expense	22,500				22,500			
Freight Out Expense	5,740				5,740			
Advertising Expense	10,000				10,000			
Office Salaries Expense	26,900				26,900			
	406,611	406,611						
Insurance Expense, Selling			(a) 1,600		1,600			
Insurance Expense, General			(a) 4,200		4,200			
Store Supplies Expense			(b) 1,540		1,540			
Office Supplies Expense			(c) 1,204		1,204			
Depreciation Expense, Building			(d) 2,600		2,600			
Depreciation Expense, Office Equipment			(e) 2,200		2,200			
			13,344	13,344	272,945	302,426	186,766	157,285
Net Income					29,481			29,481
					302,426	302,426	186,766	186,766

equipment (adjustments **d** and **e**). No adjusting entry is made for merchandise inventory. After the adjusting entries are entered on the work sheet, the columns are totaled to prove the equality of the debits and credits.

Omission of Adjusted Trial Balance Columns. These two columns, which appeared in the work sheet for a service company in Chapter 4, may be omitted. See the discussion under the adjusting entry method.

Income Statement and Balance Sheet Columns. After the Trial Balance columns have been totaled, the adjustments entered, and the equality of the columns proved, the balances are extended to the statement columns. This process is accomplished most efficiently by beginning with the Cash account at the top of the work sheet and moving sequentially down the work sheet one account at a time. Each account balance is entered in the proper Income Statement or Balance Sheet column.

The extension that may not be obvious is in the Merchandise Inventory row. The beginning inventory balance of $52,800 (which is already in the trial balance) is first extended to the debit column of the income statement, as illustrated in Exhibit 5-5. This procedure has the effect of adding beginning inventory to net purchases because the Purchases account is also in the debit column of the income statement. The ending inventory balance of $48,300 (which is determined by the physical inventory and is not in the trial balance) is then inserted in the credit column of the income statement. This procedure has the effect of subtracting the ending inventory from goods available for sale in order to calculate the cost of goods sold. Finally, the ending merchandise inventory ($48,300) is then inserted in the debit column of the balance sheet because it will appear on the balance sheet.

After all the items have been extended into the proper statement columns, the four columns are totaled. The net income or net loss is determined as the difference in the debit and credit Income Statement columns. In this case, Fenwick Fashions Company has earned a net income of $29,481, which is extended to the credit column of the Balance Sheet. The four columns are then added to prove the equality of the debits and credits.

Adjusting Entries. The adjusting entries are now entered from the work sheet into the general journal and posted to the ledger as they would be in a service company. Under the closing entry method, there is no difference in this procedure between a service company and a merchandising company.

Closing Entries. The closing entries for Fenwick Fashions Company under the closing entry method appear in Exhibit 5-6. Note that Merchandise Inventory is credited in the first entry for the amount of beginning inventory ($52,800) and debited in the second entry for the amount of the ending inventory ($48,300), as shown on pages 200–201. Otherwise, these closing entries are very similar to those for a service company except that the new merchandising accounts introduced in this

Exhibit 5-6. Closing Entries for a Merchandising Concern: Closing Entry Method				
General Journal				**Page 1**
Date		**Description**	**Post. Ref.**	**Debit**	**Credit**

Date		Description	Post. Ref.	Debit	Credit
19xx		*Closing entries:*			
Dec.	31	Income Summary		272,945	
		Merchandise Inventory			52,800
		Sales Returns and Allowances			2,750
		Sales Discounts			4,275
		Purchases			126,400
		Freight In			8,236
		Sales Salaries Expense			22,500
		Freight Out Expense			5,740
		Advertising Expense			10,000
		Office Salaries Expense			26,900
		Insurance Expense, Selling			1,600
		Insurance Expense, General			4,200
		Store Supplies Expense			1,540
		Office Supplies Expense			1,204
		Depreciation Expense, Building			2,600
		Depreciation Expense, Office Equipment			2,200
		To close temporary expense and revenue accounts having debit balances			
	31	Merchandise Inventory		48,300	
		Sales		246,350	
		Purchases Returns and Allowances		5,640	
		Purchases Discounts		2,136	
		Income Summary			302,426
		To close temporary expense and revenue accounts having credit balances			
	31	Income Summary		29,481	
		Joseph Fenwick, Capital			29,481
		To close the Income Summary account			
	31	Joseph Fenwick, Capital		20,000	
		Joseph Fenwick, Withdrawals			20,000
		To close the Withdrawals account			

Exhibit 5-7. Income Statement for Fenwick Fashions Company

Fenwick Fashions Company
Income Statement
For the Year Ended December 31, 19xx

Revenues from Sales

Gross Sales			$246,350
Less: Sales Returns and Allowances		$ 2,750	
Sales Discounts		4,275	7,025
Net Sales			$239,325

Cost of Goods Sold

Merchandise Inventory, January 1, 19xx		$ 52,800	
Purchases		$126,400	
Less: Purchases Returns and Allowances	$5,640		
Purchases Discounts	2,136	7,776	
		$118,624	
Freight In		8,236	
Net Purchases		126,860	
Goods Available for Sale		$179,660	
Less Merchandise Inventory, December 31, 19xx		48,300	
Cost of Goods Sold			131,360

Gross Margin from Sales $107,965

Operating Expenses

Selling Expenses

Sales Salaries Expense	$ 22,500		
Freight Out Expense	5,740		
Advertising Expense	10,000		
Insurance Expense, Selling	1,600		
Store Supplies Expense	1,540		
Total Selling Expenses		$ 41,380	

General and Administrative Expenses

Office Salaries Expense	$ 26,900		
Insurance Expense, General	4,200		
Office Supplies Expense	1,204		
Depreciation Expense, Building	2,600		
Depreciation Expense, Office Equipment	2,200		
Total General and Administrative Expenses		37,104	
Total Operating Expenses			78,484

Net Income $ 29,481

chapter must also be closed to Income Summary. All income statement accounts with debit balances, for instance, Sales Returns and Allowances, Sales Discounts, Purchases, and Freight In, are credited in the first entry. The total of these accounts equals the total of the debit column in the Income Statement columns of the work sheet. All income statement accounts with credit balances, namely, Sales, Purchases Returns and Allowances, and Purchases Discounts, are debited in the second entry. The total of these accounts equals the total of the Income Statement credit column in the work sheet. The third and fourth entries are used to close the Income Summary account and transfer net income to the Capital account and to close the Withdrawals account to the Capital account.

Income Statement Illustrated

OBJECTIVE 9
Prepare an income statement for a merchandising concern

Earlier in this chapter, the parts of the income statement for a merchandising concern were presented and the transactions pertaining to each part were discussed. Exhibit 5-7 (page 209) pulls the parts together and shows the complete income statement for Fenwick Fashions Company. The statement may be prepared by referring to the accounts in the ledger that pertain to the income statement; or when a work sheet is prepared, the accounts and their balances may be taken from the Income Statement columns of the work sheet. In practice, the statement of owner's equity and balance sheet would also be prepared. They are not presented here because they are like those of service companies with the exception that merchandise inventory would be listed among the assets on the balance sheet.

Chapter Review

Review of Learning Objectives

1. **Compare the income statements for service and merchandising concerns.**
   The merchandising company differs from the service company in that it attempts to earn income by buying and selling merchandise rather than by offering services. In the simplest case, the income statement for a service company consists only of services and revenues. The income statement for a merchandising company has three major parts: (1) revenues from sales, (2) cost of goods sold, and (3) operating expenses. The cost of goods sold section is necessary for the computation of gross margin from sales made on the merchandise that has been sold. Merchandisers must sell their merchandise for more than cost to pay operating expenses and have an adequate profit remaining.

2. **Record transactions involving revenues for merchandising concerns.**
   Revenues from sales consist of gross sales less sales returns and allowances and sales discounts. The amount of a sales discount can be determined from the terms of the sale. Revenue transactions for merchandising firms may be summarized as follows:

	Related Accounting Entries	
Transaction	**Debit**	**Credit**
Sell merchandise to customer.	Cash (or Accounts Receivable)	Sales
Collect for merchandise sold on credit.	Cash (and Sales Discounts, if applicable)	Accounts Receivable
Permit customers to return merchandise or grant a reduction on original price.	Sales Returns and Allowances	Cash (or Accounts Receivable)

3. **Calculate cost of goods sold.**
   To compute cost of goods sold, add beginning merchandise inventory to the net purchases to determine goods available for sale. Then subtract ending merchandise inventory from the total, as follows:

$$\text{Beginning Merchandise Inventory} + \text{Net Purchases} = \text{Goods Available for Sale}$$

$$\text{Goods Available for Sale} - \text{Ending Merchandise Inventory} = \text{Cost of Goods Sold}$$

Net purchases are calculated by subtracting the purchases discounts and purchases returns and allowances from gross purchases and then adding any freight-in charges on the purchases, as follows:

$$\text{Gross Purchases} - \text{Purchases Discounts} - \text{Purchases Returns and Allowances} + \text{Freight In} = \text{Net Purchases}$$

The Purchases account is debited only for merchandise purchased for resale. Its sole purpose is to accumulate the total cost of merchandise purchased during an accounting period.

4. **Record transactions involving purchases of merchandise.**
   The transactions involving purchases of merchandise may be summarized as follows:

Transaction	Related Accounting Entries	
	Debit	**Credit**
Purchase merchandise for resale.	Purchases	Cash (or Accounts Payable)
Incur transportation charges on merchandise purchased for resale.	Freight In	Cash (or Accounts Payable)
Return unsatisfactory merchandise to supplier, or obtain a reduction from original price.	Cash (or Accounts Payable)	Purchases Returns and Allowances
Pay for merchandise purchased on credit.	Accounts Payable	Cash (and Purchases Discounts, if applicable)

5. **Differentiate the perpetual inventory method from the periodic inventory method.**

   Merchandise inventory may be determined by one of two methods. (1) Under the perpetual inventory method, records are kept of the quantity and usually the cost of individual items of inventory throughout the year as items are bought and sold. (2) Under the periodic inventory method, the company usually waits until the end of the accounting period to take a physical inventory and does not maintain detailed records of physical inventory on hand during the period. Merchandise inventory includes all salable goods owned, regardless of where they are located.

6. **Explain the objectives of handling merchandise inventory at the end of the accounting period and two approaches to achieving them.**

   At the end of the accounting period under a periodic inventory method, it is necessary to (1) remove the beginning balance from the Merchandise Inventory account, (2) enter the ending balance in the Merchandise Inventory account, and (3) enter these two amounts in the Income Summary account so the proper calculation of net income results. These objectives are accomplished by crediting Merchandise Inventory and debiting Income Summary for the beginning balance and debiting Merchandise Inventory and crediting Income Summary for the ending balance, as shown:

Inventory Procedures at End of Period	Related Accounting Entries	
	Debit	**Credit**
Transfer the balance of the beginning inventory to the Income Summary account.	Income Summary	Merchandise Inventory
Take a physical inventory of goods on hand at the end of the period, and establish the balance of ending inventory.	Merchandise Inventory	Income Summary

There are two ways of accomplishing these effects. Under the adjusting entry method, the entries are included among the adjusting entries. Under the closing entry method, the entries are included among the closing entries.

7. **Prepare a work sheet for a merchandising concern under one of two alternative methods.**

   The major difference between preparing a work sheet for a merchandising concern and preparing one for a service company is in the accounts relating to merchandising transactions. The accounts necessary to compute cost of goods sold appear in the Income Statement columns. Merchandise inventory is treated differently under each of the following two methods:

   Adjusting entry method: Under this method, Merchandise Inventory and Income Summary are adjusted in the Adjustments columns, the ending inventory is extended to the Balance Sheet debit column, and the two adjustments to Income Summary are extended to the Income Statement columns.

   Closing entry method: Under this method, the beginning inventory from the trial balance is extended to the debit column of the Income Statement and the ending balance of Merchandise Inventory is inserted in both the credit column of the Income Statement and the debit column of the Balance Sheet.

8. **Prepare adjusting and closing entries for a merchandising concern.**

   The adjusting and closing entries for a merchandising concern are similar to those for a service business. The greatest difference is the handling of merchandise inventory which is summarized in the following table:

Method	Adjusting Entries	Closing Entries

Adjusting entry method	Dr. Income Summary
	Cr. Merchandise Inventory
	  for amount of beginning
	  inventory
	Dr. Merchandise Inventory
	Cr. Income Summary for
	  the amount of ending
	  inventory
		Follow procedures for
		  service companies

Closing entry method	Follow procedures for
	  service companies
		Include among closing
		  entries the following:
		Dr. Income Summary
		Cr. Merchandise
		  Inventory for amount
		  of beginning inventory
		Dr. Merchandise
		  Inventory for amount
		  of ending inventory
		Cr. Income Summary

9. **Prepare an income statement for a merchandising concern.**

   The income statement of a merchandising company comprises three major sections. The revenues from sales section will show gross sales, with contra revenue accounts deducted from it to arrive at net sales. The cost of goods sold section will show the accounts that make up goods available for sale. The operating expenses section will divide the expenses into useful categories such as selling expenses and general and administrative expenses. Net income is revenues from sales less cost of goods sold less operating expenses.

Review of Concepts and Terminology

The following concepts and terms were introduced in this chapter:

(L.O. 5) **Beginning inventory:**   Merchandise on hand for sale to customers at the beginning of the accounting period.

(L.O. 1) **Cost of goods sold:**   The amount paid for goods that were sold during an accounting period.

(L.O. 5) **Ending inventory:**   Merchandise on hand for sale to customers at the end of the accounting period.

(L.O. 4) **FOB destination:**   Term relating to transportation charges meaning that the seller bears the transportation costs to the destination.

(L.O. 4) **FOB shipping point:**   Term relating to transportation charges meaning that the buyer bears the transportation costs from the point of origin.

(L.O. 4) **Freight in (transportation in):**   Transportation charges on merchandise purchased for resale.

(L.O. 3) **Goods available for sale:**   The total goods during the year that could have been sold to customers; the beginning merchandise inventory plus net purchases.

(L.O. 1) **Gross margin from sales (or gross profit):**   The amount of revenues from sales, after deducting cost of goods sold, that is available for operating expenses.

(L.O. 4) **Gross method:**   The system of initially recording purchases at the gross purchase price.

(L.O. 2) **Gross sales:**   Total sales for cash and on credit for a given accounting period.

(L.O. 3) **Merchandise inventory:**   Goods on hand available for sale to customers.

(L.O. 1) **Net income:**   The net increase in owner's equity resulting from the profit-seeking operations of a company; net income = revenue – expenses. For merchandising companies, what is left after deducting operating expenses from gross margin.

(L.O. 4) **Net method:**   A method of recording purchases which, in order to identify the discounts that are lost, requires that purchases be recorded initially at the net price.

(L.O. 4) **Net purchases:**   Under the periodic inventory method, gross purchases less purchases discounts and purchases returns and allowances plus any freight charges on the purchases.

(L.O. 2) **Net sales:**   Gross proceeds from sales of merchandise less sales returns and allowances and sales discounts.

(L.O. 1) **Operating expenses:**   Those expenses, other than cost of goods sold, that are incurred in running the business.

(L.O. 5) **Periodic inventory method:**   Determination of cost of goods sold by deducting the ending inventory, which has been determined by a physical count of the physical inventory, from total of purchases plus beginning merchandise inventory.

(L.O. 5) **Perpetual inventory method:** Determination of cost of goods sold by keeping continuous records of the physical inventory as goods are bought and sold.

(L.O. 4) **Purchases:** An account used under the periodic inventory system in which the cost of all merchandise bought for resale is recorded.

(L.O. 4) **Purchases discounts:** Allowances made for prompt payment for merchandise purchased for resale; a contra purchases account.

(L.O. 4) **Purchases returns and allowances:** Account used to accumulate cash refunds and other allowances made by suppliers on merchandise originally purchased for resale; a contra purchases account.

(L.O. 1) **Revenues from sales:** Sales of goods by a merchandising company.

(L.O. 2) **Sales discounts:** Discounts given to customers for early payment for sales made on credit; a contra revenue account.

(L.O. 2) **Sales returns and allowances:** Account used to accumulate amount of cash refunds granted to customers or other allowances related to prior sales; a contra revenue account.

(L.O. 5) **Taking a physical inventory:** The act of making a physical count of all merchandise on hand at the end of an accounting period.

(L.O. 2) **Trade discounts:** Prices for merchandise quoted at a discount (usually 30 percent or more) when manufacturers and wholesalers wish to avoid reprinting catalogues and price lists every time there is a price change.

(L.O. 2) **2/10, n/30:** Credit terms enabling the debtor to take a 2 percent discount if the invoice is paid within ten days after the invoice date; otherwise, the debtor must pay the full amount of the invoice within thirty days.

Self-Test

Test your knowledge of the chapter by choosing the best answer for each item below.

1. A net income will always result if
   a. cost of goods sold exceeds operating expenses.
   b. revenues exceed cost of goods sold.
   c. revenues exceed operating expenses.
   d. gross margin from sales exceeds operating expenses. *(L.O. 1)*

2. A sale is made on June 1 for $200, terms 2/10, n/30, on which a sales return of $50 is granted on June 7. The dollar amount received for payment in full on June 9 is
   a. $200. c. $147.
   b. $150. d. $196. *(L.O. 2)*

3. If beginning and ending merchandise inventories are $400 and $700, respectively, and cost of goods sold is $3,400, net purchases are
   a. $3,700. c. $3,100.
   b. $3,400. d. Cannot be determined. *(L.O. 3)*

4. The entry to record the payment within the discount period for a purchase of $1,000 under terms of 2/10, n/30 on which a purchase return of $300 was made would include a credit to Cash for
   a. $980. c. $686.
   b. $700. d. $680. *(L.O. 4)*

5. A purchase of merchandise for $750 including freight of $50 under terms of 2/10, n/30, FOB shipping point would include
   a. a debit to Freight In of $50.
   b. a debit to Purchases of $750.
   c. a credit to Accounts Payable of $700.
   d. a credit to Freight Payable of $50.   *(L.O. 4)*

6. Which of the accounts that follow can only result from using the net method of recording purchases?
   a. Purchases Returns and Allowances
   b. Purchases Discounts Lost
   c. Purchases
   d. Purchases Discounts   *(L.O. 4)*

7. Under which of the following inventory methods would a wholesaler most likely know the exact quantity in inventory of a particular item on hand in the middle of a month?
   a. Periodic inventory method
   b. Perpetual inventory method
   c. Either the periodic or perpetual inventory method
   d. Neither the periodic nor perpetual inventory method   *(L.O. 5)*

8. Samuel's Company has beginning merchandise inventory of $12,000 and ending merchandise inventory of $14,000. Under the periodic inventory method, the Merchandise Inventory account at the end of the accounting period would have the following balances, respectively, before and after adjusting and closing entries:
   a. $12,000 and $14,000.   c. $14,000 and $14,000.
   b. $14,000 and $12,000.   d. $12,000 and $12,000.   *(L.O. 6, 7)*

9. The closing entries for a merchandising concern would contain a debit to
   a. Sales Discounts.   c. Freight In.
   b. Purchases.   d. Purchases Discounts.   *(L.O. 8)*

10. Which of the following would appear as an operating expense on the income statement of a merchandising concern?
    a. Freight In
    b. Freight Out
    c. Sales Returns and Allowances
    d. Purchases Returns and Allowances   *(L.O. 9)*

Answers to Self-Test are at the end of this chapter.

Review Problem
Methods of Recording Purchases and Sales Contrasted

(L.O. 2, 4)   Newcomb Discount Warehouse Corporation purchased $80,000 of merchandise, terms 2/10, n/30, from Videotex Corporation on September 14.

Required   1. Give the entries in Newcomb's records to record the purchase and payment under each of the following situations.
   a. Purchases are recorded at gross amount, and payment is made on September 24.

b. Purchases are recorded at gross amount, and payment is made on October 14.

c. Purchases are recorded at net amount, and payment is made on September 24.

d. Purchases are recorded at net amount, and payment is made on October 14.

2. Give the entries on Videotex's records to record the sale and its collection under each of the four situations above. Assume all sales are recorded at their gross amounts.

Answer to Review Problem

Situation	Date	1. Newcomb's Records			2. Videotex's Records		

a.	Sept. 14	Purchases
		  Accounts Payable
		    To record purchase—
		    gross method
			80,000	80,000	Accounts Receivable
					  Sales
					    To record sales
						80,000	80,000

	Sept. 24	Accounts Payable
		  Purchases Discount
		  Cash
		    To record payment—
		    gross method
			80,000	1,600
				78,400
					Cash
					Sales Discounts
					  Accounts Receivable
					    To record collection
						78,400
						1,600
							80,000

b.	Sept. 14	Purchases
		  Accounts Payable
		    To record purchase—
		    gross method
			80,000	80,000	Accounts Receivable
					  Sales
					    To record sales
						80,000	80,000

	Oct. 14	Accounts Payable
		  Cash
		    To record payment—
		    gross method
			80,000	80,000	Cash
					  Accounts Receivable
					    To record collection
						80,000	80,000

c.	Sept. 14	Purchases
		  Accounts Payable
		    To record purchase—
		    net method
			78,400	78,400	Accounts Receivable
					  Sales
					    To record sales
						80,000	80,000

	Sept. 24	Accounts Payable
		  Cash
		    To record payment—
		    net method
			78,400	78,400	Cash
					Sales Discounts
					  Accounts Receivable
					    To record collection
						78,400
						1,600
							80,000

d.	Sept. 14	Purchases
		  Accounts Payable
		    To record purchase—
		    net method
			78,400	78,400	Accounts Receivable
					  Sales
					    To record sales
						80,000	80,000

	Oct. 14	Accounts Payable
		Purchases Discounts Lost
		  Cash
		    To record payment—
		    net method
			78,400
			1,600
				80,000	Cash
					  Accounts Receivable
					    To record collection
						80,000	80,000

Chapter Assignments

Discussion Questions and Writing Assignments

1. What is the primary difference between the operations of a merchandising concern and those of a service concern, and how are they reflected on the income statement?
2. What is the source of revenues for a merchandising concern?
3. Define gross margin from sales. Why is it important?
4. Kumler Nursery had a cost of goods sold during its first year of $64,000 and a gross margin from sales equal to 40 percent of sales. What was the dollar amount of the company's sales?
5. Could Kumler Nursery (in question 4) have a net loss for the year? Explain your answer.
6. Why is it advisable to maintain an account for Sales Returns and Allowances when the same result could be obtained by debiting each return or allowance to the Sales account?
7. What is a sales discount? If the terms are 2/10, n/30, what is the length of the credit period? What is the length of the discount period?
8. What two related transactions are reflected in the T accounts below?

Cash			Accounts Receivable		
(b)	980		(a)	1,000	(b) 1,000

Sales			Sales Discounts		
	(a)	1,000	(b)	20	

9. What is the normal balance of the Sales Discounts account? Is it an asset, liability, expense, or contra revenue account?
10. In counting the ending inventory, a clerk counts a $200 item of inventory twice. What effect does this error have on the balance sheet and income statement?
11. Hornberger Hardware purchased the following items: (a) a delivery truck, (b) two dozen hammers, (c) supplies for its office workers, (d) a broom for the janitor. Which item(s) should be debited to the Purchases account?
12. What three related transactions are reflected in the T accounts that are shown below?

Cash			Accounts Payable		
	(c)	441	(b) 50	(a)	500
			(c) 450		

Purchases			Purchases Returns and Allowances		
(a)	500			(b)	50

Purchases Discounts		
	(c)	9

13. How would the transactions in **12** differ if the net method of recording purchases were used?
14. Is Freight In an operating expense? Explain.
15. Prices and terms are quoted by two companies on fifty units of product, as follows: Supplier A—50 at $20 per unit, FOB shipping point; Supplier B—50 at $21 per unit, FOB destination. Which supplier has quoted the best deal? Explain.
16. Does the beginning or ending inventory appear in the year-end unadjusted trial balance prepared by a company that uses the periodic inventory method?
17. Under the periodic inventory method, how is the amount of inventory at the end of the year determined?
18. What is your assessment of the following statement: "The perpetual inventory method is the best method because management always needs to know how much inventory it has"?
19. Why is the handling of merchandise inventory at the end of the accounting period of special importance in the determination of net income? What must be achieved in the account?
20. What are the principal differences between the work sheet for a merchandising company and that for a service company? Discuss in terms of both the closing and adjusting entry methods.

Classroom Exercises

Exercise 5-1.
Computation of
Net Sales
(L.O. 2)

During 19xx, the Nexus Corporation had total credit sales of $220,000. Of this amount, $180,000 was collected during the year. In addition, the corporation had cash sales of $120,000. Furthermore, customers returned merchandise for credit of $8,000, and cash discounts of $4,000 were allowed. How much would 19xx net sales be for the Nexus Corporation?

Exercise 5-2.
Sales Transactions
(L.O. 2)

On June 15, the Jackson Company sold merchandise for $2,600 on terms of 2/10, n/30 to Clement Company. Give the entries to record (1) the sale, (2) a return of merchandise of $600, June 20, (3) receipt of the balance from Clement Company assuming payment on June 25, (4) balance from Clement Company assuming receipt of a check on July 15.

Exercise 5-3.
Parts of the
Income Statement:
Missing Data
(L.O. 2, 3, 4)

Compute the dollar amount of each item indicated by a letter in the table below. Treat each horizontal row of numbers as a separate problem.

Sales	Beginning Inventory	Net Purchases	Ending Inventory	Cost of Goods Sold	Gross Margin	Operating Expenses	Income (or Loss)
$125,000	$ a	$ 35,000	$10,000	$ b	$40,000	$ c	$12,000
d	12,000	e	18,000	108,000	60,000	40,000	20,000
230,000	22,000	167,000	f	g	50,000	h	(1,000)
390,000	40,000	i	60,000	j	k	120,000	40,000

Exercise 5-4.
Gross Margin
from Sales
Computation:
Missing Data
(L.O. 3)

Determine the amount of gross purchases by preparing a partial income statement showing the calculation of gross margin from sales from the following data: Purchases Discounts, $3,500; Freight In, $13,000; Cost of Goods Sold, $185,000; Sales, $275,000; Beginning Inventory, $25,000; Purchases Returns and Allowances, $4,000; Ending Inventory, $12,000.

Exercise 5-5.
Purchases and
Sales Involving
Discounts
(L.O. 2, 4)

The Orosco Company purchased $4,600 of merchandise, terms 2/10, n/30, from the Garber Company and paid for the merchandise within the discount period. Give the entries (1) by the Orosco Company to record purchase and payment, assuming purchases are recorded at gross purchase price, and (2) by the Garber Company to record the sale and receipt.

Exercise 5-6.
Gross and Net
Methods of
Recording
Purchases
Contrasted
(L.O. 4)

Westland Corporation purchased $9,400 of merchandise, terms 2/10, n/30, on June 10. Give the entries to record purchase and payment under each of the four assumptions below.

1. Purchases are recorded at gross amount, and payment is made June 20.
2. Purchases are recorded at gross amount, and payment is made July 10.
3. Purchases are recorded at net amount, and payment is made June 20.
4. Purchases are recorded at net amount, and payment is made July 20.

Exercise 5-7.
Recording
Purchases: Gross
and Net Methods
(L.O. 4)

Give the entries to record each of the following transactions, first using the gross method and then using the net method:

1. Purchased merchandise on credit, terms 2/10, n/30, FOB shipping point, $2,500.
2. Paid freight on shipment in transaction 1, $135.
3. Purchased merchandise on credit, terms 2/10, n/30, FOB destination, $1,400.
4. Purchased merchandise on credit, terms 2/10, n/30, FOB shipping point, $2,600, which includes freight paid by supplier of $200.
5. Returned merchandise pertaining to transaction 3, $500.
6. Paid the amount owed on the purchases in transactions 1 and 4, respectively, within the discount periods. Record as two transactions.
7. Paid the amount owed on the purchase in transaction 3 less return, but not within the discount period.

Exercise 5-8.
Preparation of
Work Sheet
(L.O. 7)

Simplified trial balance accounts and their balances follow in alphabetical order: Accounts Payable, $3; Accounts Receivable, $25; Accumulated Depreciation, Store Equipment, $6; Betty Guthrie, Capital, $67; Betty Guthrie, Withdrawals, $12; Cash, $12; Freight In, $2; General Expenses, $15; Merchandise Inventory (Beginning), $8; Prepaid Insurance, $2; Purchases, $35; Purchases Returns and Allowances, $2; Sales, $97; Sales Discounts, $3; Selling Expenses, $22; Store Equipment, $30; Store Supplies, $9.

Copy the trial balance accounts and amounts onto a work sheet in the same order as they appear above. Complete the work sheet, using either the adjusting entry method or the closing entry method and the following information: (a) estimated depreciation on store equipment, $3; (b) ending inventory of store supplies, $2; (c) expired insurance, $1; (d) ending merchandise inventory, $7.

Exercise 5-9.
Preparation of
Income Statement
from Work Sheet
(L.O. 9)

Selected items from the Income Statement columns of the December 31, 19xx work sheet of the Mill Pond General Store for the year ended December 31, 19xx appear below:

Account Name	Income Statement Debit	Credit
Sales		297,000
Sales Returns and Allowances	11,000	
Sales Discounts	4,200	
Purchases	114,800	
Purchases Returns and Allowances		1,800
Purchases Discounts		2,200
Freight In	5,600	
Selling Expenses	48,500	
General and Administrative Expenses	37,200	

Beginning merchandise inventory was $26,000 and ending merchandise inventory is $22,000. From the information given, prepare a 19xx income statement for the company.

Exercise 5-10.
Preparation of
Closing Entries
(L.O. 8)

Using either the adjusting entry method or the closing entry method, prepare closing entries from the information given in Exercise 5-9, assuming that Mill Pond General Store is owned by Ed Pioutek and that he made withdrawals of $34,000 during the year.

Exercise 5-11.
Merchandising
Income Statement:
Missing Data,
Multiple Years
(L.O. 9)

Determine the missing data for each letter in the following three income statements for Belden Wholesale Paper Company (in thousands):

	19x3	19x2	19x1
Gross Sales	$ p	$ h	$286
Sales Returns and Allowances	19	12	14
Sales Discounts	5	7	a
Net Sales	q	317	b
Merchandise Inventory, Jan. 1	r	i	38
Purchases	192	169	c
Purchases Returns and Allowances	23	j	13
Purchases Discounts	8	5	4
Freight In	s ·	29	22
Net Purchases	189	k	d
Goods Available for Sale	222	212	182
Merchandise Inventory, Dec. 31	39	l	42
Cost of Goods Sold	t	179	e
Gross Margin from Sales	142	m	126
Selling Expenses	u	78	f
General and Administrative Expenses	39	n	33
Total Operating Expenses	130	128	g
Net Income	v	o	27

Interpreting Accounting Information

Sears vs. K mart*
(L.O. 1)

Sears, Roebuck and Co. and K mart Corporation, the two largest retailers in the United States, have very different approaches to retailing. Sears operates a chain of full-service department stores, whereas K mart is known as a discounter. Selected information from their annual reports for the year ended December 31, 1988, and January 31, 1989, respectively, is presented below. (All amounts are in millions and, for Sears, only data for the Merchandise Group are shown.)

Sears: Net Sales, $27,755; Cost of Goods Sold, $19,184; Operating Expenses, $8,930; Ending Inventory, $3,716.

K mart: Net Sales, $27,301; Cost of Goods Sold, $19,914; Operating Expenses, $6,184; Ending Inventory, $5,671.

In an attempt to improve its competitive position, Sears announced in 1989 a change in its merchandising policies. Instead of sales on selected items at various times during the year, Sears adopted the "everyday low prices" policy and reduced the regular prices of more than 30,000 items.

Required

1. Prepare a schedule computing gross margin from sales and net income (ignore income taxes) for both companies as dollar amounts and as percentages of net sales. Also, compute inventory as a percentage of cost of goods sold.
2. From what you know about the different retailing approaches of these two companies, do the gross margin and net income computations from **1** seem compatible with these approaches? What is it about the nature of K mart's operations that results in less gross margin from sales and operating expenses in percentages than Sears? Which company's approach is more successful for this year? Explain.
3. Assuming it is successful, what might be the effects of Sears' new pricing policy?
4. K mart chooses a fiscal year that ends on January 31. Why do you suppose the company made this choice? How realistic do you think the inventory figures are as indicators of inventory levels during the rest of the year?

Problem Set A

Problem 5A-1.
Merchandising
Transactions
(L.O. 2, 4)

Dawkins Company, which uses the periodic inventory method, engaged in the following transactions:

Oct.   1   Sold merchandise to Ernie Devlin on credit, terms 2/10, n/30, $1,050.
      2   Purchased merchandise on credit from Ruland Company, terms 2/10, n/30, FOB shipping point, $1,900.
      2   Paid Custom Freight $145 for freight charges on merchandise received.
      6   Purchased office supplies on credit from Arizin Supply House, terms n/20, $318.

---

* Excerpts from the 1988 and 1989 annual reports used by permission of Sears. Excerpts from the 1988 annual report used by permission of K mart. Copyright © 1988. Data is used with the permission of K mart Corporation, Troy, Michigan.

Oct. 8 Purchased merchandise on credit from PG Company, terms 2/10, n/30, FOB shipping point, $1,200.

8 Paid Custom Freight $97 for freight charges on merchandise received.

9 Purchased merchandise on credit from LNP Company, terms 2/10, n/30, FOB shipping point, $1,800, including $100 freight costs paid by LNP Company.

11 Received full payment from Ernie Devlin for his October 1 purchase.

12 Paid Ruland Company for purchase of October 2.

13 Sold merchandise on credit to Otis King, terms 2/10, n/30, $600.

14 Returned for credit $300 of merchandise received on October 8.

15 Returned for credit $100 of office supplies purchased on October 6.

16 Sold merchandise for cash, $500.

19 Paid LNP Company for purchase of October 9.

22 Paid PG Company for purchase of October 8 less return of October 14.

23 Received full payment from Otis King for his October 13 purchase.

26 Paid Arizin Supply House for purchase of October 6, less return on October 15.

31 Sold merchandise for cash, $675.

Required

1. Prepare general journal entries to record the transactions, assuming purchases are recorded initially at the gross purchase price.
2. Which entries would differ if the purchases were recorded initially at net purchase price and purchases discounts lost were recognized? What advantages does this method have over the gross method?

Problem 5A-2.
Income
Statement for
a Merchandising
Concern
(L.O. 9)

The following data comes from Rafi's Camera Store's adjusted trial balance as of June 30, 19x3:

Rafi's Camera Store Partial Adjusted Trial Balance June 30, 19x3		
Sales		433,912
Sales Returns and Allowances	11,250	
Purchases	221,185	
Purchases Returns and Allowances		26,450
Purchases Discounts		3,788
Freight In	10,078	
Store Salaries Expense	107,550	
Office Salaries Expense	26,500	
Advertising Expense	18,200	
Rent Expense	14,400	
Insurance Expense	2,800	
Utility Expense	18,760	
Store Supplies Expense	464	
Office Supplies Expense	814	
Depreciation Expense, Store Equipment	1,800	
Depreciation Expense, Office Equipment	1,850	

The company's beginning inventory was $81,222 and the ending merchandise inventory is $76,664.

Required

1. Prepare an income statement for Rafi's Camera Store. Store Salaries Expense; Advertising Expense; Store Supplies Expense; Depreciation Expense, Store Equipment are considered to be selling expenses. The other expenses are considered to be general and administrative expenses.
2. Based on your knowledge at this point in the course, how might you use Rafi's income statement to evaluate the company's profitability?

Problem 5A-3.
Work Sheet,
Financial
Statements, and
Closing Entries for
a Merchandising
Company
(L.O. 7, 8, 9)

The following trial balance was taken from the ledger of Conner Book Store at the end of its annual accounting period:

Conner Book Store Trial Balance June 30, 19x2		
Cash	$ 6,025	
Accounts Receivable	9,280	
Merchandise Inventory	29,450	
Store Supplies	1,911	
Prepaid Insurance	1,600	
Store Equipment	37,200	
Accumulated Depreciation, Store Equipment		$ 15,600
Accounts Payable		12,300
Judy Conner, Capital		41,994
Judy Conner, Withdrawals	12,000	
Sales		102,250
Sales Returns and Allowances	987	
Purchases	63,200	
Purchases Returns and Allowances		19,655
Purchases Discounts		1,356
Freight In	2,261	
Sales Salaries Expense	21,350	
Rent Expense	3,600	
Other Selling Expenses	2,614	
Utility Expense	1,677	
	$193,155	$193,155

Required

1. Enter the trial balance on a work sheet, and complete the work sheet using the following information: (a) ending merchandise inventory, $33,227; (b) ending store supplies inventory, $304; (c) prepaid insurance, $200; (d) estimated depreciation on store equipment, $4,300; (e) sales salaries payable, $80; (f) accrued utility expense, $150. Use the adjusting entry method or the closing entry method.

2. Prepare an income statement, a statement of owner's equity, and a balance sheet. Sales Salaries Expense; Other Selling Expenses; Store Supplies Expense; and Depreciation Expense, Store Equipment are to be considered selling expenses.

3. From the work sheet, prepare closing entries.

Problem 5A-4.
Journalizing Transactions of a Merchandising Company
(L.O. 2, 4)

Following is a list of transactions for the month of January 19xx.

Jan. 2 Purchased merchandise on credit from DEF Company, terms 2/10, n/30, FOB destination, $7,400.

3 Sold merchandise on credit to A. Molina, terms 1/10, n/30, FOB shipping point, $1,000.

5 Sold merchandise for cash, $700.

6 Purchased and received merchandise on credit from Stockton Company, terms 2/10, n/30, FOB shipping point, $4,200.

7 Received freight bill from Eastline Express for shipment received on January 6, $570.

9 Sold merchandise on credit to C. Parish, terms 1/10, n/30, FOB destination, $3,800.

10 Purchased merchandise from DEF Company, terms 2/10, n/30, FOB shipping point, $2,650, including freight costs of $150.

11 Received freight bill from Eastline Express for sale to C. Parish on January 9, $291.

12 Paid DEF Company for purchase of January 2.

13 Received payment in full for A. Molina's purchase of January 3.

14 Returned faulty merchandise worth $300 to DEF Company for credit against purchase of January 10.

15 Purchased office supplies from Quaker Co. for $478, terms, n/10.

16 Paid Stockton Company one-half of the amount owed from purchase of January 6.

17 Sold merchandise to D. Healy on credit, terms 2/10, n/30, FOB shipping point, $780.

18 Returned for credit several items of office supplies received on Jan. 15, $128.

19 Received payment from C. Parish for one-half of the purchase of January 9.

20 Paid DEF Company in full for amount owed on purchase of January 10, less return on January 14.

22 Gave credit to D. Healy for returned merchandise, $180.

25 Paid for purchase of January 15, less return on January 18.

26 Paid freight company for freight charges, January 7 and 11.

27 Received payment of amount owed by D. Healy from purchase of January 17, less credit of January 22.

28 Paid Stockton Company for balance of January 6 purchase.

31 Sold merchandise for cash, $973.

Required

1. Prepare general journal entries to record the transactions, assuming that the periodic inventory method is used and that purchases are recorded initially at gross purchase price.

2. Tell how the entries would differ if the net method of recording purchases were used.

**Problem 5A-5.
Work Sheet,
Income Statement,
and Closing
Entries for a
Merchandising
Concern**
(L.O. 7, 8, 9)

The year-end trial balance for Lima's Shoe Store appears below:

Lima's Shoe Store Trial Balance June 30, 19x2		
Cash	$ 5,215	
Accounts Receivable	19,307	
Merchandise Inventory	26,500	
Store Supplies	951	
Prepaid Insurance	2,600	
Store Equipment	32,000	
Accumulated Depreciation, Store Equipment		$ 18,400
Accounts Payable		22,366
Manny Lima, Capital		63,601
Manny Lima, Withdrawals	15,000	
Sales		105,540
Sales Returns and Allowances	2,150	
Purchases	60,015	
Purchases Returns and Allowances		17,310
Purchases Discounts		1,300
Freight In	2,144	
Rent Expense	4,800	
Store Salaries Expense	41,600	
Advertising Expense	14,056	
Utility Expense	2,179	
	$228,517	$228,517

Required

1. Copy the trial balance amounts into the Trial Balance columns of a work sheet, and complete the work sheet using the following information: (a) ending merchandise inventory, $30,640; (b) ending store supplies inventory, $288; (c) expired insurance, $2,400; (d) estimated depreciation, store equipment, $8,800; (e) advertising expenses include $1,470 for July clearance sale advertisements, which will begin appearing on July 2; (f) accrued store salaries, $320. Use either the adjusting entry method or the closing entry method.
2. Prepare an income statement for the shoe store. Store Salaries Expense; Advertising Expense; Store Supplies Expense; and Depreciation Expense, Store Equipment are to be considered selling expenses. The other expenses are to be considered general and administrative expenses.
3. From the work sheet you prepared for Lima's Shoe Store in **1** above, derive closing entries.

Problem Set B

Lazzer Company, which uses the periodic inventory method, engaged in the following transactions:

March 1 Purchased merchandise on credit from Rivers Company, terms 2/10, n/30, FOB shipping point, $1,950.

        1 Paid Oakley Company $109 for shipping charges on merchandise received.

        3 Sold merchandise on credit to Wes Short, terms 2/10, n/60, $1,500.

        6 Purchased merchandise on credit from North Company, terms 2/10, n/30, FOB shipping point, $4,800, including $300 freight costs paid by North.

        7 Purchased merchandise on credit from Sun Company, terms 1/10, n/30, FOB shipping point, $3,000.

        7 Paid Oakley Company $127 for shipping charges on merchandise received.

        8 Purchased office supplies on credit from La Russo Company, terms n/10, $1,200.

     10 Sold merchandise on credit to Steven Wong, terms 2/10, n/30, $1,200.

     11 Paid Rivers Company for purchase of March 1.

     12 Returned for credit $300 of damaged merchandise received from Sun Company on March 7.

     13 Received check from Wes Short for his purchase of merchandise on March 3.

     14 Returned a portion of the office supplies received on March 8 for credit because the wrong items were received, $200.

     15 Sold merchandise for cash, $900.

     16 Paid North Company for purchase of March 6.

     19 Paid Sun Company the balance from transactions of March 7 and March 12.

     20 Received payment in full from Steven Wong for sale of merchandise on March 10.

     23 Paid La Russo Company for purchase of March 8, less the return on March 14. The terms were n/10.

     31 Sold merchandise for cash, $750.

Required

1. Prepare general journal entries to record the transactions, assuming purchases are recorded initially at the gross purchase price.
2. Which entries would differ if the purchases were recorded initially at net purchase price and discounts lost were recognized? What advantages does this method have over the gross method?

Problem 5B-2.
Income Statement
for a
Merchandising
Concern
(L.O. 9)

At the end of the fiscal year, August 31, 19x2, selected accounts from the adjusted trial balance for Irma's Fashion Shop appeared as shown on the top of the following page.

Irma's Fashion Shop
Partial Adjusted Trial Balance
August 31, 19x2

Sales		165,000
Sales Returns and Allowances	2,000	
Purchases	70,200	
Purchases Returns and Allowances		1,400
Purchases Discounts		1,200
Freight In	2,300	
Store Salaries Expense	32,625	
Office Salaries Expense	12,875	
Advertising Expense	24,300	
Rent Expense	2,400	
Insurance Expense	1,200	
Utility Expense	1,560	
Store Supplies Expense	2,880	
Office Supplies Expense	1,175	
Depreciation Expense, Store Equipment	1,050	
Depreciation Expense, Office Equipment	800	

In addition to the figures shown in the partial adjusted trial balance, the merchandise inventory for Irma's Fashion Shop was $38,200 at the beginning of the year and $29,400 at the end of the year.

Required

1. Using the information given, prepare an income statement for Irma's Fashion Shop. Store Salaries Expense; Advertising Expense; Store Supplies Expense; and Depreciation Expense, Store Equipment are considered to be selling expenses. The other expenses are considered to be general and administrative expenses.
2. Based on your knowledge at this point in the course, how might you use the income statement for Irma's Fashion Shop to evaluate the company's profitability?

**Problem 5B-3.
Work Sheet,
Financial
Statements, and
Closing Entries for
a Merchandising
Company
(L.O. 7, 8, 9)**

The year-end trial balance shown on the following page was taken from the ledger of Kirby Party Costumes Company at the end of its annual accounting period on June 30, 19x2.

Kirby Party Costumes Company
Trial Balance
June 30, 19x2

Cash	$ 7,050	
Accounts Receivable	24,830	
Merchandise Inventory	71,400	
Store Supplies	3,800	
Prepaid Insurance	4,800	
Store Equipment	51,300	
Accumulated Depreciation, Store Equipment		$ 25,500
Accounts Payable		38,950
Mark Kirby, Capital		161,350
Mark Kirby, Withdrawals	24,000	
Sales		375,250
Sales Returns and Allowances	4,690	
Sales Discounts	3,790	
Purchases	251,600	
Purchases Returns and Allowances		3,150
Purchases Discounts		2,900
Freight In	10,400	
Sales Salaries Expense	64,600	
Rent Expense	48,000	
Other Selling Expenses	32,910	
Utility Expense	3,930	
	$607,100	$607,100

Required

1. Enter the trial balance on a work sheet, and complete the work sheet using the following information: (a) ending merchandise inventory, $88,900; (b) ending store supplies inventory, $550; (c) expired insurance, $2,400; (d) estimated depreciation on store equipment, $5,000; (e) sales salaries payable, $650; (f) accrued utility expense, $100. Use the adjusting entry method or the closing entry method.
2. Prepare an income statement, a statement of owner's equity, and a balance sheet. Sales Salaries Expense; Other Selling Expenses; Store Supplies Expense; and Depreciation Expense, Store Equipment are to be considered selling expenses.
3. From the work sheet, prepare closing entries.

Problem 5B-4.
Journalizing
Transactions of a
Merchandising
Company
(L.O. 2, 4)

Following is a list of transactions for the month of June 19xx.

June 1 Sold merchandise on credit to B. Holder, terms 2/10, n/60, FOB shipping point, $1,100.
2 Purchased merchandise on credit from Eagle Company, terms 2/10, n/30, FOB shipping point, $6,400.
3 Received freight bill for shipment received on June 2, $450.

4   Sold merchandise for cash, $550.
5   Sold merchandise on credit to T. Kuo, terms 2/10, n/60, $1,200.
6   Purchased merchandise from Reliable Company, terms 1/10, n/30, FOB shipping point, $3,090, including freight costs of $200.
7   Sold merchandise on credit to A. Rodriguez, terms 2/10, n/20, $2,200.
8   Purchased merchandise from Eagle Company, terms 2/10, n/30, FOB shipping point, $8,200.
9   Received freight bill for shipment of June 8, $730.
10 Received check from B. Holder for payment in full for sale of June 1.
11 Returned for credit merchandise of the June 6 shipment that was the wrong size and color, $290.
12 Paid Eagle Company for purchase of June 2.
13 A. Rodriguez returned some of merchandise sold to him on June 7 for credit, $200.
15 Received payment from T. Kuo for one-half of his purchase on June 5. A discount is allowed on partial payment.
16 Paid Reliable Company balance due on account from transactions on June 6 and 11.
17 In checking the purchase of June 8 from Eagle Company, the accounting department found an overcharge of $400. Eagle agreed to give credit.
20 Paid freight company for freight charges of June 3 and 9.
22 Purchased on credit cleaning supplies from Goldman Company, terms n/5, $250.
23 Discovered that $50 of the cleaning supplies purchased on June 22 were items not ordered. Returned to Goldman Company for credit.
25 Sold merchandise for cash, $800.
26 Paid Goldman Company for the June 22 purchase less the June 23 return.
27 Received payment in full from A. Rodriguez for transactions on June 7 and 13.
28 Paid Eagle Company for purchase of June 8, less allowance of June 17.
30 Received payment for balance of amount owed from T. Kuo from transactions of June 5 and 15.

Required

1. Prepare general journal entries to record the transactions, assuming that the periodic inventory method is used and that purchases are recorded initially at gross purchase price.
2. Tell how the entries would differ if the net method of recording purchases were used.

**Problem 5B-5.
Work Sheet,
Income Statement,
and Closing
Entries for a
Merchandising
Concern
(L.O. 7, 8, 9)**

A year-end trial balance for Dumars Sporting Goods Store appears at the top of the following page.

Dumars Sporting Goods Store
Trial Balance
May 31, 19x2

Cash	$ 8,250	
Accounts Receivable	6,322	
Merchandise Inventory	93,750	
Store Supplies	7,170	
Prepaid Insurance	5,400	
Store Equipment	151,800	
Accumulated Depreciation, Store Equipment		$ 42,200
Accounts Payable		53,670
Charles Dumars, Capital		126,337
Charles Dumars, Withdrawals	27,000	
Sales		985,710
Sales Returns and Allowances	8,100	
Purchases	703,475	
Purchases Returns and Allowances		12,375
Purchases Discounts		11,850
Freight In	4,800	
Rent Expense	37,200	
Store Salaries Expense	113,250	
Advertising Expense	56,655	
Utility Expense	8,970	
	$1,232,142	$1,232,142

Required

1. Copy the trial balance amounts into the Trial Balance columns of a work sheet, and complete the work sheet using the following information: (a) ending merchandise inventory, $86,240; (b) ending store supplies inventory, $870; (c) insurance unexpired at end of period, $2,700; (d) estimated depreciation, store equipment, $15,900; (e) accrued store salaries, $375. Use the adjusting entry method or the closing entry method.
2. Prepare an income statement for the store. Store Salaries Expense; Advertising Expense; Store Supplies Expense; and Depreciation Expense, Store Equipment are selling expenses. The other expenses are general and administrative expenses.
3. From the work sheet, prepare closing entries.

Financial Decision Case

Jefferson Jeans Company
(L.O. 3)

In 19x1, Joseph "JJ" Jefferson opened a small retail store in a suburban mall. Called Jefferson Jeans Company, the shop sold designer jeans. JJ worked fourteen hours a day and controlled all aspects of the operation. All sales were for cash or bank credit card. The business was such a success that in 19x2, JJ decided to expand by opening a second store in another mall. Since the new shop needed his attention, he hired a manager to work in the original store with the two sales clerks. During 19x2, the new store was successful, but the operations of the original store did not match the first year's performance. Concerned about this turn of events, JJ compared the two years' results for the original store. The figures are as follows:

	19x2	19x1
Net Sales	$325,000	$350,000
Cost of Goods Sold	225,000	225,000
Gross Margin from Sales	$100,000	$125,000
Operating Expenses	75,000	50,000
Net Income	$ 25,000	$ 75,000

In addition, JJ's analysis revealed that the cost and selling price of jeans were about the same in both years and that the level of operating expenses was roughly the same in both years except for the $25,000 salary of the new manager. Sales returns and allowances were insignificant amounts in both years. Studying the situation further, JJ discovered the following facts about cost of goods sold:

	19x2	19x1
Gross Purchases	$200,000	$271,000
Total Purchases Allowances and Discounts	15,000	20,000
Freight In	19,000	27,000
Physical Inventory, end of year	32,000	53,000

Still not satisfied, JJ went through all the individual sales and purchase records for the year. Both sales and purchases were verified. However, the 19x2 ending inventory should have been $57,000, given the unit purchases and sales during the year. After puzzling over all this information, JJ comes to you for accounting help.

Required

1. Using JJ's new information, recompute cost of goods sold for 19x1 and 19x2, and account for the difference in net income between 19x1 and 19x2.
2. Suggest at least two reasons that might have caused the difference. (Assume that the new manager's salary is proper.) How might JJ improve his management of the original store?

Answers to Self-Test

1. d	3. a	5. a	7. b	9. d
2. c	4. c	6. b	8. a	10. b

1. Identify the phases of systems installation and the principles of systems design.
2. Identify the basic elements of computer systems in mainframe and microcomputer contexts.
3. Explain the objectives and uses of special-purpose journals.
4. Construct and use the following types of special-purpose journals: sales journal, purchases journal, cash receipts journal, cash payments journal, and others as needed.
5. Explain the purposes and relationships of controlling accounts and subsidiary ledgers.

CHAPTER 6

Accounting Systems and Special-Purpose Journals

Knowledge of accounting systems for processing information is very important today because of the many different systems in use and the rapidly changing needs of businesses. In this chapter, you first study the key ideas and principles of accounting systems design. You then learn about the major kinds of data processing, from manual systems to computer systems. Because the idea behind special-purpose journals is basic to all accounting systems, particular attention is given to the way these journals are used in manual data processing. After studying this chapter, you should be able to meet the learning objectives listed on the left.

As you learned earlier, **accounting systems** gather data from all parts of a business, put them in useful form, and communicate the results to management. Thus accounting systems are essential to business managers. As businesses have become larger and more complicated, the role and importance of accounting systems have grown. With the development of computers, the need for a total information system with accounting as its base has become more pressing. For this reason, today's accountant must understand all phases of a company's operations as well as the latest developments in systems design and technology.

Accounting Systems Installation

The installation of an accounting system has three phases: investigation, design, and implementation. Each of these phases is necessary whether the system is a new one or an existing one that must be changed. The constant changes in a business's operations and environment call for continuous review of the current accounting system to make sure that it will always be responsive to management's need for information.

The aim of a **system investigation** is to discover the needs of a new system or to judge an existing system. This phase involves studying the information needs of managers, seeking the sources of this information, and outlining the steps and processes needed that will put the data into the correct form for use. Included in this phase are a review of the organization itself and of job descriptions and a study of forms, records, reports, procedures, data processing methods, and controls presently in use.

Some companies have handbooks that give all of this information in great detail. In existing systems, there is the further task of seeing that procedures are really followed. This task is done by tracing test transactions through the system and watching and talking to people as they do the work itself.

The new system or the changes in the current system are formulated in the **system design** phase and are based on the studies made during the investigation phase. For a major system, the design phase may call for accountants as well as computer experts, engineers, personnel managers, and other specialists. The design must take into account the people who work with and run the system, the documents and records used, the operational procedures, the reports to be prepared, and the equipment to be used in the system. The interaction of all these components must conform to the principles of systems design that are outlined below.

If management accepts a new system's design, the next phase, **system implementation**, follows. This phase depends on careful planning and communication to make sure that the new system is understood and accepted, properly installed, and well run. The people responsible for the operation of the new system should take an active part in the actual implementation. This task involves scheduling all activities of the installation. For large systems, implementation may take months or even years. The people working with the new system must be chosen and trained. The equipment, forms, and records must be bought. The new system must be tested and then changed as suggested by the tests. After implementation, it is important to review the new system regularly as part of the system investigation.

Principles of Systems Design

In designing an accounting system, it is very important to follow four general principles: (1) the cost-benefit principle, (2) the control principle, (3) the compatibility principle, and (4) the flexibility principle.

Cost-Benefit Principle

The most important systems principle, the **cost-benefit principle**, holds that the value or benefits received from a system and its information output must be equal to or greater than its cost. Beyond certain routine tasks of an accounting system, such as payroll and tax reports, preparing financial statements, and maintaining good internal control, management may want or need other information. To be beneficial, this information must be reliable, timely, and useful to management. These benefits of additional information must be weighed against both the tangible and intangible costs of gathering it. Among the tangible costs are those for personnel, forms, and equipment. One of the intangible costs is the cost of wrong decisions stemming from lack of good information. For instance, wrong decisions may lead to loss of sales, production stoppages, or inventory losses. In some cases, companies have spent thousands of dollars on computer systems that have not offered enough benefits. On the other hand, some managers have failed to realize important benefits that could be gained from investing in more advanced systems. It is the job of the accountant as systems analyst to weigh the opposing factors of costs and benefits.

Control Principle

The **control principle** requires that an accounting system provide all the features of internal control needed to protect assets and make sure of the reliability of data. For example, expenditures should be approved by a responsible member of management before they are made. Chapter 7 covers the subject of internal control in detail.

Compatibility Principle

The **compatibility principle** holds that the design of a system must be in harmony with the organizational and human factors of a business. An organization is made up of people working in different jobs and groups. The organizational factors have to do with the organization's kind of business and how the different units of the business are formally related in meeting its objectives. For example, a company may organize its marketing efforts by region or by product. If a company is organized by region, major reports will present revenues and expenses by region. A company organized by product, on the other hand, should have a system that will report revenues and expenses first by product and then by region.

The human factors of business have to do with the people within the organization and their abilities, behaviors, and personalities. The interest, support, and competence of these people are very important to the success or failure of systems design. In changing systems or installing new ones, the accountant must deal with the persons presently carrying out or supervising existing procedures. These people must understand, accept, and in many cases, be trained in the new procedures. The new system cannot succeed unless the system and the people in the organization are compatible.

Flexibility Principle

The **flexibility principle** calls for an accounting system that has enough flexibility to allow the volume of transactions to grow and organizational changes to be made in the business. Businesses do not often stay the same. They grow, offer new products, add new branch offices, sell existing divisions, or make other changes that require adjustments in the accounting system. A carefully designed system will allow a business to grow and change without making major alterations. For example, the chart of accounts should be designed to allow for adding new asset, liability, owner's equity, revenue, or expense accounts without destroying the usefulness of the accounts.

Data Processing: Three Perspectives

Data processing is the means by which the accounting system gathers data, organizes them into useful forms, and issues the resulting information to users. It can be viewed from three perspectives or points of view—functional, content, and mechanical—as shown in Figure 6-1. The functional and content points of view are closely related. The functional perspective deals with what is done, and the content perspective has to do with the data or material acted upon. The origin of the input is a bill, a report, or some other kind of document. This document, of course, is the data content. The processing function organizes the data into useful forms by handling and storing them until they are needed. The output is information presented to users by means of reports. The mechanical view has to do with the devices used in carrying out data processing. In any data processing system, there must be a means of originating the data, a device for data input, a processor and memory unit for storing and dealing with the data, a device for output of information, and a means of distributing the information.

From the mechanical point of view, the two extremes of data processing systems are manual systems and computer systems, both of which do the same job. The accountant must be able to work with many different kinds of accounting systems, and may also have a voice in choosing the right sort of data processing for a business. The basic ways of handling a large amount of data using manual data processing are described in the last part of this chapter. The main features of computer systems and their use in data processing are presented in the next part.

Figure 6-1. Data Processing from Three Perspectives

Computer Data Processing

Most data processing in business today is done by computer. Computers are able to process large volumes of data very quickly. The development of large mainframe computer systems has allowed the largest companies to centralize their accounting operations and eliminate much of the work that used to be done by hand. The development of minicomputers and microcomputers has now made it possible for even the smallest company to keep its accounting records on a computer.

Elements of a Computer System

OBJECTIVE 2
Identify the basic elements of computer systems in mainframe and microcomputer contexts

Regardless of the size of a computer data processing system, it consists of three basic elements: hardware, software, and personnel.

Hardware. **Hardware** is all the equipment needed to operate a computer data processing system. Figure 6-2 shows the hardware in a typical mainframe computer system and Figure 6-3 shows the hardware in a typical microcomputer system. In both cases, there are devices that assist in inputting data to the system, processing and storing data, and outputting information. In a mainframe system, for example, data related to a purchase transaction might be input through a remote data entry device to the central processor where it is recorded for future processing on a magnetic tape using a magnetic disk drive or on a disk using a disk drive. After processing the data, accounting reports may be prepared on an output device such as a printer. In a microcomputer

Figure 6-2. Mainframe Computer System

Source: Courtesy of IBM.

system, the day's transactions may be input through the keyboard and monitor onto a floppy disk or a hard disk. A daily transaction report may then be printed.

Software. Instead of recording transactions with a pencil in a journal, posting to a ledger, and then preparing a trial balance and financial statements, the computer performs these steps internally. To do this, the computer must be instructed to follow the proper steps. The set of instructions and steps that bring about the desired results are called **programs**. Programs are known collectively as **software**. Several programs are needed to instruct the computer to record and post transactions and prepare financial statements. On a mainframe computer, these programs are written in languages that are understood by the computer such as FORTRAN, COBOL, or PL/1, whereas programs for microcomputers are often written in BASIC or PASCAL. In addition, many programs are available commercially to do specialized accounting tasks, such as LOTUS® 1-2-3 for financial analysis; dBASE IV for organizing, storing, and retrieving large quantities of data; and general accounting systems for keeping the records and preparing financial statements.

Personnel. Important personnel in a computer system are the systems analyst, the programmer, and the computer operator. The **systems analyst** designs the system on the basis of information needs. The **programmer** writes instructions for the computer, and the **computer operator**

Figure 6-3. Microcomputer System

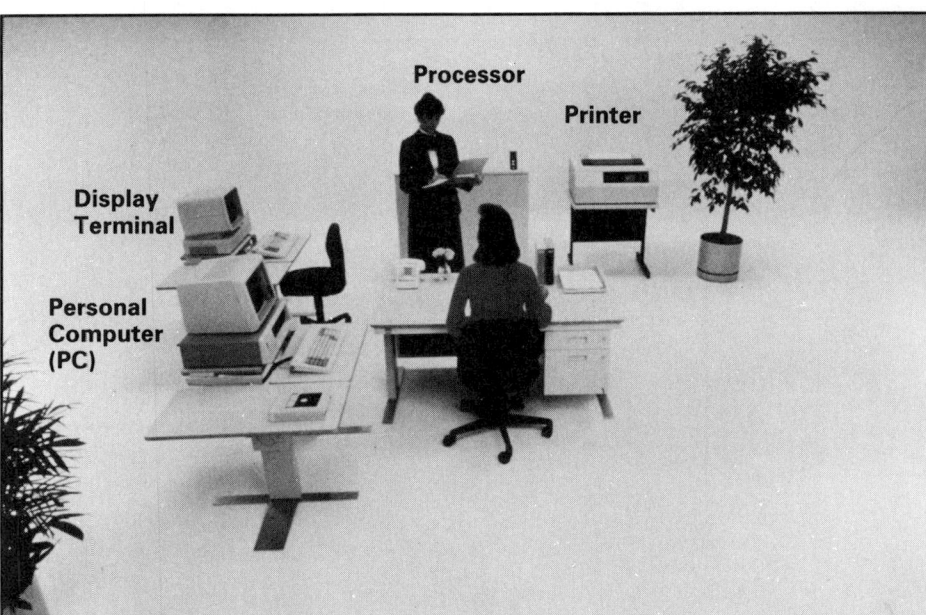

Source: Courtesy of IBM.

runs the computer. In large organizations, the accountant works closely with the systems analyst to make sure that accounting data processing systems are designed in accordance with the principles of systems design discussed in the first part of this chapter. In smaller organizations that may use a microcomputer system and not have computer experts for all these positions, the company's owners or management will often work with their certified public accountant in the purchase and installation of commercial software that will meet the company's needs.

Mainframe Accounting Systems

The parts of a computer data processing system can be put together in many different ways, and companies use their computers for many purposes besides accounting. Overall, the company's goal is to meet all its computing needs at the lowest cost. For the accounting system, it is important to coordinate all tasks so as to provide management with the reports and statements it needs on a timely basis.

Most mainframe computer systems take two approaches in processing business transactions and preparing financial reports. The first is called **batch processing**, in which processing tasks are scheduled in a logical order. For example, a set of transactions for a day or a week are all processed together (as a batch). Later, a separate program will be run to update the ledger and prepare the trial balance and financial statements. The processing of the employee timecards, the preparation of the company's payroll, and printing the paychecks on a specific day each week or month is another example of batch processing.

Most mainframe systems also provide for **on-line processing**, in which remote terminals are linked to the central processor, and the files are updated virtually as soon as the transactions occur. For example, at the time it occurs a credit sale may be entered into a remote terminal that records and posts the transaction in the appropriate accounts and updates the trial balance.

Microcomputer Accounting Systems

Most small businesses purchase commercial accounting systems that are already programmed to perform accounting functions. Most of these systems rely on a variation of batch processing in which a part of the software performs each major task of the accounting system. Although the configuration of such systems differs from system to system, a typical configuration appears in Figure 6-4, in which there is a software program for each major accounting function—sales/accounts receivable, purchases/accounts payable, cash receipts, cash disbursements, payroll, and general journal.

The transactions for these functions are based on **source documents**, which are the written evidence that supports the transaction. Source documents verify the fact that a transaction occurred and provide the details of the transaction. For example, a customer's invoice should support each sale on account and a vendor's invoice should support each purchase. Even though the transactions are recorded by the

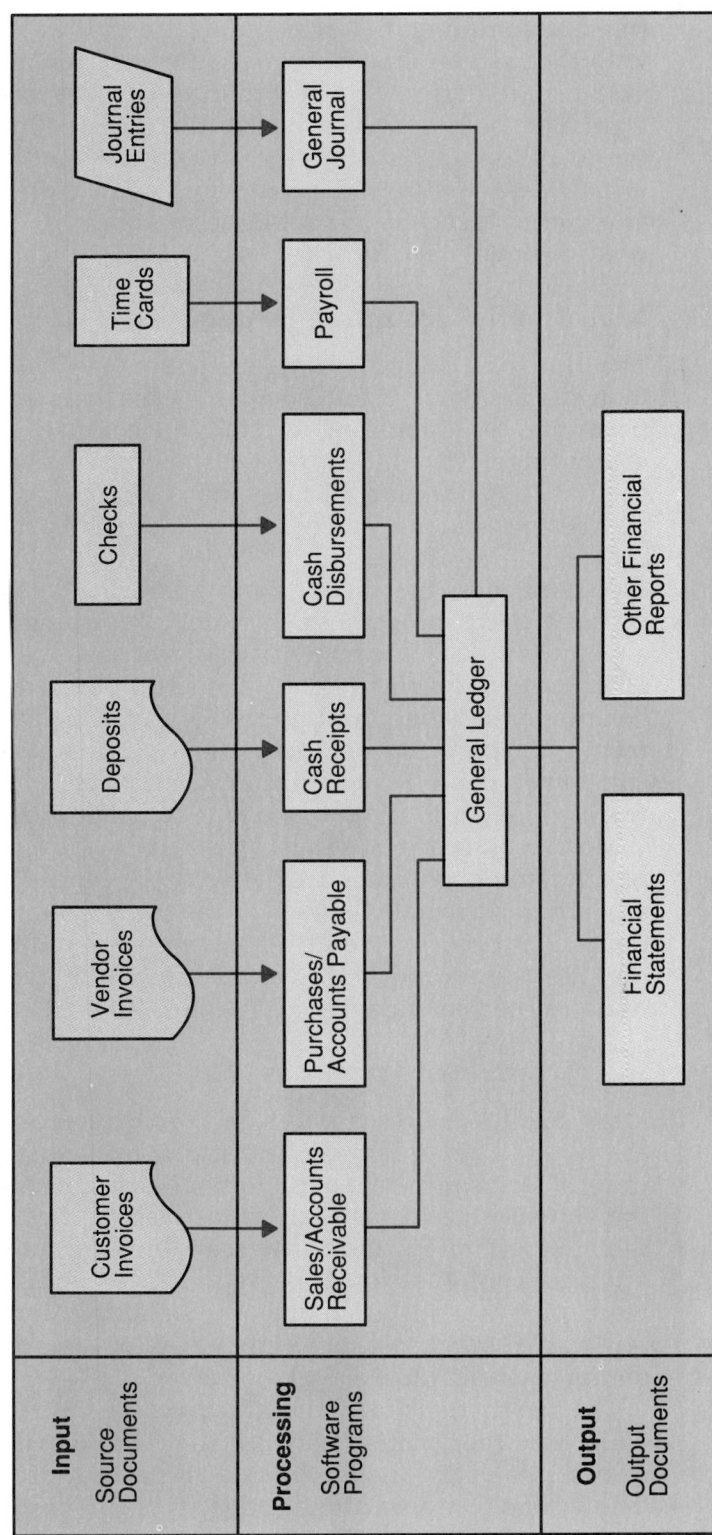

Figure 6-4. Microcomputer Accounting System

computer on floppy disks or hard disks, the documents should be kept so that they can be examined at a later date if a question arises about the accuracy of the accounting records. The source documents for each function are gathered together in a batch and processed in an orderly fashion with the appropriate program. The scheduling of these programs depends on the function. For example, cash transactions and sales are usually processed daily, whereas payroll may be processed only once every week or two weeks.

After the transactions are processed, a procedure is then followed to update the general ledger, post to the subsidiary ledgers (see page 240), and prepare the trial balance. Finally, the financial statements and other accounting reports are prepared.

The batch processing systems used in these microcomputer accounting systems very closely resemble manual accounting systems using special-purpose journals that have been in existence for many decades. In fact, their basic idea is to computerize existing accounting systems to make them less time consuming and more accurate and dependable. However, it is important for the beginning student to understand, in principle, just what the computer is accomplishing. Such knowledge of the underlying accounting process is helpful in ensuring that the accounting records are accurate, in protecting the assets of the business, and in understanding the company's financial statements. For this reason, we turn in the next section to manual data processing.

Manual Data Processing: Journals and Procedures

The system of accounting described so far in this book, and presented in Figure 6-5, is a form of **manual data processing**. This application of the mechanical view from Figure 6-1 (page 236) has been a useful way to present basic accounting theory and practice in small businesses. The recording is done manually by entering each transaction from a source document, such as an invoice, in the general journal (input device in a computer system) and posting each debit and credit to the correct

Figure 6-5. Steps and Devices in a Manual Accounting System

Source Documents	Data Input	Processing	Information Output	Distribution
Invoices and other documents	Journalize in book of original entry	Post to ledger, prepare trial balance, and make adjusting entries	Prepare work sheet and financial statements	Distribute financial statements to users

ledger account (processor and memory device). A work sheet (output device) is then used as an aid in preparing financial statements (output devices) to be presented to users. This system, while useful for explaining the basic ideas of accounting, is limited in practice to only the smallest of companies.

OBJECTIVE 3
Explain the objectives and uses of special-purpose journals

Companies that are faced with larger numbers of transactions, perhaps hundreds or thousands every week or every day, must have a more efficient and economical way of recording transactions in the journal and posting entries to the ledger. The easiest approach is to group the company's typical transactions into common categories and use an input device, called a **special-purpose journal**, for each category. The objectives of special-purpose journals are efficiency, economy, and control. In addition, although manual special-purpose journals are used by companies that have not yet computerized their systems, the concepts underlying special-purpose journals are found in computer systems.

Most business transactions, usually 90 to 95 percent, fall into one of four categories. Each kind of transaction may be recorded in a special-purpose journal as shown below.

Transaction	Special-Purpose Journal	Posting Abbreviation
Sales of merchandise on credit	Sales journal	S
Purchases on credit	Purchases journal	P
Receipts of cash	Cash receipts journal	CR
Disbursements of cash	Cash payments journal	CP

The general journal is used for recording transactions that do not fall into any of the special categories. For example, purchase returns, sales returns, and adjusting and closing entries are recorded in the general journal. (When transactions are posted from the general journal to the ledger accounts, the posting abbreviation used is J.)

It is important to note that use of these four journals reduces the amount of detailed work. For example, the amount of posting is greatly reduced because, instead of posting every debit and credit for each transaction, in most cases only column totals, which represent many transactions, are posted. In addition, the labor can be divided, assigning each journal to a different employee. This division of labor is important in establishing good internal control, as shown in Chapter 7. It is also important to note that these special-purpose journals correspond closely to the accounting functions shown in the microcomputer system in Figure 6-4, except for payroll, which is discussed in Chapter 11.

Sales Journal

Special-purpose journals are designed to record particular kinds of transactions. Thus all transactions in a special-purpose journal result in debits and credits to the same accounts. The **sales journal**, for example, is designed to handle all credit sales, and only credit sales. Cash sales are recorded in the cash receipts journal, which is explained later.

OBJECTIVE 4
Construct and use the following types of special-purpose journals: sales journal, purchases journal, cash receipts journal, cash payments journal, and others as needed

Exhibit 6-1 illustrates a typical sales journal. Six sales transactions involving five people are recorded in this sales journal. As each sale takes place, several copies of the sales invoice are made. The accounting department of the seller uses one copy to make the entry in the sales journal. The date, the customer's name, the invoice number, the amount of the sale, and possibly the credit terms are copied from the invoice. These data correspond to the columns of the sales journal.

Note the following time-saving features of the sales journal:

1. Only one line is needed to record each transaction. Each entry consists of a debit to each customer in Accounts Receivable. The corresponding credit to Sales is understood.
2. Account names do not have to be written out because account names occurring most frequently are used as column headings. Thus entry in a column has the effect of debiting or crediting the account.
3. No explanations are necessary, because the function of the special-purpose journal is to record just one type of transaction. Only credit sales are recorded in the sales journal. Sales for cash must be recorded in the cash receipts journal, which is described in detail later in this chapter.

Exhibit 6-1. Sales Journal and Related Ledger Accounts

Sales Journal   Page 1

Date		Account Debited	Invoice Number	Post. Ref.	Debit / Credit Accounts Receivable / Sales
July	1	Peter Clark	721	✓	750
	5	Georgetta Jones	722	✓	500
	8	Eugene Cumberland	723	✓	335
	12	Maxwell Gertz	724	✓	1,165
	18	Peter Clark	725	✓	1,225
	25	Michael Powers	726	✓	975
					4,950
					(114/411)

Post total at **end of month**.

Accounts Receivable   114

Date	Post. Ref.	Debit	Credit	Balance Debit	Balance Credit
July 31	S1	4,950		4,950	

Sales   411

Date	Post. Ref.	Debit	Credit	Balance Debit	Balance Credit
July 31	S1		4,950		4,950

4. Only one amount—the total credit sales for the month—needs to be posted. It is posted twice: once as a debit to Accounts Receivable and once as a credit to Sales. Instead of the six sales entries in the example, there might be hundreds of actual sales transactions in a more realistic situation. Thus one can see the saving in posting time.

Controlling Accounts and Subsidiary Ledgers. Every entry in the sales journal represents a debit to a customer's account in Accounts Receivable. In previous chapters, all such transactions have been posted to Accounts Receivable. However, this single Accounts Receivable entry does not readily tell how much each customer bought and paid for or how much each customer still owes. In practice, almost all companies that sell to customers on credit keep an individual accounts receivable record for each customer. If the company has 6,000 credit customers, there are 6,000 accounts receivable. To include all these accounts in the ledger with the other assets, liabilities, and owner's equity accounts would make it very bulky. Consequently, most companies take the individual customers' accounts out of the general ledger, which contains the financial statement accounts, and place them in a separate ledger called a **subsidiary ledger**. The customers' accounts are either filed alphabetically in this accounts receivable ledger or they are filed numerically if account numbers are used.

When a company puts its individual customers' accounts in an accounts receivable ledger, there is still a need for an Accounts Receivable account in the general ledger to maintain its balance. This Accounts Receivable account in the general ledger is said to control the subsidiary ledger and is called a **controlling** or **control account**. It is a controlling account in the sense that its balance should equal the total of the individual account balances in the subsidiary ledger. This is true because in transactions involving accounts receivable, such as credit sales, there must be postings to the individual customer accounts every day. Postings to the controlling account in the general ledger in total should be made at least each month and sometimes daily if the company has a large number of credit sales and collections. If a wrong amount has been posted, the sum of all customer account balances in the subsidiary accounts receivable ledger will not equal the balance of the Accounts Receivable controlling account in the general ledger. When these amounts do not match, the accountant knows that there is an error to find and correct.

The concept of controlling accounts is shown in Exhibit 6-2, where boxes used for the accounts receivable ledger and the general ledger are presented. The principle involved is that the single controlling account in the general ledger summarizes all the individual accounts in the subsidiary ledger. Note that since the individual accounts are recorded daily and the controlling account is posted monthly, the total of the individual accounts in the accounts receivable ledger will equal the controlling account only after the monthly posting. The monthly trial balance is prepared using only the general ledger accounts.

Most companies, as you will see, use an accounts payable subsidiary ledger as well. It is also possible to use a subsidiary ledger for almost

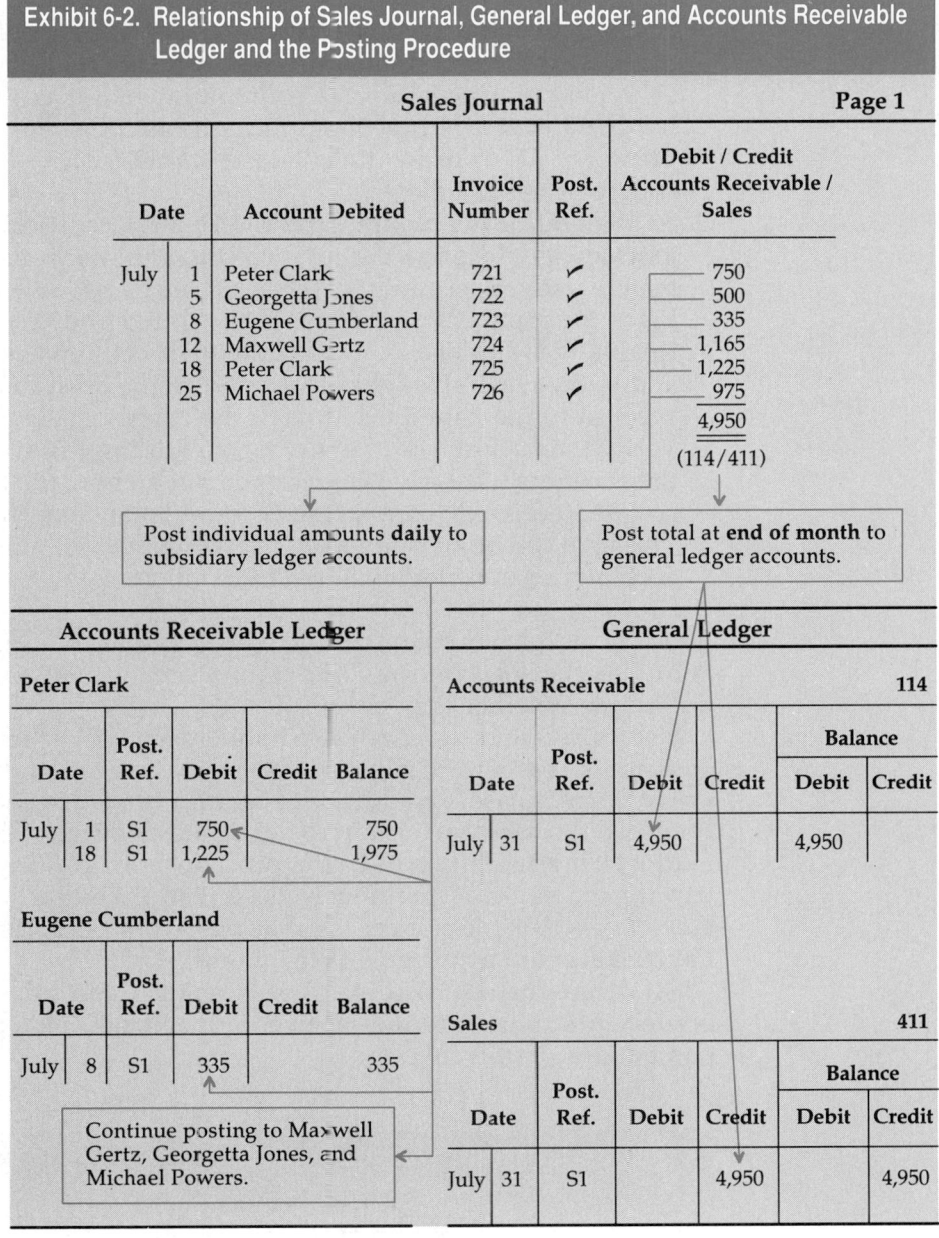

Exhibit 6-2. Relationship of Sales Journal, General Ledger, and Accounts Receivable Ledger and the Posting Procedure

any account in the general ledger where management wants a specific account for individual items, such as Merchandise Inventory, Notes Receivable, Temporary Investments, and Equipment.

Summary of the Sales Journal Procedure. Observe from Exhibit 6-2 that the procedures for using a sales journal are as follows:

1. Enter each sales invoice in the sales journal on a single line, recording date, customer's name, invoice number, and amount.

2. At the end of each day, post each individual sale to the customer's account in the accounts receivable ledger. As each sale is posted, place a check mark in the Post. Ref. (posting reference) column of the sales journal (or customer account number, if used) to indicate that it has been posted. In the Post. Ref. column of each customer account, place an S1 (representing Sales Journal—Page 1) to indicate the source of the entry.

3. At the end of the month, sum the Debit/Credit column in the sales journal to determine the total credit sales, and post the total to the general ledger accounts (debit Accounts Receivable and credit Sales). Place the numbers of the accounts debited and credited beneath the total in the sales journal to indicate that this step has been completed, and in the general ledger place an S1 in the Post. Ref. column of each account to indicate the source of the entry.

4. Verify the accuracy of the posting by adding the account balances of the accounts receivable ledger and by matching the total with the Accounts Receivable controlling account balance in the general ledger. This step can be accomplished by listing the accounts in a schedule of accounts receivable, as shown in Exhibit 6-3.

Sales Taxes. Other columns, such as a column for credit terms, can be added to the sales journal. The nature of the company's business will determine whether they are needed.

Many cities and states require retailers to collect a sales tax from their customers and periodically remit the total amount of the tax to the state or city. In this case, an additional column is needed in the sales journal to record the necessary credit to Sales Taxes Payable. The required entry is illustrated in Exhibit 6-4. The procedure for posting to the ledger is exactly the same as previously described except that the total of the Sales Taxes Payable column must be posted as a credit to the Sales Taxes Payable account at the end of the month.

Most companies also make cash sales. Cash sales are usually recorded in a column of the cash receipts journal. This procedure is discussed later in the chapter.

Exhibit 6-3. Schedule of Accounts Receivable	
Mitchell's Used Car Sales **Schedule of Accounts Receivable** **July 31, 19xx**	
Peter Clark	$1,975
Eugene Cumberland	335
Maxwell Gertz	1,165
Georgetta Jones	500
Michael Powers	975
Total Accounts Receivable	$4,950

Exhibit 6-4. Section of a Sales Journal with a Column for Sales Taxes						
Sales Journal						Page 7
				Debit	Credits	
Date	Account Debited	Invoice Number	Post. Ref.	Accounts Receivable	Sales Taxes Payable	Sales
Sept. 1	Ralph P. Hake	727	✓	206	6	200

Purchases Journal

The techniques associated with the sales journal are very similar to those of the purchases journal. The **purchases journal** is used to record all purchases on credit and may take the form of either a single-column journal or a multicolumn journal. In the single-column journal, shown in Exhibit 6-5, only credit purchases of merchandise for resale to customers are recorded. This kind of transaction is recorded with a debit to Purchases and a credit to Accounts Payable. When the single-column purchases journal is used, credit purchases of things other than merchandise are recorded in the general journal. Also, cash purchases are not recorded in the purchases journal but in the cash payments journal, which is explained later

As with Accounts Receivable, the Accounts Payable account in the general ledger is used by most companies as a controlling account. So that the company will know how much it owes each supplier, it keeps a separate account for each supplier in an accounts payable subsidiary ledger. The ideas and techniques described above for the accounts receivable subsidiary ledger and general ledger account apply also to the accounts payable subsidiary ledger and general ledger account. Thus the total of the separate accounts in the accounts payable subsidiary ledger will equal the balance of the Accounts Payable controlling account in the general ledger. The reason is that the monthly total of the credit purchases posted to the individual accounts each day is equal to the total credit purchases posted to the controlling account each month.

The steps for using a purchases journal, as shown in Exhibit 6-5, are as follows:

1. Enter each purchase invoice in the purchases journal on a single line, recording date, supplier's name, invoice date, terms if given, and amount.
2. At the end of each day, post each individual purchase to the supplier's account in the accounts payable subsidiary ledger. As each purchase is posted, place a check in the Post. Ref. column of the purchases journal to show that it has been posted. Also place a P1 (representing Purchases Journal—Page 1) in the Post. Ref. column of each supplier's account to show the source of the entry.

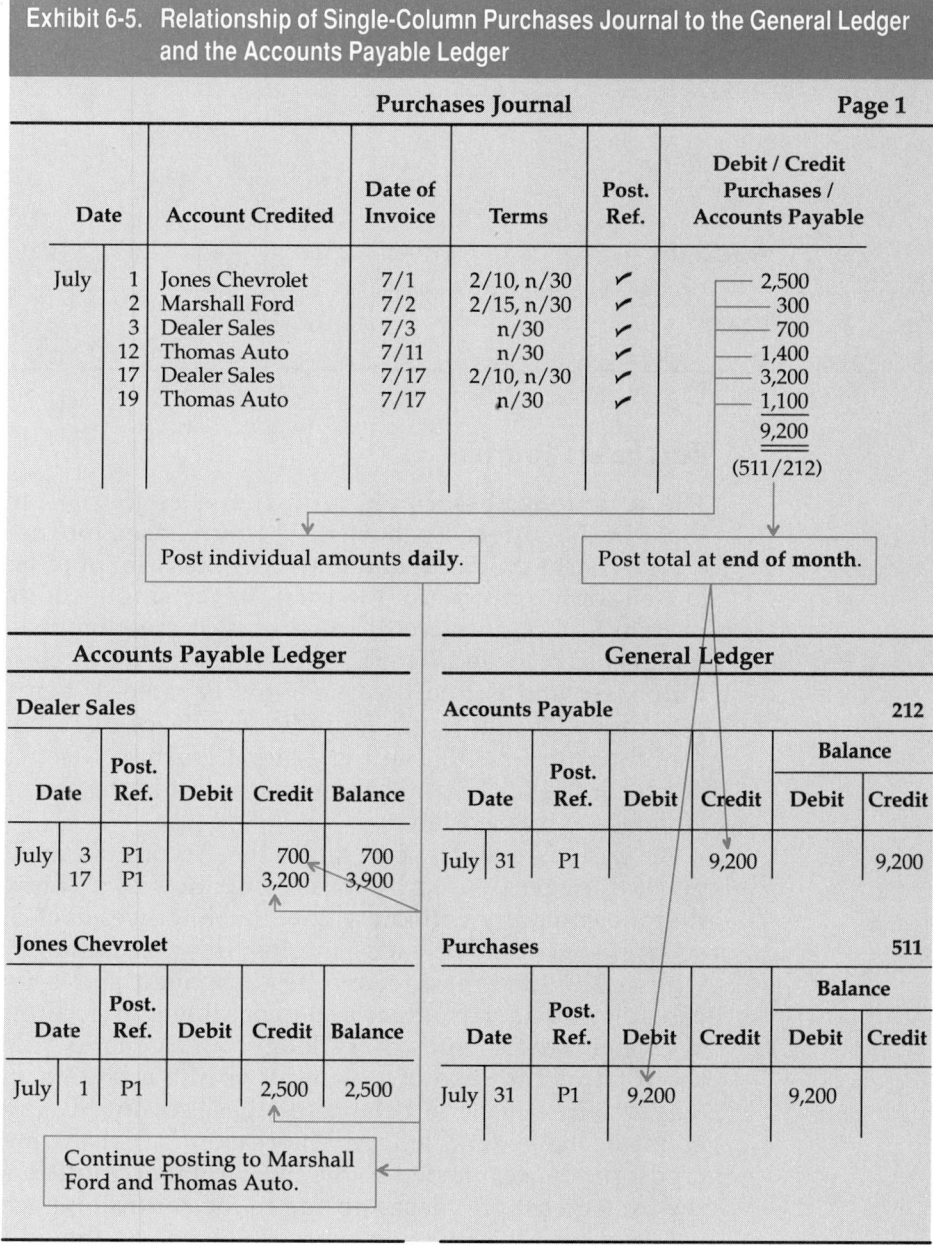

Exhibit 6-5. Relationship of Single-Column Purchases Journal to the General Ledger and the Accounts Payable Ledger

3. At the end of the month, sum the credit purchases, and post the amount in the general ledger accounts (Accounts Payable and Purchases). Place the numbers of the accounts debited and credited beneath the totals in the purchases journal to show that this step has been carried out.

4. Check the accuracy of the posting by adding the balances of the accounts payable ledger accounts and matching the total with the Accounts Payable controlling account balance in the general ledger. This step may be carried out by preparing a schedule of accounts payable.

The single-column purchases journal may be expanded to record credit purchases of things other than merchandise by adding a separate column for other debit accounts that are often used. For example, the multicolumn purchases journal in Exhibit 6-6 has columns for Freight In, Store Supplies, Office Supplies, and Other. Here the total credits to Accounts Payable ($9,437) equal the total debits to Purchases, Freight In, Store Supplies, and Office Supplies ($9,200 + $50 + $145 + $42 = $9,437). As in the procedure already described, the individual transactions in the Accounts Payable column are posted regularly to the accounts payable subsidiary ledger, and the totals of each column in the journal are posted monthly to the correct general ledger accounts. Some credit purchases call for a debit to an account that has no special column (that is, no place to record the debit) in the purchases journal. These transactions are recorded in the Other Accounts column with an indication of the account to which the debit is to be made.

Cash Receipts Journal

All transactions involving receipts of cash are recorded in the **cash receipts journal**. Examples of such transactions are cash from cash sales, cash from credit customers in payment of their accounts, and cash from other sources. To be most efficient, the cash receipts journal must be multicolumn. Several columns are necessary because, though all cash receipts are alike in that they require a debit to Cash, they are different in that they require a variety of credit entries. Thus you should be alert to several important differences between the cash receipts journal and the journals previously presented. Among these differences are an Other Accounts column, use of account numbers in the Post. Ref. column, and daily posting of the credits to Other Accounts.

Exhibit 6-6. A Multicolumn Purchases Journal

Purchases Journal — Page 1

Date	Account Credited	Date of Invoice	Terms	Post. Ref.	Credit — Accounts Payable	Purchases	Freight In	Store Supplies	Office Supplies	Other Accounts — Account	Post. Ref.	Amount
July 2	Jones Chevrolet	7/1	2/10, n/30	✓	2,500	2,500						
2	Marshall Ford	7/2	2/15, n/30	✓	300	300						
2	Shelby Car Delivery	7/2	n/30	✓	50		50					
3	Dealer Sales	7/3	n/30	✓	700	700						
12	Thomas Auto	7/11	n/30	✓	1,400	1,400						
17	Dealer Sales	7/17	2/10, n/30	✓	3,200	3,200						
19	Thomas Auto	7/17	n/30	✓	1,100	1,100						
25	Osborne Supply	7/21	n/10	✓	187			145	42			
					9,437	9,200	50	145	42			
					(212)	(511)	(514)	(132)	(133)			

The cash receipts journal illustrated in Exhibit 6-7 is based on the following selected transactions for July:

July 1 Henry Mitchell invested $20,000 in a used-car business.
      5 Sold a used car for $1,200 cash.
      8 Collected $500 from Georgetta Jones, less 2 percent sales discount.
     13 Sold a used car for $1,400 cash.
     16 Collected $750 from Peter Clark.
     19 Sold a used car for $1,000 cash.
     20 Sold some equipment not used in the business for $500 cash. The carrying value of the equipment was $500.
     24 Signed a note at the bank for a loan of $5,000.
     26 Sold a used car for $1,600 cash.
     28 Collected $600 from Peter Clark, less 2 percent sales discount.

The cash receipts journal, as illustrated in Exhibit 6-7, has three debit columns and three credit columns. The three debit columns record Cash, Sales Discounts, and Other Accounts.

1. *Cash* Each entry must have an amount in this column because each transaction must be a receipt of cash.
2. *Sales Discounts* The company in the illustration allows a 2 percent discount for prompt payment. Therefore, it is useful to have a column for sales discounts. Note that in the transactions of July 8 and 28, the debits to Cash and Sales Discounts are equal to the credit to Accounts Receivable.
3. *Other Accounts* The Other Accounts column is sometimes called Sundry Accounts and is used in the case of transactions that involve both a debit to Cash and a debit to some other account besides Sales Discounts.

The credit columns are the following:

1. *Accounts Receivable* This column is used to record collections on account from customers. The customer's name is written in the space entitled Account Credited so that the payment can be entered in his or her account in the accounts receivable subsidiary ledger. The postings to the individual accounts receivable accounts are usually done daily so that the customer's account balance will be known in case of an inquiry.
2. *Sales* This column is used to record all cash sales during the month. Retail firms that normally use cash registers would make an entry at the end of each day for the total sales from each cash register for that day. The debit, of course, is in the Cash debit column.
3. *Other Accounts* This column is used for the credit portion of any entry that is neither a cash collection from accounts receivable nor a cash sale. The name of the account to be credited is indicated in the Account Credited column. For example, the transactions of July 1, 20, and 24 involved credits to accounts other than Accounts Receivable or Sales. These individual postings should be done daily (or weekly if there are few of them). If a company finds that it is consistently

Exhibit 6-7. Relationship of the Cash Receipts Journal to the General Ledger and the Accounts Receivable Ledger

Cash Receipts Journal — Page 1

				Debits			Credits		
Date	Account Debited / Credited	Post. Ref.	Cash	Sales Discounts	Other Accounts	Accounts Receivable	Sales	Other Accounts
July 1	Henry Mitchell, Capital	311	20,000					20,000
5	Sales		1,200				1,200	
8	Georgetta Jones	✓	490	10		500		
13	Sales		1,400				1,400	
16	Peter Clark	✓	750			750		
19	Sales		1,000				1,000	
20	Equipment	151	500					500
24	Notes Payable	213	5,000					5,000
26	Sales		1,600				1,600	
28	Peter Clark	✓	588	12		600		
			32,528	22		1,850	5,200	25,500
			(111)	(412)		(114)	(411)	(✓)

Post individual amounts in Accounts Receivable credit columns **daily**.

Post totals at **end of month**.

Total not posted.

Post individual amounts in Other Accounts column **daily**.

General Ledger

Cash   111

Date	Post. Ref.	Debit	Credit	Balance Debit	Balance Credit
July 31	CR1	32,528		32,528	

Accounts Receivable   114

Date	Post. Ref.	Debit	Credit	Balance Debit	Balance Credit
July 31	S1	4,950		4,950	
31	CR1		1,850	3,100	

Equipment   151

Date	Post. Ref.	Debit	Credit	Balance Debit	Balance Credit
July 20	CR1		500	500 —	

Accounts Receivable Ledger

Peter Clark

Date	Post. Ref.	Debit	Credit	Balance
July 1	S1	750		750
16	CR1		750	—
18	S1	1,225		1,225
28	CR1		600	625

Georgetta Jones

Date	Post. Ref.	Debit	Credit	Balance
July 5	S1	500		500
8	CR1		500	—

Continue posting to Notes Payable and Henry Mitchell, Capital.

Continue posting to Sales and Sales Discounts.

crediting a certain account in the Other Accounts column, it may be appropriate to add another credit column to the cash receipts journal for that particular account.

The posting of the cash receipts journal, as illustrated in Exhibit 6-7, can be summarized as follows:

1. Post the Accounts Receivable column daily to each individual account in the accounts receivable subsidiary ledger. A check mark in the Post. Ref. column of the cash receipts journal indicates that the amount has been posted, and a CR1 (representing Cash Receipts Journal—Page 1) in the Post. Ref. column of each ledger account indicates the source of the entry.
2. Post the debits/credits in the Other Accounts columns daily or at convenient short intervals during the month to the general ledger accounts. Write the account number in the Post. Ref. column of the cash receipts journal as the individual items are posted to indicate that the posting has been done, and write CR1 in the Post. Ref. column of each ledger account to indicate the source of the entry.
3. At the end of the month, total the columns in the cash receipts journal. The sum of the debit column totals must equal the sum of the credit column totals, as follows:

Debit Column Totals		Credit Column Totals	
Cash	$32,528	Accounts Receivable	$ 1,850
Sales Discounts	22	Sales	5,200
Other Accounts	0	Other Accounts	25,500
Total Debits	$32,550	Total Credits	$32,550

This step is called crossfooting—a procedure we encountered earlier.
4. Post the column totals as follows:

   a. Cash debit column—posted as a debit to the Cash account.
   b. Sales Discounts debit column—posted as a debit to the Sales Discounts account.
   c. Accounts Receivable credit column—posted as a credit to the Accounts Receivable controlling account.
   d. Sales credit column—posted as a credit to the Sales account.
   e. The account numbers are written below each column in the cash receipts journal as they are posted to indicate that this step has been completed. A CR1 is written in the Post. Ref. column of each account to indicate the source of the entry.
   f. Note that the Other Accounts column totals are not posted by total because each entry was posted separately when the transaction occurred. The individual accounts were posted in step 2 above. Accountants place a check mark at the bottom of the column to show that appropriate postings in that column have been made and that the total is not posted.

Cash Payments Journal

All transactions involving payments of cash are recorded in the **cash payments journal** (also called the cash disbursements journal). Examples of such transactions are cash purchases, payments of obligations resulting from earlier purchases on credit, and other cash payments. As with the cash receipts journal, the cash payments journal must be multicolumn and is similar in design to the cash receipts journal.

The cash payments journal illustrated in Exhibit 6-8 is based on the following selected transactions of Mitchell's Used Car Sales for July:

July 2 Purchased merchandise (a used car) from Sondra Tidmore for cash, $400.
6 Paid for newspaper advertising in the *Daily Journal*, $200.
8 Paid one month's land and building rent to Siviglia Agency, $250.
11 Paid Jones Chevrolet for July 1 invoice (previously recorded in purchases journal in Exhibit 6-5), $2,500, less 2 percent purchase discount earned for payment in ten days or less.
16 Paid Charles Kunz, a salesperson, his salary, $600.
17 Paid Marshall Ford invoice of July 2 (previously recorded in purchases journal in Exhibit 6-5), $300, less 2 percent discount earned for payment in fifteen days or less.
24 Paid Grabow & Company for two-year insurance policy, $480.
27 Paid Dealer Sales invoice of July 17 (previously recorded in purchases journal in Exhibit 6-5), $3,200, less 2 percent purchase discount for payment in ten days or less.
30 Purchased office equipment for $400 and service equipment for $500 from A&B Equipment Company. Issued one check for the total amount.
31 Purchased land for $15,000 from Burns Real Estate. Issued check for $5,000 and note payable for $10,000.

The cash payments journal, as illustrated in Exhibit 6-8, has three credit columns and two debit columns. The credit columns for the cash payments journal are as follows:

1. *Cash* Each entry must have an amount in this column because each transaction must involve a payment of cash.
2. *Purchases Discounts* When purchases discounts are taken, they are recorded in this column.
3. *Other Accounts* This column is used to record credits other than Cash or Purchases Discounts. Note that the July 31 transaction shows a purchase of Land for $15,000 through the issuance of a check for $5,000 and a Note Payable for $10,000.

The debit columns are as follows:

1. *Accounts Payable* This column total is used to record payments to suppliers that have extended credit to the company. The supplier's name is written in the space entitled Payee so that the payment can be entered in his or her account in the accounts payable ledger.

Exhibit 6-8. Cash Payments Journal

Cash Payments Journal   Page 1

Date	Ck. No.	Payee	Account Credited / Debited	Post. Ref.	Credits			Debits	
					Cash	Purchases Discounts	Other Accounts	Accounts Payable	Other Accounts
July 2	101	Sondra Tidmore	Purchases	511	400				400
6	102	Daily Journal	Advertising Expense	612	200				200
8	103	Siviglia Agency	Rent Expense	631	250				250
11	104	Jones Chevrolet		✓	2,450	50		2,500	
16	105	Charles Kuntz	Salary Expense	611	600				600
17	106	Marshall Ford		✓	294	6		300	
24	107	Grabow & Company	Prepaid Insurance	119	480				480
27	108	Dealer Sales		✓	3,136	64		3,200	
30	109	A&B Equipment Company	Office Equipment Service Equipment	144 146	900				400 500
31	110	Burns Real Estate	Notes Payable Land	213 141	5,000		10,000		15,000
					13,710	120	10,000	6,000	17,830
					(111)	(512)	(✓)	(212)	(✓)

Post individual amounts in Other Accounts column **daily**.

Post individual amounts in Accounts Payable column **daily**.

Post totals at **end of month**.

Totals not posted.

General Ledger

Cash   111

				Balance	
Date	Post. Ref.	Debit	Credit	Debit	Credit
July 31	CR1	32,528		32,528	
31	CP1		13,710	18,818	

Prepaid Insurance   119

				Balance	
Date	Post. Ref.	Debit	Credit	Debit	Credit
July 24	CP1	480		480	

Continue posting to Land, Office Equipment, Service Equipment, Notes Payable, Purchases, Salary Expense, Advertising Expense, and Rent Expense.

Continue posting to Purchases Discounts and Accounts Payable.

Accounts Payable Ledger

Jones Chevrolet

Date	Post. Ref.	Debit	Credit	Balance
July 1	P1		2,500	2,500
11	CP1	2,500		—

Marshall Ford

Date	Post. Ref.	Debit	Credit	Balance
July 2	P1		300	300
17	CP1	300		—

Dealer Sales

Date	Post. Ref.	Debit	Credit	Balance
July 3	P1		700	700
17	P1		3,200	3,900
27	CP1	3,200		700

2. *Other Accounts* Cash can be expended for many reasons. Thus an Other Accounts or Sundry Accounts column is needed in the cash payments journal. The title of the account to be debited is written in the Account Debited column, and the amount is entered in the Other Accounts debit column. If a company finds that a particular account occurs often in the Other Accounts column, it may be desirable to add another debit column to the cash payments journal.

The posting of the cash payments journal, as illustrated in Exhibit 6-8, can be summarized as follows:

1. The Accounts Payable column should be posted daily to each individual account in the accounts payable subsidiary ledger. A check mark is placed in the Post. Ref. column of the cash payments journal to indicate that the posting is accomplished.
2. The debits/credits in the Other Accounts debit/credits columns should be posted to the general ledger daily or at convenient short intervals during the month. The account number is written in the Post. Ref. column of the cash payments journal as the individual items are posted in order to indicate that the posting has been completed, and a CP1 (representing Cash Payments Journal—Page 1) is written in the Post. Ref. column of each ledger account.
3. At the end of the month, the columns are totaled and crossfooted. That is, the sum of the credit column totals must equal the sum of the debit column totals, as follows:

Credit Column Totals		Debit Column Totals	
Cash	$13,710	Accounts Payable	$ 6,000
Purchases Discounts	120	Other Accounts	17,830
Other Accounts	10,000	Total Debits	$23,830
Total Credits	$23,830		

4. The column totals for Cash, Purchases Discounts, and Accounts Payable are posted at the end of the month to their respective accounts in the general ledger. The account numbers are written below each column in the cash payments journal as they are posted to indicate that this step has been completed, and a CP1 is written in the Post. Ref. column of each ledger account. A check mark is placed under the total of each Other Accounts column in the cash payments journal to indicate that appropriate postings in the column have been made and that the total is not posted.

General Journal

Transactions that do not involve sales, purchases, cash receipts, or cash payments should be recorded in the general journal. Usually there are only a few such transactions. The two examples that follow are entries that do not fit in a special-purpose journal: a return of merchandise, and an allowance from a supplier for credit. Adjusting and closing entries are also recorded in the general journal.

July 25   Returned one of the two used cars purchased on credit from Thomas
           Auto for $700 on July 11. Each car cost $700.
      26   Agreed to give Maxwell Gertz a $35 allowance on his account because
           a tire blew out on the car he purchased.

These entries are shown in Exhibit 6-9. The entries on July 25 and 26
include a debit or a credit to a controlling account (Accounts Payable or
Accounts Receivable). The name of the customer or supplier is also
given here. When such a debit or credit is made to a controlling account
in the general journal, the entry must be posted twice: once in the controlling account and once in the individual account in the subsidiary
ledger. This procedure keeps the subsidiary ledger equal to the controlling account. Note that the July 26 transaction is posted by a debit to
Sales Returns and Allowances in the general ledger (shown by the account number 413), by a credit to the Accounts Receivable controlling
account in the general ledger (shown by the account number 114), and
by a credit to the Maxwell Gertz account in the accounts receivable subsidiary ledger (shown by the check mark).

Flexibility of Special-Purpose Journals

The functions of special-purpose journals are to reduce and simplify the
work in accounting and to allow for the division of labor. These journals
should be designed to fit the business in which they are used. As noted
earlier, if certain accounts show up often in the Other Accounts column
of a journal, it may be wise to add a column for those accounts when a
new page of a special-purpose journal is prepared.

Exhibit 6-9. Transactions Recorded in the General Journal

General Journal				Page 1
Date	**Description**	**Post. Ref.**	**Debit**	**Credit**
July 25	Accounts Payable, Thomas Auto	212/✓	700	
	Purchases Returns and			
	Allowances	513		700
	Returned used car for credit;			
	invoice date: 7/11			
26	Sales Returns and Allowances	413	35	
	Accounts Receivable, Maxwell			
	Gertz	114/✓		35
	Allowance given because of			
	faulty tire			

Also, if certain transactions appear over and over again in the general journal, it may be a good idea to set up a new special-purpose journal. For example, if Mitchell's Used Car Sales finds that it must often give allowances to customers, it may want to set up a sales returns and allowances journal specifically for these transactions. Sometimes, a purchases returns and allowances journal may be in order. In short, special-purpose journals should be designed to take care of the kinds of transactions a company commonly encounters.

Chapter Review

Review of Learning Objectives

1. **Identify the phases of systems installation and the principles of systems design.**

   The phases of systems installation are system investigation, system design, and system implementation. In designing an accounting system, the system designer must keep in mind the four principles of systems design: the cost-benefit principle, the control principle, the compatibility principle, and the flexibility principle.

2. **Identify the basic elements of computer systems in mainframe and microcomputer contexts.**

   Computer data processing systems are the most advanced type of data processing systems, in which recording, posting, and other bookkeeping tasks are done with the aid of a computer. The typical computer system consists of hardware, software, and personnel. The internal processing is specified in the form of programs, which may be designed to allow batch processing (grouping of similar transactions to be done at a specified time) or on-line processing (recording transactions and updating records as they occur). Commercial accounting packages for microcomputer systems typically use a batch processing approach.

3. **Explain the objectives and uses of special-purpose journals.**

   The typical manual data processing system consists of several special-purpose journals, each of which is designed to record one kind of transaction. Recording all transactions of one kind in each journal reduces and simplifies the bookkeeping work and allows a division of labor. This division of labor is important for internal control purposes.

4. **Construct and use the following types of special-purpose journals: sales journal, purchases journal, cash receipts journal, cash payments journal, and others as needed.**

   A special-purpose journal is constructed by devoting a single column to a particular account (for example, debit cash in the cash receipts journal and credit cash in the cash payments journal). Other columns in such a journal depend on the kinds of transactions in which the company normally engages. The special-purpose journals also have columns for the transaction dates, explanations or subsidiary account names, and reference columns.

5. **Explain the purposes and relationships of controlling accounts and subsidiary ledgers.**

Subsidiary ledgers contain the individual accounts of a certain kind such as customer accounts (accounts receivable) or supplier accounts (accounts payable). The individual account records are kept separately in a subsidiary ledger to avoid making the general ledger too bulky. The total of the balances of the subsidiary accounts will equal the total of the controlling or general ledger account because the individual items are posted daily to the subsidiary accounts and the column totals are posted to the general ledger account monthly from the special-purpose journal.

Review of Concepts and Terminology

The following concepts and terms were introduced in this chapter:

(L.O. 1) **Accounting systems**:   All steps in the accounting process including analyzing and recording transactions, posting entries, adjusting and closing the accounts, and preparing financial statements.

(L.O. 2) **Batch processing**:   The approach in the computer processing of business transactions and preparation of financial reports in which processing tasks are scheduled in a logical order.

(L.O. 4) **Cash payments journal**:   A multicolumn special-purpose journal in which payments or disbursements of cash are recorded.

(L.O. 4) **Cash receipts journal**:   A multicolumn special-purpose journal in which transactions involving receipts of cash are recorded.

(L.O. 1) **Compatibility principle**:   A principle requiring that the design of an accounting system be in harmony with the organizational and human factors of a business.

(L.O. 2) **Computer operator**:   The person who runs a computer.

(L.O. 5) **Controlling or control account**:   An account in the general ledger that summarizes the total balance of a group of related accounts in a subsidiary ledger.

(L.O. 1) **Control principle**:   A principle requiring that the design of an accounting system provides all the features of internal control needed to protect assets and ensure the reliability of data.

(L.O. 1) **Cost-benefit principle**:   A principle holding that the benefits to be derived from providing new accounting information should equal or exceed the costs of providing it.

(L.O. 1) **Data processing**:   The means by which an accounting system gathers data, organizes them into useful forms, and issues the resulting information to users.

(L.O. 1) **Flexibility principle**:   A principle holding that the design of an accounting system has enough flexibility to allow the volume of transactions to grow and organizational changes to be made in the business.

(L.O. 2) **Hardware**:   All the equipment needed to operate a computerized data processing system.

(L.O. 2) **Manual data processing**:   A system of accounting in which each transaction is entered manually from a source document into the general journal

(input device) and each debit and credit is posted manually to the correct ledger account (processor and memory device) for the eventual preparation of financial statements (output device).

(L.O. 2) **On-line processing:** The approach in the computer processing of business transactions and preparation of financial reports in which remote terminals are linked to the central processor, and the files are updated virtually as the transactions occur

(L.O. 2) **Programmer:** The person who writes the instructions for a computer.

(L.O. 2) **Programs:** The set of instructions and steps that bring about the desired results in a computer data processing system.

(L.O. 4) **Purchases journal:** A single-column or multicolumn special-purpose journal used to record all purchases on credit.

(L.O. 4) **Sales journal:** A type of special-purpose journal used to record credit sales.

(L.O. 2) **Software:** The programs in a computer data processing system.

(L.O. 2) **Source documents:** The written evidence that supports the transactions for each major accounting function.

(L.O. 3) **Special-purpose journal:** An input device in an accounting system that is used to record a single type of transaction.

(L.O. 5) **Subsidiary ledger:** A ledger separate from the general ledger; contains a group of related accounts the total of whose balances equals the balance of a controlling account in the general ledger.

(L.O. 1) **System design:** The phase in the installation of an accounting system in which the new system or the changes in the current system are formulated.

(L.O. 1) **System implementation:** The phase in which a new accounting system or changes in the current system are properly installed.

(L.O. 1) **System investigation:** The phase in the installation of an accounting system whose aim is to discover the needs of a new system or to judge an existing system.

(L.O. 2) **Systems analyst:** The person who designs a computer data processing system on the basis of information needs.

Self-Test

Test your knowledge of the chapter by choosing the best answer for each item below and on the next page.

1. A systems analyst would most likely discover the system needs of an organization during
   a. system investigation.   c. system implementation.
   b. system design.   d. system use.   *(L.O. 1)*

2. A decision to go ahead with a costly computer system because of potential sales loss and customer discontent is probably a result of application of the·
   a. cost-benefit principle.   c. compatibility principle.
   b. control principle.   d. flexibility principle.   *(L.O. 1)*

3. In a microcomputer system, an example of a hardware output device would be a
   a. hard disk.
   b. computer program.
   c. central processor.
   d. printer. *(L.O. 2)*

4. Special-purpose journals have come into existence primarily because most businesses have many transactions that
   a. are difficult to classify.
   b. fall into a few categories.
   c. use only a very few ledger accounts.
   d. are easy to classify. *(L.O. 3)*

5. The total of a one-column sales journal would be posted as a
   a. debit to Sales and a credit to Accounts Receivable.
   b. debit to Accounts Receivable and a credit to Sales.
   c. debit to Cash and a credit to Sales.
   d. debit to Sales and a credit to Cash. *(L.O. 4)*

6. Each entry in the purchases journal requires that an entry be made in
   a. the general journal.
   b. the accounts payable ledger.
   c. the general ledger.
   d. the purchases account. *(L.O. 4)*

7. The daily total of sales for cash is recorded in the
   a. sales journal.
   b. purchases journal.
   c. cash disbursements journal.
   d. cash receipts journal. *(L.O. 4)*

8. One advantage of a multicolumn purchases journal is that it
   a. minimizes use of the general journal.
   b. eliminates the need for the accounts payable subsidiary ledger.
   c. includes purchases on credit and for cash.
   d. records only credit sales. *(L.O. 4)*

9. A company that has four special journals and a general journal would probably record which of the following in the general journal?
   a. A sale on credit
   b. A purchase on credit
   c. A sales return
   d. A purchases discount *(L.O. 4)*

10. Failure to post the receipt of a customer's payment in the customer's account in the subsidiary ledger will most likely be discovered when
    a. the cash receipts journal is totaled and crossfooted.
    b. the trial balance is prepared.
    c. the total of the subsidiary ledger is compared to the balance of the accounts receivable controlling account.
    d. the assets are compared with the liabilities and owner's equity on the balance sheet. *(L.O. 5)*

Answers to Self-Test are at the end of this chapter.

Review Problem
Purchases Journal

(L.O. 1, 3, 4) Caraban Company is a retail seller of hiking and camping gear. The company is installing a manual accounting system, and the accountant is trying to

decide whether to use a single-column or a multicolumn purchases journal. Some transactions related to purchases follow:

Jan. 5   Received a shipment of merchandise from Simons Corporation, $2,875, terms 2/10, n/30, FOB shipping point.

    10   Received a bill from Allied Freight for the freight charges on the January 5 shipment, $416, terms n/30.

    15   Returned some of the merchandise received from Simons Corporation because it was not what was ordered, $315.

    20   Purchased store supplies of $56 and office supplies of $117 from Mason Company, terms n/30.

    25   Received a shipment from Thomas Manufacturing, with the bill for $1,882, including freight charges of $175, terms n/30, FOB shipping point.

Required

1. Record the transactions above, using a single-column purchases journal and a general journal.
2. Record the transactions above, using a multicolumn purchases journal and a general journal, rule and total the purchases journal, and show the posting reference for each journal. Use the following accounts: Store Supplies (116), Office Supplies (117), Accounts Payable (211), Purchases (611), Purchases Returns and Allowances (612), and Freight In (613).
3. Using the principles of systems design as a basis for your answer, compare the two systems as to number of journal entries and postings and in terms of the cost-benefit, control, compatibility, and flexibility principles.

Answer to Review Problem

1. Transactions recorded in a single-column purchases journal and the general journal are shown below.

Purchases Journal					Page 1
Date	Account Credited	Date of Invoice	Terms	Post. Ref.	Amount
Jan. 5	Simons Corporation	1/5	2/10, n/30	✓	2,875

General Journal				Page 1
Date	Description	Post. Ref.	Debit	Credit
Jan. 10	Freight In	613	416	
	Accounts Payable, Allied Freight	211/✓		416
	Freight charges on Simons			
	Corporation shipment, terms n/30			

(continued)

General Journal				Page 1
Date	**Description**	**Post. Ref.**	**Debit**	**Credit**
Jan. 15	Accounts Payable, Simons Corporation	211/✓	315	
	Purchases Returns and	612		
	Allowances			315
	Returned merchandise not			
	ordered			
20	Store Supplies	116	56	
	Office Supplies	117	117	
	Accounts Payable, Mason	211		
	Company			173
	Purchased supplies, terms n/30			
25	Purchases	611	1,707	
	Freight In	613	175	
	Accounts Payable, Thomas	211/✓		
	Manufacturing			1,882
	Purchased merchandise, terms			
	n/30			

2. Transactions recorded in a multicolumn purchases journal and the general journal are shown below.

Purchases Journal									Page 1
					Credit	**Debits**			
Date	**Account Credited**	**Date of Invoice**	**Terms**	**Post. Ref.**	**Accounts Payable**	**Purchases**	**Freight In**	**Store Supplies**	**Office Supplies**
Jan. 5	Simons Corporation	1/5	2/10, n/30	✓	2,875	2,875			
10	Allied Freight	1/10	n/30	✓	416		416		
20	Mason Company	1/20	n/30	✓	173			56	117
25	Thomas Manufacturing	1/25	n/30	✓	1,882	1,707	175		
					5,346	4,582	591	56	117
					(211)	(611)	(613)	(116)	(117)

Each of these accounts is posted **daily** to the appropriate account in the subsidiary ledger.

Each of these totals is posted **monthly** to the applicable general ledger account.

	General Journal				Page 1
Date	**Description**	**Post. Ref.**	**Debit**	**Credit**

Jan. 15	Accounts Payable, Simons Corporation
	Purchases Returns and
	Allowances
	   Returned merchandise
	   not ordered
		211
		
		612
			315	315

This amount is posted both to the controlling account and to the subsidiary account.

This amount is posted to the general ledger account.

3. The first system (single-column purchases journal) requires four general journal entries plus one purchases journal entry, or fifteen separate lines, including explanations, to be written. In addition, fifteen postings to the general ledger and the accounts payable subsidiary ledger are necessary. (Also, the total of the purchases journal must be posted twice at the end of the month.) The second system (multicolumn purchases journal) calls for only one general journal entry and four purchases journal entries. Only seven lines need to be written, and only seven postings must be made (in addition, the column totals in the purchases journal must be posted at the end of the month).

In applying the cost-benefit principle, the benefits of the expanded purchases journal in terms of journalizing and posting time saved are clear from the analysis above. In addition, there are fewer chances for error when using the expanded purchases journal. So this aspect of achieving the control principle is better under the second system. It is not possible to decide which system better meets the compatibility principle because we do not know the relative proportion of transaction types. For instance, if the number of transactions like the one for January 5 outnumber all the others by ten to one, the first system may be more compatible with the needs of the company. On the other hand, if there are great numbers of transactions like those for January 10, 20, and 25, the second system may be more compatible. Finally, in terms of the flexibility principle, the multicolumn purchases journal is obviously more flexible because it can handle more kinds of transactions and may be expanded to include columns for other accounts if necessary.

Chapter Assignments

Discussion Questions and Writing Assignments

1. What are the three phases of system installation?
2. What are the four principles of system design? Explain the essence of each in a sentence.
3. What is the function of data processing?
4. What are three ways of viewing data processing?
5. What are the elements of a computer data processing system?
6. What is the difference between hardware and software?
7. What is the purpose of a computer program?
8. What is the difference between batch processing and on-line processing?
9. Data are the raw material of a computer system. Trace the flow of data through the different parts of a microcomputer system.
10. How do special-purpose journals save time in entering and posting transactions?
11. Long Transit had 1,700 sales on credit during the current month.
    a. If the company uses a two-column general journal to record sales, how many times will the word *Sales* be written?
    b. How many postings to the Sales account will have to be made?
    c. If the company uses a sales journal, how many times will the word *Sales* be written?
    d. How many postings to the Sales account will have to be made?
12. What is the purpose of the Accounts Receivable controlling account? What is its relationship to the accounts receivable subsidiary ledger?
13. Why are the cash receipts journal and cash payments journal cross-footed? When is this step performed?
14. A company has the following numbers of accounts with balances: 18 asset accounts, including the Accounts Receivable account but not the individual customer accounts; 200 customer accounts; 8 liability accounts, including the Accounts Payable account but not the individual creditor accounts; 100 creditor accounts; 35 owner's equity accounts, including income statement accounts. The total is 361 accounts. How many accounts in total would appear in the general ledger?

Classroom Exercises

Exercise 6-1.
Matching
Transactions to
Special-Purpose
Journals
(L.O. 3)

A company uses a one-column sales journal, a one-column purchases journal, a cash receipts journal, a cash payments journal, and a general journal.

Indicate in which journal each of the following transactions would be recorded: (1) sold merchandise on credit; (2) sold merchandise for cash; (3) gave a customer credit for merchandise purchased on credit and returned; (4) paid a creditor; (5) paid office salaries; (6) customer paid for merchandise previously purchased on credit; (7) recorded adjusting and closing entries; (8) purchased merchandise on credit; (9) purchased sales department supplies on credit; (10) purchased office equipment for cash; (11) returned merchandise purchased on credit; (12) paid taxes.

Exercise 6-2.
Characteristics of
Special-Purpose
Journals
(L.O. 3)

Sanchez Corporation uses a single-column sales journal, a single-column purchases journal, a cash receipts journal, a cash payments journal, and a general journal.

1. In which of the journals listed above would you expect to find the fewest transactions recorded?
2. At the end of the accounting period, to which account or accounts should the total of the purchases journal be posted as a debit and/or credit?
3. At the end of the accounting period, to which account or accounts should the total of the sales journal be posted as a debit and/or credit?
4. What two subsidiary ledgers would probably be associated with the journals listed above? From which journals would postings normally be made to each of the two subsidiary ledgers?
5. In which of the journals are adjusting and closing entries made?

Exercise 6-3.
Identifying the
Content of a
Special-Purpose
Journal
(L.O. 4)

Shown below is a page from a special journal.

1. What kind of journal is this?
2. Give an explanation for each of the following transactions: (a) August 27, (b) August 28, (c) August 29, (d) August 30.
3. Explain the following: (a) the numbers under the bottom lines, (b) the checks entered in the Post. Ref. column, (c) the numbers 115 and 715 in the Post. Ref. column, and (d) the check below the Other Accounts column.

Date		Account Credited	Post. Ref.	Debits		Credits		
				Cash	Sales Discount	Other Accounts	Accounts Receivable	Sales
		Balance Forward	✓	39,799	787	26,100	10,204	4,282
Aug.	27	Betsy McCray	✓	490	10		500	
	28	Notes Receivable	115			1,000		
		Interest Income	715	1,120		120		
	29	Cash Sale		960				960
	30	Michael Harper	✓	200			200	
				42,569	797	27,220	10,904	5,242
				(111)	(412)	(✓)	(114)	(411)

Exercise 6-4.
Finding Errors in
Special-Purpose
Journals
(L.O. 4, 5)

A company records purchases in a one-column purchases journal and records purchases returns in its general journal. During the past month an accounting clerk made each of the errors described below. Explain how each error might be discovered.

1. Correctly recorded an $86 purchase in the purchases journal but posted it to the creditor's account as a $68 purchase.
2. Made an additional error in totaling the Amount column of the purchases journal.

3. Posted a purchases return recorded in the general journal to the Purchases Returns and Allowances account and to the Accounts Payable account but did not post it to the creditor's account.
4. Made an error in determining the balance of a creditor's account.
5. Posted a purchases return to the Accounts Payable account but did not post to the Purchases Returns and Allowances account.

Exercise 6-5.
Posting from a
Sales Journal
(L.O. 4, 5)

Grammas Corporation began business on September 1. The company maintained a sales journal, which appeared at the end of the month as presented below.

Sales Journal				Page 1
Date	Account Debited	Invoice Number	Post. Ref.	Amount
Sept. 4	Yung Moon	1001		172
10	Stacy Kravitz	1002		317
15	Arthur Hillman	1003		214
17	Yung Moon	1004		97
25	Juan Robles	1005		433
				1,233

1. On a sheet of paper, open general ledger accounts for Accounts Receivable (account number 112) and Sales (account number 411) and an accounts receivable subsidiary ledger with an account for each customer. Make the appropriate postings from the sales journal. State the posting references that you would place in the sales journal above.
2. Prove the accounts receivable subsidiary ledger by preparing a schedule of accounts receivable.

Exercise 6-6.
Multicolumn
Purchases Journal
(L.O. 4)

Jablouski Company uses a multicolumn purchases journal similar to the one illustrated in Exhibit 6-6.

During the month of October, Jablouski made the following purchases:

Oct. 1 Purchased merchandise from Cowen Company on account for $2,700, invoice dated October 1, terms 2/10, n/30.

      2 Received freight bill dated October 1 from Riker Freight for above merchandise, $175, terms n/30.

     23 Purchased supplies from Zimmer, Inc. for $120; allocated one-half each to store and office; invoice dated October 20, terms n/30.

     27 Purchased merchandise from Fleming Company on account for $987; total included freight in of $87; invoice dated October 25, terms n/30, FOB shipping point.

Oct. 30   Purchased office supplies from Zimmer, Inc. for $48, invoice dated October 30, terms n/30.
   31   Purchased a one-year insurance policy from Greenspan Agency, $240, terms n/30.

1. Draw a multicolumn purchases journal similar to the one in Exhibit 6-6.
2. Enter the above transactions in the purchases journal. Then foot and crossfoot the columns.

Interpreting Accounting Information

B. Dalton and Waldenbooks
(L.O. 1)

In the mid-1960s a new and tempting mass market was emerging. Americans were becoming better educated and more affluent. Also, the increasing number of shopping centers provided the perfect setting for a chain of national bookstores. To take advantage of this opportunity, Minneapolis-based Dayton-Hudson launched its B. Dalton Bookseller, and Los Angeles-based Carter Hawley Hale began expanding its Waldenbooks division. By 1982, these two chains were by far the biggest book retailers in the country and were very competitive with each other. Dalton had 575 stores and planned to add 556 more by 1987. Waldenbooks had 750 outlets and planned to add 80 to 90 more each year.

   Forbes magazine reported that although Waldenbooks had more outlets, Dalton "looks like the leader in the fight." Each chain had roughly $250 million in sales in 1980, but Dalton sold an estimated $132 worth of books per square foot of store space to Walden's $114. *Forbes* stated that "A computerized inventory system installed in 1966 is what gives Dalton its edge—and is a key to why its 10% pretax profits are well above Walden's." In the book business today, "Success depends far more on fast, high efficiency distribution than on any fundamental appreciation of literature. . . . Order a little of everything and remain secure in your capabilities to restock quickly those titles the computer says are selling fast."[1]

Required

1. Describe in your own words how you believe Dalton used the four principles of systems design in 1966 to design its computerized inventory system so that it was able to grow rapidly and to become more profitable than Waldenbooks.
2. Describe in your own words the following parts of the computerized inventory system that would allow Dalton to restock fast-selling books quickly: source documents, data input, processing, information output, and distribution.

Problem Set A

Problem 6A-1. Identification of Transactions
(L.O. 4, 5)

Chin Company uses a general journal, purchases journal, sales journal, cash receipts journal, and cash payments journal similar to those illustrated in the text. On September 30, the P. Quaid account in the accounts receivable subsidiary ledger appeared as shown on the top of the following page.

1. "Dalton, Walden and the Amazing Money Machine," by Jeff Blyskal. Excerpted by permission of *Forbes* magazine, January 18, 1982, p. 47. © Forbes, Inc., 1982.

P. Quaid

Date		Item	Post. Ref.	Debit	Credit	Balance
Aug.	31		S4	816		816
Sept.	4		J7		64	752
	10		CR5		200	552
	15		S6	228		780

On September 30, the account of Diaz Company in the accounts payable subsidiary ledger appeared as follows:

Diaz Company

Date		Item	Post. Ref.	Debit	Credit	Balance
Sept.	16		P7		2,026	2,026
	21		J9	212		1,814
	28		CP8	1,814		—

Required

1. Write an explanation of each entry affecting the P. Quaid account receivable including the journal from which the entry was posted.
2. Write an explanation of each entry affecting the Diaz Company account payable including the journal from which the entry was posted.

Problem 6A-2.
Cash Receipts and
Cash Payments
Journals
(L.O. 4)

The items below detail all cash transactions by Baylor Company for the month of July. The company uses multicolumn cash receipts and cash payments journals similar to those illustrated in the chapter.

July 1 The owner, Eugene Baylor, invested $50,000 cash and $24,000 in equipment in the business.
2 Paid rent to Leonard Agency, $600, with check no. 75.
3 Cash sales, $2,200.
6 Purchased store equipment for $5,000 from Gilmore Company, with check no. 76.
7 Purchased merchandise for cash, $6,500, from Pascual Company, with check no. 77.
8 Paid Audretti Company invoice, $1,800, less 2 percent with check no. 78.
9 Paid advertising bill, $350, to WOSU, with check no. 79.
10 Cash sales, $3,910.
12 Received $800 on account from B. Erring.

July 13 Purchased used truck for cash, $3,520, from Pettit Company, with check no. 80.

19 Received $4,180 from Monroe Company, in settlement of a $4,000 note plus interest.

20 Received $1,078 ($1,100 less $22 cash discount) from Young Lee.

21 Paid Baylor $2,000 from business for personal use by issuing check no. 81.

23 Paid Dautley Company invoice, $2,500, less 2 percent discount, with check no. 82.

26 Paid Haywood Company for freight on merchandise received, $60, with check no. 83.

27 Cash sales, $4,800.

28 Paid C. Murphy for monthly salary, $1,400, with check no. 84.

31 Purchased land from N. Archibald for $20,000, paying $5,000 with check no. 85 and signing a note payable for $15,000.

Required

1. Enter the preceding transactions in the cash receipts and cash payments journals.
2. Foot, crossfoot, and rule the journals.

**Problem 6A-3.
Purchases and
General Journals**
(L.O. 4, 5)

The following items represent the credit transactions for McGarry Company during the month of August. The company uses a multicolumn purchases journal and a general journal similar to those illustrated in the text.

Aug. 2 Purchased merchandise from Alvarez Company, $1,400.

5 Purchased van from Meriweather Company, $8,000.

8 Purchased office supplies from Daudridge Company, $400.

12 Purchased filing cabinets from Daudridge Company, $550.

14 Purchased merchandise, $1,400, and store supplies, $200, from Petrie Company.

17 Purchased store supplies from Alvarez Company, $100, and office supplies from Hollins Company, $50.

20 Purchased merchandise from Petrie Company, $1,472.

24 Purchased merchandise from Alvarez Company, $2,452; the $2,452 invoice total included shipping charges, $232.

26 Purchased office supplies from Daudridge Company, $150.

30 Purchased merchandise from Petrie Company, $290.

31 Returned defective merchandise purchased from Petrie Company on August 20 for full credit, $432.

Required

1. Enter the preceding transactions in the purchases journal and the general journal. Assume that all terms are n/30 and that invoice dates are the same as the transaction dates.
2. Foot, crossfoot, and rule the purchases journal.
3. Open the following general ledger accounts: Store Supplies (116); Office Supplies (117); Trucks (142); Office Equipment (144); Accounts Payable (211); Purchases (611); Purchases Returns and Allowances (612); and Freight In (613). Open accounts payable subsidiary ledger accounts as needed. Post from the journals to the ledger accounts.

Problem 6A-4.
Comprehensive
Use of
Special-Purpose
Journals
(L.O. 4, 5)

Chung Refrigerating Company completed the following transactions:

May   1   Received merchandise from Costello Company, $2,500, invoice dated April 29, terms 2/10, n/30, FOB shipping point.
   2   Issued check no. 230 to Roundfield Agency for May rent, $2,000.
   3   Received merchandise from Vranes Manufacturing, $5,400, invoice dated May 1, terms 2/10, n/30, FOB shipping point.
   5   Issued check no. 231 to Dukes Company for repairs, $560.
   6   Received $400 credit memorandum pertaining to May 3 shipment from Vranes Manufacturing for unsatisfactory merchandise returned to Vranes Manufacturing.
   7   Issued check no. 232 to Orta Company for freight charges on May 1 and May 3 shipments, $184.
   8   Sold merchandise to C. Share, $1,000, terms 1/10, n/30, invoice no. 725.
   9   Issued check no. 233 to Costello Company in full payment less discount.
   10   Sold merchandise to R. Bell for $1,250, terms 1/10, n/30, invoice no. 726.
   11   Issued check no. 234 to Vranes Manufacturing for balance of account less discount.
   12   Purchased advertising on credit from WXYR, $450, terms n/20.
   14   Issued credit memorandum to R. Bell for $50 for merchandise returned.
   15   Cash sales for the first half of the month, $9,670. (To shorten these problems, cash sales are recorded only twice a month instead of daily, as they would be in actual practice.)
   16   Sold merchandise to L. Stokes, $700, terms 1/10, n/30, invoice no. 727.
   17   Received check from C. Share for May 8 sale less discount.
   19   Received check from R. Bell for balance of account less discount.
   20   Received merchandise from Costello Company, $2,800, invoice dated May 19, terms 2/10, n/30, FOB shipping point.
   21   Received freight bill on merchandise purchased from Noh Company, $570, terms n/5.
   22   Issued check no. 235 for advertising purchase of May 12.
   23   Received merchandise from Vranes Manufacturing, $3,600, invoice dated May 22, terms 2/10, n/30, FOB shipping point.
   24   Issued check no. 236 for freight charge of May 21.
   26   Sold merchandise to C. Share, $800, terms 1/10, n/30, invoice no. 728.
   27   Received credit memorandum from Vranes Manufacturing for defective merchandise received May 23, $300.
   28   Issued check no. 237 to Espinoza Company for purchase of office equipment, $350.
   29   Issued check no. 238 to Costello Company for one-half of May 20 purchase less discount.
   30   Received check in full from L. Stokes, discount not allowed.
   31   Cash sales for the last half of month, $11,560.
   31   Issued check no. 239, payable to Payroll Account for monthly sales salaries, $4,300.

Required   1. Prepare a sales journal, a multicolumn purchases journal, a cash receipts journal, a cash payments journal, and a general journal for Chung Refrigerating Company similar to the ones illustrated in this chapter. Use one as the page number for each journal.

2. Open the following general ledger accounts: Cash (111); Accounts Receivable (112); Office Equipment (141); Accounts Payable (211); Sales (411); Sales Discounts (412); Sales Returns and Allowances (413); Purchases (511); Purchases Discounts (512); Purchases Returns and Allowances (513); Freight In (514); Sales Salaries Expense (521); Advertising Expense (522); Rent Expense (531); and Repairs Expense (532).

3. Open the following accounts receivable subsidiary ledger accounts: R. Bell, C. Share, and L. Stokes.

4. Open the following accounts payable subsidiary ledger accounts: Costello Company, Noh Company, Vranes Manufacturing, and WXYR.

5. Enter the transactions in the journals and post as appropriate.

6. Foot and crossfoot the journals, and make end-of-month postings.

7. Prepare a trial balance of the general ledger and prove the control balances of Accounts Receivable and Accounts Payable by preparing schedules of accounts receivable and accounts payable.

Problem 6A-5.
Comprehensive
Use of
Special-Purpose
Journals
(L.O. 4, 5)

The following transactions were completed by Lezcano's Men's Wear during the month of July, its first month of operation:

July 2 Carlos Lezcano deposited $20,000 in the new company's bank account.

3 Issued check no. 101 to Rollins Corporation for one month's rent, $1,200.

4 Received merchandise from Garnett Company, $7,000, invoice dated July 3, terms 2/10, n/60, FOB shipping point.

5 Received freight bill on merchandise purchased from Wiggins Company, $964, terms n/20.

6 Issued check no. 102 to Bagley Company for store equipment, $7,400.

7 Borrowed $8,000 from bank on a ninety-day, 9 percent note.

8 Cash sales for the first week, $1,982.

10 Sold merchandise to Midlands School, $900, terms 2/10, n/30, invoice no. 1001.

11 Sold merchandise to Charlotte Soo, $300, terms n/20, invoice no. 1002.

12 Purchased advertising in *The Journal-Citizen*, $150, terms n/15.

13 Issued check no. 103 for purchase of July 4 less discount.

14 Issued a credit memorandum for merchandise returned by Charlotte Soo, $30.

15 Cash sales for the second week, $3,492.

17 Received merchandise from Garnett Company, $1,900, invoice dated July 16, terms 2/10, n/60, FOB shipping point.

18 Received freight bill on merchandise purchased from Wiggins Company, $262, terms n/20.

19 Received merchandise from Law Company, $1,400, invoice dated July 17, terms 1/10, n/60, FOB destination.

20 Received payment in full, less discount from Midlands School.

21 Received a credit memorandum from Garnett Company of $100 for merchandise returned.

22 Cash sales for third week, $2,912.

July 24   Issued check no. 104 for total amount owed Wiggins Company.
      25   Sold merchandise to Midlands School, $684, terms 2/10, n/30, invoice no. 1003.
      26   Issued check no. 105 in payment of amount owed Garnett Company less discount.
      27   Sold merchandise to Al Kaiser, $372, terms n/20, invoice no. 1004.
      28   Issued check no. 106 for amount owed *The Journal-Citizen.*
      29   Cash sales for the fourth week, $1,974.
      31   Issued check no. 107 to Payroll account for sales salaries for the month of July, $3,600.

Required

1. Prepare a sales journal, a purchases journal, a cash receipts journal, a cash payments journal, and a general journal. Use one as the page number for each journal.
2. Open the following general ledger accounts: Cash (111); Accounts Receivable (112); Store Equipment (141); Accounts Payable (211); Notes Payable (212); Carlos Lezcano, Capital (311); Sales (411); Sales Discounts (412); Sales Returns and Allowances (413); Purchases (511); Purchases Discounts (512); Purchases Returns and Allowances (513); Freight In (514); Sales Salaries Expense (611); Advertising Expense (612); and Rent Expense (613).
3. Open the following accounts receivable subsidiary ledger accounts: Al Kaiser, Midlands School, and Charlotte Soo.
4. Open the following accounts payable subsidiary ledger accounts: Garnett Company, *The Journal-Citizen,* Law Company, and Wiggins Company.
5. Enter the transactions in the journals and post as appropriate.
6. Foot and crossfoot the journals, and make end-of-month postings.
7. Prepare a trial balance of the general ledger and prove the control balances of Accounts Receivable and Accounts Payable by preparing schedules of accounts receivable and accounts payable.

Problem Set B

Problem 6B-1.
Identification of
Transactions
(L.O. 4, 5)

The manual accounting system of Stokes Company contains a general journal, purchases journal, cash receipts journal, and cash payments journal similar to those illustrated in the text.

On May 31, the Sales account in the general ledger appeared as follows:

Sales   **Account No. 411**

Date		Item	Post. Ref.	Debit	Credit	Balance Debit	Balance Credit
May	31		S11		37,421		37,421
	31		CR7		21,207		58,628
	31		J17	58,628			—

On May 31, the L. Gomez account in the accounts receivable subsidiary ledger appeared as shown on the top of the following page:

L. Gomez Account No. 10012

Date		Item	Post. Ref.	Debit	Credit	Balance
May	5		S10	2,108		2,108
	9		J14		282	1,826
	15		CR6		500	1,326

Required

1. Write an explanation of each entry in the Sales account, including the journal from which the entry was posted.
2. Write an explanation of each entry in the L. Gomez account receivable, including the journal from which the entry was posted.

**Problem 6B-2.
Cash Receipts and
Cash Payments
Journals**
(L.O. 4)

Horton Company is a small retail business that uses a manual data processing system similar to the one illustrated in the chapter. Among its special-purpose journals are multicolumn cash receipts and cash payments journals. All cash transactions for Horton Company for the month of June follow:

June 1 Paid June rent to P. Nguyen, $500, with check no. 782.
2 Paid Moritz Wholesale on account, $1,150, less a 2 percent discount, with check no. 783.
3 Received $490 net a 2 percent discount, on account from B. Fischer.
4 Cash sales, $1,315.
7 Paid Jarvis Freight on account, $299, with check no. 784.
8 The owner, Willis Horton, invested an additional $5,000 in cash and a truck valued at $7,000 in the business.
10 Paid Clear Supply on account, $142, with check no. 785.
11 Cash sales, $1,417.
14 Paid Jarvis Freight $155 with check no. 786 for a shipment of merchandise received today.
15 Paid Marks Company on account, $784, net of a 2 percent discount, with check no. 787.
16 Received payment on account from G. Derby, $60.
19 Cash sales, $987.
20 Received payment on a note receivable of $900 plus $18 interest.
21 Purchased office supplies from Clear Supply, $54, with check no. 788.
22 Paid a note payable in full to Midwest Bank, $2,050, including $50 interest, with check no. 789.
26 Cash sales, $1,482.
27 Paid $250 less a 2 percent discount to Moritz Wholesale, with check no. 790.
28 Paid Mary Dillard, a sales clerk, $550 for her monthly salary, with check no. 791.
29 Purchased equipment from Sands Corporation for $8,000, paying $2,000 with check no. 792 and signing a note payable for the difference.
30 Willis Horton withdrew $600 from the business, using check no. 793.

1. Enter the above transactions in the cash receipts and cash payments journals.
2. Foot and rule the journals.

Problem 6B-3.
Purchases and
General Journals
(L.O. 4, 5)

Milner Lawn Supply Company uses a multicolumn purchases journal and general journal similar to those illustrated in the text. The company also maintains an accounts payable subsidiary ledger. The items below represent the company's credit transactions for the month of October.

Oct. 3 Purchased merchandise from Hong Fertilizer Company, $1,320.
4 Purchased office supplies of $83 and store supplies of $104 from Ferrara Supply, Inc.
7 Purchased cleaning equipment from Sinclair Company, $928.
10 Purchased display equipment from Ferrara Supply, Inc. for $2,350.
14 Purchased lawn mowers from Medina Lawn Equipment Company, for resale, $4,200 (including transportation charges of $175).
15 Purchased merchandise from Hong Fertilizer Company, $1,722.
19 Purchased a lawn mower from Medina Lawn Equipment Company to be used in the business, $475 (including transportation charges of $35).
24 Purchased store supplies from Ferrara Supply, Inc. for $27.
25 Returned a defective lawn mower purchased on October 14 for full credit, $375.

Required

1. Enter the above transactions in a multicolumn purchases journal and the general journal. Assume that all terms are n/30 and that invoice dates are the same as the transaction dates.
2. Foot, crossfoot, and rule the purchases journal.
3. Open the following general ledger accounts: Store Supplies (116); Office Supplies (117); Lawn Equipment (142); Display Equipment (144); Cleaning Equipment (146); Accounts Payable (211); Purchases (611); Purchases Returns and Allowances (612); and Freight In (613). Open accounts payable subsidiary ledger accounts as needed. Post from the journals to the ledger accounts.

Problem 6B-4.
Comprehensive
Use of
Special-Purpose
Journals
(L.O. 4, 5)

Capitol Office Supply Company completed the following transactions:

Nov. 1 Issued check no. 2101 to McHenry Rentals, Inc. for November rent, $1,100.
2 Received merchandise from Sutter Company, $3,350, invoice dated Nov. 2, terms 2/10, n/30, FOB shipping point.
3 Received freight bill from Fueutes Transit for previous shipment, $276, terms n/10.
4 Sold merchandise to K. Nham, $800, terms 2/10, n/30, invoice no. 3219.
5 Received a bill from WTVN for radio commercials, $317, terms n/25th of this month.
6 Received a credit memorandum from Sutter Company for merchandise returned, $250.

Nov. 7 Issued check no. 2102 to Boswell Insurance for a two-year fire and casualty policy, $487.

8 Sold merchandise to B. Haas, $840, terms 2/10, n/30, invoice no. 3220.

9 Received merchandise from Sutter Company, $1,850, invoice dated Nov. 7, terms 2/10, n/30, FOB shipping point.

10 Received freight bill from Fueutes Transit for previous shipment, $206, terms n/10.

11 Issued a credit memorandum to B. Haas for merchandise returned, $40.

12 Issued check no. 2103 to Sutter Company for balance owed for the November 2 purchase, less discount.

13 Issued check no. 2104 to Fueutes Transit for balance owed.

14 Received payment in full less discount from K. Nham.

15 Cash sales for first half of month, $10,425. (To shorten these problems, cash sales are recorded only twice a month instead of daily, as they would be in actual practice.)

16 Issued check no. 2105 to Berwyn Gas Co. for monthly heating bill, $119.

17 Issued check no. 2106 to Sutter Company for $1,000 less discount, in partial payment of amount owed.

18 Received payment from B. Haas for one-half amount owed less discount.

19 Sold merchandise to J. Kowolski, $350, terms 2/10, n/30, invoice no. 3221.

20 Received a credit memorandum from WTVN because two scheduled commercials were not played, $62.

21 Sold merchandise to B. Haas, $159, terms 2/10, n/30, invoice no. 3222.

22 Issued check no. 2107 to Central Power Co. for monthly utilities, $283.

23 Sold merchandise to K. Nham, $496, terms 2/10, n/30, invoice no. 3223.

24 Received payment in full, less discount, from J. Kowolski.

25 Issued check no. 2108 to WTVN for balance of account.

26 Received merchandise from Crane, Inc., $2,700, invoice dated Nov. 22, terms 2/10, n/30, FOB shipping point.

27 Issued check no. 2109 to Acme Freight for transportation on previous shipment, $319.

28 Issued check no. 2110 to Sutter Company for balance of amount owed.

29 Issued check no. 2111, payable to Payroll Account for monthly salaries, $4,200.

30 Cash sales for the last half of month, $10,213.

Required

1. Prepare a sales journal, a multicolumn purchases journal, a cash receipts journal, a cash payments journal, and a general journal similar to the ones illustrated in this chapter. Use one as the page number for each journal.

2. Open the following general ledger accounts: Cash (111); Accounts Receivable (112); Prepaid Insurance (113); Accounts Payable (211); Sales (411); Sales Discounts (412); Sales Returns and Allowances (413); Purchases (511); Purchases Discounts (512); Purchases Returns and Allowances

(513); Freight In (514); Salaries Expense (521); Advertising Expense (522); Rent Expense (531); and Utility Expense (532).

3. Open the following accounts receivable subsidiary ledger accounts: B. Haas, J. Kowolski, and K. Nham.

4. Open the following accounts payable subsidiary ledger accounts: Crane, Inc.; Fueutes Transit; Sutter Company; and WTVN.

5. Enter the transactions in the journals and post as appropriate.

6. Foot and crossfoot the journals, and make end-of-month postings.

7. Prepare a trial balance of the general ledger, and prove the control balances of Accounts Receivable and Accounts Payable by preparing schedules of accounts receivable and accounts payable.

Problem 6B-5.
Comprehensive
Use of
Special-Purpose
Journals
(L.O. 4, 5)

Scott Book Store opened its doors for business on September 1. During September the following transactions occurred:

Sept. 1 Cynthia Scott began business by depositing $21,000 in the new company's bank account.

2 Issued check no. C001 to Page Rentals for one month's rent, $500.

3 Received a shipment of books from Gray Books, Inc., $7,840, invoice dated September 2, terms 5/10, n/60, FOB shipping point.

4 Received a bill for freight from All Points Shippers for previous day's shipment, $395, terms n/30.

5 Received a shipment from Choice Books, $5,650, invoice dated September 5, terms 2/10, n/30, FOB shipping point.

6 Issued check no. C002 to Selby Freight, Inc. for transportation charges on previous day's shipment, $287.

8 Issued check no. C003 to Urban Equipment Company for store equipment, $5,200.

9 Sold books to Spectrum Center, $782, terms 5/10, n/30, invoice no. 1001.

10 Returned books to Gray Books, Inc. for credit, $380.

11 Issued check no. C004 to WBNS for radio commercials, $235.

12 Issued check no. C005 to Gray Books, Inc. for balance of amount owed less discount.

13 Cash sales for the first two weeks, $2,009.

15 Issued check no. C006 to Choice Books, $3,000 less discount.

16 Signed a 90-day, 10 percent note for a bank loan and received the $10,000 in cash.

17 Sold books to Joe Prokop, $130, terms n/30, invoice no. 1002.

18 Issued a credit memorandum to Spectrum Center for returned books, $62.

19 Received payment in full for balance owed, less discount, from Spectrum Center.

20 Sold books to Joyce Monsoya, $97, terms n/30, invoice no. 1003.

22 Received a shipment from Temple Publishing Company, $2,302, invoice dated September 21, terms 5/10, n/60.

23 Returned additional books purchased on Sept. 3 to Gray Books, Inc. for credit at gross price, $718.

24 Sold books to Spectrum Center, $817, terms 5/10, n/30, invoice no. 1004.

25 Received a shipment from Gray Books, Inc., $1,187, invoice dated September 22, terms 5/10, n/60, FOB shipping point.

Sept. 26   Issued check no. C007 to All Points Shippers for balance owed on account plus shipping charges of S97 on previous day's shipment.
27   Cash sales for the second two weeks, $3,744.
29   Issued check no. C008 to Payroll Account for sales salaries for first four weeks of the month, $700.
30   Cash sales for the last two days of the month, $277.

Required

1. Prepare a sales journal, a multicolumn purchases journal, a cash receipts journal, a cash payments journal, and a general journal.
2. Open the following general ledger accounts: Cash (111); Accounts Receivable (112); Store Equipment (141); Accounts Payable (211); Notes Payable (212); Cynthia Scott, Capital (311); Sales (411); Sales Discounts (412); Sales Returns and Allowances (413); Purchases (511); Purchases Discounts (512); Purchases Returns and Allowances (513); Freight In (514); Sales Salaries Expense (611); Advertising Expense (612); and Rent Expense (613).
3. Open the following accounts receivable subsidiary ledger accounts: Joyce Monsoya, Joe Prokop, and Spectrum Center.
4. Open the following accounts payable subsidiary ledger accounts: All Points Shippers; Choice Books; Gray Books, Inc.; and Temple Publishing Company.
5. Enter the transactions in the journals and post as appropriate.
6. Foot and crossfoot the journals, and make end-of-month postings.
7. Prepare a trial balance of the general ledger, and prove the control balances of Accounts Receivable and Accounts Payable by preparing schedules of accounts receivable and accounts payable.

Financial Decision Case

Buy-Rite Foods Company
(L.O. 3, 4, 5)

Buy-Rite Foods Company, owned by Taylor Haskins, is a local grocery store that accepts cash or checks in payment for food. Known for its informality, the store has been very successful and has grown with the community. Along with the growth, however, has come an increase in the number of bad checks that are written for purchases by customers. Because Taylor is concerned about the difficulty of accounting for these returned checks, he asks you to look into the problem.

In addition to a purchases journal and a cash payments journal, the company has a combination one-column sales and cash receipts journal. This combination journal has been acceptable in the past because all sales are for cash (including checks) and almost all cash receipts represent sales transactions. Thus the one column represents a debit to Cash and a credit to Sales.

The bad checks are recorded individually in the general journal by debiting Accounts Receivable and crediting Cash. When a customer pays off a bad check, another entry is made in the general journal debiting Cash and crediting Accounts Receivable. Taylor keeps the returned checks in an envelope, and when a customer comes in to pay one off, he gives the check back. No other records of the returned checks are maintained.

In studying the problem, you discover that the company is averaging ten returned checks per day totaling $500. As part of the solution, you recommend to Taylor that he establish a policy of issuing check-cashing cards to customers whose credit is approved in advance. The card must be presented when a customer offers a check in payment for groceries. You recommend further that a special journal be established for the returned checks, that a subsidiary ledger be maintained, and that the combination sales/cash receipts journal be expanded.

Required

1. Draw and label the columns for the new returned checks journal and the expanded sales/cash receipts journal. Assume that there are 300 returned checks and 280 collections per month and that the records are closed each month. How many written lines will be saved each month in recording returned checks and subsequent collections in the special journals? How many postings will be saved each month? (Ignore the effect of the subsidiary ledger.)
2. Describe the nature and use of the subsidiary ledger. What advantages do you see in having this subsidiary ledger?
3. Assuming that it takes approximately two and one-half minutes to make each entry and related postings under the old system and one minute to make each entry and related postings under the new system, what are the monthly savings if the cost is $10 an hour? What further, and possibly more significant, savings may be realized by using the suggested system?

Answers to Self-Test

| 1. a | 3. d | 5. b | 7. d | 9. c |
| 2. a | 4. b | 6. b | 8. a | 10. c |

Comprehensive Problem: Fenwick Fashions Company

Fenwick Fashions Company was introduced in Chapter 5. This chapter continues the Fenwick Fashions example by completing the accounting cycle for the month of January, 19x2, using special-purpose journals.

The chart of accounts and December 31, 19x1, post-closing trial balance for Fenwick Fashions Company appears as follows:

Account Name	Account Number	Debit	Credit
Cash	111	$ 29,410	
Accounts Receivable	112	42,400	
Merchandise Inventory	113	48,300	
Prepaid Insurance	114	11,600	
Store Supplies	115	1,060	
Office Supplies	116	636	
Land	141	4,500	
Building	142	20,260	
Accumulated Depreciation. Building	143		$ 8,250
Office Equipment	144	8,600	
Accumulated Depreciation. Office Equipment	145		5,000
Accounts Payable	211		25,683
Joseph Fenwick, Capital	311		127,833
Joseph Fenwick, Withdrawals	312		
Income Summary	314		
Sales	411		
Sales Returns and Allowances	412		
Sales Discounts	413		
Purchases	511		
Purchases Returns and Allowances	512		
Purchases Discounts	513		
Freight In	514		
Sales Salaries Expense	611		
Freight Out Expense	612		
Advertising Expense	613		
Insurance Expense, Selling	614		
Store Supplies Expense	621		
Office Salaries Expense	622		
Insurance Expense, General	623		
Office Supplies Expense	624		
Telephone Expense	625		
Utility Expense	626		
Depreciation Expense, Building	627		
Depreciation Expense, Office Equipment	628		
Totals		$166,766	$166,766

The Company's account receivable and accounts payable subsidiary ledgers had the following accounts and amounts on December 31, 19x1:

Schedule of Accounts Receivable

Carolyn Harrington	$ 2,300
Sara Kradich	1,800
Henry Montin	—
Turnstyle Apparel Centers	38,300
Total Accounts Receivable	$42,400

Schedule of Accounts Payable

Daily Herald	—
Drake Freight	$ 350
Jason Styles	4,500
Jones Supply House	—
Modern Fashions	8,900
Thompson Shoes	11,933
Total Accounts Payable	$25,683

During the month of January, 19x2, Fenwick Fashions engaged in the following transactions:

Jan. 2 Sold merchandise to Sara Kradich on credit, terms 2/10, net/30, F.O.B. destination, invoice no. 2330, $1,200.

2 Received bill for shipping costs on above merchandise from Drake Freight, dated today, terms, n/30, $70.

4 Received payment on account from Turnstyle Apparel Centers, no discount allowed, $10,000.

5 Accepted defective merchandise back from Carolyn Harrington and gave full credit on account, $1,100.

6 Paid amount owed to Jason Styles, less 2 percent discount for payment within 10 days, check no. 1441.

8 Returned merchandise to Thompson Shoes for full credit, $753.

9 Received payment on account in full from Sara Kradich, less 2 percent discount allowed, for sale in December.

10 Received a shipment of merchandise from Modern Fashions, invoice dated January 8, terms 2/10, n/30, F.O.B. shipping point, $1,900.

10 Received bill for shipping costs on above merchandise from Drake Freight, dated today, terms, n/30, $180.

11 Paid Drake Freight for amount owed at the beginning of the month, check no. 1442, $350.

12 Received payment in full for sale of January 2, to Sara Kradich, less 2 percent discount.

13 Made partial payment on account to Thompson Shoes, no discount allowed, check no. 1443, $6,000.

15 Sold merchandise to Turnstyle Apparel Centers on account, terms n/30, F.O.B. shipping point, invoice no. 2331, $5,000.

16 Cash sales for the first half of January were $8,320.

Jan. 16 Paid salaries for the first half of January by making a check payable to Payroll Account for the total payroll, check no. 1444, $2,000. Salaries are allocated $1,100 to sales salaries; and $900 to office salaries.

17 Paid in full Modern Fashions amount owed on account at December 31 (no discount allowed) and for purchase received January 10, dated January 8, less discount, check no. 1445.

19 Sold merchandise to Henry Montin on credit, terms 2/10, n/30, F.O.B. destination, invoice no. 2332, $900.

19 Received bill for shipping costs on above merchandise from Drake Freight, dated today, terms, n/30, $50.

20 Received bill from Daily Herald for advertisements, dated January 15, terms n/30, $850.

21 Received a shipment of supplies from Jones Supply House, dated January 18, terms, n/30, F.O.B. destination, $360. The supplies are allocated $200 to store supplies and $160 to office supplies.

22 Paid MidBell for January telephone bill, check no. 1446, $120.

23 Received a shipment of merchandise from Jason Styles, invoice dated January 22, terms 2/10, n/30, F.O.B. shipping point, $3,500.

23 Received bill for shipping costs on above merchandise from Drake Freight, dated today, terms, n/30, $220.

25 Sold merchandise to Sara Kradich on credit, terms 2/10, n/30, F.O.B. destination, invoice no. 2333, $1,400.

25 Received bill for shipping costs on above merchandise from Drake Freight, dated today, terms, n/30, $90.

26 Made a check payable to Joseph Fenwick for his monthly withdrawal, check no. 1447, $1,900.

27 Paid Common Utility for January utilities, check no. 1448, $330.

28 Received payment from Henry Montin for one-half of the sale on January 19, less discount.

31 Paid salaries for the last half of January by making a check payable to Payroll Account for the total payroll, check no. 1449, $2,000. Salaries are allocated $1,100 to sales salaries; and $900 to office salaries.

31 Cash sales for the last half of January were $7,350.

Fenwick Fashions Company uses a single column sales journal, a multi-column purchases journal, a cash receipts journal, a cash payments journal, and a general journal. It also has subsidiary ledgers for accounts receivable and accounts payable. General ledger accounts are maintained for each account in the trial balance. Assume all journals begin January on page 13, except for the general journal, which is page 20.

Required

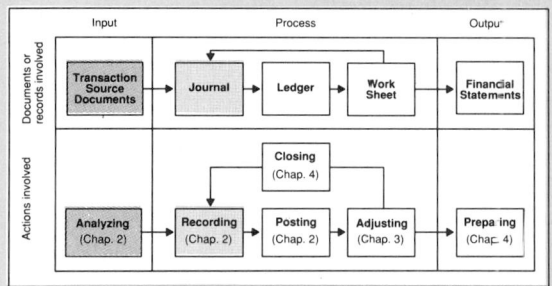

1. Record the above transactions in the journals and make individual postings as appropriate.

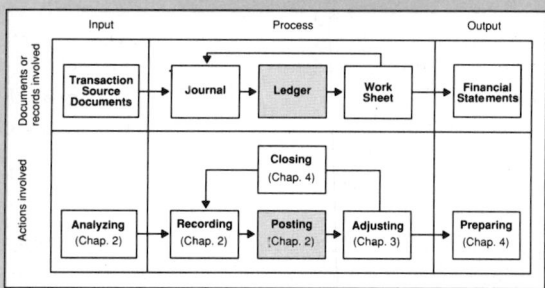

2. Foot and crossfoot the journals and make end-of-month postings.

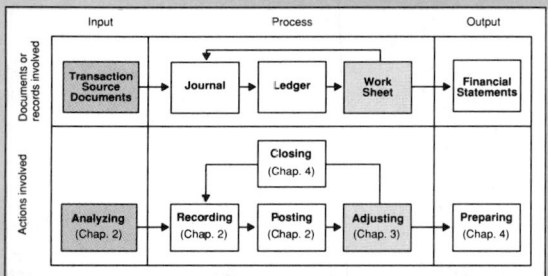

3. Prepare a trial balance in the Trial Balance columns of a work sheet, and complete the work sheet using the following information:
   a. Ending merchandise inventory, $41,900.
   b. Expired insurance (allocated 30 percent to selling and 70 percent to general), $900.
   c. Ending store supplies inventory, $620.
   d. Ending office supplies inventory, $310.
   e. Estimated depreciation on building, $220.
   f. Estimated depreciation on office equipment, $200.

   In preparing the work sheet, use either the adjusting entry or the closing entry method.

4. From the work sheet, prepare an income statement, statement of owner's equity, and a balance sheet.

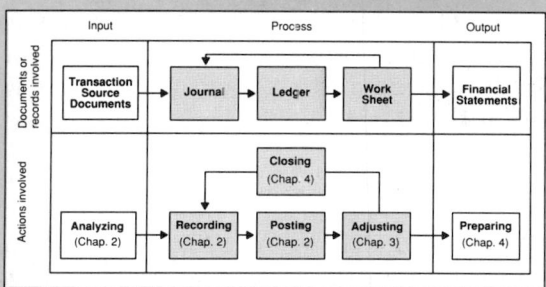

5. Prepare a schedule of accounts receivable and a schedule of accounts payable to prove the balances of the controlling accounts.
6. From the work sheet, record and post adjusting entries.
7. From the work sheet, record and post closing entries.
8. Prepare a post-closing trial balance.

This Comprehensive Problem covers all of the Learning Objectives in Chapter 5 and Learning Objectives 3 through 5 in Chapter 6.

LEARNING OBJECTIVES

1. Define internal control and identify the three elements of the internal control structure, including seven examples of control procedures.
2. Describe the inherent limitations of internal control.
3. Apply control procedures to certain merchandising transactions.
4. Describe a bank account and demonstrate control of cash by preparing a bank reconciliation.
5. Describe and record the related entries for a simple petty cash system.
6. Define a voucher system, and describe its components.
7. State and perform the five steps in operating a voucher system.

CHAPTER 7

Internal Control and Merchandising Transactions

One of the four principles of systems design identified in Chapter 6 was the concept of control. Effective control is maintained in an accounting system through a network of checks and procedures known as the internal control structure, or simply, internal control. This chapter is an introduction to the concept of internal control and its application to certain merchandising transactions, including banking transactions and voucher system transactions. After studying this chapter, you should be able to meet the learning objectives listed on the left.

This chapter has five main parts. The first part presents the general principles and characteristics of internal control. In the second part, these principles are applied to certain merchandising transactions. The third and fourth parts explain the role of banking transactions and petty cash procedures in the control of cash. The fifth part describes the voucher system, a common means of controlling purchases and cash disbursements.

All of the control techniques used in this chapter are also applicable to other types of businesses, such as service organizations and manufacturers. The application of these control techniques to merchandising transactions is simply a convenient introduction.

Internal Control Structure: Basic Elements and Procedures

Accounting for merchandising companies, as you have seen, focuses on buying and selling. These transactions involve asset accounts—Cash, Accounts Receivable, and Merchandise Inventory—that are vulnerable to theft or embezzlement. There are two reasons for this vulnerability. One is that cash and inventory are fairly easy to steal. The other is that these assets involve a large number of transactions—cash sales, receipts on account, payments for purchases, receipts and shipments of inventory, and so on. A merchandising company can have high losses of cash and inventory if it does not take steps to protect the assets.

The best way to do so is to set up and maintain a good internal control structure.

Internal Control Defined

OBJECTIVE 1
Define internal control and identify the three elements of the internal control structure, including seven examples of control procedures

Internal control has traditionally been defined as all the policies and procedures by which management protects the assets and assures the accuracy and reliability of the accounting records. It includes controls that deal with operating efficiency and adherence to management policies. In other words, management wants not only to safeguard assets and have reliable records, but also to maintain an efficient operation that follows its policies. To achieve this, management should establish an **internal control structure** consisting of three elements: the control environment, the accounting system, and the control procedures.[1]

The **control environment** reflects the overall attitude, awareness, and actions of the owners and management of the business. It includes such things as management's philosophy and operating style, the company's organizational structure, methods of assigning authority and responsibility, and personnel policies and practices. Personnel should be qualified to handle responsibilities, which means that employees must be trained and informed. For example, the manager of a retail store should train employees to follow prescribed procedures for handling cash sales, credit card sales, and returns and refunds. It is clear that an accounting system, no matter how well designed, is only as good as the people who run it. The control environment also includes regular reviews for compliance with procedures. For example, large companies often have a staff of internal auditors who review the company's system of internal control to see that it is working properly and that procedures are being followed. In smaller businesses, the owners and managers should conduct such reviews.

The **accounting system** consists of methods and records established by management to identify, assemble, analyze, classify, and report a company's transactions, and to provide assurance that the objectives of internal control are achieved. Many **control procedures** are in management's toolbox to ensure the safeguarding of the company's assets and the reliability of the accounting records. Examples of these control procedures are presented below:

1. **Authorization** All transactions and activities should be properly authorized by management. In a retail store, for example, some transactions, such as normal cash sales, are routinely authorized, but others, such as issuing a refund, may require the manager's approval.
2. **Recording of transactions** All transactions should be recorded to facilitate preparation of financial statements and to establish accountability for assets. In a retail store, for example, the cash register records sales, refunds, and other transactions internally on a paper tape or computer disk so that the cashier may be held responsible for the cash that has been received, as well as merchandise that has been removed, during his or her shift.

1. *Professional Standards* (New York: American Institute of Certified Public Accountants, June 1, 1989), Vol. 1, Sec. AU 319.06–.11.

3. **Documents and records** Design and use of adequate documents help ensure the proper recording of transactions. For example, to ensure that all transactions are recorded, invoices should be prenumbered and all numbers accounted for.
4. **Limited access** Access to assets should be permitted only in accordance with management's authorization. For example, retail stores should use cash registers and only the cashier responsible for the cash in the register should have access to it. Other employees should not be able to open the cash drawer if the cashier is not present. Likewise, warehouses and storerooms should be accessible only to authorized personnel. Access to accounting records, including company computers, should also be controlled.
5. **Periodic independent verification** The records should be checked against the assets by someone other than the person responsible for the records and the assets. For example, at the end of each shift or day, the owner or store manager should count the cash in the cash drawer and compare the amount to the amounts recorded in the cash register on the tape or computer disk. Other examples of independent verification are the monthly bank reconciliation (described later in this chapter) and periodic counts of physical inventory.
6. **Separation of duties** Separation of duties means that the plan of organization should describe proper separation of functional responsibilities. Authorizing transactions, operating a department, handling assets, and keeping the records of assets for the department should not be the responsibility of one person. For example, in an appliance or stereo store, each employee will oversee only a single part of a transaction. A sales employee will take the order and write out an invoice. Another employee will receive the customer's money or credit card. Once the customer has a paid receipt, and only then, a third employee will obtain the item from the warehouse and give it to the customer. A person in the accounting department will subsequently record the sales from the tape in the cash register, comparing them to the sales invoices and updating the inventory in the records. In other words, separation of duties should mean that a mistake, honest or not, cannot be made without having been seen by at least one other person.
7. **Sound personnel procedures** Sound practices should be followed in managing the people who carry out the duties and functions of each department. Among these practices are good supervision, rotation of key people among different jobs, insistence that employees take vacations, and bonding of personnel who handle cash or inventories. **Bonding** means carefully checking on an employee's background and insuring the company against any theft by that person. Bonding will not prevent theft, but it will prevent or reduce economic loss if theft occurs.

Limitations of Internal Control

No system of internal control is without certain weaknesses. As long as people must carry out control procedures, the internal control system is open to human error. Errors may arise because of misunderstanding instructions, mistakes in judgment, carelessness, distraction, or fatigue. The separation of duties can be defeated through collusion—that is, when employees secretly agree to deceive the company. Also, procedures designed by management may be ineffective against employee errors or dishonesty. Or, controls that may have been effective at first may become ineffective because of changing conditions.[2] In some cases, the costs of establishing and maintaining elaborate systems may exceed the benefits. In a small business, for example, active involvement by the owner may be a practical substitute for certain separation of duties.

Internal Control Over Merchandising Transactions

Sound internal control procedures are needed in all aspects of a business, but particularly when assets are involved. Assets are especially vulnerable when they enter or leave the business. When sales are made, for example, cash or other assets enter the business, and goods or services leave the business. Procedures must be set up to prevent theft during these transactions. Likewise, purchases of assets and payments of liabilities must be controlled. The majority of these transactions can be safeguarded by adequate purchasing and payroll systems. In addition, assets on hand such as cash, investments, inventory, plant, and equipment must be protected.

In this and the following sections, internal control procedures will be applied to such merchandising transactions as sales, cash receipts, purchases, and cash payments. Internal control for other kinds of transactions will be covered later in the book. As mentioned previously, similar procedures are applicable to service and manufacturing businesses.

When a system of internal control is applied effectively to merchandising transactions, it can achieve important goals for accounting as well as for general management. Examples of two goals for accounting follow:

1. To prevent losses of cash or inventory from theft or fraud
2. To provide accurate records of merchandising transactions and account balances

Examples of broader management goals are as follows:

1. To keep just enough inventory on hand to sell to customers without overstocking
2. To keep enough cash on hand to pay for purchases in time to receive purchases discounts
3. To keep credit losses as low as possible by restricting credit sales to those customers who are likely to pay on time

One control to meet broad management goals is the cash budget, which projects future cash receipts and disbursements. By maintaining

2. Ibid., Sec. AU 320.35.

adequate cash balances, the company is able to take advantage of discounts on purchases, prepare for borrowing money when necessary, and avoid the damaging effects of not being able to pay bills when they are due. On the other hand, if the company has excess cash at a particular time, it can be invested, earning interest until needed.

A more specific accounting control is the separation of duties involving the control of cash. This separation means that theft without detection is impossible except through the collusion of two or more employees. The subdivision of duties is easier in large businesses than in small ones, where one person may have to carry out several duties. The effectiveness of internal control over cash will vary depending on the size and nature of the company. Most firms, however, should use the following procedures:

1. The functions of authorization, recordkeeping, and the custodianship of cash should be kept separate.
2. The number of persons who have access to cash should be limited.
3. Persons who are to have responsibility for handling cash should be specifically designated.
4. Banking facilities should be used as much as possible, and the amount of cash on hand should be kept to a minimum.
5. All employees having access to cash should be bonded.
6. Cash on hand should be protected physically by the use of such devices as cash registers, cashiers' cages, and safes.
7. Surprise audits of cash on hand should be made by a person who does not handle or record cash.
8. All cash receipts should be recorded promptly.
9. All cash receipts should be deposited promptly.
10. All cash payments should be made by check.
11. The cash account should be reconciled monthly by a person who does not authorize, handle, or record cash.

Note that each of the above procedures helps to safeguard cash by making it more difficult for any one person to have access to cash and to steal or misuse it undetected. These procedures may be specifically related to the control of cash receipts and cash disbursements.

Control of Cash Sales Receipts

Cash receipts for sales of goods and services may be received by mail or over the counter in the form of checks or currency. Whatever the source, cash should be recorded immediately upon receipt. This is generally done by making an entry in a cash receipts journal. As shown in the last chapter, this step establishes a written record of the receipt of cash and should prevent errors and make theft more difficult.

Control of Cash Received Through the Mail. Cash receipts received through the mail are vulnerable to being stolen by employees who receive them. This way of doing business is increasing, however, due to the expansion of mail order sales. To control these receipts, customers should always be urged to pay in the form of checks instead of currency.

Second, cash that comes in through the mail should be handled by two or more employees. The employee who opens the mail should make a list in triplicate of the money received. This list should contain each payer's name, the purpose for which the money was sent, and the amount. One copy goes with the cash to the cashier, who deposits the money. The second copy goes to the accounting department to be recorded in the cash receipts journal. The person who opens the mail keeps the third copy of the list. Errors can be caught easily because the amount deposited by the cashier must agree with the amount received and the amount recorded in the cash receipts journal.

Control of Cash Sales Received Over the Counter. Two common means of controlling cash sales are through the use of cash registers and prenumbered sales tickets. Amounts from cash sales should be rung up on a cash register at the time of each sale. The cash register should be placed so that the customer can see the amount recorded. Each cash register should have a locked-in tape on which it prints the day's transactions. At the end of the day, the cashier counts the cash in the cash register and turns it in to the cashier's office. Another employee takes the tape out of the cash register and records the cash receipts for the day in the cash receipts journal. The amount of cash turned in and the amount recorded on the tape should be in agreement; if not, any differences must be accounted for. Large retail chains commonly perform this function by having each cash register tied directly into a computer. In this way each transaction is recorded as it occurs. The separation of duties involving cash receipts, cash deposits, and record-keeping is thus achieved, ensuring good internal control.

In some stores, internal control is strengthened further by the use of prenumbered sales tickets and a central cash register or cashier's office, where all sales are rung up and collected by a person who does not participate in the sale. Under this procedure, the salesperson completes a prenumbered sales ticket at the time of sale, giving one copy to the customer and keeping a copy. At the end of the day, all sales tickets must be accounted for, and the sales total computed from the sales tickets should equal the total sales recorded on the cash register.

Cash Short or Over. When there are numerous transactions involving cash receipts, small mistakes are bound to occur. For example, cash registers in grocery and retail stores will often have a cash shortage or overage at the end of the day. When the shortages are consistent or large for a particular cash register, they should, of course, be investigated. If at the end of a day a cash register shows recorded cash sales of $675 but contains only $670 in cash, the following entry would record the sales:

Cash	670	
Cash Short or Over	5	
Sales		675
To record cash sales; a cash shortage		
of $5 was discovered		

The **Cash Short or Over** account is debited for shortages and credited for overages. The use of a separate account to record cash short or over calls management's attention to irregular activity. If at the end of an accounting period a debit balance appears in Cash Short or Over, it would be reported as a general operating expense on the income statement. A credit balance would be reported as other revenue.

Control of Purchases and Cash Disbursements

Cash disbursements are very vulnerable to fraud and embezzlement. In a recent and notable case, the treasurer of one of the nation's largest jewelry retailers was charged with having stolen over one-half million dollars by systematically overpaying federal income taxes and pocketing the refund checks as they came back to the company.

To avoid this kind of theft, cash should be paid only on the basis of specific authorization that is supported by documents establishing the validity and amount of the claim. In addition, maximum possible use should be made of the principle of separation of duties in the purchase of goods and services and the payments for them. The amount of separation of duties will vary depending on the size of the business. Figure 7-1 shows how this kind of control can be achieved in companies large

Figure 7-1. Internal Control for Purchasing and Paying for Goods and Services

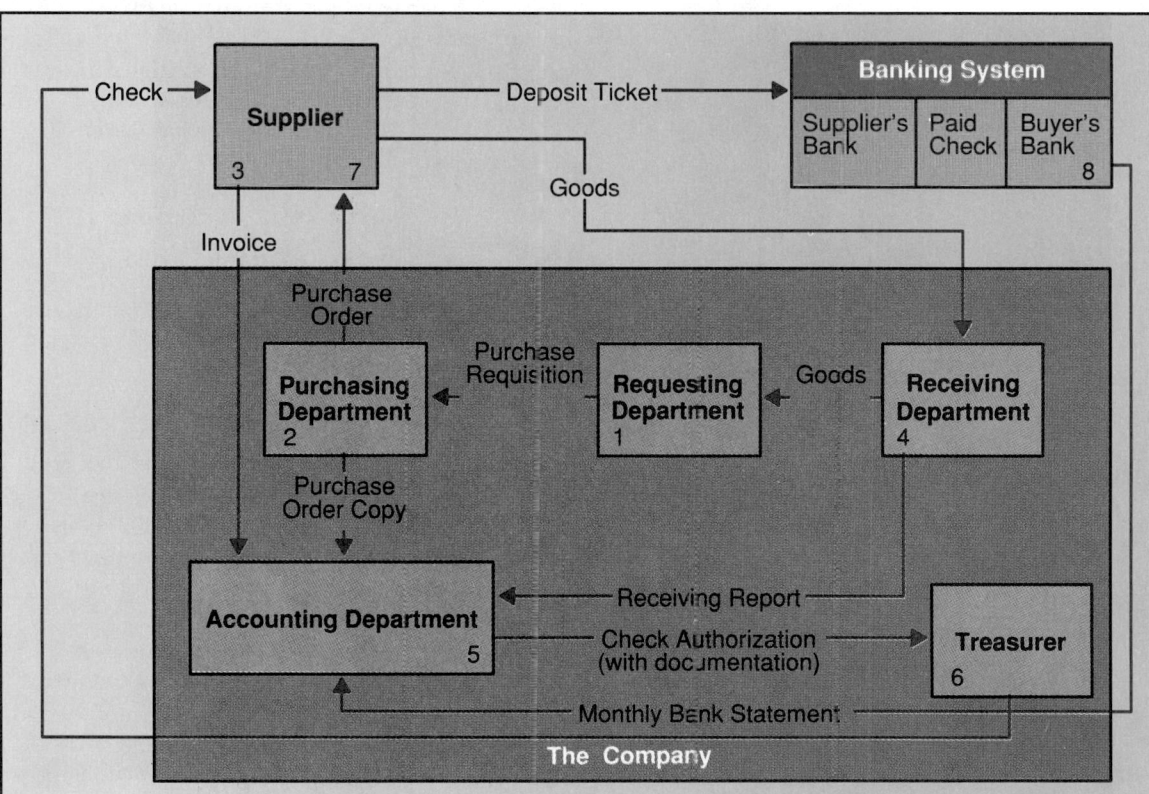

enough for maximum separation of duties. In this example, five internal units (the requesting department, the purchasing department, the accounting department, the receiving department, and the treasurer) and two external contacts (the supplier and the banking system) all play a role in the internal control plan. Note that business documents also play an important role in the plan. The plan is summarized in Table 7-1. Under this plan, every action is documented and subject to verification by at least one other person. For instance, the requesting department cannot work out a kickback scheme with the supplier because the receiving department independently records receipts and the accounting

Table 7-1. Internal Control Plan for Cash Disbursements

Business Document	Prepared by	Sent to	Verifications and Related Procedures
1. Purchase requisition	Requesting department	Purchasing department	Purchasing verifies authorization.
2. Purchase order	Purchasing department	Supplier	Supplier sends goods or services in accordance with purchase order.
3. Invoice	Supplier	Accounting department	Accounting receives invoice from supplier.
4. Receiving report	Receiving department	Accounting department	Accounting compares invoice, purchase order, and receiving report. Accounting verifies prices.
5. Check authorization (or voucher)	Accounting department	Treasurer	Accounting attaches check authorization to invoice, purchase order, and receiving report.
6. Check	Treasurer	Supplier	Treasurer verifies all documents before preparing check.
7. Deposit ticket	Supplier	Supplier's bank	Supplier compares check with invoice. Bank deducts check from buyer's account.
8. Bank statement	Buyer's bank	Accounting department	Accounting compares amount and payee's name on returned check with check authorization.

department verifies prices. The receiving department cannot steal goods because the receiving report must equal the invoices. For the same reason, the supplier cannot bill for more goods than were shipped. The accounting department's work is verified by the treasurer, and the treasurer is ultimately checked by the accounting department.

Figures 7-2 through 7-6, which show typical documents used in this plan, serve as an example of purchasing twenty boxes of typewriter ribbons. In Figure 7-2 the credit office of Martin Maintenance Company fills out a **purchase requisition** for twenty boxes of typewriter ribbons. The department head approves it and forwards it to the purchasing department. The people in the purchasing department prepare a **purchase order**, as illustrated in Figure 7-3. The purchase order is addressed to the vendor (seller) and contains a description of the items ordered; their expected price, terms, and shipping date; and other shipping instructions. Martin Maintenance Company will not pay any bill that is not accompanied by a purchase order number.

After receiving the purchase order, the vendor, Henderson Supply Company, ships the goods (in this case delivers them) and sends an **invoice**, or bill (Figure 7-4, page 289) to Martin Maintenance Company. The invoice gives the quantity and a description of the goods delivered and the terms of payment. If all goods cannot be shipped immediately, the estimated date for shipment of the remainder is indicated.

When the goods reach the receiving department of Martin Maintenance Company, an employee of this department writes the description,

Figure 7-2. Purchase Requisition

PURCHASE REQUISITION		No. 7077
Martin Maintenance Company		

From: Credit Office	Date September 6, 19xx	
To: Purchasing Department	Suggested Vendor: Henderson Supply	
Please purchase the following items:	Company	

Quantity	Number	Description
20 boxes	X 144	Typewriter ribbons

Reason for Request	To be filled in by Purchasing Department
Six months' supply for office	Date ordered 9/8/xx P.O. No. J 102
Approved B.M.	

Figure 7-3. Purchase Order

PURCHASE ORDER				No.	J 102	

Martin Maintenance Company
8428 Rocky Island Avenue
Chicago, Illinois 60643

To: Henderson Supply Company   Date   September 8, 19xx
    2525 25th Street
    Mesa, Illinois 61611   FOB   Destination

    Ship by September 12, 19xx

Ship to: Martin Maintenance Company   Terms   2/10, n/30
    Above Address

Please ship the following:

Quantity	✓	Number	Description	Price	Per	Amount
20 boxes		X 144	Typewriter ribbons	12.00	box	$240.00

Purchase order number must appear on all shipments and invoices.	Ordered by *Marsha Owen*

quantity, and condition of the goods on the **receiving report**. The receiving department does not receive a copy of the purchase order or invoice, so the people in it do not know what is to be received. Thus they are not tempted to steal any excess that may have been delivered.

The receiving report is sent to the accounting department, where it is compared with the purchase order and the invoice. If all is correct, the accounting department completes a **check authorization** and attaches it to the three supporting documents. The check authorization form shown in Figure 7-5 has a space for each item to be checked off as it is examined. Note that the accounting department has all the documentary evidence for the transaction but does not have access to the assets purchased. Nor does it write the checks for payment. For this reason, the people performing the accounting function cannot gain by falsifying documents in an effort to conceal fraud.

Finally, the treasurer again examines all the evidence and issues a **check** (Figure 7-6, page 290) for the amount of the invoice less any appropriate discount. In some systems, the accounting department fills out the check so that all the treasurer has to do is inspect and sign it. The check is then sent to the supplier, with remittance advice, which shows what the check is paying. A supplier who is not paid the proper amount will complain, of course, thus providing a form of outside control over the payment. The supplier will deposit the check in the bank, which will

Figure 7-4. Invoice

| | INVOICE | | No. _0468_ |

Henderson Supply Company
2525 25th Street
Mesa, Illinois 61611

Date ___September 12, '19xx___

Your Order No. ___J 102___

Sold to:

Ship to:

Martin Maintenance Company
8428 Rocky Island Avenue
Chicago, Illinois 60543

Same

Sales Representative: Joe Jacobs

Quantity					
Ordered	Shipped	Description	Price	Per	Amount
20	20	X 144 Typewriter ribbons	12.00	box	$240.00

| FOB Delivered | Terms: 2/10, n/30 | Date Shipped: 9/12/xx Via: Self |

Figure 7-5. Check Authorization

CHECK AUTHORIZATION

	NO.	CHECK
Requisition	7077	✓
Purchase Order	J 102	✓
Receiving Report	JR 065	✓
INVOICE	0468	
Price		✓
Calculations		✓
Terms		✓
Approved for Payment	*F Joseph*	

return the canceled check with Martin Maintenance Company's next bank statement. If the treasurer has made the check for an incorrect amount (or altered a prefilled-in check), it will show up at this point.

There are many variations of the system just described. This example is offered as a simple system that provides adequate internal control.

Figure 7-6. Check with Attached Remittance Advice

			NO. 1787
PAY TO THE ORDER OF	Henderson Supply Company	9/21 19 xx	$ 235.20

Two hundred thirty-five and 20/100------------------- Dollars

THE LAKE PARK NATIONAL BANK
    Chicago, Illinois

Martin Maintenance Company

⑆0313015321⑆ ⑈8030 647 4⑈ by *Arthur Martin*

Remittance Advice

Date	P.O. No.	DESCRIPTION	AMOUNT
9/21/xx	J 102	20 boxes typewriter ribbons Supplied Inv. No. 0468 Less 2% discount Net Martin Maintenance Company	$240.00 4.80 $235.20

Banking Transactions

Banking facilities are also an important aid to businesses in controlling both cash receipts and cash disbursements. Banks are safe depositories of cash, negotiable instruments, and other valuable business documents such as stocks and bonds. The use of bank checks for disbursements improves a company's control by minimizing the amount of currency on hand and by providing a permanent record of all cash payments. Furthermore, banks can serve as agents for a company in a variety of important transactions such as the collection and payment of certain kinds of debts and the exchange of foreign currencies.

Bank Account

OBJECTIVE 4
Describe a bank account and demonstrate control of cash by preparing a bank reconciliation

A bank account is an account a business opens with a bank, into which cash is deposited for safekeeping and from which cash is withdrawn by writing checks. The procedure for establishing a bank account varies. In some small towns where the bank personnel are familiar with local activities, it may be very easy to open an account. In other cases, particularly in large metropolitan areas, the bank may require financial information and references.

The evidence used for the bank account is a **signature card**. When a business opens an account, this card must be signed by the depositor in exactly the same way that he or she expects to sign the checks. This signature card is required so that a bank teller can authenticate the signature on checks. When a business opens an account, the owners must sign an authorization giving a particular official or officials the right to sign checks. The bank receives a copy of the authorization.

Deposits

When making a deposit, the depositor fills out a **deposit ticket** (usually in duplicate), as illustrated in Figure 7-7. Space is provided for listing each check and the amounts of coin and currency deposited.

Bank Statement

Once a month the bank sends a statement to each depositor and returns the canceled checks that it has paid and charged to the depositor's account. The returned checks are said to be "canceled" because the bank stamps, or cancels, them to show that they have been paid. The **bank statement** shows the balance at the beginning of the month, the deposits, the checks paid, other debits and credits during the month, and the

Figure 7-7. Deposit Ticket

DEPOSIT TICKET
THE LAKE PARK NATIONAL BANK
Chicago, Illinois

Date 10/6/xx

Name   Martin Maintenance Company
Address 8428 Rocky Island Avenue
         Chicago, Illinois

CASH	CURRENCY	22	00
	COIN	2	50
	CHECKS – LIST SINGLY		
	G. Mason	30	00
	R Enterprises	39	00
	Preston Company	206	50
TOTAL		300	00
Less Cash Received			—
NET DEPOSIT		300	00

balance at the end of the month. A bank statement is illustrated in
Figure 7-8.

Preparing a Bank Reconciliation

Rarely will the balance of a company's Cash account exactly equal the
cash balance as shown on the bank statement. Certain transactions
shown in the company's records may not be recorded by the bank, and
certain bank transactions may not appear in the company's records.
Therefore, a necessary step in internal control is to prove both the bal-

Figure 7-8. Bank Statement

Statement of Account with
THE LAKE PARK NATIONAL BANK
Chicago, Illinois

Martin Maintenance Company
8428 Rocky Island Avenue
Chicago, Illinois 60643

Checking Acct No
8030-647-4
Period covered
Sept.30-Oct.31,19xx

Previous Balance	Checks/Debits—No.	Deposits/Credits—No.	S.C.	Current Balance
$2,645.78	$4,319.33 --15	$5,157.12 --7	$12.50	$3,471.07

CHECKS/DEBITS			DEPOSITS/CREDITS		DAILY BALANCES	
Posting Date	Check No.	Amount	Posting Date	Amount	Date	Amount
					09/30	2,645.78
10/01	564	100.00	10/01	586.00	10/01	2,881.78
10/01	565	250.00	10/05	1,500.00	10/04	2,825.60
10/04	567	56.18	10/06	300.00	10/05	3,900.46
10/05	566	425.14	10/16	1,845.50	10/06	4,183.34
10/06	568	17.12	10/21	600.00	10/12	2,242.34
10/12	569	1,705.80	10/24	300.00CM	10/16	3,687.84
10/12	570	235.20	10/31	25.62IN	10/17	3,589.09
10/16	571	400.00			10/21	4,189.09
10/17	572	29.75			10/24	3,745.59
10/17	573	69.00			10/25	3,586.09
10/24	574	738.50			10/28	3,457.95
10/24		5.00DM			10/31	3,471.07
10/25	575	7.50				
10/25	577	152.00				
10/28		128.14NSF				
10/31		12.50SC				

Explanation of Symbols:

CM – Credit Memo   SC – Service Charge   The last amount
DM – Debit Memo   EC – Error Correction   in this column
NSF – Non-Sufficient Funds   OD – Overdraft   is your balance.
                          IN – Interest on Average Balance

Please examine; if no errors are reported within ten (10) days, the account will be
considered to be correct.

ance of the bank and the balance of Cash in the accounting records. A **bank reconciliation** is the process of accounting for the differences between the balance appearing on the bank statement and the balance of Cash according to the company's records. This process involves making additions to and subtractions from both balances to arrive at the adjusted cash balance.

The most common examples of transactions shown in the company's records but not entered in the bank's records are the following:

1. **Outstanding checks** These are checks issued and recorded by the company, but do not yet appear on the bank statement.
2. **Deposits in transit** These are deposits mailed or taken to the bank but not received in time to be recorded on the statement.

Transactions that may appear on the bank statement but have not been recorded by the company include the following:

1. **Service Charges (SC)** Banks cannot profitably handle small accounts without making a service charge. Many banks base the service charge on a number of factors, such as the average balance of the account during the month or the number of checks drawn.
2. **NSF (Non-Sufficient Funds) checks** An NSF check is a check deposited by the company that is not paid when the company's bank presents it to the maker's bank. The bank charges the company's account and returns the check so that the company can try to collect the amount due. If the bank has deducted the NSF check from the bank statement but the company has not deducted it from its book balance, an adjustment must be made in the bank reconciliation. The depositor usually reclassifies the NSF check from Cash to Accounts Receivable because the company must now collect from the person or company that wrote the check.
3. **Interest income** It is very common for banks to pay interest on a company's average balance. These accounts are sometimes called N.O.W. or money market accounts but can take other forms. Such interest is reported on the bank statement.
4. **Miscellaneous charges and credits** Banks also charge for other services such as collection and payment of promissory notes, stopping payment on checks, and printing checks. The bank notifies the depositor of each deduction by including a debit memorandum with the monthly statement. A bank will sometimes serve as an agent in collecting on promissory notes for the depositor. In such a case, a credit memorandum will be included.

An error by either the bank or the depositor will, of course, require immediate correction.

Steps in Reconciling the Bank Balance. The steps to be followed in achieving a bank reconciliation are as follows:

1. Compare the deposits listed on the bank statement with deposits shown in the accounting records. Any deposits in transit should be added to the bank balance. (Immediately investigate any deposits in transit from last month still not listed on the bank statement.)

2. Trace returned checks to the bank statement, making sure that all checks have been issued by the company, properly charged to the company's account, and properly signed.
3. Arrange the canceled checks returned with the bank statement in numerical order, and compare them with the record of checks issued. List checks issued but not on the bank statement. (Be sure to include any checks still outstanding from prior months; investigate any checks outstanding for more than a few months.) Deduct outstanding checks from the bank balance.
4. Deduct from the balance per books any debit memoranda issued by the bank such as NSF checks and service charges that are not yet recorded on the company's records.
5. Add to the balance per books any interest earned or credit memoranda issued by the bank such as collection of a promissory note that is not yet recorded on the company's books.
6. Make journal entries for any items on the bank statement that have not been recorded in the company's books.

Exhibit 7-1. Bank Reconciliation

Martin Maintenance Company
Bank Reconciliation
October 31, 19xx

Balance per bank, October 31		$3,471.07
① Add deposit of October 31 in transit		276.00
		$3,747.07
② Less outstanding checks:		
No. 551	$150.00	
No. 576	40.68	
No. 578	500.00	
No. 579	370.00	
No. 580	130.50	1,191.18
Adjusted bank balance, October 31		**$2,555.89**
Balance per books, October 31		$2,405.91
Add:		
④ Notes receivable collected by bank, including $20.00 of interest income	$300.00	
⑦ Interest income	25.62	325.62
		$2,731.53
Less:		
③ Overstatement of deposit of October 6	$ 30.00	
④ Collection fee	5.00	
⑤ NSF check of Arthur Clubb	128.14	
⑥ Service charge	12.50	175.64
Adjusted book balance, October 31		**$2,555.89**

Note: The circled numbers refer to the items listed in the text on page 295.

Illustration of a Bank Reconciliation. The October bank statement for Martin Maintenance Company, as shown in Figure 7-8, indicates a balance on October 31 of $3,471.07. We shall assume that Martin Maintenance Company has a cash balance in its records on October 31 of $2,405.91. The purpose of a bank reconciliation is to identify the items that make up the difference between these amounts and to determine the correct cash balance. The bank reconciliation for Martin Maintenance Company is given in Exhibit 7-1. The numbered items in the exhibit refer to the following:

1. A deposit in the amount of $276.00 was mailed to the bank on October 31 and had not been recorded by the bank.
2. Five checks issued in October or prior months have not yet been paid by the bank, as follows:

Check No.	Date	Amount
551	Sept. 14	$150.00
576	Oct. 30	40.68
578	Oct. 31	500.00
579	Oct. 31	370.00
580	Oct. 31	130.50

3. The deposit for cash sales of October 6 was incorrectly recorded in Martin Maintenance Company's records as $330.00. The bank correctly recorded the deposit as $300.00.
4. Among the returned checks was a credit memorandum showing that the bank had collected a promissory note from A. Jacobs in the amount of $280.00, plus $20.00 in interest on the note. A debit memorandum was also enclosed for the $5.00 collection fee. No entry had been made on Martin Maintenance Company's records.
5. Also returned with the bank statement was an NSF check for $128.14. This check had been received from a customer named Arthur Clubb. The NSF check from Clubb was not reflected in the company's accounting records.
6. A debit memorandum was enclosed for the regular monthly service charge of $12.50. This charge was not yet recorded by Martin Maintenance Company.
7. Interest earned by the company on the average balance was reported as $25.62.

Note in Exhibit 7-1 that, starting from their separate balances, the bank and book amounts are adjusted to the amount of $2,555.89. This adjusted balance is the amount of cash owned by the company on October 31 and thus is the amount that should appear on its October 31 balance sheet.

Recording Transactions After Reconciliation. The adjusted balance of cash differs from both the bank statement and Martin Maintenance Company's records. The bank balance will automatically become correct when outstanding checks are presented for payment and when the deposit in transit is received and recorded by the bank. Entries are necessary, however, to reflect in the company's records the transactions necessary to correct the book balance. All the items reported by the bank but not yet recorded by the company must be recorded in the general journal by means of the following entries:

Oct. 31	Cash		300.00	
	Notes Receivable			280.00
	Interest Income			20.00
	Note receivable of $280.00 and interest of $20.00 collected by bank from A. Jacobs			
31	Cash		25.62	
	Interest Income			25.62
	Interest on average bank account balance			
31	Sales		30.00	
	Cash			30.00
	Correction of error in recording a $300.00 deposit as $330.00			
31	Accounts Receivable, Arthur Clubb		128.14	
	Cash			128.14
	NSF check of Arthur Clubb returned by bank			
31	Bank Service Charges Expense		17.50	
	Cash			17.50
	Bank service charge ($12.50) and collection fee ($5.00) for October			

It is acceptable to record these entries in one or two compound entries to save time and space, as follows:

Oct. 31	Cash		149.98	
	Sales		30.00	
	Accounts Receivable, Arthur Clubb		128.14	
	Bank Service Charges Expense		17.50	
	Notes Receivable			280.00
	Interest Income			45.62
	To record items from bank reconciliation			

Petty Cash Procedures

OBJECTIVE 5
Describe and record the related entries for a simple petty cash system

Under some circumstances, it is not practical to make all disbursements by check. In most businesses, for example, it is sometimes necessary to make small payments of cash for such things as a few postage stamps, incoming postage, shipping charges due, or minor purchases of supplies such as pens, paper, and the like.

For situations when it is inconvenient to pay with a check, most companies set up a **petty cash fund**. One of the best methods to use is the **imprest system**. Under this system, a petty cash fund is established for a fixed amount and is periodically reimbursed for the exact amount necessary to bring it back to the fixed amount.

Establishing the Petty Cash Fund

Some companies have a regular cashier, secretary, or receptionist to administer the petty cash fund. To establish the petty cash fund, the company issues a check for an amount that is intended to cover two to four weeks of small expenditures. The check is cashed, and the money is placed in the petty cash box, drawer, or envelope.

The only entry required when the fund is established is to record the issuance of the check, as follows:

Oct. 14	Petty Cash	100.00	
	Cash		100.00
	To establish petty cash fund		

Making Disbursements from the Petty Cash Fund

The custodian of the petty cash fund should prepare a **petty cash voucher**, or written authorization, for each expenditure, as illustrated in Figure 7-9. On each petty cash voucher the custodian enters the date, amount, and purpose of the expenditure. The voucher is signed by the person receiving the payment.

The custodian should be informed that surprise audits of the fund will be made occasionally. The cash in the fund plus the sum of the petty cash vouchers should equal the amount shown in the Petty Cash account at all times.

Reimbursing the Petty Cash Fund

At specified intervals, when the fund becomes low, and at the end of an accounting period, the petty cash fund is replenished by a check issued

Figure 7-9. Petty Cash Voucher

PETTY CASH VOUCHER	
	No. X 744
	Date Oct. 23, 19xx
For Postage due	
Charge to Postage Expense	
Amount	$2.86
_____	_____
Approved by	Received by

to the custodian for the exact amount of the expenditures. From time to time there may be minor discrepancies in the amount of cash left in the fund at the time of reimbursement. In these cases, the amount of the discrepancy should be recorded in Cash Short or Over as a debit if short or as a credit if over.

Assume that after two weeks the petty cash fund established earlier had a cash balance of $14.27 and petty cash vouchers as follows: postage, $25.00; supplies, $30.55; freight in, $30.00. The entry to replenish, or replace, the fund is as follows:

Oct. 28	Postage Expense	25.00	
	Supplies	30.55	
	Freight In	30.00	
	Cash Short or Over	.18	
	Cash		85.73
	To replenish petty cash fund		

Note that the Petty Cash account is debited only when the fund is first established. Expense or asset accounts will be debited each time the fund is replenished. In most cases, no further entries to the Petty Cash account are needed unless there is a desire to change the original fixed amount of the fund.

The petty cash fund should be replenished at the end of an accounting period to bring it up to its fixed amount and ensure that the other accounts involved will be properly reflected in the current period's financial statements. If through an oversight the petty cash fund is not replenished at the end of the period, expenditures for the period must still appear on the income statement. They are shown through an adjusting entry debiting the expense accounts and crediting Petty Cash. The result is a reduction in the petty cash fund and the Petty Cash account by the amount of the adjusting entry. For financial statement presentation, the balance of the Petty Cash account is usually combined with other cash accounts.

The Voucher System

OBJECTIVE 6
Define a voucher system, and describe its components

A voucher system is any system giving documentary proof of and written authorization for business transactions. Here, a voucher system for a company's expenditures is presented. It consists of records and procedures for systematically gathering, recording, and paying a company's expenditures. It is much like the control of cash because its goal is to keep the tightest possible control over expenditures. Under this system there is strong internal control because duties and responsibilities in the following functions are separated:

1. Authorization of expenditures
2. Receipt of goods and services

3. Validation of liability by examination of invoices from suppliers for correctness of prices, extensions, shipping costs, and credit terms
4. Payment of expenditure by check, taking discounts when possible

Under the voucher system, every liability must be recorded as soon as it is incurred. A written authorization, called a voucher, is prepared for each expenditure, and checks are written only for approved vouchers. No one person has authority both to incur expenses and to issue checks. In large companies, the duties of authorizing expenditures, verifying receipt of goods and services, checking invoices, recording liabilities, and issuing checks are divided among different people. So for both accounting and management control, every expenditure must be carefully and routinely reviewed and verified before payment. For each transaction, the written approval leaves a trail of documentary evidence, or an audit trail.

Though there is more than one way to set up a voucher system, most systems would use (1) vouchers, (2) voucher checks, (3) a voucher register, and (4) a check register.

Vouchers

Vouchers may be used by any business to control expenditures. A voucher is a written authorization for each expenditure, and serves as the basis of an accounting entry. A separate voucher is attached to each bill as it comes in, and it is given a number. Vouchers are prenumbered in order. In the cash disbursement system introduced earlier in this chapter, a voucher would replace the check authorization form. On the face of a typical voucher (see Figure 7-10), there is important information about the expenditure. The voucher must be signed by authorized individuals before payment is made. On the reverse side of the voucher is information about the accounts and amounts to be debited and credited. The voucher identifies the transaction by voucher number and check number and is recorded in the voucher register and check register, as described below.

Voucher Checks

Although regular checks can be used effectively with a voucher system, many businesses use a form of voucher check that tells the payee the reason for issuing the check. This information may be written either on the check itself or on a detachable stub.

Voucher Register

The voucher register is the book of original entry in which vouchers are recorded after they have been properly approved. The voucher register takes the place of the purchases journal shown in the preceding chapter. However, a major difference between the two journals is that all expenditures—expenses, payroll, plant, and equipment, as well as purchases of merchandise—are recorded in the voucher register. Only purchases of merchandise are recorded in the single-column purchases journal.

Figure 7-10. Front and Back of a Typical Voucher Form

FACE OF VOUCHER

Thomas Appliance Company				

Payee __Belmont Products__ Voucher No. __704__

Address __Gary, Indiana__ Date Due __7/13__

Date Paid __7/13__

Terms __2/10, n/30__ Check No. __205__

Date	Invoice No.	Description	Amount
7/3	XL1066	10 cases Model 70X14	1,200--

Approved ___M.N.___ Approved ___A. Thomas___

　　　　　Controller　　　　　　　　　　　　　　Treasurer

BACK OF VOUCHER

Account Debited	Acct. No.	Amount
Purchases	511	1,200.00
Freight In	512	
Rent Expense	631	
Salary Expense	611	
Utility Expense	635	
Total		$1,200.00

Voucher No. __704__

Payee __Belmont Products__

Address __Gary, Indiana__

Invoice Amount 1,200.00

Less Discount 24.00

Net 1,176.00

Date Due 7/13

Date Paid 7/13

Check No. 205

A voucher register appears in Exhibit 7-2 (see pages 302 and 303). Note that in a voucher system, instead of the Accounts Payable column there is a new column called Vouchers Payable. As you can see, the first entry in the voucher register records the receipt of a utility bill. It is recorded as a debit to Utility Expense and a credit to Vouchers Payable (not Accounts Payable). Note that the utility bill was later paid by check number 203 on July 6.

Check Register

In a voucher system, the check register replaces the cash payments journal because it is the journal in which the checks are listed as they are written, as shown in Exhibit 7-3 (page 304). Study carefully the connection between the voucher register and the check register. The incurring of a liability is recorded in the voucher register; its payment is recorded in the check register.

Operation of a Voucher System

OBJECTIVE 7
State and perform the five steps in operating a voucher system

There are five steps in the operation of a voucher system, presented as follows:

1. Preparing the voucher
2. Recording the voucher
3. Paying the voucher
4. Posting the voucher and check registers
5. Summarizing unpaid vouchers

1. **Preparing the Voucher**   A voucher is prepared for each expenditure. All evidence such as purchase orders, invoices, receiving reports, and/or authorization statements should be attached to the voucher when it is submitted for approval.

   Many companies pay their employees out of a separate bank account or payroll account. A voucher is prepared to cover the total payroll. The check for this voucher is then deposited in the special payroll account, and individual payroll checks are drawn on that bank account.
2. **Recording the Voucher**   All approved vouchers should be recorded in the voucher register, as shown in Exhibit 7-2. Vouchers that do not have appropriate approvals or supporting documents should be investigated immediately. In this illustration, all purchases are recorded at gross purchase price. If the net method were used, the purchases would be recorded at the net purchase price after deducting the anticipated discount.
3. **Paying the Voucher**   After a voucher has been recorded, it is placed in an unpaid voucher file. Many companies file the vouchers by due date and by vendor within due date so that checks can be drawn each day to cover all vouchers due on that day. In this way, all discounts for prompt payment can be taken without risk of missing the discount date.

   On the date the voucher is due, a check for the correct amount, accompanied by the voucher and supporting documents, is presented to the individual authorized to sign checks. The check is then entered in the check register, as shown in Exhibit 7-3. Both the date of payment and the check number are then entered in the voucher register on the same line as the corresponding voucher, which aids in the preparation of a schedule of unpaid vouchers, as explained later.

Exhibit 7-2. Voucher Register

						Payment	Credit		Debits	
Date		Voucher No.	Payee	Date	Check No.	Vouchers Payable	Purchases	Freight In	Store Supplies
19xx July	1	701	Common Utility	7/6	203	75			
	2	702	Ade Realty	7/2	201	400			
	2	703	Buy Rite Supplies	7/6	202	25			
	3	704	Belmont Products	7/13	205	1,200	1,200		
	6	705	M&M Freight			60		60	
	7	706	J. Jay, Petty Cash	7/7	204	50			
	8	707	Belmont Products	7/18	208	600	600		
	11	708	M&M Freight			30		30	
	11	709	Mack Truck			5,600			
	12	710	Livingstone Wholesale	7/22	209	785	750	35	
	14	711	Payroll	7/14	206	2,200			
	17	712	First National Bank	7/17	207	4,250			
	20	713	Livingstone Wholesale			525	500	25	
	21	714	Belmont Products			400	400		
	24	715	M&M Freight			18		18	
	30	716	Payroll	7/30	210	2,200			
	31	717	J. Jay, Petty Cash	7/31	211	47		17	
	31	718	Maintenance Company			175			
	31	719	Store Supply Company			350			350
						18,990	3,450	185	350
						(211)	(511)	(512)	(116)

However, if the net method of recording purchases were illustrated instead of the gross method, a Discounts Lost (Debit) column would replace the Purchases Discounts (Credit) column.

A problem arises in paying a voucher when there has been a purchase return or allowance that applies to the voucher. For example, suppose that part of a shipment of merchandise is defective and is returned to the supplier for credit. At the time the merchandise is returned or the allowance is given, an entry should be made in the gen-

Exhibit 7-2. (continued)

			Debits					
Office Supplies	**Sales Salaries Expense**	**Office Salaries Expense**	**Maintenance, Selling**	**Maintenance, Office**	**Utility Expense**	**Other Accounts**		
						Name	**No.**	**Amount**
25					75	Rent Expense	631	400
						Petty Cash	121	50
						Trucks	148	5,600
	1,400	800				Notes Payable	212	4,000
						Interest Expense	645	250
20	1,400	800				Misc. Exp.	649	10
			100	75				
45	2,800	1,600	100	75	75			10,310
(117)	(611)	(612)	(621)	(622)	(635)			(✓)

eral journal debiting Vouchers Payable and crediting Purchases Returns and Allowances and a notation should be made on the voucher in the voucher file. At the time of payment, only the net amount of the voucher (original amount less return or allowance and any applicable discount) should be paid and recorded in the check register. Rather than noting the change on the voucher, some companies cancel the original voucher and prepare a new one for the amount to be paid.

Exhibit 7-3. Check Register

Check Register

Check No.	Date		Payee	Voucher No.	Debit Vouchers Payable	Credits Purchases Discounts	Cash
	19xx						
201	July	2	Ade Realty	702	400		400
202		6	Buy Rite Supplies	703	25		25
203		6	Common Utility	701	75		75
204		7	J. Jay, Petty Cash	706	50		50
205		13	Belmont Products	704	1,200	24	1,176
206		14	Payroll	711	2,200		2,200
207		17	First National Bank	712	4,250		4,250
208		18	Belmont Products	707	600	12	588
209		22	Livingstone Wholesale	710	785	15	770
210		30	Payroll	716	2,200		2,200
211		31	J. Jay, Petty Cash	717	47		47
					11,832	51	11,781
					(211)	(513)	(111)

4. **Posting the Voucher and Check Registers** Posting of the voucher and check registers is very similar to the posting of the purchases journal and cash payments journal, as illustrated in Chapter 6. The only exception is that the Vouchers Payable account is substituted for the Accounts Payable account.

5. **Summarizing Unpaid Vouchers** At any particular time, the sum of the vouchers in the unpaid vouchers file equals the credit balance of the Vouchers Payable account. So a subsidiary ledger like that described in Chapter 6 is unnecessary. At the end of each accounting period, the unpaid voucher file should be totaled to prove the balance of the Vouchers Payable account. Exhibit 7-4, a schedule of unpaid vouchers, is prepared by listing all unpaid vouchers shown in Exhibit 7-2. A reconciliation of the voucher register (Exhibit 7-2) and check register (Exhibit 7-3) can be accomplished by simple subtraction:

Vouchers Payable credit from voucher register	$18,990
Vouchers Payable debit from check register	11,832
Vouchers Payable credit balance from schedule of unpaid vouchers	$ 7,158

Exhibit 7-4. Schedule of Unpaid Vouchers		
Thomas Appliance Company		
Schedule of Unpaid Vouchers		
July 31, 19xx		
Payee	**Voucher Number**	**Amount**
M&M Freight	705	$ 60
M&M Freight	708	30
Mack Truck	709	5,600
Livingstone Wholesale	713	525
Belmont Products	714	400
M&M Freight	715	18
Maintenance Company	718	175
Store Supply Company	719	350
Total Unpaid Vouchers		$7,158

Sometimes the account title Vouchers Payable appears on a company's balance sheet. It is, however, the preferred practice to use the more widely known and accepted term Accounts Payable, even when a voucher system is in use.

Chapter Review

Review of Learning Objectives

1. **Define internal control and identify the three elements of the internal control structure, including seven examples of control procedures.**
   Internal controls are the methods and procedures employed primarily to protect assets and ensure the accuracy and reliability of the accounting records, but also to achieve efficient operation and compliance with management policies. The internal control structure consists of three elements: the control environment, the accounting system, and control procedures. Examples of control procedures are proper authorization of transactions; recording of transactions to facilitate preparation of financial statements and to establish accountability for assets; use of well-designed documents and records; limited access to assets by authorized personnel; periodic independent comparison of records and assets; appropriate separation of duties into the functions of authorization, operations and custody of assets, and recordkeeping; and use of sound personnel policies.

2. **Describe the inherent limitations of internal control.**

   To be effective, a system of internal control must rely on the people who perform the duties assigned. Thus, the effectiveness of internal control is limited by the people involved. Human errors, collusion, management interference, and failure to recognize changed conditions can all contribute to a system failure.

3. **Apply control procedures to certain merchandising transactions.**

   Internal control over sales, cash receipts, purchases, and cash disbursements is strengthened if the attributes of effective internal control are applied. First, the functions of authorization, recordkeeping, and custody should be kept separate. Second, the accounting system should provide for physical protection of assets (especially cash and merchandise inventory), prompt recording and depositing of cash receipts, and payment by check only on the basis of documentary support. Third, persons who have access to cash and merchandise inventory should be specifically designated and their number limited. Fourth, personnel should be trained and bonded. Fifth, the Cash account should be reconciled monthly, and surprise audits of cash on hand should be made by an individual who does not handle or record cash.

4. **Describe a bank account and demonstrate control of cash by preparing a bank reconciliation.**

   A bank account is an account a company opens with a bank, into which cash is deposited for safekeeping and from which cash is withdrawn primarily by writing checks. The term *bank reconciliation* means accounting for the differences between the balance appearing on the bank statement and the balance of cash according to the company's records. It involves adjusting both balances to arrive at the adjusted cash balance. The bank balance is adjusted for outstanding checks and deposits in transit. The depositor's book balance is adjusted for service charges, NSF checks, interest earned, and miscellaneous charges and credits.

5. **Describe and record the related entries for a simple petty cash system.**

   A petty cash system is established by a debit to Petty Cash and a credit to Cash. It is replenished by debits to various expense or asset accounts and a credit to Cash. Each expenditure should be supported by a petty cash voucher.

6. **Define a voucher system, and describe its components.**

   A voucher system is any system giving documentary proof of and written authorization for business transactions. It consists of authorizations called vouchers; voucher checks; a special journal to record the vouchers, called the voucher register; and a special journal to record the voucher checks, called the check register.

7. **State and perform the five steps in operating a voucher system.**

   The five steps in operating a voucher system are:
   (1) preparing the voucher,
   (2) recording the voucher,
   (3) paying the voucher,
   (4) posting the voucher and check registers, and
   (5) summarizing unpaid vouchers.

Review of Concepts and Terminology

The following concepts and terms were introduced in this chapter:

(L.O. 1) Accounting system: The methods and records established to identify, assemble, analyze, classify, record, and report a company's transactions and to provide assurance that the objectives of internal control are achieved.

(L.O. 6) Audit trail: The documentary evidence of written approval by key people in a business in routinely reviewing and verifying expenditures before payment is made.

(L.O. 4) Bank reconciliation: A procedure to account for the difference between the cash balance appearing on the bank statement and the balance of the Cash account in the depositor's record.

(L.O. 4) Bank statement: A statement showing the balance in a bank account at the beginning of the month, the deposits, the checks paid, other debits and credits during the month, and the balance at the end of the month.

(L.O. 1) Bonding: The careful checking of an employee's background and insuring the company against theft by that person.

(L.O. 3) Cash short or over: An account debited for cash shortages and credited for overages in order to call management's attention to irregular activity.

(L.O. 3) Check: A written order to a bank to pay the amount specified from funds on deposit.

(L.O. 3) Check authorization: A form prepared by the accounting department after it has compared the receiving report for goods received with the purchase order and the invoice.

(L.O. 6) Check register: The journal in a voucher system in which the checks are listed as they are written.

(L.O. 1) Control environment: The overall attitude, awareness, and actions of the owners and management of a business, as reflected in philosophy and operating style, organizational structure, methods of assigning authority and responsibility, and personnel policies and practices.

(L.O. 1) Control procedures: Additional procedures and policies established by management to provide assurance that the objectives of internal control are achieved.

(L.O. 4) Deposit ticket: A form filled out by a depositor listing each check and the amounts of coin and currency being deposited in the bank.

(L.O. 5) Imprest system: A system for controlling cash by establishing a fund at a fixed amount and periodically reimbursing the fund by the amount necessary to bring the fund back to the fixed amount.

(L.O. 1) Internal control: Plan of organization and all policies and procedures adopted within a company to safeguard its assets, check the accuracy and reliability of its accounting data, promote operational efficiency, and encourage adherence to prescribed managerial policies.

(L.O. 1) Internal control structure: A structure established to safeguard the assets of a business and provide reliable accounting records; consists of the control environment, the accounting system, and the control procedures.

(L.O. 3)   **Invoice:**   A form sent or delivered to the purchaser by the vendor (seller) giving the quantity and price as well as a description of goods delivered and the terms of payment.

(L.O. 5)   **Petty cash fund:**   A system established by a business for making small payments of cash for minor purchases when it is inconvenient to pay with a check.

(L.O. 5)   **Petty cash voucher:**   A form signed by each person receiving a cash payment from a business, listing the date, amount, and purpose of the expenditure.

(L.O. 3)   **Purchase order:**   A form addressed by the purchasing department of a company to a vendor (seller) containing a description of the items ordered; their expected price, terms, and shipping date; and other shipping instructions.

(L.O. 3)   **Purchase requisition:**   A formal written request for a purchase.

(L.O. 3)   **Receiving report:**   A form prepared by the receiving department of a company giving the description, quantity, and condition of goods received.

(L.O. 4)   **Signature card:**   A card signed by a depositor in exactly the same way he or she expects to sign checks; used as evidence in the opening of a bank account.

(L.O. 6)   **Voucher:**   A written authorization prepared for each expenditure made by a business as soon as it occurs; checks are written only for approved vouchers.

(L.O. 6)   **Voucher check:**   The form of check used in the voucher system to tell the payee the reason for issuing the check; includes remittance advice to the payee.

(L.O. 6)   **Voucher register:**   The book of original entry in which vouchers are recorded after they have been properly approved.

(L.O. 6)   **Voucher system:**   Any system giving documentary proof of and written authorization for business transactions.

Self-Test

Test your knowledge of the chapter by choosing the best answer for each item below and on the following page.

1. The internal control structure encompasses all the following items except the
   a. attitude of management toward controls.
   b. accounting records and system.
   c. amount of autonomy held by various divisions within a company.
   d. specific procedures for controlling transactions.   *(L.O. 1)*

2. The separation of duties means that with regard to a particular asset or transaction, separate individuals should be responsible for authorization, custody, and
   a. approval.   c. control.
   b. recordkeeping.   d. protection.   *(L.O. 1)*

3. Which of the following is least likely to lead to a breakdown in internal control?
   a. Human errors and mistakes
   b. Employees carrying out duties as prescribed
   c. Management taking full control of an operation
   d. Two employees working together to steal assets   *(L.O. 2)*

4. Which of the following documents should be presented and agreed upon before check authorization is prepared?
   a. Purchase requisition and purchase order
   b. Purchase order and receiving report
   c. Purchase requisition, purchase order, and invoice
   d. Purchase order, invoice, and receiving report   *(L.O. 3)*

5. On a bank reconciliation, which of the following would be added to the balance per bank?
   a. Outstanding checks   c. Service charge
   b. Deposits in transit   d. Interest on balance   *(L.O. 4)*

6. Which of the following items appearing on a bank reconciliation would require a journal entry?
   a. Outstanding checks   c. Interest on balance
   b. Deposits in transit   d. Adjusted cash balance   *(L.O. 4)*

7. The entry to replenish a $50 petty cash fund that has $20 cash and a receipt for $30 of postage would include a credit to
   a. Cash.   c. Postage Expense.
   b. Petty Cash.   d. Prepaid Postage.   *(L.O. 5)*

8. The voucher system strengthens internal control by requiring that a voucher be prepared to authorize payment of a liability at the time that it is
   a. paid.   c. planned.
   b. incurred.   d. audited.   *(L.O. 6)*

9. To assist in making timely payments, the unpaid vouchers are filed by
   a. voucher number.   c. due date.
   b. date of authorization.   d. check number.   *(L.O. 7)*

10. Under the voucher system, at the end of the accounting period the amount of Accounts Payable on the balance sheet would equal the
    a. total of the schedule of unpaid vouchers.
    b. amounts paid to creditors during the accounting period.
    c. the total of the subsidiary accounts payable file.
    d. none of the above.   *(L.O. 7)*

Answers to Self-Test are at the end of this chapter.

Review Problem
Bank Reconciliation

(L.O. 4) The information that appears on the next page comes from the records of Maynard Company:

From the Cash Receipts Journal		Page 14
Date		Debit Cash
Apr. 1		560
10		1,440
17		780
30		2,900
		5,680

From the Cash Payments Journal		Page 18
Date	Check Number	Credit Cash
Apr. 4	1716	580
6	1717	800
17	1718	1,050
25	1719	110
		2,540

From the General Ledger

Cash   Account No. 111

Date		Item	Post. Ref.	Debit	Credit	Balance Debit	Balance Credit
Mar.	31	Balance				4,200	
Apr.	30		CR14	5,680		9,880	
	30		CP18		2,540	7,340	

From the Company's Bank Statement

Checks and Other Debits

Date	Check Number	Amount	Deposits		Balance	
					4/1	4,480
4/5	1714	210	4/2	560	4/2	5,040
4/5	1716	580	4/11	1,440	4/5	4,250
4/12	1717	800	4/15	1,500CM	4/11	5,690
4/28		20SC	4/17	780	4/12	4,890
			4/28	220IN	4/15	6,390
					4/17	7,170
					4/28	7,370

CM–Credit Memo   SC–Service Charge   IN–Interest

The credit memo on April 15 is for the collection of a note, including $100 in interest. Checks no. 1714 for $210 and no. 1715 for $70 were outstanding on April 1.

Required
1. Prepare a bank reconciliation as of April 30, 19xx.
2. Prepare appropriate entries in general journal form.

Answer to Review Problem

1. Bank reconciliation prepared

Maynard Company Bank Reconciliation April 30, 19xx		
Balance per bank, April 30, 19xx		$ 7,370
Add deposit of April 30 in transit		2,900
		$10,270
Less outstanding checks		
No. 1715	$ 70	
1718	1,050	
1719	110	1,230
Adjusted bank balance, April 30, 19xx		$ 9,040
Balance per books, April 30, 19xx		$ 7,340
Add: Note collected by bank, including		
$100 of interest	$1,500	
Interest Income	220	1,720
		$ 9,060
Less service charge		20
Adjusted book balance, April 30, 19xx		$ 9,040

2. Journal entries prepared

April 30	Cash	1,500	
	Notes Receivable		1,400
	Interest Income		100
	Collection of note by bank		
30	Cash	220	
	Interest Income		220
	Interest on bank account		
30	Bank Service Charges Expense	20	
	Cash		20
	Service charge from bank statement		

Chapter Assignments

Discussion Questions and Writing Assignments

1. Most people think of internal control as making fraud harder to commit and easier to detect. Can you think of some other important purposes of internal control?
2. What are the three elements of the internal control structure?
3. What are some examples of control procedures?
4. Why is a separation of duties policy necessary to ensure sound internal control?
5. At Thrifty Variety Store, each sales clerk counts the cash in his or her cash drawer at the end of the day and then removes the cash register tape and prepares the daily cash form, noting any discrepancies. This information is checked by an employee of the cashier's office, who counts the cash, compares the total with the form, and takes the cash to the cashier's office. What is the weakness in this system of internal control?
6. How does a movie theater control cash receipts?
7. What does a credit balance in the Cash Short or Over account indicate?
8. One of the basic principles of internal control is separation of duties. What does this principle assume about the relationships of employees in a company and the possibility of two or more of them stealing from the company?
9. Why is a bank reconciliation prepared?
10. Assume that each of the numbered items below appeared on a bank reconciliation. Which item would be (a) an addition to the balance on the bank statement? (b) a deduction from the balance on the bank statement? (c) an addition to the balance on the books? (d) a deduction from the balance on the books? Write the correct letter after each numbered item.
    (1) Outstanding checks
    (2) Deposits in transit
    (3) Bank service charge
    (4) NSF check returned with statement
    (5) Note collected by bank
    Which of the above items require a journal entry?
11. In a small business, it is sometimes impossible to obtain complete separation of duties. What are three other practices that a small business can follow to achieve the objectives of internal control over cash?
12. Explain how each of the following can contribute to internal control over cash: (a) a bank reconciliation, (b) a petty cash fund, (c) a cash register with printed receipts, (d) printed, prenumbered cash sales receipts, (e) a regular vacation for the cashier, (f) two signatures on checks, and (g) prenumbered checks.
13. At the end of the day, the combined count of cash for all cash registers in a store reveals a cash shortage of $17.20. In what account would this cash shortage be recorded? Would the account be debited or credited?
14. What is the purpose of a petty cash fund, and, from the standpoint of internal control, what is the significance of the total of the fund (the level at which the fund is established)?
15. What account or accounts are debited when a petty cash fund is established? What account or accounts are debited when a petty cash fund is replenished?

16. Should a petty cash fund be replenished as of the last day of the accounting period? Explain.
17. What is the greatest advantage of the voucher system?
18. Before a voucher for the purchase of merchandise is approved for payment, three documents should be compared to verify the amount of the liability. What are the three documents?
19. When the voucher system is used, is there an Accounts Payable controlling account and an accounts payable subsidiary ledger? Be prepared to explain your answer.
20. A company that presently uses a general journal, a sales journal, a cash receipts journal, a cash payments journal, and a purchases journal decides to adopt the voucher system. Which of the five journals would be changed or replaced? What would replace them?
21. What is the correct order to use for filing (a) unpaid vouchers? (b) paid vouchers?

Classroom Exercises

Exercise 7-1.
Use of Accounting Records in Internal Control
(L.O. 1)

Careful scrutiny of the accounting records and financial statements may lead to the discovery of fraud or embezzlement. Each of the following situations may indicate a breakdown in internal control. Indicate what the possible fraud or embezzlement may be in each situation.

a. Wages Expense for a branch office was 30 percent higher in 19x2 than in 19x1, even though the office was authorized to employ only the same four employees and raises were only 5 percent in 19x2.
b. Sales Returns and Allowances increased from 5 percent to 20 percent of sales in the first two months of 19x2, after record sales in 19x1 resulted in large bonuses being paid to the sales staff.
c. Gross Margin decreased from 40 percent of net sales to 30 percent even though there was no change in pricing. Ending Inventory was 50 percent less than it was at the beginning of the year. There is no immediate explanation for the decrease in inventory.
d. A review of daily cash register receipts records shows that one cashier consistently accepts more discount coupons for purchases than other cashiers.

Exercise 7-2.
Control Procedures
(L.O. 1)

Sean O'Mara, who operates a small grocery store, has established the following policies with regard to the check-out cashiers:

_____ 1. Each cashier has his or her own cash drawer, to which no one else has access.
_____ 2. Each cashier may accept checks for purchases under $50 with proper identification. Checks over $50 must be approved by O'Mara before they are accepted.
_____ 3. Every sale must be rung up on the cash register and a receipt given to the customer. Each sale is recorded on a tape inside the cash register.
_____ 4. At the end of each day O'Mara counts the cash in the drawer and compares it to the amount on the tape inside the cash register.

Identify by letter which of the following conditions for internal control apply to each of the above policies:

a. Transactions are executed in accordance with management's general or specific authorization.
b. Transactions are recorded as necessary to (1) permit preparation of financial statements and (2) maintain accountability for assets.
c. Access to assets is permitted only as allowed by management.
d. The recorded accountability for assets is compared with the existing assets at reasonable intervals.

Exercise 7-3.
Internal Control
Procedures
(L.O. 1)

Ruth's Video Store maintains the following policies with regard to purchases of new video tapes at each of its branch stores:

_____ 1. Employees are required to take vacations, and duties of employees are rotated periodically.

_____ 2. Once each month a person from the home office visits each branch to examine the receiving records and to compare the inventory of tapes with the accounting records.

_____ 3. Purchases of new tapes must be authorized by purchase order in the home office and paid for by the treasurer in the home office. Receiving reports are prepared in each branch and sent to the home office.

_____ 4. All new personnel receive a one-hour training orientation on receiving and cataloging new tapes.

_____ 5. The company maintains a perpetual inventory system which keeps track of all tapes purchased, sold, and on hand.

Indicate by letter which of the following control procedures apply to each of the above policies:

a. Authorization
b. Recording
c. Documents and records
d. Limited access

e. Periodic independent verification
f. Separation of duties
g. Sound personnel policies

Exercise 7-4.
Internal Control
Evaluation
(L.O. 1)

Developing a convenient means of providing sales representatives with cash for their incidental expenses, such as entertaining a client at lunch, is a problem many companies face. One company has a plan whereby the sales representatives receive advances in cash from the petty cash fund. Each advance is supported by an authorization from the sales manager. The representative returns the receipt for the expenditure and any unused cash, which is replaced in the petty cash fund. The cashier of the petty cash fund is responsible for seeing that the receipt and the cash returned equal the advance. At the time that the petty cash fund is reimbursed, the amount of the representative's expenditure is debited to Direct Sales Expense.

What is the weak point of the procedure, and what fundamental principle of internal control has been ignored? What improvement in the procedure can you suggest?

Exercise 7-5.
Internal Control
Evaluation
(L.O. 3)

An accountant and his assistants are responsible for the following procedures: (a) receipt of all cash; (b) maintenance of the general ledger; (c) maintenance of the accounts receivable ledger; (d) maintenance of the journals for recording sales, cash receipts, and purchases; and (e) preparation of monthly statements to be sent to customers. As a service to customers and employees, the company allows the accountant to cash checks of up to $50 with money from the cash receipts. The accountant may approve the cashing of such a check for current employees and customers. When the deposits are made, the checks are included in place of the cash receipts.

What weakness in internal control exists in this system?

Exercise 7-6.
Bank
Reconciliation
(L.O. 4)

Prepare a bank reconciliation from the following information:

a. Balance per bank statement as of May 31, $4,227.27
b. Balance per books as of May 31, $3,069.02
c. Deposits in transit, $567.21
d. Outstanding checks, $1,727.96
e. Bank service charge, $2.50

Exercise 7-7.
Bank
Reconciliation:
Missing Data
(L.O. 4)

Compute the correct amounts to replace each letter in the following table:

Balance per bank statement	$ a	$8,900	$315	$1,990
Deposits in transit	600	b	50	125
Outstanding checks	1,500	1,000	c	75
Balance per books	3,450	9,400	225	d

Exercise 7-8.
Collection of Note
by Bank
(L.O. 4)

Nicks Corporation received a notice with its bank statement that the bank had collected a note for $2,000.00 plus $10.00 interest from R. Maggio and credited Nicks Corporation's account for the total less a collection charge of $15.00.

Explain the effect that these items have on the bank reconciliation. Prepare a general journal entry to record the information on the books.

Exercise 7-9.
Petty Cash Entries
(L.O. 5)

The petty cash fund of Martinez Company appeared as follows on December 31, 19xx (the end of the accounting period):

Cash on Hand		$ 61.23
Petty Cash vouchers		
Freight In	$22.86	
Postage	21.19	
Flowers for a sick employee	18.50	
Office Supplies	26.22	88.77
Total		$150.00

Because there is cash on hand, is there a need to replenish the petty cash fund on December 31? Explain. Prepare in general journal form an entry to replenish the fund.

Exercise 7-10.
Voucher System
Entries (including
Petty Cash)
(L.O. 5, 7)

Karim Company uses a voucher system to control expenditures. The following transactions occurred recently:

a. Voucher no. 700 prepared to purchase merchandise from Runge Corp., $800.
b. Check no. 401 issued in payment of voucher no. 700.
c. Voucher no. 701 prepared to establish petty cash fund of $100.
d. Check no. 402 issued to S. Kay, petty cashier, in payment of voucher no. 701.
e. Voucher no. 702 prepared to replenish the petty cash fund, which contains cash of $30 and the following receipts: supplies, $27; postage, $36; miscellaneous expense, $7.
f. Check no. 403 issued to S. Kay, petty cashier, in payment of voucher no. 702.

Record each of the above transactions in a voucher register or check register, and foot and crossfoot the journals.

Exercise 7-11.
Voucher System
Entries
(L.O. 7)

Crissman Company uses a voucher system. Some related transactions are as follows:

Aug. 1 Voucher no. 352 prepared to purchase office equipment from Sanders Equipment Company, $720, terms n/30.
       4 Voucher no. 353 prepared to purchase merchandise from Hubbard Corporation, $1,400, terms 2/10, n/30, FOB shipping point.
       5 Voucher no. 354 prepared to pay freight charge to Floyd Freight for August 4 shipment, $175, terms n/10.
      14 Issued check no. 846 to pay voucher no. 353.
      15 Issued check no. 847 to pay voucher no. 354.
      30 Issued check no. 848 to pay voucher no. 352.

Record each of the preceding transactions in a voucher register or check register, and foot and crossfoot the journals.

Interpreting Accounting Information

J. Walter
Thompson
(L.O. 1, 3)

J. Walter Thompson Co. (JWT) is one of the world's largest advertising agencies, with more than $1 billion in billings per year. One of its smaller units is a television syndication unit that acquires rights to distribute television programming and sells those rights to local television stations, receiving in exchange advertising time that is sold to the agency's clients. Cash rarely changes hands between the unit and the television station, but the unit is supposed to recognize revenue when the television programs are exchanged for advertising time that will later be used by clients.

The Wall Street Journal reported on February 17, 1982, that the company "had discovered 'fictitious' accounting entries that inflated revenue at the television program syndication unit." The article went on to say that "the syndication unit booked revenue of $29.3 million over a five-year period, but that $24.5 million of that amount was fictitious" and that "the accounting irregularities didn't involve an outlay of cash . . . and its (JWT's) advertising clients weren't improperly billed. . . . The fictitious sales were recorded in such a manner as to prevent the issuance of billings to advertising clients. The sole effect of these transactions was to overstate the degree to which the unit was achieving its revenue and profit objectives."

The chief financial officer of JWT indicated that "the discrepancies began to surface . . . when the company reorganized so that all accounting functions reported to the chief financial officer's central office. Previously, he said, 'we had been decentralized in accounting,' with the unit keeping its own books."

Required

1. Show an example entry to recognize revenue from the exchange of the right to televise a show for advertising time and an example entry to bill a client for using the advertising time. Explain how the fraud was accomplished.
2. What would motivate the head of the syndication unit to perpetrate this fraud if no cash or other assets were stolen?
3. What principles of internal control were violated that would allow this fraud to exist for five years, and how did correction of the weaknesses in internal control allow the fraud to be discovered?

Problem Set A

**Problem 7A-1.
Petty Cash
Transactions
(L.O. 5)**

The UpTown Theater Company established a petty cash fund in its snack bar so that payment can be made for small deliveries upon receipt. The following transactions occurred:

Oct. 1 The fund was established in the amount of $200.00 from the proceeds of a check drawn for that purpose.

31 The petty cash fund has cash of $15.71 and the following receipts on hand: for merchandise received, $102.15; freight in, $32.87; laundry service, $42.00; and miscellaneous expense, $7.27. A check was drawn to replenish the fund.

Nov. 30 The petty cash fund has cash of $27.50 and the following receipts on hand: merchandise, $98.42; freight in, $38.15; laundry service, $42.00; and miscellaneous expense, $3.93. The petty cash custodian cannot account for the excess cash in the fund. A check is drawn to replenish the fund.

Required

In general journal form, prepare the entries necessary to record each transaction above.

**Problem 7A-2.
Bank
Reconciliation
(L.O. 4)**

The following information is available for Jorge Mendoza Company as of October 31, 19xx.

a. Cash on the books as of October 31 amounted to $21,327.08. Cash on the bank statement for the same date was $26,175.73.

b. A deposit of $2,610.47, representing cash receipts of October 31, did not appear on the bank statement.

c. Outstanding checks totaled $1,968.40.

d. A check for $960.00 returned with the statement was recorded incorrectly in the check register as $690.00. The check was made for a cash purchase of merchandise.

e. Bank service charges for October amounted to $12.50.

f. The bank collected for Jorge Mendoza Company $6,120.00 on a note. The face value of the note was $6,000.00.

g. An NSF check for $91.78 from a customer, Beth Franco, was returned with the statement.

h. The bank mistakenly charged to the company account a check for $425.00 drawn by another company.

i. The bank reported that it had credited the account for $170.00 in interest on the average balance for October.

Required

1. Prepare a bank reconciliation for Jorge Mendoza Company as of October 31, 19xx.

2. Prepare the journal entries necessary to adjust the accounts.

3. State the amount that should appear on the balance sheet as of October 31.

Problem 7A-3.
Internal Control
(L.O. 1, 2)

Greenwood Company, a small concern, is attempting to organize its accounting department to achieve maximum internal control, subject to the constraint of limited resources. There are three employees (1, 2, and 3) in the accounting department, each of whom has some accounting experience. The accounting department must accomplish the following functions: (a) maintain the general ledger, (b) maintain the accounts payable ledger, (c) maintain the accounts receivable ledger, (d) prepare checks for signature, (e) maintain the cash payments journal, (f) issue credits on returns and allowances, (g) reconcile the bank account, and (h) handle and deposit cash receipts.

Required

1. Assuming that each employee will do only the jobs assigned, assign the functions to the three employees in a way that will ensure the highest degree of internal control possible.

2. Identify four possible unsatisfactory combinations of functions.

Problem 7A-4.
Voucher System
Transactions
(L.O. 7)

In January, M and S Company had the following transactions affecting vouchers payable:

Jan. 2 Prepared voucher no. 7901, payable to Banyan Realty, for January rent, $700.

2 Issued check no. 5501 for voucher no. 7901.

3 Prepared voucher no. 7902, payable to Fishman Company for merchandise, $4,200, invoice dated January 2, terms 2/10, n/30, FOB destination.

Jan. 5 Prepared voucher no. 7903, payable to Holiday Supply House, for supplies, $650, to be allocated $450 to Store Supplies and $200 to Office Supplies, terms n/10.

6 Prepared voucher no. 7904, payable to City Power and Light, for monthly service, $314.

6 Issued check no. 5502 for voucher no. 7904.

9 Prepared voucher no. 7905, payable to Crandall Company, for merchandise, $1,700, invoice dated January 7, terms 2/10, n/60, FOB shipping point. Crandall Company prepaid freight charges of $146 and added them to the invoice, for a total of $1,846.

12 Issued check no. 5503 for voucher no. 7902.

15 Issued check no. 5504 for voucher no. 7903.

16 Prepared voucher no. 7906, payable to Lopez Company, for merchandise, $970, invoice dated January 14, terms 2/10, n/30, FOB shipping point.

16 Prepared voucher no. 7907, payable to Kidd Freight Company, for shipment from Lopez Company, $118, terms n/10 eom.

17 Issued check no. 5505 for voucher no. 7905.

18 Returned $220 in defective merchandise to Lopez Company for credit.

22 Prepared voucher no. 7908, payable to Holiday Supply House, for supplies, $375, to be allocated $200 to Store Supplies and $175 to Office Supplies, terms n/10.

23 Prepared voucher no. 7909, payable to Expo National Bank, for 90-day note that is due, $5,000 plus $150 interest.

23 Issued check no. 5506 for voucher no. 7909.

24 Issued check no. 5507 for voucher no. 7906, less the return on January 18.

26 Prepared voucher no. 7910, payable to Crandall Company, for merchandise, $2,100, invoice dated January 25, terms 2/10, n/30, FOB shipping point. Crandall Company prepaid freight charges of $206 and added them to the invoice, for a total of $2,306.

27 Prepared voucher no. 7911, payable to Telephone Company, $37. Payments for telephone are considered a utility expense.

27 Issued check no. 5508 for voucher no. 7911.

30 Prepared voucher no. 7912, payable to Payroll account, for monthly payroll, $17,200, to be allocated $13,300 to Sales Salaries Expense and $3,900 to Office Salaries Expense.

30 Issued check no. 5509 for voucher no. 7912.

31 Prepared voucher no. 7913, payable to Maintenance Company, $360, to be allocated two-thirds to Maintenance Expense, Selling, and one-third to Maintenance Expense, Office.

Required

1. Record the transactions in a voucher register, a check register, and a general journal using the gross method.
2. Prepare a Vouchers Payable account (number 211), and post the appropriate portions of the journal and register entries. Assume that the December 31 balance of Vouchers Payable was zero.
3. Prove the balance of the Vouchers Payable account by preparing a schedule of unpaid vouchers.

Problem 7A-5.
Bank
Reconciliation
(L.O. 4)

The information presented below comes from the records of the Janesville Company:

From the Cash Receipts Journal	Page 22
Date	Debit Cash
Feb. 1	1,416
8	14,486
15	13,214
22	10,487
28	7,802
	47,405

From the Cash Payments Journal	Page 106	
Date	Check Number	Credit Cash
Feb. 1	2076	1,218
3	2077	22
6	2078	6
7	2079	19,400
8	2080	2,620
12	2081	9,135
16	2082	14
17	2083	186
18	2084	5,662
		38,263

From the General Ledger

Cash   **Account No. 111**

Date		Item	Post. Ref.	Debit	Credit	Balance Debit	Balance Credit
Jan.	31	Balance				10,570	
Feb.	28		CR22	47,405		57,975	
	28		CP106		38,263	19,712	

The bank statement for Janesville Company is shown on page 321. The NSF check was received from customer T. Lambeth for merchandise. The credit memorandum represents a $1,600 note, plus interest collected by the bank. The February 2 deposit, recorded by Janesville as $1,416 in cash sales, was recorded correctly by the bank as $1,614. On February 1, there were the following outstanding checks: no. 2056 at $510, no. 2072 at $4, no. 2073 at $35, no. 2074 at $1,265, and no. 2075 at $32.

Required

1. Prepare a bank reconciliation as of February 28, 19xx.
2. Prepare journal entries to update the accounts.
3. What amount should appear on the balance sheet for cash as of February 28?

| FIRST NATIONAL BANK | | | | | Statement of Janesville Company | |
| | | | | | | Janesville, OH |

Checks/Debits			Deposits/Credits		Daily Balances	
Posting Date	Check No.	Amount	Posting Date	Amount	Date	Amount
02/02	2056	510.00	02/02	1,614.00	02/01	12,416.00
02/02	2075	32.00	02/09	14,486.00	02/02	13,488.00
02/03	2076	1,218.00	02/12	1,654.00CM	02/03	12,266.00
02/03	2072	4.00	02/16	13,214.00	02/05	12,244.00
02/05	2077	22.00	02/23	10,487.00	02/09	26,730.00
02/10	2079	19,400.00	02/28	101.00IN	02/10	6,065.00
02/10	2074	1,265.00			02/11	3,445.00
02/11	2080	2,620.00			02/12	5,099.00
02/17	2081	9,135.00			02/16	18,313.00
02/17	2082	14.00			02/17	9,164.00
02/18		40.00NSF			02/18	9,124.00
02/24	2084	5,662.00			02/23	19,611.00
02/28		17.00SC			02/24	13,949.00
					02/28	14,033.00

| Code: | CM–Credit Memo | IN–Interest | NSF–Non-Sufficient |
| | DM–Debit Memo | SC–Service Charge | Funds |

Problem Set B

Problem 7B-1.
Petty Cash
Transactions
(L.O. 5)

A small company maintains a petty cash fund for minor expenditures. The following transactions occurred:

a. The fund was established in the amount of $100.00 on September 1 from the proceeds of check no. 2707.
b. On September 30, the petty cash fund had cash of $15.46 and the following receipts on hand: postage, $40.00; supplies, $24.94; delivery service, $12.40; and rubber stamp, $7.20. Check no. 2778 was drawn to replenish the fund.
c. On October 31, the petty cash fund had cash of $22.06 and the following receipts on hand: postage, $34.20; supplies, $32.84; and delivery service, $6.40. The petty cash custodian could not account for the shortage. Check no. 2847 was written to replenish the fund.

Required

Prepare the general journal entries necessary to record each transaction.

Problem 7B-2.
Bank
Reconciliation
(L.O. 4)

The following information is available for Pagan Company as of June 30, 19xx:

a. Cash on the books as of June 30 amounted to $56,837.64. Cash on the bank statement for the same date was $70,858.54.

b. A deposit of $7,124.92, representing cash receipts of June 30, did not appear on the bank statement.
c. Outstanding checks totaled $3,646.82.
d. A check for $1,210.00 returned with the statement was recorded in the cash payments journal as $1,012.00. The check was for advertising.
e. Bank service charges for June amounted to $13.00.
f. The bank collected for Pagan Company $18,200.00 on a note left for collection. The face value of the note was $18,000.00.
g. An NSF check for $570.00 from a customer, Louise Bryant, was returned with the statement.
h. The bank mistakenly deducted a check for $400.00 drawn by Sherod Corporation.
i. The bank reported a credit of $480.00 for interest on the average balance.

Required

1. Prepare a bank reconciliation for Pagan Company as of June 30, 19xx.
2. Prepare the journal entries necessary from the reconciliation.
3. State the amount of cash that should appear on the balance sheet as of June 30.

Problem 7B-3.
Internal Control
(L.O. 1, 2)

Ostrowski Company, a large merchandising concern that stocks over 85,000 different items in inventory, has just installed a new computer system for inventory control. The computer's data storage system has random access processing and carries all pertinent data relating to individual items of inventory. The system is equipped with fifteen remote computer terminals, distributed at various locations throughout the warehouse and sales areas. Using these terminals, employees can obtain information from the computer system about the status of any inventory item. To make an inquiry, they use a keyboard similar to a typewriter's. The answer is relayed back instantaneously on the screen. As inventory is received, shipped, or transferred, employees update the inventory records in the computer system by means of the remote terminals.

Required

1. What potential weakness in internal control exists in the system?
2. What suggestions do you have for improving the internal control?

Problem 7B-4.
Voucher System
Transactions
(L.O. 7)

During the month of March, Starr Toy Center had the following transactions affecting vouchers payable:

Mar. 1 Prepared voucher no. 125, payable to the petty cash cashier, to establish a petty cash fund, $250.
      1 Issued check no. 262 for voucher no. 125.
      2 Prepared voucher no. 126, payable to Turner Distributing, for a shipment of merchandise, $800, invoice dated March 1, terms 2/10, n/60, FOB shipping point. Turner prepaid freight of $60 and added it to the invoice, for a total of $860.
      3 Prepared voucher no. 127, payable to Morales Realty, for March rent, $1,200.
      3 Issued check no. 263 for voucher no. 127.

Mar. 5 Prepared voucher no. 128, payable to Cheeks Distributors, for merchandise, $1,000, invoice dated March 3, terms 2/10, n/60, FOB shipping point.

   6 Prepared voucher no. 129, payable to Compass Express, for freight in on March 5 shipment, $64, terms n/10.

   7 Prepared voucher no. 130, payable to Atlas Hardware, for office equipment, $400, terms n/30.

   8 Received credit memorandum from Cheeks Distributors for damaged merchandise returned, $100.

   9 Prepared voucher no. 131, payable to Cheeks Distributors, for merchandise, $1,300, invoice dated March 8, terms 2/10, n/60, FOB shipping point.

  10 Prepared voucher no. 132, payable to Compass Express, for freight in on March 9, $94, terms n/10.

  11 Issued check no 264 for voucher no. 126.

  12 Prepared voucher no. 133, payable to the company's owner, Estelle Sierra, for her personal expenses, $1,000.

  12 Issued check no. 265 for voucher no. 133.

  13 Issued check no. 266 for voucher no. 128. There was a return on March 8.

  15 Issued check no. 267 for voucher no. 129.

  17 Prepared vouchers no. 134, 135, 136, and 137, payable to Chung Furniture, for office furniture having an invoice price of $2,400, terms, one-fourth down and one-fourth each month for three months.

  17 Issued check no. 268 for voucher no. 134.

  18 Issued check no. 269 for voucher no. 131.

  19 Issued check no. 270 for voucher no. 132.

  20 Prepared voucher no. 138, payable to Kellogg Supply, $270 ($190 to be charged to Store Supplies and $80 to Office Supplies), terms n/10 eom.

  22 Prepared voucher no. 139, payable to Toney Videocassettes, for merchandise, $630, invoice dated March 19, terms 2/10, n/30, FOB shipping point. Freight paid by shipper and included in invoice total, $30.

  23 Prepared voucher no. 140, payable to Lakeview National Bank, in payment of a $4,000 note plus interest, $100; total, $4,100.

  23 Issued check no. 271 for voucher no. 140.

  24 Prepared voucher no. 141, payable to Liu Insurance Company, for a one-year policy, $480.

  24 Issued check no. 272 for voucher no. 141.

  26 Prepared voucher no. 142, payable to Cheeks Distributors, for merchandise, $600, invoice dated March 25, terms 2/10, n/60, FOB shipping point.

  27 Prepared voucher no. 143, payable to Compass Express, for freight in on shipment of March 26, $38.

  28 Prepared voucher no. 144, payable to Payroll Account, for monthly salaries, $7,900 (to be divided as follows: Sales Salaries Expense, $4,400, and Office Salaries Expense, $3,500).

  28 Issued check no. 273 for voucher no. 144.

  29 Issued check no. 274 for voucher no. 139.

Mar. 31 Prepared voucher no. 145 to reimburse the petty cash fund. A count of the fund revealed cash on hand, $50, and the following receipts: postage, $44; office supplies, $34; collect telegram, $6; flowers for sick employee, $30; and delivery service, $54. The total of cash on hand and receipts was $32 less than the book balance of petty cash.

31 Issued check no. 275 for voucher no. 145.

Required

1. Record the transactions in a voucher register, a check register, and a general journal using the gross method.
2. Prepare a Vouchers Payable account (number 211) and post those portions of the journal and register entries that affect this account. Assume the Vouchers Payable account had a zero balance on February 28.
3. Prove the balance of the Vouchers Payable account by preparing a schedule of unpaid vouchers.

Problem 7B-5.
Bank
Reconciliation
(L.O. 4)

The information presented below comes from the records of the Lightman Company:

From the Cash Receipts Journal	Page 9		From the Cash Payments Journal	Page 12
Date	Debit Cash		Date / Check Number	Credit Cash

Date	Debit Cash
Nov. 1	1,828
7	2,024
14	6,480
21	5,292
30	3,884
	19,508

Date	Check Number	Credit Cash
Nov. 1	721	28
2	722	566
3	723	832
4	724	54
	725 (voided)	
5	726	10
10	727	11,492
11	728	1,418
20	729	2,492
21	730	152
		17,044

From the General Ledger

Cash   **Account No. 111**

Date		Item	Post. Ref.	Debit	Credit	Balance Debit	Balance Credit
Oct.	31	Balance				4,930	
Nov.	30		CR9	19,508		24,438	
	30		CP12		17,044	7,394	

SHORELINE NATIONAL BANK					Statement of Lightman Company Davis and Wells Streets	
Checks/Debits			**Deposits/Credits**		**Daily Balances**	
Posting Date	Check No.	Amount	Posting Date	Amount	Date	Amount
11/02	700	200.00	11/02	1,828.00	11/01	7,570.00
11/02	707	1,000.00	11/08	2,024.00	11/02	8,198.00
11/04	720	920.00	11/15	6,480.00	11/04	7,250.00
11/04	721	28.00	11/22	5,292.00	11/06	6,418.00
11/06	723	832.00	11/26	816.00CM	11/08	8,388.00
11/08	724	54.00	11/30	84.00IN	11/12	8,348.00
11/12	726	10.00			11/14	6,534.00
11/12		30.00NSF			11/15	13,014.00
11/14	728	1,814.00			11/22	18,306.00
11/24	727	11,492.00			11/24	6,814.00
11/26	730	152.00			11/26	7,478.00
11/30		8.00SC			11/30	7,554.00

Code:	CM–Credit Memo	IN–Interest	NSF–Non-Sufficient
	DM–Debit Memo	SC–Service Charge	Funds

The NSF check was received from customer G. Soto for merchandise. The credit memorandum represents an $800 note, plus interest, collected by the bank. Check number 725 was prepared improperly and has been voided. Check number 728 for a purchase of merchandise was incorrectly recorded in the cash payments journal as $1,418 instead of $1,814. On November 1, there were the following outstanding checks: no. 700 at $200, no. 707 at $1,000, no. 719 at $520, and no. 720 at $920.

Required

1. Prepare a bank reconciliation as of November 30, 19xx.
2. Prepare the general journal entries.
3. What amount should appear on the balance sheet for cash as of November 30?

Financial Decision Case

Gabhart's
(L.O. 1, 2, 3)

Gabhart's is a retail department store with several departments. Its internal control procedures for cash sales and purchases are described below.

Cash sales. Every cash sale is rung up on the department cash register by the sales clerk assigned to a particular department. The cash register produces a sales slip to be given to the customer with the merchandise. A carbon copy of the sales ticket is made on a continuous tape locked inside the machine. At the end of each day, a "total" key is pressed, and the machine prints the total sales for the day on the continuous tape. Then the sales clerk unlocks the machine, takes off the total sales figure, makes the entry in the accounting records for the day's cash sales, counts the cash in the drawer, retains the basic $50 change fund, and gives the cash received to the cashier. The sales clerk then files the cash register tape and is ready for the next day's business.

Purchases. All goods are ordered by the purchasing agent upon the request of the various department heads. When the goods are received, the receiving clerk prepares a receiving report in triplicate. One copy is sent to the purchasing agent, one copy is forwarded to the department head, and one copy is kept by the receiving clerk. Invoices are forwarded immediately to the accounting department to ensure payment before the discount period elapses. After payment, the invoice is forwarded to the purchasing agent for comparison with the purchase order and the receiving report and is then returned to the accounting office for filing.

Required

For each of the above situations, identify at least one major internal control weakness. What would you suggest to improve the system?

Answers to Self-Test

1. c	3. b	5. b	7. a	9. c
2. b	4. d	6. c	8. b	10. a

CHAPTER 8

Accounting Concepts and Classified Financial Statements

Financial statements are the most important means of communicating accounting information to decision makers. For decision makers external to the business, the financial statements, which are usually audited by independent accountants, are often the only information available directly from the company. As a result, it is essential that all business students have a thorough knowledge of the objectives and concepts underlying financial reporting, as well as the forms and evaluation of financial statements. This knowledge provides the foundation for the further study of accounting.

Since those outside the business who have a financial interest in it have no direct access to the accounting records, they must depend on what is presented to them. For them to understand and interpret these external financial reports, certain rules and standards must be followed in preparing the financial statements. This chapter begins by describing the objectives of financial information. It then discusses some qualities that accounting information ought to have and some conventions helpful in interpreting it. It also summarizes the financial accounting concepts presented to this point in the text and relates them to ethical reporting practices. After studying this chapter, you should be able to meet the learning objectives on the left.

One way of making financial statements more useful is to break the information into special categories. After dividing the balance sheet and income statement into useful categories, this chapter explains how to use the categories to analyze a business. Financial statements prepared in this way are also useful to the management of a company. Finally, the annotated financial statements of a major U.S. corporation are presented as an example of how corporations report to their stockholders.

Objectives of Financial Information[1]

The United States has a highly developed exchange economy. In such an economy, most goods and services are exchanged for

---

1. This discussion is based on *Statement of Financial Accounting Concepts No. 1*, "Objectives of Financial Reporting by Business Enterprises" (Stamford, Conn.: Financial Accounting Standards Board, 1978), pars. 6–16 and 28–40.

money or claims to money instead of being used or bartered by their producers. Much business is done by sole proprietorships and partnerships. As noted in Chapter 1, however, most business is carried on through investor-owned companies that are called corporations, including many large ones that buy, sell, and obtain financing in U.S. and world markets.

OBJECTIVE 1
State the objectives of financial reporting

By issuing stocks and bonds that are traded in the market, businesses can raise capital for production and marketing activities through financial institutions, small groups, and the public at large. Investors are interested mainly in returns from dividends and in the market prices of their investments, rather than in managing the company's business. Creditors want to know if the business can repay a loan according to its terms. Thus, investors and creditors both need to know if a company can generate favorable cash flows. Financial statements are important to both groups in making this judgment. They offer valuable information that helps investors and creditors judge a company's ability to pay dividends and repay debts with interest. In this way, the market puts scarce resources to work in companies that can use them most efficiently.

The needs of users and the general business environment described above are the basis for the Financial Accounting Standards Board's three objectives of financial reporting:[2]

1. *To furnish information useful in making investment and credit decisions* Financial reporting should offer information that is useful to present and potential investors and creditors as well as to others in making rational investment and credit decisions. The reports should be in a form that makes sense to those who have some understanding of business and are willing to study the information carefully.
2. *To provide information useful in assessing cash flow prospects* Financial reporting should supply information to help present and potential investors (owners), creditors, and others judge the amounts, timing, and risk of expected cash receipts from dividends or interest and the proceeds from the sale, redemption, or maturity of stocks or loans.
3. *To provide information about business resources, claims to those resources, and changes in them* Financial reporting should give information about the assets of a company, the liabilities and owner's equity of a company, and the effects of transactions that change its assets, liabilities, and owner's equity.

General-purpose external financial statements are the most important way of periodically presenting to parties outside the business the information that has been gathered and processed in the accounting system. For this reason, these statements—the balance sheet, the income statement, the statement of owner's equity, and the statement of cash flows—are the most important output of the accounting system. These financial statements are called "general purpose" because of their wide audience. They are "external" because the users are outside the business. Because of a potential conflict of interest between manag-

2. Ibid., pars. 32–54.

ers, who must prepare the statements, and the investors or creditors, who invest in or lend money to the businesses, these statements are often audited by outside accountants to increase confidence in their reliability.

Qualitative Characteristics of Accounting Information[3]

OBJECTIVE 2
State the qualitative characteristics of accounting information and describe their interrelationships

It is easy for a student in the first accounting course to get the idea that accounting is 100 percent accurate. This idea is reinforced by the fact that all the problems in this and other introductory books can be solved. The numbers all add up, what is supposed to equal something else does, and so forth. Accounting seems very much like mathematics in its perfection. In this course, the basics of accounting are presented in a simple form at first to promote better understanding. In practice, however, accounting information is neither simple nor perfect and rarely satisfies all criteria. The FASB emphasizes this fact in the following statement:

The information provided by financial reporting often results from approximate, rather than exact, measures. The measures commonly involve numerous estimates, classifications, summarizations, judgments and allocations. The outcome of economic activity in a dynamic economy is uncertain and results from combinations of many factors. Thus, despite the aura of precision that may seem to surround financial reporting in general and financial statements in particular, with few exceptions the measures are approximations, which may be based on rules and conventions, rather than exact amounts.[4]

The goal of accounting information—to provide the basic data that different users need to make informed decisions—is an ideal. The gap, however, between the ideal and the actual provides much of the interest and controversy in accounting. The information needs to be both useful and understandable. Therefore, the burden for interpreting and using the information falls partly on the decision maker. The decision maker not only must judge what information to use and how to use it but also must understand it. How useful and understandable accounting information is depends on both the decision maker and the accountant. The accountant prepares the financial statements in accordance with accepted practices and presents information that is believed to be generally useful. But the decision maker must interpret the information and use it in making the decision. To aid in understanding this process of interpretation, the FASB has described the qualitative characteristics of accounting information. **Qualitative characteristics** are the standards for judging the information. In addition, there are generally accepted

---

3. The discussion in this section is based on *Statement of Financial Accounting Concepts No. 2,* "Qualitative Characteristics of Accounting Information" (Stamford, Conn.: Financial Accounting Standards Board, 1980). Copyright by Financial Accounting Standards Board, High Ridge Park, Stamford, CT 06905, USA. Reprinted with permission. Copies of the complete document are available from the FASB.
4. *Statement of Financial Accounting Concepts No. 1,* par. 20.

conventions for recording and reporting that facilitate interpretation. The relationships among these concepts are shown in Figure 8-1.

If accounting information is to be useful, it must have two major qualitative characteristics: relevance and reliability. **Relevance** means that the information makes a difference to the outcome of a decision. In other words, another decision would be made if the relevant information were not available. To be relevant, information must provide feedback, give help in predicting future conditions, and be timely. For example, the income statement provides information about how a company did in the past year (feedback), and it helps in making plans for the next year (prediction). To be useful, however, it must also be communicated soon enough after the first year to affect the operations of the second year (timeliness).

In addition to being relevant, accounting information must have **reliability**. In other words, the user must be able to depend on the information. It must represent what it is meant to represent. It must be regarded as credible or verifiable by independent parties using the same methods of measuring. It must also be neutral or objective. Accounting should convey business activity as faithfully as possible without coloring the picture being presented in order to influence anyone in a certain direction. For example, the balance sheet should represent the economic resources, obligations, and owner's equity of a business as faithfully as possible in accordance with generally accepted accounting principles, and this balance sheet should be verifiable by an auditor.

Figure 8-1. Qualitative Characteristics and Conventions of Accounting Information

Conventions to Aid Interpretation of Financial Information

OBJECTIVE 3
Define and describe the use of the conventions of comparability and consistency, materiality, conservatism, full disclosure, and cost-benefit

To a large extent, financial statements are based on estimates and rather arbitrary rules of recognition and allocation. In this book we point out a number of difficulties that financial statements may have. One is failing to recognize the changing value of the dollar due to inflation. Another is treating intangibles, like research and development costs, as assets only if purchased outside the company, but treating them as expenses if developed within the company. These problems do not mean that financial statements are useless; they are, of course, essential. However, users must know how to interpret them. To help in this interpretation, accountants depend on five conventions or rules of thumb that aid in recording transactions and preparing financial statements: (1) comparability and consistency, (2) materiality, (3) conservatism, (4) full disclosure, and (5) cost-benefit.

Comparability and Consistency

A characteristic that adds to the usefulness of accounting information is comparability. Information about a company is more useful if it can be compared with similar facts about the same company over several time periods or about another company for the same time period. **Comparability** means that the information is presented in such a way that the decision maker can recognize similarities, differences, and trends between different companies or between different time periods.

Consistent use of accounting measures and procedures is important in achieving comparability. The **consistency** convention requires that a particular accounting procedure, once adopted by a company, remain in use from one period to the next unless users are informed of the change. Thus, without a statement to the contrary, users of financial statements may assume that there has been no arbitrary change in the treatment of a particular account or item that may affect the interpretation of the statements.

If management decides that a certain procedure is not appropriate and should be changed, generally accepted accounting principles require that the change and its dollar effect be described in the notes to the financial statements:

The nature of and justification for a change in accounting principle and its effect on income should be disclosed in the financial statements of the period in which the change is made. The justification for the change should explain clearly why the newly adopted accounting principle is preferable.[5]

For example, during the current year, a company might report that it had changed its method of accounting for inventories because management felt the new method reflected actual cost flows more realistically.

---

5. Accounting Principles Board, *Opinion No. 20*, "Accounting Changes" (New York: American Institute of Certified Public Accountants, 1971), par. 17.

Materiality

The term **materiality** refers to the relative importance of an item or event. If an item or event is material, it is likely to be relevant to the user of the financial statements. In other words, an item is material if the user would have done something differently if he or she had not known about the item. The accountant is often faced with many small items or events that make little difference to users no matter how they are handled. For example, in Chapter 12 it is suggested that it is more practical to charge small tools as expenses than to depreciate them. Also, small capital expenditures of less than $100 or $500 may be charged as an expense rather than recorded as equipment and depreciated.

In general, an item is material if there is a reasonable expectation that knowing about it would influence the decisions of users of financial statements. The materiality of an item is normally determined by relating its dollar value to parts of the financial statements, such as net income or total assets. However, the materiality of an item also depends on the nature of the item as well as the amount. For example, in a multi-million-dollar company, a mistake in recording an item of $5,000 may not be important, but discovering a $5,000 bribe or theft may be very significant. Also, a great many small errors combined may result in a material amount. Accountants judge the materiality of many things, and the users of financial statements depend on their judgment to be fair and accurate.

Conservatism

Accountants try to base their decisions on logic and evidence that will lead to the fairest report of what happened. In judging and estimating, however, accountants are often faced with uncertainties or doubts. In these cases, they look to the convention of **conservatism**. This convention means that when accountants face major uncertainties as to which accounting procedure to use, they generally choose the one that will be least likely to overstate assets and income.

One of the most common applications of the conservatism convention is the use of the lower-of-cost-or-market method in accounting for short-term investments, described in Chapter 9, and for inventories, presented in Chapter 10. Under this method, if the market value is greater than cost, the more conservative cost figure is used. If the market value is less than cost, then the more conservative market value is used.

Conservatism can be a useful tool in doubtful cases, but the abuse of this convention will certainly lead to incorrect and misleading financial statements. Suppose that someone incorrectly applied the conservatism convention by expensing a long-term asset in the period of purchase. In this case, there is no uncertainty. Income and assets for the current period would be understated, and income of future periods would be overstated. For this reason, accountants depend on the conservatism convention only as a last resort.

Full Disclosure

The convention of full disclosure requires that financial statements and their footnotes present all information relevant to the user's understanding of the case. In other words, accounting information should offer any explanation that is needed to keep it from being misleading. Such explanations in the notes are considered an integral part of the financial statements. For instance, as noted in the previous section on consistency, a change from one accounting procedure to another should be reported. In general, the form of the financial statements, as described later in this chapter, may affect their usefulness in making certain decisions. Also, certain items are considered essential to financial statement readers, such as the amount of depreciation expense on the income statement and the accumulated depreciation on the balance sheet.

Other examples of disclosures required by the Financial Accounting Standards Board and other official bodies are the accounting procedures used in preparing the statements, important terms of the company's debt, commitments and contingencies, and important events taking place after the date of the statements. However, there is a point where the statements become so cluttered that they impede rather than aid understanding. Beyond required disclosures, the application of the full-disclosure convention is based not on definite standards, but on the judgment of management and of the accountants who prepare the financial statements.

The principle of full disclosure has also been influenced by users of accounting information in recent years. To protect the investor, independent auditors, the stock exchanges, and the SEC have made more demands for disclosure by publicly owned companies. The SEC has been pushing especially hard for the enforcement of full disclosure. So today more and better information about corporations is available to the public than ever before.

Cost-Benefit

The cost-benefit convention underlies all the qualitative characteristics and conventions. It holds that the benefits to be gained from providing new accounting information should be greater than the costs of providing it. Of course, certain minimum levels of relevance and reliability must be reached for accounting information to be useful. Beyond these minimum levels, however, it is up to the FASB and the SEC, which require the information, and the accountant, who provides the information, to judge the costs and benefits in each case. Most of the costs of providing information fall at first on the preparers, though the benefits are reaped by both preparers and users. Finally, both the costs and the benefits are passed on to society in the form of prices and social benefits from more efficient allocation of resources. The costs and benefits of a particular requirement for an accounting disclosure are both direct and indirect, immediate and deferred. For example, it is hard to judge the final costs and benefits of a far-reaching and costly regulation. The FASB, for instance, allows certain large companies to make a supplemental disclosure in their financial statements of the effects of changes on current costs (presented in Chapter 21). Most companies have chosen not to present this information because they view their costs of producing and providing it as exceeding the benefits to the readers of their financial statements. Cost-benefit is a question faced by all regulators, including the FASB and the SEC. Even though there are no definitive ways of measuring costs and benefits, much of an accountant's work deals with these concepts.

Financial Accounting Concepts and Ethical Reporting

OBJECTIVE 4
Summarize the concepts underlying financial accounting and their relationship to ethical financial reporting

In the presentation of accounting thus far, the relationships of financial accounting concepts to accounting techniques and procedures as well as the judgment underlying their application have been emphasized. The next sections summarize the financial accounting concepts presented to this point and make clear that the use of judgment in their application places an ethical responsibility on the preparer.

Summary of Financial Accounting Concepts

In Chapter 1, Figure 1-1 introduced accounting as an information system for business decision making. That information system is expanded in Figure 8-2 to include the financial accounting concepts introduced thus far. In overview, Figure 8-2 shows the information system as a circular, continuous process. People make decisions and take actions; these decisions and actions affect economic activities that in turn are measured, processed, and communicated back to the decision makers in the form of financial statements in accordance with their information needs or objectives.

The decision makers consist of internal users (management) and direct and indirect external users of accounting information. Present and potential investors and creditors are direct users; and taxing authorities, regulatory agencies, citizens and citizen groups, and economic planners are indirect users. Accountants measure some but not all economic activities for various economic entities (businesses, government units, not-for-profit organizations, and individuals). In the case of specific business entities, accountants measure business transactions in terms of money.

The measurement, processing, and communication of accounting information is governed by generally accepted accounting principles (GAAP) that encompass all the rules, procedures, and conventions necessary to define accounting practices at a given point in time. The most important source of GAAP is the Financial Accounting Standards Board

Figure 8-2. Summary of Financial Accounting Concepts

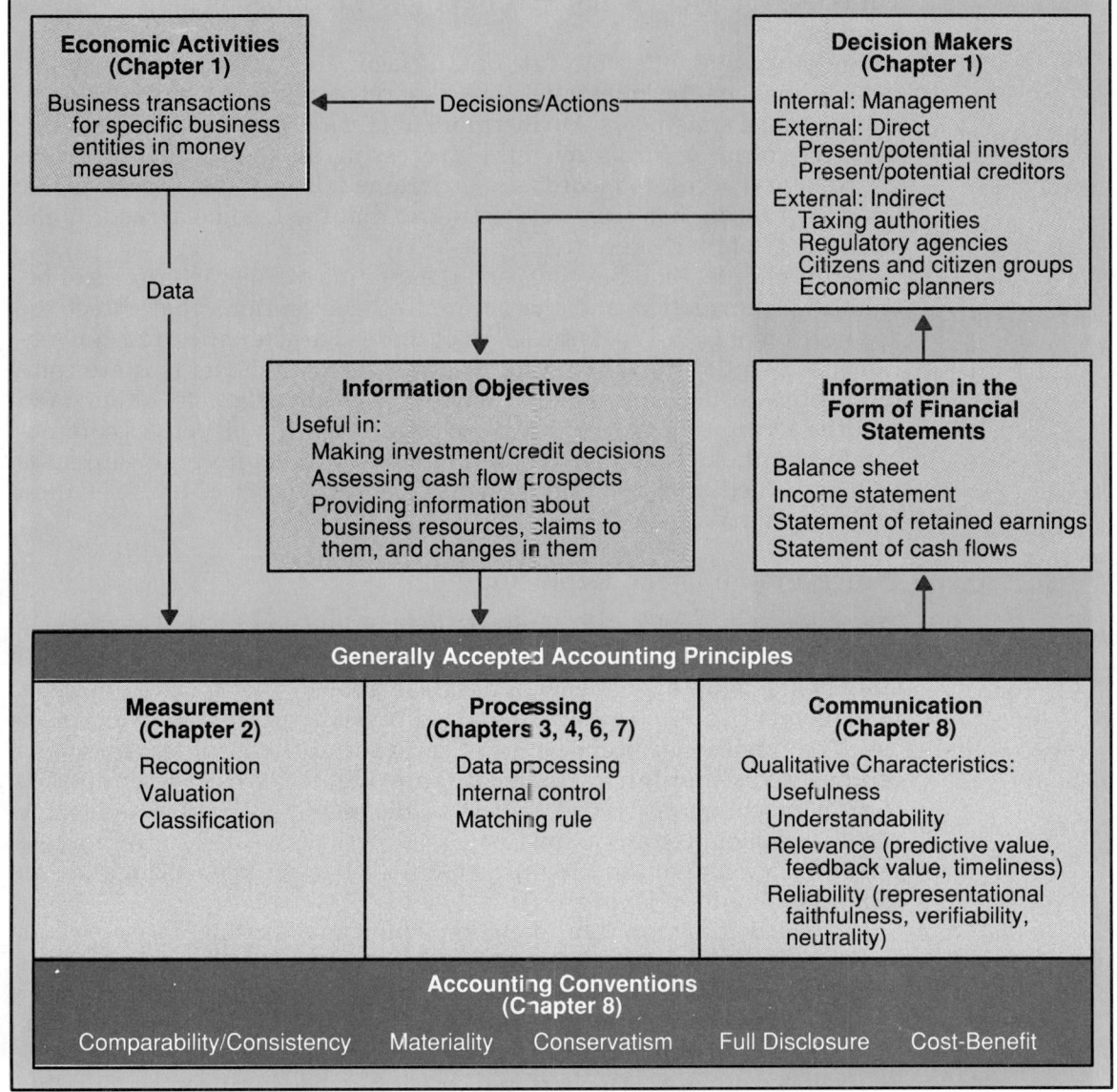

(FASB), but other sources include authoritative bodies such as the American Institute of CPAs (AICPA), as well as traditional practices.

In measuring a business transaction, three characteristics must be identified. First, recognition focuses on when a transaction took place. Second, valuation focuses on what value to place on the transaction. The usual value assigned to a transaction is cost (the value exchanged at the time the transaction is recognized). Third, classification requires the identification of the specific accounts in which the transaction is to be recorded. When these three determinations are made in accordance with GAAP, the transaction may be properly recorded in the accounting records.

The processing of accounting data is facilitated if the data are stored in a manner that permits quick and easy retrieval for preparing reports and financial statements. Furthermore, it is important to establish internal accounting controls over the processing so that assets are safeguarded and accurate records are maintained. Lastly, the matching rule is applied through accrual accounting so that the income earned by the business is properly reported.

In this chapter, you have learned the qualitative characteristics of accounting information and the accounting conventions that direct the application of GAAP. A knowledge of these characteristics and conventions is essential to interpreting the financial statements that are communicated to decision makers. Finally, it is important to understand that the accounting process is driven by information objectives communicated by the decision makers to accountants. This link reinforces the primary function of accounting, which is to provide useful information to decision makers.

Ethics and Financial Reporting

The users of financial statements depend on the good judgment of preparers in applying accounting concepts to the preparation of financial statements. This dependence places a responsibility on a company's management and its accountants to act ethically in the reporting process. The intentional preparation of misleading financial statements is referred to as **fraudulent financial reporting**[6] and can result from distortion of company records, such as the manipulation of inventory records; falsified transactions, such as fictitious sales or orders; or misapplication of accounting principles, such as treating as an asset an item that should be expensed.

The motivation for fraudulent reporting may spring from various sources, for instance the desire to obtain a higher price in the sale of the company, meet the expectations of the owners, or obtain a loan. Other times the incentive is personal gain, such as additional compensation, promotion, or avoidance of penalties for poor performance by the managers or accountants. The personal costs of such actions can be high due to the fact that criminal penalties and financial loss can fall to the individuals who authorize or prepare the financial statements. Others, including investors and lenders to the company, other employees, and customers, suffer from fraudulent financial reporting as well.

The motivations for fraudulent financial reporting exist to some extent in every company. It is the responsibility of management to insist upon honest financial reporting, but it is also the responsibility of the

6. National Commission on Fraudulent Financial Reporting, *Report of the National Commission on Fraudulent Financial Reporting* (Washington, D.C., 1987), p. 2.

accountants within the organization to maintain high ethical standards in the performance of their duties to avoid being linked to fraudulent financial statements. To be ethical in financial reporting, the accountant should seek to apply financial accounting concepts in a way that will present a fair view of the operations and financial position of the company and not mislead the readers of the financial statements.

Classified Balance Sheet

OBJECTIVE 5
Identify and describe the basic components of a classified balance sheet

So far in this book, balance sheets have listed the accounts in categories of assets, liabilities, and owner's equity. Because even a fairly small company may have hundreds of accounts, simply listing accounts by these broad categories is not particularly helpful to a statement user. Setting up subcategories within the major categories will often make the financial statements much more useful. Investors and creditors study and evaluate the relationships among the subcategories. When general-purpose external financial statements are divided into useful subcategories, they are called **classified financial statements**.

The balance sheet presents the financial position of a company at a particular time. The classified balance sheet shown in Exhibit 8-1 has subdivisions that are typical of most companies in the United States. The subdivisions under owner's equity, of course, depend on the form of business.

Assets

The assets of a company are often divided into four categories: (1) current assets; (2) investments; (3) property, plant, and equipment; and (4) intangible assets. Some companies use a fifth category called other assets if there are miscellaneous assets that do not fall into any of the other groups. These categories are listed in the order of their presumed liquidity (the ease with which an asset can be converted into cash). For example, current assets are considered more liquid than property, plant, and equipment.

Current Assets. **Current assets** are cash or other assets that are reasonably expected to be realized in cash, sold, or consumed during the next year or during a normal operating cycle of a business, if the cycle is longer than a year. The normal operating cycle of a company is the average time that is needed to go from cash to cash. As illustrated in Figure 8-3, cash is used to buy merchandise inventory, which is sold for cash or for a promise of cash (a receivable) if the sale is made on account (for credit). If the sales are on account, the resulting receivables must be collected before the cycle is completed.

The normal operating cycle for most companies is less than one year, but there are exceptions. Tobacco companies, for example, must cure the tobacco for two or three years before their inventory can be sold. The tobacco inventory is still considered a current asset because it will

Exhibit 8-1. Classified Balance Sheet for Shafer Auto Parts Company

Shafer Auto Parts Company
Balance Sheet
December 31, 19xx

Assets

Current Assets			
Cash		$10,360	
Short-Term Investments		2,000	
Notes Receivable		8,000	
Accounts Receivable		35,300	
Merchandise Inventory		60,400	
Prepaid Insurance		6,600	
Store Supplies		1,060	
Office Supplies		636	
Total Current Assets			$124,356
Investments			
Land Held for Future Use			5,000
Property, Plant, and Equipment			
Land		$ 4,500	
Building	$20,650		
Less Accumulated Depreciation	8,640	12,010	
Delivery Equipment	$18,400		
Less Accumulated Depreciation	9,450	8,950	
Office Equipment	$ 8,600		
Less Accumulated Depreciation	5,000	3,600	
Total Property, Plant, and Equipment			29,060
Intangible Assets			
Trademark			500
Total Assets			$158,916

Liabilities

Current Liabilities			
Accounts Payable		$25,683	
Notes Payable		15,000	
Salaries Payable		2,000	
Total Current Liabilities			$ 42,683
Long-Term Liabilities			
Mortgage Payable			17,800
Total Liabilities			$ 60,483

Owner's Equity

Fred Shafer, Capital	98,433
Total Liabilities and Owner's Equity	$158,916

Figure 8-3. The Operating Cycle

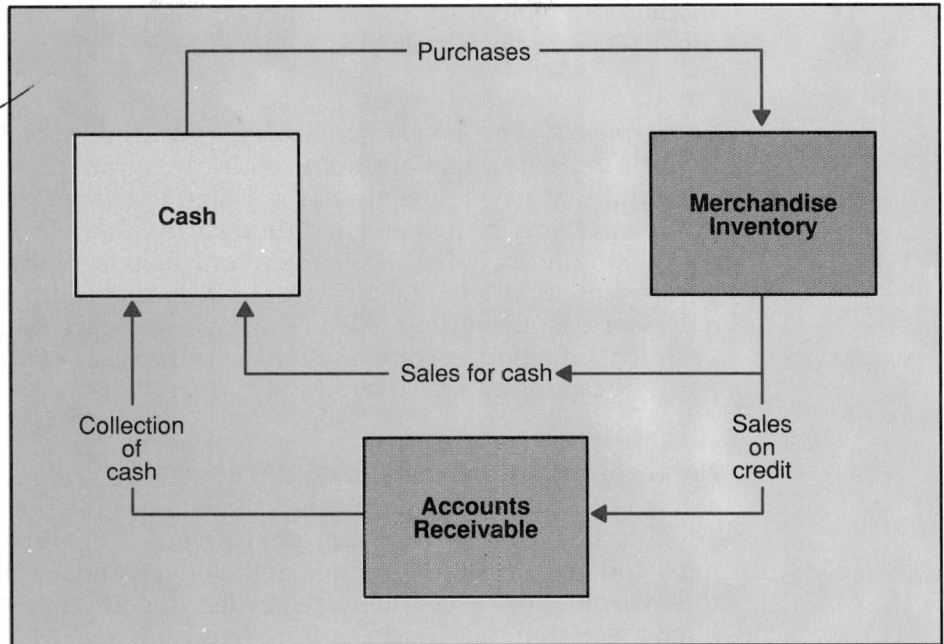

be sold within the normal operating cycle. Another example is a company that sells on the installment basis. The collection payments for a television set or stove may be extended over twenty-four or thirty-six months, but these receivables are still considered current assets.

Cash is obviously a current asset. Temporary investments, accounts and notes receivable, and inventory are also current assets because they are expected to be converted to cash within the next year or during the normal operating cycle of most firms, if the cycle is longer than one year. They are listed in the order of the ease of their conversion into cash. Accounting for these short-term assets is presented in Chapter 9.

Prepaid expenses, such as rent and insurance paid for in advance, and inventories of various supplies bought for use rather than for sale should also be classified as current assets. These kinds of assets are current in the sense that, if they had not been bought earlier, a current outlay of cash would be needed to obtain them. They are an exception to the current asset definition presented earlier.[7]

In deciding whether or not an asset is current or noncurrent, the idea of "reasonable expectation" is important. For example, short-term investments represent an account used for temporary investments of idle cash or cash not immediately required for operating purposes. Management can reasonably expect to sell these securities as cash needs arise

7. *Accounting Research and Terminology Bulletin,* Final Edition (New York: American Institute of Certified Public Accountants, 1961), p. 20.

over the next year or operating cycle. Investments in securities that management does not expect to sell within the next year and that do not involve the temporary use of idle cash should be shown in the investments category of a classified balance sheet.

Investments. The investments category includes assets, generally of a long-term nature, that are not used in the normal operation of a business and that management does not plan to convert to cash within the next year. Items in this category are securities held for long-term investment, long-term notes receivable, land held for future use, plant or equipment not used in the business, and special funds such as to pay off a debt or buy a building. Also in this category are large permanent investments in another company for the purpose of controlling that company. These topics are covered in Chapter 20.

Property, Plant, and Equipment. The property, plant, and equipment category includes long-term assets that are used in the continuing operation of the business. They represent a place to operate (land and buildings) and equipment to produce, sell, deliver, and service its goods. For this reason, these assets are often called operating assets or sometimes fixed assets, tangible assets, or long-lived assets. We have seen earlier in the book that, through depreciation, the cost of these assets (except land) is spread over the periods they benefit. Past depreciation is recorded in the accumulated depreciation accounts. The exact order in which property, plant, and equipment are listed is not the same everywhere in practice and often various accounts are combined to make the financial statement less cluttered, perhaps in the following manner:

Property, Plant, and Equipment

Land		$ 4,500
Buildings and Equipment	$47,650	
Less Accumulated Depreciation	23,090	24,560
Total Property, Plant, and Equipment		$29,060

Property, plant, and equipment also includes natural resources owned, such as forest lands, oil and gas properties, or coal mines. Assets of this type not used in the regular course of business should be listed in the investments category, as noted above. Chapters 12 and 13 are devoted largely to property, plant, and equipment.

Intangible Assets. Intangible assets are long-term assets that have no physical substance but have a value based on rights or privileges that belong to the owner. Examples are patents, copyrights, goodwill, franchises, and trademarks. These assets are recorded at cost, which is spread over the expected life of the right or privilege. These assets are explained further in Chapter 13.

Other Assets. Some companies use the category **other assets** to group all the assets owned by a company other than current assets and property, plant, and equipment. Other assets might include investments and intangible assets.

Liabilities

Liabilities are divided into two categories: current liabilities and long-term liabilities.

Current Liabilities. The category **current liabilities** consists of obligations due within the normal operating cycle of the business or within a year, whichever is longer. These liabilities are generally paid from current assets or by incurring new short-term liabilities. Under this heading are notes payable, accounts payable, the current portion of long-term debt, wages payable, taxes payable, and customer advances (unearned revenues). Current liabilities are presented in more detail in Chapter 11.

Long-Term Liabilities. Debts of a business that fall due more than one year ahead or beyond the normal operating cycle, or that are to be paid out of noncurrent assets are **long-term liabilities.** Mortgages payable, long-term notes, bonds payable, employee pension obligations, and long-term lease liabilities generally fall in this category. Long-term liabilities are presented in Chapter 17.

Owner's Equity

The terms *owner's equity, proprietorship, capital,* and *net worth* are used interchangeably. They all stand for the owner's interest in the company. The first three terms are felt to be better usage than *net worth* because most assets are recorded at original cost rather than at current value. For this reason, the ownership section will not represent "worth." It is really a claim against the assets.

The accounting treatment of assets and liabilities is not generally affected by the form of business organization. However, the owner's equity section of the balance sheet will be different depending on whether the business is a sole proprietorship, a partnership, or a corporation.

Sole Proprietorship. You are already familiar with the owner's equity section of a sole proprietorship as shown in the balance sheet for Shafer Auto Parts Company:

Owner's Equity

Fred Shafer, Capital $98,433

Partnership. The owners' equity section of the balance sheet for a partnership is called partners' equity and is much like that of the sole proprietorship. It might appear as follows:

Partners' Equity

A. J. Martin, Capital	$21,666
R. C. Moore, Capital	35,724
Total Partners' Equity	$57,390

Corporation. Corporations are by law separate and legal entities. The owners are the stockholders. The owners' equity section of a balance sheet for a corporation is called stockholders' equity and has two parts: contributed or paid-in capital and earned capital or retained earnings. It might appear as follows:

Stockholders' Equity

Contributed Capital		
Common Stock—$10 par value, 5,000 shares		
authorized, issued, and outstanding	$50,000	
Paid-in Capital in Excess of Par Value	10,000	
Total Contributed Capital		$60,000
Retained Earnings		37,500
Total Stockholders' Equity		$97,500

As you will remember, owner's equity accounts show the sources of and claims on assets. Of course, these claims are not on any particular asset but rather on the assets as a whole. It follows, then, that contributed and earned capital accounts of a corporation measure stockholders' claims on assets and also indicate the sources of the assets. Contributed or paid-in capital accounts reveal the amounts of assets invested by stockholders themselves. Generally, contributed capital is shown on corporate balance sheets by two amounts: (1) the face or par value of issued stock, and (2) amounts paid in or contributed in excess of the face or par value per share. In the illustration above, stockholders invested amounts equal to par value of the outstanding stock (5,000 × $10) plus $10,000 more.

The **Retained Earnings** account is sometimes called Earned Capital because it represents the stockholders' claim to the assets earned during profitable operations and plowed back into, or reinvested in, corporate operations. Distributions of assets to shareholders, called dividends, reduce the Retained Earnings account balance just as withdrawals of assets by the owner of a business lower his or her capital account balance. Thus the Retained Earnings account balance, in its simplest form, represents the earnings of the corporation less dividends paid to stockholders over the life of the business.

Forms of the Income Statement

For internal management, a detailed income statement such as the one you learned about in Chapter 5 and the one for Shafer Auto Parts Company in Exhibit 8-2 is helpful in analyzing the company's performance.

Exhibit 8-2. Income Statement for Shafer Auto Parts Company

Shafer Auto Parts Company
Income Statement
For the Year Ended December 31, 19xx

Revenues from Sales			
Sales			$299,156
Less: Sales Returns and Allowances	$ 6,300		
Sales Discounts	3,200		9,500
Net Sales			$289,656
Cost of Goods Sold			
Merchandise Inventory, January 1, 19xx		$ 64,800	
Purchases	$168,624		
Freight In	8,236	176,860	
Goods Available for Sale		$241,660	
Merchandise Inventory, December 31, 19xx		60,400	
Cost of Goods Sold			181,260
Gross Margin from Sales			$108,396
Operating Expenses			
Selling Expenses			
Sales Salaries Expense	$ 22,500		
Rent Expense, Store Fixtures	5,600		
Freight Out Expense	5,740		
Advertising Expense	10,000		
Insurance Expense, Selling	1,600		
Store Supplies Expense	1,540		
Depreciation Expense, Building	2,600		
Depreciation Expense, Delivery Equipment	5,200		
Total Selling Expenses		$ 54,780	
General and Administrative Expenses			
Office Salaries Expense	$ 26,900		
Insurance Expense, General	4,200		
Office Supplies Expense	1,204		
Depreciation Expense, Office Equipment	2,200		
Total General and Administrative Expenses		34,504	
Total Operating Expenses			89,284
Income from Operations			$ 19,112
Other Revenues and Expenses			
Interest Income		$ 1,400	
Less Interest Expense		2,631	
Excess of Other Expenses over Other Revenues			1,231
Net Income			$ 17,881

In the Shafer statement, gross margin from sales less operating expenses is called **income from operations**, and a new section, **other revenues and expenses**, is added to the statement to include nonoperating revenues and expenses. This latter section includes revenues from investments (such as dividends and interest from stocks and bonds and savings accounts) and interest earned on credit or notes extended to customers. It also includes interest expense and other expenses that result from borrowing money or from credit being extended to the company. If the company has other revenues and expenses unrelated to normal business operations, they too are classified in this part of the income statement. Thus, an analyst wanting to compare two companies independent of their financing methods, that is, before considering other revenues and expenses, would focus on income from operations. Income taxes expense and earnings per share information do not appear on the income statement for Shafer Auto Parts Company because they apply to corporation accounting.

OBJECTIVE 6
Prepare the multistep and single-step types of classified income statements

For external reporting purposes, the income statement is usually presented in condensed form. **Condensed financial statements** present only the major categories of the financial statement. There are two common forms of the condensed income statement, the multistep form and the single-step form. The **multistep form**, illustrated in Exhibit 8-3, derives net income in the same step-by-step fashion as the detailed income statement for Shafer Auto Parts Company in Exhibit 8-2 except that only the totals of significant categories are given. Usually, some breakdown is shown for operating expenses such as the totals for selling expenses and for general and administrative expenses. Other reve-

---

Exhibit 8-3. Condensed Multistep Income Statement for Shafer Auto Parts Company

Shafer Auto Parts Company
Income Statement
For the Year Ended December 31, 19xx

Revenues from Sales		$289,656
Cost of Goods Sold		181,260
Gross Margin from Sales		$108,396
Operating Expenses		
Selling Expenses	$54,780	
General and Administrative Expenses	34,504	
Total Operating Expenses		89,284
Income from Operations		$ 19,112
Other Revenues and Expenses		
Interest Income	$ 1,400	
Less Interest Expense	2,631	
Excess of Other Expenses over Other Revenues		1,231
Net Income		$ 17,881

nues and expenses are also usually broken down. The **single-step form,** illustrated in Exhibit 8-4, derives net income in a single step by putting the major categories of revenues in the first part of the statement and the major categories of costs and expenses in the second part. Each of these forms has its advantages. The multistep form shows the components used in deriving net income, while the single-step form has the advantage of simplicity. About an equal number of large U.S. companies use each form in their public reports.

Other Financial Statements

Two other statements that are necessary to an understanding of a company's financial operations are the statement of owner's equity and the statement of cash flows.

The statement of owner's equity for Shafer Auto Parts Company is shown in Exhibit 8-5. The statement of retained earnings for a corporation is very similar. In place of the beginning and ending balances of capital are the beginning and ending balances of retained earnings. Instead of withdrawals there are dividends paid to stockholders. Net income is added in a similar way in the statement of retained earnings. Later in this chapter, the statement related to the owners' equity of a major corporation is presented. Chapters 15 and 16 deal with the special problems of the equity section of the balance sheet for corporations.

A simple form of the statement of cash flows was shown in Chapter 1. A more complicated one appears in Figure 8-7 near the end of this chapter. This important statement is explained in detail in Chapter 18.

Exhibit 8-4. Condensed Single-Step Income Statement for Shafer Auto Parts Company

Shafer Auto Parts Company
Income Statement
For the Year Ended December 31, 19xx

Revenues		
Net Sales	$289,656	
Interest Income	1,400	
Total Revenues		$291,056
Costs and Expenses		
Cost of Goods Sold	$181,260	
Selling Expenses	54,780	
General and Administrative Expenses	34,504	
Interest Expense	2,631	
Total Costs and Expenses		273,175
Net Income		$ 17,881

Exhibit 8-5. Statement of Owner's Equity for Shafer Auto Parts Company	
Shafer Auto Parts Company	
Statement of Owner's Equity	
For the Year Ended December 31, 19xx	
Fred Shafer, Capital, January 1, 19xx	$100,552
Net Income for the Year	17,881
	$118,433
Less Withdrawals	20,000
Fred Shafer, Capital, December 31, 19xx	$ 98,433

Using Classified Financial Statements

OBJECTIVE 7
Use classified financial statements for the simple evaluation of liquidity and profitability

A major reason for classifying financial statements is to aid in evaluating a business. Though the analysis and interpretation of financial statements is the subject of Chapter 19, it is helpful at this point to explain briefly how classified financial statements can be used to show meaningful relationships. Earlier in this chapter you learned that the objectives of financial reporting, according to the Financial Accounting Standards Board, are to provide information that is useful in making investment and credit decisions, in judging cash flow prospects, and in understanding business resources, claims to those resources, and changes in them. These objectives are related to two of the more important goals of management (explained in Chapter 1)—those of (1) maintaining adequate liquidity and (2) achieving satisfactory profitability—because the decisions made by investors and creditors are based largely on their assessment of the company's potential liquidity and profitability. The following analysis focuses on these two important goals.

Evaluation of Liquidity

Liquidity means having enough money on hand to (1) pay a company's bills when they are due and (2) take care of unexpected needs for cash. Two measures of liquidity are working capital and the current ratio.

Working Capital. The first measure, **working capital**, is the amount by which total current assets exceed total current liabilities. This is an important measure of liquidity, because current liabilities are debts to be paid within one year and current assets are assets to be realized in cash or used up within one year or one operating cycle, whichever is longer. By definition, current liabilities will be paid out of current assets. So the excess of current assets over current liabilities is, in fact, the net current assets on hand to continue business operations. It is the funds or working capital that can be used to buy inventory, obtain credit, and finance expanded sales. Lack of working capital can lead to the failure of a company. For Shafer Auto Parts Company, the working capital is computed as follows:

Current Assets	$124,356
Less Current Liabilities	42,683
Working Capital	$ 81,673

Current Ratio. The second measure of liquidity, called the current ratio, is closely related to working capital and is believed by many bankers and other creditors to be a good indicator of a company's ability to pay its bills and to repay outstanding loans. The **current ratio** is the ratio of current assets to current liabilities. For Shafer Auto Parts Company, it would be computed as follows:

$$\text{Current ratio} = \frac{\text{current assets}}{\text{current liabilities}} = \frac{\$124,356}{\$42,683} = 2.9$$

Based on this result, Shafer has $2.90 of current assets for each $1.00 of current liabilities. Judging whether this rate is good or bad involves comparing this year's ratio with those of earlier years and with similar measures of successful companies in the same industry. A very low current ratio can, of course, be unfavorable, but so can a very high one. The latter may indicate that the company is not using its assets effectively.

Evaluation of Profitability

Equally important as paying one's bills on time is the goal of **profitability**—the ability to earn a satisfactory level of earnings. As a goal, profitability competes with liquidity for managerial attention because liquid assets, while important, are not the best profit-producing resources. Cash, for example, means purchasing power, but a satisfactory profit will result only if purchasing power is used to buy profit-producing (and less liquid) assets such as inventory and long-term assets.

Among the common measures that have to do with a company's ability to earn an income are (1) profit margin, (2) asset turnover, (3) return on assets, (4) debt to equity, and (5) return on equity. To evaluate a company meaningfully, one must relate a company's profit performance to its past and prospects for the future as well as to the norms (averages) of other companies competing in the same industry.

Profit Margin. The **profit margin** shows the percentage of each sales dollar that results in net income. It is figured by dividing net income by net sales. It should not be confused with gross margin, which is not a ratio, but rather the amount by which revenues exceed cost of goods sold. For Shafer Auto Parts Company, the profit margin is as follows:

$$\text{Profit margin} = \frac{\text{net income}}{\text{net sales}} = \frac{\$17,881}{\$289,656} = .062 \ (6.2\%)$$

On each dollar of sales, Shafer Auto Parts Company made 6.2¢. A difference of 1 or 2 percent in a company's profit margin may mean the difference between a fair year and a very profitable one.

Asset Turnover. **Asset turnover** measures how efficiently assets are used to produce sales. It is computed by dividing net sales by average total assets and shows how many dollars of sales were generated by each dollar of assets. A company with a higher asset turnover uses its assets more productively than one with a lower asset turnover. Average total assets is computed by adding total assets at the beginning of the year to total assets at the end of the year and dividing by 2. Assuming that total assets for Shafer Auto Parts Company were $148,620 at the beginning of the year, the asset turnover is computed as follows:

$$\text{Asset turnover} = \frac{\text{net sales}}{\text{average total assets}}$$

$$= \frac{\$289,656}{(\$148,620 + \$158,916)/2}$$

$$= \frac{\$289,656}{\$153,768} = 1.88 \text{ times}$$

Shafer Auto Parts Company produces $1.88 in sales for each dollar in average total assets. This ratio shows the relationship between an income statement figure and a balance sheet figure.

Return on Assets. Both the profit margin and asset turnover ratios have deficiencies. The profit margin ratio does not take into consideration the assets necessary to produce income, and the asset turnover ratio does not take into account the amount of income produced. The **return on assets** ratio overcomes these deficiencies by relating net income to average total assets. It is computed as follows:

$$\text{Return on assets} = \frac{\text{net income}}{\text{average total assets}}$$

$$= \frac{\$17,881}{(\$148,620 + \$158,916)/2}$$

$$= \frac{\$17,881}{\$153,768} = .116 \text{ (or 11.6\%)}$$

For each dollar invested, Shafer Auto Parts Company's assets generated 11.6¢ of net income. This ratio indicates the income-generating strength (profit margin) of the company's resources and how efficiently the company is using all its assets (asset turnover). This conclusion may be demonstrated as follows:

$$\text{Profit margin} \times \text{asset turnover} = \text{return on assets}$$
$$6.2\% \quad \times \quad 1.88 \text{ times} \quad = \quad 11.6\%$$

Thus a company's management may improve overall profitability by increasing the profit margin or the asset turnover or both. Similarly, in evaluating a company's overall profitability, the financial statement user must consider the interaction of both ratios to produce return on assets.

Debt to Equity. Another useful measure is the debt to equity ratio, which shows the proportion of the company financed by creditors in comparison to that financed by the owner. This ratio is computed by dividing total liabilities by owner's equity. A debt to equity ratio of 1.0 means that total liabilities equal owner's equity and that one-half of the company's assets are financed by creditors. A ratio of .5 would mean that one-third of the assets were financed by creditors. A company with a high debt to equity ratio is more vulnerable in poor economic times because it must continue to repay creditors. Owner's investments, on the other hand, do not have to be repaid and withdrawals can be deferred if the company is suffering because of a poor economy. The debt to equity ratio for Shafer Auto Parts Company is computed as follows:

$$\text{Debt to equity} = \frac{\text{total liabilities}}{\text{owner's equity}} = \frac{\$60,483}{\$98,433} = .614 \text{ (or } 61.4\%)$$

Because its ratio of debt to equity is 61.4 percent, about 40 percent of Shafer Auto Parts Company is financed by creditors and roughly 60 percent is financed by Fred Shafer.

The debt to equity ratio does not fit neatly into either the liquidity or profitability category. It is clearly very important to liquidity analysis because it relates to debt and its repayment. However, it is also relevant to profitability for two reasons. First, creditors are interested in the proportion of the business that is debt financed because the more debt a company has, the more profit it must earn to protect the payment of interest to the creditors. Second, owners are interested in the proportion of the business that is debt financed. The amount of interest that must be paid on the debt affects the amount of profit that is left to provide a return on owner's investment. The debt to equity ratio also shows how much expansion might be possible by borrowing additional long-term funds.

Return on Equity. Of course, Fred Shafer is interested in how much he as the owner earned on his investment in the business. His return on equity is measured by the ratio of net income to average owner's equity. The beginning and ending owner's equity needed to compute average owner's equity are found on the statement of owner's equity (Exhibit 8-5, page 346). The return on equity for the company is computed as follows:

$$\text{Return on equity} = \frac{\text{net income}}{\text{average owner's equity}}$$

$$= \frac{\$17,881}{(\$100,552 + \$98,433)/2}$$

$$= \frac{\$17,881}{\$99,492.50} = .180 \text{ (or 18.0\%)}$$

So in 19xx Shafer Auto Parts Company has earned 18¢ for every dollar invested by the owner, Fred Shafer. Judging whether or not this is an acceptable return will depend on several factors such as how much the company earned in prior years and how much other companies in the same industry earned.

The Annual Report of a Major Corporation

OBJECTIVE 8

Identify the major components of a corporate annual report

So far, simple financial statements have been presented. Statements for major corporations, however, can be quite complicated and have many other features. The management of a corporation has a responsibility each year to report to the stockholders on the company's performance. This report, called the **annual report**, contains the annual financial statements, the notes related to these financial statements, and other information about the company. In addition to the financial statements and related notes, the annual report usually contains a letter to the stockholders, a multi-year summary of financial highlights, a description of the business, management's discussion of operating results and financial condition, a report of management's responsibility, the auditors' report, and a list of directors and officers of the company. This report and other data must also be filed annually with the Securities and Exchange Commission.

To illustrate the annual report of a major corporation, excerpts from the 1989 annual report of Toys "R" Us, Inc. will be used in the following sections of this chapter. Toys "R" Us, Inc. is one of the most successful retailers of this generation and is famous for its stores filled with huge inventories of toys and other items for children. In recent years, the company has opened a chain of stores that sell children's clothes, called Kids "R" Us.

Letter to the Stockholders

Traditionally, the top officers of corporations address the stockholders about the performance and prospects for the company in a letter at the beginning of the annual report. The President and the Chairman of the Board for Toys "R" Us wrote to the stockholders about the highlights of the past year, the outlook for the new year, human resources, and expansion plans. For example, they reported on the prospects for the 1989 season as follows:

After visiting the February Toy Fair, we are confident that 1989 will be another Toys "R" Us kind of year. There are many new, exciting products and line extensions, particularly in the infants, pre-school, dolls, electronic music, outdoor play, die-cast and action figure categories. Also the electronics category was very strong in 1988 and we expect further strong growth in electronics in 1989.

Financial Highlights (Figure 8-4)

The financial highlights section of the annual report presents key financial statistics for a ten-year period and is often accompanied by graphical presentations. Note, for example, that Figure 8-4 shows key figures for operations, financial position, and number of stores at year end for Toys "R" Us. Net sales and earnings per share are presented graphically. Note that the financial highlights section often includes nonfinancial data such as number of stores or number of employees. In addition to the financial highlights, the annual report will contain a detailed description of the products and divisions of the company. Some analysts scoff at this section of the annual report because of the glossy photographs, but many companies provide useful information about past results and future plans.

Statements of Consolidated Earnings (Figure 8-5)

1. Toys "R" Us calls its income statements the statements of consolidated earnings. The word **consolidated** used in the title means that Toys "R" Us consists of several companies that are combined for financial reporting purposes.
2. The statements of consolidated earnings contain data for the years ended in 1989, 1988, and 1987, shown in the columns at the right, to aid in the evaluation of the company over the years. Financial statements presented in this fashion are called **comparative financial statements**. This form of reporting is in accordance with generally accepted accounting principles. For Toys "R" Us, the fiscal year ends on the Sunday nearest the end of January.
3. Toys "R" Us uses the single-step form of the income statement and so includes all costs and expenses as a deduction from sales to arrive at Earnings Before Taxes on Income.
4. **Income taxes** are the expense for federal and state tax on Toys "R" Us's corporate income. Income taxes for corporations are substantial, often exceeding 35 percent of the income before income taxes, and thus have a significant effect on company decisions. Most other taxes, such as property taxes and employment taxes, are shown among the operating expenses.
5. Earnings per share is reported by Toys "R" Us as **net earnings per share**, a term used by some companies to emphasize that the figure is based on net earnings. Its calculation is based on the average number of common shares outstanding during the year.
6. At the bottom of each page of financial statements, the company reminds the reader in a footnote that the notes accompanying the

Figure 8-4. Financial Highlights for Toys "R" Us, Inc.

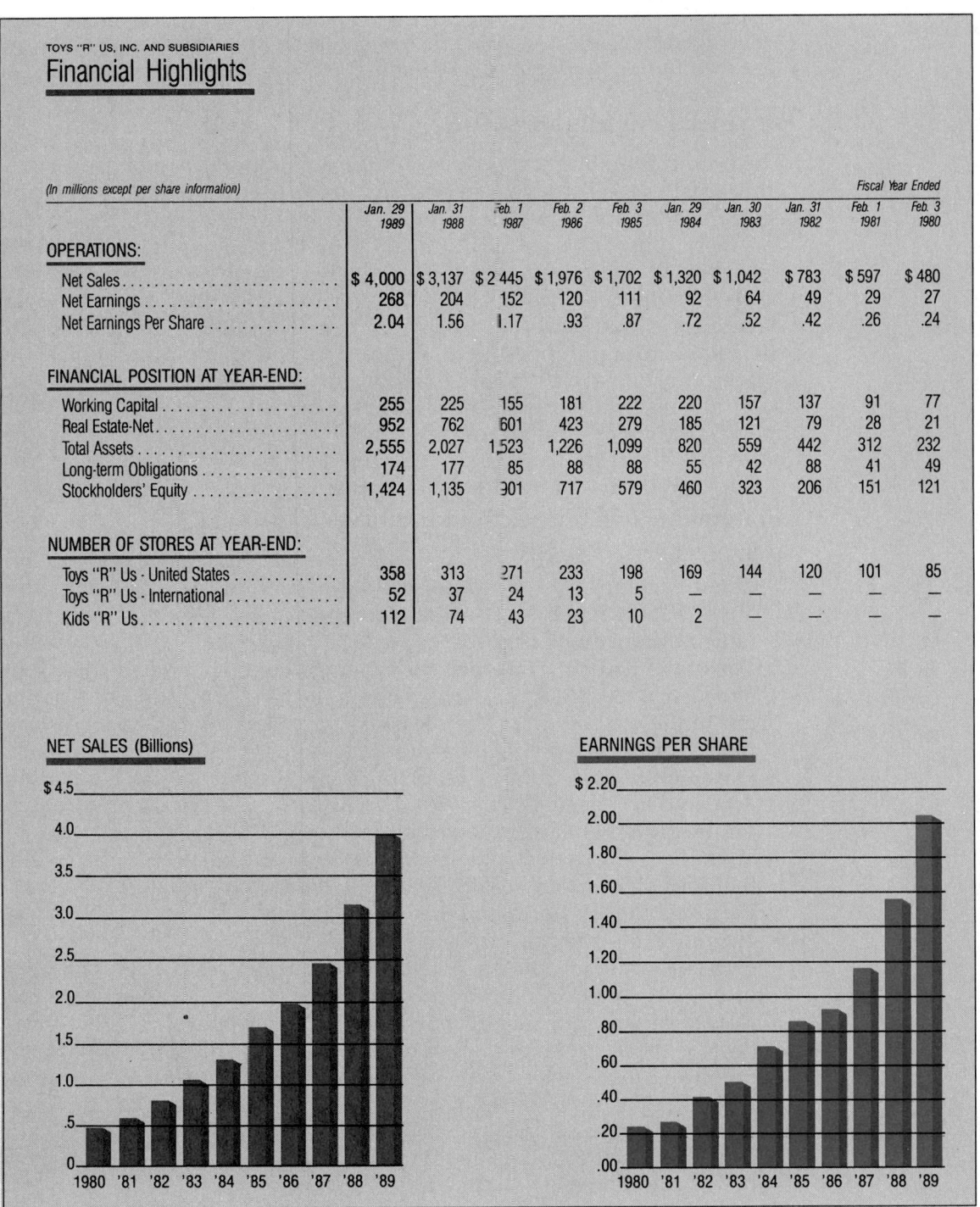

TOYS "R" US, INC. AND SUBSIDIARIES
Financial Highlights

(In millions except per share information)   *Fiscal Year Ended*

	Jan. 29 1989	Jan. 31 1988	Feb. 1 1987	Feb. 2 1986	Feb. 3 1985	Jan. 29 1984	Jan. 30 1983	Jan. 31 1982	Feb. 1 1981	Feb. 3 1980
OPERATIONS:										
Net Sales	$ 4,000	$ 3,137	$ 2,445	$ 1,976	$ 1,702	$ 1,320	$ 1,042	$ 783	$ 597	$ 480
Net Earnings	268	204	152	120	111	92	64	49	29	27
Net Earnings Per Share	2.04	1.56	1.17	.93	.87	.72	.52	.42	.26	.24
FINANCIAL POSITION AT YEAR-END:										
Working Capital	255	225	155	181	222	220	157	137	91	77
Real Estate-Net	952	762	601	423	279	185	121	79	28	21
Total Assets	2,555	2,027	1,523	1,226	1,099	820	559	442	312	232
Long-term Obligations	174	177	85	88	88	55	42	88	41	49
Stockholders' Equity	1,424	1,135	901	717	579	460	323	206	151	121
NUMBER OF STORES AT YEAR-END:										
Toys "R" Us - United States	358	313	271	233	198	169	144	120	101	85
Toys "R" Us - International	52	37	24	13	5	—	—	—	—	—
Kids "R" Us	112	74	43	23	10	2	—	—	—	—

NET SALES (Billions)

EARNINGS PER SHARE

Reprinted courtesy of Toys "R" Us, Inc. The footnotes to the financial statement, which are an integral part of the report, are not included.

Figure 8-5. Statements of Consolidated Earnings for Toys "R" Us, Inc.

TOYS "R" US, INC. AND SUBSIDIARIES

Statements of Consolidated Earnings

(In thousands except per share information)	Fiscal Year Ended		
	January 29 1989	January 31 1988	February 1 1987
Net sales	$ 4,000,192	$ 3,136,568	$ 2,444,903
Costs and expenses:			
Cost of sales	2,766,543	2,157,017	1,668,209
Selling, advertising, general and administrative	736,329	584,120	458,528
Depreciation and amortization	54,564	43,716	33,288
Interest expense	25,812	13,849	7,890
Interest and other income	(11,880)	(8,056)	(7,229)
	3,571,368	2,790,646	2,160,686
Earnings before taxes on income	428,824	345,922	284,217
Taxes on income (Note 6)	160,800	142,000	132,000
Net earnings	$ 268,024	$ 203,922	$ 152,217
Net earnings per share (Note 8)	$2.04	$1.56	$1.17

See notes to consolidated financial statements.

Reprinted courtesy of Toys "R" Us, Inc. The footnotes to the financial statement, which are an integral part of the report, are not included.

financial statements are an integral part of the statements and must be consulted in interpreting the financial statements.

Consolidated Balance Sheets (Figure 8-6)

1. Toys "R" Us also presents consolidated balance sheets in comparative form. In contrast to the statements of consolidated earnings, only two years of comparative data are used for the balance sheet.
2. Toys "R" Us has a typical set of current assets for a merchandising company.
3. Toys "R" Us has a large investment in property and equipment. Note that the contra account Accumulated Depreciation and Amortization is handled here in the same way as the contra account Allowance for Doubtful Accounts in the current asset section. More details on property and equipment are provided in the notes.
4. Toys "R" Us has some leased property that is recorded on the balance sheet as an asset. Also, in place of an investment category and an intangible asset category, Toys "R" Us has a catchall group named other assets.

Figure 8-6. Consolidated Balance Sheets for Toys "R" Us, Inc.

TOYS "R" US, INC. AND SUBSIDIARIES

Consolidated Balance Sheets

(In thousands except shares information)

①

Fiscal Year Ended

	January 29 1989	January 31 1988
ASSETS		
Current Assets:		
② Cash and short-term investments	$ 122,912	$ 45,996
Accounts and other receivables, less allowance for doubtful accounts of $1,510 and $1,386	68,030	62,144
Merchandise inventories (Note 1)	931,120	772,833
Prepaid expenses	10,822	5,050
Total Current Assets	1,132,884	886,023
③ *Property and Equipment (Notes 1, 2 and 3):*		
Real estate, net of accumulated depreciation of $42,781 and $31,238	951,788	762,082
Other, net of accumulated depreciation and amortization of $147,440 and $116,980	436,264	351,037
④ *Leased Property Under Capital Leases,* net of accumulated depreciation of $12,262 and $16,840 (Note 4)	8,910	11,397
Other Assets	25,114	16,520
	$ 2,554,960	$ 2,027,059
LIABILITIES AND STOCKHOLDERS' EQUITY		
Current Liabilities:		
Short-term notes payable to banks	$ 76,133	$ 17,657
Accounts payable	505,370	403,105
⑤ Accrued expenses, taxes and other liabilities	240,928	169,227
Income taxes (Note 6)	55,839	71,003
Total Current Liabilities	878,270	660,992
⑥ *Deferred Income Taxes (Note 6)*	78,819	53,356
Long-Term Debt (Note 3)	159,888	159,788
Obligations Under Capital Leases (Note 4)	14,296	17,602
Commitments (Note 4)		
⑦ *Stockholders' Equity (Note 5):*		
Common stock par value $.10 per share:		
Authorized 350,000,000 shares		
Issued 131,637,038 and 130,530,467	13,164	13,053
Additional paid-in capital	305,739	252,493
Retained earnings	1,122,445	854,421
Foreign currency translation adjustments	23,049	23,586
Treasury shares, at cost	(43,407)	(5,929)
Receivable from exercise of stock options	(2,303)	(2,303)
	1,423,687	1,135,321
	$ 2,554,960	$ 2,027,059

See notes to consolidated financial statements.

Reprinted courtesy of Toys "R" Us, Inc. The footnotes to the financial statement, which are an integral part of the report, are not included.

5. The current liabilities section contains, among other typical current liabilities, the amount of long-term debt and capital leases that must be paid within one year.
6. Another liability in the Toys "R" Us balance sheet is long-term debt and obligations under capital leases (excluding the current portions). Also included is Deferred Income Taxes, an account that is sometimes hard to understand. In general, deferred income taxes are income tax expenses that will not have to be paid until sometime in the future. The subject of deferred income taxes is covered in Chapter 16. Commitments refers to future rental payments and is explained in Note 4 to the Toys "R" Us financial statements.
7. There are several items in the stockholders' equity section. You are familiar with Common Stock and Retained Earnings. Additional paid-in capital represents amounts invested by stockholders in excess of the par value of the common stock. The cumulative foreign currency adjustment occurs because Toys "R" Us has foreign operations (see Chapter 21). Treasury shares is a contra shareholders' equity account that represents the cost of previously issued shares that have been bought back by the company. Finally, the receivable from exercise of stock options represents stock purchased by management and employees but not yet paid for.

The Statement of Consolidated Stockholders' Equity

Instead of a simple statement of retained earnings, Toys "R" Us presents a statement of stockholders' equity. This statement, which is too complex to present at this point in the text, explains the changes in each of the six components of stockholders' equity. The statement is covered in Chapter 16.

The Statements of Consolidated Cash Flows (Figure 8-7)

1. The preparation of the statements of consolidated cash flows is presented in Chapter 18. However, its importance makes it worthwhile for you to look at its major sections at this point. Whereas the income statement reflects the profitability of the company, the statement of cash flows reflects the liquidity of the company. The statement provides information about a company's cash receipts and cash payments and about its investing and financing activities during an accounting period. Three years of comparative statements are presented in Figure 8-7.
2. The first section of the statements of consolidated cash flows shows cash flows from operating activities. It begins with the net income (earnings) from the statement of consolidated earnings (Figure 8-5) and adjusts the figure, which is based on accrual accounting, to a figure that represents the net cash flows provided by operating activities. Among the adjustments are increases for depreciation and amortization, which are expenses that do not require the use of cash, and increases and decreases for the changes in the various working capital accounts. In the year ended January 29, 1989, Toys "R" Us had

Figure 8-7. Statements of Consolidated Cash Flows for Toys "R" Us, Inc.

TOYS "R" US, INC. AND SUBSIDIARIES
Statements of Consolidated Cash Flows

(In thousands)   ①   Fiscal Year Ended

	January 29 1989	January 31 1988	February 1 1987
CASH FLOWS FROM OPERATING ACTIVITIES			
Net income	$ 268,024	$ 203,922	$ 152,217
Adjustments to reconcile net income to net cash provided by operating activities:			
Depreciation and amortization.	54,564	43,716	33,288
Deferred taxes	25,463	13,035	14,184
Change in operating assets and liabilities:			
Accounts and other receivables	(5,886)	(24,642)	(11,531)
Merchandise inventories	(158,287)	(243,894)	(115,446)
Prepaid expenses	(5,772)	(1,484)	(320)
Accounts payable, accrued expenses and taxes	158,802	144,364	102,382
Total adjustments.	68,884	(68,905)	22,557
Net cash provided by operating activities	336,908	135,017	174,774
CASH FLOWS FROM INVESTING ACTIVITIES			
Capital expenditures-net.	(327,010)	(314,827)	(259,388)
Other-net.	(4,131)	13,792	10,952
Net cash used in investing activities	(331,141)	(301,035)	(248,436)
CASH FLOWS FROM FINANCING ACTIVITIES			
Short-term borrowings-net.	58,476	17,663	(1,136)
Long-term borrowings	693	96,611	—
Long-term debt repayments	(3,899)	(1,860)	(2,027)
Exercise of stock options	52,429	15,221	25,033
Share repurchase program	(36,550)	—	—
Net cash provided by financing activities	71,149	127,635	21,870
CASH AND SHORT-TERM INVESTMENTS			
Increase/(decrease) during year	76,916	(38,383)	(51,792)
Beginning of year	45,996	84,379	136,171
End of year	$ 122,912	$ 45,996	$ 84,379

SUPPLEMENTAL DISCLOSURES OF CASH FLOW INFORMATION

⑥   The Company considers all highly liquid investments purchased as part of its daily cash management activities to be short-term investments.

During the years ended January 29, 1989, January 31, 1988 and February 1, 1987, the Company made income tax payments of $110,079,000, $119,722,000 and $79,934,000 and interest payments (net of amounts capitalized) of $25,738,000, $9,610,000 and $8,044,000 respectively.

See notes to consolidated financial statements.

Reprinted courtesy of Toys "R" Us, Inc. The footnotes to the financial statement, which are an integral part of the report, are not included.

net income of $268,024,000, and its net cash inflow from these operations was $336,908,000. The main reason cash flow exceeded net income is that the company had depreciation and amortization of $54,564,000, expenses that do not require the use of cash. Also note that the cash used to increase inventories ($158,287,000) was provided by an increase in Accounts Payable of almost the same amount ($158,802,000).

3. The second major section of the statements of consolidated cash flows is cash flows from investing activities. The main item in this category is capital expenditures, net, of $327,010,000. This shows that Toys "R" Us is a growing company.

4. The third major section of the statements of consolidated cash flows is cash flows from financing activities. You can see here that the primary sources of cash from financing activities are short-term borrowings of $58,476,000 and exercise of stock options of $52,429,000, which was helpful in paying for part of the capital expenditures in the investing activities section. In total, the company raised $71,149,000 from financing activities during the year.

5. At the bottom of the statement of consolidated cash flows, the net effect of the operating, investing, and financing activities on the cash balance may be seen. Toys "R" Us had an increase in cash (and short-term investments) during the year of $76,916,000 and ended the year with $122,912,000 of cash (and short-term investments) on hand.

6. The supplemental disclosures of cash flow information explain that Toys "R" Us intends the word cash to include not only cash but also highly liquid short-term investments, which earn a return on cash that is not needed at the moment. This section also explains other significant investing and financing transactions.

Notes to Consolidated Financial Statements

To meet the requirements of full disclosure, the company must add **notes to the financial statements** to help the user interpret some of the more complex items in the published financial statements. The notes are considered an integral part of the financial statements. In recent years, the need for explanation and further details has become so great that the notes often take more space than the statements themselves. The notes to the financial statements can be put into three broad groups: summary of significant accounting policies, explanatory notes, and supplementary information notes.

Summary of Significant Accounting Policies. In its *Opinion No. 22*, the Accounting Principles Board requires that the financial statements include a **summary of significant accounting policies**. In most cases, this summary is presented in the first note to the financial statements or as a separate part just before the notes. In this part, the company tells which generally accepted accounting principles it has followed in preparing the statements. For example, in the Toys "R" Us report the company states the principles followed for property and equipment:

Property and equipment are recorded at cost. Depreciation and amortization are provided using the straight-line method over the estimated useful lives of the assets, or where applicable, the terms of the respective leases, whichever is shorter.

Other important accounting policies listed by Toys "R" Us deal with principles of consolidation, merchandise inventories, preopening costs, and capitalized interest.

Explanatory Notes. Other notes explain some of the items in the financial statements. For example, Toys "R" Us showed the details of its Property and Equipment account in Note 2, as follows:

(In thousands)	Useful Life (In years)	January 29, 1989	January 31, 1988
Land		$ 333,856	$ 275,012
Buildings	20–50	610,882	473,397
Furniture and equipment	5–15	387,125	320,491
Leaseholds and leasehold improvements	12½–50	196,579	147,526
Construction in progress		49,831	44,911
		1,578,273	1,261,337
Less accumulated depreciation and amortization		190,221	148,218
		$1,388,052	$1,113,119

Other notes had to do with long-term debt, leases, stock options, stock option plan, taxes on income, profit sharing plan, net earnings per share, and foreign operations.

Supplementary Information Notes. In recent years, the FASB and SEC have ruled that certain supplemental information must be presented with financial statements. An example is the quarterly report that most companies make to their stockholders and to the Securities and Exchange Commission. These quarterly reports, which are called **interim financial statements**, are in most cases reviewed but not audited by the company's independent CPA firm. In its annual report, Toys "R" Us presented unaudited quarterly financial data from its 1989 quarterly statements, which are shown in the following table (dollars in thousands, except per share amounts).

Year ended January 29, 1989:

Quarter	Net Sales	Cost of Sales	Net Earnings	Net Earnings per Share
1st	$ 647,195	$ 450,718	$ 22,509	$ .17
2nd	686,760	481,752	23,103	.18
3rd	776,831	541,646	25,823	.20
4th	1,889,406	1,292,427	196,589	1.50
Year	$4,000,192	$2,766,543	$268,024	$2.04

Interim data were presented for 1988 as well. Toys "R" Us also provides supplemental information on the market price of its common stock during the years. Other companies that are engaged in more than one line or type of business may present information for each business segment.

Report of Management's Responsibilities

A statement of management's responsibility for the financial statements and the system of internal control may accompany the financial statements. A part of the statement by Toys "R" Us management is as follows:

Responsibility for the integrity and objectivity of the financial information presented in this Annual Report rests with Toys "R" Us management. The accompanying financial statements have been prepared from accounting records which management believes fairly and accurately reflect the operations and financial position of the Company. Management has established a system of internal controls to provide reasonable assurance that assets are maintained and accounted for in accordance with its policies and that transactions are recorded accurately on the Company's books and records.

Management's Discussion and Analysis

A discussion and analysis of financial conditions and results of operations by management is also presented. In this section, management explains the difference from one year to the next. For example, the management of Toys "R" Us describes the company's sales performance in the following way:

The Company has experienced strong sales growth in each of its last three years; sales were up 27.5% in fiscal 1989, 28.3% in fiscal 1988, and 23.7% in fiscal 1987. Part of the growth is attributable to the opening of 125 new U.S. toy stores, 39 international toy stores and 89 children's clothing stores during the three-year period, and a portion of the increase is due to comparable U.S. toy store sales increases as follows: fiscal 1989—11.3%, fiscal 1988—10.1%, fiscal 1987—8.5%.

Its management of cash flows is described as follows:

Because of the seasonal nature of the business (approximately 47% of sales take place in the fourth quarter), cash typically declines from the beginning of the year through October as inventory is built up for the Christmas season and funds are used for land purchases and construction of new stores which usually open in the first nine months of the year. In this connection, the Company has commitments and backup lines from numerous financial institutions to adequately support its short-term financing needs. The Company expects that seasonal cash requirements will continue to be met primarily through operations, issuance of short-term commercial paper, and bank borrowings for its foreign subsidiaries.

Report of Certified Public Accountants (Figure 8-8)

1. The **accountants' report** (or auditors' report) deals with the credibility of the financial statements. This report by independent public accountants gives the accountants' opinion about how fairly these statements have been presented. Using financial statements prepared by managers without an independent audit would be like having a judge hear a case in which he or she was personally involved or having a member of a team taking part in a football game act as a referee. Management, through its internal accounting system, is logically responsible for recordkeeping because it needs similar information for its own use in operating the business. The certified public

Figure 8-8. Auditors' Report for Toys "R" Us, Inc.

Auditors' Report

(1) Board of Directors and Stockholders
Toys "R" Us, Inc.
Paramus, New Jersey

(2) We have audited the accompanying consolidated balance sheets of Toys "R" Us, Inc. and subsidiaries as of January 29, 1989 and January 31, 1988, and the related consolidated statements of earnings, stockholders' equity and cash flows for the three years then ended. These financial statements are the responsibility of the Company's management. Our responsibility is to express an opinion on these financial statements based on our audits.

(3) We conducted our audits in accordance with generally accepted auditing standards. Those standards require that we plan and perform the audit to obtain reasonable assurance about whether the financial statements are free of material misstatement. An audit includes examining, on a test basis, evidence supporting the amounts and disclosures in the financial statements. An audit also

includes assessing the accounting principles used and significant estimates made by management, as well as evaluating the overall financial statement presentation. We believe that our audits provide a reasonable basis for our opinion.

(4) In our opinion, the consolidated financial statements referred to above present fairly, in all material respects, the financial position of Toys "R" Us, Inc. and subsidiaries as of January 29, 1989 and January 31, 1988, and the results of its operations and its cash flows for each of the three years in the period ended January 29, 1989 in conformity with generally accepted accounting principles.

Touche Ross & Co.

Certified Public Accountants
March 15, 1989
New York, New York

Reprinted courtesy of Toys "R" Us, Inc. The footnotes to the financial statement, which are an integral part of the report, are not included.

accountant, acting independently, adds the necessary credibility to management's figures for interested third parties. Note that the certified public accountant reports to the board of directors and the stockholders rather than to management.

In form and language, most auditors' reports are like the ones shown in Figure 8-8. Usually such a report is short, but its language is very important. The report is divided into three parts.

2. The first paragraph identifies the financial statements subject to the auditors' report. This paragraph also identifies responsibilities. Management is responsible for financial statements, and the auditor is responsible for expressing an opinion on the financial statements based on the audit.

3. The second paragraph or **scope section** states that the examination was made in accordance with generally accepted auditing standards. These standards call for an acceptable level of quality in ten areas established by the American Institute of Certified Public Accountants. This paragraph also contains a brief description of the objectives and nature of the audit.

4. The third paragraph or **opinion section** states the results of the auditors' examination. The use of the word *opinion* is very important, because the auditor does not certify or guarantee that the statements are absolutely correct. To do so would go beyond the truth, because many items such as depreciation are based on estimates. Instead, the auditors simply give an opinion as to whether, overall, the financial statements "present fairly" the financial position and results of operations. This means that the statements are prepared in accordance with generally accepted accounting principles. If in the auditors' opinion they are not, the auditors must explain why and to what extent they do not meet the standards.

This report reflects a change made by the American Institute of Certified Public Accountants in the language of the auditors' report to emphasize management's responsibility for the financial statements and to clarify the nature and purpose of the audit.

Chapter Review

Review of Learning Objectives

1. **State the objectives of financial reporting.**
   The objectives of financial reporting are that financial statements should provide (1) information useful in making investment and credit decisions, (2) information useful in assessing cash flow prospects, and (3) information about business resources, claims to those resources, and changes in them.

2. **State the qualitative characteristics of accounting information and describe their interrelationships.**
Understandability depends on the knowledge of the user and the ability of the accountant to provide useful information. Usefulness is a function of two primary characteristics, relevance and reliability. Relevance depends on the information's predictive value, feedback value, and timeliness. Reliability depends on the information's representational faithfulness, verifiability, and neutrality.

3. **Define and describe the use of the conventions of comparability and consistency, materiality, conservatism, full disclosure, and cost-benefit.**
Because accountants' measurements are not exact, certain conventions have come to be applied in current practice to aid in interpreting the financial statements. One of these conventions is consistency, which requires the use of the same accounting procedures from period to period and enhances the comparability of financial statements. Second is materiality, which involves the relative importance of an item. Third is conservatism, which entails using the procedure that will be least likely to overstate assets and income. Fourth is full disclosure, which means including all relevant information in the financial statements. Fifth is cost-benefit, which suggests that after providing a minimum level of information, additional information should be provided only if the benefits derived from the information exceed the costs of providing it.

4. **Summarize the concepts underlying financial accounting and their relationship to ethical financial reporting.**
Accounting is an information system that facilitates the making of business decisions by measuring, processing, and communicating to decision makers information in the form of financial statements about the transactions of a business entity. To interpret and use the financial statements, it is important to understand the generally accepted accounting principles (GAAP), qualitative characteristics, and accounting conventions that underlie the accounting information system. Ethical financial reporting means that these concepts are applied with the intent to enlighten, not to mislead.

5. **Identify and describe the basic components of a classified balance sheet.**
The classified balance sheet is subdivided as follows:

Assets	**Liabilities**
Current Assets	Current Liabilities
Investments	Long-Term Liabilities
Property, Plant, and Equipment	
Intangible Assets	**Owner's Equity**
(Other Assets)	
	(Category depends on form of business)

A current asset is an asset that can reasonably be expected to be realized in cash during the next year or normal operating cycle. In general, assets are listed in the order of the ease of their conversion into cash. A current liability is a liability that can reasonably be expected to be paid during the next year or normal operating cycle, whichever is longer. The owners' (stockholders') equity section for a corporation differs from that of a proprietorship in that it has subdivisions of contributed capital and retained earnings.

6. **Prepare the multistep and single-step types of classified income statements.**

   Condensed income statements for external reporting may be in multistep or single-step form. The multistep form arrives at net income through a series of steps, whereas the single-step form arrives at net income in a single step. There is usually a separate section in the multistep form for other revenues and expenses.

7. **Use classified financial statements for the simple evaluation of liquidity and profitability.**

   One major use of classified financial statements is to evaluate the company's liquidity and profitability. Two simple measures of liquidity are working capital and the current ratio. Five simple measures of profitability are profit margin, asset turnover, return on assets, debt to equity, and return on equity.

8. **Identify the major components of a corporate annual report.**

   A corporation's annual report is the mechanism by which management reports to the stockholders the company's financial results for the year. The annual report has the following principal components: letter to the stockholders, financial highlights, the four basic financial statements, notes to the financial statements, report of management's responsibilities, management's discussion and analysis of earnings, and the report of the certified public accountant.

Review of Concepts and Terminology

The following concepts and terms were introduced in this chapter:

(L.O. 8) **Accountants' (auditors') report:** The medium by which the independent public accountants communicate to the users of the financial statements the nature of the audit (scope section) and the conclusion as to the fair presentation of the financial statements (opinion section).

(L.O. 8) **Annual report:** The medium by which the general-purpose external financial statements of a business are communicated once a year to stockholders and other interested parties.

(L.O. 7) **Asset turnover:** A ratio that measures how efficiently assets are used to produce sales; net sales divided by average total assets.

(L.O. 5) **Classified financial statements:** General-purpose external financial statements that are divided into useful subcategories.

(L.O. 3) **Comparability:** The convention of presenting information in such a way that decision makers can recognize similarities, differences, and trends.

(L.O. 8) **Comparative financial statements:** Financial statements in which data for two or more years are presented in adjacent columnar form.

(L.O. 6) **Condensed financial statements:** Financial statements for external reporting purposes that present only the major categories of information.

(L.O. 3)   **Conservatism:** The convention that mandates that, in the face of two equally acceptable alternatives, the accountant will choose the one less likely to overstate assets and income.

(L.O. 3)   **Consistency:** The convention that an accounting procedure, once adopted, will not be changed from one period to another unless users are informed of the change.

(L.O. 8)   **Consolidated (financial statements):** The combined financial statements of a parent company and its subsidiaries.

(L.O. 3)   **Cost-benefit:** The convention that benefits gained from providing accounting information should be greater than the costs of providing that information.

(L.O. 5)   **Current assets:** Cash or other assets that are reasonably expected to be realized in cash, sold, or consumed during a normal operating cycle of a business or within one year if the operating cycle is shorter than one year.

(L.O. 5)   **Current liabilities:** Obligations due within the normal operating cycle of the business or within one year, whichever is longer.

(L.O. 7)   **Current ratio:** A measure of liquidity; current assets divided by current liabilities.

(L.O. 7)   **Debt to equity ratio:** A ratio that measures the relationship of assets provided by creditors to those provided by owners; total liabilities divided by owner's equity.

(L.O. 8)   **Earnings per share (net earnings per common share or net income per share):** Item on corporate income statements that shows the net income earned on each share of common stock; net income divided by the weighted average of common shares outstanding.

(L.O. 4)   **Fraudulent financial reporting:** The intentional preparation of misleading financial statements.

(L.O. 3)   **Full disclosure:** The convention that requires financial statements and the notes to them to present all information relevant to the users' understanding of the company's financial condition.

(L.O. 1)   **General-purpose external financial statements:** The medium through which information gathered and processed in the accounting system is periodically communicated to investors, creditors, and other interested parties outside the business.

(L.O. 6)   **Income from operations:** The excess of gross margin from sales over operating expenses.

(L.O. 8)   **Income taxes (income taxes expense or provision for income taxes):** An account that represents the expense for federal and state income tax on corporate income; this account appears only on income statements of corporations.

(L.O. 5)   **Intangible assets:** Long-term assets that have no physical substance but have a value based on rights or privileges accruing to the owner.

(L.O. 8)   **Interim financial statements:** Financial statements prepared on a condensed basis for an accounting period of less than one year.

(L.O. 5)   **Investments:** Assets, generally of a long-term nature, that are not used in the normal operation of a business and that management does not intend to convert to cash within the next year.

(L.O. 7) **Liquidity:** Having enough money on hand to (1) pay a company's bills when they are due and (2) take care of unexpected needs for cash.

(L.O. 5) **Long-term liabilities:** Debts of a business that fall due more than one year ahead or beyond the normal operating cycle, or are to be paid out of noncurrent assets.

(L.O. 3) **Materiality:** The convention that requires an item or event in a financial statement to be important to the decisions made by users of the financial statements.

(L.O. 6) **Multistep form:** Form of the income statement that arrives at net income in steps.

(L.O. 8) **Notes to the financial statements:** A section of a corporate annual report containing notes that aid the user in interpreting the financial statements.

(L.O. 8) **Opinion section:** Section of auditors' report that states the results of the examination.

(L.O. 5) **Other assets:** All of the assets owned by a company other than current assets and property, plant, and equipment.

(L.O. 6) **Other revenues and expenses:** The section of a classified income statement that includes nonoperating revenues and expenses.

(L.O. 7) **Profitability:** The ability of a business to earn a satisfactory level of earnings.

(L.O. 7) **Profit margin:** A measure of profitability; the percentage of each sales dollar that results in net income; net income divided by net sales.

(L.O. 5) **Property, plant, and equipment:** Tangible assets of a long-term nature used in the continuing operation of the business.

(L.O. 2) **Qualitative characteristics:** Standards for judging the information that accountants give to decision makers.

(L.O. 2) **Relevance:** A qualitative characteristic of accounting information that makes a difference to or bears directly on the economic outcome of a decision for which it is used.

(L.O. 2) **Reliability:** The qualitative characteristic of accounting information that has the traits of representational faithfulness, verifiability, and neutrality.

(L.O. 5) **Retained earnings:** The account representing the stockholders' claim to the assets earned during profitable operations and plowed back into, or reinvested in, corporate operations.

(L.O. 7) **Return on assets:** A measure of profitability that shows how efficiently a company is using its assets; net income divided by average total assets.

(L.O. 7) **Return on equity:** A measure of profitability related to the amount earned by a business in relation to the owner's investment in the business; net income divided by average owner's equity.

(L.O. 8) **Scope section:** Part of auditors' report that tells that the examination was made in accordance with generally accepted auditing standards.

(L.O. 6) **Single-step form:** Form of the income statement that arrives at net income in a single step.

(L.O. 8) **Summary of significant accounting policies:** Section of a corporate annual report that discloses which generally accepted accounting principles the company has followed in preparing the financial statements.

(L.O. 7)   **Working capital**:   The amount by which total current assets exceed total current liabilities.

Self-Test

Test your knowledge of the chapter by choosing the best answer for each item below:

1. Financial reporting provides information that is useful in each of the following situations except
   a. making investment and credit decisions.
   b. assessing cash flow prospects.
   c. making employment decisions.
   d. assessing business resources, claims to, and changes in them.   *(L.O. 1)*

2. Accounting information is said to be useful if it is
   a. timely and biased.   c. relevant and uncertain.
   b. relevant and reliable.   d. accurate and faithful.   *(L.O. 2)*

3. To ignore an amount because it is small in relation to the financial statements taken as a whole is an application of
   a. materiality.   c. full disclosure.
   b. conservatism.   d. comparability.   *(L.O. 3)*

4. Accounting is concerned with providing information to decision makers. The overall framework of rules within which accountants work to provide this information is best described as
   a. business transactions.
   b. data processing.
   c. generally accepted accounting principles.
   d. income tax laws.   *(L.O. 4)*

5. A note receivable due in two years would normally be classified as
   a. a current asset.
   b. an investment.
   c. property, plant, and equipment.
   d. an intangible asset.   *(L.O. 5)*

6. The current portion of long-term debt is normally classified as
   a. current assets.   c. long-term liabilities.
   b. current liabilities.   d. owner's equity.   *(L.O. 5)*

7. A disadvantage of the single-step income statement is that
   a. gross margin from sales is not separately disclosed.
   b. other revenues and expenses is separated from operating items.
   c. interest expense is not disclosed.
   d. cost of goods sold cannot be determined.   *(L.O. 6)*

8. Which of the following ratios is a measure of liquidity?
   a. Return on equity   c. Profit margin
   b. Return on assets   d. Current ratio   *(L.O. 7)*

9. Net income is a component in determining each of the following ratios except
   a. profit margin.   c. debt to equity.
   b. return on assets.   d. return on equity.   *(L.O. 7)*

10. A good source of detailed financial information about a major public corporation is the
    a. company's local office.
    b. company's annual report.
    c. company's product catalog.
    d. *The Wall Street Journal.*   *(L.O. 8)*

Answers to Self-Test can be found at the end of this chapter.

Review Problem
Analyzing Liquidity and Profitability Using Ratios

(L.O. 7)   Flavin Shirt Company has faced increased competition from imported shirts in recent years.
        Presented below is summary information for the past two years:

	19x2	19x1
Current Assets	$ 200,000	$ 170,000
Total Assets	880,000	710,000
Current Liabilities	90,000	50,000
Long-Term Liabilities	150,000	50,000
Owner's Equity	640,000	610,000
Sales	1,200,000	1,050,000
Net Income	60,000	80,000

Total assets and owner's equity at the beginning of 19x1 were $690,000 and $590,000, respectively.

Required   Use liquidity and profitability analyses to document the declining financial position of Flavin Shirt Company.

Answer to Review Problem

Liquidity analysis:

	Current Assets	Current Liabilities	Working Capital	Current Ratio
19x1	$170,000	$50,000	$120,000	3.40
19x2	200,000	90,000	110,000	2.22
Increase (decrease) in working capital			$ (10,000)	
Decrease in current ratio				1.18

Both working capital and the current ratio declined because, although current assets increased by $30,000 ($200,000 – $170,000), current liabilities increased by the greater amount of $40,000 ($90,000 – $50,000) from 19x1 to 19x2.

	Sales			Average Total Assets			Average Owner's Equity	
	Net Income	Sales	Profit Margin	Amount	Asset Turnover	Return on Assets	Amount	Return on Equity
19x1	$ 80,000	$1,050,000	7.6%	$700,000[1]	1.50	11.4%	$600,000[3]	13.3%
19x2	60,000	1,200,000	5.0%	795,000[2]	1.51	7.5%	625,000[4]	9.6%
Increase (Decrease)	$(20,000)	$ 150,000	(2.6)%	$ 95,000	0.01	(3.9)%	$ 25,000	(3.7)%

[1] ($690,000 + $710,000) ÷ 2   [3] ($590,000 + $610,000) ÷ 2
[2] ($710,000 + $880,000) ÷ 2   [4] ($610,000 + $640,000) ÷ 2

Net income decreased by $20,000 in spite of an increase in sales of $150,000 and an increase in average total assets of $95,000. The results were decreases in profit margin from 7.6 percent to 5.0 percent and in return on assets from 11.4 percent to 7.5 percent. Asset turnover had almost no change and thus did not contribute to the decline in profitability. The decrease in return on equity from 13.3 percent to 9.6 percent was not as much as the decrease in return on assets because the growth in total assets was financed by debt instead of owner's equity, as shown by the capital structure analysis that is presented as follows:

	Total Liabilities	Owner's Equity	Debt to Equity Ratio
19x1	$100,000	$610,000	16.4%
19x2	240,000	640,000	37.5%
Increase	$140,000	$ 30,000	21.1%

Total liabilities increased by $140,000 while owner's equity increased by $30,000. As a result, the amount of the business financed by debt in relation to owner's equity increased from 16.4 percent to 37.5 percent.

Chapter Assignments

Discussion Questions and Writing Assignments

1. What are the three objectives of financial reporting?
2. What are the qualitative characteristics of accounting information, and what is their significance?

3. What are the accounting conventions, and how does each aid in the interpretation of financial information?
4. What is the relationship among objectives of financial information, financial statements, decision makers, economic activities, and ethical financial reporting?
5. What is the purpose of classified financial statements?
6. What are four common categories of assets?
7. What criteria must an asset meet to be classified as current? Under what condition will an asset be considered current even though it will not be realized as cash within a year? What are two examples of assets that fall into this category?
8. In what order should current assets be listed?
9. What is the difference between a short-term investment in the current assets section and a security in the investments section of the balance sheet?
10. What is an intangible asset? Give at least three examples.
11. Name the two major categories of liabilities.
12. What are the primary differences between the owner's equity section for a sole proprietorship or partnership and the corresponding section for a corporation?
13. Explain the difference found between contributed capital and retained earnings.
14. Explain how the multistep form of the income statement differs from the single-step form. What are the relative merits of each?
15. Why are other revenues and expenses separated from operating revenues and expenses on the multistep income statement?
16. Define liquidity and name two measures.
17. How is the current ratio computed and why is it important?
18. Which is the more important goal—liquidity or profitability? Explain.
19. Name five measures of profitability.
20. Evaluate this statement: "Return on assets is a better measure of profitability than profit margin."
21. What are some of the differences between the income statement for a sole proprietorship and for a corporation?
22. Explain earnings per share and how this figure appears on the income statement.
23. What is the purpose of the accountants' report?
24. Why are notes to financial statements necessary?

Classroom Exercises

**Exercise 8-1.
Accounting
Concepts and
Conventions
(L.O. 3)**

Each of the statements below violates a convention in accounting. State which of the following concepts or conventions is illustrated: comparability and consistency, materiality, conservatism, full disclosure, or cost-benefit.

1. A series of reports that are time-consuming and expensive to prepare are presented to the board of directors each month even though the reports are never used.
2. A company changes its method of accounting for depreciation.
3. The company in 2 does not indicate in the financial statements that the method of depreciation was changed, nor does it specify the effect of the change on net income.

4. A new office building next to the factory is debited to the Factory account because it represents a fairly small dollar amount in relation to the factory.

5. The asset account for a pickup truck still used in the business is written down to salvage value even though the carrying value under conventional depreciation methods is higher.

Exercise 8-2.
Financial
Accounting
Concepts
(L.O. 1, 2, 3, 4)

The lettered items below represent a classification scheme for the concepts of financial accounting. Match each term with the letter indicating in which category it belongs.

a. Decision makers (users of accounting information)
b. Business activities or entities relevant to accounting measurement
c. Objectives of accounting information
d. Accounting measurement considerations
e. Accounting processing considerations
f. Qualitative characteristics
g. Accounting conventions
h. Financial statements

_____ 1. Conservatism
_____ 2. Verifiability
_____ 3. Statement of cash flows
_____ 4. Materiality
_____ 5. Reliable
_____ 6. Recognition
_____ 7. Cost-benefit
_____ 8. Understandable
_____ 9. Business transactions
_____ 10. Consistency
_____ 11. Full disclosure
_____ 12. To furnish information useful to investors and creditors

_____ 13. Specific business entities
_____ 14. Classification
_____ 15. Management
_____ 16. Neutral (objective)
_____ 17. Internal accounting control
_____ 18. Valuation
_____ 19. Investors
_____ 20. Timely
_____ 21. Relevance
_____ 22. To furnish information useful in assessing cash flow prospects

Exercise 8-3.
Classification of
Accounts: Balance
Sheet
(L.O. 5)

The lettered items below represent a classification scheme for a balance sheet, and the numbered items are account titles. Match each account with the letter indicating in which category it belongs.

a. Current assets
b. Investments
c. Property, plant, and equipment
d. Intangible assets
e. Current liabilities
f. Long-term liabilities
g. Owner's equity
h. Not on balance sheet

_____ 1. Patent
_____ 2. Building Held for Sale
_____ 3. Prepaid Rent
_____ 4. Wages Payable
_____ 5. Note Payable in Five Years
_____ 6. Building Used in Operations
_____ 7. Fund Held to Pay Off Long-Term Debt
_____ 8. Inventory

_____ 9. Prepaid Insurance
_____ 10. Depreciation Expense
_____ 11. Accounts Receivable
_____ 12. Interest Expense
_____ 13. Revenue Received in Advance
_____ 14. Short-term Investments
_____ 15. Accumulated Depreciation
_____ 16. M. Cepeda, Capital

Exercise 8-4.
Classification of
Accounts: Income
Statement
(L.O. 6)

Using the classification scheme below for a multistep income statement, match each account with the category in which it belongs.

a. Revenue
b. Cost of goods sold
c. Selling expenses
d. General and administrative expenses
e. Other revenue or expense
f. Not on income statement

———— 1. Purchases
———— 2. Sales Discounts
———— 3. Beginning Merchandise Inventory
———— 4. Dividend Income
———— 5. Advertising Expense
———— 6. Office Salaries Expense
———— 7. Freight Out Expense
———— 8. Prepaid Insurance
———— 9. Utility Expense
———— 10. Sales Salaries Expense
———— 11. Rent Expense
———— 12. Purchases Returns and Allowances
———— 13. Freight In
———— 14. Depreciation Expense, Delivery Equipment
———— 15. Taxes Payable
———— 16. Interest Expense

Exercise 8-5.
Classified Balance
Sheet Preparation
(L.O. 5)

The following data pertain to a corporation: Cash, $31,200; Investment in Six-Month Government Securities, $16,400; Accounts Receivable, $38,000; Inventory, $40,000; Prepaid Rent, $1,200; Investment in Corporate Securities (long-term), $20,000; Land, $8,000; Building, $70,000; Accumulated Depreciation, Building, $14,000; Equipment, $152,000; Accumulated Depreciation, Equipment, $17,000; Copyright, $6,200; Accounts Payable, $51,000; Revenue Received in Advance, $2,800; Bonds Payable, $60,000; Common stock—$10 par, 10,000 shares authorized, issued, and outstanding, $100,000; Paid-in Capital in Excess of Par Value, $50,000; and Retained Earnings, $88,200.

Prepare a classified balance sheet; omit the heading.

Exercise 8-6.
Preparation of
Income
Statements
(L.O. 6)

The following data pertain to a sole proprietorship: Sales, $810,000; Cost of Goods Sold, $440,000; Selling Expenses, $180,000; General and Administrative Expenses, $120,000; Interest Expense, $8,000; and Interest Income, $6,000.

1. Prepare a condensed single-step income statement.
2. Prepare a condensed multistep income statement.

Exercise 8-7.
Condensed
Multistep Income
Statement
(L.O. 6)

A condensed single-step income statement appears on the following page. Present this information in a condensed multistep income statement, and tell what insights may be obtained from the multistep form as opposed to the single-step form.

Dawson Furniture Company
Income Statement
For the Year Ended December 31, 19xx

Revenues		
Net Sales	$598,566	
Interest Income	2,860	
Total Revenues		$601,426
Costs and Expenses		
Cost of Goods Sold	$388,540	
Selling Expenses	101,870	
General and Adminstrative Expenses	50,344	
Interest Expense	6,780	
Total Costs and Expenses		547,534
Net Income		$ 53,892
Earnings per Share		$5.39

Exercise 8-8.
Liquidity Ratios
(L.O. 7)

The following accounts and balances are taken from the general ledger of West Hills Company:

Accounts Payable	$16,600
Accounts Receivable	10,200
Cash	1,500
Current Portion of Long-Term Debt	10,000
Long-Term Investments	10,400
Marketable Securities	12,600
Merchandise Inventory	25,400
Notes Payable, 90 days	15,000
Notes Payable, 2 years	20,000
Notes Receivable, 90 days	26,000
Notes Receivable, 2 years	10,000
Prepaid Insurance	400
Property, Plant, and Equipment	60,000
Retained Earnings	28,300
Salaries Payable	850
Supplies	350
Property Taxes Payable	1,250
Unearned Revenue	750

Compute (1) working capital and (2) the current ratio.

Exercise 8-9.
Profitability Ratios
(L.O. 7)

The following end-of-year amounts are taken from the financial statements of Lewiston Company: Total Assets, $426,000; Total Liabilities, $172,000; Owner's Equity, $254,000; Net Sales. $782,000; Cost of Goods Sold, $486,000; Operating Expenses, $202,000; and Withdrawals, $40,000. During the past year, total assets increased by $75,000. Total owner's equity was affected only by net income and withdrawals.

Compute (1) profit margin, (2) asset turnover, (3) return on assets, (4) debt to equity, and (5) return on equity.

Exercise 8-10.
Computation of
Ratios
(L.O. 7)

The simplified balance sheet and income statement for a sole proprietorship appear as follows:

Balance Sheet
December 31, 19xx

Assets		Liabilities	
Current Assets	$100,000	Current Liabilities	$ 40,000
Investments	20,000	Long-Term Liabilities	60,000
Property, Plant, and		Total Liabilities	$100,000
Equipment	293,000		
Intangible Assets	27,000	**Owner's Equity**	
Total Assets	$440,000	S. Carroll, Capital	$340,000
		Total Liabilities and	
		Owner's Equity	$440,000

Income Statement
For the Year Ended December 31, 19xx

Revenue from Sales (net)	$820,000
Cost of Goods Sold	500,000
Gross Margin from Sales	$320,000
Operating Expenses	270,000
Net Income	$ 50,000

Total assets and owner's equity at the beginning of 19xx were $360,000 and $280,000, respectively.

1. Compute the following liquidity measures: (a) working capital and (b) current ratio.
2. Compute the following profitability measures: (a) profit margin, (b) asset turnover, (c) return on assets, (d) debt to equity, and (e) return on equity.

Interpreting Accounting Information

Toys "R" Us, Inc.*
(L.O. 5, 6, 7, 8)

The questions in this exercise pertain to the financial statements of Toys "R" Us, Inc. in Figures 8-4 to 8-8. (Note that 1989 refers to the year ended January 29, 1989, and 1988 refers to the year ended January 31, 1988.)

* Excerpts from the 1989 annual report used by permission of Toys "R" Us, Inc. Copyright © 1989.

Required

1. Consolidated balance sheets: (a) Did the amount of working capital increase or decrease from 1988 to 1989? By how much? (b) Did the current ratio improve from 1988 to 1989? (c) Does the company have long-term investments or intangible assets? (d) Did the capital structure of Toys "R" Us change from 1988 to 1989? (e) What is the contributed capital for 1989? How does it compare with retained earnings?
2. Statements of consolidated earnings: (a) Did Toys "R" Us use a multistep or single-step form of income statement? (b) Is it a comparative statement? (c) What is the trend of net earnings? (d) How significant are income taxes for Toys "R" Us? (e) What is the trend of net earnings per share? (f) Did the profit margin increase from 1988 to 1989? (g) Did asset turnover improve from 1988 to 1989? (h) Did the return on assets increase from 1988 to 1989? (i) Did the return on equity increase from 1988 to 1989? Total assets and total stockholders' equity for 1989 may be obtained from Figure 8-6.
3. Statements of cash flows: (a) Compare net income with cash provided by operating activities. Why is there a difference? (b) What are the most important investment activities in 1989? (c) What are the most important financing activities in 1989? (d) How did these investing and financing activities compare with those in prior years? (e) Where did Toys "R" Us get cash to pay for the capital expenditures? (f) How did the change in Cash and Short-Term Investments in 1989 compare to that in other years?
4. Auditors' report: (a) What was the name of Toys "R" Us's independent auditor? (b) Who is responsible for the financial statements? (c) What is the auditor's responsibility? (d) Does the auditor examine all the company's records? (e) Did the accountants think that the financial statements presented fairly the financial situation of the company? (f) Did the company comply with generally accepted accounting principles?

Problem Set A

Problem 8A-1.
Accounting
Conventions
(L.O. 3)

In each case below, accounting conventions may have been violated.

1. Figuero Manufacturing Company uses the cost method for computing the balance sheet amount of inventory unless the market value of the inventory is less than the cost, in which case the market value is used. At the end of the current year, the market value is $77,000 and the cost is $80,000. Figuero uses the $77,000 figure to compute net income because management feels it is the more cautious approach.
2. Margolis Company has annual sales of $5,000,000. It follows the practice of charging any items costing less than $100 to expenses in the year purchased. During the current year, it purchased several chairs for the executive conference rooms at $97 each, including freight. Although the chairs were expected to last for at least ten years, they were charged as an expense in accordance with company policy.
3. Choi Company closed its books on December 31, 19x8, before preparing its annual report. On December 30, 19x8, a fire destroyed one of the company's two factories. Although the company had fire insurance and would not suffer a loss on the building, a significant decrease in sales in 19x9 was expected because of the fire. The fire damage was not reported in the 19x8 financial statements because the operations for that year were not affected by the fire.

4. Shumate Drug Company spends a substantial portion of its profits on research and development The company has been reporting its $2,500,000 expenditure for research and development as a lump sum, but management recently decided to begin classifying the expenditures by project even though the recordkeeping costs will increase.
5. During the current year, McMillan Company changed from one generally accepted method of accounting for inventories to another method.

Required

In each case, state the convention that is applicable, and explain briefly whether or not the treatment is in accord with the convention and generally accepted accounting principles.

**Problem 8A-2.
Forms of the
Income Statement
(L.O. 6)**

Income statement accounts from the June 30, 19x2 year-end adjusted trial balance of Tasheki Hardware Company appear as follows. Beginning merchandise inventory was $175,200 and ending merchandise inventory is $157,650. The company is a sole proprietorship.

Account Name	Debit	Credit
Sales		541,230
Sales Discounts	5,070	
Sales Returns and Allowances	10,228	
Purchases	212,336	
Purchases Discounts		1,877
Purchases Returns and Allowances		4,282
Freight In	11,221	
Sales Salaries Expense	102,030	
Sales Supplies Expense	1,642	
Rent Expense, Selling Space	18,000	
Utility Expense, Selling Space	11,256	
Advertising Expense	21,986	
Depreciation Expense, Selling Fixtures	6,778	
Office Salaries Expense	47,912	
Office Supplies Expense	782	
Rent Expense, Office Space	4,000	
Depreciation Expense, Office Equipment	3,251	
Utility Expense, Office Space	3,114	
Postage Expense	626	
Insurance Expense	2,700	
Miscellaneous Expense	481	
Interest Expense	3,600	
Interest Income		800

Required

From the information provided, prepare the following:

1. A detailed income statement.
2. A condensed income statement in multistep form.
3. A condensed income statement in single-step form.

Problem 8A-3.
Classified Balance Sheet
(L.O. 5)

Accounts from the June 30, 19x2 post-closing trial balance of Tasheki Hardware Company appear below.

Account Name	Debit	Credit
Cash	24,000	
Short-Term Investments	13,150	
Notes Receivable	45,000	
Accounts Receivable	76,570	
Merchandise Inventory	156,750	
Prepaid Rent	2,000	
Prepaid Insurance	1,200	
Sales Supplies	426	
Office Supplies	97	
Land Held for Future Expansion	11,500	
Selling Fixtures	72,400	
Accumulated Depreciation, Selling Fixtures		22,000
Office Equipment	24,100	
Accumulated Depreciation, Office Equipment		12,050
Trademark	4,000	
Accounts Payable		109,745
Salaries Payable		787
Interest Payable		600
Notes Payable (due in three years)		36,000
Thomas Tasheki, Capital		250,011

Required

From the information provided, prepare a classified balance sheet.

Problem 8A-4.
Ratio Analysis: Liquidity and Profitability
(L.O. 7)

A summary of data taken from the income statements and balance sheets for Heard Construction Supply for the past two years appears as follows.

	19x2	19x1
Current Assets	$ 183,000	$ 155,000
Total Assets	1,160,000	870,000
Current Liabilities	90,000	60,000
Long-Term Liabilities	400,000	290,000
Owner's Equity	670,000	520,000
Net Sales	2,300,000	1,740,000
Net Income	150,000	102,000

Total assets and owner's equity at the beginning of 19x1 were $680,000 and $420,000, respectively.

Required

1. Compute the following liquidity measures for 19x1 and 19x2: (a) working capital and (b) current ratio. Comment on the differences between the years.
2. Compute the following measures of profitability for 19x1 and 19x2: (a) profit margin, (b) asset turnover, (c) return on assets, (d) debt to equity,

and (e) return on equity. Comment on the change in performance from 19x1 to 19x2.

Problem 8A-5.
Classified
Financial
Statement
Preparation and
Evaluation
(L.O. 5, 6, 7)

The following accounts (in alphabetical order) and amounts were taken or calculated from the December 31, 19x2 year-end adjusted trial balance of Blossom Lawn Equipment Center: Accounts Payable, $36,300; Accounts Receivable, $84,700; Accumulated Depreciation, Building, $26,200; Accumulated Depreciation, Equipment, $17,400; Building, $110,000; Cash, $10,640; Cost of Goods Sold, $246 000; Depreciation Expense, Building, $4,500; Depreciation Expense, Equipment, $6,100; Dividend Income, $1,280; Equipment, $75,600; Interest Expense, $12,200; Inventory, $56,150; Investment in General Motors, 100 shares (short-term), $6,500; Land Held for Future Use, $20,000; Land Used in Operations, $29,000; Mortgage Payable, $90,000; Nancy Gregorio, Capital, $211,210; Nancy Gregorio, Withdrawals, $23,900; Notes Payable (short-term), $25,000; Notes Receivable, $12,000; Operating Expenses Excluding Depreciation, $151,350; Sales (net), $448,000; and Trademark, $6,750. Total assets on December 31, 19x1 were $343,950.

Required

1. From the information above, prepare (a) an income statement in condensed multistep form, (b) a statement of owner's equity, and (c) a classified balance sheet.
2. Calculate the following measures of liquidity: (a) working capital and (b) current ratio.
3. Calculate the following measures of profitability: (a) profit margin, (b) asset turnover, (c) return on assets, (d) debt to equity, and (e) return on equity.

Problem Set B

Problem 8B-1.
Accounting
Conventions
(L.O. 3)

In each case below, accounting conventions may have been violated.

1. After careful study, Hawthorne Company, which has offices in forty states, has determined that, in the future, the depreciation of its office furniture should be changed. The new method is adopted for the current year, and the change is noted in the financial statements.
2. Regalado Corporation has in the past recorded operating expenses in general accounts for each classification, such as Salaries Expense, Depreciation Expense, and Utility Expense. Management has determined that in spite of the additional recordkeeping costs, the company's income statement should break down each operating expense into its selling expense and administrative expense components.
3. Watts, the auditor of Burleson Corporation, discovered that an official of the company may have authorized the payment of a $1,000 bribe to a local official. Management argued that, because the item was so small in relation to the size of the company ($1,000,000 in sales), the illegal payment should not be disclosed.
4. Kuberski's Book Store built a small addition to the main building to house a new computer games division. Because of uncertainty about whether the computer games division would succeed or not, a conservative approach was taken by recording the addition as expense.

5. Since its origin ten years ago, Hsu Company has used the same generally accepted inventory method. Because there has been no change in the inventory method, the company does not declare in its financial statements what inventory method it uses.

Required

In each case, state the convention that is applicable, explain briefly whether or not the treatment is in accord with the convention and generally accepted accounting principles, and explain why.

Problem 8B-2.
Forms of the
Income Statement
(L.O. 6)

The March 31, 19x2 year-end income statement accounts that follow are for O'Dell Hardware Company. Beginning merchandise inventory was $86,400 and ending merchandise inventory is $72,500. The O'Dell Hardware Company is a sole proprietorship.

Account Name	Debit	Credit
Sales		461,100
Sales Discounts	5,700	
Sales Returns and Allowances	21,200	
Purchases	224,500	
Purchases Discounts		3,800
Purchases Returns and Allowances		8,120
Freight In	17,400	
Sales Salaries Expense	62,160	
Sales Supplies Expense	1,640	
Rent Expense, Selling Space	7,200	
Utility Expense, Selling Space	2,960	
Advertising Expense	16,800	
Depreciation Expense, Delivery Equipment	4,400	
Office Salaries Expense	29,240	
Office Supplies Expense	9,760	
Rent Expense, Office Space	2,400	
Utility Expense, Office Space	1,000	
Postage Expense	2,320	
Insurance Expense	2,680	
Miscellaneous Expense	1,440	
General Management Salaries Expense	42,000	
Interest Expense	5,600	
Interest Income		420

Required

From the information provided, prepare the following:

1. A detailed income statement.
2. A condensed income statement in multistep form.
3. A condensed income statement in single-step form.

Problem 8B-3.
Classified Balance
Sheet
(L.O. 5)

Accounts from the March 31, 19x2 post-closing trial balance of O'Dell Hardware Company appear below.

Account Name	Debit	Credit
Cash	15,500	
Short-Term Investments	16,500	
Notes Receivable	5,000	
Accounts Receivable	138,000	
Merchandise Inventory	72,500	
Prepaid Rent	800	
Unexpired Insurance	2,400	
Sales Supplies	640	
Office Supplies	220	
Deposit for Future Advertising	1,840	
Building, Not in Use	24,800	
Land	11,200	
Delivery Equipment	20,600	
Accumulated Depreciation, Delivery Equipment		14,200
Franchise Fee	2,000	
Accounts Payable		57,300
Salaries Payable		2,600
Interest Payable		420
Long-Term Notes Payable		40,000
Bill O'Dell, Capital		197,480

Required

From the information provided, prepare a classified balance sheet.

Problem 8B-4.
Ratio Analysis:
Liquidity and
Profitability
(L.O. 7)

Sambito Products Company has been disappointed with its operating results for the past two years. As accountant for the company, you have the following information available:

	19x2	19x1
Current Assets	$ 90,000	$ 70,000
Total Assets	290,000	220,000
Current Liabilities	40,000	20,000
Long-Term Liabilities	40,000	—
Owner's Equity	210,000	200,000
Net Sales	524,000	400,000
Net Income	32,000	22,000

Total assets and owner's equity at the beginning of 19x1 were $180,000 and $160,000, respectively.

Required

1. Compute the following measures of liquidity for 19x1 and 19x2: (a) working capital and (b) current ratio. Comment on the differences between the years.

2. Compute the following measures of profitability for 19x1 and 19x2: (a) profit margin, (b) asset turnover, (c) return on assets, (d) debt to equity, and (e) return on equity. Comment on the change in performance from 19x1 to 19x2.

Problem 8B-5.
Classified
Financial
Statement
Preparation and
Evaluation
(L.O. 5, 6, 7)

Wedman Company sells outdoor sports equipment. At the end of the year 19x2, the following financial information was available from the income statement: Administrative Expenses, $87,800; Cost of Goods Sold, $350,420; Interest Expense, $22,640; Interest Income, $2,800; Net Sales, $714,390; and Selling Expenses, $220,200.

The following information was available from the balance sheet (after closing entries): Accounts Payable, $32,600; Accounts Receivable, $104,800; Accumulated Depreciation, Delivery Equipment, $17,100; Accumulated Depreciation, Store Fixtures, $42,220; Cash, $28,400; Charles Wedman, Capital, $359,300; Delivery Equipment, $88,500; Inventory, $136,540; Investment in Gray Corporation (long-term), $56,000; Investment in U.S. Government Securities (short-term), $39,600; Notes Payable (long-term), $100,000; Notes Payable (short-term), $50,000; Short-Term Prepaid Expenses, $5,760; and Store Fixtures, $141,620.

Total assets at December 31, 19x1 were $524,400 and withdrawals during 19x2 were $60,000.

Required

1. From the information above, prepare the following: (a) an income statement in single-step form, (b) a statement of owner's equity, and (c) a classified balance sheet.
2. From the two statements you have prepared, compute the following measures: (a) for liquidity—working capital and current ratio, and (b) for profitability—profit margin, asset turnover, return on assets, debt to equity, and return on equity.

Financial Decision Case

Josephina
Tapestries
Company
(L.O. 7)

Josephina Mancilla is the principal stockholder and president of Josephina Tapestries Company, which wholesales fine tapestries to retail stores. Because Josephina was not satisfied with the earnings of the company in 19x2, she raised prices in 19x3 so that gross margin from sales is 35 percent in 19x3, as opposed to 30 percent in 19x2. Josephina is pleased that net income did in fact go up from 19x2 to 19x3, as shown in the following comparative income statements:

	19x3	19x2
Revenues		
Net Sales	$1,222,600	$1,386,400
Costs and Expenses		
Cost of Goods Sold	794,690	970,480
Selling and Administrative Expenses	308,398	305,008
Total Costs and Expenses	$1,103,088	$1,275,488
Net Income	$ 119,512	$ 110,912

Total assets for Josephina Tapestries Company for 19x1, 19x2, and 19x3 were $1,246,780, $1,386,810, and $1,536,910, respectively.

Required

1. Has Josephina Tapestries' profitability really improved? **Hint:** Compute profit margin and return on assets, and comment.
2. What factors has Josephina overlooked in evaluating the profitability of the company? **Hint:** Compute asset turnover, and comment on the role it plays in profitability.

Answers to Self-Test

1. c	3. a	5. b	7. a	9. c
2. b	4. c	6. b	8. d	10. b

PRINCIPLES OF ACCOUNTING

FINANCIAL ACCOUNTING

PART ONE
The Basic Accounting Model

PART TWO
Extensions of the Basic Accounting Model

PART THREE
Measuring and Reporting Assets and Current Liabilities

Chapter 9
  Short-Term Liquid Assets

Chapter 10
  Inventories

Chapter 11
  Current Liabilities and Payroll Accounting

Chapter 12
  Long-Term Assets: Acquisition and Depreciation

Chapter 13
  Long-Term Assets: Other Issues and Types

PART FOUR
Accounting for Partnerships and Corporations

PART FIVE
Special Reports and Analyses of Accounting Information

MANAGERIAL ACCOUNTING

PART SIX
Basic Concepts of Management Accounting

PART SEVEN
Accounting for Management Decision Making

Part Three considers each of the major types of assets as well as the category of current liabilities and payroll accounting, with particular emphasis on the effect of their measurement on net income and their presentation in the financial statements. It also provides an overview of revenue and expense issues and accounting for natural resources and intangible assets.

PART THREE

Measuring and Reporting Assets and Current Liabilities

Chapter 9 focuses on the major types of short-term liquid assets: cash and short-term investments, accounts receivable, and notes receivable.

Chapter 10 presents the accounting concepts and techniques associated with inventories and discusses their importance to income measurement.

Chapter 11 deals with current liabilities and payroll accounting.

Chapter 12 discusses the acquisition of property, plant, and equipment, and the concept and techniques of depreciation.

Chapter 13 discusses in more detail application of the matching rule to capital and revenue expenditures and to disposal of depreciable assets. In addition, accounting for long-term assets such as natural resources and for intangible assets is covered.

1. Account for cash
and short-term
investments.
2. Define accounts re-
ceivable, and explain
the relationships
among credit policies,
sales, and uncollect-
ible accounts.
3. Apply the percentage
of net sales method
and the accounts re-
ceivable aging method
to estimate uncollect-
ible accounts.
4. Record entries involv-
ing the allowance
method of account-
ing for uncollectible
accounts.
5. Recognize types of
receivables not classi-
fied as accounts re-
ceivable and specify
their balance sheet
presentation.
6. Define and describe
a promissory note.
7. Make calculations
involving promissory
notes.
8. Journalize entries
involving notes
receivable.

CHAPTER 9

Short-Term Liquid Assets

In Chapters 1 and 8, profitability and liquidity were identified as two major concerns of management. In this chapter you will study the assets that are most closely associated with the liquidity of business. **Short-term liquid assets** are financial assets that arise from cash transactions, the investment of cash, and the extension of credit. They include cash, short-term investments, accounts receivable, and notes receivable. They are useful because they are usually quickly available for paying current obligations. Other assets such as inventories, property, plant, and equipment, natural resources, and intangibles, are less liquid. After studying this chapter, you should be able to meet the learning objectives listed on the left.

Accounting for Cash and Short-Term Investments

Cash, of all the short-term liquid assets, is the most liquid and the most readily available to pay debts. We discussed the control of cash receipts and payments in Chapter 7, but we did not deal with the content of the Cash account on the balance sheet. Cash normally consists of coin and currency on hand, checks and money orders received from customers, and deposits in bank checking accounts. Cash may also include an amount that is not entirely free to be spent called a **compensating balance**. A compensating balance is a minimum amount that a bank requires a company to keep in its bank account as part of a credit-granting arrangement. This arrangement restricts cash and may reduce a company's liquidity. Therefore, the SEC requires companies to disclose in a note to the financial statements the amount of any compensating balance.

Sometimes during the year, a company may find that it has more cash on hand than it needs to pay current obligations. It is not wise to allow this excess cash to lie idle, especially in periods of high interest rates. Therefore the company may invest in time deposits or certificates of deposit in banks and other financial institutions, in government securities such as U.S. Treasury notes, or in other securities. Such investments are called **short-term investments** or **marketable securities** and are considered current assets because the intent is to hold the investments only until the cash is needed for current obligations.

OBJECTIVE 1
Account for cash and short-term investments

The term *marketable securities* is used widely. However, it is preferable to call them short-term investments because long-term investments may also contain securities that are just as marketable as the short-term investments. The difference is that management intends to hold the long-term investments for longer than one year.

Some companies accumulate large amounts of cash from operating activities that they put into short-term investments. For example, on December 31, 1987, General Motors Corporation's balance sheet contained the following information (in millions):

Current Assets

Cash	$ 431.9
U.S. government and other marketable securities and time deposits—at cost, which approximates market of $4,275.6	4,274.5
Total Cash and Marketable Securities	$4,706.4

Short-term investments are first recorded at cost. Suppose that on March 1, ST Company purchased U.S. Treasury bills, which are short-term debt of the U.S. government, for $97,000. The bills will mature in 120 days at $100,000. The following entry would be made by ST Company:

Mar. 1	Short-Term Investments	97,000	
	Cash		97,000
	Purchase of U.S. Treasury bills that mature in 120 days at $100,000		

Income on short-term investments is recorded as received. For example, dividends and interest on stocks and bonds held as short-term investments would be recorded as Dividend Income or Interest Income when it is received. In the case of the investment by ST Company, the interest is received when the bills are paid at maturity, as shown in the entry below:

June 29	Cash	100,000	
	Interest Income		3,000
	Short-Term Investments		97,000
	Receipt of cash on U.S. Treasury bills and recognition of related income		

When short-term investments are sold, a gain or loss usually results. Suppose that ST Company sells 5,000 shares of an investment in Mobil Corporation on December 5. It bought the shares for $35 per share, including broker's commission. When it sells them at $25 per share net of (after) broker's commissions, the entry presented at the top of the following page results:

Dec. 5	Cash	125,000	
	Loss on Sale of Investments	50,000	
	Short-Term Investments		175,000
	Sale of 5,000 shares of Mobil Corporation at $25, net of commissions		

In *Statement of Financial Accounting Standards No. 12*, the Financial Accounting Standards Board requires that investments in debt securities such as U.S. Treasury bills or corporate debt be listed at cost, unless there is reason to believe the value of the security is permanently impaired. However, the board requires that investments in equity securities such as capital stock be reported at the lower of historical cost or the market value determined at the balance sheet date.[1] For example, assume that at its year end of December 31, ST Company still owns 10,000 shares of Mobil Corporation that it purchased for $35 per share and that are now worth $25 per share. An adjusting entry is made to recognize the loss in value and to reduce the asset amount by means of a contra account, as follows:

Dec. 31	Loss on Decline in Short-Term Investments	100,000	
	Allowance to Reduce Short-Term Investments to Market		100,000
	To recognize decline in market value of short-term investments		

The loss is reported on the income statement, and although it is not usually shown as a separate item, the allowance account is reflected in the value assigned to short-term investments on the balance sheet, as follows:

Current Assets

| Short-Term Investments (at lower of cost or market; cost equals $350,000) | $250,000 |

Subsequent increases in the market value of the investment in Mobil may be recorded, but only to the extent of bringing the short-term investment back up to cost. Increases in market value per share above cost are not recorded. When investments that previously have been written down are sold, as was done in this case, the gain or loss is measured by the difference between the sale price and the original purchase cost regardless of any balance in Allowance to Reduce Short-Term Investments to Market. For instance, if ST Company sells 2,000 of the Mobil shares it owned at year end on January 15 for $27 per share, the entry would be:

1. *Statement of Financial Accounting Standards No. 12*, "Accounting for Certain Marketable Securities" (Stamford, Conn.: Financial Accounting Standards Board, 1975).

Jan. 15	Cash	54,000	
	Loss on Sale of Investments	16,000	
	Short-Term Investments		70,000
	Sale of 2,000 shares of Mobil at a loss:		
	2,000 shares × ($35 − $27) = $16,000		

The balance in the allowance account at the end of the next accounting period is adjusted up or down to reflect any difference between the cost and the lower market value of any short-term investments held at the end of the accounting period. The credit balance in the allowance account may be reduced to zero (resulting in a gain) if the market value exceeds the cost of the short-term investments. In no case, however, are short-term investments increased to a value above cost. If the company has more than one investment, then these rules are applied to the total value of the investments at the end of each accounting period.

Note that accounting for investments is inconsistent with the concept of historical cost. Under historical cost the cost value would be maintained on the balance sheet until the asset is sold. Accountants justify this inconsistency on the basis of the conservatism convention. That is, they recognize the potential loss immediately but put off recognition of any potential gain until it is actually realized.

Accounting for Accounts Receivable

OBJECTIVE 2
Define accounts receivable, and explain the relationships among credit policies, sales, and uncollectible accounts

The other major types of short-term liquid assets are accounts receivable and notes receivable. Both result from credit sales to customers. Retail companies such as Sears, Roebuck and Company have made credit available to nearly every responsible person in the United States. Every field of retail trade has expanded by allowing customers the right to make payments a month or more after the date of sale. What is not so apparent is that credit in the wholesale and manufacturing industries has expanded even more than at the retail level. The rest of this chapter shows the accounting for accounts receivable and notes receivable, which play a key role in this credit expansion.

Accounts receivable are short-term liquid assets that arise from sales on credit to customers by wholesalers or retailers. This type of credit is often called **trade credit.**

Credit Policies and Uncollectible Accounts

Companies that sell on credit naturally want customers who will pay. Therefore, most companies develop control procedures to increase the likelihood of selling only to customers who will pay when they are supposed to. As a result of these procedures, a company generally has a credit department. This department's responsibilities include the examination of each person or company that applies for credit and the approval or rejection of a credit sale to that customer. Typically, the credit department will ask for information on the customer's financial resources and debts. In addition, it may check personal references and established credit bureaus, which may have information about the customer. On the basis of this information, the credit department will decide whether to sell on credit to that customer. It may recommend the amount of payment, limit the amount of credit, or ask the customer to put up certain assets as security.

Regardless of how thorough and efficient its credit control system is, a company will always have some customers who will not pay. The accounts owed by such customers are called **uncollectible accounts**, or bad debts, and are a loss or an expense of selling on credit. Why does a company sell on credit if it expects that some of its accounts will not be paid? The answer is that the company expects to sell much more than it would if it did not sell on credit and, as a result, increase its earnings.

Matching Losses on Uncollectible Accounts with Sales

Accounting for uncollectible accounts depends on the matching rule. Expenses should be matched against the sales they help to produce. If bad debt losses are incurred in the process of increasing sales revenues, they should be charged against those sales revenues. A company does not know at the time of a credit sale that the debt will not be collected. In fact, it may take a year or more to exhaust every possible means of collection. Even though the loss may not be specifically identified until a later accounting period, it is still an expense of the period of the sale. Therefore, losses from the uncollectible accounts must be estimated, and this estimate becomes an expense in that fiscal year.

For example, let us assume that Cottage Sales Company made most of its sales on credit during its first year of operation. At the end of the year, accounts receivable amounted to $100,000. On this date, management reviewed the collectible status of the accounts receivable. Approximately $6,000 of the $100,000 of accounts reviewed were estimated to be uncollectible. Thus the uncollectible accounts expense for the first year of operation amounted to $6,000. The following adjusting entry would be made on December 31 of that year:

Dec. 31	Uncollectible Accounts Expense	6,000	
	Allowance for Uncollectible Accounts		6,000
	To record the estimated		
	uncollectible accounts expense		
	for the year 19xx		

The Uncollectible Accounts Expense appears on the income statement as an operating expense. The **Allowance for Uncollectible Accounts** appears in the balance sheet as a contra account that is deducted from the face value of accounts receivable.[2] It reduces the accounts receivable to the amount that is expected to be realized, or collected in cash, as follows:

2. Note that although the purpose of the Allowance for Uncollectible Accounts is to reduce the gross accounts receivable to the amount collectible (estimated value), the purpose of another contra account, the Accumulated Depreciation account, is not to reduce the gross plant and equipment accounts to realizable value. The purpose of the Accumulated Depreciation account is to show how much of the cost of the plant and equipment has been allocated as an expense to previous accounting periods.

Current Assets		
Cash		$ 10,000
Short-Term Investments		15,000
Accounts Receivable	$100,000	
Less Allowance for Uncollectible Accounts	6,000	94,000
Inventory		56,000
Total Current Assets		$175,000

The allowance method of accounting for uncollectible accounts argues that in accordance with the matching rule, a business should assume that losses from an uncollectible account occur at the moment the sale is made to the customer. The Allowance for Uncollectible Accounts is used because the company does not know until after the sale that the customer will not pay. Since the amount of the loss must be estimated if it is to be matched against the sales or revenue for the period, it is not possible to credit the account of any particular customer. Also, it is not possible to credit the Accounts Receivable controlling account in the general ledger because doing so would cause the controlling account to be out of balance with the total of customers' accounts in the subsidiary ledger.

The Allowance for Uncollectible Accounts will often have other titles such as Allowance for Doubtful Accounts or Allowance for Bad Debts. Once in a while, the older phrase Reserve for Bad Debts will be seen, but in modern practice it should not be used. Bad Debts Expense is often used as another title for Uncollectible Accounts Expense.

Estimating Uncollectible Accounts Expense

Because it is impossible to know which accounts will be uncollectible at the time financial statements are prepared, it is necessary to estimate the expense to cover the expected losses for the year. Of course, estimates can vary widely. If one takes an optimistic view and projects a small loss from uncollectible accounts, the resulting net accounts receivable will be larger than if one takes a pessimistic view. Also, the net income will be larger under the optimistic view because the estimated expense will be smaller. The company's accountant makes an estimate based on past experience, modified by current economic conditions. For example, losses from uncollectible accounts are normally expected to be greater in a recession than during a period of economic growth. The final decision of what the expense will be, made by management, will depend on objective information such as the accountant's analyses and on certain qualitative factors such as how investors, bankers, creditors, and others may view the performance of the company. Regardless of the qualitative considerations, the estimated losses from uncollectible accounts should be realistic.

The accountant has two common methods available for estimating uncollectible accounts expense for an accounting period: the first is the percentage of net sales method, and the second is the accounts receivable aging method.

OBJECTIVE 3
Apply the
percentage of net
sales method and
the accounts
receivable aging
method to estimate
uncollectible
accounts

Percentage of Net Sales Method. The percentage of net sales method asks the question, How much of this year's net sales will not be collected? The answer determines the amount of uncollectible accounts expense for the year.

For example, assume that the following balances represent the ending figures for Hassel Company for the year 19x9:

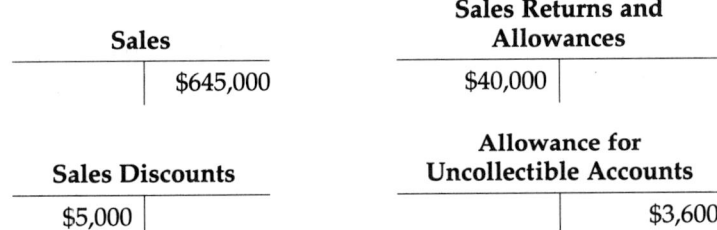

Sales		Sales Returns and Allowances
	$645,000	$40,000

Sales Discounts		Allowance for Uncollectible Accounts
$5,000		$3,600

Assume that actual losses from uncollectible accounts for the past three years have been as follows:

Year	Net Sales	Losses from Uncollectible Accounts	Percentage
19x6	$ 520,000	$10,200	1.96
19x7	595,000	13,900	2.34
19x8	585,000	9,900	1.69
Total	$1,700,000	$34,000	2.00

Management believes that uncollectible accounts will continue to average about 2 percent of net sales. The uncollectible accounts expense for the year 19x9 is therefore estimated to be:

$$.02 \times (\$645,000 - \$40,000 - \$5,000) = .02 \times \$600,000 = \$12,000$$

OBJECTIVE 4
Record entries
involving the
allowance method
of accounting for
uncollectible
accounts

The entry to record this estimate is:

Dec. 31	Uncollectible Accounts Expense	12,000	
	Allowance for Uncollectible Accounts		12,000
	To record uncollectible accounts expense at 2 percent of $600,000 net sales		

The Allowance for Uncollectible Accounts will have a balance of $15,600 after the above entry is posted, as follows:

Allowance for Uncollectible Accounts				Balance	
Date	Item	Debit	Credit	Debit	Credit
Dec. 31	Balance				3,600
31	Adjustment		12,000		15,600

The balance consists of the $12,000 estimated uncollectible accounts receivable from 19x9 sales and the $3,600 estimated uncollectible accounts receivable from previous years. The latter have not yet been matched with specific uncollectible accounts receivable resulting from sales in those years.

Accounts Receivable Aging Method. The **accounts receivable aging method** asks the question, How much of the year-end balance of accounts receivable will not be collected? The answer determines the year-end balance of Allowance for Uncollectible Accounts. The difference between this amount and the actual balance of the Allowance for Uncollectible Accounts is the expense for the year. In theory, this method should produce the same result as the percentage of net sales method, but in practice it rarely does in any one year.

The **aging of accounts receivable** is the process of listing each accounts receivable customer according to the due date of the account. If a customer is past due on the account, there is a possibility that the account will not be paid. The further past due an account is, the greater the likelihood that the customer will not pay. The aging of accounts receivable is useful to management in evaluating its credit and collection policies and alerting it to possible problems. The aging of accounts receivable for Myer Company is shown in Exhibit 9-1. Each account receivable is classified as being not yet due, or 1–30 days, 31–60 days, 61–90 days, or over 90 days past due. The percentage uncollectible in each category is also shown.

The aging of accounts receivable method is useful to the accountant in determining the proper balance of the Allowance for Uncollectible

Exhibit 9-1. Analysis of Accounts Receivable by Age

Myer Company
Analysis of Accounts Receivable by Age
December 31, 19xx

Customer	Total	Not Yet Due	1–30 Days Past Due	31–60 Days Past Due	61–90 Days Past Due	Over 90 Days Past Due
A. Arnold	$ 150		$ 150			
M. Benoit	400			$ 400		
J. Connolly	1,000	$ 900	100			
R. DiCarlo	250				$ 250	
Others	42,600	21,000	14,000	3,800	2,200	$1,600
Totals	$44,400	$21,900	$14,250	$4,200	$2,450	$1,600
Percentage Uncollectible		1.0	2.0	10.0	30.0	50.0

Accounts. In Exhibit 9-2, estimates based on past experience show that only 1 percent of the accounts not yet due and 2 percent of the 1–30 days past due accounts will not be collected. Past experience also indicates that of the 31–60 days, 61–90 days, and over 90 days accounts, 10 percent, 30 percent, and 50 percent, respectively, will not be collected. In total, it is estimated that $2,459 of the $44,400 in accounts receivable will not be collected.

Let us assume that the December 31 credit balance of the Allowance for Uncollectible Accounts for Myer Company is $800. Thus the estimated uncollectible accounts expense for the year is $1,659, which is calculated as follows:

Estimated Uncollectible Accounts	$2,459
Less Credit Balance—Allowance for Uncollectible Accounts	800[3]
Uncollectible Accounts Expense	$1,659

The uncollectible accounts expense is recorded as follows:

Dec. 31 Uncollectible Accounts Expense	1,659	
Allowance for Uncollectible Accounts		1,659
To increase the allowance		
for uncollectible accounts		
to the level of expected losses		

The resulting balance of the Allowance for Uncollectible Accounts is $2,459, as follows:

Allowance for Uncollectible Accounts				Balance	
Date	Item	Debit	Credit	Debit	Credit
Dec. 31	Balance				800
31	Adjustment		1,659		2,459

Since an $800 credit balance in this account carried over due to the fact that fewer accounts had been written off thus far than anticipated, an adjustment of only $1,659 is needed to bring the Allowance for Uncollectible Accounts to its estimated level. However, if we assume the same facts except that the balance of the Allowance for Uncollectible Accounts for Meyer Company is a debit balance of $800, the estimated uncollectible accounts expense for the year will be $3,259, calculated as follows:

Estimated Uncollectible Accounts	$2,459
Plus Debit Balance—Allowance for Uncollectible Accounts	800
Uncollectible Accounts Expense	$3,259

3. If the Allowance for Uncollectible Accounts had a debit balance, the amount of the debit balance would have to be added to the estimated uncollectible accounts to obtain the uncollectible accounts expense.

Exhibit 9-2. Calculation of Estimated Uncollectible Accounts

Myer Company
Estimated Uncollectible Accounts
December 31, 19xx

	Amount	Percentage Considered Uncollectible	Allowance for Uncollectible Accounts
Not yet due	$21,900	1	$ 219
1–30 days	14,250	2	285
31–60 days	4,200	10	420
61–90 days	2,450	30	735
Over 90 days	1,600	50	800
	$44,400		$2,459

The uncollectible accounts expense is recorded as follows:

Dec. 31	Uncollectible Accounts Expense	3,259	
	Allowance for Uncollectible Accounts		3,259
	To increase the allowance for uncollectible accounts to the level of expected losses		

After this entry, the balance of the Allowance for Uncollectible Accounts is a credit of $2,459, as follows:

Allowance for Uncollectible Accounts — **Balance**

Date	Item	Debit	Credit	Debit	Credit
Dec. 31	Balance			800	
31	Adjustment		3,259		2,459

In the latter case, $800 more in accounts were written off due to uncollectibility than had been provided by the adjustment for estimated uncollectible accounts in the prior period. In order to bring the Allowance for Uncollectible Accounts to the new estimate of $2,459, the uncollectible accounts expense for the period had to be $3,259.

Comparison of the Two Methods. Both methods of estimation try to determine the uncollectible accounts expense for the current period in accordance with the matching rule, but they do so in different ways. The percentage of net sales method represents an income statement viewpoint. It is based on the proposition that of each dollar of sales a certain proportion will not be collected, and this proportion is the expense for the year. Because this method matches expenses against revenues, it is in accordance with the matching rule. However, this way of determining expense is independent of the current balance of the Allowance for Uncollectible Accounts. The estimated proportion of net sales not expected to be collected is added to the current balance of the allowance account.

The aging of accounts receivable represents a balance sheet viewpoint and is a more direct valuation method. It is based on the proposition that of each dollar of accounts receivable outstanding, a certain proportion will not be collected, and this proportion should be the balance of the allowance account at the end of the year. This method also agrees with the matching rule because the expense is the difference between what the account is and what it should be. The difference is assumed to be applicable to the current year.

Writing Off an Uncollectible Account

When it becomes clear that a specific account will not be collected, the amount should be written off to the Allowance for Uncollectible Accounts. Remember that it was already accounted for as an expense when the allowance was established. For example, assume that R. Deering, who owes the Myer Company $250, is declared bankrupt by a federal court. The entry to *write off* this account is as follows:

Jan. 15	Allowance for Uncollectible Accounts	250	
	Accounts Receivable, R. Deering		250
	To write off receivable from		
	R. Deering as uncollectible;		
	Deering declared bankruptcy		
	on January 15		

Note that the write-off does not affect the estimated net amount of accounts receivable because there is no expense involved and because the related allowance for uncollectible accounts has already been deducted from the receivables. The write-off simply reduces R. Deering's account to zero and reduces the Allowance for Uncollectible Accounts by a similar amount, as the following table shows:

	Balances Before Write-off	Balances After Write-off
Accounts Receivable	$44,400	$44,150
Less Allowance for Uncollectible Accounts	2,459	2,209
Estimated Net Value of Accounts Receivable	$41,941	$41,941

Why Accounts Written Off Will Differ from Estimates. The total of accounts receivable written off in any given year will rarely equal the estimated amount credited to the Allowance for Uncollectible Accounts. The allowance account will show a credit balance when the accounts written off are less than the estimated uncollectible accounts. The allowance account will show a debit balance when the accounts written off are greater than the estimated uncollectible accounts. The adjusting entry that is made to record the estimated uncollectible accounts expense for the current year will eliminate any debit balance at the end of the accounting period.

If the percentage of net sales method is used, the new balance of the allowance account after the adjusting entry will equal the percentage of sales estimated to be uncollectible minus the old debit balance. If the accounts receivable aging method is used, the amount of the adjustment must equal the estimated uncollectible accounts plus the debit balance in the Allowance for Uncollectible Accounts. Of course, if the estimates are consistently wrong, the balance of the allowance account will become unusually large and will indicate that management should reexamine the company's estimation rates.

Recovery of Accounts Receivable Written Off. Sometimes a customer whose account has been written off as uncollectible will later be able to pay the amount in full or in part. When this happens, it is necessary to make two journal entries: one to reverse the earlier write-off, which is now incorrect; and another to show the collection of the account.

For example, assume that on September 1, R. Deering, after his bankruptcy on January 15, notified the company that he would be able to pay $100 of his account and sent a check for $50. The entries to record this transaction are as follows:

Sept. 1	Accounts Receivable, R. Deering		100	
	Allowance for Uncollectible Accounts			100
		To reinstate the portion of the account of R. Deering now considered collectible, which had been written off January 15		
	1	Cash	50	
		Accounts Receivable, R. Deering		50
		To record collection from R. Deering		

The collectible portion of R. Deering's account must be restored to his account and credited to the Allowance for Uncollectible Accounts for two reasons. First, it was an error in judgment to write off the full $250 on January 15 because only $150 was actually uncollectible. Second, the accounts receivable subsidiary account for R. Deering should reflect his ability to pay a portion of the money he owed in spite of his bankruptcy. Documentation of this action will give a clear picture of his credit record for future credit action.

Other Issues Related to Receivables

Direct Charge-off Method. Some companies record uncollectible accounts by debiting expenses directly when bad debts are discovered instead of using the Allowance for Uncollectible Accounts. The **direct**

charge-off method is not in accordance with good accounting theory because it makes no attempt to match revenues and expenses. Uncollectible accounts are charged to expenses in the accounting period in which they are discovered rather than in the period of the sale. On the balance sheet the accounts receivable are shown at gross value, not realizable value, because there is no Allowance for Uncollectible Accounts. Only the direct charge-off method, however, is allowable in computing taxable income under federal income tax regulations. The allowance method is still used for financial reporting because it is better from the standpoint of accounting theory.

OBJECTIVE 5
Recognize types of receivables not classified as accounts receivable and specify their balance sheet presentation

Credit Balances in Accounts Receivable. Sometimes customers overpay their accounts because of mistakes or in anticipation of future purchases. When customer accounts show credit balances in the accounts receivable ledger, the balance of the Accounts Receivable controlling account should not appear on the balance sheet as the amount of the accounts receivable. The total of the customers' accounts with credit balances should be shown as a current liability because the company is liable to these customers for their overpayments.

Installment Accounts Receivable. Installment sales make up a significant portion of the accounts receivable of many retail companies. Department stores, appliance stores, and retail chains all sell goods that are paid for in a series of time payments. Companies such as J. C. Penney and Sears have millions of dollars in these **installment accounts receivable.** Although the payment period may be twenty-four months or more, installment accounts receivable are classified as current assets if such credit policies are customary in the industry. There are special accounting rules that apply to installment sales. Because these rules can be very complicated, their study is usually deferred until a more advanced accounting course.

Credit Card Sales. Many retailers allow customers to charge their purchases to a third-party company that the customer will pay later. These transactions are normally handled with credit cards. The five most widely used credit cards are American Express, Carte Blanche, Diners Club, MasterCard, and VISA. The customer establishes credit with the lender and receives a plastic card to use in making charge purchases. If the seller accepts the card, an invoice is made that is imprinted by the charge card and signed by the customer at the time of the sale. The seller then sends the invoice to the lender and receives cash. Because the seller does not have to establish the customer's credit, collect from the customer, or tie money up in accounts receivable, the seller receives an economic benefit that is provided by the lender (credit card company). For this reason, the credit card company does not pay 100 percent of the total amount of the invoices. The lender takes a discount of 2 to 6 percent on the credit card sales invoices.

One of two procedures is used in accounting for credit card sales, depending on whether the merchant must wait for collection from the credit card company or may deposit the sales invoices in a checking account immediately. The following example illustrates the procedure used in the first case. Assume that, at the end of the day, a restaurant has American Express invoices totaling $1,000 and that the discount charged by American Express is 5 percent. These sales are recorded as follows:

Accounts Receivable, American Express	950	
Credit Card Discount Expense	50	
Sales		1,000
Sales made on American Express		
cards; discount fee is 5 percent		

The seller sends the American Express invoices to American Express and later receives payment for them at 95 percent of their face value. When cash is received, the entry is as follows:

Cash	950	
Accounts Receivable, American Express		950
Receipt of payment from American		
Express for invoices at 95 percent of		
face value		

The second case is typical of sales made through bank credit cards such as VISA and MasterCard. For example, assume that the restaurant made sales of $1,000 on VISA credit cards and that VISA takes a 5 percent discount on the sales. Assume also that the sales invoices can be deposited in a special VISA bank account in the name of the company in much the same way that checks from cash sales are deposited. These sales are recorded as follows:

Cash	950	
Credit Card Discount Expense	50	
Sales		1,000
Sales on VISA cards		

Other Accounts Receivable. The title Accounts Receivable on the balance sheet should be reserved for sales made to regular customers in the ordinary course of business. If loans or sales that do not fall in this category are made to employees, officers of the corporation, or owners, they should be shown separately on the balance sheet with an asset title such as Receivables from Employees and Officers.

Accounting for Notes Receivable

OBJECTIVE 6
Define and describe a promissory note

A **promissory note** is an unconditional promise to pay a definite sum of money on demand or at a future date. The person who signs the note and thereby promises to pay is called the *maker* of the note. The person to whom payment is to be made is called the *payee*. The promissory note in Figure 9-1 is dated May 20, 19x1, and is an unconditional promise by the maker, Samuel Mason, to pay a definite sum or principal ($1,000) to the payee, Cook County Bank & Trust Company, at the future date of August 18, 19x1. The promissory note bears an interest rate of 8 percent. The payee regards all promissory notes it holds that are due in less than a year as notes receivable in the current asset section of the balance sheet. The makers regard them as notes payable in the current liability section of the balance sheet.

In this chapter, we are concerned primarily with notes received from customers. The nature of a business generally determines how frequently promissory notes are received from customers. Firms selling durable goods of high value, such as farm machinery and automobiles, will often accept promissory notes. Among the advantages of promissory notes are that they produce interest income and represent a stronger legal claim against the creditor than accounts receivable. In addition, promissory notes can be resold to banks as a financing method. Almost all companies will occasionally receive a note, and many companies obtain notes receivable in settlement of past-due accounts.

Computations for Promissory Notes

OBJECTIVE 7
Make calculations involving promissory notes

In accounting for promissory notes, several terms are important to remember. These terms are (1) maturity date, (2) duration of note, (3) interest and interest rate, (4) maturity value, (5) discount, and (6) proceeds from discounting.

Maturity Date. The maturity date is the date on which the note must be paid. It must either be stated on the promissory note or be determinable

Figure 9-1. A Promissory Note

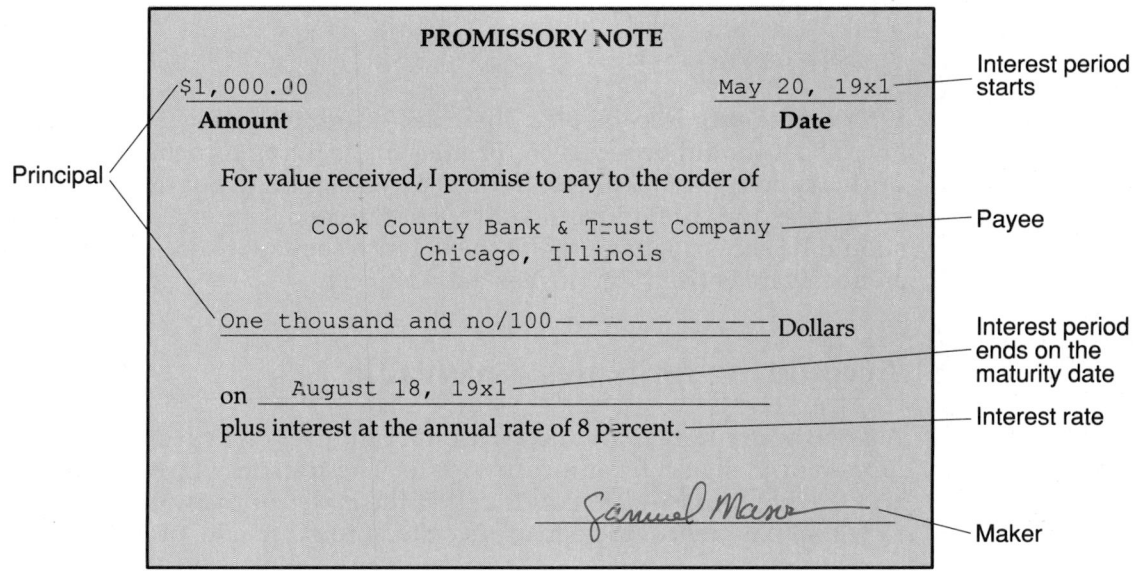

from the facts stated on the note. Among the most common statements of maturity date are the following:

1. A specific date, such as "November 14, 19xx"
2. A specific number of months after the date of the note, for example, "3 months after date"
3. A specific number of days after the date of the note, for example, "60 days after date"

There is no problem in determining the maturity date when it is stated. When the maturity date is a number of months from date of note, one simply uses the same day in the appropriate future month. For example, a note dated January 20 that is due in two months would be due on March 20.

When the maturity date is stated in a specific number of days, it must be based on the exact number of days. In computing the maturity, it is important to exclude the date of the note and to include the maturity day. For example, a note dated May 20, and due in 90 days, would be due on August 18, computed as follows:

Days remaining in May (31 – 20)	11
Days in June	30
Days in July	31
Days in August	18
Total days	90

Duration of Note. Determining the **duration of note**, or its length of time in days, is the opposite problem from determining the maturity date. This calculation is important because interest must be calculated on the basis of the exact number of days. There is no problem when the maturity date is based on the number of days from date of note. However, if the maturity date is a specified date, the exact number of days must be determined. Assume that the length of time of a note is from May 10 to August 10. The length of time is 92 days, determined as follows:

Days remaining in May (31 – 10)	21
Days in June	30
Days in July	31
Days in August	10
Total days	92

Interest and Interest Rate. The **interest** is the cost of borrowing money or the return for lending money, depending on whether one is the borrower or the lender. The amount of interest is based on three factors: the principal (the amount of money borrowed or lent), the rate of interest, and the loan's length of time. The formula used in computing interest is as follows:

Principal × rate of interest × time = interest

Interest rates are usually stated on an annual basis. For example, the interest on a $1,000, one-year, 8 percent note is computed as follows: $1,000 × 8/100 × 1 = $80.

If the term of the note were three months instead of a year, the interest charge would be $20, computed as follows: $1,000 × 8/100 × 3/12 = $20.

When the terms of a note are expressed in days, the exact number of days must be used in computing the interest. To keep the computation simple, let us compute interest on the basis of 360[4] days per year. Therefore, if the term of the above note were 45 days, the interest would be $10, computed as follows: $1,000 × 8/100 × 45/360 = $10.

Maturity Value. It is necessary to determine the **maturity value** of a note or the total proceeds of the note at maturity date. Maturity value is the face value of the note plus interest. The maturity value of a 90-day, 8 percent, $1,000 note is computed as follows:

$$\begin{aligned} \text{Maturity value} &= \textbf{principal + interest} \\ &= \$1{,}000 + (\$1{,}000 \times 8/100 \times 90/360) \\ &= \$1{,}000 + \$20 \\ &= \$1{,}020 \end{aligned}$$

Occasionally, one will encounter a so-called noninterest-bearing note. The maturity value is the face value or principal amount. In this case, the principal amount includes an implied interest cost.

Discount. To **discount** a note means to take out the interest in advance. The **discount** is the amount of interest deducted. It is very common for banks to use this method when lending money on promissory notes. The amount of the discount is computed as follows:

Discount = maturity value × interest rate × time

For example, assume that a note has a maturity value of $1,000, is due in 90 days, and is discounted at a 10 percent rate of interest:

$$\text{Discount} = \$1{,}000 \times 10/100 \times 90/360 = \$25$$

Proceeds from Discounting. Normally when someone borrows money on a note, the amount he or she receives or borrows is the face value or principal. But when a note receivable is discounted, the amount the borrower receives is called the **proceeds from discounting** and must be computed as follows:

Proceeds = maturity value – discount

Thus, in the preceding example, the proceeds would be computed as shown on the top of the following page.

---

4. Practice varies in the computation of interest. Many banks use a 360-day year for commercial loans and a 365-day year for consumer loans. Other banks use a 365-day year for all loans. In Europe, use of a 360-day year is common. In this book, we use 360 days in a year to keep the computations simple.

$$\text{Proceeds} = \$1,000 - (\$1,000 \times 10/100 \times 90/360)$$
$$= \$1,000 - \$25$$
$$= \$975$$

This calculation is very simple when the maturity value is given, as illustrated here. However, the calculation is more complicated when the maturity value must be calculated, as when an interest-bearing note from a customer is discounted to the bank. In this situation, the maturity value must first be computed under the formula described for computing maturity value. Then the discount must be computed on the basis of the maturity value. Finally, the proceeds are determined by deducting the discount from the maturity value. For example, the proceeds of a $2,000, 8 percent, 90-day note, discounted on the date it is drawn at the bank at 10 percent, would be $1,989:

$$\text{Maturity value} = \text{principal} + \text{interest}$$
$$= \$2,000 + (\$2,000 \times 8/100 \times 90/360)$$
$$= \$2,000 + \$40$$
$$= \$2,040$$

$$\text{Discount} = \text{maturity value} \times \text{discount rate} \times \text{time}$$
$$= \$2,040 \times 10/100 \times 90/360$$
$$= \$51$$

$$\text{Proceeds} = \text{maturity value} - \text{discount}$$
$$= \$2,040 - \$51$$
$$= \$1,989$$

In this example, the note was discounted to the bank on the same day it was written. Usually time will pass between the date the note is written and the date it is discounted. In such a case, the number of days used in computing the discount should be the days remaining until the maturity date of the note, because that is the length of time for which the bank is lending the money to the company holding the note. For example, assume the same facts as above except that the company holding the note waits 30 days to discount the note to the bank. In other words, at the date of discounting, there are 60 (90 – 30) days remaining until the maturity date. The proceeds are determined as follows:

$$\text{Maturity value} = \text{principal} + \text{interest}$$
$$= \$2,040 \text{ (from above)}$$

$$\text{Discount} = \text{maturity value} \times \text{discount rate} \times \text{time}$$
$$= \$2,040 \times 10/100 \times 60/360$$
$$= \$34$$

$$\text{Proceeds} = \text{maturity value} - \text{discount}$$
$$= \$2,040 - \$34$$
$$= \$2,006$$

The difference in discount of $17 ($51 – $34) between the two cases is equal to the discount on the 30 days that have lapsed between writing and discounting the note ($2,040 × 10/100 × 30/360 = $17).

Illustrative Accounting Entries

OBJECTIVE 8
Journalize entries
involving notes
receivable

The accounting entries for promissory notes receivable fall into five groups: (1) receipt of a note, (2) collection on a note, (3) recording a dishonored note, (4) discounting a note, and (5) recording adjusting entries.

Receipt of a Note. Assume that a 12 percent, 30-day note is received from a customer, J. Halsted, in settlement of an existing account receivable of $4,000, on June 1. The entry for this transaction is as follows:

June 1	Notes Receivable	4,000	
	Accounts Receivable, J. Halsted		4,000
	Received 12 percent, 30-day note in payment of account		

Collection on a Note. When the note plus interest is collected 30 days later, the entry is as follows:

July 1	Cash	4,040	
	Notes Receivable		4,000
	Interest Income		40
	Collected 12 percent, 30-day note from J. Halsted		

Recording a Dishonored Note. When the maker of a note does not pay the note at maturity, the note is said to be dishonored. In the case of a **dishonored note**, an entry should be made by the holder or payee to transfer the total amount due from the Notes Receivable account to an account receivable from the debtor. If J. Halsted did not pay his note on July 1 but dishonored it, the following entry would be made:

July 1	Accounts Receivable, J. Halsted	4,040	
	Notes Receivable		4,000
	Interest Income		40
	To record 12 percent, 30-day note dishonored by J. Halsted		

The interest earned is recorded because although J. Halsted did not pay the note, he is still obligated to pay both the principal amount and the interest.

Two things are accomplished by transferring dishonored notes receivable into an accounts receivable account. First, it leaves the Notes Receivable account with only notes that have not matured and are presumably negotiable and collectible. Second, it establishes a record in the borrower's account receivable that he or she has dishonored a note receivable. This information may be helpful in deciding whether to extend future credit to this customer.

Discounting a Note. Many companies raise money for operations by selling unmatured notes receivable to banks or finance companies for cash. This type of financing is common in the sales of equipment and other products where the customer does not have a strong credit rating, as in sales of videogame machines to convenience stores. It is usually called discounting because the bank deducts the interest from the maturity value of the note to determine the proceeds. The holder of the note (usually the payee) signs his or her name on the back of the note (as in endorsing a check) and delivers the note to the bank. The bank expects to collect the maturity value of the note (principal plus interest) on the maturity date but also has recourse against the endorser or seller of the note. Therefore, if the maker fails to pay, the endorser is liable to the bank for payment.

For example, assume that we take a $1,000, 12 percent, 90-day note to the bank 60 days before maturity and that the bank discounts it at 15 percent for cash. The cash to be received (proceeds from discounting) is calculated as the maturity value less the discount, recorded as follows:

Cash	1,004.25	
Notes Receivable		1,000.00
Interest Income		4.25
To record discounting of a 12 percent, 90-day note with 60 days left at 15 percent		

Maturity value:		
$1,000 + ($1,000 \times 12/100 \times 90/360)$	=	\$1,030.00
Less discount:		
$1,030 \times 15/100 \times 60/360$	=	25.75
Proceeds from discounted note receivable		\$1,004.25

Since the interest to be received of $30 exceeds the interest cost or discount, the difference of $4.25 is credited to Interest Income. If the proceeds had been less than the note receivable, the difference would have been recorded as a debit to Interest Expense. For example, if the proceeds had been $995.75 instead of $1,004.25, Interest Expense would have been debited for $4.25, and there would have been no entry to Interest Income.

Note that neither the length of the discounting period nor the discount rate is the same as the term or the rate of interest of the note. This situation is typical. Also, notice that the account Notes Receivable is credited. Although this entry removes the note from the records, remember that if the maker cannot or will not pay the bank, the endorser is liable to the bank for the note. In accounting terminology, the endorser is said to be contingently liable to the bank. A contingent liability is a potential liability that can develop into a real liability if a possible subsequent event occurs. In this case, the subsequent event would be the nonpayment of the note by the maker.

Before the maturity date of the discounted note, the bank will notify the maker that it is holding the note and that payment should be made directly to the bank. If the maker pays the bank as agreed, then no entry is required in the records of the endorser. If the maker does not pay the note and interest on the due date, the note is dishonored. To hold the endorser liable for the note, the bank must notify the endorser that the note is dishonored. The bank will normally notify the endorser by protesting the note. The bank does this by preparing and mailing a notice of protest to the endorser. The **notice of protest** is a sworn statement that the note was presented to the maker for payment and the maker refused to pay. The bank typically charges a **protest fee** for protesting the note, which must be paid when the endorser pays the bank the amount due on the dishonored note.

If the note discounted in the example above is dishonored by the maker on the maturity date, the following entry should be made by the endorser when paying the obligation:

Accounts Receivable, Name of Maker	1,040	
Cash		1,040
To record payment of principal and interest on discounted note (maturity value of $1,030), plus a protest fee of $10 to bank; the note was dishonored by the maker		

Additional interest accrues on the maturity value plus the protest fee until the note is paid or written off as uncollectible.

Recording Adjusting Entries. A promissory note received in one period might not be due until a following accounting period. Because the interest on the note accrues by a small amount each day of the note's duration, it is necessary, according to the matching rule, to apportion the interest earned to the period in which it belongs. For example, assume that on August 31 a 60-day, 8 percent, $2,000 note was received and that the company prepares financial statements monthly. The following adjusting entry on September 30 is necessary to show how the interest earned for September has accrued:

Sept. 30 Interest Receivable	13.33	
Interest Income		13.33
To accrue 30 days' interest earned on note receivable $2,000 \times 8/100 \times 30/360 = \$13.33$		

The account Interest Receivable is a current asset on the balance sheet. Upon receiving payment of the note plus interest on October 30, the following entry is made:[5]

Oct. 30 Cash	2,026.67	
Note Receivable		2,000.00
Interest Receivable		13.33
Interest Income		13.34
To record receipt of note receivable plus interest		

5. Some firms may follow the practice of reversing the September 30 adjusting entry. Here we assume that a reversing entry is not made.

As seen from the transactions on the previous page, both September and October receive the benefit of one-half the interest earned.

Chapter Review

Review of Learning Objectives

1. **Account for cash and short-term investments.**
   Cash consists of coin and currency on hand, checks and money orders received from customers, and deposits in bank accounts. Short-term investments, sometimes called marketable securities, including time deposits, certificates of deposit, government securities, stocks, and other securities intended to be held for short periods of time (usually less than a year), are first recorded at cost. Afterwards, investments in debt securities are carried at cost unless there is a permanent drop in the market value. Investments in equity securities are reported at the lower of cost or market. If cost exceeds market value of equity securities, an allowance to reduce short-term investments to market value is established.

2. **Define accounts receivable, and explain the relationships among credit policies, sales, and uncollectible accounts.**
   Accounts receivable are amounts still to be collected from credit sales to customers. The amounts still owed by individual customers are found in the subsidiary ledger.
   Because credit is offered to increase sales, bad debts associated with the sales should be charged as expenses in the period in which the sales are made. However, because of the time lag between the sales and the time the accounts are judged to be uncollectible, the accountant must estimate the amount of bad debts in any given period.

3. **Apply the percentage of net sales method and the accounts receivable aging method to estimate uncollectible accounts.**
   Uncollectible accounts expense is estimated by either the percentage of net sales method or the accounts receivable aging method. When the first method is used, bad debts are judged to be a certain percentage of sales during the period. When the second method is used, certain percentages are applied to groups of the accounts receivable that have been arranged by due dates. A third method, the direct charge-off method, is required when filing federal income tax returns but is not used in the accounting records because it does not follow the matching rule.

4. **Record entries involving the allowance method of accounting for uncollectible accounts.**
   Allowance for Uncollectible Accounts is a contra account to Accounts Receivable. When the estimate of uncollectible accounts is made, debit the Uncollectible Accounts Expense and credit the allowance account. When an individual account is determined to be uncollectible, it is removed from Accounts Receivable by debiting the allowance account and crediting Accounts Receivable. If this account should later be collected, the earlier entry should be reversed and the collection recorded in the normal way.

5. **Recognize types of receivables not classified as accounts receivable and specify their balance sheet presentation.**
   Accounts of customers with credit balances should not be classified as negative accounts receivable but as current liabilities on the balance sheet. Installment accounts receivable are classified as current assets if such credit policies are followed in the industry. Receivables from credit card companies should be classified as current assets. Receivables from employees, officers, stockholders, and others made outside the normal course of business should not be listed among accounts receivable. They may be either short- or long-term assets depending on when collection is expected to take place.

6. **Define and describe a promissory note.**
   A promissory note is an unconditional promise to pay a definite sum of money on demand or at a future date. Companies selling durable goods of high value such as farm machinery and automobiles will often take promissory notes, which can be sold to banks as a financing method.

7. **Make calculations involving promissory notes.**
   In accounting for promissory notes, it is important to know how to calculate the following: maturity date, duration of note, interest and interest rate, maturity value, discount, and proceeds from discounting. Discounting is the act by which the lender takes out the interest in advance when making a loan on a note.

8. **Journalize entries involving notes receivable.**
   The accounting entries for promissory notes receivable fall into five groups: receipt of a note, collection on a note, recording a dishonored note, discounting a note, and recording adjusting entries.

Review of Concepts and Terminology

The following concepts and terms were introduced in this chapter:

(L.O. 2) **Accounts receivable:** Short-term liquid assets that arise from sales on credit at the wholesale or the retail level.

(L.O. 3) **Accounts receivable aging method:** A method of estimating uncollectible accounts based on the assumption that a predictable portion of accounts receivable will not be collected.

(L.O. 3) **Aging of accounts receivable:** The process of listing each customer in accounts receivable according to the due date of the account.

(L.O. 2) **Allowance for uncollectible accounts:** A contra account that serves to reduce accounts receivable to the amount that is expected to be collected in cash.

(L.O. 1) **Compensating balance:** A minimum amount required by a bank to be kept in an account as part of a credit-granting arrangement.

(L.O. 8) **Contingent liability:** A potential liability that can develop into a real liability if a possible subsequent event occurs.

(L.O. 4) **Direct charge-off method:** A method of accounting for uncollectible accounts by debiting expenses directly when bad debts are discovered instead of using the allowance method; a method that violates the matching rule but is required for federal income tax computations.

(L.O. 7) **Discount**: (Verb) to take out interest in advance; (noun) the interest amount deducted in advance.

(L.O. 8) **Dishonored note**: A promissory note that the maker cannot or will not pay at the maturity date.

(L.O. 7) **Duration of note**: Length of time in days between the making of a promissory note and its maturity date.

(L.O. 5) **Installment accounts receivable**: Accounts receivable that are payable in a series of time payments.

(L.O. 7) **Interest**: The cost of borrowing money or the return for lending money, depending on whether one is the borrower or the lender.

(L.O. 7) **Maturity date**: The due date of a promissory note.

(L.O. 7) **Maturity value**: The total proceeds of a promissory note including principal and interest at the maturity date.

(L.O. 6) **Notes payable**: Collective term for promissory notes owed by the maker to other entities.

(L.O. 6) **Notes receivable**: Collective term for promissory notes held by the entity (payee) to whom payment is promised.

(L.O. 8) **Notice of protest**: A sworn statement that a promissory note was presented to the maker for payment and the maker refused to pay.

(L.O. 3) **Percentage of net sales method**: A method of estimating uncollectible accounts based on the assumption that a predictable portion of sales will not be collected.

(L.O. 7) **Proceeds from discounting**: The amount received by the borrower when a promissory note is discounted; proceeds = maturity value − discount.

(L.O. 6) **Promissory note**: An unconditional promise to pay a definite sum of money on demand or at a future date.

(L.O. 8) **Protest fee**: The charge made by a bank for preparing and mailing a notice of protest.

(L.O. 1) **Short-term investments (marketable securities)**: Temporary investments of excess cash, invested until needed to pay current obligations.

(L.O. 1) **Short-term liquid assets**: Financial assets that arise from cash transactions, the investment of cash, and the extension of credit.

(L.O. 2) **Trade credit**: Credit granted to customers by wholesalers or retailers.

(L.O. 2) **Uncollectible accounts**: Accounts receivable from customers who cannot or will not pay.

Self-Test

Test your knowledge of the chapter by choosing the best answer for each item below and on the next pages.

1. A $100,000 U.S. Treasury bill due in ninety days is purchased for $97,000. When cash in the amount of $100,000 is received, the entry in the general journal would contain
   a. a credit to Interest Income for $3,000.
   b. a debit to Gain on Investment for $3,000.
   c. a credit to Investment Loss for $3,000.
   d. a credit to Gain on Investment for $3,000. *(L.O. 1)*

2. The matching rule
   a. necessitates the recording of an estimated amount for bad debts.
   b. is violated when the allowance method is employed.
   c. results in the recording of an exact amount for bad debt losses.
   d. requires that bad debt losses be recorded when an individual customer defaults. *(L.O. 2)*

3. Which of the following methods of recording uncollectible accounts expense would best be described as an income statement method?
   a. Accounts receivable aging method
   b. Direct charge-off method
   c. Percentage of net sales method
   d. Both **a** and **b** above *(L.O. 3)*

4. One might infer from a debit balance in Allowance for Uncollectible Accounts that
   a. the account has overestimated bad debt losses.
   b. more has been written off than has been estimated.
   c. the accounts receivable aging method is apparently being used.
   d. a posting error has been made. *(L.O. 3)*

5. Using the percentage of net sales method, uncollectible accounts expenses for the year are estimated to be $54,000. If the balance of the allowance for uncollectible accounts is a $16,000 credit before adjustment, what is the balance after adjustment?
   a. $16,000   c. $54,000
   b. $38,000   d. $70,000 *(L.O. 4)*

6. Using the accounts receivable aging method, estimated uncollectible accounts are $74,000. If the balance of the allowance for uncollectible accounts is an $18,000 credit before adjustment, what is the balance after adjustment?
   a. $18,000   c. $74,000
   b. $56,000   d. $92,000 *(L.O. 4)*

7. A retailer accepted VISA charge sales totaling $400 and deposited the charge slips in the bank. Assuming a credit card discount expense of 5 percent, what would be the debit to Cash and the credit to Sales for this transaction?
   a. $400 and $400   c. $380 and $380
   b. $380 and $400   d. $400 and $380 *(L.O. 5)*

8. Each of the following is a characteristic of a promissory note, with the exception of
   a. a payee who has an unconditional right to receive a definite amount on a definite date.
   b. an amount to be paid that can be determined on the date the note is signed.
   c. a due date that can be determined on the date the note is signed.
   d. a maker who agrees to pay a definite sum subject to other conditions to be determined at a later date. *(L.O. 6)*

9. The maturity value of a $6,000, 90-day note at 10 percent is
   a. $600.   c. $6,600.
   b. $5,850.   d. $6,150. *(L.O. 7)*

10. A $1,000 interest-bearing note is discounted at the bank, generating $1,024 in proceeds. The endorser's (payee's) entry to record this would include a
    a. debit to Cash for $1,024.
    b. debit to Interest Income for $24.
    c. credit to Notes Receivable for $1,024.
    d. debit to Notes Receivable for $1,000. *(L.O. 8)*

Answers to Self-Test are at the end of this chapter.

Review Problem
Entries for Uncollectible Accounts
Expense and Notes Receivable Transactions

(L.O. 3, 4, 7, 8) The Farm Implement Company sells merchandise on credit and also accepts notes for payment, which are discounted to the bank. During the year ended June 30, the company had net credit sales of $1,200,000 and at the end of the year had Accounts Receivable of $400,000 and a debit balance in the Allowance for Uncollectible Accounts of $2,100. In the past, approximately 1.5 percent of net sales have proved uncollectible. Also, an aging analysis of accounts receivable reveals that $17,000 in accounts receivable appears to be uncollectible.

The Farm Implement Company sold a tractor to R. C. Sims. Payment was received in the form of a $15,000, 9 percent, 90-day note dated March 16. On March 31, the note was discounted to the bank at 10 percent. On June 14, the bank notified the company that Sims had dishonored the note. The company paid the bank the maturity value of the note plus a fee of $15. On June 29, the company received payment in full from Sims plus additional interest from the date of the dishonored note.

Required 1. Prepare journal entries to record uncollectible accounts expense using (a) the percentage of net sales method and (b) the accounts receivable aging method.
2. Prepare journal entries relating to the note received from R. C. Sims.

Answer to Review Problem

1. Journal entries for uncollectible accounts prepared:

   a. Percentage of net sales method:

June 30	Uncollectible Accounts Expense	18,000	
	Allowance for Uncollectible Accounts		18,000
	To record estimated uncollectible accounts expense at 1.5 percent of $1,200,000		

b. Accounts receivable aging method:

June 30	Uncollectible Accounts Expense	19,100	
	Allowance for Uncollectible Accounts		19,100
	To record estimated uncollectible accounts expense. The debit balance in the allowance account must be added to the estimated uncollectible accounts: $2,100 + $17,000 = $19,100		

2. Journal entries related to note prepared:

March 16	Notes Receivable	15,000.00	
	Sales		15,000.00
	Tractor sold to R. C. Sims; terms of note: 9 percent, 90 days		
31	Cash	15,017.97	
	Notes Receivable		15,000.00
	Interest Income		17.97
	To record note discounted at bank at 10 percent		

Maturity value:

$$\$15,000 + (\$15,000 \times 9/100 \times 90/360) \quad = \quad \$15,337.50$$

Less discount:

$$\$15,337.50 \times 10/100 \times 75/360 \quad = \quad 319.53$$

$$\text{Proceeds from discounted note receivable} \quad \$15,017.97$$

June 14	Accounts Receivable, R. C. Sims	15,352.50	
	Cash		15,352.50
	To record payment of principal and interest on discounted note (maturity value $15,337.50), plus a $15 fee to bank; the note was dishonored by Sims		
29	Cash	15,410.07	
	Accounts Receivable, R. C. Sims		15,352.50
	Interest Income		57.57
	Received payment in full from R. C. Sims $15,352.50 + ($15,352.50 × 9/100 × 15/360) $15,352.50 + $57.57 = $15,410.07		

Chapter Assignments

Discussion Questions and Writing Assignments

1. What items are included in the cash account? What is a compensating balance?

2. Why does a business need short-term liquid assets? Why is it acceptable to account for certain short-term investments by the lower-of-cost-or-market method?

3. Why does a company sell on credit if it expects that some of the accounts will not be paid? What role does a credit department play in selling on credit?

4. According to generally accepted accounting principles, at what point in the cycle of selling and collecting does the bad debt loss occur?

5. If management estimates that $5,000 of the year's sales will not be collected, what entry should be made at year end?

6. After adjusting and closing entries at the end of the year, suppose that Accounts Receivable is $176,000 and the Allowance for Uncollectible Accounts is $14,500. (a) What is the collectible value of Accounts Receivable? (b) If the $450 account of a bankrupt customer is written off in the first month of the new year, what will be the resulting collectible value of Accounts Receivable?

7. What is the effect on net income of an optimistic versus a pessimistic view by management of estimated uncollectible accounts?

8. In what ways is the Allowance for Uncollectible Accounts similar to Accumulated Depreciation? In what ways is it different?

9. What procedure for estimating uncollectible accounts also gives management a view of the status of collections and the overall quality of accounts receivable?

10. What is the underlying reasoning behind the percentage of net sales method and the accounts receivable aging method of estimating uncollectible accounts?

11. Are the following terms different in any way: allowance for bad debts, allowance for doubtful accounts, allowance for uncollectible accounts?

12. Why should the entry for an account that has been written off as uncollectible be reinstated if the amount owed is subsequently collected?

13. What accounting rule is violated by the direct charge-off method of recognizing uncollectible accounts? Why?

14. Which of the lettered items below should be in Accounts Receivable? For those that do not belong in Accounts Receivable, tell where they do belong on the balance sheet: (a) installment accounts receivable from regular customers, due monthly for three years; (b) debit balances in customers' accounts; (c) receivables from employees; (d) credit balances in customers' accounts; (e) receivables from officers of the company; (f) accounts payable to a company that are less than accounts receivable from the same company.

15. What is a promissory note? Who is the maker? Who is the payee?

16. What are the due dates of the following notes: (a) a 3-month note dated August 16, (b) a 90-day note dated August 16, (c) a 60-day note dated March 25?

17. What is the difference between a cash discount and a discount on a note?
18. What is the difference between the interest on a note and the discount on a note?

Classroom Exercises

**Exercise 9-1.
Accounting for
Short-Term
Investments in
Equities
(L.O. 1)**

On October 16, 19x1, Jetline Corporation acquired the following short-term securities:

100 shares of IBM	$15,000
200 shares of General Motors	14,000
Total acquisition cost	$29,000

Jetline received dividends from IBM of $4.40 per share and from General Motors of $5.00 per share on December 15. IBM stock is selling for $155 per share and General Motors is selling for $60 at the end of the year. On January 9, 19x2 Jetline sells the General Motors shares for $13,000.

1. Prepare the journal entry to record the acquisition.
2. Prepare the journal entry to record receipt of the dividends.
3. Calculate the market value of the portfolio on December 31, 19x1 and prepare the journal entry to record the loss.
4. Prepare the balance sheet presentation for short-term investments on the December 31, 19x1 balance sheet.
5. Prepare the journal entry for January 9, 19x2, to record the sale.

**Exercise 9-2.
Accounting for
Short-Term
Investments
(L.O. 1)**

During certain periods of its fiscal year, Nicks Company invests its excess cash until it is needed. On January 16, the company invested $146,000 in 90-day U.S. Treasury bills that had a maturity value of $150,000. On April 15, Nicks purchased 10,000 shares of Goodrich Paper common stock at $40 per share and 5,000 shares of Keuron Power common stock at $30 per share. The Treasury bills matured on April 16, and the company received $150,000 in cash. On May 15, it received quarterly dividends of 92.25 cents per share from Keuron Power and 60 cents per share from Goodrich Paper. On June 15, the company sold all the shares of Goodrich Paper for $48 per share. On June 30, the value of the Keuron Power stock was $28 per share.

Prepare journal entries to record the transactions on January 16, April 15, April 16, May 15, June 15, and June 30. Also, show the balance sheet presentations of short-term investments on June 30. Round to the nearest whole dollar.

**Exercise 9-3.
Adjusting Entries:
Accounts
Receivable Aging
Method
(L.O. 3, 4)**

Accounts Receivable of Herrera Company shows a debit balance of $104,000 at the end of the year. An aging method analysis of the individual accounts indicates estimated uncollectible accounts to be $6,700.

Give the general journal entry to record the uncollectible accounts expense under each of the following independent assumptions: (a) The Allowance for Uncollectible Accounts has a credit balance of $800 before adjustment. (b) The Allowance for Uncollectible Accounts has a debit balance of $800 before adjustment.

Exercise 9-4.
Adjusting Entry:
Percentage of Net
Sales Method
(L.O. 3, 4)

At the end of the year, Marin Enterprises estimates the uncollectible accounts expense to be .7 percent of net sales of $10,100,000. The current credit balance of the Allowance for Uncollectible Accounts is $17,200. Give the general journal entry to record the uncollectible accounts expense.

Exercise 9-5.
Aging Method and
Net Sales Method
Contrasted
(L.O. 3, 4)

At the beginning of 19xx, the balances for Accounts Receivable and the Allowance for Uncollectible Accounts were $860,000 and $62,800, respectively. During the current year, credit sales were $6,400,000 and collections on account were $5,900,000. In addition, $70,000 in uncollectible accounts were written off. Using T accounts, determine year-end balances of Accounts Receivable and Allowance for Uncollectible Accounts. Then, make the year-end adjusting entry to record the uncollectible accounts expense, and show the year-end balance sheet presentation of Accounts Receivable and the Allowance for Uncollectible Accounts under each of the following conditions:

a. Management estimates the percentage of uncollectible credit sales to be 1.2 percent of total credit sales.
b. Based on an aging of accounts receivable, management estimates the end-of-year uncollectible accounts receivable to be $77,400.

Post the results of each entry to the Allowance for Uncollectible Accounts.

Exercise 9-6.
Entries for
Uncollectible
Accounts Expense
(L.O. 3, 4)

The Schumacker Office Supply Company sells merchandise on credit. During the year ended December 31, the company had net credit sales of $2,300,000. At the end of the year it had Accounts Receivable of $600,000 and a debit balance in the Allowance for Uncollectible Accounts of $3,400. In the past, approximately 1.4 percent of net sales have proved uncollectible. Also, an aging analysis of accounts receivable reveals that $30,000 of the receivables appear to be uncollectible. Prepare journal entries to record uncollectible accounts expense using (a) the percentage of net sales method and (b) the accounts receivable aging method.

What is the resulting balance of the Allowance for Uncollectible Accounts under each method? How would your answers change if the Allowance for Uncollectible Accounts had begun with a credit balance of $3,400 instead of a debit balance?

Exercise 9-7.
Accounts
Receivable
Transactions
(L.O. 4)

Assuming that the allowance method is being used, prepare journal entries to record the following transactions:

May 17, 19x8   Sold merchandise to Holly Fox for $900, terms n/10.
Sept. 20, 19x8   Received $300 from Holly Fox on account.
June 25, 19x9   Wrote off as uncollectible the balance of the Holly Fox account when she was declared bankrupt.
July 27, 19x9   Unexpectedly received a check for $100 from Holly Fox.

Exercise 9-8.
Credit Card Sales
Transactions
(L.O. 5)

Prepare journal entries to record the following transactions for Maggie's Specialty Shop:

Dec. 4 A tabulation of invoices at the end of the day showed $1,100 in American Express invoices and $600 in Diners Club invoices. American Express takes a discount of 4 percent, and Diners Club takes a 5 percent discount.

   8 Received payment from American Express at 96 percent of face value and from Diners Club at 95 percent of face value.

   9 A tabulation of invoices at the end of the day showed $400 in VISA invoices, which are deposited in a special bank account at full value less 5 percent discount.

Exercise 9-9.
Interest
Computations
(L.O. 7)

Determine the interest on the following notes:

a. $11,400 at 10 percent for 90 days
b. $8,000 at 12 percent for 60 days
c. $9,000 at 9 percent for 30 days
d. $15,000 at 15 percent for 120 days
e. $5,400 at 6 percent for 60 days

Exercise 9-10.
Discounting Notes
(L.O. 7)

In an effort to raise cash, Chao Company discounted two notes at the bank on September 15. The bank charged a discount rate of 15 percent applied to the maturity value. Compute the proceeds from discounting of each of the following notes:

Date of Note	Amount	Interest Rate	Life of Note
a. Aug. 1	$ 9,500	10	120 days
b. July 20	$18,000	12	90 days

Exercise 9-11.
Notes Receivable
Transactions
(L.O. 8)

Prepare general journal entries to record the following transactions:

Jan. 16 Sold merchandise to Brighton Corporation on account for $36,000, terms n/30.

Feb. 15 Accepted a $36,000, 10 percent, 90-day note from Brighton Corporation in lieu of payment on account.

Mar. 17 Discounted Brighton Corporation note at bank at 12 percent.

May 16 Received notice that Brighton dishonored the note. Paid the bank the maturity value of the note plus a protest fee of $15.

June 15 Received payment in full from Brighton Corporation, including interest at 10 percent from the date the note was dishonored.

Exercise 9-12.
Adjusting Entries:
Interest Expense
(L.O. 8)

Prepare journal entries (assuming reversing entries were not made) to record the following:

Dec. 1 Received a 90-day, 12 percent note for $5,000 from a customer for a sale of merchandise.

   31 Made end-of-year adjustment for interest income.

Mar. 1 Received payment in full for note and interest.

Exercise 9-13.
Comprehensive
Notes Receivable
Transactions
(L.O. 8)

Prepare general journal entries to record these transactions:

Jan. 5 Accepted a $2,400, 60-day, 10 percent note dated this day in granting a time extension on the past-due account of A. Jones.

Mar. 6 A. Jones paid the maturity value of his $2,400 note.

9 Accepted a $1,500, 60-day, 12 percent note dated this day in granting a time extension on the past-due account of S. Smith.

May 8 S. Smith dishonored his note when presented for payment.

12 Accepted a $1,800, 90-day, 12 percent note in granting a time extension on the past-due account of R. Johnson.

16 Discounted the R. Johnson note at the bank at 15 percent.

Aug. 14 Since notice protesting the R. Johnson note had not been received, assumed that it had been paid.

14 Accepted a $1,200, 60-day, 10 percent note dated August 14 in granting a time extension on the past-due account of E. Cummings.

Sept. 6 Discounted the E. Cummings note at the bank at 15 percent.

Oct. 13 Received notice protesting the E. Cummings note. Paid the bank the maturity value of the note plus a $20 protest fee.

14 Received a $3,000, 60-day, 12 percent note dated this day from J. Carlos in granting a time extension on his past-due account.

Nov. 13 Discounted the J. Carlos note at the bank at 15 percent.

Dec. 14 Received notice protesting the J. Carlos note. Paid the bank the maturity value of the note plus a $20 protest fee.

25 Received payment from J. Carlos of the maturity value of his dishonored note, the protest fee, and the interest on both for 12 days beyond maturity at 15 percent.

31 Wrote off the account of S. Smith against the allowance for uncollectible accounts.

Interpreting Accounting Information

Winton Sharrer Co.
(L.O. 3, 4)

Winton Sharrer Co. is a major consumer goods company that sells over 3,000 products in 135 countries. From the company's annual report to the Securities and Exchange Commission, data pertaining to net sales and accounts related to accounts receivable for 1987, 1988, and 1989 were as follows (in thousands):

	1989	1988	1987
Net Sales	$4,910,000	$4,865,000	$4,888,000
Accounts Receivable	523,000	524,000	504,000
Allowance for Doubtful Accounts	18,600	21,200	24,500
Uncollectible Accounts Expense	15,000	16,700	15,800
Uncollectible Accounts Written Off	19,300	20,100	17,700
Recoveries of Accounts Previously Written Off	1,700	100	1,000

Required

1. Compute the ratios of Uncollectible Accounts Expense to Net Sales and Accounts Receivable and of the Allowance for Doubtful Accounts to Accounts Receivable for 1987, 1988, and 1989. What appears to be management's attitude with respect to the collectibility of accounts receivable over the three-year period?

2. Make the general journal entries related to the Allowance for Doubtful Accounts for 1989.

Problem Set A

Problem 9A-1.
Percentage of Net
Sales Method
(L.O. 3, 4)

Chappell Company had an Accounts Receivable balance of $320,000 and a credit balance in the Allowance for Uncollectible Accounts of $16,700 at January 1, 19xx. During the year, the company recorded the following transactions:

a. Sales on account, $1,052,000.
b. Sales returns and allowances by credit customers, $53,400.
c. Collections from customers, $993,000.
d. Worthless accounts written off, $19,800.
e. Written-off accounts collected, $4,200.

The company's past history indicates that, in addition, 2.5 percent of net credit sales will not be collected.

Required

1. Open ledger accounts for the Accounts Receivable controlling account (112) and the Allowance for Uncollectible Accounts (113). Then enter the beginning balances in these accounts.
2. Record a single general journal entry for each of the five items listed above, summarizing the year's activity.
3. Record the general journal entry on December 31 for the estimated uncollectible accounts expense for the year.
4. Post the appropriate parts of the transactions in **2** and **3** to Accounts Receivable and the Allowance for Uncollectible Accounts.

Problem 9A-2.
Accounts
Receivable Aging
Method
(L.O. 3, 4)

The DiPalma Jewelry Store uses the accounts receivable aging method to estimate uncollectible accounts. The balances of Accounts Receivable and Allowance for Uncollectible Accounts were $446,341 and $43,000, respectively, at February 1, 19x1. During the year, the store had sales on account of $3,724,000, sales returns and allowances of $63,000, worthless accounts written off of $44,300, and collections from customers of $3,214,000. As part of end-of-year (January 31, 19x2) procedures, an aging analysis of accounts receivable is prepared. The analysis is partially complete. The totals of the analysis appear below.

Customer Account	Total	Not Yet Due	1–30 Days Past Due	31–60 Days Past Due	61–90 Days Past Due	Over 90 Days Past Due
Balance Forward	$793,791	$438,933	$149,614	$106,400	$57,442	$41,402

The accounts at the top of the following page remain to be classified in order to finish the analysis:

Account	Amount	Due Date
H. Caldwell	$10,977	January 15
D. Carlson	9,314	February 15 (next fiscal year)
M. Guokas	8,664	December 20
F. Javier	780	October 1
B. Loo	14,810	January 4
S. Qadri	6,316	November 15
A. Rosenthal	4,389	March 1 (next fiscal year)
	$55,250	

From past experience, the company has found that the following rates for estimating uncollectible accounts produce an adequate balance for the Allowance for Uncollectible Accounts:

Time Past Due	Percentage Considered Uncollectible
Not yet due	2
1–30 days	5
31–60 days	15
61–90 days	25
Over 90 days	50

Required

1. Complete the aging analysis of accounts receivable.
2. Determine the end-of-year balances (before adjustments) of the Accounts Receivable controlling account and the Allowance for Uncollectible Accounts.
3. Prepare an analysis, computing the estimated uncollectible accounts.
4. Prepare a general journal entry to record the estimated uncollectible accounts expense for the year (round the adjustment to the nearest whole dollar).

Problem 9A-3.
Notes Receivable
Transactions
(L.O. 7, 8)

Sharman Manufacturing Company sells truck beds to various companies. To improve its liquidity, Sharman discounts any promissory notes it receives. The company engaged in the following transactions involving promissory notes:

Jan. 10 Sold beds to Hudson Company for $30,000, terms n/10.
　　　20 Accepted a 90-day, 12 percent promissory note in settlement of the account from Hudson.
　　　31 Discounted the note from Hudson Company at the bank at 14 percent.
Apr. 20 Having received no notice that the note had been dishonored, assumed Hudson Company paid the bank.
May 5 Sold beds to Monroe Company for $20,000, terms n/10.
　　　15 Received $4,000 cash and a 60-day, 13 percent note for $16,000 in settlement of the Monroe account.
　　　25 Discounted the note from Monroe to the bank at 14 percent.

July 14   Received notice that Monroe dishonored the note. Paid the bank the maturity value of the note plus a protest fee of $20.

Aug. 2   Wrote off the Monroe account as uncollectible after news that the company declared bankruptcy.

5   Received a 90-day, 11 percent note for $15,000 from Circle Company in settlement of an account receivable.

15   Discounted the note from Circle at the bank at 14 percent.

Nov. 3   Received notice that Circle dishonored the note. Paid the bank the maturity value of the note plus a protest fee of $20.

9   Received payment in full from Circle, including 15 percent interest for the 6 days since the note was dishonored.

Required   Prepare general journal entries to record the above transactions.

Problem 9A-4.
Notes Receivable
Transactions
(L.O. 7, 8)

The Alvarado Company accepts notes as payment for sales to key customers. The transactions involving notes for August and October are presented below.

Aug. 6   Accepted a $9,000, 60-day, 10 percent note from Cronin Company in payment for merchandise.

8   Accepted a $7,000, 60-day, 11 percent note from La Russo's Electronics in payment for merchandise.

13   Discounted the Cronin Company note at the bank at 15 percent.

23   Discounted the La Russo's Electronics note at the bank at 15 percent.

28   Accepted a $21,000, 60-day, 9 percent note from Ramsey Company in payment for purchase of merchandise.

30   Accepted a $14,000, 60-day, 12 percent note from Lee Company in payment for merchandise.

Oct. 5   Receiving no notice of dishonor by Cronin Company, Alvarado Company assumed Cronin paid its obligation to the bank.

7   Received notice from the bank that La Russo's Electronics dishonored its note. Paid the bank the maturity value plus a protest fee of $18.

27   Ramsey Company paid its note and interest.

29   Lee Company dishonored its note.

Required   Prepare general journal entries to record the above transactions.

Problem 9A-5.
Short-Term
Financing by
Discounting
Customers' Notes
(L.O. 7, 8)

The management of Gerrin Lawn Products sells its goods to distributors 120 days before the summer season. Mr. Gerrin has worked out a plan with his bank to finance receivables from sales. The plan calls for the company to receive a 120-day, 10 percent note for each sale to a distributor. Each note will be discounted at the bank at the rate of 12 percent. This plan will provide Gerrin with adequate cash flow to operate his company.

During January and February, Gerrin made the following sales under the plan:

Company	Amount of Note	Date of Note	Discount Date*
Gold Hardware	$460,000	Jan. 7	Jan. 9
Kedzie Stores	820,000	12	15
Howell's Markets	290,000	19	Feb. 18

*Assume 28 days in February

During May, all the distributors paid on their respective due dates except Kedzie Stores, which defaulted on its note. The note was paid in full 30 days late, including additional interest at 9 percent and a bank protest fee of $50.

Required

1. Prepare general journal entries to record Gerrin Lawn Product's transactions (round calculations to nearest dollar) for January 7, 9, 12, 15, 19 and February 18.
2. What was the total amount of cash generated in January by discounting the notes receivable?
3. Prepare general journal entries to record the transactions on Gerrin Lawn Products' records for May 12 and June 11.
4. What is your evaluation of the plan? What risk is management taking?

Problem Set B

Problem 9B-1.
Percentage of Net
Sales Method
(L.O. 3, 4)

On December 31 of last year, the balance sheet of Marzano Company had Accounts Receivable of $298,000 and a credit balance in the Allowance for Uncollectible Accounts of $20,300. During the current year, the company's records included the following selected activities: sales on account, $1,195,000; sales returns and allowances, $73,000; collections from customers, $1,150,000; accounts written off as worthless, $16,000; written-off accounts unexpectedly collected, $2,000. In the past, the company had found that 1.6 percent of net sales would not be collected.

Required

1. Open ledger accounts for the Accounts Receivable controlling account (112) and the Allowance for Uncollectible Accounts (113). Then enter the beginning balances in these accounts.
2. Give a single general journal entry to record in summary form each of the five items listed above.
3. Give the general journal entry on December 31 of the current year to record the estimated uncollectible accounts expense for the year.
4. Post the appropriate parts of the transactions in 2 and 3 to these accounts.

Problem 9B-2.
Accounts
Receivable Aging
Method
(L.O. 3, 4)

Pokorny Company uses the accounts receivable aging method to estimate uncollectible accounts. The Accounts Receivable controlling account and the Allowance for Uncollectible Accounts had balances of $88,430 and $7,200, respectively, at the beginning of the year. During the year, the company had sales on account of $473,000, sales returns and allowances of $4,200, worthless accounts written off of $7,900, and collections from customers of $450,730. At the end of the year (December 31), a junior accountant for the company was preparing an aging analysis of accounts receivable. At the top of page 6 of his report, his totals appeared as follows:

Customer Account	Total	Not Yet Due	1–30 Days Past Due	31–60 Days Past Due	61–90 Days Past Due	Over 90 Days Past Due
Balance Forward	$89,640	$49,030	$24,110	$9,210	$3,990	$3,300

He had the following accounts remaining to finish the analysis:

Account	Amount	Due Date
K. Foust	$ 930	Jan. 14 (next year)
K. Groth	620	Dec. 24
R. Mejias	1,955	Sept. 28
C. Polk	2,100	Aug. 16
M. Spears	375	Dec. 14
J. Yong	2,685	Jan. 23 (next year)
A. Zorr	295	Nov. 5
	$8,960	

The company has found from past experience that the following rates of estimated uncollectible accounts produce an adequate balance for the Allowance for Uncollectible Accounts:

Time Past Due	Percentage Considered Uncollectible
Not yet due	2
1–30 days	4
31–60 days	20
61–90 days	30
Over 90 days	50

Required

1. Complete the aging analysis of accounts receivable.
2. Determine the end-of-year balances (before adjustments) of the Accounts Receivable controlling account and the Allowance for Uncollectible Accounts.
3. Prepare an analysis computing the estimated uncollectible accounts.
4. Prepare a general journal entry to record the estimated uncollectible accounts expense for the year. (Round adjustment to the nearest dollar.)

Problem 9B-3.
Notes Receivable
Transactions
(L.O. 7, 8)

Hopson Manufacturing Company engaged in the following transactions involving promissory notes:

Jan. 14 Sold merchandise to Barbara Reid Company for $18,500, terms n/30.
Feb. 13 Received $4,200 in cash from Barbara Reid Company and received a 90-day, 8 percent promissory note for the balance of the account.
       23 Discounted the note at the bank at 15 percent.

May 14 Because no notice that the note had been dishonored was received, it was assumed that Barbara Reid Company paid the bank.

15 Received a 60-day, 12 percent note from Ralph Sarkis Company in payment of a past-due account, $6,000.

30 Discounted the note at the bank at 15 percent.

July 14 Received notice that Ralph Sarkis Company dishonored the note. Paid the bank the maturity value of the note plus a protest fee of $20.

20 Received a check from Ralph Sarkis Company for payment of the maturity value of the note, the $20 protest fee, and interest at 12 percent for the six days beyond maturity.

25 Sold merchandise to James Flowers Company for $18,000, with payment of $3,000 cash down and the remainder on account.

31 Received a $15,000, 45-day, 10 percent promissory note from James Flowers Company for the outstanding account.

Aug. 5 Discounted the note at the bank at 15 percent.

Sept. 14 Received notice that James Flowers Company dishonored the note. Paid the bank the maturity value of the note plus a protest fee of $20.

25 Wrote off the James Flowers Company account as uncollectible following news that the company had been declared bankrupt.

Required   Prepare general journal entries to record the above transactions.

Problem 9B-4.
Notes Receivable
Transactions
(L.O. 7, 8)

Roman's Auto Store engaged in the following transactions:

Jan. 2 Accepted a $9,400, 90-day, 14 percent note from Willis Daniels as an extension on his past-due account.

5 Accepted a $2,900, 90-day, 12 percent note from Sharon Kelly in payment of a past-due account receivable.

10 Accepted a $4,500, 90-day, 10 percent note from Charles Suggs as an extension of a past-due account.

12 Discounted Willis Daniels' note at the bank at 14 percent.

25 Discounted Charles Suggs' note at the bank at 14 percent.

30 Accepted a $5,200, 90 day, 12 percent note from Linda Pate in lieu of payment of a past-due account.

Apr. 2 Received notice that Willis Daniels had dishonored his note. Paid the bank the maturity value plus a protest fee of $25.

5 Sharon Kelly dishonored her note.

10 Received no notice of dishonor by Charles Suggs and assumed he paid his obligation to the bank.

22 Received payment from Willis Daniels for the total amount owed including maturity value, protest fee, and interest at 15 percent for the twenty days past maturity.

25 Wrote off the Sharon Kelly account as uncollectible because she could not be located.

30 Linda Pate paid her note plus interest in full.

Required   Prepare general journal entries to record the above transactions.

Problem 9B-5.
Short-Term
Financing by
Discounting
Customers' Notes
(L.O. 7, 8)

The Ling Company is faced with a severe cash shortage because of slowing sales and past-due accounts. The financial vice president has studied the situation and has found a number of large past-due accounts. He makes the following recommendations: (a) that the company seek promissory notes from past-due accounts to encourage the customers to pay on time and to earn interest on these accounts, and (b) that the company generate cash by discounting the notes at the bank at the going rate of interest. During the first month of this program, the company was successful, as indicated by the following table:

Company	Amount of Note	Length of Note	Date of Note	Interest Rate	Discount Date	Discount Rate
Blue Manufac-						
turing Company	$210,000	60 days	Apr. 5	15%	Apr. 7	15%
Norris Company	170,000	60 days	Apr. 10	12%	Apr. 13	15%
Lazaro						
Corporation	110,000	60 days	Apr. 15	14%	Apr. 20	15%

Blue Manufacturing Company and Norris Company paid their notes on the due dates. Lazaro Corporation dishonored its note on the due date. The latter note was paid by Ling Company, including a bank protest fee of $50.

Required

1. Prepare appropriate general journal entries for April 5, 7, 10, 13, 15, and 20.
2. What was the total cash generated during April by the vice president's plan?
3. Prepare appropriate general journal entries for June 4, 9, 14.
4. What is your evaluation of the plan? What offsetting factors occur in later months such as June?

Financial Decision Case

Golina Christmas
Tree Company
(L.O. 1)

The Golina Christmas Tree Company engages in a seasonal business, the growing and selling of Christmas trees. By January 1, after a successful season, the company has cash on hand that will not be needed for several months. The company has minimal expenses from January to October and heavy expenses during the harvest and shipping months of November and December. The company's management follows the practice of investing the idle cash in marketable securities, which can be sold as the funds are needed for operations. The company's fiscal year ends on June 30. On January 10 of the current year the company has cash of $372,800 on hand. It keeps $20,000 on hand for operating expenses and invests the rest as follows:

$100,000 3-month Treasury bill	$ 97,800
1,000 shares of Ford Motor Co. ($40 per share)	40,000
2,500 shares of McDonald's ($40 per share)	100,000
1,000 shares of IBM ($115 per share)	115,000
Total of short-term investments	$352,800

During the next few months the company receives quarterly cash dividends of $1 per share from Ford, $.125 from McDonald's, and $1.10 from IBM twice from each company (assume February 10 and May 10). The Treasury bill is redeemed at face value on April 10. On June 1 management sells 500 shares of McDonald's at $45 per share. On June 30 the market values of the investments are as follows:

Ford Motor Co.	$ 51 per share
McDonald's	$ 36 per share
IBM	$105 per share

Another quarterly dividend is received from each company (assume August 10). All the remaining shares are sold on November 1 at the following prices:

Ford Motor Co.	$ 45 per share
McDonald's	$ 34 per share
IBM	$126 per share

Required
1. Record the investment transactions that occurred on January 10, February 10, April 10, May 10, and June 1. Prepare the required adjusting entry on June 30, and record the investment transactions on August 10 and November 1.
2. How would the short-term investments be shown on the balance sheet on June 30?
3. After November 1, what is the balance of the account called Allowance to Reduce Short-Term Investments to Market, and what will happen to this account next June?
4. What is your assessment of Golina Christmas Tree Company's strategy with regard to idle cash?

Answers to Self-Test

1. a	3. c	5. d	7. b	9. d
2. a	4. b	6. c	8. d	10. a

LEARNING OBJECTIVES

1. *Define merchandise inventory, and show how inventory measurement affects income determination.*
2. *Define inventory cost, and relate it to goods flow and cost flow.*
3. *Calculate the pricing of inventory, using the cost basis according to the (a) specific identification method; (b) average-cost method; (c) first-in, first-out (FIFO) method; (d) last-in, first-out (LIFO) method.*
4. *State the effects of each method on income determination and income taxes in periods of changing prices.*
5. *Apply the perpetual inventory system to accounting for inventories and cost of goods sold.*
6. *Apply the lower-of-cost-or-market rule to inventory valuation.*
7. *Estimate the cost of ending inventory using (a) the retail inventory method and (b) the gross profit method.*

CHAPTER 10

Inventories

The major source of revenues for retail and wholesale businesses is the sale of merchandise. In terms of dollars, the inventory of goods held for sale is one of the largest assets of a merchandising business. The cost of goods sold is the largest deduction from sales because merchandise is continually bought and sold by these companies. In fact, this cost is often larger than the total of other expenses. Inventories are also important to manufacturing companies. These companies have three kinds of inventory: raw materials to be used in making products, partly complete products (often called work in process), and finished goods ready for sale. This chapter deals with inventory measurement, emphasizing its importance to income determination and explaining several different ways of determining, valuing, and estimating inventories. Although the examples used in this chapter mostly relate to merchandising businesses, the concepts and techniques are also applicable to manufacturing companies. After studying this chapter, you should be able to meet the learning objectives listed on the left.

Assets may be divided into two categories. There are financial assets, such as those studied in Chapter 9, including cash, short-term investments, accounts receivable, and notes receivable. These assets represent a right to cash or can be easily converted into cash. The second type of asset represents an unexpired cost that has not yet been matched against revenues. Among these assets are prepaid expenses, inventories, property, plant, and equipment, natural resources, and intangibles.

The most important accounting problem that arises in connection with the latter type of assets is the application of the matching rule for the purpose of measuring income. In applying the matching rule, two important questions must be answered: (1) How much of the asset is used up or has expired during the current accounting period and should be shown as an expense on the income statement? (2) How much of the asset is still unused or unexpired and should remain on the balance sheet as an asset? Chapter 12 will apply the matching rule to long-term assets including property, plant, and equipment, natural resources, and intangibles.

Inventories and Income Determination

Merchandise inventory consists of all goods that are owned and held for sale in the regular course of business, including goods in transit. Because it will normally be converted into cash within a year's time, merchandise inventory is considered a current asset. It is shown on the balance sheet just below Accounts Receivable because it is less liquid.

OBJECTIVE 1
Define merchandise inventory, and show how inventory measurement affects income determination

The American Institute of Certified Public Accountants states, "A major objective of accounting for inventories is the proper determination of income through the process of matching appropriate costs against revenues."[1] Note that the objective is to determine the best measure of income, not the most realistic inventory value. As you will see, the two objectives are sometimes incompatible, in which case the objective of income determination takes precedence over a realistic inventory figure for the balance sheet.

Review of Gross Margin and Cost of Goods Sold Computations

A review should show how the cost assigned to inventory is related to the computations of gross margin and cost of goods sold. The gross margin on sales is computed by deducting cost of goods sold from the net sales of the period. Cost of goods sold is measured by deducting ending inventory from cost of goods available for sale. Because of these relationships, the higher the cost of ending inventory, the lower the cost of goods sold will be and the higher the resulting gross margin. Conversely, the lower the value assigned to ending inventory, the higher the cost of goods sold will be and the lower the gross margin. *In effect, the value assigned to the ending inventory determines what portion of the cost of goods originally available for sale will be deducted from net sales as cost of goods sold and what portion will be carried to the next period as beginning inventory.* Remember that the amount of goods available for sale includes the beginning inventory (unexpired costs passed from the last period to this period) plus net purchases during this period. The effects on income of errors in the cost of ending inventory are demonstrated in the next section.

Effects of Errors in Inventory Measurement

As seen above, the basic problem of separating goods available for sale into the two components, goods sold and goods not sold, is that of assigning a cost to the goods not sold, the ending inventory. This, in turn, determines the cost of goods sold because whatever portion of the goods available for sale is assigned to the ending inventory, the remainder is cost of goods sold.

For this reason, an error made in determining the inventory figure at the end of the period will cause an equal error in gross margin and net income in the income statement. The amount of assets and owner's equity in the balance sheet will also be misstated by the same amount. The consequences of overstatement and understatement of inventory are illustrated in the three simplified examples on the next page. In each

1. American Institute of Certified Public Accountants, *Accounting Research Bulletin No. 43* (New York: AICPA, 1953), Ch. 4.

case, beginning inventory, purchases, and cost of goods available for sale are correctly stated. In the first example, ending inventory has been stated correctly. In the second example, inventory is overstated by $6,000, and in the third example, inventory is understated by $6,000.

Example 1. Ending Inventory Correctly Stated at $10,000

Cost of Goods Sold for the Year		Income Statement for the Year	
Beginning Inventory	$12,000	Net Sales	$100,000
Net Purchases	58,000	Cost of Goods Sold	60,000
Cost of Goods Available		Gross Margin from Sales	$ 40,000
for Sale	$70,000	Operating Expenses	32,000
Ending Inventory	10,000	Net Income	$ 8,000
Cost of Goods Sold	$60,000		

Example 2. Ending Inventory Overstated by $6,000

Cost of Goods Sold for the Year		Income Statement for the Year	
Beginning Inventory	$12,000	Net Sales	$100,000
Net Purchases	58,000	Cost of Goods Sold	54,000
Cost of Goods Available		Gross Margin from Sales	$ 46,000
for Sale	$70,000	Operating Expenses	32,000
Ending Inventory	16,000	Net Income	$ 14,000
Cost of Goods Sold	$54,000		

Example 3. Ending Inventory Understated by $6,000

Cost of Goods Sold for the Year		Income Statement for the Year	
Beginning Inventory	$12,000	Net Sales	$100,000
Net Purchases	58,000	Cost of Goods Sold	66,000
Cost of Goods Available		Gross Margin from Sales	$ 34,000
for Sale	$70,000	Operating Expenses	32,000
Ending Inventory	4,000	Net Income	$ 2,000
Cost of Goods Sold	$66,000		

In these examples, the total cost of goods available for sale amounted to $70,000 in each case. The difference in net income resulted from how this $70,000 was divided between ending inventory and cost of goods sold.

Because the ending inventory in one period becomes the beginning inventory in the following period, it is important to recognize that an error in inventory valuation affects not only the current period but also the following period. Using the same figures in Examples **1** and **2** above, the income statements for two successive years in Exhibit 10-1 illustrate this carryover effect.

Exhibit 10-1. Effect of Error in Ending Inventory on Current and Succeeding Year

Effect of Error in Inventory
Income Statement
For the Year Ended December 31, 19x1

	Correct Statement of Ending Inventory		Overstatement of Ending Inventory	
Net Sales		$100,000		$100,000
Cost of Goods Sold				
Beginning Inventory, Jan. 1, 19x1	$12,000		$12,000	
Net Purchases	58,000		58,000	
Cost of Goods Available for Sale	$70,000		$70,000	
Less Ending Inventory, Dec. 31, 19x1	10,000		16,000	
Cost of Goods Sold		60,000		54,000
Gross Margin from Sales		$ 40,000		$ 46,000
Operating Expenses		32,000		32,000
Net Income		$ 8,000		$ 14,000

Effect on Succeeding Year
Income Statement
For the Year Ended December 31, 19x2

	Correct Statement of Beginning Inventory		Overstatement of Beginning Inventory	
Net Sales		$130,000		$130,000
Cost of Goods Sold				
Beginning Inventory, Jan. 1, 19x2	$10,000		$16,000	
Net Purchases	68,000		68,000	
Cost of Goods Available for Sale	$78,000		$84,000	
Less Ending Inventory, Dec. 31, 19x2	13,000		13,000	
Cost of Goods Sold		65,000		71,000
Gross Margin from Sales		$ 65,000		$ 59,000
Operating Expenses		50,000		50,000
Net Income		$ 15,000		$ 9,000

Note that over a period of two years the errors in net income will off-set or counterbalance each other. In Exhibit 10-1, for example, the overstatement of ending inventory in 19x1 caused a $6,000 overstatement of beginning inventory in the following year, resulting in an understatement of income by $6,000 in the second year. This offsetting effect is shown as follows:

	With Inventory Correctly Stated	With Inventory at Dec. 31, 19x1 Overstated	
		Reported Net Income Will Be	Reported Net Income Will Be Overstated (Understated)
Net Income for 19x1	$ 8,000	$14,000	$ 6,000
Net Income for 19x2	15,000	9,000	(6,000)
Total Net Income for Two Years	$23,000	$23,000	—

Because the total income for the two years is the same, there may be a tendency to think that one does not need to worry about inventory errors. This idea is not correct because it violates the matching rule, and many management decisions as well as creditor and investor decisions are made on an annual basis and depend on the accountant's determination of net income. The accountant has an obligation to make the net income figure for each year as useful as possible.

The effects of errors in inventory on net income are as follows:

Effect on Net Income

	Overstated	Understated
Beginning Inventory:		
Overstated		×
Understated	×	
Ending Inventory:		
Overstated	×	
Understated		×

If we assume no income tax effects, a change or error in inventory results in a change or error in net income of the same amount. Thus the measurement of inventory is an important problem and is the subject of the remainder of this chapter.

Inventory Measurement

The cost assigned to ending inventory depends on two measurements: quantity and price. At least once each year, a business must take an actual physical count of all items of merchandise held for sale. This process is called taking a physical inventory, or simply taking inventory, as described in Chapter 5. Although companies may take inventory at other times during the year, most companies take inventory only at the end of each year. Taking the inventory consists of (1) counting, weighing, or measuring the items on hand, (2) pricing each item, and (3) extending (multiplying) to determine the total.

Merchandise in Transit

Because merchandise inventory includes items owned by the company and held for sale, purchased merchandise in transit should be included in the inventory count if title to the goods has passed. As explained in Chapter 5, the terms of the shipping agreement must be examined to determine if title has passed. For example, outgoing goods shipped FOB destination would be included in merchandise inventory, whereas those shipped FOB shipping point would not. Conversely, incoming goods shipped FOB shipping point would be included in merchandise inventory, but those shipped FOB destination would not.

Merchandise on Hand Not Included in Inventory

At the time a physical inventory is taken, there may be merchandise on hand to which the company does not hold title. One category of such goods is an order for a customer on which the sale is completed and the goods in question now belong to the buyer and await delivery. This sale should be recorded and the goods segregated for delivery. A second category is goods held on consignment. A **consignment** is the placing of goods by the owner of the goods (known as the *consignor*) on the premises of another company (the *consignee*). Title to consigned goods remains with the consignor until the consignee sells the goods. Thus if consigned goods are on hand, they should not be included in the physical inventory because they still belong to the consignor.

Pricing the Inventory at Cost

OBJECTIVE 2
Define inventory cost, and relate it to goods flow and cost flow

The pricing of inventory is one of the most interesting and most widely debated problems in accounting. As demonstrated, the value placed on ending inventory may have a dramatic effect on net income for each of two consecutive years. Federal income taxes are based on income, so the valuation of inventory may also have a considerable effect on the income taxes to be paid. Federal income tax authorities have, therefore, been interested in the effects of various inventory valuation procedures and have specific regulations about the acceptability of different methods. So the accountant is sometimes faced with the problem of balancing the goals of proper income determination with those of minimizing income taxes.

There are a number of acceptable methods of valuing inventories on the financial statements. Most are based either on cost or on the lower of cost or market. Both methods are acceptable for income tax purposes. We will first explain variations of the cost basis of inventory valuation and then turn to the lower-of-cost-or-market method.

Cost Defined

According to the AICPA, "The primary basis of accounting for inventories is cost, which has been defined generally as the price paid or consideration given to acquire an asset."[2] This definition of **inventory cost** has generally been interpreted to include the following costs: (1) invoice price less purchases discounts; (2) freight or transportation in, including insurance in transit; and (3) applicable taxes and tariffs. Other costs, such as those for purchasing, receiving, and storing, should in principle also be included in inventory cost. In practice, however, it is so hard to allocate these costs to specific inventory items that they are usually considered an expense of the accounting period instead of an inventory cost.

Methods of Pricing Inventory at Cost

The prices of most kinds of merchandise vary during the year. Identical lots of merchandise may have been purchased at different prices. Also, when identical items are bought and sold, it is often impossible to tell which have been sold and which are still in inventory. For this reason, it is necessary to make an assumption about the order in which items have been sold. Because the assumed order of sale may or may not be the same as the actual order of sale, the assumption is really an assumption about the *flow of costs* rather than the *flow of physical inventory*.

Thus the term **goods flow** refers to the actual physical movement of goods in the operations of the company, and the term **cost flow** refers to the association of costs with their *assumed* flow in the operations of the company. The assumed cost flow may or may not be the same as the actual goods flow. Though this statement may seem strange at first, there is nothing wrong with it. Several assumed cost flows are available under generally accepted accounting principles. In fact, it is sometimes preferable to use an assumed cost flow that bears no relationship to goods flow because it gives a better estimate of income, which, as stated earlier, is the major goal of inventory valuation.

Accountants usually price inventory by using one of the following generally accepted methods, each based on a different assumption of cost flow: (1) specific identification method; (2) average-cost method; (3) first-in, first-out method (FIFO); and (4) last-in, first-out method (LIFO).

To illustrate the four methods, the following data for the month of June will be used:

Inventory Data, June 30

June	1	Inventory	50 units @ $1.00	$ 50
	6	Purchased	50 units @ $1.10	55
	13	Purchased	150 units @ $1.20	180
	20	Purchased	100 units @ $1.30	130
	25	Purchased	150 units @ $1.40	210
Goods Available for Sale			500 units	$625
Sales			280 units	
On hand June 30			220 units	

2. Ibid.

Note that the total available for sale is 500 units, at a total cost of $625. Stated simply, the problem of inventory pricing is to divide the $625 between the 280 units sold and the 220 units on hand.

OBJECTIVE 3a
Calculate the pricing of inventory, using the cost basis according to the specific identification method

Specific Identification Method. If the units in the ending inventory can be identified as coming from specific purchases, the **specific identification method** may be used to price the inventories. For instance, assume that the June 30 inventory consisted of 50 units from the inventory on hand June 1, 100 units of the purchase of June 13, and 70 units of the purchase of June 25. The cost to be assigned to the inventory under the specific identification method would be $268, and it can be determined as follows:

Inventory, June 30—Specific Identification Method

50 units @ $1.00	$ 50	Cost of Goods Available	
100 units @ $1.20	120	for Sale	$625
70 units @ $1.40	98	Less June 30 Inventory	268
220 units at cost of	$258	Cost of Goods Sold	$357

The specific identification method might be used in the purchase and sale of high-priced articles such as automobiles, heavy equipment, and works of art. Although this method may appear logical, it is not used by many companies because it has two definite disadvantages. First, it is difficult and impractical in most cases to keep track of the purchase and sale of individual items. Second, when a company deals in items of an identical nature, deciding which items are sold becomes arbitrary; thus the company can raise or lower income by choosing to sell the high- or low-cost items.

OBJECTIVE 3b
Calculate the pricing of inventory, using the cost basis according to the average-cost method

Average-Cost Method. Under the **average-cost method**, it is assumed that the cost of inventory is the average cost of goods on hand at the beginning of the period plus all goods purchased during the period. Average cost is computed by dividing the total cost of goods available for sale by the total units available for sale. This gives a weighted-average unit cost that is applied to the units in the ending inventory. The ending inventory in our illustration would be $1.25 per unit, or a total of $275, determined as follows:

Inventory, June 30—Average-Cost Method

June	1	Inventory	50 @ $1.00	$ 50
	6	Purchased	50 @ $1.10	55
	13	Purchased	150 @ $1.20	180
	20	Purchased	100 @ $1.30	130
	25	Purchased	150 @ $1.40	210
Totals			500 units	$625

(continued)

Average unit cost: $625 ÷ 500 = $1.25
→ **Ending inventory: 220 units @ $1.25 = $275**

Cost of Goods Available for Sale	$625
→ **Less June 30 Inventory**	275
Cost of Goods Sold	$350

The cost figure obtained for the ending inventory under the average-cost method is influenced by all the prices paid during the year and thus tends to level out the effects of cost increases and decreases. Some, however, criticize the average-cost method because they feel that recent costs should receive more attention and are more relevant for income measurement and decision making.

OBJECTIVE 3c
Calculate the pricing of inventory, using the cost basis according to the first-in, first-out (FIFO) method

First-In, First-Out (FIFO) Method. The **first-in, first-out (FIFO) method** is based on the assumption that the costs of the first items acquired should be assigned to the first items sold. The costs of the goods on hand at the end of a period are assumed to be from the most recent purchases, and the costs assigned to goods that have been sold are assumed to be from the earliest purchases. The FIFO method of determining inventory cost may be adopted by any business, regardless of the actual physical flow of goods, because the assumption is made regarding the flow of costs and not the flow of goods.

In our illustration, the June 30 inventory would be $301 when the FIFO method is used. It is computed as follows:

Inventory, June 30—First-In, First-Out Method

150 units at $1.40 from the purchase of June 25	$210
70 units at $1.30 from the purchase of June 20	91
→ **220 units at a cost of**	$301

Cost of Goods Available for Sale	$625
→ **Less June 30 Inventory**	301
Cost of Goods Sold	$324

The effect of the FIFO method is to value the ending inventory at the most recent costs and include earlier ones in cost of goods sold. During periods of consistently rising prices, the FIFO method yields the highest possible amount of net income, since cost of goods sold will show costs closer to the price level at the time the goods were purchased. Another reason for this result is that businesses tend to increase selling prices as costs rise, regardless of the fact that inventories may have been purchased before the price rise. The reverse effect occurs in periods of price decreases. For these reasons a major criticism of FIFO is that it magnifies the effects of the business cycle on income.

Last-In, First-Out (LIFO) Method. The **last-in, first-out (LIFO) method** of costing inventories is based on the assumption that the costs of the last items purchased should be assigned to the first items used or sold and that the cost of the ending inventory is the cost of merchandise purchased earliest.

Under this method, the June 30 inventory would be $249, computed as follows:

OBJECTIVE 3d
Calculate the pricing of inventory, using the cost basis according to the last-in, first-out (LIFO) method

Inventory, June 30—Last-In, First-Out Method

50 units at $1.00 from June 1 inventory	$ 50
50 units at $1.10 from purchase of June 6	55
120 units at $1.20 from purchase of June 13	144
220 units at a cost of	**$249**
Cost of Goods Available for Sale	$625
Less June 30 Inventory	249
Cost of Goods Sold	$376

The effect of LIFO is to value inventory at earliest prices and to include in cost of goods sold the cost of the most recently purchased goods. This assumption, of course, does not agree with the actual physical movement of goods in most businesses.

However, there is a strong logical argument to support this method, based on the fact that a certain size inventory is necessary in a going concern. When inventory is sold, it must be replaced with more goods. The supporters of LIFO reason that the fairest determination of income occurs if the current costs of merchandise are matched against current sales prices, regardless of which physical units of merchandise are sold. When prices are moving either upward or downward, LIFO will mean that the cost of goods sold will show costs closer to the price level at the time the goods were sold. As a result, the LIFO method tends to show a smaller net income during inflationary times and a larger net income during deflationary times than other methods of inventory valuation. Thus the peaks and valleys of the business cycle tend to be smoothed out. The important factor here is that in inventory valuation the flow of costs and hence income determination is more important than the physical movement of goods and balance sheet valuation.

An argument may also be made against the LIFO method. Because the inventory valuation on the balance sheet reflects earlier prices, this value is often unrealistic with respect to the current value of the inventory. Thus such balance sheet measures as working capital and current ratio may be distorted and must be interpreted carefully.

Comparison and Effects of the Alternative Methods of Pricing Inventory

The specific identification, average-cost, FIFO, and LIFO methods of pricing inventory have now been illustrated. The specific identification method is based on actual costs, whereas the other three methods are based on assumptions regarding the flow of costs. Let us now compare the effects of the four methods on net income using the same data as before and assuming sales during June of $500.

	Specific Identification Method	Average-Cost Method	First-In, First-Out Method	Last-In, First-Out Method
Sales	$500	$500	$500	$500
Cost of Goods Sold				
Beginning Inventory	$ 50	$ 50	$ 50	$ 50
Purchases	575	575	575	575
Cost of Goods				
Available for Sale	$625	$625	$625	$625
Less Ending Inventory	268	275	301	249
Costs of Goods Sold	$357	$350	$324	$376
Gross Margin from Sales	$143	$150	$176	$124

OBJECTIVE 4
State the effects of each method on income determination and income taxes in periods of changing prices

Keeping in mind that in the illustration June was a period of rising prices, we can see that LIFO, which charges the most recent and in this case the highest prices to cost of goods sold, resulted in the lowest gross margin. Conversely, FIFO, which charges the earliest and in this case the lowest prices to cost of goods sold, produced the highest gross margin. The gross margin under the average-cost method is somewhere between those computed under LIFO and FIFO. Thus it is clear that this method has a less pronounced effect.

During a period of declining prices, the reverse would occur. The LIFO method would produce a higher gross margin than the FIFO method. It is apparent that the method of inventory valuation has the greatest importance during prolonged periods of price changes in one direction, either up or down.

Effect on the Financial Statements. Each of the four methods of inventory pricing presented above is acceptable for use in published financial statements. The FIFO, LIFO, and average-cost methods are widely used, as can be seen in Figure 10-1, which shows the inventory cost methods used by six hundred large companies. Each has its advantages and disadvantages, and none can be considered best or perfect. The factors that should be considered in choosing an inventory method are the effects of each method on the balance sheet, the income statement, income taxes, and management decisions.

A basic problem in determining the best inventory measure for a particular company is that inventory appears on both the balance sheet and the income statement. As we have seen, the LIFO method is best suited

Figure 10-1. Inventory Cost Methods Used by 600 Large Companies

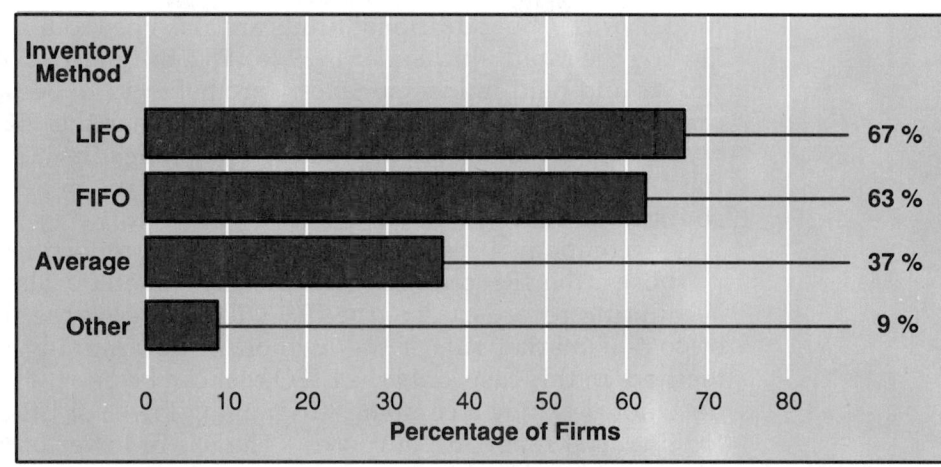

Total percentage exceeds 100 because some companies used different methods for different types of inventory.
Source: American Institute of Certified Public Accountants, *Accounting Trends and Techniques* (New York: AICPA, 1985).

for the income statement because it matches revenues and cost of goods sold. But it is not the best measure of the current balance sheet value of inventory, particularly during a prolonged period of price increases or decreases. The FIFO method, on the other hand, is best suited to the balance sheet because the ending inventory is closest to current values and thus gives a more realistic view of the current financial assets of a business. Readers of financial statements must be alert to inventory methods and be able to assess their effects.

Effect on Income Taxes. The Internal Revenue Service has developed several rules for valuing inventories for federal income tax purposes. A company has a wide choice of methods, including cost (or lower of cost or market) and FIFO or LIFO. But once a method is chosen, it must be used consistently from one year to the next. The IRS must approve any changes in inventory valuation method for income tax purposes.[3] This requirement is in agreement with the rule of consistency in accounting in that changes in inventory method would cause income to fluctuate too much and would make income statements hard to interpret from year to year. A company can change its inventory method if there is a good reason for doing so. The nature and effect of the change must be shown on its financial statements.

Many accountants believe that the use of FIFO or average-cost methods in periods of rising prices causes businesses to report more than their true profit, resulting in the payment of excess income taxes. The

3. A single exception to this rule is that taxpayers must notify the IRS of a change to LIFO from another method, but do not have to have advance IRS approval.

profit is overstated because cost of goods sold is understated, relative to current prices. The company must buy replacement inventory at higher prices, but additional funds are also needed to pay income taxes. During the rapid inflation of 1979 to 1982, billions of dollars reported as profits and paid in income taxes were believed to be the result of poor matching of current costs and revenues under the FIFO and average-cost methods. Consequently, many companies have since switched to the LIFO inventory method encouraged by the belief that prices will continue to rise.

If a company uses the LIFO method in reporting income for tax purposes, the IRS requires that the LIFO method also be used in the accounting records. Also, the IRS will not allow the use of the lower-of-cost-or-market rule if the method of determining cost is the LIFO method. In this case, only the LIFO cost can be used. This rule, however, does not preclude a company from using lower of LIFO cost or market for financial reporting purposes. (The use of lower of cost or market is discussed later in this chapter.)

Over a period of rising prices, a business that uses the LIFO basis may find that its inventory is valued for balance sheet purposes at a cost figure far below what it currently pays for the same items. Management must monitor this situation carefully, because, if it should let the inventory quantity fall at year end below the beginning-of-the-year level, it will find itself paying income taxes on the difference between the current cost and the old LIFO cost in the records. When this occurs, it is called a **LIFO liquidation** because sales have reduced inventories below the levels established in prior years. A LIFO liquidation may be prevented by making enough purchases prior to year end to restore the desired inventory level. Sometimes a LIFO liquidation cannot be avoided because the products are discontinued or supplies are interrupted, as in the case of a strike.

Application of the Perpetual Inventory System

OBJECTIVE 5
Apply the perpetual inventory system to accounting for inventories and cost of goods sold

The system of inventories used so far in this book has been the **periodic inventory system**. Under this system no detailed record of inventory is kept during the year and a physical inventory must be taken at the end of the year to establish ending inventory. The cost of goods sold cannot be determined until the physical inventory is completed. Cost of goods sold is computed by adding the net cost of purchases to beginning inventory and then subtracting the ending inventory.

Periodic inventory systems are used in many retail and wholesale businesses because they do not require a large amount of clerical work. The primary disadvantage of periodic inventory systems is the lack of detailed records as to what items of inventory are on hand at a point in time. Such detailed data would enable management to respond to customers' inquiries concerning product availability, order inventory more effectively to avoid being out of stock, and control the financial costs associated with the money invested in the inventory. The system that provides this type of data is the **perpetual inventory system**. Under this system, a continuous record of the inventory is maintained by keeping detailed records of the purchases and sales of inventory. As a result, the amount of inventory on hand and the cost of goods sold are known throughout the accounting period. In the past, the high clerical cost of maintaining this type of system meant that it was used primarily for goods of high value and low volume. However, with the advent of the computer and of electronic tags and markings, the perpetual inventory system has become easier and less expensive to operate and, consequently, much more prevalent. For example, the electronic markings of grocery items enable grocery stores to maintain perpetual inventory records; and the tags attached to products sold by clothing, department, and discount stores such as Sears and K mart enable them to have tight controls over inventory and ordering.

Handling the Perpetual Inventory System in the Accounting Records

The primary difference in accounting between the perpetual and the periodic inventory systems is that under the perpetual inventory system, the Merchandise Inventory account is continuously adjusted by entering purchases, sales, and other inventory transactions as they occur. Under the periodic inventory system, on the other hand, the Merchandise Inventory account stays at the beginning level until the physical inventory is recorded at the end of the period. As a result, accounts you are familiar with under the periodic inventory system such as Purchases, Purchases Returns and Allowances, Purchases Discounts, and Freight In are not used under the perpetual system. Also, under the perpetual system, as sales occur, the Cost of Goods Sold account is used to accumulate the cost of goods sold to customers. To illustrate these differences, the transactions of an office supply wholesaler are recorded under both the periodic and perpetual inventory systems as follows:

1. Received 100 cases of floppy disks for word processors at a cost of $12,000; terms 2/10, n/30, FOB destination. The net method of recording purchases is used.

Perpetual Inventory System		**Periodic Inventory System**	
Merchandise Inventory 11,760		Purchases 11,760	
Accounts Payable	11,760	Accounts Payable	11,760
Purchase of merchandise at net purchase price; (terms 2/10, n/30, FOB destination)		Purchase of merchandise at net purchase price; (terms 2/10, n/30, FOB destination)	

2. Sold 20 cases of floppy disks to a retailer at a total price of $3,000, terms n/10, FOB shipping point.

Perpetual Inventory System			Periodic Inventory System		
Accounts Receivable	3,000		Accounts Receivable	3,000	
Sales		3,000	Sales		3,000
Sales of 20 cases;			Sales of 20 cases;		
terms n/10, FOB			terms n/10, FOB		
shipping point			shipping point		
Cost of Goods Sold	2,352				
Merchandise Inventory		2,352			
To record cost of					
goods sold					
20 cases × $117.60 = $2,352					

3. Arranged to return 10 cases of the floppy disks to supplier for full credit.

Perpetual Inventory System			Periodic Inventory System		
Accounts Payable	1,176		Accounts Payable	1,176	
Merchandise Inventory		1,176	Purchases Returns		
To record purchase return			and Allowances		1,176
10 cases × $117.60 = $1,176			To record purchase return		

4. Paid supplier in full within the discount period.

Perpetual Inventory System			Periodic Inventory System		
Accounts Payable	10,584		Accounts Payable	10,584	
Cash		10,584	Cash		10,584
Payment to supplier			Payment to supplier		
$11,760 − $1,176 = $10,584			$11,760 − $1,176 = $10,584		

Note the differences in the first three transactions. In each case, under the perpetual inventory method, the Merchandise Inventory account is updated for the effect on the physical inventory; the Purchases and Purchases Returns and Allowances accounts are not used. Also, in transaction 2, the Cost of Goods Sold account is updated at the time of a sale.

At the end of the year, neither adjustments to Merchandise Inventory nor corresponding debits or credits to Income Summary are needed under the perpetual inventory system. Because the Merchandise Inventory account has been continually updated during the year, there is no need to establish the ending inventory in the records. The required entry closes Cost of Goods Sold to Income Summary.

Maintaining the Detailed Perpetual Inventory Records

To keep track of the quantities and costs of the individual items stocked in merchandise inventory under the perpetual inventory system, it is necessary to maintain an individual record for each type of inventory. The Merchandise Inventory account is a controlling account for a subsidiary file of individual inventory records. This mechanism is similar to the Accounts Receivable controlling account and its subsidiary ledger. In the inventory subsidiary file, each item has a card (or file in a computer system) on which purchases and sales are entered as they take place. A sample perpetual inventory card is shown in Exhibit 10-2 for another item held for sale by our office supply wholesaler. At any time, the card will show the number of pencil sharpeners on hand, and the total of all the cards is equal to the merchandise inventory.

As shown in Exhibit 10-2, on June 1 there is a balance of 60 pencil sharpeners that cost $5 each. A sale on June 4 reduces the balance by 10 pencil sharpeners. On June 10, 100 pencil sharpeners are purchased at $6 each. Now the inventory consists of 50 pencil sharpeners purchased at $5 each and 100 pencil sharpeners purchased at $6 each. The method of inventory valuation in Exhibit 10-2 is first-in, first-out, as can be determined by looking at the June 20 sale. The entire sale of 30 pencil sharpeners is taken from the 50 sharpeners still left from the beginning inventory. If the LIFO method were used, the sale would be deducted from the latest purchase of 100 pencil sharpeners at $6 each. Under LIFO the resulting balance would be $670 [(50 × $5) + (70 × $6)]. An example showing both the FIFO and LIFO methods appears in the review problem at the end of this chapter.

Need for Physical Inventories
Under the Perpetual Inventory System

The use of the perpetual inventory system does not eliminate the need for a physical inventory at the end of the accounting period. The perpetual inventory records show what should be on hand, not necessarily what is on hand. There may be losses due to spoilage, employee pilferage, theft, or other causes. If a loss has occurred, it is reflected in the accounts by a debit to Inventory Shortage Expense and a credit to Merchandise Inventory. The individual inventory cards, which may also be the subsidiary ledger, must also be adjusted.

Exhibit 10-2. Perpetual Inventory Record Card, FIFO

Item: Pencil Sharpener, Model D-222

Date	Purchased			Sold			Balance		
	Units	Cost	Total	Units	Cost	Total	Units	Cost	Balance
June 1							60	5.00	300.00
4				10	5.00	50.00	50	5.00	250.00
10	100	6.00	600.00				50 100	5.00 6.00	850.00
20				30	5.00	150.00	20 100	5.00 6.00	700.00

Valuing the Inventory at the Lower of Cost or Market (LCM)

OBJECTIVE 6
Apply the lower-of-cost-or-market rule to inventory valuation

Although cost is usually the most appropriate basis for valuation of inventory, there are times when inventory may properly be shown in the financial statements at less than its cost. If by reason of physical deterioration, obsolescence, or decline in price level the market value of the inventory falls below the cost, a loss has occurred. This loss may be recognized by writing the inventory down to market. The term **market** is used here to mean current replacement cost. For a merchandising company, market is the amount that the company would pay at the present time for the same goods, purchased from the usual suppliers and in the usual quantities. It may help in applying the **lower-of-cost-or-market (LCM) rule** by thinking of it as the "lower-of-cost-or-replacement-cost" rule.[4]

Methods of Applying LCM

There are three basic methods of valuing inventories at the lower of cost or market, as follows: (1) the item-by-item method, (2) the major category method, and (3) the total inventory method.

For example, a stereo shop could determine lower of cost or market for each kind of speaker, receiver, and turntable (item by item); for all speakers, all receivers, and all turntables (major categories); or for all speakers, receivers, and turntables together (total inventory).

Item-by-Item Method. When the **item-by-item method** is used, cost and market are compared for each item in the inventory. The individual items are then valued at their lower price.

Lower of Cost or Market with Item-by-Item Method				
		Per Unit		**Lower of**
	Quantity	**Cost**	**Market**	**Cost or Market**
Category I				
Item a	200	$1.50	$1.70	$ 300
Item b	100	2.00	1.80	180
Item c	100	2.50	2.60	250
Category II				
Item d	300	5.00	4.50	1,350
Item e	200	4.00	4.10	800
Inventory at the lower of cost or market				**$2,880**

4. In some cases, *market value* is determined by the *realizable value* of the inventory—the amount for which the goods can be sold rather than the amount for which the goods can be replaced. The circumstances in which realizable value determines market value are only occasionally encountered in practice and the valuation procedures are technical enough to be addressed in a more advanced accounting course.

Major Category Method. Under the **major category method**, the total cost and total market for each category of items are compared. Each category is then valued at its lower amount.

		Per Unit		Total		Lower of
	Quantity	Cost	Market	Cost	Market	Cost or Market
Category I						
Item a	200	$1.50	$1.70	$ 300	$ 340	
Item b	100	2.00	1.80	200	180	
Item c	100	2.50	2.60	250	260	
Totals				$ 750	$ 780	$ 750
Category II						
Item d	300	5.00	4.50	$1,500	$1,350	
Item e	200	4.00	4.10	800	820	
Totals				$2,300	$2,170	$2,170
Inventory at the lower of cost or market						$2,920

Total Inventory Method. Under the **total inventory method**, the entire inventory is valued at both cost and market, and the lower price is used to value inventory. Since this method is not acceptable for federal income tax purposes, it is not illustrated here.

Valuing Inventory by Estimation

It is sometimes necessary or desirable to estimate the value of ending inventory. The methods most commonly used for this purpose are the retail method and the gross profit method.

Retail Method of Inventory Estimation

OBJECTIVE 7a
Estimate the cost of ending inventory using the retail inventory method

The **retail method**, as its name implies, is used in retail merchandising businesses. There are two principal reasons for the use of the retail method. First, management usually requires that financial statements be prepared at least once a month and, as it is time-consuming and expensive to take a physical inventory each month, the retail method is used to estimate the value of inventory on hand. Second, because items in a retail store normally have a price tag, it is a common practice to take the physical inventory at retail from these price tags and reduce the total value to cost through use of the retail method. The term *at retail* means the amount of the inventory at the marked selling prices of the inventory items.

When the retail method is used to estimate an ending inventory, the records must show the beginning inventory at cost and at retail. The records must also show the amount of goods purchased during the period both at cost and at retail. The net sales at retail are, of course, the balance of the Sales account less returns and allowances. A simple example of the retail method is shown below.

The Retail Method of Inventory Valuation		
	Cost	Retail
Beginning Inventory	$ 40,000	$ 55,000
Net Purchases for the Period (excluding Freight In)	107,000	145,000
Freight In	3,000	
Merchandise Available for Sale	$150,000	$200,000
Ratio of Cost to Retail Price: $\frac{\$150,000}{\$200,000} = 75\%$		
Net Sales During the Period		160,000
Estimated Ending Inventory at Retail		$ 40,000
Ratio of Cost to Retail	75%	
Estimated Cost of Ending Inventory	$ 30,000	

Merchandise available for sale is determined both at cost and at retail by listing beginning inventory and net purchases for the period at cost and at the expected selling price of the goods, adding freight to the cost column, and totaling. The ratio of these two amounts (cost to retail price) provides an estimate of the cost of each dollar of retail sales value. The estimated ending inventory at retail is then determined by deducting sales for the period from the retail price of the goods that were available for sale during the period. The inventory at retail is now converted to cost on the basis of the ratio of cost to retail.

The cost of ending inventory may also be estimated by applying the ratio of cost to retail to the total retail value of the physical count of the inventory. Applying the retail method in practice is often more difficult than this simple example because of certain complications such as changes in the retail price that take place during the year, different markups on different types of merchandise, and varying volumes of sales for different types of merchandise.

Gross Profit Method of Inventory Estimation

The **gross profit method** assumes that the ratio of gross margin for a business remains relatively stable from year to year. It is used in place of the retail method when records of the retail prices of beginning inventory and purchases are not kept. It is considered acceptable for estimating the cost of inventory for interim reports, but is not an acceptable method for valuing inventory in the annual financial statements. It is also useful in estimating the amount of inventory lost or destroyed by theft, fire, or other hazards. Insurance companies often use this method to verify loss claims.

OBJECTIVE 7b
Estimate the cost of ending inventory using the gross profit method

The gross profit method is very simple to use. First, figure the cost of goods available for sale in the usual way (add purchases to beginning inventory). Second, estimate the cost of goods sold by deducting the estimated gross margin from sales. Third, deduct the estimated cost of goods sold from the goods available for sale in order to estimate the cost of ending inventory. This method is shown below.

The Gross Profit Method of Inventory Valuation		
1. Beginning Inventory at Cost		$ 50,000
Purchases at Cost		290,000
Cost of Goods Available for Sale		$340,000
2. Less Estimated Cost of Goods Sold		
Sales at Selling Price	$400,000	
Less Estimated Gross Margin of 30%	120,000	
Estimated Cost of Goods Sold		280,000
3. Estimated Cost of Ending Inventory		$ 60,000

Chapter Review

Review of Learning Objectives

1. **Define merchandise inventory and show how inventory measurement affects income determination.**

   Merchandise inventory consists of all goods owned and held for sale in the regular course of business. The objective of accounting for inventories is the proper determination of income. If the value of ending inventory is understated or overstated, a corresponding error—dollar for dollar—will be made in net income. Furthermore, because the ending inventory of one period is the beginning inventory of the next, the misstatement affects two accounting periods, although the effects are opposite.

2. **Define inventory cost, and relate it to goods flow and cost flow.**

   The cost of inventory includes (1) invoice price less purchases discounts, (2) freight or transportation in, including insurance in transit, and (3) applicable taxes and tariffs. Goods flow relates to the actual physical flow of merchandise, whereas cost flow refers to the assumed flow of costs in the operation of the business.

3. **Calculate the pricing of inventory, using the cost basis according to the (a) specific identification method; (b) average-cost method; (c) first-in, first-out (FIFO) method; (d) last-in, first-out (LIFO) method.**

The value assigned to the ending inventory is the result of two measurements: quantity and price. Quantity is determined by taking a physical inventory. The pricing of inventory is usually based on the assumed cost flow of the goods as they are bought and sold. One of four assumptions is usually made regarding cost flow. These assumptions are represented by four inventory methods. Inventory pricing could be determined by the specific identification method, which associates the actual cost with each item of inventory but is rarely used. The average-cost method assumes that the cost of inventory is the average cost of goods available for sale during the period. The first-in, first-out (FIFO) method assumes that the costs of the first items acquired should be assigned to the first items sold. The last-in, first-out (LIFO) method assumes that the costs of the last items acquired should be assigned to the first items sold. The inventory method chosen may or may not be equivalent to the actual physical flow of goods.

4. **State the effects of each method on income determination and income taxes in periods of changing prices.**

During periods of rising prices, the LIFO method will show the lowest net income; FIFO, the highest; and average cost, in between. The opposite effects occur in periods of falling prices. No generalization can be made regarding the specific identification method. The Internal Revenue Service requires that if LIFO is used for tax purposes, it must also be used for book purposes, and that the lower-of-cost-or-market rule cannot be applied to the LIFO method.

5. **Apply the perpetual inventory system to accounting for inventories and cost of goods sold.**

Under the periodic inventory system, the one used earlier in this book, inventory is determined by a physical count at the end of the accounting period. Under the perpetual inventory system, the inventory control account is constantly updated as sales and purchases are made during the accounting period. Also, as sales are made the Cost of Goods Sold account is used to accumulate the costs of those sales.

6. **Apply the lower-of-cost-or-market (LCM) rule to inventory valuation.**

The lower-of-cost-or-market rule can be applied to the above methods of determining inventory at cost. This rule states that if the replacement cost (market) of the inventory is lower than what the inventory cost, the lower figure should be used.

7. **Estimate the cost of ending inventory using (a) the retail inventory method and (b) the gross profit method.**

Two methods of estimating the value of inventory are the retail inventory method and the gross profit method. Under the retail inventory method, inventory is determined at retail prices and is then reduced to estimated cost by applying a ratio of cost to retail price. Under the gross profit method, cost of goods sold is estimated by reducing sales by estimated gross margin. The estimated cost of goods sold is then deducted from cost of goods available for sale to estimate the inventory.

Review of Concepts and Terminology

The following concepts and terms were introduced in this chapter:

(L.O. 3)   **Average-cost method:** An inventory cost method which assumes that the cost of inventory is the average cost of all goods available for sale.

(L.O. 1)   **Consignment:** The placing of goods by the owner of the goods (known as the consignor) on the premises of another company (the consignee).

(L.O. 2)   **Cost flow:** Association of costs with their assumed flow within the operations of the company.

(L.O. 3)   **First-in, first-out (FIFO) method:** An inventory cost method based on the assumption that the cost of the first items acquired should be assigned to the first items sold.

(L.O. 2)   **Goods flow:** The actual physical movement of goods in the operations of the company.

(L.O. 7)   **Gross profit method:** A method of inventory estimation that assumes the ratio of gross margin for a business remains relatively stable from year to year.

(L.O. 2)   **Inventory cost:** The price paid or consideration given to acquire an asset; includes invoice price less purchases discounts, plus freight or transportation in, and applicable taxes or tariffs.

(L.O. 6)   **Item-by-item method:** A lower-of-cost-or-market method of valuing inventory in which cost and market are compared for each item in the inventory, with each item then valued at its lower price.

(L.O. 3)   **Last-in, first-out (LIFO) method:** An inventory cost method that assumes that the costs of the last items purchased should be assigned to the first items sold.

(L.O. 4)   **LIFO liquidation:** The reduction of inventory below previous levels so that income is increased by the amount current prices exceed the historical cost of the inventory under LIFO.

(L.O. 6)   **Lower-of-cost-or-market (LCM) rule:** A method of valuing inventory at an amount below cost if the replacement (market) value is less than cost.

(L.O. 6)   **Major category method:** A lower-of-cost-or-market method for valuing inventory in which the total cost and total market for each category of items are compared, with each category then valued at its lower amount.

(L.O. 6)   **Market:** Current replacement cost of inventory.

(L.O. 1)   **Merchandise inventory:** All goods that are owned and held for sale in the regular course of business.

(L.O. 5)   **Periodic inventory system:** The method of accounting for the physical quantity of inventory by taking a count at the end of the period and then adjusting the inventory account for the new balance.

(L.O. 5)   **Perpetual inventory system:** The method of accounting for the physical quantity and costs of inventory by keeping continuous detailed records of purchases and sales.

(L.O. 7)   **Retail method:** Method of inventory estimation used in retail businesses; inventory at retail value is reduced by the ratio of cost to retail price.

(L.O. 3) **Specific identification method**: Determining the cost of inventory by identifying the cost of each item.

(L.O. 6) **Total inventory method**: The entire inventory is valued at both cost and market, and the lower price :s used; not an acceptable method for federal income tax purposes.

Self-Test

Test your knowledge of the chapter by choosing the best answer for each item below.

1. An overstatement of ending inventory in one period results in
   a. an overstatement of the ending inventory of the next period.
   b. an understatement of net income of the next period.
   c. an overstatement of net income of the next period.
   d. no effect on net income of the next period.   *(L.O. 1)*

2. Which of the following costs would *not* be included in the cost of inventory?
   a. Goods held on consignment
   b. Purchased goods in transit, FOB shipping point
   c. Freight In
   d. Invoice price   *(L.O. 2)*

3. September   1   Inventory   1⊃ @ $4.00
            8   Purchased 4⊅ @ $4.40
           17   Purchased 20 @ $4.20
           25   Purchased 30 @ $4.80   Sold 70

   Using the above information, cost of goods sold under the average-cost method is
   a. $133.20.   c. $310.80.
   b. $444.00.   d. $304.50.   *(L.O. 3)*

4. Assuming the same facts as in **3**, cost of goods sold under the first-in, first-out (FIFO) method is
   a. $144.00.   c. $388.50.
   b. $300.00.   d. $444.00.   *(L.O. 3)*

5. Assuming the same facts as in **3**, ending inventory under the last-in, first-out (LIFO) method is
   a. $316.   c. $300.
   b. $444.   d. $128.   *(L.O. 3)*

6. In a period of rising prices, which of the following inventory methods generally results in the lowest net income figure?
   a. Average-cost method
   b. FIFO method
   c. LIFO method
   d. Cannot tell without more information   *(L.O. 4)*

7. Under the perpetual inventory method, a purchase of merchandise results in a debit to
   a. Income Summary.   c. Purchases.
   b. Cost of Goods Sold.   d. Merchandise Inventory.   *(L.O. 5)*

8. When applying the lower-of-cost-or-market method to inventory, "market" generally means
a. original cost, less physical deterioration.
b. resale value.
c. original cost.
d. replacement cost. *(L.O. 6)*

9. Which of the following companies would be most likely to use the retail inventory method?
a. A farm supply company
c. A dealer in heavy machinery
b. A TV repair company
d. A men's clothing shop *(L.O. 7)*

10. A retail company has goods available for sale of $1,000,000 at retail and $600,000 at cost and ending inventory of $100,000 at retail. What is the estimated cost of goods sold?
a. $60,000
c. $900,000
b. $100,000
d. $540,000 *(L.O. 7)*

Answers to Self-Test are at the end of this chapter.

Review Problem
Periodic and Perpetual Inventory Methods

(L.O. 3, 5) The following table summarizes the beginning inventory, purchases, and sales of Psi Company's single product during January.

Date	Beginning Inventory			Purchases			Sales Units
	Units	Cost	Total	Units	Cost	Total	
Jan. 1	1,400	$19	$26,600				
4							300
8				600	$20	$12,000	
10							1,300
12				900	21	18,900	
15							150
18				500	22	11,000	
24				800	23	18,400	
31							1,350
Totals	1,400		$26,600	2,800		$60,300	3,100

Required

1. Assuming that the company uses the periodic inventory method, compute the cost that should be assigned to ending inventory using (a) a FIFO basis and (b) a LIFO basis.
2. Assuming that the company uses the perpetual inventory method, compute the cost that should be assigned to ending inventory using (a) a FIFO

basis and (b) a LIFO basis. (**Hint:** It is helpful to use a form similar to the perpetual inventory card in Exhibit 10-2.)

Answer to Review Problem

	Units	Dollars
Beginning Inventory	1,400	$26,600
Purchases	2,800	60,300
Available for Sale	4,200	$86,900
Sales	3,100	
Ending Inventory	1,100	

1. Periodic inventory method
   a. FIFO basis
      Ending inventory consists of

January 24 purchases (800 × $23)	$18,400	
January 18 purchases (300 × $22)	6,600	$25,000

   b. LIFO basis
      Ending inventory consists of

Beginning inventory (1,100 × $19)	$20,900

2. Perpetual inventory method
   a. FIFO basis

Date	Purchased			Sold			Balance		
	Units	Cost	Total	Units	Cost	Total	Units	Cost	Total
Jan. 1							1,400	$19	$26,600
4				300	$19	$ 5,700	1,100	19	20,900
8	600	$20	$12,000				1,100	19	
							600	20	32,900
10				1,100	19		400	20	8,000
				200	20	24,900			
12	900	21	18,900				400	20	
							900	21	26,900
15				150	20	3,000	250	20	
							900	21	23,900
18	500	22	11,000				250	20	
							900	21	
							500	22	34,900
24	800	23	18,400				250	20	
							900	21	
							500	22	
							800	23	53,300
31				250	20		300	22	
				900	21		800	23	25,000
				200	22	28,300			

b. LIFO basis

Date	Purchased			Sold			Balance		
	Units	Cost	Total	Units	Cost	Total	Units	Cost	Total
Jan. 1							1,400	$19	$26,600
4				300	$19	$ 5,700	1,100	19	20,900
8	600	$20	$12,000				1,100	19	
							600	20	32,900
10				500	20				
				700	19	25,300	400	19	7,600
12	900	21	18,900				400	19	
							900	21	26,500
15				150	21	3,150	400	19	
							750	21	23,350
18	500	22	11,000				400	19	
							750	21	
							500	22	34,350
24	800	23	18,400				400	19	
							750	21	
							500	22	
							800	23	52,750
31				800	23				
				500	22		400	19	
				50	21	30,450	700	21	22,300

Chapter Assignments

Discussion Questions and Writing Assignments

1. How does inventory differ from short-term liquid assets, and what measurements of inventory must be taken to make a proper income determination? What is the relationship of inventory to the matching rule?
2. What is merchandise inventory, and what is the primary objective of inventory measurement?
3. If the merchandise inventory is mistakenly overstated at the end of 19x8, what is the effect on (a) 19x8 net income, (b) 19x8 year-end balance sheet value, (c) 19x9 net income, and (d) 19x9 year-end balance sheet value?
4. Fargo Sales Company is very busy at the end of its fiscal year on June 30. There is an order for 130 units of product in the warehouse. Although the shipping department tries, it cannot ship the product by June 30, and title has not yet passed. Should the 130 units be included in the year-end count of inventory? Why or why not?
5. What does the term *taking a physical inventory* mean?
6. What items are included in the cost of inventory?

7. In periods of steadily rising prices, which of the three inventory methods—average-cost, FIFO, or LIFO—will give the (a) highest inventory cost, (b) lowest inventory cost, (c) highest net income, and (d) lowest net income?

8. May a company change its inventory costing method from year to year? Explain.

9. Do the FIFO and LIFO inventory methods result in different quantities of ending inventory?

10. Under which method of cost flow are (a) the earliest costs assigned to inventory, (b) the latest costs assigned to inventory, (c) the average costs assigned to inventory?

11. What are the relative advantages and disadvantages of FIFO and LIFO from management's point of view?

12. Which is more expensive to maintain: a perpetual inventory system or a periodic inventory system? Why?

13. What differences occur in recording sales, purchases, and closing entries under the perpetual and periodic inventory systems?

14. In the phrase "lower of cost or market," what is meant by the word "market"?

15. What methods can be used to determine lower of cost or market?

16. What effects do income taxes have on inventory valuation?

17. What are some reasons management may use the gross profit method of determining inventory?

18. Does using the retail inventory method mean that inventories are measured at retail value on the balance sheet? Explain.

19. Which of the following inventory systems do not require taking a physical inventory: (a) perpetual, (b) periodic, (c) retail, (d) gross profit?

Classroom Exercises

Exercise 10-1.
Effects of
Inventory Errors
(L.O. 1)

Condensed income statements for Rodriguez Company for two years are shown below.

	19x2	19x1
Sales	$42,000	$35,000
Cost of Goods Sold	25,000	18,000
Gross Margin on Sales	$17,000	$17,000
Operating Expenses	10,000	10,000
Net Income	$ 7,000	$ 7,000

After the end of 19x2, it was discovered that an error had been made that resulted in a $3,000 understatement of the 19x1 ending inventory.

Compute the corrected net income for 19x1 and 19x2. What effect will the error have on net income and owner's equity for 19x3?

Exercise 10-2.
Inventory Cost
Methods
(L.O. 3)

Helen's Farm Store had the purchases and sales of fertilizer during the year that are presented at the top of the following page:

Jan. 1	Beginning Inventory	250 cases @ $23	$ 5,750
Feb. 25	Purchased	100 cases @ $26	2,600
June 15	Purchased	400 cases @ $28	11,200
Aug. 15	Purchased	100 cases @ $26	2,600
Oct. 15	Purchased	300 cases @ $28	8,400
Dec. 15	Purchased	200 cases @ $30	6,000
Total Goods Available for Sale		1,350	$36,550
Total Sales		1,000 cases	
Dec. 31	Ending Inventory	350 cases	

Assume that all of the June 15 purchase and 200 cases each from the January 1 beginning inventory, the October 15 purchase, and the December 15 purchase were sold.

Determine the costs that should be assigned to ending inventory and cost of goods sold under each of the following assumptions: (1) costs are assigned by the specific identification method; (2) costs are assigned on an average-cost basis; (3) costs are assigned on a FIFO basis; (4) costs are assigned on a LIFO basis. What conclusions can be drawn as to the effect of each method on the income statement and the balance sheet of Helen's Farm Store?

Exercise 10-3.
Inventory Cost
Methods
(L.O. 3)

During its first year of operation, Jefferson Company purchased 5,600 units of a product at $21 per unit. During the second year, it purchased 6,000 units of the same product at $24 per unit. During the third year, it purchased 5,000 units at $30 per unit. Jefferson Company managed to have an ending inventory each year of 1,000 units. The company sells goods at a 100 percent markup over cost.

Prepare cost of goods sold statements that compare the value of ending inventory and the cost of goods sold for each of the three years using (1) the FIFO method and (2) the LIFO method. What conclusions can you draw from the resulting data about the relationships between changes in unit price and changes in the value of ending inventory?

Exercise 10-4.
Perpetual and
Periodic Inventory
Methods
(L.O. 5)

Record general journal entries using the net purchase method to record the following transactions under (1) the perpetual inventory system and (2) the periodic inventory system.

March 11   Received 4,000 cases of chloride tablets at a cost of $200 per case, terms 2/10, n/30, FOB destination.

15   Sold 200 cases of tablets for $300 per case, terms n/10, FOB shipping point.

17   Returned 50 cases of tablets that were damaged to suppliers for full credit.

20   Paid the supplier in full for the amount owed on the purchase of March 11.

Exercise 10-5.
Periodic Inventory
Method and
Inventory Cost
Methods
(L.O. 3, 4)

In chronological order, the inventory, purchases, and sales of a single product for a recent month appear as follows:

		Units	Amount per Unit
June 1	Beginning Inventory	300	$10
4	Purchase	800	11
8	Sale	400	20
12	Purchase	1,000	12
16	Sale	700	20
20	Sale	500	22
24	Purchase	1,200	13
28	Sale	600	22
30	Sale	400	22

Using the periodic inventory system, compute the cost of ending inventory,
cost of goods sold, and gross margin from sales. Use the FIFO and LIFO inventory costing methods. Explain the difference in gross margin from sales
produced by the two methods.

Exercise 10-6.
Perpetual
Inventory Method
and Inventory Cost
Methods
(L.O. 3, 5)

Using the data provided in Exercise 10-5 and assuming the perpetual inventory system, compute the cost of ending inventory, cost of goods sold and
gross margin from sales. Use the FIFO and LIFO inventory costing methods. Explain the difference in gross margin from sales produced by the two
methods.

Exercise 10-7.
Lower-of-Cost-or-
Market Method
(L.O. 6)

Tillman Company values its inventory, shown below, at the lower of cost or
market. Compute Tillman's inventory value using (1) the item-by-item
method and (2) the major category method.

	Quantity	Per Unit Cost	Per Unit Market
Category I			
Item aa	200	$1.00	$0.90
Item bb	240	2.00	2.20
Item cc	400	4.00	3.75
Category II			
Item dd	300	6.00	6.50
Item ee	400	9.00	9.10

Exercise 10-8.
Retail Method
(L.O. 7)

Jamie's Dress Shop had net retail sales of $250,000 during the current year.
The following additional information was obtained from the accounting
records:

	At Cost	At Retail
Beginning Inventory	$ 40,000	$ 60,000
Net Purchases (excluding Freight In)	140,000	220,000
Freight In	10,400	

1. Estimate the company's ending inventory at cost using the retail method.
2. Assume that a physical inventory taken at year end revealed an inventory on hand of $18,000 at retail value. What is the estimated amount of inventory shrinkage (loss due to theft, damage, and so forth) at cost?
3. Prepare the journal entry to record the inventory shrinkage.

Interpreting Accounting Information

General Motors*
(L.O. 4)

General Motors Corporation experienced in 1985 and 1986 what is called a LIFO liquidation, as explained in its 1986 annual report: "Certain LIFO inventories carried at lower costs prevailing in prior years, as compared with the costs of current purchases, were liquidated in 1986 and 1985. These inventory adjustments favorably affected income before income taxes by approximately $38.2 million in 1986 and $20.9 million in 1985." General Motors average income tax rate for 1985 and 1986 was 22 percent.

Required

1. Explain why a reduction in the quantity of inventory resulted in favorable effects on income before income taxes. Would the same result have occurred if the FIFO method had been used by General Motors to value inventory? Explain your answer.
2. What is the income tax effect of the LIFO liquidation? Is it really a "favorable" outcome?

Problem Set A

Problem 10A-1.
Inventory Cost
Methods
(L.O. 3)

Palaggi Company merchandises a single product called Compak. The following data represent beginning inventory and purchases of Compak during the past year: January 1 inventory, 68,000 units at $11.00; February purchases, 80,000 units at $12.00; March purchases, 160,000 units at $12.40; May purchases, 120,000 units at $12.60; July purchases, 200,000 units at $12.80; September purchases, 160,000 units at $12.60; and November purchases, 60,000 units at $13.00. Sales of Compak totaled 786,000 units at $20 per unit. Selling and administrative expenses totaled $5,102,000 for the year, and Palaggi Company uses a periodic inventory method.

Required

1. Prepare a schedule to compute the cost of goods available for sale.
2. Prepare an income statement under each of the following assumptions: (a) costs are assigned to inventory on an average-cost basis; (b) costs are assigned to inventory on a FIFO basis; (c) costs are assigned to inventory on a LIFO basis.

* Excerpts from the 1986 annual report used by permission of General Motors. Copyright 1986.

Problem 10A-2.
Lower-of-Cost-or-
Market Method
(L.O. 6)

After taking the physical inventory, the accountant for McFarlane Company prepared the inventory schedule shown below:

| | | Per Unit | |
	Quantity	Cost	Market
Product line 1			
Item 11	190	$ 9	$10
Item 12	270	4	5
Item 13	210	8	7
Product line 2			
Item 21	160	15	17
Item 22	400	21	20
Item 23	70	18	20
Product line 3			
Item 31	290	26	20
Item 32	310	30	28
Item 33	120	34	39

Required

Determine the value of the inventory at lower of cost or market using (1) the item-by-item method and (2) the major category method.

Problem 10A-3.
Periodic Inventory
System
(L.O. 3)

The beginning inventory of Product M and data on purchases and sales for a two-month period are presented below. The company closes its books at the end of each month. It uses a periodic inventory system.

Apr.	1	Inventory	50 units @ $102
	5	Sale	30 units
	10	Purchase	100 units @ $110
	17	Sale	60 units
May	2	Purchase	100 units @ $108
	8	Sale	110 units
	14	Purchase	50 units @ $112
	18	Sale	40 units
	22	Purchase	60 units @ $117
	26	Sale	30 units
	31	Sale	20 units

Required

1. Compute the value of the ending inventory of Product M on April 30 and May 31 on a FIFO basis. In addition, determine cost of goods sold for April and May.
2. Compute the value of the ending inventory of Product M on April 30 and May 31 on a LIFO basis. In addition, determine cost of goods sold for April and May.
3. Prepare a general journal entry to record the sale on May 31 to Alou Corporation on credit for $4,000.

**Problem 10A-4.
Perpetual
Inventory System**
(L.O. 3, 5)

Assume the data presented in Problem 10A-3, except that the company uses a perpetual inventory system.

Required

1. Assume that the company maintains inventory on a FIFO basis and uses perpetual inventory cards similar to the one illustrated in Exhibit 10-2. Record the transactions on a card using two or more lines as needed. Also, determine cost of goods sold for April and May.
2. Assuming that the company keeps its records on a LIFO basis, record the transactions on a second record card and determine cost of goods sold for both months.
3. Assuming that the May 31 sale was made to Alou Corporation on credit for $4,000, prepare a general journal entry to record the sale and cost of goods sold on a LIFO basis.
4. Assuming that the company takes a periodic physical inventory on May 31, that the value of the Product M inventory was $6,900, and that the FIFO basis of evaluating inventory is used, record an inventory shrinkage if necessary.

**Problem 10A-5.
Retail Inventory
Method**
(L.O. 7)

Ramirez Company operates a large discount store and uses the retail inventory method to estimate the cost of ending inventory. Management suspects that in recent weeks there have been unusually heavy losses from shoplifting or employee pilferage. To estimate the amount of the loss, the company has taken a physical inventory and will compare the results with the estimated cost of inventory. Data from the accounting records of Ramirez Company are as follows:

	At Cost	At Retail
October 1 Beginning Inventory	$51,488	$ 74,300
Purchases	71,733	108,500
Purchases Returns and Allowances	(2,043)	(3,200)
Freight In	950	
Sales		109,183
Sales Returns and Allowances		(933)
October 31 Physical Inventory		62,450

Required

1. Prepare a schedule to estimate the dollar amount of the store's year-end inventory using the retail method.
2. Use the store's cost ratio to reduce the retail value of the physical inventory to cost.
3. Calculate the estimated amount of inventory shortage at cost and at retail.

**Problem 10A-6.
Gross Profit
Method**
(L.O. 7)

Holmes Brothers is a large retail furniture company that operates in two adjacent warehouses. One warehouse is a showroom, and the other is used for storage of merchandise. On the night of April 22, a fire broke out in the storage warehouse and destroyed the merchandise. Fortunately, the fire did not reach the showroom, so all the merchandise on display was saved.

Although the company maintained a perpetual inventory system, its records were rather haphazard, and the last reliable physical inventory was taken on December 31. In addition, there was no control of the flow of the goods between the showroom and the warehouse. Thus it was impossible to tell what goods should be in either place. As a result, the insurance company required an independent estimate of the amount of loss. The insurance company examiners were satisfied when they were provided with the following information:

1. Merchandise Inventory on December 31	$ 727,400
2. Purchases, January 1 to April 22	1,206,100
3. Purchases Returns, January 1 to April 22	(5,353)
4. Freight In, January 1 to April 22	26,550
5. Sales, January 1 to April 22	1,979,525
6. Sales Returns, January 1 to April 22	(14,900)
7. Merchandise inventory in showroom on April 22	201,480
8. Average gross profit margin	44 percent

Required   Prepare a schedule that estimates the amount of the inventory lost in the fire.

Problem Set B

**Problem 10B-1.
Inventory Cost
Methods
(L.O. 3)**

The Highland Door Company sold 2,200 doors during 19x8 at $160 per door. Its beginning inventory on January 1 was 130 doors at $56. Purchases during the year were as follows:

February	225 doors @ $62
April	350 doors @ $65
June	700 doors @ $70
August	300 doors @ $66
October	400 doors @ $68
November	250 doors @ $72

The company's selling and administrative costs for the year were $101,000, and the company uses the periodic inventory method.

Required

1. Prepare a schedule to compute the cost of goods available for sale.
2. Prepare an income statement under each of the following assumptions: (a) costs are assigned to inventory on an average-cost basis; (b) costs are assigned to inventory on a FIFO basis; (c) costs are assigned to inventory on a LIFO basis.

**Problem 10B-2.
Lower-of-Cost-or-
Market Method
(L.O. 6)**

The employees of Garland's Shoes completed their physical inventory as shown at the top of the following page.

	Pairs of Shoes	Per Unit	
		Cost	Market
Men			
Black	400	$22	$24
Brown	325	21	21
Blue	100	25	23
Tan	200	19	10
Women			
White	300	26	32
Red	150	23	20
Yellow	100	30	25
Blue	250	25	33
Brown	100	20	30
Black	150	20	25

Required

Determine the value of inventory at lower of cost or market using (1) the item-by-item method and (2) the major category method.

**Problem 10B-3.
Periodic Inventory
System**
(L.O. 3)

The beginning inventory, purchases, and sales of Product SLT for August and September are presented below. The company closes its books at the end of each month. It uses a periodic inventory system.

Aug.	1	Beginning Inventory	60 units @ $49
	7	Sales	20 units
	10	Purchases	100 units @ $52
	19	Sales	70 units
Sept.	4	Purchases	120 units @ $53
	11	Sales	110 units
	15	Purchases	50 units @ $54
	23	Sales	80 units
	25	Purchases	100 units @ $55
	27	Sales	100 units

Required

1. Compute the cost of the ending inventory on August 31 and September 30 on a FIFO basis. In addition, determine cost of goods sold for August and September.
2. Compute the cost of the ending inventory on August 31 and September 30 on a LIFO basis. In addition, determine cost of goods sold for August and September.
3. Prepare a general journal entry to record the sale on September 27 to Karimi Company on credit for $9,100.

**Problem 10B-4.
Perpetual
Inventory System**
(L.O. 3, 5)

Assume the data presented in Problem 10B-3, except the company uses a perpetual inventory system.

Required

1. Assume that the company maintains inventory on a FIFO basis and uses perpetual inventory cards similar to the one illustrated in Exhibit 10-2. Record the transactions on a card using two or more lines as needed. Also, determine cost of goods sold for August and September.
2. Assuming that the company keeps its records on a LIFO basis, record the transactions on a second record card and determine cost of goods sold for both months.
3. Prepare general journal entries to record the credit purchase on September 15 and the credit sale on September 27 for $9,100, assuming the LIFO basis of costing inventory. What is the amount and LIFO cost of the inventory at the end of September?
4. On September 30, the company counted a physical inventory of 22 units. Record any inventory shrinkage necessary, assuming a LIFO basis.

Problem 10B-5.
Retail Inventory
Method
(L.O. 7)

Steelcraft switched recently to the retail inventory method to estimate the cost of ending inventory. To test this method, the company took a physical inventory one month after its implementation. Cost, retail, and the physical inventory data are presented below:

	At Cost	At Retail
March 1 Beginning Inventory	$236,066	$311,400
Purchases	375,000	504,200
Purchases Returns and Allowances	(12,600)	(17,400)
Freight In	4,175	
Sales		530,000
Sales Returns and Allowances		(14,000)
March 31 Physical Inventory		254,100

Required

1. Prepare a schedule to estimate the dollar amount of Steelcraft's March 31 inventory using the retail method.
2. Use Steelcraft's cost ratio to reduce the retail value of the physical inventory to cost.
3. Calculate the estimated amount of inventory shortage at cost and at retail.

Problem 10B-6.
Gross Profit
Method
(L.O. 7)

Raleigh Oil Products warehouses its oil field products in a West Texas warehouse. The warehouse and most of its inventory were completely destroyed by a tornado on May 11. The company found some of its records, but it does not keep perpetual inventory records. The warehouse manager must estimate the amount of the loss. He found the information presented below in the records:

Beginning Inventory January 1	$660,000
Purchases, January 2 to May 11	390,000
Purchases Returns, January 2 to May 11	(15,000)
Freight In since January 2	8,000
Sales, January 2 to May 11	920,000
Sales Returns, January 2 to May 11	(20,000)

Inventory costing $210,000 was recovered and could be sold. The manager remembers that the average gross margin on oil field products is 48 percent.

Required

Prepare a schedule to estimate the inventory destroyed by the tornado.

Financial Decision Case

RTS Company
(L.O. 3, 4)

Refrigerated Truck Sales Company (RTS Company) buys large refrigerated trucks from the manufacturer and sells them to companies and independent truckers who haul perishable goods for long distances. RTS has been successful in this specialized niche of the industry because it provides a unique product and service. Because of the high cost of these trucks and of financing inventory, RTS tries to maintain as small an inventory as possible. In fact, at the beginning of March, the company had no inventory or liabilities, as shown by the following balance sheet:

RTS Company
Balance Sheet
March 1, 19xx

Assets		Owner's Equity	
Cash	$400,000	Robert Trinker, Capital	$400,000
		Total Owner's	
Total Assets	$400,000	Equity	$400,000

On March 5, RTS takes delivery of a truck at a price of $150,000. On March 15 after a rise in price, an identical truck is delivered to the company at a price of $160,000. On March 25, the company sells one of the trucks for $195,000. During March, expenses totaled $15,000. All transactions were paid in cash.

Required

1. Prepare income statements and balance sheets for RTS on March 31 using (a) the FIFO method of inventory valuation and (b) the LIFO method of inventory valuation. Explain the effects that each method has on the financial statements.
2. Assume that Robert Trinker, owner of RTS Company, follows the policy of withdrawing cash each period that is exactly equal to net income. What effect does this action have on each balance sheet prepared in **1**, and how do they compare with the balance sheet at the beginning of the month? Which inventory method, if either, do you feel is more realistic in representing RTS's income?
3. Assume that RTS receives notice of another price increase of $10,000 on refrigerated trucks, to take effect on April 1. How does this information relate to the withdrawal policy of the owner, and how will it affect next month's operations?

Answers to Self-Test

1. b	3. c	5. d	7. d	9. d
2. a	4. b	6. c	8. d	10. d

LEARNING OBJECTIVES

1. Explain how the issues of recognition, valuation, and classification apply to liabilities.
2. Identify, compute, and record definitely determinable and estimated current liabilities.
3. Define a contingent liability.
4. Identify and compute the liabilities associated with payroll accounting.
5. Record transactions associated with payroll accounting.

CHAPTER 11

Current Liabilities and Payroll Accounting

Liabilities are one of the three major parts of the balance sheet. The two major kinds of liabilities are current and long-term liabilities. This chapter deals with the nature and measurement of current liabilities. The subject of long-term liabilities is covered in Chapter 17. Because a number of current liabilities arise through the payroll process, the fundamentals of payroll accounting are also presented in this chapter. After studying this chapter, you should be able to meet the learning objectives listed on the left.

Nature and Measurement of Liabilities

Liabilities are the result of a company's past transactions and are legal obligations for the future payment of assets or the future performance of services. They are more than monetary obligations. For example, revenues received in advance are for goods or services that must be provided to customers. In most cases, the amount and due date are definite or subject to reasonable estimation. The problems of recognition, valuation, and classification apply equally to liabilities and assets.

Recognition of Liabilities

Timing is important in the recognition of liabilities. Very often failure to record a liability in an accounting period goes along with failure to record an expense. Thus it leads to an understatement of expense and an overstatement of income. Liabilities are recorded when an obligation occurs. This rule is harder to apply than it appears to be on the surface. When a transaction obligates the company to make future payments, a liability arises and is recognized, as when goods are bought on credit. However, current liabilities often are not represented by a direct transaction. One of the major reasons for adjusting entries at the end of an accounting period is to recognize unrecorded liabilities. Among these accrued liabilities are salaries payable and interest payable. Other liabilities that can only be estimated, such as taxes payable, must also be recognized by adjusting entries.

OBJECTIVE 1
Explain how the issues of recognition, valuation, and classification apply to liabilities

On the other hand, a company may sometimes enter into an agreement for future transactions. For instance, a company may agree to pay an executive $50,000 a year for a period of three years, or a public utility may agree to buy an unspecified quantity of coal at a certain price over the next five years. These contracts, though they are definite commitments, are not considered liabilities because they are for future—not past—transactions. As there is no current obligation, no liability is recognized.

Valuation of Liabilities

Liabilities are generally valued at the amount of money needed to pay the debt or at the fair market value of goods or services to be delivered. For most liabilities the amount is definitely known, but for some it must be estimated. For example, an automobile dealer who sells a car with a one-year warranty must provide parts and services during the year. The obligation is definite because the sale of the car has occurred, but the amount must be estimated.

Classification of Liabilities

Current liabilities are debts and obligations that are expected to be satisfied in one year or within the normal operating cycle, whichever is longer. In most cases, they are paid out of current assets or by taking on another short-term liability. The classification of current liabilities directly matches the classification of current assets. In Chapter 8, we noted that two important measures of liquidity are working capital (current assets less current liabilities) and the current ratio (current assets divided by current liabilities). Liabilities that will not be due during the next year or during the normal operating cycle are listed as **long-term liabilities**.

Disclosure of Liabilities

In addition to proper recognition, valuation, and classification, sufficient details about a company's liabilities should be disclosed to allow the statement reader to assess the ultimate effects of the liabilities on the liquidity and profitability of the company and whatever risks the company may be facing. Because it believes that disclosure practices in the past have been inadequate, the Financial Accounting Standards Board is proposing significant increases in the disclosures that corporations must make about all their financial instruments. **Financial instruments** include any contract that results in an asset in one entity's records and a liability in another entity's records. As such, they include financial assets like cash, investments, and receivables (see Chapter 9). However, the FASB is more concerned with the disclosure practices of financial instruments related to **financial liabilities** such as loans, mortgages, bonds, leases, and more sophisticated forms of debt financing, and with **financial equities** such as common stock and other forms of ownership.

Common Categories of Current Liabilities

Current liabilities fall into two major groups: (1) definitely determinable liabilities and (2) estimated liabilities. Discussions of each follow.

Definitely Determinable Liabilities

OBJECTIVE 2
Identify, compute, and record definitely determinable and estimated current liabilities

Current liabilities that are set by contract or by statute and can be measured exactly are called **definitely determinable liabilities.** The accounting problems connected with these liabilities are to determine the existence and amount of the liability and to see that the liability is recorded properly. Definitely determinable liabilities include trade accounts payable, notes payable, dividends payable, sales and excise taxes payable, current portions of long-term debt, accrued liabilities, payroll liabilities, and deferred revenues.

Trade Accounts Payable. Trade accounts payable are short-term obligations to suppliers for goods and services. The amount in the Trade Accounts Payable account is generally supported by an accounts payable subsidiary ledger, which contains an individual account for each person or company to whom money is owed. Under the voucher system, this account is called Vouchers Payable. Accounting for trade accounts payable has been treated at length earlier in the book.

Notes Payable. Short-term notes payable, which also arise out of the ordinary course of business, are obligations represented by promissory notes. The two major sources of notes payable are bank loans and payments to suppliers for goods and services. As with notes receivable, presented in Chapter 9, the interest on notes may be stated separately on the face of the note (Case 1 in Figure 11-1), or it may be deducted in advance by discounting it from the face value of the note (Case 2). The entries to record the note in each case are as follows:

Case 1—Interest stated separately

Aug. 31	Cash	5,000	
	Notes Payable		5,000
	To record 60-day, 12% promissory note with interest stated separately		

Case 2—Interest in face amount

Aug. 31	Cash	4,900	
	Prepaid Interest	100	
	Notes Payable		5,000
	To record 60-day, 12% promissory note with prepaid interest included in face amount		

$$\$5,000 \times \frac{60}{360} \times .12 = \$100$$

Figure 11-1. Two Promissory Notes: One with Interest Stated Separately; One with Interest in Face Amount

Note that in Case 1 the money borrowed equaled the face value of the note, whereas in Case 2 the money borrowed ($4,900) was less than the face value ($5,000) of the note. The amount of the discount equals the amount of the interest for sixty days. Since the obligation to pay the interest is incurred on August 31, it is treated as prepaid interest that will become an expense over the next sixty days. Prepaid interest is a current asset.

On October 30, when the note is paid, each alternative is recorded as follows:

Case 1—Interest stated separately

Oct. 30	Notes Payable	5,000	
	Interest Expense	100	
	Cash		5,100
	Payment of note with interest stated separately		

Case 2—Interest in face amount

Oct. 30	Notes Payable	5,000	
	Cash		5,000
	Payment of note with interest included in face amount		
30	Interest Expense	100	
	Prepaid Interest		100
	To record interest expense on matured note		

Dividends Payable. Cash dividends are a distribution of earnings by a corporation. The payment of dividends is solely the decision of the corporation's board of directors. A liability does not exist until the board declares the dividends. There is usually a short time between the date of declaration and the date of payment of dividends. During that short time, the dividends declared are current liabilities of the corporation. Accounting for dividends is treated extensively in Chapter 16.

Sales and Excise Taxes Payable. Most states and many cities levy a sales tax on retail transactions. There are federal excise taxes on some products, such as automobile tires. The merchant who sells goods subject to these taxes must collect the taxes and remit, or pay, them periodically to the appropriate government agency. The amount of tax collected represents a current liability until it is remitted to the government. For example, assume that a merchant makes a $100 sale that is subject to a 5 percent sales tax and a 10 percent excise tax. Assuming that the sale took place on June 1, the correct entry to record the sale is as follows:

June 1	Cash	115	
	Sales		100
	Sales Tax Payable		5
	Excise Tax Payable		10
	To record sale of merchandise and collection of sales and excise taxes		

The sale is properly recorded at $100, and the tax collections are recorded as liabilities to be remitted at the proper time to the appropriate government agency.

Current Portions of Long-Term Debt. If a portion of long-term debt is due within the next year and is to be paid from current assets, then the current portion of long-term debt is properly classified as a current liability. For example, suppose that a $500,000 debt is to be paid in installments of $100,000 per year for the next five years. The $100,000 installment due in the current year should be classified as a current liability. The remaining $400,000 should be classified as a long-term liability. Note that no journal entry is necessary. The total debt of $500,000 is simply reclassified when the financial statements are prepared, as follows:

Current Liabilities	
Current Portion of Long-Term Debt	$100,000
Long-Term Liabilities	
Long-Term Debt	400,000

Accrued Liabilities. A principal reason for adjusting entries at the end of an accounting period is to recognize and record liabilities that are not already recorded in the accounting records. This practice applies to any type of liability. For example, in previous chapters, adjustments relating to salaries payable were made. As you will see, accrued liabilities can also include estimated liabilities.

Here the focus is on interest payable, a definitely determinable liability. Interest accrues daily on interest-bearing notes. At the end of the accounting period, an adjusting entry should be made in accordance with the matching rule to record the interest obligation up to that point in time. Let us again use the example of the two notes presented earlier in this chapter. If we assume that the accounting period ends on September 30, or thirty days after the issuance of the sixty-day notes, the adjusting entries for each case would be as follows:

Case 1—Interest stated separately

Sept. 30	Interest Expense	50	
	Interest Payable		50
	To record interest expense for		
	30 days on note with interest		
	stated separately		

$$\$5,000 \times \frac{30}{360} \times .12 = \$50$$

Case 2—Interest in face amount

Sept. 30	Interest Expense	50	
	Prepaid Interest		50
	To record interest expense for		
	30 days on note with interest		
	included in face amount		

$$\$5,000 \times \frac{30}{360} \times .12 = \$50$$

In Case 2, Prepaid Interest will now have a debit balance of $50, which will become interest expense during the next thirty days.

Payroll Liabilities. A number of current liabilities are associated with payroll accounting. These liabilities are discussed in a major section at the end of this chapter.

Unearned or Deferred Revenues. **Unearned** or **deferred revenues** represent obligations for goods or services that the company must provide or deliver in a future accounting period in return for an advance payment from a customer. For example, a publisher of a monthly magazine who receives annual subscriptions totaling $240 would make the following entry:

Cash	240	
Unearned Subscriptions		240
Receipt of annual subscriptions		
in advance		

The publisher now has a liability of $240 that will be gradually reduced as monthly issues of the magazine are mailed, as follows:

Unearned Subscriptions	20	
Subscription Revenues		20
Delivery of monthly magazine issues		

Many businesses such as repair companies, construction companies, and special-order firms ask for a deposit or advance from a customer before they will begin work. These advances are also current liabilities until the goods or services are delivered.

Estimated Liabilities

Estimated liabilities are a company's definite debts or obligations for which the exact amount canrot be known until a later date. Since there is no doubt as to the existence of the legal obligation, the primary accounting problem is to estimate and record the amount of the liability. Examples of estimated liabilities are income taxes, property taxes, product warranties, and vacation pay.

Income Tax. The income of a corporation is taxed by the federal government, most state governments, and some cities and towns. The amount of income tax liability depends on the results of operations. Often it is not certain until after the end of the year. However, because income taxes are an expense in the year in which income is earned, an adjusting entry is necessary to record the estimated tax liability. An example of this entry follows:

Dec. 31	Federal Income Tax Expense	53,000	
	Federal Income Tax Payable		53,000
	To record estimated federal income tax		

Remember that the income of sole proprietorships and partnerships is *not* subject to income taxes. Their owners must report their share of the firm's income on their individual tax returns.

Property Taxes Payable. Property taxes are taxes levied on real property such as land and buildings and on personal property such as inventory and equipment. Property taxes are a main source of revenue for local governments. Usually they are assessed annually against the property involved. Because the fiscal years of local governments and their assessment dates rarely correspond to those of the firm, it is necessary to estimate the amount of property taxes that applies to each month of the year. Assume, for instance, that a local government has a fiscal year of July 1 to June 30, that its assessment date is November 1 for the current fiscal year that began on July 1, and that its payment date is December 15. Assume also that on July 1, Janis Corporation estimates that its property tax assessment will be $24,000 for the coming year. The adjusting entry to be made on July 31, which would be repeated on August 31, September 30, and October 31, would be as follows:

```
July 31   Property Taxes Expense              2,000
             Estimated Property Taxes Payable          2,000
                To record estimated property taxes
                expense for the month
                $24,000 ÷ 12 months = $2,000
```

On November 1, the firm receives a property tax bill for $24,720. The estimate made in July was too low. The monthly charge should have been $2,060 per month. Because the difference between the actual and the estimate is small, the company decides to absorb in November the amount undercharged in the previous four months. Therefore, the property tax expense for November is $2,300 [$2,060 + 4($60)] and is recorded as follows:

```
Nov. 30   Property Taxes Expense              2,300
             Estimated Property Taxes Payable          2,300
                To record estimated property taxes
```

The Estimated Property Taxes Payable account now has a balance of $10,300. The entry to record payment on December 15 would be made as follows:

```
Dec. 15   Estimated Property Taxes Payable    10,300
          Prepaid Property Taxes              14,420
             Cash                                      24,720
                To record payment of property taxes
```

Beginning December 31 and each month afterward until June 30, property tax expense is recorded by a debit to Property Taxes Expense and a credit to Prepaid Property Taxes in the amount of $2,060. The total of these seven entries will reduce the Prepaid Property Taxes account to zero on June 30.

Product Warranty Liability. When a firm places a warranty or guarantee on its product at the time of sale, a liability exists for the length of the warranty. The cost of the warranty is properly debited to an expense account in the period of sale because it is a feature of the product or service sold and thus was one of the reasons the customer made the purchase. On the basis of experience, it should be possible to estimate the amount the warranty will cost in the future. Some products or services will require little warranty service; others may require much. Thus there will be an average cost per product or service.

For example, assume that a muffler company guarantees that it will replace any muffler free of charge if it fails any time as long as you own your car. The company charges a small service fee for replacing the muffler. This guarantee is an important selling feature for the firm's mufflers. In the past, 6 percent of the mufflers sold have been returned for replacement under the guarantee. The average cost of a muffler is $25. Assume that during July, 350 mufflers were sold. This accrued liability would be recorded as an adjustment at the end of July as follows:

July 31	Product Warranty Expense	525	
	Estimated Product Warranty Liability		525
	To record estimated product warranty expense:		
	Number of units sold	350	
	Rate of replacements under warranty	× .06	
	Estimated units to be replaced	21	
	Estimated cost per unit	×$ 25	
	Estimated liability for product warranty	$525	

When a muffler is returned for replacement under the product warranty, the cost of the muffler is charged against the estimated product warranty liability account. For example, assume that a customer returns on December 5 with a defective muffler and pays a $10 service fee to have the muffler replaced. Assume that this particular muffler cost $20. The entry is as follows:

Dec. 5	Cash	10	
	Estimated Product Warranty Liability	20	
	Service Revenue		10
	Merchandise Inventory		20
	To record replacement of muffler under warranty		

Vacation Pay Liability. In most companies, employees earn the right to paid vacation days or weeks as they work during the year. For example, an employee may earn two weeks of paid vacation for each fifty weeks of work. Therefore, she or he is paid fifty-two weeks' salary for fifty weeks' work. Theoretically, the cost of the two weeks' vacation should be allocated as expense over the whole year so that month-to-month costs will not be distorted. So vacation pay represents 4 percent (two weeks' vacation divided by fifty weeks) of a worker's pay. Every week worked earns the employee a small fraction (4 percent) of his or her vacation pay. Vacation pay liability can amount to a substantial amount of money. For example, Delta Airlines reported at its year end in 1985 a vacation pay liability of $82,844,000.

Suppose that a company with this policy has a weekly payroll of $20,000. Since not all employees in every company will collect vacation pay because of turnover and rules regarding term of employment, it is assumed that 75 percent of employees will ultimately collect vacation pay. The computation of vacation pay expense is as follows: $20,000 × 4 percent × 75 percent = $600.

The entry to record vacation pay expense for the week ended April 20 is as follows:

Apr. 20 Vacation Pay Expense 600
      Estimated Liability for Vacation Pay 600
        To record estimated vacation pay expense

At the time that a person receives his or her vacation pay, an entry is made debiting Estimated Liability for Vacation Pay and crediting Cash or Wages Payable. For example, assume that an employee is paid $550 during a two-week vacation ending August 31; the entry is as follows:

Aug. 31 Estimated Liability for Vacation Pay 550
      Cash (or Wages Payable) 550
        To record wages of employee on
        vacation

The treatment presented here for vacation pay may also be applied to other payroll costs such as bonus plans and contributions to pension plans.

Contingent Liabilities

OBJECTIVE 3
Define a contingent liability

A **contingent liability** is not an existing liability. Rather, it is a potential liability because it depends on a future event arising out of a past transaction. For instance, a construction company that built a bridge may have been sued by the state for using poor materials. The past transaction is the building of the bridge under contract. The future event whose outcome is not known is the suit against the company. Two conditions have been established by the FASB for determining when a contingency should be entered in the accounting records. They are that the liability must be probable and that it must be reasonably estimated.[1] Estimated liabilities such as the estimated income taxes liability, warranty liability, and vacation pay liability that were described earlier in this chapter meet these conditions. So they are accrued in the accounting records. Potential liabilities that do not meet both conditions are reported in the notes to the financial statements. Losses from such potential liabilities are recorded when the conditions set by the FASB are met. The following example comes from the notes in a recent annual report of Humana Inc., one of the largest health services organizations:

The company continuously evaluates contingencies based upon the best available evidence. In addition, allowances for loss are provided currently for disputed items that have continuing significance, such as certain third-party reimbursements and tax deductions and credits that continue to be claimed in current cost reports and tax returns. Management believes that allowances for

1. *Statement of Financial Accounting Standards No. 5,* "Accounting for Contingencies" (Stamford, Conn.: Financial Accounting Standards Board, 1975).

loss have been provided to the extent necessary and that its assessment of contingencies is reasonable. To the extent that resolution of contingencies results in amounts that vary from management's estimates, future earnings will be charged or credited. The principal contingencies are described below:

Third-Party Revenues. Cost reimbursements and certain other third-party payments are subject to examination by agencies administering the programs. The Company is contesting certain issues raised in audits of prior-year cost reports.

Income Taxes. The Internal Revenue Service has proposed additional taxes for prior years. The more significant issues include current deductibility of liability insurance premiums paid to an insurance subsidiary, cash-basis tax accounting, depreciable lives and investment tax credits. Settlement of these issues is not expected to have a material adverse effect on earnings. However, deferred tax credits could be reduced as a result of any such resolution.

Insurance Activities. Certain levels of professional liability risks have been underwritten by a subsidiary. Company hospitals have paid premiums, and the subsidiary has provided loss allowances, based upon actuarially-determined estimates. In addition, the Company's Group Health Division has entered into group accident and health contracts that involve actuarial estimation of medical claims reserves. Actual claim settlements and expenses incident thereto may differ from the provisions for loss.

Litigation. Various suits and claims arising in the ordinary course of business are pending against the Company.[2]

Contingent liabilities may also arise from failure to follow government regulations, from discounted notes receivable, and from guarantees of the debt of other companies.

Introduction to Payroll Accounting

OBJECTIVE 4
Identify and compute the liabilities associated with payroll accounting

A major expense of most companies is the cost of labor and related payroll taxes. In some industries such as banking and airlines, payroll costs represent more than half the operating costs. Payroll accounting is important because of the amounts of money involved and because the employer must conform to many complex laws governing taxes on payrolls. The employer is liable for meeting reporting requirements and for the money withheld from employees' salaries and for payroll taxes.

Also, the payroll accounting system is subject to complaints and to possible fraud. Every employee must be paid on time and receive a detailed explanation of the amount of his or her pay. The payroll system calls for strong internal control and efficient processing and distribution of checks, as well as accurate reporting to government agencies.

This section will focus on the liabilities, the records, and the control requirements of payroll accounting. The three general kinds of liabilities associated with payroll accounting are (1) liabilities for employee

2. Excerpts from the 1988 annual report used by permission of Humana Inc.

compensation, (2) liabilities for employee payroll withholdings, and (3) liabilities for employer payroll taxes.

It is important to distinguish between employees and independent contractors. Payroll accounting applies only to employees of the company. Employees are paid a wage or salary by the company and are under its direct supervision and control. Independent contractors are not employees of the company, so they are not accounted for under the payroll system. They offer services to the firm for a fee, but are not under its direct control or supervision. Some examples of independent contractors are certified public accountants, advertising agencies, and lawyers.

Liabilities for Employee Compensation

The employer is liable to employees for wages and salaries. The term **wages** refers to payment for the services of employees at an hourly rate or on a piecework basis. The term **salaries** refers to the compensation for employees who are paid at a monthly or yearly rate. Generally, these employees are administrators or managers.

Besides setting minimum wage levels, the federal Fair Labor Standards Act (also called the Wages and Hours Law) regulates overtime pay. Employers who take part in interstate commerce must pay overtime for hours worked beyond forty hours a week or more than eight hours a day. This overtime pay must be at least one and one-half times the regular rate. Work on Saturdays, Sundays, or holidays may also call for overtime pay under separate wage agreements. Overtime pay under union or other employment contracts may exceed these minimums.

For example, suppose that the employment contract of Robert Jones calls for a regular wage of $8 an hour, one and one-half times the regular rate for work over eight hours in any weekday, and twice the regular rate for work on Saturdays, Sundays, or holidays. He works the following days and hours during the week of January 18, 19xx:

Day	Total Hours Worked	Regular Time	Overtime
Monday	10	8	2
Tuesday	8	8	0
Wednesday	8	8	0
Thursday	9	8	1
Friday	10	8	2
Saturday	2	0	2
	47	40	7

Jones's wages would be figured as follows:

Regular time	40 hours × $8	$320.00
Overtime, weekdays	5 hours × $8 × 1.5	60.00
Overtime, weekend	2 hours × $8 × 2	32.00
Total wages		$412.00

Liabilities for Employee Payroll Withholdings

The amount paid to employees is generally less than the wages they earned because the employer is required by law to withhold certain amounts from the employees' wages and send them directly to government agencies to pay taxes owed by the employees. In this group are FICA taxes, federal income taxes, and state income taxes. Also, certain withholdings are made for the employees' benefit, often at their request. These include pension payments, medical insurance premiums, life insurance premiums, union dues, and charitable contributions. No matter the reason for the withholding from employees' wages, the employer is liable for payment to the proper agency, fund, or organization.

FICA Tax. With the passage of the United States social security program in the 1930s, the federal government began to take more responsibility for the well-being of its citizens. The social security program offers retirement and disability benefits, survivor's benefits, and hospitalization and other medical benefits. One of the major extensions of the program provides hospitalization and medical insurance for persons over sixty-five.

The social security program is financed by taxes on employees, employers, and the self-employed. About 90 percent of the people working in the United States fall under the provisions of this program.

The Federal Insurance Contributions Act (FICA) set up the tax to pay for this program. The tax is paid by *both* employee and employer and is based on the following schedule (for 1989):

FICA tax rate (paid by employee and employer)	7.51%
Maximum wage taxed under present law	$48,000.00
Present maximum tax (on employee and employer)	$ 3,604.80

This current schedule is subject to frequent amendments by Congress. We will use these figures throughout the text.[3]

The FICA tax applies to the pay of each employee up to a certain level. In 1989, it applies up to the level of $48,000. There is no tax on individual earnings above this amount, so the largest possible FICA tax for each employee is $3,604.80 ($48,000 × .0751). Since the employee and the employer must each pay the tax, the total maximum paid by both is $7,209.60. The employer deducts the tax from the employee's wages and sends the amount, along with other employees' withholdings of FICA taxes and the employer's FICA taxes, to the government. Because of inflation and rising benefits under the social security system, these provisions are under constant study by Congress. They are subject to change and should be verified each year.

As an example of the FICA tax, suppose that Robert Jones will earn less than $48,000 this year and that the FICA withholding for taxes on his paycheck this week is $30.94 ($412.00 × .0751). The employer must pay an equal tax of $30.94 and remit a total of $61.88.

3. The 1990 FICA tax rate is 7.65% and the maximum wage taxed is $50,400, making a present maximum tax on employee and employer of $3855.60.

Federal Income Tax. The largest deduction from many employees' earnings is their estimated liability for federal income taxes. The system of tax collection for federal income taxes is to "pay as you go." The employer is required to withhold the amount of the taxes from employees' paychecks and turn it over to the Internal Revenue Service.

The amount to be withheld depends in part on the amount of each employee's earnings and on the number of the employee's exemptions. All employees are required by law to indicate exemptions by filing a Form W-4 (Employee's Withholding Exemption Certificate). Each employee is entitled to one exemption for himself and one for each dependent.

The Internal Revenue Service provides employers with tables to aid them in computing the amount of withholdings. For example, Figure 11-2 is a withholding table for married employees who are paid weekly. The withholding from Robert Jones's $412.00 weekly earnings is $31.00. The amount is shown in the intersection of columns for four withholding allowances (one for Robert and each of his three dependents) and the $410–420 wage bracket. (This table is presented for illustrative purposes only. Actual withholding tables change periodically as changes occur in tax rates and laws.)

State Income Tax. Most states have income taxes, and in most cases the procedures for withholding are similar to those for federal income taxes.

Figure 11-2. Wage Bracket Table

Weekly Payroll Period–Employee Married											
	And the number of withholding allowances claimed is–										
And the wages are–	0	1	2	3	4	5	6	7	8	9	10 or more
At least / But less than	The amount of income tax to be withheld shall be–										
$300 – $310	$37	$31	$26	$20	$14	$9	$3	$0	$0	$0	$0
310 – 320	38	33	27	22	16	10	5	0	0	0	0
320 – 330	40	34	29	23	17	12	6	1	0	0	0
330 – 340	41	36	30	25	19	13	8	2	0	0	0
340 – 350	43	37	32	26	20	15	9	4	0	0	0
350 – 360	44	39	33	28	22	16	11	5	0	0	0
360 – 370	46	40	35	29	23	18	12	7	1	0	0
370 – 380	47	42	36	31	25	19	14	8	2	0	0
380 – 390	49	43	38	32	26	21	15	10	4	0	0
390 – 400	50	45	39	34	28	22	17	11	5	0	0
400 – 410	52	46	41	35	29	24	18	13	7	1	0
410 – 420	53	48	42	37	31	25	20	14	8	3	0
420 – 430	55	49	44	38	32	27	21	16	10	4	0

Other Withholdings. Some of the other withholdings, such as for a retirement or pension plan, are required of each employee. Others, such as withholdings for insurance premiums or savings plans, may be requested by the employee. The payroll system must allow for treating each employee separately with regard to withholdings and the records of those withholdings. The employer is liable to account for all withholdings and to make proper remittances.

Computation of an Employee's Take-Home Pay: An Illustration

OBJECTIVE 5
Record transactions associated with payroll accounting

To continue with the example of Robert Jones, let us now compute his take-home pay. We know that his total earnings for the week of January 18 are $412.00, that his FICA tax rate at 7.51 percent is $30.94 (he has not earned over $48,000), and that his federal income tax withholding is $31.00. Assume also that his union dues are $2.00, his medical insurance premiums are $7.60, his life insurance premium is $6.00, he places $15.00 per week in savings bonds, and he contributes $1.00 per week to United Charities. His net (take-home) pay is computed as follows:

Gross earnings		$412.00
Deductions		
FICA tax	$30.94	
Federal income tax withheld	31.00	
Union dues	2.00	
Medical insurance	7.60	
Life insurance	6.00	
Savings bonds	15.00	
United Charities contribution	1.00	
Total deductions		93.54
Net (take-home) pay		$318.46

Employee Earnings Record. Each employer must keep a record of earnings and withholdings for each employee. Many companies today use computers to maintain these records, but small companies use manual records. The manual form of **employee earnings record** used for Robert Jones is shown in Exhibit 11-1. This form is designed to help the employer meet legal reporting requirements. Each deduction must be shown to have been paid to the proper agency and the employee must receive a report of the deductions made each year. Most columns are self-explanatory. Note, however, the column on the far right, where cumulative earnings (earnings to date) are recorded. This record helps the employer comply with the rule of applying FICA taxes only up to the maximum wage level. At the end of the year, the employer reports to the employee on Form W-2, the Wage and Tax Statement, the totals of earnings and tax deductions for the year, so that the employee can complete his or her individual tax return. The employer sends a copy of the

Exhibit 11-1. Employee Earnings Record

Employee Earnings Record

Employee's Name Robert Jones **Social Security Number** 444-66-9999

Address 777 20th Street **Sex** Male   **Employee No.** 705

   Marshall, Michigan 52603 **Single** **Married** X **Weekly Pay Rate**

Date of Birth September 20, 1962 **Exemptions (W-4)** 4 **Hourly Rate** $8

Position Sales Assistant **Date of Employment** July 15, 1988 **Date Employment Ended**

| 19xx | | Earnings | | | Deductions | | | | | | | Payment | | |
Period Ended	Total Hours	Regular	Overtime	Gross	FICA Tax	Federal Income Tax	Union Dues	Medical Insurance	Life Insurance	Savings Bonds	Other: A—United Charities	Net Earnings	Check No.	Cumulative Gross Earnings
Jan. 4	40	320.00	0	320.00	24.03	17.00	2.00	7.60	6.00	15.00	A 1.00	247.37	717	320.00
11	44	320.00	48.00	368.00	27.64	23.00	2.00	7.60	6.00	15.00	A 1.00	285.76	822	688.00
18	47	320.00	92.00	412.00	30.94	31.00	2.00	7.60	6.00	15.00	A 1.00	318.46	926	1,100.00

W-2 to the Internal Revenue Service. Thus the IRS can check on whether the employee has reported all income earned from that employer.

Payroll Register. The **payroll register** is a detailed listing of the firm's total payroll that is prepared each payday. A payroll register is presented in Exhibit 11-2. Note that the name, hours, earnings, deductions, and net pay of each employee are listed. Compare the January 18 entry in the employee earnings record of Robert Jones (Exhibit 11-1) with the entry for Robert Jones in the payroll register. Except for the first column, which lists the employee names, and the last column, which shows the wage or salary as either sales or office expense, the columns are the same. The columns help employers to record the payroll in the accounting records and to meet legal reporting requirements as noted above. The last two columns are needed to divide the expenses on the income statement into selling and administrative categories.

Exhibit 11-2. Payroll Register

Payroll Register Pay Period: Week ended January 18

| | | Earnings | | | Deductions | | | | | | | Payment | | Distribution | |
Employee	Total Hours	Regular	Overtime	Gross	FICA Tax	Federal Income Tax	Union Dues	Medical Insurance	Life Insurance	Savings Bonds	Other: A—United Charities	Net Earnings	Check No.	Sales Wages Expense	Office Wages Expense
Linda Duval	40	160.00		160.00	12.02	11.00		5.80				131.18	923		160.00
John Franks	44	160.00	24.00	184.00	13.82	14.00	2.00	7.60			A 10.00	136.58	924	184.00	
Samuel Goetz	40	400.00		400.00	30.04	53.00		10.40	14.00		A 3.00	289.56	925	400.00	
Robert Jones	47	320.00	92.00	412.00	30.94	31.00	2.00	7.60	6.00	15.00	A 1.00	318.46	926	412.00	
Billie Matthews	40	160.00		160.00	12.02	14.00		5.80				128.18	927		160.00
Rosaire O'Brian	42	200.00	20.00	220.00	16.52	22.00	2.00	5.80				173.68	928	220.00	
James Van Dyke	40	200.00		200.00	15.02	20.00		5.80				159.18	929		200.00
		1,600.00	136.00	1,736.00	130.38	165.00	6.00	48.80	20.00	15.00	14.00	1,336.82		1,216.00	520.00

Recording the Payroll. The journal entry for recording the payroll is based on the total of the columns from the payroll register. The journal entry to record the payroll of January 18 follows. Note that each account debited or credited is a total from the payroll register. If the payroll register is considered a special-purpose journal like those in Chapter 6, the column can be entered directly in the ledger accounts with the correct account numbers shown at the bottom of each column.

Jan. 18	Sales Wages Expense	1,216.00	
	Office Wages Expense	520.00	
	FICA Tax Payable		130.38
	Employees' Federal Income Tax Payable		165.00
	Union Dues Payable		6.00
	Medical Insurance Premiums Payable		48.80
	Life Insurance Premiums Payable		20.00
	Savings Bonds Payable		15.00
	United Charities Payable		14.00
	Wages Payable		1,336.82
	To record weekly payroll		

Liabilities for Employer Payroll Taxes

The payroll taxes discussed so far were deducted from the employee's gross earnings, to be remitted by the employer. There are three major taxes on salaries that the employer must pay in addition to gross wages: the FICA tax, the federal unemployment insurance tax, and state unemployment compensation tax. These taxes are considered operating expenses.

FICA Tax. The employer must pay FICA tax equal to the amount paid by the employees. That is, from the payroll register in Exhibit 11-2, the employer would have to pay FICA tax of $130.38, equal to that paid by the employees.

Federal Unemployment Insurance Tax. The Federal Unemployment Tax Act (FUTA) is another part of the U.S. social security system. It is intended to pay for operating programs to help unemployed workers. In this way, it is different from FICA taxes and state unemployment taxes. The dollars paid through FUTA provide for unemployment compensation. Unlike the FICA tax, which is levied on both employees and employers, the FUTA is assessed only against employers.

The amount of tax can vary. Recently it has been 6.2 percent of the first $7,000 earned by each employee. The employer, however, is allowed a credit against this federal tax for unemployment taxes paid to the state. The maximum credit is 5.4 percent of the first $7,000 of each employee's earnings. Most states set their rate at this maximum. Thus, the FUTA paid would be 0.8 percent (6.2 percent – 5.4 percent) of the taxable wages.

State Unemployment Insurance Tax. All state unemployment plans provide for unemployment compensation to be paid to eligible unemployed workers. This compensation is paid out of the fund provided by the 5.4 percent of the first $7,000 earned by each employee. In some states, employers with favorable employment records may be entitled to pay less than the 5.4 percent.

Recording Payroll Taxes. According to Exhibit 11-2, the gross payroll for the week ended January 18 was $1,736.00. Because it was the first month of the year, all employees had accumulated less than the $48,000 and $7,000 maximum taxable salaries. Therefore, the total FICA tax was $130.38 (equal to tax on employees); the total FUTA was $13.89 (.008 × $1,736.00); and the total state unemployment tax was $93.74 (.054 × $1,736.00). The entry to record this expense and related liability in the general journal is as follows:

Jan. 18	Payroll Tax Expense	238.01	
	FICA Tax Payable		130.38
	Federal Unemployment Tax Payable		13.89
	State Unemployment Tax Payable		93.74
	To record weekly payroll taxes expense		

Payment of Payroll and Payroll Taxes

After the weekly payroll is recorded, as illustrated earlier, a liability of $1,336.82 exists for wages payable. How this liability will be paid depends on the system used by the company. Many companies use a special payroll account against which payroll checks are drawn. Under this system, a check must first be drawn on the regular checking account for total net earnings for this payroll, or $1,336.82, and deposited in the special payroll account before the payroll checks are issued to the employees. If a voucher system is combined with a special payroll account, a voucher for the total wages payable is prepared and recorded in the voucher register as a debit to Payroll Bank Account and a credit to Vouchers Payable.

The combined FICA taxes (both employees' and employer's share) and the federal income taxes must be paid to the Internal Revenue Service at least quarterly. Monthly payments are necessary if more than a certain amount of money is involved. The federal unemployment insurance taxes are paid yearly if the amount is less than $100. If it is more than $100, quarterly payments are necessary. Payment dates vary among the states. Other payroll deductions must be paid according to the particular contracts or agreements involved.

Chapter Review

Review of Learning Objectives

1. **Explain how the issues of recognition, valuation, and classification apply to liabilities.**
   Liabilities represent present legal obligations of the firm for future payment of assets or the future performance of services. They result from past

transactions, and should be recognized when there is a transaction that obligates the company to make future payments. Liabilities are valued at the amount of money necessary to satisfy the obligation or the fair market value of goods or services that must be delivered. Liabilities are classified as current or long term.

2. **Identify, compute, and record definitely determinable and estimated current liabilities.**
   Two principal categories of current liabilities are definitely determinable liabilities and estimated liabilities. Although definitely determinable liabilities such as accounts payable, notes payable, dividends payable, accrued liabilities, and the current portion of long-term debt can be measured exactly, the accountant must still be careful not to overlook existing liabilities in these categories. Estimated liabilities such as liabilities for income taxes, property taxes, product warranties, and others definitely exist, but the amounts must be estimated and recorded properly.

3. **Define a contingent liability.**
   A contingent liability is a potential liability arising from a past transaction and dependent on a future event. Examples are lawsuits, income tax disputes, discounted notes receivable, guarantees of debt, and the potential cost of changes in government regulations.

4. **Identify and compute the liabilities associated with payroll accounting.**
   Labor costs are a large segment of the total cost of most businesses. In addition, three important categories of liabilities are associated with the payroll. The employer is liable for the compensation to the employee, for withholdings from the employee's gross pay, and for the employer portion of payroll taxes. The most common payroll withholdings are the FICA tax, federal and state income taxes, and employee-requested withholdings. The principal employer-paid taxes are FICA (an amount equal to that of the employee) and federal and state unemployment compensation taxes.

5. **Record transactions associated with payroll accounting.**
   The salary and deductions for each employee are recorded each pay period in the payroll register. From the payroll register the details of each employee's earnings are transferred to the employee's earnings record. The column totals of the payroll register are used to prepare a general journal entry that records the payroll and accompanying liabilities. One further general journal entry is needed to record the employer's share of the FICA taxes and the federal and state unemployment taxes.

Review of Concepts and Terminology

The following concepts and terms were introduced in this chapter:

(L.O. 3) **Contingent liability:** A potential liability that depends on a future event arising out of a past transaction.

(L.O. 1) **Current liabilities:** Debts and obligations that are expected to be satisfied in one year or within the normal operating cycle, whichever is longer.

(L.O. 2) **Definitely determinable liabilities:** Current liabilities that are set by contract or by statute and can be measured exactly.

(L.O. 5) **Employee earnings record:** A record of earnings and withholdings for a single employee.

(L.O. 2) **Estimated liabilities:** Definite debts or obligations for which the exact amounts cannot be known until a later date.

(L.O. 1) **Financial equities:** Common stock and other forms of ownership.

(L.O. 1) **Financial instruments:** Any contract that results in an asset in one entity's records and a liability in another entity's records.

(L.O. 1) **Financial liabilities:** Loans, mortgages, bonds, leases, and other forms of debt financing.

(L.O. 1) **Liabilities:** Legal obligations for the future payment of assets or the future performance of services that result from past transactions.

(L.O. 1) **Long-term liabilities:** Debts or obligations that will not be due during the next year or the normal operating cycle.

(L.O. 5) **Payroll register:** A detailed listing of a firm's total payroll that is prepared each payday.

(L.O. 4) **Salaries:** Compensation to employees who are paid at a monthly or yearly rate.

(L.O. 4) **Wages:** Payment for services of employees at an hourly rate or on a piece-meal basis.

(L.O. 2) **Unearned or deferred revenues:** Revenues received in advance for which the goods will not be delivered or the services performed during the current accounting period.

Self-Test

Test your knowledge of the chapter by choosing the best answer for each item below and on the next page.

1. Failure to record a liability will probably
   a. have no effect on net income.
   b. result in overstated net income.
   c. result in overstated total assets.
   d. result in overstated total liabilities and owner's equity. *(L.O. 1)*

2. Which of the following is most likely to be a definitely determinable liability?
   a. Property taxes payable   c. Income taxes payable
   b. Product warranty liability   d. Interest payable   *(L.O. 2)*

3. Which of the following is most likely to be an estimated liability?
   a. Deferred revenues
   b. Vacation pay liability
   c. Current portion of long-term debt
   d. Payroll liabilities   *(L.O. 2)*

4. The amount received by a borrower on a one-year, $3,000, 10 percent note with interest included in the face value is
   a. $3,000.   c. $3,300.
   b. $2,700.   d. $2,990.   *(L.O. 2)*

5. If product J cost $100 and had a 2 percent failure rate, the estimated warranty expense in a month in which 1,000 units were sold would be
   a. $2,000.   c. $20.
   b. $100.   d. $20,000.   *(L.O. 2)*

6. Of a company's employees, 70 percent typically qualify to receive two weeks' paid vacation per year. The amount of estimated vacation pay liability for a week in which the total payroll is $3,000 is
   a. $2,100.   c. $84.
   b. $42.   d. $120.   *(L.O. 2)*

7. A contingent liability would be recorded in the accounting records if it is
   a. not probable but can be reasonably estimated.
   b. not probable but cannot be estimated.
   c. probable and can be reasonably estimated.
   d. probable but cannot be reasonably estimated.   *(L.O. 3)*

8. Which of the following is a payroll tax borne by both employee and employer?
   a. Excise tax   c. FUTA tax
   b. Income tax   d. FICA tax   *(L.O. 4)*

9. An employee has gross earnings of $500 and withholdings of $30 for FICA and $60 for income taxes. The employer pays $30 for FICA and $20 for FUTA. The total cost of the employee to the employer is
   a. $410.   c. $550.
   b. $500.   d. $580.   *(L.O. 4)*

10. Payroll Tax expense includes all the following except
    a. Federal unemployment tax payable
    b. FICA tax payable
    c. Federal income tax payable
    d. State unemployment tax payable   *(L.O. 5)*

Answers to Self-Test are at the end of this chapter.

Review Problem
Notes Payable Transactions and End-of-Period Entries

(L.O. 2)   McLaughlin, Inc., whose fiscal year ends June 30, completed the following transactions involving notes payable:

May 11   Purchased a small crane by issuing a sixty-day, 12 percent note for $54,000. The face of the note does not include interest.

16   Obtained a $40,000 loan from the bank to finance a temporary increase in receivables by signing a ninety-day, 10 percent note. The face value includes interest.

June 30   Made end-of-year adjusting entry to accrue interest expense.

30   Made end-of-year adjusting entry to recognize prepaid interest expired.

30   Made end-of-year closing entry pertaining to interest expense.

July 1   Made appropriate reversing entry.

10   Paid the note plus interest on the crane purchase.

Aug. 14   Paid off the note to the bank.

Required

1. Prepare general journal entries for the above transactions (journal Page 36).
2. Open general ledger accounts for Prepaid Interest (114), Notes Payable (212), Interest Payable (214), and Interest Expense (721). Post the relevant portions of the entries to these general ledger accounts.

Answer to Review Problem

1. Journal entries prepared

General Journal					Page 36
Date		**Description**	**Post. Ref.**	**Debit**	**Credit**
19xx					
May	11	Equipment		54,000	
		Notes Payable	212		54,000
		Purchase of crane with 60-day, 12% note			
	16	Cash		39,000	
		Prepaid Interest	114	1,000	
		Notes Payable	212		40,000
		Loan from bank obtained by signing 90-day, 10% note; discount $40,000 \times .1 \times 90/360 = \$1,000$			
June	30	Interest Expense	721	900	
		Interest Payable	214		900
		To accrue interest expense $54,000 \times .12 \times 50/360 = \$900$			
	30	Interest Expense	721	500	
		Prepaid Interest	114		500
		To recognize prepaid interest expired $\$1,000 \times 45/90 = \$500$			
	30	Income Summary		1,400	
		Interest Expense	721		1,400
		To close interest expense			
July	1	Interest Payable	214	900	
		Interest Expense	721		900
		To reverse interest expense accrual			
	10	Notes Payable	212	54,000	
		Interest Expense	721	1,080	
		Cash			55,080
		Payment of note on equipment $\$54,000 \times .12 \times 60/360 = \$1,080$			
Aug.	14	Notes Payable	212	40,000	
		Cash			40,000
		Payment of bank loan			
	14	Interest Expense	721	500	
		Prepaid Interest	114		500
		To recognize prepaid interest expired $\$1,000 - \$500 = \$500$			

2. Accounts opened and amounts posted

Prepaid Interest   Account No. 114

Date		Item	Post. Ref.	Debit	Credit	Balance	
						Debit	Credit
May	16		J36	1,000		1,000	
June	30		J36		500	500	
Aug.	14		J36		500	—	

Notes Payable   Account No. 212

Date		Item	Post. Ref.	Debit	Credit	Balance	
						Debit	Credit
May	11		J36		54,000		54,000
	16		J36		40,000		94,000
July	10		J36	54,000			40,000
Aug.	14		J36	40,000			—

Interest Payable   Account No. 214

Date		Item	Post. Ref.	Debit	Credit	Balance	
						Debit	Credit
June	30		J36		900		900
July	1		J36	900			—

Interest Expense   Account No. 721

Date		Item	Post. Ref.	Debit	Credit	Balance	
						Debit	Credit
June	30		J36	900		900	
	30		J36	500		1,400	
	30		J36		1,400	—	
July	1		J36		900		900
	10		J36	1,080		180	
Aug.	14		J36	500		680	

Chapter Assignments

Discussion Questions and Writing Assignments

1. What are liabilities?
2. Why is the timing of liability recognition important in accounting?
3. At the end of the accounting period, Janson Company had a legal obligation to accept delivery and pay for a truckload of hospital supplies the following week. Is this legal obligation a liability?
4. Ned Johnson, a star college basketball player, received a contract from the Midwest Blazers to play professional basketball. The contract calls for a salary of $300,000 a year for four years, dependent on his making the team in each of those years. Should this contract be considered a liability and recorded on the books of the basketball team?
5. What is the rule for determining a current liability?
6. Where should the Prepaid Interest account appear on the balance sheet?
7. When can a portion of long-term debt be classified as a current liability?
8. Why are deferred revenues classified as liabilities?
9. What is definite about an estimated liability?
10. Why are income taxes payable considered to be estimated liabilities?
11. When does a company incur a liability for a product warranty?
12. What is a contingent liability, and how does it differ from an estimated liability?
13. What are some examples of contingent liabilities, and why is each a contingent liability?
14. Why is payroll accounting important?
15. How does an employee differ from an independent contractor?
16. Who pays the FICA tax?
17. What role does the W-4 form play in determining the withholding for estimated federal income taxes?
18. What withholdings might an employee voluntarily request?
19. Why is an employee earnings record necessary, and how does it relate to the W-2 form?
20. How can the payroll register be used as a special-purpose journal?
21. What are three types of employer-related payroll liabilities?
22. A bank is offering Diane Wedge two alternatives for borrowing $2,000. The first alternative is a $2,000, 12 percent, thirty-day note. The second alternative is a $2,000, thirty-day note discounted at 12 percent. (a) What entries are required by Diane Wedge to record the two loans? (b) What entries are needed by Diane to record the payment of the two loans? (c) Which alternative favors Diane, and why?

Classroom Exercises

Exercise 11-1.
Interest Expense:
Interest Not
Included in Face
Value of Note
(L.O. 2)

On the last day of October, Gross Company borrows $60,000 on a bank note for sixty days at 12 percent interest. Assume that interest is not included in the face amount. Prepare the following general journal entries: (1) October 31, recording of note; (2) November 30, accrual of interest expense; (3) November 30, closing entry; (4) December 1, reversing entry; (5) December 30, payment of note plus interest.

Exercise 11-2.
Interest Expense:
Interest Included
in Face Value of
Note
(L.O. 2)

Assume the same facts as in Exercise 11-1, except that interest is included in the face amount of the note and the note is discounted at the bank on October 31. Prepare the following general journal entries: (1) October 31, recording of note; (2) November 30, recognize prepaid interest expired; (3) November 30, closing entry; (4) December 30, payment of note and recording of interest expense.

Exercise 11-3.
Sales and Excise
Taxes
(L.O. 2)

Quik Dial Service billed its customers for a total of $490,200 for the month of May, including 9 percent federal excise tax and 5 percent sales tax.

1. Determine the proper amount of revenue to report for the month.
2. Prepare a general journal entry to record the revenue and related liabilities for the month.

Exercise 11-4.
Product Warranty
Liability
(L.O. 2)

Rainbow manufactures and sells electronic games. Each game costs $50 to produce and sells for $90. In addition, each game carries a warranty that provides for free replacement if it fails for any reason during the two years following the sale. In the past, 7 percent of the games sold had to be replaced under the warranty. During October, Rainbow sold 52,000 games and 2,800 games were replaced under the warranty.

1. Prepare a general journal entry to record the estimated liability for product warranties during the month.
2. Prepare a general journal entry to record the games replaced under warranty during the month.

Exercise 11-5.
Vacation Pay
Liability
(L.O. 2)

Outland Corporation currently allows each employee three weeks' paid vacation after working at the company for one year. On the basis of studies of employee turnover and previous experience, management estimates that 65 percent of the employees will qualify for vacation pay this year.

1. Assume that the August payroll for Outland is $300,000. Figure the estimated employee benefit for the month.
2. Prepare a general journal entry to record the employee benefit for August.

Exercise 11-6.
Estimated Liability
(L.O. 2)

Southeast Airways has initiated a frequent flyer program in which enrolled passengers accumulate miles of travel which may be redeemed for rewards such as free trips or upgrades from coach to first class. Southeast estimates that approximately 2 percent of its passengers are traveling for free as a result of this program. During 19x3, Southeast Airways had total revenues of $8,000,000,000.

In January 19x4, passengers representing tickets of $150,000 flew free. Prepare the December year-end adjusting entry to record the estimated liability for this program and the January entry for the free tickets. Can you suggest how these transactions would be recorded if the estimate of the free tickets were to be considered a deferred revenue (revenue received in advance) rather than an estimated liability? How is each treatment an application of the matching rule?

**Exercise 11-7.
FICA and
Unemployment
Taxes
(L.O. 4)**

Ultra Company is subject to a 5.4 percent state unemployment insurance tax and a 0.8 percent federal unemployment insurance tax after credits. Currently, both federal and state unemployment taxes apply to the first $7,000 earned by each employee. FICA taxes in effect at this time are 7.51 percent for both employee and employer on the first $48,000 earned by each employee during this year. During the current year, the cumulative earnings for each employee of the company are as follows:

Employee	Cumulative Earnings	Employee	Cumulative Earnings
Brown, E.	$28,620	Lavey, M.	$16,760
Caffey, B.	5,260	Lehman, L.	6,420
Evett, C.	32,820	Massie, M.	51,650
Harris, D.	30,130	Neal, M.	32,100
Hester, J.	52,250	Pruesch, R.	36,645
Jordan, M.	5,120	Widmer, J.	5,176

1. Prepare and complete a schedule with the following columns: Employee Name, Cumulative Earnings, Earnings Subject to FICA Taxes, and Earnings Subject to Unemployment Taxes. Total the columns.
2. Compute the FICA taxes and the federal and state unemployment taxes for Ultra Company.

**Exercise 11-8.
Net Pay
Calculation and
Payroll Entries
(L.O. 4, 5)**

Lynn Karas is an employee whose overtime pay is regulated by the Fair Labor Standards Act. Her hourly rate is $8, and during the week ended July 11, she worked forty-two hours. Lynn claims two exemptions, which include one for herself, on her W-4 form. So far this year she has earned $8,650. Each week $12 is deducted from her paycheck for medical insurance.

1. Compute the following items related to the pay for Lynn Karas for the week of July 11: (a) gross pay, (b) FICA taxes (assume a rate of 7.51 percent), (c) federal income tax withholding (use Figure 11-2), and (d) net pay.
2. Prepare a general journal entry to record the wages expense and related liabilities for Lynn Karas for the week ended July 11.

**Exercise 11-9.
Payroll
Transactions
(L.O. 4, 5)**

Monroe Howard earns a salary of $60,000 per year. FICA taxes are 7.51 percent up to $48,000. Federal unemployment insurance taxes are 6.2 percent of the first $7,000; however, a credit is allowed equal to the state unemployment insurance taxes of 5.4 percent on the $7,000. During the year, $15,000 was withheld for federal income taxes.

1. Prepare a general journal entry summarizing the payment of $60,000 to Howard during the year.
2. Prepare a general journal entry summarizing the employer payroll taxes on Howard's salary for the year.
3. Determine the total cost paid by Monroe Howard's employer to employ Howard for the year.

Interpreting Accounting Information

Texaco, Inc.*
(L.O. 3)

Texaco, one of the largest oil companies in the world, reported its loss of the largest damage judgment in history in its 1986 annual report as follows:

Note 17. Contingent Liabilities
Pennzoil Litigation
State Court Action. On December 10, 1985, the 151st District Court of Harris County, Texas entered judgment for Pennzoil Company of $7.5 billion actual damages, $3 billion punitive damages, and approximately $600 million prejudgment interest in *Pennzoil Company v. Texaco, Inc.,* an action in which Pennzoil claims that Texaco, Inc., tortiously interfered with Pennzoil's alleged contract to aquire 3/7ths interest in Getty. Interest began accruing on the judgment at the simple rate of 10% per annum from the date of the judgment. Texaco, Inc., believes that there is no legal basis for the judgment, which it believes is contrary to the evidence and applicable law. Texaco, Inc., is pursuing all available remedies to set aside or to reverse the judgment.

*   *   *

The outcome of the appeal on the preliminary injunction and the ultimate outcome of the Pennzoil litigation are not presently determinable, but could have a material adverse effect on the consolidated financial position and the results of the consolidated operations of Texaco, Inc.

On December 31, 1986, Texaco's retained earnings were $12.882 billion, and its cash and marketable securities totalled $3.0 billion. The company's net income for 1986 was $.725 billion.

After a series of court reversals and filing for bankruptcy in 1987, Texaco announced in December, 1987, an out-of-court settlement with Pennzoil for $3.0 billion. Although less than the original amount, it is still the largest damage payment in history.

Required

1. The FASB has established two conditions that a contingent liability must meet before it is recorded in the accounting records. What are the two conditions? Does the situation described in "Note 17: Contingent Liabilities" meet those conditions? Explain your answer.
2. Do the events of 1987 change your answer to part 1? Explain your answer.
3. What will be the effect of the settlement on Texaco's retained earnings, cash and marketable securities, and net income?

Problem Set A

**Problem 11A-1.
Notes Payable
Transactions and
End-of-Month
Period Entries**
(L.O. 2)

Prentiss Paper Company, whose fiscal year ends December 31, completed the following transactions involving notes payable:

Nov. 25 Purchased a new loading cart by issuing a sixty-day, 10 percent note for $21,600.
Dec. 16 Borrowed $25,000 from the bank to finance inventory by signing a ninety-day, 12 percent note. The face value of the note includes interest. Proceeds received were $24,250.
      31 Made end-of-year adjusting entry to accrue interest expense.
      31 Made end-of-year adjusting entry to recognize prepaid interest expired.

* Excerpts from the 1986 annual report used by permission of Texaco, Inc. Copyright 1986.

Dec. 31 Made end-of-year closing entry pertaining to interest expense.
Jan. 2 Made appropriate reversing entry.
      24 Paid off the loading cart note.
Mar. 16 Paid off the inventory note to the bank.

Required

1. Prepare general journal entries for these transactions (journal Page 41).
2. Open general ledger accounts for Prepaid Interest (114), Notes Payable (212), Interest Payable (214), and Interest Expense (721). Post the relevant portions of the entries to these general ledger accounts.

Problem 11A-2.
Property Tax and
Vacation Pay
Liabilities
(L.O. 2, 4, 5)

Chin Corporation accrues estimated liabilities for property taxes and vacation pay. The company's fiscal year ends June 30. The property taxes for the previous year were $36,000 and they are expected to increase 6 percent this year. Two weeks' vacation pay is given to each employee after one year of service. Chin management estimates that 75 percent of its employees will qualify for this benefit in the current year. In addition, the following information is available:

The property tax bill of $39,552 was received in September and paid on November 1.

Total payroll for July was $98,200. This amount includes $9,016 paid to employees on paid vacations.

Required

1. Prepare the monthly journal entries to record accrued property taxes for July through November and actual property taxes paid. (Round to nearest dollar.)
2. a. Prepare a general journal entry to record the vacation accrual expense for July.
   b. Prepare a general journal entry to record the wages of employees on vacation in July (ignore payroll deductions and taxes).

Problem 11A-3.
Product Warranty
Liability
(L.O. 2)

The Citation Company manufactures and sells food processors. The company guarantees the processors for five years. If a processor fails, the customer is charged a percentage of the retail price for replacement. That percentage is based on the age of the processor. In the past, management found only 3 percent of the processors sold required replacement under the warranty. Of those replaced, an average of 20 percent of the cost is collected under the replacement pricing policy. The average food processor costs the company $120. At the beginning of September, the account for estimated liability for product warranties had a credit balance of $104,000. During September, 250 processors were returned under the warranty. The cost of replacement was $27,000, of which $4,930 was recovered under the replacement pricing policy. During the month, the company sold 2,800 food processors.

Required

1. Prepare general journal entries to record the cost of food processors replaced under warranty and the estimated liability for product warranties for processors sold during the month.
2. Compute the balance of the estimated product warranty liabilities at the end of the month.

Problem 11A-4.
Payroll Entries
(L.O. 4, 5)

At the end of October, the payroll register for Mejias Corporation contained the following totals: sales salaries, $88,110; office salaries, $40,440; administrative salaries, $57,120; FICA taxes withheld, $13,108; federal income taxes withheld, $47,442; state income taxes withheld, $7,818; medical insurance deductions, $6,435; life insurance deductions, $5,856; union dues deductions, $684; and salaries subject to unemployment taxes, $28,620.

Required

Prepare general journal entries to record the following: (1) accrual of the monthly payroll, (2) payment of the net payroll, (3) accrual of employer's payroll taxes (assuming FICA tax equal to the amount for employees, a federal unemployment insurance tax of 0.8 percent, and a state unemployment tax of 5.4 percent), and (4) payment of all liabilities related to the payroll (assuming that all are settled at the same time).

Problem 11A-5.
Payroll Register
and Related
Entries
(L.O. 4, 5)

Huff Manufacturing Company employs seven people in the Drilling Division. All employees are paid an hourly wage except the foreman, who receives a monthly salary. Hourly employees are paid once a week and receive a set hourly rate for regular hours plus time-and-a-half for overtime. The employees and employer are subject to a 7.51 percent FICA tax on the first $48,000 earned by each employee. The unemployment insurance tax rates are 5.4 percent for the state and 0.3 percent for the federal government. The unemployment insurance tax applies to the first $7,000 earned by each employee and is levied only on the employer.

Each employee qualifies for the Huff Manufacturing Profit Sharing Plan. Under this plan each employee may contribute up to 10 percent of his or her gross income as a payroll withholding, and Huff Manufacturing Company matches this amount. The data for the last payday of October are presented below:

	Hours			Cumulative Gross Pay Excluding Current Pay	Percentage Contribution to Profit	Income Tax to Be
Employee	Regular	Overtime	Pay Rate	Period	Sharing Plan	Withheld
Branch, W.	40	4	$ 9.00	$14,350.00	2	$ 40.00
Choy, T.	40	2	8.50	6,275.00	5	48.00
Duran, P.	40	5	12.70	16,510.00	7	35.00
Finnegan, M.*	Salary	—	5,000.00	45,000.00	9	760.00
Patel, B.	40	—	12.50	15,275.00	3	60.00
Sammuals, J.	40	7	9.00	11,925.00	—	23.00
Tobin, R.	40	3	7.50	10,218.00	—	20.00

*Supervisory

Required

1. Prepare a payroll register for the pay period ended October 31. The payroll register should have the following columns:

Employee	Deductions
Total Hours	FICA Tax
Earnings	Federal Income Tax
Regular	Profit Sharing Plan
Overtime	Net Pay
Gross	Distribution
Cumulative	Drilling Wages Expense
	Supervisory Salaries Expense

2. Prepare a general journal entry to record the payroll and related liabilities for deductions for the period ended October 31.
3. Prepare general journal entries to record the expenses and related liabilities for the employer's payroll taxes (FICA, federal and state unemployment) and contribution to the profit sharing plan.
4. Prepare the October 31 entries for the transfer of sufficient cash from the company's regular checking account to a special Payroll Disbursement account and for the subsequent payment of employees.

Problem Set B

Problem 11B-1.
Notes Payable
Transactions and
End-of-Period
Entries
(L.O. 2)

Fairbrooks Corporation, whose fiscal year ends June 30, completed the following transactions involving notes payable:

May 11   Signed a ninety-day, 12 percent, $132,000 note payable to Village Bank for a working capital loan. The face value included interest. Proceeds received were $128,040.
21   Obtained a sixty-day extension on a $36,000 trade account payable owed to a supplier by signing a sixty-day, $36,000 note. Interest is in addition to the face value, at the rate of 14 percent.
June 30   Made end-of-year adjusting entry to accrue interest expense.
30   Made end-of-year adjusting entry to recognize prepaid interest expense.
30   Made end-of-year closing entry pertaining to interest expense.
July   1   Made appropriate reversing entry.
20   Paid off the note plus interest due the supplier.
Aug.   9   Paid amount due bank on ninety-day note.

Required

1. Prepare general journal entries for the above transactions (journal Page 28).
2. Open general ledger accounts for Prepaid Interest (114), Notes Payable (212), Interest Payable (214), and Interest Expense (721). Post the relevant portions of the entries to these general ledger accounts.

Problem 11B-2.
Property Tax and
Vacation Pay
Liabilities
(L.O. 2, 4, 5)

Brett Corporation prepares monthly financial statements and ends its fiscal year on June 30. In July, your first month as accountant for the company, you find that the company has not previously accrued estimated liabilities. In the past, the company, which has a large property tax bill, has charged property taxes to the month in which the bill is paid. The tax bill for last year was $36,000, and it is estimated that the tax will increase by 8 percent in the coming year. The tax bill is usually received on September 1, to be paid November 1.

You also discover that the company allows employees who have worked for the company for one year to take two weeks' paid vacation each year. The cost of these vacations had been charged to expense in the month of payment. Approximately 80 percent of the employees qualify for this benefit. You suggest to management that proper accounting treatment of these expenses is to spread their cost over the entire year. Management agrees and asks you to make the necessary adjustments.

Required

1. Figure the proper monthly charge to property taxes expense, and prepare general journal entries for the following:

   July 31 Accrual of property tax expense
   Aug. 31 Accrual of property tax expense
   Sept. 30 Accrual of property tax expense (assume actual bill is $40,860)
   Oct. 31 Accrual of property tax expense
   Nov. 1 Payment of property tax
   Nov. 30 Accrual of property tax expense

2. Assume that the total payroll for July is $568,000. This amount includes $21,300 paid to employees on paid vacations. (a) Compute the vacation pay expense for July. (b) Prepare a general journal entry to record the accrual of vacation pay expense for July. (c) Prepare a general journal entry to record the wages of employees on vacation in July (ignore payroll deductions and taxes).

Problem 11B-3.
Product Warranty
Liability
(L.O. 2)

Lighthouse Company is engaged in the retail sale of washing machines. Each machine has a twenty-four-month warranty on parts. If a repair under warranty is required, a charge for the labor is made. Management has found that 20 percent of the machines sold require some work before the warranty expires. Furthermore, the average cost of replacement parts has been $80 per repair. At the beginning of February, the account for the estimated liability for product warranties had a credit balance of $14,300. During February, 112 machines were returned under the warranty. The cost of the parts used in repairing the machines was $8,765, and $9,442 was collected as service revenue for the labor involved. During the month, Lighthouse Company sold 450 new machines.

Required

1. Prepare general journal entries to record each of the following: (a) the warranty work completed during the month, including related revenue; (b) the estimated liability for product warranties for machines sold during the month.
2. Compute the balance of the estimated product warranty liabilities at the end of the month.

Problem 11B-4.
Payroll Entries
(L.O. 4, 5)

The following payroll totals for the month of April were taken from the payroll register of Tobias Corporation: sales salaries, $58,200; office salaries, $28,500; general salaries, $24,840; FICA taxes withheld, $8,377; income taxes withheld, $15,720; medical insurance deductions, $3,290; life insurance deductions, $1,880; salaries subject to unemployment taxes, $78,300.

Required

Prepare general journal entries to record the following: (1) accrual of the monthly payroll, (2) payment of the net payroll, (3) accrual of employer's payroll taxes (assuming FICA tax equal to the amount for employees, a federal unemployment insurance tax of 0.8 percent, and a state unemployment tax of 5.4 percent), and (4) payment of all liabilities related to the payroll (assuming that all are settled at the same time).

**Problem 11B-5.
Payroll Register
and Related
Entries
(L.O. 4, 5)**

DiGregorio Pasta Company has seven employees. The salaried employees are paid on the last biweekly payday of each month. Employees paid hourly receive a set rate for regular hours plus one-half times their hourly rate for overtime hours. They are paid every two weeks. The employees and company are subject to 7.51 percent FICA taxes on the first $48,000 earned by each employee. The unemployment insurance tax rates are 5.4 percent for the state and 0.8 percent for the federal government. The unemployment insurance tax applies to the first $7,000 earned by each employee and is levied only on the employer.

The company maintains a supplemental benefits plan that includes medical insurance, life insurance, and additional retirement funds for employees. Under the plan, each employee contributes 4 percent of his or her gross income as a payroll withholding, and the company matches the amount. Data for the November 30 payroll, the last payday of November, follow:

| Employee | Hours | | Pay Rate | Cumulative Gross Pay Excluding Current Pay Period | Federal Income Tax to Be Withheld |
	Regular	Overtime			
Antonelli, J.	80	5	$ 8.00	$ 4,867.00	$ 71.00
Bertelli, A.	80	4	6.50	3,954.00	76.00
DiGregorio, G.*	Salary	—	5,000.00	50,000.00	985.00
Falcone, P.	80	—	5.00	8,250.00	32.00
Greco, B.*	Salary	—	2,000.00	20,000.00	294.00
Parilli, T.	80	20	10.00	12,000.00	103.00
Rosario, A.*	Salary	—	1,500.00	15,000.00	210.00

*Denotes administrative; the rest are sales

Required

1. Prepare a payroll register for the pay period ended November 30. The payroll register should have the following columns:

Employee	Deductions
Total Hours	FICA Tax
Earnings	Federal Income Tax
Regular	Supplemental Benefits Plan
Overtime	Net Pay
Gross	Distribution
Cumulative	Sales Expense
	Administrative Expense

2. Prepare a general journal entry to record the payroll and related liabilities for deductions for the period ended November 30.
3. Prepare general journal entries to record the expenses and related liabilities for the employer's payroll taxes and contribution to the supplemental benefits plan.
4. Prepare the entries on November 30 to transfer sufficient cash from the company's regular checking account to a special Payroll Disbursement account and for the subsequent payment of the employees.

Financial Decision Case

**Highland
Television Repair
(L.O. 1, 2, 4)**

Jerry Highland opened a small television repair shop on January 2, 19xx. He also sold a small line of television sets. Jerry's wife, Jane, was the sole salesperson for the television sets, and Jerry was the only person doing repairs. (Jerry had worked for another television repair store for twenty years, where he was the supervisor for six repairpersons.) The new business was such a success that he hired two assistants on March 1, 19xx. In October, Jerry received a letter from the Internal Revenue Service informing him that he had failed to file any tax reports for his business since its inception, and probably owed a considerable amount of taxes. Since Jerry has limited experience in maintaining business records, he has brought the letter and all his business records to you for help. The records include a checkbook, canceled checks, deposit slips, invoices from his suppliers, notice of annual property taxes of $4,620 due to the city November 1, 19xx, and a promissory note to his father-in-law for $5,000. He wants you to determine what his business owes to the government and other parties.

You analyze all his records and determine the following:

Unpaid supplies invoices	$ 3,160
Sales (excluding sales tax)	88,540
Workers' salaries	20,400
Repair revenues	120,600

You learn that the shop workers are each paid $300 per week. Each is married and claims four income tax exemptions. The current FICA tax is 7.51 percent. The FUTA tax is 5.4 percent to the state and 0.8 percent to the federal government on the first $7,000 earned by each employee. Jerry has not filed a sales tax report to the state (5 percent of sales).

Required

1. Given these limited facts, determine Highland Television Repair's liabilities as of October 31, 19xx. (For employee income tax withholding, use Figure 11-2. Compute payroll-related liabilities on the two assistants only.)
2. What additional information would you want from Jerry to satisfy yourself that all liabilities have been identified?

Answers to Self-Test

1. b	3. b	5. a	7. c	9. c
2. d	4. b	6. c	8. d	10. c

LEARNING OBJECTIVES

1. Describe the nature, types, and issues of accounting for long-term assets.
2. Account for the cost of property, plant, and equipment.
3. Define depreciation, state the factors that affect its computation, and show how to record it.
4. Compute periodic depreciation under the (a) straight-line method, (b) production method, and (c) accelerated methods, including (1) sum-of-the-years'-digits method and (2) declining-balance method.
5. Apply depreciation methods to problems of partial years, revised rates, items of low unit cost, groups of similar items, and accelerated cost recovery.
6. Record property, plant, and equipment transactions in the plant asset records.

CHAPTER 12

Long-Term Assets: Acquisition and Depreciation

In this chapter, you will begin the study of long-term assets. The focus will be on the major categories of long-term assets and accounting for their acquisition cost. You will also study the allocation of the costs of plant assets over their useful life through depreciation and the control of plant assets. Chapter 13 will continue the study of long-term assets. After studying this chapter, you should be able to meet the learning objectives listed on the left.

Long-Term Assets

Let us take a closer look at long-term assets, which were defined briefly in Chapter 10. **Long-term assets** are assets that (1) have a useful life of more than one year, (2) are acquired for use in the operation of the business, and (3) are not intended for resale to customers. For many years, it was common to refer to long-term assets as **fixed assets**, but use of this term is declining because the word *fixed* implies that they last forever.

Although there is no strict minimum length of time for an asset to be classified as long term, the most common criterion is that the asset must be capable of repeated use for a period of at least a year. Included in this category is equipment that is used only in peak or emergency periods, such as a generator.

Assets not used in the normal course of business should not be included in this category. Thus, land held for speculative reasons or buildings that are no longer used in ordinary business operations should not be included in the property, plant, and equipment category. Instead, they should be classified as long-term investments.

Finally, if an item is held for resale to customers, it should be classified as inventory—not plant and equipment—no matter how durable it is. For example, a printing press held for sale by a printing press manufacturer would be considered inventory, whereas the same printing press would be plant and equipment for a printing company that buys the press to use it in its operations.

Life of Long-Term Assets

OBJECTIVE 1
Describe the
nature, types,
and issues of
accounting for
long-term assets

The primary accounting issue in dealing with short-term assets such as inventory and prepaid assets was to determine how much of the asset benefited the current period and how much should be carried forward as an asset to benefit future periods. Costs must be allocated to the periods that benefit from the use of the asset due to the matching rule. Note that exactly the same matching issue applies to long-term assets since they are long-term unexpired costs.

It is helpful to think of a long-term asset as a bundle of services that are to be used in the operation of the business over a period of years. A delivery truck may provide 100,000 miles of service over its life. A piece of equipment may have the potential to produce 500,000 parts. A building may provide shelter for fifty years. As each of these assets is purchased, the company is paying in advance (prepaying) for 100,000 miles, 500,000 parts, or fifty years of service. In essence, each of these assets is a type of long-term prepaid expense. The accounting problem is to spread the cost of these services over the useful life of the asset. As the services benefit the company over the years, the cost becomes an expense rather than an asset.

Types of Long-Term Assets

Long-term assets are customarily divided into the following categories:

Asset	Expense
Tangible Assets	
Land	None
Plant, buildings, and equipment (plant assets)	Depreciation
Natural resources	Depletion
Intangible Assets	Amortization

Tangible assets have physical substance. Land is a tangible asset, and because it has an unlimited life it is the only tangible asset not subject to depreciation or other expense. Plant, buildings, and equipment (referred to hereafter as plant assets) are subject to depreciation. **Depreciation** is the periodic allocation of the cost of a tangible long-lived asset over its useful life. The term applies to manmade assets only. Note that accounting for depreciation is an allocation process, not a valuation process. This point is discussed in more detail later.

Natural resources differ from land in that they are purchased for the substances that can be taken from the land and used up rather than for the value of their location. Among natural resources are ore from mines, oil and gas from oil and gas fields, and lumber from forests. Natural resources are subject to depletion rather than to depreciation. The term **depletion** refers to the exhaustion of a natural resource through mining, cutting, pumping, or otherwise using up the resource, and to the way in which the cost is allocated.

Intangible assets are long-term assets that do not have physical substance and in most cases have to do with legal rights or advantages held.

Among them are patents, copyrights, trademarks, franchises, organization costs, leaseholds, leasehold improvements, and goodwill. The allocation of the cost of intangible assets to the periods that they benefit is called **amortization**. Even though the current assets accounts receivable and prepaid expenses do not have physical substance, they are not intangible assets because they are not long term.

The unexpired part of the cost of an asset is generally called its book value or *carrying value*. The latter term is used in this book when referring to long-term assets. The carrying value of plant assets, for instance, is cost less accumulated depreciation.

Issues of Accounting for Long-Term Assets

As with inventories and prepaid expenses, there are two important accounting problems connected with long-term assets. The first is determining how much of the total cost should be allocated to expense in the current accounting period. The second is figuring how much should remain on the balance sheet as an asset to benefit future periods. To solve these problems, four important questions (shown in Figure 12-1) must be answered:

1. How is the cost of the long-term assets determined?
2. How should the expired portion of the cost of the long-term assets be allocated against revenues over time?
3. How should later expenditures such as repairs, maintenance, and additions be treated?

Figure 12-1. Issues of Accounting for Long-Term Assets

4. How should disposal of long-term assets be recorded?

The remainder of this chapter deals with the answers to questions **1** and **2**. The discussion of questions **3** and **4** will be postponed until Chapter 13. Specific discussion of natural resources and intangibles is also included in Chapter 13.

Acquisition Cost of Property, Plant, and Equipment

OBJECTIVE 2
Account for the cost of property, plant, and equipment

The acquisition cost of property, plant, and equipment includes all expenditures reasonable and necessary to get them in place and ready for use. For example, the cost of installing and testing a machine is a legitimate cost of the machine. However, if the machine is damaged during installation, the cost of repairing the machine is an operating expense and not a cost of the machine.

Cost is easiest to determine when a transaction is made for cash. In this case, the cost of the asset is equal to the cash paid for the asset plus expenditures for freight, insurance while in transit, installation, and other necessary related costs. If a debt is incurred in the purchase of the asset, the interest charges are not a cost of the asset but a cost of borrowing the money to buy the asset. They are therefore an expense for the period. An exception to this principle is that interest costs during the construction of an asset are properly included as a cost of the asset.[1]

Expenditures such as freight, insurance while in transit, and installation are included in the cost of the asset because these expenditures are necessary for the asset to function. In accordance with the matching rule, they are allocated to the useful life of the asset rather than charged as an expense in the current period.

Some of the problems of determining the cost of a long-lived asset are demonstrated in the illustrations for land, buildings, equipment, land improvements, and group purchases presented in the next few sections.

Land

There are often expenditures in addition to the purchase price of the land that should be debited to the Land account. Some examples are commissions to real estate agents; lawyers' fees; accrued taxes paid by the purchaser; cost of draining, clearing, and grading; and assessments for local improvements such as streets and sewage systems. The cost of landscaping is usually debited to the land account also because these improvements are relatively permanent.

Let us assume that a company buys land for a new retail operation. It pays a net purchase price of $170,000, pays brokerage fees of $6,000 and legal fees of $2,000, pays $10,000 to have an old building on the site torn

---

1. "Capitalization of Interest Cost," *Statement of Financial Accounting Standards No. 34* (Stamford, Conn.: Financial Accounting Standards Board, 1979), par. 9–11.

down, receives $4,000 salvage from the old building, and pays $1,000 to have the site graded. The cost of the land will be $185,000, determined as follows:

Net purchase price		$170,000
Brokerage fees		6,000
Legal fees		2,000
Tearing down old building	$10,000	
Less salvage	4,000	6,000
Grading		1,000
		$185,000

Land Improvements

Improvements to real estate such as driveways, parking lots, and fences have a limited life and so are subject to depreciation. They should be recorded in an account called Land Improvements rather than in the Land account.

Buildings

When an existing building is purchased, its cost includes the purchase price plus all repairs and other expenses required to put it in usable condition. When a business constructs its own building, the cost includes all reasonable and necessary expenditures, such as those for materials, labor, part of the overhead and other indirect costs, the architects' fees, insurance during construction, interest on construction loans during the period of construction, the lawyers' fees, and building permits. If outside contractors are used in the construction, the net contract price plus other expenditures necessary to put the building in usable condition are included.

Equipment

The cost of equipment includes all expenditures connected with purchasing the equipment and preparing it for use. These expenditures include invoice price less cash discounts; freight or transportation, including insurance; excise taxes and tariffs; buying expenses; installation costs; and test runs to ready the equipment for operation.

Group Purchases

Sometimes land and other assets will be purchased for a lump sum. Because land is a nondepreciable asset and has an unlimited life, separate ledger accounts must be kept for land and the other assets. For this reason, the lump-sum purchase price must be apportioned between the land and the other assets. For example, assume that a building and the land on which it is situated are purchased for a lump-sum payment of $85,000. The apportionment can be made by determining the price of each if purchased separately and applying the appropriate percentages to the lump-sum price. Assume that appraisals yield estimates of $10,000 for the land and $90,000 for the building, if purchased separately. In that case, 10 percent, or $8,500, of the lump-sum price would be allocated to the land and 90 percent, or $76,500, would be allocated to the building, as follows:

	Appraisal	Percentage	Apportionment
Land	$ 10,000	10	$ 8,500
Building	90,000	90	76,500
Totals	$100,000	100	$85,000

Accounting for Depreciation

OBJECTIVE 3
Define depreciation, state the factors that affect its computation, and show how to record it

Depreciation accounting is described by the AICPA as follows:

The cost of a productive facility is one of the costs of the services it renders during its useful economic life. Generally accepted accounting principles require that this cost be spread over the expected useful life of the facility in such a way as to allocate it as equitably as possible to the periods during which services are obtained from the use of the facility. This procedure is known as depreciation accounting, a system of accounting which aims to distribute the cost or other basic value of tangible capital assets, less salvage (if any), over the estimated useful life of the unit . . . in a systematic and rational manner. It is a process of allocation, not of valuation.[2]

This description contains several important points. First, all tangible assets except land have a limited useful life. Because of the limited useful life, the cost of these assets must be distributed as expenses over the years they benefit. Physical deterioration and obsolescence are the major causes of the limited useful life of a depreciable asset. The **physical deterioration** of tangible assets results from use and from exposure to the elements, such as wind and sun. Periodic repairs and a sound maintenance policy may keep buildings and equipment in good operating order and extract the maximum useful life from them, but every machine or building at some point must be discarded. The need for depreciation is not eliminated by repairs. **Obsolescence** is the process of becoming out of date. With fast-changing technology as well as fast-changing demands, machinery and even buildings often become obsolete before they wear out. Accountants do not distinguish between physical deterioration and obsolescence because they are interested in the length of the useful life of the asset regardless of what limits that useful life.

Second, the term *depreciation*, as used in accounting, does not refer to the physical deterioration of an asset or the decrease in market value of

2. *Financial Accounting Standards: Original Pronouncements as of July 1, 1977* (Stamford, Conn.: Financial Accounting Standards Board, 1977), ARB No. 43, Chapt. 9, Sec. C, par. 5.

an asset over time. Depreciation means the allocation of the cost of a plant asset to the periods that benefit from the services of the asset. The term is used to describe the gradual conversion of the cost of the asset into an expense.

Third, depreciation is not a process of valuation. Accounting records are kept in accordance with the cost principle and thus are not meant to be indicators of changing price levels. It is possible that, through an advantageous buy and specific market conditions, the market value of a building may rise. Nevertheless, depreciation must continue to be recorded because it is the result of an allocation, not a valuation, process. Eventually the building will wear out or become obsolete regardless of interim fluctuations in market value.

Factors That Affect the Computation of Depreciation

Four factors affect the computation of depreciation. They are: (1) cost, (2) residual value, (3) depreciable cost, and (4) estimated useful life.

Cost. As explained above, cost is the net purchase price plus all reasonable and necessary expenditures to get the asset in place and ready for use.

Residual Value. The residual value of an asset is its estimated net scrap, salvage, or trade-in value as of the estimated date of disposal. Other terms often used to describe residual value are **salvage value** and **disposal value.**

Depreciable Cost. The **depreciable cost** of an asset is its cost less its residual value. For example, a truck that costs $12,000 and has a residual value of $3,000 would have a depreciable cost of $9,000. Depreciable cost must be allocated over the useful life of the asset.

Estimated Useful Life. The **estimated useful life** of an asset is the total number of service units expected from the asset. Service units may be measured in terms of years the asset is expected to be used, units expected to be produced, miles expected to be driven, or similar measures. In computing the estimated useful life of an asset, the accountant should consider all relevant information including (1) past experience with similar assets, (2) the asset's present condition, (3) the company's repair and maintenance policy, (4) current technological and industry trends, and (5) local conditions such as weather.

As introduced in Chapter 3, depreciation is recorded at the end of the accounting period by an adjusting entry that takes the following form:

Depreciation Expense, Asset Name   xxx
   Accumulated Depreciation, Asset Name   xxx
     To record depreciation for the period

Methods of Computing Depreciation

OBJECTIVE 4
Compute periodic depreciation under each of four methods

Many methods are used to allocate the cost of plant and equipment to accounting periods through depreciation. Each of them is proper for certain circumstances. The most common methods are (1) the straight-line method, (2) the production method, and (3) two accelerated methods known as the sum-of-the-years'-digits method and the declining-balance method.

Straight-Line Method

OBJECTIVE 4a
Compute periodic depreciation under the straight-line method

When the **straight-line method** is used to allocate depreciation, the depreciable cost of the asset is spread evenly over the life of the asset. The straight-line method is based on the assumption that depreciation depends only on the passage of time. The depreciation expense for each period is computed by dividing the depreciable cost (cost of the depreciating asset less its estimated residual value) by the number of accounting periods in the estimated useful life. The rate of depreciation is the same in each year. Suppose, for example, that a delivery truck costs $10,000 and has an estimated residual value of $1,000 at the end of its estimated useful life of five years. In this case, the annual depreciation would be $1,800 under the straight-line method. This calculation is as follows:

$$\frac{\text{Cost} - \text{residual value}}{\text{Useful life}} = \frac{\$10,000 - \$1,000}{5} = \$1,800$$

The depreciation for the five years would be as follows:

Depreciation Schedule, Straight-Line Method

	Cost	Yearly Depreciation	Accumulated Depreciation	Carrying Value
Date of purchase	$10,000	—	—	$10,000
End of first year	10,000	$1,800	$1,800	8,200
End of second year	10,000	1,800	3,600	6,400
End of third year	10,000	1,800	5,400	4,600
End of fourth year	10,000	1,800	7,200	2,800
End of fifth year	10,000	1,800	9,000	1,000

There are three important points to note from the schedule for the straight-line depreciation method. First, the depreciation is the same each year. Second, the accumulated depreciation increases uniformly. Third, the carrying value decreases uniformly until it reaches the estimated residual value.

Production Method

The **production method** of depreciation is based on the assumption that depreciation is solely the result of use and that the passage of time plays no role in the depreciation process. If we assume that the delivery truck from the previous example has an estimated useful life of 90,000 miles, the depreciation cost per mile would be determined as follows:

$$\frac{\text{Cost} - \text{residual value}}{\text{Estimated units of useful life}} = \frac{\$10,000 - \$1,000}{90,000 \text{ miles}} = \$.10 \text{ per mile}$$

OBJECTIVE 4b
Compute periodic depreciation under the production method

If we assume that the mileage use of the truck was 20,000 miles for the first year, 30,000 miles for the second, 10,000 miles for the third, 20,000 miles for the fourth, and 10,000 miles for the fifth, the depreciation schedule for the delivery truck would appear as follows:

Depreciation Schedule, Production Method

	Cost	Miles	Yearly Depreciation	Accumulated Depreciation	Carrying Value
Date of purchase	$10,000	—	—	—	$10,000
End of first year	10,000	20,000	$2,000	$2,000	8,000
End of second year	10,000	30,000	3,000	5,000	5,000
End of third year	10,000	10,000	1,000	6,000	4,000
End of fourth year	10,000	20,000	2,000	8,000	2,000
End of fifth year	10,000	10,000	1,000	9,000	1,000

Note the direct relation between the amount of depreciation each year and the units of output or use. Also, the accumulated depreciation increases each year in direct relation to units of output or use. Finally, the carrying value decreases each year in direct relation to units of output or use until it reaches the estimated residual value.

Under the production method, the unit of output or use that is used to measure estimated useful life for each asset should be appropriate for that asset. For example, the number of items produced may be appropriate for one machine, whereas the number of hours of use may be a better indicator of depreciation for another. The production method should only be used when the output of an asset over its useful life can be estimated with reasonable accuracy.

Accelerated Methods

Accelerated methods of depreciation result in relatively large amounts of depreciation in the early years and smaller amounts in later years. These methods, which are based on the passage of time, assume that many kinds of plant assets are most efficient when new, so they provide more and better service in the early years of useful life. It is consistent with the matching rule to allocate more depreciation to the early years than to later years if the benefits or services received in the early years are greater.

The accelerated methods also recognize that changing technologies make some equipment lose service value rapidly. Thus it is realistic to allocate more to depreciation in current years than in future years. New inventions and products result in obsolescence of equipment bought earlier, making it necessary to replace equipment sooner than if our technology changed more slowly.

Another argument in favor of accelerated methods is that repair expense is likely to be greater in future years than in current years. Thus the total of repair and depreciation expense remains fairly constant over a period of years. This result naturally assumes that the services received from the asset are roughly equal from year to year.

OBJECTIVE 4c(1)
Compute periodic depreciation under the sum-of-the-years'-digits method

Sum-of-the-Years'-Digits Method. Under the **sum-of-the-years'-digits method**, the years in the service life of an asset are added. Their sum becomes the denominator of a series of fractions that are applied against the depreciable cost of the asset in allocating the total depreciation over the estimated useful life. The numerators of the fractions are the individual years in the estimated useful life of the asset in their reverse order.

For the delivery truck used in the illustrations above, the estimated useful life is five years. The sum of the years' digits is as follows:[3]

$$1 + 2 + 3 + 4 + 5 = 15$$

The annual depreciation is then determined by multiplying the depreciable cost of $9,000 ($10,000 − $1,000) by each of the following fractions: 5/15, 4/15, 3/15, 2/15, 1/15. The depreciation schedule for the sum-of-the-years'-digits method is as follows:

Depreciation Schedule, Sum-of-the-Years'-Digits Method

	Cost	Yearly Depreciation		Accumulated Depreciation	Carrying Value
Date of purchase	$10,000	—		—	$10,000
End of first year	10,000	(5/15 × $9,000)	$3,000	$3,000	7,000
End of second year	10,000	(4/15 × $9,000)	2,400	5,400	4,600
End of third year	10,000	(3/15 × $9,000)	1,800	7,200	2,800
End of fourth year	10,000	(2/15 × $9,000)	1,200	8,400	1,600
End of fifth year	10,000	(1/15 × $9,000)	600	9,000	1,000

From the schedule, note that the yearly depreciation is greatest in the first year and declines each year after that. Also, the accumulated depreciation increases by a smaller amount each year. Finally, the carrying

---

3. The denominator used in the sum-of-the-years'-digits method can be computed quickly from the following formula:

$$S = \frac{N(N + 1)}{2}$$

where S equals the sum of the digits and N equals the number of years in the estimated useful life. For example, for an asset with an estimated useful life of ten years, the sum of the digits equals 55, calculated as follows:

$$S = \frac{10(10 + 1)}{2} = \frac{110}{2} = 55$$

value decreases each year by the amount of depreciation until it reaches the residual value.

OBJECTIVE 4c(2)
Compute periodic depreciation under the declining-balance method

Declining-Balance Method. The **declining-balance method** is an accelerated method of depreciation in which depreciation is computed by applying a fixed rate to the carrying value (the declining balance) of a long-lived asset. It is based on the same assumption as the sum-of-the-years'-digits method. Both methods result in higher depreciation charges during the early years of an asset's life. Though any fixed rate might be used under the method, the most common rate is a percentage equal to twice the straight-line percentage. When twice the straight-line rate is used, the method is usually called the **double-declining-balance method.**

In our earlier example, the delivery truck had an estimated useful life of five years. Consequently, under the straight-line method, the percentage depreciation for each year was 20 percent (100 percent ÷ 5 years).

Under the double-declining-balance method, the fixed percentage rate is therefore 40 percent (2 × 20 percent). This fixed rate of 40 percent is applied to the *remaining carrying value* at the end of each year. Estimated residual value is not taken into account in figuring depreciation except in the last year of an asset's useful life, when depreciation is limited to the amount necessary to bring the carrying value down to the estimated residual value. The depreciation schedule for this method is as follows:

Depreciation Schedule, Double-Declining-Balance Method

	Cost	Yearly Depreciation		Accumulated Depreciation	Carrying Value
Date of purchase	$10,000	—		—	$10,000
End of first year	10,000	(40% × $10,000)	$4,000	$4,000	6,000
End of second year	10,000	(40% × $6,000)	2,400	6,400	3,600
End of third year	10,000	(40% × $3,600)	1,440	7,840	2,160
End of fourth year	10,000	(40% × $2,160)	864	8,704	1,296
End of fifth year	10,000		296*	9,000	1,000

*Depreciation limited to amount necessary to reduce carrying value to residual value.
$296 = $1,296 (previous carrying value) – $1,000 (residual value)

Note that the fixed rate is always applied to the carrying value of the previous year. Next, the depreciation is greatest in the first year and declines each year after that. Finally, the depreciation in the last year is limited to the amount necessary to reduce carrying value to residual value.

Comparing the Four Methods

A visual comparison may provide a better understanding of the four depreciation methods described above. Figure 12-2 compares periodic depreciation and carrying value under the four methods. In the graph that

Figure 12-2. Graphical Comparison of Four Methods of Determining Depreciation

shows yearly depreciation, straight-line depreciation is uniform over the five-year period at $1,800. However, both accelerated depreciation methods (sum-of-the-years'-digits and declining-balance) begin at amounts greater than straight-line ($3,000 and $4,000, respectively), and decrease each year to amounts less than straight-line ($600 and $296, respectively). The production method does not produce a regular pattern of depreciation because of the random fluctuation of the depreciation from year to year. These yearly depreciation patterns are reflected in the carrying value graph. For instance, the carrying value for the straight-line method is always greater than that for the accelerated methods. However, in the latter graph, each method starts in the same place (cost of $10,000) and ends at the same place (residual value of $1,000). It is the patterns during the useful life of the asset that differ for each method.

The depreciation methods used by six hundred large companies are illustrated in Figure 12-3.

Special Problems of Depreciating Plant Assets

The illustrations used so far in this chapter have been simplified to explain the concepts and methods of depreciation. In real business practice, there is often a need to (1) calculate depreciation for partial years, (2) revise depreciation rates on the basis of new estimates of the useful

Figure 12-3. Depreciation Methods Used by 600 Large Companies

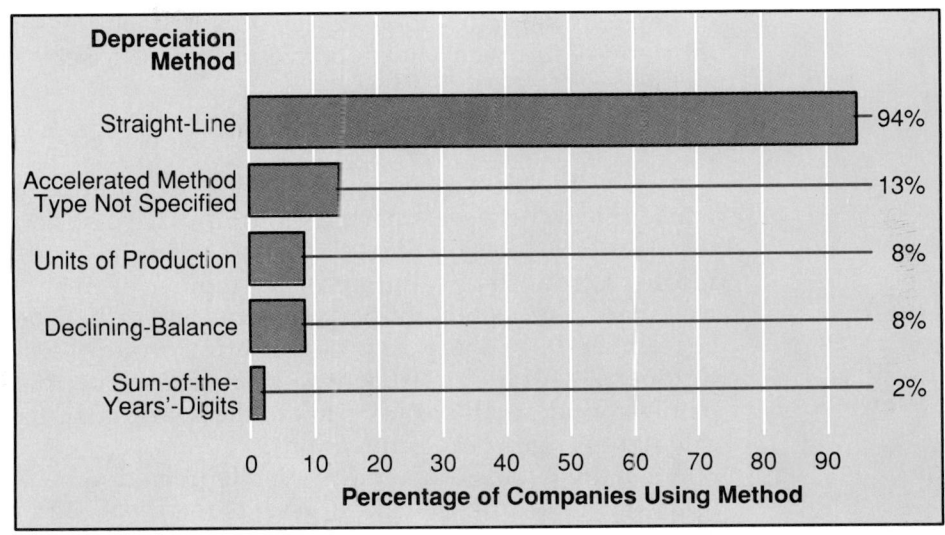

Total percentage exceeds 100 because some companies used different methods for different types of depreciable assets.

Source: American Institute of Certified Public Accountants, *Accounting Trends and Techniques* (New York: AICPA, 1987), p. 296.

life or residual value, (3) develop more practical ways of depreciating items of low unit cost, (4) group together items that are alike in order to calculate depreciation, and (5) use the accelerated cost recovery method for tax purposes. The next sections discuss these five cases.

Depreciation for Partial Years

OBJECTIVE 5
Apply depreciation methods to problems of partial years, revised rates, items of low unit cost, groups of similar items, and accelerated cost recovery

So far, the illustrations of the depreciation methods have assumed that the plant assets were purchased at the beginning or end of the accounting period. However, business people do not often buy assets exactly at the beginning or end of the accounting period. In most cases, they buy the assets when they are needed and sell or discard them when they are no longer useful or needed. The time of the year is normally not a factor in the decision. Consequently, it is often necessary to calculate depreciation for partial years.

For example, assume that a piece of equipment is purchased for $3,500 and that it has an estimated useful life of six years, with an estimated residual value of $500. Assume also that it is purchased on September 5 and that the yearly accounting period ends on December 31. Depreciation must be recorded for four months, or four-twelfths of the year. This factor is applied to the calculated depreciation for the entire year. The four months' depreciation under the straight-line method is calculated as follows:

$$\frac{\$3,500 - \$500}{6 \text{ years}} \times 4/12 = \$167$$

For the other depreciation methods, most companies will compute the first year's depreciation and then multiply by the partial year factor. For example, if the company used the double-declining-balance method on the above equipment, the depreciation on the asset would be computed as follows:

$$\$3,500 \times .33 \times 4/12 = \$385$$

Typically, the depreciation calculation is rounded off to the nearest whole month because a partial month's depreciation is not usually material and it makes the calculation easier. In this case, depreciation was recorded from the beginning of September even though the purchase was made on September 5. If the equipment had been purchased on September 16 or thereafter, depreciation would be charged beginning October 1, as if the equipment were purchased on that date. Some companies round off all partial years to the nearest one-half year for ease of calculation (half-year convention).

When an asset is disposed of, the depreciation on it must be brought up to date. For example, if the asset is not disposed of at the beginning or end of the year, depreciation must be recorded for a partial year, reflecting the time to the date of disposal. The accounting treatment of disposals is covered in Chapter 13.

Revision of Depreciation Rates

Because depreciation rates are based on an estimate of the useful life of an asset, the periodic depreciation charge is seldom precisely accurate. Sometimes it is very inadequate or excessive. This situation may result from an underestimate or overestimate of the asset's useful life or perhaps from a wrong estimate of the residual value. What action should be taken when it is found, after using a piece of equipment for several years, that the equipment will not last as long as—or will last longer than—originally thought? Sometimes it is necessary to revise the estimate of the useful life, so that the periodic depreciation expense increases or decreases. In such a case, the method for correcting depreciation is to spread the undepreciated cost of the asset over the years of remaining useful life.

Under this method, the annual depreciation expense is increased or decreased so that the remaining depreciation of the asset will reduce its carrying value to residual value at the end of the remaining useful life. To illustrate, assume that a delivery truck was purchased for a price of $7,000, with a residual value of $1,000. At the time of the purchase, it was thought that the truck would last six years, and it was depreciated on the straight-line basis. However, after two years of intensive use, it is determined that the delivery truck will last only two more years and will continue to carry an estimated residual value of $1,000 at the end of the two years. In other words, at the end of the second year, the estimated useful life has been reduced from six years to four years. At that time, the asset account and its related accumulated depreciation account would appear as follows:

Delivery Truck		Accumulated Depreciation, Delivery Truck	
Cost 7,000		Depreciation, year 1	1,000
		Depreciation, year 2	1,000

The remaining depreciable cost is computed as follows:

$$\underbrace{\text{cost}} \quad \text{minus} \quad \underbrace{\text{depreciation already taken}} \quad \text{minus} \quad \underbrace{\text{residual value}}$$

$$\$7,000 \quad - \quad \$2,000 \quad - \quad \$1,000 \quad = \$4,000$$

The new annual periodic depreciation charge is computed by dividing the remaining depreciable cost of $4,000 by the remaining useful life of two years. Therefore, the new periodic depreciation charge is $2,000. The annual adjusting entry for depreciation for the next two years would be as follows:

Dec. 31	Depreciation Expense, Delivery Truck	2,000	
	Accumulated Depreciation, Delivery Truck		2,000
	To record depreciation expense for the year		

This method of revising depreciation is used widely in industry. It is also supported by the Accounting Principles Board of the AICPA in Accounting Principles Board *Opinion No. 9* and *Opinion No. 20*.

Accounting for Assets of Low Unit Cost

Some classes of plant assets are made up of many individual items of low unit cost. In this category are included small tools such as hammers, wrenches, and drills, as well as dies, molds, patterns, and spare parts. Because of their large numbers, hard usage, breakage, and pilferage, assets such as these are relatively short-lived and require constant replacement. It is impractical to use the ordinary depreciation methods for such assets, and it is often costly to keep records of individual items.

There are two basic methods for accounting for plant assets of low unit cost. The first method is simply to charge the items as expenses when they are purchased. This method assumes that the annual loss on these items from use, depreciation, breakage, and other causes will approximately equal the amount of these items purchased during the year.

The second method used for plant assets of low unit cost is to account for them on an inventory basis. This method is best used when the amounts of items purchased vary greatly from year to year. The inventory basis of accounting for items of low unit cost is very similar to the method of accounting for supplies, which you already know. Let us assume that a company's asset account for Spare Parts on hand at the beginning of the accounting period is represented by a debit balance. As spare parts are purchased during the accounting period, their cost is debited to this account. At the end of the period, a physical inventory of usable spare parts on hand in the factory is taken. This inventory amount is subtracted from the end-of-period balance in the Spare Parts account to determine the cost of spare parts lost, broken, and used during this period. This cost, assumed in this case to be $700, is then charged to an expense account as a work sheet adjustment with the adjusting entry as follows:

Dec. 31	Spare Parts Expense	700	
	Spare Parts		700
	To record cost of spare parts used or lost during the period		

Group Depreciation

To say that the estimated useful life of an asset, such as a piece of equipment, is six years means that the average piece of equipment of that type is expected to last six years. In reality, some equipment may last only two or three years, and other equipment may last eight or nine years, or longer. For this reason and also for reasons of convenience, large companies will group items of similar assets such as trucks, power lines, office equipment, or transformers together for purposes of calculating depreciation. This method is called **group depreciation.** Group depreciation is used widely in all fields of industry and business. A recent survey of large businesses indicated that 65 percent used group depreciation for all or part of their plant assets.[4]

Cost Recovery for Federal Tax Purposes

In 1981, Congress dramatically changed the rules for tax depreciation by substituting for depreciation methods similar to those used for financial reporting a new method called **Accelerated Cost Recovery System (ACRS).** ACRS was a completely new and mandatory cost recovery system that for tax purposes discarded the concepts of estimated useful life and residual value and instead required that a cost recovery allowance be computed (1) on the unadjusted cost of property being recovered, and (2) over a period of years prescribed by the law for all property of similar types. Recovery allowances could be calculated by the straight-line method or by prescribed percentages that approximated 150 percent of the declining-balance method with a half-year convention. ACRS recovery property is generally defined as tangible property subject to depreciation and placed in service after December 31, 1980, and before January 1, 1987. Property purchased before January 1, 1981 is subject to the accounting depreciation methods presented earlier in this chapter.

4. Edward P. McTague, "Accounting for Trade-Ins of Operational Assets," *The National Public Accountant* (January 1986), p. 39.

In 1986, Congress passed the Tax Reform Act of 1986, arguably the most sweeping revision of federal tax laws since the original enactment of the Internal Revenue Code in 1913. The new Modified Accelerated Cost Recovery System (MACRS) retains the ACRS concepts of prescribed recovery periods for different classes of property, calculation of recovery allowances on the basis of the unadjusted cost of property, and elective use of the straight-line method or an accelerated method of cost recovery. The accelerated method prescribed under MACRS for most property other than real estate is 200 percent declining balance with a half-year convention (only one half-year's depreciation is allowed in the year of purchase and one half-year is taken in the last year). In addition, the period over which the cost may be recovered has been increased. Recovery of the cost of property placed in service after December 31, 1986 will be calculated as prescribed in the new law. Recovery of the cost of property placed in service before January 1, 1987 will continue to be calculated under ACRS. There is one exception. For property placed in service after July 31, 1986, the new law can be elected based on a property-by-property evaluation. In summary,

Date Property Purchased	Applicable Methods
Before January 1, 1981	Accounting depreciation methods
After December 31, 1980 but before January 1, 1987	ACRS
January 1, 1987 or after	MACRS

The intent of Congress, in both ACRS and MACRS, was to encourage businesses to invest in new plant and equipment by allowing them to write the assets off rapidly. Both ACRS and MACRS accelerate the write-off of these investments in two ways. First, the recovery periods they prescribe are often shorter than the estimated useful lives used for calculating book depreciation. Second, the accelerated methods allowed under ACRS and the new law provide for recovery of most of the cost of the investments early in the recovery period. Recovery will generally be more rapid under MACRS than under ACRS because of the faster accelerated method allowed. In some cases, however, MACRS provides longer recovery periods. For example, automobiles, light trucks, and light tools were classified as three-year property under ACRS. Under the new law, light tools continue to be three-year property, but automobiles and light trucks are five-year property. Table 12-1 shows the percentages of asset costs that can be written off under ACRS and MACRS.

The use of ACRS may be demonstrated using a delivery truck with a cost of $7,000, an estimated useful life of six years, and an estimated residual value of $1,000. Under ACRS, the delivery truck is a three-year property. The depreciation expense for federal income tax purposes is determined for each year as follows:

Table 12-1. Old and New Depreciation Rates for Federal Income Tax Purposes				
	ACRS		MACRS*	
Year	3-Year Property	5-Year Property	3-Year Property	5-Year Property
1	25%	15%	33.33%	20%
2	38	22	44.45	32
3	37	21	14.81	19.2
4		21	7.41	11.52
5		21		11.52
6				5.76

* Because of the half-year convention, an additional year is added on to each property year category (e.g., there are four depreciation percentages in the three-year category).

Year	Computation	Depreciation Expense	Accumulated Depreciation	Carrying Value
				$7,000
1	(25% × $7,000)	$1,750	$1,750	5,250
2	(38% × $7,000)	2,660	4,410	2,590
3	(37% × $7,000)	2,590	7,000	0

Note that three years, rather than the estimated useful life of six years, is used to calculate depreciation under ACRS. In addition, the estimated residual value is ignored, and the truck is depreciated to a carrying value of zero. No fractional year computations are made, regardless of when during the year the truck was put into service.

Under MACRS, the truck is five-year property and is depreciated for tax purposes using the 200 percent declining-balance method with a half-year convention. Depreciation expense for federal income tax purposes is calculated as follows:

Year	Computation	Depreciation Expense*	Accumulated Depreciation	Carrying Value
				7,000
1	($7,000 × 20%)	$1,400	$1,400	5,600
2	($7,000 × 32%)	2,240	3,640	3,360
3	($7,000 × 19.2%)	1,344	4,984	2,016
4	($7,000 × 11.52%)	806	5,790	1,210
5	($7,000 × 11.52%)	806	6,596	404
6	($7,000 × 5.76%)	404	7,000	0

* Rounded to nearest dollar

Note that cost recovery under the new law is less rapid, despite the use of the 200 percent declining-balance method, because the truck is now classified as five-year property. Also note that six years are required to write off the five-year property due to the half-year convention that allowed only a half-year's recovery in the first year.

Tax methods of depreciation are not usually acceptable for financial reporting under generally accepted accounting principles because the recovery periods used are shorter than the depreciable assets' estimated useful lives. Accounting for the effects of differences between tax and book depreciation is discussed in Chapter 16.

Control of Plant Assets

OBJECTIVE 6
Record property, plant, and equipment transactions in the plant asset records

Most businesses divide their plant assets into functional groups and have separate asset and accumulated depreciation control accounts for each group. For example, a company will usually have separate controlling accounts for Store Equipment, Office Equipment, and Delivery Truck, with an Accumulated Depreciation controlling account for each of these groups. All transactions affecting any one of the functional groups are recorded in the asset and the Accumulated Depreciation controlling accounts of that group. The purchase, depreciation, exchange, or sale of all delivery equipment will therefore be recorded in one Delivery Equipment account and its related Accumulated Depreciation account. Most businesses must have a subsidiary ledger with a detailed record for each asset, just as they do for each account receivable and account payable, but it is possible that a very small business may be able to function without it. Today's complicated income tax rules require most businesses to give evidence of depreciation and gains and losses from sales of assets by means of such detailed records. Normally a subsidiary ledger is the source of these records.

There are many ways to devise these records. One way is illustrated in Exhibit 12-1. In this simple example, the company has only two delivery trucks. The information on the subsidiary records is self-evident. But note that when the two subsidiary records for plant assets 1 and 2 are combined, they equal the balance in the general ledger accounts for both delivery trucks and accumulated depreciation on the delivery trucks.

This method of using subsidiary ledgers for plant assets is very much like the one you have already learned in accounting for accounts receivable and accounts payable. Subsidiary ledgers for plant assets are useful to the accounting department in (1) determining the periodic depreciation expense, (2) recording disposal of individual items, (3) preparing tax returns, and (4) preparing insurance claims in the event of insured losses. Forms may be expanded to provide spaces for gathering data on the operating efficiency of the assets. Such information as the frequency of breakdowns, the length of time out of service, and the cost of repairs is useful in evaluating equipment.

Plant assets, of course, represent a significant investment on the part of a company. Most companies identify each plant asset with a number when it is purchased. Periodically, an inspection and inventory of plant

Exhibit 12-1. Illustration of Plant Asset Subsidiary Records and Controlling Accounts

Controlling Accounts in General Ledger

Delivery Truck   **Account No. 132**

Date		Item	Post. Ref.	Debit	Credit	Balance Debit	Balance Credit
19x5 Jan.	1	Delivery Truck T4862	J1	5,400		5,400	
19x6 Jan.	1	Delivery Truck ST74289	J20	6,200		11,600	

Accumulated Depreciation   **Account No. 133**

Date		Item	Post. Ref.	Debit	Credit	Balance Debit	Balance Credit
19x5 Dec.	31	Delivery Truck T4862	J19		800		800
19x6 Dec.	31	Delivery Truck T4862	J40		800		1,600
	31	Delivery Truck ST74289	J40		900		2,500

Subsidiary Plant Asset and Depreciation Record   **Plant Asset No. 1**

Item: Delivery Truck   Serial No: T4862
General Ledger Account: Delivery Truck   Purchased from:
                                                 GMR Corporation

Where Located: Warehouse
Person Responsible for Asset: Delivery foreman
Estimated Life: 6 years   Estimated Residual Value: $600.00
Depreciation Method: SL   Depreciation per Year: $800.00
                                  Mo.: $ 66.67

Date	Explanation	Post. Ref.	Asset Record Dr.	Asset Record Cr.	Asset Record Bal.	Depreciation Dr.	Depreciation Cr.	Depreciation Bal.
Jan. 1, 19x5		J1	5,400		5,400			
Dec. 31, 19x5		J19					800	800
Dec. 31, 19x6		J40					800	1,600

Exhibit 12-1. Illustration of Plant Asset Subsidiary Records and Controlling Accounts (continued)

Subsidiary Plant Asset and Depreciation Record — Plant Asset No. 2

Item: Delivery Truck   Serial No: ST74289

General Ledger Account: Delivery Truck   Purchased from: AMG Corporation

Where Located: Warehouse

Person Responsible for Asset: Warehouse foreman

Estimated Life: 6 years   Estimated Residual Value: $800

Depreciation Method: SL   Depreciation per Year: $900

                        Mo.: $ 75

Date	Explanation	Post. Ref.	Asset Record			Depreciation		
			Dr.	Cr.	Bal.	Dr.	Cr.	Bal.
Jan. 1, 19x6		J20	6,200		6,200			
Dec. 31, 19x6		J40					900	900

assets should be made and compared with the information on the subsidiary records. Such an inventory should disclose changes in use of the plant assets, unusual wear and tear, and loss from theft, damage, or negligence.

Chapter Review

Review of Learning Objectives

1. **Describe the nature, types, and issues of accounting for long-term assets.**

   Long-term assets are unexpired costs that are used in the operation of the business, are not intended for resale, and have a useful life of more than one year. Long-term assets are either tangible or intangible. In the former category are land, plant assets, and natural resources. In the latter are trademarks, patents, franchises, goodwill, and other rights. The issues associated with accounting for long-term assets are the determination of cost, the allocation of expired cost, and the handling of repairs, maintenance, additions, and disposals.

2. **Account for the cost of property, plant, and equipment.**

   The acquisition cost of property, plant, and equipment includes all expenditures reasonable and necessary to get the asset in place and ready for use. These expenditures include such payments as purchase price, installation cost, freight charges, and insurance.

3. **Define depreciation, state the factors that affect its computation, and show how to record it.**
   Depreciation is the periodic allocation of the cost of a plant asset over its estimated useful life. It is recorded by debiting Depreciation Expense and crediting a related contra-asset account called Accumulated Depreciation. Factors that affect its computation are its cost, residual value, depreciable cost, and estimated useful life.

4. **Compute periodic depreciation under the (a) straight-line method, (b) production method, and (c) accelerated methods, including (1) sum-of-the-years'-digits method and (2) declining-balance method.**
   Depreciation is commonly computed by the straight-line method, the production method, or one of the accelerated methods. The two most widely used accelerated methods are the sum-of-the-years'-digits method and the declining-balance method. The straight-line method is related directly to the passage of time, whereas the production method is related directly to use. Accelerated methods, which result in relatively large amounts of depreciation in the early years and reduced amounts in later years, are based on the assumption that plant assets provide greater economic benefit in their early years than in later years.

5. **Apply depreciation methods to problems of partial years, revised rates, items of low unit cost, groups of similar items, and accelerated cost recovery.**
   In the application of depreciation methods, it may be necessary to calculate depreciation for partial years and to revise depreciation rates. In addition, it may be practical to apply these methods to groups of similar assets and to apply an inventory method to items of low unit cost. For income tax purposes, rapid write-offs of depreciable assets are allowed through the accelerated cost recovery system.

6. **Record property, plant, and equipment transactions in the plant asset records.**
   The use of controlling accounts and subsidiary plant ledgers detailing acquisitions, subsequent transactions, depreciation, and disposals is usually necessary to provide adequate control over long-term assets.

Review of Concepts and Terminology

The following concepts and terms were introduced in this chapter:

(L.O. 5) **Accelerated Cost Recovery System (ACRS):** A mandatory system enacted by Congress in 1981 that requires that a cost recovery allowance be computed (1) on the unadjusted cost of property being recovered, and (2) over a period of years prescribed by the law for all property of similar types.

(L.O. 4) **Accelerated methods:** Methods of depreciation that allocate relatively large amounts of the depreciable cost of the asset to earlier years and reduced amounts to later years.

(L.O. 1) **Amortization:** The periodic allocation of the cost of an intangible asset over its useful life.

(L.O. 4) **Declining-balance method:** An accelerated method of depreciation in which depreciation is computed by applying a fixed rate to the carrying value (the declining balance) of a tangible long-lived asset.

(L.O. 1) **Depletion:** The proportional allocation of the cost of a natural resource to the units removed; the exhaustion of a natural resource through mining, cutting, pumping, or otherwise using up the resource.

(L.O. 3) **Depreciable cost:** The cost of an asset less its residual value.

(L.O. 1) **Depreciation:** The periodic allocation of the cost of a tangible long-lived asset over its estimated useful life.

(L.O. 4) **Double-declining-balance method:** An accelerated method of depreciation that applies a fixed rate percentage equal to twice the straight-line percentage to the carrying value of a tangible long-term asset.

(L.O. 3) **Estimated useful life:** The total number of service units expected from a long-term asset.

(L.O. 1) **Fixed assets:** Another name, no longer in wide use, for long-term assets.

(L.O. 5) **Group depreciation:** The grouping of items of similar plant assets together for purposes of calculating depreciation.

(L.O. 1) **Intangible assets:** Long-term assets that have no physical substance but have a value based on rights or privileges accruing to the owner.

(L.O. 1) **Long-term assets:** Assets that (1) have a useful life of more than one year, (2) are acquired for use in the operation of the business, and (3) are not intended for resale to customers.

(L.O. 5) **Modified Accelerated Cost Recovery System (MACRS):** A modification made by the Tax Reform Act of 1986 in the accelerated cost recovery system (ACRS).

(L.O. 1) **Natural resources:** Long-term assets purchased for the physical substances that can be taken from the land and used up rather than for the value of their location.

(L.O. 3) **Obsolescence:** The process of becoming out of date; a contributor, together with physical deterioration, to the limited useful life of tangible assets.

(L.O. 3) **Physical deterioration:** Limitations on the useful life of a depreciable asset resulting from use and from exposure to the elements.

(L.O. 4) **Production method:** A method of depreciation that bases the depreciation charge for a period of time solely on the amount of use of the asset during the period of time.

(L.O. 3) **Residual value (salvage value or disposal value):** The estimated net scrap, salvage, or trade-in value of a tangible asset at the estimated date of disposal.

(L.O. 4) **Straight-line method:** A method of depreciation which assumes that depreciation is dependent on the passage of time and which allocates an equal amount of depreciation to each period of time.

(L.O. 4) **Sum-of-the-years'-digits method:** An accelerated method of depreciation in which the years in the service life of an asset are added; their sum becomes the denominator of a series of fractions that are applied against the depreciable cost of the asset in allocating the total depreciation over the estimated useful life.

(L.O. 1) **Tangible assets:** Long-term assets that have physical substance.

(L.O. 5) **Tax Reform Act of 1986:** Arguably the most sweeping revision of federal tax laws since the original enactment of the Internal Revenue Code in 1913.

Self-Test

Test your knowledge of the chapter by choosing the best answer for each item below.

1. The unexpired cost of a plant asset is referred to as its
   a. depreciable cost.
   b. original cost.
   c. accumulated depreciation.
   d. carrying value.   *(L.O. 1)*

2. Which of the following is *not* a characteristic of all long-term assets?
   a. Used in operations of business
   b. Possess physical substance
   c. Useful life of more than a year
   d. Not for resale   *(L.O. 1)*

3. Which of the following would *not* be included in the cost of land?
   a. Cost of paving the land for parking
   b. Assessment from local government for sewer
   c. Cost of clearing an unneeded building from the land
   d. Commission to real estate agent   *(L.O. 2)*

4. Which of the following most appropriately describes depreciation?
   a. Allocation of cost of plant asset
   b. Decline in value of plant asset
   c. Gradual obsolescence of plant asset
   d. Physical deterioration of plant asset   *(L.O. 3)*

5. If an asset cost $48,000 and has a residual value of $6,000 and a useful life of six years, the depreciation in the second year, using the sum-of-the-years'-digits method, would be
   a. $13,714.
   b. $12,000.
   c. $11,428.
   d. $10,000.   *(L.O. 4)*

6. Assuming a useful life of six years, which of the following methods would result in the most depreciation in the first year?
   a. Cannot tell from data given
   b. Double-declining-balance
   c. Sum-of-the-years'-digits
   d. Straight-line   *(L.O. 4)*

7. A truck was purchased for $50,000. It had a six-year life and an $8,000 residual value. Under the straight-line method, what is the asset's carrying value after $2^1/2$ years?
   a. $17,500
   b. S24,500
   c. $29,166
   d. $32,500   *(L.O. 4)*

8. ACRS depreciation
   a. carefully considers the estimated useful life of an asset.
   b. is a variation on straight-line depreciation.
   c. requires that buildings be written off over a five-year period.
   d. cannot be used for financial reporting purposes. *(L.O. 5)*

9. Equipment costing $27,000 with a residual value of $3,000 and an estimated life of six years has been depreciated using the straight-line

method for two years. Assuming a revised estimated total life of four years and the same estimated residual value, the depreciation expense for the third year will be

a. $4,000.   c. $8,000.

b. $4,750.   d. $9,500.   *(L.O. 5)*

10. An important way of maintaining control over plant assets is to maintain a separate record card on each plant asset in

a. the depreciation ledger.   c. a subsidiary ledger.

b. the controlling account.   d. the general ledger.   *(L.O. 6)*

Answers to Self-Test can be found at the end of this chapter.

Review Problem
Depreciation Methods and Partial Years

(L.O. 3, 4, 5)   Norton Construction Company purchased a cement mixer for $14,500. The mixer is expected to have a useful life of five years and a residual value of $1,000. The company engineers estimate the mixer will have a useful life of 7,500 hours, of which 2,625 hours were used in 19x2. The company's year end is December 31.

Required

1. Compute the depreciation expense for 19x2 assuming the cement mixer was purchased on January 1, 19x1, using the following four methods: (a) straight-line, (b) production, (c) sum-of-the-years'-digits, (d) double-declining-balance.
2. Compute the depreciation expense for 19x2 assuming the cement mixer was purchased on July 1, 19x1, using the following methods: (a) straight-line, (b) production, (c) sum-of-the-years'-digits, (d) double-declining-balance.
3. Prepare the adjusting entry to record the depreciation calculated in **1 (a)**.
4. Show the balance sheet presentation for the cement mixer after the entry in **3** on December 31, 19x2.

Answer to Review Problem

1. Depreciation expense for 19x2 assuming purchase on January 1, 19x1:
   a. Straight-line method
   ($14,500 − $1,000) ÷ 5 = $2,700
   b. Production method

   $$(\$14,500 - \$1,000) \times \frac{2,625}{7,500} = \$4,725$$

   c. Sum-of-the-years'-digits method

   $$(\$14,500 - \$1,000) \times \frac{4}{15} = \$3,600$$

   d. Double-declining-balance method
   First year: $14,500 × .4 = $5,800
   Second year: ($14,500 − $5,800) × .4 = $3,480

2. Depreciation expense for 19x2 assuming purchase on July 1, 19x1:
   a. Straight-line method
      First half: [($14,500 − $1,000) ÷ 5] × ½ = $1,350
      Second half: [($14,500 − $1,000) ÷ 5] × ½ = 1,350
         19x2 Total $2,700

      (Note that depreciation is the same for each half-year under the straight-line method.)
   b. Production method

      $$(\$14,500 - \$1,000) \times \frac{2,625}{7,500} = \$4,725$$

   c. Sum-of-the-years'-digits method
      First half: ($14,500 − $1,000) × 5/15 × ½ = $2,250
      Second half: ($14,500 − $1,000) × 4/15 × ½ = 1,800
         19x2 Total $4,050

   d. Double-declining-balance method
      First half: ($14,500 × .4) × ½   = $2,900
      Second half: [($14,500 − $5,800*) × .4] × ½ = 1,740
         19x2 Total $4,640

      *First full year's depreciation: $14,500 × .4 = $5,800

3. Adjusting entry for depreciation prepared:

   19x2
   Dec. 31   Depreciation Expense, Cement Mixer   2,700
                  Accumulated Depreciation,
                     Cement Mixer   2,700
                        To record depreciation for 19x2
                        under the straight-line method

4. Balance sheet presentation shown for December 31, 19x2:

   Cement Mixer $14,500
   Less Accumulated Depreciation   5,400
                                             $ 9,100

Chapter Assignments

Discussion Questions and Writing Assignments

1. What are the characteristics of long-term assets?
2. Which of the following items would be classified as plant assets on the balance sheet: (a) a truck held for sale by a truck dealer, (b) an office building that was once the company headquarters but is now to be sold, (c) a typewriter used by a secretary of the company, (d) a machine that is used in the manufacturing operations but is now fully depreciated, (e) pollution-control equipment that does not reduce the cost or improve the efficiency of the factory, (f) a parking lot for company employees?
3. Why is it useful to think of plant assets as a bundle of services?
4. Why is land different from other long-term assets?
5. What in general is included in the cost of a long-term asset?

6. Which of the following expenditures incurred in connection with the purchase of a computer system would be charged to the asset account? (a) Purchase price of the equipment, (b) interest on debt incurred to purchase the equipment, (c) freight charges, (d) installation charges, (e) cost of special communications outlets at the computer site, (f) cost of repairing door that was damaged during installation, (g) cost of adjustments to the system during first month of operation.

7. Hale's Grocery obtained bids on the construction of a dock for receiving goods at the back of its store. The lowest bid was $22,000. The company, however, decided to build the dock itself and was able to do it for $20,000, which it borrowed. The activity was recorded as a debit to Buildings for $22,000 and credits to Notes Payable for $20,000 and Gain on Construction for $2,000. Do you agree with the entry?

8. What do accountants mean by the term *depreciation*, and what is its relationship to depletion and amortization?

9. A firm buys a piece of technical equipment that is expected to last twelve years. Why might the equipment have to be depreciated over a shorter period of time?

10. A company purchased a building five years ago. The market value of the building is now greater than it was when the building was purchased. Explain why the company should continue depreciating the building.

11. Evaluate the following statement: "A parking lot should not be depreciated because adequate repairs will make it last forever."

12. Is the purpose of depreciation to determine the value of equipment? Explain your answer.

13. Contrast the assumptions underlying the straight-line depreciation method with the assumptions underlying the production depreciation method.

14. What is the principal argument supporting accelerated depreciation methods?

15. What does the balance of the Accumulated Depreciation account represent? Does it represent funds available to purchase new plant assets?

16. If a plant asset is sold during the year, why should depreciation be computed for the partial year prior to the date of the sale?

17. What basic procedure should be followed in revising a depreciation rate?

18. Explain why and how plant assets of low unit cost can be accounted for on a basis similar to handling supplies inventory.

19. On what basis can depreciation be taken on a group of assets rather than on individual items?

20. What is the difference between depreciation for accounting purposes and accelerated cost recovery for income tax purposes?

21. What records are usually necessary for good control over plant assets?

Classroom Exercises

Exercise 12-1.
Determining Cost of Long-Term Assets
(L.O. 2)

Rosemond Manufacturing purchased land next to its factory to be used as a parking lot. Expenditures incurred by the company were as follows: purchase price, $75,000; broker's fees, $6,000; title search and other fees, $550; demolition of a shack on the property, $2,000; general grading of property, $1,050; paving parking lots, $10,000; lighting for parking lots, $8,000; and signs for parking lots, $1,600. Determine the amount that should be debited to the Land account and to the Land Improvements account.

Exercise 12-2.
Cost of Long-Term
Asset and
Depreciation
(L. O. 2, 3, 4)

Jason Farm purchased a used tractor for $17,500. Before the tractor could be used it required new tires which cost $1,100 and an overhaul which cost $1,400. Its first tank of fuel cost $75. The tractor is expected to last six years and have a residual value of $2,000. Determine the cost and depreciable cost of the tractor and calculate the first year's depreciation under the straight-line method.

Exercise 12-3.
Group Purchase
(L.O. 2)

Ellen Briggs went into business by purchasing a car wash business for $240,000. The car wash assets included land, building, and equipment. If purchased separately, the land would have cost $60,000, the building $135,000, and the equipment $105,000. Determine the amount that should be recorded by Briggs in the new business's records for land, building, and equipment.

Exercise 12-4.
Depreciation
Methods
(L.O. 3, 4)

Logan Oil Corporation purchased a drilling truck for $45,000. The company expected the truck to last five years or 200,000 miles, with an estimated residual value of $7,500 at the end of that time. During 19x2, the truck was driven 48,000 miles. The company's year end is December 31.

Compute the depreciation for 19x2 under each of the following methods, assuming that the truck was purchased on January 13, 19x1: (1) straight-line, (2) production, (3) sum-of-the-years'-digits, and (4) double-declining-balance. Using the amount computed in **4**, prepare the general journal entry to record depreciation expense for the second year and show how drilling trucks would appear on the balance sheet.

Exercise 12-5.
Depreciation
Methods: Partial
Years
(L.O. 4, 5)

Using the same data given for Logan Oil Corporation in Exercise 12-4, compute the depreciation for 19x2 under each of the following methods, assuming that the truck was purchased on July 1, 19x1: (1) straight-line, (2) production, (3) sum-of-the-years'-digits, (4) double-declining-balance.

Exercise 12-6.
Declining-Balance
Method
(L.O. 4)

Quadri Burglar Alarm Systems Company purchased a word processor for $4,480. It has an estimated useful life of four years and an estimated residual value of $480. Compute the depreciation charge for each of the four years using the double-declining-balance method.

Exercise 12-7.
Straight-Line
Method: Partial
Years
(L.O. 4, 5)

Strauss Manufacturing Corporation purchased three machines during the year, as follows:

February 10	Machine 1	$ 1,800
July 26	Machine 2	12,000
October 11	Machine 3	21,600

The machines are assumed to last six years and have no estimated residual value. The company's fiscal year corresponds to the calendar year. Using the straight-line method, compute the depreciation charge for each machine for the year.

**Exercise 12-8.
Revision of
Depreciation Rates**
(L.O. 4, 5)

Eastmoor Hospital purchased a special x-ray machine for its operating room. The machine, which cost $155,780, was expected to last ten years, with an estimated residual value of $15,780. After two years of operation (and depreciation charges using the straight-line rate), it became evident that the x-ray machine would last a total of only seven years. At that time, the estimated residual value would remain the same. Given this information, determine the new depreciation charge for the third year on the basis of the new estimated useful life.

**Exercise 12-9.
Accounting for
Items of Low Unit
Cost**
(L.O. 5)

Newgard Air Conditioner Service Company maintains a large supply of small tools for servicing air conditioners. The company uses the inventory basis for accounting for the tools and assumes that annual expense is approximately equal to the cost of tools lost and discarded during the year. At the beginning of the year, the company had an inventory of small tools on hand in the amount of $8,765. During the year, small tools were purchased in the amount of $4,780. At the end of the year (December 31), a physical inventory revealed small tools in the amount of $6,585 on hand. Prepare a general journal entry to record small tools expense for the year for Newgard Air Conditioner Service Company.

Interpreting Accounting Information

Inland Steel*
(L.O. 5)

Depreciation expense is a significant expense for companies in industries that have a high proportion of plant assets to other assets. Also, the amount of depreciation expense in a given year is affected by estimates of useful life and by choice of depreciation method. In 1982, Inland Steel, a major integrated steel producer, changed both the estimates of depreciable lives for major production assets and the method of depreciation from straight-line to the production method for other steel-making assets.

The company's 1982 annual report states, "Management review indicates that, on average, the major production assets continue in service significantly beyond their assigned depreciable lives. . . . Equipment lives which formerly ranged from 10 to 28 years have been increased to between 12 and 34 years." The report goes on to explain that the new production method of depreciation "recognizes that depreciation of production assets is substantially related to physical wear as well as the passage of time. This method, therefore, more appropriately allocates the cost of these facilities to the periods in which products are manufactured."

* Excerpts from the 1982 annual report used by permission of Inland Steel. Copyright © 1982.

The report also summarized the effects of both actions on the year 1982 as follows:

Incremental Increase in Net Income	In Millions	Per Share
Lengthened lives	$15.7	$ .74
Production method		
Current year	10.5	.49
Prior years	4.0	.19
Total increase	$30.2	$1.42

During 1982, Inland Steel reported a net loss of $118,795,000 ($5.60 per share). Depreciation expense for 1982 was $125,296,000.

In explaining the changes, the controller of Inland Steel was quoted in an article in *Forbes* on November 22, 1982, as follows: "Why should we put ourselves at a disadvantage by depreciating more conservatively than other steel companies do?" But the article quotes a certified public accountant who argues that when a company slows its method of depreciation it "might be viewed by some people as reporting . . . lower quality earnings."

Required

1. Explain the accounting treatment when there is a change in the estimated lives of depreciable assets. What circumstances must exist for the production method to produce the effect it did in relation to the straight-line method? What would have been Inland's net income or loss if the changes had not been made? What may have motivated management to make the changes?
2. What does the controller of Inland Steel mean when he says that Inland had been "depreciating more conservatively than other steel companies"? Why might the changes at Inland indicate, as the accountant asserts, "lower quality earnings"? What risks might Inland face as a result of its decision to use the production method of depreciation?

Problem Set A

**Problem 12A-1.
Determining Cost
of Assets
(L.O. 2, 3, 4, 5)**

Flair Corporation began operation on January 1 of the current year. At the end of the year, the company's auditor discovered that all expenditures involving long-term assets were debited to an account called Fixed Assets. An analysis of the account, which has a balance at the end of the year of $2,644,972, disclosed that it contained the items presented at the top of the following page.

The timber that was cleared from the land was sold to a firewood dealer for $5,000. This amount was credited to Miscellaneous Income. During the construction period, two supervisors devoted their full time to the construction project. These people earn annual salaries of $48,000 and $42,000, respectively. They spent two months on the purchase and preparation of the land, six months on the construction of the building (approximately one-sixth of which was devoted to improvements on the grounds), and one month on installation of machinery. The plant began operation on October 1, and the supervisors returned to their regular duties. Their salaries were debited to Factory Salary Expense.

Cost of land	$ 316,600
Surveying costs	4,100
Transfer of title and other fees required by the county	920
Broker's fees	21,144
Attorney's fees associated with land acquisition	7,048
Cost of removing unusable timber from land	50,400
Cost of grading land	4,200
Cost of digging building foundation	34,600
Architect's fee for building and land improvements (80 percent building)	64,800
Cost of building	710,000
Cost of sidewalks	11,400
Cost of parking lots	54,400
Cost of lighting for grounds	80,300
Cost of landscaping	11,800
Cost of machinery	989,000
Shipping cost on machinery	55,300
Cost of installing machinery	176,200
Cost of testing machinery	22,100
Cost of changes in building due to safety regulations required because of machinery	12,540
Cost of repairing building that was damaged in the installation of machinery	8,900
Cost of medical bill for injury received by employee while installing machinery	2,400
Cost of water damage to building during heavy rains prior to opening the plant for operation	6,820
Account Balance	$2,644,972

Required

1. Prepare a schedule with the following column headings: Land, Land Improvements, Buildings, Machinery, and Losses. List the items appropriate to these accounts and sort them out into their proper accounts. Negative amounts should be shown in parentheses. Total the columns.
2. Prepare an entry to adjust the accounts based on all the information given, assuming that the company's accounts have not been closed at the end of the year.
3. Assume that the plant was in operation for three months during the year. Prepare an adjusting entry to record depreciation expense, assuming that the land improvements are depreciated over twenty years with no residual value, that the buildings are depreciated over thirty years with no estimated residual value, and that the machinery is depreciated over twelve years with the estimated residual value equal to 10 percent of cost. The company uses the straight-line method. Round your answers to the nearest dollar.

**Problem 12A-2.
Comparison of
Depreciation
Methods
(L.O. 3, 4)**

Riggio Construction Company purchased a new crane for $360,500. The crane has an estimated residual value of $35,000 and an estimated useful life of six years. The crane is expected to last 10,000 hours. It was used 1,800 hours in year 1; 2,000 in year 2; 2,500 in year 3; 1,500 in year 4; 1,200 in year 5; and 1,000 in year 6.

Required

1. Compute the annual depreciation and carrying value for the new crane for each of the six years (round to nearest dollar where necessary) under each of the following methods: (a) straight-line, (b) production, (c) sum-of-the-years'-digits, (d) double-declining-balance.
2. Prepare the adjusting entry that would be made each year to record the depreciation calculated under the straight-line method.
3. Show the balance sheet presentation for the crane after the adjusting entry in year 2 using the straight-line method.
4. What conclusions can you draw from the patterns of yearly depreciation and carrying value in 1?

Problem 12A-3.
Depreciation
Methods and
Partial Years
(L.O. 4, 5)

Wu Corporation operates four types of equipment. Because of their varied functions, company accounting policy requires the application of four different depreciation methods to the equipment. Data on this equipment are summarized below.

Equip-ment	Date Purchased	Cost	Installation Cost	Estimated Residual Value	Estimated Life	Depreciation Method
1	1/12/x1	$57,000	$3,000	$ 6,000	10 years	Double-declining-balance
2	1/7/x1	76,675	2,750	7,500	6 years	Sum-of-the-years'-digits
3	7/9/x1	63,700	5,300	7,000	10 years	Straight-line
4	10/2/x1	96,900	2,700	11,200	20,000 hours	Production

Required

Assuming that the fiscal year ends December 31, compute the depreciation charges for 19x1, 19x2, and19x3 by filling in a table with the headings shown below.

		Depreciation		
Equipment No.	Computations	19x1	19x2	19x3

Assume that production for Equipment 4 was 2,000 hours in 19x1; 4,200 hours in 19x2; and 3,200 hours in 19x3. Show your computations.

Problem 12A-4.
Plant Asset
Transactions,
Revised
Depreciation, and
Spare Parts
(L.O. 2, 3, 4, 5)

Rita Carrasquel entered the jewelry refinishing business in January 19x1. She was able to purchase refinishing equipment for $59,275 on January 2. It cost her $6,400 to have the equipment moved to her building and $2,340 to have it installed. It cost another $1,585 to adjust the equipment. She estimated that the equipment would have a useful life of ten years and a residual value of $6,000. Small tools were purchased on May 14 at a cost of $580, and regular maintenance of the equipment on September 16 came to $1,485. At the end of the year, an inventory revealed that $240 in small tools were still on hand. During 19x2, small tools of $725 were purchased on April 18, and the physical inventory disclosed $230 on hand at the end of the year. Regular maintenance costs expended on October 4 were $2,070. Soon it became apparent that the equipment would last a total of only six years instead of the originally estimated ten years, and the estimated residual value at the end of six years would be only $2,500.

Required

1. Prepare general journal entries for 19x1 to record the purchase of the equipment, the costs associated with the purchase, the transaction involving small tools, the upkeep costs, the year-end depreciation charge, and the small tools expense. Carrasquel's company uses the inventory method of recording small tools expense and the straight-line method for computing depreciation expense. Assume that all purchases are made with cash.
2. Prepare general journal entries for 19x2 for small tools, maintenance, and depreciation expense. The depreciation expense should be based on the new estimates regarding the equipment.

Problem 12A-5.
Plant Asset
Transactions and
Record Cards
(L.O. 2, 3, 4, 5, 6)

Kamal's Bakery Company completed the following transactions involving its delivery trucks. These trucks are under the control of the delivery supervisor:

19x1
Mar. 1 Purchased a delivery truck on credit from Palambo Chevrolet, serial number B253651, for $17,250. The truck has an estimated useful life of five years and an estimated residual value of $2,250. The delivery truck is assigned Plant Asset No. T5-01.

July 2 Purchased a delivery truck on credit from Lynch Dodge, serial number LW53711429, for $15,750. The truck has an estimated useful life of five years and an estimated residual value of $2,000. The delivery truck is assigned Plant Asset No. T5-02.

Dec. 31 Recorded 19x1 depreciation on delivery equipment using the straight-line method.

19x2
Oct. 1 Purchased a delivery truck on credit from Swoboda Ford, serial number R683271, for $11,125. The truck has an estimated useful life of five years and an estimated residual value of $1,875. The delivery truck is assigned Plant Asset No. T6-01.

Dec. 31 Recorded 19x2 depreciation on delivery equipment using the straight-line method.

Required

1. Prepare general journal entries to record transactions in 19x1 and 19x2.
2. Open ledger accounts for Delivery Equipment (143) and Accumulated Depreciation, Delivery Equipment (144), and prepare three plant asset record cards. Post to the general ledger accounts and plant asset cards, recording all available information. All plant assets are the responsibility of the site foreman. Round to the nearest dollar.
3. Prepare a schedule for the end of 19x2 listing the cost and accumulated depreciation to date for each item of delivery equipment, and compare the balances of the delivery equipment and related accumulated depreciation accounts.

Problem Set B

Problem 12B-1.
Determining Cost
of Assets
(L.O. 2, 3, 4, 5)

Moline Computers, Incorporated constructed a new training center in 19x7. You have been hired to manage the training center. A review of the accounting records lists the following expenditures debited to the Training Center account:

Attorney's fee, land acquisition	$ 17,450
Cost of land	299,000
Architect's fee, building design	51,000
Contractor's cost, building	510,000
Contractor's cost, parking lot and sidewalk	67,800
Contractor's cost, electrical	82,000
Landscaping	27,500
Costs of surveying land	4,600
Training equipment, tables, and chairs	68,200
Contractor's cost, installing training equipment	34,000
Cost of grading the land	7,000
Cost of changes in building to soundproof rooms	29,600
Total Account Balance	$1,198,150

During the center's construction, someone from Moline Computers, Incorporated worked full time on the project. He spent two months on the purchase and preparation of the site, six months on the construction, one month on land improvements, and one month on equipment installation and training room furniture purchase and set-up. His salary of $32,000 during this ten-month period was charged to Administrative Expense. The training center was placed in operation on November 1.

Required

1. Prepare a schedule with the following four column (Account) headings: Land, Land Improvements, Building, and Equipment. Place each item in the appropriate column. Total the columns.
2. Prepare an entry on December 31 to correct the accounts associated with the training center, assuming that the company's accounts have not been closed at the end of the year.
3. Assume that the center was in operation for two months during the year. Prepare an adjusting entry to record depreciation expense, assuming that the land improvements are depreciated over twenty years with no residual value, that the buildings are depreciated over thirty years with no residual value, and that the equipment is depreciated over twelve years with the estimated residual value equal to 10 percent of cost. The company uses the straight-line method. Round your answers to the nearest dollar.

Problem 12B-2.
Comparison of
Depreciation
Methods
(L.O. 3, 4)

Hoekstra Manufacturing Company purchased a robot for its manufacturing operations at a cost of $720,000 at the beginning of year 1. The robot has an estimated useful life of four years and an estimated residual value of $60,000. The robot is expected to last 20,000 hours. The robot was operated 6,000 hours in year 1; 8,000 hours in year 2; 4,000 hours in year 3; and 2,000 hours in year 4.

Required

1. Compute the annual depreciation and carrying value for the robot for each year assuming the following depreciation methods: (a) straight-line, (b) production, (c) sum-of-the-years'-digits, and (d) double-declining-balance.
2. Prepare the adjusting entry that would be made each year to record the depreciation calculated under the straight-line method.
3. Show the balance sheet presentation for the robot after the adjusting entry in year 2 using the straight-line method.
4. What conclusions can you draw from the patterns of yearly depreciation and carrying value in 1?

Problem 12B-3.
Depreciation
Methods and
Partial Years
(L.O. 4, 5)

Ada Pinkston purchased a laundry company that caters to young college students. In addition to the washing machines, Ada installed a tanning machine, a video game machine, and a bar. Because each type of asset performs a different function, she has decided to use different depreciation methods. Data on each type of asset are summarized below:

Asset	Date Purchased	Cost	Installation Cost	Residual Value	Estimated Life	Depreciation Method
Washing machines	3/5/x7	$15,000	$2,000	$2,600	4 years	Straight-line
Tanning machine	4/1/x7	34,000	3,000	1,000	7,500 hours	Production
Video game	6/30/x7	10,000	1,000	800	4 years	Sum-of-the-years'-digits
Bar	10/1/x7	3,400	600	600	10 years	Double-declining-balance

The tanning machine was operated 2,100 hours in 19x7, 3,000 hours in 19x8, and 2,400 hours in 19x9.

Required

Assuming the fiscal year ends December 31, compute the depreciation charges for 19x7, 19x8, and 19x9. Round your answers to the nearest dollar and present them by filling in a table with the headings shown below:

Asset	Computations	Depreciation		
		19x7	19x8	19x9

Problem 12B-4.
Plant Asset
Transactions,
Revised
Depreciation, and
Spare Parts
(L.O. 2, 3, 4, 5)

Fernandez Auto Repair Company installed auto repair equipment on January 2, 19x7, which was purchased for $94,000. Delivery cost was $3,500, and installation cost was $2,500. Mr. Fernandez estimated the equipment would have a useful life of six years and a residual value of $10,000. On April 2, small tools for auto repairs were purchased for $1,475. Regular maintenance in 19x7 was $480, expended on November 1. At the end of the year, an inventory revealed $760 of small tools still on hand. Regular maintenance for the equipment was $750 in 19x8. This expenditure was made on May 10. Mr.

Fernandez determined that the equipment would last only four years instead of the originally estimated six years. The new estimated residual value would be only $5,000. On June 10, 19x8, $420 of small tools were purchased, and the inventory of small tools showed $1,020 on hand at the end of the year.

Required

1. Prepare general journal entries for 19x7 to record the purchase of the equipment, costs associated with the purchase, maintenance costs, the transactions involving small tools, and year-end depreciation assuming the straight-line method of depreciation. Assume that all purchases are made with cash.
2. Prepare general journal entries for 19x8 for maintenance, small tools, and depreciation expense using Mr. Fernandez's revised estimates.

Problem 12B-5.
Plant Asset
Transactions and
Record Cards
(L.O. 2, 3, 4, 5, 6)

Pinto Sprinkler System Company completed these transactions:

19x8
Feb. 25 Purchased trench digging machine from Horwitz Equipment on credit, serial number K363, for $12,600. The machine has an estimated life of five years and a residual value of $800. Pinto assigned the machine asset number 47.
Apr. 4 Purchased a larger trench digging machine on credit from Overstreet Machinery, serial number RT569, for $23,000. This machine has an estimated life of six years and a residual value of $2,000. The machine was assigned asset number 48.
Dec. 31 Recorded 19x8 depreciation on digging machinery using the straight-line method.

19x9
Mar. 2 Purchased another trench digging machine on credit from Waldron Equipment Co., serial number J652W, for $15,600. The machine has an estimated useful life of seven years and a residual value of $1,600. It was assigned asset number 49.
Dec. 31 Recorded 19x9 depreciation on machines using the straight-line method.

Required

1. Prepare journal entries to record transactions in 19x8 and 19x9.
2. Open ledger accounts for Machinery (141), and Accumulated Depreciation, Machinery (142). Prepare three plant asset record cards. Post to the general ledger accounts and plant asset cards, recording all available information. All plant assets are the responsibility of the site foreman. Round to the nearest dollar.
3. Prepare a schedule for the end of 19x9, listing both cost and accumulated depreciation to date for each item of machinery. Compare the delivery equipment and related accumulated depreciation accounts.

Financial Decision Case

Hyde Computer
Company
(L.O. 4)

The Hyde Computer Company manufactures computers for sale or rent. On January 2, 19x1, the company completed the manufacture of a computer for a total cost of $190,000. A customer leased the computer on the same day for a five-year period at a monthly rental of $5,000. Although the computer will last longer than five years, it is likely that it will be technologically obsolete by the end of the five-year period. However, it is still possible that the computer will not be obsolete. Hyde's management estimates that if the computer is obsolete, it can be sold for $20,000 at the end of the lease, and if it is not obsolete, it can be sold for S40,000 because it would probably last for another two years. On the basis of its experience in leasing many computers, management estimates that the expenses associated with the lease of this computer will be as follows:

	Insurance and Property Taxes	Repairs and Maintenance
19x1	$7,000	S3,000
19x2	6,400	4,500
19x3	5,800	6,000
19x4	5,200	7,500
19x5	4,600	9,000

Required

1. What estimated useful life and estimated residual value do you recommend that Hyde use for the computer? Explain.
2. Prepare two schedules that show for each year the lease revenue, expenses, and income before income taxes. Also, show on each schedule for each year the carrying value of the computer at the end of the year, and compute the ratio of income before income taxes to carrying value (return on assets). Round components to one decimal point. The first schedule should compute depreciation by using the straight-line method, and the second schedule should use the sum-of-the-years'-digits method.
3. Compare the two schedules in 2, and discuss the results. Which of the methods do you feel produces the most realistic pattern of income before taxes, and why?
4. If you were asked to determine the amount of cash generated each year from this lease (cash received minus cash disbursed), what effect, if any, would the method of depreciation have on your computations?

Answers to Self-Test

1. d	3. a	5. d	7. d	9. c
2. b	4. a	6. b	8. d	10. c

LEARNING OBJECTIVES

1. Apply the matching rule to the allocation of expired costs for capital expenditures and revenue expenditures.
2. Account for disposal of depreciable assets not involving exchanges.
3. Account for disposal of depreciable assets involving exchanges.
4. Identify natural resource accounting issues and compute depletion.
5. Apply the matching rule to intangible asset accounting issues, including research and development costs and goodwill.

CHAPTER 13

Long-Term Assets: Other Issues and Types

In Chapter 12 you learned about the acquisition of long-term assets and the depreciation and control of plant assets. In this chapter, the study of long-term assets continues with an explanation of capital and revenue expenditures, disposal of plant assets, natural resources, and intangible assets. After studying this chapter, you should be able to meet the learning objectives listed on the left.

Capital Expenditures and Revenue Expenditures

The term **expenditure** refers to a payment or incurrence of an obligation to make future payment for an asset, such as a truck, or a service received, such as a repair. When the payment or debt is for an asset or a service, it is correctly called an expenditure. A **capital expenditure** is an expenditure for the purchase or expansion of long-term assets and is recorded in the asset accounts. Expenditures for repairs, maintenance, fuel, or other things needed to maintain and operate plant and equipment are called **revenue expenditures** because they are immediately charged as expenses against revenues. They are recorded by debits to expense accounts. Revenue expenditures are charged to expense because the benefits from the expenditures will be used up in the current period. For this reason, they will be deducted from the revenues of the current period in determining net income. In summary, any expenditure that will benefit several accounting periods is considered a capital expenditure. Any expenditure that will benefit only the current accounting period is called a revenue expenditure.

It is important to note this careful distinction between capital and revenue expenditures. In accordance with the matching rule, expenditures of any type should be charged to the period that they benefit. For example, if the purchase of an automobile is mistakenly charged as a revenue expenditure, the expense for the current period is overstated on the income statement. As a result, current net income is understated, and in future periods net income will be overstated. If, on the other hand, a revenue expenditure such as the painting of a building were charged to an asset account, the expense of the current period would be understated. Current net income would be overstated by the same amount, and net income of future periods would be understated.

OBJECTIVE 1
Apply the matching rule to the allocation of expired costs for capital expenditures and revenue expenditures

For practical purposes many companies establish policies stating what constitutes a revenue or capital expenditure. For example, small expenditures for items that normally would be treated as capital expenditures may be treated as revenue expenditures because the amounts involved are not material in relation to net income. Thus a wastebasket, which might last for years, would be recorded as a supplies expense rather than as a depreciable asset.

In addition to acquisition of plant assets, natural resources, and intangible assets, capital expenditures also include additions and betterments. **Additions** are enlargements to the physical layout of a plant asset. If a new wing is added to a building, the benefits from the expenditure will be received over several years, and the amount paid for it should be debited to the asset account. **Betterments** are improvements to plant assets that do not add to the physical layout of the asset. Installation of an air-conditioning system is an example of an expenditure for a betterment or improvement that will offer benefits over a period of years and so should be charged to an asset account.

Among the more usual kinds of revenue expenditures relating to plant equipment are the ordinary repairs, maintenance, lubrication, cleaning, and inspection necessary to keep an asset in good working condition.

Repairs fall into two categories: ordinary repairs and extraordinary repairs. **Ordinary repairs** are expenditures that are necessary to maintain an asset in good operating condition. Trucks must have tune-ups, tires and batteries must be replaced regularly, and other ordinary repairs must be made. Offices and halls must be painted regularly and have broken tiles or woodwork replaced. Ordinary repairs consist of any expenditures needed to maintain a plant asset in its normal state of operation. Such repairs are a current expense.

Extraordinary repairs are repairs of a more significant nature—they affect the estimated residual value or estimated useful life of an asset. For example, a boiler for heating a building may receive a complete overhaul, at a cost of several thousand dollars, that will extend the useful life of the boiler five years.

Typically, extraordinary repairs are recorded by debiting the Accumulated Depreciation account, under the assumption that some of the depreciation previously recorded has now been eliminated. The effect of this reduction in the Accumulated Depreciation account is to increase the book or carrying value of the asset by the cost of the extraordinary repair. Consequently, the new carrying value of the asset should be depreciated over the new estimated useful life. Let us assume that a machine costing $10,000 had no estimated residual value and an original estimated useful life of ten years. After eight years, the accumulated depreciation (straight-line method assumed) would be $8,000, and the carrying value would be $2,000 ($10,000 − $8,000). Assume that, at this point in time, the machine was given a major overhaul costing $1,500.

This expenditure extends the useful life three years beyond the original ten years. The entry for extraordinary repair would be as follows:

Mar. 14   Accumulated Depreciation, Machinery   1,500
              Cash   1,500
                  To record extraordinary repair
                  to machinery

The annual periodic depreciation for each of the five years remaining in the machine's useful life would be calculated as follows:

Carrying value before extraordinary repairs $2,000
Extraordinary repairs   1,500
Total $3,500

Annual periodic depreciation $= \dfrac{\$3,500}{5 \text{ years}} = \$700$

If the machine remains in use for the five years expected after the major overhaul, the annual periodic depreciation charges of $700 will exactly write off the new carrying value, including the cost of extraordinary repairs.

Disposal of Depreciable Assets

OBJECTIVE 2
Account for disposal of depreciable assets not involving exchanges

When items of plant assets are no longer useful in a business because they are worn out or obsolete, they may be discarded, sold, or traded in on the purchase of new plant and equipment. A comprehensive illustration is used in the following sections to show how these disposals are recorded in the accounting records.

Assumptions for the Comprehensive Illustration

For accounting purposes, a plant asset may be disposed of in three ways: (1) discarded, (2) sold for cash, or (3) exchanged for another asset. To illustrate how each of these cases is recorded, assume the following facts. MGC Corporation purchased a machine on January 1, 19x0, for $6,500 and depreciated it on a straight-line basis over an estimated useful life of ten years. The residual value at the end of ten years was estimated to be $500. On January 1, 19x7, the balances of the relevant accounts in the plant ledger appear as follows:

Machinery		Accumulated Depreciation, Machinery	
6,500			4,200

On September 30, management disposes of the asset. The next few sections illustrate the accounting treatment to record depreciation for the partial year and the disposal under several assumptions.

Depreciation for Partial Year Prior to Disposal

When items of plant assets are discarded or disposed of in some other way, it is necessary to record depreciation expense for the partial year up to the date of disposal. This step is required because the asset was used until that date and under the matching rule the accounting period should receive the proper allocation of depreciation expense.

The depreciation expense for the partial year before disposal is calculated in exactly the same way as it is calculated for the partial year after purchase illustrated in Chapter 12.

In this comprehensive illustration, MGC Corporation disposes of the machinery on September 30. The entry to record the depreciation for the first nine months of 19x7 is as follows:

Sept. 30   Depreciation Expense, Machinery   450
     Accumulated Depreciation, Machinery   450
       To record depreciation up to date of
       disposal:
$$\frac{\$6,500 - \$500}{10} \times \frac{9}{12} = \$450$$

The relevant accounts in the plant ledger accounts appear as follows after the entry is posted:

Machinery		Accumulated Depreciation, Machinery	
6,500			4,650

Recording Discarded Plant Assets

Even though it is depreciated over its estimated life, a plant asset rarely lasts exactly as long as its estimated life. If it lasts longer than its estimated life, it is not depreciated past the point that its carrying value equals its residual value. The purpose of depreciation is to spread the depreciable cost of the asset over the future life of the asset. Thus the total accumulated depreciation should never exceed the total depreciable cost. If the asset is still used in the business, this fact should be supported by its cost and accumulated depreciation remaining in the ledger accounts. Proper records will thus be available for maintaining control over plant assets. If the residual value is zero, the carrying value of a fully depreciated asset is zero until the asset is disposed of. If such an asset is discarded, no gain or loss results.

In the comprehensive illustration, however, the discarded equipment has a carrying value of $1,850 at the time of disposal. A loss equal to the carrying value should be recorded when the machine is discarded:

Sept. 30   Accumulated Depreciation, Machinery   4,650
     Loss on Disposal of Machinery   1,850
       Machinery   6,500
         Discarded machine no longer
         used in the business

Gains and losses on disposals of long-term assets are classified as other income and expenses on the income statement.

Recording Plant Assets Sold for Cash

The entries to record an asset sold for cash are similar to the one illustrated above except that the receipt of cash should also be recorded. The following entries show how to record the sale of a machine under three assumptions about the selling price. In the first case, the $1,850 of cash received is exactly equal to the carrying value of the machine ($1,850), so no gain or loss results:

Sept. 30	Cash	1,850	
	Accumulated Depreciation, Machinery	4,650	
	Machinery		6,500
	Sale of machine at carrying		
	value; no gain or loss		

In the second case, the $1,000 cash received is less than the carrying value of $1,850, so a loss of $850 is recorded:

Sept. 30	Cash	1,000	
	Accumulated Depreciation, Machinery	4,650	
	Loss on Sale of Machinery	850	
	Machinery		6,500
	Sale of machine at less than carrying		
	value; loss of $850 ($1,850 − $1,000)		
	recorded		

In the third case, the $2,000 cash received exceeds the carrying value of $1,850, so a gain of $150 is recorded:

Sept. 30	Cash	2,000	
	Accumulated Depreciation, Machinery	4,650	
	Gain on Sale of Machinery		150
	Machinery		6,500
	Sale of machine at more than the		
	carrying value, gain of $150		
	($2,000 − $1,850) recorded		

Recording Exchanges of Plant Assets

OBJECTIVE 3
Account for disposal of depreciable assets involving exchanges

Businesses also dispose of plant assets by trading them in on the purchase of other plant assets. Exchanges may involve similar assets, for example, an old machine traded in on a newer model, or dissimilar assets, such as a machine being traded in on a truck. In either case, the purchase price is reduced by the amount of the trade-in allowance given for the asset traded in.

The basic accounting for exchanges of plant assets is similar to accounting for sales of plant assets for cash. If the trade-in allowance received is greater than the carrying value of the asset surrendered, there has been a gain. If the allowance is less, there has been a loss. There are special rules for recognizing these gains and losses depending on the nature of the assets exchanged.

Exchange	Losses Recognized	Gains Recognized
For financial accounting purposes		
Of dissimilar assets	Yes	Yes
Of similar assets	Yes	No
For income tax purposes		
Of dissimilar assets	Yes	Yes
Of similar assets	No	No

Both gains and losses are recognized when a company exchanges dissimilar assets. Assets are dissimilar when they perform different functions and are similar when they perform the same function. For financial accounting purposes, gains on exchanges of similar assets are not recognized because the earning lives of the assets surrendered are not considered to be completed. When a company trades in an older machine on a newer machine of the same type, the economic substance of the transaction is the same as a major renovation and upgrading of the older machine. One can think of the trade-in as an extension of the life and usefulness of the original machine. Instead of recognizing a gain at the time of the exchange, the company records the new machine at the sum of the book value of the older machine plus any cash paid.[1]

Accounting for exchanges of similar assets is complicated by the fact that neither gains nor losses are recognized for income tax purposes. This is important because many companies choose to follow this practice in their accounting records. The reason usually given is for convenience. Thus, in practice, accountants face cases where both gains and losses are recognized (exchanges of dissimilar assets), where losses are recognized and gains are not (exchanges of similar assets), and where neither gains nor losses are recognized (income tax exchanges of similar assets). Since all these options are used in practice, they are all illustrated in the following paragraphs.

Loss Recognized on the Exchange. A loss is recognized for accounting purposes on all exchanges in which a material loss occurs. To illustrate the recognition of a loss, let us assume that the firm in our comprehensive example exchanges the machine for a newer, more modern machine on the following terms:

Price of new machine	**$12,000**
Trade-in allowance for old machine	(1,000)
Cash payment required	$11,000

1. Accounting Principles Board, *Opinion No. 29*, "Accounting for Nonmonetary Transactions" (New York: American Institute of Certified Public Accountants, 1973); also see James B. Hobbs and D. R. Bainbridge, "Nonmonetary Exchange Transactions: Clarification of APB Opinion No. 29," *The Accounting Review* (January 1982).

In this case the trade-in allowance ($1,000) is less than the carrying value ($1,850) of the old machine. Thus there is a loss on the exchange of $850 ($1,850 – $1,000). The following journal entry records this transaction under the assumption that the loss is to be recognized:

Sept. 30	**Machinery (new)**	12,000	
	Accumulated Depreciation, Machinery	4,650	
	Loss on Exchange of Machinery	850	
	Machinery (old)		6,500
	Cash		11,000
	Exchange of machines—cost		
	of old machine and its accumulated		
	depreciation removed from the		
	records; new machine recorded		
	at list price; loss recognized		

Loss Not Recognized on the Exchange. In the previous example in which a loss was recognized, the new asset was recorded at the purchase price of $12,000 and a loss of $850 was recorded. If the transaction is for similar assets and is to be recorded for income tax purposes, the loss should not be recognized. In this case, the cost basis of the new asset will reflect the effect of the unrecorded loss. The cost basis is computed by adding the cash payment to the carrying value of the old asset:

Carrying value of old machine	$ 1,850
Cash paid	11,000
Cost basis of new machine	**$12,850**

Note that no loss is recognized in the entry to record this transaction:

Sept. 30	**Machinery (new)**	12,850	
	Accumulated Depreciation, Machinery	4,650	
	Machinery (old)		6,500
	Cash		11,000
	Exchange of machines—cost of		
	old machine and its accumulated		
	depreciation removed from the		
	records; new machine recorded at		
	amount equal to carrying value of		
	old machine plus cash paid; no		
	loss recognized		

Note that the new machinery is reported at the purchase price of $12,000 plus the unrecognized loss of $850. The nonrecognition of the loss on the exchange is, in effect, a postponement of the loss. Since depreciation of the new machine will be computed based on a cost of $12,850 instead of $12,000, the "unrecognized" loss is reflected by more depreciation each year than if the loss had been recognized.

Gain Recognized on the Exchange. Gains are recognized for accounting purposes on exchanges when dissimilar assets are exchanged. To illustrate the recognition of a gain, we will continue with the same example, assuming the following terms for the exchange in which the machines serve different functions:

Price of new machine	$12,000
Trade-in allowance for old machine	(3,000)
Cash payment required	$ 9,000

Here the trade-in allowance ($3,000) exceeds the carrying value ($1,850) of the old machine by $1,150. Thus there is a gain on the exchange if we assume that the price of the new machine is not a figure that has been inflated for the purpose of allowing an excessive trade-in value. In other words, a gain exists if the trade-in allowance represents the fair market value of the old machine Assuming that this condition is true, the entry to record the transaction is as follows:

Sept. 30	Machinery (new)	12,000	
	Accumulated Depreciation, Machinery	4,650	
	Gain on Exchange of Machinery		1,150
	Machinery (old)		6,500
	Cash		9,000
	Exchange of machines—cost of old machine and its accumulated depreciation removed from the records; new machine recorded at sales price; gain recognized		

Gain Not Recognized on the Exchange. A gain on an exchange should not be recognized in the accounting records if the machines perform similar functions. The cost basis of the new machine must indicate the effect of the unrecorded gain. This cost basis is computed by adding the cash payment to the carrying value of the old asset:

Carrying value of old machine	$ 1,850
Cash paid	9,000
Cost basis of new machine	$10,850

The entry to record the transaction is as follows:

Sept. 30	Machinery (new)	10,850	
	Accumulated Depreciation, Machinery	4,650	
	Machinery (old)		6,500
	Cash		9,000
	Exchange of machine—cost of old machine and its accumulated depreciation removed from the records; new machine recorded at amount equal to carrying value of old machine plus cash paid; no gain recognized		

Similar to the nonrecognition of losses, the nonrecognition of the gain on exchange is, in effect, a postponement of the gain. In the illustration above, when the new machine is eventually discarded or sold, its cost basis will be $10,850 instead of its original price of $12,000. Since depreciation will be computed on the cost basis of $10,850, the "unrecognized" gain is reflected in less depreciation each year than if the gain had been recognized.

Accounting for Natural Resources

OBJECTIVE 4
Identify natural resource accounting issues and compute depletion

Natural resources are also known as **wasting assets**. Examples of natural resources are standing timber, oil and gas fields, and mineral deposits. The distinguishing characteristic of these wasting assets is that they are converted into inventory by cutting, pumping, or mining. For example, an oil field is a reservoir of unpumped oil, and a coal mine is a deposit of unmined coal.

Natural resources are shown on the balance sheet as long-term assets with descriptive titles such as Timber Lands, Oil and Gas Reserves, and Mineral Deposits. When the timber is cut, the oil is pumped, or the coal is mined, it becomes an inventory of the product to be sold. Natural resources are recorded at acquisition cost, which may also include some costs of development. As the resource is converted through the process of cutting, pumping, or mining, the asset account must be proportionally reduced. The carrying value of oil reserves on the balance sheet, for example, is reduced by a small amount for each barrel of oil pumped. As a result, the original cost of the oil reserves is gradually reduced, and depletion is recognized by the amount of the decrease.

Depletion

The term **depletion** is used to describe not only the exhaustion of a natural resource but also the proportional allocation of the cost of a natural resource to the units extracted. The costs are allocated in a way that is much like the production method used for depreciation. When a natural resource is purchased or developed, there must be an estimate of the total units that will be available, such as barrels of oil, tons of coal, or board-feet of lumber. The depletion cost per unit is determined by dividing the cost (less residual value, if any) of the natural resource by the estimated number of units available. The amount of the depletion cost for each accounting period is then computed by multiplying the depletion cost per unit by the number of units pumped, mined, or cut. For example, for a mine having an estimated 1,500,000 tons of coal, a cost of $1,800,000, and an estimated residual value of $300,000, the depletion charge per ton of coal is $1. Thus, if 115,000 tons of coal are mined and sold during the first year, the depletion charge for the year is $115,000. It is recorded as follows:

```
Dec. 31   Depletion Expense, Coal Mine           115,000
              Accumulated Depletion, Coal Mine              115,000
                To record depletion of coal mine:
                115,000 tons mined and sold at
                $1 per ton
```

On the balance sheet, the mine would be presented as follows:

Coal Mine	$1,800,000	
Less Accumulated Depletion	115,000	$1,685,000

A natural resource that is extracted in one year may sometimes not be sold until a later year. It is important to note that it would then be recorded as a depletion *expense* in the year it is *sold*. The part not sold is considered inventory.

Depreciation of Closely Related Plant Assets

Natural resources often require special on-site buildings and equipment such as conveyors, roads, tracks, and drilling and pumping devices that are necessary to extract the resource. If the useful life of these assets is longer than the estimated time it will take to deplete the resource, a special problem arises. Because these long-term assets are often abandoned and have no useful purpose beyond the time when the resources are extracted, they should be depreciated on the same basis as the depletion is computed. For example, if machinery with a useful life of ten years is installed on an oil field that is expected to be depleted in eight years, the machinery should be depreciated over the eight-year period using the production method. In other words, each year's depreciation charge should be proportional to the depletion charge. If one-sixth of the oil field's total reserves is pumped in one year, then the depreciation should be one-sixth of the machinery's cost minus the scrap value. If the useful life of a long-term asset is less than the expected life of the depleting asset, the shorter life should be used to compute depreciation. In this case or when an asset is not to be abandoned when the reserves are fully depleted, other depreciation methods such as straight-line or accelerated methods are appropriate.

Development and Exploration Costs in the Oil and Gas Industry

The costs of exploration and development of oil and gas resources can be accounted for under either of the following methods. Under **successful efforts accounting**, successful exploration—for example, the cost of a producing oil well—is a cost of the resource. This cost should be recorded as an asset and depleted over the estimated life of the resource. On the other hand, an unsuccessful exploration—such as the cost of a dry well—is written off immediately as a loss. Because of these immediate write-offs, successful efforts accounting is considered the more conservative method and is used by most large oil companies.

Exploration-minded independent oil companies, on the other hand, argue that the cost of the dry wells is part of the overall cost of the systematic development of the oil field and thus a part of the cost of producing wells. Under this **full-costing** method, all costs including the cost of dry wells are recorded as assets and depleted over the estimated life of the producing resources. This method tends to improve earnings performance in the early years of companies using it. Either method is permitted by the Financial Accounting Standards Board.[2]

Accounting for Intangible Assets

OBJECTIVE 5

Apply the matching rule to intangible asset accounting issues, including research and development costs and goodwill

The purchase of an intangible asset is a special kind of capital expenditure. An intangible asset is long term, but it has no physical substance. Its value comes from the long-term rights or advantages that it offers to the owner. Among the most common examples are patents, copyrights, leaseholds, leasehold improvements, trademarks and brand names, franchises, licenses, formulas, processes, and goodwill. Some current assets such as accounts receivable and certain prepaid expenses have no physical nature, but they are not called intangible assets because they are short term. Intangible assets are both long term and nonphysical.

Intangible assets are accounted for at acquisition cost, that is, the amount paid for them. Some intangible assets such as goodwill or trademarks may have been acquired at little or no cost. Even though they may have great value and are needed for profitable operations, they should not appear on the balance sheet unless they have been purchased from another party at a price established in the marketplace.

The accounting issues connected with intangible assets are the same as those connected with other long-lived assets. The Accounting Principles Board, in its *Opinion No. 17*, lists them as follows:

1. Determining an initial carrying amount
2. Accounting for that amount after acquisition under normal business conditions—that is, through periodic write-off or amortization—in a manner similar to depreciation
3. Accounting for that amount if the value declines substantially and permanently[3]

Besides these three problems, an intangible asset has no physical qualities and so in some cases may be impossible to identify. For these reasons, its value and its useful life may be quite hard to estimate.

The Accounting Principles Board has decided that a company should record as assets the costs of intangible assets acquired from others. However, the company should record as expenses the costs of developing intangible assets. Also, intangible assets that have a determinable

---

2. *Statement of Financial Accounting Standards No. 25*, "Suspension of Certain Accounting Requirements for Oil and Gas Producing Companies" (Stamford, Conn.: Financial Accounting Standards Board, 1979).
3. Adapted from Accounting Principles Board, *Opinion No. 17*, "Intangible Assets" (New York: American Institute of Certified Public Accountants, 1970), par. 2.

life, such as patents, copyrights, and leaseholds, should be written off through periodic amortization over that useful life in much the same way that plant assets are depreciated. Even though some intangible assets, such as goodwill and trademarks, have no measurable limit on their lives, they should also be amortized over a reasonable length of time (not to exceed forty years).

To illustrate these procedures, assume that Soda Bottling Company purchases a patent on a unique bottle cap for $18,000. The entry to record the patent would be

Patent	18,000	
Cash		18,000
Purchase of bottle cap patent		

Note that if this company had developed the bottle cap internally instead of purchasing it from a third party, the costs of developing the cap, such as salaries of researchers, supplies used in testing, and costs of equipment, would have been expensed as incurred.

Assume now that Soda's management determines that, although the patent for the bottle cap will last for seventeen years, the product using the cap will be sold only for the next six years. The entry to record the annual amortization would be

Amortization of Patent	3,000	
Patent		3,000
Annual amortization of patent:		
$18,000 \div 6$ years $= \$3,000$		

Note that the Patent account is reduced directly by the amount of the amortization expense. This is in contrast to other long-term asset accounts in which depreciation or depletion is accumulated in a separate contra account.

If the patent becomes worthless before it is fully amortized, the remaining carrying value is written off as a loss. For instance, assume that after the first year Soda's chief competitor offers a bottle with a new type of cap that makes Soda's cap obsolete. The entry to record the loss would be

Loss on Patent	15,000	
Patent		15,000
To record loss resulting from patent's		
becoming worthless		

Accounting for the different types of intangible assets is outlined in Table 13-1.

Research and Development Costs

Most successful companies carry out activities, possibly within a separate department, involving research and development. Among these activities are development of new products, testing of existing and

Table 13-1. Accounting for Intangible Assets

Type	Description	Special Accounting Problems
Patent	An exclusive right granted by the federal government for a period of 17 years to make a particular product or use a specific process.	The cost of successfully defending a patent in a patent infringement suit is added to the acquisition cost of the patent. Amortize over the useful life, which may be less than the legal life of 17 years.
Copyright	An exclusive right granted by the federal government to the possessor to publish and sell literary, musical, and other artistic materials for a period of the author's life plus 50 years. Includes computer programs.	Record at acquisition cost and amortize over the useful life, but not to exceed 40 years which is often much shorter than the legal life. For example, the cost of paperback rights to a popular novel would typically be amortized over a useful life of two to four years.
Leasehold	A right to occupy land or buildings under a long-term rental contract. For example, Company A, which owns but does not want to use a prime retail location, sells Company B the right to use it for ten years in return for one or more rental payments. Company B has purchased a leasehold.	Debit Leasehold for the amount of the payment, and amortize it over the remaining life of the lease. Payments to the lessor during the life of the lease should be debited to Lease Expense.
Leasehold Improvements	Improvements to leased property that become the property of the lessor (the person who owns the property) at the end of the lease.	Debit Leasehold Improvements for the cost of improvements, and amortize the cost of the improvements over the remaining life of the lease.
Trademark, Brand Name	A registered symbol or name giving the holder the right to use it to identify a product or service.	Debit the trademark or brand name for the acquisition cost, and amortize it over a reasonable life, not to exceed 40 years.
Franchise, License, Formula, Process	A right to an exclusive territory or to exclusive use of a formula, technique, or design.	Debit the franchise, license, formula, or process for the acquisition cost, and amortize it over a reasonable life, not to exceed 40 years.
Goodwill	The excess of the cost of a group of assets (usually a business) over the market value of the assets individually.	Debit Goodwill for the acquisition cost, and amortize it over a reasonable life, not to exceed 40 years.

proposed products, and pure research. In the past, some companies would record as an asset those costs of research and development that could be directly traced to the development of certain patents, formulas, or other rights. Other costs, such as those for testing and pure research, were treated as expenses of the accounting period and deducted from income.

The Financial Accounting Standards Board has stated that all research and development costs should be treated as revenue expenditures and charged to expense in the period when incurred.[4] The board argues that it is too hard to trace specific costs to specific profitable developments. Also, the costs of research and development are continuous and necessary for the success of a business and so should be treated as current expenses. To support this conclusion, the board cites studies showing that 30 to 90 percent of all new products fail and that three-fourths of new product expenses go to unsuccessful products. Thus, their costs do not represent future benefits.

Goodwill

The term **goodwill** is widely used by business people, lawyers, and the public to mean different things. In most cases one thinks of goodwill as meaning the good reputation of a company. From an accounting standpoint, goodwill exists when a purchaser pays more for a business than the fair market value of the assets if purchased separately. Because the purchaser has paid more than the fair market value of the physical assets, there must be intangible assets. If the company being purchased does not have patents, copyrights, trademarks, or other identifiable intangible assets of value, one must conclude that the excess payment is for goodwill. One would pay for goodwill because most businesses are worth more as going concerns than as collections of assets. Goodwill reflects all the factors, including customer satisfaction, good management, manufacturing efficiency, the advantages of holding a monopoly, good locations, and good employee relations, that allow a company to earn a higher than market rate of return on its assets. The payment above and beyond the fair market value of the tangible assets and other specific intangible assets is properly recorded in the Goodwill account.

In *Opinion No. 17*, the Accounting Principles Board states that the benefits arising from purchased goodwill will in time disappear. It is hard for a company to keep having above-average earnings unless new factors of goodwill replace the old ones. For this reason, goodwill should be amortized or written off by systematic charges to income over a reasonable number of future time periods. The time period should in no case be more than forty years.[5]

Goodwill, as stated above, should not be recorded unless it is paid for in connection with the purchase of a whole business. The amount to be recorded as goodwill can be determined by writing the identifiable net

4. *Statement of Financial Accounting Standards No. 2,* "Accounting for Research and Development Costs" (Stamford, Conn.: Financial Accounting Standards Board, 1974), par. 12.
5. Accounting Principles Board, *Opinion No. 17,* par. 29.

assets up to their fair market values at the time of purchase and subtracting the total from the purchase price. For example, assume that the owners of Company A agree to sell the company for $11,400,000. If the net assets (total assets – total liabilities) are fairly valued at $10,000,000, then the amount of the goodwill is $1,400,000 ($11,400,000 – $10,000,000). If the fair market value of the net assets is later determined to be more or less than $10,000,000, an entry is made in the accounting records to adjust the assets to the fair market value. The goodwill would then represent the difference between the adjusted net assets and the purchase price of $11,400,000.

It is sometimes difficult to determine the fair market value of individual assets. In such cases, the accountant may want to determine the going concern value of the purchased business, in order to estimate what the amount of goodwill must be. Several methods are available for determining a business's going concern value. One method is to determine the business's superior earning power. For instance, assume that Company A is able to demonstrate that it earns a higher rate of return on its net assets than other companies do in the same industry, as follows:

	Company A	Average of Similar Companies in Same Industry
Net assets other than goodwill	$10,000,000	$10,000,000
Normal rate of return	10%	10%
Normal net income	$ 1,000,000	$ 1,000,000
Actual net income (five-year average)	1,200,000	1,000,000
Above average earnings	$ 200,000	—

Based on this analysis, the buyer and seller could agree on a price of the net assets plus some additional amount for goodwill equal to a multiple of the earnings above the average for the industry. For example, if they agree on a multiple of 4 times the above-average earnings, the price of the business would be the net asset price of $10,000,000 plus goodwill of $800,000 ($200,000 × 4), or $10,800,000.

Another way to measure going concern value is to capitalize expected earnings in excess of the average at a rate that is normal in the industry. Expected above-average earnings are capitalized by dividing them by the average rate of return. For example, in the case of Company A, the above-average earnings are $200,000 and the average rate of return is 10 percent. Estimated goodwill may then be calculated as $2,000,000 ($200,000 ÷ .1), and the price of the business is $12,000,000 ($10,000,000 + $2,000,000). This is the most theoretically correct way to estimate goodwill because, in effect, it answers the question of how many dollars the company would need to invest to earn the $200,000 of above-average earnings derived from the goodwill. It also means that the same rate of return (in this case, 10 percent) applies to all assets (net assets plus goodwill).

Computer Software Costs

Many companies develop computer programs or software to be sold or leased to individuals and companies. The costs incurred in creating a computer software product are considered research and development costs until the product has been proved to be technologically feasible. As a result, costs incurred to this point in the process should be charged to expense as incurred. A product is deemed to be technologically feasible when a detailed working program has been designed. After the working program is developed, all software production costs are recorded as assets and amortized as expense over the estimated economic life of the product using the straight-line method. If at any time the company cannot expect to realize from the software product the amount of its unamortized costs on the balance sheet, the asset should be written down to the amount expected to be realized.[6]

Chapter Review

Review of Learning Objectives

1. **Apply the matching rule to the allocation of expired costs for capital expenditures and revenue expenditures.**
   It is important to distinguish between capital expenditures, which are recorded as assets, and revenue expenditures, which are recorded as expenses. The error of classifying one as the other will have an important effect on net income. Expenditures for plant assets, additions, betterments, and intangible assets are capital expenditures. Extraordinary repairs, which increase the residual value or extend the life of an asset, are also treated as capital expenditures, whereas ordinary repairs are revenue expenditures.

2. **Account for disposal of depreciable assets not involving exchanges.**
   Long-term assets may be disposed of by being discarded, sold, or exchanged. In the disposal of long-term assets, it is necessary to bring the depreciation up to the date of disposal and to remove the carrying value from the accounts by removing the cost from the asset account and the depreciation to date from the accumulated depreciation account. If a long-term asset is sold at a price different from carrying value, there is a gain or loss that should be recorded and reported on the income statement.

6. *Statement of Financial Accounting Standards No. 86,* "Accounting for the Costs of Computer Software to Be Sold, Leased, or Otherwise Marketed" (Stamford, Conn.: Financial Accounting Standards Board, 1985).

3. **Account for disposal of depreciable assets involving exchanges.**
In recording exchanges of similar plant assets, a gain or loss may also arise. According to the Accounting Principles Board, losses, but not gains, should be recognized at the time of the exchange (as long as no money is received). When a gain is not recognized, the new asset is recorded at the carrying value of the old asset plus any cash paid. For income tax purposes, neither gains nor losses are recognized in the exchange of similar assets. When dissimilar assets are exchanged, gains and losses are recognized under both accounting and income tax rules.

4. **Identify natural resource accounting issues and compute depletion.**
Natural resources are wasting assets, which are converted to inventory by cutting, pumping, mining, or other forms of extraction. Natural resources are recorded at cost as long-term assets. They are allocated as expenses through depletion charges as the resources are sold. The depletion charge is based on the ratio of the resource extracted to the total estimated resource. A major issue related to this subject is accounting for oil and gas reserves.

5. **Apply the matching rule to intangible asset accounting issues, including research and development costs and goodwill.**
Purchases of intangible assets should be treated as capital expenditures and recorded at acquisition cost, which in turn should be amortized over the useful life of the assets (but not more than forty years). The FASB requires that research and development costs be treated as revenue expenditures and charged as expense in the period of the expenditure. Goodwill is the excess of the amount paid over the fair market value of the net assets in the purchase of a business and is usually related to the superior earning potential of the business. It should be recorded only if purchased in connection with the purchase of a business and should be amortized over a period not to exceed forty years.

Review of Concepts and Terminology

The following concepts and terms were introduced in this chapter:

(L.O. 1) **Additions:** Enlargements to the physical layout of a plant asset.

(L.O. 1) **Betterments:** Improvements to plant assets that do not add to the physical layout of the asset.

(L.O. 1) **Capital expenditure:** An expenditure for the purchase or expansion of long-term assets, recorded in the asset accounts.

(L.O. 5) **Copyright:** An exclusive right granted by the federal government to the possessor to publish and sell literary, musical, and other artistic materials for a period of the author's life plus fifty years.

(L.O. 4) **Depletion:** The proportional allocation of the cost of a natural resource to the units extracted; the exhaustion of a natural resource through mining, cutting, pumping, or otherwise using up the natural resource.

(L.O. 1) **Expenditure:** A payment or incurrence of an obligation to make future payment for an asset or a service received.

(L.O. 1) **Extraordinary repairs**: Repairs that affect the estimated residual value or estimated useful life of an asset.

(L.O. 5) **Franchise**: The right to an exclusive territory or market.

(L.O. 4) **Full-costing**: Method of accounting for the costs of exploration and development of oil and gas resources in which all costs are recorded as assets and depleted over the estimated life of the producing resources.

(L.O. 5) **Goodwill**: The excess of the cost of a group of assets (usually a business) over the market value of the assets individually.

(L.O. 5) **Leasehold**: A right to occupy land or buildings under a long-term rental contract.

(L.O. 5) **Leasehold improvement**: An improvement to leased property that becomes the property of the lessor at the end of the lease.

(L.O. 5) **License**: Official or legal permission to do or own a specific thing.

(L.O. 1) **Ordinary repairs**: Expenditures, usually of a recurring nature, that are necessary to maintain an asset in good operating condition.

(L.O. 5) **Patent**: An exclusive right granted by the federal government to make a particular product or use a specific process.

(L.O. 1) **Revenue expenditure**: An expenditure for repairs, maintenance, or other services needed to maintain or operate plant assets.

(L.O. 4) **Successful efforts accounting**: Method of accounting in which successful exploration of oil and gas resources is recorded as an asset and depleted over the estimated life of the resource and all unsuccessful efforts are immediately written off as a loss.

(L.O. 5) **Trademark**: A registered symbol that gives the holder the right to use it to identify a product or service.

(L.O. 4) **Wasting assets**: Another term for natural resources; long-term assets purchased for the physical substances that can be taken from the land and used up rather than for the value of their location.

Self-Test

Test your knowledge of the chapter by choosing the best answer for each item below and on the next page.

1. An expenditure for which of the following items would be considered a revenue expenditure?
   a. Betterment
   b. Addition
   c. Ordinary repair
   d. Plant assets   *(L.O. 1)*

2. The primary difference between ordinary and extraordinary repairs is that extraordinary repairs
   a. extend the useful life of the asset.
   b. are an expense of the current period.
   c. are necessary in order to maintain the asset in good operational condition.
   d. are periodic in nature.   *(L.O. 1)*

3. The sale of equipment costing $16,000, with accumulated depreciation of $13,400 and sale price of $4,000, would result in a
   a. gain of $4,000.
   b. gain of $1,400.
   c. loss of $1,400.
   d. loss of $12,000.   (L.O. 2)

4. When an asset is sold, a gain occurs when
   a. the sale price exceeds the depreciable cost of the asset sold.
   b. the carrying value exceeds the sale price of the asset sold.
   c. the sale price exceeds the original cost of the asset sold.
   d. the sale price exceeds the carrying value of the asset sold.   (L.O. 2)

5. A truck that cost $16,800 and on which $12,600 of accumulated depreciation has been recorded was disposed of on January 1, the first day of the year. Assume the truck was traded for a similar truck having a price of $19,600, that a $2,000 trade-in was allowed, and that the balance was paid in cash. Following APB rules, the amount of the gain or loss recognized on this transaction would be
   a. $2,200 gain.
   b. $2,200 loss.
   c. no gain or loss recognized.
   d. none of the above.   (L.O. 3)

6. Assume the same facts as in 5, except that the truck was traded for a similar truck having a price of $19,600, that a $6,000 trade-in was allowed, and that the balance was paid in cash. Following income tax rules, the amount of gain or loss recognized on this transaction would be
   a. $1,800 gain.
   b. $1,800 loss.
   c. no gain recognized.
   d. none of the above.   (L.O. 3)

7. A specialized piece of equipment closely associated with a mine is most likely to be depreciated over a shorter-than-normal useful life because
   a. management wants to increase expenses.
   b. the equipment contains certain defects.
   c. the mine is expected to be fully depleted in the shorter length of time.
   d. the equipment will be fully utilized.   (L.O. 4)

8. Which of the following items is not classified as a natural resource?
   a. Timber land
   b. Gas reserve
   c. Goodwill
   d. Oil well   (L.O. 5)

9. According to generally accepted accounting principles, the proper accounting treatment for the cost of a trademark that management feels will retain its value indefinitely is to
   a. amortize the cost over a period not to exceed forty years.
   b. amortize the cost over five years.
   c. carry the cost of an asset indefinitely.
   d. write the cost off immediately.   (L.O. 5)

10. According to generally accepted accounting principles, the proper accounting treatment of the cost of most research and development expenditures is to
    a. amortize the cost over a period not to exceed forty years.
    b. amortize the cost over five years.
    c. carry the cost as an asset indefinitely.
    d. write the cost off immediately as an expense.   *(L.O. 5)*

Answers to Self-Test are at the end of this chapter.

Review Problem
Comprehensive Capital and Revenue
Expenditure Entries

(L.O. 1, 2) The Haywood Haberdashery, Inc. operates several stores featuring men's fashions. The following transactions describe the capital and revenue expenditures that relate to one of the company's stores. All expenditures are made in cash. The company records a full month of depreciation for the month of purchase on depreciable assets.

The building was purchased on January 1, 1975, for $117,000. At that time the building was repaired and renovated for use as a clothing store at a cost of $63,000. It was estimated that the building would have a useful life of forty years and a residual value after that time of $20,000.

On April 15, 1979, the front windows were replaced because they were cracked, and the roof was repaired because it was leaking. The repairs cost a total of $9,800.

On January 10, 1980, a new addition to the building was completed at a cost of $115,000. The addition did not add to the estimated useful life of the building but did increase the residual value by $10,000.

On August 3, 1983, the building was painted at a cost of $17,500.

On January 7, 1985, a complete overhaul of the heating and cooling system was completed at a cost of $20,000. It was estimated that this work would add ten years to the useful life of the building but would not increase its residual value.

Because of a decline in business, the building was sold on January 1, 1990, for $260,000 in cash.

Required
1. Prepare general journal entries for the following dates: (a) January 1, 1975; (b) April 15, 1979; (c) January 10, 1980; (d) August 3, 1983; and (e) January 7, 1985.
2. Open ledger accounts for Building (141) and for Accumulated Depreciation, Building (142), and post the relevant portions of the entries in 1.
3. Compute depreciation expense for each year until the date of sale, assuming that the straight-line method is used and that the company's fiscal year ends on December 31. Enter the amounts in the account for Accumulated Depreciation, Building.
4. Prepare a general journal entry to record the sale of the building on January 1, 1990. Post the relevant portions of the entry to the two accounts opened in 2.

Answer to Review Problem

1. and 4. Journal entries prepared:

		General Journal			Page
Date		Description	Post. Ref.	Debit	Credit
1975 Jan.	1	Building 　Cash 　　Purchase of building: 　　Cost　　　　　　　　$117,000 　　Repair and renovation　　63,000 　　Total cost　　　　　　$180,000	141	180,000	180,000
1979 Apr.	15	Repair Expense 　Cash 　　Replacement of windows and repair of roof		9,800	9,800
1980 Jan.	10	Building 　Cash 　　Addition to building	141	115,000	115,000
1983 Aug.	3	Repair Expense 　Cash 　　Painting of building		17,500	17,500
1985 Jan.	7	Accumulated Depreciation, Building 　Cash 　　Overhaul of heating and cooling system	142	20,000	20,000
1990 Jan.	1	Cash Accumulated Depreciation, Building 　Building 　Gain on Sale of Building 　　Sale of building	142 141	260,000 63,750	295,000 28,750

2. Ledger accounts opened and posted:

Building						Account No. 141	
						Balance	
Date		Item	Post. Ref.	Debit	Credit	Debit	Credit
1975 Jan.	1		J	180,000		180,000	
1980 Jan.	10		J	115,000		295,000	
1990 Jan.	1		J		295,000	—	

Accumulated Depreciation, Building					Account No. 142	
		Post.			Balance	
Date	Item	Ref.	Debit	Credit	Debit	Credit
1975		J		4,000		4,000
1976		J		4,000		8,000
1977		J		4,000		12,000
1978		J		4,000		16,000
1979		J		4,000		20,000
1980		J		7,000		27,000
1981		J		7,000		34,000
1982		J		7,000		41,000
1983		J		7,000		48,000
1984		J		7,000		55,000
1985						
Jan. 7			20,000			35,000
Dec. 31		J		5,750		40,750
1986		J		5,750		46,500
1987		J		5,750		52,250
1988		J		5,750		58,000
1989		J		5,750		63,750
1990						
Jan. 1		J	63,750			—

3. Depreciation expense computed:

January 1, 1975 to December 31, 1979—five years

($180,000 − $20,000) ÷ 40 years = $4,000 per year

January 1, 1980 to December 31, 1984—five years

($295,000 − $30,000 − $20,000) ÷ 35 years = $7,000 per year

January 1, 1985 to December 31, 1989—five years

Book value before extraordinary repair:

Building Account	$295,000	
Accumulated Depreciation	55,000	$240,000
Extraordinary repair		20,000
New carrying value		$260,000
Less residual value		30,000
Depreciable cost		$230,000
Divide by years remaining in useful life:		
Years remaining before extraordinary item	30	
Years added by extraordinary item	10	40
Depreciation per year		$ 5,750

Chapter Assignments

Discussion Questions and Writing Assignments

1. What is the distinction between revenue expenditures and capital expenditures, and why is this distinction important?
2. What will be the effect on future years' income of charging an addition to a building as repair expense?
3. In what ways do an addition, a betterment, and an extraordinary repair differ?
4. How does an extraordinary repair differ from an ordinary repair? What is the accounting treatment for each?
5. If a plant asset is discarded before the end of its useful life, how is the amount of loss measured?
6. When similar assets are exchanged, at what amount is the new asset recorded for federal income tax purposes?
7. When an exchange of similar assets occurs in which there is an unrecorded loss, is the taxpayer ever able to deduct or receive federal income tax credit for the loss?
8. Old Stake Mining Company computes the depletion rate to be $2 per ton. During 19xx, the company mined 400,000 tons of ore and sold 370,000 tons. What is the total depletion for the year?
9. Under what circumstances can a mining company depreciate its plant assets over a period of time that is less than their useful lives?
10. Because accounts receivable have no physical substance, can they be classified as intangible assets?
11. Under what circumstances can a company have intangible assets that do not appear on the balance sheet?
12. When the Accounting Principles Board indicates that accounting for intangible assets involves the same problem as accounting for tangible assets, what problem is it referring to?
13. How does the Financial Accounting Standards Board recommend that research and development costs be treated?
14. Under what conditions should goodwill be recorded? Should it remain in the records permanently once it is recorded?

Classroom Exercises

**Exercise 13-1.
Capital and
Revenue
Expenditures
(L.O. 1)**

For each of the following transactions related to an office building, tell whether each transaction is a revenue expenditure (RE) or capital expenditure (CE). In addition, indicate whether each transaction is an ordinary repair (OR), extraordinary repair (ER), addition (A), betterment (B), or none of these (N).

_____ a. The hallways and ceilings in the building are repainted at a cost of $8,300.
_____ b. The hallways, which have tile floors, are carpeted at a cost of $28,000.
_____ c. A new wing is added to the building at a cost of $175,000.

_____ d. Furniture is purchased for the entrance to the building at a cost of $16,500.

_____ e. The air conditioning system is overhauled at a cost of $28,500. The overhaul extends the useful life of the air conditioning system by 10 years.

_____ f. A cleaning firm is paid $200 per week to clean the newly installed carpets.

Exercise 13-2.
Extraordinary
Repairs
(L.O. 1)

Sharif Manufacturing has an incinerator that originally cost $93,600 and now has accumulated depreciation of $66,400. The incinerator just completed its fifteenth year of service in an estimated useful life of twenty years. At the beginning of the sixteenth year, the company spent $21,400 repairing and modernizing the incinerator to comply with pollution control standards. Therefore, instead of five years, the incinerator is now expected to last ten more years. It will not, however, have more capacity than it did in the past or a residual value at the end of its useful life.

1. Prepare the entry to record the cost of the repairs.
2. Compute the book value of the incinerator after the entry.
3. Prepare the entry to record the depreciation (assuming straight-line method) for the current year.

Exercise 13-3.
Disposal of Plant
Assets
(L.O. 2, 3)

A piece of equipment that cost $32,400 and on which $18,000 of accumulated depreciation had been recorded was disposed of on January 2, the first day of business of the current year. Give general journal entries to record the disposal under each of the following assumptions:

1. It was discarded as having no value.
2. It was sold for $6,000 cash.
3. It was sold for $18,000 cash.
4. The equipment was traded in on dissimilar equipment having a list price of $48,000. A $15,600 trade-in was allowed, and the balance was paid in cash. Gains and losses are to be recognized.
5. The equipment was traded in on dissimilar equipment having a list price of $48,000. A $7,200 trade-in was allowed, and the balance was paid in cash. Gains and losses are to be recognized.
6. Same as 5 except that the items are similar and gains and losses are not to be recognized.

Exercise 13-4.
Disposal of Plant
Assets
(L.O. 2, 3)

A commercial vacuum cleaner costing $4,900, with accumulated depreciation of $3,600, was traded in on a new model that had a list price of $6,100. A trade-in allowance of $1,000 was given.

1. Compute the carrying value of the old vacuum cleaner.
2. Determine the amount of cash required to purchase the new vacuum cleaner.
3. Compute the amount of loss on the exchange.
4. Determine the cost basis of the new vacuum cleaner assuming (a) the loss is recognized and (b) the loss is not recognized.

5. Compute the yearly depreciation on the new vacuum cleaner for both assumptions in **4**, assuming a useful life of five years, a residual value of $1,600, and straight-line depreciation.

Exercise 13-5.
Disposal of Plant
Assets
(L.O. 2, 3)

A microcomputer was purchased by Juniper Company on January 1, 19x1 at a cost of $5,000. It is expected to have a useful life of five years and a residual value of $500. Assuming the computer is disposed of on July 1, 19x4, record the partial year's depreciation for 19x4, and record the disposal under each of the following assumptions:

1. The microcomputer is discarded.
2. The microcomputer is sold for $800.
3. The microcomputer is sold for $2,200.
4. The microcomputer is exchanged for a new microcomputer with a list price of $9,000. A $1,200 trade-in is allowed on the cash purchase. The accounting approach to gains and losses is followed.
5. Same as **4** except a $2,400 trade-in is allowed.
6. Same as **4** except the income tax approach is followed.
7. Same as **5** except the income tax approach is followed.
8. Same as **4** except the microcomputer is exchanged for dissimilar office equipment.
9. Same as **5** except the microcomputer is exchanged for dissimilar office equipment.

Exercise 13-6.
Natural Resource
Depletion and
Depreciation of
Related Plant
Assets
(L.O. 4)

Church Mining Corporation purchased land containing an estimated 10 million tons of ore for a cost of $8,800,000. The land without the ore is estimated to be worth $1,600,000. The company expects that all the usable ore can be mined in ten years. Buildings costing $800,000 with an estimated useful life of thirty years were erected on the site. Equipment costing $960,000 with an estimated useful life of ten years was installed. Because of the remote location, neither the buildings nor the equipment has an estimated residual value. During its first year of operation, the company mined and sold 800,000 tons of ore.

1. Compute the depletion charge per ton.
2. Compute the depletion expense that Church Mining Corporation should record for the year.
3. Determine the annual depreciation expense for the buildings, making it proportional to the depletion.
4. Determine the annual depreciation expense for the equipment under two alternatives: (a) using the straight-line method and (b) making the expense proportional to the depletion.

Exercise 13-7.
Amortization of
Copyrights and
Trademarks
(L.O. 5)

1. Fortunato Publishing Company purchased the copyright to a basic computer textbook for $20,000. The usual life of a textbook is about four years. However, the copyright will remain in effect for another fifty years. Calculate the annual amortization of the copyright.
2. Guzman Company purchased a trademark from a well-known supermarket for $160,000. The management of the company argued that the trade-

mark value would last forever and might even increase and so no amortization should be charged. Calculate the minimum amount of annual amortization that should be charged, according to guidelines of the appropriate Accounting Principles Board opinion.

Exercise 13-8.
Computation of
Goodwill
(L.O. 5)

Loften Corporation has assets of $760,000 and liabilities of $200,000. In Loften Corporation's industry, the typical return is 10 percent of net assets. Over the last five years, Loften Corporation has earned $70,000 per year, with net assets similar to those throughout the industry. Bibbs Corporation has offered to buy out Loften Corporation for a cash payment equal to net assets plus five times the excess earnings over industry average.

1. Determine the net assets for Loften Corporation.
2. Determine how much Loften Corporation's earnings exceed the industry average.
3. Calculate how much cash Bibbs Corporation is offering to buy out Loften Corporation.
4. Compute the value of goodwill. (Assume that the book value of assets equals fair market value.)

Interpreting Accounting Information

Ocean Drilling
and Exploration
Company
(ODECO)*
(L.O. 1)

Selected accounting policies involving long-term assets of ODECO, one of the largest oil and gas contract drilling companies, appear below:

1. Provisions are made for major repairs on the company's drilling barges by monthly charges to expense. The cost of major repairs incurred is charged against the related allowance created by the monthly provisions.
2. All other maintenance and repair costs are charged to expense.
3. Renewals (extraordinary repairs) are capitalized by reducing accumulated depreciation, and betterments are capitalized by increasing the asset account.

The following data apply to the year 1986:

Major Barge Repairs

Provisions	$ 4,451,000
Charges	2,588,000
Repairs and maintenance	27,165,000
Renewals to drilling barges (estimated)	10,000,000
Betterments to drilling barges (estimated)	20,000,000

Required

1. Explain the reasoning behind each of the accounting policies listed above.
2. Prepare journal entries to record each of the amounts listed (assume that expenditures are made in cash).

**Excerpts from the 1986 annual report used by permission of Ocean Drilling and Exploration Company. Copyright © 1986.

Problem Set A

Problem 13A-1.
Comprehensive
Capital and
Revenue
Expenditure
Entries
(L.O. 1, 2)

Nieman's, Inc. operates a chain of self-service gasoline stations in several southern states. The transactions below describe the capital and revenue expenditures for one station.

Construction on the station was completed on July 1, 1970, at a cost of $355,000. It was estimated that the station would have a useful life of thirty-five years and a residual value of $40,000. On September 15, 1974, scheduled painting and minor repairs affecting the appearance of the station were completed at a cost of $4,650. On July 9, 1975, a new gasoline tank was added at a cost of $80,000. The tank did not add to the useful life of the station, but it did add $11,000 to its estimated residual value. On October 22, 1979, the driveway of the station was resurfaced at a cost of $1,900. The cost of major repairs and renovation, as part of the company's planned maintenance completed on July 3, 1980, was $55,000. It was estimated that this work would extend the life of the station by five years and would not increase the residual value. A change in the routing of a major highway led to the sale of the station on January 2, 1983, for $230,000. The company received $30,000 in cash and a note for the balance of the $230,000.

Required

1. Prepare general journal entries for the following dates: (a) July 1, 1970; (b) September 15, 1974; (c) July 9, 1975; (d) October 22, 1979; and (e) July 3, 1980.
2. Open ledger accounts for Station (143) and for Accumulated Depreciation, Station (144), and post the relevant portions of the entries in 1.
3. Compute depreciation expense for each year and partial year until the date of sale, assuming that the straight-line method is used and that the company's fiscal year ends on June 30. Enter the amounts in the account for Accumulated Depreciation, Station.
4. Prepare a general journal entry to record the sale of the station on January 2, 1983. Post the relevant portions of the entries to the two accounts opened in 2.

Problem 13A-2.
Recording
Disposals
(L.O. 2, 3)

Robles Construction Company purchased a road grader for $29,000. The road grader is expected to have a useful life of five years and a residual value of $2,000 at the end of that time.

Required

Prepare journal entries to record the disposal of the road grader at the end of the second year, assuming that the straight-line method is used and making the following additional assumptions:

a. The road grader is sold for $20,000 cash.
b. It is sold for $16,000 cash.
c. It is traded in on a dissimilar item (machinery) having a price of $33,000, a trade-in allowance of $20,000 is given, the balance is paid in cash, and gains or losses are recognized.
d. It is traded in on a dissimilar item (machinery) having a price of $33,000, a trade-in allowance of $16,000 is given, the balance is paid in cash, and gains or losses are recognized.

e. Same as **c** except it is traded for a similar road grader and Robles Construction Company follows APB accounting rules with regard to the recognition of gains or losses.

f. Same as **d** except it is traded for a similar road grader and Robles Construction Company follows APB accounting rules with regard to the recognition of gains or losses.

g. Same as **c** except it is traded for a similar road grader and gains or losses are not recognized (income tax purposes).

h. Same as **d** except it is traded for a similar road grader and gains or losses are not recognized (income tax purposes).

Problem 13A-3.
Comprehensive
Disposals
(L.O. 2, 3)

Waynesboro Tool and Stamp Company manufactures custom-designed metal parts for stereo component systems. During the past several years of operation, the company has owned several of the machines needed for this type of specialized metal shaping. The transactions related to four of these machines are presented below:

Machine	Cost	Facts Regarding Disposal	Accumulated Depreciation to Date of Disposal
1	$17,000	Exchanged for new machine No. 3., $5,000 trade-in allowed	$ 9,000
2	$20,000	Exchanged for new machine No. 4., $8,000 trade-in allowed	$16,000
3	$21,000	Sold for $10,500 cash	$13,000
4	$16,000	Sold for $1,000 cash	$10,000
5	$19,000	Exchanged for dissimilar equipment with a price of $26,000, $9,500 trade-in allowed	$12,000
6	$22,000	Exchanged for dissimilar equipment with a price of $27,000, $3,000 trade-in allowed	$15,000

Required

1. Prepare the general journal entries to record the disposal of each machine applying the APB rules applicable to exchanges.
2. Prepare the general journal entries to record the disposal of machines 1 and 2 applying the income tax rules applicable to exchanges.

Problem 13A-4.
Comprehensive
Natural Resources
Entries
(L.O. 4)

Ben Green is a gravel man from New Mexico. On January 3, 19x2, Green purchased a piece of property with gravel deposits for $6,510,000. He estimated that the gravel deposits contained 4,700,000 cubic yards of gravel. The gravel is used for making roads. After the gravel is gone, the land, which is in the desert, will be worth only about $400,000. The equipment required to extract the gravel cost $1,452,000. In addition, Green decided to build a small frame building to house the mine office and a small dining hall for the workers. The building cost $152,000 and would have no residual value after its estimated useful life of ten years. It cannot be moved from the mine site. The equipment has an estimated useful life of six years (with no residual value and it cannot be removed from the mine site). Trucks for the project cost $308,000 (estimated life, six years; residual value, $20,000). The trucks, of course, can be used at a different site. Green estimated that in five years all the gravel would be mined and the mine would be shut down. During 19x2, 1,175,000 cubic yards of gravel were mined and sold.

Required

1. Prepare general journal entries to record the purchase of the property and all the buildings and equipment associated with the mine.
2. Prepare adjusting entries to record depletion and depreciation for the first year of operation (19x2). Assume that the depreciation rate is equal to the percentage of the total gravel sold during the year unless the asset is movable. For movable assets, use the straight-line method.

Problem 13A-5.
Amortization of
Exclusive License,
Leasehold, and
Leasehold
Improvements
(L.O. 5)

Part 1
On January 1, Future Play, Inc. purchased the exclusive license to make dolls based on the characters in a new hit series on television called "Sky Pirates." The exclusive license cost $2,100,000, and there was no termination date on the rights. Immediately after signing the contract, the company sued a rival firm that claimed it had already received the exclusive license to the series characters. Future Play successfully defended its rights at a cost of $360,000. During the first year and the next, Future Play marketed toys based on the series. Because a successful television series lasts about five years, the company felt it could market the toys for three more years. However, before the third year of the series could get under way, a controversy arose between the two stars of the series and the producer. As a result, the stars refused to do the third year and the show was canceled, rendering exclusive rights worthless.

Required

Prepare journal entries to record the following: (a) purchase of the exclusive license; (b) successful defense of the license; (c) amortization expense, if any, for the first year; and (d) news of the series cancellation.

Part 2
Pamela Newell purchased a six-year sublease on a building from the estate of the former tenant, who had died suddenly. It was a good location for her business, and the annual rent of $3,600, which had been established ten years before, was low for such a good location. The cost of the sublease was $9,450. To use the building, Newell had to make certain alterations. First she moved some panels at a cost of $1,700 and installed others for $6,100. Then she added carpet, lighting fixtures, and a sign at costs of $2,900, $3,100, and $1,200, respectively. All items except the carpet would last for at least twelve years. The expected life of the carpet was six years. None of the improvements would have a residual value at the end of those times.

Required

Prepare general journal entries to record the following: (a) the payment for the sublease; (b) the payments for the alterations, panels, carpet, lighting fixtures, and sign; (c) the lease payment for the first year; (d) the expense, if any, associated with the sublease; and (e) the expense, if any, associated with the alterations, panels, carpet, lighting fixtures, and sign.

Problem Set B

**Problem 13B-1.
Capital and
Revenue
Expenditure
Entries
(L.O. 1, 2)**

Gary Kubiak operates several low-budget motels in the Midwest. The transactions below describe the capital and revenue expenditures for the first motel he purchased:

Dec. 21, 19x1   Purchased the motel at a cost of $940,000. The estimated life of the motel is twenty years, and the residual value is $140,000.

Dec. 31, 19x1   The motel was repainted and some minor roof problems were corrected at a cost of $40,000. These costs were necessary before the motel was opened to the public.

Jan. 12, 19x5   Made a small addition to the motel at a cost of $38,250. This cost did not impact on the life or residual value of the motel.

May 20, 19x5   Minor repairs were made to the doors of each room for $5,300.

Sept. 17, 19x5   Minor resurfacing was performed on the parking lot at a cost of $6,100.

Jan. 9, 19x8   Major repairs and renovation of $74,500 were completed. It was estimated that this work would extend the life of the motel by five years and increase the residual value by $10,000.

Required

1. Prepare general journal entries for each transaction. Assume that all transactions are made with cash.
2. Open ledger accounts for Motel (150) and Accumulated Depreciation, Motel (151), and post the relevant entries in 1 and other necessary entries above through 19x8.
3. Compute depreciation expense for each year and partial year assuming that the straight-line method is used and the company's fiscal year ends on December 31. Enter the amounts in the accounts for Accumulated Depreciation, Motel.
4. Prepare general journal entries to record the partial year's depreciation and the sale of the motel on June 30, 19x9, for $880,000, including $80,000 in cash and the remaining amount as a mortgage note. Post the relevant portions of the entry to the two accounts opened in 2.

**Problem 13B-2.
Recording
Disposals
(L.O. 2, 3)**

Ingram Designs, Inc. purchased a computer that will assist it in designing factory layouts. The cost of the computer was $47,000. The expected useful life is six years. The company can probably sell the computer for $5,000 at the end of six years.

Required

Prepare journal entries to record the disposal of the computer at the end of the third year, assuming that it was depreciated using the straight-line method and making the assumptions listed at the top of the next page:

a. The computer is sold for $38,000.
b. It is sold for $20,000.
c. It is traded in on a dissimilar item (equipment) costing $72,000, a trade-in allowance of $35,000 is given, the balance is paid in cash, and gains and losses are recognized.
d. Same as **c**, except the trade-in allowance is $22,000.
e. Same as **c** except it is traded for a similar computer and APB accounting rules are followed with regard to the recognition of gains or losses.
f. Same as **d** except it is traded for a similar computer and APB accounting rules are followed with regard to the recognition of gains or losses.
g. Same as **c**, except it is traded for a similar computer and gains and losses are not recognized (income tax method).
h. Same as **d**, except it is traded for a similar computer and gains and losses are not recognized (income tax method).

Problem 13B-3.
Comprehensive
Disposals
(L.O. 2, 3)

Otto Printing Company prints predesigned multiple-copy forms for use in a wide variety of businesses. During the past four years of operation, the company has owned a number of the printers needed for this type of specialized printing. The transactions related to six of these printers are presented as follows:

Printer	Cost	Facts Regarding Disposal	Accumulated Depreciation to Date of Disposal
1	$28,000	Exchanged for new printer No. 3, $7,000 trade-in allowed	$18,000
2	$32,000	Exchanged for new printer No. 4, $6,000 trade-in allowed	$28,000
3	$33,000	Sold for $9,000 cash	$25,000
4	$27,000	Sold for $3,000 cash	$22,000
5	$31,000	Exchanged for dissimilar equipment with a price of $38,000, $8,000 trade-in allowed	$24,000
6	$34,000	Exchanged for dissimilar equipment with a price of $39,000, $4,000 trade-in allowed	$23,000

Required

1. Prepare the general journal entries to record the disposal of each printer applying the APB rules applicable to exchanges.
2. Prepare the general journal entries to record the disposal of printers 1 and 2 applying the income tax rules applicable to exchanges.

Problem 13B-4.
Comprehensive
Natural Resources
Entries
(L.O. 4)

Ramon Munoz purchased property for the Munoz Coal Company that is estimated to contain 50,000,000 tons of coal. Munoz paid $6,000,000 for the property on January 2, 19x3. The property should be worth $1,000,000 after all the coal is extracted. At the same time Munoz purchased equipment costing $1,196,000 to extract the coal. The equipment has an eight-year useful life with a residual value of $96,000 and can be moved to a new site when this site is depleted. Also, an on-site office had to be constructed for $120,000. The office has an estimated useful life of ten years with no residual value. The office will be abandoned when the site is depleted. The coal extracted from this site will be sold to retail companies that will load and deliver the coal directly from Munoz's property. Munoz estimates all the coal will be mined in four years, and the mine will be closed. During 19x3, 13,000,000 tons of coal were mined and sold.

Required

1. Prepare general journal entries to record the purchase of the property, equipment, and office construction.
2. Prepare adjusting entries to record depreciation and depletion for 19x3. Assume that the depreciation rate is equal to the percentage of the total coal mined during the year unless the asset is movable and that the straight-line method of depreciation is used for the movable assets.

Problem 13B-5.
Leasehold,
Leasehold
Improvements,
and Amortization
of Patent
(L.O. 5)

Part 1

At the beginning of the fiscal year, Dempsey Company purchased an eight-year sublease on a warehouse in Nashville for $24,000. Dempsey will also pay rent of $500 a month. The warehouse needs the following improvements to meet Dempsey's needs:

Lighting fixtures	$ 9,000	Heating system	$15,000
Replacement of a wall	12,500	Break room	6,100
Office carpet	7,200	Loading dock	4,200

The expected life of the loading dock and carpet is eight years. The other items are expected to last ten years. None of the improvements will have a residual value.

Required

Prepare general journal entries to record the following: (a) payment for the sublease; (b) first-year lease payment; (c) payments for the improvements; (d) amortization of leasehold for the year; (e) leasehold improvement amortization for the year.

Part 2

At the beginning of the fiscal year, Fellner Company purchased a patent for $515,000 that applies to the manufacture of a unique tamper-proof lid for medicine bottles. Fellner incurred legal costs of $225,000 in successfully defending the patent against use of the lid by a competitor. Fellner estimated that the patent would be valuable for at least ten years. During the first two years of operation, Fellner successfully marketed the lid. At the beginning of the third year, a study appeared in a consumers' magazine showing that the lid could, in fact, be removed by children. As a result, all orders for the lids were canceled, and the patent was rendered worthless.

Required

Prepare journal entries to record the following: (a) purchase of the patent; (b) successful defense of the patent; (c) amortization expense for the first year; and (d) write-off of the patent as worthless.

Financial Decision Case

Stan Johnson, president of Johnson Company, has been looking for a good business to purchase. He found one in Conway Enterprises, which has earned an average of $46,000 a year for the last five years. Johnson proposed that he purchase all the assets, except for cash, of Conway Enterprises and assume the liabilities of Conway. He will pay $150,000 cash and give a one-year note for the balance. He is willing to pay for goodwill equal to four times those earnings that exceed the industry average earnings of 10 percent of net tangible assets, excluding cash.

Information from the current balance sheet for Conway Enterprises is as follows:

Conway Enterprises Balance Sheet		
Cash		$ 22,000
Other Current Assets		164,000
Plant Assets		
Land		5,000
Buildings	$124,000	
Less Accumulated Depreciation	42,000	82,000
Equipment	$289,000	
Less Accumulated Depreciation	106,000	183,000
Trademark		22,000
Franchise		17,000
Total Assets		$495,000
Current Liabilities		$ 46,000
Long-Term Note Payable		100,000
Bob Conway, Capital		349,000
Total Liabilities and Owner's Equity		$495,000

Stan Johnson and Bob Conway agree to adjust the Conway Enterprises books in two ways. First of all, the land, which had been purchased many years before by the Conway family, was not realistically valued and should have a value of $25,000. Second, the trademark and franchise that had been on the books for many years without being amortized should not be considered to have any value.

Required

1. Prepare a general journal entry to adjust the Conway Enterprises books in accordance with the agreement.
2. Compute the net tangible assets exclusive of cash.
3. Compute the amount of goodwill to be purchased.
4. Prepare a general journal entry in Johnson Company's records to show the purchase of Conway Enterprises.

Answers to Self-Test

1. c
2. a
3. b
4. d
5. b

6. c
7. c
8. c
9. a
10. d

PRINCIPLES OF ACCOUNTING

FINANCIAL ACCOUNTING

PART ONE
The Basic Accounting Model

PART TWO
Extensions of the Basic Accounting Model

PART THREE
Measuring and Reporting Assets and Current Liabilities

PART FOUR
Accounting for Partnerships and Corporations

Chapter 14
 Accounting for
 Partnerships

Chapter 15
 Contributed Capital

Chapter 16
 Retained Earnings
 and Corporate
 Income Statements

Chapter 17
 Long-Term
 Liabilities

PART FIVE
Special Reports and Analyses of Accounting Information

MANAGERIAL ACCOUNTING

PART SIX
Basic Concepts of Management Accounting

PART SEVEN
Accounting for Management Decision Making

In the earlier parts of this book, except for the demonstration using financial statements from Toys "R" Us (Chapter 8), the sole proprietorship has been the major form of business organization discussed. In Part Four, introductory accounting concepts and practices of partnerships and corporations are presented.

PART FOUR

Accounting for Partnerships and Corporations

Chapter 14 deals with the formation and liquidation of partnerships, as well as with how income and losses are distributed among partners.

Chapter 15 introduces accounting for the corporate form of business, including the issuance of capital stock, cash dividends, and other transactions.

Chapter 16 focuses on accounting for retained earnings, a number of other transactions that affect the stockholders' equity of a corporation, and the parts that make up the corporate income statement.

Chapter 17 introduces the long-term liabilities of corporations, with special attention to accounting for bonds payable.

LEARNING OBJECTIVES

1. *Identify the major characteristics, advantages, and disadvantages of the partnership form of business.*
2. *Record investments of cash and of other assets by the partners in forming a partnership.*
3. *Compute and record the income or losses that partners share, based on a stated ratio, the capital investment ratio, and salaries and interest to partners.*
4. *Record a person's admission to a partnership.*
5. *Record a person's withdrawal from a partnership.*
6. *Compute the distribution of assets to partners when they liquidate their partnership.*

CHAPTER 14

Accounting for Partnerships

In the first half of this book, we used the sole proprietorship to illustrate the basic principles and practices of accounting. This chapter will focus on accounting for the partnership form of business organization. The Uniform Partnership Act, which has been adopted by most of the states, defines a **partnership** as "an association of two or more persons to carry on as co-owners of a business for profit." Generally, partnerships are formed when owners of small businesses wish to combine capital or managerial talents for some common business purpose. After studying this chapter, you should be able to meet the learning objectives listed on the left.

Partnership Characteristics

Partnerships, which are treated as separate entities in accounting, differ in many ways from other forms of business. The next few paragraphs describe some of the important characteristics of a partnership.

Voluntary Association

A partnership is a voluntary association of individuals rather than a legal entity in itself. Therefore, a partner is responsible under the law for his or her partner's business actions within the scope of the partnership. A partner also has unlimited liability for the debts of the partnership. Because of these potential liabilities, an individual must be allowed to choose the people who will join the partnership. A person should select as partners individuals who share his or her business objectives.

Partnership Agreement

A partnership is easy to form. Two or more competent people simply agree to be partners in some common business purpose. This agreement is known as the **partnership agreement** and does not have to be in writing. However, good business practice calls for a written document that clearly states the details of the partnership. The contract should include the name, location, and purpose of the business; the partners and their respective duties; the investments of each partner; the methods for distributing profits and losses; the admission or withdrawal of partners; the withdrawals of assets allowed each partner; and procedures for dissolving, or ending. the business.

Limited Life

OBJECTIVE 1
Identify the major characteristics, advantages, and disadvantages of the partnership form of business

Because a partnership is formed by a contract between partners, it has **limited life**: anything that ends the contract dissolves the partnership. A partnership is dissolved when (1) a partner withdraws, (2) a partner goes bankrupt, (3) a partner is incapacitated (as when a partner becomes so ill that he or she cannot perform as obligated), (4) a partner dies, (5) a new partner is admitted, (6) a partner retires, or (7) the partnership ends according to the partnership agreement (as when a major project is completed). However, the partnership agreement can be written to cover each of these situations. This would allow the partnership to continue legally. For example, if a partner dies, the partnership agreement may state that the remaining partner or partners will purchase the deceased partner's capital at book value from the surviving beneficiaries.

Mutual Agency

Each partner is an agent of the partnership within the scope of the business. Because of this **mutual agency** feature, any partner can bind the partnership to a business agreement as long as he or she acts within the scope of normal operations of the business. For example, a partner in a used-car business can bind the partnership through the purchase or sale of used cars. This partner cannot bind the partnership, however, to a contract for buying men's clothing or any other goods unrelated to the used-car business. Because of this mutual agency characteristic, it is very important for an individual to choose business partners who have integrity and business objectives similar to his or her own.

Unlimited Liability

Each partner is personally liable for all the debts of the partnership. If a partnership is in poor financial condition and cannot pay its debts, the creditors must first satisfy their claims from the assets of the partnership. When the assets of the business are not enough to pay all debts, the creditors may seek payment from the personal assets of each partner. If a partner's personal assets are used up before the debts are paid, the creditors may claim additional assets from the remaining partners who are able to pay the debts. Each partner could conceivably be required by law to pay all the debts of the partnership; therefore, all the partners have **unlimited liability** for their company's debt.

An exception to the unlimited liability rule is the **limited partnership**, which is a partnership formed for a specific purpose such as the development of a shopping center or an apartment complex. In a limited partnership, there is a general partner who runs the partnership business and has generally unlimited liability, and there are limited partners who are investors in the project whose liability is generally limited to their investment in the partnership.

Co-ownership of Partnership Property

When individuals invest property into a partnership, they give up the right to their separate use of the property. The property becomes an asset of the partnership and is owned jointly by all the partners.

Participation in Partnership Income

Each partner has the right to share in the company's profits and the responsibility to share in its losses. The partnership agreement should state the method of distributing profits and losses to each partner. If the agreement describes how profits are to be shared but does not mention losses, the losses are distributed in the same way as profits. If the partners fail to describe the method of profit and loss distribution in the partnership agreement, the law states that profits and losses must be shared equally.

Summary of the Advantages and Disadvantages of Partnerships

Partnerships have both advantages and disadvantages. Several of the advantages are that the partnership is easy to form and to dissolve; it is able to pool capital resources and individual talents; it has no corporate tax burden (because the partnership is not a legal entity, it does not have to pay an income tax but must file an informational return); and it gives freedom and flexibility to its partners' actions.

Several of the disadvantages of a partnership are that its life is limited; one partner can bind the partnership to a contract (mutual agency); the partners have unlimited personal liability; and it is hard in a partnership to raise large amounts of capital and to transfer ownership interest.

Accounting for Partners' Equity

OBJECTIVE 2
Record investments of cash and of other assets by the partners in forming a partnership

Accounting for a partnership is very similar to accounting for a sole proprietorship. A major difference is that the owners' equity of a partnership is called **partners' equity**. In accounting for partners' equity, it is necessary to maintain separate capital and withdrawal accounts for each partner and to divide the profits and losses of the company among the partners. The differences in the capital accounts of a sole proprietorship and a partnership are shown in the following illustration.

Sole Proprietorship	Partnership	
Blake, Capital	**Desmond, Capital**	**Frank, Capital**
50,000	30,000	40,000
Blake, Withdrawals	**Desmond, Withdrawals**	**Frank, Withdrawals**
12,000	5,000	6,000

In the partners' equity section of the balance sheet, the balance of each partner's capital account is listed separately, as shown in the partial balance sheet that follows.

Liabilities and Partners' Equity

Total Liabilities		$28,000
Partners' Equity		
Desmond, Capital	$25,000	
Frank, Capital	34,000	
Total Partners' Equity		59,000
Total Liabilities and Partners' Equity		$87,000

Each partner invests cash, other assets, or a combination in the partnership according to the agreement. When other assets are invested, the partners must agree on their value. The value of noncash assets should be their fair market value on the date they are transferred to the partnership. The assets invested by a partner are debited to the proper accounts, and the total amount is credited to the partner's capital account.

To illustrate the recording of partners' investments, we shall assume that Jerry Adcock and Rose Villa agree to combine their capital and equipment in a partnership for the purpose of operating a jewelry store. Adcock will invest $28,000 cash and $37,000 of furniture and displays, and Villa will invest $40,000 cash and $20,000 of equipment, according to the partnership agreement. The general journal entries that record the initial investments of Adcock and Villa are as follows:

July 1	Cash	28,000	
	Furniture and Displays	37,000	
	Jerry Adcock, Capital		65,000
	To record the initial investment		
	of Jerry Adcock in Adcock and Villa		
1	Cash	40,000	
	Equipment	20,000	
	Rose Villa, Capital		60,000
	To record the initial investment		
	of Rose Villa in Adcock and Villa		

The values assigned to the assets in the above illustration would have had to be included in the partnership agreement. These values may differ from those carried on the partners' personal books. For example, the equipment that Rose Villa contributed may have had a value of only $12,000 on her books. However, after she purchased the equipment, its market value increased considerably. Regardless of book value, Villa's investment should be recognized at the fair market value of the equipment at the time of transfer, because that value represents the amount of money that Villa has put into the partnership.

Further investments are recorded in the same way. The partnership may also assume liabilities that are related to investments. For example, suppose that after seven months Rose Villa invests additional equipment with a fair market value of $45,000 into the partnership. Related to the equipment is a note payable for $37,000, which the partnership assumes. The entry that records the transaction is as follows:

Feb. 1	Equipment	45,000	
	Notes Payable		37,000
	Rose Villa, Capital		8,000
	To record additional investment		
	by Rose Villa in Adcock and Villa		

Distribution of Partnership Income and Losses

OBJECTIVE 3
Compute and record the income or losses that partners share, based on a stated ratio, the capital investment ratio, and salaries and interest to partners

A partnership's income and losses can be distributed according to any method that the partners specify in the partnership agreement. The agreement should be specific and clear to avoid disputes among partners over later distributions of income and losses. However, if the partnership agreement does not mention the distribution of income and losses, the law requires that they be shared equally by all partners. Also, if the partnership agreement mentions only the distribution of income, the law requires that losses be distributed in the same ratio as income.

The income of a partnership normally has three components: (1) return to the partners for the use of their capital (referred to as interest on partners' capital), (2) compensation for services that the partners have rendered (referred to as partners' salaries), and (3) further economic income for the business risks the partners have taken. The breakdown of total income into its three components helps clarify how much each partner has contributed to the firm.

If all partners are spending the same amount of time, are contributing equal capital, and have similar managerial talents, then an equal sharing of income and losses would be fair. However, if one partner works full time in the firm whereas another partner devotes only one-fourth of his or her time, then the distribution of income or losses should reflect this difference. This arrangement would apply to any situation in which the partners contribute unequally to the business.

Several ways for partners to share income are (1) by stated ratio, (2) by capital investment ratio, and (3) by salaries to the partners and interest on partners' capital, with the remaining income shared according to a stated ratio. "Salaries" and "interest" are not regarded as salaries expense or interest expense in the ordinary sense of the terms. Rather, they refer to ways of determining each partner's share of net income or loss on the basis of time spent and money invested in the partnership.

Stated Ratio

One method of distributing income and losses is to give each partner a stated ratio of the total. If each partner is making an equal contribution to the firm, each may assume the same share of the income and losses. The equal contribution of the partners may take many forms. For example, each partner may have made an equal investment in the firm. On the other hand, one partner may be devoting more time and talent to the firm, whereas the second partner may make a larger capital investment. Also, if the partners contribute unequally to the firm, unequal stated ratios can be appropriate, such as 60 percent and 40 percent.

To illustrate this method, we shall assume that Adcock and Villa had a net income last year of $30,000. The partnership agreement states that the percentages of income and losses distributed to Adcock and Villa will be 60 percent and 40 percent, respectively. The computation of each partner's share of the income and the journal entry to show the distribution are as follows:

Adcock ($30,000 × 60%)	$18,000
Villa ($30,000 × 40%)	12,000
Net Income	$30,000

June 30	Income Summary	30,000	
	Jerry Adcock, Capital		18,000
	Rose Villa, Capital		12,000
	To distribute the income for the year to the partners' capital accounts		

Capital Investment Ratio

If the invested capital produces the most income for the partnership business, then income and losses may be distributed according to capital investment. One way of distributing income and losses in this case is to use a ratio based on the capital balance of each partner at the beginning of the year. Another way is to use the average capital balance of each partner during the year.

To show how the first method works, we will assume the following balances for the capital accounts of Adcock and Villa for their first year of operation, which was July 1, 19x1 through June 30, 19x2. Income for the year was $140,000.

Jerry Adcock, Capital		Jerry Adcock, Withdrawals
	7/1 65,000	1/1 10,000

Rose Villa, Capital		Rose Villa, Withdrawals
	7/1 60,000	11/1 10,000
	2/1 8,000	

Beginning capital balances for Adcock and Villa were as follows:

	Capital	Capital Ratio
Jerry Adcock	$ 65,000	65/125
Rose Villa	60,000	60/125
	$125,000	

The income that each partner will receive when distribution is based on beginning capital investment ratios is figured by multiplying the total income by each partner's capital ratio:

Jerry Adcock	$140,000 × 65/125 =	$ 72,800
Rose Villa	$140,000 × 60/125 =	$ 67,200
		$140,000

The entry showing distribution of income to Jerry Adcock and Rose Villa is as follows:

June 30	Income Summary	140,000	
	Jerry Adcock, Capital		72,800
	Rose Villa, Capital		67,200
	To distribute the income for the		
	year to the partners' capital accounts		

If Adcock and Villa use their beginning capital investments to determine the ratio for distributing income, they do not consider any withdrawals or further investments made during the year. However, such investments and withdrawals usually change the partners' capital ratio. Therefore, the partnership agreement should state which capital balances will determine the ratio for distributing income and losses.

If partners believe their capital balances will change very much during the year, they may select their average capital balances as a fairer means of distributing income and losses. To illustrate this method, we will assume that, during the first year, Jerry Adcock withdrew $10,000 on January 1, 19x2, and Rose Villa withdrew $10,000 on November 1, 19x1, and invested the additional $8,000 of equipment on February 1, 19x2. The income for the year's operation was $140,000. The calculations for the average capital balances and the distribution of income are as follows:

Average Capital Balances

Partner	Date	Capital Balance	×	Months Unchanged	=	Total	Average Capital
Adcock	7/x1–12/x1	$65,000	×	6	=	$390,000	
	1/x2–6/x2	55,000	×	6	=	330,000	
				12		$720,000 ÷ 12 =	$ 60,000
Villa	7/x1–10/x1	$60,000	×	4	=	$240,000	
	11/x1–1/x2	50,000	×	3	=	150,000	
	2/x2–6/x2	58,000	×	5	=	290,000	
				12		$680,000 ÷ 12 =	$ 56,667
						Total average capital	$116,667

Average Capital Balance Ratios

$$\text{Adcock} = \frac{\text{Adcock's average capital balance}}{\text{total average capital}} = \frac{\$60,000}{\$116,667} = 51.4\%$$

$$\text{Villa} = \frac{\text{Villa's average capital balance}}{\text{total average capital}} = \frac{\$56,667}{\$116,667} = 48.6\%$$

Distribution of Income

Partner	Income × Ratio	=	Share of Income
Adcock	$140,000 × 51.4%	=	$ 71,960
Villa	$140,000 × 48.6%	=	68,040
		Total income	$140,000

Note that this calculation calls for determining (1) average capital balances, (2) average capital balance ratios, and (3) each partner's share of income or loss. To compute a partner's average capital balance, it is necessary to examine the changes that have taken place during the year in each partner's capital balance. These changes result from further investments and withdrawals. The partner's beginning capital is multiplied by the number of months the balance remains unchanged. After the balance changes, the new balance is multiplied by the number of months it remains unchanged. This process continues until the end of the year. The totals of these computations are added together, then divided by twelve, to determine the average capital balances. Once the average capital balances are determined, the method of figuring capital balance ratios for sharing income and losses is the same as that used for beginning capital balances.

The entry showing how the earnings for the year are distributed to the partners' capital accounts is as follows:

June 30	Income Summary	140,000	
	Jerry Adcock, Capital		71,960
	Rose Villa, Capital		68,040
	To distribute the income for the year to the partners' capital accounts		

Salaries, Interest, and Stated Ratio

Partners generally do not contribute equally to a firm. To make up for these unequal contributions, some partnership agreements will allow for partners' salaries interest on partners' capital balances, or a combination of both in the distribution of income. Salaries and interest of this kind are not deducted as expenses before the partnership income is determined. They represent a method of arriving at an equitable distribution of the income or loss.

To illustrate an allowance for partners' salaries, we shall assume that Adcock and Villa agree to the following salaries: $8,000 for Adcock and $7,000 for Villa. Any remaining income will be divided equally between the two partners. Each salary is charged to the appropriate partner's withdrawal account when paid. If we assume the same $140,000 income for the first year, the calculations and journal entry for Adcock and Villa are as follows.

| | Income of Partner | | Income Distributed |
	Adcock	Villa	
Total Income for Distribution			$140,000
Distribution of Salaries			
Adcock	$ 8,000		
Villa		$ 7,000	15,000
Remaining Income after Salaries			$125,000
Equal Distribution of Remaining Income			
Adcock	62,500		
Villa		62,500	125,000
Remaining Income			—
Income of Partners	$70,500	$69,500	$140,000

June 30	Income Summary	140,000	
	Jerry Adcock, Capital		70,500
	Rose Villa, Capital		69,500
	To distribute the income for the year to the partners' capital accounts		

Salaries allow for differences in the services that partners provide to the business. However, they do not consider differences in invested capital. To allow for capital differences, each partner may receive, in addition to salary, a stated interest on his or her invested capital. To illustrate, we will assume that Adcock and Villa agree to receive 10 percent interest on their beginning capital balances as well as annual salaries of $8,000 for Adcock and $7,000 for Villa. They will share any remaining income equally. The calculations for Adcock and Villa, if we assume income of $140,000, are at the top of the next page. The journal entry is

June 30	Income Summary	140,000	
	Jerry Adcock, Capital		70,750
	Rose Villa, Capital		69,250
	To distribute the income for the year to the partners' capital accounts		

	Income of Partner		Income Distributed
	Adcock	Villa	
Total Income for Distribution			$140,000
Distribution of Salaries			
Adcock	$ 8,000		
Villa		$ 7,000	15,000
Remaining Income after Salaries			$125,000
Distribution of Interest			
Adcock ($65,000 × 10%)	6,500		
Villa ($60,000 × 10%)		6,000	12,500
Remaining Income after Salaries and Interest			$112,500
Equal Distribution of Remaining Income			
Adcock	56,250		
Villa		56,250	112,500
Remaining Income			—
Income of Partners	$70,750	$69,250	$140,000

If the partnership agreement allows for distributing salaries or interest or both, these amounts must be allocated to the partners even if the profits are not enough to cover the salaries and interest. Such a situation would result in the partners sharing a negative amount after salaries and interest are paid. If the company has a loss, these allocations must still occur. The negative amount after allocation of salaries and interest must be distributed according to the stated ratio in the partnership agreement, or equally if the agreement does not mention a ratio.

To illustrate this situation, we will assume that the partnership of Adcock and Villa agreed to the following conditions for the distribution of income and losses:

	Salaries	Interest	Beginning Capital Balance
Adcock	$70,000	10 percent of beginning	$65,000
Villa	60,000	capital balances	60,000

The income for the first year of operation was $140,000. The computation for the distribution of the income and loss is shown at the top of the next page. The journal entry is

June 30	Income Summary	140,000	
	Jerry Adcock Capital		75,250
	Rose Villa, Capital		64,750
	To distribute the income for the year to the partners' capital accounts		

| | Income of Partner | | Income Distributed |
	Adcock	Villa	
Total Income for Distribution			$140,000
Distribution of Salaries			
Adcock	$70,000		
Villa		$60,000	130,000
Remaining Income after Salaries			$ 10,000
Distribution of Interest			
Adcock ($65,000 × 10%)	6,500		
Villa ($60,000 × 10%)		6,000	12,500
Negative Amount after Distribution of Salaries and Interest			$ (2,500)
Adcock*	(1,250)		
Villa*		(1,250)	2,500
Remaining Income			—
Income of Partners	$75,250	$64,750	$140,000

* Notice that the negative amount was distributed equally because the agreement did not indicate how income and losses would be distributed after salaries and interest were paid.

On the income statement for the partnership, the distribution of income or losses is shown below the net income figure. Exhibit 14-1 illustrates this point using the last example.

Dissolution of a Partnership

Dissolution of a partnership occurs whenever there is a change in the original association of the partners. When a partnership is dissolved, the partners lose their authority to continue the business as a going concern. This does not mean that the business operation is necessarily ended or interrupted, but it does mean from a legal and accounting standpoint that the separate entity will cease to exist. The remaining partners can act for the partnership in finishing the affairs of the business or in forming a new partnership that will be a new accounting entity. The dissolution of a partnership through admission of a new partner, withdrawal of a partner, and death of a partner is discussed in the following sections of this chapter.

Admission of a New Partner

OBJECTIVE 4
Record a person's admission to a partnership

Admission of a new partner will dissolve the old partnership because a new association has been formed. Dissolving the old partnership and creating a new one requires the consent of all the old partners and the ratification of a new partnership agreement. When a new partner is ad-

Exhibit 14-1. Partial Income Statement for Adcock and Villa

Adcock and Villa
Partial Income Statement
For the Year Ended June 30, 19x2

Net Income		$140,000
Distribution to the partners		
Adcock		
Salary distribution	$70,000	
Interest on beginning capital balance	6,500	
Total	$76,500	
One-half of remaining negative amount	(1,250)	
Share of net income		$ 75,250
Villa		
Salary distribution	$60,000	
Interest on beginning capital balance	6,000	
Total	$66,000	
One-half of remaining negative amount	(1,250)	
Share of net income		64,750
Net Income Distributed		$140,000

mitted, a new partnership agreement should describe the new agreement in detail.

An individual may be admitted into a firm in one of two ways: (1) by purchasing an interest in the partnership from one or more of the original partners, or (2) by investing assets in the partnership.

Purchase Interest from Partner. When an individual is admitted to a firm by purchasing an interest from an old partner, each partner must agree to the change. The transaction is a personal one between the old and new partners, but the interest purchased must be transferred from the capital account of the selling partner to the capital account of the new partner.

For example, assume that Jerry Adcock of Adcock and Villa decides to sell his $70,000 interest in the business to Richard Davis for $100,000 on August 31, 19x3. Rose Villa agrees to the sale. The entry that records the sale on the partnership books would be:

Aug. 31	Jerry Adcock, Capital	70,000	
	Richard Davis, Capital		70,000
	To record the transfer of		
	Jerry Adcock's equity to		
	Richard Davis		

Note that the entry above records the book value of the equity and not the amount paid by Davis. The amount that Davis paid is a personal matter between him and Adcock. Because the amount paid did not affect the assets or liabilities of the firm, it should not be entered into the records.

For another example of a purchase, assume that Richard Davis purchases one-half of Jerry Adcock's $70,000 and one-half of Rose Villa's $80,000 interest in the partnership by paying a total of $100,000 to the two partners on August 31, 19x3. The entry that records this transaction on the partnership books would be:

Aug. 31	Jerry Adcock, Capital	35,000	
	Rose Villa, Capital	40,000	
	Richard Davis, Capital		75,000
	To record the transfer of one-half of Jerry Adcock's and Rose Villa's equity to Richard Davis		

Investment of Assets in Partnership. When a new partner is admitted by an investment in the partnership, both the assets and the partners' equity of the firm are increased. This is so because, in contrast to the case of buying a partner out, the assets that the new partner invests become partnership assets, and this increase in assets creates a corresponding increase in partners' equity. For example, assume that Richard Davis wished to invest $75,000 for a one-third interest in the partnership of Adcock and Villa. The capital accounts of Adcock and Villa are $70,000 and $80,000, respectively. The assets of the firm are correctly valued. Thus the partners agree to admit Davis to a one-third interest in the firm for a $75,000 investment. Davis's $75,000 investment will equal a one-third interest in the firm after the investment is added to the previously existing capital, as shown below:

Jerry Adcock, Capital	$ 70,000
Rose Villa, Capital	80,000
Davis's investment	75,000
Total capital after Davis's investment	$225,000

$$\text{One-third interest} = \frac{\$225,000}{3} = \qquad \$75,000$$

The entry to record this investment is:

Aug. 31	Cash	75,000	
	Richard Davis, Capital		75,000
	To record the admission of Richard Davis to a one-third interest in the company		

Bonus to Old Partners. Sometimes a partnership is so profitable or otherwise advantageous that a new investor will be willing to pay more than the actual dollar interest that he or she receives in the partnership. An individual may have to pay $100,000 for an $80,000 interest in a partnership. The $20,000 excess of the payment over the interest purchased is considered a bonus to the original partners. The bonus should be distributed to the original partners according to the partnership agreement. When the agreement does not cover the distribution of a bonus, it should be distributed to the original partners in accordance with the method of distributing income and losses.

As an illustration of the bonus method, assume that the Adcock and Villa Company has operated for several years and that the partners' capital balances and the new ratio for distribution of income and loss are as follows.

Partners	Capital Balances	Stated Ratio
Adcock	$160,000	55%
Villa	140,000	45%
	$300,000	100%

Richard Davis wishes to join the firm, and he offers to invest $100,000 on December 1 for a one-fifth interest in the business and income. The original partners agree to the offer. The computation of the bonus to the original partners is as follows:

Partners' equity in the original partnership		$300,000
Cash investment by Richard Davis		100,000
Partners' equity in the new partnership		$400,000
Partners' equity assigned to Richard Davis ($400,000 × ⅕)		$ 80,000
Bonus to the original partners		
Investment by Richard Davis	$100,000	
Less equity assigned to Richard Davis	80,000	$ 20,000
Distribution of bonus to original partners		
Jerry Adcock ($20,000 × 55%)	$ 11,000	
Rose Villa ($20,000 × 45%)	9,000	$ 20,000

The journal entry that records the admission of Davis to the partnership is as follows:

Dec. 1	Cash	100,000	
	Jerry Adcock, Capital		11,000
	Rose Villa, Capital		9,000
	Richard Davis, Capital		80,000
	To record the sale of one-fifth interest in the firm to Richard Davis and the bonus he paid to the original partners		

Bonus to New Partner. There are several reasons why a partnership might seek a new partner. For example, a firm in financial trouble might seek additional cash from a new partner. Or the original partners, wishing to expand the firm's markets, might require more capital than they themselves can provide. Also, the partners might know a person who would add a unique talent to the firm. Under these conditions, a new partner may be admitted to the partnership with the understanding that part of the original partners' capital will be transferred (credited) to the new partner's capital as a bonus.

For example, assume that Adcock and Villa have invited Richard Davis to join the firm. Davis is to invest $60,000 on December 1 for a one-fourth interest in the company's capital and income. The capital balances of Adcock and Villa are $160,000 and $140,000, respectively. If Davis is to receive a one-fourth interest in the firm, the interest of the original partners represents a three-fourths interest in the business. The computation of the bonus to Davis follows.

Total equity in partnership		
Jerry Adcock, Capital		$160,000
Rose Villa, Capital		140,000
Investment by Richard Davis		60,000
Partners' equity in the new partnership		$360,000
Partners' equity assigned to Richard Davis		
($360,000 × ¼)		$ 90,000
Bonus		
One-fourth interest, Richard Davis	$90,000	
Cash investment by Richard Davis	60,000	$ 30,000
Distribution from original partners		
Jerry Adcock ($30,000 × 55%)	$16,500	
Rose Villa ($30,000 × 45%)	13,500	$ 30,000

The journal entry that records the admission of Davis to the partnership is as follows:

Dec. 1	Cash	60,000	
	Jerry Adcock, Capital	16,500	
	Rose Villa, Capital	13,500	
	Richard Davis, Capital		90,000
	To record the investment by		
	Richard Davis of cash and a		
	bonus		

Withdrawal of a Partner

OBJECTIVE 5
Record a person's withdrawal from a partnership

Generally, a partner has the right to withdraw from a partnership in accord with legal requirements. However, to avoid any disputes when a partner does decide to withdraw or retire from the firm, the partnership agreement should describe the appropriate actions to be taken. The agreement may specify (1) whether or not an audit will be performed by CPAs, (2) how the assets will be reappraised, (3) how a bonus is to be determined, and (4) by what method the withdrawing partner will be paid.

There are several ways in which a partner may withdraw from a partnership. A partner may (1) sell his or her interest to an outsider with the consent of the remaining partners, (2) sell his or her interest to another partner with the consent of the remaining partners, (3) withdraw assets that are equal to his or her capital balance, (4) withdraw assets that are greater than his or her capital balance (in this case the withdrawing partner will receive a bonus), or (5) withdraw assets that are less than his or her capital balance (in this case the remaining partners will receive a bonus). These alternatives are illustrated in Figure 14-1.

Withdrawal by Selling Interest. When a partner sells his or her interest to an outsider or to another partner with the consent of the other partners, the transaction is personal and does not change the partnership assets or the partnership equity. For example, we will assume that the capital balances of Adcock, Villa, and Davis are $140,000, $100,000, and $60,000, respectively, for a total of $300,000.

Villa is withdrawing from the partnership and is reviewing two offers for her interest. The offers are to (1) sell her interest to Judy Jones for $120,000 or (2) sell her interest to Davis for $110,000. The remaining partners have agreed to either potential transaction. Because Jones and Davis will pay for Villa's interest from their personal assets, the partnership accounting records will show only the transfer of Villa's interest to

Figure 14-1. Alternative Ways for a Partner to Withdraw

Jones or Davis. The entries that record these possible transfers are as follows:

1. If Villa's interest is purchased by Jones:

Rose Villa, Capital	100,000	
Judy Jones, Capital		100,000
To record sale of Villa's partnership interest to Jones		

2. If Villa's interest is purchased by Davis:

Rose Villa, Capital	100,000	
Richard Davis, Capital		100,000
To record sale of Villa's partnership interest to Davis		

Withdrawal by Removing Assets. A partnership agreement may state that a withdrawing partner is allowed to remove assets from the firm equal to his or her capital balance. Assume that Richard Davis decides to withdraw from Adcock, Villa, Davis & Company. Davis's capital balance is $60,000. The partnership agreement states that he may withdraw cash from the firm equal to his capital balance. If there is not enough cash, he is to accept a promissory note from the new partnership for the balance. The remaining partners request that Davis take only $50,000 in cash because of a cash shortage at the time of his withdrawal. He agrees. The journal entry recording Davis's withdrawal follows:

Jan. 21	Richard Davis, Capital	60,000	
	Cash		50,000
	Notes Payable, Richard Davis		10,000
	To record the withdrawal of Richard Davis from the partnership		

When a withdrawing partner takes assets greater than his or her capital balance, the excess may be treated as a bonus to the withdrawing partner. The remaining partners absorb the bonus according to their stated ratios. On the other hand, the withdrawing partner may take out assets that represent less than his or her capital balance. A partner who withdraws under these conditions leaves a part of his or her capital in the business. The remaining partners will divide the remaining equity according to their stated ratios. This distribution is considered a bonus to the remaining partners. Alternative arrangements may exist through prior agreement in the partnership contract.

Death of a Partner

When a partner dies, the partnership is dissolved because the original association has changed. The partnership agreement should state the action to be taken upon the death of a partner. Normally the books are closed and financial statements prepared. These actions are necessary to determine the capital balance of each partner at the date of the death.

The agreement may also indicate whether an audit should be conducted, assets appraised and a bonus recorded as well as the procedures for settling with the heirs of the deceased partner. The conditions for settling with the heirs may be that the remaining partners purchase the deceased's equity, sell it to outsiders, or deliver certain business assets to the estate. If the firm intends to continue, a new partnership must be formed.

Liquidation of a Partnership

OBJECTIVE 6
Compute the distribution of assets to partners when they liquidate their partnership

Liquidation of a partnership is the process of ending a business, which entails selling enough assets to pay the liabilities and distributing any remaining assets among the partners. Unlike the case of dissolution, if a partnership is liquidated, the business will not continue.

The partnership agreement should indicate the procedures to be followed in the case of liquidation. Normally, the books should be adjusted and closed, with the income or loss being distributed to the partners. As the assets of the business are sold, any gain or loss should be distributed among the partners according to the established stated ratio. As cash becomes available, it must be applied first to outside creditors, then to partners' loans, and finally to the partners' capital balances.

The process of liquidation may have a variety of financial results. However, we will describe only the following three: (1) assets sold for a gain, (2) assets sold for a loss but absorbed by capital balances, and (3) assets sold for a loss when a partner's capital balance is insufficient to absorb the loss. For each alternative we will assume that the books have been closed for Adcock, Villa, Davis & Company and that the following balance sheet exists prior to liquidation:

Adcock, Villa, Davis & Company
Balance Sheet
February 2, 19x4

Assets		Liabilities	
Cash	$ 60,000	Accounts Payable	$120,000
Accounts Receivable	40,000		
Merchandise Inventory	100,000	**Partners' Equity**	
Plant Assets (net)	200,000		
Total Assets	$400,000	Adcock, Capital	85,000
		Villa, Capital	95,000
		Davis, Capital	100,000
		Total Liabilities and Partners' Equity	$400,000

The stated ratios of Adcock, Villa, and Davis are 30, 30, and 40, respectively.

Gain on Sale of Assets

Let us assume that the following transactions occurred in the liquidation of Adcock, Villa, Davis & Company. The accounts receivable were collected for $35,000, and the inventory and plant assets were sold for $110,000 and $200,000, respectively. After the accounts payable were paid off, the resulting gain or loss from realization of the assets is distributed according to the partners' stated ratio. Then, the partners shared the remaining cash in accordance with the resulting balances of their capital accounts. These transactions are summarized in the statement of liquidation in Exhibit 14-2. The journal entries that record the transactions are shown as follows.

	Journal Entries	Explanation on Statement of Liquidation		
Feb. 13	Cash	35,000		1
	Gain or Loss from Realization	5,000		
	Accounts Receivable		40,000	
	To record collection of accounts receivable			
14	Cash	110,000		2
	Merchandise Inventory		100,000	
	Gain or Loss from Realization		10,000	
	To record the sale of inventory			
16	Cash	200,000		3
	Plant Assets		200,000	
	To record the sale of plant assets			
16	Accounts Payable	120,000		4
	Cash		120,000	
	To record the payment of accounts payable			
20	Gain or Loss from Realization	5,000		5
	Jerry Adcock, Capital		1,500	
	Rose Villa, Capital		1,500	
	Richard Davis, Capital		2,000	
	To record the distribution of the gain on assets ($10,000 gain minus $5,000 loss) to the partners			
20	Jerry Adcock, Capital	86,500		6
	Rose Villa, Capital	96,500		
	Richard Davis, Capital	102,000		
	Cash		285,000	
	To record the distribution of cash to the partners			

Exhibit 14-2. Statement of Liquidation Showing Gain on Sale of Assets

Adcock, Villa, Davis & Company
Statement of Liquidation
February 2–20, 19x4

Explanation	Cash	Other Assets	Accounts Payable	Adcock, Capital (30%)	Villa, Capital (30%)	Davis, Capital (40%)	Gain (or Loss) from Realization
Balance 2/2	$ 60,000	$340,000	$120,000	$85,000	$95,000	$100,000	
1. Collection of Accounts Receivable	35,000	(40,000)					$ (5,000)
	$ 95,000	$300,000	$120,000	$85,000	$95,000	$100,000	$ (5,000)
2. Sale of Inventory	110,000	(100,000)					10,000
	$205,000	$200,000	$120,000	$85,000	$95,000	$100,000	$ 5,000
3. Sale of Plant Assets	200,000	(200,000)					
	$405,000	—	$120,000	$85,000	$95,000	$100,000	$ 5,000
4. Payment of Liabilities	(120,000)		(120,000)				
	$285,000		—	$85,000	$95,000	$100,000	$ 5,000
5. Distribution of Gain or Loss from Realization				1,500	1,500	2,000	(5,000)
	$285,000			$86,500	$96,500	$102,000	—
6. Distribution to Partners	(285,000)			(86,500)	(96,500)	(102,000)	
	—			—	—	—	

Note that cash distributed to the partners is the balance in their respective capital accounts. Cash is not distributed according to the partners' stated ratio.

Loss on Sale of Assets

We will discuss two cases involving losses on the sale of the company's assets. In the first case, the losses are small enough to be absorbed by the partners' capital balances. In the second case, one partner's share of the losses is too large for his or her capital balance to absorb.

When a firm's assets are sold at a loss, the partners share the loss on liquidation according to their stated ratio. For example, assume that during the liquidation of Adcock, Villa, Davis & Company, the total cash received from the collection of accounts receivable and the sale of inventory and plant assets was $140,000. The statement of liquidation appears in Exhibit 14-3, and the journal entries for the transaction are shown below.

	Journal Entries	Explanation on Statement of Liquidation		
Feb. 15	Cash	140,000		1
	Gain or Loss from Realization	200,000		
	Accounts Receivable		40,000	
	Merchandise Inventory		100,000	
	Plant Assets		200,000	
	To record the collection of accounts receivable and the sale of the other assets			
16	Accounts Payable	120,000		2
	Cash		120,000	
	To record the payment of accounts payable			
20	Jerry Adcock, Capital	60,000		3
	Rose Villa, Capital	60,000		
	Richard Davis, Capital	80,000		
	Gain or Loss from Realization		200,000	
	To record the distribution of the loss on assets to the partners			
20	Jerry Adcock, Capital	25,000		4
	Rose Villa, Capital	35,000		
	Richard Davis, Capital	20,000		
	Cash		80,000	
	To record the distribution of cash to the partners			

In some liquidation cases, a partner's share of the losses is greater than his or her capital balance. In this situation, due to the concept of unlimited liability, the partner must make up the deficit in his or her capital account from personal assets. For example, assume that after the sale of assets and the payment of liabilities, the following conditions exist during the liquidation of Adcock, Villa, Davis & Company:

Assets		
Cash		$30,000
Partners' Equity		
Adcock, Capital	$25,000	
Villa, Capital	20,000	
Davis, Capital	(15,000)	$30,000

Exhibit 14-3. Statement of Liquidation Showing Loss on Sale of Assets

Adcock, Villa, Davis & Company
Statement of Liquidation
February 2–20, 19x4

Explanation	Cash	Other Assets	Accounts Payable	Adcock, Capital (30%)	Villa, Capital (30%)	Davis, Capital (40%)	Gain (or Loss) from Realization
Balance 2/2	$ 60,000	$340,000	$120,000	$85,000	$95,000	$100,000	
1. Collection of Accounts Receivable and Sale of Inventory and Plant Assets	140,000	(340,000)					($200,000)
	$200,000	—	$120,000	$85,000	$95,000	$100,000	($200,000)
2. Payment of Liabilities	(120,000)		(120,000)				
	$ 80,000		—	$85,000	$95,000	$100,000	($200,000)
3. Distribution of Gain or Loss from Realization				(60,000)	(60,000)	(80,000)	200,000
	$ 80,000			$25,000	$35,000	$ 20,000	—
4. Distribution to Partners	(80,000)			(25,000)	(35,000)	(20,000)	
	—			—	—	—	

Richard Davis must pay $15,000 into the partnership from personal funds to cover his deficit. If we assume that he paid cash to the partnership, the following entry would record his cash contribution:

Feb. 20	Cash	15,000	
	Richard Davis, Capital		15,000
	To record the additional investment of Richard Davis to cover his liquidation losses		

After Davis's payment of $15,000, there is sufficient cash to pay Adcock and Villa their capital balances and thus to complete the liquidation. This transaction is recorded as follows:

Feb. 20	Jerry Adcock, Capital	25,000	
	Rose Villa, Capital	20,000	
	Cash		45,000
	To record the distribution		
	of cash to the partners		

During liquidation, a partner might not have any additional cash to cover his or her obligations to the partnership, so the remaining partners must share the loss according to their established stated ratio. This procedure is necessary because all partners have unlimited liability, which is characteristic of a partnership. Assume that Richard Davis cannot pay the $15,000 deficit in his capital account. Adcock and Villa must share the deficit according to the stated ratio. Their percentages are 30 and 30, respectively. Therefore, each will incur 50 percent of the losses that Davis cannot pay. The new stated ratio is computed as follows:

	Old Ratios	**New Ratios**
Adcock	30%	30/60 = 50%
Villa	30%	30/60 = 50%
	60%	100%

The journal entries that record these transactions are as follows:

Feb. 20	Jerry Adcock, Capital	7,500	
	Rose Villa, Capital	7,500	
	Richard Davis, Capital		15,000
	To record the transfer of Davis's		
	deficit to Adcock and Villa		
20	Jerry Adcock, Capital	17,500	
	Rose Villa, Capital	12,500	
	Cash		30,000
	To record the cash distribution		
	to the partners		

Richard Davis's inability to meet his obligations at the time of liquidation does not relieve him of his liabilities to Adcock and Villa. If he is able to pay his liabilities sometime in the future, Adcock and Villa may collect the amounts of Davis's deficit that they absorbed.

Chapter Review

Review of Learning Objectives

1. **Identify the major characteristics, advantages, and disadvantages of the partnership form of business.**
   A partnership has several major characteristics that distinguish it from other forms of business. It is a voluntary association of two or more per-

sons who combine their talents and resources to carry on a business for a profit. This joint effort should be supported by a partnership agreement, specifying details of operation for the partnership. A partnership is dissolved by a partner's admission, withdrawal, or death, and therefore has a limited life. Each partner acts as an agent of the partnership within the scope of normal operations and is personally liable for the partnership's debts.

The advantages of a partnership are ease of formation and dissolution, the opportunity to pool several individuals' talents and resources, the freedom of action each partner enjoys, and no tax burden. The disadvantages are the limited life of the partnership, the unlimited personal liability of the partners, the difficulty of transferring partners' interest and of raising large amounts of capital, and the risk inherent in each partner's capacity to bind the partnership to a contract.

2. **Record investments of cash and of other assets by the partners in forming a partnership.**

Normally a partnership is formed when the partners contribute cash, other assets, or a combination of both to the business in accordance with the partnership agreement. The recording of initial investments entails a debit to the Cash or other asset account and a credit to the investing partner's capital account. The recorded amount of the other assets should be their fair market value on the date of transfer to the partnership. In addition, a partnership may assume the investing partner's liabilities. When this occurs, the partner's capital account is credited with the difference between the assets invested and the liabilities assumed.

3. **Compute and record the income or losses that partners share, based on a stated ratio, the capital investment ratio, and salaries and interest to partners.**

The partners should share income and losses in accordance with the partnership agreement. If the agreement says nothing about income and loss distributions, the partners will share them equally. Common methods used for distributing income and losses to partners include the use of stated ratios or capital investment ratios, the payment of salaries, and interest on capital investments. Each method tries to measure each partner's contribution to the operations of the business. A stated ratio is usually based on the partners' relative contribution of effort to the partnership. If the capital investment ratio is used, the income (or losses) is divided strictly on the amount of capital provided to the partnership by each partner. The use of salaries and interest on capital investment takes into account both efforts (salary) and capital investment (interest) in dividing income (or losses) among the partners.

4. **Record a person's admission to a partnership.**

An individual is admitted to a partnership by purchasing a partner's interest or by contributing additional assets. When an interest is purchased, the old partner's capital is transferred to the new partner. When the new partner contributes assets to the partnership, it may be necessary to recognize a bonus to be shared or borne by the old partners.

5. **Record a person's withdrawal from a partnership.**

When a partner withdraws from a partnership, the partner either sells his or her interest in the business or withdraws company assets. When assets are withdrawn, the amount can be equal to, greater than, or less than the partner's capital interest. When assets that have a value greater than or less than the partner's interest are withdrawn, a bonus is recognized and distributed among the appropriate partners.

6. **Compute the distribution of assets to partners when they liquidate their partnership.**
   Liquidation of a partnership entails selling the assets necessary to pay the company's liabilities, then distributing any remaining assets to the partners. Any gain or loss on the sale of the assets is shared by the partners according to their stated ratio. When a partner has a deficit balance in a capital account, that partner must contribute personal assets equal to the deficit. When a partner does not have personal assets to cover a capital deficit, the deficit must be absorbed by the solvent partners according to their stated ratio.

Review of Concepts and Terminology

The following concepts and terms were introduced in this chapter:

(L.O. 4)   **Bonus:** An amount that accrues to the original partners when a new partner pays more to the partnership than the interest received or that accrues to the new partner when the amount paid to the partnership is less than the interest received.

(L.O. 4)   **Dissolution:** A change in the original association of the partners in a partnership resulting from such events as the admission, withdrawal, or death of a partner.

(L.O. 1)   **Limited life:** The characteristic of a partnership shown when certain events such as the admission, withdrawal, or death of a partner terminate the partnership.

(L.O. 1)   **Limited partnership:** A partnership formed for a specific objective in which a general partner with unlimited liability operates the partnership business and the investors or limited partners generally have their liabilities limited to their investments in the partnership.

(L.O. 6)   **Liquidation:** The process of ending a business; entails selling assets, paying liabilities, and distributing any remaining assets to the partners.

(L.O. 1)   **Mutual agency:** The authority of each partner to act as an agent of the partnership within the scope of normal operations of the business.

(L.O. 2)   **Partners' equity:** The owners' equity section of the balance sheet in a partnership.

(L.O. 1)   **Partnership:** An association of two or more persons to carry on as co-owners of a business for profit.

(L.O. 1)   **Partnership agreement:** The contractual relationship between partners that identifies the details of the partnership.

(L.O. 1)   **Unlimited liability:** Each partner has a personal liability for all debts of the partnership.

Self-Test

Test your knowledge of the chapter by choosing the best answer for each item that follows.

1. The ability of a partner to enter into a contract on behalf of all partners is called
   a. unlimited liability.   c. mutual agency.
   b. the partnership agreement.   d. voluntary association.   (L.O. 1)

2. Which of the following partnership characteristics is a disadvantage?
   a. Voluntary association
   b. Participation in partnership income
   c. Mutual agency
   d. Co-ownership of partnership property   (L.O. 2)

3. A partner invests in a partnership a building with an $80,000 carrying value and a $100,000 fair market value. The related mortgage payable of $40,000 is assumed by the partnership. As a result of the investment, the partner's capital account will be credited for
   a. $40,000.   c. $80,000.
   b. $60,000.   d. $100,000.   (L.O. 3)

4. Shoemaker and Taylor are forming a partnership. Taylor will invest cash of $15,000 and a building with a book value of $40,000, a fair market value of $60,000, and a mortgage of $30,000, which the partners will assume. What amount should be recorded in Taylor's capital account?
   a. $25,000   c. $55,000
   b. $45,000   d. $75,000   (L.O. 3)

5. Tom and Jane are partners in a business. Tom's original capital was $40,000 and Jane's was $60,000. They agreed to share profits and losses as follows:

	Tom	Jane
As salaries	$14,000	$20,000
As interest on original capital	10%	10%
Remaining profits or losses	2/5	3/5

   If the profits for the year were $80,000, what share of the profits would Tom receive?
   a. $14,400   c. $21,600
   b. $18,000   d. $32,400   (L.O. 4)

6. Assuming the same facts as in 5, if the profits for the year were $40,000, what share of the profits would Jane receive?
   a. $20,000   c. $23,600
   b. $22,000   d. $26,000   (L.O. 4)

7. Assuming the same facts as in 5, if the losses for the year were $10,000, what share of the loss would Tom receive?
   a. $15,000   c. $(3,600)
   b. $26,000   d. $(6,400)   (L.O. 3)

8. O and P are partners who share profits and losses in the ratio of 3:2 and have the following capital balances on December 31, 19xx:

O, Capital	P, Capital
$500,000	$200,000

Assume that the partners agree to let Q into the partnership if he invests $300,000 for one-fourth interest. Q's capital balance would be
a. $250,000.
c. $500,000.
b. $300,000.
d. $1,000,000.   (L.O. 5)

9. Assume the same facts as in 8, except that P withdraws from the partnership by selling his interest in the partnership to Q for $300,000. Q's capital balance in the partnership will be
a. $500,000.
c. $200,000.
b. $300,000.
d. $100,000.   (L.O. 5)

10. In a partnership liquidation
a. the last journal entry credits the partners' capital accounts.
b. gains and losses on the sale of assets are allocated to the partners based on their current capital balances.
c. the partners' accounts are settled based on their stated ratios.
d. creditors should be paid before partners.   (L.O. 6)

Answers to Self-Test are at the end of this chapter.

Review Problem
Distribution of Income and Admission of Partner

(L.O. 3, 4)   Jack Holder and Dan Williams reached an agreement in 19x7 to pool their resources for the purpose of forming a partnership to manufacture and sell university T-shirts. In forming the partnership, Holder and Williams contributed $100,000 and $150,000, respectively. They drafted a partnership agreement stating that Holder was to receive an annual salary of $6,000 and Williams was to receive 3 percent interest annually on his original investment in the business. Income and losses after salary and interest were to be shared by Holder and Williams in a 2:3 ratio.

Required   1. Compute the income or loss that Holder and Williams share, and prepare the required journal entries, assuming the following income and loss before salary and interest: 19x7—$27,000 income; 19x8—$2,000 loss.
2. Assume that Jean Ratcliffe offers Holder and Williams $60,000 for a 15 percent interest in the partnership on January 1, 19x9. Holder and Williams agree to Ratcliffe's offer because they need her resources to expand the business. The capital balances of Holder and Williams are $113,600 and $161,400, respectively, on January 1, 19x9. Record the admission of Ratcliffe to the partnership, assuming that her investment is to represent a 15 percent interest in the total partners' capital and that a bonus is to be given to Holder and Williams in the ratio of 2:3.

Answer to Review Problem

1. Income distribution to partners computed:

	Income of Partner		Income Distributed
	Holder	Williams	
19x7			
Total Income for Distribution			$ 27,000
Distribution of Salary			
Holder	$ 6,000		(6,000)
Remaining Income After Salary			$ 21,000
Distribution of Interest			
Williams ($150,000 × 3%)		$ 4,500	(4,500)
Remaining Income After Salary and Interest			$ 16,500
Distribution of Remaining Income			
Holder ($16,500 × 2/5)	6,600		
Williams ($16,500 × 3/5)		9,900	(16,500)
Remaining Income			—
Income of Partners	$12,600	$14,400	
19x8			
Total Income for Distribution			$ (2,000)
Distribution of Salary			
Holder	$ 6,000		(6,000)
Remaining Loss After Salary			$ (8,000)
Distribution of Interest			
Williams ($150,000 × 3%)		$ 4,500	(4,500)
Negative Amount After Distribution of Salary and Interest			$(12,500)
Distribution of Remaining Loss in Profit/Loss Ratio			
Holder ($12,500 × 2/5)	(5,000)		
Williams ($12,500 × 3/5)		(7,500)	12,500
Remaining Income			—
Income of Partners	$ 1,000	$ (3,000)	

Journal entry—19x7

Income Summary	27,000	
Jack Holder, Capital		12,600
Dan Williams, Capital		14,400
To record the distribution (based on salary, interest, and stated ratio) of $27,000 profit for 19x7		

Journal entry—19x8

Dan Williams, Capital	3,000	
Income Summary		2,000
Jack Holder, Capital		1,000
To record the distribution (based on salary, interest, and stated ratio) of $2,000 loss for 19x8		

2. Admission of new partner recorded:

Journal entry

19x9
Jan. 1	Cash	60,000	
	Jack Holder, Capital		3,900
	Dan Williams, Capital		5,850
	Jean Ratcliffe, Capital		50,250
	To record the $60,000 cash investment by Jean Ratcliffe for a 15 percent interest in the partnership, a bonus being allocated to original partners		

Computation

$$\text{Ratcliffe, Capital} = \text{(original partners' capital + investment)} \times 15 \text{ percent}$$
$$= (\$113,600 + \$161,400 + \$60,000) \times 15\% = \$50,250$$
$$\text{Bonus} = \text{investment} - \text{Ratcliffe, Capital} = \$60,000 - \$50,250$$
$$= \$9,750$$

Distribution of bonus:

$$\text{Holder} = \$9,750 \times 2/5 = \$3,900$$
$$\text{Williams} = \$9,750 \times 3/5 = \underline{\$5,850}$$
$$\text{Total bonus } \underline{\underline{\$9,750}}$$

Chapter Assignments

Discussion Questions and Writing Assignments

1. Briefly define a partnership, and list several major characteristics of the partnership form of business.
2. What is the meaning of unlimited liability when applied to a partnership? What exception exists to this characteristic?
3. Abe and Bill are partners in a drilling operation. Abe purchased a drilling rig to be used in the partnership's operations. Is this purchase binding on Bill even though he was not involved in it?

4. The partnership agreement for Karla and Jean's partnership does not disclose how they will share income and losses. How would the income and losses be shared in this partnership?
5. What are several major advantages of a partnership? What are some possible disadvantages?
6. Edward contributes $10,000 in cash and a building with a book value of $40,000 and fair market value of $50,000 to the Edward and Francis partnership. What is the balance of Edward's capital account in the partnership if the building is recorded at its fair market value?
7. Gayle and Henry share income and losses in their partnership in a 3:2 ratio. The firm's net income for the current year is $80,000. How would the distribution of income be recorded in the journal?
8. Irene purchases Jane's interest in the Jane and Kane partnership for $62,000. Jane has a $57,000 capital interest in the partnership. How would this transaction be recorded in the partnership books?
9. Larry and Madison each own a $50,000 interest in a partnership. They agree to admit Nancy as a partner by selling her a one-third interest for $80,000. How large a bonus will be distributed to Larry and Madison?
10. Opel and Paul share income in their partnership in a 2:4 ratio. Opel and Paul receive salaries of $6,000 and $10,000, respectively. How would they share a net income before salaries of $22,000?
11. In the liquidation of a partnership, Robert's capital account showed a $5,000 deficit balance after all the creditors were paid. What obligation does Robert have to the partnership?
12. Describe how a dissolution of a partnership may differ from a liquidation of a partnership.
13. Tom Howard and Sharon Thomas are forming a partnership. What are some of the factors they should consider in deciding how income might be divided?

Classroom Exercises

Exercise 14-1.
Partnership
Formation
(L.O. 2)

Beau Buckner and Rudy Alvaro are watch repairmen who wish to form a partnership and open a jewelry store. They have their attorney prepare their partnership agreement, which indicates that assets invested in the partnership will be recorded at their fair market value and liabilities will be assumed at book value. The assets contributed by each partner, the liabilities assumed, and their fair market and book values are as follows.

Assets	Beau Buckner	Rudy Alvaro	Total
Cash	$20,000	$15,000	$35,000
Accounts Receivable	26,000	10,000	36,000
Allowance for Uncollectible			
Accounts	2,000	1,500	3,500
Supplies	500	250	750
Equipment	10,000	5,000	15,000
Liabilities			
Accounts Payable	$16,000	$ 4,500	$20,500

Prepare the journal entry necessary to record the original investments of Buckner and Alvaro in the partnership.

Exercise 14-2.
Distribution of
Income and
Losses
(L.O. 3)

Elmore Davis and Jan Johnson agreed to form a partnership. Davis contributed $100,000 in cash, and Johnson contributed assets with a fair market value of $200,000. The partnership, in its initial year, reported income of $60,000.

Determine how the partners would share the first year's income, and prepare the journal entry to distribute the income to the partners under each of the following conditions: (1) Davis and Johnson failed to include stated ratios in the partnership agreement. (2) Davis and Johnson agreed to share the income and losses in a 3:2 ratio. (3) Davis and Johnson agreed to share the income and losses in the ratio of original investments. (4) Davis and Johnson agreed to share the income and losses by allowing 10 percent interest on original investments and sharing any remainder equally.

Exercise 14-3.
Distribution of
Income: Salary
and Interest
(L.O. 3)

Assume that the partnership agreement of Davis and Johnson in Exercise 14-2 states that Davis and Johnson are to receive salaries of $10,000 and $12,000, respectively; that Davis is to receive 6 percent interest on his capital balance at the beginning of the year; and that the remainder of income and losses are to be shared equally.

Prepare the journal entries for distributing the income under the following conditions: (1) Income totaled $60,000 before deductions for salaries and interest. (2) Income totaled $24,000 before deductions for salaries and interest. (3) There was a loss of $1,000. (4) There was a loss of $20,000.

Exercise 14-4.
Distribution of
Income: Average
Capital Balance
(L.O. 3)

Ron and Jed operate a furniture rental business. Their capital balances on January 1, 19x7 were $80,000 and $120,000, respectively. Ron withdrew cash of $16,000 from the business on April 1, 19x7. Jed withdrew $30,000 cash on October 1, 19x7. Ron and Jed distribute partnership income based on their average capital balances each year. Income for 19x7 was $80,000. Compute the income to be distributed to Ron and Jed using their average capital balances in 19x7.

Exercise 14-5.
Admission of New
Partner: Bonus to
Old Partners
(L.O. 4)

Ted, Dave, and Reg have equities in a partnership of $20,000, $20,000, and $30,000, respectively, and they share income and losses in a ratio of 1:1:3. The partners have agreed to admit Chet to the partnership.

Prepare journal entries to record the admission of Chet to the partnership under the following assumptions: (1) Chet invests $30,000 for a one-fifth interest in the partnership, and a bonus is recorded for the original partners. (2) Chet invests $30,000 for a 40 percent interest in the partnership, and a bonus is recorded for Chet.

Exercise 14-6.
Withdrawal of
Partner
(L.O. 5)

Scott, Bill, and Louis are partners who share income and losses in the ratio of 3:2:1. Louis's capital account has a $60,000 balance. Scott and Bill have agreed to let Louis take $80,000 of the company's cash when he retires from the business.

What journal entry must be made on the partnership's books when Louis retires, assuming that a bonus to Louis is recognized and absorbed by the remaining partners?

Exercise 14-7.
Partnership
Liquidation
(L.O. 6)

Assume the following assets, liabilities, and owner's equity of the Toney and Cheeks partnership on December 31, 19xx:

Assets = Liabilities + Toney, Capital + Cheeks, Capital
$80,000 = $5,000   + $45,000   + $30,000

The partnership has no cash. When the partners agree to liquidate the business, the assets are sold for $60,000 and the liabilities are paid. Toney and Cheeks share income and losses in a ratio of 3:1.

1. Prepare a schedule to determine the final cash distribution to the partners after liquidation.
2. Prepare journal entries for the sale of assets, payment of liabilities, distribution of loss from realization, and final distribution of cash to Toney and Cheeks.

Exercise 14-8.
Partnership
Liquidation
(L.O. 6)

Barbara, Ruth, and Meg are partners in a tanning salon. The assets, liabilities, and capital balances as of July, 19x7 are:

Assets $240,000
Liabilities   80,000
Barbara, Capital   70,000
Ruth, Capital   20,000
Meg, Capital   70,000

Because competition is strong, business is declining, and the partnership has no cash, they have decided to sell the business. Barbara, Ruth, and Meg share income and losses in a ratio of 3:1:1, respectively. The assets were sold for $130,000, and the liabilities were paid. Ruth has no other assets and will not be able to cover any deficits in her capital account. How will the ending cash balance be distributed to the partners?

Interpreting Accounting Information

Burlington Clinic
(L.O. 1, 3)

The Burlington Clinic is owned and operated by ten local doctors as a partnership. Recently, a paralyzed patient has sued the clinic for malpractice for a total of $20,000,000. The clinic carries malpractice liability insurance in the amount of $10,000,000. There is no provision for the possible loss from this type of lawsuit in the partnership's financial statements. The condensed balance sheet for 19xx is presented on the following page.

Required

1. How should information on this type of lawsuit be disclosed in the December 31, 19xx financial statements of the partnership?
2. Assume that the clinic and its insurance company settle out of court by agreeing to pay a total of $10,100,000, of which $100,000 must be paid by

the partnership. What will be the effect of this payment on the clinic's December 31, 19xx financial statements? Discuss the effect of the settlement on the doctors' personal financial situations.

Burlington Clinic
Condensed Balance Sheet
December 31, 19xx

Assets

Current Assets	$246,000	
Property, Plant, and Equipment (net)	750,000	
Total Assets		$996,000

Liabilities and Partners' Equity

Current Liabilities	$180,000	
Long-Term Debt	675,000	
Total Liabilities		$ 855,000
Partners' Equity		141,000
Total Liabilities and Partners' Equity		$996,000

Problem Set A

Problem 14A-1.
Partnership
Formation and
Distribution of
Income
(L.O. 2, 3)

On January 1, 19x1, Joyce Chan and Kim Nichols agreed to form a partnership to establish an educational consulting business. Chan and Nichols invested cash of $90,000 and $60,000, respectively, in the partnership. The business had normal first-year problems, but during the second year the operation was very successful. For 19x1 they reported a $30,000 loss, and for 19x2 an $80,000 income.

Required

1. Prepare the journal entry to record the investment of both partners in the partnership.
2. Determine Chan's and Nichols's share of the income or loss for each year, assuming each of the following methods of sharing income and losses: (a) The partners agreed to share income and losses equally. (b) The partners agreed to share income and losses in the ratio of 7:3 for Chan and Nichols, respectively. (c) The partners agreed to share income according to their original capital investment ratio, but the agreement did not mention losses. (d) The partners agreed to share income and losses in the ratio of their capital investments at the beginning of each year. (e) The partners agreed to share income and losses by allowing interest of 10 percent on original investments and dividing the remainder equally. (f) The partners agreed to share income and losses by allowing interest of 10 percent on original investments, paying salaries of $20,000 to Chan and $15,000 to Nichols, and dividing the remainder equally.

**Problem 14A-2.
Distribution of
Income: Salaries
and Interest**
(L.O. 3)

Gregory, Jerome, and Owen are partners in the Custom Tech Company. The partnership agreement states that Gregory is to receive 8 percent interest on his capital investment at the beginning of the year, Jerome is to receive a salary of $50,000 a year, and Owen will be paid interest of 6 percent on his average capital balance during the year. Gregory, Jerome, and Owen will share any income or loss after salaries and interest in a 5:3:2 ratio. Gregory's capital investment at the beginning of the year was $300,000, and Owen's average capital balance for the year was $360,000.

Required

Determine each partner's share of income and losses under each of the following assumptions. In each case the income or loss is stated before distribution of salary and interest.

1. The income was $272,600.
2. The income was $77,800.
3. The loss was $28,400.

**Problem 14A-3.
Admission and
Withdrawal of a
Partner**
(L.O. 4, 5)

Alicia, Roberta, and Joanne are partners in the Image Gallery. The balances in the capital accounts of Alicia, Roberta, and Joanne as of November 30, 19xx are $50,000, $60,000, and $90,000, respectively. The partners share income and losses in a ratio of 2:3:5.

Required

Prepare journal entries for each of the following conditions: (a) Luke pays Joanne $100,000 for four-fifths of Joanne's interest. (b) Luke is to be admitted to the partnership with a one-third interest for a $100,000 cash investment. (c) Luke is to be admitted to the partnership with a one-third interest for a $160,000 investment. A bonus is to be distributed to the original partners when Luke is admitted. (d) Luke is to be admitted to the partnership with a one-third interest for an $82,000 cash investment. A bonus is to be given to Luke upon admission. (e) Alicia withdraws from the partnership, taking $66,000 in cash. (f) Alicia withdraws from the partnership by selling her interest directly to Luke for $70,000.

**Problem 14A-4.
Partnership
Liquidation**
(L.O. 6)

The balance sheet of the GDL Partnership as of July 31, 19xx follows.

**GDL Partnership
Balance Sheet
July 31, 19xx**

Assets		Liabilities	
Cash	$ 6,000	Accounts Payable	$480,000
Accounts Receivable	120,000	**Partners' Equity**	
Inventory	264,000		
Equipment (net)	462,000	Gary, Capital	72,000
		Dawn, Capital	180,000
		Leslie, Capital	120,000
		Total Liabilities and	
Total Assets	$852,000	Partners' Equity	$852,000

Gary, Dawn, and Leslie share income and losses in the ratio of 5:3:2. Because of a mutual disagreement, the partners have decided to liquidate the business.

Assume that Gary cannot contribute any additional personal assets to the company during liquidation and that the following transactions occurred during liquidation: (a) Accounts receivable were sold for 60 percent of their book value. (b) Inventory was sold for $276,000. (c) Equipment was sold for $300,000. (d) Accounts payable were paid in full. (e) Gain or loss from realization was distributed to the partners' capital accounts. (f) Gary's deficit was transferred to the remaining partners in their new profit and loss ratio. (g) The remaining cash was distributed to the partners.

Required

1. Prepare a statement of liquidation.
2. Prepare journal entries to liquidate the partnership and distribute any remaining cash.

**Problem 14A-5.
Comprehensive
Partnership
Transactions**
(L.O. 2, 3, 4, 6)

Sam Flippo and Henry McCovey formed a partnership on January 1, 19x1, to operate a computer software store. To begin the partnership, Sam transferred cash totaling $116,000 and office equipment valued at $84,000 to the partnership. Henry transferred cash of $56,000, land valued at $36,000, and a building valued at $300,000. In addition, the partnership assumed the mortgage of $232,000 on the building.

For the first year, the partnership reported a loss of $16,000 on December 31. In the partnership agreement, the owners had specified the distribution of income and losses by allowing interest of 10 percent on beginning capital, salaries of $20,000 to Sam and $48,000 to Henry, and the remaining amount to be divided in the ratio of 3:2.

On January 1, 19x2, the partners brought Mel Sanford, who was experienced in the software business, into the partnership. Mel invested $56,000 in the partnership for a 20 percent interest. The bonus to Mel was transferred from the original partners' accounts in the ratio of 3:2.

During 19x2, the partnership earned an income of $108,000. The new partnership agreement required that income and losses be divided by providing interest of 10 percent on beginning capital balances and salaries of $20,000, $48,000, and $60,000 for Sam, Henry, and Mel, respectively. Remaining amounts were to be divided equally.

Because of the lack of sufficient income, the partners decided to liquidate the partnership on January 1, 19x3. On that date, the assets and liabilities of the partnership were as follows: Cash, $244,000; Accounts Receivable, $152,000; Land, $36,000; Building (net), $280,000; Office Equipment (net), $108,000; Accounts Payable, $108,000; Mortgage Payable, $204,000.

The office equipment was sold for $72,000, and the accounts receivable were valued at $128,000. The accounts payable were paid. The losses were distributed equally to the partners' capital accounts. Sam agreed to accept the accounts receivable plus cash in payment for his partnership interest. Henry accepted the land, building, and mortgage payable at book value plus cash for his share in the liquidation. Mel was paid in cash.

Required

Prepare general journal entries to record all the above facts. Support your computations with schedules, and prepare a statement of liquidation in connection with the January 1, 19x3 entries.

Problem Set B

**Problem 14B-1.
Partnership
Formation and
Distribution of
Income**
(L.O. 2, 3)

Lew Sanders and Irwin Thau agreed in January 19x1 to produce and sell printed T-shirts. Lew contributed $120,000 in cash to the business. Irwin contributed the building and equipment with values of $110,000 and $70,000, respectively. The partnership had an income of $42,000 during 19x1 but was less successful during 19x2, when the income was only $20,000.

Required

1. Prepare the journal entry to record the investment of both partners in the partnership.
2. Determine the share of income for each partner in 19x1 and 19x2 under each of the following conditions: (a) The partners agreed to share income equally. (b) The partners failed to agree on an income-sharing arrangement. (c) The partners agreed to share income according to the ratio of their original investments. (d) The partners agreed to share income by allowing interest of 10 percent on original investments and dividing the remainder equally. (e) The partners agreed to share income by allowing salaries of $20,000 to Sanders and $14,000 to Thau, and dividing the remainder equally. (f) The partners agreed to share income by allowing interest of 9 percent on original investments, paying salaries of $20,000 to Sanders and $14,000 to Thau, and dividing the remainder equally.

**Problem 14B-2.
Distribution of
Income: Salaries
and Interest**
(L.O. 3)

Gloria and Dennis are partners in a tennis shop. They have agreed that Gloria will operate the store and receive a salary of $52,000 per year. Dennis will receive 10 percent interest on his average capital balance during the year of $250,000. The remaining income or losses are to be shared by Gloria and Dennis in a 2:3 ratio.

Required

Determine each partner's share of income and losses under each of the following conditions. In each case, the income or loss is stated before distribution of salary and interest.

1. The income was $84,000.
2. The income was $44,000.
3. The loss was $12,800.

**Problem 14B-3.
Admission and
Withdrawal of a
Partner**
(L.O. 4)

Renee, Esther, and Jane are partners in Seabury Woodwork Company. Their capital balances as of July 31, 19x4 are as follows:

Renee, Capital	Esther, Capital	Jane, Capital
90,000	30,000	60,000

Each partner has agreed to admit Maureen to the partnership.

Required

Prepare the journal entries to record Maureen's admission to or Renee's withdrawal from the partnership under each of the following conditions: (a) Maureen pays Renee $25,000 for one-fifth of her interest. (b) Maureen invests $40,000 cash in the partnership. (c) Maureen invests $60,000 cash in the partnership for a 20 percent interest in the business. A bonus is to be recorded for the original partners on the basis of their capital balances. (d) Maureen invests $60,000 cash in the partnership for a 40 percent interest in the business. The original partners give Maureen a bonus according to the ratio of their capital balances on July 31, 19x4. (e) Renee withdraws from the partnership, taking $105,000. The excess of assets over the partnership interest are distributed according to the balances of the capital accounts. (f) Renee withdraws by selling her interest directly to Maureen for $120,000.

Problem 14B-4.
Partnership
Liquidation
(L.O. 6)

Nguyen, Waters, and Leach are partners in a retail lighting store and share income and losses in the ratio of 2:2:1, respectively. The partners have agreed to liquidate the partnership. The partnership balance sheet prior to liquidation follows.

Nguyen, Waters, and Leach Partnership
Balance Sheet
August 31, 19x7

Cash	$140,000	Accounts Payable	$180,000
Other Assets	440,000	Nguyen, Capital	200,000
		Waters, Capital	120,000
		Leach, Capital	80,000
	$580,000		$580,000

The other assets were sold on September 1, 19x7 for $360,000. Accounts Payable were paid on September 4, 19x7. The remaining cash was distributed to the partners on September 11, 19x7.

Required

1. Prepare a statement of liquidation.
2. Prepare the following journal entries: (a) Sale of the other assets. (b) Payment of the accounts payable. (c) Distribution of the partners' gain or loss on liquidation. (d) Distribution to the partners of the remaining cash.

Problem 14B-5.
Comprehensive
Partnership
Transactions
(L.O. 2, 3, 4, 6)

The following events pertain to a partnership formed by Luis Mota and Ken Sabo to operate a floor cleaning company.

19x1

Feb. 14 The partnership was formed. Mota transferred to the partnership $40,000 cash, land worth $40,000, a building worth $240,000, and a mortgage on the building of $120,000. Sabo transferred to the partnership $20,000 cash and equipment worth $80,000.

Dec. 31 During 19x1, the partnership had an income of only $42,000. The partnership agreement specified that income and losses were to be divided by allowing 8 percent interest on beginning capital investments, paying salaries of $20,000 to Mota and $30,000 to Sabo, and dividing any remainder equally.

19x2

Jan. 1 To improve the prospects for the company, the partners decided to take in a new partner, Gail Shiner, who had experience in the floor cleaning business. Shiner invested $78,000 for a 25 percent interest in the business. A bonus was transferred in equal amounts from the previous partners' capital accounts to Shiner's capital account.

Dec. 31 During 19x2, the company earned an income of $43,600. The new partnership agreement specified that income and losses would be divided by allowing 8 percent interest on beginning capital balances after Shiner's admission, paying salaries of $30,000 to Sabo and $40,000 to Shiner (no salary to Mota), and dividing the remainder equally.

19x3

Jan. 1 Because it appeared that the business could not support the three partners, the partners decided to liquidate the partnership. The asset and liability accounts of the partnership were as follows: Cash, $203,600; Accounts Receivable, $34,000; Land, $40,000; Building (net), $224,000; Equipment (net), $118,000; Accounts Payable, $44,000; Mortgage Payable, $112,000. The equipment was sold for $100,000. The accounts payable were paid. The loss was distributed equally to the partners' accounts. A statement of liquidation was prepared, and the remaining assets and liabilities were distributed. Mota agreed to accept cash plus the land and buildings at book value and the mortgage payable as payment for his share. Sabo accepted cash and the accounts receivable for his share. Shiner was paid in cash.

Required Prepare general journal entries to record all the above facts. Support your computations with schedules, and prepare a statement of liquidation in connection with the January 1, 19x3 entries.

Financial Decision Case

Perfect Fitness Center
(L.O. 4, 5)

The Perfect Fitness Center is owned by James Zorn and Larry Carson. The business has been very successful since its inception five years ago. James and Larry work ten to eleven hours a day at the business. They have decided to expand by opening up another fitness center in the north part of town. James has approached you about becoming a partner in their business. They are interested in you because of your past experience in operating a small gym. In addition, they will need additional funds to expand their business.

Projected income after the expansion but before partner salaries for the next five years is

19x1	19x2	19x3	19x4	19x5
$100,000	$120,000	$130,000	$140,000	$150,000

Currently, James and Larry each draw a $25,000 salary and share remaining profits equally. They are willing to give you an equal share of the business for $142,000. You will receive a $25,000 salary and ⅓ of the remaining profits. You would work the same hours as James and Larry. Your salary for the next five years where you currently work is expected to be:

19x1	19x2	19x3	19x4	19x5
$34,000	$38,000	$42,000	$45,000	$50,000

Financial information for the Perfect Fitness Center is as follows:

Current assets	$ 45,000
Fixed assets	365,000
Current liabilities	50,000
Long-term liabilities	100,000
Zorn, Capital	140,000
Carson, Capital	120,000

Required

1. Compute your capital balance if you decide to join James and Larry in the partnership.
2. Analyze your expected income for the next five years. Should you invest in the Perfect Fitness Center?
3. Assume that you do not consider James and Larry's offer to be very attractive. Develop a counter offer that you would be willing to accept to join the partnership (be realistic in your proposed arrangement).

Answers to Self-Test

1. c	3. b	5. d	7. c	9. c
2. c	4. b	6. c	8. a	10. d

LEARNING OBJECTIVES

1. *Define a corporation, and state the advantages and disadvantages of the corporate form of business.*
2. *Account for organization costs.*
3. *Identify the components of stockholders' equity.*
4. *Account for cash dividends.*
5. *Calculate the division of dividends between common and preferred stockholders.*
6. *Account for the issuance of common and preferred stock for cash and other assets.*
7. *Account for stock subscriptions.*
8. *Account for the exercise of stock options.*

CHAPTER 15

Contributed Capital

There are fewer corporations than sole proprietorships and partnerships in the United States. However, the corporate form of business dominates the economy in total dollars of assets and output of goods and services. The major reason for this dominance is that it is easier for a corporation to amass a large amount of capital. The corporate form of business is also well suited to today's trends toward large organizations, international trade, and professional management.

This chapter begins by outlining some of the important characteristics of the corporate form of business. Then it explains accounting for organization costs and describes the components of stockholders' equity. The rest of the chapter focuses on accounting for the issuance of stock and other stock transactions. After studying this chapter, you should be able to meet the learning objectives listed on the left.

The Corporation

A **corporation** is defined as "a body of persons granted a charter legally recognizing them as a separate entity having its own rights, privileges, and liabilities distinct from those of its members."[1] In other words, the corporation is a legal entity separate and distinct from its owners. For this reason, corporate accounting is different in some ways from that for proprietorships and partnerships.

Formation of a Corporation

To form a corporation in most states an application is filed with the proper state official. The application contains the **articles of incorporation**. If approved by the state, these articles become, in effect, a contract between the state and the incorporators, called the company charter. After the charter is approved, the company is authorized to do business. The incorporators first hold a meeting to elect a board of directors and pass a set of bylaws to guide the operations of the corporation. The board of directors then holds a meeting to elect officers of the corporation. Finally, when beginning capital is raised through the issuance of shares of stock, the corporation is ready to begin operating.

1. Copyright © 1985 Houghton Mifflin Company. Adapted and reprinted by permission from *The American Heritage Dictionary, Second College Edition.*

Organization of a Corporation

OBJECTIVE 1
Define a corporation, and state the advantages and disadvantages of the corporate form of business

The authority to manage the corporation is given by the stockholders to the board of directors and by the board of directors to the corporate officers (see Figure 15-1). That is, the stockholders elect the board of directors, which sets company policies and chooses the corporate officers. The officers in turn carry out the corporate policies by managing the business.

Stockholders. A unit of ownership in a corporation is called a share of stock. The articles of incorporation state the maximum or authorized number of shares of a stock that the corporation will be allowed to issue. The number of shares held by stockholders is the outstanding capital stock, and it may be less than the number of authorized shares. To invest in a corporation, a stockholder transfers cash or other resources to the corporation. In return, the stockholder receives shares of stock representing a proportionate share of ownership in the corporation. Afterward, the stockholder may transfer the shares at will. Corporations may have more than one kind of capital stock, but the first part of this chapter will refer only to common stock.

Individual stockholders do not normally take part in the day-to-day management of a corporation. However, a stockholder may serve as a member of the board if elected or as an officer of the company if appointed. But, in general, stockholders participate in management only through electing the board of directors and voting on particular issues at stockholders' meetings.

Stockholders will normally meet once a year to elect directors and carry on other business as provided for in the company's bylaws. Business transacted at these meetings may include the election of auditors, review of proposed mergers and acquisitions, changes in the charter, stock option plans, and issuance of additional stock and of long-term debt. Each stockholder has one vote for each share of voting stock held. Today, ownership of large corporations is spread over the entire world. As a result, only a few stockholders may be able to attend the annual stockholders' meeting. A stockholder who cannot attend the meeting may vote by proxy. The proxy is a legal document, signed by the stockholder, giving another party the right to vote his or her shares. Normally, this right is given to the current management of the corporation.

Figure 15-1. The Corporate Form of Business

Board of Directors. As noted, the stockholders elect the board of directors, which in turn decides on the major business policies of the corporation. Among the duties of the board are authorizing contracts, deciding on executive salaries, and arranging major loans with banks. The declaration of dividends is also an important function of the board of directors. Only the board has the authority to declare dividends. Dividends are distributions of resources, generally in the form of cash, to the stockholders. They are one way of rewarding stockholders for their investment in the corporation when it has been successful in earning a profit. (The other way is a rise in the market value of the stock.) There is usually a delay of two or three weeks between the time when the board declares a dividend and the date of the actual payment.

The make-up of the board of directors is different from company to company. In most cases, though, it contains several officers of the corporation and several outsiders. Today, it is common to form an **audit committee** with several outside directors to make sure that the board will be objective in judging management's performance. One of the audit committee's tasks is to hire the company's independent auditors and review their work.

Management. The board of directors appoints the managers of a corporation to carry out the company's policies and to run the day-to-day operations. The management consists of the operating officers, who are generally the president vice presidents, controller, treasurer, and secretary. Besides being responsible for running the business, management has the duty to report the financial results of its administration to the board of directors and to the stockholders. Though management may and generally does report more often, it must report at least once a year. For large public corporations, these annual reports are available to the public. Parts of many of them have been used in this book.

Advantages of a Corporation

The corporate form of business organization has several advantages over the sole proprietorship and the partnership. Among these advantages are separate legal entity, limited liability, ease of capital generation, ease of transfer of ownership, lack of mutual agency, continuous existence, centralized authority and responsibility, and professional management.

Separate Legal Entity. A corporation is a separate legal entity that has most of the rights of a person except those of voting and marrying. As such, it may buy, sell, or own property, sue and be sued, enter into contracts with all parties, hire and fire employees, and be taxed.

Limited Liability. Because a corporation is a separate legal entity, it is responsible for its own actions and liabilities. For this reason, a corporation's creditors generally cannot look beyond the assets of the company to satisfy their claims. In other words, the creditors can satisfy their claims only against the assets of the corporation, not against the personal property of the owners of the company. Because owners of a corporation are not responsible for the debts of the company, their liability is limited to the amount of their investment. The personal property of sole proprietors and partners, however, may be available to creditors.

Ease of Capital Generation. It is fairly easy for a corporation to raise money because many people can take part in the ownership of the business by investing small amounts of money. As a result, a single corporation may be owned by many people.

Ease of Transfer of Ownership. The ownership of a corporation is represented by a transferable unit called a share of stock. The owner of the share of stock, or the stockholder, can normally buy and sell shares of stock without affecting the activities of the corporation or needing the approval of other owners.

Lack of Mutual Agency. There is no mutual agency with the corporate form of business. If a stockholder, acting as an owner, tries to enter into a contract for the corporation, the corporation will not be bound by the contract. But a partnership, where there is mutual agency, can be bound by a partner's actions.

Continuous Existence. Another advantage of the corporation being a legal entity separate from its owners is that an owner's death, incapacity, or withdrawal does not affect the life of the corporation. The life of a corporation is set by its charter and regulated by state laws.

Centralized Authority and Responsibility. The board of directors represents the stockholders and delegates the responsibility and authority for the day-to-day operation of the corporation to a single person, usually the president of the organization. This power is not divided among the many owners of the business. The president may delegate authority for certain segments of the business to others, but he or she is held accountable to the board of directors for the business. If the board is dissatisfied with the performance of the president, he or she can be replaced.

Professional Management. Large corporations are owned by many people who probably do not have the time or training to make timely operating decisions for the business. So, in most cases, management and ownership are separated in the manner described in the previous paragraph. This arrangement allows the corporation to hire the best talent available for managing the business.

Disadvantages of a Corporation

The corporate form of business has its disadvantages. Among the more important ones are government regulation, taxation, limited liability, and separate ownership and control.

Government Regulation. When corporations are created, they must meet the requirements of state laws. For this reason, they are said to be "creatures of the state" and are subject to greater control and regulation by the state than other forms of business. Corporations must file many reports with the states in which they are chartered. Also, corporations that are publicly held must file reports with the Securities and Exchange Commission and with the stock exchanges. Meeting these requirements becomes very costly.

Taxation. A major disadvantage of a corporation is **double taxation.** Because the corporation is a separate legal entity, its earnings are subject to federal and state income taxes. These taxes may approach 35 percent of the corporate earnings. If the corporation's after-tax earnings are then paid out to its stockholders as dividends, these earnings are again taxed as income to the stockholders who receive them. Taxation is different for the sole proprietorship and the partnership, whose earnings are taxed only as personal income to the owners.

Limited Liability. Earlier, limited liability was listed as an advantage of a corporation. This same feature, however, may limit the ability of a small corporation to borrow money. Credit of a small corporation is reduced because the stockholders have limited liability and the creditors will have claims only to the assets of the corporation. In such cases, the creditors will limit their loans to the level secured by the assets of the corporation or ask the stockholders to personally guarantee the loans.

Separation of Ownership and Control. Just as limited liability may be a drawback, so may the separation of ownership and control. Sometimes management makes decisions that are not good for the corporation as a whole. Poor communication can also make it hard for stockholders to exercise control over the corporation or even to recognize that management's decisions are harmful.

Organization Costs

OBJECTIVE 2
Account for organization costs

The costs of forming a corporation are called **organization costs.** These costs, which are incurred prior to the start of the corporation, include such items as state incorporation fees and attorneys' fees for drawing up the articles of incorporation to establish the corporation. They also include the cost of printing stock certificates, accountants' fees for services rendered in registering the firm's initial stock, and other expenditures necessary for forming the corporation.

Theoretically, these costs benefit the entire life of the organization. For this reason, a case can be made to record organization costs as intangible assets and to amortize them over the years of the life of the corporation. However, the life of a corporation is normally unknown, so accountants amortize these costs over the early years of a corporation's life. Because federal income tax regulations allow organization costs to be amortized over five years or more, most companies amortize these costs over a five-year (sixty months) period, although the FASB will allow a period up to forty years. Organization costs normally appear as Other Assets or as Intangible Assets on the balance sheet.

To illustrate accounting practice for organization costs, we will assume that a corporation pays a lawyer $5,000 for services rendered in July in preparing the application for a charter with the state. The entry to record this cost would be as follows:

```
19x0
July  1   Organization Costs                   5,000
              Cash                                       5,000
                  To record $5,000 lawyer's fee for
                  services rendered in corporate
                  organization
```

If the corporation amortizes the organization costs over a five-year period, the entry to record the amortization at the end of the fiscal year on June 30, 19x1, would be:

```
19x1
June 30   Amortization Expense, Organization Costs   1,000
              Organization Costs                              1,000
                  To record one year's
                  costs:
                  $5,000 ÷ 5 years = $1,000
```

The Components of Stockholders' Equity

OBJECTIVE 3
Identify the components of stockholders' equity

The major difference in accounting for corporations and accounting for sole proprietorships or partnerships involves the owners' equity. The assets and liabilities of a corporation are handled in the same way as they are for other forms of business. In a corporation's balance sheet, the owners' claims to the business are called **stockholders' equity**, as follows:

Stockholders' Equity		
Contributed Capital		
Preferred Stock—$50 par value, 1,000 shares authorized and issued		$ 50,000
Common Stock—$5 par value, 30,000 shares authorized, 20,000 shares issued	$100,000	
Paid-in Capital in Excess of Par Value, Common	50,000	150,000
Total Contributed Capital		$200,000
Retained Earnings		60,000
Total Stockholders' Equity		$260,000

This equity section is different from the balance sheet presentation of a proprietorship and partnership in that it is divided into two parts: (1) contributed capital and (2) retained earnings. **Contributed capital** represents the investments made by the stockholders in the corporation. The retained earnings are the earnings of the business that have not been distributed to the stockholders. Instead, the retained earnings have been reinvested in the business.

The contributed capital part of stockholders' equity on the balance sheet, in keeping with the convention of full disclosure, gives a great deal of information about the stock of a corporation. For example, the kinds of stock, their par value, and the number of shares authorized and issued are reported in this part of stockholders' equity. This information in the contributed capital part of stockholders' equity is the subject of the rest of this chapter. Retained earnings will be explained fully in Chapter 16.

Capital Stock

A unit of ownership in a corporation is called a share of stock. A **stock certificate** will be issued to the owner. It shows the number of shares of the corporation's stock owned by the stockholder. Stockholders can transfer their ownership at will, but they must sign their stock certificate and send it to the corporation's secretary. In large corporations listed on the organized stock exchanges, it is hard to maintain stockholders' records. Such companies may have millions of shares of stock, several thousand of which may change ownership every day. Therefore, these corporations often appoint independent registrars and transfer agents to aid in performing the secretary's duties. The registrars and the transfer agents are usually banks and trust companies. They are responsible for transferring the corporation's stock, maintaining stockholders' records, preparing a list of stockholders for stockholders' meetings, and paying the dividends. To help with the initial issue of capital stock, corporations often engage an underwriter. The underwriter is an intermediary, or contact, between the corporation and the investing public. For a fee—usually less than one percent of the selling price—the underwriter guarantees the sale of the stock. The corporation records the amount of the net proceeds of the offering—what the public paid less the underwriter's fee, legal and printing expenses, and any other direct costs of the offering—in its capital stock and additional paid-in capital accounts.

Authorization of Stock. When a corporation applies for a charter, the articles of incorporation indicate the maximum number of shares of stock a corporation will be allowed to issue. This number represents **authorized stock.** Most corporations get an authorization to issue more shares of stock than are necessary at the time of organization. This action enables the corporation to issue stock in the future to raise additional capital. For example, if a corporation is planning to expand later, a possible source of capital would be the unissued shares of stock that were authorized in its charter. If all authorized stock is issued immediately, the corporation must change its charter by applying to the state to increase the number of shares of authorized stock. The charter also shows the par value of the stock that has been authorized. The **par value** is an arbitrary amount to be printed on each share of stock. It must be recorded in the capital stock accounts and constitutes the legal capital of a corporation. It usually bears little if any relationship to the market value or book value of the shares. When the corporation is formed, a memorandum entry may be made in the general journal giving the number and description of authorized shares.

Issued and Outstanding Stock. The **issued stock** of a corporation is the shares sold or otherwise transferred to the stockholders. For example, a corporation may have been authorized to issue 500,000 shares of stock but chose to issue only 300,000 shares when the company was organized. The 300,000 shares represent the issued stock. The holders of those shares own 100 percent of the corporation. The remaining 200,000 shares of stock are unissued shares. No rights or privileges are associated with them until they are issued. Shares of stock are said to be **outstanding stock** if they have been issued and are still in circulation. A share of stock would not be outstanding if it had been repurchased by the issuing corporation or given back to the company that issued it by a stockholder. In such cases, a company can have more shares issued than are currently outstanding or held by the stockholders. Issued shares that are bought back and still held by the corporation are called *treasury stock*, which is explained in Chapter 16.

Common Stock

A corporation may issue two basic types of stock: common stock and preferred stock. If only one kind of stock is issued by the corporation, it is called **common stock**. The common stock is the **residual equity** of a company. This term means that all other creditor and preferred stockholder claims to the company's assets rank ahead of those of the common stockholders in case of liquidation. Because common stock is generally the only stock carrying voting rights, it represents the means of controlling the corporation.

Dividends

OBJECTIVE 4
Account for cash dividends

A **dividend** is a distribution of assets of a corporation to its stockholders. Each stockholder receives assets, usually cash, in proportion to the number of shares of stock held. The board of directors has sole authority to declare dividends.

Dividends may be paid quarterly, semiannually, annually, or at other times decided on by the board. Most states do not allow the board to declare a dividend that exceeds retained earnings. Where such a dividend is declared, the corporation is essentially returning to the stockholders a part of their paid-in capital. This is called a **liquidating dividend** and is normally paid when a company is going out of business or is reducing its operations. However, having sufficient retained earnings does not in itself justify the distribution of a dividend. Cash or other readily distributable assets may not be available for distribution. In such a case the company might have to borrow money in order to pay a dividend. This is an action the board of directors may want to avoid.

There are three important dates associated with dividends. In order of occurrence, these are (1) the date of declaration, (2) the date of record, and (3) the date of payment. The date of declaration is the date the board of directors takes formal action declaring that a dividend will be paid. The date of record is the date on which ownership of the stock of a company, and therefore of the right to receive a dividend, is determined. Those individuals who own the stock on the date of record will be the ones to receive the dividend. After that date, the stock is said to be **ex-dividend** because if the shares of stock are sold from one person to another the right to the cash dividend remains with the first person and does not transfer with the shares to the second person. The date of payment is the date the dividend will be paid to the stockholders of record.

Cash Dividends. To illustrate the accounting for cash dividends, we will assume that the board of directors has decided that sufficient cash is available to pay a $56,000 cash dividend to the common stockholders. To do this, a two-step process is followed. First, the dividend is declared by the board of directors for stockholders as of a certain date. Second, the dividend is paid. Assume that the dividend is declared on February 21, 19xx, for stockholders of record on March 10, 19xx, to be paid on March 31, 19xx. The entries to record the declaration and payment of the cash dividend follow:

Date of Declaration

Feb. 21	Dividends Declared	56,000	
	Dividends Payable		56,000
	To record the declaration of a cash dividend to common stockholders		

Date of Record

Mar. 10 No entry is required because this date is used simply to determine the owners of the stock who will receive the dividends. After this date (starting March 11) the shares are ex-dividend.

Date of Payment

Mar. 31	Dividends Payable	56,000	
	Cash		56,000
	To record the payment of cash dividends		

Note that the liability for the dividend was recorded on the date of declaration because the legal obligation to pay the dividend was established on that date. No entry was required on the date of record, and the liability was liquidated, or settled, on the date of payment. At the end of the accounting period, the Dividends Declared account is a stockholders' equity account that is closed by debiting Retained Earnings and crediting Dividends Declared. Retained earnings are thereby reduced by the total dividends declared during the period.

Some companies do not pay dividends very often. For one reason, the company may not have any earnings. For another, the company may be growing and thus the assets generated by the earnings are kept in the company for business purposes such as expansion of the plant. Investors in such growth companies expect a return on their investment in the form of an increased market value of their stock. Stock dividends, another kind of return, will be discussed in Chapter 16.

Preferred Stock

The second kind of stock, called **preferred stock**, may be issued so that the company can obtain money from investors who have different investment goals. Preferred stock has preference over common stock in one or more areas. There may be several different classes of preferred stock, each with distinctive characteristics to attract different investors. Most preferred stock has one or more of the following characteristics: preference as to dividends, preference as to assets of the business in liquidation, convertibility or nonconvertibility, and callable option.

OBJECTIVE 5
Calculate the division of dividends between common and preferred stockholders

Preference as to Dividends. Preferred stocks ordinarily have a *preference* over common stock in the receipt of dividends; that is, the holders of preferred shares must receive a certain amount of dividends before the holders of common shares may receive dividends. The amount that preferred stockholders must be paid before common stockholders may be paid is usually stated in dollars per share or in a percentage of the face value of the preferred shares. For example, a corporation may issue a preferred stock and pay a dividend of $4 per share, or it might issue a preferred stock of $50 par value and pay a yearly dividend of 8 percent of par value, which amounts to a $4 annual dividend.

Preferred stockholders have no guarantee of ever receiving dividends; the company must have earnings and the board of directors must declare dividends on preferred shares before any liability to pay them arises. The consequences of not declaring a dividend to preferred stockholders in the current year vary, however, according to the exact terms under which the shares were issued. To have **noncumulative** preferred shares means that if the board of directors fails to declare a dividend to preferred stockholders in a given year, it is under no obligation to make up the missed dividend in future years. If the shares are **cumulative**, however, the fixed preference amount per preferred share accumulates from year to year, and the whole amount must be paid before any common dividends may be paid. The dividends that are not paid in the year they are due are called **dividends in arrears**.

Assume that the preferred stock of a corporation is as follows: preferred stock, 5 percent cumulative, 10,000 shares authorized, issued, and outstanding, $100 par value, $1,000,000. If in 19x1 no dividends were paid, at the end of that year there would be preferred dividends of $50,000 in arrears (10,000 shares × $100 × 5% = $50,000). Thus if dividends are paid next year, the preferred stockholders' dividends in arrears plus the 19x2 preferred dividends must be paid before any dividends can be paid in 19x2 on common stock.

Dividends in arrears are not recognized as liabilities of a corporation because there is no liability until the board declares a dividend. A corporation cannot be sure of making a profit. So, of course, it cannot promise dividends to stockholders. However, if a company has dividends in arrears, they should be reported either in the body of the financial statements or in a footnote. It is important to give this information to the users of these statements. The following footnote appeared in a steel company's annual report a few years ago:

On January 1, 19xx, the company was in arrears by $37,851,000 ($1.25 per share) on dividends to its preferred stockholders. The company must pay all dividends in arrears to preferred stockholders before paying any dividends to common stockholders.

As an illustration, let us assume the following facts. On January 1, 19x1, a corporation issued 10,000 shares of $10 par, 6 percent cumulative preferred stock and 50,000 shares of common stock. The first year's operations resulted in income of only $4,000. The board of directors declared a $3,000 cash dividend to the preferred stockholders. The dividend picture at the end of 19x1 appears as follows:

19x1 dividends due preferred stockholders	
($100,000 × 6%)	$6,000
19x1 dividends declared to preferred stockholders	(3,000)
Preferred stock dividends in arrears	$3,000

Let us suppose that in 19x2 the company earned income of $30,000 and wished to pay dividends to both the preferred and the common stockholders. But the preferred stock is cumulative. So the corporation must pay the $3,000 in arrears on the preferred stock, plus the current year's dividends, before the common stockholders can receive a dividend. For example, assume that the corporation's board of directors declared a $12,000 dividend to be distributed to the preferred and common stockholders. Under these circumstances, the distribution of the dividend would be as follows:

19x2 declaration of dividends	$12,000	
Less 19x1 preferred stock dividends in arrears	**3,000**	
Available for 19x2 dividends		$9,000
Less 19x2 preferred stock dividend		
($100,000 × 6%)		**6,000**
Remainder available to common stockholders		$3,000

The entry presented at the top of the next page is made when the dividend is declared:

Dec. 31	Dividends Declared	12,000	
	Dividends Payable		12,000

            To record declaration of a $9,000 cash
            dividend to preferred stockholders
            and a $3,000 cash dividend to
            common stockholders

Preference as to Assets. Many preferred stocks have preference as to the assets of the corporation in the case of liquidation of the business. So when the business is ended, the preferred stockholders have a right to receive the par value of their stock or a larger stated liquidation value per share before the common stockholders receive any share of the company's assets. This preference may also include any dividends in arrears owed to the preferred stockholders.

Convertible Preferred Stock. A corporation may make its preferred stock more attractive to investors by adding a convertibility feature. Those who hold **convertible preferred stock** can exchange their shares of preferred stock, if they wish, for shares of the company's common stock at a ratio stated in the preferred stock contract. Convertibility is attractive to investors for two reasons. (1) Like all preferred stockholders, owners of convertible stock can be surer of regular dividends than can common stockholders. (2) If the market value of a company's common stock rises, the conversion feature will allow the preferred stockholders to share in this increase. The rise in value would come either through equal increases in the value of the preferred stock or through conversion to common stock.

For example, suppose that a company issues 1,000 shares of 8 percent, $100 par value convertible preferred stock for $100 per share. Each share of stock can be converted into five shares of the company's common stock at any time. The market value of the common stock is now $15 a share. In the past, dividends on the common stock had been about $1 per share per year. The stockholder owning one share of preferred stock, on the other hand, now holds an investment that is worth about $100 on the market, and the probability of dividends is higher than with common stock.

Assume that in the next several years the corporation's earnings increase, and the dividends paid to common stockholders also increase, to $3 per share. In addition, the market value of a share of common stock increases from $15 to $30. The preferred stockholders can convert each of their preferred shares into five common shares and increase their dividends from $8 on each preferred share to the equivalent of $15 ($3 on each of five common shares). Furthermore, the market value of each share of preferred stock will be close to the $150 value of the five shares of common stock because the share may be converted into the five shares of common stock.

Callable Preferred Stock. Most preferred stocks are **callable preferred stocks**. That is, they may be redeemed or retired at the option of the issuing corporation at a certain price stated in the preferred stock contract. The stockholder must surrender a nonconvertible preferred stock to the corporation when requested to do so. If the preferred stock is convertible, the stockholder may either surrender the stock to the corporation or convert it into common stock when the corporation calls the stock. The call price, or redemption price, is usually higher than the par value of the stock. For example, a $100 par value preferred stock might be callable at $103 per share. When preferred stock is called and surrendered, the stockholder is entitled to (1) the par value of the stock, (2) the call premium, (3) the dividends in arrears, and (4) a prorated (by the proportion of the year to the call date) portion of the current period's dividend.

There are several reasons why a corporation may call its preferred stock. First, it may wish to force conversion of the preferred stock to common because the cash dividend to be paid on the equivalent common stock is less than the dividend being paid on the preferred shares. Second, it may be possible to replace the outstanding preferred stock on the current market with a preferred stock at a lower dividend rate or with long-term debt which may have a lower after-tax cost. Third, the company may simply be profitable enough to retire the preferred stock.

Retained Earnings

Retained earnings, the other component of stockholders' equity, represents the claim of stockholders to the assets of the company resulting from profitable operations. Chapter 16 focuses on the retained earnings section of the balance sheet.

Accounting for Stock Issuance

OBJECTIVE 6
Account for the issuance of common and preferred stock for cash and other assets

A share of capital stock is either a par or a no-par stock. If the capital stock is par stock, the corporation charter states the par value, and this value must be printed on each share of stock. Par value may be 10¢, $1, $5, $100, or any other amount worked out by the organizers of the corporation. The par values of common stocks tend to be lower than those of preferred stocks.

Par value is the amount per share that is entered into the corporation's Capital Stock account and makes up the **legal capital** of the corporation. Legal capital equals the number of shares issued times the par value and is the minimum amount that can be reported as contributed capital. A corporation may not declare a dividend that would cause stockholders' equity to fall below the legal capital of the firm. Therefore, the par value is a minimum cushion of capital that protects creditors. Any amount received in excess of par value from the issuance of stock is recorded as Paid-in Capital in Excess of Par Value and represents a portion of the company's contributed capital.

No-par stock is capital stock that does not have a par value. There are several reasons for issuing stock without a par value. One is that some investors have confused par value with the market value of stock instead of recognizing it as an arbitrary figure. Another reason is that most states will not allow an original issuance of stock below par value and thereby limit a corporation's flexibility in obtaining capital.

No-par stock may be issued with or without a stated value. The board of directors of the corporation issuing the no-par stock may be required by state law to place a **stated value** on each share of stock or may wish to do so as a matter of convenience. The stated value can be any value set by the board, but some states do indicate a minimum stated value per share. The stated value may be set before or after the shares are issued if the state law does not specify this point.

If a company issues a no-par stock without a stated value, then all proceeds of the stock's issuance are recorded in the Capital Stock account. This amount becomes the corporation's legal capital unless the amount is specified by state law. Because additional shares of the stock may be issued at different prices, the credit to the Capital Stock account will not be uniform per share. In this way it differs from par value stock or no-par stock with a stated value.

When no-par stock with a stated value is issued, the shares are recorded in the Capital Stock account at the stated value. Any amount received in excess of the stated value is recorded as Paid-in Capital in Excess of Stated Value. The excess of the stated value is a part of the corporation's contributed capital. However, the stated value is normally considered to be the legal capital of the corporation.

Issuance of Par Value Stock

When par value stock is issued, the appropriate capital stock account (usually Common Stock or Preferred Stock) is credited for the par value (legal capital) regardless of whether the proceeds are more or less than the par value. For example, assume that Bradley Corporation is authorized to issue 20,000 shares of $10 par value common stock and actually issues 10,000 shares at $10 per share on January 1. The entry to record the issuance of the stock at par value would be as follows:

Jan. 1	Cash	100,000	
	Common Stock		100,000
	Issued 10,000 shares of $10 par value common stock for $10 per share		

Cash is debited for $100,000 (10,000 shares × $10), and Common Stock is credited for an equal amount because the stock was sold for par value (legal capital). If the stock had been issued for a price greater than par, the proceeds in excess of par would be credited to a capital account entitled Paid-in Capital in Excess of Par Value, Common. For example, assume that the 10,000 shares of Bradley common stock were sold for $12 per share on January 1. The entry to record the issuance of the stock at the price in excess of par value would be as follows:

Jan. 1	Cash	120,000	
	Common Stock		100,000
	Paid-in Capital in Excess		
	of Par Value, Common		20,000
	Issued 10,000 shares of $10 par		
	value common stock for $12 per		
	share		

Cash is debited for the proceeds of $120,000 (10,000 shares × $12), and Common Stock is credited at total par value of $100,000 (10,000 shares × $10). Paid-in Capital in Excess of Par Value, Common, is credited for the difference of $20,000 (10,000 shares × $2). The latter amount is a part of the corporation's contributed capital and will be added to Common Stock in the stockholders' equity section of the balance sheet. The stockholders' equity secton for Bradley Corporation immediately following the stock issue would appear as follows:

Contributed Capital	
Common Stock—$10 par value, 20,000 shares	
authorized, 10,000 shares issued and outstanding	$100,000
Paid-in Capital in Excess of Par Value, Common	20,000
Total Contributed Capital	$120,000
Retained Earnings	—
Total Stockholders' Equity	$120,000

If a corporation issues stock for less than par, an account entitled Discount on Capital Stock should be debited for the discount. The issuance of stock at a discount rarely occurs because it is illegal in many states and is thus not illustrated in this text.

Issuance of No-Par Stock

As mentioned earlier, stock may be issued without a par value. However, most states require that all or part of the proceeds from the issuance of no-par stock be designated as legal capital not subject to withdrawal, except in liquidation. The purpose is to protect the corporation's assets for the creditors. Assume that the Bradley Corporation's capital stock is no-par common and that 10,000 shares are issued on January 1, 19xx, at $15 per share. The $150,000 (10,000 shares at $15) in proceeds would be recorded as shown in the following entry:

Jan. 1	Cash	150,000	
	Common Stock		150,000
	Issued 10,000 shares of no-par		
	common stock for $15 per share		

Since the stock does not have a stated or par value, all proceeds of the issue are credited to Common Stock and are part of the company's legal capital.

Most states allow the board of directors to put a stated value on no-par stock, and this value represents the legal capital. Assume that Bradley's board puts a $10 stated value on its no-par stock. The entry to record the issue of 10,000 shares of no-par common stock with a $10 stated value for $15 per share would change from that in the last paragraph to the following:

Jan. 1	Cash	150,000	
	Common Stock		100,000
	Paid-in Capital in Excess of		
	Stated Value, Common		50,000
	Issued 10,000 shares of no-par		
	common stock of $10 stated value		
	for $15 per share		

Note that the legal capital credited to Common Stock is the stated value as decided by the board of directors. Note also that the account Paid-in Capital in Excess of Stated Value, Common, is credited for $50,000. The $50,000 is the difference between the proceeds ($150,000) and the total stated value ($100,000). Paid-in Capital in Excess of Stated Value, Common, is presented on the balance sheet in the same way that Paid-in Capital in Excess of Par Value, Common, is presented on the balance sheet for par value stock.

Issuance of Stock for Noncash Assets

In many stock transactions, stock is issued for assets or services other than cash. As a result, a problem arises as to what dollar amount should be recorded for the exchange. The generally preferred rule for such a transaction is to record the transaction at the fair market value of what is given up—in this case, the stock. If the fair market value of the stock cannot be determined, the fair market value of the assets or services may be used to record the transaction. Transactions of this kind usually include the use of stock to pay for land or buildings or for services of attorneys and others who helped organize the company.

Where there is an exchange of stock for noncash assets, the board of directors has the right to determine the fair market value of the property. Thus, when the Bradley Corporation was formed on January 1, its attorney agreed to accept 100 shares of its $10 par value common stock for services rendered. At the time of the issuance, the market value of the stock could not be determined. However, for similar services the attorney would have billed the company for $1,500. The entry to record the noncash transaction follows:

Jan. 1	Organization Costs	1,500	
	Common Stock		1,000
	Paid-in Capital in Excess of		
	Par Value, Common		500
	Issued 100 shares of $10 par value		
	common stock for attorney's services		

Assume further that the Bradley Corporation exchanged 1,000 shares of its $10 par value common stock for a piece of land two years later. At the time of the exchange the stock was selling on the market for $16 per share and the value of the land could not be determined. The entry to record this exchange would be:

Jan. 1	Land	16,000	
	Common Stock		10,000
	Paid-in Capital in Excess of		
	Par Value, Common		6,000
	Issued 1,000 shares of $10 par value common stock for a piece of land; market value of the stock $16 per share		

Stock Subscriptions

In some states, corporations may sell stock on a subscription basis. In a **stock subscription**, the investor agrees to pay for the stock on some future date or in installments at an agreed price. When a subscription is received, a contract exists and the corporation acquires an asset, Subscriptions Receivable, which represents the amount owed on the stock, and a capital item, Capital Stock Subscribed. The latter account is used because it represents the par or stated value of the stock not yet fully paid for and issued. The Common Stock account is reserved for the par value of stock that has been issued. The Subscriptions Receivable account should be identified as either common or preferred stock. The Capital Stock Subscribed account should also be identified as either common or preferred stock. Whether or not the subscriber is entitled to dividends on the subscribed stock depends on the laws of the state in which the company is incorporated. In certain states, the stock is considered to be legally issued when a subscription contract is accepted, thereby making the subscriber a legal stockholder. However, in accounting for stock subscriptions, capital stock is not issued and recorded until the subscriptions receivable pertaining to the shares are collected in full and the stock certificate is delivered to the stockholder. Likewise, it may be assumed that dividends are not paid on common stock subscribed until it is fully paid for and the certificates issued.

To illustrate stock subscriptions, we will assume that on January 1, 19xx, the Bradley Corporation received subscriptions for 15,000 shares of $10 par value common stock at $15 per share. The entry to record the subscriptions would be as follows:

Jan. 1	Subscriptions Receivable, Common	225,000	
	Common Stock Subscribed		150,000
	Paid-in Capital in Excess of		
	Par Value, Common		75,000
	Received subscriptions for 15,000 shares of $10 par value common stock for $15 per share		

If the full subscription price for 10,000 shares was collected on January 21, 19xx, the entry for the collection of the subscription would be as shown below:

```
Jan. 21   Cash                                        150,000
              Subscriptions Receivable, Common                    150,000
              Collected subscriptions in full
              for 10,000 shares of $10 par
              value common stock at $15
              per share
```

Because the 10,000 shares are fully paid for, it is appropriate to issue the common stock, as follows:

```
Jan. 21   Common Stock Subscribed               100,000
              Common Stock                                      100,000
              Issued 10,000 shares of $10
              par value common stock
```

Note that since the paid-in capital in excess of par value was recorded in the January 1 entry, there is no need to record it again.

Assume that the financial statements are prepared on January 31, 19xx, before the remaining subscriptions are collected. The Subscriptions Receivable account of $75,000 ($225,000 – $150,000) would be classified as a current asset unless there was some reason why it would not be collected in the next year. The balance of $50,000 ($150,000 – $100,000) in the Common Stock Subscribed account represents the par value of the stock yet to be issued and is a temporary capital account. As such, it is properly shown as a part of stockholders' equity under Contributed Capital, as in the following illustration:

```
Contributed Capital
  Common Stock—$10 par value, 80,000
    shares authorized
    Issued and outstanding, 10,000 shares     $100,000
    Subscribed but not issued, 5,000 shares      50,000    $150,000
  Paid-in Capital in Excess of Par Value,
  Common                                                      75,000
Total Contributed Capital                                   $225,000
```

Assume that one-half payment of $37,500 is received on February 5 for the remaining subscriptions receivable. The entry for the collection would be as follows:

```
Feb. 5   Cash                                        37,500
              Subscriptions Receivable, Common                    37,500
              Collected one-half payment for
              subscriptions to 5,000 common
              shares
```

In this case, there is no entry to issue common stock because the subscription for the stock is not paid in full. If the subscriptions receivable are paid in full on February 20 the entries are as follows:

Feb. 20	Cash	37,500	
	Subscriptions Receivable, Common		37,500
	Collected remaining subscriptions in full for 5,000 shares of $10 par value common stock for $15 per share		

Because the subscriptions are now paid in full, the common stock can be issued as follows:

Feb. 20	Common Stock Subscribed	50,000	
	Common Stock		50,000
	Issued 5,000 shares of $10 par value common stock		

Exercise of Stock Options

OBJECTIVE 8
Account for the exercise of stock options

Many companies encourage the ownership of the company's common stock through a **stock option plan**. A stock option plan is an agreement to issue stock to employees according to the terms of the plan. Under some plans, the option to purchase stock may apply to all employees equally, and the purchase of stock is made at a price that is approximately market value at the time of purchase. When this situation exists, the issuance of stock is recorded in the same way any stock issue to an outsider is recorded. If, for example, we assume that on March 30 the employees of a company purchased 2,000 shares of $10 par value common stock at the current market value of $25 per share, the entry would be as follows:

Mar. 30	Cash	50,000	
	Common Stock		20,000
	Paid-in Capital in Excess of Par Value, Common		30,000
	Issue 2,000 shares of $10 par value common stock under employee stock option plan		

In other cases, the stock option plan may give the employee the right to purchase stock in the future at a fixed price. This type of plan, which usually applies to management personnel, serves to compensate and motivate the employee, because if the company's performance is such that the market value of the stock goes up, the employee can purchase the stock at the option price and sell it at the higher market price. The amount of compensation to the employee is measured by the difference between the option price and the market price on the date of granting the option, not on the date of issuing the stock. If no difference exists between the option price and the market price on the date of grant, no compensation exists. When the option is eventually exercised on the stock and it is issued, the entry is similar to the previous entry. For example, assume that a company grants to key management personnel on July 1, 19x1 the option to purchase 50,000 shares of $10 par value common stock at the market value of $15 per share on that date. Assume that a company vice president exercises the option to purchase 2,000 shares on March 30, 19x2, when the market price is $25 per share. The entry to record the issue would be

Mar. 30	Cash	30,000	
	Common Stock		20,000
	Paid-in Capital in Excess of Par		
	Value, Common		10,000
	Issue 2,000 shares of $10 par value common stock under employee stock option plan		

Although the vice president has a gain of $20,000 ($50,000 market value minus $30,000 option price), no compensation expense is recorded. Compensation expense would have been recorded only if the option price were less than the $15 market price on July 1, 19x1, the date of grant. The handling of compensation when this situation exists is covered in more advanced courses.[2] Information pertaining to the employee stock option plans should be discussed in the notes to the financial statements.

Chapter Review

Review of Learning Objectives

1. **Define a corporation, and state the advantages and disadvantages of the corporate form of business.**

   Corporations, whose ownership is represented by shares of stocks, are separate entities for both legal and accounting purposes. The corporation is a separate legal entity having its own rights, privileges, and liabilities distinct from its owners. Like other forms of business entities, it has several advantages and disadvantages. The more common advantages are that (a) a corporation is a separate legal entity, (b) stockholders have limited liability, (c) it is easy to generate capital for a corporation, (d) stockholders can buy and sell shares of stock with ease, (e) there is a lack of mutual agency, (f) the corporation has a continuous existence, (g) authority and responsibility are centralized, and (h) it is run by a professional management team. Disadvantages of corporations include (a) a large amount of government regulation, (b) double taxation, (c) limited liability, and (d) the separation of ownership and control.

2. Stock options are discussed here in the context of employee compensation. They can also be important features of complex corporate capitalization arrangements.

2. **Account for organization costs.**

The costs of organizing a corporation are recorded on a historical cost basis. As an intangible asset, organization costs are amortized over a reasonable period of time, usually five years but not more than forty years.

3. **Identify the components of stockholders' equity.**

Stockholders' equity consists of contributed capital and retained earnings. Contributed capital may include more than one type of stock. Two of the most common types of stock are common stock and preferred stock. When only one type of security is issued, it is common stock. The holders of common stock have the right to elect the board of directors and vote on key issues of the corporation. In addition, common stockholders share in the earnings of the corporation, share in the assets of the corporation in case of liquidation, and maintain their percentage ownership.

Preferred stock is issued to investors whose investment objectives differ from those of common stockholders. To attract these investors, corporations give them a preference as to certain items. Preferred stockholders' rights normally include the privilege of receiving dividends ahead of common stockholders and the right to assets in liquidation ahead of common stockholders. Sometimes they have the right of convertibility to common stock.

Retained earnings, the other component of stockholders' equity, represents the claim of stockholders to the assets of the company resulting from profitable operations.

4. **Account for cash dividends.**

A liability for payment of cash dividends arises on the date of declaration by the board of directors. The date of record, on which no entry is required, establishes the stockholders who will receive the cash dividend on the date of payment.

5. **Calculate the division of dividends between common and preferred stockholders.**

Most preferred stock is preferred as to dividends. This preference means that in allocating total dividends between common and preferred stockholders, the amount for the preferred stock is figured first. Then the remainder goes to common stock. If the preferred stock is cumulative and in arrears, the amount in arrears also has to be allocated to preferred before any allocation is made to common.

6. **Account for the issuance of common and preferred stock for cash and other assets.**

A corporation's stock will normally be issued for cash and other assets or by subscription. The majority of states require that stock be issued at a minimum value called legal capital. Legal capital is represented by the par or stated value of the stock.

When stock is issued for cash or other assets, the par or stated value of the stock is recorded as common or preferred stock. When the stock is sold at an amount greater than the par or stated value, the excess is recorded as Paid-in Capital in Excess of Par or Stated Value.

Sometimes stock is issued for noncash assets. In these transactions, it is necessary to decide what value to use in recording the issuance of the stock. The general rule is to record the stock at the market value of the stock issued. If this value cannot be determined, then the fair market value of the asset received will be used to record the transaction.

7. **Account for stock subscriptions.**

   When stock is not fully paid for at the time of sale, it is not issued. However, the transaction is recorded by debiting Subscriptions Receivable (a current asset) and crediting Capital Stock Subscribed (a stockholders' equity account) for the par or stated value and crediting Paid-in Capital in Excess of Par or Stated Value for any difference. When the stock has been fully paid for and is issued, Capital Stock Subscribed is debited and Capital Stock is credited.

8. **Account for the exercise of stock options.**

   Stock option plans are established to allow a company's employees to own a part of the company. Usually the issue of stock to employees under stock option plans is recorded in a manner similar to the issue of stock to any outsider.

Review of Concepts and Terminology

The following concepts and terms were introduced in this chapter:

(L.O. 1) **Articles of incorporation:** A contract between the state and the incorporators forming the corporation.

(L.O. 1) **Audit committee:** A committee of the board of directors of a corporation usually made up of outside directors, whose functions include engaging and monitoring the work of the external auditors.

(L.O. 3) **Authorized stock:** The maximum number of shares a corporation may issue without changing its charter with the state.

(L.O. 5) **Callable preferred stock:** Preferred stock that may be redeemed and retired by the corporation at its option.

(L.O. 3) **Common stock:** The stock representing the most basic rights to ownership of a corporation.

(L.O. 3) **Contributed capital:** The part of the owners' equity section of a corporation's balance sheet representing the investments made by the stockholders in the corporation.

(L.O. 5) **Convertible preferred stock:** Preferred stock that may be exchanged at the option of the holder for common stock.

(L.O. 1) **Corporation:** A body of persons granted a charter legally recognizing it as a separate entity having its own rights, privileges, and liabilities distinct from those of its members.

(L.O. 5) **Cumulative stock:** Preferred stock on which unpaid dividends accumulate over time and must be satisfied in any given year before a dividend may be paid to common stockholders.

(L.O. 4) **Dividend:** A distribution of assets (usually cash) of a corporation to its stockholders.

(L.O. 5) **Dividends in arrears:** The accumulated unpaid dividends on cumulative preferred stock from prior years.

(L.O. 1) **Double taxation:** A term referring to the fact that earnings of a corporation are taxed twice, both as the net income of the corporation and as the dividends distributed to the stockholders.

(L.O. 4) **Ex-dividend:** A description of capital stock when the right to a dividend already declared on the stock remains with the person who sells the stock and does not transfer to the person who buys it.

(L.O. 3) **Issued stock:** The shares of stock sold or otherwise transferred to stockholders.

(L.O. 6) **Legal capital:** The minimum amount that can be reported as contributed capital; usually equal to par value or stated value.

(L.O. 4) **Liquidating dividend:** A dividend that exceeds retained earnings.

(L.O. 5) **Noncumulative:** Preferred stock on which the dividend may lapse and does not have to be paid if not paid within a given year.

(L.O. 6) **No-par stock:** Capital stock that does not have a par value.

(L.O. 2) **Organization costs:** The costs of forming a corporation.

(L.O. 3) **Outstanding stock:** The shares of a corporation's stock held by stockholders.

(L.O. 3) **Par value:** The amount printed on each share of stock, which must be recorded in the capital stock accounts; used in determining the legal capital of a corporation.

(L.O. 4) **Preferred stock:** A type of stock that has some preference over common stock, usually including dividends.

(L.O. 1) **Proxy:** A legal document, signed by the stockholder, giving another party the right to vote his or her shares.

(L.O. 3) **Residual equity:** The common stock of a corporation.

(L.O. 1) **Share of stock:** A unit of ownership in a corporation.

(L.O. 6) **Stated value:** A value assigned by the board of directors of a corporation to no-par stock.

(L.O. 3) **Stock certificate:** A document issued to a stockholder in a corporation indicating the number of shares of stock owned by the stockholder.

(L.O. 3) **Stockholders' equity:** The owners' equity section of a corporation's balance sheet representing the owners' claims to the business.

(L.O. 8) **Stock option plan:** An agreement to issue stock to employees according to the terms of the plan.

(L.O. 7) **Stock subscription:** An issuance of stock where the investor agrees to pay for the stock on some future date or in installments at an agreed price.

Self-Test

Test your knowledge of the chapter by choosing the best answer for each item below and following.

1. A disadvantage of the corporate form of business is
   a. government regulation.
   b. centralized authority and responsibility.
   c. its being a separate legal entity.
   d. continuous existence. *(L.O. 1)*

2. The organization costs of a corporation should be
   a. recorded and maintained as an intangible asset for the life of a corporation.
   b. recorded as an intangible asset and amortized over a reasonable length of time.
   c. written off as expense when incurred.
   d. avoided before receiving a charter from the state.   (L.O. 3)

3. All of the following are normally found in a corporation's stockholders' equity section except
   a. paid-in capital in excess of par value.
   b. retained earnings.
   c. dividends payable.
   d. common stock.   (L.O. 3)

4. The board of directors of the Birch Corporation declared a cash dividend on January 18, 19x8, to be paid on February 18, 19x8, to shareholders holding stock on February 2, 19x8. Given these facts, the date February 2, 19x8 is referred to as the
   a. date of declaration.
   b. date of record.
   c. payment date.
   d. ex-dividend date.   (L.O. 4)

5. The journal entry to record the declaration of a cash dividend will
   a. reduce assets.
   b. increase liabilities.
   c. increase total stockholders' equity.
   d. not affect total stockholders' equity.   (L.O. 5)

6. Dividends in arrears are dividends on
   a. noncumulative preferred stock, which have not been declared for some specific period of time.
   b. cumulative preferred stock, which have been declared but have not been paid.
   c. cumulative preferred stock, which have not been declared for some specific period of time.
   d. common stock, which may never be declared.   (L.O. 5)

7. The par value of the common stock represents
   a. an amount entered into the corporation's Common Stock account when shares are issued.
   b. the exact amount always received by the corporation when the stock was issued.
   c. the liquidation value of a share of stock.
   d. the market value of a share of stock.   (L.O. 6)

8. The Paid-in Capital in Excess of Stated Value account normally arises in the accounting records when
   a. the par value of capital stock is greater than the stated value.
   b. capital stock is sold at an amount greater than stated value.
   c. the market value of the stock rises above stated value.
   d. the number of shares issued exceeds stated value.   (L.O. 6)

9. Which of the following is properly classified as an asset?
   a. Subscriptions receivable
   b. Common stock subscribed
   c. Dividends in arrears
   d. Paid-in capital   *(L.O. 7)*

10. A plan under which employees are allowed to purchase shares of stock in a company at a specified price is called a
    a. stock option plan.
    b. stock subscription plan.
    c. stock dividend plan.
    d. stock compensation plan.   *(L.O. 8)*

Answers to Self-Test are at the end of this chapter.

Review Problem
Stock Journal Entries and Stockholders' Equity

(L.O. 4, 5, 6, 7) The Beta Corporation was organized in 19xx in the state of Arizona. The charter of the corporation authorized the issuance of 1,000,000 shares of $1 par value common stock and an additional 25,000 shares of 4 percent, $20 par value cumulative convertible preferred stock. Transactions that relate to the stock of the company for 19xx are as follows:

Feb. 12 Issued 100,000 shares of common stock for $125,000.
      20 Issued 3,000 shares of common stock for accounting and legal services. The services were billed to the company at $3,600.
Mar. 15 Issued 120,000 shares of common stock to Edward Jackson in exchange for a building and land that had an appraised value of $100,000 and $25,000, respectively.
Apr. 2 Accepted subscriptions on 200,000 shares of common stock for $1.30 per share.
July 1 Issued 25,000 shares of preferred stock for $500,000.
Sept. 30 Collected in full subscriptions related to 60 percent of the common stock subscribed, and issued the appropriate stock to common stock subscribers. Make two separate entries.
Dec. 31 The company reported net income of $40,000 for 19xx, and the board declared dividends of $25,000, payable on January 15 to stockholders of record on January 8. Dividends include preferred stock cash dividends for one-half year.

Required
1. Prepare the journal entries necessary to record these stock-related transactions, including closing net income and Dividends Declared to Retained Earnings. Following the December 31 entry to record dividends, show dividends payable for each class of stock.
2. Prepare the stockholders' equity section of the Beta Corporation balance sheet as of December 31, 19xx.

Answer to Review Problem

1. Journal entries prepared:

Feb.	12	Cash	125,000	
		Common Stock		100,000
		Paid-in Capital in Excess of Par		
		Value, Common		25,000
		To record the sale of 100,000		
		shares of $1 par value common		
		stock for $1.25 per share		
	20	Organization Costs	3,600	
		Common Stock		3,000
		Paid-in Capital in Excess of Par Value,		
		Common		600
		To record issuance of 3,000		
		shares of $1 par value common stock		
		for billed accounting and legal		
		services of $3,600		
Mar.	15	Building	100,000	
		Land	25,000	
		Common Stock		120,000
		Paid-in Capital in Excess of Par		
		Value, Common		5,000
		To record issuance of 120,000 shares		
		of $1 par value common stock for a		
		building and tract of land appraised		
		at $100,000 and $25,000		
Apr.	2	Subscriptions Receivable, Common		
		Stock	260,000	
		Common Stock Subscribed		200,000
		Paid-in Capital in Excess of Par		
		Value, Common		60,000
		To record subscription for 200,000		
		shares of $1 par value stock at $1.30		
		a share		
July	1	Cash	500,000	
		Preferred Stock		500,000
		To record sale of 25,000 shares		
		of $20 par value preferred stock		
		for $20 per share		
Sept.	30	Cash	156,000	
		Subscriptions Receivable, Common		
		Stock		156,000
		To record collection in full of		
		60 percent of subscriptions		
		receivable:		
		$260,000 × .60 = $156,000		
	30	Common Stock Subscribed	120,000	
		Common Stock		120,000
		To record issuance of		
		common stock		
		$200,000 × .60 = $120,000		

Dec. 31	Income Summary	40,000	
	Retained Earnings		40,000
	To close net income to Retained Earnings		

31	Dividends Declared	25,000	
	Dividends Payable		25,000

To record the declaration
of a $25,000 cash dividend
to preferred and common
stockholders:

Total dividend	$25,000
Less preferred stock cash dividend:	
$500,000 × .04 × .5 =	10,000
Common stock cash dividend	$15,000

31	Retained Earnings	25,000	
	Dividends Declared		25,000
	To close the Dividends Declared account for the year ended Dec. 31, 19xx		

2. Stockholders' equity section of balance sheet prepared:

Beta Corporation
Stockholders' Equity
December 31, 19xx

Contributed Capital		
4% Cumulative Convertible Preferred Stock— $20 par value, 25,000 shares authorized, issued, and outstanding		$ 500,000
Common Stock—$1 par value, 1,000,000 shares authorized, 343,000 shares issued and outstanding	$343,000	
Common Stock Subscribed	80,000	
Paid-in Capital in Excess of Par Value, Common	90,600	513,600
Total Contributed Capital		$1,013,600
Retained Earnings		15,000
Total Stockholders' Equity		$1,028,600

Chapter Assignments

Discussion Questions and Writing Assignments

1. What is a corporation, and how is it formed?
2. What is the role of the board of directors in a corporation, and how does it differ from the role of management?
3. What are the typical officers in the management of a corporation and their duties?
4. What are several advantages of the corporate form of business? Explain.
5. What are several disadvantages of the corporate form of business? Explain your answer.
6. What are organization costs of a corporation?
7. What is the proper accounting treatment of organization costs?
8. What is the legal capital of a corporation, and what is its significance?
9. How is the value determined for recording stock issued for noncash assets?
10. Explain the accounting treatment of cash dividends.
11. What are stock subscriptions, and how are Subscriptions Receivable and Common Stock Subscribed classified on the balance sheet?
12. What does it mean for preferred stock to be cumulative, convertible, and/or callable?
13. What are dividends in arrears, and how should they be disclosed in the financial statements?
14. What is the proper classification of the following accounts on the balance sheet? (a) Organization Costs; (b) Common Stock; (c) Subscriptions Receivable, Preferred; (d) Preferred Stock Subscribed; (e) Paid-in Capital in Excess of Par Value, Common; (f) Paid-in Capital in Excess of Stated Value, Common; (g) Discount on Common Stock; (h) Retained Earnings.
15. What reasons can you think of for a corporation to have a stock option plan? Why would an employee want to participate in one?

Classroom Exercises

Exercise 15-1.
Journal Entries for Organization Costs
(L.O. 2)

The Korman Corporation was organized during 19x7. At the beginning of the fiscal year, the company incurred the following costs in organizing the company: (1) Attorney's fees, market value of services $3,000; paid with 2,000 shares of $1 par common stock. (2) Incorporation fees paid to the state, $2,500. (3) Accountant's services that would normally be billed at $1,500 paid with 1,100 shares of $1 par value common stock.

Prepare the separate journal entries necessary to record these transactions and to amortize organization costs for the first year, assuming that the company elects to write off organization costs over five years.

Exercise 15-2.
Journal Entries and Stockholders' Equity
(L.O. 3, 6)

The Winkler Hospital Supply Corporation was organized in 19xx. The company was authorized to issue 100,000 shares of no-par common stock with a stated value of $5 per share, and 20,000 shares of $100 par value, 6 percent noncumulative preferred stock. On March 1 the company sold 60,000 shares of its common stock for $15 per share and 8,000 shares of its preferred stock for $100 per share.

1. Prepare the journal entries to record the sale of the stock.
2. Prepare the company's stockholders' equity section of the balance sheet immediately after the common and preferred stock were issued.

Exercise 15-3.
Stockholders'
Equity
(L.O. 3)

The accounts and balances that follow were taken from the records of Aguilar Corporation on December 31, 19xx.

| | | Balance | |
Account Name		Debit	Credit
Preferred Stock—$100 par value, 9% cumulative, 10,000 shares authorized, 6,000 shares issued and outstanding			$600,000
Common Stock—$12 par value, 60,000 shares authorized, 30,000 shares issued and outstanding			360,000
Common Stock Subscribed, 2,000 shares			24,000
Paid-in Capital in Excess of Par Value, Common			170,000
Retained Earnings			23,000
Subscriptions Receivable, Common		$30,000	

Prepare a stockholders' equity section for Aguilar Corporation's balance sheet.

Exercise 15-4.
Cash Dividends
(L.O. 4)

Downey Corporation has authorized 200,000 shares of $10 par value common stock. There are 160,000 shares issued and 140,000 shares outstanding. On June 5, the board of directors declares a $.50 per share cash dividend to be paid on June 25 to stockholders of record on June 15. Prepare the journal entries necessary to record these events.

Exercise 15-5.
Preferred Stock
Dividends with
Dividends in
Arrears
(L.O. 5)

The Matsuta Corporation has 10,000 shares of its $100, 7 percent cumulative preferred stock outstanding, and 50,000 shares of its $1 par value common stock outstanding. In its first four years of operation, the board of directors of Matsuta Corporation paid cash dividends as follows: 19x1, none; 19x2, $120,000; 19x3, $140,000; 19x4, $140,000.

Determine the total cash dividends and dividends per share paid to the preferred and common stockholders during each of the four years.

Exercise 15-6.
Preferred and
Common Stock
Dividends
(L.O. 5)

The Goss-Carterly Corporation pays dividends at the end of each year. The dividends paid for 19x1, 19x2, and 19x3 were $40,000, $30,000, and $90,000, respectively.

Calculate the total amount of dividends paid each year to the common and preferred stockholders if each of the following capital structures is assumed: (1) 10,000 shares of $100 par, 6 percent noncumulative preferred stock and 30,000 shares of $10 par common stock. (2) 5,000 shares of $100 par, 7 percent cumulative preferred stock and 30,000 shares of $10 par common stock. There were no dividends in arrears at the beginning of 19x1.

Exercise 15-7.
Journal Entries:
Stated Value Stock
(L.O. 6)

The Sayre Corporation is authorized to issue 100,000 shares of no-par stock. The company recently sold 40,000 shares for $13 per share.

1. Prepare the journal entry to record the sale of the stock if there is no stated value.
2. Prepare the entry if a $10 stated value is authorized by the company's board of directors.

Exercise 15-8.
Issuance of Stock
for Noncash
Assets
(L.O. 6)

On July 1, 19xx, Wayside, a new corporation, issued 20,000 shares of its common stock for a corporate headquarters building. The building has a fair market value of $300,000 and a book value of $200,000. Because the corporation is new, it is not possible to establish a market value for the common stock.

Record the issuance of stock for the building, assuming the following conditions: (a) the par value of the stock is $5 per share; (b) the stock is no-par stock; and (c) the stock is no-par stock but has a stated value of $2 per share.

Exercise 15-9.
Issuance of Stock
for Noncash
Assets
(L.O. 6)

The Probst Corporation issued 2,000 shares of its $10 par value common stock for some land. The land had a fair market value of $30,000.

Prepare the journal entries necessary to record the issuance of the stock for the land under each of the following conditions: (1) the stock was selling for $14 per share on the day of the transaction; and (2) management attempted to place a value on the common stock but could not do so.

Exercise 15-10.
Stock
Subscriptions
(L.O. 7)

The Spangler Corporation sold 15,000 shares of its $2 par value common stock by subscription for $8 per share on February 15, 19xx. Cash was received in installments from the purchasers: 50 percent on April 1 and 50 percent on June 1.

Prepare the entries necessary to record these transactions.

Exercise 15-11.
Exercise of Stock
Options
(L.O. 8)

Record the following equity transaction of the Evans Company in 19xx:

May 5   Walter Evans exercised his option to purchase 10,000 shares of $1 par value common stock at an option price of $12. The market price per share on the grant date was $12, and it was $24 on the exercise date.

Interpreting Accounting Information

United Airlines*
(L.O. 3, 6)

United Airlines (UAL, Inc.) is one of the largest domestic airlines, with destinations in all fifty states plus the Orient. On February 18, 1986, the airline announced an issuance of common stock in *The Wall Street Journal*, as shown on the following page:

*Excerpts from the 1985 annual report used by permission of United Airlines. Copyright © 1985.

4,400,000 Shares
UAL, Inc.
Common Stock
($5 par value)
Price $56¾ per share[3]

A portion of the stockholders' equity section of the balance sheet from UAL's 1985 annual report appeared as follows:

	1985	1984
	(in thousands)	
Common stock, $5 par value; authorized 50,000,000 shares; outstanding 34,484,544 shares in 1985 and 29,609,734 shares in 1984	172,423	148,049
Additional Paid-in Capital	555,427	421,100
Retained earnings	681,383	555,954

Required

1. Assuming all the shares are issued at the price indicated and that UAL receives the full proceeds, prepare the entry in UAL's accounting records to record the stock issue.
2. Prepare the portion of the stockholders' equity section of the balance sheet shown above after the issue of the common stock. Did UAL have to increase the authorized shares to undertake this stock issue?
3. How do you think the above results would differ if UAL's underwriter kept a fee of $.50 per share to assist it in issuing the stock so that UAL receives $56.25 per share?

Problem Set A

**Problem 15A-1.
Organization
Costs, Stock and
Dividend Journal
Entries, and
Stockholders'
Equity**
(L.O. 2, 3, 4, 6)

On March 1, 19xx, Benson Corporation began operations with a charter from the state that authorized 100,000 shares of $2 par value common stock and engaged in the following transactions:

Mar. 1 Issued 30,000 shares of common stock, $100,000.
     2 Paid fees associated with obtaining the charter and organizing the corporation, $12,000.
Apr. 10 Issued 13,000 shares of common stock, $65,000.
May 31 Closed the Income Summary account. Net income earned during the first quarter, $12,000.
     31 The board of directors declared a $.10 per share cash dividend to be paid on June 15 to shareholders of record on June 10. Closed Dividends Declared to Retained Earnings.

Required

1. Prepare general journal entries to record the above transactions and closing entries as indicated.
2. Prepare the stockholders' equity section of Benson Corporation's balance sheet on May 31, 19xx.

3. Reprinted by permission of *The Wall Street Journal*, © Dow Jones & Co., Inc., 1986. All rights reserved.

3. Assuming that the paymen.t for organization costs on March 2 was to be amortized over five years, what adjustment was made on May 31 to record three months' amortization? Describe the resulting balance sheet presentation of organization costs.

**Problem 15A-2.
Stock Journal
Entries and
Stockholders'
Equity**
(L.O. 3, 6, 7)

The Lau Company, Inc. has been authorized by the state of Indiana to issue 1,000,000 shares of $1 par value common stock. The company began issuing its common stock in May of 19xx.

During May the company had the following stock transactions:

May 10   Issued 30,000 shares of stock for a building and land with fair market value of $32,C00 and $7,000, respectively.
     15   Accepted subscriptions to 500,000 shares of its stock for $650,000.
     20   Collected full payment on 200,000 shares of the common stock subscribed on May 15. Issued the appropriate shares.
     23   Sold 15,000 shares of stock for $20,000 cash.
     27   Collected full payment on 100,000 shares of the common stock subscribed on May 15 and issued the shares.

Required

1. Prepare the general journal entries to record the stock transactions of Lau Company, Inc. for the month of May.
2. Prepare the stockholders' equity section of Lau's balance sheet as of May 31. Assume the company had net income of $18,000 for May and paid no dividends.

**Problem 15A-3.
Preferred and
Common Stock
Dividends**
(L.O. 5)

The Sabatino Corporation had the following stock outstanding for 19x1 through 19x4:

Preferred stock—$50 par value, 8 percent cumulative, 10,000 shares authorized, issued, and outstanding

Common stock—$5 par value, 200,000 shares authorized, issued, and outstanding

The company paid $30,000, $30,000, $94,000, and $130,000 in dividends during 19x1, 19x2, 19x3, and 19x4, respectively.

Required

1. Determine the dividend per share paid to common stockholders and preferred stockholders in 19x1, 19x2, 19x3, and 19x4.
2. Perform the same computations assuming that the preferred stock is noncumulative.

**Problem 15A-4.
Comprehensive
Stockholders'
Equity
Transactions**
(L.O. 2, 3, 4, 6, 7)

Cabrini, Inc. was organized and authorized to issue 10,000 shares of $100 par value 9 percent preferred stock and 100,000 shares of no-par, $5 stated value common stock on July 1, 19xx. Stock-related transactions for Cabrini are as follows:

July   1   Issued 20,000 shares of common stock at $11 per share.
       1   Issued 1,000 shares of common stock at $11 per share for services rendered in connection with the organization of the company.

July 2 Issued 2,000 shares of preferred stock at par value for cash.

10 Received subscriptions for 10,000 shares of common stock at $12 per share.

10 Issued 5,000 shares of common stock for land on which the asking price was $60,000. Market value of stock was $12. Management wishes to record the land at full market value of the stock.

31 Closed the Income Summary account. Net income earned during July was $13,000.

Aug. 2 Received payment in full for 6,000 shares of the stock subscriptions of July 10. Issued the appropriate stocks.

10 Declared a cash dividend for one month on the outstanding preferred stock and $.02 per share on common stock outstanding, payable on August 22 to stockholders of record on August 12.

12 Date of record for cash dividends.

22 Paid cash dividends.

31 Closed the Income Summary and Dividends Declared accounts. Net income during August was $12,000.

Required

1. Prepare general journal entries to record the above transactions.
2. Prepare the stockholders' equity section of the balance sheet as it would appear on August 31, 19xx.

**Problem 15A-5.
Comprehensive
Stockholders'
Equity
Transactions**
(L.O. 2, 3, 4, 6, 7, 8)

In January 19xx, the Abelman Corporation was organized and authorized to issue 2,000,000 shares of no-par common stock and 50,000 shares of 5 percent, $50 par value, noncumulative preferred stock. The stock-related transactions of the first year's operations follow.

Jan. 19 Sold 15,000 shares of the common stock for $31,500. State law requires a minimum of $1 stated value per share.

21 Issued 5,000 shares of common stock to attorneys and accountants for services valued at $11,000 provided during the organization of the corporation.

26 Accepted subscriptions for 20,000 shares of the common stock for $2.50 per share.

Feb. 7 Issued 30,000 shares of common stock for a building that had an appraised value of $78,000.

Mar. 22 Collected full payment for 12,000 shares of the common stock subscribed on January 26, 19xx, and issued the stock.

June 30 Closed the Income Summary account. Reported $80,000 income for the first six months of operations, ended June 30.

July 15 Issued 5,000 shares of common stock to employees under a stock option plan that allows any employee to buy shares at the current market price, which today is $3 per share.

Aug. 1 Collected the full amount on the remaining 8,000 shares of common stock subscribed and issued the stock.

Sept. 1 Declared a cash dividend of $.15 per common share to be paid on September 25 to stockholders of record on September 15.

15 Cash dividend date of record.

25 Paid cash dividend to stockholders of record on September 15.

Oct. 30 Issued 4,000 shares of common stock for a piece of land. The stock is selling for $3 per share, and the land has a fair market value of $12,500.

Nov. 10   Accepted subscriptions for 10,000 shares of the common stock for $3.50 per share.

Dec. 15   Issued 2,200 shares of preferred stock for $50 per share.

    31   Closed the Income Summary account and Dividends Declared account. Reported $20,000 income for the past six months of operations.

Required

1. Prepare the journal entries to record all of the above transactions of Abelman Corporation during 19xx.
2. Prepare the stockholders' equity section of Abelman Corporation's balance sheet as of December 31, 19xx.

Problem Set B

**Problem 15B-1.
Organization
Costs, Stock and
Dividend Journal
Entries, and
Stockholders'
Equity**
(L.O. 2, 3, 4, 6)

Forsyth Corporation began operations on September 1, 19xx. The corporation's charter authorized 300,000 shares of $4 par value common stock. Forsyth Corporation engaged in the following transactions during the first quarter:

Sept. 1   Issued 50,000 shares of common stock, $250,000.
       1   Paid an attorney $16,000 to assist in organizing the corporation and obtaining the corporate charter from the state.

Oct.   2   Issued 80,000 shares of common stock, $480,000.

Nov. 30   The board of directors declared a cash dividend of $.20 per share to be paid on December 15 to stockholders of record on December 10.

    30   Closed the Income Summary and Dividends Declared accounts for the first quarter. Revenues were $210,000 and expenses $170,000. (Assume revenues and expenses have already been closed to Income Summary.)

Required

1. Prepare general journal entries to record the first-quarter transactions and closing entries as indicated.
2. Prepare the stockholders' equity section of Forsyth Corporation's November 30, 19xx balance sheet.
3. Assuming that the payment to the attorney on September 1 was to be amortized over five years, what adjusting entry was made on November 30? Also, describe the resulting balance sheet presentation.

**Problem 15B-2.
Stock Journal
Entries and
Stockholders'
Equity**
(L.O. 3, 6, 7)

The corporate charter for Waldman Corporation states the company is authorized to issue 500,000 shares of $3 par value common stock. The company was involved with several stock transactions during June 19x8 as shown in the following list. Assume no prior transactions.

June 3   Accepted subscriptions for 200,000 shares of its common stock at $5.50 per share.

    12   Issued 24,000 shares of stock for land and warehouse. The land and warehouse had a fair market value of $25,000 and $100,000, respectively.

    22   Sold 50,000 shares of stock for $325,000.

    25   Collected full payment on 60,000 shares of the common stock subscribed on June 3 and issued the shares.

Required

1. Prepare the general journal entries to record the June transactions of Waldman Corporation.
2. Prepare the stockholders' equity section of the Waldman Corporation's balance sheet as of June 30, 19x8. Assume the company had net income of $8,000 during June and paid no dividends (and all necessary entries have been made).

Problem 15B-3.
Preferred and
Common Stock
Dividends
(L.O. 5)

The Jefferson Corporation had both common stock and preferred stock outstanding from 19x4 through 19x6. Information about each stock for the three years is as follows:

Type	Par Value	Shares Outstanding	Other
Preferred	$100	20,000	7 percent cumulative
Common	10	600,000	

The company paid $70,000, $400,000, and $550,000 in dividends for 19x4 through 19x6, respectively.

Required

1. Determine the dividend per share paid to the common and preferred stockholders each year.
2. Repeat the computation performed in **1**, assuming the preferred stock was noncumulative.

Problem 15B-4.
Comprehensive
Stockholders'
Equity
Transactions
(L.O. 2, 3, 4, 6, 7)

The Specialty Plastics Corporation was chartered in the state of Michigan. The company was authorized to issue 10,000 shares of $100 par value 6 percent preferred stock and 100,000 shares of no-par common stock. The common stock has a $1 stated value. The stock-related transactions for March and April, 19xx, were as follows:

Mar. 3 Issued 10,000 shares of common stock for $60,000 worth of services rendered in organizing and chartering the corporation.
      10 Received subscriptions for 40,000 shares of common stock at $6 a share.
      15 Issued 16,000 shares of common stock for land, which has an asking price of $100,000. The common stock has a market value of $6 per share.
      22 Issued 5,000 shares of preferred stock for $500,000.
      30 Closed the Income Summary account. Net income for March was $9,000.
Apr. 4 Issued 10,000 shares of common stock for $60,000.
      10 Received payment in full for 30,000 shares of the stock subscriptions of March 10 and issued the appropriate stock.
      15 Declared a cash dividend for one month on the outstanding preferred stock and $.05 per share on common stock outstanding, payable on April 30 to stockholders of record on April 25.
      25 Date of record for cash dividends.
      30 Paid cash dividends.
      30 Closed the Income Summary and Dividends Declared accounts. Net income for April was $14,000.

Required

1. Prepare general journal entries for March and April.
2. Prepare the stockholders' equity section of the company's balance sheet as of April 30, 19xx.

Problem 15B-5.
Comprehensive
Stockholders'
Equity
Transactions
(L.O. 2, 3, 4, 6, 7, 8)

The Sun Lighting Corporation was organized and authorized to issue 100,000 shares of 6 percent, $100 par value, noncumulative preferred stock and 3,000,000 shares of $5 par value common stock. The stock-related transactions for the first six months of 19xx operations are as follows:

Apr. 3 Issued 12,000 shares of common stock for legal and other organizational fees valued at $60,000.
     29 Sold 300,000 shares of common stock for $6 a share.
May   5 Issued 40,000 shares of common stock for a building and land appraised at $150,000 and $80,000, respectively.
     17 Received subscriptions for 300,000 shares of common stock at $8 a share.
June 17 Received full payment for 200,000 shares of common stock subscribed on May 17 and issued the stock.
     30 Closed the Income Summary account for the first quarter of operations. Net income for the first quarter was $200,000. (Assume the revenues and expenses have already been closed into Income Summary.)
July 10 Issued 2,000 shares of common stock to employees under a stock option plan. The plan allows employees to purchase the stock at the current market price, which was $6.
     17 Collected the full amount for the remaining 100,000 shares of common stock subscribed on May 17 and issued the stock.
Aug. 8 Issued 10,000 shares of common stock for $8 a share.
Sept.11 Declared a cash dividend of $.10 per common share to be paid on September 25 to stockholders of record on September 18.
     18 Cash dividend date of record.
     25 Paid the cash dividend to stockholders of record on September 18.
     26 Issued 5,000 shares of preferred stock at par value.
     29 Accepted subscriptions for 20,000 shares of common stock at $9 per share.
     30 Closed the Income Summary account and Dividends Declared for the second quarter of operations. Net income for the second quarter was $125,000.

Required

1. Prepare general journal entries to record the stock-related transactions of the Sun Lighting Corporation.
2. Prepare the stockholders' equity section of Sun Lighting Corporation's balance sheet as of September 30.

Financial Decision Case

Northeast
Servotech
Corporation
(L.O. 3)

The companies offering services to the computer technology industry are growing quickly. Participating in this growth, Northeast Servotech Corporation has expanded rapidly in recent years. Because of its profitability, the company has been able to grow without obtaining external financing. This fact is reflected in its current balance sheet, which contains no long-term debt. The liability and stockholders' equity sections of the balance sheet are as follows.

Northeast Servotech Corporation
Partial Balance Sheet

Liabilities

Current Liabilities	$ 500,000

Stockholders' Equity

Common Stock, $10 par value, 500,000 shares authorized, 100,000 shares issued and outstanding	$1,000,000	
Paid-in Capital in Excess of Par Value, Common	1,800,000	
Retained Earnings	1,700,000	
Total Stockholders' Equity		4,500,000
Total Liabilities and Stockholders' Equity		$5,000,000

The company is now faced with the possibility of doubling its size by purchasing the operations of a rival company for $4,000,000. If the purchase goes through, Northeast will become the top company in its specialized industry in the northeastern part of the country. The problem for management is how to finance the purchase. After much study and discussion with bankers and underwriters, management prepares three financing alternatives to present to the board of directors, which must authorize the purchase and the financing.

Alternative A: The company could issue $4,000,000 of long-term debt. Given the company's financial rating and the current market rates, it is believed that the company will have to pay an interest rate of 17 percent on the debt.

Alternative B: The company could issue 40,000 shares of 12 percent, $100 par value preferred stock.

Alternative C: The company could issue 100,000 additional shares of $10 par value common stock at $40.

Management explains to the board that the interest on the long-term debt is tax deductible and that the applicable income tax rate is 40 percent. The board members know that a dividend of $.80 per share of common stock was paid last year, up from $.60 and $.40 per share in the two years before that. The board has had a policy of regular increases in dividends of $.20 per share. The board feels that each of the three financing alternatives is feasible and now wishes to study the financial effects of each alternative.

Required

1. Prepare a schedule to show how the liability and stockholders' equity side of Northeast Servotech's balance sheet will look under each alternative, and figure the debt to equity ratio (total liabilities ÷ total stockholders' equity) for each.

2. Compute and compare the cash needed to pay the interest or dividend for each kind of financing net of income taxes in the first year. How may this requirement change in future years?
3. Evaluate the alternatives, giving the arguments for and against each one.

Answers to Self-Test

1. a	3. c	5. b	7. a	9. a
2. b	4. b	6. c	8. b	10. a

CHAPTER 16

Retained Earnings and Corporate Income Statements

This chapter continues the study of the stockholders' equity section of the balance sheet. It first covers the retained earnings of a corporation, the transactions that affect them, and the statement of stockholders' equity. The rest of the chapter examines the components of the corporate income statement. After studying this chapter, you should be able to meet the learning objectives listed on the left.

Retained Earnings Transactions

Stockholders' equity, as presented earlier, has two parts: contributed capital and retained earnings. The **retained earnings** of a company are the part of the stockholders' equity that represents claims to assets arising from the earnings of the business. Retained earnings equal the profits of a company since the date of its beginning less any losses, dividends to stockholders, or transfers to contributed capital. Exhibit 16-1 shows a statement of retained earnings of Caprock Corporation for 19x2. The beginning balance of retained earnings of $854,000 is increased by net income of $76,000 and decreased by cash dividends of $30,000, so that the ending balance is $900,000. This statement may also disclose other transactions that are explained in the chapter.

It is important to note that retained earnings are not the assets themselves, but the existence of retained earnings means that assets generated by profitable operations have been kept in the company to help it grow or to meet other business needs. However, a credit balance in Retained Earnings does *not* mean that cash or any designated set of assets is directly associated with retained earnings. The fact that earnings have been retained means that assets as a whole have been increased.

Retained Earnings may carry a debit balance. Generally, this happens when a company's losses and distributions to stockholders are greater than its profits from operations. In such a case, the firm is said to have a **deficit** (debit balance) in retained earnings. This is shown in the stockholders' equity section of the balance sheet as a deduction from contributed capital.

Exhibit 16-1. A Statement of Retained Earnings

Caprock Corporation
Statement of Retained Earnings
For the Year Ended December 31, 19x2

Retained Earnings, December 31, 19x1	$854,000
Net Income, 19x2	76,000
Subtotal	$930,000
Less Cash Dividends, Common	30,000
Retained Earnings, December 31, 19x2	$900,000

OBJECTIVE 1
Define retained earnings, and prepare a statement of retained earnings

Accountants have used various terms for the retained earnings of a business. One term is *surplus,* which implies that there are excess assets available for dividends. This is poor terminology as the existence of retained earnings carries no connotation of "excess" or "surplus." Because of possible misinterpretation, the American Institute of Certified Public Accountants recommends more fitting terms, such as *retained income, retained earnings, accumulated earnings,* or *earnings retained for use in the business.*[1]

Prior period adjustments are events or transactions that relate to earlier accounting periods but were not determinable in the earlier period. When they occur, they are shown on the statement of retained earnings as an adjustment in the account's beginning balance. The Financial Accounting Standards Board identifies only two kinds of prior period adjustments. The first is to correct an error in the financial statements of a prior year. The second is needed if a company realizes an income tax gain from carrying forward a preacquisition operating loss of a purchased subsidiary.[2] Prior period adjustments are rare in accounting.

Stock Dividends

OBJECTIVE 2
Account for stock dividends and stock splits

A **stock dividend** is a proportional distribution of shares of the company's stock to the corporation's stockholders. The distribution of stock does not change the assets and liabilities of the firm because there is not a distribution of assets as in a cash dividend. The board of directors may declare a stock dividend for several reasons:

1. It may wish to give stockholders some evidence of the success of the company without paying a cash dividend, which would affect the firm's working capital position.
2. The board's aim may be to reduce the market price of the stock by increasing the number of shares outstanding, though this goal is more often met by stock splits.

1. Committee on Accounting Terminology, *Accounting Terminology Bulletin No. 1*, "Review and Resume" (New York: American Institute of Certified Public Accountants, 1953), par. 69.
2. *Statement of Financial Accounting Standards No. 16*, "Prior Period Adjustments" (Stamford, Conn.: Financial Accounting Standards Board, 1977), par. 11.

3. It may want to make a nontaxable distribution to stockholders. Stock dividends that meet certain conditions are not considered income, so a tax is not levied on this type of transaction.
4. It communicates that the permanent capital of the company has increased by transferring an amount from retained earnings to contributed capital.

The total stockholders' equity is not affected by a stock dividend. The effect of a stock dividend is to transfer a dollar amount from Retained Earnings to the contributed capital section on the date of declaration. The amount to be transferred is the fair market value (usually market price) of the additional shares to be issued. The laws of most states state the minimum value of each share to be transferred under a stock dividend, which is normally the minimum legal capital (par or stated value). However, generally accepted accounting principles state that market value reflects the economic effect of small stock distributions (less than 20 or 25 percent of a company's outstanding common stock) better than the par or stated value does. For this reason, the market price should be used for proper accounting of small stock dividends.[3]

To illustrate the accounting for a stock dividend, we will assume that Caprock Corporation has the following stockholders' equity structure:

Contributed Capital
Common Stock—$5 par value, 100,000 shares	
authorized, 30,000 issued and outstanding	$ 150,000
Paid-in Capital in Excess of Par Value, Common	30,000
Total Contributed Capital	$ 180,000
Retained Earnings	900,000
Total Stockholders' Equity	$1,080,000

Assume further that the board of directors declares a 10 percent stock dividend on February 24, distributable on March 31 to stockholders of record on March 15. The market price of the stock on February 24 was $20 per share. The entries to record the stock dividend declaration and distribution are as follows:

Date of Declaration

Feb. 24	Retained Earnings	60,000	
	Common Stock Distributable		15,000
	Paid-in Capital in Excess of Par		
	Value, Common		45,000

To record the declaration of a
10% stock dividend on common
stock, distributable on March 31
to stockholders of record on March 15:
30,000 shares × 10% = 3,000 shares
3,000 shares × $20/share = $60,000
3,000 shares × $5/share = $15,000

3. *Accounting Research Bulletin No. 43* (New York: American Institute of Certified Public Accountants, 1953), Chapter 7, Section B, par. 10.

Note that Retained Earnings is reduced directly rather than through a Dividends Declared account as was done for cash dividends in Chapter 15. The reason for this treatment is that cash dividends are usually declared on several occasions during the year. The Dividends Declared account is useful in accumulating the total cash dividends declared during the year. Stock dividends are usually declared only once per year, if at all.

Date of Record

Mar. 15   No entry required

Date of Distribution

Mar. 31	Common Stock Distributable	15,000	
	Common Stock		15,000
	To record the distribution of		
	stock dividend of 3,000 shares		

The effect of the above stock dividend is to transfer permanently the market value of the stock, $60,000, from Retained Earnings to Contributed Capital and to increase the number of shares outstanding by 3,000. Common Stock Distributable is credited for the par value of the stock to be distributed (3,000 × $5 = $15,000). In addition, when the market value is greater than the par value of the stock, Paid-in Capital in Excess of Par Value, Common, must be credited for the amount by which market value exceeds par value. In this case, total market value of the stock dividend ($60,000) exceeds the total par value ($15,000) by $45,000. No entry is required on the date of record. On the distribution date, the common stock is issued by debiting Common Stock Distributable and crediting Common Stock for the par value of the stock ($15,000).

Common Stock Distributable is not a liability because there is no obligation to distribute cash or other assets. The obligation is to distribute additional shares of capital stock. If financial statements are prepared between the date of declaration and the distribution of stock, Common Stock Distributable should be reported as part of Contributed Capital, as follows:

Contributed Capital	
Common Stock—$5 par value, 100,000 shares	
authorized, 30,000 issued and outstanding	$ 150,000
Common Stock Distributable, 3,000 shares	15,000
Paid-in Capital in Excess of Par Value, Common	75,000
Total Contributed Capital	$ 240,000
Retained Earnings	840,000
Total Stockholders' Equity	$1,080,000

Three points can be made from this example. First, the total stockholders' equity is unchanged before and after the stock dividend. Second, the assets of the corporation are not reduced as in the case of a cash dividend. Third, the proportionate ownership in the corporation of any individual stockholder is unchanged before and after the stock dividend. To illustrate these points, we will assume that a stockholder owns 1,000 shares before the stock dividend. After the 10 percent stock dividend is distributed, this stockholder would own 1,100 shares.

Stockholders' Equity	Before Dividend	After Dividend
Common Stock	$ 150,000	$ 165,000
Paid-in Capital in Excess of Par Value	30,000	75,000
Total Contributed Capital	$ 180,000	$ 240,000
Retained Earnings	900,000	840,000
Total Stockholders' Equity	$1,080,000	$1,080,000
Shares Outstanding	30,000	33,000
Book Value per Share	$36.00	$32.73

Stockholders' Investment		
Shares owned	1,000	1,100
Shares outstanding	30,000	33,000
Percentage of ownership	3⅓%	3⅓%
Book value of investment		
(3⅓% × $1,080,000)	$ 36,000	$ 36,000

Both before and after the stock dividend, the stockholders' equity totals $1,080,000 and the stockholder owns 3⅓ percent of the company. Book value of the investment stays at $36,000.

All stock dividends have an effect on the market price of a company's stock. But some stock dividends are so large that they have a material effect on the price per share of the stock. For example, a 50 percent stock dividend would cause the market price of the stock to drop about 33 percent. The AICPA has arbitrarily decided that large stock dividends, those greater than 20 to 25 percent, should be accounted for by transferring the par or stated value of the stock on the date of declaration from Retained Earnings to Contributed Capital.[4]

Stock Splits

A **stock split** occurs when a corporation increases the number of issued shares of stock and reduces the par or stated value proportionally. A company may plan a stock split when it wishes to lower the market value per share of its stock and increase the liquidity of the stock. This action may be necessary if the market value per share has become so high that it hinders the trading of the company's stock on the market. For example, suppose that the Caprock Corporation has 30,000 shares of $5.00 par value stock outstanding. The market value is $70.00 per share. The corporation plans a 2 for 1 split. This split will lower the par value to $2.50 and increase the number of shares outstanding to 60,000.

4. Ibid., par. 13.

If a stockholder previously owned 400 shares of the $5.00 par stock, he or she would own 800 shares of the $2.50 par stock after the split. When a stock split occurs, the market value tends to fall in proportion to the increase in outstanding shares of stock. For example, a 2 for 1 stock split would cause the price of the stock to drop by approximately 50 percent to about $35.00. The lower price plus the increase in shares tends to promote the buying and selling of shares.

A stock split does not, in itself, increase the number of shares authorized. Nor does it change the balances in the stockholders' equity section. It simply changes the par value and number of shares outstanding. Therefore, an entry is not necessary. However, it is appropriate to document the change by making a memorandum entry in the general journal, as follows:

July 15   The 30,000 shares of $5 par value common stock that are issued and outstanding were split 2 for 1, resulting in 60,000 shares of $2.50 par value common stock issued and outstanding.

The change for the Caprock Corporation is as follows:

Before Stock Split (from page 645)

Contributed Capital	
Common Stock—$5 par value, 100,000 shares	
authorized, 30,000 issued and outstanding	$ 150,000
Paid-in Capital in Excess of Par Value, Common	30,000
Total Contributed Capital	$ 180,000
Retained Earnings	900,000
Total Stockholders' Equity	$1,080,000

After Stock Split

Contributed Capital	
Common Stock—$2.50 par value, 100,000 shares	
authorized, 60,000 issued and outstanding	$ 150,000
Paid-in Capital in Excess of Par Value, Common	30,000
Total Contributed Capital	$ 180,000
Retained Earnings	900,000
Total Stockholders' Equity	$1,080,000

In cases where the number of split shares will exceed the number of authorized shares, the board of directors will have to authorize, with appropriate state approval, additional shares at the time of the split.

Treasury Stock Transactions

Treasury stock is capital stock, either common or preferred, that has been issued and reacquired by the issuing company but has not been sold or retired. The company normally gets the stock back by purchasing the shares on the market or through donations by stockholders.

There are several reasons why a company purchases its own stock. (1) It may want to have stock available to distribute to employees through stock option plans. (2) It may be trying to maintain a favorable market for the company's stock. (3) It may want to increase the company's earnings per share. (4) It may want to have additional shares of the company's stock available for such activities as purchasing other companies. (5) It may be used as a strategy to prevent a hostile takeover.

OBJECTIVE 3
Account for treasury stock transactions

The effect of a treasury stock purchase is to reduce the assets and stockholders' equity of the company. It is not considered a purchase of assets, as purchase of the shares in another company would be. The treasury stock is capital stock that has been issued but is no longer outstanding. Treasury shares may be held for an indefinite period of time, reissued, or retired. Thus treasury stock is somewhat similar to unissued stock. That is, it has no rights until the stock is reissued. Treasury stock does not have voting rights, preemptive rights, rights to cash dividends, or rights to share in assets during liquidation of the company, and it is not considered to be outstanding in the calculation of book value. However, there is one major difference between unissued shares and treasury shares. If a share of stock was originally issued at par value or greater and fully paid for, and then reacquired as treasury stock, it may be reissued at less than par value without a discount liability attaching to it.

Purchase of Treasury Stock. When treasury stock is purchased, it is normally recorded at cost. The transaction reduces both the assets and stockholders' equity of the firm. For example, assume that on September 15 the Caprock Corporation purchases 1,000 shares of its common stock on the market at a price of $50 per share. The purchase would be recorded as follows:

Sept. 15	Treasury Stock, Common	50,000	
	Cash		50,000
	Acquired 1,000 shares of company's common stock for $50 per share		

Note that the treasury shares are recorded at cost. Any par value, stated value, or original issue price of the stock is ignored.

The stockholders' equity section of Caprock's balance sheet shows the cost of the treasury stock as a deduction from the total of Contributed Capital and Retained Earnings, as follows:

Contributed Capital	
Common Stock—$5 par value, 100,000 shares authorized,	
30,000 shares issued, 29,000 shares outstanding	$ 150,000
Paid-in Capital in Excess of Par Value, Common	30,000
Total Contributed Capital	$ 180,000
Retained Earnings	900,000
Total Contributed Capital and Retained Earnings	$1,080,000
Less Treasury Stock, Common (1,000 shares at cost)	**50,000**
Total Stockholders' Equity	$1,030,000

Note that the number of shares issued, and thus the legal capital, has not changed, although the number of outstanding shares has decreased as a result of the transaction.

Sale of Treasury Stock. The treasury shares may be sold at cost, above cost, or below cost. For example, assume that on November 15 the 1,000 treasury shares of the Caprock Corporation are sold for $50 per share. The entry to record this transaction is

Nov. 15	Cash	50,000	
	Treasury Stock, Common		50,000
	Reissued 1,000 shares of treasury stock for $50 per share		

When treasury shares are sold for an amount greater than their cost, the excess of the sales price over cost should be credited to Paid-in Capital, Treasury Stock. No gain should be recorded. For example, suppose that on November 15 the 1,000 treasury shares of the Caprock Corporation are sold for $60 per share. The entry for the reissue would be

Nov. 15	Cash	60,000	
	Treasury Stock, Common		50,000
	Paid-in Capital, Treasury Stock		10,000
	To record the sale of 1,000 shares of treasury stock for $60 per share; cost was $50 per share		

If the treasury shares are sold below their cost, the difference should be deducted from Paid-in Capital, Treasury Stock. When this account does not exist or is insufficient to cover the excess of cost over re-issuance price, Retained Earnings should absorb the excess. No loss should be recorded. For example, suppose that on September 15 the Caprock Corporation bought 1,000 shares of its common stock on the market at a price of $50 per share. The company sold 400 shares of its stock on October 15 for $60 per share and the remaining 600 shares on December 15 for $42 per share. The entries to record these transactions are presented as follows:

Sept. 15	Treasury Stock, Common	50,000	
	Cash		50,000
	To record the purchase of 1,000 shares of treasury stock at $50 per share		
Oct. 15	Cash	24,000	
	Treasury Stock, Common		20,000
	Paid-in Capital, Treasury Stock		4,000
	To record the sale of 400 shares of treasury stock for $60 per share; cost was $50 per share		

Dec. 15	Cash	25,200	
	Paid-in Capital, Treasury Stock	4,000	
	Retained Earnings	800	
	Treasury Stock, Common		30,000
	To record the sale of 600 shares of treasury stock for $42 per share; cost was $50 per share		

In the December 15 entry, Retained Earnings is debited for $800 because the 600 shares were sold for $4,800 less than cost. That amount is $800 greater than the $4,000 of paid-in capital generated by the sale of the 400 shares on October 15.

Retirement of Treasury Stock. If a company determines that it will not reissue stock it has purchased, it may, with the approval of its stockholders, decide to retire the stock. When shares of stock are retired, all items related to those shares should be removed from the related capital accounts. When stock that cost less than the original contributed capital is retired, the difference is recognized as Paid-in Capital, Retirement of Stock. However, if stock that cost more than was received when the shares were first issued is retired, the difference is a reduction in stockholders' equity and is debited to Retained Earnings. For instance, suppose that instead of selling the 1,000 shares of treasury stock purchased for $50,000, Caprock decides to retire the shares on November 15. Assuming the $5 par value common stock was originally issued at $6 per share, the entry to record the retirement is

Nov. 15	Common Stock	5,000	
	Paid-in Capital in Excess of Par Value	1,000	
	Retained Earnings	44,000	
	Treasury Stock		50,000
	To record the retirement of 1,000 shares that cost $50 per share and were originally issued at $6 per share		

Restrictions on Retained Earnings

OBJECTIVE 4
Describe the disclosure of restrictions on retained earnings

A corporation may wish or be required to restrict all or a portion of retained earnings. A **restriction on retained earnings** means that dividends may be declared only to the extent of the *unrestricted* retained earnings. The following are several reasons why it might do so:

1. *A contractual agreement.* For example, bond indentures may place a limitation on the dividends to be paid by the company.
2. *State law.* Many states will not allow dividends or the purchase of treasury stock if doing so impairs the legal capital of a company.
3. *Voluntary action by the board of directors.* Many times a board will decide to retain assets in the business for future needs. For example, the company may be planning to build a new plant and may wish to

show that dividends will be limited to save enough money for the building. The company may also restrict retained earnings to show the possible future loss of assets resulting from a lawsuit.

There are two ways of reporting retained earnings restrictions to readers of financial statements. First, the restriction of retained earnings may be shown in the stockholders' equity section of the balance sheet. Second, the restricted retained earnings may be disclosed by means of a note to the financial statements.

A restriction on retained earnings does not change the total retained earnings or stockholders' equity of the company. It simply divides retained earnings into two parts, restricted and unrestricted. The restricted part indicates that assets in that amount may not be used for payment of dividends. The unrestricted amount represents earnings kept in the business that could be used for dividends and other purposes. Assuming that Caprock's board of directors has decided to restrict retained earnings for $300,000 because of plans for plant expansion, the disclosure in Caprock's stockholders' equity section would be as follows:

Contributed Capital		
Common Stock—$5 par value, 100,000 shares authorized, 30,000 shares issued and outstanding		$ 150,000
Paid-in Capital in Excess of Par Value, Common		30,000
Total Contributed Capital		$ 180,000
Retained Earnings		
Restricted for Plant Expansion	**$300,000**	
Unrestricted	600,000	
Total Retained Earnings		900,000
Total Stockholders' Equity		$1,080,000

The same facts about restricted retained earnings could also be presented by reference to a note to the financial statements. For example:

Retained Earnings (Note 15) $900,000

Note 15:
Because of plans for expanding the capacity of the clothing division, the board of directors has restricted retained earnings available for dividends by $300,000.

Note that the restriction of retained earnings does not restrict cash in any way. It simply explains to the readers of the financial statements that a certain amount of assets generated by earnings will remain in the business for the purpose stated. It is still management's job to make sure that there is enough cash or assets on hand to satisfy the restriction, and the subsequent removal of the restriction does not necessarily mean that the board of directors will now be able to declare a dividend.

Statement of Stockholders' Equity

OBJECTIVE 5
Prepare a statement of stockholders' equity

The **statement of stockholders' equity**, also called the statement of changes in stockholders' equity, summarizes the changes in the components of the stockholders' equity section of the balance sheet. Companies are increasingly using this statement in place of the statement of retained earnings because it reveals much more about the year's stockholders' equity transactions. In Exhibit 16-2, for example, note that in the Tri-State Corporation's statement of stockholders' equity, the first line contains the beginning balances (last period's ending balances) of each account in the stockholders' equity section. Each additional line in the statement discloses the effects of transactions that affect the accounts. It is possible to determine from this statement that during 19x2 Tri-State Corporation issued 5,000 shares of common stock for $250,000, had a conversion of $100,000 of preferred stock into common stock, declared and issued a 10 percent stock dividend on common stock, had a net purchase of treasury shares of $24,000, earned net income of

---

Exhibit 16-2. A Statement of Stockholders' Equity

Tri-State Corporation
Statement of Stockholders' Equity
For the Year Ended December 31, 19x2

	Preferred Stock $100 Par Value 8% Convertible	Common Stock $10 Par Value	Paid-in Capital in Excess of Par Value	Retained Earnings	Treasury Stock	Total
Balance, December 31, 19x1	$400,000	$300,000	$300,000	$600,000	—	$1,600,000
Issuance of 5,000 Shares of Common Stock		50,000	200,000			250,000
Conversion of 1,000 Shares of Preferred Stock into 3,000 Shares of Common Stock	(100,000)	30,000	70,000			—
10 Percent Stock Dividend on Common Stock, 3,800 Shares		38,000	152,000	(190,000)		—
Purchase of 500 Shares of Treasury Stock					$(24,000)	(24,000)
Net Income				270,000		270,000
Cash Dividends						
Preferred Stock				(33,000)		(33,000)
Common Stock				(38,600)		(38,600)
Balance, December 31, 19x2	$300,000	$418,000	$722,000	$608,400	$(24,000)	$2,024,400

$270,000, and paid cash dividends on both preferred and common stock. The ending balances of the accounts are presented at the bottom of the statement. These accounts and balances will make up the stockholders' equity section of Tri-State's balance sheet at December 31, 19x2, as shown below. Also, note that the Retained Earnings column has the same components as would the statement of retained earnings, if it were prepared separately.

Tri-State Corporation		
Stockholders' Equity		
December 31, 19x2		
Contributed Capital		
Preferred Stock, $100 par value, 8% convertible,		
10,000 shares authorized, 3,000 shares outstanding		$ 300,000
Common Stock, $10 par value, 100,000 shares		
authorized, 41,800 shares issued, 41,300 shares outstanding	$418,000	
Paid-in Capital in Excess of Par Value, Common	722,000	1,140,000
Total Contributed Capital		$1,440,000
Retained Earnings		608,400
Total Contributed Capital and Retained Earnings		$2,048,400
Less Treasury Stock, Common (500 shares)		24,000
Total Stockholders' Equity		$2,024,400

Stock Values

The word *value* is associated with shares of stock in several ways. The terms *par value* and *stated value* have already been explained. They are each values per share that establish the legal capital of a company. Par value or stated value is arbitrarily set when the stock is authorized. Neither has any relationship to the book value or to the market value.

Book Value

OBJECTIVE 6
Calculate book value per share, and distinguish it from market value

The **book value** of a company's stock represents the total assets of the company less liabilities. Thus, it is simply the owners' equity of the company or, to look at it another way, the company's net assets. The book value per share, therefore, represents the equity of the owner of one share of stock in the net assets of the corporation. This value, of course, does not necessarily equal the amount the shareholders would receive if the company were sold or liquidated. It is probably different, because most assets are recorded at historical cost, not at the current value at which they could be sold. To learn the book value per share when the company has only common stock outstanding, divide the total stockholders' equity by the total common shares outstanding. In computing shares outstanding, shares subscribed but not issued are included, but treasury stock (shares previously issued now held by the company) are not included. For example, on page 649, Caprock Corporation has total stockholders' equity of $1,030,000 and 29,000 shares outstanding after recording the purchase of treasury shares. The book value per share of Caprock's common stock is $35.52 ($1,030,000 ÷ 29,000 shares).

If a company has both preferred and common stock, the determination of book value per share is not so simple. The general rule is that the call value (or par value, if a call value is not specified) of the preferred stock plus any dividends in arrears is subtracted from total stockholders' equity to figure the equity pertaining to common stock. As an illustration, refer to the stockholders' equity section for Tri-State Corporation on page 654. Assuming there are no dividends in arrears and the preferred stock is callable at $105, the equity pertaining to common stock is figured as follows:

Total stockholders' equity	$2,024,400
Less equity allocated to preferred shareholders ($105 × 3,000 shares)	315,000
Equity pertaining to common shareholders	**$1,709,400**

There are 41,300 shares of common stock outstanding (41,800 shares issued less 500 shares of treasury stock). The book values per share would be as follows:

Preferred Stock: $315,000 ÷ 3,000 shares = $105 per share
Common Stock: $1,709,400 ÷ 41,300 shares = $41.39 per share

If we assume the same facts except that the preferred stock is cumulative and that one year of dividends is in arrears, the stockholders' equity would be allocated as follows:

Total Stockholders' Equity		$2,024,400
Less: Call value of outstanding preferred shares	$315,000	
Dividends in arrears (8% × $300,000)	24,000	
Equity allocated to preferred shareholders		339,000
Equity pertaining to common shareholders		**$1,685,400**

The book values per share under this assumption are:

Preferred Stock: $339,000 ÷ 3,000 shares = $113 per share
Common Stock: $1,685,400 ÷ 41,300 shares = $40.81 per share

Undeclared preferred dividends fall into arrears on the last day of the fiscal year (the date when the financial statements are prepared). Also, dividends in arrears do not apply to unissued preferred stock.

Market Value

The **market value** is the price that investors are willing to pay for a share of stock on the open market. While the book value is based on historical cost, the market value is usually determined by investors' expectations for the particular company and general economic conditions. That is, what people expect about the company's future profitability and dividends per share, how risky they view the company and its current financial condition, as well as the state of the money market, all will play a part in determining the market value of a corporation's stock. Although the book value per share often has little relationship to the market value per share, some investors use the relationship of the two measures as rough indicators of relative values of shares. For example, in July 1986 one major oil company, Texaco, had a market value per share of $31 compared with a book value per share of $55. At the same time, another large oil company, Exxon, had a market value per share of $61 and a book value per share of $40.

Corporate Income Statement

OBJECTIVE 7
Prepare a corporate income statement

This chapter and the one before it have shown how certain transactions are reflected in the stockholders' equity section of the corporate balance sheet and in the retained earnings statement. Chapter 18 deals with the statement of cash flows. The following sections will briefly describe some of the features of the corporate income statement.

The format of the income statement has not been specified by the accounting profession because flexibility has been considered more important than a standard format. Either the single-step or multistep form may be used (see Chapter 8). However, the accounting profession has taken the position that income for a period shall be an all-inclusive or **comprehensive income**.[5] This rule means that income or loss for a period should include all revenues, expenses, gains, and losses of the period, except for prior period adjustments. This approach to the measurement of income has resulted in several items being added to the income statement. These items include discontinued operations, extraordinary items, and accounting changes. In addition, earnings per share figures should be disclosed. Exhibit 16-3 illustrates the corporate income statement and the disclosures required. The following sections discuss these components of the corporate income statement, beginning with income taxes expense.

Income Taxes Expense

OBJECTIVE 8
Show the relationships among income taxes expense, deferred income taxes, and net of taxes

Corporations determine their taxable income (the amount on which taxes will be paid) by subtracting allowable business deductions from includable gross income. The federal tax laws determine what business deductions are allowed and what must be included in gross income.[6]

The tax rates that apply to a corporation's taxable income are shown in Table 16-1. A corporation with a taxable income of $70,000 would

5. *Statement of Financial Accounting Concepts No. 6*, "Elements of Financial Statements" (Stamford, Conn.: Financial Accounting Standards Board, 1985), pars. 70–77.
6. Rules for calculating and reporting taxable income in specialized industries such as banking, insurance, mutual funds, and cooperatives are highly technical and may vary significantly from those shown in this chapter.

Exhibit 16-3. A Corporate Income Statement

Junction Corporation
Income Statement
For the Year Ended December 31, 19xx

Revenues		$925,000
Less Costs and Expenses		500,000
Income from Continuing Operations Before Taxes		$425,000
Income Taxes Expense		119,000
Income from Continuing Operations		$306,000
Discontinued Operations		
Income from Operations of Discontinued Segment		
(net of taxes, $35,000)	$90,000	
Loss on Disposal of Segment (net of taxes, $42,000)	(73,000)	17,000
Income Before Extraordinary Items and		
Cumulative Effect of Accounting Change		$323,000
Extraordinary Gain (net of taxes, $17,000)		43,000
Subtotal		$366,000
Cumulative Effect of a Change in Accounting		
Principle (net of taxes, $5,000)		(6,000)
Net Income		$360,000
Earnings per Common Share:		
Income from Continuing Operations		$3.06
Discontinued Operations (net of taxes)		.17
Income Before Extraordinary Items		$3.23
Extraordinary Gain (net of taxes)		.43
Cumulative Effect of Accounting Change		
(net of taxes)		(.06)
Net Income		$3.60

Table 16-1. Tax Rate Schedule for Corporations

Taxable Income		Tax Liability	
Over	But Not Over		Of the Amount Over
—	$ 50,000	0 + 15%	—
$ 50,000	75,000	S 7,500 + 25%	$ 50,000
75,000	100,000	13,750 + 34%	75,000
100,000	335,000	22,250 + 39%	100,000
335,000	—	113,900 + 34%	335,000

have a federal income tax liability of $12,500. This amount is computed by adding $7,500 (the tax on the first $50,000 of taxable income) to $5,000 (25 percent times the $20,000 earned in excess of $50,000).

Income Taxes Expense is the expense recognized in the accounting records on an accrual basis to be applicable to income from continuing operations. This expense may or may not be equal to the amount of taxes actually paid by the corporation. The amount payable is determined from taxable income, which is measured according to the rules and regulations of the income tax code. For most small businesses, it is convenient to keep accounting records on the same basis as tax records so that the income taxes expense on the income statement equals the income taxes liability to be paid to the Internal Revenue Service (IRS). This practice is usually acceptable when there is not a material difference between the income on an accounting basis and income on an income tax basis. However, the purpose of accounting is to determine net income in accordance with generally accepted accounting principles, whereas the purpose of the tax code is to determine taxable income and tax liability.

Management has an incentive to use methods that will minimize the tax liability, but accountants, who are bound by accrual accounting and the materiality concept, cannot let the tax procedures dictate the method of preparing financial statements if the result would be misleading. As a consequence, a material difference can occur between accounting and taxable incomes, especially in larger businesses. This difference in accounting and taxable incomes may result from a difference in the timing of the recognition of revenues and expenses because of different methods used in determining the respective incomes. Some possible alternatives are as follows:

	Accounting Method	Tax Method
Expense recognition	Accrual or deferral	At time of expenditure
Accounts receivable	Allowance	Direct charge-off
Inventories	Average-cost	FIFO
Depreciation	Straight-line	Accelerated cost recovery system (see Chapter 12)

Accounting for the difference between income taxes expense based on accounting income and the actual income taxes payable based on taxable income is accomplished by an accounting technique called **income tax allocation**. The amount by which income taxes expense differs from income taxes payable is reconciled in an account called **Deferred Income Taxes**. For example, if the Junction Corporation had income taxes expense of $119,000 shown on the income statement and actual income taxes payable to the IRS of $92,000, the entry to record the Income Taxes Expense applicable to income from continuing operations using the income tax allocation procedure would be as follows:

Dec. 31	Income Taxes Expense	119,000	
	Income Taxes Payable		92,000
	Deferred Income Taxes		27,000
	To record current and deferred income taxes		

In other years, it is possible for Income Taxes Payable to exceed Income Taxes Expense, in which case the same entry is made except that the Deferred Income Taxes account is debited.

The Financial Accounting Standards Board has issued new rules for recording, measurement and classification of deferred income taxes.[7] When the Deferred Income Taxes account has a credit balance, which is the normal situation, it is classified as a liability on the balance sheet. Whether or not it is classified as a current or long-term (noncurrent) liability depends on when the timing difference is expected to reverse or have the opposite effect. For instance, if an income taxes deferral is caused by an expenditure that is deducted for income tax purposes in one year but is not an expense for accounting purposes until the next year, an income taxes deferral is present in the first year that will reverse in the second year. The income tax deferral in the first year is classified as a current liability. On the other hand, if the deferral is not expected to reverse for more than one year, the deferred income taxes are classified as a long-term (noncurrent) liability. This latter situation may occur, for example, when the income tax deferral is caused by a difference in depreciation methods for items of plant and equipment that have useful lives of more than one year. In other words, the income tax liability is classified as short-term or long-term based on the nature of the transactions that gave rise to the deferrals and their corresponding expected date of reversal.

The Deferred Income Taxes account may at times have a debit balance, in which case it should be classified as an asset. In this situation, the company has prepaid its income taxes because total income taxes paid have exceeded income taxes expensed. Classification of the debit balance as a current asset or as a long-term asset follows the same rules as for liabilities, but the amount of the asset is subject to certain limitations that are reserved for more advanced courses.

Each year the balance of the deferred taxes account is evaluated to determine if it represents the expected asset or liability in light of the legislated changes in income tax laws and regulations in the current year. If changes have occurred in the income tax laws, an adjusting entry is required to bring the account balance into line with the current laws. For example, a decrease in corporate income tax rates, as occurred in 1987, means that companies with deferred income tax liabilities will pay less taxes in future years than indicated by the credit balances of their Deferred Income Taxes accounts. As a result, they would debit Deferred Income Taxes to reduce the liability and credit Gain from Reduction in Income Taxes Rates. The latter amount increases the reported

7. *Statement of Financial Accounting Standards No. 96*, "Accounting for Income Taxes" (Stamford, Conn.: Financial Accounting Standards Board, 1987).

income on the income statement. If there are tax increases in future years, a loss would be recorded and the deferred income tax liability increased.

In any given year the amount of a company's income taxes paid is determined by subtracting (or adding, as the case may be) the Deferred Income Taxes for that year (as reported in the notes to the financial statements) from (or to) the Income Taxes Expense, which is also reported in the notes to the financial statements. In subsequent years, the amount of deferred income taxes can vary based on changes in the income tax laws and rates.

Some understanding of the importance of deferred income taxes to financial reporting may be gained from studying the financial statements of six hundred large companies surveyed in a recent year. About 82 percent reported Deferred Income Taxes with a credit balance in the noncurrent long-term liability section.[8] About 8 percent reported deferred income taxes as a current liability.[9]

Net of Taxes

The phrase **net of taxes**, as used in Exhibit 16-3 and in the discussion below, means that the effect of applicable taxes (usually income taxes) has been considered when determining the overall effect of the item on the financial statements. The phrase is used on the corporate income statement when a company has items (such as those explained below) that must be disclosed in a separate section of the income statement. Each of these items should be reported at net of the income taxes applicable to that item to avoid distorting the net operating income figure. For example, assume that a corporation with $120,000 operating income before taxes has a total tax liability of $66,000 based on taxable income, which is higher because it includes a capital gain of $100,000 on which a tax of $30,000 is due. Assume also that the gain is an extraordinary item (see Extraordinary Items, page 662) and must be disclosed as such. Thus,

Operating Income Before Taxes	$120,000
Income Taxes Expense **(actual taxes are $66,000, of which $30,000 is applicable to extraordinary gain)**	36,000
Income Before Extraordinary Item	$ 84,000
Extraordinary Gain (net of taxes) **($100,000 − $30,000)**	70,000
Net Income	$154,000

If all the taxes payable were deducted from operating income before taxes, both the income before extraordinary items and the extraordinary gain would be distorted. A company follows the same procedure in the case of an extraordinary loss. For example, assume the same facts

8. *Accounting Trends and Techniques* (New York: American Institute of Certified Public Accountants, 1987), p. 207.
9. Ibid., p. 182.

as before except that total tax liability is only $6,000 because of a $100,000 extraordinary loss, which results in a $30,000 tax saving, as shown below.

Operating Income Before Taxes	$120,000
Income Taxes Expense **(actual taxes of $6,000 as a result**	
of an extraordinary loss)	36,000
Income Before Extraordinary Item	$ 84,000
Extraordinary Loss (net of taxes) **($100,000 − $30,000)**	(70,000)
Net Income	$ 14,000

If we apply these ideas to Junction Corporation in Exhibit 16-3, the total of the income tax items is $124,000. This amount is allocated among five statement components, as follows:

Income Taxes Expense on Income from Continuing Operations	$119,000
Income Tax on Income of Discontinued Segment	35,000
Income Tax Saving on Loss on Disposal of Segment	(42,000)
Income Tax on Extraordinary Gain	17,000
Income Tax Saving on Cumulative Effect of Change	
in Accounting Principle	(5,000)
Total Income Taxes Expense	$124,000

Discontinued Operations

OBJECTIVE 9
Describe the disclosure on the income statement of discontinued operations, extraordinary items, and accounting changes

Large companies in the United States usually have many segments. A segment of a business may be a separate major line of business or a separate class of customer. For example, a company that makes heavy drilling equipment may also have another line of business, such as the manufacturing of mobile homes. These large companies may discontinue or otherwise dispose of certain segments of their business that are not profitable. **Discontinued operations** are segments of a business that are no longer part of the ongoing operations of the company. Generally accepted accounting principles require that gains and losses from discontinued operations be reported separately in the income statement. The reasoning for the separate disclosure requirement is that the income statement will be more useful in evaluating the ongoing activities of the business if results from continuing operations are reported separately from discontinued operations.

In Exhibit 16-3, the disclosure of discontinued operations has two parts. One part shows that the income during the year from operations of the segment of business that has been disposed of (or will be disposed of) after the decision date to discontinue was $90,000 (net of $35,000 taxes). The other part shows that the loss from disposal of the segment of business was $73,000 (net of $42,000 tax savings). The computation of the gains or losses will be covered in more advanced accounting courses. The disclosure has been described, however, to give a complete view of the content of the corporate income statement.

Extraordinary Items

The Accounting Principles Board, in its *Opinion No. 30*, defines **extraor-dinary items** as those "events or transactions that are distinguished by their unusual nature *and* by the infrequency of their occurrence."[10] As stated in the definition, the major criteria for these extraordinary items are that they must be unusual and they must not happen very often. Unusual and infrequent occurrences are explained in the opinion as follows:

Unusual Nature—the underlying event or transaction should possess a high de-gree of abnormality and be of a type clearly unrelated to, or only incidentally related to, the ordinary and typical activities of the entity, taking into account the environment in which the entity operates.

Infrequency of Occurrence—the underlying event or transaction should be of a type that would not reasonably be expected to recur in the foreseeable future, taking into account the environment in which the entity operates.[11]

If these items are both unusual and infrequent (and material in amount), they should be reported separately from continuing opera-tions on the income statement. This disclosure will allow the reader of the statement to identify those gains or losses shown in the computation of income that would not be expected to happen again soon. Examples of items that usually are treated as extraordinary are (1) uninsured losses from floods, earthquakes, fires, and theft; (2) gains and losses re-sulting from the passing of a new law; (3) expropriation (taking) of property by a foreign government; and (4) gains or losses from early retirement of debt. These items should be reported in the income state-ment after discontinued operations. Also, the gain or loss should be shown net of applicable taxes. In a recent year, 107 (18 percent) of six hundred large companies reported extraordinary items on the income statement.[12] In Exhibit 16-3, the extraordinary gain was $43,000 after applicable taxes of $17,000.

Accounting Changes

Consistency, one of the basic conventions of accounting, means that, for accounting purposes, companies apply the same accounting principles from year to year. However, a company is allowed to make accounting changes if current procedures are incorrect or inappropriate. For exam-ple, a change from the FIFO to the LIFO inventory method may be made if there is adequate justification for the change. Adequate justification usually means that, if the change occurs, the financial statements will

10. Accounting Principles Board, *Opinion No. 30*, "Reporting the Results of Opera-tions" (New York: American Institute of Certified Public Accountants, 1973), par. 20.
11. Ibid.
12. *Accounting Trends and Techniques* (New York: American Institute of Certified Public Accountants, 1987), p. 322.

better show the financial activities of the company. A company's desire to lower the amount of income taxes to be paid is not seen as an adequate justification for an accounting change. If justification does exist and an accounting change is made during an accounting period, generally accepted accounting principles require the disclosure of the change in the financial statements.

The **cumulative effect of an accounting change** is the effect that the new accounting principle would have had on net income of prior periods if it, instead of the old principle, had been applied in past years; this effect is shown on the income statement immediately after extraordinary items.[13] For example, assume in Exhibit 16-3 that for the prior five years the Junction Corporation has used the straight-line method in depreciating its machinery. The company changes to the sum-of-the-years'-digits method of depreciation this year. The following depreciation charges (net of taxes) were arrived at by the controller:

Cumulative, 5-year sum-of-the-years'-digits depreciation	$16,000
Less cumulative, 5-year straight-line depreciation	10,000
Cumulative effect of accounting change	$ 6,000

Relevant information about the accounting change is shown in the notes to the financial statements. The $6,000 difference (net of $5,000 income taxes) is the cumulative effect of the change in depreciation methods. The change results in an additional $6,000 (net of taxes) depreciation expense for prior years being deducted in the current year in addition to the current year's depreciation costs included in the $500,000 costs and expenses section of the Income Statement. It must be shown in the current year's income statement as a reduction in income (see Exhibit 16-3). In a recent year, 164 (27 percent) of six hundred large companies reported changes in accounting procedures.[14] Further study of accounting changes is left up to more advanced accounting courses.

Earnings per Share

OBJECTIVE 10
Compute earnings per share

Readers of financial statements use earnings per share information to judge the performance of the company and to compare its performance with that of other companies. The Accounting Principles Board recognized the importance of this information in its *Opinion No. 15*. There it concluded that earnings per share of common stock should be presented on the face of the income statement.[15] As shown in Exhibit 16-3, the information is generally disclosed just below the net income figure.

13. Accounting Principles Board, *Opinion No. 20*, "Accounting Changes" (New York: American Institute of Certified Public Accountants, 1971), par. 20.
14. *Accounting Trends and Techniques* (New York: American Institute of Certified Public Accountants, 1987), p. 435.
15. Accounting Principles Board, *Opinion No. 15*, "Earnings per Share" (New York: American Institute of Certified Public Accountants, 1969), par. 12.

An earnings per share amount is always shown for (1) income from continuing operations, (2) income before extraordinary items and cumulative effect of accounting changes, (3) cumulative effect of accounting changes, and (4) net income. If the statement has a gain or loss from discontinued operations or a gain or loss on extraordinary items, earnings per share amounts may also be presented for these items.

A basic earnings per share amount is found when a company has only common stock and the same number of shares outstanding during the year. For example, it is assumed in Exhibit 16-3 that Junction Corporation, with a net income of $360,000, had 100,000 shares of common stock outstanding for the entire year. The earnings per share of common stock were computed as follows:

$$\text{Earnings per share} = \frac{\text{net income}}{\text{shares outstanding}}$$

$$= \frac{\$360,000}{100,000 \text{ shares}}$$

$$= \$3.60 \text{ per share}$$

If, however, the number of shares outstanding changes during the year, it is necessary to figure a weighted-average number of shares outstanding for the year. Let us now suppose some different facts about Junction Corporation's outstanding shares. Let us assume that the common shares outstanding during various periods of the year were as follows: January–March, 100,000 shares; April–September, 120,000 shares; and October–December, 130,000 shares. The weighted-average number of common shares outstanding and earnings per share would be found as shown:

100,000 shares × ¼ year	25,000
120,000 shares × ½ year	60,000
130,000 shares × ¼ year	32,500
Weighted-average shares outstanding	117,500

$$\text{Earnings per share} = \frac{\$360,000}{117,500 \text{ shares}}$$

$$= \$3.06 \text{ per share}$$

If a company has nonconvertible preferred stock outstanding, the dividend for this stock must be subtracted from net income before computing earnings per share for common stock. If we suppose that Junction Corporation has preferred stock on which the annual dividend is $23,500, earnings per share on common stock would be $2.86 [($360,000 – $23,500) ÷ 117,500 shares].

Companies with a capital structure in which there are no bonds, stocks, or stock options that could be converted into common stock are said to have a **simple capital structure**. The earnings per share for these companies are computed as shown on the previous page. Many companies, however, have a **complex capital structure**, which includes convertible stock and bonds. These convertible securities have the potential of diluting the earnings per share of common stock. Potential dilution means that a person's proportionate share of ownership in the company may be reduced by an increase in total shares outstanding through a conversion of stocks or bonds, or exercise of stock options. For example, suppose that a person owns 10,000 shares of a company, which equals 2 percent of the outstanding shares of 500,000. Now suppose that holders of convertible bonds convert the bonds into 100,000 shares of stock. The person's 10,000 shares would then be only 1.67 percent (10,000 ÷ 600,000) of the outstanding shares. In addition, the added shares outstanding would result in lower earnings per share and most likely a lower market price per share.

Since stock options and convertible preferred stocks or bonds have the potential to dilute earnings per share, they are referred to as **potentially dilutive securities**. A special subset of these convertible securities is called **common stock equivalents** because these securities are considered to be similar to common stock. A convertible stock or bond is considered a common stock equivalent if the conversion feature is an important part of determining its original issue price. Special rules are applied by the accountant to determine if a convertible stock or bond is a common stock equivalent. A stock option, on the other hand, is by definition a common stock equivalent. The significance of common stock equivalents is that, when they exist, they are used in the earnings per share calculations explained in the next paragraph.

When a company has a complex capital structure, it must present two earnings per share figures. The company must report **primary earnings per share** and **fully diluted earnings per share**. Primary earnings per share are calculated by including in the denominator the total of weighted-average common shares outstanding and common stock equivalents. On the other hand, fully diluted earnings per share are calculated by including in the denominator the additional potentially dilutive securities that are not common stock equivalents. The latter figure thus shows stockholders the maximum potential effect of dilution of their ownership in the company. An example of this type of disclosure is as follows:

	19x2	19x1
Net Income	$280,000	$200,000
Earnings per Share of Common Stock		
Primary	$2.25	$1.58
Fully Diluted	$2.00	$1.43

The computation of these figures is a complex process reserved for more advanced courses.

Chapter Review

Review of Learning Objectives

1. **Define retained earnings, and prepare a statement of retained earnings.**
   Retained earnings are the part of stockholders' equity that comes from retaining assets earned in business operations. They are the claims of the stockholders against the assets of the company that arise from profitable operations. This account is different from contributed capital, which represents the claims against assets brought about by the initial and later investments by the stockholders. Both are claims against the general assets of the company, not against any specific assets that may have been set aside. It is important not to confuse the assets themselves with the claims against the assets. The statement of retained earnings will always show the beginning and ending balance of retained earnings, net income or loss, and cash dividends. It may also show prior period adjustments, stock dividends, and other transactions affecting retained earnings.

2. **Account for stock dividends and stock splits.**
   A dividend is a distribution of assets, usually cash, by a corporation to its stockholders in proportion to the number of shares of stock held by each owner. A summary of the key dates and accounting treatment of stock dividends follows:

Key Date	Stock Dividend
Declaration date	Debit Retained Earnings for the market value of the stock to be distributed, if it is a small stock dividend, and credit Common Stock Distributable (par value) and Paid-in Capital in Excess of Par Value for the excess of market value over the stock's par value.
Record date	No entry.
Payment date	Debit Common Stock Distributable and credit Common Stock for the par value of the stock that was distributed.

A stock split is usually undertaken to reduce the market value and improve the liquidity of a company's stock. Since there is normally a decrease in the par value of the stock proportionate to the number of additional shares issued, there is no effect on the dollar amounts in the stockholders' equity accounts. The split should be recorded in the general journal by a memorandum entry only.

3. **Account for treasury stock transactions.**
   The treasury stock of a company is stock that has been issued and reacquired but not resold or retired. A company acquires its own stock for reasons such as creating stock option plans, maintaining a favorable market for the stock, increasing earnings per share, and purchasing other companies. Treasury stock is similar to unissued stock in that it does not have rights until it is reissued. However, treasury stock can be resold at

less than par value without incurring a discount liability. The accounting treatment for treasury stock is summarized as follows:

Treasury Stock Transaction	Accounting Treatment
Purchase of treasury stock	Debit Treasury Stock and credit Cash for the cost of the shares.
Sale of treasury stock at cost	Debit Cash and credit Treasury Stock for the cost of the shares.
Sale of treasury stock at an amount greater than the cost of the shares	Debit Cash for the reissue price of the shares, and credit Treasury Stock for the cost of the shares, and Paid-in Capital, Treasury Stock for the excess.
Sale of treasury stock at an amount less than the cost of the shares	Debit Cash for the reissue price; debit Paid-in Capital, Treasury Stock for the difference between reissue price and the cost of the shares; and credit Treasury Stock for the cost of the shares. If Paid-in Capital, Treasury Stock does not exist or is not large enough to cover the difference, Retained Earnings should absorb the difference.

4. **Describe the disclosure of restrictions on retained earnings.**

    For reasons such as plant expansion, a company may need to retain a portion of its assets in the business rather than distribute them to the stockholders as dividends. Management may communicate the plans to stockholders and other users of the company's financial statements by restricting retained earnings. This restriction may be disclosed in two ways: in the stockholders' equity section of the balance sheet, or more commonly as a note to the financial statements. When the reason for the restriction no longer exists, its disclosure may be removed from the financial statements.

5. **Prepare a statement of stockholders' equity.**

    The statement of stockholders' equity shows the changes during the year in each component of the stockholders' equity section of the balance sheet.

6. **Calculate book value per share, and distinguish it from market value.**

    Book value per share is the owners' equity per share, calculated by dividing stockholders' equity by the number of common shares outstanding plus shares subscribed and shares distributable. When preferred stock exists, the call or par value plus any dividends in arrears are deducted first from total stockholders' equity before dividing by common shares outstanding plus shares subscribed. Market value per share is the price investors are willing to pay based on their expectations about general economic conditions and the future earning ability of the company.

7. **Prepare a corporate income statement.**

The corporate income statement is prepared under the all-inclusive or comprehensive income philosophy and thus includes all revenues, expenses, gains, and losses for the accounting period, except for prior period adjustments. The top part of the corporate income statement includes all revenues, costs and expenses, and income taxes that pertain to continuing operations. The bottom part of the statement may contain any or all of the following: discontinued operations, extraordinary items, and cumulative effect of a change in accounting principle. Earnings per share data should be shown below the statement.

8. **Show the relationships among income taxes expense, deferred income taxes, and net of taxes.**

Income taxes expense are the taxes applicable to income from operations on an accrual basis. Income tax allocation is necessary when differences between accrual-based accounting income and taxable income cause a material difference in income taxes expense as shown on the income statement and the actual income tax liability. The difference between the income taxes payable and income taxes expense is debited or credited to an account called Deferred Income Taxes. Net of taxes is a phrase used to indicate that the effect of taxes has been considered when showing an item on the income statement.

9. **Describe the disclosure on the income statement of discontinued operations, extraordinary items, and accounting changes.**

There are several accounting items that must be disclosed separately from continuing operations and net of income taxes on the income statement because of their unusual nature. These items include a gain or loss on discontinued operations, extraordinary items, and the cumulative effect of accounting changes.

10. **Compute earnings per share.**

Stockholders and other users of financial statements use earnings per share data to evaluate the performance of a company, estimate future earnings, and evaluate their investment opportunities. Therefore, earnings per share data are presented on the face of the income statement. The amounts are computed by dividing the income applicable to common stock by the common shares outstanding for the year. If the number of shares outstanding has varied during the year, then the weighted-average shares outstanding should be used in the computation. When the company has a complex capital structure, a dual presentation of primary and fully diluted earnings per share data must be disclosed on the face of the income statement.

Review of Concepts and Terminology

The following concepts and terms were introduced in this chapter:

(L.O. 6) **Book value:**   Total assets of a company less total liabilities; owners' equity.

(L.O. 10) **Common stock equivalents:**   Convertible stocks or bonds whose conversion feature is an important part of determining the original issue price.

(L.O. 10) **Complex capital structure:**   A capital structure with additional securities (convertible stocks and bonds) that can be converted into common stock.

(L.O. 7) **Comprehensive income**:   The change in equity (net assets) of an entity during a period from transactions and other events and circumstances from nonowner sources. It includes all changes in equity during a period except those resulting from investments by the owners and distributions to or withdrawals by owners.

(L.O. 9) **Cumulative effect of an accounting change**:   The effect that a new accounting principle would have had on net income of prior periods if it had been used instead of the old principle.

(L.O. 8) **Deferred Income Taxes**:   An account used to record the difference between Income Taxes Expense and current Income Taxes Payable accounts.

(L.O. 1) **Deficit**:   A debit balance in the Retained Earnings account.

(L.O. 9) **Discontinued operations**:   Segments of a business that are no longer part of the ongoing operations of the company.

(L.O. 9) **Extraordinary items**:   Events or transactions that are distinguished by their unusual nature and by the infrequency of their occurrence.

(L.O. 10) **Fully diluted earnings per share**:   Net income applicable to common stock divided by the sum of the weighted-average common stock and common stock equivalents and other potentially dilutive securities.

(L.O. 8) **Income tax allocation**:   An accounting method designed to accrue income tax expense on the basis of accounting income whenever there are differences in accounting and taxable income.

(L.O. 6) **Market value**:   The price investors are willing to pay for a share of stock on the open market.

(L.O. 8) **Net of taxes**:   The effect of applicable taxes (usually income taxes) on an item when used in determining the overall effect of the item on the financial statements.

(L.O. 10) **Potentially dilutive securities**:   Term referring to stock options and convertible preferred stocks or bonds because of their potential to dilute earnings per share.

(L.O. 10) **Primary earnings per share**:   Net income applicable to common stock divided by the sum of the weighted-average common shares and common stock equivalents.

(L.O. 1) **Prior period adjustments**:   Events or transactions that relate to an earlier accounting period but were not determinable in the earlier period.

(L.O. 4) **Restriction on retained earnings**:   A restriction of retained earnings that indicates that a portion of a company's assets are to be used for purposes other than paying dividends.

(L.O. 1) **Retained earnings**:   The stockholders' equity that has arisen from retaining assets from earnings in the business; the accumulated earnings of a corporation from its inception minus any losses, dividends, or transfers to contributed capital.

(L.O. 10) **Simple capital structure**:   A capital structure with no other securities (either stocks or bonds) that can be converted into common stock.

(L.O. 5) **Statement of stockholders' equity**:   A financial statement that summarizes changes in the components of the stockholders' equity section of the balance sheet; also called a statement of changes in stockholders' equity.

(L.O. 2) **Stock dividend**:   A proportional distribution of shares of a corporation's stock to the corporation's stockholders.

(L.O. 2) **Stock split:**   An increase in the number of outstanding shares of stock accompanied by a proportionate reduction in the par or stated value.

(L.O. 3) **Treasury stock:**   Capital stock, either common or preferred, that has been issued and reacquired by the issuing company but has not been sold or retired.

Self-Test

Test your knowledge of the chapter by choosing the best answer for each item below.

1. The balance of the Retained Earnings account represents
   a. an excess of revenues over expenses for the most current operating period.
   b. profits of a company since the date of its beginning less any losses, dividends to stockholders, or transfers to contributed capital.
   c. cash set aside for specific future uses.
   d. cash available for daily operations.   *(L.O. 1)*

2. A corporation should account for the declaration of a 3% stock dividend by
   a. transferring from retained earnings to contributed capital an amount equal to the market value of the dividend shares.
   b. transferring from retained earnings to contributed capital an amount equal to the legal capital represented by the dividend shares.
   c. making only a memorandum entry in the general journal.
   d. transferring from retained earnings to contributed capital whatever amount the board of directors deems appropriate.   *(L.O. 2)*

3. Which of the following reduces total stockholders' equity?
   a. Stock split
   b. Restriction of retained earnings
   c. Treasury stock
   d. Stock dividend   *(L.O. 3)*

4. When retained earnings are restricted, total retained earnings
   a. increase.
   b. decrease.
   c. may increase or decrease.
   d. are unaffected.   *(L.O. 4)*

5. The purpose of a statement of stockholders' equity is to
   a. summarize the changes in the components of stockholders' equity for a period of time.
   b. disclose the computation of book values per share of stock.
   c. budget the transactions expected to occur during the forthcoming period.
   d. replace the statement of retained earnings.   *(L.O. 5)*

6. All of the following terms related to a corporation's common stock may be determined from the accounting records except
   a. par value.   c. book value.
   b. stated value.   d. market value.   *(L.O. 6)*

7. Which of the following items appears on the corporate income statement before Income from Continuing Operations?
   a. Income from Operations of a Discontinued Segment
   b. Income Taxes Expense
   c. Cumulative Effect of a Change in Accounting Principle
   d. Extraordinary Gain *(L.O. 7)*

8. When there is a difference in the timing of revenues and expenses for accounting and for income tax purposes, it is usually necessary to
   a. prepare an adjusting entry.
   b. adjust figures on the corporate tax return.
   c. perform income tax allocation procedures.
   d. do nothing, because such differences are a result of two different sets of rules. *(L.O. 8)*

9. A loss due to discontinued operations should be reported in the income statement
   a. before both extraordinary items and cumulative effect of an accounting change.
   b. before cumulative effect of an accounting change and after extraordinary items.
   c. after both extraordinary items and cumulative effect of an accounting change.
   d. after cumulative effect of an accounting change and before extraordinary items. *(L.O. 9)*

10. Which of the following would be involved in the computation of earnings per share for a company with a simple capital structure?
    a. Common shares authorized
    b. Dividends declared on nonconvertible preferred stock
    c. Number of shares of nonconvertible preferred stock
    d. Common stock equivalents *(L.O. 10)*

Answers to Self-Test are at the end of this chapter.

Review Problem
Comprehensive Stockholders' Equity Transactions

(L.O. 1, 2, 3, 4, 5) The stockholders' equity on June 30, 19x5 of the Szatkowski Company is as follows:

Contributed Capital	
Common Stock—no par value, $6 stated value, 1,000,000 shares authorized, 250,000 shares issued and outstanding	$1,500,000
Paid-in Capital in Excess of Stated Value, Common	820,000
Total Contributed Capital	$2,320,000
Retained Earnings	970,000
Total Stockholders' Equity	$3,290,000

Stockholders' equity transactions for the next fiscal year were as follows:

a. The board of directors declared a 2 for 1 split.
b. The board of directors obtained authorization to issue 50,000 shares of $100 par value 6 percent noncumulative preferred stock that is callable at $104.
c. Issued 12,000 shares of common stock for a building appraised at $96,000.
d. Purchased 8,000 shares of the company's common stock for $64,000.
e. Issued 20,000 shares of the preferred stock for $100 per share.
f. Sold 5,000 shares of the treasury stock for $35,000.
g. Declared cash dividends of $6 per share on the preferred stock and $.20 per share on the common stock.
h. Date of record.
i. Paid the preferred and common stock cash dividends.
j. Declared a 10 percent stock dividend on the common stock. The market value was $10 per share. The stock dividend is distributable after the end of the fiscal year.
k. Net income for the year was $340,000.
l. Closed Dividends Declared to Retained Earnings.

Due to a loan agreement, the company is not allowed to reduce retained earnings below $100,000. The board of directors determined that this restriction should be disclosed in the notes to the financial statements.

Required

1. Make the general journal entries as appropriate to record the transactions above.
2. Prepare the company's statement of retained earnings at June 30, 19x6.
3. Prepare the stockholders' equity section of the company's balance sheet at June 30, 19x6, including appropriate disclosure of the restriction on retained earnings.
4. Compute the book values per share of common stock on June 30, 19x5 and 19x6 and preferred stock on June 30, 19x6.

Answer to Review Problem

1. Journal entries prepared:

   a. Memorandum entry: 2 for 1 stock split, common, resulting in 500,000 shares issued and outstanding of no par value common stock with a stated value of $3

   b. No entry required

   c. Building 96,000
       Common Stock 36,000
       Paid-in Capital in Excess of Stated Value,
       Common 60,000
         To record issuance of 12,000 shares of common stock for a building appraised at $96,000

d. Treasury Stock, Common 64,000

    Cash 64,000

      To record the purchase of 8,000 shares
of common stock for the treasury for
$8.00 per share

e. Cash 2,000,000

    Preferred Stock 2,000,000

      To record the sale of 20,000 shares of
$100 par value preferred stock at $100

f. Cash 35,000

    Retained Earnings 5,000

      Treasury Stock, Common 40,000

      To record the sale of 5,000 shares of
treasury stock for $35,000, originally
purchased for $8.00 per share

g. Dividends Declared 221,800

    Dividends Payable 221,800

      To record the declaration of cash
dividends of $6 per share on 20,000
shares of preferred stock and
$.20 per share on 509,000 shares
of common stock:

      $6 × 20,000   = $120,000

      $.20 × 509,000 =   101,800

               $221,800

h. No entry required

i. Dividends Payable 221,800

    Cash 221,800

      Paid cash dividend to preferred and
common stockholders

j. Retained Earnings 509,000

    Common Stock Distributable 152,700

    Paid-in Capital in Excess of Stated Value,

      Common 356,300

      To record the declaration of a 50,900
share stock dividend (10% × 509,000)
on $3 stated value common stock at
market value of $509,000 (50,900 × $10)

k. Income Summary 340,000

    Retained Earnings 340,000

      To close Income Summary

l. Retained Earnings 221,800

    Dividends Declared 221,800

      To close Dividends Declared to
Retained Earnings

2. Statement of Retained Earnings prepared:

Szatkowski Company Statement of Retained Earnings For the Year Ended June 30, 19x6		
Retained Earnings, June 30, 19x5		$ 970,000
Net Income, 19x6		340,000
Subtotal		$1,310,000
Less: Cash Dividends		
Preferred	$120,000	
Common	101,800	
Stock Dividends	509,000	
Treasury Stock Transaction	5,000	735,800
Retained Earnings, June 30, 19x6		$ 574,200

3. Stockholders' equity section of balance sheet prepared:

Szatkowski Company Stockholders' Equity June 30, 19x6		
Contributed Capital		
Preferred Stock, $100 par value, 6% noncumulative, 50,000 shares authorized, 20,000 shares outstanding		$2,000,000
Common Stock, no par value, $3 stated value, 1,000,000 shares authorized, 512,000 shares issued, 509,000 shares outstanding	$1,536,000	
Common Stock Distributable, 50,900 shares	152,700	
Paid-in Capital in Excess of Stated Value, Common	1,236,300	2,925,000
Total Contributed Capital		$4,925,000
Retained Earnings (Note x)		574,200
Total Contributed Capital and Retained Earnings		$5,499,200
Less Treasury Stock, Common (3,000 shares at cost)		24,000
Total Stockholders' Equity		$5,475,200

Note x: The board of directors has restricted retained earnings available for dividends by the amount of $100,000 as required under a loan agreement.

4. Book values computed:

June 30, 19x5
   Common Stock: $3,290,000 ÷ 250,000 shares = $13.16 per share
June 30, 19x6
   Preferred Stock:
      Call price of $104 per share equals book value per share

Common Stock:
($5,475,200 − $2,080,000) ÷ (509,000 shares + 50,900 shares) =
$3,395,200 ÷ 559,900 shares = $6.06 per share

Chapter Assignments

Discussion Questions and Writing Assignments

1. What are retained earnings, and how do they relate to the assets of a corporation?
2. When does a company have a deficit in retained earnings?
3. What items are identified by generally accepted accounting principles as prior period adjustments?
4. Describe the significance of the following dates as they relate to dividends: (a) date of declaration, (b) date of record, and (c) date of payment.
5. How does the accounting treatment of stock dividends differ from that of cash dividends?
6. What is the difference between a stock dividend and a stock split? What is the effect of each on the capital structure of a corporation?
7. What is the purpose of restricting retained earnings?
8. Define treasury stock and explain why a company would purchase its own stock.
9. What is the difference between the statement of stockholders' equity and the stockholders' equity section of the balance sheet?
10. Would you expect a corporation's book value per share to equal its market value per share? Why or why not?
11. "Accounting income should be geared to the concept of taxable income because the public understands the concept of taxable income." Comment on this statement, and tell why income tax allocation is necessary.
12. Santa Fe Southern Pacific Railroad had about $1.8 billion of deferred income taxes in 1982, equal to about 31 percent of total liabilities. By 1984, deferred income taxes had reached almost $2.3 billion, or about 38 percent of total liabilities. Given management's desire to put off the payment of taxes as long as possible, the long-term growth of the economy and inflation, and the definition of a liability (probable future sacrifices of future benefits arising from present obligations), can you give an argument for not accounting for deferred income taxes?
13. Explain the two major criteria for extraordinary items. How should extraordinary items be disclosed in financial statements?
14. How are earnings per share disclosed in financial statements?
15. When an accounting change occurs, what financial statement disclosures are necessary?
16. When does a company have a simple capital structure? a complex capital structure?
17. What is the difference between primary and fully diluted earnings per share?
18. Why should the gain or loss on discontinued operations be disclosed separately on the income statement?

Classroom Exercises

Exercise 16-1.
Statement of
Retained Earnings
(L.O. 1)

The Snadhu Corporation had a Retained Earnings balance on January 1, 19x2 of $260,000. During 19x2, the company reported a profit of $112,000 after taxes. In addition, the company located a $44,000 (net of taxes) error that resulted in an overstatement of prior years' income and meets the criteria of a prior period adjustment. During 19x2, the company declared cash dividends totaling $16,000.

Prepare the company's statement of retained earnings for the year ended December 31, 19x2.

Exercise 16-2.
Journal Entries:
Stock Dividends
(L.O. 2)

The Geyer Company has 30,000 shares of its $1 par value common stock outstanding. Record the following transactions as they relate to the company's common stock:

July 17   Declared a 10 percent stock dividend on common stock to be distributed on August 10 to stockholders of record on July 31. Market value of the stock was $5 per share on this date.
      31   Record date.
Aug. 10   Distributed the stock dividend declared on July 17.
Sept. 1   Declared a $.50 per share cash dividend on common stock to be paid on September 16 to stockholders of record on September 10.

Exercise 16-3.
Stock Split
(L.O. 2)

The Colson Company currently has 200,000 shares of $1 par value common stock outstanding. The board of directors declared a 2 for 1 split on May 15, when the market value of the common stock was $2.50 per share. The Retained Earnings balance on May 15 was $700,000. Paid-in Capital in Excess of Par Value, Common Stock, on this date was $20,000.

Prepare the stockholders' equity section of the company's balance sheet before and after the stock split. What journal entry, if any, would be necessary to record the stock split?

Exercise 16-4.
Treasury Stock
Transactions
(L.O. 3)

Prepare the journal entries necessary to record the following stock transactions of the Henderson Company during 19xx:

May 5   Purchased 400 shares of its own $1 par value common stock for $10, the current market price.
     17   Sold 150 shares of treasury stock purchased on May 5 for $11 per share.
     21   Sold 100 shares of treasury stock purchased on May 5 for $10 per share.
     28   Sold the remaining 150 shares of treasury stock purchased on May 5 for $9.50 per share.

Exercise 16-5.
Restriction of
Retained Earnings
(L.O. 4)

The board of directors of the Hollander Company has approved plans to acquire another company during the coming year. The acquisition should cost approximately $550,000. The board has taken action to restrict retained earnings of the company in the amount of $550,000 on July 17, 19x1. On July 31, the company has retained earnings of $975,000.

1. Show two ways the restriction of retained earnings may be disclosed.
2. Assuming the purchase takes place as planned, what effect will it have on retained earnings and future disclosures?

Exercise 16-6.
Statement of Stockholders' Equity
(L.O. 5)

The stockholders' equity section of Network Corporation's balance sheet on December 31, 19x2 appears as follows:

Contributed Capital	
Common Stock—$1 par value, 500,000 shares	
authorized, 400,000 issued and outstanding	$ 400,000
Paid-in Capital in Excess of Par Value, Common	600,000
Total Contributed Capital	$1,000,000
Retained Earnings	2,100,000
Total Stockholders' Equity	$3,100,000

Prepare a statement of stockholders' equity at December 31, 19x3, assuming the following transactions occurred in sequence during 19x3:

a. Issued 5,000 shares of $100 par value, 9 percent cumulative preferred stock at par after obtaining authorization from the state.
b. Issued 40,000 shares of common stock in connection with the conversion of bonds having a carrying value of $300,000.
c. Declared and issued a 2 percent common stock dividend. The market value on the date of declaration is $7 per share.
d. Purchased 10,000 shares of common stock for the treasury at a cost of $8 per share.
e. Earned net income of $230,000.
f. Paid the full year's dividend on preferred stock and a dividend of $.20 per share on common stock outstanding at the end of the year.

Exercise 16-7.
Book Value for Preferred and Common Stock
(L.O. 6)

The stockholders' equity section of the Colombo Corporation's balance sheet is shown below.

Contributed Capital		
Preferred Stock—$100 per share, 6 percent		
cumulative, 10,000 shares authorized, 200		
shares issued and outstanding*		$ 20,000
Common Stock—$5 par value, 100,000 shares		
authorized, 10,000 shares issued, 9,000		
outstanding	$50,000	
Paid-in Capital in Excess of Par Value, Common	28,000	78,000
Total Contributed Capital		$ 98,000
Retained Earnings		95,000
Total Contributed Capital and Retained Earnings		$193,000
Less Treasury Stock, Common (1,000 shares at cost)		15,000
Total Stockholders' Equity		$178,000

*The preferred stock is callable at $105 per share, and one year's dividends are in arrears.

Determine the book value per share for both the preferred and the common stock.

Exercise 16-8.
Corporate Income
Statement
(L.O. 7)

Assume that the Jaeger Furniture Company's chief financial officer gave you the following information: Net Sales, $1,900,000; Cost of Goods Sold, $1,050,000; Extraordinary Gain (applicable income tax on gain of $3,500), $16,000; Loss from Discontinued Operations (applicable income tax benefit of $30,000), $82,000; Loss on Disposal of Discontinued Operations (applicable income tax benefit of $13,000), $48,000; Selling Expenses, $50,000; Administrative Expenses, $40,000; Income Taxes Expense on Continuing Operations, $300,000.

From this information, prepare the company's income statement for the year ended June 30, 19xx. (Ignore earnings per share information.)

Exercise 16-9.
Use of Corporate
Income Tax Rate
Schedule
(L.O. 8)

Using the corporate tax rate schedule on page 657, compute the income tax liability for the following situations:

Situation	Taxable Income
A	$ 70,000
B	85,000
C	320,000

Exercise 16-10.
Income Tax
Allocation
(L.O. 8)

The Theus Corporation reported the following accounting income before income taxes, income taxes expense, and net income for 19x2 and 19x3:

	19x2	19x3
Accounting income before taxes	$140,000	$140,000
Income taxes expense	44,150	44,150
Net income	$ 95,850	$ 95,850

Also on the balance sheet, deferred income taxes liability increased by $19,200 in 19x2 and decreased by $9,400 in 19x3.

1. How much did Theus Corporation actually pay in income taxes in 19x2 and 19x3?
2. Prepare journal entries to record income taxes expense in 19x2 and 19x3.

Exercise 16-11.
Earnings per
Share
(L.O. 10)

During 19x1, the Heath Corporation reported a net income of $1,529,500. On January 1, Heath had 700,000 shares of common stock outstanding. The company issued an additional 420,000 shares of common stock on October 1. In 19x1, the company had a simple capital structure. During 19x2, there were no transactions involving common stock, and the company reported net income of $2,016,000.

1. Determine the weighted-average number of common shares outstanding each year.
2. Compute earnings per share for each year.

Exercise 16-12.
Corporate Income
Statement
(L.O. 7, 8, 9, 10)

During 19x3 Dasbol Corporation engaged in a number of complex transactions to restructure the business by selling off a division, retiring bonds, and changing accounting methods. The company has always issued a simple single-step income statement, and the accountant has accordingly prepared the following December 31 year-end income statement for 19x3 and 19x2:

Dasbol Corporation
Income Statement
For the Years Ended December 31, 19x3 and 19x2

	19x3	19x2
Sales	$1,000,000	$1,200,000
Cost of Goods Sold	(550,000)	(600,000)
Operating Expenses	(225,000)	(150,000)
Income Taxes Expense	(164,700)	(135,000)
Income from Operations of a Discontinued Segment	160,000	
Gain on Disposal of Segment	140,000	
Extraordinary Gain on Retirement of Bonds	72,000	
Cumulative Effect of a Change in Accounting Principle	(48,000)	
Net Income	$ 384,300	$ 315,000
Earnings per Share	$1.92	$1.58

The president of the company, Joseph Dasbol, is pleased to see that net income and earnings per share increased by 22 percent from 19x2 to 19x3 and intends to announce to the stockholders that the restructuring is a success.

1. Recast the 19x3 income statement in proper multistep form, including allocating income taxes to appropriate items (assume a 30 percent income tax rate) and showing earnings per share figures (200,000 shares outstanding).
2. What is your assessment of the restructuring plan?

Interpreting Accounting Information

Lockheed
Corporation
(L.O. 7, 9)

Presented below are several excerpts from an article that appeared in the February 2, 1982, *Wall Street Journal* entitled "Lockheed Had Loss in 4th Quarter, Year; $396 Million TriStar Write-Off is Cited."

As expected, Lockheed Corp. took a $396 million write-off to cover expenses of its production phase-out of L-1011 TriStar commercial jets, resulting in a net loss of . . . $289 million for the year.

Roy A. Anderson, Lockheed Chairman, said he believed the company had "recognized all costs, including those yet to be incurred, that are associated with the phase-out of the TriStar program." He said he thinks the company now is in a sound position to embark on a program of future growth and earnings improvement.

Included in the $396 million total write-off are remaining deferred production start-up costs, adjustments for redundant inventories, and provisions for losses and other costs expected to be incurred while TriStar production is completed. In addition to the write-off, discontinued operations include a S70 million after-tax loss associated with 1981 L-1011 operations. The comparable 1980 L-1011 loss was $108 million.

The $289 million 1981 net loss consists of the TriStar losses, reduced by the previously reported [extraordinary after-tax] gain of $23 million from the exchange of debentures.

For the year, Lockheed had earnings from continuing operations of $154 million, a 14% gain from $135 million in 1980. In 1981 the company had a $466 million loss from discontinued operations, resulting in a net loss of $289 million. A year earlier, the concern had a $108 million loss from discontinued operations, resulting in a net profit of $28 million.[16]

Required

1. Interpret the financial information from *The Wall Street Journal* by preparing a partial income statement for Lockheed for 1981, beginning with "income from continuing operations." Be prepared to explain the nature of each item on the income statement.
2. How do you explain the fact that on the New York Stock Exchange, Lockheed common stock closed at $50 per share, up 75¢ on the day after the quoted announcement of a net loss of $289 million and up from $41 per share two months earlier?

Problem Set A

**Problem 16A-1.
Treasury Stock
Transactions
(L.O. 3)**

The following treasury stock transactions occurred during 19xx for the Arroyo Company: (a) Purchased 26,000 shares of its $1 par value common stock on the market for $20 per share. (b) Sold 8,000 shares of the treasury stock for $21 per share. (c) Sold 6,000 shares of the treasury stock for $19 per share. (d) Sold 10,000 shares of the treasury stock remaining for $17 per share. (e) Purchased an additional 4,000 shares for $18 per share. (f) Retired all the remaining shares of treasury stock. All shares were originally issued at $4 per share.

Required

Record these transactions in general journal form.

**Problem 16A-2.
Stock Dividend
and Treasury
Stock
Transactions
(L.O. 2, 3, 5)**

The stockholders' equity section of Linden Cotton Mills, Inc. as of December 31, 19x2 is as follows:

Contributed Capital	
Common Stock—$6 par value, 500,000 shares authorized, 80,000 shares issued and outstanding	$ 480,000
Paid-in Capital in Excess of Par Value, Common	150,000
Total Contributed Capital	$ 630,000
Retained Earnings	480,000
Total Stockholders' Equity	$1,110,000

16. "Lockheed Had Loss in 4th Quarter, Year; $396 Million TriStar Write-Off is Cited," *The Wall Street Journal* (February 2, 1982). Reprinted by permission of *The Wall Street Journal*, © Dow Jones & Company, Inc. 1982. All Rights Reserved Worldwide.

A review of the stockholders' equity records of Linden Cotton Mills, Inc. disclosed the following transactions during 19x3:

Jan. 30 Purchased 20,000 shares of the company's $6 par value common stock for $10.50. The stock was originally issued at $9.

Feb. 16 Sold 6,000 shares of the company's stock purchased on January 30 for $12 per share.

Mar. 25 The board of directors declared a 5 percent stock dividend to stockholders of record on April 20 to be distributed on May 1. The market value of common stock is $11 per share.

Apr. 20 Date of record for stock dividend.

May 1 Issued stock dividend.

Aug. 17 Sold 1,000 shares of the company's stock purchased on January 30 for $9 per share.

Sept. 10 Declared a 3 for 1 stock split. Assume the stock split applies to shares held in the treasury.

Oct. 5 Sold 6,000 shares of the company's stock purchased on January 30 for $2 per share. (**Hint:** Note effect of stock split on cost of shares.)

Nov. 20 Decided to retire, effective immediately, 20,000 of the remaining shares held in the treasury.

Dec. 15 Declared a 10 percent stock dividend to stockholders of record on January 15 to be distributed on February 15. The market price on this date is $3.50 per share.

Required

1. Record the transactions for Linden Cotton Mills, Inc. in general journal form.
2. Prepare the stockholders' equity section of the company's balance sheet as of December 31, 19x3. Assume net income for 19x3 is $47,000.

**Problem 16A-3.
Dividend
Transactions,
Retained Earnings,
and Stockholders'
Equity
(L.O. 1, 2, 4, 5)**

The balance sheet of the Shimer Clothing Company disclosed the following stockholders' equity as of September 30, 19x1:

Contributed Capital	
Common Stock—$2 par value, 1,000,000 shares	
authorized, 300,000 shares issued and outstanding	$ 600,000
Paid-in Capital in Excess of Par Value, Common	370,000
Total Contributed Capital	$ 970,000
Retained Earnings	350,000
Total Stockholders' Equity	$1,320,000

The following stockholders' equity transactions were completed during the next fiscal year in the order presented:

19x1

Dec. 17 Declared a 10 percent stock dividend to be distributed January 20 to stockholders of record on January 1. The market value per share on the date of declaration was $4.

19x2

Jan. 1 Date of record.

20 Distributed the stock dividend.

Apr. 14 Declared a 25¢ per share cash dividend. Cash dividend payable May 15 to stockholders of record on May 1.

May 1 Date of record.

     15 Paid the cash dividend.

June 17 Split its stock 2 for 1.

Sept. 15 Declared a cash dividend of 10¢ per share payable October 10 to stockholders of record October 1.

     30 Closed Income Summary with a credit balance of $150,000 to Retained Earnings.

     30 Closed Dividends Declared to Retained Earnings.

On September 14, the board of directors restricted retained earnings for plant expansion in the amount of $150,000. The restriction is shown within the balance sheet.

Required

1. Record the above transactions in general journal form.
2. Prepare a statement of retained earnings.
3. Prepare the stockholders' equity section of the company's balance sheet as of September 30, 19x2, with appropriate disclosure of the restriction of retained earnings.

Problem 16A-4.
Corporate Income Statement
(L.O. 7, 8, 9, 10)

Information concerning operations of the Daniels Shoe Corporation during 19xx is as follows: (a) administrative expenses, $90,000; (b) cost of goods sold, $420,000; (c) cumulative effect of an accounting change in depreciation methods that increased income (net of taxes, $20,000), $42,000; (d) extraordinary loss from earthquake (net of taxes, $36,000), $60,000; (e) sales (net), $900,000; (f) selling expenses, $80,000; and (g) income taxes expense applicable to continuing operations, $105,000.

Required

Prepare the corporation's income statement for the year ended December 31, 19xx, including earnings per share information. Assume a weighted average of 100,000 common stock shares outstanding during the year.

Problem 16A-5.
Stockholders' Equity and Comprehensive Stockholders' Equity Transactions
(L.O. 1, 2, 3, 4, 5, 6)

On December 31, 19x1, the stockholders' equity section of the Skolnick Company's balance sheet appeared as follows:

Contributed Capital

Common Stock—$4 par value, 200,000 shares authorized,

    60,000 shares issued and outstanding $ 240,000

  Paid-in Capital in Excess of Par Value, Common   640,000

  Total Contributed Capital $ 880,000

Retained Earnings   412,000

Total Stockholders' Equity $1,292,000

Selected transactions involving stockholders' equity in 19x2 are as follows: On January 4, the board of directors obtained authorization for 20,000 shares of $20 par value noncumulative preferred stock that carried an indicated dividend rate of $2 per share and was callable at $21 per share. On January

14, the company sold 12,000 shares of the preferred stock at $20 per share and issued another 2,000 in exchange for a building valued at $40,000. On March 8, the board of directors also declared a 2 for 1 stock split on the common stock. On April 20, after the stock split, the company purchased 3,000 shares of common stock for the treasury at an average price of $6 per share; 1,000 of these shares were subsequently sold on May 4 at an average price of $8 per share. On July 15, the board of directors declared a cash dividend of $2 per share on preferred stock and $.20 per share on common stock. The date of record was July 25. The dividends were paid on August 15. The board of directors declared a 15 percent stock dividend on November 28 when the common stock was selling for $10. The record date for the stock dividend was December 15, and the dividend was to be distributed on January 5. Net loss for 19x2 was $109,000 On December 31, Income Summary and Dividends Declared were closed. The board of directors noted that footnote disclosure must be made due to a bank loan agreement that requires minimum retained earnings. No cash dividends may be declared or paid if retained earnings falls below $50,000.

Required

1. Prepare journal entries to record the above transactions.
2. Prepare the company's statement of retained earnings for the year ended December 31, 19x2.
3. Prepare the stockholders' equity section of the company's balance sheet as of December 31, 19x2, including appropriate disclosure of the restrictions on retained earnings.
4. Compute book value per share for preferred and common stock on December 31, 19x1 and 19x2.

Problem Set B

Problem 16B-1.
Treasury Stock
Transactions
(L.O. 3)

The Oliva Corporation was involved in the following treasury stock transactions during 19x7: (a) purchased 40,000 shares of its $1 par value common stock at $2.50 per share; (b) purchased 8,000 shares of its common stock at $2.80 per share; (c) sold 22,000 shares purchased in a for $65,500; (d) sold the other 18,000 shares purchased in a for $36,000; (e) sold 3,000 of the remaining shares of treasury stock for $1.60 per share; and (f) retired all the remaining shares of treasury stock. All shares were originally issued at $1.50 per share.

Required

Record the treasury stock transactions in general journal form.

Problem 16B-2.
Stock Dividend
and Treasury
Stock
Transactions
(L.O. 2, 3, 5)

The stockholders' equity section of the balance sheet of Packer Corporation as of December 31, 19x6, is as follows:

Contributed Capital	
Common Stock—$2 par value, 500,000 shares authorized, 200,000 shares issued and outstanding	$ 400,000
Paid-in Capital in Excess of Par Value, Common	500,000
Total Contributed Capital	$ 900,000
Retained Earnings	600,000
Total Stockholders' Equity	$1,500,000

The following transactions occurred in 19x7 for Packer Corporation:

Jan. 21   Purchased 10,000 shares of the company's $2 par value common stock at $6 per share.

Feb. 28   The board of directors declared a 10 percent stock dividend to stockholders of record on March 25 to be distributed on April 5. The market value on this date is $8.

Mar. 25   Date of record for stock dividend.

Apr. 5   Issued stock dividend.

May 16   Sold 4,000 shares of the treasury stock purchased on January 21 for $7 per share.

June 15   Sold 5,000 shares of the treasury stock purchased on January 21 for $3.50 per share.

July 15   Decided to retire, effective immediately, the remaining shares held in the treasury. The shares were originally issued at $3 per share.

Aug. 3   Declared a 2 for 1 stock split.

Nov. 20   Purchased 20,000 shares of the company's common stock at $4 per share for the treasury.

Dec. 31   Declared a 5 percent stock dividend to stockholders of record on January 25 to be distributed on February 5. The market value per share is $4.50.

Required

1. Record the transactions for Packer Corporation in general journal form.
2. Prepare the stockholders' equity section of the company's balance sheet as of December 31, 19x7. Assume net income for 19x7 is $54,000.

**Problem 16B-3.
Dividend
Transactions,
Retained Earnings,
and Stockholders'
Equity**
(L.O. 1, 2, 4, 5)

The stockholders' equity section of the Hughes Blind and Awning Company's balance sheet as of December 31, 19x6 is as follows:

Contributed Capital	
Common Stock—$1 par value, 3,000,000 shares authorized, 500,000 issued and outstanding	$ 500,000
Paid-in Capital in Excess of Par Value, Common	200,000
Total Contributed Capital	$ 700,000
Retained Earnings	540,000
Total Stockholders' Equity	$1,240,000

The company was involved in the following stockholders' equity transactions during 19x7:

Mar. 5   Declared a $.20 per share cash dividend to be paid on April 6 to stockholders of record on March 20.

20   Date of record.

Apr. 6   Paid the cash dividend.

June 17   Declared a 10 percent stock dividend to be distributed August 17 to stockholders of record on August 5. The market value of the stock was $7 per share.

Aug. 5   Date of record.

17   Distributed the stock dividend.

Oct. 2   Split its stock 3 for 1.

Dec. 27 Declared a cash dividend of $.05 payable January 27, 19x8 to stock-holders of record on January 14, 19x8.

31 Closed Income Summary with a credit balance of $200,000 to Retained Earnings.

31 Closed Dividends Declared to Retained Earnings.

On December 9, the board of directors restricted retained earnings for a pending lawsuit in the amount of $100,000. The restriction is to be shown within the balance sheet.

Required

1. Record the 19x7 transactions in general journal form.
2. Prepare a statement of retained earnings.
3. Prepare the stockholders' equity section of the company's balance sheet as of December 31, 19x7.

Problem 16B-4.
Corporate Income Statement
(L.O. 7, 8, 9, 10)

Income statement information for the Walker Corporation during 19x1 is as follows: (a) administrative expenses, $110,000; (b) cost of goods sold, $440,000; (c) cumulative effect of accounting change in inventory methods that decreased income (net of taxes, $28,000), $60,000; (d) extraordinary loss from storm (net of taxes, $10,000), $20,000; (e) income taxes expense, continuing operations, $42,000; (f) net sales, $890,000; and (g) selling expenses, $190,000.

Required

Prepare Walker Corporation's income statement for 19x1, including earnings per share information assuming a weighted average of 200,000 shares of common stock outstanding for 19x1.

Problem 16B-5.
Comprehensive Stockholders' Equity Transactions
(L.O. 1, 2, 3, 4, 5)

The stockholders' equity on June 30, 19x5 of the Roper Company is as shown below:

Contributed Capital	
Common Stock—no par value, $2 stated value,	
500,000 shares authorized, 200,000 shares issued	
and outstanding	$ 400,000
Paid-in Capital in Excess of Stated Value, Common	640,000
Total Contributed Capital	$1,040,000
Retained Earnings	420,000
Total Stockholders' Equity	$1,460,000

Stockholders' equity transactions for the next fiscal year are as follows:

a. The board of directors declared a 2 for 1 split.
b. The board of directors obtained authorization to issue 100,000 shares of $100 par value $4 noncumulative preferred stock that is callable at $105.
c. Issued 10,000 shares of common stock for a building appraised at $22,000.
d. Purchased 6,000 shares of the company's common stock for $15,000.
e. Issued 15,000 shares of the preferred stock for $100 per share.
f. Sold 4,000 shares of the treasury stock for $9,000.

g. Declared cash dividends of $4 per share on the preferred stock and $.10 per share on the common stock.

h. Date of record.

i. Paid the preferred and common stock cash dividends.

j. Declared a 5 percent stock dividend on the common stock. The market value was $9 per share. The stock dividend was distributable after the end of the fiscal year.

k. Net income for the year was $210,000.

l. Closed dividends declared to Retained Earnings. Due to a loan agreement, the company is not allowed to reduce retained earnings below $100,000. The board of directors determined that this restriction should be disclosed in the notes to the financial statements.

Required

1. Make the appropriate general journal entries to record the transactions.
2. Prepare the company's statement of retained earnings at June 30, 19x6.
3. Prepare the stockholders' equity section of the company's balance sheet at June 30, 19x6, including appropriate disclosure of the restriction on retained earnings.
4. Compute the book values per share of preferred and common stock (including common stock distributable) on June 30, 19x5 and 19x6.

Financial Decision Case

Metzger Steel Corporation
(L.O. 2, 3, 6)

Metzger Steel Corporation (MSC) is a small specialty steel manufacturer located in northern Alabama that has been owned by the Metzger family for several generations. Arnold Metzger III is a major shareholder in MSC by virtue of having inherited 200.000 shares of common stock in the company. Previously, Arnold has not shown much interest in the business because of his enthusiasm for archaeology, which takes him to far parts of the world. However, when he received minutes of the last board of directors meeting, he questioned a number of transactions involving the stockholders' equity of MSC. He asks you, as a person with a knowledge of accounting, to help him interpret the effect of these transactions on his interest in MSC.

First, you note that at the beginning of 19xx the stockholders' equity of MSC appeared as follows:

Metzger Steel Corporation	
Stockholders' Equity	
January 1, 19xx	
Contributed Capital	
Common Stock—$10 par value, 5,000,000 shares authorized, 1,000,000 shares issued and outstanding	$10,000,000
Paid-in Capital in Excess of Par Value, Common	25,000,000
Total Contributed Capital	$35,000,000
Retained Earnings	20,000,000
Total Stockholders' Equity	$55,000,000

Then you read the relevant parts of the minutes of the December 15 meeting of the board of directors of MSC:

Item A: The president reported the following transactions involving the company's stock during the last quarter:

October 15. Sold 500,000 shares of authorized common stock through the investment banking firm of A. B. Abbott at a net price of $50 per share.

November 1. Purchased 100,000 shares for the corporate treasury from Sharon Metzger at a price of $55 per share.

Item B: The board declared a 2 for 1 stock split (accomplished by halving the par value, doubling each stockholder's shares, and increasing authorized shares to 10,000,000), followed by a 10 percent stock dividend. The board then declared a cash dividend of $2.00 per share on the resulting shares. All these transactions are applicable to stockholders of record on December 20 and are payable on January 10. The market value of Metzger stock on the board meeting date after the stock split was estimated to be $30.

Item C: The chief financial officer stated that he expected the company to report a net income for the year of $4,000,000.

Required

1. Prepare a stockholders' equity section of MSC's balance sheet as of December 31, 19xx that reflects the above transactions. (**Hint:** Use T accounts to analyze the transactions. Also, use a T account to keep track of the shares of common stock outstanding.)
2. Compute the book value per share and Arnold's percentage of ownership of the company at the beginning and at the end of the year. Explain the differences. Would you say that Arnold's position has improved or not during the year?

Answers to Self-Test

1. b	3. c	5. a	7. b	9. a
2. a	4. d	6. d	8. c	10. b

Comprehensive Problem: Sundial Corporation

Sundial Corporation filed articles of incorporation and obtained authorization for 500,000 shares of no-par common stock with a stated value of $1 per share and 10,000 shares of 9 percent cumulative preferred stock with a par value of $100 and a call price of $104. The company began business on January 1, 19xx, as a high-tech startup in the business of making sophisticated time measuring devices. The company's first year of operation was an exciting and profitable one in which the company engaged in a number of transactions involving its stockholders' equity, which are listed below.

19xx

Jan. 1 Issued for cash 100,000 shares of common stock at a price of $5 per share.

2 Issued 12,000 shares of common stock to attorneys and others who assisted with the organization of the corporation. The value of these services was put at $60,000.

3 Issued for cash 10,000 shares of preferred stock at par value.

Feb. 6 Accepted subscriptions for 60,000 shares of common stock at a price of $6 per share.

Mar. 7 Issued 8,000 shares of common stock in exchange for a patent that had a value set at $50,000.

Apr. 2 Received full payment for half the stock subscription of February 6 and issued the stock.

May 5 Purchased 30,000 common shares from a stockholder for $8 per share.

19 Sold 13,000 of the common shares purchased on May 5 for $9 per share.

June 30 Transferred by a closing entry the net income for the first half of the year to retained earnings, $250,000.

July 8 Sold 7,000 more of the common shares purchased on May 5 for $7.

Aug. 4 Declared a 10 percent common stock dividend distributable on Aug. 24 to stockholders of record Aug. 14. At this time the company's common stock is selling for $8 per share.

14 Date of record for stock dividend.

24 Date of distribution for stock dividend.

Sept. 9 Issued common stock for cash in connection with the exercise by management of employee stock options on 40,000 shares of common stock at $5 per share.

Oct. 10 Purchased 10,000 shares of common stock from a stockholder for $9 per share.

20 Retired the shares purchased on October 10. The shares were originally issued at $6 per share.

Nov. 1 Declared cash dividends representing the annual dividend on preferred stock and $0.25 per share on common stock to stockholders of record November 11, payable on November 21.

11 Date of record for cash dividends.

21 Date of payment for cash dividends.

Dec. 16 Declared a 2 for 1 stock split. Assume the stock split applies to treasury stock and common stock subscribed.

Dec. 31   Transferred by closing entry the net income for the second half of the year of $230,000 to retained earnings and closed dividends to retained earnings.

31   Due to litigation and potential loss under a law suit over patent infringement, the Board of Directors voted to restrict retained earnings to the extent of $100,000 and to disclose this information in a note to the financial statements.

Required

1. Record the above entries for Sundial Corporation in the general journal.

2. Prepare the statement of retained earnings for 19xx for Sundial Corporation.
3. Prepare the stockholders' equity section of Sundial's balance sheet on December 31, 19xx, including proper disclosure of the restriction of retained earnings.
4. Compute book value for preferred stock and common stock at year end.

This Comprehensive Problem covers all of the Learning Objectives in Chapter 15 and Learning Objectives 1 through 6 in Chapter 16.

1. *Identify and contrast the major characteristics of bonds.*
2. *Record the issuance of bonds at face value and at a discount or premium.*
3. *Determine the value of bonds using present values.*
4. *Amortize (a) bond discounts and (b) bond premiums by using the straight-line and effective interest methods.*
5. *Account for bonds issued between interest dates and make year-end adjustments.*
6. *Account for the retirement of bonds and the conversion of bonds into stock.*
7. *Explain the basic features of mortgages payable, long-term leases, and pensions as long-term liabilities.*

CHAPTER 17

Long-Term Liabilities

This chapter introduces long-term liabilities. It describes the nature of bonds and the accounting treatment for bonds payable and other long-term liabilities such as mortgages, long-term leases, and pension liabilities. After studying this chapter, you should be able to meet the learning objectives listed on the left.

A corporation has many sources of funds from which to finance operations and expansion. As you learned earlier, corporations acquire cash and other assets by conducting profitable operations, obtaining short-term credit, and issuing stock. Another source of funds for a business is long-term debt in the form of bonds or notes. When a company issues bonds or notes, it promises to pay the creditor periodic interest plus the principal of the debt on a certain date in the future. Notes and bonds are long-term if they are due more than one year from the balance sheet date. In practice, long-term notes can range from two to ten years to maturity and long-term bonds and mortgages from ten to fifty years to maturity.

Nature of Bonds

A **bond** is a security, usually long-term, representing money borrowed by a corporation from the investing public. (Other kinds of bonds are issued by the United States government, state and local governments, and foreign companies and countries to raise money.) Bonds must be repaid at a certain time and require periodic payments of interest. Interest is usually paid semiannually, or twice a year. Bonds must not be confused with stocks. Because stocks are shares of ownership, stockholders are owners. Bondholders, however, are creditors. Bonds are promises to repay the amount borrowed, called the principal, and a certain rate of interest at specified future dates.

The holder of a bond receives a **bond certificate** as evidence of the company's debt to the bondholder. In most cases, the face value (denomination) of the bond is $1,000 or some multiple of $1,000. A **bond issue** is the total number of bonds that are issued at one time. For example, a $1,000,000 bond issue may consist of a thousand $1,000 bonds. The issue may be bought and held by many investors. So the corporation usually enters into a supplementary agreement, called a **bond indenture**. The bond indenture defines the rights, privileges, and limitations of bondholders. The bond indenture will generally describe such things as the maturity date of the bonds, interest payment dates, interest rate, and characteristics of the bonds such as call features. Repayment plans and restrictions may also be covered.

OBJECTIVE 1
Identify and contrast the major characteristics of bonds

The prices of bonds are stated in terms of a percentage of face value. If a bond issue is quoted at $103\frac{1}{2}$, this means that a $1,000 bond would cost $1,035 ($1,000 × $103\frac{1}{2}$%). When a bond sells at exactly 100, it is said to sell at face or par value. When it sells above 100, it is said to sell at a premium; below 100, at a discount. A $1,000 bond quoted at 87.62 would be selling at a discount and would cost the buyer $876.20.

A bond indenture can be written to fit the financing needs of an individual company. As a result, the bonds being issued by corporations in today's financial markets have many different features. Several of the more important ones are described here.

Secured or Unsecured Bonds

Bonds may be either secured or unsecured. If issued on the general credit of the company, they are unsecured bonds (also called debenture bonds). Secured bonds give the bondholders a pledge of certain assets of the company as a guarantee of repayment. The security identified by a secured bond may be any specific asset of the company or a general category such as property, plant, and equipment.

Term or Serial Bonds

When all the bonds of an issue mature at the same time, they are called term bonds. For example, a company may issue $1,000,000 worth of bonds, all due twenty years from the date of issue. If the maturity dates of a bond issue are spread over several different dates, the bonds are serial bonds. A company may issue serial bonds to ease the task of retiring its debt. An example of serial bonds would be a $1,000,000 issue that calls for retiring $200,000 of the principal every five years. This arrangement means that after the first $200,000 payment is made, $800,000 of the bonds would remain outstanding for the next five years. In other words, $1,000,000 is outstanding for the first five years, $800,000 for the second five years, and so on.

Registered or Coupon Bonds

Most bonds that are issued today are registered bonds. These bonds require the name and address of the owner to be recorded with the issuing company. In this way the company keeps a register of the owners and pays interest by check to the bondholders of record on the interest payment date. Coupon bonds generally are not registered with the corporation, but instead bear interest coupons stating the amount of interest due and the payment date. The coupons are removed from the bond on the interest payment dates and presented at a bank for collection. In this way the interest is paid to the holder of the coupon.

Accounting for Bonds Payable[1]

OBJECTIVE 2
Record the issuance of bonds at face value and at a discount or premium

When the board of directors decides to issue bonds, it generally presents the proposal to the stockholders. If the stockholders agree to the issue, the company prints the certificates and draws up a deed of trust. The bonds are then authorized for issuance. It is not necessary to make a journal entry for the authorization, but most companies prepare a memorandum in the Bonds Payable account describing the issue. This note gives the amount of bonds authorized, interest rate, interest payment dates, and life of the bonds.

Once the bonds are issued, the corporation must pay interest to the bondholders during the life of the bonds (in most cases semiannually) and the principal of the bonds at maturity.

Balance Sheet Disclosure of Bonds

Bonds payable and either unamortized discount or premium (which will be explained later) are generally shown on a company's balance sheet as long-term liabilities. However, as explained in Chapter 11, if the maturity date of the bond issue is one year or less and the bonds will be retired by the use of current assets, bonds payable should be listed as current liabilities. If the issue is to be paid with segregated assets or replaced by another bond issue, then bonds should still be shown as long-term liabilities.

Important provisions of the bond indenture are reported in the notes to the financial statements. Often reported with them is a list of all bond issues, the kind of bond, interest rate, any security connected with the bonds, interest payment dates, maturity date, and effective interest rate.

Bonds Issued at Face Value

As an example, suppose that the Vason Corporation has authorized the issuance of $100,000 of 9 percent, five-year bonds on January 1, 19x0. Interest is to be paid on January 1 and July 1 of each year. Assume that the bonds are sold on January 1, 19x0, for their face value. The entry to record the issuance is as follows:

Jan. 1	Cash	100,000	
	Bonds Payable		100,000
	Sold $100,000 of 9%, 5-year bonds at face value		

As stated above, interest is paid on July 1 and January 1 of each year. Thus the corporation would owe the bondholders $4,500 interest on July 1, 19x0. The interest computation would be:

---

1. At the time this chapter was being written, the market interest rates on corporate bonds were volatile. Therefore, the examples and problems in this chapter use a variety of interest rates that are convenient for demonstrating the concepts.

$$interest = principal \times rate \times time$$
$$= \$100,000 \times .09 \times \frac{1}{2} \ year$$
$$= \$4,500$$

The interest paid to the bondholders on each semiannual interest payment date (January 1 or July 1) would be recorded as follows:

Bond Interest Expense	4,500	
Cash (or Interest Payable)		4,500
Paid (or accrued) semiannual interest		
to bondholders of 9%, 5-year bonds		

Face Interest Rate and Market Interest Rate

When issuing bonds, most companies try to set the face interest rate as close as possible to the market interest rate. The **face interest rate** is the rate of interest paid to the bondholders based on the face value or principal of the bonds. The rate and amount are fixed over the life of the bond. The **market interest rate** is the rate of interest paid in the market by bond investors for bonds of similar risk. The market interest rate fluctuates on a day-by-day basis. However, a company must decide in advance what the face interest rate will be to allow time to file with regulatory bodies, publicize the issue, and print the certificates. Since the company has no control over the market rate of interest, there is often a difference between the market or effective rate of interest and the face rate of interest on the issue date. The result is that the issue price of the bond does not always equal the principal or face value of the bond. If the market rate of interest is greater than the face interest rate, the issue price will be less than the face value and the bonds are said to be issued at a **discount**. The discount equals the excess of face value over issue price. On the other hand, if the market rate of interest is less than the face interest rate, the issue price will be more than the face value and the bonds are said to be issued at a **premium**. The premium is equal to the excess of the issue price over the face value.

Bonds Issued at a Discount

Suppose that the Vason Corporation issues its $100,000 of five-year, 9 percent bonds at 96.149 on January 1, 19x0 when the market rate of interest is 10 percent. In this case a discount exists, because the market rate of interest exceeds the face interest rate. The entry to record the issuance of the bonds at a discount is:

Jan. 1 Cash		96,149	
Unamortized Bond Discount		3,851	
Bonds Payable			100,000
Sold $100,000 of 9%, 5-year bonds			
Face Amount of Bonds	$100,000		
Less Purchase Price of Bonds			
($100,000 × .96149)	96,149		
Unamortized Bond Discount	$ 3,851		

As shown, Cash is debited for the amount received ($96,149), Bonds Payable is credited for the face amount ($100,000) of the bond liability, and the difference ($3,851) is debited to Unamortized Bond Discount. If a balance sheet is prepared right after this issuance of bonds at a discount, the liability for bonds payable is as follows:

Long-Term Liabilities
   9% Bonds Payable, due 1/1/x5 $100,000
   Less Unamortized Bond Discount   3,851 $96,149

The unamortized bond discount is a contra liability account that is deducted from the face amount of the bonds to arrive at the carrying value or present value of the bonds. The bond discount is described as unamortized because it will be amortized (written off) over the life of the bonds.

Bonds Issued at a Premium

When bonds have a face interest rate that is above the market rate for similar investments, they will be issued at a price above the face value, or at a premium. For example, assume that the Vason Corporation issues $100,000 of 9 percent, five-year bonds for $104,100 on January 1, 19x0, when the market rate of interest is 8 percent. This means that they will be purchased by investors at 104.1 percent of their face value. The entry to record their issuance would be as follows:

Jan. 1   Cash   104,100
         Unamortized Bond Premium   4,100
         Bonds Payable   100,000
            Sold $100,000 of 9%, 5-year
            bonds at 104.1

Right after this entry is made, bonds payable would be presented on the balance sheet as follows:

Long-Term Liabilities
   9% Bonds Payable, due 1/1/x5 $100,000
   Unamortized Bond Premium   4,100 $104,100

The carrying value of the bonds payable is $104,100, which is equal to the face value of the bonds plus the unamortized bond premium. The cash received from the issuance of the bonds is also $104,100. This means that the purchasers were willing to pay a premium of $4,100 to get these bonds because the face interest on them was greater than the market rate.

Bond Issue Costs

Most bonds are sold through underwriters, who receive a fee for taking care of the details of marketing the issue or for taking a chance on getting the selling price. These costs are connected with the issuance of bonds. Since bond issue costs benefit the whole life of the bond issue, it makes sense to spread these costs over that period. It is generally accepted practice to establish a separate account for bond issue costs and amortize them over the life of the bonds. However, issue costs decrease the amount of money received by the company for the bond issue. Thus they have the effect of raising the discount or lowering the premium on the issue. As a result, bond issue costs may be spread over the life of the bonds through the amortization of discount or premium. Because this method simplifies the recordkeeping, it is assumed in the text and problems of this book that all bond issue costs increase discounts or decrease premiums of the bond issues.

Using Present Value to Value a Bond[2]

OBJECTIVE 3
Determine the value of bonds using present values

Present value is relevant here because the value of bonds is based on the present value of two components of cash flow: (1) a series of fixed interest payments and (2) a single payment at maturity. The amount of interest that a bond pays is fixed over its life. During its life, however, the market rate of interest varies from day to day. Thus the amount that investors are willing to pay for the bond changes as well.

Assume, for example, that a particular bond has a face value of $10,000 and pays a fixed amount of interest of $450 (9 percent annual rate) every six months. The bond is due in five years. If the market rate of interest today is 14 percent, what is the present value of the bond?

To determine the present value of the bond, we use Tables B-3 and B-4 in Appendix B. Because the compounding period is shorter than a year, it is necessary to convert the annual rate to a semiannual rate of 7 percent (14 percent divided by two six-month periods per year) and to use ten periods (five years multiplied by two six-month periods per year). Using this information, we compute the present value of the bond:

Present value of 10 periodic payments at 7% (from Table B-4): $450 × 7.024	=	$3,160.80
Present value of a single payment at end of 10 periods at 7% (from Table B-3): $10,000 × 0.508	=	5,080.00
Present value of $10,000 bond	=	$8,240.80

The market rate of interest has increased so much since the bond was issued (from 9 percent to 14 percent) that the value of the bond is only $8,240.80 today. This amount is all that investors would be willing to pay at this time for an income from this bond of $450 every six months and return of the $10,000 principal in five years.

If the market rate of interest falls below the face interest rate, say to 8 percent, the present value of the bond will be greater than the face value of $10,000, as shown in the calculation on the next page.

---

2. A knowledge of present value concepts, as presented in Appendix A, is necessary to an understanding of this section.

Present value of 10 periodic payments at 4%
(from Table B-4): $450 × 8.111   = $ 3,649.95
Present value of a single payment at end of 10
periods at 4% (from Table B-3): $10,000 × .676 = 6,760.00
Present value of $10,000 bond   = $10,409.95

Amortizing Bond Discount

OBJECTIVE 4a
Amortize bond discounts by using the straight-line and effective interest methods

Recall that in the first illustration on page 691 Vason Corporation is-sued $100,000 of five-year bonds at a discount because the market inter-est rate of 10 percent exceeded the face interest rate of 9 percent. The bonds were sold for $96,149, resulting in an unamortized bond discount of $3,851. Since this discount, as we will see, affects interest expense in each year of the bond issue, the bond discount should be amortized or reduced gradually over the life of the bond issue. As a result, the un-amortized bond discount will gradually decrease over time and the car-rying value of the bond issue (face value less unamortized discount) will gradually increase. By the maturity date of the bond, the carrying value of the issue will equal its face value and the unamortized bond discount will be zero.

In the next two sections the calculation of total interest cost is ex-plained and the straight-line and effective interest methods of amortiz-ing bond discount are presented.

Calculation of Total Interest Cost

When bonds are issued at a discount, the effective interest rate paid by the company is greater than the face interest rate on the bonds. The rea-son is that the interest cost to the company is the stated interest pay-ments *plus* the amount of the bond discount. That is, though the company does not receive the full face value of the bonds upon issue, it must still pay back the full face amount at maturity. The difference be-tween the issue price and the face value must be added to the total in-terest payments to arrive at the actual interest expense. The full cost to the Vason Corporation of issuing the bonds at a discount is as follows:

Cash to be paid to bondholders	
Face value at maturity	$100,000
Interest payments ($100,000 × .09 × 5 years)	45,000
Total cash paid to bondholders	$145,000
Less cash received from bondholders	96,149
Total interest cost	$ 48,851 ←

Or alternatively:

Interest payments ($100,000 × .09 × 5 years)	$ 45,000
Bond discount	3,851
Total interest cost	$ 48,851 ←

The total interest cost of $48,851 is made up of $45,000 in interest payments and the $3,851 bond discount. So the bond discount increases the interest paid on the bonds from the stated to the effective interest rate. The effective interest rate is the real interest cost of the bond over its life.

In order for each year's interest expense to reflect the effective interest rate, the discount must be spread or allocated over the remaining life of the bonds as an increase in the interest expense each period. This process of allocation is called amortization of the bond discount. Thus interest expense for each period will exceed the actual payment of interest by the amount of bond discount amortized during the period.

It is interesting to note that some companies and governmental units have begun to issue bonds that do not have periodic interest payments. These bonds, called **zero coupon bonds**, are simply a promise to pay a fixed amount at the maturity date. They are issued at a large discount, because the only interest earned by the buyer or paid by the issuer is the discount. For example, a five-year, $100,000 bond issued at a time when the market rate is 14 percent, compounded semiannually, would sell for only $50,800. This amount is the present value of a single payment of $100,000 at the end of five years (from Table B-3: 7 percent for ten periods equals 0.508). The discount of $49,200 ($100,000 – $50,800) is the total interest cost and is amortized over the life of the bond. Methods of amortizing a discount are shown in the following sections.

Methods of Amortizing the Bond Discount

There are two ways of amortizing bond discounts or premiums: the straight-line method and the effective interest method. These methods are first applied to the amortization of bond discounts.

Straight-Line Method. The **straight-line method** is the easier of the two, with equal amortization of the discount for each interest period. In this case, suppose that the interest payment dates for the Vason bond issue are January 1 and July 1. The amount of the bond discount amortized and the interest cost for each semiannual period are figured in four steps, as follows:

1. Total interest payments = interest payments per year × life of bonds
   = 2 × 5 = 10

2. Amortization of bond discount per interest payment
   $$= \frac{\text{bond discount}}{\text{total interest payments}} = \frac{\$3,851}{10} = \$385^*$$

3. Regular cash interest payment
   = face value × face interest rate × time
   = $100,000 × .09 × ½ = $4,500

4. Total interest cost per interest date
   = interest payment + amortization of bond discount
   = $4,500 + $385 = $4,885

* Rounded

On July 1, 19x0, the semiannual interest date, the entry would be as follows:

July 1	Bond Interest Expense	4,885	
	Unamortized Bond Discount		385
	Cash (or Interest Payable)		4,500
	Paid (or accrued) semiannual interest to bondholders and amortized discount on 9%, 5-year bonds		

Note that the bond interest expense is $4,885, but the amount paid to the bondholder is the $4,500 face interest payment. The difference of $385 is the credit to Unamortized Bond Discount. This will lower the debit balance of the Unamortized Bond Discount and raise the carrying value of the bonds payable by $385 each interest period. Assuming that no changes occur in the bond issue, this entry will be made every six months for the life of the bond. When the bond issue matures, there will be no balance in the Unamortized Bond Discount account, and the carrying value of the bonds will be $100,000. This is exactly equal to the amount due the bondholder.

Though the straight-line method has long been used, it has a certain weakness. Because the carrying value goes up each period and the bond interest expense stays the same, the straight-line method leads to a decreasing rate of interest over time. Conversely, using the straight-line method to amortize a premium leads to a rising rate of interest over time. For this reason, the APB has ruled that the straight-line method can be used only when it does not lead to a material difference from the effective interest method.[3] As will be seen, the effective interest rate method presupposes a constant rate of interest over the life of the bond. This rate will be constant if the total interest expense changes a little each interest period in response to the changing carrying value of the bond.

Alternative Method

Effective Interest Method. To compute the interest and amortization of bond discount for each interest period under the **effective interest method**, one must apply a constant interest rate to the carrying value of the bonds at the beginning of the interest period. This constant rate is equal to the market rate at the time the bonds are issued and is called the **effective rate**. The amount to be amortized becomes the difference between the interest computed by using the effective rate and the actual interest paid to the bondholders.

As an example of this method, let us use the same facts presented earlier (a $100,000 bond issued at 9 percent, with a five-year maturity, interest to be paid twice a year). The market or effective rate of interest at the time was 10 percent. The bonds were sold for $96,149, at a discount of

3. Accounting Principles Board, *Opinion No. 21*, "Interest on Receivables and Payables" (New York: American Institute of Certified Public Accountants, 1971), par. 15.

$3,851. The resulting amounts of interest and amortization of the bond discount are shown in Table 17-1.

Note the following explanations of how the amounts in the table are computed:

Column A: The carrying value of the bonds is the face value of the bonds less unamortized bond discount ($100,000 – $3,851 = $96,149).

Column B: The interest expense to be recorded is the effective interest. It is found by multiplying the carrying value of the bonds by the effective interest rate for one-half year ($96,149 × .10 × ½ = $4,807).

Column C: The interest paid in the period is the face value of the bonds multiplied by the face interest rate for the bonds multiplied by the interest time period ($100,000 × .09 × ½ = $4,500).

Column D: The discount amortized is the difference between the effective interest expense to be recorded and the interest to be paid on the interest payment date ($4,807 – $4,500 = $307).

Column E: The unamortized bond discount is the balance of the bond discount at the beginning of the period less the current period amortization of the discount ($3,851 – $307 = $3,544). The unamortized discount

Table 17-1. Interest and Amortization of Bond Discount: Effective Interest Method

	A	B	C	D	E	F
Semi-annual Interest Period	Carrying Value at Beginning of Period	Semiannual Interest Expense at 10% to Be Recorded* (5% × A)	Semiannual Interest to Be Paid to Bondholders (4½% × $100,000)	Amortization of Discount (B – C)	Unamortized Bond Discount at End of Period	Carrying Value at End of Period (A + D)
0					$3,851	$ 96,149
1	$96,149	$4,807	$4,500	$307	3,544	96,456
2	96,456	4,823	4,500	323	3,221	96,779
3	96,779	4,839	4,500	339	2,882	97,118
4	97,118	4,856	4,500	356	2,526	97,474
5	97,474	4,874	4,500	374	2,152	97,848
6	97,848	4,892	4,500	392	1,760	98,240
7	98,240	4,912	4,500	412	1,348	98,652
8	98,652	4,933	4,500	433	915	99,085
9	99,085	4,954	4,500	454	461	99,539
10	99,539	4,961 **	4,500	461	—	100,000

* Rounded to nearest dollar
** Error due to rounding

decreases each interest payment period because it is amortized as a portion of interest expense.

Column F: The carrying value of the bonds at the end of the period is the carrying value at the beginning of the period plus the amortization during the period ($96,149 + $307 = $96,456). Notice that the sum of the carrying value and unamortized discount (column F + column E) always equals the face value of the bonds ($96,456 + $3,544 = $100,000).

The entry to record the interest expense is exactly like the one used when the straight-line method is applied. However, the amounts debited and credited to the various accounts are different. The entry for July 1, 19x0, using the effective interest method, would be:

July 1	Bond Interest Expense	4,807	
	Unamortized Bond Discount		307
	Cash (or Interest Payable)		4,500
	Paid (or accrued) semiannual interest to bondholders and amortized discount on 9%, 5-year bonds		

Note that an interest and amortization table does not have to be prepared to determine the amortization of discount for any one interest payment period. It is necessary only to multiply the carrying value by the effective interest rate and subtract the interest payment from the result. For example, the amount of discount to be amortized in the seventh interest payment period equals $412 [($98,240 × .05) − $4,500].

Visual Summary of Effective Interest Method. The effect of the amortization of bond discount using the effective interest method on carrying value and interest expense may be seen visually in Figure 17-1 (based on the data from Table 17-1). Note that initially the carrying value (issue price) is less than face value, but that it gradually increases toward face value over the life of the bond issue. Note also that interest expense exceeds interest payments by the amount of the discount amortized. Interest expense increases gradually over the life of the bond because it is based on the gradually increasing carrying value (multiplied by the market interest rate).

Amortizing Bond Premium

OBJECTIVE 4b
Amortize bond premiums by using the straight-line and effective interest methods

Recall that in a second assumption (page 692) Vason Corporation issued $100,000 of five-year bonds at a premium because the market rate of interest of 8 percent was less than the face interest rate of 9 percent. The bonds were sold for $104,100, resulting in an unamortized bond premium of $4,100. In a manner similar to the methods shown for amortizing bond discounts, the bond premium must be amortized over the life

Figure 17-1. Carrying Value and Interest Expense—Bonds Issued at a Discount

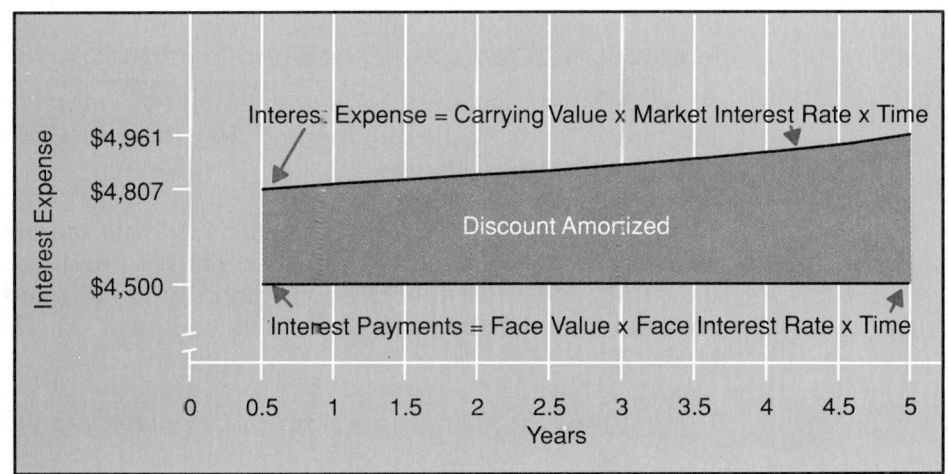

of the bond in order that it may be matched to its effects on interest expense during that period. In the following sections, the total interest cost is calculated and the bond premium is amortized using the straight-line and effective interest methods.

Calculation of Total Interest Cost

Since the bondholders paid in excess of face value for the bonds, the premium of $4,100 ($104,100 – $100,000) represents an amount that the bondholders will not receive at maturity. The premium is in effect a reduction, in advance, of the total interest paid on the bonds over the life of the bond issue. The total interest cost over the issue's life may be computed as follows:

Cash to be paid to bondholders

Face value at maturity	$100,000
Interest payments ($100,000 × .09 × 5 years)	45,000
Total cash paid to bondholders	$145,000
Less cash received from bondholders	104,100
Total interest cost	$ 40,900

Or alternatively:

Interest payments ($100,000 × .09 × 5 years)	$ 45,000
Less bond premium	4,100
Total interest cost	$ 40,900

Note that total interest payments of $45,000 exceed total interest costs of $40,900 by $4,100, or the amount of the bond premium.

Methods of Amortizing the Bond Premium

As with bond discounts, the two methods of amortizing the bond premium are the straight-line method and the effective interest method. Both are discussed below.

Straight-Line Method. Under the straight-line method, the bond premiums are spread evenly over the life of the bond issue. As with bond discounts, the amount of the bond premium amortized and the interest cost for each semiannual period are computed in the following four steps:

1. Total interest payments = interest payments per year × life of bonds
$$= 2 \times 5$$
$$= 10$$

2. Amortization of bond premium per interest payment
$$= \frac{\text{bond premium}}{\text{total interest payments}} = \frac{\$4,100}{10} = \$410$$

3. Regular cash interest payment
$$= \text{face value} \times \text{face interest rate} \times \text{time}$$
$$= \$100,000 \times .09 \times \tfrac{1}{2}$$
$$= \$4,500$$

4. Total interest cost per interest date
$$= \text{interest payment} - \text{amortization of bond premium}$$
$$= \$4,500 - \$410 = \$4,090$$

On July 1, 19x0, the semiannual interest date, the entry would be as follows:

July 1	Bond Interest Expense	4,090	
	Unamortized Bond Premium	410	
	Cash (or Interest Payable)		4,500
	Paid (or accrued) semiannual interest to bondholders and amortized premium on 9%, 5-year bonds		

Note that the bond interest expense is $4,090, but the amount received by the bondholder is the $4,500 face interest payment. The difference of $410 is the debit to Unamortized Bond Premium. This will lower the credit balance of the Unamortized Bond Premium and the carrying value of the bonds payable by $410 each interest period. Assuming that the bond issue remains unchanged, the same entry will be made every six months over the life of the bond issue. When the bond issue matures, there will be no balance in the Unamortized Bond Premium account, and the carrying value of the bonds payable will be $100,000. This is exactly equal to the amount due the bondholder. As noted before, the straight-line method should be used only when it does not lead to a material difference from the effective interest method.

Alternative Method

Effective Interest Method. Under the straight-line method, the real or effective interest rate is constantly changing even though the interest expense is fixed, because the effective interest rate is determined by comparing the fixed interest expense with a carrying value that is changing due to amortization of the discount or premium. To apply a fixed interest rate over the life of the bonds based on the actual market rate at the time of the bond issue requires the use of the effective interest method, as was shown previously in regard to the amortization of bond discounts. Under this method the interest expense decreases slightly each period (see Table 17-2, column B) because the amount of the bond premium amortized increases slightly (column D). This occurs because a fixed rate is applied each period to the gradually decreasing carrying value (column A).

The first interest payment is recorded as follows:

July 1	Bond Interest Expense	4,164	
	Unamortized Bond Premium	336	
	Cash (or Interest Payable)		4,500
	Paid (or accrued) semiannual interest to bondholders and amortized premium on 9%, 5-year bonds		

Note that the unamortized bond premium (column E) decreases gradually to zero as the carrying value decreases to the face value (column F). To find the amount of premium amortization in any one interest payment period we subtract the effective interest expense (the

Table 17-2. Interest and Amortization of Bond Premium: Effective Interest Method						
	A	B	C	D	E	F
Semi-annual Interest Period	Carrying Value at Beginning of Period	Semiannual Interest Expense at 8% to Be Recorded* (4% × A)	Semiannual Interest to Be Paid to Bondholders (4½% × $100,000)	Amortization of Premium (C – B)	Unamortized Bond Premium at End of Period	Carrying Value at End of Period (A – D)
0					$4,100	$104,100
1	$104,100	$4,164	$4,500	$336	3,764	103,764
2	103,764	4,151	4,500	349	3,415	103,415
3	103,415	4,137	4,500	363	3,052	103,052
4	103,052	4,122	4,500	378	2,674	102,674
5	102,674	4,107	4,500	393	2,281	102,281
6	102,281	4,091	4,500	409	1,872	101,872
7	101,872	4,075	4,500	425	1,447	101,447
8	101,447	4,058	4,500	442	1,005	101,005
9	101,005	4,040	4,500	460	545	100,545
10	100,545	3,955 **	4,500	545	—	100,000

 * Rounded to nearest dollar
** Error due to rounding

carrying value times the effective interest rate, column B) from the interest payment (column C). In semiannual interest period 5, for example, the amortization of premium equals $393 [$4,500 – ($102,674 × .04)].

Visual Summary of Effective Interest Method. The effect of the amortization of bond premium using the effective interest method on carrying value and interest expense may be seen visually in Figure 17-2 (based on data from Table 17-2). Note that initially the carrying value (issue price) is greater than face value, but that it gradually decreases toward face value over the life of the bond issue. Note also that interest payments exceed interest expense by the amount of the premium amortized, and that interest expense decreases gradually over the life of the bond because it is based on the gradually decreasing carrying value (multiplied by the market interest rate).

Other Bonds Payable Issues

Several other issues arise in accounting for bonds payable. Among these are sales of bonds between interest payment dates, year-end accrual of bond interest expense, retirement of bonds, and conversion of bonds into common stock.

Figure 17-2. Carrying Value and Interest Expense—Bonds Issued at a Premium

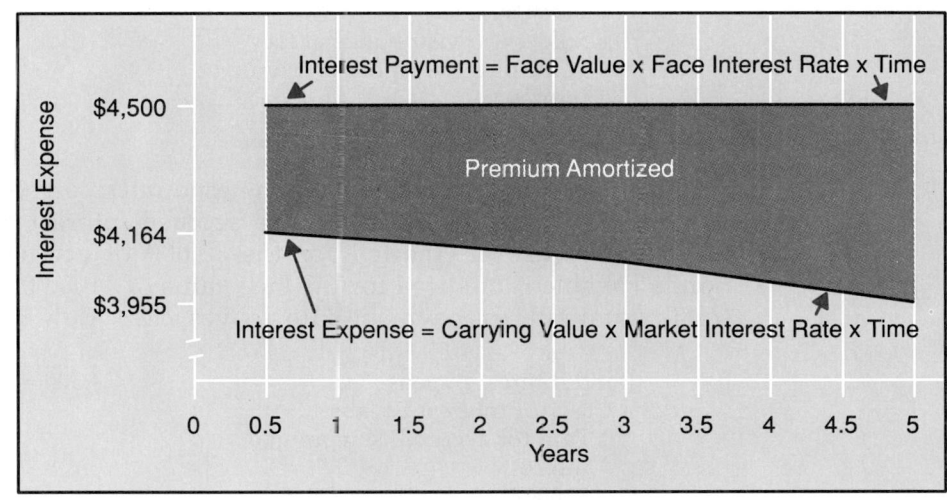

Sales of Bonds Between Interest Dates

OBJECTIVE 5
Account for bonds issued between interest dates and make year-end adjustments

Bonds may be issued on their interest date, as in the example above, but many times they are issued between interest payment dates. The generally accepted method of handling bonds issued in this manner is to collect from the investor the interest that has accrued since the last interest payment date. Then when the next interest period arrives, the corporation pays the investor the interest for the entire period. Thus the interest collected when bonds are sold is returned to the investor on the next interest payment date.

There are two reasons for following this procedure. The first is a practical one. If a company were to issue bonds on several different days and did not collect the accrued interest, records would have to be maintained for each bondholder and date of purchase. In such a case, the interest due each bondholder would have to be computed on the basis of different time periods. Clearly, large bookkeeping costs would be incurred under such a system. On the other hand, if accrued interest is collected when the bonds are sold, then on the interest payment date the corporation can pay the interest due for the entire period, eliminating the extra computations and costs.

The second reason for collecting accrued interest in advance is that when this amount is netted against the full interest paid on the interest payment date, the resulting interest expense is the amount for the time the money has been borrowed.

For example, assume that the Vason Corporation sold $100,000 of 9 percent, five-year bonds for face value on May 1, 19x0, rather than on January 1, 19x0, the issue date. The entries to record the sale of the bonds and payment of interest on July 1, 19x0 follow:

May 1	Cash	103,000	
	Bond Interest Expense		3,000
	Bonds Payable		100,000
	Sold 9%, 5-year bonds at face value plus four months' accrued interest		
	$100,000 \times .09 \times \frac{4}{12} = \$3,000$		

As shown, Cash is debited for the amount received, $103,000 (face value of $100,000 plus four months' accrued interest of $3,000). Bond Interest Expense is credited for the $3,000 of accrued interest, and Bonds Payable is credited for the face value of $100,000. When the first semiannual interest payment date arrives, the following entry is made:

July 1	Bond Interest Expense	4,500	
	Cash (or Interest Payable)		4,500
	Paid (or accrued) semiannual interest		
	$100,000 \times .09 \times \frac{1}{2} = \$4,500$		

Note that here the entire half-year interest is both debited to Bond Interest Expense and credited to Cash, because the corporation only pays bond interest once every six months, in full six-month amounts. Also note that the actual interest expense for the two months that the bonds were outstanding is $1,500. This amount is the net balance of the $4,500 debit to Bond Interest Expense on July 1 less the $3,000 credit to Bond Interest Expense on May 1. We can see these steps clearly in the posted entries in the ledger account for Bond Interest Expense on the next page.

Year-End Accrual for Bond Interest Expense

It is not often that bond interest payment dates will correspond to a company's fiscal year. An adjustment therefore must be made at the end of the accounting period to accrue the interest expense on the bonds from the last payment date to the end of the fiscal year. Further, if there

Bond Interest Expense						Account No. 723
					Balance	
Date	Item	Post. Ref.	Debit	Credit	Debit	Credit
19x0 May 1				3,000		3,000
July 1			4,500		1,500	

is any discount or premium on the bonds it must also be amortized for the fractional period.

Remember that in an earlier example, Vason Corporation issued $100,000 in bonds on January 1, 19x0 at 104.1 (see page 692). The company's fiscal year ends September 30, 19x0. In the period since the interest payment and amortization of premium on July 1, three months' interest has accrued, and the following adjusting entry under the effective interest method must be made:

Sept. 30	Bond Interest Expense	2,075.50	
	Unamortized Bond Premium	174.50	
	Interest Payable		2,250.00
	Accrued interest on 9% bonds payable for 3 months and amortized one-half of the premium for second interest payment period		

This entry covers one-half of the second interest period. Unamortized Bond Premium is debited for $174.50, which is one-half of $349, the amortization of premium for the second period from Table 17-2. Interest Payable is credited for $2,250, three months' interest on the face value of the bonds ($100,000 × .09 × ¼). The net debit figure of $2,075.50 ($2,250 − $174.50) is the bond interest expense for the three-month period.

When the January 1, 19x1 payment date arrives, the entry to pay the bondholders and amortize the premium is as follows:

Jan. 1	Bond Interest Expense	2,075.50	
	Interest Payable	2,250.00	
	Unamortized Bond Premium	174.50	
	Cash		4,500.00
	Paid semiannual interest including interest previously accrued and amortized the premium for the period since the end of the fiscal year		

As shown here, one-half ($2,250) of the amount paid ($4,500) was accrued on September 30. Unamortized Bond Premium is debited for the remaining amount to be amortized for the period ($349.00 − $174.50 = $174.50). The resulting bond interest expense is the amount that applies to the three-month period from September 30 to January 1.

Bond discounts are recorded at year end in the same way as bond premiums. The difference is that the amortization of bond discounts will increase interest expense instead of decreasing it as a premium does.

Retirement of Bonds

OBJECTIVE 6
Account for the retirement of bonds and the conversion of bonds into stock

Most bond issues provide a call feature. This feature gives the corporation a chance to buy back and retire the bonds at a given price, usually above face value, before maturity. Such bonds are known as **callable bonds**. They give the corporation flexibility in financing its operations. For example, if bond interest rates drop, the company can call its bonds and reissue debt at a lower interest rate. The bond indenture will state the time period and the prices at which the bonds can be redeemed. When a bond issue is retired before its maturity date, it is called **early extinguishment of debt**.

As an illustration of this feature, assume that Vason Corporation may call or retire the $100,000 bond issued at a premium (page 692) at 105, and that it decides to do so on July 1, 19x3. To avoid complexity, this illustration assumes retirement on an interest payment date. Because the bonds were issued on January 1, 19x0, the retirement takes place on the seventh interest payment date. Assume that the entry for the interest payment (which must be made) and the amortization of premium have been made. The entry to retire the bonds is as follows:

19x3			
July 1	Bonds Payable	100,000	
	Unamortized Bond Premium	1,447	
	Loss on Retirement of Bonds	3,553	
	Cash		105,000
	Retired 9% bonds at 105		

In this entry, the cash paid is the face value times the call price ($100,000 × 1.05 = $105,000). The unamortized bond premium can be found in column E of Table 17-2. The loss on retirement of bonds occurs because the call price of the bonds is greater than the carrying value ($105,000 − $101,447 = $3,553). The loss, if material, is presented as an extraordinary item on the income statement, as explained in Chapter 16.

Sometimes a rise in the market interest rate will cause the market value of the bonds to fall considerably below the face amount of the bond. If it has the cash to do so, the company may find it advantageous to purchase the bonds on the open market and retire them, rather than wait and pay them off at face value. An extraordinary gain is recognized in the difference between the purchase price of the bonds and the face value of the retired bonds. For example, assume that due to a rise in interest rates, Vason Corporation was able to purchase the $100,000 bond issue on the open market at 85, making it unnecessary to call the bonds at the higher price of 105. Then the entry would be as follows:

```
19x3
July 1   Bonds Payable                            100,000
            Unamortized Bond Premium                1,447
               Cash                                                85,000
               Gain on Retirement                                  16,447
                  of Bonds
                  Purchased and retired
                  9% bonds at 85
```

Conversion of Bonds into Common Stock

Bonds that may be exchanged for other securities of the corporation (in most cases common stock) are called **convertible bonds**. The conversion feature gives the investor a chance to make more money, because if the market price of the common stock rises, the value of the bond rises. However, if the price of the common stock does not rise, the investor still holds the bond and receives the periodic interest payment as well as the principal at the maturity date.

When a bondholder wishes to convert bonds into common stock, the rule is that the common stock is recorded at the carrying value of the bonds. The bond liability and associated unamortized discount or premium are written off the books. For this reason, no gain or loss is recorded on the transaction. For example, suppose that Vason Corporation's bonds are not called on July 1, 19x3. Instead, the corporation's bondholders decide to convert all the bonds to $8 par value common stock under a convertible provision of 40 shares of common stock for each $1,000 bond. The entry would be:

```
19x3
July 1   Bonds Payable                            100,000
            Unamortized Bond Premium                1,447
               Common Stock                                        32,000
               Paid-in Capital in Excess of Par
                  Value, Common                                    69,447
                  Converted 9% bonds payable
                  into common stock at a rate
                  of 40 shares for each $1,000 bond
```

The unamortized bond premium is found in column E of Table 17-2. At a rate of 40 shares for each $1,000 bond, 4,000 shares will be issued at a total par value of $32,000 (4,000 × $8). The Common Stock account is credited for the amount of the par value of the stock issued. Another account, called Paid-in Capital in Excess of Par Value, Common, is credited for the difference between the carrying value of the bonds and the par value of the stocks issued ($101,447 – $32,000 = $69,447). No gain or loss is recorded.

Other Long-Term Liabilities

A company may have other long-term liabilities besides bonds. The most common are mortgages payable, long-term leases, and pensions.

Mortgages Payable

OBJECTIVE 7
Explain the basic
features of
mortgages payable,
long-term leases,
and pensions as
long-term liabilities

A **mortgage** is a long-term debt secured by real property. It is usually paid in equal monthly installments. Each monthly payment includes interest on the debt and a reduction in the debt. To illustrate this point, Table 17-3 shows the first three monthly payments on a $50,000, 12 percent mortgage. The mortgage was obtained on June 1 and the monthly payments are $800. According to the table, the entry to record the July 1 payment would be as follows:

July 1	Mortgage Payable	300	
	Mortgage Interest Expense	500	
	Cash		800
	Made monthly mortgage payment		

Note from the entry and from Table 17-3 that the July 1 payment represents interest expense of $500 ($50,000 × .12 × $\frac{1}{12}$) and a reduction in the debt of $300 ($800 − $500). Therefore, the unpaid balance is reduced by the July payment to $49,700. The interest expense for August is slightly less than July's because of this decrease in the debt.

Long-Term Leases

There are several ways in which a company may obtain new operating assets. One way is to borrow the money and buy the asset. Another is to rent the equipment on a short-term lease. A third way is to obtain the

Table 17-3. Monthly Payment Schedule on $50,000, 12 Percent Mortgage

	A	B	C	D	E
Payment Date	Unpaid Balance at Beginning of Period	Monthly Payment	Interest for 1 Month at 1% on Unpaid Balance* (1% × A)	Reduction in Debt (B − C)	Unpaid Balance at End of Period (A − D)
June 1					$50,000
July 1	$50,000	$800	$500	$300	49,700
Aug. 1	49,700	800	497	303	49,397
Sept. 1	49,397	800	494	306	49,091

* Rounded to nearest dollar

equipment on a long-term lease. The first two methods cause no unusual accounting problems. In the first case, the asset and liability are recorded at the amount paid, and the asset is subject to periodic depreciation. In the second case, the lease is short-term or cancelable, and the risks of ownership lie with the lessor. This type of lease is called an **operating lease**. It is proper accounting to treat operating lease payments as an expense and to debit the amount of each monthly payment to Rent Expense.

The third case, a long-term lease, is one of the fastest-growing ways of financing operating equipment in the U.S. today. It has several advantages. For instance, it requires no immediate cash payment. The rental payment is deducted in full for tax purposes. And it costs less than a short-term lease. Acquiring the use of a plant asset under a long-term lease does cause several accounting problems, however. Often, such leases may not be canceled. Also, their length may be about the same as the useful life of the asset. Finally, they may provide for the lessee to buy the asset at a nominal price at the end of the lease. The lease is much like an installment purchase because the risks of ownership lie with the lessee. Not only the lessee company's available assets but its legal obligations (liabilities) increase, because it must make a number of payments over the life of the asset.

Noting this problem, the Financial Accounting Standards Board has described such a long-term lease as a **capital lease**. This term reflects the provisions of the lease, which make the transaction more like a purchase or sale on installment. The FASB has ruled that in the case of a capital lease, the lessee must record an asset and a long-term liability equal to the present value of the total lease payments during the lease term. In doing so, the lessee must use the present value at the beginning of the lease.[4] In much the same way as the mortgage payments above, each lease payment becomes partly interest expense and partly a repayment of debt. Further, depreciation expense is figured on the asset and entered on the records of the lessee.

Suppose, for example, that Isaacs Company enters into a long-term lease for a machine used in its manufacturing operations. The lease terms call for an annual payment of $4,000 for six years, which approximates the useful life of the machine. (See Table 17-4.) At the end of the lease period, the title to the machine passes to Isaacs. This lease is clearly a capital lease and should be recorded according to FASB *Statement No. 13*.

A lease is a periodic payment for the right to use an asset or assets. Present value techniques, explained in Appendix A, can be used to value the asset and the corresponding liability associated with a capital lease. If Isaacs' usual interest cost is 16 percent, the present value of the lease payments may be computed as follows:

Periodic payment × factor (Table B-4: 16%, 6 years) = present value
$4,000 × 3.685 = $14,740

---

4. *Statement of Financial Accounting Standards No. 13*, "Accounting for Leases" (Stamford, Conn.: Financial Accounting Standards Board, 1976), par. 10.

Table 17-4. Payment Schedule on 16 Percent Capital Lease				
	A	B	C	D
Year	Lease Payment	Interest (16%) on Unpaid Obligation (D × 16%)	Reduction of Lease Obligation (A – B)	Balance of Lease Obligation
Beginning				$14,740.00
1	$ 4,000	$2,358.40	$ 1,641.60	13,098.40
2	4,000	2,095.74	1,904.26	11,194.14
3	4,000	1,791.06	2,208.94	8,985.20
4	4,000	1,437.63	2,562.37	6,422.83
5	4,000	1,027.65	2,972.35	3,450.48
6	4,000	549.52 *	3,450.48	—
	$24,000	$9,260.00	$14,740.00	

* The last year's interest equals the lease payment minus the remaining balance of the lease obligation ($549.52 = $4,000 – $3,450.48) and does not exactly equal $552.08 ($3,450.48 × 0.16) because of cumulative rounding errors.

The entry to record the lease contract is

Equipment Under Capital Lease	14,740	
Obligations Under Capital Lease		14,740

Equipment Under Capital Lease is classified as a long-term asset; Obligations Under Capital Lease is classified as a long-term liability. Each year, Isaacs must record depreciation on the leased asset. If we assume straight-line depreciation, a six-year life, and no salvage value, the entry will be

Depreciation Expense	2,456.67	
Accumulated Depreciation, Leased Equipment Under Capital Lease		2,456.67

The amount of interest expense for each year would be computed by multiplying the interest rate (16 percent) by the amount of the remaining lease obligation. Table 17-4 shows these calculations. Using the data presented in Table 17-4, the first lease payment would be recorded as follows:

Interest Expense (col. B)	2,358.40	
Obligations Under Capital Lease (col. C)	1,641.60	
Cash		4,000.00

Pensions

Most employees who work for medium-sized and large companies are covered by some sort of pension plan. A **pension plan** is a contract between the company and its employees wherein the company agrees to pay benefits to employees after retirement. Most companies contribute the full cost of the pension, but sometimes the employees also pay part of their salary or wages toward their pension. The contributions from both parties are generally paid into a **pension fund**, from which benefits are paid out to retirees. In most cases, pension benefits consist of monthly payments to employees after retirement and other payments on death or disability.

There are two kinds of pension plans. Under *defined contribution plans*, the employer is required to contribute an annual amount determined in the current year on the basis of agreements between the company and its employees or resolution of the board of directors. Retirement payments will depend on the amount of pension payments the accumulated contributions can support. Under *defined benefit plans*, the employer's required annual contribution is the amount required to fund pension liabilities that arise as a result of employment in the current year but whose amount will not be finally determined until the retirement and death of the persons currently employed. Here the amount of the contribution required in the current year depends on a fixed amount of future benefits but uncertain current contributions; whereas under a defined contribution plan, the uncertain future amount of pension liabilities depends on the cumulative amounts of fixed current contributions.

Accounting for annual pension expense under defined contribution plans is simple. After determining what contribution is required, Pension Expense is debited and a liability (or Cash) is credited.

Accounting for annual expense under defined benefit plans is one of the most complex topics in accounting; thus, the intricacies are reserved for advanced courses. In concept, however, the procedure is simple.

First, the amount of pension expense is determined. Then, if the amount of cash contributed to the fund is less than the pension expense, a liability results which is reported on the balance sheet. If the amount of cash paid to the pension plan exceeds the pension expense, a prepaid expense arises and appears on the asset side of the balance sheet. For example, the December 31, 1986 annual report for Goodyear Tire & Rubber Company included among other assets on the balance sheet deferred pension plan costs of $320.2 million.

In accordance with *Statement No. 87*, all companies should use the same actuarial method to compute pension expense.[5] However, because many estimates, such as average remaining service life of active employees, expected long-run return on pension plan assets, and expected future salary increases, must be estimated, the computation of

---

5. *Statement of Financial Accounting Standards No. 87*, "Employers' Accounting for Pensions" (Stamford, Conn.: Financial Accounting Standards Board, 1985).

pension expense is not simple. In addition, actuarial terminology further complicates pension accounting. In nontechnical terms, the pension expense for the year includes not only the cost of the benefits earned by people working during the year but interest costs on the total pension obligation (which is calculated on the present value of future benefits to be paid) and other adjustments. These costs are reduced by the expected return on the pension fund assets.

Beginning in 1989, all employers whose pension plans do not have sufficient assets to cover the present value of their pension benefit obligations (on a termination basis) must record the amount of the shortfall as a liability on their balance sheets. The investor will no longer have to read the notes to the financial statements to learn whether the pension plan is fully funded. However, if a pension plan does have sufficient assets to cover its obligations, then no balance sheet reporting is required or permitted.

Chapter Review

Review of Learning Objectives

1. **Identify and contrast the major characteristics of bonds.**
   When bonds are issued, the corporation enters into a contract with the bondholders, called a bond indenture. The bond indenture identifies the major conditions of the bonds. A corporation may issue several types of bonds, each having different characteristics. For example, a bond issue may or may not require security (secured versus unsecured). It may be payable at a single time (term) or at several times (serial). The holder may receive interest automatically (registered) or may have to return coupons to receive interest payable (coupon bond). The bond may be callable or convertible into other securities.

2. **Record the issuance of bonds at face value and at a discount or premium.**
   When bonds are issued, the bondholders will pay an amount equal to, greater than, or less than the face value of the bond. A bondholder will pay face value for the bonds when the interest rate on the bonds approximates the market rate for similar investments. The issuing corporation records the issuance of bonds as a long-term liability, called Bonds Payable, equal to the face value of the bonds.

   Bonds are issued at a rate less than face value when the bond interest rate is below the market rate for similar investments. The difference between face value and issue price is called a discount and is debited to Unamortized Bond Discount.

   If the interest rate on bonds is greater than the return on similar investments, investors will be willing to pay more than face value for the bonds. The difference between issue price and face value is called a premium and is credited to Unamortized Bond Premium.

3. **Determine the value of bonds using present values.**
   The value of a bond may be determined by summing the present values of (a) the series of fixed interest payments of a bond issue and (b) the single

payment of the face value at maturity. Tables B-4 and B-3 in Appendix B should be used in making those computations.

4. **Amortize (a) bond discounts and (b) bond premiums by using the straight-line and effective interest methods.**

When bonds are sold at a premium or discount, the result is an adjustment of the interest rate on the bonds from the face rate to an effective rate that is close to the market rate when the bonds were issued. Therefore, bond premiums or discounts have the effect of increasing or decreasing the interest paid on the bonds over their life. Under these conditions, it is necessary to amortize the premium or discount over the life of the bonds by either the straight-line or effective interest method. The straight-line method allocates a fixed portion of the bond discount or premium each interest period to adjust the interest payment to interest expense.

The effective interest method, which is used when the effects of amortization are material, results in a constant rate of interest on the carrying value of the bonds. To find interest and the amortization of premiums or discounts we apply the effective interest rate to the carrying value (face value plus premium or minus discount) of the bonds at the beginning of the interest period. The amount of premium or discount to be amortized is the difference between the interest figured by using the effective rate and that obtained by using the stated or face rate. The effects of the effective interest method on bonds issued at par value, at a discount, and at a premium may be summarized as follows:

	Bonds Issued at		
	Face Value	**Discount**	**Premium**
Trend in Carrying Value over Bond Term	constant	increasing	decreasing
Trend in Interest Expense over Bond Term	constant	increasing	decreasing
Interest Expense vs. Interest Payments	expense = interest expense payments	expense > interest expense payments	expense < interest expense payments
Classification of Bond Discount or Premium		contra liability (deducted from Bonds Payable)	liability (added to Bonds Payable)

5. **Account for bonds issued between interest dates and make year-end adjustments.**

If the bonds are sold on dates between the interest payment dates, the issuing corporation collects from the investor the interest that has accrued since the last interest payment date. When the next interest payment date arrives, the corporation pays the bondholder interest for the entire interest period.

When the end of a corporation's fiscal year does not agree with interest payment dates, the corporation must accrue bond interest expense from the last interest payment date to the end of the company's fiscal year. This accrual results in the inclusion of the interest expense in the year incurred.

6. **Account for the retirement of bonds and the conversion of bonds into stock.**

   Callable bonds may be retired before maturity at the option of the issuing corporation. The call price is usually an amount greater than the face value of the bonds so the corporation usually recognizes a loss on the retirement of the bonds. An extraordinary gain may also be recognized on early extinguishment of debt, which results when a company purchases its bonds on the open market. This retirement method can be used when a rise in the market interest rate causes the market value of the bonds to fall.

   Convertible bonds allow the bondholder to convert bonds to stock in the issuing corporation. In this case, the common stocks issued are recorded at the carrying value of the bonds being converted. No gain or loss is recognized.

7. **Explain the basic features of mortgages payable, long-term leases, and pensions as long-term liabilities.**

   A mortgage is a type of long-term debt secured by real property. It is usually paid in equal monthly installments. Each payment is partly interest expense and partly debt repayment. If a long-term lease is a capital lease, the risks of ownership lie with the lessee. Like a mortgage payment, each lease payment is partly interest and partly reduction of debt. For a capital lease, then, both an asset and a long-term liability should be recorded. The liability should be equal to the present value at the beginning of the lease of the total lease payments during the lease term. The recorded asset is subject to depreciation. Pension expense must be recorded in the current period.

Review of Concepts and Terminology

The following concepts and terms were introduced in this chapter:

(L.O. 1)   **Bond:**   A security, usually long-term, representing money borrowed by a corporation from the investing public.

(L.O. 1)   **Bond certificate:**   Evidence of a company's debt to the bondholder.

(L.O. 1)   **Bond indenture:**   A supplementary agreement to a bond issue that defines the rights, privileges, and limitations of bondholders.

(L.O. 1)   **Bond issue:**   The total number of bonds that are issued at one time.

(L.O. 6)   **Callable bonds:**   Bonds that a corporation may buy back and retire at a given price, usually above face value, before maturity.

(L.O. 7)   **Capital lease:**   A long-term lease in which the risk of ownership lies with the lessee, and whose terms resemble a purchase or sale.

(L.O. 6)   **Convertible bonds:**   Bonds that may be exchanged for other securities of the corporation, usually common stock.

(L.O. 1) **Coupon bonds:** Bonds that generally are not registered with the issuing corporation but instead bear interest coupons stating the amount of interest due and the payment date.

(L.O. 2) **Discount:** The amount by which the face value of a bond exceeds the issue price; for bonds issued when the market rate of interest is greater than the face interest rate.

(L.O. 6) **Early extinguishment of debt:** The purchase by a company of its own bonds on the open market in order to retire the debt at less than face value.

(L.O. 4) **Effective interest method:** A method of amortizing bond discount or premium in which a constant interest rate, the effective rate (market rate) at the time the bonds were issued, is applied to the carrying value of the bonds at the beginning of each interest period.

(L.O. 4) **Effective rate:** The interest rate used to amortize bond interest discounts and premiums under the effective interest rate method; equal to the market rate of interest at the time the bonds are issued.

(L.O. 2) **Face interest rate:** The rate of interest paid to the bondholders based on the face value or principal of the bonds.

(L.O. 2) **Market interest rate:** The rate of interest paid in the market by bond investors for bonds of similar risk.

(L.O. 7) **Mortgage:** A type of long-term debt secured by real property that is usually paid in equal monthly installments.

(L.O. 7) **Operating lease:** A short-term, cancelable lease for which the risks of ownership lie with the lessor, and whose payments are recorded as a rent expense.

(L.O. 7) **Pension fund:** A fund established through contributions from an employer and sometimes employees that pays pension benefits to employees after retirement or on their death or disability.

(L.O. 7) **Pension plan:** A contract between a company and its employees under which the company agrees to pay benefits to employees after their retirement.

(L.O. 2) **Premium:** The amount by which the issue price of a bond exceeds the face value; for bonds issued when the market rate of interest is less than the face interest rate.

(L.O. 1) **Registered bonds:** Bonds for which the name and address of the bond owner are recorded with the issuing company.

(L.O. 1) **Secured bonds:** Bonds that give the bondholders a pledge of certain assets of the company as a guarantee of repayment.

(L.O. 1) **Serial bonds:** A bond issue with several different maturity dates.

(L.O. 4) **Straight-line method:** A method of amortizing bond discount or premium in which amortization of the discount or premium is equal for each interest period over the life of the bond.

(L.O. 1) **Term bonds:** Bonds of a bond issue that all mature at the same time.

(L.O. 1) **Unsecured bonds (debenture bonds):** Bonds issued on the general credit of a company.

(L.O. 4) **Zero coupon bonds:** Bonds that do not pay periodic interest, but are simply a promise to pay a fixed amount at the maturity date. The only interest earned by the buyer or paid by the issuer is the discount on the issue date.

Self-Test

Test your knowledge of the chapter by choosing the best answer for each item below.

1. A bond indenture is
   a. a bond which has past due interest payments.
   b. a bond which is secured by specific assets of the issuing corporation.
   c. an agreement between the issuing corporation and the bondholders.
   d. a bond which is unsecured.   *(L.O. 1)*

2. Ten $1,000 bonds issued at 98.5 on the interest date result in a debit to the Cash account for
   a. $9,850.00.   c. $985.00.
   b. $980.50.   d. $10,000.00.   *(L.O. 2)*

3. The current value of a bond may be determined by calculating the present value of
   a. the face value of the bond.
   b. the interest payments.
   c. the interest payments plus any discount or minus any premium.
   d. the interest payments plus the face value of the bond.   *(L.O. 3)*

4. When the straight-line method of amortization is used for a bond discount, the amount of interest expense for an interest period is calculated by
   a. deducting the amount of discount amortization for the period from the amount of cash paid for interest during the period.
   b. adding the amount of discount amortization for the period to the amount of cash paid for interest during the period.
   c. multiplying the face value of the bonds by the face interest rate.
   d. multiplying the carrying value of the bonds by the effective interest rate.   *(L.O. 4)*

5. The total interest cost on a ten-year, 9 percent, $1,000 bond that is issued at 95 is
   a. $50.00.   c. $900.00.
   b. $140.00.   d. $950.00.   *(L.O. 4)*

6. If the market rate of interest is lower than the face interest rate at the date of issuance, bonds
   a. will sell at a discount.
   b. will sell at a premium.
   c. will sell at face value.
   d. will not sell until the face interest rate is adjusted.   *(L.O. 4)*

7. Medco Corporation issued a ten-year, 10 percent bond payable in 19x4 at a premium. During 19x5, the company's accountant failed to amortize any of the bond premium. The omission of the premium amortization will
   a. not affect net income reported for 19x5.
   b. cause net income for 19x5 to be overstated.
   c. cause net income for 19x5 to be understated.
   d. cause retained earnings at the end of 19x5 to be overstated. *(L.O. 4)*

8. The Kuger Corporation has authorized a bond issue with interest payment dates of January 1 and July 1. If the bonds are sold at face amount on March 1, the amount of cash to be received by the issuer is equal to the face amount of the bonds
   a. plus the interest accrued from March 1 to July 1.
   b. plus the interest accrued from January 1 to March 1.
   c. minus the interest accrued from March 1 to July 1.
   d. minus the interest accrued from January 1 to March 1.   *(L.O. 5)*

9. Bonds which contain a provision that allows the holders to exchange the bonds for other securities of the issuing corporation are called
   a. secured bonds.   c. debenture bonds.
   b. callable bonds.   d. convertible bonds.   *(L.O. 6)*

10. Which of the following is most likely a capital lease?
    a. A five-year lease on a new building
    b. A two-year lease on a truck with an option to renew for one more year
    c. A five-year lease on a computer with an option to buy for a small amount at the end of the lease
    d. A monthly lease on a building that can be canceled with ninety days' notice   *(L.O. 7)*

Answers to Self-Test are at the end of this chapter.

Review Problem
Interest and Amortization
of Bond Discount, Bond Retirement, and Bond Conversion

(L. O. 2, 4, 6)   When the Merrill Manufacturing Company was expanding its metal window division in Utah, the company did not have enough capital to finance the expansion. Thus, management sought and received approval from the board of directors to issue bonds for the activity. The company planned to issue $5,000,000 of 8 percent, five-year bonds in 19x1. Interest would be paid on December 31 and June 30 of each year. The bonds would be callable at 104, and each $1,000 bond would be convertible into 30 shares of $10 par value common stock.

The bonds were sold at 96 on January 1, 19x1 because the market rate for similar investments was 9 percent. The company decided to amortize the bond discount by using the effective interest method. On July 1, 19x3, management called and retired half the bonds, and investors converted the other half into common stock.

Required   1. Prepare an interest and amortization schedule for the first five interest payment dates.
2. Prepare the journal entries to record the sale of the bonds, the first two interest payments, the bond retirement, and the bond conversion.

Answer to Review Problem

1. Schedule for first five periods prepared

				Interest and Amortization of Bond Discount			

Semiannual Interest Payment	Carrying Value at Beginning of Period	Semi-annual Interest Expense* (9% × ½)	Semi-annual Interest Paid per Period (8% × ½)	Amortiza-tion of Discount	Unamortized Bond Discount at End of Period	Carrying Value at End of Period
Jan. 1, 19x1					$200,000	$4,800,000
June 30, 19x1	$4,800,000	$216,000	$200,000	$16,000	184,000	4,816,000
Dec. 31, 19x1	4,816,000	216,720	200,000	16,720	167,280	4,832,720
June 30, 19x2	4,832,720	217,472	200,000	17,472	149,808	4,850,192
Dec. 31, 19x2	4,850,192	218,259	200,000	18,259	131,549	4,868,451
June 30, 19x3	4,868,451	219,080	200,000	19,080	112,469	4,887,531

* Rounded to nearest dollar

2. Journal entries prepared

```
19x1
Jan.   1  Cash                                      4,800,000
          Unamortized Bond Discount                   200,000
             Bond Payable                                        5,000,000
                Sold $5,000,000
                of 8% bonds at 96

June 30  Bond Interest Expense                        216,000
            Unamortized Bond Discount                             16,000
            Cash                                                 200,000
               Paid semiannual interest and
               amortized discount on 8%,
               five-year bonds

Dec. 31  Bond Interest Expense                        216,720
            Unamortized Bond Discount                             16,720
            Cash                                                 200,000
               Paid semiannual interest and
               amortized discount on 8%,
               five-year bonds

19x3
July   1  Bonds Payable                              2,500,000
          Loss on Retirement of Bonds Payable          156,235
             Unamortized Bond Discount                            56,235
             Cash                                              2,600,000
                Called $2,500,000 of 8% bonds
                and retired them at 104
                $112,469 × ½ = $56,235*
```

        * Rounded

July 1 Bonds Payable	2,500,000	
Unamortized Bond Discount		56,234
Common Stock		750,000
Paid-in Capital in Excess of Par Value		1,693,766

Converted $2,500,000 of 8% bonds
into common stock:
2,500 × 30 shares = 75,000 shares
75,000 shares × $10 = $750,000
$112,469 − $56,235 = $56,234*

* Rounded

Chapter Assignments

Discussion Questions and Writing Assignments

1. What is the difference between a bond certificate, a bond issue, and a bond indenture? What are some examples of items found in a bond indenture?
2. What are the essential differences between (a) secured versus debenture bonds, (b) term versus serial bonds, and (c) registered versus coupon bonds?
3. Napier Corporation sold $500,000 of 5 percent bonds on the interest payment date. What would the proceeds from the sale be if the bonds were issued at 95, at 100, and at 102?
4. If you were buying a bond on which the face interest rate was less than the market interest rate, would you expect to pay more or less than par value for the bonds? Why?
5. Why does the amortization of a bond discount increase interest expense to an amount above that of interest paid? Why does a premium have the opposite effect?
6. When the effective interest rate method of amortizing bond discount or premium is used, why does the amount of interest expense change from period to period?
7. When bonds are issued between interest dates, why is it necessary for the issuer to collect an amount equal to accrued interest from the buyer?
8. Why would a company want to exercise the callable provision of a bond when it can wait longer to pay off the debt?
9. What are the advantages of convertible bonds to the company issuing them and to the investor?
10. What are the two components of a uniform monthly mortgage payment?
11. Under what conditions is a long-term lease called a capital lease? Why should the accountant record both an asset and a liability in connection with this type of lease? What items should appear on the income statement as the result of such a lease?
12. What is a pension plan? What assumptions must be made to account for the expenses of such a plan?
13. What is the difference between a defined contribution plan and a defined benefit plan? In general, how is expense determined under each?

Classroom Exercises[6]

Exercise 17-1.
Journal Entries for
Interest Using the
Straight-Line
Method
(L.O. 2, 4)

Plantation Corporation issued $2,000,000 in 10 1/2 percent, ten-year bonds on February 1, 19x1, at 104. The semiannual interest payment dates are February 1 and August 1.

Prepare journal entries for the issue of bonds by Plantation on February 1, 19x1, and the first two interest payments on August 1, 19x1 and February 1, 19x2, using the straight-line method (ignore year-end accruals).

Exercise 17-2.
Journal Entries for
Interest Using the
Straight-Line
Method
(L.O. 2, 4)

Brennan Corporation issued $4,000,000 in 8 1/2 percent, five-year bonds on March 1, 19x1, at 96. The semiannual interest payment dates are March 1 and September 1.

Prepare journal entries for the issue of the bonds by Brennan on March 1, 19x1, and the first two interest payments on September 1, 19x1 and March 1, 19x2, using the straight-line method (ignore year-end accruals).

Exercise 17-3.
Journal Entries for
Interest Using the
Effective Interest
Method
(L.O. 2, 4)

The Mayfair Drapery Company sold $500,000 of its 9 1/2 percent, twenty-year bonds on April 1, 19xx, at 106. The semiannual interest payment dates are April 1 and October 1. The effective interest rate is approximately 8.9 percent. The company's fiscal year ends September 30.

Prepare journal entries to record the sale of the bonds on April 1, the accrual of interest and amortization of premium on September 30, and the first interest payment on October 1. Use the effective interest method to amortize the premium.

Exercise 17-4.
Journal Entries for
Interest Using the
Effective Interest
Method
(L.O. 2, 4)

On March 1, 19x1, the Clayton Corporation issued $600,000 of five-year, 10 percent bonds. The semiannual interest payment dates are March 1 and September 1. Because the market rate for similar investments was 11 percent, the bonds had to be issued at a discount. The discount on the issuance of the bonds was $24,335. The company's fiscal year ends February 28.

Prepare journal entries to record the bond issue on March 1, 19x1; the payment of interest and amortization of the discount on September 1, 19x1; the accrual of interest and amortization of discount on February 28, 19x2; and the payment of interest on March 1, 19x2. Use the effective interest method.

Exercise 17-5.
Journal Entries for
Interest Payments
Using the Effective
Interest Method
(L.O. 4)

The long-term debt section of the Discovery Corporation's balance sheet at the end of its fiscal year, December 31, 1988, is as follows:

Long-Term Liabilities
    Bonds Payable—8%, interest payable

1/1 and 7/1, due 12/31/03	$500,000	
Less Unamortized Bond Discount	40,000	$460,000

6. Bond interest rates are most often quoted in eighths of a percent. Some exercises and problems in this chapter quote the rates in tenths of a percent to ease the burden of computation.

Prepare the journal entries relevant to the interest payments on July 1, 1989, December 31, 1989, and January 1, 1990. Assume an effective interest rate of 10 percent.

Exercise 17-6.
Valuing Bonds
Using Present
Value
(L.O. 3)

Lakeshore, Inc. is considering two bond issues. (a) One is a $400,000 bond issue that pays semiannual interest of $32,000 and is due in twenty years. (b) The other is a $400,000 bond issue that pays semiannual interest of $30,000 and is due in fifteen years. Assume that the market rate of interest for each bond is 12 percent.

Calculate the amount that Lakeshore, Inc. will receive if both bond issues occur. (Calculate the present value of each bond issue and sum.)

Exercise 17-7.
Coupon
Bonds
(L.O. 3)

Using the present value tables in Appendix B, calculate the issue price of a $600,000 bond issue in each of the following independent cases, assuming that interest is paid semiannually:

a. a ten-year, 8% bond issue; market rate of interest is 10%.
b. a ten-year, 8% bond issue; market rate of interest is 6%.
c. a ten-year, 10% bond issue; market rate of interest is 8%.
d. a twenty-year, 10% bond issue; market rate of interest is 12%.
e. a twenty-year, 10% bond issue; market rate of interest is 6%.

Exercise 17-8.
Zero Coupon
Bonds
(L.O. 3)

The Commonwealth of Kentucky needs to raise $50,000,000 for highway repairs. Officials are considering issuing zero coupon bonds, which have no periodic interest payments. The current market rate of interest for the bonds is 10 percent. What face value of bonds must be issued to raise the needed funds, assuming the bonds will be due in thirty years and compounded annually? How would your answer change if the bonds were due in fifty years?

How would both answers change if the market rate of interest were 8 percent instead of 10 percent?

Exercise 17-9.
Time Value of
Money and Early
Extinguishment of
Debt
(L.O. 3, 6)

Nelson, Inc. has a $700,000, 8 percent bond issue that was issued a number of years ago at face value. There are now ten years left on the bond issue, and the market rate of interest is 16 percent. Interest is paid semiannually.

1. Figure the current market value of the bond issue, using present value tables.
2. Record the retirement of the bonds, assuming the company purchases the bonds on the open market at the calculated value.

Exercise 17-10.
Bond Issue Entries
(L.O. 2, 5)

Microfilm is authorized to issue $900,000 in bonds on June 1. The bonds carry a face interest rate of 9 percent, which is to be paid on June 1 and December 1.

Prepare journal entries for the issue of the bonds by Microfilm under the assumptions that (a) the bonds are issued on September 1 at 100 and (b) the bonds are issued on June 1 at 105.

Exercise 17-11.
Sales of Bonds
Between Interest
Dates
(L.O. 5)

Tripp Corporation sold $200,000 of 12 percent, ten-year bonds for face value on September 1, 19xx. The issue date of the bonds was May 1, 19xx.

1. Record the sale of the bonds on September 1 and the first semiannual interest payment on November 1, 19xx.
2. The company's fiscal year ends on December 31 and the above is its only bond issue. What is the bond interest expense for the year ending December 31, 19xx?

Exercise 17-12.
Year-End Accrual
of Bond Interest
(L.O. 2, 4, 5)

Rex Corporation issued $500,000 of 9 percent bonds on October 1, 19x1, at 96. The bonds are dated October 1 and pay interest semiannually. The market rate of interest is 10 percent and the company's year end is December 31.

Prepare the entries to record the issuance of the bonds, the accrual of the interest on December 31, 19x1, and the payment of the first semiannual interest on April 1, 19x2. Assume the company does not use reversing entries and uses the effective interest method to amortize bond discount.

Exercise 17-13.
Bond Retirement
Journal Entry
(L.O. 6)

The Figaro Corporation has outstanding $800,000 of 8 percent bonds callable at 104. On September 1, immediately after recording the payment of the semiannual interest and amortization of discount, the unamortized bond discount equaled $21,000. On that date, $480,000 of the bonds were called and retired.

Prepare the entry to record the retirement of the bonds on September 1.

Exercise 17-14.
Bond Conversion
Journal Entry
(L.O. 6)

The Gallery Corporation has $400,000 of 6 percent bonds outstanding. There is $20,000 of unamortized discount remaining on these bonds after the July 1, 19x8 semiannual interest payment. The bonds are convertible at the rate of 40 shares of $5 par value common stock for each $1,000 bond. On July 1, 19x8, bondholders presented $300,000 of the bonds for conversion.

Prepare the journal entry to record the conversion of the bonds.

Exercise 17-15.
Mortgage Payable
(L.O. 7)

Inland Corporation purchased a building by signing a $150,000 long-term mortgage with monthly payments of $2,000. The mortgage carries an interest rate of 12 percent.

1. For the first three months, prepare a monthly payment schedule showing the monthly payment, the interest for the month, the reduction in debt, and the unpaid balance. (Round to the nearest dollar.)
2. Prepare a journal entry to record the purchase and the first two monthly payments.

Exercise 17-16.
Recording Lease
Obligations
(L.O. 7)

Profile Corporation has leased a piece of equipment that has a useful life of twelve years. The terms of the lease are $21,500 per year for twelve years. Profile is currently able to borrow money at a long-term interest rate of 15 percent.

1. Calculate the present value of the lease.
2. Prepare the journal entry to record the lease agreement.
3. Prepare the entry to record depreciation of the equipment for the first year using the straight-line method.
4. Prepare the entries to record the lease payment for the first two years.

Interpreting Accounting Information

Franklin Savings Association
(L.O. 2, 3, 4)

A notice appeared in the November 16, 1984, *Wall Street Journal* stating that Franklin Savings Association of Kansas was issuing $2.9 billion in zero coupon bonds. "The Bonds do not pay interest periodically. The only scheduled payment to the holder of a Bond will be the amount at maturity," the ad read. The details of two components of the issue were as follows:

$500,000,000 Bonds due December 12, 2014, at 3.254%
$500,000,000 Bonds due December 12, 2024, at 1.380%

plus accrued amortization. if any, of the original issue discount from December 12, 1984, to date of delivery.

Required

1. Assuming all the bonds were issued on December 12, 1984, make the general journal entry to record each component shown above.
2. Determine the approximate effective interest rate on each of the two components of the bond issue. Assume that interest is compounded annually. **Hint:** Use Table B-3.
3. Prepare general journal entries to record bond interest expense for each of the first two years (December 12, 1985 and 1986) on the component of the bond due in 2014 (ignore effects of fiscal year ends). What advantages or disadvantages are there to Franklin in issuing zero coupon bonds?

Problem Set A

**Problem 17A-1.
Bond Transactions—Straight-Line Method**
(L.O. 2, 4, 5)

Marconi Corporation has $10,000,000 of 10½ percent, twenty-year bonds dated June 1, with interest payment dates of May 30 and November 30. The company's fiscal year ends December 31. It uses the straight-line method to amortize premium or discount.

Required

1. Assume the bonds were issued at 103 on June 1. Prepare general journal entries for June 1, November 30, and December 31.
2. Assume the bonds were issued at 97 on June 1. Prepare general journal entries for June 1, November 30, and December 31.
3. Assume the bonds are issued at face value plus accrued interest on August 1. Prepare general journal entries for August 1, November 30, and December 31.

**Problem 17A-2.
Bond Transactions—Effective Interest Method**
(L.O. 2, 4, 5)

Aparicio Corporation has $8,000,000 of 9½ percent, twenty-five-year bonds dated March 1, with interest payable on March 1 and September 1. The company's fiscal year ends on November 30. It uses the effective interest method to amortize premium or discount. Round amounts to nearest dollar.

Required

1. Assume the bonds were issued at 102.5 on March 1, to yield an effective interest rate of 9.2 percent. Prepare general journal entries for March 1, September 1, and November 30.

2. Assume the bonds were issued at 97.5 on March 1, to yield an effective interest rate of 9.8 percent. Prepare general journal entries for March 1, September 1, and November 30.
3. Assume the bonds were issued on June 1 at face value plus accrued interest. Prepare general journal entries for June 1, September 1, and November 30.

Problem 17A-3.
Bonds Issued at
Discount and
Premium
(L.O. 2, 4, 5)

Chambliss Corporation sold bonds twice during 19x2. A summary of the transactions involving these bonds follows.

19x2
Jan. 1   Issued $3,000,000 of 9%/10 percent, ten-year bonds dated January 1, 19x2, with interest payable on December 31 and June 30. The bonds were sold at 102.6, resulting in an effective interest rate of 9.4 percent.

Mar. 1   Issued $2,000,000 of 9⅕ percent, ten-year bonds dated March 1, 19x2, with interest payable March 1 and September 1. The bonds were sold at 98.2, resulting in an effective interest rate of 9.5 percent.

June 30   Paid semiannual interest on the January 1 issue and amortized the premium, using the effective interest method.

Sept. 1   Paid semiannual interest on the March 1 issue and amortized the discount, using the effective interest method.

Dec. 31   Paid the semiannual interest on the January 1 issue and amortized the premium, using the effective interest method.

31   Made an end-of-year adjusting entry to accrue the interest on the March 1 issue and amortize two-thirds of the discount applicable to the second interest period.

19x3
Mar. 1   Paid the semiannual interest on the March 1 issue and amortized the remainder of the discount applicable to the second interest period.

Required

Prepare general journal entries to record the bond transactions. Round amounts to nearest dollar.

Problem 17A-4.
Bond and
Mortgage
Transactions
Contrasted
(L.O. 2, 4, 5, 7)

Munson Grocery Stores, Inc. is expanding its operations by buying a chain of four outlets in another city. To finance this purchase of land and buildings, Munson is getting a $2,000,000 mortgage that carries an interest rate of 12 percent and requires monthly payments of $27,000. To finance the rest of the purchase, Munson is issuing $2,000,000 of 12½ percent unsecured bonds due in twenty years, with interest payable December 31 and June 30.

The company's fiscal year ends March 31. Selected transactions related to these two financing activities are as follows:

Jan. 1   Issued the bonds for cash at 104 to yield an effective rate of 12 percent.

Feb. 1   Issued the mortgage in exchange for land and buildings. The land represents 15 percent of the purchase price.

Mar. 1   Made first mortgage payment.

31   Made the year-end adjusting entry to accrue interest on the bonds and amortize the premium, using the effective interest method.

Apr. 1 Made second mortgage payment.
May 1 Made third mortgage payment.
June 1 Made fourth mortgage payment.
      30 Made the first semiannual interest payment on the bonds and amortized the premium for the time period since the end of the fiscal year.
July 1 Made fifth mortgage payment.
Dec. 1 Made tenth mortgage payment.
      31 Made the second semiannual interest payment on the bonds and amortized the premium for the time period since the last payment.

Required

1. Prepare a payment schedule for the mortgage for ten months using these headings (round amounts to the nearest dollar): Payment Date, Unpaid Balance at Beginning of Period, Monthly Payment, Interest for One Month at 1% on Unpaid Balance, Reduction in Debt, and Unpaid Balance at End of Period.
2. Prepare the journal entries for the selected transactions. (Ignore the mortgage payments for August 1 through November 1.)

Problem 17A-5.
Bond Interest and
Amortization Table
and Bond
Retirements
(L.O. 2, 4, 6)

In 19x1 Sharief Corporation was authorized to issue 3,000,000 of unsecured bonds, due March 31, 19x6. The bonds carried a face interest rate of $11\frac{3}{5}$ percent, payable semiannually on March 31 and September 30, and were callable at 104 any time after March 31, 19x4. All the bonds were issued on April 1, 19x1 at 102.261, a price that yielded an effective interest of 11 percent.

On April 1, 19x4, Sharief Corporation called one-half of the outstanding bonds and retired them.

Required

1. Prepare a table similar to Table 17-2 to show the interest and amortization of the bond premium for ten interest payment periods, using the effective interest method (round results to nearest dollar).
2. Prepare general journal entries for the bond issue, interest payments and amortization of bond premium, and bond retirement on the following dates: April 1, 19x1; September 30, 19x1; March 31, 19x4; April 1, 19x4; and September 30, 19x4.

Problem 17A-6.
Comprehensive
Bond Transactions
(L.O. 2, 4, 5, 6)

Over a period of three years, Henley Corporation, a company with a December 31 year end, engaged in the following transactions involving two bond issues:

19x1
July 1 Issued $10,000,000 of 12 percent convertible bonds at 96. The bonds are convertible into $20 par value common stock at the rate of 20 shares of stock for each $1,000 bond. Interest is payable on June 30 and December 31, and the market rate of interest is 13 percent.
Dec. 31 Made semiannual interest payment and amortized bond discount.

19x2
June 1 Issued $20,000,000 of 9 percent bonds at face value plus accrued interest. Interest is payable on February 28 and August 31. The bonds are callable at 105, and the market rate of interest is 9 percent.

June 30 Made semiannual interest payment on 12 percent bonds and amortized the bond discount.

Aug. 31 Made semiannual interest payment on 9 percent bonds.

Dec. 31 Made semiannual interest payment on 12 percent bonds, amortized discount, and accrued interest on 9 percent bonds.

19x3

Feb. 28 Made semiannual interest payment on 9 percent bonds.

June 30 Made semiannual interest payment on 12 percent bonds and amortized the bond discount.

July   1 Accepted for conversion into common stock all 12 percent bonds.

July 31 Called and retired all 9 percent bonds, including accrued interest.

Required Prepare general journal entries to record the bond transactions, making all necessary accruals and using the effective interest method. (Round calculations to the nearest dollar.)

Problem Set B

Problem 17B-1.
Bond
Transactions—
Straight-Line
Method
(L.O. 2, 4, 5)

Dunston Corporation has $4,000,000 of 9½ percent, twenty-five-year bonds dated March 1, with interest payable on March 1 and September 1. The company's fiscal year ends on November 30. It uses the straight-line method to amortize premium or discount.

Required

1. Assume that the bonds were issued at 103.5 on March 1. Prepare general journal entries for March 1, September 1, and November 30.
2. Assume that the bonds were issued at 96.5 on March 1. Prepare general journal entries for March 1, September 1, and November 30.
3. Assume that the bonds were issued on June 1 at face value plus accrued interest. Prepare general journal entries for June 1, September 1, and November 30.

Problem 17B-2.
Bond
Transactions—
Effective Interest
Method
(L.O. 2, 4, 5)

Marino Corporation has $10,000,000 of 10½ percent, twenty-year bonds dated June 1, with interest payment dates of May 30 and November 30. The company's fiscal year ends December 31. It uses the effective interest method to amortize premium or discount. Round amounts to nearest dollar.

Required

1. Assume the bonds were issued at 103 on June 1, to yield an effective interest rate of 10.1 percent. Prepare general journal entries for June 1, November 30, and December 31.
2. Assume the bonds were issued at 97 on June 1, to yield an effective interest rate of 10.9 percent. Prepare general journal entries for June 1, November 30, and December 31.
3. Assume the bonds are issued at face value plus accrued interest on August 1. Prepare general journal entries for August 1, November 30, and December 31.

**Problem 17B-3.
Bonds Issued at
Discount and
Premium**
(L.O. 2, 4, 5)

Perenial Corporation issued bonds twice during 19x1. The transactions were as follows:

19x1

Jan. 1 Issued $1,000,000 of 9⅕ percent, ten-year bonds dated January 1, 19x1, with interest payable on June 30 and December 31. The bonds were sold at 98.1, resulting in an effective interest rate of 9.5 percent.

Apr. 1 Issued $2,000,000 of 9⅘ percent, ten-year bonds dated April 1, 19x1, with interest payable on March 31 and September 30. The bonds were sold at 102, resulting in an effective interest rate of 9.5 percent.

June 30 Paid semiannual interest on the January 1 issue and amortized the discount, using the effective interest method.

Sept. 30 Paid semiannual interest on the April 1 issue and amortized the premium, using the effective interest method.

Dec. 31 Paid semiannual interest on the January 1 issue and amortized the discount, using the effective interest method.

31 Made an end-of-year adjusting entry to accrue interest on the April 1 issue and amortize one-half the premium applicable to the second interest period

19x2

Mar. 31 Paid semiannual interest on the April 1 issue and amortized the premium applicable to the second half of the second interest period.

Required

Prepare general journal entries to record the bond transactions. Round amounts to nearest dollar.

**Problem 17B-4.
Bond and
Mortgage
Transactions
Contrasted**
(L.O. 2, 4, 5, 7)

Shah Manufacturing Company, a company with a June 30 fiscal year, is expanding its operations by building and equipping a new plant. It is financing the building and land with a $10,000,000, thirty-year mortgage, which carries an interest rate of 12 percent and requires monthly payments of $118,000. The company is financing the equipment and working capital for the new plant with a $10,000,000, twenty-year bond, which carries a face interest rate of 11 percent, payable semiannually on March 31 and September 30. To date, selected transactions related to these two issues have been as follows:

19x1

Jan. 1 Signed mortgage in exchange for land and building. Land represents 10 percent of total price.

Feb. 1 Made first mortgage payment.

Mar. 1 Made second mortgage payment.

31 Issued bonds for cash at 96, resulting in an effective interest rate of 11.5 percent.

Apr. 1 Made third mortgage payment.

May 1 Made fourth mortgage payment.

June 1 Made fifth mortgage payment.

30 Made end-of-year adjusting entry to accrue interest on bonds and amortize the discount, using the effective interest method.

July 1 Made sixth mortgage payment.

Aug. 1 Made seventh mortgage payment.

Sept. 1 Made eighth mortgage payment.

Sept. 30   Made first interest payment on bonds and amortized the discount for the time period since the end of the fiscal year.

19x2
Mar. 31   Made second interest payment on bonds and amortized the discount for the time period since the last interest payment.

Required

1. Prepare a monthly payment schedule for the mortgage for ten months using these headings (round amounts to the nearest dollar): Payment Date, Unpaid Balance at Beginning of Period, Monthly Payment, Interest for One Month at 1% on Unpaid Balance, Reduction in Debt, and Unpaid Balance at End of Period.
2. Prepare the journal entries for the selected transactions. (Ignore mortgage payments made after September 1, 19x1.)

**Problem 17B-5.
Bond Interest and
Amortization Table
and Bond
Retirements
*(L.O. 2, 4, 6)***

In 19x1 the Vallejo Corporation was authorized to issue $30,000,000 of six-year unsecured bonds. The bonds carried a face interest rate of 9 percent, payable semiannually on June 30 and December 31. Each $2,000 bond was convertible into 40 shares of $20 par value common stock. The bonds were callable at 105 any time after June 30, 19x4. All bonds were issued on July 1, 19x1, at 95.568, a price yielding an effective interest rate of 10 percent. On July 1, 19x4 the company called and retired one-half the outstanding bonds.

Required

1. Prepare a table similar to Table 17-1, showing the interest and amortization of bond discount for twelve interest payment periods. Use the effective interest method (round results to the nearest dollar).
2. Prepare general journal entries for the bond issue, interest payments and amortization of bond discount, and bond retirement on the following dates: July 1, 19x1; December 31, 19x1; June 30, 19x4; July 1, 19x4; and December 31, 19x4.

**Problem 17B-6.
Comprehensive
Bond Transactions
*(L.O. 2, 4, 5, 6)***

The Ozaki Corporation, a company with a June 30 fiscal year end, engaged in the following long-term bond transactions over a three-year period:

19x5
Nov. 1   Issued $20,000,000 of 12 percent debenture bonds at face value plus accrued interest. Interest is payable on January 31 and July 31, and the bonds are callable at 104.

19x6
Jan. 31   Made the semiannual interest payment on the 12 percent bonds.
June 30   Made the year-end accrual of interest payment on the 12 percent bonds.
July 31   Issued $10,000,000 of 10 percent, fifteen-year convertible bonds at 105 plus accrued interest. Interest is payable on June 30 and December 31, and each $1,000 bond is convertible into 30 shares of $10 par value common stock. The market rate of interest is 9 percent.
      31   Made the semiannual interest payment on the 12 percent bonds.
Dec. 31   Made the semiannual interest payment on the 10 percent bonds and amortized the bond premium.

19x7
Jan. 31   Made the semiannual interest payment on the 12 percent bonds.

Feb. 28   Called and retired all the 12 percent bonds, including accrued interest.

June 30   Made the semiannual interest payment on the 10 percent bonds and amortized the bond premium.

July   1   Accepted for conversion into common stock all the 10 percent bonds.

Required

Prepare general journal entries to record the bond transactions, making all necessary accruals and using the effective interest method. (Round all calculations to the nearest dollar.)

Financial Decision Case

Gianni Chemical Corporation
(L.O. 2, 4, 7)

The Gianni Chemical Corporation plans to build a new plant that will produce liquid fertilizer for the agricultural market. The plant is expected to cost $200,000,000 and will be located in the southwestern part of the United States. The company's chief financial officer, Julio Bassi, has spent the last several weeks studying different means of financing the plant's construction. From his talks with bankers and other financiers, he has decided that there are two basic choices. The plant can be financed through the issuance of a long-term bond or a long-term lease. The two options follow:

a. Issuance of a $200,000,000, twenty-five-year, 16 percent bond secured by the new plant. Interest on the bonds would be payable semiannually.

b. Signing of a twenty-five-year lease calling for semiannual lease payments of $16,350,000.

Bassi wants to know what the effect of each choice will be on the company's financial statements. He estimates that the useful life of the plant is twenty-five years, at which time it is expected to have an estimated residual value of $20,000,000.

Required

1. Prepare the entries to record issuance of the bonds at face value in exchange for the fertilizer plant. Assume that the transaction occurs on the first day of the fiscal year, which is July 1. Also prepare entries to pay the interest expense and interest payable and to record depreciation on the plant during the first year. Assume that the straight-line method is used. Describe the effects that these transactions will have on the balance sheet and income statement.

2. Prepare the entries required to treat the long-term lease as a capital lease. Assume that the plant is occupied on the first day of the fiscal year, July 1, and that an interest rate of 16 percent applies. Also prepare entries to record the lease payments and to record depreciation during the first year. Describe the effects that these transactions will have on the balance sheet and income statement. (A knowledge of present value, which is dealt with in Appendix A and in Table B-4 in Appendix B, is necessary to do this part of the question.)

3. What factors would you consider important in deciding which alternative to choose? Contrast the annual cash requirement of the two alternatives.

Answers to Self-Test

1. c	3. d	5. d	7. c	9. d
2. a	4. b	6. b	8. b	10. c

PRINCIPLES OF ACCOUNTING

FINANCIAL ACCOUNTING

PART ONE
The Basic Accounting Model

PART TWO
Extensions of the Basic Accounting Model

PART THREE
Measuring and Reporting Assets and Current Liabilities

PART FOUR
Accounting for Partnerships and Corporations

PART FIVE
Special Reports and Analyses of Accounting Information

Chapter 18
  The Statement of Cash Flows

Chapter 19
  Financial Statement Analysis

Chapter 20
  Intercompany Investments

Chapter 21
  International Accounting and Inflation Accounting

MANAGERIAL ACCOUNTING

PART SIX
Basic Concepts of Management Accounting

PART SEVEN
Accounting for Management Decision Making

B ecause business organizations are so complex today, special reports are needed to present important information about their activities. To understand and evaluate financial statements, it is necessary to learn how to analyze them. Part Five deals with these important special reports and with the analysis of financial statements.

PART FIVE

Special Reports and Analyses of Accounting Information

Chapter 18 presents the statement of cash flows, which explains the major operating, financing, and investing activities of a business. The chapter presents this statement using both the direct approach and the indirect approach.

Chapter 19 explains the objectives and techniques of financial statement analysis from the standpoint of the financial analyst.

Chapter 20 examines the accounting issues of companies that invest in other companies. One is by investment in the capital stocks of other companies, which often calls for consolidated financial statements. The other way is by investment in the bonds of other companies.

Chapter 21 describes progress toward international accounting standards and addresses the accounting issues that result from the changing value of the dollar. These issues involve accounting for the effects of general and specific price changes and for changes in the rate at which the dollar may be exchanged for foreign currencies.

CHAPTER 18

The Statement
of Cash Flows

Earlier in this book you studied the balance sheet, the income statement, and the statement of stockholders' equity. In this chapter you will learn to prepare a fourth major financial statement, the statement of cash flows. After studying this chapter, you should be able to meet the learning objectives listed on the left.

Each financial statement is useful in specific ways. The balance sheet shows, at a point in time, how management has invested a company's resources in assets, and how those assets are financed by liabilities and owners' equity. The income statement reports how much net income a company earned during the accounting period. The statement of stockholders' equity shows changes in the status of the ownership of a business during the accounting period, including the cumulative income retained in the business.

These financial statements are useful, but there are important questions that they do not answer. For instance, did a company's operations generate enough cash to pay its dividends? If a company lost money during the year, does it still generate enough cash to pay its liabilities? What new financing and investing activities did the company engage in during the year? In what new assets did the company invest this year? If liabilities were reduced, how were they reduced? Or if liabilities increased during the year, where were the proceeds invested? Did the company issue common stock during the year, and if so, what was done with the proceeds?

Why can these questions not be answered by the income statement, the balance sheet, or the statement of stockholders' equity? First, because the income statement is prepared on an accrual basis, the effect of operating activities on the cash or liquidity position of the business is not shown. Second, because the balance sheet is a static financial statement, the financing and investing activities that caused changes from one year to the next are not presented. Third, the statement of stockholders' equity discloses only transactions that affect stockholders' equity. To correlate all this information, another major financial statement is required.

Until recently, the need was met by the statement of changes in financial position. The statement, which could be prepared in two ways based on two different definitions of funds, showed the sources of funds received by the business and the use of those funds in the business. Historically, the most common way of preparing the statement was to define funds as working capital (current assets minus current liabilities) and to show the sources and uses of working capital. Another way, which had rapidly become more popular, defined funds as cash and showed the sources and uses of cash. Figure 18-1 shows the change in popularity from 1981 to 1986 from the working capital approach to the cash approach. In 1988, it was estimated that 90 percent of the companies surveyed followed the cash approach. Because of the lack of a single definition of funds and the existence of various formats for the statement used, reporting practices by businesses have varied greatly.

To remedy the confusion and lack of comparability that result from the existence of different approaches, in November 1987 the Financial Accounting Standards Board adopted a new statement called the statement of cash flows.[1] This statement is in accord with the FASB's long-held position that a primary objective of financial statements is to provide information to investors and creditors on a business's cash

Figure 18-1. Use of Working Capital and Cash Flow Bases by 600 Large Companies

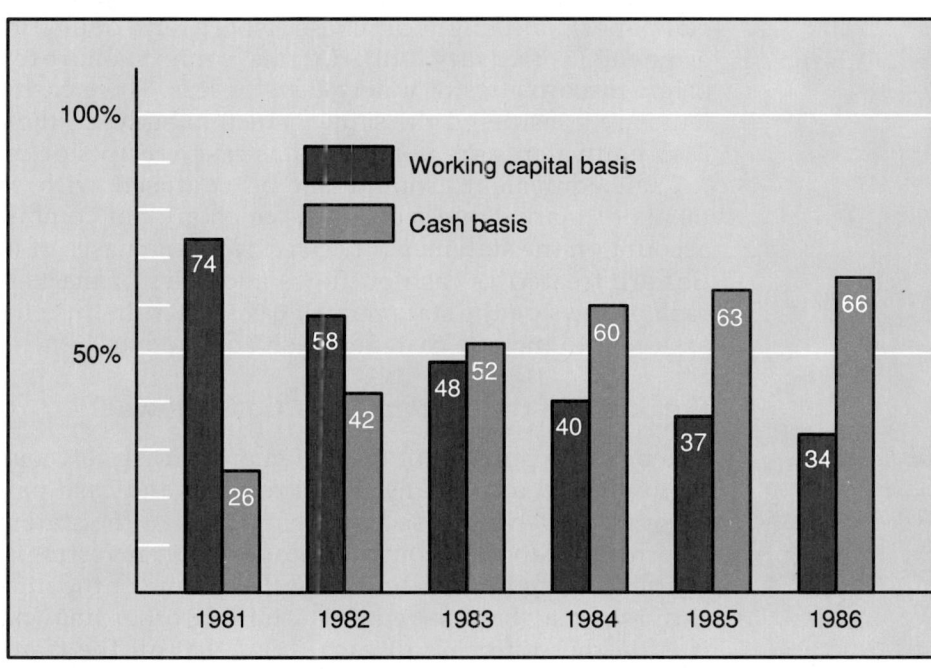

Source: American Institute of Certified Public Accountants, *Accounting Trends and Techniques* (New York: AICPA, 1986 and 1987), p. 364 and p. 392.

1. *Statement of Financial Accounting Standards No. 95,* "Statement of Cash Flows" (Stamford, Conn.: Financial Accounting Standards Board, 1987).

flows.[2] This new statement, which replaced the statement of changes in financial position, is prepared using a uniform format. The statement of cash flows is required every time a company prepares an income statement. The effective date of the requirement is for fiscal years ending after July 15, 1988.

Purposes, Uses, and Components of the Statement of Cash Flows

OBJECTIVE 1
Describe the statement of cash flows, and define cash and cash equivalents

The **statement of cash flows** shows the effect on cash of the operating, investing, and financing activities of a company for an accounting period. It explains the net increase (or decrease) in cash during the accounting period. For purposes of preparing this statement, **cash** is defined to include both cash and cash equivalents. **Cash equivalents** are defined by the FASB as short-term, highly liquid investments, including money market accounts, commercial paper, and U.S. Treasury bills. A company maintains cash equivalents in order to earn interest while cash temporarily lies idle. Suppose, for example, that a company has $1,000,000 that it will not need for thirty days. To earn a return on this sum, the company may place the cash in an account that earns interest (for example, a money market account); it may loan the cash to another corporation by purchasing that corporation's short-term note (commercial paper); or it might purchase a short-term obligation of the U.S. government (a Treasury bill). In this context, short-term is defined as original maturities of ninety days or less. Since cash and cash equivalents are considered the same, transfers between the cash account and cash equivalents are not treated as cash receipts or cash payments.

Cash equivalents should not be confused with short-term investments or marketable securities, which are not combined with the cash account on the statement of cash flows. Purchases of marketable securities are treated as cash outflows and sales of marketable securities as cash inflows on the statement of cash flows. In this chapter, cash will be assumed to include cash and cash equivalents.

Purposes of the Statement of Cash Flows

OBJECTIVE 2
State the principal purposes and uses of the statement of cash flows

The primary purpose of the statement of cash flows is to provide information about a company's cash receipts and cash payments during an accounting period. A secondary purpose of the statement is to provide information about a company's operating, investing, and financing activities during the accounting period. Some of the information on these activities may be inferred by examining other financial statements, but it is on the statement of cash flows that all the transactions affecting cash are summarized.

2. *Statement of Financial Accounting Concepts No. 1*, "Objectives of Financial Reporting for Business Enterprises" (Stamford, Conn.: Financial Accounting Standards Board, 1978), par. 37–39.

Internal and External Uses of the Statement of Cash Flows

The statement of cash flows is useful internally to management and externally to investors and creditors. Management may use the statement of cash flows to assess the liquidity of the business, to determine dividend policy, and to evaluate the effects of major policy decisions involving investments and financing. In other words, management will use the statement of cash flows to determine whether or not short-term financing is needed to pay current liabilities, to decide whether to raise or lower dividends, and to plan for investing and financing needs.

Investors and creditors will find the statement useful in assessing the company's ability to manage cash flows, to generate positive future cash flows, to pay its liabilities, and to pay dividends, as well as its need for additional financing. In addition, they may use the statement to explain the differences between net income on the income statement and the net cash flows generated from operations. The statement shows both the cash and noncash effects of investing and financing activities during the accounting period.

Classification of Cash Flows

OBJECTIVE 3
Identify the principal components of the classifications of cash flows, and state the significance of noncash investing and financing transactions

The statement of cash flows classifies cash receipts and cash payments into the categories of operating, investing, and financing activities. The components of these activities are illustrated in Figure 18-2 and are summarized as follows:

1. **Operating activities** include the cash effects of transactions and other events that enter into the determination of net income. Included in this category as cash inflows are cash receipts received from customers for goods and services and interest and dividends received on loans and investments. Included as cash outflows are cash payments for wages, goods and services, interest, and taxes applied to employees, suppliers, government bodies, and others. In effect, the income statement is changed from an accrual to a cash basis.

2. **Investing activities** include the acquiring and selling of long-term assets, the acquiring and selling of marketable securities other than cash equivalents, and the making and collecting of loans. Cash inflows include the cash received from selling long-term assets and marketable securities and from collecting loans. Cash outflows include the cash expended for purchases of long-term assets and marketable securities and the cash loaned to borrowers.

3. **Financing activities** include (1) obtaining or returning resources from or to owners and providing them with a return on their investment and (2) obtaining resources from creditors and repaying the amounts borrowed, or otherwise settling the obligation. Cash inflows include the proceeds from issues of stocks and from short-term and long-term borrowing. Cash outflows include the repayments of loans and payments to owners, including cash dividends. Treasury

Figure 18-2. Classification of Cash Inflows and Cash Outflows

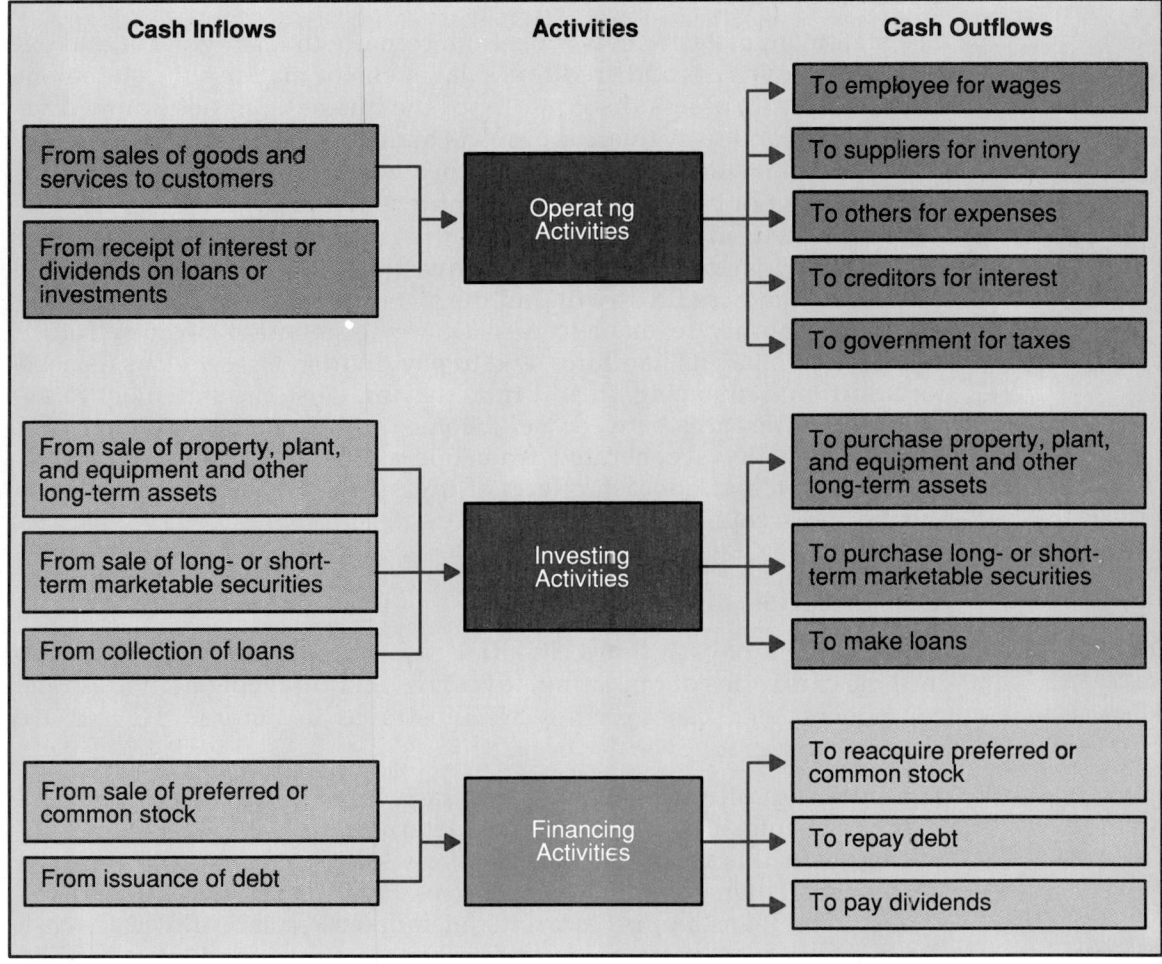

stock transactions are also considered financing activities. Repayments of accounts payable or accrued liabilities are not considered repayments of loans under financing activities, but are classified as cash outflows under operating activities.

A company will occasionally engage in significant **noncash investing and financing transactions** involving only long-term assets, long-term liabilities, or stockholders' equity, such as the exchange of a long-term asset for a long-term liability or the settlement of a debt by issuing capital stock. For instance, a company might issue a long-term mortgage for the purchase of land and a building. Or it might convert long-term bonds into common stock. These transactions represent significant investing and financing activities, but they would not be reflected on the statement of cash flows because they do not involve either cash inflows or cash outflows. However, since one purpose of the statement of cash flows is to show investing and financing activities, and since transactions like these will have future effects on cash flows, the FASB has determined that they should be disclosed in a separate schedule as part of the statement of cash flows. In this way, the reader of the statement will see clearly the company's investing and financing activities.

Format of the Statement of Cash Flows

The general format of the statement of cash flows, shown in Exhibit 18-1, is divided into three categories corresponding to the three activities discussed above. The cash flows from operating activities are followed by cash flows from investing activities and cash flows from financing activities. The individual inflows and outflows from investing and financing activities are shown separately in their respective categories. For instance, cash inflows from sale of property, plant, and equipment are shown separately from the cash outflows for the purchase of property, plant and equipment. Similarly, cash inflows from borrowing are shown separately from cash outflows to retire loans. A reconciliation of the beginning and ending balances of cash is shown at the end of the statement. A list of noncash transactions appears in the schedule at the bottom of the statement.

Exhibit 18-1. Format for the Statement of Cash Flows

Company Name
Statement of Cash Flows
Period Covered

Cash Flows from Operating Activities		
(List of individual inflows and outflows)	xxx	
Net Cash Flows from Operating Activities		xxx
Cash Flows from Investing Activities		
(List of individual inflows and outflows)	xxx	
Net Cash Flows from Investing Activities		xxx
Cash Flows from Financing Activities		
(List of individual inflows and outflows)	xxx	
Net Cash Flows from Financing Activities		xxx
Net Increase (Decrease) in Cash		xx
Cash at Beginning of Year		xx
Cash at End of Year		xx

Schedule of Noncash Investing and Financing Transactions

(List of individual transactions)		xxx

Preparing the Statement of Cash Flows

To demonstrate the preparation of the statement of cash flows, we will work an example step by step. The data for this example are presented in Exhibits 18-2 and 18-3 (Exhibit 18-3 is on page 740). They are the Ryan Corporation's balance sheets for December 31, 19x1 and 19x2, and its 19x2 income statement, with additional data about transactions affecting noncurrent accounts during 19x2. Since the changes in the balance sheet accounts will be used in analyzing the various accounts, those changes are shown in Exhibit 18-2. For each individual account, an indication is made as to whether the change is an increase or a decrease.

There are four steps in preparing the statement of cash flows:

1. Determine cash flows from operating activities.
2. Determine cash flows from investing activities.
3. Determine cash flows from financing activities.
4. Present the information obtained in the first three steps in the form of the statement of cash flows.

Determining Cash Flows from Operating Activities

The income statement indicates the success or failure of a business in earning an income from its operating activities, but it does not reflect the inflow and outflow of cash from those activities. The reason for this is that the income statement is prepared on an accrual basis. Revenues are recorded even though the cash for them may not have been received, and expenses are incurred and recorded even though cash may not yet have been expended for them. As a result, to arrive at cash flows from operations, one must convert the figures on the income statement from an accrual basis to a cash basis by adjusting earned revenues to cash received from sales and incurred costs and expenses to cash expended, as shown in Figure 18-3 (see page 740).

OBJECTIVE 4a
Determine cash flows from operating activities using the direct method

There are two methods of converting the income statement from an accrual basis to a cash basis: the direct method and the indirect method. The **direct method** is accomplished by adjusting each item in the income statement in turn from the accrual basis to the cash basis. The result is a statement that begins with cash receipts from sales and then deducts cash payments for purchases, operating expenses, interest payments, and income taxes, to arrive at net cash flows from operating activities:

Cash Flows from Operating Activities		
Cash Receipts from		
Sales	xxx	
Interest and Dividends Received	<u>xxx</u>	xxx
Cash Payments for		
Purchases	xxx	
Operating Expenses	xxx	
Interest Payments	xxx	
Income Taxes	<u>xxx</u>	<u>xxx</u>
Net Cash Flows from Operating Activities		xxx

Exhibit 18-2. Balance Sheet with Changes in Accounts Indicated for Ryan Corporation

Ryan Corporation
Balance Sheets
December 31, 19x2 and 19x1

	19x2	19x1	Change	Increase or Decrease
Assets				
Current Assets				
Cash	$ 46,000	$ 15,000	$ 31,000	Increase
Accounts Receivable (net)	47,000	55,000	(8,000)	Decrease
Inventory	144,000	110,000	34,000	Increase
Prepaid Expenses	1,000	5,000	(4,000)	Decrease
Total Current Assets	$238,000	$185,000	$ 53,000	
Investments	$115,000	$127,000	$(12,000)	Decrease
Plant Assets				
Plant Assets	$715,000	$505,000	$210,000	Increase
Accumulated Depreciation	(103,000)	(68,000)	(35,000)	Increase
Total Plant Assets	$612,000	$437,000	$175,000	
Total Assets	$965,000	$749,000	$216,000	
Liabilities				
Current Liabilities				
Accounts Payable	$ 50,000	$ 43,000	$ 7,000	Increase
Accrued Liabilities	12,000	9,000	3,000	Increase
Income Taxes Payable	3,000	5,000	(2,000)	Decrease
Total Current Liabilities	$ 65,000	$ 57,000	$ 8,000	
Long-Term Liabilities				
Bonds Payable	$295,000	$245,000	$ 50,000	Increase
Total Liabilities	$360,000	$302,000	$ 58,000	
Stockholders' Equity				
Common Stock, $5 par value	$276,000	$200,000	$ 76,000	Increase
Paid-in Capital in Excess of Par Value	189,000	115,000	74,000	Increase
Retained Earnings	140,000	132,000	8,000	Increase
Total Stockholders' Equity	$605,000	$447,000	$158,000	
Total Liabilities and Stockholders' Equity	$965,000	$749,000	$216,000	

Exhibit 18-3. Income Statement and Other Information on Noncurrent Accounts for Ryan Corporation

Ryan Corporation
Income Statement
For the Year Ended December 31, 19x2

Sales		$698,000
Cost of Goods Sold		520,000
Gross Margin		$178,000
Operating Expenses (including Depreciation Expense of $37,000)		147,000
Operating Income		$ 31,000
Other Income (Expenses)		
Interest Expense	$(23,000)	
Interest Income	6,000	
Gain on Sale of Investments	12,000	
Loss on Sale of Plant Assets	(3,000)	(8,000)
Income before Taxes		$ 23,000
Income Taxes		7,000
Net Income		$ 16,000

Other transactions affecting noncurrent accounts during 19x2:

1. Purchased investments in the amount of $78,000.
2. Sold investments for $102,000. These investments cost $90,000.
3. Purchased plant assets in the amount of $120,000.
4. Sold plant assets that cost $10,000 with accumulated depreciation of $2,000 for $5,000.
5. Issued $100,000 of bonds at face value in a noncash exchange for plant assets.
6. Repaid $50,000 of bonds at face value at maturity.
7. Issued 15,200 shares of $5 par value common stock for $150,000.
8. Paid cash dividends in the amount of $8,000.

Figure 18-3. Relationship of Accrual and Cash Bases of Accounting

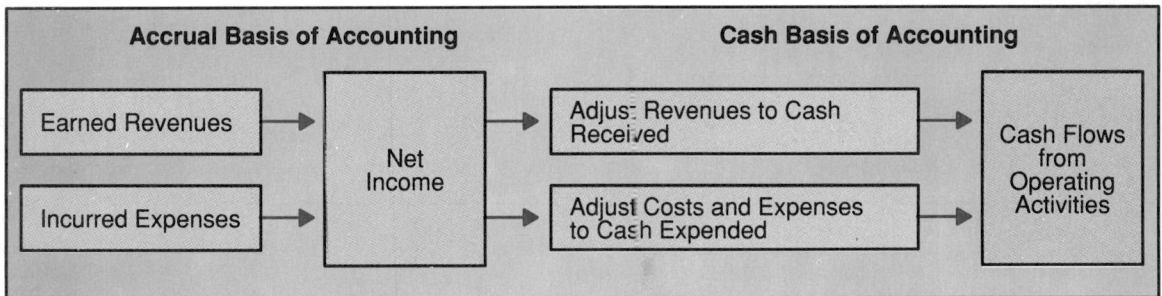

OBJECTIVE 4b
Determine cash flows from operating activities using the indirect method

The **indirect method**, on the other hand, does not involve adjustment of each item in the income statement individually, but lists only those adjustments necessary to convert net income to cash flows from operations, as follows:

Cash Flows from Operating Activities
Net Income		xxx
Adjustments to Reconcile Net Income to Net Cash		
Flows from Operating Activities		
(List of individual items)	xxx	xxx
Net Cash Flows from Operating Activities		**xxx**

Both approaches produce the same result, and the FASB accepts both methods. However, the FASB recommends that the direct method be used, with a supplemental reconciliation to the indirect method. In the paragraphs that follow, the direct method will be used to illustrate the conversion of the income statement to a cash basis. The process will be summarized using the indirect method.

Cash Receipts from Sales. Sales result in a positive cash flow for a company. Cash sales are direct increases in the cash flows of the company. Credit sales are not, because they are recorded originally as accounts receivable. When they are collected, they become inflows of cash. One cannot, however, assume that credit sales are automatically inflows of cash, because the collections of accounts receivable in any one accounting period are not likely to equal credit sales. Receivables may prove to be uncollectible, sales from a prior period may be collected in the current period, or sales from the current period may be collected next period. For example, if accounts receivable increases from one accounting period to the next, cash receipts from sales will not be as great as sales. On the other hand if accounts receivable decreases from one accounting period to the next, cash receipts from sales will exceed sales.

The relationships among sales, changes in accounts receivable, and cash receipts from sales are reflected in the following formula.

$$\text{Cash Receipts from Sales} = \text{Sales} \begin{cases} + \textbf{Decrease in accounts receivable} \\ \text{or} \\ - \textbf{Increase in accounts receivable} \end{cases}$$

Refer to the balance sheets and income statement for Ryan Corporation in Exhibits 18-2 and 18-3. Note that sales were $698,000 in 19x2, and accounts receivable decreased by $8,000. Thus, cash received from sales is $706,000, calculated as follows:

$$\$706,000 = \$698,000 + \$8,000$$

Ryan Corporation collected $8,000 more from sales than it sold during the year. This relationship may be illustrated as follows:

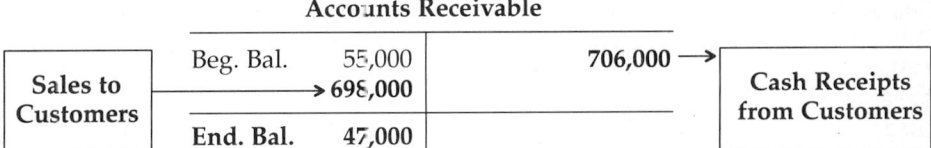

Accounts Receivable

Sales to Customers	Beg. Bal.	55,000		706,000 →	Cash Receipts from Customers
	→	698,000			
	End. Bal.	47,000			

If Ryan Corporation had unearned revenues or advances from customers, an adjustment would be made for changes in those items as well.

Cash Receipts from Interest and Dividends Received. Although interest and dividends received are most closely associated with investment activity and are often called investment income, the FASB has decided to classify the cash received from these items as operating activities. To simplify the examples in this text, it is assumed that interest income equals interest received and that dividend income equals dividends received. Thus, from Exhibit 18-3, cash received from interest received by Ryan Corporation is assumed to equal $6,000, which is the amount of interest income.

Cash Payments for Purchases. Cost of goods sold (from the income statement) must be adjusted for changes in two balance sheet accounts to arrive at cash payments for purchases. First, cost of goods sold must be adjusted for changes in inventory to arrive at net purchases. Then, net purchases must be adjusted for the change in accounts payable to arrive at cash payments for purchases. If inventory has increased from one accounting period to another, net purchases will be greater than cost of goods sold; if inventory has decreased, net purchases will be less than cost of goods sold. Conversely, if accounts payable has increased, cash payments for purchases will be less than net purchases; if accounts payable has decreased, cash payments for purchases will be greater than net purchases.

These relationships may be stated in equation form as follows:

$$\text{Cash Payments for Purchases} = \text{Cost of Goods Sold} \begin{cases} + \text{ Increase in Inventory} \\ \text{or} \\ - \text{ Decrease in Inventory} \end{cases} \begin{cases} + \text{ Decrease in Accounts Payable} \\ \text{or} \\ - \text{ Increase in Accounts Payable} \end{cases}$$

From Exhibits 18-2 and 18-3, cost of goods sold is $520,000, inventory increased by $34,000, and accounts payable increased by $7,000. Thus, cash payments for purchases is $547,000, as the following calculation shows:

$$\$547,000 = \$520,000 + \$34,000 - \$7,000$$

In this example, Ryan Corporation purchased $34,000 more inventory than it sold and paid out $7,000 less in cash than it purchased. The net result is that cash payments for purchases exceeded cost of goods sold by $27,000 ($547,000 − $520,000). These relationships may be visualized as follows:

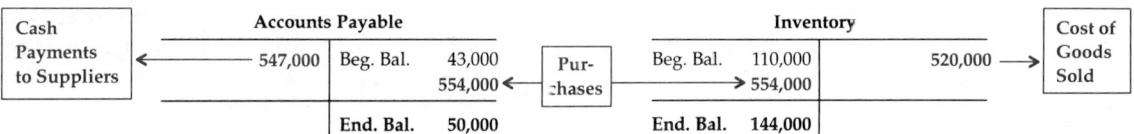

Cash Payments for Operating Expenses. Just as cost of goods sold does not represent the amount of cash paid for purchases during an accounting period, operating expenses will not match the amount of cash paid to employees, suppliers, and others for goods and services. Three adjustments must be made to operating expenses to arrive at the cash flows. The first adjustment is for changes in prepaid expenses, such as prepaid insurance or prepaid rent. If prepaid assets increase during the accounting period, more cash will have been paid out than appears on the income statement in the form of expenses. If prepaid assets decrease, more expenses will appear on the income statement than cash was spent.

The second adjustment is for changes in liabilities resulting from accrued expenses, such as wages payable and payroll taxes payable. If accrued liabilities increase during the accounting period, operating expenses on the income statement will exceed the cash spent. And if accrued liabilities decrease, operating expenses will fall short of cash spent.

The third adjustment is made because certain expenses do not require a current outlay of cash, so they must be subtracted from operating expenses to arrive at cash payments for operating expenses. The most common expenses in this category are depreciation expense, amortization expense, and depletion expense. Expenditures for plant assets, intangibles, and natural resources occur when they are purchased and are classified as an investing activity at that time. Depreciation expense, amortization expense, and depletion expense are simply allocations of the costs of those original purchases to the current accounting period, and do not affect cash flows in the current period. For example, Ryan Corporation recorded 19x2 depreciation expense as follows:

Depreciation Expense	37,000	
Accumulated Depreciation		37,000
To record depreciation on plant assets		

No cash payment is made in this transaction. Thus, to the extent that operating expenses include depreciation and similar items, an adjustment is needed to reduce operating expenses to the amount of cash expended.

The three adjustments to operating expenses are summarized in the following equation.

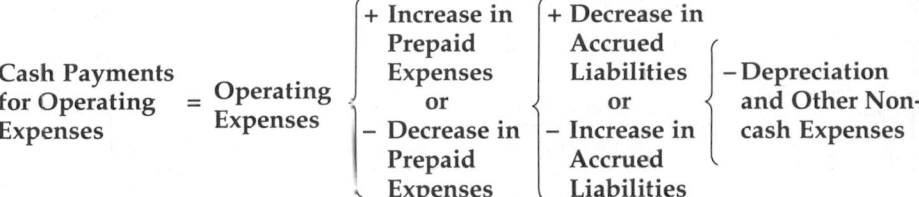

From Exhibits 18-2 and 18-3, Ryan's operating expenses (including depreciation of $37,000) were $147,000; prepaid expenses decreased by $4,000; and accrued liabilities increased by $3,000. As a result, Ryan Corporation's cash payments for operating expenses are $103,000, computed as follows:

$$\$103,000 = \$147,000 - \$4,000 - \$3,000 - \$37,000$$

If prepaid expenses and accrued liabilities that are *not* related to specific operating expenses exist, they are not to be used in these computations. An example of such a case is income taxes payable, which is the accrued liability related to income taxes expense. The cash payment for income taxes is discussed in a later section.

Cash Payments for Interest. The FASB classifies cash payments for interest as operating activities in spite of the fact that some authorities argue that they should be considered financing activities because of their association with loans incurred to finance the business. The FASB feels that interest expense is a cost of operating the business. We follow the FASB position in this text. Also, for the sake of simplicity, all examples in this text assume interest payments are equal to interest expense on the income statement. Thus, from Exhibit 18-3, Ryan Corporation's interest payments are assumed to be $23,000 in 19x2.

Cash Payments for Income Taxes. The amount of income taxes expense that appears on the income statement rarely equals the amount of income taxes actually paid during the year. One reason for this difference is that the final payments for the income taxes of one year are not due until some time in the following year. A second reason is that there may be differences between what is deducted from, or included in, income for accounting purposes and what is included or deducted for purposes of calculating income tax liability. The latter reason often results in a deferred income tax liability. Its effects on cash flows were discussed in Chapter 16. Here, we deal only with the changes that result from increases or decreases in income taxes payable.

To determine cash payments for income taxes, income taxes expense (from the income statement) is adjusted by the change in income taxes payable. If income taxes payable increased during the accounting period, cash payments for taxes will be less than the expense shown on the income statement. If income taxes payable decreased, cash payments for taxes will exceed income taxes on the income statement. In other words, the following equation is applicable.

$$\text{Cash Payments for Income Taxes} = \text{Income Taxes} \begin{cases} + & \text{Decrease in Income Taxes Payable} \\ & \text{or} \\ - & \text{Increase in Income Taxes Payable} \end{cases}$$

In 19x2, Ryan Corporation showed income taxes of $7,000 on its income statement and a decrease of $2,000 in income taxes payable on its balance sheets (see Exhibits 18-2 and 18-3). As a result, cash payments for income taxes during 19x2 were $9,000, calculated as follows:

$$\$9,000 = \$7,000 + \$2,000$$

Other Income and Expenses. In computing cash flows from operations, some items classified on the income statement as other income and expenses are not considered operating items because they are more closely related to financing and investing activities than to operating activities. Items must be analyzed individually to determine their proper classification on the statement of cash flows. For instance, we have already dealt with interest income and interest expense as operating activities. Unlike interest, however, the effects on cash flows of gains and losses are considered with the item that gave rise to the gain or loss. The effects of gains or losses on the sale of assets are considered with investing activities, and the effects of gains and losses related to liabilities are considered with financing activities. Consequently, the effects of the gain on sale of investments and of the loss on sale of plant assets reported on Ryan Corporation's income statement (Exhibit 18-3) are considered under cash flows from investing activities.

Schedule of Cash Flows from Operating Activities—Direct Method. It is now possible to prepare a schedule of cash flows from operations using the direct method and the calculations made in the preceding paragraphs. In Exhibit 18-4, Ryan Corporation had Cash Receipts from Sales and Interest Received of $712,000 and Cash Payments for Purchases, Operating Expenses, Interest Payments, and Income Taxes of $682,000, resulting in Net Cash Flows from Operating Activities of $30,000 in 19x2.

Schedule of Cash Flows from Operating Activities—Indirect Method. It is also possible to calculate net cash flows from operations using the indirect method, as shown in Exhibit 18-5. Note that the amount for Net Cash Flows from Operating Activities is the same as it was under the direct method (Exhibit 18-4). Under the indirect method, the same adjustments for the changes in current assets and current liabilities are made as under the direct method, except that they are made as additions to or subtractions from net income instead of as adjustments to the individual income statement items. For instance, under the direct method,

Exhibit 18-4. Schedule of Cash Flows from Operating Activities—Direct Method

Ryan Corporation
Schedule of Cash Flows from Operating Activities
For the Year Ended December 31, 19x2

Cash Flows from Operating Activities
Cash Receipts from

Sales	$706,000	
Interest Received	6,000	$712,000
Cash Payments for		
Purchases	$547,000	
Operating Expenses	103,000	
Interest Payments	23,000	
Income Taxes	9,000	682,000
Net Cash Flows from Operating Activities		$ 30,000

Exhibit 18-5. Schedule of Cash Flows from Operating Activities—Indirect Method

Ryan Corporation
Schedule of Cash Flows from Operating Activities
For the Year Ended December 31, 19x2

Cash Flows from Operating Activities

Net Income		$16,000
Adjustments to Reconcile Net Income to Net		
Cash Flows from Operating Activities		
Depreciation	$ 37,000	
Gain on Sale of Investments	(12,000)	
Loss on Sale of Plant Assets	3,000	
Decrease in Accounts Receivable	8,000	
Increase in Inventory	(34,000)	
Decrease in Prepaid Expenses	4,000	
Increase in Accounts Payable	7,000	
Increase in Accrued Liabilities	3,000	
Decrease in Income Taxes Payable	(2,000)	14,000
Net Cash Flows from Operating Activities		$30,000

the decrease in accounts receivable was added to Sales to adjust sales from an accrual basis to a cash basis. Since sales is included in the computation of net income, the same effect is achieved by adding the decrease in Accounts Receivable to Net Income. The same logic applies to adjustments to Cost of Goods Sold, Operating Expenses, and Income Taxes, except that the signs will be opposite for these adjustments. The following table summarizes these adjustments.

	Adjustments to Convert Net Income to Net Cash Flows from Operating Activities	
	Add to Net Income	**Deduct from Net Income**
Current Assets		
Accounts Receivable (net)	Decrease	Increase
Inventory	Decrease	Increase
Prepaid Expenses	Decrease	Increase
Current Liabilities		
Accounts Payable	Increase	Decrease
Accrued Liabilities	Increase	Decrease
Income Taxes Payable	Increase	Decrease

Net income must also be adjusted for expenses such as depreciation expense, amortization expense, depletion expense, and other income and expenses such as gains and losses in accordance with the same logic. These items are added or deducted as follows:

	Adjustments to Convert Net Income to Net Cash Flows from Operating Activities
	Add to (Deduct from) Net Income
Depreciation Expense	Add
Amortization Expense	Add
Depletion Expense	Add
Losses	Add
Gains	Deduct

Note that these adjustments to net income are made for several reasons. Depreciation expense is added because it is a noncash expense that was deducted in the income statement to arrive at net income. Adjustments are made for gains and losses because of reasons that will become clear when investing and financing activities are discussed in the next section. Finally, the additions or deductions for increases and decreases in current assets and current liabilities are included because each is necessary to adjust an income statement item from an accrual basis to a cash basis.

Determining Cash Flows from Investing Activities

The second step in preparation of the statement of cash flows is to determine cash flows from investing activities. The procedure followed in this step is to examine individually the accounts that involve cash receipts and cash payments from investing activities. The objective in each case is to explain the change in the account balance from one year to the next.

Investing activities center on the long-term assets shown on the balance sheet, but they also include transactions affecting short-term investments from the current asset section of the balance sheet and investment income from the income statement. From the balance sheet in Exhibit 18-2, we can see that Ryan Corporation has long-term assets including investments and plant, but no short-term investments. From the income statement in Exhibit 18-3, we see that it has investment income in the form of interest income, a gain on sale of investments, and a loss on sale of plant assets. Also, from the schedule at the bottom of Exhibit 18-3, we find the following five items pertaining to investing activities in 19x2:

1. Purchased investments in the amount of $78,000.
2. Sold investments that cost $90,000 for $102,000, resulting in a gain of $12,000.
3. Purchased plant assets in the amount of $120,000.
4. Sold plant assets that cost $10,000 with accumulated depreciation of $2,000 for $5,000, resulting in a loss of $3,000.
5. Issued $100,000 of bonds at face value in a noncash exchange for plant assets.

The following paragraphs analyze the accounts related to investing activities for the purpose of determining their effects on Ryan Corporation's cash flows.

Investments. The objective here is to explain the $12,000 decrease in investments (from Exhibit 18-2) by analyzing the increases and decreases in investments to determine the effects on the Cash account. Purchases increase investments and sales decrease investments. Item 1 in the list of Ryan's investing activities shows purchases of $78,000 during 19x2. This transaction is recorded as follows:

Investments	78,000	
Cash		78,000
To record purchase of investments		

As we can see from the entry, the effect of this transaction is a $78,000 decrease in cash flows.

Item 2 in the list shows a sale of investments at a gain. It is recorded as follows:

Cash	102,000	
Investments		90,000
Gain on Sale of Investments		12,000
To record sale of investments for a gain		

The effect of this transaction is a $102,000 increase in cash flows. Note that the gain on sale of investments is included in the $102,000. This is the reason it was excluded earlier in computing cash flows from operations. If it had been included in that section, it would have been counted twice.

The $12,000 decrease in the Investments account during 19x2 has now been explained, as may be seen in the following T account:

Investments			
Beg. Bal.	127,000	Sales	90,000
Purchases	78,000		
End. Bal.	115,000		

The cash flow effects from these transactions will be shown under the Cash Flows from Investing Activities section on the statement of cash flows, as follows:

Purchase of Investments	$ (78,000)
Sale of Investments	102,000

Note that purchases and sales are disclosed separately as cash outflows and cash inflows. They are not netted against each other into a single figure. This disclosure gives the reader of the statement a more complete view of investing activity.

If Ryan Corporation had short-term investments or marketable securities, the analysis of cash flows would be the same.

Plant Assets. In the case of plant assets, it is necessary to explain the changes in both the asset account and the related accumulated depreciation account. From Exhibit 18-2, Plant Assets increased by $210,000 and Accumulated Depreciation increased by $35,000. Purchases increase plant assets and sales decrease plant assets. Accumulated Depreciation is increased by the amount of depreciation expense and decreased by the removal of the accumulated depreciation associated with plant assets that are sold. Three items listed in Exhibit 18-3 affect plant assets. Item 3 in the list on page 748 indicates that Ryan Corporation purchased plant assets in the amount of $120,000 during 19x2, as shown by this entry:

Plant Assets	120,000	
Cash		120,000
To record purchase of plant assets		

This transaction results in a cash outflow of $120,000.

Item 4 states that Ryan Corporation sold plant assets for $5,000 that had cost $10,000 and had accumulated depreciation of $2,000. The entry to record this transaction is

Cash	5,000	
Accumulated Depreciation	2,000	
Loss on Sale of Plant Assets	3,000	
Plant Assets		10,000
To record sale of plant assets at a loss		

Note that in this transaction the positive cash flow is equal to the amount of cash received, or $5,000. The loss on sale of plant assets is considered here rather than in the operating activities section, where it was deleted from the income statement when computing cash flows from operating activities. The amount of loss or gain on the sale of an asset is determined by the amount of cash received.

The disclosure of these two transactions in the investing activities section of the statement of cash flows is as follows:

Purchase of Plant Assets	**$(120,000)**
Sale of Plant Assets	5,000

As with investments, cash outflows and cash inflows are not netted, but are presented separately to give full information to the statement reader.

Item **5** on the list of Ryan's investing activities is a noncash exchange that affects two long-term accounts, Plant Assets and Bonds Payable. It is recorded as follows:

Plant Assets	100,000	
Bonds Payable		100,000
Issued bonds at face value for plant assets		

Although this transaction is not an inflow or outflow of cash, it is a significant transaction involving both an investing activity (the purchase of plant assets) and a financing activity (the issue of bonds payable). Because one purpose of the statement of cash flows is to show important investing and financing activities, it is listed in a separate schedule at the bottom of the statement of cash flows or accompanying the statement, as follows:

Schedule of Noncash Investing and Financing Transactions

Issue of Bonds Payable for Plant Assets	**$100,000**

Through our analysis of these transactions and the depreciation expense for plant assets of $37,000, all the changes in the plant assets accounts have now been accounted for, as shown in these T accounts:

Plant Assets

Beg. Bal.	505,000	Sale	10,000
Purchase	120,000		
Noncash Purchase	100,000		
End. Bal.	715,000		

Accumulated Depreciation

Sale	2,000	Beg. Bal.	68,000
		Dep. Exp.	37,000
		End. Bal.	103,000

If the balance sheet had included specific plant asset accounts such as Buildings and Equipment and their related accumulated depreciation accounts, or other long-term asset accounts such as intangibles or natural resources, the analysis would be the same.

Determining Cash Flows from Financing Activities

OBJECTIVE 5b
Determine cash flows from financing activities

The third step in preparation of the statement of cash flows is to determine cash flows from financing activities. The procedure followed in this step is the same as that applied to the analysis of investing activities, including related gains and/or losses. The only difference between the two is that the accounts to be analyzed are the long-term liability and stockholders' equity accounts. Also to be taken into account are cash dividends from the statement of stockholders' equity. The following items from Exhibit 18-3 pertain to Ryan Corporation's financing activities in 19x2:

5. Issued $100,000 of bonds at face value in a noncash exchange for plant assets.
6. Repaid $50,000 of bonds at face value at maturity.
7. Issued 15,200 shares of $5 par value common stock for $150,000.
8. Paid cash dividends in the amount of $8,000.

Bonds Payable. Exhibit 18-2 shows that Bonds Payable increased by $50,000 in 19x2. This account is affected by items **5** and **6**. Item **5** was analyzed in connection with plant assets. It is reported on the schedule of noncash investing and financing transactions (see Exhibit 18-6), but must be remembered here in preparing the T account for Bonds Payable. Item **6** results in a cash outflow, a point that can be seen in the following transaction:

Bonds Payable	50,000	
Cash		50,000
To record repayment of bonds at face value at maturity		

This cash outflow is shown in the financing activities section of the statement of cash flows as follows:

Repayment of Bonds	$(50,000)

From these transactions, the change in the Bonds Payable account can be explained as follows:

Bonds Payable

Repayment	50,000	Beg. Bal.	245,000
		Noncash Issue	100,000
		End. Bal.	295,000

If Ryan Corporation had notes payable, either short-term or long-term, the analysis would be the same.

Common Stock. As with plant assets, related stockholders' equity accounts should be analyzed together. For example, Paid-in Capital in Excess of Par Value should be examined together with Common Stock. In 19x2 Ryan Corporation's Common Stock account increased by $76,000 and Paid-in Capital in Excess of Par Value increased by $74,000. These increases are explained by item **7**, which states that Ryan Corporation issued 15,200 shares of stock for $150,000. The entry to record this cash inflow is as follows:

Cash	150,000	
Common Stock		76,000
Paid-in Capital in Excess of Par Value		74,000
Issue of 15,200 shares of $5 par value common stock		

This cash inflow is shown in the financing activities section of the statement of cash flows as follows:

Issue of Common Stock	**$150,000**

The analysis of this transaction is all that is needed to explain the changes in the two accounts during 19x2, as follows:

Common Stock

	Beg. Bal.	200,000
	Issue	**76,000**
	End. Bal.	276,000

Paid-in Capital in Excess of Par Value

	Beg. Bal.	115,000
	Issue	**74,000**
	End. Bal.	189,000

Retained Earnings. At this point in the analysis, several items that affect Retained Earnings have already been dealt with. For instance, in the case of Ryan Corporation, net income was used as part of the analysis of cash flows from operating activities. The only other item affecting the retained earnings of Ryan Corporation is the payment of $8,000 in cash dividends (item 8 on the list on page 751), as reflected by the following transaction:

Retained Earnings	8,000	
Cash		8,000
To record cash dividends for 19x2		

Ryan Corporation may have declared the dividend before paying it and debited the Dividends Declared account instead of Retained Earnings, but after paying the dividend and closing the Dividends Declared account to Retained Earnings, the effect is as shown. Cash dividends are displayed in the financing activities section of the statement of cash flows as follows:

Dividends Paid $(8,000)

The change in the Retained Earnings account is explained in the T account below:

Retained Earnings

Dividends	8,000	Beg. Bal.	132,000
		Net Income	16,000
		End. Bal.	**140,000**

Presenting the Information in the Form of the Statement of Cash Flows

OBJECTIVE 6
Prepare a statement of cash flows using the (a) direct and (b) indirect methods

At this point in the analysis, all income statement items have been analyzed, all balance sheet changes have been explained, and all additional information has been taken into account. The resulting information may now be assembled into a statement of cash flows for Ryan Corporation, as shown in Exhibit 18-6. The direct approach is used because the operating activities section contains the data from Exhibit 18-4, which shows the net cash flows from operating activities as determined by the direct approach. The statement is just as easily prepared using the indirect approach and the data in Exhibit 18-5, as presented in Exhibit 18-7 (located on page 755). The only difference in these two statements is the approach used in the operating activities section. The Schedule of Noncash Investing and Financing Transactions is presented at the bottom of each statement.

In *Statement No. 95,* the FASB states a preference for the direct method of preparing the statement of cash flows, but allows companies to use the indirect method if they wish. When the direct method is used, a schedule explaining the difference between reported net income and cash flows from operating activities must be provided. An acceptable format for this schedule is the cash flows from operating activities section of the indirect method form of the statement, as shown in Exhibits 18-5 and 18-7.

Exhibit 18-6. The Statement of Cash Flows—Direct Method

Ryan Corporation
Statement of Cash Flows
For the Year Ended December 31, 19x2

Cash Flows from Operating Activities		
Cash Receipts from		
Sales	$706,000	
Interest Received	6,000	$712,000
Cash Payments for		
Purchases	$547,000	
Operating Expenses	103,000	
Interest Payments	23,000	
Income Taxes	9,000	682,000
Net Cash Flows from Operating Activities		$ 30,000
Cash Flows from Investing Activities		
Purchase of Investments	$ (78,000)	
Sale of Investments	102,000	
Purchase of Plant Assets	(120,000)	
Sale of Plant Assets	5,000	
Net Cash Flows from Investing Activities		(91,000)
Cash Flows from Financing Activities		
Repayment of Bonds	$ (50,000)	
Issue of Common Stock	150,000	
Dividends Paid	(8,000)	
Net Cash Flows from Financing Activities		92,000
Net Increase (Decrease) in Cash		$ 31,000
Cash at Beginning of Year		15,000
Cash at End of Year		$ 46,000

Schedule of Noncash Investing and Financing Transactions

Issue of Bonds Payable for Plant Assets	$100,000

Interpretation of the Statement of Cash Flows

OBJECTIVE 7
Interpret the statement of cash flows

Now that the statement is prepared, it is important to know how to interpret and use it. What can one learn about Ryan Corporation and its management by reading its statement of cash flows?

Starting with the first section of the statement in Exhibits 18-6 and 18-7, note that Ryan Corporation generated net cash flows from operating activities of $30,000, which compares very favorably with its net income of $16,000. We can see from Exhibit 18-7 that the largest positive factor is the depreciation expense of $37,000. This expense did not require a current cash outlay, and is thus an important cause of the difference between net income and cash flows from operating activities.

Exhibit 18-7. Statement of Cash Flows—Indirect Method

Ryan Corporation
Statement of Cash Flows
For the Year Ended December 31, 19x2

Cash Flows from Operating Activities		
Net Income		$ 16,000
Adjustments to Reconcile Net Income to Net		
Cash Flows from Operating Activities		
Depreciation	$ 37,000	
Gain on Sale of Investments	(12,000)	
Loss on Sale of Plant Assets	3,000	
Decrease in Accounts Receivable	8,000	
Increase in Inventory	(34,000)	
Decrease in Prepaid Expenses	4,000	
Increase in Accounts Payable	7,000	
Increase in Accrued Liabilities	3,000	
Decrease in Income Taxes Payable	(2,000)	14,000
Net Cash Flows from Operating Activities		$ 30,000
Cash Flows from Investing Activities		
Purchase of Investments	$ (78,000)	
Sale of Investments	102,000	
Purchase of Plant Assets	(120,000)	
Sale of Plant Assets	5,000	
Net Cash Flows from Investing Activities		(91,000)
Cash Flows from Financing Activities		
Repayment of Bonds	$ (50,000)	
Issue of Common Stock	150,000	
Dividends Paid	(8,000)	
Net Cash Flows from Financing Activities		92,000
Net Increase (Decrease) in Cash		$ 31,000
Cash at Beginning of Year		15,000
Cash at End of Year		$ 46,000
Schedule of Noncash Investing and Financing Transactions		
Issue of Bonds Payable for Plant Assets		$100,000

The largest drain on cash in the operating activities section is the $34,000 increase in inventory. Management may want to explore ways of reducing inventory during the next year, unless this increase was for increased sales activities next year. Other changes in current assets and current liabilities, except for the small decrease in income taxes payable, have positive effects on cash flows in this section.

Investors and creditors may want to compare net cash flows from operating activities to dividends paid in the financing activities section to determine if the company has adequate cash flows from operations to cover its payments to investors. Ryan Corporation is in good condition in this regard. Dividends paid are $8,000, compared to $30,000 in net cash flows from operating activities. The remaining $22,000 is available for other purposes and provides a cushion for payment of dividends.

Moving to the investing activities, it is apparent that the company is expanding because there is a net cash outflow of $91,000 in this section. The company has expanded by purchasing plant assets of $120,000. Various other investing activities have reduced the cash need to $91,000. This is not the whole story on the expansion of the business, however, because the schedule of noncash investing and financing transactions reveals that the company bought another $100,000 in plant assets by issuing bonds. In other words, total purchases of plant assets were $220,000. Part of this expansion was financed by issuing bonds in exchange for plant assets and most of the rest was financed through other activities.

Net cash inflows of $92,000 were provided by financing activities to offset the $91,000 net cash outflows needed for investing activities. The company looked to its owners for financing by issuing common stock for $150,000 while repaying $50,000 in bonds payable. Taking into account the noncash transaction, bonds payable increased by $50,000.

In summary, Ryan Corporation has paid for its expansion with a combination of cash flows from operating activities, net sales of investment assets, issuance of common stock, and a net increase in bonds payable.

Preparing the Work Sheet

OBJECTIVE 8
Prepare a work sheet for the statement of cash flows

Previous sections illustrated the preparation of the statement of cash flows for Ryan Corporation, a relatively simple company. To assist in preparing the statement of cash flows in more complex companies, accountants developed a work sheet approach. The work sheet approach employs a special format that allows for the systematic analysis of all the changes in the balance sheet accounts to arrive at the statement of cash flows. In this section, the work sheet approach is demonstrated using the statement of cash flows for Ryan Corporation. The work sheet approach uses the indirect method of determining cash flows from operating activities because of its basis in changes in the balance sheet accounts.

Procedures in Preparing the Work Sheet

Alternative Method

The work sheet for Ryan Corporation is presented in Exhibit 18-8. The work sheet has four columns, labeled as follows:

Column A: Description

Column B: Account balances for the end of the prior year (19x1)

Column C: Analysis of transactions for the current year

Column D: Account balances for the end of the current year (19x2)

Five steps are followed in the preparation of the work sheet. As you read each one, refer to Exhibit 18-8.

Exhibit 18-8. Work Sheet for the Statement of Cash Flows

Ryan Corporation
Work Sheet for Statement of Cash Flows
For the Year Ended December 31, 19x2

C   D

Description	Account Balances 12/31/x1	Analysis of Transactions		Account Balances 12/31/x2
		Debit	Credit	
Debits				
Cash	15,000	(x) 31,000		46,000
Accounts Receivable (net)	55,000		(b) 8,000	47,000
Inventory	110,000	(c) 34,000		144,000
Prepaid Expenses	5,000		(d) 4,000	1,000
Investments	127,000	(h) 78,000	(i) 90,000	115,000
Plant Assets	505,000	(j) 120,000	(k) 10,000	715,000
		(l) 100,000		
Total Debits	817,000			1,068,000
Credits				
Accumulated Depreciation	68,000	(k) 2,000	(m) 37,000	103,000
Accounts Payable	43,000		(e) 7,000	50,000
Accrued Liabilities	9,000		(f) 3,000	12,000
Income Taxes Payable	5,000	(g) 2,000		3,000
Bonds Payable	245,000	(n) 50,000	(l) 100,000	295,000
Common Stock	200,000		(o) 76,000	276,000
Paid-in Capital	115,000		(o) 74,000	189,000
Retained Earnings	132,000	(p) 8,000	(a) 16,000	140,000
Total Credits	817,000	425,000	425,000	1,068,000
Cash Flows from Operating Activities				
Net Income		(a) 16,000		
Decrease in Accounts Receivable		(b) 8,000		
Increase in Inventory			(c) 34,000	
Decrease in Prepaid Expenses		(d) 4,000		
Increase in Accounts Payable		(e) 7,000		
Increase in Accrued Liabilities		(f) 3,000		
Decrease in Income Taxes Payable			(g) 2,000	
Gain on Sale of Investments			(i) 12,000	
Loss on Sale of Plant Assets		(k) 3,000		
Depreciation Expense		(m) 37,000		
Cash Flows from Investing Activities				
Purchase of Investments			(h) 78,000	
Sale of Investments		(i) 102,000		
Purchase of Plant Assets			(j) 120,000	
Sale of Plant Assets		(k) 5,000		
Cash Flows from Financing Activities				
Repayment of Bonds			(n) 50,000	
Issue of Common Stock		(o) 150,000		
Dividends Paid			(p) 8,000	
		335,000	304,000	
Net Increase in Cash			(x) 31,000	
		335,000	335,000	

A   B

1. Enter the account names from the balance sheet (Exhibit 18-2 on page 739) in column A. Note that all accounts with debit balances are listed first, followed by all accounts with credit balances.
2. Enter the account balances for 19x1 in column B and the account balances for 19x2 in column D. In each column, total the debits and the credits. The total debits should equal the total credits in each column. (This is a check of whether all accounts were transferred from the balance sheet correctly.)
3. Below the data entered in Step 2, insert the captions: Cash Flows from Operating Activities; Cash Flows from Investing Activities; and Cash Flows from Financing Activities, leaving several lines of space between each one. As you do the analysis in Step 4, write the results in the appropriate categories.
4. Analyze the changes in each balance sheet account using information from both the income statement (see Exhibit 18-3) and from other appropriate transactions. (The procedures for this analysis are presented in the next section.) Enter the results in the debit and credit columns in column C. Identify each item with a letter. On the first line identify the change in cash with an (x). In a complex situation, these letters will reference a list of explanations on another working paper.
5. When all the changes in the balance sheet accounts have been explained, add the debit and credit columns in both the top and bottom portions of column C. The debit and credit columns in the top portion should equal each other. They should *not* be equal in the bottom portion. If no errors have been made, the difference between columns in the bottom portion should equal the increase or decrease in the cash account identified with an (x) on the first line of the work sheet. Add this difference to the lesser of the two columns, and identify it as either an increase or decrease in cash. Label the change with an (x) and compare it with the change in cash on the first line of the work sheet, also labeled (x). The amounts should be equal, as they are in Exhibit 18-8, where the net increase in cash is $31,000.

When the work sheet is complete, the statement of cash flows may be prepared using the information in the lower half of the work sheet, as shown previously in Exhibit 18-7.

Analyzing the Changes in Balance Sheet Accounts

The most important step in the preparation of the work sheet is the analysis of the changes in the balances of the balance sheet accounts (Step 4). Although there are a number of transactions and reclassifications to analyze and record, the overall procedure is systematic and not overly complicated. It is as follows:

1. Record net income.
2. Account for changes in current assets and current liabilities.
3. Account for changes in noncurrent accounts using the information about other transactions.
4. Reclassify any other income and expense items not already dealt with. In the following explanations, the identification letters refer

to the corresponding transactions and reclassifications in the work sheet.

a. **Net Income.** Net income results in an increase in Retained Earnings. It is also the starting point under the indirect method for determining cash flows from operating activities. Under this method, additions and deductions are made to net income to arrive at cash flows from operating activities. Work sheet entry **a** is as follows:

| (a) Cash Flows from Operations: Net Income | 16,000 | |
| Retained Earnings | | 16,000 |

b–g. **Changes in Current Assets and Current Liabilities.** Entries **b** to **g** record the effects of the changes in current assets and current liabilities on cash flows. In each case, there is a debit or credit to the current asset or current liability to account for the change in the year and a corresponding debit or credit in the operating activities section of the work sheet. Recall that in the prior analysis, each item on the accrual-based income statement was adjusted for the change in the related current asset or current liability to arrive at the cash-based figure. The same reasoning applies in recording these changes in accounts as debits or credits in the operating activities section. For example, work sheet entry **b** records the decrease in Accounts Receivable as a credit (decrease) to Accounts Receivable and as a debit in the operating activities section because the decrease has a positive effect on cash flows, as follows:

(b) Cash Flows from Operating Activities:		
Decrease in Accounts Receivable	8,000	
Accounts Receivable		8,000

Work sheet entries **c–g** reflect the effects of the changes in the other current assets and current liabilities on cash flows from operating activities. As you study these entries, note how the effects of each entry on cash flows are automatically determined by debits or credits reflecting changes in the balance sheet accounts.

(c) Inventory	34,000	
Cash Flows from Operating Activities:		
Increase in Inventory		34,000
(d) Cash Flows from Operating Activities:		
Decrease in Prepaid Expenses	4,000	
Prepaid Expenses		4,000
(e) Cash Flows from Operating Activities:		
Increase in Accounts Payable	7,000	
Accounts Payable		7,000
(f) Cash Flows from Operating Activities:		
Increase in Accrued Liabilities	3,000	
Accrued Liabilities		3,000
(g) Income Taxes Payable	2,000	
Cash Flows from Operating Activities:		
Decrease in Income Taxes Payable		2,000

h–i. *Investments.* Among the other transactions affecting noncurrent accounts during 19x2 (see Exhibit 18-3), two items pertain to investments. One is the purchase for $78,000 and the other is the sale at $102,000. The purchase is recorded on the work sheet as a cash flow in the investing activities section, as follows:

(h) Investments	78,000	
Cash Flows from Investing Activities:		
Purchase of Investments		78,000

Note that instead of crediting Cash, a credit entry with the appropriate designation is made in the appropriate section in the lower half of the work sheet. The sale transaction is more complicated because it involves a gain that appears on the income statement and is included in net income. The work sheet entry accounts for this gain as follows:

(i) Cash Flows from Investing Activities:		
Sale of Investments	102,000	
Investments		90,000
Cash Flows from Operating Activities:		
Gain on Sale of Investments		12,000

This entry records the cash inflow in the investing activities section, accounts for the remaining difference in the Investments account, and removes the gain on sale of investments from its inclusion in net income.

j–m. *Plant Assets and Accumulated Depreciation.* Four transactions affect plant assets and the related accumulated depreciation. These are the purchase of plant assets, the sale of plant assets at a loss, the noncash exchange of plant assets for bonds, and the depreciation expense for the year. Because these transactions may appear complicated, it is important to work through them systematically when preparing the work sheet. First, the purchase of plant assets for $120,000 is entered (entry j) in the same way the purchase of investments was entered in entry h. Second, the sale of plant assets is similar to the sale of investments, except that instead of a gain, a loss is involved, as follows:

(k) Cash Flows from Investing Activities:		
Sale of Plant Assets	5,000	
Cash Flows from Operating Activities:		
Loss on Sale of Plant Assets	3,000	
Accumulated Depreciation	2,000	
Plant Assets		10,000

The cash inflow from this transaction is $5,000. The rest of the entry is necessary to add the loss back into net income in the operating activities section of the statement (since it was deducted to arrive at net income) and to record the effects on plant assets and accumulated depreciation.

The third transaction (entry l) is the noncash issue of bonds for the purchase of plant assets, as follows:

(l) Plant Assets	100,000	
Bonds Payable		100,000

Note that this transaction does not affect cash. Still, it needs to be recorded because the objective is to account for all the changes in the balance sheet accounts. It is listed at the end of the statement of cash flows (Exhibit 18-7) in the schedule of noncash investing and financing transactions.

At this point the increase of $210,000 ($715,000 – $505,000) in plant assets has been explained by the two purchases less the sale ($120,000 + $100,000 – $10,000 = $210,000), but the change in Accumulated Depreciation has not been completely explained. The depreciation expense for the year needs to be entered, as follows:

(m) Cash Flows from Operating Activities:		
Depreciation Expense	37,000	
Accumulated Depreciation		37,000

The debit is to the operating activities section of the work sheet because, as explained earlier in the chapter, no current cash outflow is required for depreciation expense. The effect of this debit is to add the amount for depreciation expense back into net income. The $35,000 increase in Accumulated Depreciation has now been explained by the sale transaction and the depreciation expense (– $2,000 + $37,000 = $35,000).

n. **Bonds Payable.** Part of the change in Bonds Payable was explained in entry l when a noncash transaction, a $100,000 issue of bonds in exchange for plant assets, was entered. All that remains is to enter the repayment, as follows:

(n) Bonds Payable	50,000	
Cash Flows from Financing Activities:		
Repayment of Bonds		50,000

o. **Common Stock and Paid-in Capital in Excess of Par Value.** One transaction affects both these accounts. It is an issue of 15,200 shares of $5 par value common stock for a total of $150,000. The work sheet entry is:

(o) Cash Flows from Financing Activities:		
Issue of Common Stock	150,000	
Common Stock		76,000
Paid-in Capital in Excess of Par Value		74,000

p. *Retained Earnings.* Part of the change in Retained Earnings was recognized when net income was entered (entry **a**). The only remaining effect to be recognized is that of the $8,000 in cash dividends paid during the year, as follows:

(p) Retained Earnings	8,000	
Cash Flows from Financing Activities:		
Dividends Paid		8,000

x. The final step is to total the debit and credit columns in the top and bottom portions of the work sheet and then to enter the net change in cash at the bottom of the work sheet. The columns in the upper half equal $425,000. In the lower half, the debit column totals $335,000 and the credit column totals $304,000. The credit difference of $31,000 (entry **x**) equals the debit change in cash on the first line of the work sheet.

Chapter Review

Review of Learning Objectives

1. **Describe the statement of cash flows, and define *cash* and *cash equivalents*.**

   The statement of cash flows explains the changes in cash and cash equivalents from one accounting period to the next by showing cash outflows and cash inflows from the operating, investing, and financing activities of a company for an accounting period. For purposes of preparing the statement of cash flows, *cash* is defined to include cash and cash equivalents. *Cash equivalents* are short-term (ninety days or less) highly liquid investments, including money market accounts, commercial paper, and U.S. Treasury bills.

2. **State the principal purposes and uses of the statement of cash flows.**

   The primary purpose of the statement of cash flows is to provide information about a company's cash receipts and cash payments during an accounting period. Its secondary purpose is to provide information about a company's operating, investing, and financing activities. It is useful to management as well as to investors and creditors in assessing the liquidity of a business, including the ability of the business to generate future cash flows and to pay its debts and dividends.

3. **Identify the principal components of the classifications of cash flows, and state the significance of noncash investing and financing transactions.**

   Cash flows may be classified as operating activities, which include the cash effects of transactions and other events that enter into the determination of net income; as investing activities, which include the acquiring and selling of long- and short-term marketable securities, property, plant, and equipment, and the making and collecting of loans, excluding interest; or as financing activities, which include the obtaining and returning or repaying of resources, excluding interest to owners and creditors. Noncash investing and financing transactions are particularly important because they are exchanges of assets and/or liabilities that are of interest to investors and creditors when evaluating the financing and investing activities of the business.

4. **Determine cash flows from operating activities using the (a) direct and (b) indirect methods.**
   The direct method of determining cash flows from operating activities is accomplished by adjusting each item in the income statement from an accrual basis to a cash basis, in the following form:

Cash Flows from Operating Activities		
Cash Receipts from		
Sales	xxx	
Interest and Dividends Received	<u>xxx</u>	xxx
Cash Payments for		
Purchases	xxx	
Operating Expenses	xxx	
Interest Payments	xxx	
Income Taxes	<u>xxx</u>	<u>xxx</u>
Net Cash Flows from Operating Activities		xxx

In the indirect method, net income is adjusted for all noncash effects to arrive at a cash flow basis, as follows:

Cash Flows from Operating Activities		
Net Income		xxx
Adjustments to Reconcile Net Income to Net Cash		
Flows from Operating Activities		
(List of individual items)	<u>xxx</u>	<u>xxx</u>
Net Cash Flows from Operating Activities		xxx

5. **Determine cash flows from (a) investing activities and (b) financing activities.**
   Cash flows from investing activities are determined by identifying the cash flow effects of the transactions that affect each account relevant to investing activities. These accounts include all long-term assets and short-term marketable securities. The same procedure is followed for financing activities, except that the accounts involved are short-term notes payable, long-term liabilities, and owners' equity accounts. The effects on related accounts of gains and losses reported on the income statement must also be considered. When the change in a balance sheet account from one accounting period to the next has been explained, all the cash flow effects should have been identified.

6. **Prepare a statement of cash flows using the (a) direct and (b) indirect methods.**

   The statement of cash flows lists cash flows from operating activities, investing activities, and financing activities, in that order. The section on operating activities may be prepared using either the direct or indirect method of determining cash flows from operating activities. The sections on investing and financing activities are prepared by examining individual accounts involving cash receipts and cash payments in order to explain year-to-year changes in the account balances. Significant noncash transactions are included in a schedule of noncash investing and financing transactions that accompanies the statement of cash flows.

7. **Interpret the statement of cash flows.**

   Interpretation of the statement of cash flows begins with an examination of the cash flows from operations, to determine if they are positive and to assess the differences between net income and net cash flows from operating activities. It is usually informative to relate cash flows from operations to dividend payments in the financing section to see if the company is comfortably covering these important cash outflows. It is also useful to examine investing activities to determine if the company is expanding, and if so, in what areas of business it is investing; and if not, in what areas it is contracting. Based on the analysis of investing, one should then look at the financing section to evaluate how the company is financing its expansion, or if it is not expanding, how it is reducing its financing obligations. Finally, it is important to evaluate the impact of the noncash investing and financing transactions listed in the lower portion of the statement of cash flows.

8. **Prepare a work sheet for the statement of cash flows.**

   A work sheet is useful in preparing the statement of cash flows for complex companies. The basic procedures in the work sheet approach are to analyze the changes in the balance sheet accounts for their effects on cash flows (in the top portion of the work sheet) and to classify those effects according to the format of the statement of cash flows (in the lower portion of the work sheet). When all the changes in the balance sheet accounts have been explained and entered on the work sheet, the change in the cash account will also be explained, and the information will be available to prepare the statement of cash flows. The work sheet approach lends itself to the indirect method of preparing the statement of cash flows.

Review of Concepts and Terminology

The following concepts and terms were introduced in this chapter:

(L.O. 1) **Cash:** Cash and cash equivalents.

(L.O. 1) **Cash equivalents:** Short-term (ninety days or less), highly liquid investments, including money market accounts, commercial paper, and U.S. Treasury bills.

(L.O. 4a) **Direct method:** The procedure for converting the income statement from an accrual basis to a cash basis by adjusting each item in the income statement separately.

(L.O. 3) **Financing activities**: Business activities that involve obtaining or returning resources from or to owners and providing them with a return on their investment.

(L.O. 4b) **Indirect method**: The procedure for converting the income statement from an accrual basis to a cash basis by adjusting net income for items that do not affect cash flows, including depreciation, amortization, depletion, gains, losses, and changes in current assets and current liabilities.

(L.O. 3) **Investing activities**: Business activities that include the acquiring and selling of long-term assets, the acquiring and selling of marketable securities other than cash equivalents, and the making and collecting of loans.

(L.O. 3) **Noncash investing and financing transactions**: Significant investing and financing transactions that do not involve an actual cash inflow or outflow but involve only long-term assets, long-term liabilities, or stockholders' equity, such as the exchange of a long-term asset for a long-term liability or the settlement of a debt by the issue of capital stock.

(L.O. 3) **Operating activities**: Business activities that include the cash effects of transactions and other events that enter into the determination of net income.

(L.O. 1) **Statement of cash flows**: A primary financial statement that shows the effect on cash of the operating, investing, and financing activities of a company for an accounting period.

Self-Test

Test your knowledge of the chapter by choosing the best answer for each item below and on the following page.

1. Cash equivalents include
   a. three-month Treasury bills.
   b. short-term investments.
   c. accounts receivable.
   d. long-term investments.   *(L.O. 1)*

2. The primary purpose of the statement of cash flows is to provide information
   a. regarding the results of operations for a period of time.
   b. regarding the financial position of a company as of the end of an accounting period.
   c. about a company's operating, investing, and financing activities during an accounting period.
   d. about a company's cash receipts and cash payments during an accounting period.   *(L.O. 2)*

3. Which of the following is supplemental to the statement of cash flows?
   a. Operating activities
   b. Investing activities
   c. Significant noncash transactions
   d. Financing activities   *(L.O. 3)*

4. Which of the following would be classified as an operating activity in the statement of cash flows?
   a. Declared or paid a cash dividend
   b. Issued long-term notes for plant assets
   c. Paid interest on a long-term note
   d. Purchased a patent   (L.O. 4)

5. The direct method of preparing the operating activities section of the statement of cash flows differs from the indirect method in that it
   a. starts with the net income figure.
   b. lists the changes in current asset accounts in the operating section.
   c. begins with cash from customers, which is revenues adjusted for the change in accounts receivable.
   d. lists significant noncash transactions.   (L.O. 4)

6. Which of the following would be classified as an investing activity on the statement of cash flows?
   a. Paid a cash dividend
   b. Issued long-term notes for plant assets
   c. Paid interest on a long-term note
   d. Purchased a patent   (L.O. 5)

7. Which of the following would be classified as a financing activity on the statement of cash flows?
   a. Declared and paid a cash dividend
   b. Issued long-term notes for plant assets
   c. Paid interest on a long-term note
   d. Purchased a patent   (L.O. 5)

8. On the statement of cash flows, the net amount of the major components of cash flow will equal the increase or decrease in
   a. cash and accounts receivable.
   b. working capital.
   c. cash and cash equivalents.
   d. very short-term investments.   (L.O. 6)

9. In general, to determine where the funds came from to pay for net investing activities, it is best to focus on which of the following sections of the statement of cash flows?
   a. Operating activities and financing activities
   b. Investing activities and financing activities
   c. Operating activities
   d. Financing activities   (L.O. 7)

10. A basic feature of the work sheet approach to preparing the statement of cash flows is that entries are made on the work sheet to
    a. be used for reference for later entry in the general journal.
    b. adjust the cash amount to an accrual basis.
    c. explain the changes in income statement accounts.
    d. explain the changes in balance sheet accounts.   (L.O. 8)

Answers to Self-Test are at the end of this chapter.

Review Problem
The Statement of Cash Flows

(L.O. 4, 5, 6)   The comparative balance sheets for Northwest Corporation for the years 19x7 and 19x6 are presented below; the 19x7 income statement is shown on the following page.

	19x7	19x6	Change	Increase or Decrease
Northwest Corporation Comparative Balance Sheets December 31, 19x7 and 19x6				
Assets				
Cash	$ 115,850	$ 121,850	$ (6,000)	Decrease
Accounts Receivable (net)	296,000	314,500	(18,500)	Decrease
Inventory	322,000	301,000	21,000	Increase
Prepaid Expenses	7,800	5,800	2,000	Increase
Long-Term Investments	36,000	86,000	(50,000)	Decrease
Land	150,000	125,000	25,000	Increase
Building	462,000	462,000	—	—
Accumulated Depreciation, Building	(91,000)	(79,000)	(12,000)	Increase
Equipment	159,730	167,230	(7,500)	Decrease
Accumulated Depreciation, Equipment	(43,400)	(45,600)	2,200	Decrease
Intangible Assets	19,200	24,000	(4,800)	Decrease
Total Assets	$1,434,180	$1,482,780	$ (48,600)	
Liabilities and Stockholders' Equity				
Accounts Payable	$ 133,750	$ 233,750	$(100,000)	Decrease
Notes Payable (current)	75,700	145,700	(70,000)	Decrease
Accrued Liabilities	5,000	—	5,000	Increase
Income Taxes Payable	20,000	—	20,000	Increase
Bonds Payable	210,000	310,000	(100,000)	Decrease
Mortgage Payable	330,000	350,000	(20,000)	Decrease
Common Stock—$10 par value	360,000	300,000	60,000	Increase
Paid-in Capital in Excess of Par Value, Common	90,000	50,000	40,000	Increase
Retained Earnings	209,730	93,330	116,400	Increase
Total Liabilities and Stockholders' Equity	$1,434,180	$1,482,780	$ (48,600)	

		Northwest Corporation
		Income Statement
		For the Year Ended December 31, 19x7

Sales		$1,650,000
Cost of Goods Sold		920,000
Gross Margin		$ 730,000
Operating Expenses (including Depreciation Expense of $12,000 on Buildings and $23,100 on Equipment and Amortization Expense of $4,800)		470,000
Operating Income		$ 260,000
Other Income (Expense)		
Interest Expense	$(55,000)	
Dividend Income	3,400	
Gain on Sale of Investments	12,500	
Loss on Disposal of Equipment	(2,300)	(41,400)
Income before Taxes		$ 218,600
Income Taxes		52,200
Net Income		$ 166,400

The following additional information was taken from the company's records:

a. Long-term investments that cost $70,000 were sold at a gain of $12,500; additional long-term investments were made in the amount of $20,000.
b. Five acres of land were purchased for $25,000 for a parking lot.
c. Equipment that cost $37,500 with accumulated depreciation of $25,300 was sold at a loss of $2,300; new equipment in the amount of $30,000 was purchased.
d. Notes payable in the amount of $100,000 were repaid; an additional $30,000 was borrowed by signing notes payable.
e. Bonds payable in the amount of $100,000 were converted into 6,000 shares of common stock.
f. The Mortgage Payable account was reduced by $20,000 during the year.
g. Cash dividends declared and paid were $50,000.

Required

1. Prepare a schedule of cash flows from operating activities using the (a) direct method and (b) indirect method.
2. Prepare a statement of cash flows using the direct method.

Answer to Review Problem

1. (a) Schedule of cash flows from operating activities—direct method prepared

Northwest Corporation Schedule of Cash Flows from Operating Activities For the Year Ended December 31, 19x7		
Cash Flows from Operating Activities		
Cash Receipts from		
Sales	$1,668,500[1]	
Dividends Received	3,400	$1,671,900
Cash Payments for		
Purchases	$1,041,000[2]	
Operating Expenses	427,100[3]	
Interest Payments	55,000	
Income Taxes	32,200[4]	1,555,300
Net Cash Flows from Operating Activities		$ 116,600

[1] $1,650,000 + $18,500 = $1,668 500
[2] $920,000 + $100,000 + $21,000 = $1,041,000
[3] $470,000 + $2,000 − $5,000 − ($12,000 + $23,100 + $4,800) = $427,100
[4] $52,200 − $20,000 = $32,200

1. (b) Schedule of cash flows from operating activities—indirect method prepared

Northwest Corporation Schedule of Cash Flows from Operating Activities For the Year Ended December 31, 19x7		
Net Income		$166,400
Adjustments to Reconcile Net Income to		
Net Cash Flows from Operating Activities		
Depreciation Expense, Buildings	$ 12,000	
Depreciation Expense, Equipment	23,100	
Amortization Expense, Intangible Assets	4,800	
Gain on Sale of Investments	(12,500)	
Loss on Disposal of Equipment	2,300	
Decrease in Accounts Receivable	18,500	
Increase in Inventory	(21,000)	
Increase in Prepaid Expenses	(2,000)	
Decrease in Accounts Payable	(100,000)	
Increase in Accrued Liabilities	5,000	
Increase in Income Taxes Payable	20,000	(49,800)
Net Cash Flows from Operating Activities		$116,600

2. Statement of cash flows—direct method prepared

Northwest Corporation Statement of Cash Flows For the Year Ended December 31, 19x7		
Cash Flows from Operating Activities		
Cash Receipts from		
Sales	$1,668,500	
Dividends Received	3,400	$1,671,900
Cash Payments for		
Purchases	$1,041,000	
Operating Expenses	427,100	
Interest Payments	55,000	
Income Taxes	32,200	1,555,300
Net Cash Flows from Operating Activities		$ 116,600
Cash Flows from Investing Activities		
Sale of Long-Term Investments	$ 82,500*	
Purchase of Long-Term Investments	(20,000)	
Purchase of Land	(25,000)	
Sale of Equipment	9,900**	
Purchase of Equipment	(30,000)	
Net Cash Flows from Investing Activities		17,400
Cash Flows from Financing Activities		
Repayment of Notes Payable	$ (100,000)	
Issuance of Notes Payable	30,000	
Reduction in Mortgage	(20,000)	
Dividends Paid	(50,000)	
Net Cash Flows from Financing Activities		(140,000)
Net Increase (Decrease) in Cash		$ (6,000)
Cash at Beginning of Year		121,850
Cash at End of Year		$ 115,850
Schedule of Noncash Investing and Financing Transactions		
Conversion of Bonds Payable into Common Stock		$ 100,000

* $70,000 + $12,500 (gain) = $82,500
**$37,500 − $25,300 = $12,200 (book value)
    $12,200 − $2,300 (loss) = $9,900
(Note: When the direct method is used, a schedule explaining the difference between reported net income and cash flows from operating activities must be provided. An acceptable format for this schedule is the schedule of cash flows from operating activities under the indirect method, shown in part **1(b)**.)

Chapter Assignments

Discussion Questions and Writing Assignments

1. How has the practice in the reporting of changes in financial position and of investing and reporting activities changed during the 1980s?
2. What is the term *cash* in the statement of cash flows understood to mean and include?
3. In order to earn a return on cash on hand during 19x3, Sallas Corporation transferred $45,000 from its checking account to a money market account, purchased a $25,000 Treasury bill, and bought $35,000 in common stocks. How will each of these transactions affect the statement of cash flows?
4. What are the purposes of the statement of cash flows?
5. Why is the statement of cash flows needed when most of the information in it is available from a company's comparative balance sheets and the income statement?
6. What are the three classifications of cash flows? Give some examples of each.
7. Why is it important to disclose certain noncash transactions? How should they be disclosed?
8. Cell-Borne Corporation has a net loss of $12,000 in 19x1 but has positive cash flows from operations of $9,000. What conditions may have caused this situation?
9. What are the essential differences between the direct method and the indirect method of determining cash flows from operations?
10. Glen Corporation has the following other income and expense items: interest expense, $12,000; interest income, $3,000; dividend income, $5,000; and loss on retirement of bonds, $6,000. How does each of these items appear on or affect the statement of cash flows?
11. What are the effects of the following items on cash flows from operations: (a) an increase in accounts receivable, (b) a decrease in inventory, (c) an increase in accounts payable, (d) a decrease in wages payable, (e) depreciation expense, and (f) amortization of patents?
12. What is the proper treatment on the statement of cash flows of a transaction in which a building that cost $50,000 with accumulated depreciation of $32,000 is sold for a loss of $5,000?
13. What is the proper treatment on the statement of cash flows of (a) a transaction in which buildings and land are purchased by the issuance of a mortgage for $234,000 and (b) a conversion of $50,000 in bonds payable into 2,500 shares of $6 par value common stock?
14. In interpreting the statement of cash flows, what are some comparisons that can be made with cash flows from operations? Prepare a list of reasons why a company would have a decrease in cash flows from investing activities.
15. Why is the work sheet approach considered to be more compatible with the indirect method than the direct method of determining cash flows from operations?

16. Assuming in each of the following independent cases that only one transaction occurred, what transactions would likely cause (1) a decrease in investments and (2) an increase in common stock? How would each case be treated on the work sheet for the statement of cash flows?

Classroom Exercises

Exercise 18-1.
Classification
of Cash Flow
Transactions
(L.O. 3)

Horizon Corporation engaged in the following transactions. Identify each as (1) an operating activity, (2) an investing activity, (3) a financing activity, (4) a noncash transaction, or (5) none of the above.

a. Declared and paid a cash dividend.
b. Purchased an investment.
c. Received cash from customers.
d. Paid interest.
e. Sold equipment at a loss.
f. Issued long-term bonds for plant assets.
g. Received dividends on securities held.
h. Issued common stock.
i. Declared and issued a stock dividend.
j. Repaid notes payable.
k. Paid employees for wages.
l. Purchased a 60-day Treasury bill.
m. Purchased land.

Exercise 18-2.
Computing
Cash Flows
from Operating
Activities—
Direct Method
(L.O. 4)

Europa Corporation engaged in the following transactions in 19x2. Using the direct method, compute the various cash flows from operating activities as required.

a. During 19x2, Europa Corporation had cash sales of $41,300 and sales on credit of $123,000. During the same year, accounts receivable decreased by $18,000. Determine the cash received from customers during 19x2.
b. During 19x2, Europa Corporation's cost of goods sold was $119,000. During the same year, merchandise inventory increased by $12,500 and accounts payable decreased by $4,300. Determine the cash payments for purchases during 19x2.
c. During 19x2, Europa Corporation had operating expenses of $45,000, including depreciation of $15,600. Also during 19x2, related prepaid expenses decreased by $3,100 and relevant accrued expenses increased by $1,200. Determine the cash payments to suppliers of goods and services during 19x2.
d. Europa Corporation's income taxes expense for 19x2 was $4,300. Income Taxes Payable decreased by $230 that year. Determine the cash payment for income taxes during 19x2.

Exercise 18-3.
Computing
Cash Flows
from Operating
Activities—
Indirect Method
(L.O. 4)

During 19x1, Mayfair Corporation had a net income of $41,000. Included on the income statement was Depreciation Expense of $2,300 and Amortization Expense of $300. During the year, accounts receivable increased by $3,400, inventories decreased by $1,900, prepaid expenses decreased by $200, accounts payable increased by $5,000, and accrued liabilities decreased by $450. Determine cash flows from operating activities using the indirect method.

Exercise 18-4.
Preparing a
Schedule of
Cash Flows
from Operating
Activities—
Direct Method
(L.O. 4)

The income statement for the Ridge Corporation follows.

Ridge Corporation
Income Statement
For the Year Ended June 30, 19xx

Sales		$61,000
Cost of Goods Sold		30,000
Gross Margin from Sales		$31,000
Other Expenses		
Salaries Expense	$16,000	
Rent Expense	8,400	
Depreciation Expense	1,000	25,400
Income before Income Taxes		$ 5,600
Income Taxes		1,200
Net Income		$ 4,400

Additional information: (a) All sales were on credit, and accounts receivable increased by $2,200 during the year. (b) All merchandise purchased was on credit. Inventories increased by $3,500, and accounts payable increased by $7,000 during the year. (c) Prepaid rent decreased by $700, while salaries payable increased by $500. (d) Income taxes payable decreased by $300 during the year. Prepare a schedule of cash flows from operating activities using the direct method.

Exercise 18-5.
Preparing a
Schedule of
Cash Flows
from Operating
Activities—
Indirect Method
(L.O. 4)

Using the data provided in Exercise 18-4, prepare a schedule of cash flows from operating activities using the indirect method.

Exercise 18-6.
Computing
Cash Flows
from Investing
Activities—
Investments
(L.O. 5)

The T account for the Investments account for Krieger Company at the end of 19x3 follows.

Investments			
Beg. Bal.	38,500	Sales	39,000
Purchases	58,000		
End. Bal.	**57,500**		

In addition, Krieger's income statement shows a loss on the sale of investments of $6,500. Compute the amounts to be shown as cash flows from investing activities and show how they are to appear on the statement of cash flows.

Exercise 18-7.
Computing
Cash Flows
from Investing
Activities—
Plant Assets
(L.O. 5)

The T accounts for the Plant Assets and Accumulated Depreciation accounts for Krieger Company at the end of 19x3 are as follows:

Plant Assets

Beg. Bal.	65,000	Disposals	23,000
Purchases	33,600		
End. Bal.	75,600		

Accumulated Depreciation

Disposals	14,700	Beg. Bal.	34,500
		19x3	
		Depreciation	10,200
		End. Bal.	30,000

In addition, Krieger Company's income statement shows a gain on sale of plant assets of $4,400. Compute the amounts to be shown as cash flows from investing activities and show how they are to appear on the statement of cash flows.

Exercise 18-8.
Determining
Cash Flows
from Investing
and Financing
Activities
(L.O. 5)

All transactions involving Notes Payable and related accounts engaged in by Krieger Company during 19x3 are as follows:

Cash	18,000	
Notes Payable		18,000
Bank loan		
Patent	30,000	
Notes Payable		30,000
Purchase of patent by issuing note payable		
Notes Payable	5,000	
Interest Expense	500	
Cash		5,500
Repayment of note payable at maturity		

Determine the amounts and how these transactions are to be shown in the statement of cash flows for 19x3

**Exercise 18-9.
Preparing the
Statement of
Cash Flows
(L.O. 6)**

Javier Corporation's comparative balance sheets for June 30, 19x2 and 19x1, and its 19x2 income statement follow.

Javier Corporation
Comparative Balance Sheets
June 30, 19x2 and 19x1

	19x2	19x1
Assets		
Cash	$ 69,900	$ 12,500
Accounts Receivable (net)	21,000	26,000
Inventory	43,400	48,400
Prepaid Expenses	3,200	2,600
Furniture	55,000	60,000
Accumulated Depreciation, Furniture	(9,000)	(5,000)
Total Assets	$183,500	$144,500
Liabilities and Stockholders' Equity		
Accounts Payable	$ 13,000	$ 14,000
Income Taxes Payable	1,200	1,800
Notes Payable (long-term)	37,000	35,000
Common Stock—$5 par value	115,000	90,000
Retained Earnings	17,300	3,700
Total Liabilities and Stockholders' Equity	$183,500	$144,500

Javier Corporation
Income Statement
For the Year Ended June 30, 19x2

Sales	$234,000
Cost of Goods Sold	156,000
Gross Margin	$ 78,000
Operating Expenses	45,000
Operating Income	$ 33,000
Interest Expense	2,800
Income Before Income Taxes	$ 30,200
Income Taxes	12,300
Net Income	$ 17,900

Additional information: (a) issued $22,000 note payable for purchase of furniture; (b) sold furniture that cost $27,000 with accumulated depreciation of $15,300 at carrying value; (c) recorded depreciation on the furniture during the year, $19,300; (d) repaid a note in the amount of $20,000; issued $25,000 of common stock at par value; and (e) declared and paid dividends of $4,300. Without using a work sheet, prepare a statement of cash flows for 19x2 using the direct method.

**Exercise 18-10.
Preparing a
Work Sheet for
the Statement
of Cash Flows
(L.O. 6, 8)**

Using the information in Exercise 18-9, prepare a work sheet for the statement of cash flows for Javier Corporation for 19x2. From the work sheet, prepare a statement of cash flows using the indirect method.

Interpreting Accounting Information

**Airborne Express,
Inc.***
(L.O. 7)

Airborne Express, Inc. is an air express transportation company, providing next day, morning delivery of small packages and documents throughout the United States. Airborne Express is one of three major participants, along with Federal Express and United Parcel Service, in the air express industry. The letter to the stockholders from the company's 1988 annual report states, "Throughout 1988 Airborne Express continued to experience very strong shipment growth, but we were unable to convert that growth into significant earnings improvement due to continued downward pressure on prices." It goes on to state, "The problem we have experienced is that given competitive pressures, we have not been able to generate adequate revenues to the rapidly rising depreciation expense associated with our capital expenditures." Airborne's 1988 statement of cash flows is presented on the next page.

Required

1. What has been the trend of depreciation over the last three years and what was the relationship between net earnings and net funds (cash) provided by operations in 1988?
2. Does Airborne Express, Inc. generate enough net cash flows from operating activities to both pay dividends and provide additional funds for expansion?
3. Has Airborne Express been expanding over the last three years? If your answer is yes, what were Airborne's primary means of financing the expansion?

* Excerpts from the 1988 annual report used by permission of Airborne Express, P. O. Box 662, Seattle, Washington 98111. Copyright © 1988.

Airborne Freight Corporation and Subsidiaries
Consolidated Statements of Cash Flows
For the Years Ended December 31, 1986–1988

Year Ended December 31	1988	1987	1986
	(In thousands)		
Operating Activities			
Net Earnings	$ 7,036	$ 5,898	$ 13,215
Adjustments to Reconcile Net Earnings to Net Cash Provided by Operating Activities			
Depreciation and amortization	46,462	35,594	22,725
Provision for aircraft engine overhauls	5,823	5,230	3,545
Gain on disposition of aircraft	(1,717)	—	(2,509)
Deferred income taxes	1,795	2,595	4,297
Cash Provided by Operations	$ 59,399	$ 49,317	$ 41,273
Change in:			
Receivables	(16,874)	(18,020)	(2,714)
Inventories and prepaid expenses	(8,229)	(1,444)	(2,881)
Accounts payable	20,243	3,057	10,366
Accrued expenses, salaries and taxes payable	6,077	335	(5,156)
Net Cash Provided by Operating Activities	$ 60,616	$ 33,245	$ 40,888
Investing Activities			
Additions to property and equipment	$(85,831)	$ (85,901)	$(76,023)
Disposition of property and equipment	2,142	5,637	6,684
Expenditures for engine overhauls	(6,525)	(4,608)	(3,797)
Purchase of leased aircraft	—	(14,147)	—
Increase in other assets	(1,730)	(2,068)	(704)
Decrease in restricted construction funds	—	—	10,328
Net Cash Used in Investing Activities	$(91,944)	$(101,087)	$(63,512)
Financing Activities			
Increase (decrease) in bank notes payable	$ 37,800	$ 53,400	$(21,200)
Principal payments of long-term debt and capital lease obligations	(3,165)	(8,289)	(2,259)
Issuance of common stock	78	30,632	467
Dividends paid	(4,141)	(3,836)	(3,512)
Issuance of subordinated debt	—	—	50,000
Debt issue costs	—	—	(1,061)
Net Cash Provided by Financing Activities	$ 30,572	$ 71,907	$ 22,435
Net Increase (Decrease) in Cash	$ (756)	$ 4,065	$ (189)
Cash at Beginning of Year	$ 7,197	S 3,132	$ 3,321
Cash at End of Year	$ 6,441	S 7,197	$ 3,132

See notes to consolidated financial statements.

Problem Set A

Problem 18A-1.
Classification of
Transactions
(L.O. 3)

Analyze the transactions presented in the schedule that follows and place an X in the appropriate column to indicate the classification of each transaction and its effect on cash flows using the direct method.

Transaction	Operating Activity	Investing Activity	Financing Activity	Noncash Transac-tions	Increase	Decrease	No Effect
	Cash Flow Classification				Effect on Cash		
a. Incurred a net loss.							
b. Declared and issued a stock dividend.							
c. Paid a cash dividend.							
d. Collected accounts receivable.							
e. Purchased inventory with cash.							
f. Retired long-term debt with cash.							
g. Sold investment for a loss.							
h. Issued stock for equipment.							
i. Purchased a one-year insurance policy for cash.							
j. Purchased treasury stock with cash.							
k. Retired a fully depreciated truck (no gain or loss).							
l. Paid interest on note.							
m. Received dividend on investment.							
n. Sold treasury stock.							
o. Paid income taxes.							
p. Transferred cash to money market account.							
q. Purchased land and building with a mortgage.							

Problem 18A-2.
Cash Flows
from Operating
Activities
(L.O. 4)

The income statement for Milos Food Corporation is shown as follows:

Milos Food Corporation
Income Statement
For the Year Ended December 31, 19xx

Sales		$490,000
Cost of Goods Sold		
Beginning Inventory	$220,000	
Purchases (net)	400,000	
Goods Available for Sale	$620,000	
Ending Inventory	250,000	
Cost of Goods Sold		370,000
Gross Margin from Sales		$120,000
Selling and Administrative Expenses		
Selling and Administrative Salaries Expense	$ 50,000	
Other Selling and Administrative Expenses	11,500	
Depreciation Expense	18,000	
Amortization Expense (Intangible Assets)	1,500	81,000
Income before Income Taxes		$ 39,000
Income Taxes		12,500
Net Income		$ 26,500

Additional information: (a) accounts receivable (net) increased by $18,000, and accounts payable decreased by $26,000 during the year; (b) salaries payable at the end of the year were $7,000 more than last year; (c) the expired amount of prepaid insurance for the year is $500 and equals the decrease in the Prepaid Insurance account; and (d) income taxes payable decreased by $5,400 from last year.

Required

1. Prepare a schedule of cash flows from operating activities using the direct method.
2. Prepare a schedule of cash flows from operating activities using the indirect method.

Problem 18A-3.
Cash Flows
from Operating
Activities
(L.O. 4)

The income statement of Gardner Electronics, Inc. appears on page 780. Relevant accounts from the comparative balance sheets for February 28, 19x3 and 19x2 are as follows:

	19x3	19x2
Accounts Receivable (net)	$65,490	$ 48,920
Inventory	98,760	102,560
Prepaid Expenses	10,450	5,490
Accounts Payable	42,380	55,690
Accrued Liabilities	3,560	8,790
Income Taxes Payable	24,630	13,800

Gardner Electronics, Inc.
Income Statement
For the Year Ended February 28, 19x3

Sales		$919,000
Cost of Goods Sold		643,500
Gross Margin from Sales		$275,500
Operating Expenses (including Depreciation Expense of $21,430)		176,900
Operating Income		$ 98,600
Other Income (Expenses)		
Interest Expense	$(27,800)	
Dividend Income	14,200	
Loss on Sale of Investments	(12,100)	(25,700)
Income before Income Taxes		$ 72,900
Income Taxes		21,500
Net Income		$ 51,400

Required

1. Prepare a schedule of cash flows from operating activities using the direct method.
2. Prepare a schedule of cash flows from operating activities using the indirect method.

Problem 18A-4.
The Statement of Cash Flows—Direct Method
(L.O. 6, 7)

Meridian Corporation's 19x2 income statement and its comparative balance sheets as of December 31, 19x2 and 19x1 appear as follows.

Meridian Corporation
Income Statement
For the Year Ended December 31, 19x2

Sales		$804,500
Cost of Goods Sold		563,900
Gross Margin from Sales		$240,600
Operating Expenses (including Depreciation Expense of $23,400)		224,700
Income from Operations		$ 15,900
Other Income (Expenses)		
Gain on Disposal of Furniture and Fixtures	$ 3,500	
Interest Expense	(11,600)	(8,100)
Income before Income Taxes		$ 7,800
Income Taxes		2,300
Net Income		$ 5,500

Meridian Corporation
Comparative Balance Sheets
December 31, 19x2 and 19x1

	19x2	19x1
Assets		
Cash	$ 82,400	$ 25,000
Accounts Receivable (net)	82,600	100,000
Merchandise Inventory	175,000	225,000
Prepaid Rent	1,000	1,500
Furniture and Fixtures	74,000	72,000
Accumulated Depreciation, Furniture and Fixtures	(21,000)	(12,000)
Total Assets	$394,000	$411,500
Liabilities and Stockholders' Equity		
Accounts Payable	$ 71,700	$100,200
Notes Payable (long-term)	20,000	10,000
Bonds Payable	50,000	100,000
Income Taxes Payable	700	2,200
Common Stock—$10 par value	120,000	100,000
Paid-in Capital in Excess of Par Value	90,720	60,720
Retained Earnings	40,880	38,380
Total Liabilities and Stockholders' Equity	$394,000	$411,500

Additional information about 19x2: (a) furniture and fixtures that cost $17,800 with accumulated depreciation of $14,400 were sold at a gain of $3,500; (b) furniture and fixtures were purchased in the amount of $19,800; (c) a $10,000 note payable was paid and $20,000 was borrowed on a new note; (d) bonds payable in the amount of $50,000 were converted into 2,000 shares of common stock; and (e) $3,000 in cash dividends were declared and paid.

Required

1. Prepare a statement of cash flows using the direct method. Include a supporting schedule of noncash investing and financing transactions. (Do not use a work sheet.)
2. What are the primary reasons for Meridian Corporation's large increase in cash from 19x1 to 19x2, despite its low net income?

Problem 18A-5.
The Work Sheet and the Statement of Cash Flows— Indirect Method
(L.O. 6, 8)

Use the information for Meridian Corporation given in Problem 18A-4 to answer the requirements on the next page.

Required

1. Prepare a work sheet for gathering information for the preparation of the statement of cash flows.
2. From the information on the work sheet, prepare a statement of cash flows using the indirect approach. Include a supporting schedule of non-cash investing and financing transactions.

Problem 18A-6.
The Work Sheet
and the Statement
of Cash Flows—
Indirect Method
(L.O. 6, 7, 8)

The comparative balance sheets for Gregory Fabrics, Inc. for December 31, 19x3 and 19x2 appear as follows.

Gregory Fabrics, Inc.
Comparative Balance Sheets
December 31, 19x3 and 19x2

	19x3	19x2
Assets		
Cash	$ 38,560	$ 27,360
Accounts Receivable (net)	102,430	75,430
Inventory	112,890	137,890
Prepaid Expenses	—	20,000
Land	25,000	—
Building	137,000	—
Accumulated Depreciation, Building	(15,000)	—
Equipment	33,000	34,000
Accumulated Depreciation, Equipment	(14,500)	(24,000)
Patents	4,000	6,000
Total Assets	$423,380	$276,680
Liabilities and Stockholders' Equity		
Accounts Payable	$ 10,750	$ 36,750
Notes Payable	10,000	—
Accrued Liabilities (current)	—	12,300
Mortgage Payable	162,000	—
Common Stock	180,000	150,000
Paid-in Capital in Excess of Par Value	57,200	37,200
Retained Earnings	3,430	40,430
Total Liabilities and Stockholders' Equity	$423,380	$276,680

Additional information about Gregory Fabrics' operations during 19x3: (a) net loss, $28,000; (b) building and equipment depreciation expense amounts, $15,000 and $3,000, respectively; (c) equipment that cost $13,500 with accumulated depreciation of $12,500, sold for a gain of $5,300; (d) equipment purchases, $12,500; (e) patent amortization, $3,000; purchase of patent, $1,000; (f) borrowed funds by issuing notes payable, $25,000; notes payable repaid, $15,000; (g) land and building purchased for $162,000 by signing a mortgage for the total cost; (h) 3,000 shares of $10 par value common stock issued for a total of $50,000; and (i) cash dividend, $9,000.

Required	1. Prepare a work sheet for the statement of cash flows for Gregory Fabrics.

1. Prepare a work sheet for the statement of cash flows for Gregory Fabrics.
2. Prepare a statement of cash flows from the information in the work sheet using the indirect method.
3. Why did Gregory Fabrics have an increase in Cash in a year in which it recorded a net loss of $28,000? Discuss and interpret.

Problem Set B

**Problem 18B-1.
Classification of
Transactions
(L.O. 3)**

Analyze the transactions in the schedule below and on the next page, and place an X in the appropriate column to indicate the classification of each transaction and its effect on cash flows using the direct method.

	Cash Flow Classification				Effect on Cash		
Transaction	Operating Activity	Investing Activity	Financing Activity	Noncash Transactions	Increase	Decrease	No Effect
a. Recorded net income.							
b. Declared and paid cash dividend.							
c. Issued stock for cash.							
d. Retired long-term debt by issuing stock.							
e. Paid accounts payable.							
f. Purchased inventory.							
g. Purchased a one-year insurance policy.							
h. Purchased a long-term investment with cash.							
i. Sold marketable securities at a gain.							
j. Sold a machine for a loss.							
k. Retired fully depreciated equipment.							
l. Paid interest on debt.							
m. Purchased marketable securities.							

(continued)

Transaction	Cash Flow Classification				Effect on Cash		
	Operating Activity	Investing Activity	Financing Activity	Noncash Transactions	Increase	Decrease	No Effect
n. Received dividend income.							
o. Received cash on account.							
p. Converted bonds to common stock.							
q. Purchased short-term, ninety-day Treasury bill.							

**Problem 18B-2.
Cash Flows
from Operating
Activities
(L.O. 4)**

The income statement for Falcone Clothing Store is shown as follows.

**Falcone Clothing Store
Income Statement
For the Year Ended June 30, 19xx**

Sales		$2,450,000
Cost of Goods Sold		
Beginning Inventory	$ 620,000	
Purchases (net)	1,520,000	
Goods Available for Sale	$2,140,000	
Ending Inventory	700,000	
Cost of Goods Sold		1,440,000
Gross Margin from Sales		$1,010,000
Operating Expenses		
Sales and Administrative Salaries Expense	$ 556,000	
Other Sales and Administrative Expenses	312,000	
Total Operating Expenses		868,000
Income before Income Taxes		$ 142,000
Income Taxes		39,000
Net Income		$ 103,000

Additional information: (a) other sales and administrative expenses include depreciation expense of $52,000 and amortization expense of $18,000; (b) at the end of each year, accrued liabilities for salaries were $12,000 less than the previous year and prepaid expenses were $20,000 more than the previous year; and (c) during the year accounts receivable (net) increased by $144,000, accounts payable increased by $114,000, and income taxes payable decreased by $7,200.

Required

1. Prepare a schedule of cash flows from operating activities using the direct method.
2. Prepare a schedule of cash flows from operating activities using the indirect method.

**Problem 18B-3.
Cash Flows
from Operating
Activities
(L.O. 4)**

The income statement for Malamud Greeting Card Company follows.

Malamud Greeting Card Company Income Statement For the Year Ended December 31, 19x2		
Sales		$472,000
Cost of Goods Sold		286,700
Gross Margin from Sales		$185,300
Operating Expenses (including Depreciation Expense of $21,430)		87,400
Operating Income		$ 97,900
Other Income (Expenses)		
Interest Expense	$(8,400)	
Interest Income	4,300	
Loss on Sale of Investments	(5,800)	(9,900)
Income before Income Taxes		$ 88,000
Income Taxes		18,500
Net Income		$ 69,500

Relevant accounts from the balance sheet for December 31, 19x2 and 19x1 are as follows:

	19x2	19x1
Accounts Receivable (net)	$18,530	$23,670
Inventory	39,640	34,990
Prepaid Expenses	2,400	8,900
Accounts Payable	34,940	22,700
Accrued Liabilities	4,690	8,830
Income Taxes Payable	4,750	17,600

Required

1. Prepare a schedule of cash flows from operating activities using the direct method.
2. Prepare a schedule of cash flows from operating activities using the indirect method.

**Problem 18B-4.
The Statement of
Cash Flows—
Direct Method
(L.O. 6, 7)**

Plath Corporation's comparative balance sheets as of June 30, 19x7 and 19x6 and its 19x7 income statement appear as follows.

Plath Corporation
Comparative Balance Sheets
June 30, 19x7 and 19x6

	19x7	19x6
Assets		
Cash	$167,000	$ 20,000
Accounts Receivable (net)	100,000	120,000
Finished Goods Inventory	180,000	220,000
Prepaid Expenses	600	1,000
Property, Plant, and Equipment	628,000	552,000
Accumulated Depreciation, Property, Plant, and Equipment	(183,000)	(140,000)
Total Assets	$892,600	$773,000
Liabilities and Stockholders' Equity		
Accounts Payable	$ 64,000	$ 42,000
Notes Payable (due in 90 days)	30,000	80,000
Income Taxes Payable	26,000	18,000
Mortgage Payable	360,000	280,000
Common Stock—$5 par value	200,000	200,000
Retained Earnings	212,600	153,000
Total Liabilities and Stockholders' Equity	$892,600	$773,000

Plath Corporation
Income Statement
For the Year Ended June 30, 19x7

Sales		$1,040,900
Cost of Goods Sold		656,300
Gross Margin from Sales		$ 384,600
Operating Expenses (including Depreciation Expense of $60,000)		189,200
Income from Operations		$ 195,400
Other Income (Expenses)		
Loss on Disposal of Equipment	$ (4,000)	
Interest Expense	(37,600)	(41,600)
Income before Income Taxes		$ 153,800
Income Taxes		34,200
Net Income		$ 119,600

Additional information about 19x7: (a) equipment that cost $24,000 with accumulated depreciation of $17,000 was sold at a loss of $4,000; (b) land and building were purchased in the amount of $100,000 through an increase of $100,000 in the mortgage payable; (c) a $20,000 payment was made on the mortgage; (d) the notes were repaid, but the company borrowed an additional $30,000 through the issuance of a new note payable; and (e) a $60,000 cash dividend was declared and paid.

Required

1. Prepare a statement of cash flows using the direct method. Include a supporting schedule of noncash investing and financing transactions.
2. What are the primary reasons for Plath Corporation's large increase in cash from 19x6 to 19x7?

Problem 18B-5.
The Work Sheet
and the Statement
of Cash Flows—
Indirect Method
(L.O. 6, 8)

Use the information for Plath Corporation given in Problem 18B-4 to answer the requirements below.

Required

1. Prepare a work sheet for gathering information for the preparation of the statement of cash flows.
2. From the information on the work sheet, prepare a statement of cash flows using the indirect method. Include a supporting schedule of noncash investing and financing transactions.

Problem 18B-6.
The Work Sheet
and the Statement
of Cash Flows—
Indirect Method
(L.O. 6, 7, 8)

The comparative balance sheets for Willis Ceramics, Inc. for December 31, 19x3 and 19x2 appear on page 788. Additional information about Willis Ceramics' operations during 19x3: (a) net income, $48,000; (b) building and equipment depreciation expense amounts were $40,000 and $30,000, respectively; (c) intangible assets were amortized in the amount of $10,000; (d) investments in the amounts of $58,000 were purchased; (e) investments were sold for $75,000, on which a gain of $17,000 was made; (f) the company issued $120,000 in long-term bonds at face value; (g) a small warehouse building with the accompanying land was purchased through the issue of a $160,000 mortgage; (h) the company paid $20,000 to reduce mortgage payable during 19x7; (i) the company borrowed funds in the amount of $30,000 by issuing notes payable and repaid notes payable in the amount of $90,000; and (j) cash dividends in the amount of $18,000 were declared and paid.

Required

1. Prepare a work sheet for the statement of cash flows for Willis Ceramics.
2. Prepare a statement of cash flows from the information in the work sheet using the indirect method. Include a supporting schedule of noncash investing and financing transactions.
3. Why did Willis Ceramics experience a decrease in cash in a year in which it had a net income of $48,000? Discuss and interpret.

	19x3	19x2

Willis Ceramics, Inc.
Comparative Balance Sheets
December 31, 19x3 and 19x2

Assets

	19x3	19x2
Cash	$ 138,800	$ 152,800
Accounts Receivable (net)	369,400	379,400
Inventory	480,000	400,000
Prepaid Expenses	7,400	13,400
Long-Term Investments	220,000	220,000
Land	180,600	160,600
Building	600,000	460,000
Accumulated Depreciation, Building	(120,000)	(80,000)
Equipment	240,000	240,000
Accumulated Depreciation, Equipment	(58,000)	(28,000)
Intangible Assets	10,000	20,000
Total Assets	$2,068,200	$1,938,200

Liabilities and Stockholders' Equity

	19x3	19x2
Accounts Payable	$ 235,400	$ 330,400
Notes Payable (current)	20,000	80,000
Accrued Liabilities	5,400	10,400
Mortgage Payable	540,000	400,000
Bonds Payable	500,000	380,000
Common Stock	600,000	600,000
Paid-in Capital in Excess of Par Value	40,000	40,000
Retained Earnings	127,400	97,400
Total Liabilities and Stockholders' Equity	$2,068,200	$1,938,200

Financial Decision Case

Adams Print Gallery
(L.O. 6, 7)

Bernadette Adams, President of Adams Print Gallery, Inc., is examining the income statement presented on the next page, which has just been handed to her by her accountant, Jason Rosenberg, CPA. After looking at the statement, Ms. Adams said to Mr. Rosenberg, "Jason, the statement seems to be well done, but what I need to know is why I don't have enough cash to pay my bills this month. You show that I have earned $60,000 in 19x2, but I only have $12,000 in the bank. I know I bought a building on a mortgage and paid a cash dividend of $24,000, but what else is going on?" Mr. Rosenberg replied, "To answer your question, Bernadette, we have to look at comparative balance sheets and prepare another type of statement. Here, take a look at these balance sheets." The statements handed to Ms. Adams are shown on the next page.

Adams Print Gallery, Inc.
Income Statement
For the Year Ended December 31, 19x2

Sales	$442,000
Cost of Goods Sold	254,000
Gross Margin	$188,000
Operating Expenses (including Depreciation Expense of $10,000)	102,000
Operating Income	$ 86,000
Interest Expense	12,000
Income Before Taxes	$ 74,000
Income Taxes	14,000
Net Income	$ 60,000

Adams Print Gallery, Inc.
Comparative Balance Sheets
December 31, 19x2 and 19x1

	19x2	19x1
Assets		
Cash	$ 12,000	$ 20,000
Accounts Receivable (net)	89,000	73,000
Inventory	120,000	90,000
Prepaid Expenses	5,000	7,000
Building	200,000	—
Accumulated Depreciation	(10,000)	—
Total Assets	$416,000	$190,000
Liabilities and Stockholders' Equity		
Accounts Payable	$ 37,000	$ 48,000
Income Taxes Payable	3,000	2,000
Mortgage Payable	200,000	—
Common Stock	100,000	100,000
Retained Earnings	76,000	40,000
Total Liabilities and Stockholders' Equity	$416,000	$190,000

Required

1. To what statement is Mr. Rosenberg referring? From the information given, prepare the additional statement using the direct method.
2. Explain why Adams has a cash problem despite profitable operations.

Answers to Self-Test

1. a	3. c	5. c	7. a	9. a
2. d	4. c	6. d	8. c	10. d

CHAPTER 19

Financial Statement Analysis

This chapter presents a number of techniques intended to aid in decision making by highlighting important relationships in the financial statements. This process is called financial statement analysis. After studying this chapter, you should be able to meet the learning objectives listed on the left.

Effective decision making calls for the ability to sort out relevant information from a great many facts and to make adjustments for changing conditions. Very often, financial statements in a company's annual report run ten or more pages, including footnotes and other necessary disclosures. If these statements are to be useful in making decisions, decision makers must be able to see important relationships among figures and to make comparisons from year to year and from company to company. The many techniques that together are called **financial statement analysis** accomplish this goal.

Objectives of Financial Statement Analysis

Users of financial statements fall into two broad categories: internal and external. Management is the main internal user. The tools of financial analysis are, of course, useful in management's operation of the business. However, because those who run the company have inside information on operations, other techniques are available to them. Since these techniques are covered in managerial accounting courses, the main focus here is on the external use of financial analysis.

Creditors make loans in the form of trade accounts, notes, or bonds, on which they receive interest. They expect a loan to be repaid according to its terms. Investors buy capital stock, from which they hope to receive dividends and an increase in value. Both groups face risks. The creditor faces the risk that the debtor will fail to pay back the loan. The investor faces the risk that dividends will be reduced or not paid or that the market price of the stock will drop. In each case, the goal is to achieve a return that makes up for the risk taken. In general, the greater the risk taken, the greater the return required as compensation.

Any one loan or any one investment can turn out badly. As a result, most creditors and investors put their funds into a **port-**

folio, or group of loans or investments. The portfolio allows them to average both the return and the risk. Nevertheless, the portfolio is made up of a number of loans or stocks on which individual decisions must be made. It is in making these individual decisions that financial statement analysis is most useful. Creditors and investors use financial statement analysis in two general ways. (1) They use it to judge past performance and current position. (2) They use it to judge future potential and the risk connected with the potential.

Assessment of Past Performance and Current Position

OBJECTIVE 1
Describe and discuss the objectives of financial statement analysis

Past performance is often a good indicator of future performance. Therefore, an investor or creditor is interested in the trend of past sales, expenses, net income, cash flow, and return on investment. These trends offer a means for judging management's past performance and are a possible indicator of future performance. In addition, an analysis of current position will tell where the business stands today. For example, it will tell what assets the business owns and what liabilities must be paid. It will tell what the cash position is, how much debt the company has in relation to equity, and how reasonable the inventories and receivables are. Knowing a company's past performance and current position is often important in achieving the second general objective of financial analysis.

Assessment of Future Potential and Related Risk

The past and present information is useful only to the extent that it has bearing on future decisions. An investor judges the potential earning ability of a company because that ability will affect the value of the investment (market price of the company's stock) and the amount of dividends the company will pay. A creditor judges the potential debt-paying ability of the company.

The potentials of some companies are easier to predict than others, and so there is less risk associated with them. The riskiness of the investment or loan depends on how easy it is to predict future profitability or liquidity. If an investor can predict with confidence that a company's earnings per share will be between $2.50 and $2.60 next year, the investment is less risky than if the earnings per share are expected to fall between $2.00 and $3.00. For example, the potential associated with an investment in an established and stable electric utility, or a loan to it, is relatively easy to predict on the basis of the company's past performance and current position. The potential associated with a small minicomputer manufacturer, on the other hand, may be much harder to predict. For this reason, the investment or loan to the electric utility is less risky than the investment or loan to the small computer company.

Often, in return for taking the greater risk, the investor in the minicomputer company will demand a higher expected return (increase in market price plus dividends) than will the investor in the utility company. Also, a creditor of the minicomputer company will need a higher interest rate and possibly more assurance of repayment (a secured loan, for instance) than a creditor to the utility company. The higher interest rate is payment to the creditor for assuming a higher risk.

Standards for Financial Statement Analysis

OBJECTIVE 2
Describe and
discuss the
standards for
financial statement
analysis

In using financial statement analysis, decision makers must judge whether the relationships they have found are favorable or unfavorable. Three standards of comparison often used are (1) rule-of-thumb measurements, (2) past performance of the company, and (3) industry norms.

Rule-of-Thumb Measures

Many financial analysts and lenders use ideal or rule-of-thumb measures for key financial ratios. For example, it has long been thought that a current ratio (current assets divided by current liabilities) of 2:1 is acceptable. The credit-rating firm of Dun & Bradstreet, in its *Key Business Ratios*, offers these guidelines:

Current debt to tangible net worth. Ordinarily, a business begins to pile up trouble when this relationship exceeds 80%.

Inventory to net working capital. Ordinarily, this relationship should not exceed 80%.

Although such measures may suggest areas that need further investigation, there is no proof they are the best for any company. A company with a higher than 2:1 current ratio may have a poor credit policy (resulting in accounts receivable being too large), too much or out-of-date inventory, or poor cash management. Another company may have a lower than 2:1 ratio resulting from excellent management in these three areas. Thus, rule-of-thumb measurements must be used with great care.

Past Performance of the Company

An improvement over the rule-of-thumb method is the comparison of financial measures or ratios of the same company over a period of time. This standard will at least give the analyst some basis for judging whether the measure or ratio is getting better or worse. It may also be helpful in showing possible future trends. However, since trends do reverse at times, such projections must be made with care. Another disadvantage is that the past may not be a good measure of adequacy. In other words, past performance may not be enough to meet present needs. For example, even if return on total investment improved from 3 percent last year to 4 percent this year, the 4 percent return may not be adequate.

Industry Norms

One way of making up for the limitations of using past performance as a standard is to use industry norms. This standard will tell how the company being analyzed compares with other companies in the same industry. For example, suppose that other companies in an industry have an average rate of return on total investment of 8 percent. In such a case 3 and 4 percent returns are probably not adequate. Industry norms can also be used to judge trends. Suppose that because of a downward turn in the economy, a company's profit margin dropped from 12 to 10 percent. A finding that other companies in the same industry had an average drop in profit margin from 12 to 4 percent would indicate that the company being analyzed did relatively well.

There are three limitations to using industry norms as standards. First, two companies that seem to be in the same industry may not be strictly comparable. Consider two companies said to be in the oil industry. The main business of one may be marketing oil products it buys from other producers through service stations. The other, an international company, may discover, produce, refine, and market its own oil products. The operations of these two different companies cannot be compared.

Second, most large companies today operate in more than one industry. Some of these **diversified companies**, or **conglomerates**, operate in many unrelated industries. The individual segments of a diversified company generally have different rates of profitability and degrees of risk. In using the consolidated financial statements of these companies for financial analysis, it is often impossible to use industry norms as standards. There are simply no other companies that are closely enough related. One partial solution to this problem is a requirement by the Financial Accounting Standards Board in *Statement No. 14*. This requirement states that diversified companies must report revenues, income from operations, and identifiable assets for each of their operating segments. Depending on specific criteria, segment information may be reported for operations in different industries, in foreign markets, or to major customers.[1]

An example of reporting for industry segments is shown in Exhibit 19-1, which comes from the annual report of Eastman Kodak Company. It is interesting to compare the three reported segments, Imaging, Chemicals, and Health. The Health segment is Eastman Kodak Company's fastest growing segment due to the purchase for $5 billion in 1988 of Sterling Drugs, which makes prescription and nonprescription drugs, including Bayer Aspirin. As a result, sales from the Health segment increased 250 percent, from $1,056 million in 1986 to $3,691 million in 1988. Sales from the Imaging segment, which makes copier machines and microfilm, among many other products, have increased 26.6 percent, from $8,352 million in 1986 to $10,575 million in 1988, whereas sales from the Chemical segment increased 27.5 percent over the same time period, from $2,378 million to $3,033 million. The changes in earnings from operations are even more dramatic. Health earnings from operations increased 439 percent, from $120 million in 1986 to $647 million in 1988, due to the Sterling Drugs purchase.

1. *Statement of Financial Accounting Standards No. 14*, "Financial Reporting for Segments of a Business Enterprise" (Stamford, Conn.: Financial Accounting Standards Board, 1976).

Exhibit 19-1. Segment Information (in millions)*	1988	1987	1986
Sales, including intersegment sales			
Imaging	$10,575	$ 9,711	$ 8,352
Chemicals	3,033	2,600	2,378
Health	3,691	1,230	1,056
Intersegment sales			
Imaging	(4)	(6)	(12)
Chemicals	(261)	(230)	(224)
Sales to unaffiliated customers	$17,034	$13,305	$11,550
Earnings from operations			
Imaging	$ 1,663	$ 1,509	$ 377
Chemicals	628	388	227
Health	647	214	120
Earnings from operations	$ 2,938	$ 2,111	$ 724
Interest and other income (charges)			
Imaging	47	12	(27)
Chemicals	(4)	(12)	18
Health	(120)	15	(3)
Corporate	72	39	86
Interest expense	(697)	(181)	(200)
Earnings before income taxes	$ 2,236	$ 1,984	$ 598
Assets			
Imaging	$12,157	$10,578	$ 9,330
Chemicals	2,875	2,514	2,266
Health	7,469	1,206	1,071
Corporate (cash and marketable securities)	742	620	501
Intersegment receivables	(279)	(220)	(174)
Total assets at year end	$22,964	$14,698[†]	$12,994[†]
Depreciation expense			
Imaging	$ 713	$ 689	$ 693
Chemicals	217	202	189
Health	127	71	74
Total depreciation expense	$ 1,057	$ 962	$ 956
Amortization expense			
Imaging	$ 33	$ 33	$ 19
Health	93	—	—
Total amortization expense	$ 126	$ 33	$ 19
Capital expenditures			
Imaging	$ 1,314	$ 1,199	$ 1,082
Chemicals	475	394	314
Health	125	59	42
Total capital expenditures	S 1,914	$ 1,652	$ 1,438

* The products of each segment are manufactured and marketed in the U.S. and in other parts of the world. The Imaging segment includes film, paper, equipment, and other related products. The Chemical segment includes fibers, plastics, industrial and other chemicals. Sales between segments are made on a basis intended to reflect the market value of the products.
† Restated to include amounts from the Eastman Kodak Credit Corporation.

Imaging earnings from operations increased 341 percent, from $377 million to $1,663 million, and Chemical earnings increased 177 percent, from $227 million to $628 million.

The third limitation to industry norms is that companies in the same industry with similar operations may use different accounting procedures. That is, inventories may be valued by using different methods, or different depreciation methods may be used for similar assets. Even so, if little information is available about a company's prior performance, industry norms probably offer the best available standards for judging a company's current performance. They should be used with care.

Sources of Information

OBJECTIVE 3
State the sources of information for financial statement analysis

The external analyst is often limited to publicly available information about a company. The major sources of information about publicly held corporations are published reports, SEC reports, business periodicals, and credit and investment advisory services.

Published Reports

The annual report of a publicly held corporation is an important source of financial information. The major parts of this annual report are (1) management's analysis of the past year's operations, (2) the financial statements, (3) the notes to the statements, including the principal accounting procedures used by the company, (4) the auditors' report, and (5) a summary of operations for a five- or ten-year period. Also, most publicly held companies publish **interim financial statements** each quarter. These reports present limited information in the form of condensed financial statements, which may be subject to a limited review or a full audit by the independent auditor. The interim statements are watched closely by the financial community for early signs of important changes in a company's earnings trend.[2]

SEC Reports

Publicly held corporations must file annual reports, quarterly reports, and current reports with the Securities and Exchange Commission (SEC). All such reports are available to the public at a small charge. The SEC calls for a standard form for the annual report (Form 10-K). This report is fuller than the published annual report. Form 10-K is, for this reason, a valuable source of information. It is available, free of charge, to stockholders of the company. The quarterly report (Form 10-Q) presents important facts about interim financial performance. The current report (Form 8-K) must be filed within a few days of the date of certain major events. It is often the first indicator of important changes that may affect the company's financial performance in the future.

2. Accounting Principles Board, *Opinion No. 28*, "Interim Financial Reporting" (New York: American Institute of Certified Public Accountants, 1973); and *Statement of Financial Accounting Standards No. 3*, "Reporting Accounting Change in Interim Financial Statements" (Stamford, Conn.: Financial Accounting Standards Board, 1974).

Business Periodicals and Credit and Investment Advisory Services

Financial analysts must keep up with current events in the financial world. Probably the best source of financial news is *The Wall Street Journal*, which is published daily and is the most complete financial newspaper in the United States. Some helpful magazines, published every week or every two weeks, are *Forbes, Barron's, Fortune,* and the *Commercial and Financial Chronicle*.

For further details about the financial history of companies, the publications of such services as Moody's Investors Service and Standard & Poor's Industrial Surveys are useful. Data on industry norms, average ratios and relationships, and credit ratings are available from such agencies as Dun & Bradstreet Corporation. Dun & Bradstreet offers, among other useful services, an annual analysis using 14 ratios of 125 industry groups classified as retailing, wholesaling, manufacturing, and construction in its *Key Business Ratios*. Another important source of industry data is the *Annual Statement Studies*, published by Robert Morris Associates, which presents many facts and ratios for 223 different industries. Also, a number of private services are available to the analyst for a yearly fee.

Evaluating a Company's Quality of Earnings

OBJECTIVE 4
Identify the issues related to the evaluation of the quality of a company's earnings

It is clear from the preceding sections that the current and expected earnings of a company play an important role in the analysis of a company's prospects. In fact, a recent survey of two thousand members of the Financial Analysis Federation indicated that the two most important economic indicators in evaluating common stocks were expected changes in earnings per share and expected return on equity.[3] Net income is an important component of both measures. Because of the importance of net income, or the "bottom line," in measures of a company's prospects, interest in evaluating the quality of the net income figure, or the *quality of earnings*, has become an important topic. The quality of a company's earnings may be affected by (1) the accounting methods and estimates the company's management chooses and/or (2) the nature of nonoperating items in the income statement.

Choice of Accounting Methods and Estimates

There are two aspects to the choice of accounting methods that affect the quality of earnings. First, some accounting methods are by nature more conservative than others because they tend to produce a lower net income in the current period. Second, there is considerable latitude in the choice of the estimated useful life over which assets are written off or in the amount of estimated residual value. In general, an accounting method or estimated useful life and/or residual value that results in lower current earnings is considered to produce better quality earnings.

3. Cited in *The Week in Review* (Deloitte Haskins & Sells), February 28, 1985.

In earlier chapters, various acceptable alternative methods were used in the application of the matching rule. These methods are based on allocation procedures, which in turn are based on certain assumptions. Here are some of these procedures:

1. For estimating uncollectible accounts expense: percentage of net sales method and accounts receivable aging method
2. For pricing the ending inventory: average cost method; first-in, first-out method (FIFO); and last-in, first-out method (LIFO)
3. For estimating depreciation expense: straight-line method, production method, sum-of-the-years'-digits method, and declining-balance method
4. For estimating depletion expense: production (extraction) method
5. For estimating amortization of intangibles: straight-line method

All these procedures are designed to allocate the costs of assets to the periods in which those costs contribute to the production of revenue. They are based on a determination of the benefits to the current period (expenses) versus the benefits to future periods (assets). They are estimates, and the period or periods benefited cannot be demonstrated conclusively. They are also subjective, because in practice it is hard to justify one method of estimation over another.

For this reason, it is important for the accountant as well as the financial statement user to understand the possible effects of different accounting procedures or net income and financial position. For example, suppose that two companies have similar operations, but that one uses FIFO for inventory pricing and the straight-line (SL) method for computing depreciation and the other uses LIFO for inventory pricing and the sum-of-the-years'-digits (SYD) method for computing depreciation. The income statements of the two companies might appear as follows:

	FIFO and SL	LIFO and SYD
Sales	$500,000	$500,000
Goods Available for Sale	$300,000	$300,000
Less Ending Inventory	60,000	50,000
Cost of Goods Sold	$240,000	$250,000
Gross Margin	$260,000	$250,000
Less: Depreciation Expense	$ 40,000	$ 70,000
Other Expenses	170,000	170,000
Total Operating Expenses	$210,000	$240,000
Net Income	$ 50,000	$ 10,000

This fivefold difference in income stems only from the differences in accounting methods. Differences in the estimated lives and residual values of the plant assets could cause an even greater variation. In practice, of course, differences in net income occur for many reasons, but the user must be aware of the discrepancies that can occur as a result of the methods chosen by management.

The existence of these alternatives could cause problems in the interpretation of financial statements were it not for the conventions of full disclosure and consistency described in Chapter 8. Full disclosure requires that management explain the significant accounting policies used in preparing the financial statements in a note to the statements. Consistency requires that the same accounting procedure be followed from year to year. If a change in procedure is made, the nature of the change and its monetary effect must be explained in a note.

Nature of Nonoperating Items

As seen in Chapter 16, the corporate income statement consists of several components. The top of the statement presents earnings from current ongoing operations called income from operations. The lower part of the statement can contain such nonoperating items as discontinued operations, extraordinary gains and losses, and effects of accounting changes. These items may drastically affect the bottom line, or net income, of the company. For example, Eastman Kodak Company had an unusual charge of $520 million in 1986 that related primarily to the discontinuance of its instant camera line and the loss of a patent suit with Polaroid. The loss had a detrimental effect on reported net earnings in 1986, and the discontinuance of the instant camera may adversely affect future years' earnings.

Such nonoperating items should be taken into consideration when interpreting a company's earnings. For example, in 1983, U.S. Steel made an apparent turnaround by reporting first quarter earnings of $1.35 a share versus a deficit of $1.31 a year earlier. However, the "improved" earnings included a gain from sales of assets of $.45 per share and sale of tax benefits on newly acquired assets of $.40 per share, as well as other items totaling $.61 per share. These items total $1.46, an amount greater than the reported earnings for the year.[4] The opposite effect can also occur. For the first six months of 1984, Texas Instruments reported a loss of $112 million compared with a profit of $64.5 million the previous year. The loss was caused by write-offs of $58 million for nonoperating losses, $83 million for inventory, and $37 million for increased reserves for rebates, price protection for retailers, and returned inventory.[5] In reality this large write-off was a positive step on Texas Instruments' part because getting out of the low-profit home computer business meant TI's future cash flows would not be drained by those operations.

For practical reasons, the trends and ratios in the sections that follow are based on the assumption that net income and other components are comparable from year to year and company to company. However, the astute analyst will always look beyond the ratios to the quality of the components in making interpretations.

4. Dan Dorfman, "Three Well-Known Stocks with Earnings of Dubious Quality," *The Chicago Tribune* (June 28, 1984), p. 11.
5. "Loss at Texas Instruments Hits $119.2 Million," *The Wall Street Journal* (November 14, 1984).

Tools and Techniques of Financial Analysis

Few numbers by themselves mean very much. It is their relationship to other numbers or their change from one period to another that is important. The tools of financial analysis are intended to show relationships and changes. Among the more widely used of these financial analysis techniques are horizontal analysis, trend analysis, vertical analysis, and ratio analysis.

Horizontal Analysis

OBJECTIVE 5
Apply horizontal analysis, trend analysis, and vertical analysis to financial statements

Generally accepted accounting principles call for presenting comparative financial statements that give the current year's and past year's financial information. A common starting point for studying such statements is **horizontal analysis**, which involves the computation of dollar amount changes and percentage changes from the previous to the current year. The percentage change must be figured to show how the size of the change relates to the size of the amounts involved. A change of $1 million in sales is not so drastic as a change of $1 million in net income, because sales is a larger amount than net income.

Exhibits 19-2 and 19-3 (next two pages) present the comparative balance sheets and income statements, respectively, for Eastman Kodak Company, with the dollar and percentage changes shown. The percentage change is computed as follows:

$$\text{Percentage change} = 100 \left(\frac{\text{amount of change}}{\text{previous year amount}} \right)$$

The **base year** in any set of data is always the first year being studied. For example, from 1987 to 1988, Kodak's current assets increased by $1,893 million, from $6,791 million to $8,684 million, or by 27.9 percent, computed as follows:

$$\text{Percentage increase} = 100 \left(\frac{\$1,893 \text{ million}}{\$6,791 \text{ million}} \right) = 27.9\%$$

Care must be taken in the analysis of percentage change. For example, in analyzing the changes in the components of total assets in Exhibit 19-2, one might view the 29.5 percent increase in receivables as being about the same as the 20.8 percent increase in cash. In dollar amount, though, receivables increased by more than six times as much as cash did ($927 million versus $146 million). Dollar amounts and percentage increases must be considered together. On the liability side of the balance sheet, both long-term borrowings and payables are up substantially (by 226.6 percent and 46.0 percent). The increase in long-term borrowings was due to the Sterling Drug purchase.

In the income statements (Exhibit 19-3), the most important changes from 1987 to 1988 show a 28.0 percent growth in total sales compared to a 25.9 percent increase in total costs and expenses. When the dollar amounts of these changes are combined, they result in a 39.2 percent increase in earnings from operations. In addition, net earnings in 1988

Exhibit 19-2. Comparative Balance Sheets with Horizontal Analysis

Eastman Kodak Company
Consolidated Balance Sheets
December 25, 1988, and December 27, 1987*

	(In millions)		Increase (Decrease)	
	1988	**1987**	**Amount**	**Percentage**
Assets				
Current Assets				
Cash and cash equivalents	$ 848	$ 702	$ 146	20.8
Marketable securities	227	290	(63)	(21.7)
Receivables	4,071	3,144	927	29.5
Inventories	3,025	2,178	847	38.9
Deferred income tax charges	272	326	(54)	(16.6)
Prepaid charges applicable to future operations	241	151	90	59.6
Total Current Assets	$ 8,684	$ 6,791	$1,893	27.9
Properties				
Land, buildings, machinery, and equipment at cost	$15,667	$13,789	$1,878	13.6
Less: Accumulated depreciation	7,654	7,126	528	7.4
Net Properties	$ 8,013	$ 6,663	$1,350	20.3
Other Assets				
Unamortized goodwill	4,610	424	4,186	987.3
Long-term receivables and other noncurrent assets	1,657	820	837	102.1
Total Assets	$22,964	$14,698	$8,266	56.2
Liabilities and Shareowners' Equity				
Current Liabilities				
Payables	$ 5,277	$ 3,614	$1,663	46.0
Taxes—income and other	411	380	31	8.2
Dividends payable	162	146	16	11.0
Total Current Liabilities	$ 5,850	$ 4,140	$1,710	41.3
Other Liabilities and Deferred Credits				
Long-term borrowings	7,779	2,382	5,397	226.6
Other long-term liabilities	990	743	247	33.2
Deferred income tax credits	1,565	1,420	145	10.2
Total Liabilities and Deferred Credits	$16,184	$ 8,685	$7,499	86.3
Shareowners' Equity				
Common stock, par value $2.50 per share	$ 935	$ 933	$ 2	0.2
Retained earnings	7,904	7,139	765	10.7
	$ 8,839	$ 8,072	$ 767	9.5
Less: Treasury stock at cost	2,059	2,059	0	0.0
Total Shareowners' Equity	$ 6,780	$ 6,013	$ 767	12.8
Total Liabilities and Shareowners' Equity	$22,964	$14,698	$8,266	56.2

* Certain amounts have been restated as a result of the consolidation of the Eastman Kodak Credit Corporation

Exhibit 19-3. Comparative Income Statements with Horizontal Analysis

Eastman Kodak Company
Consolidated Statements of Earnings
For the Years Ended December 25, 1988, and December 27, 1987

	(In millions*)		Increase (Decrease)	
	1988	1987	Amount	Percentage
Sales to: Customers in the United States	$ 9,554	$ 7,611	$1,943	25.5
Customers outside the United States	7,480	5,694	1,786	31.4
TOTAL SALES	$17,034	$13,305	$3,729	28.0
Cost of goods sold	$ 9,601	$ 8,004	$1,597	20.0
Sales, advertising, distribution and administrative expenses	4,495	3,190	1,305	40.9
Total costs and expenses	$14,096	$11,194	$2,902	25.9
EARNINGS FROM OPERATIONS	$ 2,938	$ 2,111	$ 827	39.2
Investment income	132	83	49	59.0
Interest expense	(697)	(181)	(516)	285.1
Other charges	(137)	(29)	(108)	372.4
Earnings before income taxes	$ 2,236	$ 1,984	$ 252	12.7
Provision for United States, foreign, and other income taxes	839	806	33	4.1
NET EARNINGS	$ 1,397	S 1,178	$ 219	18.6
Average number of common shares outstanding	324.2	334.7	(10.5)	(3.1)
Net earnings per share	$4.31	$3.52	$0.79	22.4

* Except per share data

were adversely affected by increases of 285.1 percent in interest expense (due to the increase in long-term borrowings) and 372.4 percent in other charges. As a result of these increases, overall net earnings grew only 18.6 percent.

Trend Analysis

A variation of horizontal analysis is **trend analysis,** in which percentage changes are calculated for several successive years instead of two years. Trend analysis is important because, with its long-run view, it may point to basic changes in the nature of the business. Besides comparative financial statements, most companies give out a summary of operations and data on other key indicators for five or more years. Selected items from Kodak's summary of operations together with trend analysis are presented in Exhibit 19-4.

Trend analysis uses an index number to show changes in related items over a period of time. For index numbers, one year, the base year, is equal to 100 percent. Other years are measured in relation to that amount. For example, the 1988 index of 160.7 for sales was figured as follows:

$$\text{Index} = 100 \left(\frac{\text{index year amount}}{\text{base year amount}} \right) = \left(\frac{\$17,034}{\$10,600} \right) = 160.7$$

An index number of 160.7 means that 1988 sales are 160.7 percent or 1.607 times 1984 sales.

A study of the trend analysis in Exhibit 19-4 shows that net earnings has been more volatile than sales, which increased steadily over the five-year period. After some disappointing results in 1985 and 1986, net earnings rebounded to almost equal sales in 1988 (151.4 versus 160.7). The contrasting trends are dramatically shown when graphed as in Figure 19-1. Earnings per common share increased more rapidly than net earnings (169.7 in 1988 versus 151.4), while dividends per share increased by a modest amount each year (118.8 in 1988). Apparently, the company felt it was important to keep up a small but steady increase in dividends in spite of the volatility of income per common share.

Exhibit 19-4. Trend Analysis

Eastman Kodak Company
Summary of Operations
Selected Data
(Sales and Net Earnings in Millions)

	1988	1987	1986	1985	1984
Sales	$17,034	$13,305	$11,550	$10,631	$10,600
Net Earnings	1,397	1,178	374	332	923
Per Common Share*					
Income*	4.31	3.52	1.10	0.97	2.54
Dividends*	1.90	1.71	1.63	1.62	1.60
Trend Analysis (in percentages)					
Sales	160.7	125.5	109.0	100.3	100.0
Net Earnings	151.4	127.6	40.5	36.0	100.0
Per Common Share					
Income	169.7	138.6	43.3	38.2	100.0
Dividends	118.8	106.9	101.9	101.3	100.0

* Per share data restated to reflect 3-for-2 stock splits in 1985 and 1987

Figure 19-1. Trend Analysis for Eastman Kodak Company

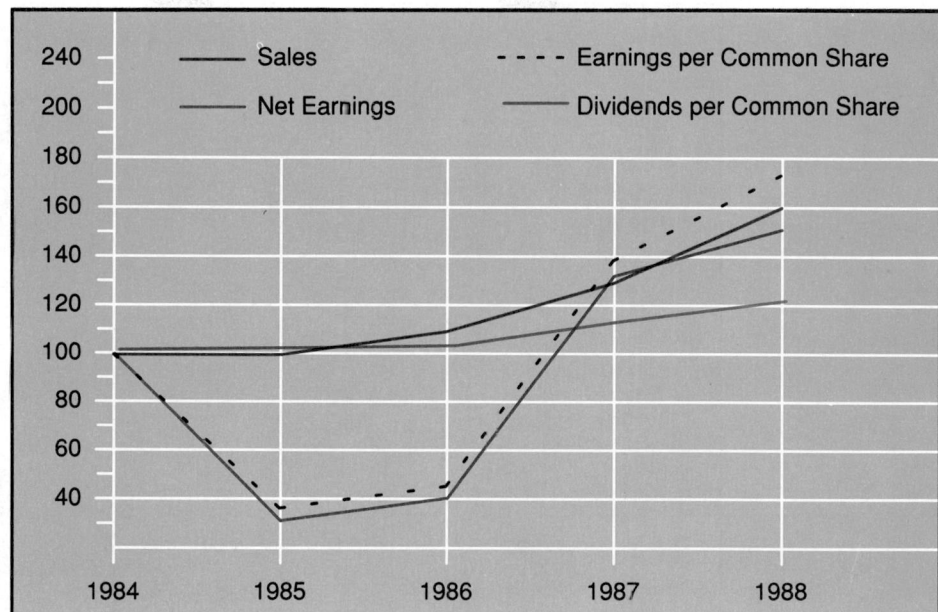

Vertical Analysis

In **vertical analysis** percentages are used to show the relationship of the different parts to the total in a single statement. The accountant sets a total figure in the statement equal to 100 percent and computes the percentage of the total of each component of that figure. (The figure would be total assets or total liabilities and stockholders' equity in the case of the balance sheet, and revenues or sales in the case of the income statement.) The resulting statement of percentages is called a **common-size statement**. Common-size balance sheets and income statements for Kodak are shown graphically in pie chart form in Figures 19-2 and 19-3, and in financial statement form in Exhibits 19-5 and 19-6 (pages 805 and 806).

Vertical analysis is useful for comparing the importance of certain components in the operation of the business. It is also useful for pointing out important changes in the components from one year to the next in comparative common-size statements. For Kodak, the composition of assets in Exhibit 19-5 changed significantly from 1987 to 1988 due to the purchase of Sterling Drugs, which resulted in an increase in other assets from 8.5 percent of total assets to 27.3 percent. As a result, proportionally fewer assets were in properties (34.9 percent versus 45.3 percent) and in current assets (37.8 percent versus 46.2 percent) in 1988 as opposed to 1987. Also, the part of total liabilities made up of current liabilities decreased from 28.2 percent to 25.5 percent. As a result of the

Figure 19-2. Common-Size Balance Sheets Presented Graphically

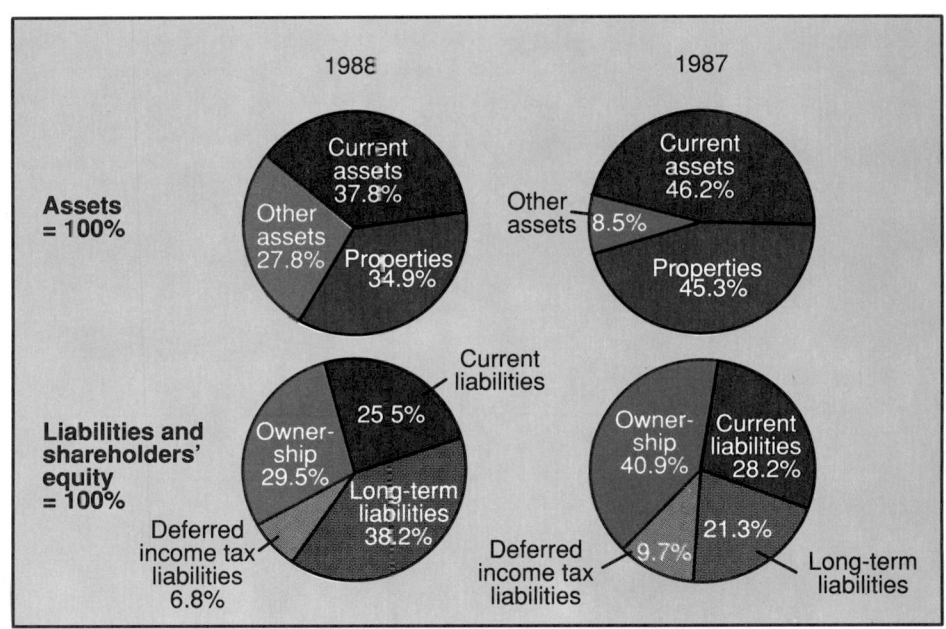

purchase, long-term liabilities increased from 21.3 percent to 38.2 percent. These two changes contributed to a much higher percentage of the company financed by total liabilities in 1988 than in 1987 (70.5 percent versus 59.2 percent).

Figure 19-3. Common-Size Income Statements Presented Graphically

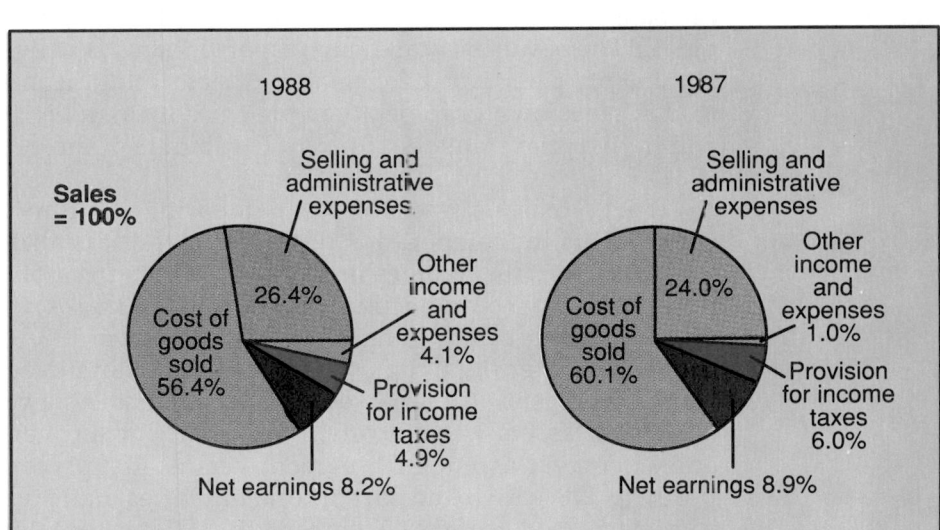

Exhibit 19-5. Common-Size Balance Sheets		
Eastman Kodak Company **Common-Size Balance Sheets** **December 25, 1988, and December 27, 1987**		
	1988	**1987**
Assets		
Current Assets	37.8%	46.2%
Properties (less Accumulated Depreciation)	34.9	45.3
Other Assets	27.3	8.5
Total Assets	100.0%	100.0%
Liabilities		
Current Liabilities	25.5%	28.2%
Long-Term Liabilities	38.2	21.3
Deferred Income Tax Liabilities	6.8	9.7
Total Liabilities	70.5%	59.2%
Ownership		
Common Stock	4.1%	6.3%
Retained Earnings	34.4	48.6
Treasury Stock at Cost	(9.0)	(14.0)
Total Ownership	29.5%	40.9%
Total Liabilities and Ownership	100.0%	100.0%

Results are rounded in some cases to equal 100%

The common-size statements of earnings (Exhibit 19-6) show the importance of the decrease in costs and expenses from 84.1 to 82.8 percent of sales. This decrease was the major cause of the increase in earnings from operations from 15.9 to 17.2 percent of sales. Note, however, the negative impact of the increase in other income and expenses from 1.0 percent of sales to 4.1 percent, which was only partially offset by the decrease in income taxes from 6.0 percent of sales to 4.9 percent. Consequently, earnings as a percent of sales actually decreased from 8.9 percent of sales in 1987 to 8.2 percent of sales in 1988.

Common-size statements are often used to make comparisons between companies. They allow an analyst to compare the operating and financing characteristics of two companies of different size in the same industry. For example, the analyst may want to compare Kodak to other companies in terms of the percentage of total assets financed by debt or the percentage of general administrative and selling expenses to sales

Exhibit 19-6. Common-Size Income Statements		
Eastman Kodak Company **Common-Size Income Statements (Statements of Earnings)** **For Years Ended December 25, 1988, and December 27, 1987**		
	1988	**1987**
Sales	100.0%	100.0%
Costs and Expenses		
Cost of Goods Sold	56.4%	60.1%
Selling and Administrative Expenses	26.4	24.0
Total Costs and Expenses	82.8%	84.1%
Earnings from Operations	17.2%	15.9%
Other Income and Expenses	(4.1)	(1.0)
Earnings before Income Taxes	13.1%	14.9%
Provision for Income Taxes	4.9	6.0
Net Earnings	8.2%	8.9%

and revenues. Common-size statements would show these and other relationships.

Ratio Analysis

Ratio analysis is an important way to state meaningful relationships between two components of a financial statement. To be most useful, a ratio must also include a study of the underlying data. Ratios are guides or short cuts that are useful in evaluating the financial position and operations of a company and in comparing them to results in previous years or other companies. The primary purpose of ratios is to point out areas needing further investigation. They should be used in connection with a general understanding of the company and its environment.

Ratios may be stated in several ways. For example, a ratio of net income of $100,000 to sales of $1,000,000 may be stated as (1) net income is 1/10 or 10 percent of sales, (2) the ratio of sales to net income is 10 to 1 (10:1) or 10 times net income, or (3) for every dollar of sales, the company has an average net income of 10 cents.

Survey of Commonly Used Ratios

In the following sections, ratio analysis is applied to four objectives, the evaluation of (1) liquidity, (2) profitability, (3) long-term solvency, and (4) market strength. Chapter 8 addressed the first two objectives in an introductory way. Here we expand the evaluation to include other ratios related to those objectives and to introduce two new objectives. Data for the analyses come from the financial statements of Kodak presented in Exhibits 19-2 and 19-3. Other data are presented as needed.

Evaluating Liquidity

OBJECTIVE 6
Apply ratio analysis to financial statements in the study of an enterprise's liquidity, profitability, long-term solvency, and market tests

Liquidity is the ability to pay bills when they are due and to meet unexpected needs for cash. The ratios that relate to this goal all have to do with working capital or some part of it, because it is out of working capital that debts are paid as they mature. Some common ratios connected with evaluating liquidity are the current ratio, the quick ratio, receivable turnover, and inventory turnover.

Current Ratio. The current ratio expresses the relationship of current assets to current liabilities. It is widely used as a broad indicator of a company's liquidity and short-term debt-paying ability. The ratio for Kodak for 1988 and 1987 is figured as follows:

Current Ratio	1988	1987
$\dfrac{\text{Current assets}}{\text{Current liabilities}}$	$\dfrac{\$8,684}{\$5,850} = 1.48$	$\dfrac{\$6,791}{\$4,140} = 1.64$

The current ratio for Kodak suggests a decrease in the company's liquidity from 1987 to 1988.

Quick Ratio. One of the current ratio's faults is that it does not take into account the make-up of current assets. They may appear to be large enough, but they may not have the proper balance. Clearly, a dollar of cash or even accounts receivable is more readily available to meet obligations than is a dollar of most kinds of inventory. The quick ratio is designed to overcome this problem by measuring short-term liquidity. That is, it measures the relationship of the more liquid current assets (cash, marketable securities or short-term investments, and receivables) to current liabilities. This ratio for Kodak for 1988 and 1987 is figured as follows:

Quick Ratio	1988	1987
$\dfrac{\text{Cash + marketable securities + receivables}}{\text{Current liabilities}}$	$\dfrac{\$848 + \$227 + \$4,071}{\$5,850}$	$\dfrac{\$702 + \$290 + \$3,144}{\$4,140}$
	$= \dfrac{\$5,146}{\$5,850} = 0.88$	$= \dfrac{\$4,136}{\$4,140} = 1.00$

This ratio too suggests a major decrease in liquidity from 1987 to 1988.

Receivable Turnover. The ability of a company to collect for credit sales in a timely way affects the company's liquidity. The **receivable turnover** ratio measures the relative size of a company's accounts receivable and the success of its credit and collection policies. It shows how many times, on average, the receivables were turned into cash during the period. However, it can also be affected by external factors, such as economic conditions and interest rates.

Turnover ratios usually consist of one balance sheet account and one income statement account. The receivable turnover is computed by dividing net sales by average accounts receivable. Theoretically, the numerator should be net credit sales, but the amount of net credit sales is rarely made available in public reports. So we will use total net sales. Further, in this ratio and others in which an average is required, we will take the beginning and ending balances and divide by 2. If we had internal financial data, it would be better to use monthly balances to find the average, because the balances of receivables, inventories, and other accounts can vary widely during the year. In fact, many companies choose a fiscal year that begins and ends at a low period of the business cycle, when inventories and receivables may be at the lowest levels of the year. When the previous year's balance is not available for computing the average, it is common practice to use the ending balance for the current year.

Using a 1986 accounts receivable ending balance of $2,553 million, Kodak's receivable turnover is computed as follows:

Receivable Turnover	1988	1987
$\dfrac{\text{Net sales}}{\text{Average accounts receivable}}$	$\dfrac{\$17,034}{(\$4,071 + \$3,144)/2}$	$\dfrac{\$13,305}{(\$3,144 + \$2,553)/2}$
	$= \dfrac{\$17,034}{\$3,607.5} = \dfrac{4.72}{\text{times}}$	$= \dfrac{\$13,305}{\$2,848.5} = \dfrac{4.67}{\text{times}}$

Within reasonable ranges, the higher the turnover ratio the better. With a higher turnover the company is turning receivables into cash at a faster pace. The speed at which receivables are turned over depends on the company's credit terms. Since a company's credit terms are usually stated in days, such as 2/10, n/30, it is helpful to convert the receivable turnover to **average days' sales uncollected**. This conversion is made by dividing the length of the accounting period (usually 365 days) by the receivable turnover (as computed above), as follows:

Average Days' Sales Uncollected	1988	1987
$\dfrac{\text{Days in year}}{\text{Receivable turnover}}$	$\dfrac{365 \text{ days}}{4.72} = 77.3 \text{ days}$	$\dfrac{365 \text{ days}}{4.67} = 78.2 \text{ days}$

In the case of Kodak, both the receivable turnover and the average days' sales uncollected were about the same in 1987 and 1988. The average accounts receivable was turned over about 4.7 times both years. This means Kodak had to wait on average about 77 or 78 days to receive payment for credit sales.

Inventory Turnover. Inventory is two steps removed from cash (sale and collection). The inventory turnover ratio measures the relative size of inventory. The proportion of assets tied up in inventory, of course, affects the amount of cash available to pay maturing debts. Inventory should be maintained at the best level to support production and sales. In general, however, a smaller, faster-moving inventory means that the company has less cash tied up in inventory. It also means that there is less chance for the inventory to become spoiled or out of date. A build-up in inventory may mean that a recession or some other factor is preventing sales from keeping pace with purchasing and production.

Using a 1986 ending inventory balance of $2,072 million, inventory turnover for 1988 and 1987 at Kodak is computed as follows:

Inventory Turnover	1988	1987
$\dfrac{\text{Cost of goods sold}}{\text{Average inventory}}$	$\dfrac{\$9,601}{(\$3,025 + \$2,178)/2}$	$\dfrac{\$8,004}{(\$2,178 + \$2,072)/2}$
	$= \dfrac{\$9,601}{\$2,601.5} = \dfrac{3.69}{\text{times}}$	$= \dfrac{\$8,004}{\$2,125} = \dfrac{3.77}{\text{times}}$

Consistent with receivable turnover, there was little change in inventory turnover from 1987 to 1988.

Evaluating Profitability

A company's long-run survival depends on its being able to earn a satisfactory income. Investors become and remain stockholders for only one reason. They believe that the dividends and capital gains they will receive will be greater than the returns on other investments of about the same risk. An evaluation of a company's past earning power may give the investor a better basis for decision making. Also, as pointed out in Chapter 8, a company's ability to earn an income usually affects its liquidity position. For this reason, evaluating profitability is important to both investors and creditors. In judging the profitability of Kodak, five ratios will be presented: profit margin, asset turnover, return on assets, return on equity, and earnings per share. Except for earnings per share, all these ratios were introduced in Chapter 8.

Profit Margin. The profit margin ratio measures the percentage of each revenue dollar that contributes to net income. It is computed for Kodak as follows:

Profit Margin[6]	1988	1987
$\dfrac{\text{Net income}}{\text{Net sales}}$	$\dfrac{\$1,397}{\$17,034} = 8.2\%$	$\dfrac{\$1,178}{\$13,305} = 8.9\%$

The ratio confirms what was clear from the common-size income statements (Exhibit 19-6): that the profit margin decreased from 1987 (8.9 percent) to 1988 (8.2 percent). Previous analysis has shown that this decrease is due primarily to a large increase in interest expense.

Asset Turnover. **Asset turnover** is a measure of how efficiently assets are used to produce sales. It shows how many dollars in sales are produced by each dollar invested in assets. In other words, it tells how many times in the period assets were "turned over" in sales. The higher the asset turnover, the more concentrated is the use of assets. Using the data for Kodak from Exhibits 19-2 and 19-3 and 1986 total assets of $12,902 million, the asset turnover for 1988 and 1987 is computed as follows:

Asset Turnover	1988	1987
$\dfrac{\text{Net sales}}{\text{Average total assets}}$	$\dfrac{\$17,034}{(\$22,964 + \$14,698)/2}$	$\dfrac{\$13,305}{(\$14,698 + \$12,902)/2}$
	$= \dfrac{\$17,034}{\$18,831} = \dfrac{.90}{\text{times}}$	$= \dfrac{\$13,305}{\$13,800} = \dfrac{.96}{\text{times}}$

Compared to other industries, Kodak needs a large investment in assets for each dollar of sales. A retailer may have an asset turnover of between 4.0 and 6.0. In Kodak's case, however, asset turnover was only .96 in 1987 and .90 in 1988. This means that Kodak makes sales of a little less than one dollar for each dollar of assets. Yet even the small decrease from 1987 to 1988 is significant because of the company's large dollar amount of sales and assets. Its effect on return on assets is striking.

Return on Assets. The best overall measure of the earning power or profitability of a company is **return on assets**, which measures the amount earned on each dollar of assets invested. The return on assets for 1988 and 1987 for Kodak is computed as follows:

Return on Assets[7]	1988	1987
$\dfrac{\text{Net income}}{\text{Average total assets}}$	$\dfrac{\$1,397}{\$18,831} = 7.4\%$	$\dfrac{\$1,178}{\$13,800} = 8.5\%$

6. In comparing companies in an industry, some analysts use net income before income taxes as the numerator to eliminate the effect of differing tax rates among firms.
7. Some authorities would add interest expense to the numerator because they view interest expense as a cost of acquiring capital rather than a cost of operations.

Kodak's return on assets decreased from 8.5 percent in 1987 to 7.4 percent in 1988, an unfavorable change.

One reason why return on assets is a good measure of profitability is that it combines the effects of profit margin and asset turnover. The 1988 and 1987 results for Kodak can be analyzed as follows:

	Profit Margin		Asset Turnover		Return on Assets
Ratios:	$\dfrac{\text{net income}}{\text{net sales}}$	$\times$	$\dfrac{\text{net sales}}{\text{average total assets}}$	$=$	$\dfrac{\text{net income}}{\text{average total assets}}$
1988	8.2%	$\times$	.90	$=$	7.4%
1987	8.9%	$\times$	.96	$=$	8.5%

From this analysis, it is clear that the decrease in return on assets in 1988 can be attributed to decreases in both profit margin and asset turnover.

Return on Equity. An important measure of profitability from the stockholders' standpoint is **return on equity**. This ratio measures how much was earned for each dollar invested by owners. For Kodak, this ratio for 1988 and 1987 is figured as follows (1986 owners' equity equals $6,388 million):

Return on Equity	1988	1987
$\dfrac{\text{Net income}}{\text{Average owners' equity}}$	$\dfrac{\$1,397}{(\$6,780 + \$6,013)/2}$	$\dfrac{\$1,178}{(\$6,013 + \$6,388)/2}$
	$= \dfrac{\$1,397}{\$6,396.5} = 21.8\%$	$= \dfrac{\$1,178}{\$6,200.5} = 19.0\%$

In contrast to the other profitability ratios, this ratio improved from 1987 to 1988, due to a small increase in average owners' equity compared to sales and average total assets.

A natural question is, Why is there a difference between return on assets and return on equity? The answer lies in the company's use of **leverage**, or debt financing. A company that has interest-bearing debt is said to be leveraged. If the company earns more with its borrowed funds than it must pay in interest for those funds, then the difference is available to increase the return on equity. Leverage may work against the company as well. Thus an unfavorable situation occurs when the return on assets is less than the rate of interest paid on borrowed funds. Because of Kodak's leverage, the return on assets in 1988 of 7.4 percent created a much larger return on equity of 21.8 percent for the same year. (The debt to equity ratio is presented later in this chapter.)

Earnings per Share. One of the most widely quoted measures of profitability is **earnings per share** of common stock. Exhibit 19-3 shows that the net earnings per share for Kodak improved from $3.52 to $4.31, reflecting the increase in net earnings from 1987 to 1988. These disclosures must be made in financial statements; calculations of this kind were presented in Chapter 16.

Evaluating Long-Term Solvency

Long-term solvency has to do with a company's ability to survive over many years. The aim of long-term solvency analysis is to point out early if a company is on the road to bankruptcy. Studies have shown that accounting ratios can show as much as five years in advance that a company may fail.[8] Declining profitability and liquidity ratios are key signs of possible business failure. Two other ratios that analysts often consider as indicators of long-term solvency are the debt to equity ratio and the interest coverage ratio.

Debt to Equity Ratio. The existence of increasing amounts of debt in a company's capital structure is thought to be risky. The company has a legal obligation to make interest payments on time and to pay the principal at the maturity date. And this obligation holds no matter what the level of the company's earnings is. If the payments are not made, the company may be forced into bankruptcy. In contrast, dividends and other distributions to equity holders are made only when the board of directors declares them. The debt to equity ratio shows the amount of the company's assets provided by creditors in relation to the amount provided by stockholders. Thus it measures the extent to which the company is leveraged. The larger the debt to equity ratio the more fixed obligations the company has, and so the riskier the situation.

The ratio is computed as follows:

Debt to Equity Ratio	1988	1987
$\dfrac{\text{Total liabilities}}{\text{Owners' equity}}$	$\dfrac{\$16,184}{\$6,780} = 2.39$	$\dfrac{\$8,685}{\$6,013} = 1.44$

From 1987 to 1988, the debt to equity ratio for Kodak went up from 1.44 to 2.39. This finding agrees with the analysis of the common-size balance sheets (Exhibit 19-5), which shows that the total liabilities of the company increased as a percentage of total assets in 1988. (Recall that long-term borrowings were up significantly as a result of the Sterling Drug purchase.)

Interest Coverage Ratio. One question that usually arises at this point is, If debt is bad, why have any? The answer is that, as with many ratios, the level of debt is a matter of balance. In spite of its riskiness, debt is a flexible means of financing certain business operations. Also, because it usually carries a fixed interest charge, it limits the cost of financing and

8. William H. Beaver, "Alternative Accounting Measures as Indicators of Failure," *Accounting Review* (January 1968); and Edward Altman, "Financial Ratios, Discriminant Analysis and the Prediction of Corporate Bankruptcy," *Journal of Finance* (September 1968).

creates a situation in which leverage can be used to advantage. Thus, if the company is able to earn a return on assets greater than the cost of the interest, it makes an overall profit.[9] However, the company runs the risk of not earning a return on assets equal to the cost of financing those assets, and thereby incurring a loss.

One measure of the degree of protection creditors have from a default on interest payments is the **interest coverage ratio**, which is computed as follows:

Interest Coverage Ratio	1988	1987
$\dfrac{\text{Net income before taxes} + \text{interest expense}}{\text{Interest expense}}$	$\dfrac{\$2{,}236 + \$697}{\$697}$	$\dfrac{\$1{,}984 + \$181}{\$181}$
	= 4.21 times	= 11.96 times

Interest coverage worsened in 1988; interest payments were protected by a ratio of only 4.21 times, versus 11.96 in 1987, due to the sharp increase in interest expense.

Market Test Ratios

The market price of a company's stock is of interest to the analyst because it represents what investors as a whole think of a company at a point in time. Market price is the price at which people are willing to buy and sell the stock. It provides information about how investors view the potential return and risk connected with owning the company's stock. This information cannot be obtained simply by considering the market price of the stock by itself, however. Companies differ in number of outstanding shares and amount of underlying earnings and dividends. Thus the market price must be related to the earnings per share, dividends per share, and price of other companies' shares. This is accomplished through the price/earnings ratio, the dividends yield, and an analysis of market risk.

Price/Earnings Ratio. The **price/earnings (P/E) ratio** measures the relationship of the current market price of a stock to the company's earnings per share. Assuming a current market price of $50 and using the 1988 earnings per share for Eastman Kodak Company of $4.31 from Exhibit 19-3, we can compute the price/earnings ratio as follows:

$$\frac{\text{Market price per share}}{\text{Earnings per share}} = \frac{\$50}{\$4.31} = 11.6 \text{ times}$$

At this time, Kodak's P/E ratio is 11.6 times its underlying earnings. The price/earnings ratio changes from day to day and from quarter to quarter as market price and earnings change. It tells how much, at any

---

9. In addition, as we will see in Chapter 21, there are advantages to being a debtor in periods of inflation because the debt, which is fixed in dollar amount, may be repaid with cheaper dollars.

particular time, the investing public as a whole is willing to pay for $1 of a company's earnings per share.

This price/earnings ratio is very useful and widely applied because it allows companies to be compared. When a company's P/E ratio is higher than the P/E ratios for other companies, it *usually* means that investors feel that the company's earnings are going to grow at a faster rate than those of the other companies. On the other hand, a lower P/E ratio *usually* means a more negative assessment by investors. To compare two well-known companies, the market was less favorable toward General Motors (6.0 times earnings per share) than it was toward IBM (13.0 times earnings per share) in 1989.

Dividends Yield. The **dividends yield** is a measure of the current return to an investor in a stock. It is found by dividing the current annual dividend by the current market price of the stock. Assuming the same $50 per share and using the 1988 dividends of $1.90 per share for Kodak from Exhibit 19-4, we can compute the dividends yield thus:

$$\frac{\text{Dividends per share}}{\text{Market price per share}} = \frac{\$1.90}{\$50} = 3.8\%$$

Thus an investor who owns Kodak stock at $50 had a return from dividends in 1988 of 3.8 percent.

The dividends yield is only one part of the investor's total return from investing in Eastman Kodak Company. The investor must add or subtract from the dividends yield the percentage change (either up or down) in the market value of the stock.

Market Risk. It was pointed out earlier that besides assessing the potential return from an investment, the investor must also judge the risk associated with the investment. Many factors may be brought into assessing risk—the nature of the business, the quality of the business, the track record of the company, and so forth. One measure of risk that has gained increased attention among analysts in recent years is market risk. **Market risk** is the volatility of (or changes up and down in) the price of a stock in relation to the volatility of the prices of other stocks.

The computation of market risk is complex, involving computers and sophisticated statistical techniques such as regression analysis. The idea, however, is simple. Consider the following data on the changes in the prices of the stocks of Company A and Company B compared to the average change in price of all stocks in the market:

Average Percentage Change in Price of All Stocks	Percentage Change in Price of Company A's Stock	Percentage Change in Price of Company B's Stock
+10	+15	+5
−10	−15	−5

In this example, when the average price of all stocks went up by 10 percent, Company A's price increased 15 percent while Company B's increased only 5 percent. When the average price of all stocks went down by 10 percent, Company A's price decreased 15 percent but Company B's decreased only 5 percent. Thus, relative to all stocks, Company A's stock is more volatile than Company B's. If the prices of stocks go down, the risk of loss is greater in the case of Company A than in the case of Company B. If the market goes up, however, the potential for gain is greater in the case of Company A than in the case of Company B.

Market risk can be approximated by dividing the percentage change in price of a particular stock by the average percentage change in the price of all stocks, as follows:

$$\text{Company A} \quad \frac{\text{specific change}}{\text{average change}} = \frac{15}{10} = 1.5$$

$$\text{Company B} \quad \frac{\text{specific change}}{\text{average change}} = \frac{5}{10} = .5$$

This means that an investor can generally expect the value of an investment in Company A to increase or decrease 1.5 times as much as the average change in the price of all stocks. An investment in Company B can be expected to increase or decrease only .5 times as much as the price of all stocks.

Analysts call this measure of market risk **beta** (β), after the mathematical symbol used in the formula for calculating the relationships of stock prices. The actual betas used by analysts are based on several years of data and are continually updated. Because the calculations require the use of computers, betas are usually provided by investment services.

The market risk or beta for U.S. Steel in a recent year was 1.01. This means that other things being equal, a person who invests in the stock of U.S. Steel can expect its volatility or risk to be about the same as the stock market as a whole (which has a beta of 1.0). When one considers that U.S. Steel is a mature company and the largest steel producer, with output closely related to the ups and downs in the economy as a whole, its near-neutral beta makes sense.

If the investor's objective is to assume less risk than that of the market as a whole, other companies in the steel industry might be considered. The second largest steel company in the United States, Bethlehem Steel, can be eliminated because its beta of 1.25 makes it riskier than U.S. Steel. National Steel, the third largest steel processor, has been more stable over the years than its competitors, with a beta of only .75. It is a less risky stock in that there is less potential for a loss in a "down" market; but there is also less potential for gain in an "up" market. National Steel's beta is very low and compares favorably with that of major utilities such as American Telephone and Telegraph, which has a beta of .65.

Typically, growth stocks and speculative stocks are riskier than the stock market as a whole. Tandy Corporation (Radio Shack), a good example of a growth company, has had a beta of 1.45 in recent years. Tandy Corporation has rewarded investors' patience over the long term, but has been much more volatile and thus riskier than the average stock with a beta of 1.00.

Investment decisions are not made on the basis of market risk alone, of course. First, other risk factors such as those indicated by the ratios discussed in this chapter, as well as industry, national, and world economic outlooks, must be considered. Second, the expected return must be considered. Further, most investors try to assemble a portfolio of stocks whose average beta corresponds to the degree of risk they are willing to assume in relation to their average expected return.

Chapter Review

Review of Learning Objectives

1. **Describe and discuss the objectives of financial statement analysis.**
   Creditors and investors, as well as managers, use financial statement analysis to judge the past performance and current position of a company. In this way they also judge its future potential and the risk associated with it. Creditors use the information gained from their analysis to make reliable loans that will be repaid with interest. Investors use the information to make investments that provide a return that is worth the risk.

2. **Describe and discuss the standards for financial statement analysis.**
   Three commonly used standards for financial statement analysis are rule-of-thumb measures, past performance of the company, and industry norms. Rule-of-thumb measures are weak because of the lack of evidence that they can be applied widely. The past performance of a company can offer a guideline for measuring improvement but is not helpful in judging performance relative to other companies. Although the use of industry norms overcomes this last problem, its disadvantage is that firms are not always comparable, even in the same industry.

3. **State the sources of information for financial statement analysis.**
   The major sources of information about publicly held corporations are published reports such as annual reports and interim financial statements, SEC reports, business periodicals, and credit and investment advisory services.

4. **Identify the issues related to the evaluation of the quality of a company's earnings.**
   Current and prospective net income is an important component in many ratios used to evaluate a company. The user should recognize that the quality of reported net income can be influenced by certain choices made by a company's management. First, management exercises judgment in choosing the accounting methods and estimates used in computing net income. Second, discontinued operations, extraordinary gains or losses, and accounting changes may affect net income positively or negatively.

5. **Apply horizontal analysis, trend analysis, and vertical analysis to financial statements.**
   Horizontal analysis involves the computation of dollar amount changes and percentage changes from year to year. Trend analysis is an extension

of horizontal analysis in that percentage changes are calculated for several years. The changes are usually computed by setting a base year equal to 100 and calculating the results for subsequent years as a percentage of that base year. Vertical analysis uses percentages to show the relationship of the component parts to the total in a single statement. The resulting statements, expressed entirely in percentages, are called common-size statements.

6. Apply ratio analysis to financial statements in the study of an enterprise's liquidity, profitability, long-term solvency, and market tests.
The following table summarizes the basic information on ratio analysis.

Ratio	Components	Use or Meaning
Liquidity Ratios		
Current ratio	$\dfrac{\text{Current assets}}{\text{Current liabilities}}$	Measure of short-term debt-paying ability
Quick ratio	$\dfrac{\text{Cash + marketable securities + receivables}}{\text{Current liabilities}}$	Measure of short-term liquidity
Receivable turnover	$\dfrac{\text{Net sales}}{\text{Average accounts receivable}}$	Measure of relative size of accounts receivable balance and effectiveness of credit policies
Average days' sales uncollected	$\dfrac{\text{Days in year}}{\text{Receivable turnover}}$	Measure of average time taken to collect receivables
Inventory turnover	$\dfrac{\text{Cost of goods sold}}{\text{Average inventory}}$	Measure of relative size of inventory
Profitability Ratios		
Profit margin	$\dfrac{\text{Net income}}{\text{Net sales}}$	Net income produced by each dollar of sales
Asset turnover	$\dfrac{\text{Net sales}}{\text{Average total assets}}$	Measure of how efficiently assets are used to produce sales
Return on assets	$\dfrac{\text{Net income}}{\text{Average total assets}}$	Overall measure of earning power or profitability of all assets employed in the business
Return on equity	$\dfrac{\text{Net income}}{\text{Average owners' equity}}$	Profitability of owners' investment
Earnings per share	$\dfrac{\text{Net income}}{\text{Weighted average outstanding shares}}$	Means of placing earnings on a common basis for comparison

(continued)

Ratio	Components	Use or Meaning
Long-Term Solvency Ratios		
Debt to equity ratio	$\dfrac{\text{Total liabilities}}{\text{Owners' equity}}$	Measure of relationship of debt financing to equity financing
Interest coverage ratio	$\dfrac{\text{Net income before taxes + interest expense}}{\text{Interest expense}}$	Measure of protection of creditors from default on interest payments
Market Test Ratios		
Price/earnings (P/E) ratio	$\dfrac{\text{Market price per share}}{\text{Earnings per share}}$	Measure of amount the market will pay for a dollar of earnings
Dividends yield	$\dfrac{\text{Dividends per share}}{\text{Market price per share}}$	Measure of current return to investor
Market risk	$\dfrac{\text{Specific change in market price}}{\text{Average change in market price}}$	Measure of volatility of the market price of a stock in relation to that of other stocks

Review of Concepts and Terminology

The following concepts and terms were introduced in this chapter:

(L.O. 6) **Asset turnover:**   Net sales divided by average total assets. Used to measure how efficiently assets are used to produce sales.

(L.O. 6) **Average days' sales uncollected:**   The length of the accounting period, usually 365 days, divided by the receivable turnover. Shows the speed at which receivables are turned over—literally, the number of days, on the average, a company must wait to receive payment for credit sales.

(L.O. 5) **Base year:**   In financial analysis, the first year to be considered in any set of data.

(L.O. 6) **Beta (β):**   A measure of the market risk of an individual stock in relation to the average market risk of all stocks.

(L.O. 5) **Common-size statement:**   A financial statement in which the components of a total figure are stated in terms of percentages of the total.

(L.O. 6) **Current ratio:**   The relationship of current assets to current liabilities. Used as an indicator of a company's liquidity and short-term debt-paying ability.

(L.O. 6) **Debt to equity ratio:** Total liabilities divided by owners' equity. Used to measure the relationship of debt financing to equity financing, or the extent to which a company is leveraged.

(L.O. 2) **Diversified companies (conglomerates):** Companies that operate in more than one industry.

(L.O. 6) **Dividends yield:** The current annual dividend divided by the current market price of a stock. Used as a measure of the current return to an investor in a stock.

(L.O. 6) **Earnings per share:** Net income divided by the weighted average number of outstanding shares of common stock. Used as a measure of profitability and a means of comparison among stocks.

(L.O. 1) **Financial statement analysis:** A collective term for the techniques used to show important relationships among figures in financial statements.

(L.O. 5) **Horizontal analysis:** A technique for analyzing financial statements that involves the computation of dollar amount changes and percentage changes from the previous to the current year.

(L.O. 5) **Index number:** In trend analysis, a number against which changes in related items over a period of time are measured. Calculated by setting the base year equal to 100 percent.

(L.O. 6) **Interest coverage ratio:** Net income before taxes plus interest expense, divided by interest expense. Used as a measure of the degree of protection creditors have from a default on interest payments.

(L.O. 3) **Interim financial statements:** Financial statements issued for a period of less than one year, usually monthly or quarterly.

(L.O. 6) **Inventory turnover:** The cost of goods sold divided by average inventory. Used to measure the relative size of inventory.

(L.O. 6) **Leverage:** Debt financing. The amount of debt financing in relation to equity financing is measured by the debt to equity ratio.

(L.O. 6) **Market risk:** The volatility of the price of a stock in relation to the volatility of the prices of other stocks.

(L.O. 1) **Portfolio:** A group of loans or investments designed to average the return and risks of a creditor or investor.

(L.O. 6) **Price/earnings (P/E) ratio:** Current market price per share divided by earnings per share. Used as a measure of investor confidence in a company, and as a means of comparison among stocks.

(L.O. 6) **Profit margin:** Net income divided by net sales. Used to measure the percentage of each revenue dollar that is contributed to net income.

(L.O. 6) **Quick ratio:** The relationship of the more liquid current assets—cash, marketable securities or short-term investments, and receivables—to current liabilities. Used as a measure of short-term liquidity.

(L.O. 6) **Ratio analysis:** A technique for analyzing financial statements in which meaningful relationships are shown between components of financial statements. (For a summary of ratios see the Review of Learning Objectives, pages 817–818.)

(L.O. 6) **Receivable turnover:** The relationship of net sales to average accounts receivable. Used as a measure of the relative size of a company's accounts receivable and the success of its credit and collection policies; shows how many times, on the average, receivables were turned into cash during the period.

(L.O. 6)   **Return on assets:**   Net income divided by average total assets. Used to measure the amount earned on each dollar of assets invested. An overall measure of earning power or profitability.

(L.O. 6)   **Return on equity:**   Net income divided by average owners' equity. Used to measure how much income was earned for each dollar invested by owners.

(L.O. 5)   **Trend analysis:**   A type of horizontal analysis in which percentage changes are calculated for several successive years instead of two years.

(L.O. 5)   **Vertical analysis:**   A technique for analyzing financial statements that uses percentages to show the relationship of the different parts to the total in a single statement.

Self-Test

Test your knowledge of the chapter by choosing the best answer for each item below.

1. A general rule in choosing among alternative investments is the greater the risk taken, the
   a. greater the return required.
   b. lower the profits expected.
   c. lower the potential expected.
   d. greater the price of the investment.   *(L.O. 1)*

2. Which of the following is the most useful in evaluating whether a company has improved its position in relation to its competitors?
   a. Rule-of-thumb measures
   b. Past performance of the company
   c. Past and current performances of the company
   d. Industry averages   *(L.O. 2)*

3. One of the best places to look for early signals of change in a company's profitability is
   a. the interim financial statements.
   b. the year-end financial statements.
   c. the annual report sent to stockholders.
   d. the annual report sent to the SEC.   *(L.O. 3)*

4. The quality of a company's earnings may be affected by
   a. the countries in which the company operates.
   b. the choice of independent auditors.
   c. the industry in which the company operates.
   d. the accounting methods used by the company.   *(L.O. 4)*

5. In trend analysis, each item is expressed as a percentage of the
   a. net income figure.   c. base year figure.
   b. retained earnings figure.   d. total assets figure.   *(L.O. 5)*

6. In a common-size balance sheet for a wholesale company, the 100% figure is
   a. merchandise inventory.
   b. total current assets.
   c. total property, plant, and equipment.
   d. total assets.   *(L.O. 5)*

7. The best way to study the changes in financial statements between two years is to prepare
   a. common-size statements.
   b. a trend analysis.
   c. a horizontal analysis.
   d. a ratio analysis. *(L.O. 5)*

8. A common measure of liquidity is
   a. return on assets.
   b. profit margin.
   c. inventory turnover.
   d. interest coverage. *(L.O. 6)*

9. Asset turnover is most closely related to
   a. profit margin and return on assets.
   b. profit margin and debt to equity.
   c. interest coverage and debt to equity.
   d. earnings per share and profit margin. *(L.O. 6)*

10. Which of the following describes the computation of the interest coverage ratio?
    a. Net income minus interest expense divided by interest expense
    b. Net income plus interest expense divided by interest expense
    c. Net income before taxes plus interest expense divided by interest expense
    d. Net income divided by interest expense *(L.O. 6)*

Answers to Self-Test are at the end of this chapter.

Review Problem
Comparative Analysis of Two Companies

(L.O. 6) Maggie Washington is considering an investment in one of two fast-food restaurant chains because she believes the trend toward eating out more often will continue. Her choices have been narrowed to Quik Burger and Big Steak, whose income statements and balance sheets follow.

Income Statements (in thousands)		
	Quik Burger	**Big Steak**
Sales	$53,000	$86,000
Cost of Goods Sold (including restaurant operating expense)	37,000	61,000
Gross Margin from Sales	$16,000	$25,000
General Operating Expenses		
Selling Expenses	$ 7,000	$10,000
Administrative Expenses	4,000	5,000
Interest Expense	1,400	3,200
Income Taxes Expense	1,800	3,400
Total Operating Expenses	$14,200	$21,600
Net Income	$ 1,800	$ 3,400

Balance Sheets (in thousands)		
	Quik Burger	Big Steak
Assets		
Cash	$ 2,000	$ 4,500
Accounts Receivable (net)	2,000	6,500
Inventory	2,000	5,000
Property, Plant, and Equipment (net)	20,000	35,000
Other Assets	4,000	5,000
Total Assets	$30,000	$56,000
Liabilities and Stockholders' Equity		
Accounts Payable	$ 2,500	$ 3,000
Notes Payable	1,500	4,000
Bonds Payable	10,000	30,000
Common Stock ($1 par value)	1,000	3,000
Paid-in Capital in Excess of Par Value, Common	9,000	9,000
Retained Earnings	6,000	7,000
Total Liabilities and Stockholders' Equity	$30,000	$56,000

In addition, dividends paid were $500,000 for Quik Burger and $600,000 for Big Steak. The market prices of the stocks were $30 and $20, respectively, and their betas were 1.00 and 1.15. Financial information pertaining to prior years is not readily available to Maggie Washington. Assume that all notes payable are current liabilities and that all bonds payable are long-term liabilities.

Required

Conduct a comprehensive ratio analysis of Quik Burger and Big Steak and compare the results. The analysis should be performed using the following steps (round all ratios and percentages to one decimal point):

1. Prepare an analysis of liquidity.
2. Prepare an analysis of profitability.
3. Prepare an analysis of long-term solvency.
4. Prepare an analysis of market tests.
5. Compare the two companies by inserting the ratio calculations from the preceding four steps in a table with the following column headings: Ratio Name, Quik Burger, Big Steak, and Company with More Favorable Ratio. Indicate in the last column the company that apparently had the more favorable ratio in each case. (Consider changes of .1 or less to be indeterminate.)
6. In what ways would having access to prior years' information aid this analysis?

Answer to Review Problem

Ratio Name	Quik Burger	Big Steak
1. Liquidity analysis		

1. Liquidity analysis

a. Current ratio

$$\frac{\$2,000 + \$2,000 + \$2,000}{\$2,500 + \$1,500}$$

$$= \frac{\$6,000}{\$4,000} = 1.5$$

$$\frac{\$4,500 + \$6,500 + \$5,000}{\$3,000 + \$4,000}$$

$$= \frac{\$16,000}{\$7,000} = 2.3$$

b. Quick ratio

$$\frac{\$2,000 + \$2,000}{\$2,500 + \$1,500}$$

$$= \frac{\$4,000}{\$4,000} = 1.0$$

$$\frac{\$4,500 + \$6,500}{\$3,000 + \$4,000}$$

$$= \frac{\$11,000}{\$7,000} = 1.6$$

c. Receivable turnover

$$\frac{\$53,000}{\$2,000} = 26.5 \text{ times}$$

$$\frac{\$86,000}{\$6,500} = 13.2 \text{ times}$$

d. Average days' sales uncollected

$$\frac{365}{26.5} = 13.8 \text{ days}$$

$$\frac{365}{13.2} = 27.7 \text{ days}$$

e. Inventory turnover

$$\frac{\$37,000}{\$2,000} = 18.5 \text{ times}$$

$$\frac{\$61,000}{\$5,000} = 12.2 \text{ times}$$

2. Profitability analysis

a. Profit margin

$$\frac{\$1,800}{\$53,000} = 3.4\%$$

$$\frac{\$3,400}{\$86,000} = 4.0\%$$

b. Asset turnover

$$\frac{\$53,000}{\$30,000} = 1.8 \text{ times}$$

$$\frac{\$86,000}{\$56,000} = 1.5 \text{ times}$$

c. Return on assets

$$\frac{\$1,800}{\$30,000} = 6.0\%$$

$$\frac{\$3,400}{\$56,000} = 6.1\%$$

d. Return on equity

$$\frac{\$1,800}{\$1,000 + \$9,000 + \$6,000}$$

$$= \frac{\$1,800}{\$16,000} = 11.3\%$$

$$\frac{\$3,400}{\$3,000 + \$9,000 + \$7,000}$$

$$= \frac{\$3,400}{\$19,000} = 17.9\%$$

e. Earnings per share

$$\frac{\$1,800}{1,000} = \$1.80$$

$$\frac{\$3,400}{3,000} = \$1.13$$

3. Long-term solvency analysis

a. Debt to equity ratio

$$\frac{\$2,500 + \$1,500 + \$10,000}{\$1,000 + \$9,000 + \$6,000}$$

$$= \frac{\$14,000}{\$16,000} = 0.9$$

$$\frac{\$3,000 + \$4,000 + \$30,000}{\$3,000 + \$9,000 + \$7,000}$$

$$= \frac{\$37,000}{\$19,000} = 1.9$$

Ratio Name	Quik Burger	Big Steak
b. Interest coverage ratio	$\dfrac{\$1,800 + \$1,800 + \$1,400}{\$1,400}$	$\dfrac{\$3,400 + \$3,400 + \$3,200}{\$3,200}$
	$= \dfrac{\$5,000}{\$1,400} = 3.6$ times	$= \dfrac{\$10,000}{\$3,200} = 3.1$ times

4. Market test analysis

a. Price/earnings ratio	$\dfrac{\$30}{\$1.80} = 16.7$ times	$\dfrac{\$20}{\$1.13} = 17.7$ times
b. Dividends yield	$\dfrac{\$500,000 \div 1,000,000}{\$30} = 1.7\%$	$\dfrac{\$600,000 \div 3,000,000}{\$20} = 1.0\%$
c. Market risk	1.00	1.15

5. Comparative analysis

Ratio Name	Quik Burger	Big Steak	Company with More Favorable Ratio*
1. Liquidity analysis			
a. Current ratio	1.5	2.3	Big Steak
b. Quick ratio	1.0	1.6	Big Steak
c. Receivable turnover	26.5 times	13.2 times	Quik Burger
d. Average days' sales uncollected	13.8 days	27.7 days	Quik Burger
e. Inventory turnover	18.5 times	12.2 times	Quik Burger
2. Profitability analysis			
a. Profit margin	3.4%	4.0%	Big Steak
b. Asset turnover	1.8 times	1.5 times	Quik Burger
c. Return on assets	6.0%	6.1%	Neutral
d. Return on equity	11.3%	17.9%	Big Steak
e. Earnings per share	$1.80	$1.13	Noncomparable[†]
3. Long-term solvency analysis			
a. Debt to equity ratio	0.9	1.9	Quik Burger
b. Interest coverage ratio	3.6 times	3.1 times	Quik Burger
4. Market test analysis			
a. Price/earnings ratio	16.7 times	17.7 times	Big Steak
b. Dividends yield	1.7%	1.0%	Quik Burger
c. Market risk	1.00	1.15	Quik Burger is less risky

*This analysis indicates the company with the apparently more favorable ratio. Class discussion may focus on conditions under which different conclusions may be drawn.

†Earnings per share are noncomparable because of the considerable difference in the number of common stockholders of the two firms. If information for prior years were available, it would be helpful in determining the earnings trend of each company.

6. **Usefulness of prior years' information**

Prior years' information would be helpful in two ways. First, turnover and return ratios could be based on average amounts. Second, a trend analysis could be performed for each company.

Chapter Assignments

Discussion Questions and Writing Assignments

1. What differences and similarities exist in the objectives of investors and creditors in using financial statement analysis?
2. What role does risk play in making loans and investments?
3. What standards are commonly used to evaluate financial statements, and what are their relative merits?
4. Why would a financial analyst compare the ratios of Steelco, a steel company, to the ratios of other companies in the steel industry? What might invalidate such a comparison?
5. Where may an investor look to find information about a company in which he or she is thinking of investing?
6. What is the basis of the statement "Accounting income is a useless measurement because it is based on so many arbitrary decisions"? Is the statement true?
7. Why would an investor want to see both horizontal and trend analyses of a company's financial statements?
8. What does the following sentence mean: "Based on 1967 equaling 100, net income increased from 240 in 1983 to 260 in 1984"?
9. What is the difference between horizontal and vertical analysis?
10. What is the purpose of ratio analysis?
11. Under what circumstances would a current ratio of 3:1 be good? Under what circumstances would it be bad?
12. In a period of high interest rates, why are receivable and inventory turnover especially important?
13. The following statements were made on page 35 of the November 6, 1978 issue of *Fortune* magazine: "Supermarket executives are beginning to look back with some nostalgia on the days when the standard profit margin was 1 percent of sales. Last year the industry overall margin came to a thin 0.72 percent." How could a supermarket earn a satisfactory return on assets with such a small profit margin?
14. Company A and Company B both have net incomes of $1,000,000. Is it possible to say that these companies are equally successful? Why or why not?
15. Circo Company has a return on assets of 12 percent and a debt to equity ratio of .5. Would you expect return on equity to be more or less than 12 percent?
16. The market price of Company J's stock is the same as Company Q's. How might one determine whether investors are equally confident about the future of these companies?
17. Why is it riskier to own a stock whose market price is more changeable than the market price of other stocks? Why might it be beneficial to own such a stock?

18. "By almost any standard. Chicago-based Helene Curtis rates as one of America's worst-managed personal care companies. In recent years its return on equity has hovered between 10% and 13%, well below the industry average of 18% to 19%. Net profit margins of 2% to 3% are half that of competitors. . . . As a result, while leading names like Revlon and Avon are trading at three and four times book value, Curtis's trades at less than two-thirds book value."[10] Considering that many companies are happy with a return on equity (owners' investment) of 10 percent and 13 percent, why is this analysis so critical of Curtis's performance? Assuming that Curtis could double its profit margin, what other information would you need to project the resulting return on owners' investment? Why are Revlon's and Avon's stocks trading for more than Curtis's?

Classroom Exercises

Exercise 19-1.
Effect of Alternative Accounting Methods
(L.O. 4)

At the end of its first year of operations, a company could calculate its ending merchandise inventory according to three different accounting methods, as follows: FIFO, $47,500; weighted average, $45,000; LIFO, $43,000. If the weighted-average method is used by the company, net income for the year would be $17,000.

1. Determine net income if the FIFO method is used.
2. Determine net income if the LIFO method is used.
3. Which method is more conservative?
4. Will the consistency convention be violated if the company chooses to use the LIFO method?
5. Does the full-disclosure convention require disclosure of the inventory method selected by management in the financial statements?

Exercise 19-2.
Effect of Alternative Accounting Methods
(L.O. 4, 6)

Jeans F' All and Jeans 'R' Us are very similar companies in size and operation. Jeans F' All uses FIFO and straight-line depreciation methods, and Jeans 'R' Us uses LIFO and accelerated depreciation. Prices have been rising during the past several years. Each company has paid its taxes in full for the current year, and each uses the same method for figuring income taxes as for financial reporting. Identify which company will report the greater amount for each of the following ratios:

a. current ratio
b. inventory turnover
c. profit margin
d. return on assets

If you cannot tell which company will report the greater amount, explain why.

Exercise 19-3.
Horizontal Analysis
(L.O. 5)

Compute the amount and percentage changes for the following balance sheets, and comment on the changes from 19x1 to 19x2. (Round the percentage changes to one decimal point.)

10. *Forbes,* November 13, 1978, p. 154.

	19x2	19x1
Herrera Company		
Comparative Balance Sheets		
December 31, 19x2 and 19x1		

Assets

	19x2	19x1
Current Assets	$ 18,600	$ 12,800
Property, Plant, and Equipment (net)	109,464	97,200
Total Assets	$128,064	$110,000

Liabilities and Stockholders' Equity

Current Liabilities	$ 11,200	$ 3,200
Long-Term Liabilities	35,000	40,000
Stockholders' Equity	81,864	66,800
Total Liabilities and Stockholders' Equity	$128,064	$110,000

Exercise 19-4.
Trend Analysis
(L.O. 5)

Prepare a trend analysis of the following data using 19x1 as the base year, and tell whether the situation shown by the trends is favorable or unfavorable. (Round your answers to one decimal point.)

	19x5	19x4	19x3	19x2	19x1
Sales	$12,760	$11,990	$12,100	$11,440	$11,000
Cost of Goods Sold	8,610	7,700	7,770	7,350	7,000
General and Administrative Expenses	2 640	2,592	2,544	2,448	2,400
Operating Income	1 510	1,698	1,786	1,642	1,600

Exercise 19-5.
Vertical Analysis
(L.O. 5)

Express the comparative income statements that follow as common-size statements, and comment on the changes from 19x1 to 19x2. (Round computations to one decimal point.)

Herrera Company		
Comparative Income Statements		
For the Years Ended December 31, 19x2 and 19x1		
	19x2	19x1
Sales	$212,000	$184,000
Cost of Goods Sold	127,200	119,600
Gross Margin from Sales	$ 84,800	$ 64,400
Selling Expenses	$ 53,000	$ 36,800
General Expenses	25,440	18,400
Total Operating Expenses	$ 78,440	$ 55,200
Net Operating Income	$ 6,360	$ 9,200

Exercise 19-6.
Liquidity Analysis
(L.O. 6)

Partial comparative balance sheet and income statement information for Prange Company follows.

	19x2	19x1
Cash	$ 3,400	$ 2,600
Marketable Securities	1,800	4,300
Accounts Receivable (net)	11,200	8,900
Inventory	13,600	12,400
Total Current Assets	$30,000	$28,200
Current Liabilities	$10,000	$ 7,050
Sales	$80,640	$55,180
Cost of Goods Sold	54,400	50,840
Gross Margin from Sales	$26,240	$ 4,340

The year-end balances for Accounts Receivable and Inventory were $8,100 and $12,800, respectively, in 19x0. Compute the current ratio, quick ratio, receivable turnover, average days' sales uncollected, and inventory turnover for each year. (Round computations to one decimal point.) Comment on the change in the company's liquidity position from 19x1 to 19x2.

Exercise 19-7.
Turnover Analysis
(L.O. 6)

McEnroe's Men's Shop has been in business for four years. Because the company has recently had a cash flow problem, management wonders whether there is a problem with receivables or inventories. Here are selected figures from the company's financial statements (in thousands):

	19x4	19x3	19x2	19x1
Net Sales	$144	$112	$96	$80
Cost of Goods Sold	90	72	60	48
Accounts Receivable (net)	24	20	16	12
Merchandise Inventory	28	22	16	10

Compute receivable turnover and inventory turnover for each of the four years, and comment on the results relative to the cash flow problem that McEnroe's Men's Shop has been experiencing. Round computations to one decimal point.

Exercise 19-8.
Profitability
Analysis
(L.O. 6)

At year end, Bodes Company had total assets of $320,000 in 19x0, $340,000 in 19x1, and $380,000 in 19x2. Its debt to equity ratio was .67 in all three years. In 19x1, the company made a net income of $38,556 on revenues of $612,000. In 19x2, the company made a net income of $49,476 on revenues of $798,000. Compute the profit margin, asset turnover, return on assets, and return on equity for 19x1 and 19x2. Comment on the apparent cause of the increase or decrease in profitability. (Round the percentages and other ratios to one decimal point.)

Exercise 19-9.
Long-Term
Solvency and
Market Test Ratios
(L.O. 6)

An investor is considering investing in the long-term bonds and common stock of Companies B and C. Both companies operate in the same industry, but Company B has a beta of 1.0 and Company C has a beta of 1.2. In addition, both companies pay a dividend per share of $2, and a yield of 10 percent on their long-term bonds. Other data for the two companies follow.

	Company B	Company C
Total Assets	$1,200,000	$540,000
Total Liabilities	540,000	297,000
Net Income before Taxes	144,000	64,800
Interest Expense	48,600	26,730
Earnings per Share	1.60	2.50
Market Price of Common Stock	20	23.75

Compute the debt to equity, interest coverage, price/earnings (P/E), and dividend yield ratios, and comment on the results. (Round computations to one decimal point.)

Exercise 19-10.
Preparation
of Statements
from Ratios and
Incomplete Data
(L.O. 6)

Following are the income statement and balance sheet of Chang Corporation, with most of the amounts missing.

Chang Corporation
Income Statement
For the Year Ended December 31, 19x1
(in thousands of dollars)

Sales		$9,000
Cost of Goods Sold		?
Gross Margin from Sales		?
Operating Expenses		
Selling Expenses	$?	
Administrative Expenses	117	
Interest Expense	81	
Income Taxes Expense	310	
Total Operating Expenses		?
Net Income		$?

Chang Corporation
Balance Sheet
December 31, 19x1
(in thousands of dollars)

Assets

Cash	$?	
Accounts Receivable (net)	?	
Inventories	?	
Total Current Assets		$?
Property, Plant, and Equipment (net)		2,700
Total Assets		$?

Liabilities and Stockholders' Equity

Current Liabilities	$?	
Bond Payable, 9% interest	?	
Total Liabilities		$?
Common Stock—$10 par value	$1,500	
Paid-in Capital in Excess of Par Value, Common	1,300	
Retained Earnings	2,000	
Total Stockholders' Equity		4,800
Total Liabilities and Stockholders' Equity		$?

Chang's only interest expense is on long-term debt. Its debt to equity ratio is
.5, its current ratio 3:1, its quick ratio 2:1, the receivable turnover 4.5, and its
inventory turnover 4.0. The return on assets is 10 percent. All ratios are
based on the current year's information. Complete the financial statements
using the information presented. Show supporting computations.

Interpreting Accounting Information

Ford Motor Company I*
(L.O. 6)

Standard & Poor's Corporation (S & P) offers a wide range of financial information services to investors. One of its services is rating the quality of the
bond issues of U.S. corporations. Its top bond rating is AAA, followed by
AA, A, BBB, BB, B, and so forth. The lowest rating of C is reserved for companies that are in or near bankruptcy. *Business Week* reported on February 2,
1981, that S & P had downgraded the bond rating for Ford Motor Company,
a leading U.S. automobile maker, from AAA to AA. The cause of the down-
grading was a deterioration of Ford's financial strength as indicated by certain ratios considered important by S & P. The ratios, S & P's guidelines, and
Ford's performances are summarized in the following table.

---

* Excerpts from the 1978, 1979, and 1980 annual reports used by permission of Ford
  Motor Company. Copyright © 1978, 1979, and 1980.

Ratio	S & P Guidelines for AAA Rating	Ford's Performance		
		1980	1979	1978
Interest Coverage	15 times	Loss	6.5 times	15.3 times
Pretax Return on Assets	15% to 20%	Loss	6.6%	13.4%
Debt to Equity	50%	63.4%	37.8%	34%
Cash Flow as a Percentage of Total Debt*	100%	91%	118.5%	152.6%
Short-Term Debt as a Percentage of Total Debt	25%	52.5%	48.3%	43.1%

* Cash flow includes net income plus noncash charges to earnings

Required

1. Identify the objective (profitability, liquidity, long-term solvency) measured by each of the S & P ratios. Why is each ratio important to the rating of Ford's long-term bonds?
2. The *Business Week* article suggested several actions that Ford might take to regain its previous rating. Tell which of the ratios each of the following actions would improve: (a) "cutting operating costs"; (b) "scrapping at least part of its massive spending plans over the next several years"; (c) "eliminate cash dividends to stockholders"; (d) "sale of profitable nonautomobile-related operations such as its steelmaker, aerospace company, and electronic concerns."

Ford Motor Company II*
(L.O. 6)

Part A: By 1983, S & P had dropped the rating on Ford's bond issues to BBB. Selected data for the years ended December 31, 1982 and 1983, from Ford Motor Company's 1983 annual report follow (in millions):

	1983	1982
Balance Sheet Data		
Short-Term Debt	$10,315.9	$10,424.0
Long-Term Debt	2,712.9	2,353.3
Stockholders' Equity	7,545.3	6,077.5
Total Assets	23,868.9	21,961.7
Income Statement Data		
Income (Loss) before Income Taxes	2,166.3	(407.9)
Interest Expense	567.2	745.5
Statement of Changes in Financial Position		
Funds (Cash Basis) Provided by Operations	5,001.5	2,632.0

Required

1. Compute for 1982 and 1983 the same ratios that were used by S & P in Ford Motor Company I.
2. If you were S & P, would you raise the rating on Ford's long-term bonds in 1984? Why or why not?

* Excerpts from the 1983 and 1987 annual reports used by permission of Ford Motor Company. Copyright © 1983 and 1987.

Part B: By the end of 1986, Ford's financial situation had improved enough to warrant an A rating from Standard & Poor's. Selected data for the years ended December 31, 1985 and 1986, from Ford Motor Company's 1987 annual report follow (in millions):

	1986	1985
Balance Sheet Data		
Short-Term Debt	$15,625.6	$12,777.4
Long-Term Debt	2,137.1	2,157.2
Stockholders' Equity	14,859.5	12,268.6
Total Assets	37,993.0	31,603.6
Income Statement Data		
Income (Loss) Before Income Taxes	5,552.2	4,076.9
Interest Expense	482.9	446.6
Statement of Changes in Financial Position		
Net Cash Flows from Operating Activities	7,624.4	5,371.6

Total assets in 1984 were $27,485.6 million.

Required

1. Compute for 1985 and 1986 the same ratios that were used by Standard & Poor's in Ford Motor Company I.
2. Do you agree that Ford's performance improved enough after 1983 (see Part A) to warrant an increase to an A rating?

Problem Set A

**Problem 19A-1.
Effect of
Alternative
Accounting
Methods
(L.O. 4, 6)**

Sarrafi Company began operations by purchasing $300,000 in equipment that had an estimated useful life of nine years and an estimated residual value of $30,000.

During the year, Sarrafi Company purchased inventory as presented in the chart below:

January	2,000 units at $25	$ 50,000
March	4,000 units at $24	96,000
May	1,000 units at $27	27,000
July	5,000 units at $27	135,000
September	6,000 units at $28	168,000
November	2,000 units at $29	58,000
December	3,000 units at $28	84,000
Total	23,000 units	$618,000

During the year the company sold 19,000 units for a total of $910,000 and incurred salary expenses of $170,000 and expenses other than depreciation of $120,000.

Sarrafi's management is anxious to present its income statement fairly in its first year of operation. It realizes that alternative accounting methods are available for accounting for inventory and equipment. Management wants to determine the effect of various alternatives on this year's income. Two sets of alternatives are required.

Required

1. Prepare two income statements for Sarrafi Company: one using a FIFO basis for inventory and the straight-line method for depreciation, the other using a LIFO basis for inventory and the sum-of-the-years'-digits method for depreciation.
2. Prepare a schedule accounting for the difference in the two net income figures obtained in part 1.
3. What effect does the choice of accounting methods have on Sarrafi's inventory turnover? What conclusion can you draw?
4. What effect does the choice of accounting methods have on Sarrafi's return on assets?

Use year-end balances to compute ratios. Round all ratios and percentages to one decimal point. Assume that the only other asset in addition to plant assets and inventory is $30,000 cash. Is your evaluation of Sarrafi's profitability affected by the choice of accounting methods?

Problem 19A-2.
Horizontal and
Vertical Analysis
(L.O. 5)

The condensed comparative balance sheets and income statements for Kelso Corporation follow.

Kelso Corporation
Comparative Balance Sheets
December 31, 19x2 and 19x1

	19x2	19x1
Assets		
Cash	$ 31,100	$ 27,200
Accounts Receivable (net)	72,500	42,700
Inventory	122,600	107,800
Property, Plant, and Equipment (net)	577,700	507,500
Total Assets	$803,900	$685,200
Liabilities and Stockholders' Equity		
Accounts Payable	$104,700	$ 72,300
Notes Payable	50,000	50,000
Bonds Payable	200,000	110,000
Common Stock—$10 par value	300,000	300,000
Retained Earnings	149,200	152,900
Total Liabilities and Stockholders' Equity	$803,900	$685,200

	Kelso Corporation Comparative Income Statements For the Years Ended December 31, 19x2 and 19x1	
	19x2	**19x1**
Sales	$800,400	$742,600
Cost of Goods Sold	454,100	396,200
Gross Margin from Sales	$346,300	$346,400
Operating Expenses		
Selling Expenses	$130,100	$104,600
Administrative Expenses	140,300	115,500
Interest Expense	25,000	20,000
Income Taxes Expense	14,000	35,000
Total Operating Expenses	$309,400	$275,100
Net Income	$ 36,900	$ 71,300

Required

(Round all ratios and percentages to one decimal point.)

1. Prepare a schedule showing the amount and percentage changes from 19x1 to 19x2 for the comparative income statements and the balance sheets.
2. Prepare common-size income statements and balance sheets for 19x1 and 19x2.
3. Comment on the results of parts **1** and **2** by identifying favorable and unfavorable changes in the components and composition of the statements.

Problem 19A-3.
Analyzing
the Effects of
Transactions
on Ratios
(L.O. 6)

Estevez Corporation engaged in the transactions listed in the first column of the following table. Opposite each transaction is a ratio and space to mark the effect of each transaction on the ratio.

			Effect	
Transaction	**Ratio**	**Increase**	**Decrease**	**None**
a. Issued common stock for cash.	Asset turnover			
b. Declared cash dividend.	Current ratio			
c. Sold treasury stock.	Return on equity			
d. Borrowed cash by issuing note payable.	Debt to equity ratio			
e. Paid salary expense.	Inventory turnover			
f. Purchased merchandise for cash.	Current ratio			
g. Sold equipment for cash.	Receivable turnover			
h. Sold merchandise on account.	Quick ratio			

(continued)

		Effect		
Transaction	Ratio	Increase	Decrease	None
i. Paid current portion of long-term debt.	Return on assets			
j. Gave sales discount.	Profit margin			
k. Purchased marketable securities for cash.	Quick ratio			
l. Declared 5% stock dividend.	Current ratio			

Required

Place an X in the appropriate column to show whether the transaction increased, decreased, or had no effect on the indicated ratio.

Problem 19A-4.
Ratio Analysis
(L.O. 6)

Additional data for Kelso Corporation in 19x1 and 19x2 follow. These data should be used in conjunction with the data in Problem 19A-2.

	19x2	19x1
Dividends Paid	$31,400	$35,000
Number of Common Shares	30,000	30,000
Market Price per Share	$40	$60
Beta	1.00	.90

Balances of selected accounts at the end of 19x0 were Accounts Receivable (net), $52,700; Inventory, $99,400; Total Assets, $647,800; and Stockholders' Equity, $376,600. All of Kelso's notes payable were current liabilities; all of the bonds payable were long-term liabilities.

Required

Note: Round all answers except earnings per share to one decimal point, and consider changes of .1 or less to be indeterminate.

1. Prepare a liquidity analysis by calculating for each year the: (a) current ratio, (b) quick ratio, (c) receivable turnover, (d) average days' sales uncollected, and (e) inventory turnover. Indicate whether each ratio improved or deteriorated from 19x1 to 19x2 by adding an F for favorable or a U for unfavorable.
2. Prepare a profitability analysis by calculating for each year the: (a) profit margin, (b) asset turnover, (c) return on assets, (d) return on equity, and (e) earnings per share. Indicate whether each ratio had a favorable (F) or unfavorable (U) change from 19x1 to 19x2.
3. Prepare a long-term solvency analysis by calculating for each year the: (a) debt to equity ratio and (b) interest coverage ratio. Indicate whether each ratio had a favorable (F) or unfavorable (U) change from 19x1 to 19x2.
4. Conduct a market test analysis by calculating for each year the: (a) price/earnings ratio, (b) dividends yield, and (c) market risk. Note the market risk measure, and indicate whether each ratio had a favorable (F) or unfavorable (U) change from 19x1 to 19x2.

**Problem 19A-5.
Comprehensive
Ratio Analysis of
Two Companies
(L.O. 6)**

Louise Brown has decided to invest some of her savings in common stock. She feels that the chemical industry has good growth prospects, and has narrowed her choice to two companies in that industry. As a final step in making the choice, she has decided to make a comprehensive ratio analysis of the two companies, Morton and Pound. Balance sheet and income statement data for the two companies appear below.

	Morton	Pound
Assets		
Cash	$ 126,100	$ 514,300
Marketable Securities (at cost)	117,500	1,200,000
Accounts Receivable (net)	456,700	2,600,000
Inventories	1,880,000	4,956,000
Prepaid Expenses	72,600	156,600
Property, Plant, and Equipment (net)	5,342,200	19,356,000
Intangibles and Other Assets	217,000	580,000
Total Assets	$8,212,100	$29,362,900
Liabilities and Stockholders' Equity		
Accounts Payable	$ 517,400	$ 2,342,000
Notes Payable	1,000,000	2,000,000
Income Taxes Payable	85,200	117,900
Bonds Payable	2,000,000	15,000,000
Common Stock—$1 par value	350,000	1,000,000
Paid-in Capital in Excess of Par Value, Common	1,747,300	5,433,300
Retained Earnings	2,512,200	3,469,700
Total Liabilities and Stockholders' Equity	$8,212,100	$29,362,900

	Morton	Pound
Sales	$9,486,200	$27,287,300
Cost of Goods Sold	5,812,200	18,372,400
Gross Margin from Sales	$3,674,000	$ 8,914,900
Operating Expenses		
Selling Expense	$1,194,000	$ 1,955,700
Administrative Expense	1,217,400	4,126,000
Interest Expense	270,000	1,360,000
Income Taxes Expense	450,000	600,000
Total Operating Expenses	$3,131,400	$ 8,041,700
Net Income	$ 542,600	$ 873,200

During the year, Morton paid a total of $140,000 in dividends, and its current market price per share is $20. Pound paid a total of $600,000 in dividends during the year, and the current market price per share is $9. An investment service reports that the beta associated with Morton's stock is 1.05, while that associated with Pound's is .8. Information pertaining to prior years is not readily available. Assume that all notes payable are current liabilities and that all bonds payable are long-term liabilities.

Required

Conduct a comprehensive ratio analysis of Morton and of Pound using the current end-of-year data. Compare the results. (Round all ratios and percentages except earnings per share to one decimal point.) This analysis should be done in the following steps:

1. Prepare an analysis of liquidity by calculating for each company the: (a) current ratio, (b) quick ratio, (c) receivable turnover, (d) average days' sales uncollected, and (e) inventory turnover.
2. Prepare an analysis of profitability by calculating for each company the: (a) profit margin, (b) asset turnover, (c) return on assets, (d) return on equity, and (e) earnings per share.
3. Prepare an analysis of long-term solvency by calculating for each company the: (a) debt to equity ratio and (b) interest coverage ratio.
4. Prepare an analysis of market tests by calculating for each company the: (a) price/earnings ratio, (b) dividends yield, and (c) market risk.
5. Compare the two companies by inserting the ratio calculations from parts 1 through 4 in a table with the following column heads: Ratio Name; Morton; Pound; and Company with More Favorable Ratio. Indicate in the right-hand column of the table which company had the more favorable ratio in each case.
6. How could the analysis be improved if prior years' information were available?

Problem Set B

**Problem 19B-1.
Effect of
Alternative
Accounting
Methods
(L.O. 4, 6)**

Jewell Company began operations this year. At the beginning of the year the company purchased plant assets of $385,000, with an estimated useful life of ten years and no salvage value. During the year, the company had sales of $650,000, salary expense of $100,000, and other expenses of $40,000, excluding depreciation. In addition, Jewell Company purchased inventory as follows:

January 15	400 units at $200	$ 80,000
March 20	200 units at $204	40,800
June 15	800 units at $208	166,400
September 18	600 units at $206	123,600
December 9	300 units at $210	63,000
Total	2,300 units	$473,800

At the end of the year, a physical inventory disclosed 500 units still on hand. The managers of Jewell Company know they have a choice of accounting methods, but are unsure how they will affect net income. They have heard of the FIFO and LIFO inventory methods and the straight-line and sum-of-the-years'-digits depreciation methods.

Required

1. Prepare two income statements for Jewell Company, one using a FIFO basis and the straight-line method, the other using a LIFO basis and the sum-of-the-years'-digits method.
2. Prepare a schedule accounting for the difference in the two net income figures obtained in **1**.
3. What effect does the choice of accounting method have on Jewell's inventory turnover? What conclusions can you draw?
4. What effect does the choice of accounting method have on Jewell's return on assets?

Use year-end balances to compute ratios. Assume the only other asset in addition to plant assets and inventory is $40,000 cash. Is your evaluation of Jewell's profitability affected by the choice of accounting methods?

Problem 19B-2.
Horizontal and
Vertical Analysis
(L.O. 5)

The condensed comparative balance sheets and income statements of Jensen Corporation are presented below and on page 839. All figures are given in thousands of dollars.

Jensen Corporation
Comparative Balance Sheets
December 31, 19x2 and 19x1

	19x2	19x1
Assets		
Cash	$ 40,600	$ 20,400
Accounts Receivable (net)	117,800	114,600
Inventory	287,400	297,400
Property, Plant, and Equipment (net)	375,000	360,000
Total Assets	$820,800	$792,400
Liabilities and Stockholders' Equity		
Accounts Payable	$133,800	$238,600
Notes Payable	100,000	200,000
Bonds Payable	200,000	—
Common Stock, $5 par value	200,000	200,000
Retained Earnings	187,000	153,800
Total Liabilities and Stockholders' Equity	$820,800	$792,400

Jensen Corporation
Comparative Income Statements
For the Years Ended December 31, 19x2 and 19x1

	19x2	19x1
Sales	$1,638,400	$1,573,200
Cost of Goods Sold	1,044,400	1,004,200
Gross Margin on Sales	$ 594,000	$ 569,000
Operating Expenses		
Selling Expenses	$ 238,400	$ 259,000
Administrative Expenses	223,600	211,600
Interest Expense	32,800	19,600
Income Taxes Expense	31,200	28,400
Total Operating Expenses	$ 526,000	$ 518,600
Net Income	$ 68,000	$ 50,400

Required

(Round percentages to one decimal point.)

1. Prepare schedules showing the amount and percentage changes from 19x1 to 19x2 for Jensen s income statements and balance sheets.
2. Prepare common-size income statements and balance sheets for 19x1 and 19x2.
3. Comment on the results to parts 1 and 2 by identifying favorable and unfavorable changes in the components and composition of the statements.

Problem 19B-3.
Analyzing the
Effects of
Transactions
on Ratios
(L.O. 6)

Rader Corporation engaged in the transactions listed in the first column of the following table. Opposite each transaction is a ratio and space to indicate the effect of each transaction on the ratio.

		Effect		
Transaction	**Ratio**	**Increase**	**Decrease**	**None**
a. Sold merchandise on account.	Current ratio			
b. Sold merchandise on account.	Inventory turnover			
c. Collected on accounts receivable.	Quick ratio			
d. Wrote off an uncollectible account.	Receivable turnover			
e. Paid on accounts payable.	Current ratio			
f. Declared cash dividend.	Return on equity			
g. Incurred advertising expense.	Profit margin			

(continued)

| | | Effect | | |
Transaction	Ratio	Increase	Decrease	None
h. Issued stock dividend.	Debt to equity ratio			
i. Issued bond payable.	Asset turnover			
j. Accrued interest expense.	Current ratio			
k. Paid previously declared cash dividend.	Dividends yield			
l. Purchased treasury stock.	Return on assets			

Required   Place an X in the appropriate column to show whether the transaction increased, decreased, or had no effect on the indicated ratio.

Problem 19B-4.
Ratio Analysis
(L.O. 6)

Additional data for Jensen Corporation in 19x1 and 19x2 follow. This information should be used together with the data in Problem 19B-2 to answer the requirements below.

	19x2	19x1
Dividends Paid	$22,000,000	$17,200,000
Number of Common Shares	40,000,000	40,000,000
Market Price per Share	$9	$15
Beta	1.40	1.25

Balances of selected accounts (in thousands) at the end of 19x0 were Accounts Receivable (net), $103,400; Inventory, $273,600; Total Assets, $732,800; and Stockholders' Equity, $320,600. All of Jensen's notes payable were current liabilities; all of the bonds payable were long-term liabilities.

Required   (Round percentages and ratios except earnings per share to one decimal point, and consider changes of .1 or less to be indeterminate.)

1. Conduct a liquidity analysis by calculating for each year the: (a) current ratio, (b) quick ratio, (c) receivable turnover, (d) average days' sales uncollected, and (e) inventory turnover. Indicate whether each ratio had a favorable (F) or unfavorable (U) change from 19x1 to 19x2.
2. Conduct a profitability analysis by calculating for each year the: (a) profit margin, (b) asset turnover, (c) return on assets, (d) return on equity, and (e) earnings per share. Indicate whether each ratio had a favorable (F) or unfavorable (U) change from 19x1 to 19x2.
3. Conduct a long-term solvency analysis by calculating for each year the: (a) debt to equity ratio and (b) interest coverage ratio. Indicate whether each ratio had a favorable (F) or unfavorable (U) change from 19x1 to 19x2.
4. Conduct a market test analysis by calculating for each year the: (a) price/earnings ratio, (b) dividends yield, and (c) market risk. Note the market beta measures, and indicate whether each ratio had a favorable (F) or unfavorable (U) change from 19x1 to 19x2.

**Problem 19B-5.
Comprehensive
Ratio Analysis of
Two Companies
(L.O. 6)**

Charles Tseng is considering an investment in the common stock of a chain of retail department stores. He has narrowed his choice to two retail companies, Kemp Corporation and Russo Corporation, whose balance sheets and income statements follow.

	Kemp Corporation	Russo Corporation
Assets		
Cash	$ 80,000	$ 192,400
Marketable Securities (at cost)	203,400	84,600
Accounts Receivable (net)	552,800	985,400
Inventory	629,800	1,253,400
Prepaid Expenses	54,400	114,000
Property, Plant, and Equipment (net)	2,913,600	6,552,000
Intangibles and Other Assets	553,200	144,800
Total Assets	$4,987,200	$9,326,600
Liabilities and Stockholders' Equity		
Accounts Payable	$ 344,000	$ 572,600
Notes Payable	150,000	400,000
Accrued Liabilities	50,200	73,400
Bonds Payable	2,000,000	2,000,000
Common Stock—$10 par value	1,000,000	600,000
Paid-in Capital in Excess of Par Value, Common	609,800	3,568,600
Retained Earnings	833,200	2,112,000
Total Liabilities and Stockholders' Equity	$4,987,200	$9,326,600

	Kemp Corporation	Russo Corporation
Sales	$12,560,000	$25,210,000
Cost of Goods Sold	6,142,000	14,834,000
Gross Margin from Sales	$ 6,418,000	$10,376,000
Operating Expenses		
Sales Expense	$ 4,822,600	$ 7,108,200
Administrative Expense	986,000	2,434,000
Interest Expense	194,000	228,000
Income Taxes Expense	200,000	300,000
Total Operating Expenses	$ 6,202,600	$10,070,200
Net Income	$ 215,400	$ 305,800

During the year, Kemp Corporation paid a total of $50,000 in dividends. The market price per share of its stock is currently $30. In comparison, Russo Corporation paid a total of $114,000 in dividends, and the current market price of its stock is $38 per share. An investment service has indicated that the beta associated with Kemp's stock is 1.20, while that associated with Russo's stock is .95. Information for prior years is not readily available. Assume that all notes payable are current liabilities and all bonds payable are long-term liabilities.

Required

Conduct a comprehensive ratio analysis for each company using the available information and compare the results. (Round percentages and ratios except earnings per share to one decimal point, and consider changes of .1 or less to be indeterminate.) This analysis should be done in the following steps:

1. Prepare an analysis of liquidity by calculating for each company the: (a) current ratio, (b) quick ratio, (c) receivable turnover, (d) average days' sales uncollected, and (e) inventory turnover.
2. Prepare an analysis of profitability by calculating for each company the: (a) profit margin, (b) asset turnover, (c) return on assets, (d) return on equity, and (e) earnings per share.
3. Prepare an analysis of long-term solvency by calculating for each company the: (a) debt to equity ratio and (b) interest coverage ratio.
4. Prepare an analysis of market tests by calculating for each company the: (a) price/earnings ratio, (b) dividends yield, and (c) market risk.
5. Compare the two companies by inserting the ratio calculations from parts **1** through **4** in a table with the following column heads: Ratio Name, Kemp Corporation, Russo Corporation, and Company with More Favorable Ratio. Indicate in the right-hand column which company had the more favorable ratio in each case.
6. In what ways could the analysis be improved if prior years' information were available?

Financial Decision Case

Tedtronics Corporation (L.O. 4)

Ted Lazzerini retired at the beginning of 19x1 as president and principal stockholder in Tedtronics Corporation, a successful producer of word-processing equipment. As an incentive to the new management, Ted supported the board of directors' new executive compensation plan, which provides cash bonuses to key executives for the years in which the company's earnings per share equal or exceed the current dividends per share of $2.00, plus a $.20 per share increase in dividends for each future year. Thus for management to receive the bonuses, the company must earn per share income of $2.00 the first year, $2.20 the second, $2.40 the third, and so forth. Since Ted owns 500,000 of the one million common shares outstanding, the dividend income will provide for his retirement years. He is also protected against inflation by the regular increase in dividends. Earnings and dividends per share for the first three years of operation under the new management were as follows:

	19x3	19x2	19x1
Earnings per share	$2.50	$2.50	$2.50
Dividends per share	2.40	2.20	2.00

During this time management earned bonuses totaling more than $1 million under the compensation plan. Ted, who had taken no active part on the board of directors, began to worry about the unchanging level of earnings and decided to study the company's annual report more carefully. The notes to the annual report revealed the following information:

a. Management changed from the LIFO inventory method to the FIFO method in 19x1. The effect of the change was to decrease cost of goods sold by $200,000 in 19x1, $300,000 in 19x2, and $400,000 in 19x3.
b. Management changed from the double-declining-balance accelerated depreciation method to the straight-line method in 19x2. The effect of this change was to decrease depreciation by $400,000 in 19x2 and by $500,000 in 19x3.
c. In 19x3, management increased the estimated useful life of intangible assets from five to ten years. The effect of this change was to decrease amortization expense by $100,000 in 19x3.

Required

1. Compute earnings per share for each year according to the accounting methods in use at the beginning of 19x1.
2. Have the executives earned their bonuses? What serious effect has the compensation package apparently had on the net assets of Tedtronics? How could Ted have protected himself from what has happened?

Answers to Self-Test

1. a	3. a	5. c	7. c	9. a
2. d	4. d	6. d	8. c	10. c

LEARNING OBJECTIVES

1. Apply the cost method and the equity method to the appropriate situations in accounting for long-term investments.
2. Explain when to prepare consolidated financial statements, and describe their uses.
3. Prepare consolidated balance sheets at acquisition date for purchase at (a) book value and (b) other than book value.
4. Prepare consolidated income statements for intercompany transactions.
5. Account for bond investment transactions.

CHAPTER 20

Intercompany Investments

Corporations often find it desirable to invest in the securities of other corporations with the intent of holding them for an indefinite period. There are many reasons for making such long-term investments. One reason, of course, is simple: the prospect of earning a return on the investment. Another might be to establish a more formal business relationship with a company with which the acquiring company has ties. A further reason might be to acquire control over a company with desirable assets or other traits, such as established customers, markets, products, expertise, or operations needed by the acquiring company. Still another reason is that a company may require less capital to buy an interest in another company than to start a whole operation independently. In some states and many foreign countries it is legally easier to buy or invest in a company than to start a new business. Sometimes there are tax advantages to be derived from investing in an existing company.

The purpose of this chapter is to provide an overview of the ways in which these investments are accounted for in the corporation's records and reported in the financial statements. After studying this chapter, you should be able to meet the learning objectives listed on the left.

This chapter is organized into three major sections: accounting for long-term investments in stocks; the preparation of consolidated financial statements when one company owns more than 50 percent of the voting stock of another; and accounting for long-term investments in bonds.

Classification of Long-Term Investments

One corporation may invest in another corporation by purchasing bonds or stocks. These investments may be either short-term or long-term. In this section, we are concerned with long-term investments in stocks. Long-term investments in bonds are covered in the last section of this chapter.

All long-term investments in stocks are recorded at cost, in accordance with generally accepted accounting principles. The treatment of the investment in the accounting records after the initial purchase depends on the extent to which the investing company can exercise significant influence or control over the operating and financial policies of the other company.

OBJECTIVE 1
Apply the cost method and the equity method to the appropriate situations in accounting for long-term investments

The Accounting Principles Board defined the important terms *significant influence* and *control* in its *Opinion No. 18*. **Significant influence** is the ability to affect the operating and financial policies of the company whose shares are owned, even though the investor holds less than 50 percent of the voting stock. Ability to influence a company may be shown by representation on the board of directors, participation in policy making, material transactions between the companies, exchange of managerial personnel, and technological dependency. For the sake of uniformity, the APB decided that unless there is proof to the contrary, an investment in 20 percent or more of the voting stock should be presumed to confer significant influence. An investment of less than 20 percent of the voting stock would not confer significant influence.[1]

Control is defined as the ability of the investing company to decide the operating and financial policies of the other company. Control is said to exist when the investing company owns more than 50 percent of the voting stock of the company in which it has invested.

Thus, in the absence of information to the contrary, a noninfluential and noncontrolling investment would be less than 20 percent ownership. An influential but noncontrolling investment would be 20 to 50 percent ownership. And a controlling investment would be more than 50 percent ownership. The accounting treatment differs for each kind of investment.

Noninfluential and Noncontrolling Investment

The **cost method** of accounting for long-term investments applies when the investor owns less than 20 percent of the voting stock. Under the cost method, the investor records the investment at cost and recognizes income as dividends are received. The Financial Accounting Standards Board states that long-term investments in marketable equity securities accounted for under the cost method should be valued at the lower of cost or market after acquisition.[2] The lower-of-cost-or-market rule is used here for the same reason it was used in the valuation of inventories. It is a conservative approach that recognizes the impairment in the value of the asset when its market value is less than cost. Conversely, a rise in the market above cost is not recognized until the investment is sold.

---

1. The Financial Accounting Standards Board points out in its *Interpretation No. 35* (May 1981) that though the presumption of significant influence applies when 20 percent or more of the voting stock is held, the rule is not a rigid one. All relevant facts and circumstances should be examined in each case to find out whether or not significant influence exists. For example, the FASB notes five circumstances that may remove the element of significant influence: (1) The company files a lawsuit against the investor or complains to a government agency; (2) The investor tries and fails to become a director; (3) The investor agrees not to increase its holdings; (4) The company is operated by a small group that ignores the investor's wishes; (5) The investor tries and fails to obtain additional information from the company that is not available to other stockholders.
2. *Statement of Financial Accounting Standards No. 12*, "Accounting for Certain Marketable Securities" (Stamford, Conn.: Financial Accounting Standards Board, 1975).

At the end of each accounting period, the total cost and the total market value of these long-term stock investments must be determined. If the total market value is less than the total cost, the difference must be credited to a contra-asset account called Allowance to Reduce Long-Term Investments to Market. Because of the long-term nature of the investment, the debit part of the entry, which represents a decrease in value below cost, is treated as a temporary decrease and does not appear as a loss on the income statement. It is shown in a contra-owners' equity account called Unrealized Loss on Long-Term Investments. Thus both these accounts are balance sheet accounts. If at some later date the market value exceeds the valuation reported in the earlier period, the Long-Term Investment account is written up to the new market value, but not to more than the acquisition cost of the investments.[3]

When long-term investments in stock are sold, the difference between the sale price and what the stock cost is recorded and reported as a realized gain or loss on the income statement. Dividend income from such investments is recorded by a debit to Cash and a credit to Dividend Income in the amount received.

For example, assume the following facts about the long-term stock investments of Coleman Corporation:

June 1, 19x0   Paid cash for the following long-term investments: 10,000 shares Durbin Corporation common stock (representing 2 percent of outstanding stock) at $25 per share; 5,000 shares Kotes Corporation common stock (representing 3 percent of outstanding stock) at $15 per share.

Dec. 31, 19x0   Quoted market prices at year end: Durbin common stock, $21; Kotes common stock, $17.

Apr. 1, 19x1   Change in policy required sale of 2,000 shares of Durbin Corporation common stock at $23.

July 1, 19x1   Received cash dividend from Kotes Corporation equal to $.20 per share.

Dec. 31, 19x1   Quoted market prices at year end: Durbin common stock, $24; Kotes common stock, $13.

Entries to record these transactions follow:

Investment

19x0			
June 1	Long-Term Investments	325,000	
	Cash		325,000
	To record investments in Durbin common stock (10,000 shares × $25 = $250,000) and Kotes common stock (5,000 shares × $15 = $75,000)		

3. If the decrease in value is deemed permanent, a different procedure is followed to record the decline in market value of the long-term investment. A loss account that appears on the income statement is debited instead of the Unrealized Loss account.

Year-End Adjustment

19x0
Dec. 31   Unrealized Loss on Long-Term
            Investments   30,000
               Allowance to Reduce Long-Term
               Investments to Market   30,000
                  To record reduction of long-term
                  investment portfolio to market

Company	Shares	Market Prices	Total Market	Total Cost
Durbin	10,000	$21	$210,000	$250,000
Kotes	5,000	17	85,000	75,000
			$295,000	$325,000

Cost − market value = $325,000 − $295,000 = $30,000.

Sale

19x1
Apr. 1   Cash   46,000
            Loss on Sale of Investment   4,000
               Long-Term Investments   50,000
                  To record sale of 2,000 shares of Durbin
                  2,000 × $23 = $46,000
                  2,000 × $25 = $50,000
                  Loss $ 4,000

Dividend Received

July 1   Cash   1,000
            Dividend Income   1,000
               To record receipt of cash dividends
               from Kotes stocks
               5,000 × $.20 = $1,000

Year-End Adjustment

Dec. 31   Allowance to Reduce Long-Term
            Investments to Market   12,000
               Unrealized Loss on Long-Term
               Investments   12,000
                  To record the adjustment in long-
                  term investment so it is reported
                  at lower of cost or market

The adjustment equals the previous balance ($30,000 from the December 31, 19x0 entry) minus the new balance ($18,000), or $12,000. The new balance of $18,000 is the difference at the present time between the total market value and the total cost of all investments. It is figured as follows:

Company	Shares	Market Prices	Total Market	Total Cost
Durbin	8,000	$24	$192,000	$200,000
Kotes	5,000	13	65,000	75,000
			$257,000	$275,000

Cost – market value = $275,000 – $257,000 = $18,000.

The Allowance to Reduce Long-Term Investments to Market and the Unrealized Loss on Long-Term Investments are reciprocal contra accounts, each with the same dollar balance, as can be shown by the effects of these transactions on the T accounts:

Contra-Asset Account		Contra-Owners' Equity Account	
Allowance to Reduce Long-Term Investments to Market		**Unrealized Loss on Long-Term Investments**	
19x1 12,000	19x0 30,000	19x0 30,000	19x1 12,000
	Bal. 19x1 18,000	Bal. 19x1 18,000	

The Allowance account reduces long-term investments by the amount by which cost exceeds market of the investments; the Unrealized Loss account reduces owners' equity by a similar amount.

Influential but Noncontrolling Investment

As we have seen, ownership of 20 percent or more of a company's voting stock is considered sufficient to influence the operations of another corporation. When this is the case, the investment in the stock of a controlled company should be accounted for using the **equity method**. The equity method presumes that an investment of more than 20 percent is more than a passive investment, and that therefore the investing company should share proportionately in the success or failure of the investee company. The three main features of this method are as follows:

1. The investor records the original purchase of the stock at cost.
2. The investor records its share of the investee's periodic net income as an increase in the Investment account, with a corresponding credit to an income account. Similarly, the investor records its share of the investee's periodic loss as a decrease in the Investment account, with a corresponding debit to a loss account.
3. When the investor receives a cash dividend, the asset account Cash is increased and the Investment account decreased.

To illustrate the equity method of accounting, we will assume the following facts about an investment by the Vassor Corporation. Vassor Corporation, on January 1 of the current year, acquired 40 percent of the voting common stock of the Block Corporation for $180,000. With this share of ownership, the Vassor Corporation can exert significant influence over the operations of the Block Corporation. During the year, the Block Corporation reported net income of $80,000 and paid cash dividends of $20,000. The entries to record these transactions by the Vassor Corporation are:

Investment

Investment in Block Corporation	180,000	
Cash		180,000
To record investment in Block Corporation common stock		

Recognition of Income

Investment in Block Corporation	32,000	
Income, Block Corporation Investment		32,000
To recognize 40% of income reported by Block Corporation		
40% × $80,000 = $32,000		

Receipt of Cash Dividend

Cash	8,000	
Investment in Block Corporation		8,000
To record cash dividend from Block Corporation		
40% × $20,000 = $8,000		

The balance of the investment in the Block Corporation account after these transactions is $204,000, as shown here:

Investment in Block Corporation

Investment	180,000	Dividends received	8,000
Share of income	32,000		
Balance	204,000		

Controlling Investment

In some cases, an investor who owns less than 50 percent of the voting stock of a company may exercise such powerful influence that for all practical purposes the investor controls the policies of the other company. Nevertheless, ownership of more than 50 percent of the voting stock is required for accounting recognition of control. When a controlling interest is owned, a parent-subsidiary relationship is said to exist.

The investing company is known as the **parent company**, the other company as the **subsidiary**. Because both corporations are separate legal entities, each prepares separate financial statements. However, owing to their special relationship, they are viewed for public financial reporting purposes as a single economic entity. For this reason, they must combine their financial statements into a single set of statements called **consolidated financial statements**

Accounting for consolidated financial statements is very complex. It is usually the subject of an advanced-level course in accounting. However, most large public corporations have subsidiaries and must prepare consolidated financial statements. It is therefore important to have some understanding of accounting for consolidations.

The proper accounting treatments for long-term investments in stock are summarized in Table 20-1.

Consolidated Financial Statements

OBJECTIVE 2
Explain when to prepare consolidated financial statements, and describe their uses

Most major corporations find it convenient for economic, legal, tax, or other reasons to operate in parent-subsidiary relationships. When we speak of a large company such as Ford, IBM, or Texas Instruments, we generally think of the parent company, not of its many subsidiaries. When considering investment in one of these firms, however, the investor wants a clear financial picture of the total economic entity. The main purpose of consolidated financial statements is to give such a view of the parent and subsidiary firms by treating them as if they were one company. On a consolidated balance sheet, the Inventory account in-

Table 20-1. Accounting Treatments of Long-Term Investments in Stock		
Level of Ownership	**Percentage of Ownership**	**Accounting Treatment**
Noninfluential and noncontrolling	Less than 20%	Cost method; investment valued subsequent to purchase at lower of cost or market.
Influential but noncontrolling	Between 20% and 50%	Equity method; investment valued subsequently at cost plus investor's share of income (or minus investor's loss) minus dividends received.
Controlling	More than 50%	Financial statements consolidated.

cludes the inventory held by the parent and all its subsidiaries. Similarly, on the consolidated income statement, the Sales account is the total revenue from sales by the parent and all its subsidiaries. This overview is very useful to management and stockholders of the parent company in judging the company's progress in meeting its goals. Long-term creditors of the parent also find consolidated statements useful because of their interest in the long-range financial health of the company as a corporation.

It has been acceptable in the past not to consolidate the statements of certain subsidiaries, even though the parent owned a controlling interest, when the business of the subsidiary was not homogeneous with that of the parent. For instance, a retail company or an automobile manufacturer may have had a wholly-owned finance subsidiary that was not consolidated. However, such practices were criticized because they tended to remove certain assets (accounts and notes receivable) and certain liabilities (borrowing by the finance subsidiary) from the consolidated financial statements. For example, in 1986, General Motors' financing subsidiary, GMAC, with assets of $90 billion and liabilities of $84 billion, was carried as a long-term investment of $6 billion on GM's balance sheet. It has also been argued by those who favor consolidation that financing arrangements such as these are an integral part of the overall business. The Financial Accounting Standards Board has now ruled that all subsidiaries in which the parent owns a controlling interest (more than 50 percent) must be consolidated with the parent for financial reporting purposes.[4] As a result, with few exceptions, the financial statements of all majority-owned subsidiaries must now be consolidated with the parent company's financial statements for external reporting purposes.

Methods of Accounting for Business Combinations

Interests in subsidiary companies may be acquired by paying cash; issuing long-term bonds, other debt, or preferred stock; or working out some combination of these forms of payment, such as exchanging shares of the parent's own unissued capital stock for the outstanding shares of the subsidiary's capital stock. For parent-subsidiary relationships that arise when cash is paid or debt or preferred stock issued, it is mandatory to use the purchase method, which is explained below. For simplicity, our illustrations assume payment in cash. In the special case of establishing a parent-subsidiary relationship through an exchange of common stock, the pooling of interests method may be appropriate. The pooling of interests method is the subject of more advanced courses.

Consolidated Balance Sheet

In preparing consolidated financial statements under the **purchase method,** similar accounts from the separate statements of the parent

---

4. *Statement of Financial Accounting Standards No. 94,* "Consolidation of All Majority-Owned Subsidiaries" (Stamford, Conn.: Financial Accounting Standards Board, 1987).

and the subsidiaries are combined. Some accounts result from transactions between the parent and subsidiary. Examples are debt owed by one of the entities to the other and sales and purchases between the two entities. From the point of view of the consolidating group of companies as a single business, it is not appropriate to include these accounts in the group financial statements; the purchases and sales are only transfers between different parts of the business, and the payables and receivables do not represent amounts due to or receivable from outside parties. For this reason, it is important that certain **eliminations** be made. These eliminations avoid the duplication of accounts and reflect the financial position and operations from the standpoint of a single entity. Eliminations appear only on the work sheets used in preparing consolidated financial statements. They are never shown in the accounting records of either the parent or the subsidiary. There are no consolidated journals or ledgers.

Another good example of accounts that result from transactions between the two entities is the Investment in Subsidiary account in the parent's balance sheet and the stockholders' equity section of the subsidiary. When the balance sheets of the two companies are combined, these accounts must be eliminated to avoid duplicating these items in the consolidated financial statements.

To illustrate the preparation of a consolidated balance sheet under the purchase method, we will use the following balance sheets for Parent and Subsidiary companies:

Accounts	Parent Company	Subsidiary Company
Cash	$100,000	$25,000
Other Assets	760,000	60,000
Total Assets	$860,000	$85,000
Liabilities	$ 60,000	$10,000
Common Stock—$10 par value	600,000	55,000
Retained Earnings	200,000	20,000
Total Liabilities and Stockholders' Equity	$860,000	$85,000

100 Percent Purchase at Book Value. Suppose that Parent Company purchases 100 percent of the stock of Subsidiary Company for an amount exactly equal to the Subsidiary's book value. The book value of Subsidiary Company is $75,000 ($85,000 − $10,000). Parent Company would record the purchase as follows:

	75,000	
Investment in Subsidiary Company		
Cash		75,000
To record 100 percent purchase of		
Subsidiary Company at book value		

OBJECTIVE 3a
Prepare consolidated balance sheets at acquisition date for purchase at book value

It is helpful to use a work sheet like the one shown in Exhibit 20-1 in preparing consolidated financial statements. Note that the balance of Parent Company's Cash account is now $25,000 and that the Investment in Subsidiary Company is shown as an asset in Parent Company's balance sheet, reflecting the purchase of the subsidiary. To prepare a consolidated balance sheet, it is necessary to eliminate the investment in the subsidiary. This procedure is shown by elimination entry 1 in Exhibit 20-1. This elimination entry does two things. First, it eliminates the double counting that would take place when the net assets of the two companies are combined. Second, it eliminates the stockholders' equity section of the Subsidiary Company.

The theory underlying consolidated financial statements is that parent and subsidiary are a single entity. The stockholders' equity section of the consolidated balance sheet is the same as that of the Parent Company. So after eliminating the Investment in Subsidiary Company

Exhibit 20-1. Work Sheet for Preparation of Consolidated Balance Sheet

Parent and Subsidiary Companies
Work Sheet for Consolidated Balance Sheet
As of Acquisition Date

Accounts	Balance Sheet Parent Company	Balance Sheet Subsidiary Company	Eliminations Debit	Eliminations Credit	Consolidated Balance Sheet
Cash	25,000	25,000			50,000
Investment in Subsidiary Company	75,000			(1) 75,000	
Other Assets	760,000	60,000			820,000
Total Assets	860,000	85,000			870,000
Liabilities	60,000	10,000			70,000
Common Stock— $10 par value	600,000	55,000	(1) 55,000		600,000
Retained Earnings	200,000	20,000	(1) 20,000		200,000
Total Liabilities and Stockholders' Equity	860,000	85,000	75,000	75,000	870,000

(1) Elimination of intercompany investment

against the stockholders' equity of the subsidiary, we can take the information from the right-hand column in Exhibit 20-1 and present it in the following form:

Parent and Subsidiary Companies Consolidated Balance Sheet As of Acquisition Date			
Cash	$ 50,000	Liabilities	$ 70,000
Other Assets	820,000	Common Stock	600,000
		Retained Earnings	200,000
		Total Liabilities and	
Total Assets	$870,000	Stockholders' Equity	$870,000

Less than 100 Percent Purchase at Book Value. A parent company does not have to purchase 100 percent of a subsidiary to control it. If it purchases more than 50 percent of the voting stock of the subsidiary company, it will have legal control. In the consolidated financial statements, therefore, the total assets and liabilities of the subsidiary are combined with the assets and liabilities of the parent. However, it is still necessary to account for the interests of those stockholders of the subsidiary company who own less than 50 percent of the voting stock. These are the minority stockholders, and their **minority interest** must appear on the consolidated balance sheet as an amount equal to their percentage of ownership times the net assets of the subsidiary.

Suppose that the same Parent Company buys, for the same $67,500 only, 90 percent of Subsidiary Company's voting stock. In this case, the portion of the company purchased has a book value of $67,500 (90% × $75,000). The work sheet used for preparing the consolidated balance sheet appears in Exhibit 20-2. The elimination is made in the same way as in the case above, except that the minority interest must be accounted for. All of the Investment in Subsidiary Company ($67,500) is eliminated against all of Subsidiary Company's stockholders' equity ($75,000). The difference ($7,500, or 10% × $75,000) is set as minority interest.

There are two ways to classify minority interest on the consolidated balance sheet. One is to place it between long-term liabilities and stockholders' equity. The other is to consider the stockholders' equity section as consisting of (1) minority interest and (2) Parent Company's stockholders' equity, as shown here:

Minority Interest	$ 7,500
Common Stock	600,000
Retained Earnings	200,000
Total Stockholders' Equity	$807,500

Exhibit 20-2. Work Sheet Showing Elimination of Less than 100 Percent Ownership

Parent and Subsidiary Companies
Work Sheet for Consolidated Balance Sheet
As of Acquisition Date

Accounts	Balance Sheet Parent Company	Balance Sheet Subsidiary Company	Eliminations		Consolidated Balance Sheet
			Debit	Credit	
Cash	32,500	25,000			57,500
Investment in Subsidiary Company	67,500			(1) 67,500	
Other Assets	760,000	60,000			820,000
Total Assets	860,000	85,000			877,500
Liabilities	60,000	10,000			70,000
Common Stock—$10 par value	600,000	55,000	(1) 55,000		600,000
Retained Earnings	200,000	20,000	(1) 20,000		200,000
Minority Interest				(1) 7,500	7,500
Total Liabilities and Stockholders' Equity	860,000	85,000	75,000	75,000	877,500

(1) Elimination of intercompany investment. Minority interest equals 10 percent subsidiary's stockholders' equity.

OBJECTIVE 3b
Prepare consolidated balance sheets at acquisition date for purchase at other than book value

Purchase at More than or Less than Book Value. The purchase price of a business depends on many factors, such as the current market price, the relative strength of the buyer's and seller's bargaining positions, and the prospects for future earnings. Thus it is only by chance that the purchase price of a subsidiary will equal the book value of the subsidiary's equity. Usually, it will not. For example, a parent company may pay more than the book value of a subsidiary to purchase a controlling interest if the assets of the subsidiary are understated. In that case, the recorded historical cost less depreciation of the subsidiary's assets may not reflect current market values. The parent may also pay more than book value if the subsidiary has something that the parent wants, such as an important technical process, a new and different product, or a new market. On the other hand, the parent may pay less than book value for its share of the subsidiary's stock if the subsidiary's assets are not worth their depreciated cost. Or the subsidiary may have suffered heavy losses, causing its stock to sell at rather low prices.

The Accounting Principles Board has provided the following guidelines for consolidating a purchased subsidiary and its parent:

First, all identifiable assets acquired . . . and liabilities assumed in a business combination . . . should be assigned a portion of the cost of the acquired company, normally equal to their fair values at date of acquisition.

Second, the excess of the cost of the acquired company over the sum of the amounts assigned to identifiable assets acquired less liabilities assumed should be recorded as goodwill.[5]

To illustrate the application of these principles, we will assume that Parent Company purchases 100 percent of Subsidiary Company's voting stock for $92,500, or $17,500 more than book value. Parent Company considers $10,000 of the $17,500 to be due to the increased value of Subsidiary's other long-term assets and $7,500 of the $17,500 to be due to the overall strength that Subsidiary Company would add to Parent Company's organization. The work sheet used for preparing the consolidated balance sheet appears in Exhibit 20-3. All of the Investment in Subsidiary Company ($92,500) has been eliminated against all of the Subsidiary Company's stockholders' equity ($75,000). The excess of cost over book value ($17,500) has been debited in the amounts of $10,000 to Long-Term Assets and $7,500 to a new account called **Goodwill,** or **Goodwill from Consolidation.**

The amount of goodwill is determined as follows:

Cost of investment in subsidiary	$92,500
Book value of subsidiary	75,000
Excess of cost over book value	$17,500
Portion of excess attributable to undervalued long-term assets of subsidiary	10,000
Portion of excess attributable to goodwill	$ 7,500

Goodwill appears as an asset on the consolidated balance sheet representing the excess of cost of the investment over book value that cannot be allocated to any specific asset. Long-Term Assets appears on the consolidated balance sheet as the combined total of $830,000 ($760,000 + $60,000 + $10,000).

When the parent pays less than book value for its investment in the subsidiary, Accounting Principles Board *Opinion No. 16*, paragraph 87, requires that the excess of book value over cost of the investment be used to lower the carrying value of the subsidiary's long-term assets. The belief is that market values of long-lived assets (other than marketable securities) are among the least reliable of estimates, since a ready market does not usually exist for such assets. In other words, the APB advises against using negative goodwill, except in very special cases.

Intercompany Receivables and Payables. If either the parent or the subsidiary company owes money to the other, there will be a receivable on the creditor company's individual balance sheet and a payable on the debtor company's individual balance sheet. When a consolidated balance sheet is prepared, both the receivable and the payable should be

---

5. Accounting Principles Board, *Opinion No. 16*, "Business Combinations" (New York: Accounting Principles Board, 1970), par. 87.

Exhibit 20-3. Work Sheet Showing Elimination Where Purchase Cost is Greater than Book Value

Parent and Subsidiary Companies
Work Sheet for Consolidated Balance Sheet
As of Acquisition Date

Accounts	Balance Sheet Parent Company	Balance Sheet Subsidiary Company	Eliminations Debit	Eliminations Credit	Consolidated Balance Sheet
Cash	7,500	25,000			32,500
Investment in Subsidiary Company	92,500			(1) 92,500	
Other Long-Term Assets	760,000	60,000	(1) 10,000		830,000
Goodwill			(1) 7,500		7,500
Total Assets	860,000	85,000			870,000
Liabilities	60,000	10,000			70,000
Common Stock—$10 par value	600,000	55,000	(1) 55,000		600,000
Retained Earnings	200,000	20,000	(1) 20,000		200,000
Total Liabilities and Stockholders' Equity	860,000	85,000	92,500	92,500	870,000

(1) Elimination of intercompany investment. Excess of cost over book value ($92,500 − $75,000 = $17,500) allocated $10,000 to Long-Term Assets and $7,500 to Goodwill.

eliminated because, from the viewpoint of the consolidated entity, neither the asset nor the liability exists. In other words, it does not make sense for a company to owe money to itself. The eliminating entry would be made on the work sheet by debiting the payable and crediting the receivable for the amount of the intercompany loan.

Consolidated Income Statement

OBJECTIVE 4
Prepare consolidated income statements for intercompany transactions

The consolidated income statement is prepared for a consolidated entity by combining the revenues and expenses of the parent and subsidiary companies. The procedure is the same as in preparing a consolidated balance sheet. That is, intercompany transactions are eliminated to prevent double counting of revenues and expenses. Several intercompany transactions affect the consolidated income statement. They are (1) sales and purchases of goods and services between parent and subsidiary (purchases for the buying company and sales for the selling company); (2) income and expenses on loans, receivables, or bond indebtedness between parent and subsidiary; and (3) other income and expenses from intercompany transactions.

To illustrate the eliminating entries, we will assume the following transactions between a parent and its wholly-owned subsidiary. Parent Company made sales of $120,000 in goods to Subsidiary Company, which in turn sold all the goods to others. Subsidiary Company paid Parent Company $2,000 interest on a loan from the parent.

The work sheet in Exhibit 20-4 shows how to prepare a consolidated income statement. The purpose of the eliminating entries is to treat the two companies as a single entity. Thus it is important to include in Sales only those sales made to outsiders and to include in Cost of Goods Sold only those purchases made from outsiders. This goal is met with the first eliminating entry, which eliminates the $120,000 of intercompany sales and purchases by a debit of that amount to Sales and a credit of that amount to Cost of Goods Sold. As a result, only sales to outsiders ($510,000) and purchases from outsiders ($240,000) are included in the Consolidated Income Statement column. The intercompany interest income and expense are eliminated by a debit to Other Revenues and a credit to Other Expenses.

Other Consolidated Financial Statements

Public corporations also prepare consolidated statements of retained earnings and consolidated statements of cash flows. For examples of these statements, see the Toys "R" Us statements in Chapter 8.

Exhibit 20-4. Work Sheet Showing Eliminations for Preparing a Consolidated Income Statement

Parent and Subsidiary Companies
Work Sheet for Consolidated Income Statement
For the Year Ended December 31, 19xx

Accounts	Income Statement Parent Company	Income Statement Subsidiary Company	Eliminations		Consolidated Income Sheet
			Debit	Credit	
Sales	430,000	200,000	(1) 120,000		510,000
Other Revenues	60,000	10,000	(2) 2,000		68,000
Total Revenues	490,000	210,000			578,000
Cost of Goods Sold	210,000	150,000		(1) 120,000	240,000
Other Expenses	140,000	50,000		(2) 2,000	188,000
Total Deductions	350,000	200,000			428,000
Net Income	140,000	10,000	122,000	122,000	150,000

(1) Elimination of intercompany sales and purchases
(2) Elimination of intercompany interest income and expense

Accounting for Bond Investments

OBJECTIVE 5
Account for bond investment transactions

In Chapter 17, bond transactions and disclosures were discussed from the issuing corporation's viewpoint. Here, similar transactions will be presented from the investor's point of view. Sometimes a company buys a bond as a short-term investment to provide a return on idle cash until it is needed for operations. There are a number of reasons, however, why a company may hold another company's bonds as long-term investments. The company may be investing funds that will eventually be needed for a major capital project. Or the company may prefer to advance funds to its subsidiary by buying its bonds rather than its capital stock, because creditors will have precedence over shareholders if the subsidiary should fail. The classification and valuation problems related to short-term investments are presented in Chapter 9. Here, the focus is on transactions involving the purchase of the bonds, amortization of premium and discount, recording of receipt of interest, and sale of the bonds. In each case, there are small differences in accounting treatment from that used for the same transactions by the issuer.

Purchase of Bonds Between Interest Dates

The purchase price of bonds includes the price of the bonds plus the broker's commission. When the bonds are purchased between interest dates, the purchaser must also pay the interest that has accrued on the bonds since the last interest payment date. On the next payment date, the purchaser will receive a payment of the interest for the whole period. The payment for accrued interest should be recorded as a debit to Interest Income, to be offset later by a credit to Interest Income when the semiannual interest is received.

Suppose that on May 1 Vason Corporation purchases twenty $1,000 MGR Corporation bonds that carry a face interest rate of 9 percent at 88 plus accrued interest and a broker's commission of $400. The interest payment dates are January 1 and July 1. The following entry records this purchase transaction:

May 1	Investment in Bonds	18,000	
	Interest Income	600	
	Cash		18,600
	To record purchase of MGR Corporation		
	bonds at 88 plus $400 commission and		
	accrued interest		
	$20,000 \times 9\% \times 1/3 = \$600		

Note that the purchase is recorded at cost, as are all purchases of assets. The debit to Investment in Bonds of $18,000 equals the purchase price of $17,600 ($20,000 × .88) plus the commission of $400. Because in managing its investments, Vason Corporation will buy and sell as seems necessary and will probably not hold the bonds to maturity, the $20,000 face value of the bonds is not recorded. This case is very different from that of the issuing corporation, which must repay the bonds at the maturity date to anyone who holds them.

The debit to Interest Income of $600 represents four months' interest (one-third year from January 1 to May 1) that was paid to the seller of the bonds.

Amortization of Premium or Discount

Accounting Principles Board *Opinion No. 21* requires companies making long-term investments in bonds to amortize the difference between the cost of the investment and its maturity value over the life of the bond. The effective interest method, which results in a constant rate of return over the life of the investment, should be used.[6]

Because the investing company does not use separate accounts for the face value and any related discount or premium, the entry to amortize the premium or discount is made directly to the investment account. The amortization of a premium calls for a credit to the investment account to reduce the carrying value gradually to face value. The amortization of a discount calls for a debit to the investment account to increase the carrying value gradually to face value.

Returning to the case of Vason Corporation's purchase of bonds at a discount, we assume that the effective interest rate is $10\frac{1}{2}$ percent. Remember that the amount of amortization of a premium or discount is the difference between (1) the face interest rate times the face value and (2) the effective interest rate times the carrying value. On July 1, the first interest date after the purchase, two months will have passed. The amount of discount to be amortized is as follows:

Two months' effective interest:	
$18,000 \times 10\frac{1}{2}\% \times \frac{1}{6}$	$315
Two months' face interest:	
$20,000 \times 9\% \times \frac{1}{6}$	300
Discount to be amortized	$ 15

The entry to record the receipt of an interest check on July 1 would be as follows:

July 1	Cash	900	
	Investment in Bonds	15	
	Interest Income		915
	To record receipt of semiannual		
	interest, some of which was		
	previously accrued, and to		
	amortize discount		

6. Accounting Principles Board, *Opinion No. 21,* "Interest on Receivables and Payables" (New York: American Institute of Certified Public Accountants, 1971), par. 15.

In this entry, Cash is debited for the semiannual interest payment ($20,000 × 9% × ½ = $900), Investment in Bonds is debited for the amortization of discount, or $15, and Interest Income is credited for the sum of the two debits, or $915. Note that the net interest earned is $315, which is the net amount of the $600 debit on May 1 and the $915 credit on July 1 to Interest Income. This amount is equal to the two months' effective interest just computed.

To continue the example, assume that Vason Corporation's fiscal year corresponds to the calendar year. Although the interest payment will not be received until January, it is necessary to accrue the interest and amortize the discount for the six months since July 1 in accordance with the matching concept. The entry to record the accrual of interest on December 31 is as follows:

Dec. 31	Interest Receivable	900.00	
	Investment in Bonds	45.79	
	Interest Income		945.79
	To accrue interest income and amortize discount on bond investment		

The period covered by this entry is six months. Therefore, the amounts to be debited and credited are as follows:

Six months' effective interest:	
$18,015 × 10½% × ½	$945.79
Six months' face interest:	
$20,000 × 9% × ½	900.00
Discount to be amortized	$ 45.79

Note that the effective interest rate is applied to the new carrying value of $18,015. The next time the effective interest is calculated, the effective rate will be applied to $18,060.79 ($18,015 + $45.79). The entry to record receipt of the interest payment check on January 1 is as follows:[7]

Jan. 1	Cash	900	
	Interest Receivable		900
	To record receipt of interest on bonds		

Similar calculations are made when a company purchases bonds at a premium. The only difference is that Investment in Bonds is credited rather than debited to reduce the carrying value, and the interest earned is less than the face interest.

---

7. This entry assumes that reversing entries are not made. Some companies may prefer to use reversing entries.

Sale of Bonds

The sale of a bond investment is recorded by debiting Cash for the amount received and crediting Investment in Bonds for the carrying value of the investment. Any difference in the proceeds from the sale and the carrying value of the bonds is debited or credited to Loss or Gain on Sale of Investments. If the sale is made between interest payment dates, the company is entitled to the accrued interest from the last interest date, just as it had to pay the accrued interest when the bonds were purchased.

If we assume that Vason Corporation sells the bonds in our continuing example at 94 less commission of $400 on March 1, two entries are required. The first entry is necessary to amortize the discount for two months:

Mar. 1	Investment in Bonds	16.06	
	Interest Income		16.06

To amortize 2 months' bond discount
Effective interest:
$18,060.79 \times 10\frac{1}{2}\% \times \frac{1}{6}$ = \$316.06
Face interest:
$20,000 \times 9\% \times \frac{1}{6}$ =   300.00
Discount to be amortized $ 16.06

The second entry is to record the sale:

Mar. 1	Cash	18,700.00	
	Gain on Sale of Investments		323.15
	Investment in Bonds		18,076.85
	Interest Income		300.00

To record sale of bonds at 94
less $400 commission plus
accrued interest

The cash received is the selling price of $18,800 ($20,000 × .94) less commission of $400 plus the accrued interest for two months of $300 ($20,000 × 9% × $\frac{1}{6}$). The gain on the sale of investments is the difference between selling price less commission ($18,400) and the carrying value of $18,076.85. The carrying value represents the assigned purchase price plus all amortization of discount:

May 1 purchase	$18,000.00
July 1 amortization	15.00
Dec. 31 amortization	45.79
Mar. 1 amortization	16.06
Carrying value of bond investment	$18,076.85

Chapter Review

Review of Learning Objectives

1. **Apply the cost method and the equity method to the appropriate situations in accounting for long-term investments.**

   Long-term stock investments fall into three categories. First are noninfluential and noncontrolling investments, representing less than 20 percent ownership. To account for these investments, use the cost method, adjusting the investment to the lower of cost or market for financial statement purposes. Second are influential but noncontrolling investments, representing 20 percent to 50 percent ownership. Use the equity method to account for these investments. Third are controlling interest investments, representing more than 50 percent ownership. Account for them using consolidated financial statements.

2. **Explain when to prepare consolidated financial statements, and describe their uses.**

   The FASB requires that consolidated financial statements be prepared when an investing company has legal and effective control over another company. Control exists when the parent company owns more than 50 percent of the voting stock of the subsidiary company. Consolidated financial statements are useful to investors and others because they treat the parent company and its subsidiaries realistically, as an integrated economic unit.

3. **Prepare consolidated balance sheets at acquisition date for purchase at (a) book value and (b) other than book value.**

   At the date of acquisition, a work sheet entry is made to eliminate the investment from the parent company's financial statements and the stockholders' equity section of the subsidiary's financial statements. The assets and liabilities of the two companies are combined. If the parent owns less than 100 percent of the subsidiary, minority interest will appear on the consolidated balance sheet equal to the percentage of the subsidiary not owned by the parent multiplied by the stockholders' equity in the subsidiary. If the cost of the parent's investment in the subsidiary is greater than the subsidiary's book value, an amount equal to the excess of cost above book value will be allocated on the consolidated balance sheet to undervalued subsidiary assets and to goodwill. If the cost of the parent's investment in the subsidiary is less than book value, the excess of book value over cost should be used to reduce the book value of the long-term assets (other than long-term marketable securities) of the subsidiary.

4. **Prepare consolidated income statements for intercompany transactions.**

   When consolidated income statements are prepared, intercompany sales, purchases, interest income, and interest expense must be eliminated to avoid double counting of these items.

5. **Account for bond investment transactions.**

   When a company invests in bonds, the bonds are recorded at cost, and no separate premium or discount is recorded. If the investment is long term, the difference between the cost and face value of the investment is amortized using the effective interest method. When the bond investment is sold, the premium or discount is amortized and interest income is accrued to the date of sale. Either a gain or a loss may result from the sale of bond investments.

Review of Concepts and Terminology

The following concepts and terms were introduced in this chapter:

(L.O. 1) **Consolidated financial statements**: Financial statements that reflect the combined operations of parent company and subsidiaries.

(L.O. 1) **Control**: The ability of the investing company to decide the operating and financial policies of another company through ownership of more than 50 percent of its voting stock.

(L.O. 1) **Cost method**: A method of accounting for long-term investments in which the investor records the investment at cost and recognizes income as dividends are received. Used when the investing company owns less than 20 percent of the voting stock of the other company.

(L.O. 2) **Eliminations**: Entries made on consolidated work sheets to eliminate transactions between parent and subsidiary companies.

(L.O. 1) **Equity method**: The method of accounting for long-term investments in which the investor records its share of the investee's periodic net income or loss as an increase or decrease in the Investment account. Used when the investing company exercises significant influence over the other company.

(L.O. 3b) **Goodwill (goodwill from consolidation)**: The amount paid for a subsidiary that exceeds the fair value of the subsidiary's assets less its liabilities.

(L.O. 3a) **Minority interest**: The amount on a consolidated balance sheet that represents the holdings of stockholders who own less than 50 percent of the voting stock of a subsidiary.

(L.O. 1) **Parent company**: An investing company that owns a controlling interest in another company.

(L.O. 2) **Purchase method**: A method of accounting for parent company/subsidiary relationships in which similar accounts from separate statements are combined.

(L.O. 1) **Significant influence**: The ability of an investing company to affect the operating and financial policies of another company, even though the investor holds less than 50 percent of the voting stock.

(L.O. 1) **Subsidiary**: An investee company in which a controlling interest is owned by another company.

Self-Test

Test your knowledge of the chapter by choosing the best answer for each item on the following pages.

1. The ability to affect the operating and financial policies of a company whose shares are owned, even if the investor company holds less than 50 percent of the voting stock, is known as
   a. noninfluential.
   c. control.
   b. noninfluential control.
   d. significant influence.   *(L.O. 1)*

2. When the equity method is used to account for a long-term investment in stock of another company, the carrying value of the investment is affected by
   a. an excess of market price over cost.
   b. neither earnings nor dividends of the investee.
   c. earnings and dividends of the investee.
   d. a decline in the market value of the stock.   *(L.O. 1)*

3. Consolidated financial statements are useful because
   a. they are much more detailed than the statements for the individual companies.
   b. minority shareholders need the consolidated information in order to make good investment decisions.
   c. the parent and subsidiaries comprise a single legal entity, and the financial statements should reflect that fact.
   d. investors of the parent company want a clear financial picture of the total economic entity.   *(L.O. 2)*

4. Which of the following items would *not* require an eliminating entry during preparation of consolidated financial statements?
   a. Amount owed by subsidiary to parent
   b. Amount owed by parent to subsidiary
   c. Short-term investments
   d. Investment in subsidiary   *(L.O. 3)*

5. B Company buys all the stock of C Company for $374,000. C Company has contributed capital of $184,000 and retained earnings of $190,000. The consolidated financial statements would contain
   a. minority interest and goodwill.
   b. goodwill but not minority interest.
   c. minority interest but not goodwill.
   d. neither minority interest nor goodwill.   *(L.O. 3)*

6. B Company buys all the stock of C Company for $634,000. C Company has contributed capital of $404,000 and retained earnings of $160,000. The consolidated financial statements would contain
   a. minority interest and goodwill.
   b. goodwill but not minority interest.
   c. minority interest but not goodwill.
   d. neither minority interest nor goodwill.   *(L.O. 3)*

7. B Company buys 80 percent of the stock of C Company for $465,600. C Company has contributed capital of $304,000 and retained earnings of $278,000. The consolidated financial statements would contain
   a. minority interest and goodwill.
   b. goodwill but not minority interest.
   c. minority interest but not goodwill.
   d. neither minority interest nor goodwill.   *(L.O. 3)*

8. In preparing consolidated financial statements, all of the following commonly require eliminatior entries except
   a. intercompany sales and purchases.
   b. intercompany interest expense and income.
   c. intercompany investment.
   d. intercompany personnel transfers.   *(L.O. 4)*

9. The amortization of a premium on bonds purchased as a long-term investment will result in reporting an amount of interest income which
   a. exceeds the amount of cash received for interest.
   b. is less than the amount of cash received for interest.
   c. equals the amount of cash received for interest.
   d. has no determinable relationship with the amount of cash interest for the period.   *(L.O. 5)*

10. One way in which accounting for bond investments differs from accounting for bonds payable is that
    a. bond discounts or premiums are usually not amortized when one is recording interest received on bond investments.
    b. a separate unamortized bond discount or premium account is not used for bond investments.
    c. amortization of unamortized premium or discount on bond investments must be done using the effective interest method.
    d. bond investments are always recorded at face value.   *(L.O. 5)*

Answers to Self-Test are at the end of this chapter.

Review Problem
Consolidated Balance Sheet: Less than 100 Percent Ownership

(L.O. 3) In a cash transaction, Taylor Company purchased 90 percent of the outstanding stock of Schumacher Company for $763,200 on June 30, 19xx . Directly after the acquisition, separate balance sheets of the companies appeared as follows:

	Taylor Company	Schumacher Company
Assets		
Cash	$ 400,000	$ 48,000
Accounts Receivable	650,000	240,000
Inventory	1,000,000	520,000
Investment in Schumacher Company	763,200	—
Plant and Equipment (net)	1,500,000	880,000
Other Assets	50,000	160,000
Total Assets	$4,363,200	$1,848,000
Liabilities and Stockholders' Equity		
Accounts Payable	$ 800,000	$ 400,000
Long-Term Debt	1,000,000	600,000
Common Stock—$5 par value	2,000,000	800,000
Retained Earnings	563,200	48,000
Total Liabilities and Stockholders' Equity	$4,363,200	$1,848,000

Additional information: (a) Schumacher Company's other assets represent a long-term investment in Taylor Company's long-term debt. The debt was purchased for an amount equal to Taylor's carrying value of the debt. (b) Taylor Company owes Schumacher Company $100,000 for services rendered.

Required

Prepare a work sheet as of the acquisition date for preparing a consolidated balance sheet.

Answer to Review Problem

Taylor and Schumacher Companies **Work Sheet for Consolidated Balance Sheet** **June 30, 19xx**					
Accounts	**Balance Sheet Taylor Company**	**Balance Sheet Schumacher Company**	**Eliminations**		**Consolidated Balance Sheet**
			Debit	**Credit**	
Cash	400,000	48,000			448,000
Accounts Receivable	650,000	240,000		(3) 100,000	790,000
Inventory	1,000,000	520,000			1,520,000
Investment in					
Schumacher Company	763,200	—		(1) 763,200	
Plant and Equipment (net)	1,500,000	880,000			2,380,000
Other Assets	50,000	160,000		(2) 160,000	50,000
Total Assets	4,363,200	1,848,000			5,188,000
Accounts Payable	800,000	400,000	(3) 100,000		1,100,000
Long-Term Debt	1,000,000	600,000	(2) 160,000		1,440,000
Common Stock—					
$5 par value	2,000,000	800,000	(1) 800,000		2,000,000
Retained Earnings	563,200	48,000	(1) 48,000		563,200
Minority Interest				(1) 84,800	84,800
Total Liabilities and Stockholders' Equity	4,363,200	1,848,000	1,108,000	1,108,000	5,188,000

(1) Elimination of intercompany investment. Minority interest equals 10 percent of Schumacher Company Stockholders' Equity (10% × [$800,000 + $48,000] = $84,800).
(2) Elimination of intercompany long-term debt.
(3) Elimination of intercompany receivables and payables.

Chapter Assignments

Discussion Questions and Writing Assignments

1. Why are the concepts of significant influence and control important in accounting for long-term investments?
2. For each of the following categories of long-term investments, briefly describe the applicable percentage of ownership and accounting treatment: (a) noninfluential and noncontrolling investment, (b) influential but noncontrolling investment, and (c) controlling investment.
3. What is meant by a parent-subsidiary relationship?
4. Would the stockholders of RCA Corporation be more interested in the consolidated financial statements of RCA than in the statements of its principal subsidiaries, such as NBC, Hertz Rent-A-Car, or the electronics division? Explain.
5. The 1985 annual report for U.S. Steel Corporation included the following statement in its Summary of Principal Accounting Policies: "*Principles applied in consolidation.*—Majority-owned subsidiaries are consolidated, except for leasing and finance companies and those subsidiaries not considered to be material." How did this practice change in 1988, and why?
6. Also in U.S. Steel's annual report, in the Summary of Principal Accounting Policies, was the following statement: "*Investments.*—Investments in leasing and finance companies are at U.S. Steel's equity in the net assets and advances to such companies. Investments in other companies, in which U.S. Steel has significant influence in management and control, are also on the equity basis." What is the equity basis of accounting for investments, and why did U.S. Steel use it in this case?
7. Why should intercompany receivables, payables, sales, and purchases be eliminated in the preparation of consolidated financial statements?
8. The following item appears on a consolidated balance sheet: "Minority Interest—$50,000." Explain how this item arose and where you would expect to find it on the consolidated balance sheet.
9. Why may the price paid to acquire a controlling interest in a subsidiary company differ from the subsidiary's book value?
10. The following item appears on a consolidated balance sheet: "Goodwill from Consolidation—$70,000." Explain how this item arose and where you would expect to find it on the consolidated balance sheet.
11. Subsidiary Corporation has a book value of $100,000, of which Parent Corporation purchases 100 percent for $115,000. None of the excess of cost over book value is attributed to tangible assets. What is the amount of goodwill from consolidation?
12. Subsidiary Corporation, a wholly-owned subsidiary, has total sales of $500,000, $100,000 of which were made to Parent Corporation. Parent Corporation has total sales of $1,000,000, including sales of all items purchased from Subsidiary Corporation. What is the amount of sales on the consolidated income statement?
13. Why does the buying company record a bond investment at cost when the issuing company will record the same issue at face value and adjust a separate account for any discount or premium?
14. What special accounting problem arises when bonds are purchased between interest dates, even if the purchase is made at face value?

Classroom Exercises

Exercise 20-1.
Methods of
Accounting for
Long-Term
Investments
(L.O. 1, 2)

Diversified Corporation has the following long-term investments:

1. 60 percent of the common stock of Calcor Corporation
2. 13 percent of the common stock of Virginia, Inc.
3. 50 percent of the nonvoting preferred stock of Camrad Corporation
4. 100 percent of the common stock of its financing subsidiary, DCF, Inc.
5. 35 percent of the common stock of the French company, Maison d'Boutaine
6. 70 percent of the common stock of the Canadian company, Alberta Mining Company

For each of these investments, tell which of the following methods should be used for external financial reporting.

a. cost method
b. equity method
c. consolidation of parent and subsidiary financial statements

Exercise 20-2.
Long-Term
Investments:
Cost Method
(L.O. 1)

Heard Corporation has the following portfolio of investments at year end:

Company	Percentage of Voting Stock Held	Cost	Year-End Market Value
N Corporation	4	$160,000	$190,000
O Corporation	12	750,000	550,000
P Corporation	5	60,000	110,000
Total		$970,000	$850,000

The Unrealized Loss on Long-Term Investments account and the Allowance to Reduce Long-Term Investments to Market account both currently have a balance of $80,000 from the last accounting period. Prepare the year-end adjustment to reflect the above information.

Exercise 20-3.
Long-Term
Investments:
Cost and
Equity Methods
(L.O. 1)

On January 1, Terry Corporation purchased, as long-term investments, 8 percent of the voting stock of Holmes Corporation for $250,000 and 45 percent of the voting stock of Miles Corporation for $1 million. During the year, Holmes Corporation had earnings of $100,000 and paid dividends of $40,000. Miles Corporation had earnings of $300,000 and paid dividends of $200,000. The market value of neither investment declined during the year. Which of these investments should be accounted for using the cost method? Which with the equity method? At what amount should each investment be carried on the balance sheet at year end? Give a reason for each choice.

Exercise 20-4.
Long-Term
Investments:
Equity Method
(L.O. 1)

At the beginning of the current year, Romano Corporation acquired 40 percent of the voting stock of Burke Corporation for $2,400,000 in cash, an amount sufficient to exercise significant influence over Burke Corporation's activities. During the year, Burke paid dividends of $400,000 but incurred a net loss of $200,000. Prepare journal entries in Romano Corporation's records to reflect this information.

**Exercise 20-5.
Elimination Entry
for a Purchase at
Book Value**
(L.O. 3)

The Maki Manufacturing Company purchased 100 percent of the common stock of the Burleson Manufacturing Company for $150,000. Burleson's stockholders' equity included common stock of $100,000 and retained earnings of $50,000. Prepare the eliminating entry in general journal form that would appear on the work sheet for consolidating the balance sheets of these two entities as of the acquisition date.

**Exercise 20-6.
Elimination Entry
and Minority
Interest**
(L.O. 3)

The stockholders' equity section of the Sher Corporation's balance sheet appeared as follows on December 31:

Common Stock—$5 par value, 40,000 shares	
authorized and issued	$200,000
Retained Earnings	24,000
Total Stockholders' Equity	$224,000

Assume that Edmunds Manufacturing Company owns 80 percent of the voting stock of Sher Corporation and paid $5.60 for each share. In general journal form, prepare the entry (including minority interest) to eliminate Edmunds's investment and Sher's stockholders' equity that would appear on the work sheet used in preparing the consolidated balance sheet for the two firms.

**Exercise 20-7.
Consolidated
Balance Sheet with
Goodwill**
(L.O. 3)

On September 1, Y Company purchased 100 percent of the voting stock of Z Company for $960,000 in cash. The separate condensed balance sheets immediately after the purchase follow.

	Y Company	Z Company
Other Assets	$2,206,000	$1,089,000
Investment in Z Company	960,000	—
	$3,166,000	$1,089,000
Liabilities	$ 871,000	$ 189,000
Common Stock—$1 par value	1,000,000	300,000
Retained Earnings	1,295,000	600,000
	$3,166,000	$1,089,000

Prepare a work sheet for preparing the consolidated balance sheet immediately after Y Company acquired control of Z Company. Assume that any excess cost of the investment in the subsidiary over book value is attributable to goodwill from consolidation.

**Exercise 20-8.
Analyzing the
Effects of
Elimination Entries**
(L.O. 3)

Some of the separate accounts from the balance sheets for F Company and G Company, just after F Company purchased 85 percent of G Company's voting stock for $765,000 in cash, follow:

	F Company	G Company
Accounts Receivable	$1,300,000	$400,000
Interest Receivable, Bonds of G Company	7,200	—
Investment in G Company	765,000	—
Investment in G Company Bonds	180,000	—
Accounts Payable	530,000	190,000
Interest Payable, Bonds	32,000	20,000
Bonds Payable	800,000	500,000
Common Stock	1,000,000	600,000
Retained Earnings	560,000	300,000

Accounts Receivable and Accounts Payable included the following: G Company owed F Company $50,000 for services rendered, and F Company owed G Company $66,000 for purchases of merchandise. F bought G Company's bonds for an amount equal to G's carrying value of the bonds. Determine the amount, including minority interest, that would appear on the consolidated balance sheet for each of the accounts listed.

Exercise 20-9.
Preparation of
Consolidated
Income Statement
(L.O. 4)

Marcus Company has owned 100 percent of Green Company since 19x0. The income statements of these two companies for the year ended December 31, 19x1 follow.

	Marcus Company	Green Company
Sales	$1,500,000	$600,000
Cost of Goods Sold	750,000	400,000
Gross Margin from Sales	$ 750,000	$200,000
Less: Selling Expenses	$ 250,000	$ 50,000
General and Administrative Expenses	300,000	100,000
Total Operating Expenses	$ 550,000	$150,000
Net Income from Operations	$ 200,000	$ 50,000
Other Income	60,000	—
Net Income	$ 260,000	$ 50,000

Additional information: (a) Green Company purchased $280,000 of inventory from Marcus Company, which had been sold to Green Company customers by the end of the year. (b) Green Company leased its building from Marcus Company for $60,000 per year. Prepare a consolidated income statement work sheet for the two companies for the year ended December 31, 19x1.

Exercise 20-10.
Bond Investment
Transactions
(L.O. 5)

On November 1, Halpern Corporation purchased as a long-term investment one thousand $1,000 bonds for $1,050,000 plus accrued interest. The bonds carried a face interest rate of 10½ percent paid semiannually on July 1 and January 1. Due to a change in investment plans, management decided to sell the bonds on January 1 for $1,070,000. Prepare journal entries to record the purchase on November 1, the receipt of interest and amortization of premium on January 1, assuming an effective interest rate of 9½ percent, and the sale of the bonds on January 1.

Interpreting Accounting Information

U.S. Steel and Marathon Oil*
(L.O. 3)

In 1981 U.S. Steel Corporation fought Mobil Oil Corporation for control of Marathon Oil Company. U.S. Steel won this battle of the giants by reaching an agreement to purchase all of Marathon's stock. *The Chicago Tribune* reported on March 12, 1982 that the $6 billion merger, as approved by the stockholders of Marathon, was the second largest in history and created the twelfth largest industrial corporation in the United States.

In a note to U.S. Steel's 1981 annual report, the details of the purchase were revealed. U.S. Steel "purchased 30 million common shares of Marathon Oil Company for $125 per share . . as the first step in its planned acquisition of the entire equity of Marathon." Additional Marathon shares would be purchased by issuing $100 principal amount of 12½ percent notes due in 1994 for each share of stock. These notes were estimated by the financial press to have a fair market value of $80 per note. The total number of Marathon shares prior to these two transactions was 59.0 million. On December 31, 1981, just before the merger, the condensed balance sheets of U.S. Steel and Marathon Oil appeared as follows (in millions).

	U.S. Steel	Marathon Oil
Assets		
Current Assets, Excluding Inventories	$ 4,214	$ 907
Inventories	1,198	576
Property, Plant, and Equipment (net)	6,676	4,233
Other Assets	1,228	278
Total Assets	$13,316	$5,994
Liabilities and Stockholders' Equity		
Current Liabilities	$ 2,823	$1,475
Long-Term Debt	2,340	1,368
Deferred Income Taxes	732	588
Other Liabilities	1,161	501
Total Liabilities	$ 7,056	$3,932
Stockholders' Equity	6,260	2,062
Total Liabilities and Stockholders' Equity	$13,316	$5,994

* Excerpts from the 1981 annual report used by permission of U.S. Steel. Copyright © 1981.

Further information in U.S. Steel's annual report indicated that when consolidated financial statements were prepared using the purchase method, management would adjust Marathon's assets and liabilities in the following manner. It would (a) increase inventory by $1,244 million; (b) increase current liabilities by $392 million; and (c) decrease deferred income taxes by $588 million. After these adjustments, any remaining excess of the purchase price over book value of Marathon's shares would be attributed to property, plant, and equipment.

Required

1. Prepare the entry in U.S. Steel's journals to record the purchase of Marathon Oil.
2. Prepare the eliminating entry, including the adjustments indicated, that would be made to consolidate U.S. Steel and Marathon.
3. Prepare a consolidated balance sheet for the merged companies.
4. Did U.S. Steel pay more or less than book value for Marathon? Why would U.S. Steel take this action? Did the purchase raise or lower U.S. Steel's book value per share?

Problem Set A

**Problem 20A-1.
Long-Term
Investment
Transactions
(L.O. 1)**

On January 2, 19x0, the Durham Company made several long-term investments in the voting stock of various companies. It purchased 10,000 shares of Kang at $2.00 a share, 15,000 shares of Pearl at $3.00 a share, and 6,000 shares of Calderone at $4.50 a share. Each investment represents less than 20 percent of the voting stock of the company. The remaining transactions of Durham in securities during 19x0 were as follows:

May 15 Purchased with cash 6,000 shares of Ross stock for $3.00 per share. This investment comprises less than 20 percent of the Ross voting stock.
July 16 Sold the 10,000 shares of Kang stock for $1.80 per share.
Sept. 30 Purchased with cash 5,000 additional shares of Pearl for $3.20 per share.
Dec. 31 The market values per share of the stock in the Long-Term Investments account were as follows: Pearl, $3.25; Calderone, $4.00; and Ross, $2.00.

Durham's transactions in securities during 19x1 were as follows:

Feb. 1 Received a cash dividend from Pearl of $.10 per share.
July 15 Sold the 6,000 Calderone shares for $4.00 per share.
Aug. 1 Received a cash dividend from Pearl of $.10 per share.
Sept. 10 Purchased 3,000 shares of Jolley for $7.00 per share.
Dec. 31 The market values per share of the stock in the Long-Term Investments account were as follows: Pearl, $3.25; Ross, $2.50; and Jolley, $6.50.

Required

Prepare the journal entries to record all of Durham Company's transactions in long-term investments during 19x0 and 19x1.

Problem 20A-2.
Long-Term
Investments:
Equity Method
(L.O. 1)

The Mathis Corporation owns 35 percent of the voting stock of the Albers Corporation. The Investment account on the books of Mathis Corporation as of January 1, 19xx was $360,000. During 19xx, the Albers Corporation reported the following quarterly earnings and dividends:

Quarter	Earnings	Dividends Paid
1	$ 80,000	$ 50,000
2	120,000	50,000
3	60,000	50,000
4	(40,000)	50,000
	$220,000	$200,000

Because of the percentage of voting shares Mathis owns, it can exercise significant influence over the operations of Albers Corporation. Under these conditions the Mathis Corporation must account for the investment using the equity method.

Required

1. Prepare the journal entries that Mathis Corporation must make each quarter to record its share of earnings and dividends.
2. Prepare a ledger account for Mathis Corporation's investment in Albers, enter the beginning balance, and post the relevant entries from part **1**.

Problem 20A-3.
Consolidated
Balance Sheet:
Less than 100
Percent Ownership
(L.O. 3)

The Lobos Corporation purchased 80 percent of the outstanding voting stock of the Yost Corporation for $820,800 in cash. The balance sheets of the two companies immediately after acquisition were as follows:

	Lobos Corporation	Yost Corporation
Assets		
Cash	$ 150,000	$ 60,000
Accounts Receivable	360,000	200,000
Inventory	1,600,000	700,000
Investment in Yost	820,800	—
Property, Plant, and Equipment (net)	2,500,000	1,000,000
Other Assets	100,000	40,000
Total Assets	$5,530,800	$2,000,000
Liabilities and Stockholders' Equity		
Accounts Payable	$ 400,000	$ 150,000
Salaries Payable	50,000	20,000
Taxes Payable	20,000	4,000
Bonds Payable	1,300,000	800,000
Common Stock	2,500,000	900,000
Retained Earnings	1,260,800	126,000
Total Liabilities and Stockholders' Equity	$5,530,800	$2,000,000

Additional information: (a) The Other Assets account on the Yost balance sheet represents an investment in Lobos's Bonds Payable. The investment in Lobos was made at an amount equal to Lobos's carrying value of the bonds. (b) $50,000 of the Accounts Receivable of Lobos Corporation represents receivables due from Yost.

Required

Prepare a work sheet as of the acquisition date for the preparation of a consolidated balance sheet.

Problem 20A-4.
Consolidated
Balance Sheet:
Cost Exceeding
Book Value
(L.O. 3)

The balance sheets of Cheever and Ham Corporations as of December 31, 19xx are shown as follows.

	Cheever Corporation	Ham Corporation
Assets		
Cash	$ 600,000	$ 120,000
Accounts Receivable	700,000	600,000
Inventory	250,000	600,000
Investment in Ham Corporation	800,000	—
Property, Plant, and Equipment	1,350,000	850,000
Other Assets	20,000	50,000
Total Assets	$3,720,000	$2,220,000
Liabilities and Stockholders' Equity		
Accounts Payable	$ 750,000	$ 500,000
Salaries Payable	300,000	270,000
Bonds Payable	350,000	800,000
Common Stock	1,500,000	500,000
Retained Earnings	820,000	150,000
Total Liabilities and Stockholders' Equity	$3,720,000	$2,220,000

Required

Prepare a consolidated balance sheet work sheet for the two companies, assuming that Cheever purchased 100 percent of the common stock of Ham for $800,000 immediately prior to December 31, 19xx, and that $70,000 of the excess of cost over book value is attributable to the increased value of Ham Corporation's inventory. The rest of the excess is considered goodwill.

Problem 20A-5.
Bond Investment
Transactions
(L.O. 5)

Transactions involving long-term bond investments made by Drury Corporation follow. Drury has a June 30 year end.

19x1
July 1 Purchased $500,000 of Stellos Corporation's 12½ percent bonds at 104, a price that yields an effective interest rate of 11½ percent.

These bonds have semiannual interest payment dates of June 30 and December 31.

Nov. 1 Purchased $300,000 of Taft Company's 9 percent bonds, dated August 1, at face value plus accrued interest.

Dec. 31 Received a check from Stellos for semiannual interest and amortized the premium using the effective interest method.

19x2
Feb. 1 Received a check from Taft for the semiannual interest.
June 30 Received a check from Stellos for the semiannual interest and amortized the premium using the effective interest method.
     30 Made a year-end adjusting entry to accrue the interest on the Taft bonds.
Aug. 1 Received a check from Taft for the semiannual interest (reversing entries were not used).
Nov. 1 Sold the Taft bonds at 98 plus accrued interest.
Dec. 31 Received a check from Stellos for the semiannual interest and amortized the premium using the effective interest method.

19x3
Jan. 1 Sold one-half of the Stellos bonds at 101.

Required   Prepare general journal entries to record these transactions.

Problem Set B

**Problem 20B-1.
Long-Term
Investments
Transactions
(L.O. 1)**

Herbst Corporation made the following transactions in its Long-Term Investments account over a two-year period:

19x0
Apr. 1 Purchased with cash 20,000 shares of Babbitt Company stock for $76 per share.
June 1 Purchased with cash 15,000 shares of Kanter Corporation stock for $36 per share.
Sept. 1 Received a $.50 per share dividend from Babbitt Company.
Nov. 1 Purchased with cash 25,000 shares of Moran Corporation stock for $55 per share.
Dec. 31 Market values per share of shares held in the Long-Term Investments account were as follows: Babbitt Company, $70; Kanter Corporation, $16; and Moran Corporation, $61.

19x1
Feb. 1 Because of unfavorable prospects for Kanter Corporation, Kanter stock was sold for cash at $20 per share.
May   1 Purchased with cash 10,000 shares of Gayle Corporation for $112 per share.
Sept. 1 Received $1 per share dividend from Babbitt Company.
Dec. 31 Market values per share of shares held in the Long-Term Investments account were as follows: Babbitt Company, $80; Moran Corporation, $70; and Gayle Corporation, $100.

Required   Prepare entries to record these transactions in the Herbst Corporation records. Assume that all investments represent less than 20 percent of the voting stock of the company whose stock was acquired.

**Problem 20B-2.
Long-Term
Investment:
Equity Method**
(L.O. 1)

The Yu Company owns 40 percent of the voting stock of the Sargent Company. The Investment account for this company on the Yu Company's balance sheet had a balance of $300,000 on January 1, 19xx. During 19xx, the Sargent Company reported the following quarterly earnings and dividends paid:

Quarter	Earnings	Dividends Paid
1	$ 40,000	$20,000
2	30,000	20,000
3	80,000	20,000
4	(20,000)	20,000
	$130,000	$80,000

The Yu Company exercises a significant influence over the operations of the Sargent Company and, therefore, uses the equity method to account for its investment.

Required

1. Prepare the journal entries that the Yu Company must make each quarter in accounting for its investment in the Sargent Company.
2. Prepare a ledger account for the investment in common stock of the Sargent Company. Enter the beginning balance and post relevant portions of the entries made in part 1.

**Problem 20B-3.
Consolidated
Balance Sheet:
Less than 100
Percent Ownership**
(L.O. 3)

In a cash transaction, Alter Company purchased 70 percent of the outstanding stock of Damon Company for $296,800 cash on June 30, 19xx. Immediately after the acquisition, the separate balance sheets of the companies appeared as follows.

	Alter Company	Damon Company
Assets		
Cash	$ 160,000	$ 24,000
Accounts Receivable	260,000	120,000
Inventory	400,000	260,000
Investment in Damon Company	296,800	—
Plant and Equipment (net)	600,000	440,000
Other Assets	20,000	80,000
Total Assets	$1,736,800	$924,000
Liabilities and Stockholders' Equity		
Accounts Payable	$ 320,000	$200,000
Long-Term Debt	400,000	300,000
Common Stock—$5 par value	800,000	400,000
Retained Earnings	216,800	24,000
Total Liabilities and Stockholders' Equity	$1,736,800	$924,000

Additional information: (a) Damon Company's other assets represent a long-term investment in Alter Company's long-term debt. The debt was purchased for an amount equal to Alter's carrying value of the debt. (b) Alter Company owes Damon Company $40,000 for services rendered.

Required   Prepare a work sheet for preparing a consolidated balance sheet as of the acquisition date.

Problem 20B-4.
Consolidated
Balance Sheet:
Cost Exceeding
Book Value
(L.O. 3)

The balance sheets of Perez and Lloyd Companies as of December 31, 19xx follow.

	Perez Company	Lloyd Company
Assets		
Cash	$ 60,000	$ 40,000
Accounts Receivable	100,000	30,000
Investment in Lloyd Company	350,000	—
Other Assets	100,000	180,000
Total Assets	$610,000	$250,000
Liabilities and Stockholders' Equity		
Liabilities	$110,000	$ 30,000
Common Stock—$10 par value	400,000	200,000
Retained Earnings	100,000	20,000
Total Liabilities and Stockholders' Equity	$610,000	$250,000

Required   Prepare a consolidated balance sheet work sheet for the Perez and Lloyd Companies. Assume that the Perez Company purchased 100 percent of Lloyd's common stock for $350,000 immediately before the above balance sheet date. Also assume that $65,000 of the excess of cost over book value is attributable to the increased value of Lloyd Company's other assets. The rest of the excess is considered by the Perez Company to be goodwill.

Problem 20B-5.
Bond Investment
Transactions
(L.O. 5)

Lao Corporation purchases bonds as long-term investments. Lao's long-term bond investment transactions for 19x1 and 19x2 follow. Lao's year end is December 31.

19x1
Jan.   1   Purchased on the semiannual interest payment date $400,000 of Wilks Company 10 percent bonds at 91, a price yielding an effective interest rate of 12 percent.
Apr.   1   Purchased $200,000 of Simon Corporation 12 percent, twenty-year bonds dated March 1 at face value plus accrued interest.

July 1 Received a check from Wilks Company for semiannual interest and amortized the discount using the effective interest method.
Sept. 1 Received a check from Simon for semiannual interest.
Dec. 31 Made year-end adjusting entries to accrue interest on the Wilks and Simon bonds and to amortize the discount on the Wilks bonds using the effective interest method.

19x2
Jan. 1 Received a check from Wilks for semiannual interest (reversing entries were not made).
Mar. 1 Received a check from Simon Corporation for semiannual interest.
July 1 Received a check from Wilks for semiannual interest and amortized the discount using the effective interest method.
1 Sold one-half of the Wilks bonds at 96.
Sept. 1 Received a check from Simon for semiannual interest.
Nov. 1 Sold the Simon bonds at 98 plus accrued interest.
Dec. 31 Made year-end adjusting entry to accrue interest on the remaining Wilks bonds and to amortize the discount using the effective interest method.

Required Prepare general journal entries to record these transactions.

Financial Decision Case

San Antonio Corporation (L.O. 1)

San Antonio Corporation is a successful oil and gas exploration business in the southwestern part of the United States. At the beginning of 19xx, the company made investments in three companies that perform services in the oil and gas industry. The details of each of these investments are presented in the next three paragraphs.

San Antonio purchased 100,000 shares in Levelland Service Corporation at a cost of $4 per share. Levelland has 1.5 million shares outstanding, and during 19xx paid dividends of $.20 per share on earnings of $.40 per share. At the end of the year, Levelland's shares were selling for $6 per share.

San Antonio also purchased 2 million shares of Plainview Drilling Company at $2 per share. Plainview has 10 million shares outstanding. In 19xx Plainview paid a dividend of $.10 per share on earnings of $.20 per share. During the current year the president of San Antonio was appointed to the board of directors of Plainview. At the end of the year Plainview's stock was selling for $3 per share.

In another action, San Antonio purchased 1 million of Brownfield Oil Field Supplies Company's 5 million outstanding shares at $3 per share. The president of San Antonio sought membership on the board of directors of Brownfield but was rebuffed by Brownfield's board when shareholders representing a majority of Brownfield's outstanding stock stated that they did not want to be associated with San Antonio. Brownfield paid a dividend of $.20 per share and reported a net income of only $.10 per share for the year. By the end of the year, the price of its stock had dropped to $1 per share.

Required 1. What principal factors must you consider in order to determine how to account for San Antonio's investments? Should they be shown on the balance sheet as short-term or long-term investments? What factors affect this decision?

2. For each of the three investments make general journal entries for each of the following: (a) initial investment, (b) receipt of cash dividend, and (c) recognition of income (if appropriate).
3. What adjusting entry (if any) is required at the end of the year?
4. Assuming that San Antonio's investment in Brownfield is sold after the first of the year for $1.50 per share, what general journal entry would be made? Assuming that the market value of the remaining investments held by San Antonio is above cost at the end of the second year, what adjusting entry (if any) would be required?

Answers to Self-Test

1. d	3. d	5. d	7. c	9. b
2. c	4. c	6. b	8. d	10. b

CHAPTER 21

International Accounting and Inflation Accounting

Money is the basic unit by which accountants measure business transactions and present financial information. In Chapter 1 we noted that accountants generally assume that the monetary unit, the dollar in the United States, is a stable measuring unit. In most of the accounting methods presented so far, we have ad- hered to this assumption. This chapter is devoted to two impor- tant cases in which the stability of the monetary unit is not assumed. They are the cases of (1) changing rates at which the dollar can be exchanged for foreign currencies, or international accounting; and (2) changing price levels, or inflation account- ing. After studying this chapter, you should be able to meet the learning objectives listed on the left.

International Accounting[1]

As businesses grow, they naturally look for new sources of sup- ply and new markets in other countries. Today, it is common for businesses, called **multinational** or **transnational corporations**, to operate in more than one country, and many of them operate throughout the world. Table 21-1 shows the extent of foreign business in a few multinational corporations. IBM, for example, has operations in eighty countries and receives about half its sales and income from outside the United States. Nestlé, the giant Swiss chocolate and food products company, operates in fifteen countries and receives 98 percent of its revenues from outside Switzerland. Together, the economies of such industrial countries as the United States, Japan, Great Britain, West Ger- many, and France have given rise to numerous worldwide cor- porations. More than five hundred companies are listed on at least one stock exchange outside their home country.

In addition, sophisticated investors no longer restrict their in- vestment activities to domestic securities markets. Many Ameri- cans invest in foreign securities markets, and non-Americans invest heavily in the stock market in the United States. Figure 21-1 shows that from 1978 until 1986, the total capitalization of

---

1. At the time this chapter was written, exchange rates were fluctuating rapidly. Thus, the examples, exercises, and problems in this book use exchange rates in the general range for the countries involved.

Table 21-1. Extent of Foreign Business for Selected Companies

Company	Country	Total Revenues (Millions)	Foreign Revenues as % of Total
Exxon	U.S.A.	$86,673	68.1
Mitsubishi	Japan	70,520	64.0
General Motors	U.S.A.	96,372	16.8
British Petroleum	Britain	53,131	81.0
International Business Machines (IBM)	U.S.A.	50,056	43.0
Volkswagen Group	Germany	17,935	51.5
Bank America	U.S.A.	13,390	38.4
Nestlé	Switzerland	17,184	98.1
Procter & Gamble	U.S.A.	13,552	26.7
Xerox	U.S.A.	11,736	27.2

Source: "The 500 Largest Foreign Companies." Excerpted by permission of *Forbes* magazine, July 28, 1986, pp. 176, 183, and 207–208. © Forbes Inc., 1986.

the world's stock markets has grown almost three times, while the United States's share of the pie has declined from 52 to 43 percent.

Foreign business transactions have two major effects on accounting. First, most sales or purchases of goods and services in other countries involve different currencies. Thus, one currency needs to be translated into another, using exchange rates. An **exchange rate** is the value of one currency in terms of another. For example, an English person purchas-

Figure 21-1. Market Capitalization of the World's Stock Markets

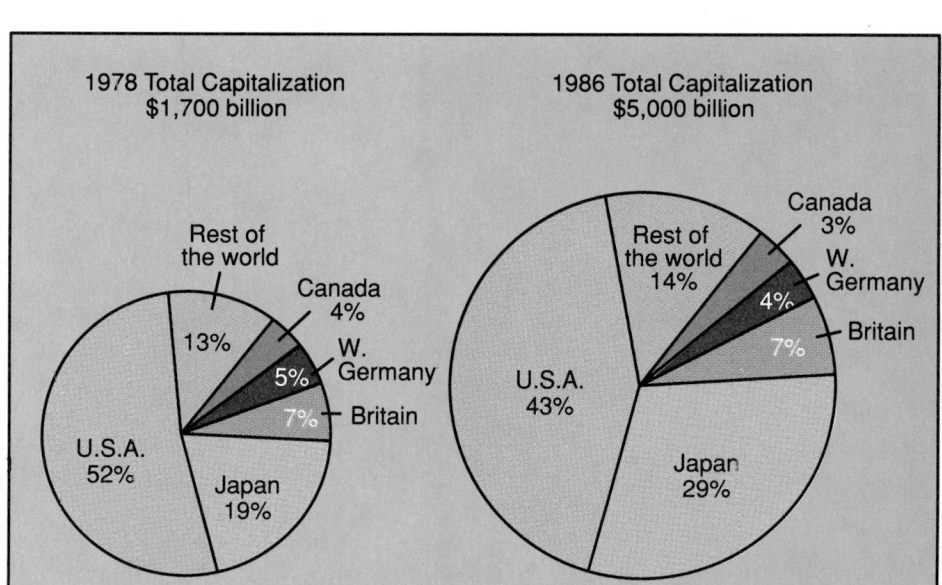

ing goods from a U.S. company and paying in U.S. dollars must exchange British pounds for U.S. dollars before making payment. In effect, currencies are goods that can be bought and sold. Table 21-2 lists the exchange rates of several currencies in terms of dollars. It shows the exchange rate for the British pound as $1.67 per pound on a particular date. Like the price of any good or service, these prices change daily according to supply and demand for the currencies. For example, less than three years earlier the exchange rate for British pounds was $1.20. Accounting for these price changes in recording foreign transactions and preparing financial statements for foreign subsidiaries is the subject of the next two sections.

The second major effect of international business on accounting is that financial standards differ from country to country, which hampers comparisons among companies from different countries. Some of the obstacles to achieving comparability and some of the progress in solving the problem are discussed later in this chapter.

Accounting for Transactions in Foreign Currencies

OBJECTIVE 1
Define exchange rate and record transactions that are affected by changes in foreign exchange rates

Among the first activities of an expanding company in the international market are the buying and selling of goods and services. For example, a maker of precision tools may try to expand by selling its product to foreign customers. Or it might try to lower its product cost by buying a less expensive part from a source in another country. In previous chapters, all transactions were recorded in dollars, and it was assumed that the dollar is a uniform measure in the same way that inches and centimeters are. But in the international marketplace, a transaction may take place in Japanese yen, British pounds, or some other currency. The values of these currencies rise and fall daily in relation to the dollar.

Foreign Sales. When a domestic company sells merchandise abroad, it may bill either in its own country's currency or in the foreign currency. If the billing and the subsequent payment are both in the domestic currency, no accounting problem arises. For example, assume that the precision toolmaker sells $170,000 worth of tools to a British company and

Table 21-2. Partial Listing of Foreign Exchange Rates			
Country	**Prices in $ U.S.**	**Country**	**Prices in $ U.S.**
Britain (pound)	1.67	Japan (yen)	.0075
Canada (dollar)	.84	Mexico (peso)	.0004
France (franc)	.16	Philippines (peso)	.049
Italy (lira)	.0007	Taiwan (dollar)	.039
Hong Kong (dollar)	.13	West Germany (mark)	.53

Source: "World Markets/Foreign Exchange," *The Wall Street Journal* (May 11, 1989). Reprinted by permission of *The Wall Street Journal*, © Dow Jones & Company, Inc., 1989. All Rights Reserved Worldwide.

bills the British company in dollars. The entry to record the sale and payment is familiar:

Date of sale

Accounts Receivable, British company	170,000	
Sales		170,000

Date of payment

Cash	170,000	
Accounts Receivable, British company		170,000

However, if the U.S. company bills the British company in British pounds and accepts payment in pounds, the U.S. company may incur an **exchange gain or loss**. A gain or loss will occur if the exchange rate of dollars to pounds changes between the date of sale and the date of payment. Exchange gains or losses are reported on the income statement. For example, assume that the sale of $170,000 above was billed as £100,000, reflecting an exchange rate of 1.70 (that is, $1.70 per pound) on the sale date. Now assume that by the date of payment, the exchange rate has fallen to 1.65. The entries to record the transactions follow:

Date of sale

Accounts Receivable, British company	170,000	
Sales		170,000
£100,000 × $1.70 = $170,000		

Date of payment

Cash	165,000	
Exchange Gain or Loss	5,000	
Accounts Receivable, British company		170,000
£100,000 × $1.65 = $165,000		

The U.S. company has incurred an exchange loss of $5,000 because it agreed to accept a fixed number of British pounds in payment, and before the payment was made, the value of each pound dropped. Had the value of the pound in relation to the dollar increased, the U.S. company would have made an exchange gain.

Foreign Purchases. Purchases are the opposite of sales. So the same logic applies to them, except that the relationship of exchange gains and losses to changes in exchange rates is reversed. For example, assume that the maker of precision tools purchases $15,000 of a certain part from a Japanese supplier. If the purchase and subsequent payment are made in U.S. dollars, no accounting problem arises.

Date of purchase

Purchases	15,000	
Accounts Payable, Japanese company		15,000

Date of payment

Accounts Payable, Japanese company	15,000	
Cash		15,000

However, the Japanese company may bill the U.S. company in yen and be paid in yen. If so, the U.S. company will incur an exchange gain or loss if the exchange rate changes between the dates of purchase and payment. For example, assume that the transaction is for 2,500,000 yen and the exchange rates on the dates of purchase and payment are $.0060 and $.0055 per yen, respectively. The entries follow.

Date of purchase

Purchases	15,000	
Accounts Payable, Japanese company		15,000
Y2,500,000 × $.0006 = $15,000		

Date of payment

Accounts Payable, Japanese company	15,000	
Exchange Gain or Loss		1,250
Cash		13,750
Y2,500,000 × $.0055 = $13,750		

In this case the U.S. company received an exchange gain of $1,250 because it agreed to pay a fixed Y2,500,000, and between the dates of purchase and payment the exchange value of the yen decreased in relation to the dollar.

Realized Versus Unrealized Exchange Gain or Loss. The preceding illustration dealt with completed transactions (in the sense that payment was completed). In each case the exchange gain or loss was recognized on the date of payment. If financial statements are prepared between the sale or purchase and the subsequent receipt or payment, and exchange rates have changed, there will be unrealized gains or losses. The Financial Accounting Standards Board, in its *Statement No. 52*, requires that exchange gains and losses "shall be included in determining net income for the period in which the exchange rate changes."[2] The requirement includes interim (quarterly) statements, and applies whether or not a transaction is complete.

This ruling has caused much debate. Critics charge that it gives too much weight to fleeting changes in exchange rates, causing random changes in earnings that hide long-run trends. Others feel the use of current exchange rates to value receivables and payables as of the balance sheet date is a major step toward economic reality (current values).

To illustrate, we will use the preceding case, in which a U.S. company buys parts from a Japanese supplier. We will assume that the transaction has not been completed by the balance sheet date, when the exchange rate is $.0051 per yen:

	Date	Exchange Rate ($ per Yen)
Date of purchase	Dec. 1	.0060
Balance sheet date	Dec. 31	.0051
Date of payment	Feb. 1	.0055

2. *Statement of Financial Accounting Standards No. 52*, "Foreign Currency Translation" (Stamford, Conn.: Financial Accounting Standards Board, 1981), par. 15.

The accounting effects of the unrealized gain are as follows:

	Dec. 1	Dec. 31	Feb. 1
Purchase recorded in U.S. dollars (billed as Y2,500,000)	$15,000	$15,000	$15,000
Dollars to be paid to equal Y2,500,000 (Y2,500,000 × exchange rate)	15,000	12,750	13,750
Unrealized gain (or loss)	—	$ ·2,250	
Realized gain (or loss)			$ 1,250

Dec. 1	Purchases	15,000	
	Accounts Payable, Japanese company		15,000
Dec. 31	Accounts Payable, Japanese company	2,250	
	Exchange Gain or Loss		2,250
Feb. 1	Accounts Payable, Japanese company	12,750	
	Exchange Gain or Loss	1,000	
	Cash		13,750

In this case, the original sale was billed in yen by the Japanese company. Following the rules of *Statement No. 52*, an exchange gain of $2,250 is recorded on December 31, and an exchange loss of $1,000 is recorded on February 1. Even though these large fluctuations do not affect the net exchange gain of $1,250 over the whole transaction, the effect on each year's income statements may be important.

Restatement of Foreign Subsidiary Financial Statements[3]

OBJECTIVE 2
Describe the restatement of a foreign subsidiary's financial statements in U.S. dollars

Growing companies often expand by setting up or buying foreign subsidiaries. If a foreign subsidiary is more than 50 percent owned and if the parent company exercises control, then the foreign subsidiary should be included in the consolidated financial statements. The consolidation procedure is the same as that for domestic subsidiaries, except that the statements of the foreign subsidiary must be restated in the reporting currency before consolidation takes place. The **reporting currency** is the currency in which the consolidated financial statements are presented. Clearly, it makes no sense to combine the assets of a Mexican subsidiary stated in pesos with the assets of the U.S. parent company stated in dollars. Most U.S. companies present their financial statements in U.S. dollars, so the following discussion assumes that the U.S. dollar is the reporting currency.

Restatement is the stating of one currency in terms of another. The method of restatement depends on the foreign subsidiary's functional

3. This section is based on the requirements of *Statement of Financial Accounting Standards No. 52,* "Foreign Currency Translation" (Stamford, Conn.: Financial Accounting Standards Board, 1981).

currency. The **functional currency** is the currency of the place where the subsidiary carries on most of its business. Generally, it is the currency in which a company earns and spends its cash. The functional currency to be used depends on the kind of foreign operation in which the subsidiary takes part. There are two broad types of foreign operation. Type I includes those that are fairly self-contained and integrated within a certain country or economy. Type II includes those that are mainly a direct and integral part or extension of the parent company's operations. As a general rule, Type I subsidiaries use the currency of the country in which they are located, while Type II subsidiaries use the currency of the parent company. If the parent company is a U.S. company, the functional currency of a Type I subsidiary will be the currency of the country where the subsidiary carries on its business, and the functional currency of a Type II subsidiary will be the U.S. dollar. *Statement No. 52* makes an exception when a Type I subsidiary operates in a country such as Brazil or Argentina, where there is hyperinflation (as a rule of thumb, more than 100 percent cumulative inflation over three years). In such a case, the subsidiary is treated as a Type II subsidiary, with the functional currency being the U.S. dollar.

The Search for Comparability of International Accounting Standards

OBJECTIVE 3
Describe progress toward international accounting standards

International investors like to compare the financial position and results of operations of companies from different countries. At present, however, few standards of accounting are recognized worldwide. A number of major problems stand in the way of setting international standards. One is that accountants and users of accounting have not been able to agree on the goals of financial statements. Some other problems are differences in the way in which the accounting profession has developed in various countries, differences in the laws regulating companies, and differences in government and other requirements. Further difficulties are the failure to deal with differences among countries in the basic economic factors affecting financial reporting, inconsistencies in practices recommended by the accounting profession in different countries, and the influence of tax laws on financial reporting.[4] In the last area, for example, a survey for a major accounting firm found widely differing requirements. In nine countries, strict adherence to tax accounting was required. In eleven countries, adherence to tax accounting was required in some areas. In four countries (including the United States), adherence to tax practice was mostly forbidden.[5]

Some efforts have been made to reach greater international understanding and uniformity of accounting practice. The Accountants International Study Group, formed in 1966 and consisting of the AICPA and

4. *Accounting Standards for Business Enterprises Throughout the World* (Chicago: Arthur Andersen, 1974), pp. 2–3.
5. *Accounting Principles and Reporting Practices: A Survey in 38 Countries* (New York: Price Waterhouse International, 1973), sec. 233.

similar bodies in Canada, England and Wales, Ireland, and Scotland, has issued reports that survey and compare accounting practices in the member countries. Probably the best hope for finding areas of agreement among all the different countries are the International Accounting Standards Committee (IASC) and the International Federation of Accountants (IFAC). The IASC was formed in 1973 as a result of an agreement by accountancy bodies in Australia, Canada, France, Germany, Japan, Mexico, the Netherlands, the United Kingdom and Ireland, and the United States. More than one hundred professional accountancy bodies from over seventy countries now support the IASC.

The role of the IASC is to contribute to the development and adoption of accounting principles that are relevant, balanced, and comparable throughout the world by formulating and publicizing accounting standards and encouraging their observance in the presentation of financial statements.[6] The standards issued by the IASC are generally followed by large multinational companies that are clients of international accounting firms. The IASC has been especially helpful to companies in developing economies that do not have the financial history or resources to develop accounting standards. The IASC is currently engaged in a major project to enhance the comparability of financial statements worldwide by reducing the number of acceptable accounting methods in twelve areas, including inventory and depreciation accounting and accounting for investments and business combinations.

The IFAC, which was formed in 1977 and also consists of most of the world's accountancy organizations, fully supports the work of the IASC and recognizes the IASC as the sole body having responsibility and authority to issue pronouncements on international accounting standards. The IFAC's objective is to develop international guidelines for auditing, ethics, education, and management accounting. Every five years an International Congress is held to judge the progress in achieving these objectives. In Europe, attempts are also being made to harmonize accounting standards. The European Economic Community has issued a directive (4th) requiring certain minimum and uniform reporting and disclosure standards for financial statements. Other directives deal with uniform rules for preparing consolidated financial statements (7th) and qualifications of auditors (8th). At present, the European Economic Community is paying considerable attention to the comparability of financial reporting as the organization moves toward the goal of a single European market in 1992.[7]

The road to international harmony is a difficult one. However, there is reason for optimism because an increasing number of countries are recognizing the appropriateness of international accounting standards in international trade and commerce.

6. "International Accounting Standards Committee Objectives and Procedures," *Professional Standards* (New York: American Institute of Certified Public Accountants, 1988) Volume B, Section 9000, par. 24–27.
7. "Comparability of Financial Statements," *Exposure Draft No. 32* (New York: International Federation of Accountants, 1989).

The Nature of Inflation

Although inflation-adjusted financial statements are not required, future accountants, managers, and users of financial statements should understand the significant effects that changing prices can have on financial reporting. A knowledge of these effects is important to understanding and interpreting financial statements. In applying the matching rule, accountants attempt to provide a basis for evaluating a company over a period of time. However, the steady and sometimes high inflation that has been occurring in this country and others for more than a generation is distorting financial statements prepared under traditional accounting methods. One of the most difficult challenges to the accounting profession is to find better ways of dealing with this chronic problem. It is an especially difficult problem because, to deal effectively with inflation, accountants must re-examine several basic ideas in accounting theory. The most important of these ideas are the concept of historical cost and the assumption of a stable measuring unit. To understand how these principles are affected by inflation, it is first necessary to examine the nature of inflation.

In a dynamic economy, the price of an electronic calculator may drop 50 percent while at the same time the price of an automobile increases 20 percent. Each of these price changes relates to inflation, but to the layperson the relationship may be confusing. Part of the confusion arises from the fact that two types of price changes are involved. First, there are changes in **specific price levels**—the price changes of very closely related groups of items or services, such as the calculator or automobile mentioned above. Second, there are changes in **general price levels**—the price changes of a broad group, or basket, of goods and services. Changes in specific price levels, which may vary widely, contribute to the overall price change reflected in the general price level. **Inflation**, in the technical sense, refers to an upward change in the general price level.

When the general price level increases, it takes more dollars to buy the same basket of goods than it did before. As a result, the dollar's **purchasing power**—its ability at a point in time to purchase goods or services—has gone down. In the opposite case of **deflation**, when a decrease occurs in the general price level, the purchasing power of the dollar increases because fewer dollars are needed to purchase the same goods and services than before. In other words, as the general price level changes, the amount of real goods and services that a single dollar can purchase also changes. Therefore, in terms of real goods and services, the dollar is an unstable measuring unit. By analogy, imagine the difficulty of expressing the distance between two cities if the number of feet in a mile was continually changing. In periods when there is little change in the general price level, the unstable dollar does not have much effect on financial statements. In periods of great change, however, the dollars quoted in financial statements soon become unrealistic measures of the items they are supposed to represent.

Price Indexes

To see how specific price changes contribute to general price changes, we will examine how a price index is constructed. A **price index** is a series of numbers, one for each period, representing the average price of a group of goods and services relative to the average price of the same group of goods and services at a beginning date. Consider the figures in Table 21-3, in which the price index for a typical basket of groceries is computed. During the year, the specific price changes of individual items ranged from a decrease of 30.2 percent in the price of sugar to an increase of 46.5 percent in the price of hamburger. Overall, the price index of the basket increased from 100 at the beginning point to 107 at the end of the first year, or 7 percent.

One must be careful in interpreting the change in an index number from one year to the next, however. For example, assume that the price index in Table 21-3 increased to 114 by the end of the next year. It would be incorrect to say that prices increased by 7 percent, because on the basis of last year's starting point of 107 the actual percentage change was less. The percentage change from the first year to the second year was 6.54 percent, calculated as follows:

$$\frac{\text{Change in index}}{\text{Previous year's index}} = \frac{114 - 107}{107} = \frac{7}{107} = 6.54 \text{ percent}$$

Table 21-3. Construction of a Price Index

Item	January 1	December 31	Percentage Change in Market Price of Individual Items
Hamburger (pound)	$1.29	$1.89	+46.5
Bread (pound loaf)	.99	1.09	+10.1
Milk (gallon)	2.20	1.95	−11.4
Lettuce (head)	.89	1.22	+37.1
Sugar (5 pounds)	1.99	1.39	−30.2
Soap (bar)	.55	.67	+21.8
Tissue (box)	.76	1.06	+39.5
	$8.67	$9.27	
Price Index (January = 100)	100	107 ($9.27 ÷ $8.67)	

Source: Reprinted by permission of *The Wall Street Journal,* © Dow Jones & Company, Inc., 1988. All Rights Reserved Worldwide.

General Price Indexes

Agencies of the U.S. government publish several general price indexes. The most widely known general price index is the Consumer Price Index for All Urban Consumers (CPI-U), published by the Bureau of Labor Statistics of the Department of Labor in *Monthly Labor Review*. The Financial Accounting Standards Board advises the use of this index when adjusting financial statements for changes in the general price level because it is readily available, is issued on a monthly basis, and is not revised after its initial publication. Also, it tends to produce a result comparable to other general price indexes.[8]

A partial listing from the CPI-U with 1967 as a base year is reproduced in Table 21-4. Note that the purchasing power of the dollar as measured by this index was about one-fourth in 1988 what it was in 1960—that is, the index almost quadrupled (88.7 to 350.4). This statistic means that it took almost four times as many dollars to buy the same good or service in 1988 as it did in 1960. For example, assume that it cost $100,000 to buy a building in 1960. A payment of $395,039 would be required in 1988 to equal the payment of $100,000 in 1960. This computation is made as follows:

$$\frac{\text{Index of year to which dollars are being converted}}{\text{Index of year from which dollars are being converted}} \times \text{dollar amount} = \text{restated amount}$$

$$\frac{1988 \text{ index}}{1960 \text{ index}} \times \text{cost of building} = \text{restated cost of building}$$

$$\frac{350.4}{88.7} \times \$100,000 = \$395,039 \text{ (rounded to nearest dollar)}$$

Reporting the Effects of Price Changes

There are two principal methods of accounting for the effects of changing prices on financial statements. One is to restate historical-cost financial statements for changes in the general price level (constant dollar accounting). The other is to develop financial statements based on changes in specific price levels (current value accounting). Descriptions of these two approaches, along with the pros and cons of each, follow.

Constant Dollar Accounting

Constant dollar accounting involves the restatement of historical cost statements for general price level changes. The objective is to state all amounts in dollars of uniform general purchasing power. As a result,

---

8. *Statement of Financial Accounting Standards No. 33*, "Financial Reporting and Changing Prices" (Stamford, Conn.: Financial Accounting Standards Board, 1979), par. 39.

Table 21-4. Consumer Price Index for All Urban Consumers			
Year	Index (1967 = 100)	Year	Index (1967 = 100)
1960	88.7	1981	272.5
1967	100.0	1982	289.6
1970	116.3	1983	298.4
1975	161.2	1984	311.0
1976	170.5	1985	322.1
1977	181.5	1986	328.4
1978	195.4	1987	340.4
1979	217.4	1988	350.4
1980	246.8		

Source: Bureau of Labor Statistics.

OBJECTIVE 5
Using constant dollar accounting, compute purchasing power gains and losses

financial statements are based on a uniform, or constant, monetary measuring unit as of the balance sheet date.

The general approach is to convert the number of dollars received or spent at various price levels (corresponding to various balance sheet dates) to an equivalent number of dollars at the price level on the latest balance sheet date. Or the company may prefer to use the average price level during the year. For instance, according to Table 21-4, the price of a building costing $100,000 in 1960 would be restated at various dates as follows:

Date	1960 Cost	Index	Conversion Factor	Restated Cost
1960	$100,000	88.7	88.7/88.7	$100,000
1970	$100,000	116.3	116.3/88.7	$131,116
1980	$100,000	246.8	246.8/88.7	$278,241
1988	$100,000	350.4	350.4/88.7	$395,039

When more than one asset is involved, the denominator of the conversion factor for each asset is the index of the year in which the asset was purchased. For example, assume that the business that owns the building that cost $100,000 in 1960 has another building that cost $200,000 in 1975. The costs of these two buildings can be restated in terms of common 1988 dollars as follows:

Item	Historical Cost	Conversions (from Table 21-4)	Restatement in Terms of 1988 Dollars
1960 building	$100,000	350.4/88.7	$395,039
1975 building	200,000	350.4/161.2	434,739
Totals	$300,000		$829,778

Note two important points about this restatement. First, restatement for general price changes is not a departure from historical cost, but from the accountant's assumption of a stable measuring unit. In this case, the $829,778 is based on an adjustment of historical cost figures totaling $300,000 to a common or constant 1988 measuring unit. Second, the $829,778 is not meant to be a contemporary or market value of the buildings. During the years in question (1960–1988), the specific price level changes and market prices for buildings of the kind used by this company may have differed radically from the general price levels. In summary, general price level restatement, or constant dollar accounting, focuses on changes in the purchasing power of the monetary unit, not on changes in the value of the asset.

It is also important to distinguish monetary from nonmonetary items because changes in the general price level affect them differently. Since monetary items, such as cash, receivables, and payables, represent ownership of cash, claims to receive it, or obligations to pay cash, their current balances are already stated in terms of current dollars. Balances for prior periods need to be restated in current equivalent dollars. **Purchasing power gains and losses** occur as a result of holding these items during periods of inflation or deflation because the amounts that must be paid or received are fixed. For instance, one who holds cash in a period of inflation will find that the cash purchases fewer goods and services as time passes. Debtors, on the other hand, will be able to retire debts with dollars that are worth less and less in terms of goods and services, while creditors will receive less for their loans. Simply stated, in times of inflation, owning monetary assets produces a loss in purchasing power, and owing liabilities produces a gain in purchasing power. These results are reversed during times of deflation.

In contrast, holding nonmonetary items, including inventories, investments, plant assets, intangibles, and owners' equity during inflationary or deflationary periods does *not* result in purchasing power gains and losses. Because these items are not tied physically or contractually to a certain dollar amount, they reflect the particular price level in effect when a transaction involving them takes place. Thus the business does not gain or lose as a result of inflation or deflation while holding or completing transactions involving nonmonetary items.

Purchasing Power Gains and Losses. Consider the following data for Town Theater, a simple company with only two monetary items.

	Dec. 31, 19x1	Dec. 31, 19x2	For the Year 19x2
Monetary items			
Cash	$10,000	$20,000	
Notes payable	10,000	10,000	
Ticket receipts			$300,000
Payments for expenses			290,000
General price index	120	144	132 (average)

The purchasing power gain or loss for Town Theater can be calculated in three steps, as shown in Exhibit 21-1. First, the purchasing power loss from holding monetary assets (cash) is calculated by restating the beginning cash balances. The December 31, 19x1 price index was 120 and the December 31, 19x2 price index was 144. Therefore, the cash balance is restated in December 31, 19x2 dollars as follows: $10,000 × 144/120 = $12,000.

Next, each increase or decrease in cash is adjusted using the price index existing at the time of the change. Since it is assumed that cash receipts and payments are uniform over time, the average price level (132) for the year 19x2 is used for the denominator of the conversion factor. Thus ticket receipts and payments for expenses are restated as shown in the exhibit. The restated ending balance is then calculated by adding the restated figures. Because the actual ending balance is already in current dollars and does not need restatement, it is deducted from the restated ending balance to obtain the purchasing power loss from holding monetary assets ($22,909 − $20,000 = $2,909).

Exhibit 21-1. Calculation of Purchasing Power Gain or Loss

Town Theater
Calculation of Purchasing Power Gain or Loss
For the Year Ended December 31, 19x2

	Recorded Amount	Conversion Factor	Restated Amount	Gain (or Loss)
Cash				
Beginning balance	$ 10,000	144/120	$ 12,000	
Ticket receipts	300,000	144/132	327,273	
Payments for expenses	(290,000)	144/132	(316,364)	
Ending balance, restated	—		$ 22,909	
Ending balance, actual	$ 20,000		(20,000)	
Purchasing power loss				$(2,909)
Notes payable				
Beginning balance	$ 10,000	144/120	$ 12,000	
Ending balance, actual	$ 10,000		(10,000)	
Purchasing power gain				2,000
Net purchasing power loss				$ (909)

The second step is to calculate the purchasing power gain from owing notes payable of $10,000 for the full year. The beginning balance is adjusted for the change in price level ($10,000 × 144/120 = $12,000). From this amount the actual ending balance of $10,000 is deducted to obtain the purchasing power gain of $2,000 from the monetary liability.

The third step is to calculate the net purchasing power gain or loss by determining the difference between the figures in the first two steps. In this case, Town Theater had a net purchasing power loss of $909.

OBJECTIVE 6
Restate a balance sheet and an income statement for changes in the general price level

Balance Sheet Restatement. To continue the case of the Town Theater, assume that the nonmonetary balance sheet items on December 31, 19x2 are as follows:

Assets		
Theater	$300,000	
Less Accumulated Depreciation	90,000	$210,000
Stockholders' Equity		
Common Stock	$150,000	
Retained Earnings	70,000	$220,000

Assume also that the theater was purchased and the capital stock issued at the same time, when the general price index was 108.

The restated balance sheet is presented in Exhibit 21-2. As can be seen, some accounts require restatement and some do not. The monetary accounts (cash and notes payable) do not require restatement because they represent a fixed number of dollars regardless of changes in

Exhibit 21-2. Restatement of Balance Sheet

Town Theater
Restatement of Balance Sheet
December 31, 19x2

	Recorded Amount	Conversion Factor	Restated Amount
Cash	$ 20,000	No restatment	$ 20,000
Theater	300,000	144/108	400,000
Accumulated Depreciation	(90,000)	144/108	(120,000)
	$230,000		$ 300,000
Notes Payable	$ 10,000	No restatement	$ 10,000
Common Stock	150,000	144/108	200,000
Retained Earnings	70,000	(See text)	90,000
	$230,000		$ 300,000

the general price level. That is the reason they are subject to purchasing power gains and losses, as has been demonstrated. In other words, $10,000 in cash will always be worth $10,000, tomorrow or next year, regardless of changes in the general price level. The other accounts on the balance sheet are nonmonetary items that *are* subject to changes in value as time passes. The $300,000 theater may or may not be worth $300,000 tomorrow or next year. Its value responds to changes in the general price level. So, in order to place the theater and other nonmonetary items on a constant dollar basis, their value must be restated for the change in general price level.

The nonmonetary items are restated by multiplying the dollar amount by the ratio of the current general price index (144) to the general price index when the transaction took place (108). The retained earnings balance is determined by inserting the amount necessary to make the balance sheet balance, as follows:

Total assets, adjusted		$300,000
Less: Notes Payable	$ 10,000	
Common Stock	200,000	210,000
Retained Earnings		$ 90,000

This retained earnings balance results from balance sheet and income statement effects as well as the purchasing power loss of $909 calculated in the section above. The details of these effects will be studied in more advanced courses.

Income Statement Restatement. All items on the income statement are nonmonetary and must be restated to year-end amounts. Most revenues and expenses are assumed to have occurred evenly throughout the year, and are thus restated to year-end amounts by using the end-of-year price index as the numerator and the average price index as the denominator. An exception is depreciation expense, which is treated the same way as in the balance sheet.

Exhibit 21-3 shows the restatement of the income statement for Town Theater. Note that although a small net income of $280 was earned under conventional accounting methods, a loss of $2,051 resulted when the figures were adjusted to constant dollars. The reason for the decrease in net income was the large increase in depreciation expense of $3,240 ($12,960 – $9,720), a result of the increase in the price index from 108 to 144 since the theater was purchased. Also observe that the purchasing power loss of $909 that was calculated in Exhibit 21-1 is placed at the bottom of the statement. The combined loss was $2,960.

Arguments For and Against Restatement. The practice of restating financial statements for changes in the general price level is controversial. Those who favor restated financial statements argue, first, that the yearly rate of inflation in the United States is often so high that the assumption of a stable measuring unit no longer holds, and unadjusted

Exhibit 21-3. Restatement of Income Statement

Town Theater
Restatement of Income Statement
For the Year Ended December 31, 19x2

	Recorded Amount	Conversion Factor	Restated Amount
Sales	$300,000	144/132	$327,273
Operating Expenses			
Expenses Other Than Depreciation	$290,000	144/132	$316,364
Depreciation Expense	9,720	144/108	12,960
Total Operating Expenses	$299,720		$329,324
Net Income (loss)	$ 280		$ (2,051)
Net Purchasing Power Gain (loss) (From Exhibit 21-1)			(909)
Net Income After Purchasing Power Gain (loss)			$ (2,960)

financial statements are unrealistic. A second argument is that because the restatement procedure is based on traditional historical cost financial statements, it is as objective, verifiable, and auditable as the traditional statement. Third, adjusted amounts, including purchasing power gains and losses, are helpful to users.

Critics of statements adjusted for price level argue, first of all, that two sets of financial statements would not be understood by most users. Second, they claim that the measures of general price level are too broad to be meaningfully applied to individual companies. A third argument is that changes in the general price level may not agree with real value changes. Finally, critics say that financial analysts and bankers do not consider the information provided by such statements useful.

Current Value Accounting

OBJECTIVE 7
Define current value accounting, *and explain its two principal approaches*

In restating financial statements for changes in general purchasing power, we relaxed the stable measuring unit assumption but did not abandon historical cost measurement. The 1975 building cost that was adjusted from $200,000 to $434,739 because of a change in the general price level from 161.2 to 350.4 may have a current market value of $50,000 or $300,000. The restated figure is not a measure of its current value. In fact, one of the strongest arguments against restatement is that the resulting financial statements do not reflect specific price changes that have affected a particular company.

For example, a lumber company, whose assets consist mostly of lumber inventory, may be much more concerned with changes in the price of lumber than with changes in the general price level. Such a company would have faced the following indexes in 1981 and 1982.[9]

Year	Consumer Price Index— Urban (1967 = 100)	Lumber Index (1967 = 100)
1981	272.5	119
1982	289.6	113

If this company had on the average $1,000,000, or three-fourths of its nonmonetary assets, invested in inventory in 1981 and 1982, one could make the following restatements:

Index	Restatement Computation	Restated Amount	Change
General	289.6/272.5 × $1,000,000	$1,062,752	$ 62,752
Specific	113/119 × $1,000,000	949,580	(50,420)
Difference due to method used			$113,172

It would be hard to convince the manager of this lumber company that the company's financial statements should show an increase of $62,752 in lumber inventory when in fact its market value dropped by $50,420.

A method of accounting that would recognize the effects of such specific price changes in financial statements is called **current value accounting**. Current value accounting represents a movement away from historical cost accounting. Its advocates call for a three-step changeover to current value statements, as follows:

Step 1. Current values of inventories, cost of goods sold, plant assets, and depreciation disclosed in footnotes

Step 2. Historical cost statements supplemented by statements expressed in current values

Step 3. Presentation of current value statements only

A major problem in current value reporting is how to measure current value. There are two main schools of thought. One school favors the use of **net realizable value**. Net realizable value is an exit value in that it represents what the company could sell its assets for. It is recommended because it is a measure of the company's ability to adapt to the marketplace. Another school of thought recommends **replacement cost**. Replacement cost is an entry value because it represents the cost of buying (or replacing), in the normal course of business, new assets of about equal operating or productive capacity. This method is favored because it relates to the need to maintain a company's productive capacity. This discussion, which must be brief, will center on replacement cost ac-

9. *Source: Statistical Abstract of the United States, 1985.*

counting because of the a tention drawn to it by the SEC's requirement in 1976 for the reporting of replacement costs[10] and its later repeal of the rule when the FASB issued *Statement No. 33.*

Arguments For Replacement Cost Disclosure. A major argument for replacement cost disclosure is that it is more realistic than historical cost statements. Specific price changes are a fact of life. If they are reflected in the financial statements, they make the information more useful. A second major argument for replacement cost is that the economy as a whole is hindered by the unrealistic depreciation rates used in historical costing. The valuation of plant assets in most cases would rise sharply if replacement costs were used, as would depreciation. These higher costs, more in line with replacing current productive capacity, offer more realistic earnings figures on which to base investment and dividend policies.

Arguments Against Replacement Cost Disclosure. On the other side of the question, critics emphasize that there are no accepted ways of measuring replacement costs. Replacement costs are not based on objective, verifiable transactions that can be audited. For this reason, the resulting information is less helpful than historical costs.

Critics also say that through wise use of current accounting techniques, income measures close to those obtained under replacement cost accounting can be found in historical cost statements. For example, by using LIFO inventory, a company in effect charges the most current inventory purchases against income. This method produces a gross margin close to that obtained by using replacement costs for inventory. Also, by using accelerated depreciation methods, a company writes off its plant assets earlier which may help offset rises in replacement costs.

The FASB Position

OBJECTIVE 8
Describe the FASB's approach to accounting for changing prices

Over the years, the Financial Accounting Standards Board has changed its stand on the question of constant dollar versus current value accounting. In 1974, it followed an earlier Accounting Principles Board recommendation that all companies put in their annual reports supplemental financial statements expressed in units of general purchasing power.[11] This proposal was not acted upon, partly because it was upstaged by the 1976 SEC release on replacement cost disclosure. By 1979, the FASB had taken a different stand in *Statement No. 33,* calling for certain large publicly held companies (those with inventories and property, plant, and equipment of more than $125 million, or total assets

10. *Accounting Series Release No. 190* (Washington: Securities and Exchange Commission, 1976).
11. *Proposed Statement of Financial Accounting Standards, Exposure Draft,* "Financial Reporting in Units of General Purchasing Power" (Stamford, Conn.: Financial Accounting Standards Board, 1974); see also Accounting Principles Board, *Statement No. 3,* "Financial Statements Restated for General Price Level Changes" (New York: American Institute of Certified Public Accountants, 1969).

after deducting accumulated depreciation of more than $1 billion) to report supplemental information on both a constant dollar and a current value basis. The current value basis used by the FASB is the lower of current cost or net realizable value at the balance sheet date. By current cost, the FASB means the lowest current buying price or production cost of an asset of the same age and in the same condition as the asset owned. So the FASB's view of current value brought together the two ideas of net realizable value and replacement cost.

The FASB recognized when it issued *Statement No. 33* that many problems in measuring the effect of changing prices remained to be solved. It therefore conducted a full review of the effects of *Statement No. 33* in 1983 and 1984. As a result of this review, the FASB issued *Statement No. 82*, which simplified the requirements for reporting the effects of changing prices by allowing companies to report supplementary information based on current cost only. Disclosure based on constant dollar accounting was required only for certain specialized assets when current cost data were not provided. In making this change the FASB followed the rationale "that reporting effects of changing prices using two different methods may detract from the usefulness of the information and that the historical cost/constant dollar information is less useful than the current cost/constant purchasing power information."[12] Late in 1986 the FASB removed the requirement to report the effects of changing prices by making disclosure voluntary. The FASB now encourages the disclosure of the effects of changing prices.[13] According to the 1987 *Accounting Trends and Techniques*, 98 of 600 large companies (16.3 percent) voluntarily disclosed or commented on the effects of changing prices in their annual reports in 1986.

Chapter Review

Review of Learning Objectives

1. **Define *exchange rate* and record transactions that are affected by changes in foreign exchange rates.**
   An *exchange rate* is the value of one currency stated in terms of another. A domestic company may make sales or purchases abroad in either its own country's currency or the foreign currency. If a transaction (sale or purchase) and its resolution (receipt or payment) are made in the domestic

---

12. *Statement of Financial Accounting Standards No. 82*, "Financial Reporting and Changing Prices: Elimination of Certain Disclosures" (Stamford, Conn.: Financial Accounting Standards Board, November 1984), par. 8. The statement is effective for fiscal years ending on or after December 15, 1984.
13. *Statement of Financial Accounting Standards No. 89*, "Changing Prices: Reporting Their Effects in the Financial Statements" (Stamford, Conn.: Financial Accounting Standards Board, 1986), par. 3.

currency, no accounting problem arises. However, if the transaction and its resolution are made in a foreign currency and the exchange rate changes between the time of the transaction and its resolution, an exchange gain or loss will occur and should be recorded.

2. **Describe the restatement of a foreign subsidiary's financial statements in U.S. dollars.**

   Foreign financial statements are converted to U.S. dollars by multiplying the appropriate exchange rates by the amounts in the foreign financial statements. In general, the rates that apply depend on whether the subsidiary is separate and self-contained (Type I) or an integral part of the parent company (Type II).

3. **Describe progress toward international accounting standards.**

   There has been some progress toward establishing international accounting standards, especially through the efforts of the International Accounting Standards Committee and the International Federation of Accountants. However, there still are serious inconsistencies in financial reporting among countries. These inconsistencies make the comparison of financial statements from different countries difficult.

4. **Define** *inflation* **and identify the two principal types of price changes.**

   Although the term *inflation* is commonly used to refer to any type of rise in prices, technically it refers to a general upward movement of prices. There are two principal types of price change that affect financial statements, general price changes and specific price changes. General price changes, or changes in the price of a group of goods or services, result in purchasing power gains or losses. Specific price changes are changes in the prices of individual items or services.

5. **Using constant dollar accounting, compute purchasing power gains and losses.**

   Holding monetary assets during periods of inflation produces purchasing power losses, while holding monetary liabilities during periods of inflation produces purchasing power gains. Thus, during a period of inflation a company will experience a purchasing power loss or gain depending on whether on average over the period it has more monetary assets than monetary liabilities or vice versa. The opposite effects occur during periods of deflation. Gains or losses in purchasing power are computed by multiplying the appropriate price indexes to monetary assets and monetary liabilities.

6. **Restate a balance sheet and an income statement for changes in the general price level.**

   Holding nonmonetary items during periods of inflation or deflation does not result in purchasing power gains or losses, because their value responds to changes in the general price level. Under constant dollar accounting, historical cost statements are therefore restated for general price level changes. Monetary items on the balance sheet do not require restatement, but each nonmonetary item must be adjusted for the change in general price level since the item's origin. Retained earnings are computed as a balancing figure. On the income statement all items except depreciation and amortization are adjusted for the average change in general price level during the year. Depreciation and amortization are adjusted using the same rate as was used to adjust related assets on the balance sheet. Any purchasing power gain or loss (see Learning Objective 5) appears on the income statement.

7. Define *current value accounting*, and explain its two principal approaches.
   Current value accounting adjusts financial statements for specific price level changes. There are various approaches to measuring these changes. Two widely accepted methods are used. The first method is net realizable value, which bases current value on what an asset would sell for. The second method is replacement cost, which bases current value on what it would cost to buy or bring to current position new assets of equal operating or productive capacity.

8. Describe the FASB's approach to accounting for changing prices.
   Although the FASB believes that historical cost financial statements should be a company's primary financial statements, after 1978, it required certain large companies to provide supplemental information, both for the current year and for a five-year period, on both a constant dollar and a current value basis. Current value is defined by the FASB as the lower of current cost or net realizable value. After a period of experimentation in reporting the effects of changing prices, the FASB decided in 1984 that companies that report on a current cost basis should not have to report on a constant dollar basis as well. In 1986, the FASB decided to make current value disclosures voluntary.

Review of Concepts and Terminology

The following concepts and terms were introduced in this chapter:

(L.O. 5) **Constant dollar accounting:**   The restatement of historical cost statements for general price level changes.

(L.O. 7) **Current value accounting:**   The recognition of the effects of specific price changes in financial statements.

(L.O. 4) **Deflation:**   A downward change in the general price level.

(L.O. 1) **Exchange gains or losses:**   Changes due to exchange rate fluctuations that are reported on the consolidated income statement.

(L.O. 1) **Exchange rate:**   The value of one currency in terms of another.

(L.O. 2) **Functional currency:**   The currency of the place where a subsidiary carries on most of its business.

(L.O. 4) **General price levels:**   The price changes of a broad group of goods and services.

(L.O. 4) **Inflation:**   An upward change in the general price level.

(L.O. 1) **Multinational (transnational) corporation:**   A company that operates in more than one country.

(L.O. 7) **Net realizable value:**   The amount for which an asset can be sold.

(L.O. 4) **Price index:**   A series of numbers, one for each period, representing an average price of a group of goods and services relative to the average price of the same group of goods and services at a beginning date.

(L.O. 4)   **Purchasing power:**   The dollar's ability at a point in time to purchase goods or services.

(L.O. 5)   **Purchasing power gains and losses:**   Gains and losses that occur as a result of holding net monetary assets (monetary assets – monetary liabilities) during periods of inflation or deflation.

(L.O. 7)   **Replacement cost:**   The cost of buying (or replacing), in the normal course of business, new assets of about equal operating or productive capacity.

(L.O. 2)   **Reporting currency:**   The currency in which consolidated financial statements are presented.

(L.O. 2)   **Restatement:**   The stating of one currency in terms of another.

(L.O. 4)   **Specific price levels:**   The price changes of very closely related groups of items or services.

Self-Test

Test your knowledge of the chapter by choosing the best answer for each item below.

1. A U. S. company makes a purchase in U. S. dollars on credit from a company in England and pays in U. S. dollars during a time when the value of the pound rises from $1.70 to $1.75. Which of the following situations is true for the U. S. company?
   a. Neither an exchange gain nor an exchange loss has occurred.
   b. An exchange gain has occurred.
   c. An exchange loss has occurred.
   d. Either an exchange gain or an exchange loss has occurred.   *(L.O. 1)*

2. A U. S. company makes a purchase on credit from a company in England. It is billed in pounds but pays in U. S. dollars at a time when the exchange rate rises from $1.70 to $1.75. Which of the following situations is true for the U. S. company?
   a. Neither an exchange gain nor an exchange loss has occurred.
   b. An exchange gain has occurred.
   c. An exchange loss has occurred.
   d. None of the above.   *(L.O. 1)*

3. A U. S. company makes a sale on credit in Japanese yen when the exchange rate is $.0078 and collects payment in Japanese yen when the exchange rate is $.0037. Which of the following situations is true for the U. S. company?
   a. Neither an exchange gain nor an exchange loss has occurred.
   b. An exchange gain has occurred.
   c. An exchange loss has occurred.
   d. None of the above.   *(L.O. 1)*

4. The currency of the place where a subsidiary carries on most of its business is called the
   a. functional currency.   c. subsidiary currency.
   b. home currency.   d. reporting currency.   *(L.O. 2)*

5. Which of the following is true with regard to adherence to uniform accounting standards by companies of different nations?
   a. Tax laws have usually not hindered the development of universally acceptable accounting standards.
   b. Efforts are being made by several international accounting organizations to identify areas of agreement in accounting standards.
   c. No progress has been made toward harmonizing international accounting standards.
   d. Most countries follow the pronouncements of the FASB.   *(L.O. 3)*

6. A change in the purchasing power of the dollar is most closely associated with
   a. changes in net realizable value.   c. general price changes.
   b. changes in replacement cost.   d. specific price changes.   *(L.O. 4)*

7. The holding of which of the following assets during a period of inflation will result in a purchasing power loss?
   a. Intangible assets   c. Inventory
   b. Plant assets   d. Cash   *(L.O. 5)*

8. Which of the following is a monetary item?
   a. Inventory   c. Franchise
   b. Equipment   d. Accounts receivable   *(L.O. 6)*

9. Replacement cost accounting is a type of
   a. net realizable value accounting.
   b. current value accounting.
   c. accounting for changes in the general price level.
   d. constant dollar accounting.   *(L.O. 7)*

10. Which of the following is true?
    a. The FASB requires supplementary reporting of price-level-adjusted statements.
    b. The FASB requires supplementary reporting of current value statements.
    c. The FASB requires supplementary reporting of either price-level-adjusted statements or current value statements.
    d. The FASB requires supplementary reporting of neither price-level-adjusted statements nor current value statements.   *(L.O. 8)*

Answers to Self-Test are at the end of this chapter.

Review Problem
Calculation of Purchasing Power Gains
and Losses and Exchange Gains and Losses

(L.O. 1, 5)   The Inflation Import Company is a conservatively operated company. The owner believes cash is the best asset to have, and the only good debt is the payables that result from delaying payment to suppliers as long as possible. The company's business is the importing of textiles from Hong Kong for sale through wholesalers in the United States. By having the textiles sent directly to the wholesalers, the company avoids carrying inventory. In fact, its modest facilities are a rented office in Manhattan.

The Inflation Import Company began the month with cash on hand of $100,000 and stockholders' equity of $100,000. During the month, the company engaged in only one transaction, but it was a large one. On March 1, the company purchased textiles from a Hong Kong company for 2 million Hong Kong dollars ($240,000) and immediately sold them to a wholesaler for $300,000. The first transaction was to be paid in Hong Kong dollars and the second in U.S. dollars. Both transactions were due to be paid on April 1 and were still owed on March 31.

March was a volatile month regarding inflation and the value of the dollar. Data regarding the consumer price index and the Hong Kong dollar are:

	CPI	Hong Kong Dollar
March 1	200	$0.12
March 31	210	$0.14

Required

1. Determine the effects of Inflation Import Company's policies by:
   a. calculating the purchasing power gain or loss for the month of March.
   b. calculating the exchange gain or loss for the month of March.
2. What recommendations would you make to Inflation Import Company to improve its performance?

Answer to Review Problem

1. a. Purchasing power gain or loss calculated

Cash			
March 1	$100,000 × 210/200	$105,000	
March 31		100,000	
Purchasing power loss			$ (5,000)
Accounts Receivable			
March 1	$300,000 × 210/200	$315,000	
March 31		300,000	
Purchasing power loss			(15,000)
Accounts Payable			
March 1	$240,000 × 210/200	$252,000	
March 31		240,000*	
Purchasing power gain			12,000
Net purchasing power gain or (loss)			$ (8,000)

*Before adjustment for exchange gain or loss; see part **1. b.**

1. b. Exchange gain or loss calculated

March 1 Purchases		$240,000
(Hong Kong $2,000,000 × 0.12 = $240,000)		
March 31 Amount owed		
(Hong Kong $2,000,000 × 0.14 = $280,000)		280,000
Exchange Loss		$(40,000)

2. Recommendations made

In an environment of rising price levels and varying exchange rates, the holding of cash and other monetary assets and liabilities, such as accounts receivable and accounts payable, can be disadvantageous. For example, if the cash and other monetary assets exceed monetary liabilities, a purchasing power loss can occur. This situation did exist in the case of Inflation Import Company, which lost $8,000 by holding net monetary assets in a period of inflation. It is usually good practice to wait as long as legally possible to pay for goods on transactions conducted solely in the United States because of the saving on financing costs. However, by waiting as long as possible to pay for the Hong Kong goods, Inflation Import Company exposed itself to an exchange loss. The company lost $40,000 due to the rise in the exchange rate for the Hong Kong dollar, from $0.12 to $0.14. This loss wiped out two-thirds of the profit on the transaction. The exchange loss also more than offset the purchasing power gain of $12,000 (see part **1. a.**) which resulted from the effects of inflation on this monetary liability. To improve performance and reduce the risk of loss from inflation and the declining value of the dollar, Inflation Import Company should:

a. invest its excess cash in nonmonetary assets, such as investments and inventory, whose value will tend to rise with inflation.
b. borrow funds for expansion to offset purchasing power losses with purchasing power gains.
c. attempt to have its purchases denominated in U.S. dollars instead of Hong Kong dollars. In this way, the Hong Kong merchant bears the risk.
d. If strategy **c** is not possible, the bill for the purchases should be paid immediately.

Chapter Assignments

Discussion Questions and Writing Assignments

1. What does it mean to say that the exchange rate of a French franc in terms of the U.S. dollar is .15? If a bottle of French perfume costs 200 francs, how much will it cost in dollars?
2. If an American firm does business with a German firm and all their transactions take place in German marks, which firm may incur an exchange gain or loss, and why?
3. What is the difference between a reporting currency and a functional currency?
4. If you as an investor were trying to evaluate the relative performance of General Motors, Volkswagen, and Toyota Motors from their published financial statements, what problem might you encounter (other than a language problem)?
5. What are some of the obstacles to uniform international accounting standards, and what efforts are being made to overcome them?

6. Why has the assumption of a stable monetary unit been questioned in recent years?

7. Distinguish specific price changes from general price changes.

8. "We love debt," says G. James Williams, vice president—finance (of Dow Chemical). "The $3 billion we have in long-term debt is one of the greatest assets of Dow Chemical Company." For forty years, Williams explained, the company has regarded inflation as a fact of American life, from which springs this corollary: borrow now to repay in cheaper dollars. (Quoted from *Barron's*, October 9, 1978, p. 4.) Why does Dow Chemical feel that it is an asset to be a debtor?

9. In what ways does current value accounting differ from constant dollar accounting?

10. What are the FASB requirements for disclosure of the effects of changing prices?

11. Why do you think the FASB at this point prefers the current cost approach to the constant dollar approach in reporting the effects of changing prices?

Classroom Exercises

Exercise 21-1.
Recording
International
Transactions:
Fluctuating
Exchange Rate
(L.O. 1)

States Corporation purchased a special-purpose machine from Hamburg Corporation on credit for 50,000 DM (marks). At the date of purchase, the exchange rate was $.55 per mark. On the date of the payment, which was made in marks, the value of the mark had increased to $.60.

Prepare journal entries to record the purchase and payment in the States Corporation's accounting records.

Exercise 21-2.
Recording
International
Transactions
(L.O. 1)

U.S. Corporation made a sale on account to U.K. Company on November 15 in the amount of £300,000. Payment was to be made in British pounds on February 15. U.S. Corporation's fiscal year is the same as the calendar year. The British pound was worth $1.70 on November 15, $1.58 on December 31, and $1.78 on February 15.

Prepare journal entries to record the sale, year-end adjustment, and collection on U.S. Corporation's books.

Exercise 21-3.
Construction
of an Index
(L.O. 4)

The following prices reflect the cost per bushel of selected farm commodities at the end of 1987, 1988, and 1989:

	1987	1988	1989
Wheat	$3.66	$3.52	$3.56
Corn	2.50	2.68	3.38
Oats	1.89	1.49	1.69
Soybeans	6.04	5.69	8.19

Construct a price index for farm commodities based on this information (1987 equals 100). What was the percentage increase or decrease in the index from 1987 to 1988? From 1988 to 1989? Would you identify this index as a specific or a general price index?

Exercise 21-4.
Application of
General Price
Index
(L.O. 4)

To achieve its plans for future expansion, Mancilla Corporation has been accumulating contiguous parcels of land as they become available. In 1975 Mancilla purchased the first parcel for $70,000. The second was purchased in 1977 for $80,000, and a third in 1979 for $110,000.

1. If each parcel of land increased in value at the same rate as prices in general, what would be the total value of all the land in 1988? (Use Table 21-4.)
2. At the end of 1988, management determines that it is inadvisable for the company to expand at this location and sells the three parcels of land for a total of $400,000. Has the company made a real gain or loss? Explain your answer.

Exercise 21-5.
Calculation of
Purchasing Power
Gains and Losses
(L.O. 5)

Assume that Company J and Company K both began operation on January 1 with $100,000 in cash. Company J raised the cash by issuing capital stock; Company K, by issuing a two-year note payable. During the year, both companies had cash receipts of $550,000 and cash payments of $440,000. Also during the year, the general price level began at 150, ended at 180, and averaged 165.

Calculate the purchasing power gain or loss for each company.

Exercise 21-6.
Restatement of
Balance Sheet
for General
Price Changes
(L.O. 6)

The Franklin Company's balance sheet, as of December 31, 19xx, appears as follows:

Franklin Company
Balance Sheet
December 31, 19xx

Cash	$ 50,000	Note Payable	$100,000
Building	210,000	Common Stock	250,000
Accumulated Depreciation	(15,000)	Retained Earnings	105,000
Equipment	300,000		
Accumulated Depreciation	(90,000)	Total Liabilities and	
Total Assets	$ 455,000	Stockholders' Equity	$455,000

The following general price level indexes are applicable:

Beginning of year	160	At the time of	
End of year	200	Building purchase	120
Average for year	180	Equipment purchase	150
		Capital stock issue	100

Restate the balance sheet of the Franklin Company for changes in the general price level.

Exercise 21-7.
Restatement of
Income Statement
(L.O. 6)

The 19x9 income statement for Geneva Car Wash is as follows:

Sales		$650,000
Operating Expenses		
Expenses Other Than Depreciation	$380,000	
Depreciation Expense	60,000	
Total Operating Expenses		440,000
Net Income		$210,000

The general price level index averaged 180 during the year and was 198 at year end. The index was 140 at the time the company's plant assets were purchased. An analysis of monetary items on the balance sheet shows a purchasing power loss of $3,800 for the year.

Restate the income statement for changes in the general price level.

Interpreting Accounting Information

Deere & Co.*
(L.O. 6, 7)

Deere & Co. engages in worldwide production and sales of farm and construction equipment. Partial income statements for recent years follow:

	Year Ended October 31		
(In thousands of dollars except per share amounts)	1988	1987	1986
Sales and Other Income			
Net sales	$5,364,810	$4,134,534	$3,516,289
Finance and interest income earned	66,131	96,254	89,300
Foreign exchange gain	532	1,232	
Miscellaneous income	22,933	21,390	19,554
Total	5,454,406	4,253,410	3,625,143
Less			
Cost of goods sold	4,366,640	3,668,563	3,270,670
Research and development expenses	215,916	213,830	224,743
Selling, administrative and general expenses	495,315	487,587	508,208
Interest expense	160,792	185,973	203,769
Foreign exchange loss			6,507
Miscellaneous charges	3,016	3,306	3,939
Total	5,241,679	4,559,259	4,217,836
Income (Loss) of Consolidated Group Before Income Taxes	212,727	(305,849)	(592,693)
Provision (credit) for income taxes	32,953	(112,681)	(283,936)
Income (Loss) of Consolidated Group	$ 179,774	$ (193,168)	$ (308,757)

Required

1. Have changes in foreign exchange rates had a positive or negative effect on Deere & Co. in 1986, 1987, and 1988? Would you consider the effects to be material?
2. Explain the conditions that might have led to the foreign exchange losses on the income statement.

* Excerpts from the 1988 annual report used by permission of Deere & Co. Copyright © 1988.

Problem Set A

Since foreign exchange rates can fluctuate widely, a variety of rates have been used in Problem Sets A and B.

Problem 21A-1.
Recording
International
Transactions
(L.O. 1)

Tsin Import/Export Company, whose year end is December 31, engaged in the following transactions (exchange rates in parentheses):

Oct. 14 Sold goods to a Mexican firm for $20,000; terms n/30 in U.S. dollars (peso = $.0004).

26 Purchased goods from a Japanese firm for $40,000; terms n/20 in yen (yen = $.0040).

Nov. 4 Sold goods to a British firm for $39,000; terms n/30 in pounds (pound = $1.30).

14 Received payment in full for October 14 sale (peso = $.0003).

15 Paid for the goods purchased on October 26 (yen = $.0044).

23 Purchased goods from an Italian firm for $28,000; terms n/10 in U.S. dollars (lira = $.0008).

30 Purchased goods from a Japanese firm for $35,200; terms n/60 in yen (yen = $.0044).

Dec. 2 Paid for the goods purchased on November 23 (lira = $.0007).

3 Received payment in full for goods sold on November 4 (pound = $1.20).

8 Sold goods to a French firm for $66,000; terms n/30 in francs (franc = $.11).

17 Purchased goods from a Mexican firm for $37,000; terms n/30 in U.S. dollars (peso = $.0004).

18 Sold goods to a German firm for $90,000; terms n/30 in marks (mark = $.30).

31 Made year-end adjusting entries for incomplete foreign exchange transactions (franc = $.09; peso = $.0003; pound = $1.10; mark = $.35; lira = $.0008; yen = $.0050).

Jan. 7 Received payment for goods sold on December 8 (franc = $.10).

16 Paid for goods purchased on December 17 (peso = $.0002).

17 Received payment for goods sold on December 18 (mark = $.40).

28 Paid for goods purchased on November 30 (yen = $.0045).

Required

Prepare general journal entries for these transactions.

Problem 21A-2.
Calculation of
Purchasing Power
Gain or Loss
(L.O. 5)

Kronos Corporation began 19x4 with $200,000 in cash. Cash transactions (including bank loans) for 19x4 and 19x5 were as follows:

	19x5	19x4
Cash Receipts	$ 920,000	$780,000
Cash Disbursements	1,040,000	710,000

Although accounts payable were immaterial in both years, the company did borrow $300,000 from the bank at the beginning of 19x5. That money was still due at the end of 19x5.

The general price levels for 19x4 and 19x5 were as follows:

	19x5	19x4
Beginning of year	240	220
End of year	260	240
Average for year	250	230

Required

1. Compute Kronos Corporation's purchasing power gain or loss for 19x4 and 19x5.
2. Comment on the reasons for the results.

Problem 21A-3.
Calculation of
Purchasing Power
Gain or Loss and
Balance Sheet
Restatement
(L.O. 5, 6)

Carousel, Inc. began on January 1, 19x1 by issuing common stock for the purchase and installation of an antique carousel in a local shopping center. Its balance sheet on December 31, 19x2 follows. The company operates strictly on a cash basis. On January 2, 19x2, the company had a cash balance of $17,000, including the proceeds from the note payable it issued on that date. During the year its cash receipts were $162,500, and its payments for expenses were $149,500. The general price level varied on different days, shown as follows:

January 1, 19x1	100
January 1, 19x2	120
December 31, 19x2	138
Average for 19x2	130

Carousel, Inc.
Balance Sheet
December 31, 19x2

Assets

Cash	$ 30,000
Carousel	260,000
Accumulated Depreciation	(39,000)
Total Assets	$251,000

Liabilities and Stockholders' Equity

Note Payable	$ 10,000
Common Stock	273,000
Retained Earnings	(32,000)
Total Liabilities and Stockholders' Equity	$251,000

Required

1. Compute the purchasing power gain or loss for Carousel, Inc. during 19x2.
2. Prepare a restated balance sheet as of December 31, 19x2.

Problem 21A-4.
Restatement of
Income Statement
(L.O. 6)

The income statement for Carousel, Inc. for the year ended December 31, 19x2 is as follows:

Revenues		$162,500
Operating Expenses		
Wages Expense	$119,500	
Utility Expense	30,000	
Depreciation Expense	19,500	
Total Operating Expenses		169,000
Net Loss		$ (6,500)

Required

1. Using the information and the purchasing power gain or loss calculation from problem 21A-3, restate Carousel's income statement for changes in the general price level.
2. Discuss the effects of inflation on Carousel's 19x2 financial position and operating results.

Problem Set B

Problem 21B-1.
Recording
International
Transactions
(L.O. 1)

Mountain States Company, whose year end is June 30, engaged in the following international transactions:

May 15 Purchased goods from a Japanese firm for $110,000; terms n/10 in U.S. dollars (yen = $.0080).

    17 Sold goods to a German company for $165,000; terms n/30 in marks (mark = $.55).

    21 Purchased goods from a Mexican company for $120,000; terms n/30 in pesos (peso = $.0004).

    25 Paid for the goods purchased on May 15 (yen = $.0085).

    31 Sold goods to an Italian firm for $200,000; terms n/60 in lira (lira = $.0005).

June 5 Sold goods to a British firm for $56,000; terms n/10 in U.S. dollars (pound = $1.30).

    7 Purchased goods from a Japanese firm for $221,000; terms n/30 in yen (yen = $.0085).

    15 Received payment for the sale made on June 5 (pound = $1.80).

    16 Received payment for the sale made on May 17 (mark = $.60).

    17 Purchased goods from a French firm for $66,000; terms n/30 in U.S. dollars (franc = $.16).

    20 Paid for the goods purchased on May 21 (peso = $.0003).

    22 Sold goods to a British firm for $108,000; terms n/30 in pounds (pound = $1.80).

    30 Made year-end adjustment for incomplete foreign exchange transactions (franc = $.17; peso = $.0003; mark = $.60; lira = $.0003; pound = $1.70; yen = $.0090).

July 7 Paid for the goods purchased on June 7 (yen = $.0085).

    19 Paid for the goods purchased on June 17 (franc = $.15).

    22 Received payment for the goods sold on June 22 (pound = $1.60).

    30 Received payment for the goods sold on May 31 (lira = $.0004).

Required

Prepare general journal entries for these transactions.

Problem 21B-2.
Calculation of
Purchasing Power
Gain or Loss
(L.O. 5)

Patterson Company began 19x2 with $50,000 in cash and $500,000 in debt. The debt was completely liquidated at the beginning of 19x3, and no more debt was incurred during that year. Cash transactions (including debt liquidation) for the two years were as follows:

	19x3	19x2
Cash receipts	$ 840,000	$1,240,000
Cash disbursements	1,260,000	760,000

General price levels during 19x2 and 19x3 were as follows:

	19x3	19x2
Beginning of year	164	150
End of year	178	164
Average for year	171	157

Required

1. Compute the purchasing power gain or loss for 19x2 and 19x3.
2. Comment on the reasons for the results.

Problem 21B-3.
Purchasing Power
Gain or Loss and
Balance Sheet
Restatement
(L.O. 5, 6)

The Emerald Parking Company operates a single parking lot. All receipts are in cash, and expenses are paid in cash. During 19x2, the company had revenues of $682,000 and expenses exclusive of depreciation of $484,000. At the end of 19x2, the company's balance sheet appeared as follows:

Emerald Parking Company
Balance Sheet
December 31, 19x2

Assets

Cash	$300,000
Land	40,000
Parking Building	600,000
Accumulated Depreciation	(120,000)
Total Assets	$820,000

Liabilities and Stockholders' Equity

Note Payable	$500,000
Common Stock	140,000
Retained Earnings	180,000
Total Liabilities and Stockholders' Equity	$820,000

The company was founded on January 1, 19x1, when the land and parking building were purchased and the capital stock was issued. The note has been outstanding during all of 19x2. The cash balance at the beginning of 19x2 was $102,000.

The general price level during the past two years varied as follows:

January 1, 19x1	200
January 1, 19x2	210
December 31, 19x2	231
Average for 19x2	220

Required

1. Compute the purchasing power gain or loss for Emerald Parking Company for 19x2.
2. Prepare a restated balance sheet as of December 31, 19x2.

Problem 21B-4.
Restatement of
Income Statement
(L.O. 6)

The income statement for Emerald Parking Company for the year ended December 31, 19x2 is as follows:

Revenues		$682,000
Operating Expenses		
Wages Expense	$412,000	
Utility Expense	72,000	
Depreciation Expense	60,000	
Total Operating Expenses		544,000
Net Income		$138,000

Required

1. Using the information and the purchasing power gain or loss calculation from problem 21B-3, restate the income statement for Emerald Parking Company for changes in the general price level.
2. Discuss the effects of inflation on Emerald's 19x2 financial position and operating results.

Financial Decision Case

Haverton's Plant
and Seed
Company
(L.O. 6, 7)

Haverton's Plant and Seed Company has been located at the corner of Routes 17 and 42 for over twenty-five years. Because of recent changes in county ordinances, the company must move. Haverton's purchased the land at this location for $120,000 in 1960. A building on the property has served as the company's place of business, but it is fully depreciated and is worthless for other uses.

Heather Haverton has been assessing the situation. Haverton has a firm offer from another business to purchase the property for $500,000. There is a piece of property two miles away that is identical to the current property with respect to its suitability for the plant and seed business. It can be purchased for $450,000. Haverton knows that the company will have to pay a corporate tax of 34 percent on the difference between what the business originally paid for the land and what the property sells for. The general price level has increased from 88.7 in 1960 to 322.1 in 1985.

Required

1. What are three alternative measures of the company's gain on the sale of the property, and the rationale behind each?
2. If Heather Haverton sells the land for $500,000, what is the taxable gain and how much tax would the company pay? Do you believe the tax is a fair one? Why or why not?

Answers to Self-Test

1. a	3. b	5. b	7. d	9. b
2. c	4. a	6. c	8. d	10. d

PRINCIPLES OF ACCOUNTING

FINANCIAL ACCOUNTING

PART ONE
The Basic Accounting Model

PART TWO
Extensions of the Basic Accounting Model

PART THREE
Measuring and Reporting Assets and Current Liabilities

PART FOUR
Accounting for Partnerships and Corporations

PART FIVE
Special Reports and Analyses of Accounting Information

MANAGERIAL ACCOUNTING

PART SIX
Basic Concepts of Management Accounting

Chapter 22
Introduction to Management Accounting

Chapter 23
Product Costing: The Job Order System

Chapter 24
Product Costing: The Process Cost Accounting System

PART SEVEN
Accounting for Management Decision Making

P art Six focuses on the basic tools of analysis used in management. Managers need specific types of information to support their day-to-day and long-term decisions. The management accountant provides these data. In Part Six you will be exposed to the development and accumulation of cost information for use in product or service costing, in the analysis of operating performance, and in reporting results of operations to management.

Basic Concepts of Management Accounting

The first five parts of this book dealt primarily with financial accounting and the measurement and reporting problems pertaining to general-purpose financial statements used by people outside the business entity, such as bankers and stockholders. The basic concepts and practices of internal or management accounting are introduced in the final two parts of this text.

Chapter 22 introduces the field of management accounting and focuses on the basic terminology used in accounting for internal operations. Reporting of manufacturing costs is also discussed and illustrated, and ethical standards of the management accountant are highlighted.

Chapters 23 and 24 describe two approaches to product costing. After defining the concept of absorption costing and describing the development and use of predetermined overhead rates, Chapter 23 focuses on product costing within the job order cost accounting system. Chapter 24 analyzes product costing in a process cost accounting environment.

LEARNING OBJECTIVES

1. Describe the field of management accounting.
2. Distinguish between management accounting and financial accounting.
3. Identify differences in accounting for manufacturing and merchandising companies.
4. State the differences among the three manufacturing cost elements: direct materials costs, direct labor costs, and factory (manufacturing) overhead costs.
5. Identify the source documents used to collect data on manufacturing cost elements.
6. Compute unit cost.
7. Describe the nature, contents, and flow of costs through the Materials, Work in Process, and Finished Goods Inventory accounts.
8. Prepare a statement of cost of goods manufactured.
9. Prepare an income statement for a manufacturing company.
10. State the standards of ethical conduct for management accountants and recognize those acts that are unethical.

CHAPTER 22

Introduction to Management Accounting

Managerial accounting is an important body of knowledge for everyone planning a career in the business world. The significance of the discipline is that the language of managerial or management accounting represents the basic communications system *within* any business enterprise. Planning (budgeting) and control (measuring performance) are vital to the success of both profit-oriented and not-for-profit organizations. Every business must manage its financial and human resources, and the field of management accounting provides the necessary mechanism.

This chapter begins your study of management accounting. In the first twenty-one chapters of this book, emphasis was placed on financial accounting issues and practices. There are fundamental differences in the two disciplines and we will outline them for you. But first we will describe the field of management accounting in professional terms. This chapter also includes basic management accounting terminology, a discussion of the cost elements of manufacturing accounting, new inventory accounts unique to production operations, cost classification and flow through the manufacturing inventory accounts to cost of goods sold, and the preparation of a statement of cost of goods manufactured. The chapter ends with a discussion of ethical considerations for management accountants. After studying this chapter, you should be able to meet the learning objectives on the left.

In this chapter, we focus on management accounting as it relates to manufacturing firms. But you should be aware that service organizations such as hospitals, accounting firms, insurance agencies, and banks are also interested in establishing the costs of their products (which are their respective services). Many of the internal accounting procedures discussed in this and future chapters can be used by such service organizations. For this reason several of the decision cases in Parts Six and Seven of the book will focus on data that support management decisions in service-oriented companies. A work sheet analysis based on periodic and perpetual inventory methods is covered in a special analysis in The Windham Company Practice Case.

The Field of Management Accounting

OBJECTIVE 1
Describe the field of management accounting

The field of management accounting consists of specific types of information gathering and reporting functions as well as related accounting techniques and procedures. When collectively applied to a company's financial, production, marketing, and distribution data, management accounting procedures will satisfy management's information needs.

All business managers require accurate, timely information for pricing, planning, and decision-making purposes. Managers of production, merchandising, government, and service-oriented enterprises all depend on management accounting information. Management accounting is often associated with large multidivisional corporations with many segments engaged in manufacturing and assembly. These large corporations need more complex accounting and reporting systems than do small, one-owner businesses such as a neighborhood grocery store or a shoe store. But small- and medium-size businesses need the same types of information as large ones to ensure efficient operating conditions.

The National Association of Accountants, in *Statement No. 1A* of its series of *Statements on Management Accounting*, defines **management accounting** as:

. . . the process of identification, measurement, accumulation, analysis, preparation, interpretation, and communication of financial (and non-financial) information used by management to plan, evaluate, and control within an organization and to assure appropriate use of and accountability for its resources.[1]

Three types of information are needed to manage a company effectively: (1) manufacturing and service-oriented companies need product (service) costing information; (2) all organizations need data to plan and control operations; and (3) managers need special reports and analyses to support their decisions.

To obtain product costing information, the management accountant uses cost accounting techniques to gather production information, assign specific costs to product batches, and calculate product unit costs. Product costing techniques are discussed in Chapters 23 and 24.

Data for planning and control should be organized in ways that help managers plan operations and their related costs. As operations continue and expected costs are incurred, the management accountant uses formal control procedures to compare planned and actual costs, so that the effectiveness of operations and management can be measured. Chapters 25, 26, and 27 focus on these planning and control functions of management accounting.

Management decisions should be supported by analyses of alternative courses of action. Special reports and analyses prepared by the management accountant help managers make decisions. Approaches

1. National Association of Accountants, *Statement No. 1A* (New York, 1982).

used by the management accountant to prepare these reports are discussed in Chapter 28.

Comparing Management Accounting with Financial Accounting

OBJECTIVE 2
Distinguish between management accounting and financial accounting

Students often have problems coping with management accounting concepts and procedures because they have first been trained in the procedures and rules governing financial accounting. Management accounting has rules too, but it is also much more open and places fewer restrictions on the accountant in his or her day-to-day work efforts. Fewer restrictions means somewhat less defined methods for doing things related to management accounting.

In this section we will take a closer look at the differences between management accounting and financial accounting. The comparison focuses chiefly on (1) primary users of information, (2) types of accounting systems, (3) restrictive guidelines, (4) units of measurement, (5) focal point for analysis, (6) frequency of reporting, and (7) degree of reliability in the information generated. These areas of comparison are summarized in Table 22-1.

Primary Users of Information

The primary users of traditional financial statements are external to the company preparing the report. Internal management is responsible for preparing the company's annual financial statements, but the information is disclosed primarily for external users.

In comparison, internal reports and analyses prepared by the management accountant are used by every member of management. The content of the reports varies, depending upon the level of management being served, the department or segment being analyzed, and the purpose underlying each report. Emphasis is placed on supplying relevant information to people responsible for particular activities. Examples of different types and uses of internally generated information include: unit cost analyses for product costing purposes; budgets for planning future operations; control reports by responsibility unit for measuring performance; relevant cost reports for short-run decision making; and capital budgeting analyses for corporate long-run planning purposes.

Types of Accounting Systems

Financial statements prepared for external use are made up of dollar totals that reflect balances of all accounts included in a company's general ledger. Before financial data are entered into the general ledger, the amounts must be coded, adjusted, and translated into a form suitable for a double-entry accounting system. Special journals, ledgers, and other analyses used to process financial accounting information are based upon the double-entry system.

Table 22-1. Comparison of Financial and Management Accounting		
Areas of Comparison	**Financial Accounting**	**Management Accounting**
1. Primary users of information	Persons and organizations outside the business entity	Various levels of internal management
2. Types of accounting systems	Double-entry system	Not restricted to double-entry system; any system that is useful
3. Restrictive guidelines	Adherence to generally accepted accounting principles	No guides or restrictions; only criterion is usefulness
4. Units of measurement	Historical dollar	Any useful monetary or physical measurement unit—labor hour, machine hour, etc.; if dollars are used, they may be historical or future dollars
5. Focal point for analysis	Business entity as a whole	Various segments of the business entity
6. Frequency of reporting	Periodically on regular basis	Whenever needed; not necessarily on a regular basis
7. Degree of reliability	Demands objectivity; historical in nature	Heavily subjective for planning purposes, though objective data are used when relevant; futuristic in nature

The analyses and flow of accounting data inside the company need not depend upon the double-entry format. Data may be gathered for small segments or large divisions of the company and may be expressed in units of measurement other than historical dollars. The information generated need not flow into and through general ledger accounts as in financial accounting. Special reports may be prepared for a particular manager's use and with the process ending there. In these situations, the information storage and retrieval system must have greater capabilities than required for financial accounting. The major criterion for the design of internal accounting systems is that the reports and analyses generated must be *useful* in meeting management's information needs.

Restrictive Guidelines

Financial accounting is concerned with analyzing, classifying, recording, and reporting on a company's financial activities. Since the financial statements are prepared primarily for people external to the company, accountants must adhere to generally accepted accounting standards and principles that govern the recording, measuring, and reporting of financial information. Although they are necessary for protection and credibility, generally accepted accounting principles confine accountants to a finite number of accounting practices. Examples of such restrictions include principles that involve matching revenues with expenses, stating inventories at lower of cost or market, reporting fixed assets at acquisition cost, recognizing revenue in appropriate periods, and reporting on a consistent basis.

Management accounting has only one restrictive guideline: The accounting practice or technique used must produce *useful* information. Before tackling a particular problem, the management accountant must decide what information will be useful to the recipient of the report. He or she then chooses the appropriate concepts, procedures, and techniques required to solve the problem. To illustrate, suppose the management of the Renée Company is deciding whether or not to purchase a specific piece of equipment. Return on investment information is relevant to the decision. Before return on investment can be computed, the financial effect of the new machine on company operations must be determined. This analysis requires estimates of the increase in product sales, changes in variable and fixed manufacturing and selling costs, and changes in administrative costs. Once these amounts have been estimated, the management accountant must then select an appropriate method for determining the machine's return on investment. Of the several approaches available, the method selected should be the most accurate under the circumstances. Since the information is only for internal use, there is no need to stay within the restrictive guidelines for recording and reporting information to people outside the company.

Units of Measurement

The fourth area of comparison between financial and management accounting is the units of measurement used as a basis for reports and analyses. Financial accounting serves a stewardship or accountability function by providing financial information of past events in a company. All information is presented in dollar amounts, the common unit of measurement being the "historical" dollar. Transactions that are summarized in the financial statements have already occurred, and the financial effects are objectively measurable.

Management accountants are not restricted to the use of the historical dollar and can employ any measurement unit that is *useful* in a particular situation. Historical dollars may be used in the short run for cost control analyses and for measuring trends for routine planning tasks. However, most of management's decisions are based upon analyses using expected "future" dollars, because projections of operating data must be based on estimates of future dollar flows. In addition to monetary units, the management accountant uses such measures as machine hours, labor hours, and product or service units as bases for analysis.

The common denominator underlying all these units of measurement is usefulness in a particular situation.

Focal Point for Analysis

Typically, financial accounting records and reports information concerning assets, equities, and net income of the *company as a whole*. Financial statements summarize transactions of the entire organization. Management accounting, on the other hand, usually involves analyses of *various segments* (cost centers, profit centers, divisions, departments) of a business or some specific aspect of its operations. Reports can range from the analysis of the revenues and expenses of an entire division to the investigation of materials used by one department or operating cell.

Frequency of Reporting

Financial statements developed for external use are usually prepared on a regular basis: monthly, quarterly, and/or annually. Periodic reporting at regular intervals is a basic concept of financial accounting. Management accounting reports may be prepared monthly, quarterly, and/or annually on a regular basis, or they may be requested daily or on an irregular basis. The key issues are that each report generated must be useful to its recipient and that information be accessible whenever needed.

Degree of Reliability

Financial information included in the financial statements prepared for external use is past data, summarized for the user as of a particular date. Because this information results from transactions that have already happened, it is *objective* and verifiable. Management accounting is concerned primarily with planning and control of internal operations, which are future-related activities. Past expense and revenue transactions, although useful for establishing trends, usually are not relevant to these activities and must be replaced by *subjective* estimates of future events.

To sum up, whereas the main emphasis in financial accounting is on full and accurate accounting for and disclosure of a company's operating results, the thrust in management accounting is on helping management accomplish its objectives. A management accountant typically is involved with non-financial data analyses that deal with units of output, machine hours, or direct labor hours in addition to reports centering on dollar amounts. Budgeted data are important to the management accountant, and the analysis of management's plans are of continual concern. Because in many cases the reports generated by the management accountant have a direct bearing on the company's profitability, they are often considered confidential to management. (Leaks of such confidential information could give the competition an unfair advantage in the marketplace.)

Merchandising Versus Manufacturing Operations

OBJECTIVE 3
Identify differences in accounting for manufacturing and merchandising companies

Much of this text has focused on the merchandising organization. Since we will now shift our emphasis to production operations, we must understand the differences in accounting for manufacturing firms and merchandising firms. Many kinds of businesses gather information on costs, but doing so is especially important in manufacturing. Figures 22-1 and 22-2 show how the computation of cost of goods sold differs between manufacturing and merchandising companies.

A merchandising company normally buys a product that is ready for resale when it is received. Nothing needs to be done to the product to make it salable, except possibly to prepare a special package or display. As shown in Figure 22-1, the total of the beginning merchandise inventory plus purchases is the basis for computing both the cost of goods sold and the ending merchandise inventory balances. Costs assigned to unsold items make up the ending inventory balance. The difference between the cost of goods available for sale and the ending inventory amount is the cost of goods sold during the period. The following example shows a typical computation:

Beginning merchandise inventory	$ 2,000
Add: total purchases of salable goods	8,000
Cost of goods available for sale	$10,000
Less ending merchandise inventory	2,700
Cost of goods sold	$ 7,300

This example and Figure 22-1 show how easy it is to figure the cost of goods sold for a merchandising company. The primary expenditure occurs when salable goods are purchased. Any items unsold at year end make up the ending inventory balance. The remainder of the purchase costs (plus any balance in beginning merchandise inventory) are reported as Cost of Goods Sold.

Computing the cost of goods sold for a manufacturing company is more complex. As shown in Figure 22-2 (page 926), instead of one inventory account, a manufacturer maintains three different types of inventory accounts: Materials Inventory, Work in Process Inventory, and Finished Goods Inventory.

Purchased raw materials and parts that are unused during the production process make up the year-end Materials Inventory balance. The cost of materials used plus the costs of labor services and factory overhead (utility costs, depreciation of factory machinery and building, and so forth) are transferred to the Work in Process Inventory account when the material, labor service, or overhead item is used in the production process.

The three kinds of costs discussed earlier are often called simply materials, labor, and overhead (abbreviated M, L, and OH). These costs are

Figure 22-1. Cost of Goods Sold: A Merchandising Company

accumulated in the Work in Process Inventory account during an accounting period. When a batch or order is completed and the products are stored in finished goods inventory, all manufacturing costs assigned to the completed units are moved to the Finished Goods Inventory account. Costs remaining in the Work in Process Inventory account belong to partly completed units. These costs make up the ending balance in the Work in Process Inventory account.

The Finished Goods Inventory account is set up in much the same way as the Merchandise Inventory account in Figure 22-1. Costs of completed goods are entered into the Finished Goods Inventory account. Then, as shown in Figure 22-2, costs attached to unsold items at year end make up the ending balance in the Finished Goods Inventory account. All costs related to units sold are added together and reported on the income statement as Cost of Goods Sold. To clarify the flow of costs, the following section will discuss the three manufacturing cost elements—direct materials, direct labor, and factory (manufacturing) overhead.

Manufacturing Cost Elements

Manufacturing costs can be classified in many different ways. Some costs can be traced directly to one product or batch of products. Other costs cannot be traced directly to products. In gathering information for

Figure 22-2. Cost of Goods Sold: A Manufacturing Company

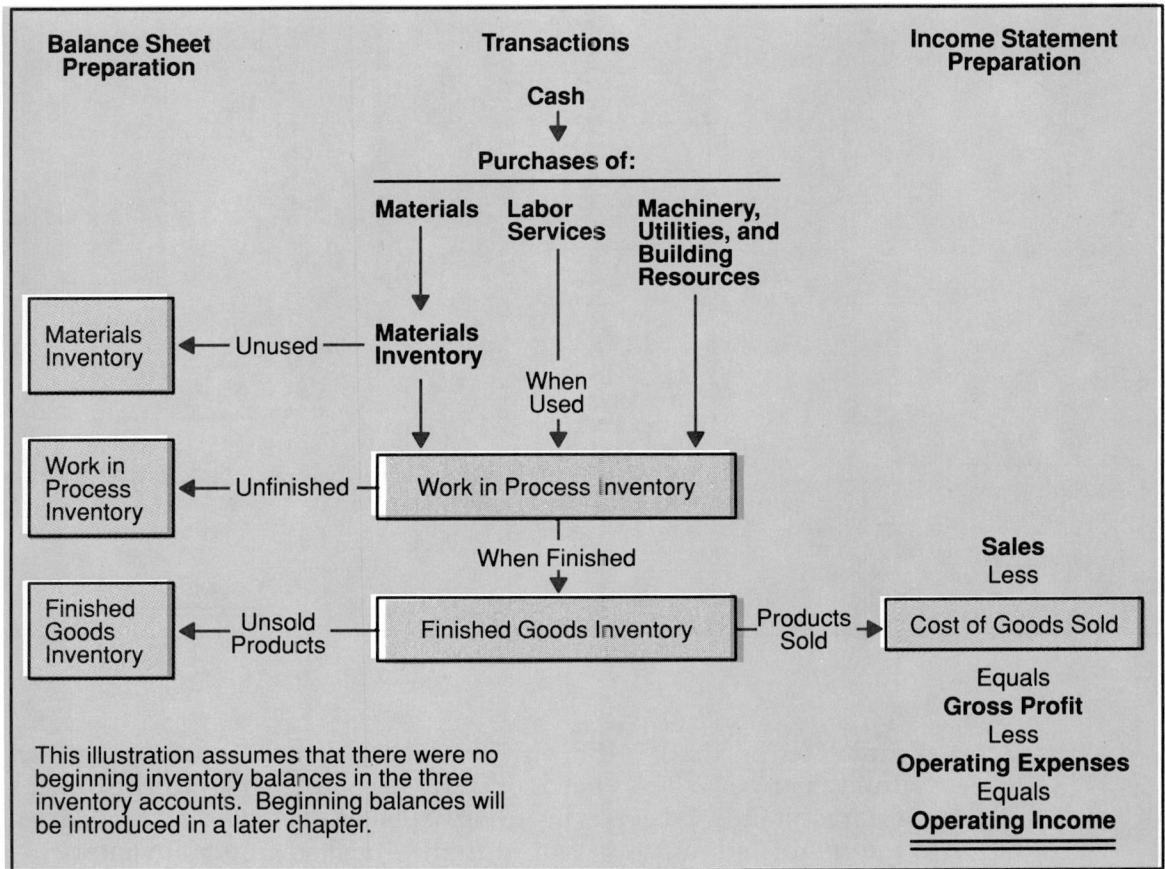

OBJECTIVE 4
*State the
differences among
the three
manufacturing cost
elements: direct
materials costs,
direct labor costs,
and factory
(manufacturing)
overhead costs*

business decisions, the accountant must bear in mind that a particular cost may be important to one type of decision but not another. In addition, some costs take on different characteristics when the accountant shifts from an external financial reporting approach to an internal or management accounting approach. In fact, manufacturing costs can be reclassified in many different ways, depending on the goal of the cost analysis.

The most common classification scheme, as mentioned before, is to group manufacturing costs into one of three classes: materials costs, labor costs, and manufacturing overhead costs. This last class of costs is often referred to as factory overhead. Materials costs and labor costs are considered direct costs, while factory overhead costs are considered indirect costs. **Direct costs** can be easily traced to specific products. **Indirect costs** must be assigned to products by some general plan for allocation.

Direct Materials Costs

Every manufactured product is made from some direct material, be it iron ore for steel, sheet steel for automobiles, or flour for bread.

Direct materials are materials that become part of the finished product and can be *conveniently and economically* traced to specific product units. In some cases, even though a material becomes part of a finished product, the expense of actually tracing the cost of the specific part is too great. Examples include nails in furniture, bolts in automobiles, and rivets in airplanes. These minor materials and other production supplies that cannot be conveniently or economically traced to specific products are accounted for as **indirect materials**. Indirect materials costs are included as part of factory overhead costs, which are discussed later in this chapter.

The way a company buys, stores, and uses its direct materials is very important. Timely purchasing is important because if the company runs out of materials, it will be forced to shut down the manufacturing process. Shutting down production results in product shortages, unhappy customers, and loss of sales and profits. Buying too many direct materials, on the other hand, can lead to high storage costs.

Proper storage of materials will avoid waste and spoilage. Sufficient storage space and orderly storage procedures are essential. Materials must be handled and stored properly to guarantee their satisfactory use in production. Proper records make it possible to find goods easily, thus reducing problems resulting from lost or misplaced items.

OBJECTIVE 5
Identify the source documents used to collect data on manufacturing cost elements

Direct Materials Purchases. Direct materials are a sizable expenditure each year, so they call for special care in purchasing. A company must be careful not only to buy proper amounts but also to ensure receipt of quality goods. An efficient purchasing system provides several important documents to account for direct materials purchases. These documents were described in Chapter 7. The **purchase requisition** (or purchase request), which starts in the production department, is used to begin the materials purchasing process. This document describes the items to be purchased and the quantities needed. It must be approved by a qualified manager or supervisor.

From the information on the purchase requisition, the purchasing department prepares a formal **purchase order**. After a number of copies are made, some of the copies are sent to the vendor or supplier, and the remaining copies are kept for internal use. When the ordered goods are received, a **receiving report** is prepared and matched with the descriptions and quantities listed on the purchase order. Usually, the materials are inspected as soon as they arrive for damage or inferior quality. The purchasing process is complete when the company receives an invoice from the vendor and approves it for payment.

Direct Materials Usage. Controlling direct materials costs does not end with the receipt and inspection of purchased goods. The materials must be stored in a safe place, counted at regular intervals, and issued into production only with the approval of a production supervisor. Keeping the materials storage areas clean and orderly and locking up valuable items are vital. Regular physical counts are necessary to see how many units are on hand and to test the inventory accounting system. Materials should be issued to production only when an approved **materials requisition** is presented to the storeroom clerk. This form, shown in Figure 22-3, is essential for controlling direct materials costs. Besides the supervisor's signature, the materials requisition includes a description of the types and quantities of goods needed and issued to production.

Direct Labor Costs

Labor services are, in essence, purchased from employees working in the factory. In addition, other types of labor are purchased from people and organizations outside the company. However, the labor cost usually

Figure 22-3. The Materials Requisition Form

Vineland Publishing Company Boston, Massachusetts				Materials Requisition	
				No. 49621	
Charge to Job No. *14-629*					
Requested by *H. Landis*			Date *4/27/89*		
Department *Binding*					
Part Number	Description	Quantity Requested	Quantity Issued	Unit Cost	Total Cost
16 T	*Glue*	*140 gallons*	*60 gallons*	*$12.40*	*$744.00*
Issued by *T. Myrtle*			Date Received *5/1/89*		
Approved by *P. Marcos*					
Received by *H. Landis*					

associated with manufacturing is that of factory personnel. These personnel include machine operators, maintenance workers, managers and supervisors, support personnel, and people who handle, inspect, and store materials. Because all of these people are connected in some way with the production process, their wages and salaries must be accounted for as production costs, and finally as costs of products. However, tracing many of these costs directly to individual products is difficult.

To help overcome this problem, the wages of machine operators and other workers involved in actually shaping the product are classified as direct labor costs. **Direct labor costs** include all labor costs for specific work performed on products that can be conveniently and economically traced to end products. Labor costs for production-related activities that cannot be connected with or conveniently or economically traced to end products are called **indirect labor costs**. These costs include the wages and salaries of such workers as machine helpers, supervisors, and other support personnel. Like indirect materials costs, indirect labor costs are accounted for as factory overhead costs.

Labor Documentation. Labor time records are important to both the employee and the company. The employee wants to be paid at the correct rate for all hours worked. The company does not wish to underpay or overpay its employees. In addition, company management wants a record kept of hours worked on particular products or batches of products made during the period. For these reasons, accounting for wages and salaries calls for careful attention.

The basic time record is called an **employee time card**. On each employee's time card, either the supervisor or a time clock records the employee's daily starting and finishing times. Normally, a company will use another set of labor cards to help verify the time recorded on the time cards and to keep track of labor costs per job or batch of goods produced. These documents, called **job time cards**, record the time spent by an employee on a certain job. Each eight-hour period recorded on a time card may be supported by several job cards. Special job cards also record machine downtime, which may stem from machine repair or changes in product design. Job cards verify the time worked by the employee and help control labor time per job.

Gross Versus Net Payroll. Accounting for direct and indirect labor costs often causes misunderstanding. People sometimes confuse gross payroll with net payroll. **Net payroll** is the amount paid to the employee after all payroll deductions have been subtracted from gross wages. Payroll deductions such as those for federal income taxes and social security taxes are paid by the employee. The employer just withholds them and pays them to the government and other organizations. **Gross payroll** is a measure of the total wages and salaries earned by employees, including payroll deductions. Gross wages and salaries are used for internal cost accounting purposes, including the computation of total manufacturing costs.

The following example shows the difference between gross and net payroll:

Gross wages earned		
40 hours at $10/hour		$400.00
Less deductions		
Federal income taxes withheld	$82.50	
FICA taxes withheld	26.00	
U.S. government savings bond	37.50	
Union dues	12.50	
Insurance premiums	21.00	
Total deductions		179.50
Net wages paid (amount of check)		$220.50

Even though the company pays $400.00 in wages and deductions, the employee receives net wages of only $220.50. The amounts withheld from the employee's gross wages are paid by the company to the taxing agencies, savings plan, union, and insurance companies. Nevertheless, it is the gross payroll cost of $400.00 that must be accounted for as a cost of production and assigned to products or jobs. Net payroll is primarily important to the employee.

Labor-Related Costs. Other labor-related manufacturing costs fall into two categories: employee benefits and employer payroll taxes. Employee benefits are considered part of an employee's compensation package. They may include paid vacations, holiday and sick pay, and an employee pension plan. Other benefits might be life and medical insurance, performance bonuses, profit sharing, and recreation facilities. Most of these costs vary in direct proportion to labor costs.

Social Security tax is one example of a payroll-related tax paid by the employer. For every dollar of social security (FICA) tax withheld from the employee's paycheck, the employer usually pays an equal amount. The company must also pay state and federal unemployment compensation taxes. Agreements between management and labor, as well as government regulations, are sources of some labor-related costs. Company management may spend other money on a voluntary basis for the benefit of its employees.

Most labor-related costs are incurred in direct proportion to wages and salaries earned by employees. As much as possible, labor-related costs that depend on direct labor costs and can be traced to them conveniently should be accounted for as part of direct labor. All other labor-related costs should be classified as factory overhead (indirect labor). However, because of the size and complexity of payroll systems, most labor-related costs are not traced to individual employees. Such costs are normally calculated from wages and salaries by means of a predetermined rate based on past history. For instance, a company may incur twelve cents of labor-related costs for every dollar of wages and salaries earned by employees. In this case, labor-related costs average 12 percent of labor costs. Therefore, if direct labor totaled $6,000 for a period of time, total direct labor cost would be $6,720 ($6,000 plus 12 percent, or $720, of labor-related costs). Total indirect labor cost would be computed in the same manner, as we will see in the next section.

Factory Overhead

The third manufacturing cost element is a catchall for manufacturing costs that cannot be classified as direct materials or direct labor costs. **Factory overhead costs** are a varied collection of production-related costs that cannot be practically or conveniently traced to end products. This collection of costs has also been called manufacturing overhead, factory burden, and indirect manufacturing costs. The following are examples of the major classifications of factory overhead costs:

Indirect materials and supplies: nails, rivets, lubricants, small tools

Indirect labor costs: lift truck driver, maintenance and inspection labor, engineering labor, machine helpers, supervisors

Other indirect factory costs: building maintenance, machinery and tool maintenance, property taxes, property insurance, pension costs, depreciation of plant and equipment, factory rent, factory utilities

Although this list is not complete, it shows how varied are the many common overhead costs.

Overhead Cost Behavior. Cost behavior is an important concept in the field of management accounting. Manufacturing costs tend either to rise and fall with the volume of production or to stay the same within certain ranges of output. **Variable manufacturing costs** increase or decrease in direct proportion to the number of units produced. Examples include direct materials costs; direct labor costs; indirect materials and supply costs; heat, light, and power costs; and small-tool costs.

Production costs that stay fairly constant during the accounting period are called **fixed manufacturing costs**. Even with changes in productive output, these costs tend to stay the same. Examples of fixed manufacturing costs are fire insurance premiums, factory rent, supervisory salaries, and depreciation of machinery. Some costs are called semivariable, because part of the cost is fixed and part varies with usage. Telephone charges (basic charge plus long-distance charges) and utility bills are generally semivariable.

A knowledge of cost behavior is essential in assigning factory overhead costs to units of output. Cost behavior will be explored further in Chapter 25.

Overhead Cost Allocation. A cost is classified as a factory overhead cost because it cannot be directly traced to an end product. Yet a product's total cost obviously includes factory overhead costs. Somehow, factory overhead costs must be identified with and assigned to specific products or jobs. Because direct materials and direct labor costs can be traced to products, assigning their costs to units of output is relatively easy. Factory overhead costs, however, have to be assigned to products by some cost allocation method. Common cost allocation methods are explained in Chapters 23 and 25.

Unit Cost Determination

OBJECTIVE 6
Compute unit cost

Direct materials, direct labor, and factory overhead costs constitute total manufacturing costs for a period of time or for a batch of products. Product unit cost for each job completed is computed by dividing the total cost of materials, labor, and factory overhead for that job by the total units produced. For example, assume that Roland Products, Inc. produced 3,000 units of output for Job KJ-1. Costs for Job KJ-1 included the following: direct materials, $5,400; direct labor, $3,000; and factory overhead, $2,700. The company's unit cost for Job KJ-1 would therefore be computed as follows:

Direct materials ($5,400 ÷ 3,000 units)	$1.80
Direct labor ($3,000 ÷ 3,000 units)	1.00
Factory overhead ($2,700 ÷ 3,000 units)	.90
Total unit cost ($11,100 ÷ 3,000 units)	$3.70

The unit cost just described above was computed when the job was completed and all the information was known. What about situations that call for this information a month before the job is started? Unit cost figures must then be estimated. Assume that accounting personnel developed the following estimates for another product: $5.50 per unit for direct materials, $2.50 per unit for direct labor, and 50 percent of direct labor cost for factory overhead. Then the unit cost would be as follows:

Direct materials	$5.50
Direct labor	2.50
Factory overhead (50% of $2.50)	1.25
Total unit cost	$9.25

This $9.25 unit cost is based on estimates. Unit cost estimates are useful for job costing and as a starting point for product pricing.

Product and Period Costs

Product costs and *period costs* are two terms commonly used in analyzing costs. **Product costs** are inventoriable production costs and include the three manufacturing cost elements: direct materials, direct labor, and factory overhead. They are incurred in making products to be sold. That is, product costs are associated with the materials, work in process, and finished goods inventories. They provide values for the ending balances of those inventories on year-end financial statements. Product costs are also considered unexpired costs because, as inventory balances, they are assets of the company. Assets, as we have already seen in earlier chapters, are economic resources expected to benefit future operations.

Period costs (expenses) are operating costs that cannot be inventoried. Period costs are linked to services consumed during a period and are not used to determine product unit cost or to establish ending inventory balances. Examples would include selling and administrative expenses, because the selling and administrative resources are used up in the same period in which they originate.

Manufacturing Inventory Accounts

Accounting for inventories is the most difficult part of manufacturing accounting as compared to merchandising accounting. Instead of dealing with one account—Merchandise Inventory—we now must use *three* accounts: Materials Inventory, Work in Process Inventory, and Finished Goods Inventory.

Materials Inventory

OBJECTIVE 7
Describe the nature, contents, and flow of costs through the Materials, Work in Process, and Finished Goods Inventory accounts

The **Materials Inventory account**, also called the Stores, Raw Materials Inventory, or Materials Inventory Control account, is made up of the balances of materials and supplies on hand at a given time. This account is maintained in much the same way as the Merchandise Inventory account. The main difference is in the way that costs of items in inventory are assigned. For the merchandising company, goods taken out of inventory are items that have been sold. When a sale is made, an entry is needed to debit Cost of Goods Sold and to credit Merchandise Inventory for the cost of the item. Materials, on the other hand, are not purchased for resale but for use in manufacturing a product. Therefore, an item taken out of Materials Inventory and requisitioned into production is transferred to the Work in Process Inventory account (not Cost of Goods Sold). Figure 22-4 compares the accounting treatment for merchandise inventory with that for materials inventory.

Work in Process Inventory

All manufacturing costs that are incurred and assigned to products being produced belong to the **Work in Process Inventory account**. This inventory account has no counterpart in merchandise accounting. A thorough understanding of the concept of Work in Process Inventory is vital in manufacturing accounting. Figure 22-5 shows the various costs that become part of Work in Process Inventory and the way costs are transferred out of the account. Accounting for work in process (products in process) really began in Figure 22-4. The requisitioning of materials into production begins the production process. These materials must be cut, molded, assembled, or in some other way changed into a

Figure 22-4. Materials Inventory Versus Merchandise Inventory Accounting (Perpetual)

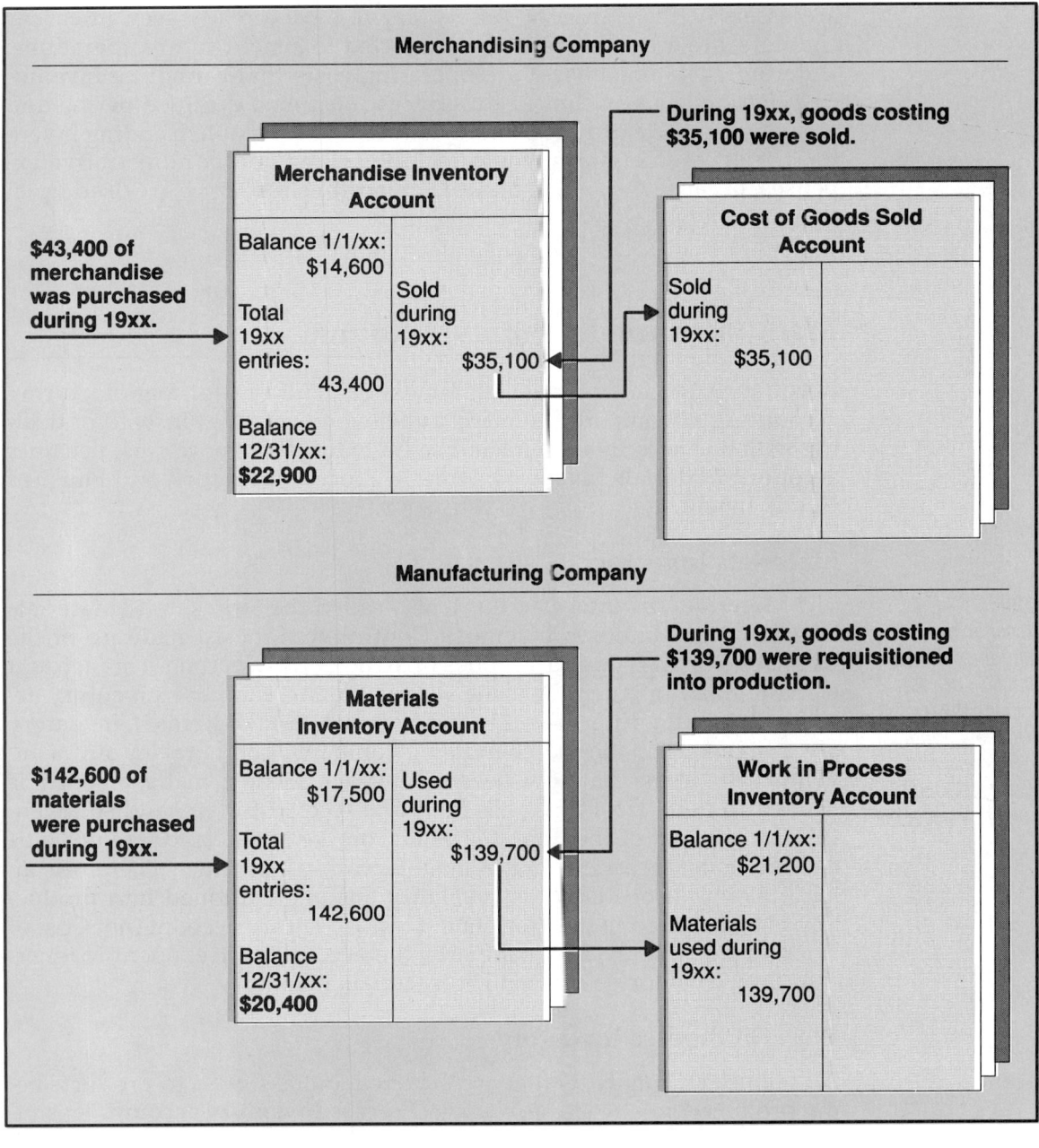

finished product. To make this change, people, machines, and other factory resources (buildings, electricity, supplies, and so on) must be used. All of these costs are manufacturing cost elements, and all of them enter into accounting for Work in Process Inventory.

Direct labor dollars earned by factory employees are also product costs. As employees work on specific products, their labor costs are as-

Figure 22-5. The Work in Process Inventory Account (Perpetual)

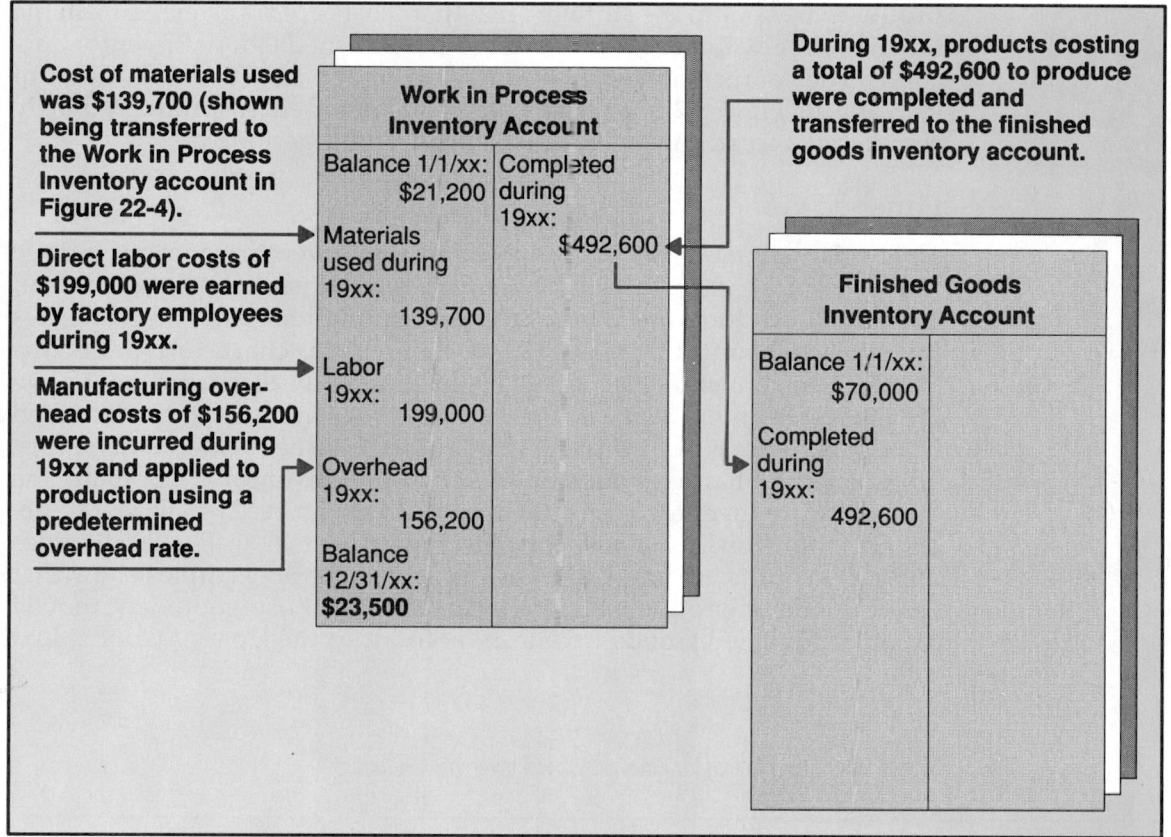

signed to those products by including the labor dollars earned as part of the Work in Process Inventory account. (Specific product costing is the topic of the next two chapters in this book. At this point, we will assume that all direct labor costs should be collected in the Work in Process Inventory account.)

Overhead costs are product costs and must be assigned to specific products. So they too are collected in the Work in Process Inventory account. As discussed earlier, there are too many overhead costs to account for on an individual basis. To reduce the amount of work needed to assign these costs to products, they are accumulated and accounted for under one account title: Factory Overhead. These costs are then assigned to products using an overhead rate. Using this rate, called a predetermined overhead rate, costs are transferred from the Factory Overhead account to the Work in Process Inventory account. In our example in Figure 22-5, factory overhead costs of $156,200 were charged to the Work in Process Inventory account. The predetermined overhead rate will be discussed in Chapter 23.

As products are completed, they are put in the finished goods storage area. They now have materials, direct labor, and factory overhead costs assigned to them. When products are completed, their costs no longer belong to work (products) in process. Therefore, when the completed products are sent to the storage area, their costs are transferred from the Work in Process Inventory account to the Finished Goods Inventory account. The balance remaining in the Work in Process Inventory account ($23,500 in Figure 22-5) represents costs assigned to products partly completed and still in process at the end of the period.

Finished Goods Inventory

The **Finished Goods Inventory account** is an inventory account unique to the manufacturing or production area where the costs assigned to all completed products are transferred and maintained. Like the Materials Inventory account, this account has some of the characteristics of the Merchandise Inventory account. We have already discussed how costs are moved from the Work in Process Inventory account to the Finished Goods Inventory account. At this point, Finished Goods Inventory takes on the characteristics of Merchandise Inventory. Compare the Merchandise Inventory account analysis in Figure 22-4 with the accounting for Finished Goods Inventory in Figure 22-6. The credit sides of both accounts are handled in the same way. Both examples show that when goods or products are sold, the costs of those goods are moved from the Finished Goods Inventory account to the Cost of Goods Sold

Figure 22-6. Accounting for Finished Goods Inventory (Perpetual)

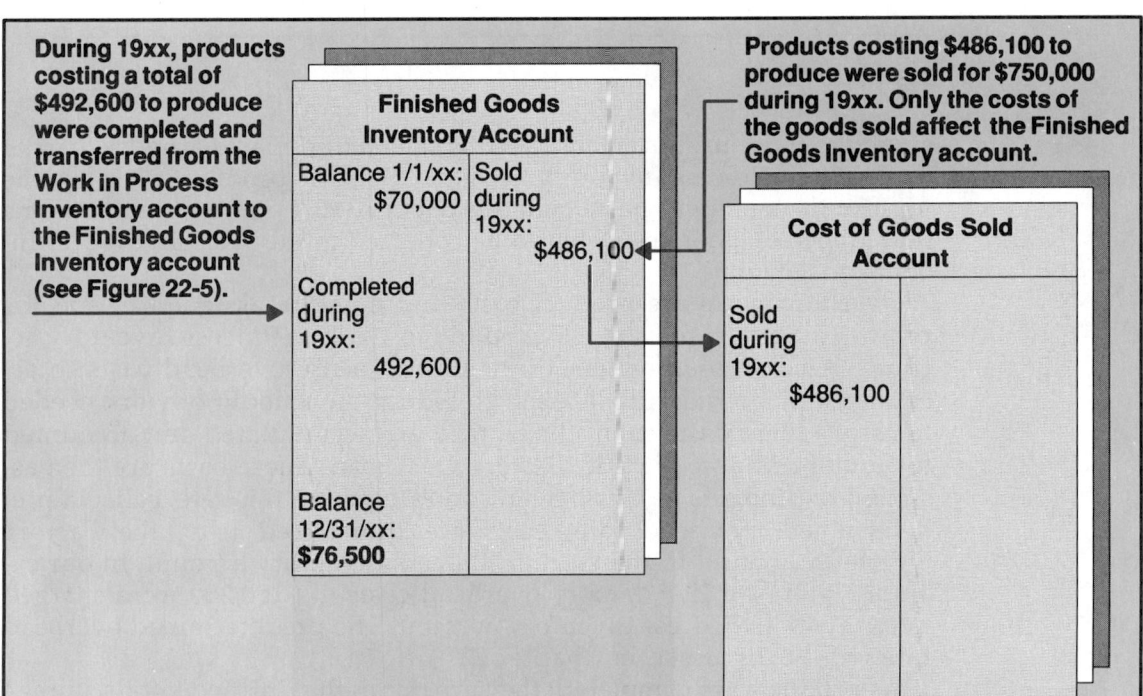

account. However, the accounting procedures affecting the debit side of the Finished Goods Inventory account differ from those for the Merchandise Inventory account. In a manufacturing firm, salable products are produced rather than purchased. All costs that are debited to Finished Goods Inventory represent transfers from the Work in Process Inventory account. At the end of an accounting period, the balance in the Finished Goods Inventory account is made up of the costs of products completed but not sold as of that date.

Periodic Versus Perpetual Inventory Methods in Manufacturing Accounting

Cost flow in accounting for manufacturing costs depends on how a company handles its inventories. In Chapter 10, we covered both the periodic and perpetual inventory methods. Since these methods relate to cost accounting systems, we include a brief discussion here. A company using the periodic inventory method records materials purchases in a separate purchases account and assigns manufacturing costs to individual labor accounts and various factory overhead cost accounts in the general ledger. Beginning inventory balances in the general ledger remain unchanged during the period. No costs flow through the Materials, Work in Process, and Finished Goods Inventory accounts during the accounting period. Year-end inventory values are found by counting the items on hand and placing a cost on these goods. Inventory accounts are then adjusted to reflect the cost of ending inventories.

If a company uses the perpetual inventory method, manufacturing costs flow through the inventory accounts as goods and services are bought and used in the production process. Inventory account balances are updated perpetually. In this way it is possible to know these account balances at any point in time. Materials purchased are debited to the Materials Inventory account. The cost of materials used, direct labor, and factory overhead items are entered into the Work in Process Inventory account. The cost of completed units is debited directly to the Finished Goods Inventory account.

The perpetual inventory method is in common use. Greater accuracy and better inventory control are the major benefits of this approach. However, a perpetual inventory system is expensive to install and maintain. For this reason, many medium- and small-size companies still use a periodic inventory approach. Most manufacturing companies utilize the perpetual inventory approach. In the remaining sections of this book, you are to assume the use of the perpetual inventory method unless otherwise indicated.

Manufacturing Cost Flow

Product costing, inventory valuation, and financial reporting depend on a defined, structured flow of manufacturing costs. This **manufacturing cost flow** was outlined in our discussion of the three manufacturing inventory accounts. Figure 22-7 sums up the entire cost flow process as

Figure 22-7. Manufacturing Cost Flow: An Example

Materials Inventory Account	
Balance 1/1/xx: $17,500	Used during 19xx: $139,700
Total 19xx entries: $142,600	
Balance 12/31/xx: **$20,400**	

Factory Payroll Account	
Direct labor earned during 19xx: $199,000	19xx: $199,000
Balance 12/31/xx: **$0**	

Manufacturing Overhead Control Account	
Total manufacturing overhead incurred during 19xx: $156,200	19xx: $156,200
Balance 12/31/xx: **$0**	

Work in Process Inventory Account	
Balance 1/1/xx: $21,200	Completed during 19xx: $492,600
Materials used during 19xx: $139,700	
Labor 19xx: $199,000	
Overhead 19xx: $156,200	
Balance 12/31/xx: **$23,500**	

Finished Goods Inventory Account	
Balance 1/1/xx: $70,000	Sold during 19xx: $486,100
Completed during 19xx: $492,600	
Balance 12/31/xx: **$76,500**	

Cost of Goods Sold Account	
Sold during 19xx: $486,100	

it relates to accounts in the general ledger. At this point, we do not need to be concerned about the actual journal entries needed to make this cost flow operational. These journal entries will be illustrated in detail in Chapter 23.

Here, we will concentrate on the general pattern of manufacturing cost flow, as shown in Figure 22-8. The cost flow begins with costs being incurred. Manufacturing costs start in a number of ways. They may be cash payments, incurrence of liabilities, fixed asset depreciation, or the expiration of prepaid expenses. Once these costs have been incurred, they are recorded as being either direct materials, direct labor, or factory overhead costs. As the resources are used up, the company transfers their costs into the Work in Process Inventory account. When production is completed, costs assigned to finished units are transferred to the Finished Goods Inventory account. In much the same way, costs attached to units sold are transferred to the Cost of Goods Sold account. Before continuing with this chapter, compare the cost flow as it moves through the general ledger accounts in Figure 22-7 with the general pattern shown in Figure 22-8. Both of these figures show the same type of cost flow.

The Manufacturing Statement

Financial statements of manufacturing companies differ very little from those of merchandising companies. Depending on the industry, the account titles found on the balance sheet (statement of financial position) are the same in most corporations. (Some examples are Cash, Accounts

Figure 22-8. Manufacturing Cost Flow: Basic Concepts

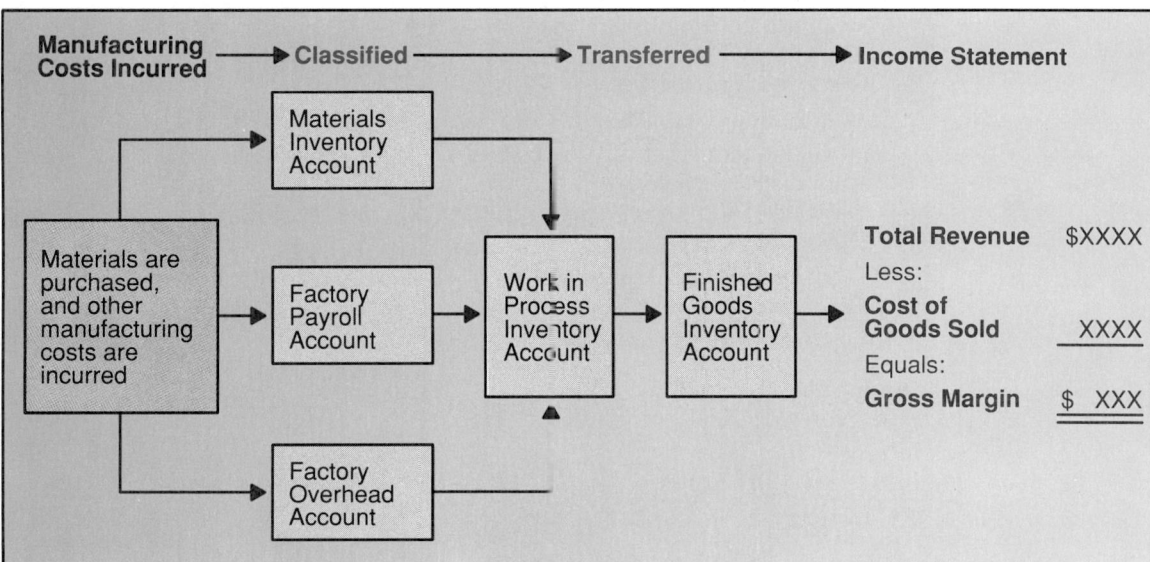

Receivable, Buildings, Machinery, Accounts Payable, and Capital Stock.) Even the income statements for the merchandiser and the manufacturer are very much alike. However, a closer look shows that the heading Cost of Goods Manufactured is used in place of Merchandise Purchases. Also, the Merchandise Inventory account is replaced by Finished Goods Inventory. Note these differences on the income statement of the Windham Company (Exhibit 22-1). The key to preparing an income statement for a manufacturing company is to determine the cost of goods manufactured. This dollar amount is the end result of a special manufacturing statement, the statement of cost of goods manufactured, which is prepared to support the figure on the income statement.

Exhibit 22-1. Income Statement for a Manufacturing Company

Windham Company
Income Statement
For the Year Ended December 31, 19xx

Net Sales			$750,000
Cost of Goods Sold			
Finished Goods Inventory, Jan. 1, 19xx		$ 70,000	
Cost of Goods Manufactured (Exhibit 22-2)		492,600	
Total Cost of Finished Goods Available for Sale		$562,600	
Less Finished Goods Inventory, Dec. 31, 19xx		76,500	
Cost of Goods Sold			486,100
Gross Margin from Sales			$263,900
Operating Expenses			
Selling Expenses			
Salaries and Commissions	$46,500		
Advertising	19,500		
Other Selling Expenses	7,400		
Total Selling Expenses		$ 73,400	
General and Administrative Expenses			
Administrative Salaries	$65,000		
Franchise and Property Taxes	72,000		
Other G & A Expenses	11,300		
Total General and Administrative Expenses		148,300	
Total Operating Expenses			221,700
Income from Operations			$ 42,200
Less Interest Expense			4,600
Income Before Taxes			$ 37,600
Less Income Tax Expense			11,548
Net Income			$ 26,052

Statement of Cost of Goods Manufactured

OBJECTIVE 8
Prepare a statement of cost of goods manufactured

The flow of manufacturing costs, pictured in Figures 22-4 through 22-8, provides the basis for accounting for manufacturing costs. In this process, all manufacturing costs incurred during the accounting period are considered product costs. They are used to compute ending inventory balances and the cost of goods sold. In the illustrations, a whole year's costs have been combined into one number to help show the basic idea. In fact, hundreds of transactions take place during a year, and each transaction affects part of the cost flow process.

At the end of the accounting period, the flow of manufacturing costs incurred during the period is summarized in the **statement of cost of goods manufactured**. This statement gives the dollar amount of costs for products completed and moved to Finished Goods Inventory during the period. The amount for cost of goods manufactured should be the same as the amount transferred from the Work in Process Inventory account to the Finished Goods Inventory account during the period.

The statement of cost of goods manufactured is shown in Exhibit 22-2. Even though the statement is rather complex, it can be pieced together in three steps. The *first step* is to compute the cost of materials used. Add the materials purchases for the period to the beginning balance in the Materials Inventory account. This subtotal represents the cost of materials available for use during the period. Then subtract the ending balance of the Materials Inventory account from the cost of materials available for use. The difference is the cost of materials used during the accounting period. The following example illustrates the computation of cost of materials used:

Computation of Cost of Materials Used

Beginning balance: Materials Inventory	$ 17,500
Plus total materials purchases (net)	142,600
Cost of materials available for use	$160,100
Less ending balance: Materials Inventory	20,400
Cost of materials used	$139,700

Before going to the next step, trace these numbers back to the Materials Inventory account in Figure 22-4 to see how that account is related to the statement of cost of goods manufactured.

Calculating total manufacturing costs for the period is the *second step*. As shown in Figure 22-5, we add the costs of materials used and direct labor to the total of all factory overhead costs incurred during the period, as follows (see also Exhibit 22-2):

Computation of Total Manufacturing Costs

Cost of materials used	$139,700
Plus direct labor costs	199,000
Plus total factory overhead costs	156,200
Total manufacturing costs	$494,900

Exhibit 22-2. Statement of Cost of Goods Manufactured

Windham Company
Statement of Cost of Goods Manufactured
For the Year Ended December 31, 19xx

Step One	Materials Used		
	Materials Inventory, Jan. 1, 19xx	$ 17,500	
	Materials Purchased (net)	142,600	
	Cost of Materials Available for		
	Use	$160,100	
	Less Materials Inventory,		
	December 31, 19xx	20,400	
	Cost of Materials Used		$139,700
	Direct Labor		199,000
Step Two	Factory Overhead Costs		
	Indirect Labor	$ 46,400	
	Power	25,200	
	Depreciation, Machinery		
	and Equipment	14,800	
	Depreciation,		
	Factory Building	16,200	
	Small Tools	2,700	
	Factory Insurance	1,600	
	Supervision	37,900	
	Other Factory Costs	11,400	
	Total Factory Overhead Costs		156,200
	Total Manufacturing Costs		$494,900
Step Three	Add: Work in Process Inventory,		
	January 1, 19xx		21,200
	Total Cost of Goods in Process During		
	the Year		$516,100
	Less Work in Process Inventory,		
	December 31, 19xx		23,500
	Cost of Goods Manufactured		$492,600

The *third step* shown in Exhibit 22-2 changes total manufacturing costs into total cost of goods manufactured for the period. Add the beginning Work in Process Inventory balance to total manufacturing costs for the period to arrive at the total cost of goods in process during the period. From this amount, subtract the ending Work in Process Inventory balance for the period to get the cost of goods manufactured. The computation follows:

Computation of Cost of Goods Manufactured

Total manufacturing costs	$494,900
Plus beginning balance: Work in Process Inventory	21,200
Total cost of goods in process during year	$516,100
Less ending balance: Work in Process Inventory	23,500
Cost of goods manufactured	$492,600

The term *total manufacturing costs* must not be confused with the cost of goods manufactured. **Total manufacturing costs** are the total costs for materials used, direct labor, and factory overhead incurred and charged to production during an accounting period. **Cost of goods manufactured** consists of the total manufacturing costs attached to units of product completed during an accounting period. To understand the difference between these two dollar amounts, review the computation just shown. Total manufacturing costs of $494,900 incurred during the current year are added to the beginning balance in Work in Process Inventory. Costs of $21,200 in the beginning balance, by definition, are costs from an earlier period. We are now mixing costs from two different accounting periods to arrive at a total cost of work in process during the year of $516,100. The costs of ending products still in process ($23,500) are then subtracted from the total cost of work in process during the year. The remainder of $492,600 is the cost of goods manufactured (completed) during the year. We assume that the items in beginning inventory were completed first. Costs attached to the ending Work in Process Inventory are part of the current period's total manufacturing costs. But they will not become part of the cost of goods manufactured until the next accounting period, when the products are completed.

Cost of Goods Sold and the Income Statement

OBJECTIVE 9
Prepare an income statement for a manufacturing company

Exhibits 22-1 and 22-2 demonstrate the relationship between the statement of cost of goods manufactured and the income statement. The total amount of cost of goods manufactured during the period is carried over to the income statement. There it is used to compute the cost of goods sold. The cost of goods manufactured is added to the beginning balance of the Finished Goods Inventory to get the total cost of goods available for sale during the period. Then the cost of goods sold is computed by subtracting the ending balance in the Finished Goods Inventory (cost of goods completed but unsold) from the total cost of goods available for sale, as follows. Cost of goods sold is considered an expense of the period in which the related products were sold.

Computation of Cost of Goods Sold

Beginning balance: Finished Goods Inventory	$ 70,000
Plus cost of goods manufactured	492,600
Total cost of finished goods available for sale	$562,600
Less ending balance: Finished Goods Inventory	76,500
Cost of goods sold	$486,100

Note that this computation is the same as the computation of the cost of goods sold in the income statement in Exhibit 22-1. The other parts of the income statement in Exhibit 22-1 should be familiar from earlier discussions in this text.

Standards of Ethical Conduct for Management Accountants[2]

OBJECTIVE 10
State the standards of ethical conduct for management accountants and recognize those acts that are unethical

The existence of the accounting profession is based on the premise that those practicing as accountants maintain high standards of ethical conduct. In Chapter 1, you studied the ethical standards that have been developed for public accountants. Following ethical standards is equally important for management accountants. On June 1, 1983, the National Association of Accountants formally adopted a set of standards of ethical conduct for management accountants that is to be followed by the over 70,000 members of the NAA. These standards are discussed below.

Competence Standards

Management accountants have a responsibility to:

1. Maintain an appropriate level of professional competence by ongoing development of their knowledge and skills.
2. Perform their professional duties in accordance with relevant laws, regulations, and technical standards.
3. Prepare complete and clear reports and recommendations after appropriate analyses of relevant and reliable information.

In our rapidly changing world, a professional's skills can become obsolete in a very short time period. Management expects accounting personnel to be knowledgeable of current management accounting issues and to possess the most current skills available. Management accountants, therefore, are expected to attend professional development and continuing education programs on an ongoing basis after they begin their professional careers.

The management accountant must be knowledgeable of all relevant laws, regulations, and technical standards that pertain to his or her duties and should perform such duties within the bounds of those defined constraints. Professional competence must be maintained at all times when dealing with the people and the resources of one's own company, the many outside entities (customers, vendors, and contractors) associated with that company, and the world marketplace in general.

Management accountants are expected to do whatever is needed to develop support information and reports for management. Researching relevant information and approaches to each task is necessary. Reports,

---

2. National Association of Accountants, *Statement No. 1C*, "Standards of Ethical Conduct for Management Accountants" (Montvale, New Jersey: June 1, 1983).

financial analyses, and statements must reveal all necessary information, follow current reporting standards, and state clearly the results of the analysis.

Confidentiality Standards

It is essential that management accountants uphold confidentiality standards. To do this, they must:

1. Refrain from disclosing confidential information acquired in the course of their work except when authorized, unless legally obligated to do so.
2. Inform subordinates as appropriate regarding the confidentiality of information acquired in the course of their work and monitor their activities to assure the maintenance of that confidentiality.
3. Refrain from using or appearing to use confidential information acquired in the course of their work for unethical or illegal advantage either personally or through third parties.

Management accountants are entrusted with information considered confidential and proprietary by the management of their company. This information is not to be communicated to anyone, inside or outside the organization, who is not authorized to receive it. Only in specific situations dealing with legal requirements is the management accountant to disclose such information.

In the conduct of their responsibilities, management accountants supervise subordinate accountants. These subordinates should be informed whenever they are dealing with confidential information and the management accountant is expected to follow the subordinates' actions closely to maintain that confidentiality.

Any confidential information acquired by the management accountant in the course of his or her work cannot be used directly or through third parties for the accountant's personal gain or to cause harm to the accountant's company, unless the accountant is legally obligated to disclose the information.

Integrity Standards

Management accountants have a responsibility to:

1. Avoid actual or apparent conflicts of interest and advise all appropriate parties of any potential conflict.
2. Refrain from engaging in any activity that would prejudice their ability to carry out their duties ethically.
3. Refuse any gift, favor, or hospitality that would influence or would appear to influence their actions.
4. Refrain from either actively or passively subverting the attainment of the organization's legitimate and ethical objectives.
5. Recognize and communicate professional limitations or other constraints that would preclude responsible judgment or successful performance of an activity.

6. Communicate unfavorable as well as favorable information and professional judgments or opinions.
7. Refrain from engaging in or supporting any activity that would discredit the profession.

A management accountant must be impartial and avoid all conflicting interest, such as owning stock in a company competing for business with his or her company. This is a potential conflict of interest if the accountant has direct input into the decision to select the vendor. Under these and similar circumstances, the management accountant is responsible for informing all appropriate parties of the potential conflict.

The management accountant should refrain from relationships with individuals (or organizations) that could cause possible conflicts of interest or put the accountant in a compromising position regarding forthcoming decision analyses. Accepting gifts, favors, or special hospitality from an individual or organization can lead to compromising one's integrity and should be avoided.

Realistic (not blind) loyalty to one's company, industry, and country is an important aspect of maintaining integrity. Performing an act or encouraging an activity that threatens the organization's legitimate and ethical objectives is unethical behavior on the part of the management accountant. If he or she gains information about disloyal, incompetent, or illegal acts of someone or some organization that imperil the existence or performance of the accountant's company in any way, that information must be communicated to management.

It is crucial that management accounting reports be accurate and truthful, regardless of whether their results have a positive or a negative impact upon the company. It is unethical to alter a report so that targets are met or expectations exceeded. Any unproven or unsubstantiated act or statement that discredits the profession is unethical.

Objectivity Standards

To be objective, management accountants must:

1. Communicate information fairly and objectively.
2. Disclose fully all relevant information that could reasonably be expected to influence an intended user's understanding of the reports, comments, and recommendations presented.

The management accountant is responsible for all financial as well as many nonfinancial reports to management; remaining objective and using the doctrine of fairness must underlie the preparation of all reports and analyses. All relevant information, both positive and negative, must be communicated to the recipient of the report.

Outsiders such as investors, creditors, vendors, and customers rely on reports prepared by the accountant. Internal managers in particular depend upon the information generated by the management accountant. Following ethical standards is critical to the successful completion of these reporting responsibilities. A familiarity with ethical standards and an ability to recognize unethical acts and avoid compromising situations should be an integral part of the knowledge and skills you possess when you begin your career in the accounting profession.

Chapter Review

Review of Learning Objectives

1. **Describe the field of management accounting.**

   Management accounting is the process of identifying, measuring, accumulating, analyzing, preparing, interpreting, and communicating information used by management. This information is used to plan, evaluate, and control the organization and to ensure that its resources are properly used and accounted for. The field of management accounting is made up of appropriate accounting techniques and procedures for information gathering and reporting. When applied to a company's financial, production, marketing, and product distribution data, management accounting procedures will satisfy management's information needs. These information needs include: (a) product costing information; (b) data for planning and control of operations; and (c) special reports and analyses to support management decisions.

2. **Distinguish between management accounting and financial accounting.**

   Management accounting and financial accounting can be contrasted in seven areas. People and organizations outside the business unit are the primary users of financial accounting information, whereas various levels of internal management use management accounting information. There is no restriction on the type of accounting system one can use in management accounting, but financial accounting requires the double-entry system. Restrictive guidelines for financial accounting are composed of all generally accepted accounting standards, whereas the only restriction in management accounting is that the information be useful to the recipient. Although the historical dollar is the main unit of measurement in financial accounting, any useful unit of measurement may be used in management accounting. The business unit as a whole is the focal point of any analysis in financial accounting, but a management accounting analysis may focus on a division, a department, or even a machine. Reporting is on a regular, periodic basis in financial accounting; in management accounting, on an as-needed basis. Financial accounting deals with past events, so it is objective and reliable; whereas management accounting often focuses on the future, and can be heavily subjective.

3. **Identify differences in accounting for manufacturing and merchandising companies.**

   Accounting methods used by a manufacturing company differ in important ways from the accounting methods used by a merchandising company. In a manufacturing company, management accountants must maintain an internal accounting system that classifies and assigns production and production-related costs to the products manufactured. The manufacturing accounting system uses three inventory accounts: Materials Inventory, Work in Process Inventory, and Finished Goods Inventory. Manufacturing costs (product costs) flow through all three inventory accounts. This flow results in a more complex internal accounting system.

Merchandise accounting concentrates on the business as a whole rather than on specific products or processes. Only one account, Merchandise Inventory, is used to record and account for items in inventory. Because the items in the merchandise inventory are purchased in salable condition, the cost flow from time of purchase to time of sale involves only three accounts: Cash or Accounts Payable, Purchases, and Cost of Goods Sold.

4. **State the differences among the three manufacturing cost elements: direct materials costs, direct labor costs, and factory (manufacturing) overhead costs.**

Direct materials are materials and parts that become part of the finished product and can be conveniently and economically traced to specific product units. Direct labor costs include all labor costs for specific work performed on products that can be conveniently and economically traced to end products. All other production-related costs are classified and accounted for as factory overhead costs. These costs cannot be practically or conveniently traced to end products, so they must be assigned to products by some cost allocation method. Classifying manufacturing costs into the three elements described above is important for product costing, inventory valuation, and product pricing purposes.

5. **Identify the source documents used to collect data on manufacturing cost elements.**

Purchase requisitions list the items or materials needed by the production departments. The purchasing department then uses the purchase order to order the items. When the items or materials come in from vendors, the receiving report is used to identify them and is then matched against purchase orders to make sure the correct items were received. The materials requisition is used to request items, and also to prove that items or materials were issued into the production process. Time cards record each employee's daily starting and finishing times. Job cards record time spent by each employee on each job. Job cards are matched against time cards to verify the time worked by each employee and to control labor time per job.

6. **Compute unit cost.**

The unit cost of a product is made up of the costs of materials, labor, and factory overhead. These three cost components are accumulated for a batch of products as they are produced. Upon completion, the number of units produced is divided into the total costs incurred to determine product unit cost.

7. **Describe the nature, contents, and flow of costs through the Materials Inventory, Work in Process Inventory, and Finished Goods Inventory accounts.**

Cost flow through the inventory accounts begins when costs are incurred for materials, direct labor, and factory overhead. Materials costs flow first into the Materials Inventory account. This account is used to record the costs of materials when they are received and again when they are issued for use in a company's production process. All manufacturing-related costs—materials, direct labor, and factory overhead—are recorded in the Work In Process Inventory account as they enter the production process. When products are completed, their costs are transferred from the Work in Process Inventory account to the Finished Goods Inventory account. Costs remain in the Finished Goods Inventory account until the products are sold. At that time their costs are transferred to the Cost of Goods Sold account.

8. **Prepare a statement of cost of goods manufactured.**

   Preparing a statement of cost of goods manufactured involves three steps. The first is to compute the cost of materials used. Total materials purchases are added to the beginning balance of the Materials Inventory account to arrive at the cost of materials available for use. From this amount, the ending balance of the Materials Inventory account is subtracted to get the cost of materials used. The second step is to compute the total manufacturing costs for the period. Costs of direct labor and factory overhead are added to the cost of materials used to arrive at this amount. The third step is the actual computation of cost of goods manufactured. Total manufacturing costs and the beginning balance in the Work in Process Inventory account are added. Their sum is called total cost of goods in process during the year. By subtracting the ending balance in the Work in Process Inventory account from the total cost of goods in process, we end up with the total cost of goods manufactured.

9. **Prepare an income statement for a manufacturing company.**

   The major change to make when preparing an income statement for a manufacturing company is that the computation of cost of goods sold requires that the cost of goods manufactured has already been determined. Cost of goods manufactured is added to the beginning balance of the Finished Goods Inventory account to arrive at the total cost of goods available for sale. When the ending balance of the Finished Goods Inventory account (cost of unsold goods) is subtracted from the total cost of goods available for sale, the difference represents the costs attached to the goods sold.

10. **State the standards of ethical conduct for management accountants and recognize those acts that are unethical.**

    Management accountants are expected to be familiar with the ethical standards relating to competence, confidentiality, integrity, and objectivity. By being knowledgeable of these ethical standards, the management accountant can recognize and avoid situations and activities that compromise his or her honesty, loyalty, and ability to supply management with accurate and relevant decision-support information.

Review of Concepts and Terminology

The following concepts and terms were introduced in this chapter:

(L.O. 8) **Cost of goods manufactured:** The total manufacturing costs attached to units of product completed during an accounting period.

(L.O. 4)   **Direct costs:**   Production costs that are easily traced to specific products.

(L.O. 4)   **Direct labor costs:**   All labor costs for specific work performed on products that can be conveniently and economically traced to end products.

(L.O. 4)   **Direct materials:**   Materials that become part of the finished product and can be conveniently and economically traced to specific product units.

(L.O. 5)   **Employee time card:**   The basic time record maintained for each employee.

(L.O. 4)   **Factory overhead costs:**   A varied collection of production-related costs that cannot be practically or conveniently traced to end products.

(L.O. 7)   **Finished Goods Inventory account:**   An inventory account unique to the manufacturing or production area where the costs assigned to all completed products are transferred and maintained.

(L.O. 4)   **Fixed manufacturing costs:**   Production costs that stay fairly constant during the accounting period.

(L.O. 5)   **Gross payroll:**   A measure of the total wages and salaries earned by employees, including payroll deductions.

(L.O. 4)   **Indirect costs:**   Production costs that are not easily traced to specific products and must be assigned using some kind of allocation method.

(L.O. 4)   **Indirect labor costs:**   Labor costs for production-related activities that cannot be connected with or conveniently or economically traced to end products.

(L.O. 4)   **Indirect materials:**   Minor materials and other production supplies that cannot be conveniently and economically traced to specific products.

(L.O. 5)   **Job time card:**   A record of the time spent by each employee on a particular job.

(L.O. 1)   **Management accounting:**   The process of identification, measurement, accumulation, analysis, preparation, interpretation, and communication of financial and non-financial information used by management to plan, evaluate, and control within the organization and to ensure appropriate use and accountability for its resources.

(L.O. 7)   **Manufacturing cost flow:**   The flow of manufacturing costs (direct materials, direct labor, and factory overhead) from their incurrence through the Materials, Work in Process, and Finished Goods Inventory accounts to the Cost of Goods Sold account.

(L.O. 7)   **Materials Inventory account:**   An inventory account made up of the balances of materials and supplies on hand at a given time. Also called the Stores, Raw Materials Inventory, or Materials Inventory Control account.

(L.O. 5)   **Materials requisition:**   A form used within the company to authorize the use of stored materials and parts in the production operation.

(L.O. 5)   **Net payroll:**   The amount paid to the employee after all payroll deductions have been subtracted from gross wages.

(L.O. 6)   **Period costs:**   Operating costs for services that are consumed during the accounting period. Period costs cannot be inventoried.

(L.O. 6)   **Product costs:**   Inventoriable production costs consisting of the three manufacturing cost elements: direct materials, direct labor, and factory overhead.

(L.O. 5) **Purchase order:** A form used to communicate a company's raw materials and/or parts needs to a supplier; contains a description of the items needed, the quantities of each, and any other distinguishing features.

(L.O. 5) **Purchase requisition:** A form used to highlight a need for raw materials or parts that begins the purchasing process.

(L.O. 5) **Receiving report:** A form used to confirm receipt of goods from a supplier; compared to purchase order data.

(L.O. 8) **Statement of cost of goods manufactured:** A formal statement summarizing the flow of all manufacturing costs incurred during an accounting period.

(L.O. 8) **Total manufacturing costs:** The total costs for materials used, direct labor, and factory overhead incurred and charged to production during an accounting period.

(L.O. 4) **Variable manufacturing costs:** Costs that increase or decrease in direct proportion to the number of units produced.

(L.O. 7) **Work in Process Inventory account:** An inventory account that includes all manufacturing costs incurred and assigned to products being produced.

Self-Test

Test your knowledge of the chapter by choosing the best answer for each item below.

1. A cost that is conveniently and economically traceable to a product is known as a
   a. product cost.
   c. direct cost.
   b. variable cost.
   d. indirect cost. *(L.O. 4)*

2. Which of the following expenditures is a product cost?
   a. Interest expense
   c. Fire insurance for factory
   b. President's salary
   d. Sales commissions *(L.O. 4)*

3. Ethical considerations in management accounting deal primarily with
   a. actions and interactions of people.
   b. cost allocation techniques.
   c. proper product costing approaches.
   d. accurate manufacturing financial statements. *(L.O. 10)*

4. Management accounting does not differ from financial accounting in which of the following categories?
   a. Primary users of information
   c. Restrictive guidelines
   b. Use of a general ledger
   d. Focal point of analysis *(L.O. 2)*

5. Which of the following is most likely an indirect cost?
   a. Factory overhead
   c. Direct materials
   b. Direct labor
   d. Labor costs for specific work on products *(L.O. 4)*

6. Manufacturing companies traditionally use how many different types of inventory accounts?
   a. Four
   c. Two
   b. Three
   d. One *(L.O. 3, 7)*

7. Which of the following is not used to account for the cost of materials?
   a. Time card   c. Receiving report
   b. Purchase order   d. Purchase requisition   (L.O. 5)

8. A management accounting system is a necessary component for
   a. only manufacturing companies.
   b. only service organizations.
   c. only not-for-profit enterprises.
   d. all types of organizations.   (L.O. 1)

9. If the beginning balance in Materials Inventory was $4,200, the ending
   balance was $3,940, and $21,560 of materials were used during the
   month, how much materials were purchased during this time period?
   a. $21,820   c. $21,790
   b. $21,300   d. $21,600   (L.O. 8)

10. If the ending Work in Process Inventory totaled $13,250, total manufac-
    turing costs for the month were $89,220, and the beginning balance in the
    Work in Process Inventory account was $11,840, how much was the cost
    of goods manufactured?
    a. $90,330   c. $90,630
    b. $87,510   d. $87,810   (L.O. 8)

Answers to Self-Test are at the end of this chapter.

Review Problem
Cost of Goods Manufactured—Three Fundamental Steps

(L.O. 8)   In addition to the year-end balance sheet and income statement, the management of the Augustana Company requires the controller to prepare a statement of cost of goods manufactured. During 19x8, $561,920 of materials
were purchased. Operating cost data and inventory account balances for
19x8 follow:

Account	Balance
Direct Labor (15,430 hours at $8.50 per hour)	$131,155
Plant Supervision	52,500
Indirect Labor (50,280 hours at $5.25 per hour)	263,970
Factory Insurance	8,100
Utility	29,220
Depreciation, Factory Building	46,200
Depreciation, Equipment	92,800
Manufacturing Supplies	9,460
Repair and Maintenance	14,980
Selling and Administrative Expenses	96,480
Materials Inventory, Jan. 1, 19x8	26,490
Work in Process Inventory, Jan. 1, 19x8	101,640
Finished Goods Inventory, Jan. 1, 19x8	148,290
Materials Inventory, Dec. 31, 19x8	24,910
Work in Process Inventory, Dec. 31, 19x8	100,400
Finished Goods Inventory, Dec. 31, 19x8	141,100

Required

To review the three basic steps for computing cost of goods manufactured, do the following:

1. Compute the cost of materials used during the year.
2. Given the cost of materials used, compute the total manufacturing costs for the year.
3. Given total manufacturing costs for the year, compute the cost of goods manufactured during the year.

Answer to Review Problem

1. Computation of cost of materials used:

Beginning balance: Materials Inventory	$ 26,490
Plus materials purchases (net)	561,920
Cost of materials available for use	$588,410
Less ending balance: Materials Inventory	24,910
Cost of materials used	$563,500

2. Computation of total manufacturing costs:

Cost of materials used		$ 563,500
Plus direct labor costs		131,155
Plus total factory overhead costs:		
Plant supervision	$ 52,500	
Indirect labor	263,970	
Factory insurance	8,100	
Utility	29,220	
Depreciation, factory building	46,200	
Depreciation, equipment	92,800	
Manufacturing supplies	9,460	
Repair and maintenance	14,980	
Total factory overhead costs		517,230
Total manufacturing costs		$1,211,885

3. Computation of cost of goods manufactured:

Total manufacturing costs	$1,211,885
Plus beginning balance: Work in Process Inventory	101,640
Total cost of goods in process during the year	$1,313,525
Less ending balance: Work in Process Inventory	100,400
Cost of goods manufactured	$1,213,125

Chapter Assignments

Discussion Questions and Writing Assignments

1. Describe the field of management accounting, including the three kinds of information needed by management.
2. Identify the differences between management accounting and financial accounting with respect to primary users of information, types of accounting systems, and restrictive guidelines.
3. Compare and contrast management accounting and financial accounting in terms of units of measurement, focal point for analysis, frequency of reporting, and degree of reliability.
4. Does the size of a business dictate the types or amount of accounting information needed by management? Explain your answer.
5. What is the difference between a merchandising company and a manufacturing company? Include in your answer a description of inventory cost flows for each type of company.
6. What are the three kinds of cost included in product cost?
7. Define a direct cost. How is it different from an indirect cost?
8. Define direct materials.
9. Describe the following: purchase requisition (request), purchase order, and receiving report.
10. How is direct labor different from indirect labor?
11. What are the two kinds of labor-related costs? Discuss each one.
12. What characteristics identify a cost as being part of factory overhead?
13. What is meant by cost behavior?
14. What is the difference between a period cost and a product cost?
15. How does the periodic inventory method differ from the perpetual inventory method?
16. Identify and describe the three inventory accounts used by a manufacturing company.
17. What is meant by manufacturing cost flow?
18. Describe how to compute the cost of materials used.
19. How do total manufacturing costs differ from the total cost of goods manufactured?
20. How is the cost of goods manufactured used in computing the cost of goods sold?
21. State the three ethical standards of competence and identify why these standards are so important to the work of the management accountant.
22. Identify four of the seven ethical standards of integrity. Why is integrity so important for the management accountant to maintain?

Classroom Exercises

**Exercise 22-1.
Definitions of
Management
Accounting
(L.O. 1)**

There are many definitions and descriptions of the field of management accounting. The National Association of Accountants, in *Statement No. 1A* of its series of *Statements on Management Accounting,* defines management accounting as

". . . the process of identification, measurement, accumulation, analysis, preparation, interpretation, and communication of financial (and non-financial) information used by management to plan, evaluate, and control within an organization and to assure appropriate use of and accountability for its resources. Management accounting also comprises the preparation of financial reports for nonmanagement groups such as shareholders, creditors, regulatory agencies, and tax authorities."[3]

In *The Modern Accountant's Handbook*, management (managerial) accounting is described as follows:

"Managerial accounting, although generally anchored to the financial accounting framework, involves a broader information-processing system. It deals in many units of measure and produces a variety of reports designed for specific purposes. Its scope encompasses the past, the present, and the future. Its purposes include short- and long-range planning, cost determination, control of activities, assessment of objectives and program performance, and provision of basic information for decision making."[4]

1. Compare and contrast these two statements about the field of management accounting.
2. "It is impossible to distinguish where financial accounting ends and management accounting begins." Explain this statement.

Exercise 22-2.
Cost Flow
(L.O. 3)

Oviedo Corporation has two divisions, the Sleek Division and the Market Division, that operate as autonomous units. Sleek Division manufactures power boats. Market Division's responsibility, as a marine supplies merchandiser, includes sales and service of Sleek's products.

1. Describe the types and flow of operating costs through the records of each division.
2. What differences will be found when the financial statements of the two divisions are compared?

Exercise 22-3.
Cost Classification
(L.O. 4, 6)

The following is a list of typical costs incurred by a garment maker: (a) gasoline and oil for salesperson's automobile; (b) telephone charges; (c) dyes for yardage; (d) seamstresses' regular hourly labor; (e) thread; (f) president's subscription to *The Wall Street Journal*; (g) sales commissions; (h) business forms used in the office; (i) buttons and zippers; (j) depreciation of sewing machines; (k) property taxes, factory; (l) advertising; (m) brand labels; (n) administrative salaries; (o) interest on business loans; (p) starch and fabric conditioners; (q) patterns; (r) hourly workers' vacation pay; (s) roof repair, office; (t) packaging.

1. At the time these costs are incurred, which ones will be classified as period costs? Which ones will be treated as product costs?
2. Of the costs identified as product costs, which are direct costs? Which are indirect costs?

3. National Association of Accountants, *Statement No. 1A* (New York, 1982).
4. Edwards and Black, *The Modern Accountant's Handbook* (Homewood, Ill.: Dow Jones-Irwin, 1976), p. 830.

Exercise 22-4.
Documentation
(L.O. 5)

St. John Company manufactures a complete line of music boxes. Seventy percent of its products are standard items and are produced in long production runs. The remaining 30 percent of the music boxes are special orders involving specific requests for tunes. These special order boxes cost from three to six times the standard product because of the use of additional materials and labor.

Erin Trease, controller, recently received a complaint memorandum from Mr. V. Johnson, production supervisor, because of the new network of source documents added to the existing cost accounting system. These new documents include a purchase requisition, a purchase order, a receiving report, and a materials requisition. Mr. Johnson claims that these forms represent extra "busy work" and interrupt the normal flow of production.

Prepare a written response from Ms. Trease that explains fully the purpose for each type of document.

Exercise 22-5.
Periodic Versus
Perpetual
Inventory Methods
(L.O. 7)

1. In as much detail as possible, discuss the differences between the periodic and the perpetual inventory methods. Be sure to describe the kinds of businesses that might use each method.
2. Would the periodic or perpetual inventory method be more suitable for each of the businesses in the following list? Be prepared to defend your answers.

a. Home appliance retailer	i. Pool supplies store
b. Grocery store	j. Paper manufacturer
c. Computer hardware company	k. Fertilizer manufacturer
d. Retailer of fine jewelry	l. Tire manufacturer
e. Sporting goods store	m. Cosmetics outlet for exclusive
f. Grain elevator	distributorship
g. Discount department store	n. Car dealer
h. Auto parts store	o. Office supplies store

Exercise 22-6.
Concept of Three
Types of Inventory
(L.O. 7)

"For manufacturing companies, the concept of the inventory account must be expanded to include three types of accounts: Materials Inventory, Work in Process Inventory, and Finished Goods Inventory."

Briefly explain how the three inventory accounts function and how they relate to each other.

Exercise 22-7.
Manufacturing
Cost Flow
(L.O. 7)

Using the ideas illustrated in Figures 22-7 and 22-8 and discussed in this chapter, describe in detail the flow of materials costs through the recording process of a cost accounting system. Include in your answer all general ledger accounts affected and all recording documents used. Prepare your answer in proper order and be as specific as you can.

Exercise 22-8.
Cost of Materials
Used
(L.O. 8)

Data for the cost of materials for the month ended July 31, 19x2 are as follows: Materials inventory on July 1, 19x2, $24,200; Materials inventory on July 31, 19x2, $51,910. During July the company purchased $220,600 of materials on account from Lakers Company and $62,200 of materials for cash from Magic Company. The company paid $45,000 on Lakers' account balance. Compute the cost of materials used during July 19x2.

Exercise 22-9.
Computing Total
Manufacturing
Costs
(L.O. 8)

The partial trial balance of Downey Millinery, Inc. follows:

Account	Debit	Credit
Accounts Receivable	$ 97,420	
Materials Inventory	78,400	
Work in Process Inventory	84,400	
Finished Goods Inventory	51,400	
Accounts Payable		$ 99,250
Sales		891,940
Materials Purchases	421,600	
Direct Labor	161,200	
Operating Supplies, Factory	31,700	
Depreciation, Machinery	74,100	
Fire Loss	82,000	
Insurance, Factory	9,700	
Indirect Labor	56,900	
Supervisory Salaries, Factory	38,700	
President's Salary	39,900	
Property Tax, Factory	9,400	
Other Indirect Manufacturing	26,500	

Inventory accounts reflect balances at the beginning of the period. Period-end balances are $77,000, $95,800, and $46,200 for the Materials Inventory, Work in Process Inventory, and Finished Goods Inventory accounts, respectively. From this information, prepare a schedule (in good form) showing the computation of total manufacturing costs for the period ending May 31, 19x1.

Exercise 22-10.
Statement of Cost
of Goods
Manufactured
(L.O. 8)

Information on the manufacturing costs incurred by the Gordon Company for the month ended August 31, 19x9, is as follows:

Purchases of materials during August totaled $139,000.

Direct labor was 3,400 hours at $8.75 per hour.

The following factory overhead costs were incurred: utilities, $5,870; supervision, $16,600; indirect supplies, $6,750; depreciation, $6,200; insurance, $1,830; miscellaneous, $1,100.

Inventory accounts on August 1 were as follows: Materials, $48,600; Work in Process, $54,250; Finished Goods, $38,500. Inventory accounts on August 31 were as follows: Materials, $50,100; Work in Process, $48,400; Finished Goods, $37,450.

From the information given above, prepare a statement of cost of goods manufactured.

**Exercise 22-11.
Computing Cost of
Goods Sold**
(L.O. 8, 9)

McCarley Distilleries, Inc. produces a deluxe line of wines and other alcoholic beverages. During 19x1 the company operated at record levels, with sales totaling $795,000. The accounting department has already determined that total manufacturing costs for the period were $464,500. Operating expenses for the year were $159,740. Inventory account balances were as follows:

Account	Jan. 1, 19x1	Dec. 31, 19x1
Materials Inventory	$25,490	$22,810
Work in Process Inventory	57,400	56,980
Finished Goods Inventory	84,820	77,320

Assuming a 34 percent tax rate, prepare an income statement for the year ended December 31, 19x1.

**Exercise 22-12.
Scenarios on
Ethics**
(L.O. 10)

For each of the two scenarios described below, identify the ethical issue or issues involved and state the appropriate solution to the problem. Be prepared to defend your answers.

1. Mac Rucker is controller for the Nashville Corporation. Mac has been with the company for seventeen years and is being considered for the job of Chief Financial Officer (CFO). His boss, the current CFO, will be the Nashville Corporation's new president. Mac has just discussed the year-end closing with his boss, who made the following statement during the conversation:

   "Mac, why are you so inflexible? I'm only asking you to postpone the write-off of the $2,500,000 of obsolete inventory for ten days so that it will not appear on this year's financial statements. Ten days! Do it. Your promotion is coming up, you know. Make sure you keep all of the possible outcomes in mind as you complete your year-end work. Oh, and keep this conversation confidential—just between you and me. OK?"

   What should Mac do?

2. Kim Wallen went to work for Vegas Industries five years ago. She was recently promoted to cost accounting manager and now has a new boss, Ted Wilcox, corporate controller. Last week, Kim and Ted went to a two-day professional development program on accounting changes in the new manufacturing environment. During the first hour of the first day's program, Ted disappeared and Kim didn't see him again until the cocktail hour. The same events took place on the second day. During the trip home, Kim asked Ted if he enjoyed the conference. He replied:

   "Kim, the golf course was excellent. You play golf. Why don't you join me during the next continuing education conference? I haven't sat in on one of those sessions in ten years. This is my R&R time. Those sessions are for the new people. My experience is enough to keep me current. Plus, I have excellent people to help me as we adjust our accounting system to the changes being implemented on the production floor."

   Does Kim have an ethical dilemma? What are her options?

Interpreting Accounting Information

Rudolph Manufacturing Company (L.O. 8, 9)

Rudolph Manufacturing Company manufactures sheet metal products for heating and air conditioning installations. For the past several years its income has been declining, and this past year, 19x1, was particularly poor. The company's statement of cost of goods manufactured and its income statement for 19x0 and 19x1 are shown below and on the following page. You have been asked to comment on why the company's profit situation has deteriorated.

Rudolph Manufacturing Company
Statements of Cost of Goods Manufactured
For the Years Ended December 31, 19x1 and 19x0

	19x1		19x0	
Materials Used				
Materials Inventory, January 1	$ 91,240		$ 93,560	
Materials Purchased	937,640		959,940	
Cost of Materials Available for Use	$1,078,880		$1,053,500	
Less Materials Inventory, December 31	95,020		91,340	
Cost of Materials Used		$ 983,860		$ 962,160
Direct Labor		571,410		579,720
Factory Overhead Costs				
Indirect Labor	$ 132,660		$ 171,980	
Power	34,990		32,550	
Insurance	22,430		18,530	
Supervision	125,330		120,050	
Depreciation	75,730		72,720	
Other Factory Costs	41,740		36,280	
Total Factory Overhead Costs		482,880		452,110
Total Manufacturing Costs		$2,038,150		$1,993,990
Add Work in Process Inventory, January 1		148,875		152,275
Total Cost of Goods in Process During the Year		$2,187,025		$2,146,265
Less Work in Process Inventory, December 31		146,750		148,875
Cost of Goods Manufactured		$2,040,275		$1,997,390

Rudolph Manufacturing Company
Income Statements
For the Years Ended December 31, 19x1 and 19x0

	19x1		19x0	
Net Sales		$2,942,960		$3,096,220
Cost of Goods Sold				
Finished Goods Inventory, January 1	$ 142,640		$ 184,820	
Cost of Goods Manufactured	2,040,275		1,997,390	
Total Cost of Finished Goods Available for Sale	$2,182,915		$2,182,210	
Less Finished Goods Inventory, December 31	186,630		192,640	
Cost of Goods Sold		1,996,285		1,989,570
Gross Margin from Sales		$ 946,675		$1,106,650
Operating Expenses				
Sales Salary and Commission Expense	$ 394,840		$ 329,480	
Advertising Expense	116,110		194,290	
Other Selling Expenses	82,630		72,930	
Administrative Expenses	242,600		195,530	
Total Operating Expenses		836,230		792,230
Income from Operations		$ 110,445		$ 314,420
Other Revenues and Expenses				
Interest Expense		54,160		56,815
Income Before Taxes		$ 56,285		$ 257,605
Less Income Taxes Expense (34%)		19,137		87,586
Net Income		$ 37,148		$ 170,019

Required

1. In preparing your comments on the decline in income, compute the following ratios for each year:
   a. Ratios of cost of materials used to total manufacturing costs, direct labor to total manufacturing costs, and total factory overhead costs to total manufacturing costs. Round to one decimal place.
   b. Ratios of gross margin from sales to sales, total operating expenses to sales, and net income to sales. Round to one decimal place.
2. From your evaluation of the ratios computed in **1**, state the probable causes of the decline in net income.
3. What other factors or ratios do you believe should be considered?

Problem Set A

**Problem 22A-1.
Direct Materials:
Cost Flow
(L.O. 4, 7)**

A good working knowledge of direct materials cost is important for understanding the elements, purpose, and operation of a management accounting system.

Required

1. Name the characteristics associated with (a) direct materials and (b) indirect materials.
2. Give at least two examples for each of the two cost categories listed in **1** above.
3. Prepare a diagram of the flow of all materials costs, both direct and indirect, for a manufacturing concern. Show which documents are used to record materials costs, and relate those documents to specific parts of the cost flow diagram.
4. If a direct materials invoice for $600 is dated September 2, terms 2/10, n/30, how much should be paid if the invoice is paid on September 8? On September 29?

**Problem 22A-2.
Unit Cost
Computation
(L.O. 6)**

Grammer Industries has recently finished production of Job Sb-15. The corporation's cost accountant is ready to calculate the unit cost for this order. Relevant information for the month ended March 31, 19x2 is as follows.

The number of units produced was 41,480. Cost information for Department F-14 included 4,410 liters at $3.00 per liter for direct materials used, 152 hours at $8.50 per hour for direct labor incurred, and $3,514 of factory overhead. Cost data for Department G-12 included 850 liters at $5.57 per liter for direct materials used, 510 hours at $7.80 per hour for direct labor incurred, and $7,470 of factory overhead. Cost data for Department H-15 included 1,980 liters at $5.00 per liter for direct materials used, 620 hours at $8.00 per hour for direct labor incurred, and $6,810 of factory overhead. Each unit produced was processed through the three departments, F-14, G-12, and H-15, in that order. There was no ending balance in the Work in Process Inventory account as of March 31, 19x2.

Required

1. Compute the unit cost for each of the three separate departments, rounding to three decimal places.
2. Compute the total unit cost.
3. Order Sb-15 was specially made for the Isman Company for a selling price of $57,125. Determine whether the selling price was appropriate. List the assumptions or computations on which you base your answer. What advice, if any, would you offer to the management of Grammer Industries on the pricing of future orders?

**Problem 22A-3.
Cost of Goods
Manufactured:
Three
Fundamental
Steps
(L.O. 8)**

Padgett Metallurgists, Inc. is a large manufacturing firm that prepares financial statements on a quarterly basis. Assume that you are working in the firm's accounting department. Preparing a statement of cost of goods manufactured is one of your regular quarterly duties. Account balances for the quarter ended March 31, 19x9, are as shown on the following page:

Account	Balance
Office Supplies	$ 4,870
Depreciation, Plant and Equipment	25,230
President's Salary	36,000
Property Taxes, Office	1,950
Equipment Repairs, Factory	4,290
Plant Supervisors' Salaries	16,750
Insurance, Plant and Equipment	2,040
Direct Labor	248,310
Utilities, Plant	6,420
Indirect Labor	16,000
Manufacturing Supplies	4,760
Small Tools	2,900
Materials Inventory, Jan. 1, 19x9	397,950
Materials Inventory, Mar. 31, 19x9	415,030
Work in Process Inventory, Jan. 1, 19x9	529,840
Work in Process Inventory, Mar. 31, 19x9	515,560
Finished Goods Inventory, Jan. 1, 19x9	375,010
Finished Goods Inventory, Mar. 31, 19x9	402,840
Materials Purchases during the Quarter	1,225,330

Required

Highlight the three basic steps in preparing the statement of cost of goods manufactured, as follows:

1. Prepare a schedule showing the computation of the cost of materials used during the quarter.
2. Using the figure calculated in **1**, prepare a schedule that determines the total manufacturing costs for the quarter.
3. From the figure derived in **2**, prepare a final schedule that derives the cost of goods manufactured for the quarter.

Problem 22A-4.
Statement of Cost of Goods Manufactured
(L.O. 8)

Bowman and Blunt Vineyards operates a large winery in California that produces a full line of varietal wines. The company, whose fiscal year begins on November 1, has just completed a record-breaking year ending October 31, 19x1. Inventory and production data for this period are as follows:

Account	Oct. 31, 19x1	Nov. 1, 19x0
Materials Inventory	$1,803,800	$2,156,200
Work in Process Inventory	2,764,500	3,371,000
Finished Goods Inventory	1,883,200	1,596,400

Materials purchased during the year amounted to $6,750,000. Direct labor hours incurred totaled 142,500, at an average labor rate of $8.20 per hour. The following factory overhead costs were incurred during the year: depreciation, plant and equipment, $685,600; operating supplies, $207,300; property tax, plant and equipment, $94,200; material handlers' labor, $83,700; small tools, $42,400; utilities, $96,500; employee benefits, $76,100.

Required

Using proper form, prepare a statement of cost of goods manufactured from the information provided.

Problem 22A-5.
Statement
Preparation:
Manufacturing
Company
(L.O. 8, 9)

The Hurlburt Pharmaceuticals Corporation manufactures a variety of drugs that are marketed internationally. Inventory information for April 19x2 was as follows:

Account	April 30	April 1
Materials:		
Natural Minerals	$ 60,600	$ 78,700
Basic Organic Compounds	101,400	114,300
Catalysts	27,900	30,500
Suspension Agents	38,200	34,900
Total Materials	$228,100	$258,400
Work in Process	$127,200	$138,800
Finished Goods	114,100	111,700

Purchases of materials for April were: natural minerals, $124,610; basic organic compounds, $250,980; catalysts, $142,670; and suspension agents, $94,340. Direct labor costs were computed on the basis of 20,000 hours at $8.00 per hour. Actual factory overhead costs incurred in April were: operating supplies, $8,700; janitorial and material-handling labor, $69,100; employee benefits, $90,800; heat, light, and power $44,000; depreciation, factory, $74,400; property taxes, $9,500; and the expired portion of insurance premiums, $7,000. Net sales for April were $2,188,400. General and administrative expenses were $362,000. Income is taxed at a rate of 34 percent.

Required

1. Compute the dollar usage of each of the four types of materials during April.
2. Using good form, prepare a statement of cost of goods manufactured for the month ended April 30.
3. Using your answer in 2, prepare an income statement for the same period.

Problem Set B

Problem 22B-1.
Factory Overhead:
Cost Flow
(L.O. 4, 5)

A working knowledge of the makeup of the factory overhead cost category is essential to understanding the elements, purpose, and operation of a cost accounting system.

Required

1. Identify the characteristics of factory overhead.
2. Are factory overhead costs always indirect costs? Why?
3. List three examples of a factory overhead cost.
4. Diagram the flow of factory overhead costs in a manufacturing environment. List the documents used to record these costs, and link the documents to specific parts of the cost flow diagram.
5. Lafite Industries in Hermann, Missouri, produces oak wine barrels. The oak wood is purchased in large slabs and milled to size. Metal barrel rings are purchased from an outside vendor. The following factory overhead costs were incurred in June: indirect mill labor, $32,620; indirect assembly labor, $16,910; supervisory salaries, $9,200; depreciation, equipment, $2,800; factory rent, $4,500; utilities, $2,200; and small tools, $1,410. Identify each of the above costs as being either a variable cost or a fixed cost. Give reasons for your answers.

Problem 22B-2.
Unit Cost
Computation
(L.O. 6)

McVan Industries, Inc. manufactures video disks for several of the leading recording studios in the United States and Europe. Department 85 is responsible for the electronic circuitry within each disk. Some parts are purchased from outside vendors and others are produced internally. Department 82 applies the plastic-like surface to the disks and packages them for shipment. A recent order for 4,000 disks from the ERV Company was produced during July. For this job the department purchased miscellaneous parts costing $7,920 from Anderson Corporation. Department 85 incurred the following costs for this job: direct materials used, $6,800; direct labor, $3,400; and factory overhead, $3,680. Costs incurred by Department 82 included $1,960 of direct materials used; $1,280 of direct labor; and $2,400 of factory overhead. All 4,000 units were completed and shipped during the month.

Required

1. Compute the unit cost for each of the two departments.
2. Compute the total unit cost for the ERV Company order.
3. The selling price for this order was $7 per unit. Was the selling price adequate? List the assumptions and/or computations upon which you based your answer. What suggestions would you make to McVan Industries' management concerning the pricing of future orders?

Problem 22B-3.
Cost of Goods
Manufactured:
Three
Fundamental
Steps
(L.O. 8)

Tanju Company manufactures a line of aquatic equipment, including a new gill-like device that produces oxygen from water and replaces the large, cumbersome pressurized air tanks. Management requires that a statement of cost of goods manufactured be prepared on a quarterly basis, along with an income statement. As the company's accountant, you have determined the following account balances for the quarter ended October 31, 19x1:

Account	Balance
Materials Purchases during Quarter	$328,000
Small Tools	18,240
Factory Insurance	3,690
Factory Utilities	7,410
Depreciation, Building	16,240
Depreciation, Equipment	12,990
Selling Expenses	42,600
Plant Supervisor's Salary	16,250
Direct Labor	194,700
Indirect Labor	81,400
Repairs and Maintenance, Factory	21,200
Miscellaneous Factory Overhead	14,120
Indirect Materials and Supplies, Factory	39,400
Materials Inventory, August 1, 19x1	55,600
Materials Inventory, October 31, 19x1	56,240
Work in Process Inventory, August 1, 19x1	44,020
Work in Process Inventory, October 31, 19x1	41,900
Finished Goods Inventory, August 1, 19x1	39,200
Finished Goods Inventory, October 31, 19x1	40,200

Required

Highlight the three basic steps used in preparing the statement of cost of goods manufactured, as follows:

1. Prepare a schedule showing the computation of the cost of materials used during the quarter.
2. Using the figure calculated in **1**, prepare a schedule that determines the total manufacturing costs for the quarter.
3. From the amount computed in **2**, prepare a final schedule that derives cost of goods manufactured for the quarter.

Problem 22B-4.
Statement of Cost
of Goods
Manufactured
(L.O. 8)

Oppedal Manufacturing Company produces a line of Viking ship replicas. These models are sold at Scandinavian gift shops throughout the world. Financial records of the company provided the following information: Inventory account balances on May 1, 19x2 were: Materials, $190,400; Work in Process, $96,250; and Finished Goods, $52,810. April 30, 19x3 inventory account balances were: Materials, $186,250; Work in Process, $87,900; and Finished Goods, $56,620.

During the 19x2–x3 fiscal year $474,630 of materials were purchased, and payroll records indicated that direct labor costs totaled $215,970. Overhead costs for the period included: indirect materials and supplies, $77,640; indirect labor, $192,710; depreciation, building, $19,900; depreciation, equipment, $14,240; heating, $19,810; electricity, $8,770; repairs and maintenance, $12,110; liability and fire insurance, $2,980; property taxes, building, $3,830; design and rework, $23,770; and supervision, $92,290. Other costs for the period included selling costs, $41,720, and administrative salaries, $102,750.

Required

Using the information provided above, prepare a statement of cost of goods manufactured for the fiscal year ended April 30, 19x3.

Problem 22B-5.
Statement
Preparation:
Manufacturing
Company
(L.O. 8, 9)

The Jessie Creek Company produces lighting fixtures. All parts are purchased, and the primary function of the company is the assembly of the fixtures. Inventory account information for the quarter ended December 31, 19x9, is as follows:

Account	December 31	October 1
Materials:		
Fixtures	$42,020	$36,810
Shades	13,940	12,660
Electrical Parts	20,470	19,890
Wire	8,840	9,250
Work in Process	80,130	77,910
Finished Goods	81,260	86,520

During the three-month period, the company purchased $92,480 of fixtures; $41,660 of shades; $52,780 of electrical parts; and $11,460 of wire. Direct labor for the period was 12,000 hours at an average wage rate of $9.50 per hour. Factory overhead costs for the period were: indirect labor, $36,870; assembly supplies, $3,930; factory rent, $2,500; insurance expense, $1,940; repairs and maintenance, $4,380; and depreciation of equipment, $2,600. Total sales for the three months were $691,770; and general, selling, and administrative expenses totaled $296,820. Assume a federal income tax rate of 34 percent.

Required

1. Compute the dollar usage of each of the four types of materials during the quarter.
2. Using good form, prepare a statement of cost of goods manufactured for the quarter ended December 31, 19x9.
3. Working from your answer in **2**, prepare an income statement for the same period.

Management Decision Case

St. Facione Municipal Hospital
(L.O. 3, 4, 6)

Hospitals exist in a highly competitive environment and they rely heavily on cost data to keep their pricing structures in line with those of competitors. St. Facione Municipal Hospital is a case in point. Located in a large city, the hospital offers three broad kinds of service. *General services* (dietary, housekeeping, maintenance, patient care coordination, and general and administrative services) are the first kind of service. *Ancillary services* (anesthesiology, blood bank, central and sterile supply, electrodiagnosis, laboratory, operating and recovery room, pharmacy, radiology, and respiratory therapy) are the second kind. *Nursing care services* (acute or intensive care units, intermediate care units, neonatal—newborn—nursery, and nursing administration) are the third kind.

The hospital's controller is Jerry Samuelson. He is reviewing the billing procedure for patients using the thirty intensive care units (ICUs) in the facility. Each unit contains a regular hospital bed and a great deal of special equipment. This includes suction equipment, oxygen flowmeters at bedside, endotracheal tubes to assist breathing, a portable respirator, back-up suction machinery, and multiple IVs (intravenous feeding lines) with automatic drip counters. An H.P. Swan Ganz machine has a cardiac catheter tube that, when inserted into the heart, constantly monitors the pressure inside the heart chambers. One of the most important pieces of equipment at each bedside in the ICU is the cardiac monitor that displays the patient's heartbeat. A set of central monitors at the nurses' station helps nurses watch for instances of tachycardia (excessively rapid heartbeat), arrhythmia (irregular heartbeat), or bradycardia (abnormally slow heartbeat). An alarm system attached to the monitor warns the nurses when the patient's heartbeat is over or under acceptable limits. To equip an ICU today costs about $185,000 per room. Use of the equipment is billed to the patient at a rate of $250 per day. This includes a 40 percent markup to cover hospital overhead and profit.

Other ICU patient costs include the following:

Doctors' care	2 hours per day @ $360 per hour (actual)
Special nursing care	4 hours per day @ $85 per hour (actual)
Regular nursing care	24 hours per day @ $28 per hour (average)
Medicines	$237 per day (average)
Medical supplies	$134 per day (average)
Room rental	$350 per day (average)
Food and service	$140 per day (average)

For billing these costs, as with the equipment charge, the hospital adds 40 percent to all costs to cover its operating costs and profit.

Required

1. From the costs listed, identify the direct costs used in computing the cost per patient day in an ICU.

2. Compute the cost per patient day.
3. Compute the billing per patient day using the hospital's existing markup rate to cover operating expenses and profit.
4. Many hospitals use separate markup rates for each cost when preparing billing statements. Industry averages revealed the following markup rates:

Equipment	30%	Medicines	50%
Doctors' care	50	Medical supplies	50
Special nursing care	40	Room rental	30
Regular nursing care	50	Food and service	25

Using these rates, recompute the billing per patient day for an ICU.
5. Using the information in **3** and **4**, which billing procedure would you recommend to the hospital's director? Why?

Answers to Self-Test

1. c	3. a	5. a	7. a	9. b
2. c	4. b	6. b	8. d	10. d

CHAPTER 23

Product Costing: The Job Order System

Determining a product's unit cost is one of the basic functions of a cost accounting system. Business success depends on product costing information in several ways. First, unit costs are an important element in determining an adequate, fair, and competitive selling price. Second, product costing information often forms the basis for forecasting and controlling operations and costs. Finally, product unit costs are needed to arrive at ending inventory balances.

One important reason for having a cost accounting system is to figure out the cost of manufacturing an individual product or batch of products. Such cost accounting systems differ from one company to another. But each system is designed to give information that company management thinks is important. In this chapter, we relate the basic information on manufacturing accounting discussed in Chapter 22 to a traditional product costing system: the job order costing system. A **job order** is a customer order for a specific number of specially designed, made-to-order products. We also learn to compute product costs in job order situations. Then we link these costs to units completed and transferred to the finished goods inventory.

However, before we can discuss a specific product cost accounting system, we need more background information. In the first part of this chapter we compare the two most common product costing systems—job order costing and process costing. Next we explain the concept of absorption costing. Finally, we discuss predetermined overhead rates and their application to specific jobs or products. Emphasis is then placed on describing and illustrating the job order cost accounting system. After studying this chapter, you should be able to meet the learning objectives listed on the left. A work sheet analysis based on perpetual inventories is covered in a special analysis in The Windham Company Practice Case.

Job Order Versus Process Costing

Job order costing and process costing are the two traditional, basic approaches to product cost accounting systems. Actual cost accounting systems may differ widely. However, all are based on one of these two product costing concepts. Once the type of system is selected, it is then adjusted to fit a particular industry, company, or operating department. The objective of the two systems is the same. They are both meant to provide product unit cost information for product pricing, cost control, inventory valuation, and income statement preparation. End-of-period values for the Cost of Goods Sold, Work in Process Inventory, and Finished Goods Inventory accounts are computed using product unit cost data.

Characteristics of Job Order Costing

OBJECTIVE 1
Identify the differences between job order costing and process costing

A **job order cost accounting system** is a product costing system used by companies making one-of-a-kind or special-order products. In such a system, direct materials, direct labor, and factory overhead costs are assigned to specific job orders or batches of products. In computing unit costs, the total manufacturing costs for each job order are divided by the number of good units produced for that order. Industries that use a job order cost accounting system include those that make ships, airplanes, large machines, and special orders. Job order costing may also be used when producing a set quantity of a product for inventory replenishment, such as a production run of 500 identical lawn mowers.

The primary characteristics of a job order cost system are as follows: (1) It collects all manufacturing costs and assigns them to specific jobs or batches of product. (2) It measures costs for each completed job, rather than for set time periods. (3) It uses just one Work in Process Inventory account in the general ledger. This account is supported by a subsidiary ledger of job order cost cards or sheets for each job still in process at period end.

Characteristics of Process Costing

A **process cost accounting system** is a product costing system used by companies that make a large number of similar products or maintain a continuous production flow. In these cases, it is more economical to account for product-related costs for a period of time (a week or a month) than to try to assign them to specific products or job orders. Unit costs are computed by dividing total manufacturing costs assigned to a particular department or work center during a week or month by the number of good units produced during that time period. If a product is routed through four departments, four unit cost amounts are added together to find the product's total unit cost. Companies producing paint, oil and gas, automobiles, bricks, or soft drinks use some form of a process costing system.

The main characteristics of a process cost accounting system are as follows: (1) Manufacturing costs are grouped by department or work center, with little concern for specific job orders. (2) It emphasizes a weekly or monthly time period rather than the time taken to complete a specific order. (3) It uses several Work in Process Inventory accounts—one for each department or work center in the manufacturing process. Process costing will be discussed in detail in Chapter 24.

The Concept of Absorption Costing

OBJECTIVE 2
Describe the concept of absorption costing

Product costing is possible only when the accounting system can define the types of manufacturing costs to be included in the analysis. For instance, should all factory overhead costs be considered costs of making the product, or only the variable factory overhead costs? Usually, we assume that product costing is governed by the concept of absorption costing. **Absorption costing** is an approach to product costing that assigns a representative portion of *all* types of manufacturing costs to individual products: direct materials, direct labor, variable factory overhead, and fixed factory overhead. The product costing systems we discuss in this chapter and in Chapter 24 apply the absorption costing concept.

Direct materials and direct labor costs are not difficult to handle in product costing because they can be conveniently and economically traced to products. Factory overhead costs, on the other hand, are not as easy to trace directly to products. For example, for a company making lawn and garden equipment, how much machine depreciation should be assigned to a single lawnmower? How about the costs of electrical power and indirect labor? One solution would be to wait until the end of the accounting period. We could then add up all the variable and fixed factory overhead costs incurred and divide the total by the number of units produced during the period. This procedure would be acceptable only if all products were alike (and required the same manufacturing operations) and managers could wait until the end of the period to learn the product unit costs. Such a situation is seldom found in industry. A company usually makes many different products, and managers need product costing information to set prices before the goods are produced. Therefore we must use a predetermined overhead rate to allocate factory overhead costs to products.

Predetermined Overhead Rates

OBJECTIVE 3
Compute a predetermined overhead rate, and use this rate to apply overhead costs to production

Factory overhead costs are a problem for the management accountant. Actual overhead costs fluctuate from month to month because of the timing of fixed overhead costs. Therefore, some method must be used to allocate overhead costs to products. How can these costs be estimated and assigned to certain products or jobs before the end of the accounting period? The most common way is to use a **predetermined overhead rate** for each department or operating unit. We can define this rate as an overhead cost factor used to assign factory overhead costs to specific products or jobs. It is based on *estimated* overhead costs and production levels for the period. The rate is computed in three steps:

1. Estimate factory overhead costs. Using various management accounting tools and analyses, estimate all factory overhead costs. Do so for each production department in the coming accounting period. (Cost behavior analysis is especially useful for this procedure and will be discussed in Chapter 25.) Add the totals for all the production

departments. For example, suppose that the total costs of rent, utilities, insurance, and so on for the coming year are expected to be $450,000.

2. Select a basis for allocating costs and estimate its amount. We must connect overhead costs to the products produced by using some measure of production activity. Common measures of production activity are machine hours, labor hours, dollars of direct labor cost, or units of output. The basis that is chosen should link the overhead cost to the product produced in a meaningful way. For instance, if an operation is more machine-hour than labor-hour intensive (as in the typical automated production line), then machine hours would be a good basis to use for overhead allocation. In our example, let us suppose that overhead per machine hour would be the most useful measure. Management believes that 50,000 machine hours will be used during the year.

3. Divide the total overhead costs estimated for the period by the total estimated basis (hours, dollars, or units). The result is the predetermined overhead rate. For our example, the computation is as follows:

$$\text{predetermined overhead rate} \atop \text{per machine hour} = \frac{\text{total estimated overhead costs}}{\text{total estimated machine hours}}$$

$$= \frac{\$450,000}{50,000 \text{ hours}}$$

$$= \$9 \text{ of overhead per machine hour}$$

Overhead costs are then applied to each product using this rate. Let us say that it takes 0.5 machine hours to produce one unit. Since the overhead rate is $9 per machine hour, that unit is assigned $4.50 of factory overhead cost. This amount is then added to the direct materials and direct labor costs already assigned to the product. Their sum is the total unit cost.

Importance of Good Estimates

The successful allocation of overhead cost depends on two factors. One is a careful estimate of the total amount of overhead. The other is a good forecast of the production activity that is used as the allocation basis.

Estimating total overhead costs is critical. If the estimate is wrong, the overhead rate will be wrong. The result will be that either too much or too little overhead cost will be assigned to the products produced. Therefore, in developing this estimate, the management accountant must be careful to include all factory overhead items and to forecast their costs accurately.

Overhead costs are generally estimated as part of the normal budgeting process. Expected overhead costs are gathered from all departments involved either directly or indirectly with the production process. The accounting department receives and totals each department's cost estimates. Since costs of supporting service departments, such as maintenance and electrical departments, have only an indirect connection with products, they are distributed among the production departments.

In this way they can be included as part of total manufacturing overhead when computing the predetermined overhead rate of the period.

Forecasting production activity is also critical to the success of overhead cost allocation. First, we must ask which activity base is most appropriate—machine hours, labor hours, labor dollars, or units of output. The basis chosen should relate to the overhead cost in a causal or beneficial way. For example, an increase in machine hours would cause higher electricity costs. Therefore, departments that are equipment intensive (for example, one person running twenty-five or thirty machines by remote control) would use machine hours as the allocation basis. The object is to pick the one activity base that varies most with total overhead costs. An appropriate activity base means that the overhead costs assigned to individual jobs or products will be closely related to the actual overhead costs incurred.

Table 23-1 sums up the process of overhead cost allocation. In Phase I we compute the predetermined overhead rate. To do so, we estimate total overhead costs and total production activity. In Phase II we use the predetermined overhead rate to compute the amount of overhead costs to be applied to products or jobs during the period.

Underapplied or Overapplied Overhead

OBJECTIVE 4
Dispose of underapplied or overapplied overhead

A lot of time and effort may be put into estimating and allocating factory overhead costs. Still, actual overhead costs and actual production activities will seldom agree with these estimates. Changes in anticipated costs or increases/decreases in the activity base will cause a difference between actual and estimated costs. Such differences will cause assigned factory overhead to be either underapplied or overapplied—

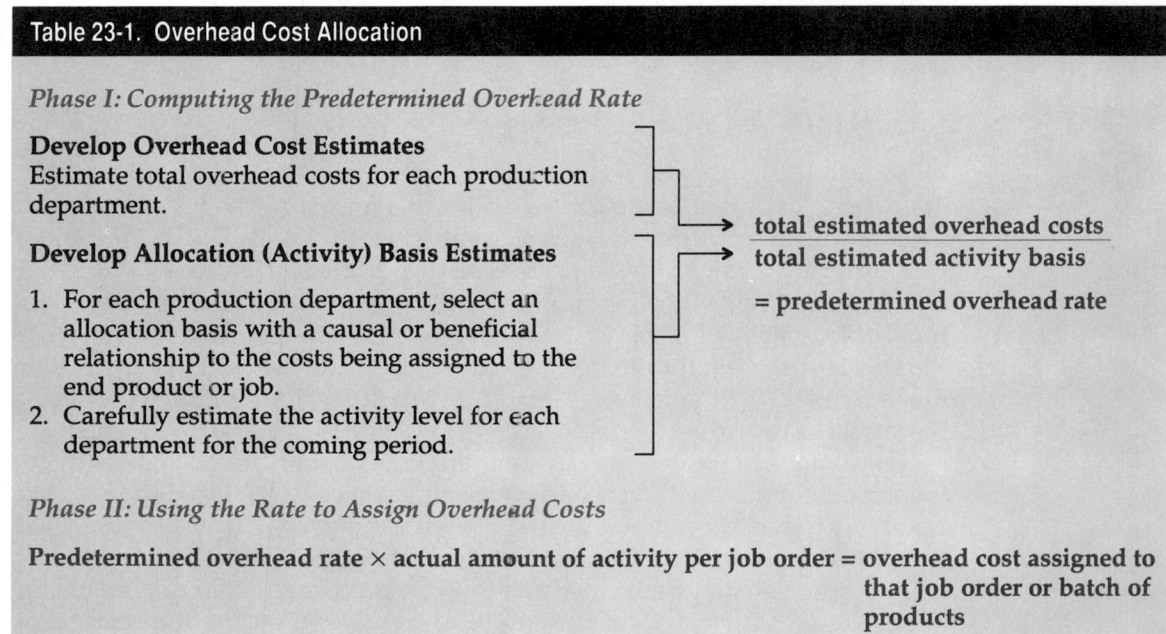

Table 23-1. Overhead Cost Allocation

Phase I: Computing the Predetermined Overhead Rate

Develop Overhead Cost Estimates
Estimate total overhead costs for each production department.

Develop Allocation (Activity) Basis Estimates

1. For each production department, select an allocation basis with a causal or beneficial relationship to the costs being assigned to the end product or job.
2. Carefully estimate the activity level for each department for the coming period.

$$\frac{\text{total estimated overhead costs}}{\text{total estimated activity basis}}$$

= predetermined overhead rate

Phase II: Using the Rate to Assign Overhead Costs

Predetermined overhead rate × actual amount of activity per job order = overhead cost assigned to that job order or batch of products that is, less or more than the actual overhead costs incurred. We account for these differences by making a quarterly or annual adjustment. Monthly differences between actual overhead incurred and overhead costs applied are normaly not adjusted. In many cases they offset one another, leaving only a small adjustment to be made at year end.

An example will illustrate the accounting problems that can occur using predetermined overhead rates. Assume that the accounting records of the Silvoso Company show the overhead transactions that follow. Assume also that all overhead costs are debited to one general ledger control account, the Factory Overhead Control account, instead of to many individual overhead accounts.

May 25 Paid utility bill for three months, $1,420.
May 27 Recorded usage of indirect materials and supplies, $940.
June 21 Paid indirect labor wages, $2,190.
Aug. 12 Paid property taxes on factory building, $620.
Sept. 9 Recorded expiratior. of prepaid insurance premium, $560.
Nov. 27 Recorded depreciation of machinery and equipment for the year, $1,210.

These transactions resulted in the following entries:

May 25	Factory Overhead Control*	1,420	
	Cash		1,420
	To record payment of three-month utility bill		
May 27	Factory Overhead Control*	940	
	Materials (or Supplies) Inventory		940
	To record usage of indirect materials and supplies		
June 21	Factory Overhead Control*	2,190	
	Factory Payroll		2,190
	To distribute indirect labor from factory payroll		
Aug. 12	Factory Overhead Control*	620	
	Cash		620
	To record payment of property taxes on factory building		
Sept. 9	Factory Overhead Control*	560	
	Prepaid Insurance		560
	To record expiration of insurance premiums		
Nov. 27	Factory Overhead Control*	1,210	
	Accumulated Depreciation, Machinery and Equipment		1,210
	To record depreciation for the year		

*When the Factory Overhead Control account is used, all types of factory overhead costs are debited to the account when incurred. A subsidiary ledger containing each individual overhead account is maintained. This procedure is illustrated later in the chapter.

These entries record actual overhead expenses of $6,940 debited to the Factory Overhead Control account. However, they do not help in assigning the costs to products nor in transferring costs to the Work in Process Inventory account. Such a transfer must take place before product unit costs can be computed.

Here the predetermined overhead rate is useful. Assume that the predetermined overhead rate for the period was $2.50 per machine hour. The following list of jobs completed during the period shows the number of machine hours for each job and the overhead cost applied to each one.

Job	Machine Hours	x	Rate	=	Overhead Applied
16-2	520		$2.50		$1,300
19-4	718		2.50		1,795
17-3	622		2.50		1,555
18-6	416		2.50		1,040
21-5	384		2.50		960
	2,660				$6,650

A journal entry like the one that follows is used to record the application of predetermined overhead costs to each job worked on during the period. This entry transfers the estimated overhead costs from the Factory Overhead Applied account to the Work in Process Inventory account. Normally the entry is made when production data is recorded, since overhead costs can be applied only after the number of machine hours used is known.

June 5	Work in Process Inventory	1,300	
	Factory Overhead Applied		1,300
	To record application of		
	overhead costs to Job 16-2		

Similar entries must be prepared for each job worked on during the period.

After posting all the actual overhead transactions discussed earlier, we can compare applied overhead costs to actual overhead costs using the general ledger account entries and balances:

Factory Overhead Control (Incurred)			**Factory Overhead Applied**	
5/25	1,420		Job 16-2	1,300
5/27	940		Job 19-4	1,795
6/21	2,190		Job 17-3	1,555
8/12	620		Job 18-6	1,040
9/9	560		Job 21-5	960
11/27	1,210			
			Bal.	6,650
Bal.	6,940			

These records show that at year end, overhead has been underapplied by $290 ($6,940 – $6,650). More overhead was incurred than applied: the predetermined overhead rate was a little low. That is, the rate used did not apply all the overhead cost incurred to the products produced. The $290 must now be added to the production costs for the period.

Two courses of action are available. First, if the $290 difference is considered small, or if most of the items worked on during the year have been sold, the entire amount can be charged to Cost of Goods Sold. This is the most common approach, because it is easy to apply.

The adjusting entry would be:

Factory Overhead Applied	6,650	
Cost of Goods Sold	290	
Factory Overhead Control		6,940
To close out overhead accounts and		
to charge underapplied overhead		
to the Cost of Goods Sold account		

Another method is used if the amount of the adjustment is large, or if a large number of products worked on during the year remain unsold at year end. Using this approach, underapplied or overapplied overhead is divided at year end among the Work in Process Inventory, Finished Goods Inventory, and Cost of Goods Sold accounts. For example, assume that at year end the products worked on during the year were located as follows: 30 percent in Work in Process Inventory, 20 percent in Finished Goods Inventory, and 50 percent sold. The following entry would be made:

Factory Overhead Applied	6,650	
Cost of Goods Sold (50 percent of $290)	145	
Work in Process Inventory (30 percent of $290)	87	
Finished Goods Inventory (20 percent of $290)	58	
Factory Overhead Control		6,940
To close out overhead accounts and		
to account for underapplied factory		
overhead		

The percentage breakdown of the $290 among the three accounts could be based on the number of units worked on during the period, the machine hours used to produce those units, or the dollar balance in each account. The review problem at the end of this chapter offers more guidance in the accounting procedures used for underapplied or overapplied overhead.

Product Costing and Inventory Valuation

One of the main goals of cost accounting is to supply management with information about production costs. This information is useful in many ways. It assists internal decision making. It helps the accountant control

OBJECTIVE 5
Explain the relationship between product costing and inventory valuation

costs. And through inventory valuation, it forms the link between financial accounting and management accounting.

All manufacturing costs incurred during a period must be accounted for in the year-end financial statements. However, not all these costs will appear on the income statement. Only those costs assigned to units sold will be reported on the income statement. Costs assigned to units sold have "expired"; they were used up in producing revenue. Costs assigned to unsold units (ending inventory) are "unexpired," or unused, costs. They are classified as assets and included in either the Work in Process Inventory or Finished Goods Inventory accounts on the balance sheet. Product unit cost information is needed both to compute the end-of-period balances in the Work in Process Inventory and the Finished Goods Inventory accounts and to compute the cost of goods sold on the income statement.

The Job Order Cost Accounting System

As we have seen, a job order cost system is designed to gather manufacturing costs for a specific order or batch of products and to aid in determining product unit costs. Price-setting decisions, production scheduling, and other management tasks depend on information from a company's cost accounting system. For these reasons, it is necessary to maintain a system that gives timely, correct data about product costs. In Chapter 22, we discussed the three main cost elements—materials, labor, and factory overhead. Here we see how these costs are accounted for in a job order cost system.

Incurrence of Materials, Labor, and Factory Overhead Costs

A basic part of a job order cost system is the set of procedures and journal entries used when the company incurs materials, labor, and factory overhead costs. To help control these costs, businesses use various documents for each transaction. The effective use of these procedures and documents promotes accounting accuracy. It also makes for a smooth, efficient flow of cost information through the accounting records. Note that all inventory balances in a job order cost system are kept on a perpetual basis.

Materials. Careful use of materials improves a company's overall efficiency. It conserves production resources and can bring about large cost savings. At the same time, good records ensure accountability and cut down on waste. Thus controlling the physical materials and keeping good records enhances profits.

To help record and control materials costs, accountants rely on a series of cost documents including the purchase requisition, purchase order, receiving report, inventory records, and materials requisition. Each of these documents was discussed in Chapter 22. Through them direct materials costs are traced to specific jobs or products and indirect materials costs are charged to factory overhead.

Labor. Labor is one production resource that cannot be stored and used later, so it must be carefully accounted for. Labor time cards and job cards are used to record labor costs as they are incurred. Direct labor costs are traceable to specific jobs or products. Indirect labor costs are routed through the Factory Overhead account.

Factory Overhead. All indirect manufacturing costs are classified as factory overhead. Unlike direct materials and direct labor, overhead costs do not call for special documents. Vendors' bills support most payments. Many factory overhead costs are charged to the Factory Overhead Control account when incurred, while others, such as factory depreciation costs and prepaid expenses, are charged to the Factory Overhead account through journal entries. Overhead costs may be accounted for in separate accounts, but that is not done in a job order cost system. Instead, they are all debited to a single Factory Overhead Control account.

A **control account**, you will recall, is a general ledger account that sums up the balances in a group of related accounts to reduce accounting detail. In the factory overhead cost area, a separate subsidiary account is kept for each type of factory overhead cost. These separate accounts make up a subsidiary ledger to the Factory Overhead Control account. In general, a subsidiary ledger is kept for each control account.

Factory overhead costs are not usually traceable directly to jobs or products. For this reason, an estimate of factory overhead costs is applied to products by means of the predetermined overhead rate. This process was discussed earlier, and will be illustrated later in the chapter (see Exhibit 23-1 on pages 980 and 981).

The Work in Process Inventory Account

OBJECTIVE 6
Describe the cost flow in a job order cost accounting system

Job order costing focuses on the flow of costs through the Work in Process Inventory account. All manufacturing costs incurred and charged to production are routed through Work in Process Inventory. Figure 23-1 shows the cost flow in a job order cost system. Direct materials costs are debited to the Work in Process Inventory account; indirect materials and supplies are debited to the Factory Overhead Control account. All labor costs that can be traced to specific jobs are debited to the Work in Process Inventory account. Indirect labor costs are charged to the Factory Overhead Control account. By means of a predetermined overhead rate, we apply overhead costs to specific jobs by debiting the Work in Process Inventory account and crediting Factory Overhead Applied.

Attaching the costs of direct materials, direct labor, and factory overhead to specific jobs and products is not accomplished automatically. Even though all manufacturing costs are debited to the Work in Process Inventory account, we need a separate accounting procedure to link those costs to specific jobs. For this purpose we use a subsidiary ledger made up of **job order cost cards**. One job order cost card exists for each job being worked on, and all costs of that job are recorded on it. As costs are debited to the Work in Process Inventory account, we reclassify them by job and add them to the job order cost cards.

Figure 23-1. Job Order Cost Flow

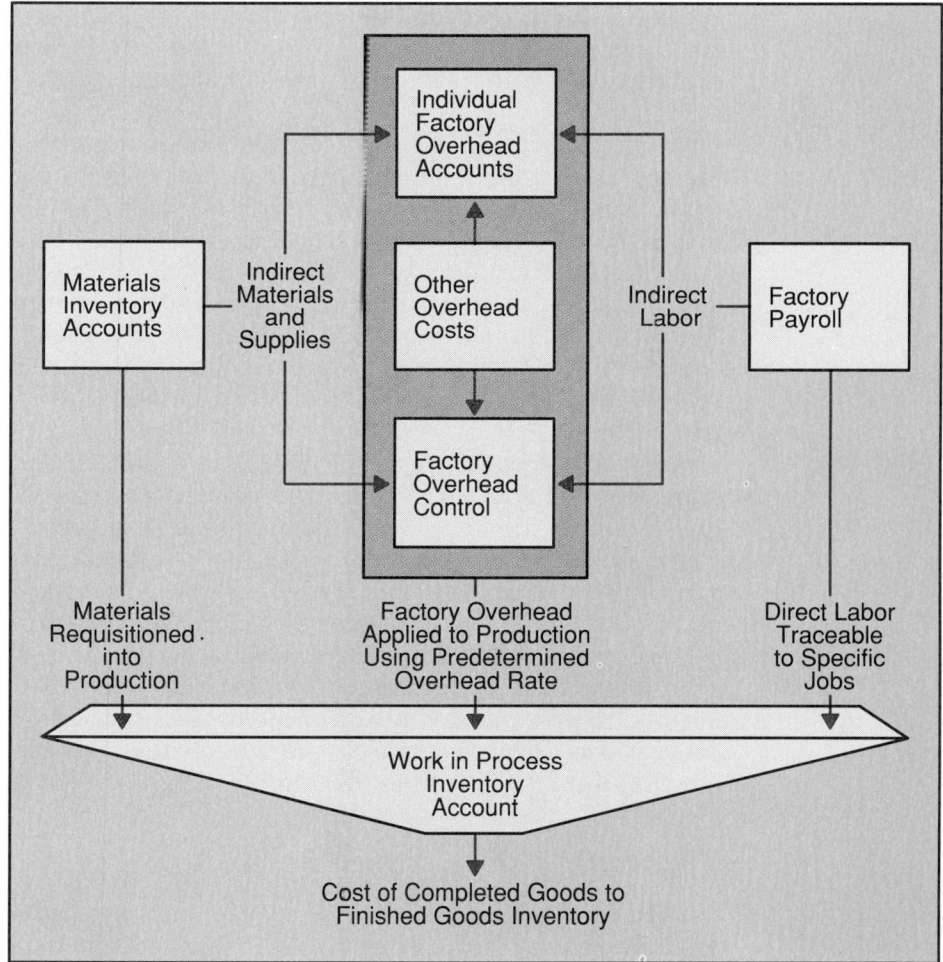

A typical job order cost card is shown in Figure 23-2. Each card has space for materials, direct labor, and factory overhead costs. The job order number, product specifications, name of customer, date of order, projected completion date, and summary cost data are also included. As each department incurs materials and labor costs, the individual job order cost cards are updated. Factory overhead, as applied, is also posted to the job order cost card. Job order cost cards for incomplete jobs make up the subsidiary ledger for the Work in Process Inventory Control account. To make sure the ending balance in the Work in Process Inventory Control account is correct, we compare it with the total of the costs shown on these job order cost cards. (See Exhibit 23-1 on pages 980 and 981.)

Figure 23-2. Job Order Cost Card

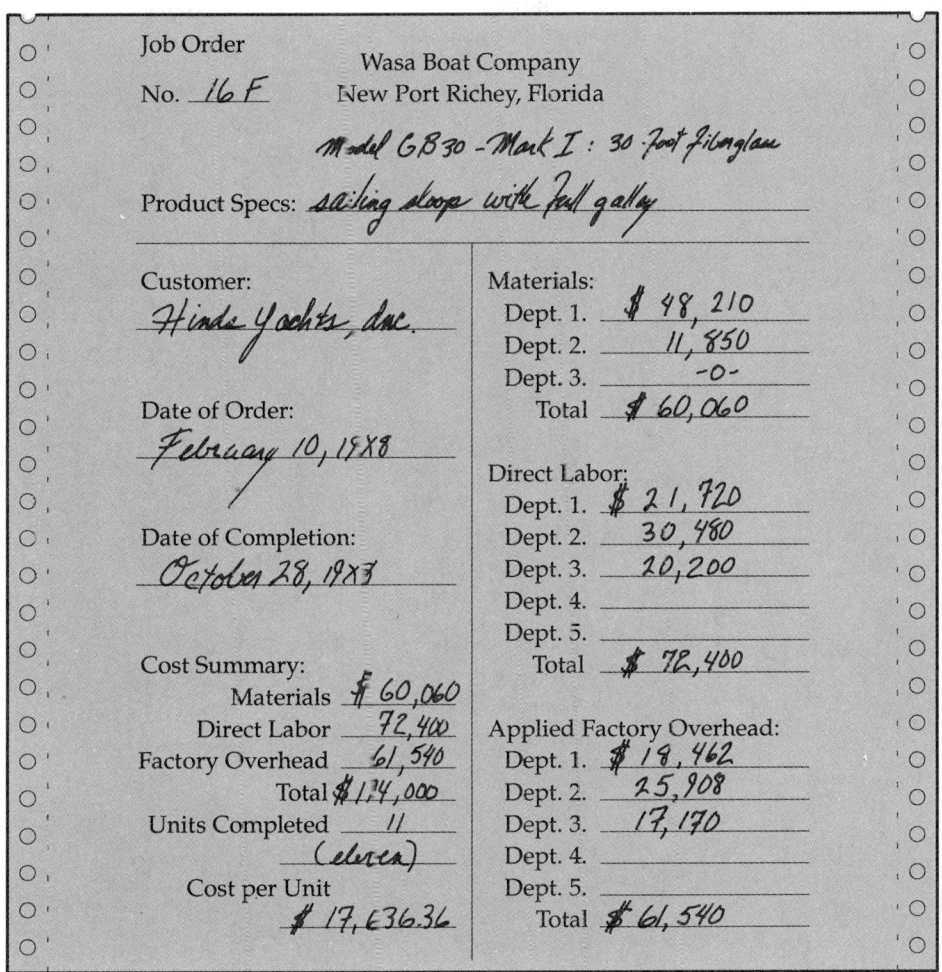

Accounting for Finished Goods

When a job has been completed, all costs assigned to that job order are transferred to the Finished Goods Inventory account by debiting the Finished Goods Inventory account and crediting the Work in Process Inventory account. When this entry is made, the job order cost card should be removed from the subsidiary ledger file. It is then used to help update the Finished Goods Inventory account records.

When goods are shipped, the order for them is recorded as a sale. We debit Accounts Receivable and credit Sales for the entire selling price. But we also need to account for the cost of the goods shipped. The proper procedure is to debit Cost of Goods Sold and credit Finished Goods Inventory for the *cost* of the goods shipped.

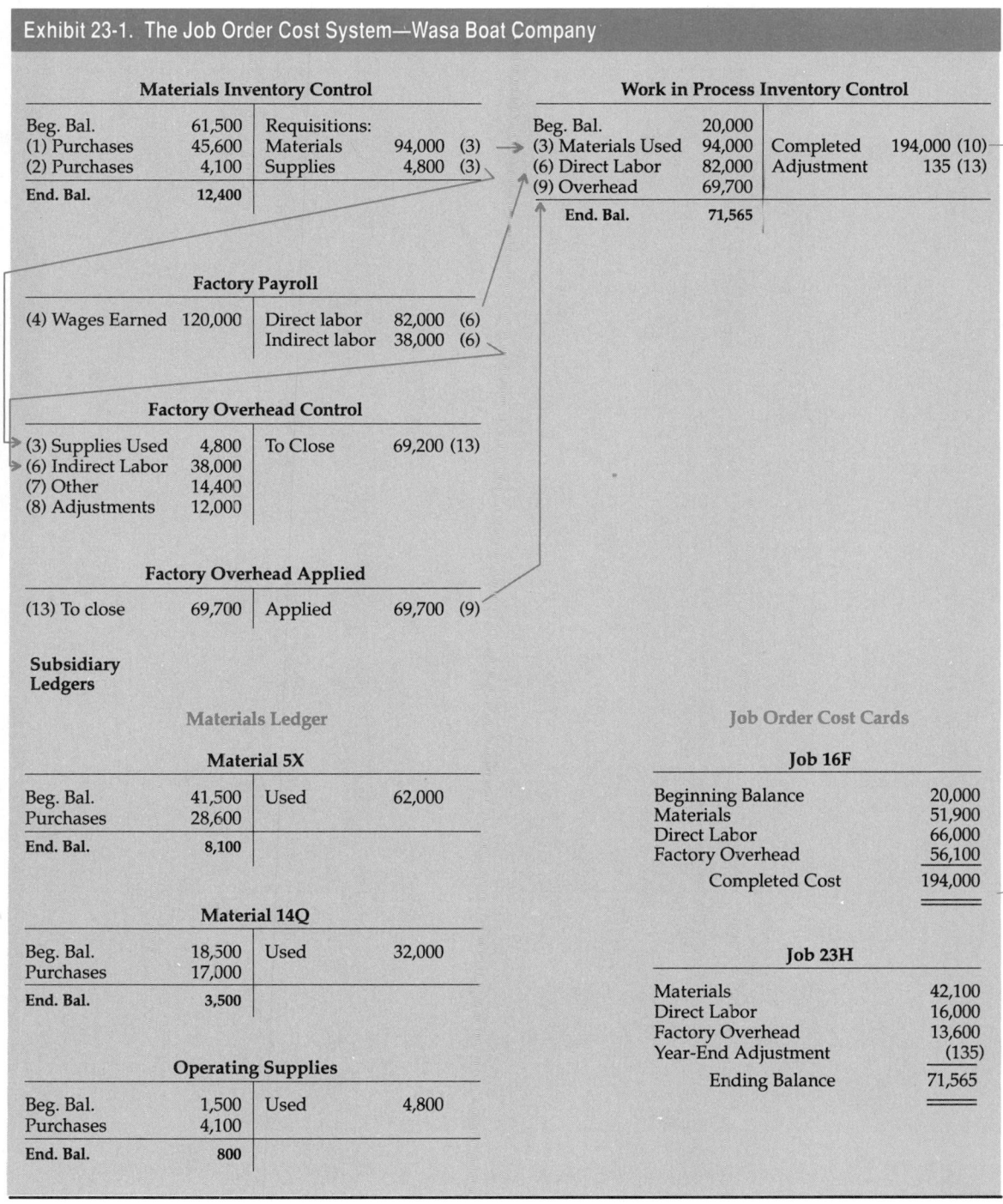

Exhibit 23-1. The Job Order Cost System—Wasa Boat Company

Materials Inventory Control

Beg. Bal.	61,500	Requisitions:		
(1) Purchases	45,600	Materials	94,000	(3)
(2) Purchases	4,100	Supplies	4,800	(3)
End. Bal.	12,400			

Work in Process Inventory Control

Beg. Bal.	20,000			
(3) Materials Used	94,000	Completed	194,000	(10)
(6) Direct Labor	82,000	Adjustment	135	(13)
(9) Overhead	69,700			
End. Bal.	71,565			

Factory Payroll

(4) Wages Earned	120,000	Direct labor	82,000	(6)
		Indirect labor	38,000	(6)

Factory Overhead Control

(3) Supplies Used	4,800	To Close	69,200	(13)
(6) Indirect Labor	38,000			
(7) Other	14,400			
(8) Adjustments	12,000			

Factory Overhead Applied

(13) To close	69,700	Applied	69,700	(9)

Subsidiary Ledgers

Materials Ledger

Material 5X

Beg. Bal.	41,500	Used	62,000
Purchases	28,600		
End. Bal.	8,100		

Material 14Q

Beg. Bal.	18,500	Used	32,000
Purchases	17,000		
End. Bal.	3,500		

Operating Supplies

Beg. Bal.	1,500	Used	4,800
Purchases	4,100		
End. Bal.	800		

Job Order Cost Cards

Job 16F

Beginning Balance	20,000
Materials	51,900
Direct Labor	66,000
Factory Overhead	56,100
Completed Cost	194,000

Job 23H

Materials	42,100
Direct Labor	16,000
Factory Overhead	13,600
Year-End Adjustment	(135)
Ending Balance	71,565

To learn the mechanics of the system just described, you really need to go through an analysis of transactions and their related journal entries. While studying the journal entry analysis that follows, review the preceding paragraphs. Try to keep in mind the cost flow concept shown in Figure 23-1.

Exhibit 23-1. *(continued)*

Finished Goods Inventory Control			
Beg. Bal.	—		
(10) Completed During Period	194,000	Sold	176,364 (12)
		Adjustment	33 (13)
End. Bal.	17,603		

Cost of Goods Sold			
(12) Sold During Period	176,364	Adjustment	332 (13)
End. Bal.	176,032		

Finished Goods Ledger

Product F			
Beg. Bal.	—	Sold	176,364
Completed	194,000	Adjustment	33
End. Bal.	17,603		

Product H	
Beg. Bal.	—

Journal Entry Analysis

OBJECTIVE 7
Journalize
transactions in a
job order cost
accounting system

Because a job order cost system emphasizes cost flow, we need to understand the journal entries that record the various costs as they are incurred. We also need to know the entries that are used to transfer costs from one account to another. In fact, these entries, along with job order cost cards and subsidiary ledgers for materials and finished goods inventories, are a major part of the job order cost system.

As we proceed through our analysis of the Wasa Boat Company, we will first describe each transaction, then supply the journal entry needed to record it. We will finish with a discussion of the unique features of the transaction or the accounts used. Exhibit 23-1 shows the entire job order cost flow through the general ledger, including supporting subsidiary ledgers. As each entry is discussed, trace its number and related debits or credits to the exhibit.

Materials Purchased. In recording direct materials purchases, we will see the differences between journal entries used in the perpetual inventory approach and those used for periodic inventories. For example, the Wasa Boat Company purchased the following materials: Material 5X for $28,600 and Material 14Q for $17,000. Materials purchases are recorded at cost in the Materials Inventory Control account:

Entry 1: Materials Inventory Control   45,600
               Accounts Payable (or Cash)   45,600
                    To record purchase of $28,600
                    of Material 5X and $17,000 of
                    Material 14Q

This procedure differs in two ways from the recording of purchases discussed before in this text. First, the debit is to an inventory account instead of a purchases account because the inventory system is perpetual. All costs of materials flow through the inventory account. Second, the inventory account used is a control account. Some companies have hundreds of items in inventory. To keep a separate account for each item in the general ledger would crowd the ledger and make it hard to work with. At the time that entry 1 is posted to the general ledger, the individual accounts in the materials ledger are also updated. See Exhibit 23-1.

Purchase of Supplies. The following transaction and entry are for the purchase of supplies for production. The company purchased $4,100 of operating supplies for the manufacturing process.

Entry 2: Materials Inventory Control   4,100
               Accounts Payable (or Cash)   4,100
                    To record the purchase of
                    operating supplies

The procedures used to account for the purchase of supplies are much like those used to record direct materials purchases. Operating Supplies Inventory, in our example, is assumed to be one subsidiary account making up the total Materials Inventory Control account. If the supplies inventory is large, a separate general ledger account may be used. Regardless of which method is selected, the accountant should be able to support the approach taken and then follow it consistently.

Requisitioning of Materials and Supplies. Upon receipt of a properly prepared materials requisition form, the following direct materials and supplies are issued from inventory to production: Material 5X for $62,000, Material 14Q for $32,000, and operating supplies for $4,800.

Entry 3: Work in Process Inventory Control   94,000
          Factory Overhead Control   4,800
              Materials Inventory Control   98,800
                  To record issuance of $62,000
                  of Material 5X, $32,000 of
                  Material 14Q, and $4,800 of
                  operating supplies into
                  production

This entry shows that $94,000 of direct materials and $4,800 of indirect materials were issued. The debit to the Work in Process Inventory Control account records the cost of direct materials issued to production. Such costs can be directly traced to specific job orders. As the direct materials costs are charged to work in process, the amounts for individual jobs are entered on the job order cost cards. As shown in Exhibit 23-1, $51,900 of materials were used on Job 16F, $42,100 of materials on Job 23H. Indirect materials costs (supplies) are debited to the Factory Overhead Control account.

Labor Costs. Chapter 11 illustrated and discussed journal entries to record payroll for a merchandising company. Recording payroll for a manufacturing company is more complex, but we use the same basic payroll documents and transactions. In accounting for factory labor costs we need some new account titles, and we assign the costs to specific products and jobs.

Recording labor costs for a manufacturing company takes three journal entries. The first labor cost entry records the total payroll liability of the company. Though only $107,640 of net earnings are to be paid to employees, the gross direct and indirect labor costs will be used for product and job costing. In the transaction described in entry 4, payroll liability for the period was recorded as follows: gross direct labor wages, $82,000; gross indirect labor wages, $38,000; gross administrative salaries, $36,000; FICA (social security) taxes withheld, $9,360; federal income taxes withheld, $39,000.

Entry 4: Factory Payroll   120,000
          Administrative Salaries Expense   36,000
              FICA Tax Payable   9,360
              Federal Income Tax Payable   39,000
              Wages and Salaries Payable   107,640
                  To record payroll liability
                  for the period

A follow-up entry is now needed to account properly for labor costs. This entry, entry 5, will record the payment of the payroll liability established in entry 4. In this transaction, payroll checks for the period were prepared and given to the employees.

Entry 5: Wages and Salaries Payable   107,640
              Cash   107,640
                  To record payment of payroll

The $120,000 first debited to the Factory Payroll account must now be moved to the production accounts. Gross direct labor costs are debited to Work in Process Inventory Control and total indirect wages (including factory supervisory salaries) are debited to Factory Overhead Control. Factory Payroll is credited to show that the total amount has been distributed to the production accounts.

Entry 6: Work in Process Inventory Control   82,000
              Factory Overhead Control   38,000
                  Factory Payroll   120,000
                      To record the distribution of factory
                      payroll to production accounts

In addition, the direct labor costs are recorded by job on the individual job order cost cards. This distribution of $66,000 to Job 16F and $16,000 to Job 23H is shown in Exhibit 23-1.

Other Factory Overhead Costs. As factory overhead costs other than indirect materials and labor charges are incurred, the sum of these costs is charged (debited) to the Factory Overhead Control account. Each cost is identified in the explanation for the journal entry. In our example, factory overhead costs were paid as follows: electricity, $3,100; maintenance and repair, $8,400; insurance, $1,300; and property taxes, $1,600.

Entry 7: Factory Overhead Control   14,400
              Accounts Payable (or Cash)   14,400
                  To record incurrence of the
                  following overhead costs:
                  electricity, $3,100; maintenance
                  and repair, $8,400; insurance,
                  $1,300; and property
                  taxes, $1,600

From the information in the explanation, individual subsidiary ledger accounts are updated. Because of the amount of information already included in Exhibit 23-1, the subsidiary ledger for the Factory Overhead Control account is not shown. However, the subsidiary ledger would include a separate account for each type of factory overhead cost. The costs would be accounted for in much the same way as in the materials ledger and job order cost cards.

The next transaction is an adjusting entry needed to record depreciation of factory equipment for the period.

Entry 8: Factory Overhead Control   12,000
              Accumulated Depreciation, Equipment   12,000
                  To record depreciation of
                  factory equipment for the
                  period

Adjusting entries are usually prepared after all transactions for the period have been recorded. We introduce the topic at this point because depreciation of factory equipment is a part of total factory overhead cost. The actual Depreciation Expense account is part of the overhead subsidiary ledger.

Factory Overhead Applied. We apply factory overhead by using a predetermined overhead rate and an allocation base (machine hours, direct labor hours, direct labor dollars, or units of output).

In this transaction, factory overhead costs were applied to production by using a rate of 85 percent of direct labor dollars.

Entry 9:   Work in Process Inventory Control   69,700
                 Factory Overhead Applied   69,700
                     To apply factory overhead
                     costs to production

The amount of overhead charged to production is found by multiplying the overhead rate by the units of the base. In our example, we multiplied 85 percent times the direct labor dollars ($82,000), which gave us $69,700 ($82,000 × .85). This amount was debited to the Work in Process Inventory Control account. Because the application of overhead is related to direct labor dollars, we can update the job order cost cards using the same procedure. Job 16F is assigned $56,100 of overhead cost ($66,000 × .85). Job 23H is assigned $13,600 ($16,000 × .85). These amounts have been posted to the job order cost cards in Exhibit 23-1.

Accounting for Completed Units. As various job orders are completed, their costs are moved to the Finished Goods Inventory Control account. In this case, goods costing $194,000, for Job 16F, were completed and transferred to Finished Goods Inventory (see the job order cost card, Figure 23-2).

Entry 10:   Finished Goods Inventory Control   194,000
                  Work in Process Inventory Control   194,000
                      To record transfer of completed
                      goods for Job 16F from Work
                      in Process Inventory to
                      Finished Goods Inventory

When a job is completed, its job order cost card is pulled from the Work in Process subsidiary ledger. It is then used to help update the Finished Goods ledger. Specifically, costs recorded on the job order cost card are used to figure unit costs and to determine the amount of the transfer entry.

Accounting for Units Sold. The final phase of the manufacturing cost flow is the transfer of costs from the Finished Goods Inventory Control account to the Cost of Goods Sold account.

At this point, ten sailing sloops from Job 16F have been shipped to the customer. The selling price for the goods shipped was $260,000. The total cost of manufacturing these products was $176,364.

Entry 11:	Accounts Receivable	260,000	
	Sales		260,000
	To record sale of portion of Job 16F		

Entry 12:	Cost of Goods Sold	176,364	
	Finished Goods Inventory Control		176,364
	To record the transfer of the cost of the shipped goods for Job 16F from Finished Goods Inventory to Cost of Goods Sold		

Both the entry to record the sale and the entry to establish the cost of the goods sold are shown here. Entry 12 is made at the time the sale is recorded. When we transfer the costs of the products sold out of the Finished Goods Inventory Control account, we should also update the finished goods ledger (subsidiary ledger), as shown in Exhibit 23-1.

Underapplied or Overapplied Overhead Disposition. At the end of an accounting period, we total the Factory Overhead Control account and the Factory Overhead Applied account. We make an entry to close these accounts and dispose of any underapplied or overapplied overhead.

Entry 13:	Factory Overhead Applied	69,700	
	Work in Process Inventory Control		135
	Finished Goods Inventory Control		33
	Cost of Goods Sold		332
	Factory Overhead Control		69,200
	To close out factory overhead account balances and to dispose of the overapplied balance		

In this transaction, we see that factory overhead was overapplied by $500. (The $500 amount in this case is assumed to be significant.) So as we closed the Factory Overhead Control and Factory Overhead Applied accounts, we distributed the $500 difference among Work in Process Inventory Control, Finished Goods Inventory Control, and Cost of Goods Sold. We did so based on each account's balance before the adjustment.

The following analysis shows how we arrived at these figures. First, we used T accounts to summarize the overhead account balances. The numbers in parentheses refer to earlier journal entries:

Factory Overhead Control				Factory Overhead Applied	
(3)	4,800			(9)	69,700
(6)	38,000				
(7)	14,400				
(8)	12,000				
Bal.	69,200			Bal.	69,700

Overhead has been overapplied by $500 ($69,700 − $69,200). This amount can be credited entirely to the Cost of Goods Sold account or distributed among the Work in Process Inventory Control, Finished Goods Inventory Control, and Cost of Goods Sold accounts. We assume that the amount is significant, so we distribute it among the three accounts on the basis of their ending balances. The following table shows how the amounts were computed:

Account	Balance Before Adjustment	Percentage of Each to Total	x	Amount to Be Allocated	=	Allocation of Overapplied Overhead
Work in Process Inventory Control	$71,700	27.0%		$500		$135
Finished Goods Inventory Control	17,636	6.6		500		33
Cost of Goods Sold	176,364	66.4		500		332
Totals	$265,700	100.0%				$500

After entry 13 has been posted to the general ledger, the accounts affected will look like those in Exhibit 23-1. In addition, all subsidiary ledgers affected by the overhead adjustment must be updated. In our example, the entire $135 of adjustment to Work in Process was credited to Job 23H. Because Job 16F had been completed, its share of the adjustment was assigned to the Finished Goods Inventory Control and Cost of Goods Sold accounts.

Computing Product Unit Costs

OBJECTIVE 8
Compute product unit cost for a specific job order

The process of computing product unit cost is fairly simple in a job order costing system. All costs of materials, direct labor, and factory overhead are recorded on the job order cost card as the job progresses to completion. When the job is finished, the costs on the job order cost card are totaled. The unit cost is then computed by dividing the total costs for the job by the number of good units produced.

Job 16F was completed in the journal entry analysis we just finished. The cost data for this job are shown on the job order cost card in Figure 23-2. Eleven sailing sloops were produced at a total cost of $194,000. This worked out to a cost of $17,636 per sloop before adjustments. Note in Exhibit 23-1 that only ten of the sloops were actually shipped during the year. One still remains in Finished Goods Inventory Control at the adjusted cost.

Fully and Partly Completed Products

In a job order costing system, as we have seen, manufacturing costs are accumulated, classified, and reclassified several times. As products near completion, all manufacturing costs are linked to them. These costs then follow the products first to the Finished Goods Inventory Control and then to Cost of Goods Sold. Exhibit 23-1 illustrated the accounting procedures and cost flows of units worked on during the period. The dollar amounts in Exhibit 23-1 came from posting the journal entries just discussed.

At period end, some costs remain in the Work in Process Inventory Control account and the Finished Goods Inventory Control account. The ending balance of $71,565 in the Work in Process Inventory Control account is from costs attached to partly completed units from Job 23H. These costs are traceable to the job order cost card in the subsidiary ledger. The Finished Goods Inventory Control account also has an ending balance. Of all units completed during the accounting period, one sloop from Job 16F has not been sold or shipped. Its cost, $17,603 after adjustment, now appears as the ending balance in the Finished Goods Inventory Control account.

Chapter Review

Review of Learning Objectives

1. **Identify the differences between job order costing and process costing.**

   Both job order costing and process costing are basic, traditional approaches to product cost accounting. However, they have different characteristics. A job order costing system is used for unique or special-order products. In such a system, materials, direct labor, and factory overhead costs are assigned to specific job orders or batches of products. In determining unit costs, the total manufacturing cost assigned to each job order is divided by the number of good units produced for that order. A process costing system is used by companies that produce a large number of similar products or have a continuous production flow. These companies find it more economical to account for product-related costs for a period of time (a week or month) than to assign them to specific products or job orders. In a process costing system unit costs are found by dividing total manufacturing costs for a department or work center during the week or month by the number of good units produced.

2. **Describe the concept of absorption costing.**

   Absorption costing is an approach to product costing in which a representative portion of *all* manufacturing costs is assigned to individual products. Thus direct materials, direct labor, variable factory overhead, and fixed factory overhead costs are all assigned to products.

3. **Compute a predetermined overhead rate, and use this rate to apply overhead costs to production.**

   A predetermined overhead rate is computed by dividing total estimated overhead costs for a period by the total expected activity basis for that period. Factory overhead costs are applied to a job order by multiplying the predetermined overhead rate by the actual amount of the activity base (such as labor hours) used for that job order.

4. **Dispose of underapplied or overapplied overhead.**

   If at year end a difference exists between the balances in the Factory Overhead Control and Factory Overhead Applied accounts, it may be disposed of in one of two ways. If the difference is small, it should be adjusted by transferring the balance to the Cost of Goods Sold account. Often, however, the amount of the adjustment is large, or the costs of the products worked on during the period are spread among the Work in Process Inventory, Finished Goods Inventory, and Cost of Goods Sold accounts. In such cases, the difference should be assigned proportionately to those three accounts.

5. **Explain the relationship between product costing and inventory valuation.**
   Product costing techniques are necessary to attach costs to job orders or to units of product worked on during a given period. At period end, when financial statements are prepared, product costs are used in costing the Work in Process and Finished Goods Inventory accounts as well as in determining the cost of goods sold.

6. **Describe the cost flow in a job order cost accounting system.**
   A job order cost accounting system presumes an absorption costing approach as well as a perpetual approach to inventory maintenance and valuation. Materials and supplies costs are first debited to the Materials Inventory Control account. Labor costs are debited to the Factory Payroll account. The various factory overhead costs are debited to the Factory Overhead Control account. As products are being manufactured, the costs of direct materials and direct labor are transferred to the Work in Process Inventory Control account. Factory overhead costs are applied and charged to the Work in Process Inventory Control account using a predetermined overhead rate. The charges are credited to the Factory Overhead Applied account. When products or jobs are completed, the costs assigned to them are transferred to the Finished Goods Inventory Control account. They are transferred to the Cost of Goods Sold account when the products are sold and shipped.

7. **Journalize transactions in a job order cost accounting system.**
   Mastery of a job order costing system requires that the user be able to prepare journal entries for each of the following transactions: (a) purchase of materials, (b) purchase of operating supplies, (c) requisition of materials and supplies into production, (d) recording of payroll liability, (e) payment of payroll to employees, (f) distribution of factory payroll to production accounts, (g) cash payment of overhead costs, (h) recording of noncash overhead costs such as depreciation of factory and equipment, (i) application of factory overhead costs to production, (j) transfer of costs of completed jobs from the Work in Process Inventory Control account to the Finished Goods Inventory Control account, (k) sale of products and transfer of related costs from the Finished Goods Inventory Control account to the Cost of Goods Sold account, and (l) disposition of underapplied or overapplied factory overhead.

8. **Compute product unit cost for a specific job order.**
   Product costs are computed by first totaling all the manufacturing costs accumulated on a particular job order cost card. This amount is then divided by the number of good units produced to find the individual unit cost for the order. The unit cost information is entered on the job order cost card and used for inventory valuation purposes.

Review of Concepts and Terminology

The following concepts and terms were introduced in this chapter:

(L.O. 2) **Absorption costing:** An approach to product costing in which all types of manufacturing costs are assigned to individual products.

(L.O. 5) **Control account:** A general ledger account that sums up the balances in a group of related accounts kept in a subsidiary ledger.

(L.O. 1) **Job order:** A customer order for a specific number of specially designed, made-to-order products.

(L.O. 1) **Job order cost accounting system:** A product costing system used by companies making one-of-a-kind or special-order products.

(L.O. 6) **Job order cost card:** A document upon which is recorded all costs incurred in the production of a particular job order. Together, the job order cost cards for unfinished jobs represent the subsidiary ledger for the Work in Process Inventory Control account.

(L.O. 3) **Predetermined overhead rate:** An overhead cost factor used to assign factory overhead costs to specific products or jobs.

(L.O. 1) **Process cost accounting system:** A product cost accounting system used by companies that make many similar products or have a continuous production flow.

(L.O. 3, 4) **Underapplied or overapplied factory overhead:** The difference in the balances of the Factory Overhead Control account and the Factory Overhead Applied account at a specific point in time.

Self-Test

Test your knowledge of the chapter by choosing the best answer for each item below and on the following page.

1. Which of the following industries is most likely to use the job order costing system?
   a. Jet aircraft company
   b. Paint producing company
   c. Soft drink producing company
   d. Oil refining company   *(L.O. 1)*

2. An approach to product costing that assigns all types of manufacturing costs to individual products is known as
   a. job order costing.
   b. process costing.
   c. absorption costing.
   d. total costing.   *(L.O. 2)*

3. To compute the predetermined overhead rate, you divide the total estimated overhead costs by
   a. number of products produced last year.
   b. total estimated activity base.
   c. number of invoices expected this year.
   d. last year's total sales.   *(L.O. 3)*

4. If actual overhead costs incurred totaled $21,780, and $22,130 of overhead was applied to products worked on during the period, which of the following situations is correct?
   a. Overhead is $350 underapplied
   b. Overhead is $350 overapplied
   c. Overhead is out of control
   d. Overhead is underspent   *(L.O. 4)*

5. If the estimated amounts listed below are for the coming year and the company uses machine hours as its activity base, what will be the predetermined overhead rate?

         7,200 direct labor hours
         14,600 machine hours
         estimated factory overhead, $49,640

a. $3.40 per direct labor hour   c. $3.40 per machine hour
b. $6.89 per direct labor hour   d. $6.89 per machine hour   *(L.O. 3)*

6. The key document used for tracking product costs in a job order costing system is a
   a. job order materials receiving report.
   b. job order cost card.
   c. job order requisition form.
   d. job order materials requisition card.   *(L.O. 6)*

7. During February, $36,400 of direct labor and $45,600 of indirect labor was paid to workers. How much labor cost should have been debited directly to the Work in Process Inventory account during the month?
   a. $36,400   c. –0–
   b. $45,600   d. $82,000   *(L.O. 7)*

8. Direct materials costing $49,200 and indirect materials and supplies totaling $14,500 were used during April. How much materials cost should be debited directly to the Work in Process Inventory account for this transaction?
   a. $49,200   c. –0–
   b. $14,500   d. $63,700   *(L.O. 7)*

9. When a control account is used in the general ledger, what special recordkeeping device is used to keep track of the balances in the accounts supporting the control account?
   a. general journal   c. subsidiary journal
   b. subsidiary ledger   d. cash payments journal   *(L.O. 6)*

10. At year end, overhead had been underapplied by $280. A total of $389,400 of manufacturing costs had been debited to the Work in Process Inventory account during the year. What account(s) should be debited to dispose of the $280 at year end?
   a. Work in Process Inventory account
   b. Finished Goods Inventory account
   c. Cost of Goods Sold account
   d. All of the above   *(L.O. 4, 7)*

Answers to Self-Test are at the end of this chapter.

Review Problem
Journal Entry Analysis: Job Order Costing System

(L.O. 4, 7, 8)   The Neilsson Manufacturing Company produces "uniframe" desk and chair assemblies and study carrels. The firm uses a job order cost system and a factory overhead application rate of 160 percent of direct labor dollars. The following transactions and events took place during September 19xx:

Sept.   4   Received direct materials costing $11,540. Purchased on account.

Sept. 7 The production department requisitioned $3,700 of materials and $950 of operating supplies.

14 Gross factory payroll of $16,000 was paid to factory personnel. Of that amount, $12,500 represented direct labor; the remaining amount, indirect labor. (Prepare only the entry to distribute factory payroll to production accounts.)

14 Factory overhead costs were applied to production.

16 Received supplies costing $5,500 and direct materials costing $18,500. Both were ordered on 9/11/xx and were purchased on account. Both can be inventoried.

20 Requisitioned $9,000 of direct materials and $1,750 of supplies for production.

26 Paid the following overhead costs: heat, light, and power, $2,400; repairs by outside firm, $3,600; property taxes, $1,700.

28 Gross factory payroll of $15,600 was earned by factory personnel. Of that amount, indirect wages and supervisory salaries totaled $5,400. (Prepare only the entry to distribute factory payroll to production accounts.)

28 Factory overhead costs were applied to production.

29 Completed units costing $67,500 were transferred to Finished Goods Inventory.

30 Depreciation of plant and equipment for September was $14,000. During the same period, $2,200 of prepaid fire insurance expired.

30 Library carrel units costing $32,750 were shipped to a customer for a total selling price of $53,710.

Required

1. Record the journal entries for all these transactions and events.
2. Assume that the beginning balance in the Materials Inventory Control account was $4,700. The beginning balance in Work in Process Inventory Control was $6,200, and the beginning balance in Finished Goods Inventory Control, $9,000. Compute the ending balances in these accounts.
3. Determine the amount of underapplied or overapplied overhead.
4. One hundred thirty-one carrels were included in the order sold and shipped on September 30. Compute the cost and selling price per carrel shipped.
5. Prepare the journal entry to dispose of the under- or overapplied factory overhead at month end. (Assume the under- or overapplied factory overhead to be immaterial in amount.)

Answer to Review Problem

1. Journal entries:

Sept. 4	Materials Inventory Control		11,540	
	Accounts Payable			11,540
	To record purchase of direct materials on account			
7	Work in Process Inventory Control		3,700	
	Factory Overhead Control		950	
	Materials Inventory Control			4,650
	To record requisition of direct materials and supplies into production			

Sept. 14	Work in Process Inventory Control	12,500	
	Factory Overhead Control	3,500	
	Factory Payroll		16,000
	To distribute payroll to production accounts		
14	Work in Process Inventory Control	20,000	
	Factory Overhead Applied		20,000
	To apply factory overhead costs to production ($12,500 × 160%)		
16	Materials Inventory Control	24,000	
	Accounts Payable		24,000
	To record purchase of $5,500 of operating supplies and $18,500 of direct materials		
20	Work in Process Inventory Control	9,000	
	Factory Overhead Control	1,750	
	Materials Inventory Control		10,750
	To record requisition of direct materials and supplies into production		
26	Factory Overhead Control	7,700	
	Cash		7,700
	To record payment of the following overhead costs: heat, light, and power, $2,400; outside repairs, $3,600; property taxes, $1,700		
28	Work in Process Inventory Control	10,200	
	Factory Overhead Control	5,400	
	Factory Payroll		15,600
	To distribute payroll to production accounts		
28	Work in Process Inventory Control	16,320	
	Factory Overhead Applied		16,320
	To apply factory overhead costs to production ($10,200 × 160%)		
29	Finished Goods Inventory Control	67,500	
	Work in Process Inventory Control		67,500
	To transfer costs of completed goods to Finished Goods Inventory		

(continued)

Sept. 30	Factory Overhead Control	16,200	
	Accumulated Depreciation,		
	Plant and Equipment		14,000
	Prepaid Insurance		2,200
	To charge Factory Overhead		
	Control with expired asset		
	costs		
30	Accounts Receivable	53,710	
	Sales		53,710
	To record sales for		
	September		
30	Cost of Goods Sold	32,750	
	Finished Goods Inventory Control		32,750
	To record transfer of costs		
	from Finished Goods Inventory		
	to Cost of Goods Sold		

2. Ending balances of inventory accounts:

Materials Inventory Control

Beg. Bal.	4,700	9/7	4,650
9/4	11,540	9/20	10,750
9/16	24,000		
	40,240		15,400
End. Bal.	24,840		

Work in Process Inventory Control

Beg. Bal.	6,200	9/29	67,500
9/7	3,700		
9/14	12,500		
9/14	20,000		
9/20	9,000		
9/28	10,200		
9/28	16,320		
	77,920		67,500
End. Bal.	10,420		

Finished Goods Inventory Control

Beg. Bal.	9,000	9/30	32,750
9/29	67,500		
	76,500		32,750
End. Bal.	43,750		

3. Underapplied or overapplied overhead:

Factory Overhead Control

9/7	950		
9/14	3,500		
9/20	1,750		
9/26	7,700		
9/28	5,400		
9/30	16,200		
Bal.	35,500		

Factory Overhead Applied

		9/14	20,000
		9/28	16,320
		Bal.	36,320

Factory overhead is overapplied by $820 ($36,320 – $35,500).

4. Cost and selling price per unit:

Cost per unit: $32,750 ÷ 131 = $250 per unit
Selling price per unit: $53,710 ÷ 131 = $410 per unit

5. Entry to dispose of the overapplied overhead at month end:

Sept. 30	Factory Overhead Applied	36,320	
	Cost of Goods Sold		820
	Factory Overhead Control		35,500
	To close the overhead applied and overhead control accounts and credit the cost of goods sold account with the overapplied amount		

Chapter Assignments

Discussion Questions and Writing Assignments

1. What is the common objective of the job order cost accounting system and the process cost accounting system?
2. What are the differences between the job order cost system and the process cost system? (Focus on the characteristics of each system.)
3. Explain the concept of absorption costing.
4. What is the connection between manufacturing cost flow and the perpetual inventory method?
5. Describe the steps used to arrive at a predetermined overhead rate based on machine hours.
6. What are the keys to successfully applying overhead to products and job orders?
7. What is meant by underapplied or overapplied overhead?
8. Describe two ways to adjust for underapplied or overapplied overhead.
9. "In any period, some direct materials costs, direct labor costs, and factory overhead costs will be reported in the company's income statement. Others will be reported on the company's balance sheet." Discuss the accuracy of this statement.
10. Cost and management accounting are often overshadowed by financial accounting, since it is better publicized. Describe the importance of a product costing system to (a) the preparation of financial statements and (b) profitability.
11. In what way is timely purchasing a "do or die" function?
12. How does materials usage influence the efficiency of operations?
13. "Purchased labor services cannot be stored." Discuss this statement.
14. Define the terms *control account* and *subsidiary ledger*. How are they related?
15. Discuss the role of the Work in Process Inventory account in a job order cost system.
16. What is the purpose of a job order cost card? Identify the types of information recorded on such a card.

Classroom Exercises

Exercise 23-1.
Cost System:
Industry Linkage
(L.O. 1)

Which of the following types of manufactured products would normally be accounted for using a job order costing system? Which would be accounted for using a process costing system? (a) paint, (b) automobiles, (c) jet aircraft, (d) bricks, (e) large milling machines, (f) liquid detergent, (g) aluminum compressed-gas cylinders of standard size and capacity, (h) aluminum compressed-gas cylinders with a special fiberglass overwrap for a Mount Everest expedition, (i) standard nails produced from wire, (j) television sets, (k) printed wedding invitations, (l) a limited edition of lithographs, (m) flea collars, (n) high-speed lathes with special-order thread drills, (o) breakfast cereal, (p) an original evening gown.

Exercise 23-2.
Concept of
Absorption
Costing
(L.O. 2)

Using the absorption costing concept, determine product unit cost from the following costs incurred during March: $2,500 in liability insurance, factory; $2,900 in rent, sales office; $6,100 in depreciation, factory equipment; $32,650 in materials used; $3,480 in indirect labor, factory; $1,080 in factory supplies; $1,910 in heat, light, and power, factory; $2,600 in fire insurance, factory; $4,250 in depreciation, sales equipment; $3,850 in rent, factory; $18,420 in direct labor; $3,100 in manager's salary, factory; $5,800 in president's salary; $8,250 in sales commissions; $2,975 in advertising expenses. The Inspection Department reported that 48,800 good units were produced during March.

Exercise 23-3.
Computation of
Predetermined
Overhead Rate
(L.O. 3)

The overhead costs used by Gerald Industries, Inc. to compute its predetermined overhead rate for 19x0 were as follows:

Indirect materials and supplies	$ 96,200
Repairs and maintenance	24,900
Outside service contracts	37,300
Indirect labor	89,100
Factory supervision	42,900
Depreciation, machinery	185,000
Factory insurance	18,200
Property taxes	6,500
Heat, light, and power	11,700
Miscellaneous factory overhead	6,045
	$517,845

A total of 55,600 machine hours were used as the 19x0 allocation base. In 19x1, all overhead costs except depreciation, property taxes, and miscellaneous factory overhead are expected to increase by 10 percent. Depreciation should increase by 12 percent, and a 20 percent increase in property taxes and miscellaneous factory overhead is expected. Plant capacity in terms of machine hours used will increase by 5,850 hours in 19x1.

1. Compute the 19x0 predetermined overhead rate.
2. Compute the predetermined overhead rate for 19x1.

Exercise 23-4.
Computation and
Application of
Overhead Rate
(L.O. 3, 7)

Gustafson Compumatics specializes in the analysis and reporting of complex inventory costing projects. Materials costs are minimal, consisting entirely of operating supplies such as data processing cards, inventory sheets, and other recording tools. Labor is the highest single expense item, totaling $645,250 for 72,400 hours of work in 19x0. Factory overhead costs for 19x0 were $825,450, and were applied to specific jobs on the basis of labor hours worked. In 19x1 the company anticipates a 25 percent increase in overhead costs. Labor costs will increase by as much as $130,000, and the number of hours worked is expected to increase 15 percent.

1. Determine the total amount of factory overhead anticipated by the company in 19x1.
2. Compute the predetermined overhead rate for 19x1. (Round your answer to the nearest penny.)
3. During April 19x1, the following jobs were completed in the following times: Job 16-A4, 2,490 hours; Job 21-C2, 5,220 hours; and Job 17-H3, 4,270 hours. Prepare the journal entry required to apply overhead costs to operations for April.

Exercise 23-5.
Disposition of
Overapplied
Overhead
(Extension of
Exercise 23-4.)
(L.O. 4)

At the end of 19x1, Gustafson Compumatics had compiled a total of 82,340 hours worked. The actual overhead incurred was $1,005,850.

1. Using the predetermined overhead rate computed in Exercise 23-4, determine the total amount of overhead applied to operations during 19x1.
2. Compute the amount of overapplied overhead for the year.
3. Prepare the journal entry needed to close out the overhead accounts and dispose of the overapplied overhead for 19x1. Assume that the amount is not significant.

Exercise 23-6.
Disposition of
Underapplied
Overhead
(L.O. 4)

The Hendel Manufacturing Company ended the year with a total of $18,200 of underapplied overhead. Because management feels that the amount is significant, this unfavorable difference should be distributed among the three appropriate accounts in proportion to their ending balances. Ending account balances were as follows: Materials Inventory Control, $214,740; Work in Process Inventory Control, $312,500; Finished Goods Inventory Control, $250,000; Cost of Goods Sold, $687,500; Factory Overhead Control, $215,400; and Factory Overhead Applied, $197,200. Using good form, close out the factory overhead accounts and dispose of the underapplied overhead. Show your work in journal entry form. Show supporting computations separately.

Exercise 23-7.
Job Order Cost
Flow
(L.O. 6)

The three manufacturing cost elements—direct materials, direct labor, and factory overhead—flow through a job order cost system in a structured, orderly fashion. Specific general ledger accounts, subsidiary ledgers, and source documents are used to verify and record cost information. In both paragraph and diagram form, describe the cost flow in a job order cost accounting system.

Exercise 23-8.
Work in Process
Inventory Account:
Journal Entry
Analysis
(L.O. 7)

On July 1, Glaser Specialty Company's Work in Process Inventory account showed a beginning balance of $39,073. Production activity for July was as follows: (a) Materials costing $238,820, along with $27,402 of operating supplies, were requisitioned into production. (b) Glaser Specialty Company's total factory payroll for July was $144,239, of which $53,989 were payments for indirect labor. (Assume that payroll has been recorded but not distributed to production accounts.) (c) Factory overhead was applied at a rate of 140 percent of direct labor cost.

1. Prepare journal entries to record the materials, labor, and factory overhead costs for July.
2. Compute the ending balance in the Work in Process Inventory Control account. Assume a transfer of $451,480 to the Finished Goods Inventory Control account during the period.

Exercise 23-9.
Computation of
Unit Cost
(L.O. 8)

Webster Corporation manufactures a full line of women's apparel. This clothing line, known the world over as Robertson Fashions, features classic tailored designs that appeal to women with sophisticated tastes. During February, Webster Corporation worked on three special orders, A-16, A-20, and B-14. Cost and production data for each order were as follows:

	Job A-16	Job A-20	Job B-14
Direct materials:			
Fabric Q	$10,840	$12,980	$17,660
Fabric Z	11,400	12,200	13,440
Fabric YB	5,260	6,920	10,900
Direct labor:			
Seamstress	8,900	10,400	16,200
Layout	6,450	7,425	9,210
Packaging	3,950	4,875	6,090
Factory overhead:			
120% of direct labor dollars	?	?	?
Number of units produced	700	775	1,482

1. Compute the total cost associated with each job. Show the subtotals for each cost category.
2. Compute the unit cost for each job. (Round your computations to the nearest penny.)

Exercise 23-10.
Computation of
Unit Cost
(L.O. 8)

During the month of January, the Lorenz Cabinet Company worked on six different orders for specialty kitchen cabinets. Job A-62, manufactured for Faber Products, Incorporated was started and completed during the month. Data from Job A-62's job order cost card are summarized in the table at the top of the following page.

	Machine Hours Used	Cost
Raw materials costs:		
Cedar wood		$8,908
Pine wood		6,120
Hardware		1,734
Assembly supplies		425
Direct labor costs:		
Sawing department	120	$2,771
Shaping department	220	3,196
Finishing department	180	2,193
Assembly department	48	2,992

A total of 34 cabinets were included in Job A-62. The current predetermined overhead rate is $21.60 per machine hour. From the information given, compute the production cost of one cabinet, assuming that all the cabinets were identical.

Interpreting Accounting Information

Internal Management Information: Earnest Company and Huband Corporation
(L.O. 3, 5)

Both Earnest Company and Huband Corporation use predetermined overhead rates for product costing, inventory pricing, and sales quotations. The two businesses are about the same size, and they compete in the corrugated box industry. Earnest Company's management believes that since the predetermined overhead rate is an estimated measure, the controller's department should spend little effort in developing it. The company computes the rate once a year based on a trend analysis of the previous year's costs, and does not monitor its accuracy.

Huband Corporation takes a much more sophisticated approach. One person in the controller's office is responsible for developing predetermined overhead rates on a monthly basis. All cost estimates are checked carefully to make sure they are realistic. Accuracy checks are done routinely during each monthly closing analysis, and forecasts of changes in business activity are taken into account.

Required

1. Describe the advantages and disadvantages of each company's approach to developing predetermined overhead rates.
2. Which company has taken the more cost-effective approach to developing predetermined overhead rates? Defend your answer.
3. Is an accurate overhead rate most important for product costing, inventory valuation, or sales quotations? Why?

Problem Set A

Problem 23A-1. Application of Factory Overhead
(L.O. 3, 4)

Crowley Cosmetics Company applies factory overhead costs on the basis of machine hours. The current predetermined overhead rate is computed by using data from the two prior years, in this case 19x0 and 19x1, adjusted to reflect expectations for the current year, 19x2. The controller prepared the overhead rate analysis for 19x2 using the information presented at the top of the next page.

	19x0	19x1
Machine hours	47,800	57,360

Factory overhead costs:

	19x0	19x1
Indirect labor	$ 18,100	$ 23,530
Employee benefits	22,000	28,600
Manufacturing supervision	16,800	18,480
Utilities	10,350	14,490
Factory insurance	6,500	7,800
Janitorial services	11,000	12,100
Depreciation, factory and machinery	17,750	21,300
Miscellaneous	5,750	7,475
Total overhead	$108,250	$133,775

For the year 19x2, each item of factory overhead cost is expected to increase by the same percentage as it did from 19x0 to 19x1. Machine hours are expected to total 68,832.

Required

1. Compute the predetermined overhead rate for 19x2.
2. Assume that the company actually surpassed its sales and operating expectations in 19x2. Jobs completed during the year and the related machine hours used were as follows:

Job No.	Machine Hours
2214	12,300
2215	14,200
2216	9,800
2217	13,600
2218	11,300
2219	8,100

   Total machine hours were 69,300. Determine the amount of factory overhead to be applied to each job and to total production during 19x2.
3. Prepare the journal entry needed to close the overhead accounts and dispose of the underapplied or overapplied overhead for 19x2. Assume that $165,845 of factory overhead was incurred during the year. Also assume that the difference between actual overhead costs and applied overhead costs was insignificant.

Problem 23A-2.
Job Order Costing:
Journal Entry
Analysis and
T Accounts
(L.O. 4, 7)

Schoenthal Manufacturing, Inc. produces electric golf carts. The carts are special-order items, so the company uses a job order cost accounting system. Factory overhead is applied at the rate of 90 percent of direct labor cost. Following is a listing of events and transactions for January.

Jan. 1 Materials costing $216,400 were purchased on account.
  2 $48,500 of operating supplies were purchased on account.
  4 Production personnel requisitioned materials costing $194,200 and operating supplies costing $37,100 into production.
  10 The following overhead costs were paid: utilities, $5,400; factory rent, $2,800; maintenance charges, $3,900.

Jan. 15 Payroll was distributed to employees. Gross wages and salaries were as follows: direct labor, $118,000; indirect labor, $62,620; sales commissions, $32,400; administrative salaries, $38,000.

15 Overhead was applied to production.

19 Operating supplies costing $27,550 and materials listed at $190,450 were purchased on account.

21 Materials costing $212,750 and operating supplies costing $33,400 were requisitioned into production.

26 Production completed during the month was transferred to Finished Goods Inventory Control. Total costs assigned to these jobs were $823,590.

31 The following gross wages and salaries were paid to employees: direct labor, $132,000; indirect labor, $66,240; sales commissions, $31,200; administrative salaries, $38,000.

31 Overhead was applied to production.

31 Products costing $804,520 were shipped to customers during the month. Total selling price of the goods was $976,800, and the sales were recorded at month end.

31 The following overhead costs (adjusting entries) were recorded: prepaid insurance expired, $3,900; property taxes (payable at year end), $3,200; depreciation, machinery, $23,500.

Required

1. Record the journal entries for all transactions and events in January. In the payroll entries, concern yourself only with the distribution of factory payroll to the production accounts.
2. Post the entries prepared in part 1 to T accounts, and determine the partial account balances. Assume no beginning inventory balances. Assume that entries made when payroll was recorded were also posted to the Factory Payroll account.
3. Compute the amount of underapplied or overapplied overhead as of January 31.

Problem 23A-3.
Job Order Costing:
Unknown Quantity
Analysis
(L.O. 6)

Partial operating data for the Duckworth Picture Company follows. Management has decided the predetermined overhead rate for the current year is 130 percent of direct labor dollars.

Account	March	April
Beginning Materials Inventory Control	$ (a)	$ (e)
Beginning Work in Process Inventory Control	89,505	(f)
Beginning Finished Goods Inventory Control	79,764	67,660
Materials Requisitioned	58,025	(g)
Materials Purchased	57,090	60,116
Direct Labor Costs	48,760	54,540
Factory Overhead Applied	(b)	(h)
Cost of Units Completed	(c)	229,861
Cost of Goods Sold	165,805	(i)
Ending Materials Inventory Control	33,014	28,628
Ending Work in Process Inventory Control	(d)	(j)
Ending Finished Goods Inventory Control	67,660	30,515

Required

Using the data provided, compute the unknown values. Show all your computations.

Problem 23A-4.
Job Order Cost
Flow
(L.O. 6, 8)

The September 1 inventory balances of Granger House, a manufacturer of high-quality children's clothing, were as follows:

Account	Balance
Materials Inventory Control	$21,360
Work in Process Inventory Control	15,112
Finished Goods Inventory Control	17,120

Job order cost cards for jobs in process as of September 30, 19x9 revealed the following:

Job No.	Materials	Direct Labor	Factory Overhead
24-A	$1,596	$1,290	$1,677
24-B	1,492	1,380	1,794
24-C	1,984	1,760	2,288
24-D	1,608	1,540	2,002

Materials purchased and received in September:
September 4	$33,120
September 16	28,600
September 22	31,920

Direct labor costs for September:
September 15 payroll	$23,680
September 29 payroll	25,960

Predetermined overhead rate:
  130 percent of direct labor dollars

Materials requisitioned into production during September:
September 6	$37,240
September 23	38,960

Finished goods with a 75 percent markup over cost were sold during September for $320,000.

Required

1. Using T accounts, reconstruct the transactions for September.
2. Compute the cost of units completed during the period.
3. What was the total cost of units sold during September?
4. Determine the ending inventory balances.
5. Jobs 24-A and 24-C were completed during the first week of October. No additional materials costs were incurred, but Job 24-A required $960 more direct labor, and Job 24-C needed additional direct labor of $1,610. Job 24-A was composed of 1,200 pairs of trousers; Job 24-C, 950 shirts. Compute the unit cost for each job.

Problem 23A-5.
Job Order Costing:
Comprehensive
Journal Entry
Analysis
(L.O. 7)

The Benz Manufacturing Company maintains a job order cost accounting system. The company is currently using an overhead application rate of 150 percent of direct labor cost. Accounting records showed that on August 1, 19x7 the Materials Inventory Control account balance was $129,150, and the materials subsidiary ledger balances were $51,800 for mixing fluid, $48,610 for MX powder, and $28,740 for operating supplies. The Work in Process Inventory Control account balance was $87,050, and job order cost card balances in the subsidiary ledger were $51,900 for Job 16-A, $29,730 for Job 18-A, and $5,420 for Job 20-A. The Finished Goods Inventory Control account balance was $66,850, and the finished goods subsidiary ledger balances were: for Product 16, none; for Product 18, $24,240; and for Product 20, $42,610. The Factory Payroll, Factory Overhead Control, and Factory Overhead Applied accounts have no balances carried forward from July because these accounts are closed at the end of each month. The following transactions and events took place during the month of August.

Aug. 1 Operating supplies totaling $28,740 were requisitioned into production.

4 Received $45,650 of mixing fluid and $26,720 of MX powder, purchased on account.

6 Paid the following factory overhead costs in cash: factory rent, $3,450; heat, light, and power, $2,290; repairs and maintenance, $4,240; outside contractual services, $8,525.

9 The following semimonthly payroll liability was recorded: gross direct labor wages, $48,250 (Job 16-A, $18,640; Job 18-A, $17,800; Job 20-A, $11,810); gross indirect labor wages, $29,420; gross administrative salaries, $9,250; FICA taxes withheld, $4,535; federal income taxes withheld, $14,320.

9 Factory payroll was distributed to the production accounts.

9 Factory overhead costs were applied to production.

12 Purchased and received $24,120 of operating supplies, on account.

13 Requisitioned $25,280 of mixing fluid and $29,960 of MX powder into production for Job 18-A.

14 Payroll checks for the liability recorded on August 9 were prepared and distributed to the employees.

15 Paid property taxes of $5,100, chargeable to factory overhead.

18 Job 16-A was completed and transferred to Finished Goods Inventory.

20 Requisitioned $31,890 of mixing fluid and $26,770 of MX powder into production for Job 20-A.

23 The following semimonthly payroll liability was recorded: gross direct wages, $32,220 (Job 18-A, $19,410; Job 20-A, $12,810); gross indirect labor wages, $22,140; gross administrative salaries, $8,250; FICA taxes payable, $3,460; federal income taxes withheld, $12,980.

23 Factory payroll was distributed to the production accounts.

23 Factory overhead costs were applied to production.

26 Job 16-A—5,000 liters—was sold and shipped to a customer for $139,840. The unit production cost was $19.70 per liter.

28 Payroll checks for the liability recorded on August 23 were prepared and distributed to the employees.

31 Recorded depreciation on machinery of $11,940 for the month.

31 The Factory Overhead Control and the Factory Overhead Applied accounts were closed out, and the difference was distributed to the Cost of Goods Sold account.

Required 1. Prepare journal entries for all the preceding transactions and events.

2. Prepare T accounts for all the general ledger and subsidiary ledger accounts relevant to the job order costing system. Enter the beginning balances where applicable, and post the journal entries prepared in part **1**.
3. To check the accuracy of ending inventory control account balances, compare them with the totals in their subsidiary ledger accounts.

Problem Set B

Problem 23B-1.
Application of
Factory Overhead
(L.O. 3, 4)

Hosseini Laser Products, Inc. uses a predetermined overhead rate in its production, assembly, and testing departments. One rate is used for the entire company and is applied based on machine hours. The current rate was determined by analyzing data from the previous two years and projecting figures for the current year, adjusted for expected changes. Mr. Roubi is about to compute the rate to be used in 19x8 using the following data:

	19x6	19x7
Machine hours	38,000	41,800
Factory overhead costs:		
Indirect materials	$ 42,500	$ 55,250
Indirect labor	21,200	25,440
Supervision	36,800	40,480
Utilities	9,400	11,280
Labor-related costs	8,100	8,910
Depreciation, factory	9,800	10,780
Depreciation, machinery	22,700	27,240
Property taxes	2,400	2,880
Insurance	1,800	2,160
Miscellaneous	4,400	4,840
Total overhead	$159,100	$189,260

Each of the factory overhead cost items is expected to increase by the same percentage in 19x8 as its 19x6 to 19x7 increase. Machine hours for 19x8 are expected to be 45,980.

Required

1. Compute the predetermined overhead rate for 19x8. (Round your answer to three decimal places.)
2. During 19x8, Hosseini Laser Products, Inc. produced the following jobs using the machine hours shown:

Job No.	Machine Hours
H-142	7,640
H-164	5,160
H-175	7,900
H-201	10,480
H-218	12,310
H-304	2,460

Determine the amount of factory overhead that was applied to each job in 19x8. What was the total overhead applied during the year?

3. Prepare the journal entry needed to close the overhead accounts and dispose of the under- or overapplied overhead. Actual factory overhead for 19x8 was $227,540. Assume that the difference between actual and applied overhead costs is insignificant.

Problem 23B-2.
Job Order Costing:
Journal Entry
Analysis and
T Accounts
(L.O. 4, 7)

Vagge, the finest name in parking attendant apparel, has been in business for over 30 years. Their colorful and stylish uniforms are special ordered by exclusive hotels and country clubs all over the world. During April 19x1, Vagge Industries, Inc. completed the following transactions. Factory overhead was applied at a rate of 120 percent of direct labor cost.

April 1 Materials costing $49,400 were purchased on account.
      3 Materials costing $26,850 were requisitioned into production.
      4 $22,830 of operating supplies were purchased for cash.
      8 The company issued checks for the following factory overhead costs: utilities, $3,310; factory insurance, $1,925; repairs, $4,640.
     10 The Cutting Department manager requisitioned $28,510 of materials and $7,480 of operating supplies into production.
     15 Payroll was distributed to the employees. Gross wages and salaries were: direct labor, $62,900; indirect labor, $31,610; factory supervision, $26,900; sales commissions, $32,980.
     15 Overhead was applied to production.
     22 Factory overhead costs were paid: utilities, $3,270; maintenance, $2,380; rent, $5,250.
     23 The receiving department recorded purchase on account and receipt of $31,940 of materials and $9,260 of operating supplies.
     27 Production requisitions of $28,870 of materials and $7,640 of operating supplies were recorded.
     30 The following gross wages and salaries were paid to employees: direct labor, $64,220; indirect labor, $29,290; factory supervision, $29,520; sales commissions, $36,200.
     30 Factory overhead was applied to production.
     30 Units completed during the month were transferred to Finished Goods Inventory Control; total cost was $322,400.
     30 Sales of $418,240 were shipped to customers. Their total production cost was $294,200.
     30 Adjusting entries for the following were recorded: Depreciation, factory equipment—$2,680; Property taxes, factory—$1,230.

Required

1. Record the journal entries for all transactions and events in April. In the payroll entries, concern yourself only with the distribution of factory payroll to the production accounts.
2. Post the entries prepared in part 1 to T accounts, and determine the partial account balances. Assume no beginning inventory balances.
3. Compute the amount of underapplied or overapplied overhead for April.

Problem 23B-3.
Job Order Costing:
Unknown Quantity
Analysis
(L.O. 6)

Baggett Enterprises makes an assortment of computer support equipment. Mr. Ruggle, the new controller for the organization, can find only partial information from the past two months, which is presented at the top of the following page. The current year's predetermined overhead rate is 80 percent of direct labor dollars.

Account	May	June
Materials Inventory Control, Beginning	$ 36,240	$ (e)
Work in Process Inventory Control, Beginning	56,480	(f)
Finished Goods Inventory Control, Beginning	44,260	(g)
Materials Purchased	(a)	96,120
Materials Requisitioned	82,220	(h)
Direct Labor Costs	(b)	71,250
Factory Overhead Applied	52,400	(i)
Cost of Units Completed	(c)	221,400
Cost of Units Sold	209,050	(j)
Materials Inventory Control, Ending	38,810	41,950
Work in Process Inventory Control, Ending	(d)	(k)
Finished Goods Inventory Control, Ending	46,940	51,180

Required

Using the information given, compute the unknown values. Show all your computations.

**Problem 23B-4.
Job Order Cost
Flow
(L.O. 6, 8)**

Alice James is chief financial officer for Meridian Industries, a company that makes special-order printers for personal computers. Her records for February 19x8 revealed the following information:

Beginning Inventory balances:
Materials Inventory Control	$26,450
Work in Process Inventory Control	22,900
Finished Goods Inventory Control	19,200

Materials purchased and received:
February 6	$ 7,200
February 12	8,110
February 24	6,890

Direct labor costs:
February 14	$12,750
February 28	13,230

Materials requisitioned into production:
February 4	$ 9,080
February 13	5,940
February 25	8,600

Job order cost cards for jobs in process on February 28 showed the following totals:

Job No.	Materials	Direct Labor	Factory Overhead
AJ-10	$3,220	$1,460	$2,044
AJ-14	3,880	2,110	2,954
AJ-30	2,980	1,640	2,296
AJ-16	4,690	2,370	3,318

The predetermined overhead rate for the month was 140 percent of direct labor dollars. Sales for February totaled $148,360, a 75 percent markup over the cost of production.

Required

1. Using T accounts, reconstruct the transactions for February.
2. Compute the cost of units completed during the month.
3. What was the total cost of units sold during February?
4. Determine the ending inventory balances.
5. During the first week of March, Jobs AJ-10 and AJ-14 were completed. No additional materials costs were incurred, but Job AJ-10 needed $720 more direct labor, and Job AJ-14 required additional direct labor of $1,140. Job AJ-10 was composed of 40 units; Job AJ-14, 55 units. Compute the unit cost for each job.

**Problem 23B-5.
Job Order Costing:
Comprehensive
Journal Entry
Analysis**
(L.O. 7)

Merriman Information Systems Company is a division of Hilbrich International, Inc. The company designs unique management information systems and produces specialty computer equipment for use in the production of heavy road construction machinery and underwater search equipment. The Accounting Department uses a job order cost accounting system. The current year's predetermined overhead rate is 90 percent of direct labor dollars.

At the beginning of business on March 1, 19x8, the Materials Inventory Control account had a balance of $246,750. Materials Inventory subsidiary records revealed the following breakdown: sheet metal, $54,820; casings, $36,110; computer components, $149,880; operating supplies, $5,940. Three jobs were in process on March 1, when job order cost cards showed the following amounts: Job P-284, $91,250; Job E-302, $56,810; and Job G-325, $17,250. The Work in Process Inventory Control account balance at March 1 was $165,310. All Finished Goods Inventory items were sold and shipped in February, so no balance existed at the beginning of March. The Factory Payroll, Factory Overhead Control, and Factory Overhead Applied accounts are closed at the end of each month, so no balances were carried forward from February. The following transactions were completed during March:

March 1 Recent purchases were received with invoices: sheet metal, $36,440, and casings, $24,980.

2 Requisitioned $3,710 of operating supplies into production.

4 Paid factory overhead costs: electricity, $3,240; water, $590; heat, $1,950; repairs and maintenance, $2,620.

5 Received new purchases along with invoices: computer components, $52,810; casings, $22,550; operating supplies, $4,070.

7 Requisitioned materials into production: Job E-302, sheet metal, $7,480; computer components, $16,270; Job G-325, casings, $5,760; computer components, $18,960; Job G-410, sheet metal, $15,420; casings, $6,130; computer components, $5,230.

9 Operating supplies costing $3,840 were requisitioned into production.

14 Semimonthly payroll liability was recorded and distributed to production accounts: total direct labor, $49,020 (Job P-284, $11,940; Job E-302, $14,720; Job G-325, $18,110; Job G-410, $4,250); indirect labor wages, $38,190; administrative salaries, $54,200; FICA taxes withheld, $10,320; federal income taxes withheld, $26,534.

14 Factory overhead costs were applied to production.

16 Purchases of materials were received along with invoices: sheet metal, $16,520; casings, $15,960; computer components, $29,280; operating supplies, $4,110.

March 18   Requisitioned materials into production: Job E-302, computer components, $14,890; Job G-325, casings, $16,780; computer components, $24,520; Job G-410, sheet metal, $13,460; casings, $13,220; computer components, $16,610; Job Y-160, sheet metal, $9,810; casings, $10,730; computer components, $6,230.

   20   Operating supplies costing $5,620 were requisitioned into production.

   23   Paid factory overhead costs: property taxes, $2,570; unemployment compensation taxes, factory, $560; repairs, $3,680; contractual indirect labor, $4,170; rent, $3,110.

   28   Recorded semimonthly payroll liability and distributed it to production accounts: total direct labor, $57,080 (Job P-284, $5,210; Job E-302, $8,760; Job G-325, $20,560; Job G-410, $16,940; Job Y-160, $5,610); indirect labor, $40,770; administrative salaries, $56,540; FICA taxes withheld, $11,090; federal income taxes withheld, $28,510.

   28   Factory overhead costs were applied to production.

   29   Completed and transferred the costs of Jobs P-284 and E-302 to Finished Goods Inventory Control.

   30   Recorded depreciation on equipment, $3,090.

   31   Job P-284 was sold and shipped to customer, selling price $267,940.

   31   The Factory Overhead Control and Factory Overhead Applied accounts were closed out, and the difference distributed to the Cost of Goods Sold account.

Required

1. Prepare journal entries for all the preceding transactions and events.
2. Prepare T accounts for all the general ledger and subsidiary ledger accounts relevant to the job order costing system. Enter the beginning balances where applicable, and post the journal entries prepared in response to part 1 to those accounts.
3. Check the accuracy of ending inventory control account balances by recording them with the totals from their respective subsidiary ledger accounts.

Management Decision Case

Fornstrom Manufacturing Company
(L.O. 5, 6, 8)

Fornstrom Manufacturing Company is a small family-owned business that makes specialty plastic products. Since it was started three years ago, the company has grown quickly, and now employs ten production people. Because of its size, the company uses a job order cost accounting system that was designed around a periodic inventory method. Work sheets and special analyses are used at Fornstrom to account for manufacturing costs and inventory valuations.

Two months ago the company's accountant quit. You have been called in to assist management. The following information has been given to you:

Beginning inventory balances (1/1/19x9):
Materials	$40,420
Work in Process (Job K-2)	59,100
Finished Goods (Job K-1)	71,700

Materials requisitioned into production during 19x9:

Job K-2	$17,000
Job K-4	42,800
Job K-6	54,500

Direct labor for the year:

Job K-2	$35,300
Job K-4	43,480
Job K-6	65,600

The company purchased materials only once during the year, for $126,500. All jobs use the same material. For the current year the company has been using an overhead application rate of 130 percent of direct labor dollars. So far two jobs, K-2 and K-4, have been completed, and Jobs K-1 and K-2 have been shipped to customers. Job K-1 contained 3,000 units, Job K-2, 5,500 units, and Job K-4, 4,800 units.

Required

1. Reconstruct the job order cost sheets for each job worked on during the period. What were the unit costs for jobs K-1, K-2, and K-4?
2. From the information given prepare a T account analysis, and compute the current balances in the three inventory accounts and the cost of goods sold.
3. The president has asked you to analyze the current job order cost accounting system. Should the system be changed? How? Why? Prepare an outline of your response to the president.

Answers to Self-Test

1. a	3. b	5. c	7. a	9. b
2. c	4. b	6. b	8. a	10. c

LEARNING OBJECTIVES

1. Explain the role of the Work in Process Inventory account(s) in a process cost accounting system.
2. Describe product flow and cost flow through a process cost accounting system.
3. Compute equivalent production for situations with and without units in the beginning work in process inventory.
4. Compute product unit cost for a specific time period (unit cost analysis schedule).
5. Prepare a cost summary schedule that assigns costs to units completed and transferred out of the department during the period, and find the ending Work in Process Inventory balance.
6. Make the journal entry(ies) needed to transfer costs of completed units out of the Work in Process Inventory account.

CHAPTER 24

Product Costing: The Process Cost System

A major goal of management accountants using any cost accounting system is to find product unit costs and to set ending values for the Materials, Work in Process, and Finished Goods Inventory accounts. In Chapter 23, we compared the characteristics of job order costing and process costing. You will remember that a process cost accounting system is used by companies in the paint, oil, fastener (screws and bolts), gas, and beverage industries. Such companies produce large amounts of similar products or have a continuous production flow. Companies employing the new just-in-time (JIT) operating philosophy also depend on process costing procedures.

A process costing system has the following characteristics: (1) Cost data are collected by department or work center, with little concern for specific job orders. (2) A weekly or monthly time period is emphasized, rather than the time it takes to complete a specific order. (3) The accounting system uses several Work in Process Inventory accounts—one for each department or work center in the manufacturing process. With this system, manufacturing costs are not traced to specific products or job orders. Instead, they are averaged over the units produced in a specific period of time.

Process costing depends on a three-schedule analysis consisting of (1) the schedule of equivalent production, (2) the unit cost analysis schedule, and (3) the cost summary schedule. From the information in these three schedules, we can tell what costs to attach to units that are completed and transferred out of the department. Then we make a journal entry to transfer those costs out of the Work in Process Inventory account. Those costs remaining in the Work in Process Inventory account belong to units still in process at period end.

This chapter will analyze the process cost accounting system and explain how to calculate product unit costs. It will also explain how to compute and verify the period-end balance for the Work in Process Inventory and the costs assigned to units completed. Those units will have been transferred either to the next department or to the Finished Goods Inventory account. After studying this chapter, you should be able to meet the learning objectives listed on the left. For a complete discussion of the just-in-time operating philosophy and its impact on product costing, see Appendix E.

Cost Flow Through Work in Process Inventory Accounts

Accounting for the costs of materials, direct labor, and factory overhead does not differ much between job order costing and process costing. Under both systems, costs must be recorded and eventually charged to production. Materials and supplies must be purchased and requisitioned into production. Direct labor wages must be paid to employees and charged to production accounts. Finally, factory overhead costs must be assigned to production. Journal entries like those described in Chapter 23 record these transactions and events. So, as you can see, the flow of costs *into* the Work in Process Inventory account is very similar in the two product costing systems.

The major difference between job order cost accounting and process cost accounting is the way in which costs are assigned to products. In a job order cost system, costs are traced to specific jobs and products. In a process cost system, an averaging technique is used. All products worked on during a specific time period (a week or a month) are used as the output base for computing unit cost. Total costs of materials, direct labor, and factory overhead accumulated in the Work in Process Inventory account (or accounts) are divided by the equivalent units for products worked on during the period. Though the concept may seem clear, technical aspects make the procedure more difficult than it first appears.

Work in Process Inventory Accounts

OBJECTIVE 1
Explain the role of the Work in Process Inventory account(s) in a process cost accounting system

The Work in Process Inventory account is the focal point of process costing. Unlike the job order system, a process cost system is not limited to one Work in Process Inventory account. In fact, process costing uses as many Work in Process Inventory accounts as there are departments or steps in the production process. The process shown in Figure 24-1 involves two departments. As shown in the figure, the three cost elements flow into the Work in Process Inventory account of Department 1. When the finished units from Department 1 become the direct materials input in Department 2, the total costs of the completed product move to Department 2 along with the completed unit. In Department 2, the units from Department 1 are processed further. No more materials are needed, but as shown in the figure, more labor is added and factory overhead is assigned, usually on the basis of labor cost or hours.

When the completed products are finished, they are transferred from the work in process inventory (Department 2) to the finished goods inventory. At that point each unit's cost is made up of five cost inputs, three from Department 1 and two from Department 2. A detailed breakdown, using *hypothetical* dollar amounts, follows.

Figure 24-1. Cost Elements and Process Cost Accounts

Total Unit Cost

Department 1		
Materials	$2.55	
Direct labor	.90	
Factory overhead	.75	
Total, Department 1		$4.20
Department 2		
Direct labor	$1.20	
Factory overhead	2.05	
Total, Department 2		3.25
Total unit cost (to Finished Goods Inventory)		$7.45

Production Flow Combinations

There are hundreds of ways in which product flows can combine with
departmental production processes. Two basic structures are illustrated
in Figure 24-2. Example 1 shows a *series* of three processes, or departments. The completed product from one department becomes the direct
materials input in the next department. (Figure 24-1 also showed a series of departments.) A department series can include two to a dozen or

Figure 24-2. Cost Flow for Process Costing

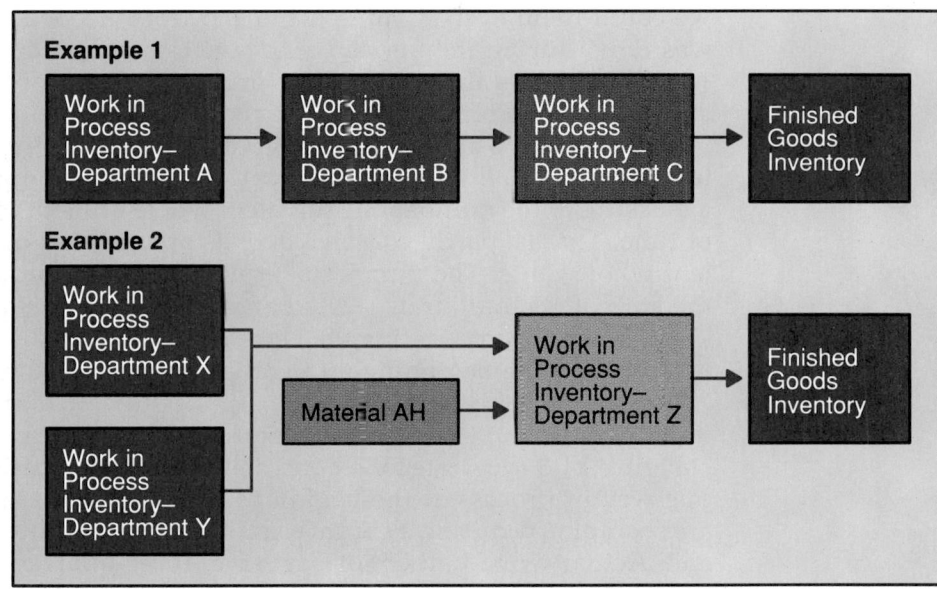

more departments. The point to remember is that the product unit cost is the sum of the cost elements added in all departments.

Example 2 in Figure 24-2 shows a different kind of production flow. Again there are three departments, but in this example the product does not flow through all departments in a simple 1–2–3 order. Instead, two separate products are developed, one in Department X and the other in Department Y. Both products then go to Department Z, where they are joined with a third direct material input, Material AH. The unit cost that is transferred to the Finished Goods Inventory account when the products are completed includes cost elements from Departments X, Y, and Z. From these two examples, you can see that the total possible combinations of product flows and production processes is limitless.

The Concept of Equivalent Production

A key feature of a process cost system is the computation of equivalent units of production for each department or process for each accounting period. This computation is needed before product unit costs can be computed. Remember that in process costing, an averaging approach is used. No attempt is made to associate costs with particular job orders. Instead, all manufacturing costs incurred in a department or production process are divided by the units produced during the period. There are, however, several important questions to answer in connection with the number of units produced. Exactly how many units were produced?

Do we count only those units completed during the period? What about partly completed units in the beginning work in process inventory? Do we count them even if only part of the work needed to complete them was done during the period? And what about products in the ending work in process inventory? Is it proper to focus only on those units started and completed during the period?

The answers to all these questions are linked to the concept of equivalent production. **Equivalent production** (also called **equivalent units**) is a measure of the number of equivalent whole units produced in a period of time. That is, partly completed units are restated in terms of equivalent whole units. The number of equivalent units produced is equal to the sum of (1) total units started and completed during the period and (2) an amount representing the work done on partially completed products in both the beginning and ending work in process inventories. A "percentage of completion" factor is applied to partially completed units to calculate the number of equivalent whole units.

Figure 24-3 illustrates the equivalent unit computation. One automobile was in process at the beginning of the month, three were started and completed during February, and one remains in process at period end. Actually, one-half (.5) of Car A and three-quarters (.75) of Car E are completed during February. We find the total equivalent units for the month by adding together those units started and completed (3.0) and

Figure 24-3. Equivalent Unit Computation

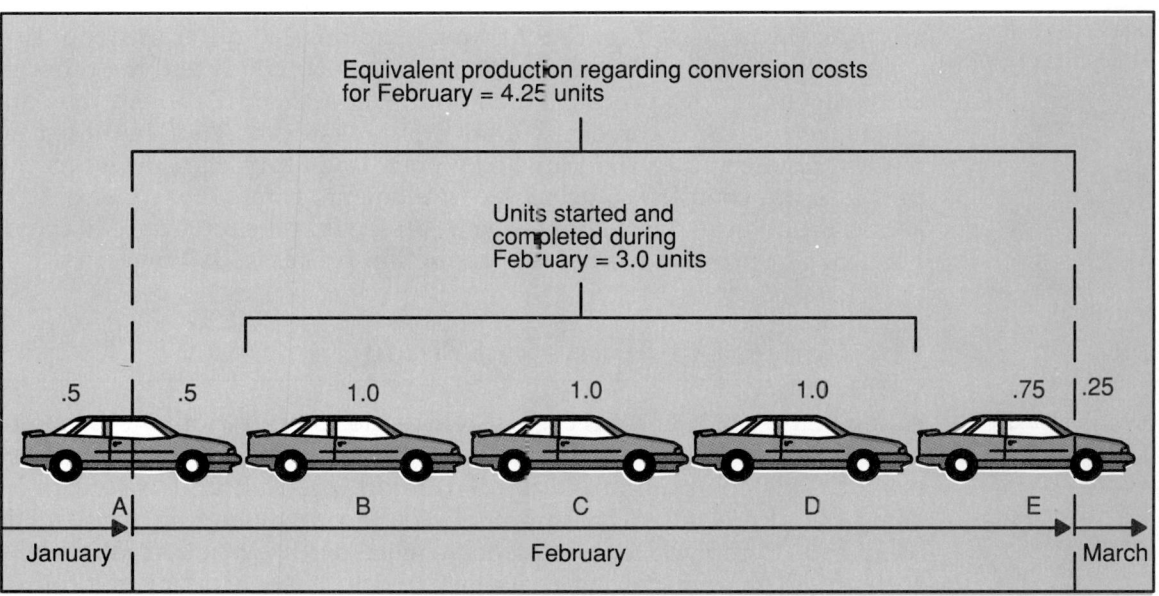

Facts: Conversion costs (those for direct labor and factory overhead) are incurred uniformly as each car moves through production. Equivalent production for February is 4.25 units as to conversion costs. But materials costs are all added to production at the beginning of the process. Since four cars entered production in February (cars B, C, D, and E), equivalent production for the month is 4.0 units as to material costs.

those units partly completed (.5 and .75). Therefore, equivalent production for February is 4.25 units.

This is the method used for determining equivalent production for direct labor and factory overhead, commonly called conversion costs. **Conversion costs** are the combined total of direct labor and factory overhead costs incurred by a production department. They are usually lumped together because they are incurred uniformly throughout the production process; combining them is convenient. Raw materials are usually added at the beginning of a process, however, so equivalent units for *materials* costs are computed in a different manner. As shown in Figure 24-3, materials for Car A were added in January and therefore do not influence equivalent units for materials in February. However, materials for Car E were all added to production in February. So we add 3.0 (units started and completed—Cars B, C, and D) to 1.0 (unit started but not completed—Car E) to get the equivalent units for materials for February, 4.0 units.

Once we know the number of equivalent units produced, we can compute unit costs for materials and conversion costs for each department in the production process. The equations for computing the unit cost amounts follow. (Note the role of equivalent units.)

$$\text{unit cost for materials} = \frac{\text{total materials costs}}{\text{equivalent units—materials}}$$

$$\text{unit cost for conversion costs} = \frac{\text{total labor and factory overhead costs}}{\text{equivalent units—conversion costs}}$$

The Average Costing Approach

We assumed in Figure 24-3 that products flow in a first-in, first-out (FIFO) manner in a process costing environment. That is, beginning inventory items are completed as new ones are brought into the production process. But cost flow and accountability do not have to follow the same assumptions that support the flow of products. Such is the case with the average costing approach to process cost accounting, in which costs are not accounted for in the same manner as actual product flow. The **average costing approach** *assumes that the items in beginning work in process inventory were started and completed during the current period.* Although a bit less accurate than the FIFO approach (an alternative approach to process costing that will be described later in this chapter), the average costing method is much easier to understand and work with. It is illustrated below.

No Beginning Work in Process Inventory. To begin our discussion of the average costing process, we will assume there are no units in beginning work in process inventory. Thus we need to consider only (1) units actually started and completed during the period and (2) units started but not completed. By definition, units started but not completed represent the balance in the ending work in process inventory.

Equivalent production is computed in parts, as follows:

Part 1: Units started and completed = (number of units) × 100 percent

Part 2: Equivalent units in ending work in process inventory = (number of units) × (percentage of completion)

The *sum* of these two amounts gives us the equivalent whole units completed during the period. (Percentage of completion figures are supplied by engineers or supervisors in the production departments.)

Earlier we noted that unit costs are computed separately for materials and conversion costs. Unlike conversion costs, materials costs generally are not incurred uniformly throughout the process. They are normally incurred either at the beginning of the process (materials input) or at the end of it (packing materials). Because of this difference, the equivalent units for materials will not always be the same as the equivalent units for conversion costs. Separate computations are necessary.

For example, assume that the records of Danelid Clothing, Inc. for January 19xx show the following information: (a) 47,500 units were started during the period; (b) 6,200 units were partly complete at period end; (c) units in ending work in process inventory were 60 percent complete; (d) materials were added at the beginning of the process; (e) conversion costs were incurred uniformly throughout the process; and (f) no units were lost or spoiled during the month. Exhibit 24-1 shows the **schedule of equivalent production**, in which equivalent units are computed for the period for both materials and conversion costs, for Danelid Clothing. Because there were no units in beginning work in process inventory, dashes are entered in that row. We see that 41,300 units were started and completed during the period (47,500 units started less 6,200 units not completed). All 41,300 have received 100 percent of the materials, labor, and overhead effort needed to complete them. Therefore, 41,300 equivalent units are recorded in both the Materials Costs and Conversion Costs columns.

So far equivalent units have been the same for materials and conversion costs. Accounting for equivalent units in ending inventory is a bit more complicated. These 6,200 units have received all materials inputs, because materials were added to each product as it entered the production process. In the Materials column, therefore, 6,200 equivalent units are entered. However, conversion costs are added uniformly as the products move through the process, and the 6,200 units in ending inventory are only 60 percent complete. So we obtain the number of equivalent whole units by multiplying the number of actual units by the percentage completed. As shown in Exhibit 24-1, 6,200 units × 60 percent completion = 3,720 equivalent units. Totaling the columns in the exhibit, we determine that there are 47,500 equivalent units for materials costs and 45,020 equivalent units for conversion costs.

With Beginning Work in Process Inventory. The case of no beginning work in process inventory is almost never found in industry. By definition, process costing techniques are used in industries where produc-

Exhibit 24-1. Equivalent Units: No Beginning Inventory

Danelid Clothing, Inc.
Schedule of Equivalent Production
For the Month Ended January 31, 19xx

Units—Stage of Completion	Units to Be Accounted For	Equivalent Units	
		Materials Costs	Conversion Costs
Beginning inventory—units completed in this period	—	—	—
Units started and completed in this period (47,500 – 6,200)	41,300	41,300	41,300
Ending inventory— units started but not completed in this period	6,200		
(Materials—100% complete)		6,200	
(Conversion costs— 60% complete)			3,720
Totals	47,500	47,500	45,020

tion flows continuously, or where there are long runs of identical products. In these cases, there is always something in process at the end of a period. So there are always units in beginning work in process inventory in the next period. We now turn to this situation, expanding the example used above.

The presence of beginning inventories makes it a little more difficult to compute equivalent units. Remember, in average costing you treat all the units in beginning work in process inventory as if they were started and completed in the current period. With the inclusion of beginning inventories, equivalent production is calculated in three parts:

Part 1: Units in beginning inventory = number of units × 100 percent

Part 2: Units started and completed = number of units × 100 percent

Part 3: Equivalent units in ending inventory:
Materials Costs = number of units × percentage of completion
Conversion Costs = number of units × percentage of completion

Exhibit 24-2 illustrates the computation of equivalent units using the average costing approach when beginning inventory items must be accounted for. During February 19xx, unit production information for Danelid Clothing, Inc. was as follows: (a) at the start of the month 6,200 units occupied the beginning work in process inventory; (b) beginning inventory items were 60 percent complete; (c) 57,500 units were started

Exhibit 24-2. Equivalent Units: With Beginning Inventory

Danelid Clothing, Inc.
Schedule of Equivalent Production
For the Month Ended February 29, 19xx

Units—Stage of Completion	Units to Be Accounted For	Equivalent Units Materials Costs	Conversion Costs
Beginning inventory—units completed in this period	6,200	6,200	6,200
Units started and completed in this period	52,500	52,500	52,500
Ending inventory— units started but not completed in this period	5,000		
(Materials—100% complete)		5,000	
(Conversion costs— 45% complete)			2,250
Totals	63,700	63,700	60,950

during the period; (d) at month end 5,000 units were in the ending work in process inventory; and (e) these ending inventory units were 45 percent complete as to conversion costs (all materials had been added).

As shown in Exhibit 24-2, the 6,200 units in beginning inventory are extended at their full amount to the materials costs and conversion costs columns of the schedule. This treatment is the same as that given to the 52,500 units started and completed during February (57,500 units started minus 5,000 unfinished units). Units started and completed receive the full amount of materials costs and conversion costs. Ending inventory is 100 percent complete as to materials (5,000 units) and 45 percent complete as to conversion costs (5,000 × .45 = 2,250). The end result is a monthly total of 63,700 equivalent units for materials costs and 60,950 equivalent units for conversion costs.

Note that this illustration covers only two of the hundreds of possible process costing situations that could arise with varying percentages of completion.

FIFO Costing Approach

Figure 24-3 on page 1014 illustrates the FIFO *product flow* normally associated with process cost accounting. With such a production flow, the first unit to enter the production process during a period is the first to be completed (automobile A in Figure 24-3). A FIFO product flow is fundamental to the process cost accounting system.

FIFO *cost flow* is an assumption underlying the FIFO method of determining product unit cost. This method, an alternative to the *average costing approach*, assigns costs to products based upon a FIFO product flow and the work performed in a given time period. It is a second method used for product costing in a process cost accounting system. Although a bit more accurate than the average costing approach, the FIFO approach is more complex, and will be left for a more advanced course in cost accounting. It is mentioned only to make you aware of an alternative to the method discussed in this chapter. All the process costing procedures illustrated in this text are based on the average costing approach.

Cost Analysis Schedules

OBJECTIVE 4
Compute product unit cost for a specific time period (unit cost analysis schedule)

So far, we have emphasized accounting for *units* of productive output. In the schedule of equivalent production, we found the total units to be accounted for. Then we computed equivalent units for materials costs and conversion costs. Once we have sorted out the unit information and arrived at equivalent unit figures, we can turn to the dollar information. Now we bring manufacturing costs, cost per equivalent unit, and inventory costing into our analysis.

Unit Cost Analysis Schedule

The **unit cost analysis schedule**, the second of the three schedules used in process costing, summarizes two computations. (1) All costs charged to the Work in Process Inventory account of each department or production process are accumulated and added together to determine total costs to be accounted for. (2) Costs per equivalent unit for materials costs and conversion costs for the period are computed. Examples of unit cost analysis schedules are shown in Exhibits 24-3 (presented on page 1020) and 24-5 (found on page 1023).

The first step in the unit cost analysis schedule is to summarize all costs for the period. These costs are made up of costs of materials and conversion costs incurred in the current period plus the costs included in the beginning Work in Process Inventory account. (The Total Costs to Be Accounted For column later serves as a check for the third schedule, the cost summary schedule.)

The second step is to divide the total costs by the number of equivalent units. Total costs for materials are divided by the equivalent units for materials. In the same way, total conversion costs are divided by the equivalent units for conversion costs. Because we are using the average cost flow assumption, units and costs in beginning inventory are included in computing this period's costs per equivalent unit.

| Exhibit 24-3. Unit Cost Determination: No Beginning Inventories |

Danelid Clothing, Inc.
Unit Cost Analysis Schedule
For the Month Ended January 31, 19xx

	Total Costs				Equivalent Unit Costs	
	Costs from Beginning Inventory	Costs from Current Period	Total Costs to Be Accounted For	÷	Equivalent Units	= Cost per Equivalent Unit
Materials costs	—	$154,375	$154,375		47,500	$3.25
Conversion costs	—	258,865	258,865		45,020	5.75
Totals	—	$413,240	$413,240			$9.00

Cost Summary Schedule

OBJECTIVE 5
Prepare a cost summary schedule that assigns costs to units completed and transferred out of the department during the period, and find the ending Work in Process Inventory balance

The final phase of the process costing analysis is to distribute the total costs accumulated during the period among all the units of output. Some costs may stay in the ending Work in Process Inventory account. Others will go with the units completed and transferred out of the department. Costs are assigned by means of the **cost summary schedule**. Information in this schedule comes from the schedule of equivalent production and the unit cost analysis schedule.

The total costs to be transferred out of the department is fairly easy to compute. Suppose that 16,500 units were completed during the period and moved to the finished goods inventory. Cost per equivalent unit was found to be $3.30. Therefore, $54,450 (16,500 × $3.30) is transferred out of the Work in Process Inventory account via a journal entry. All costs remaining in the Work in Process Inventory account after costs of completed units have been transferred out represent the cost of ending units in process. To complete the analysis, we add together the total cost of units transferred and the costs that belong to the ending work in process inventory. Then we compare the total with the total costs to be accounted for in the unit cost analysis schedule. If the two totals are not equal, an arithmetic error (in most cases because of rounding) has been made.

Illustrative Analysis

To fully explain the form and use of the three-schedule analysis, we will expand the Danelid Clothing, Inc. example. Besides the equivalent unit information we discussed earlier, the company has collected the following cost data:

January, 19xx
    Beginning Work in Process Inventory   —
    Cost of materials used $154,375
    Conversion costs for the month   258,865
February, 19xx
    Cost of materials used $190,060
    Conversion costs for the month   319,930

From these data, we will compute equivalent unit costs, total costs transferred to the Finished Goods Inventory account, and the ending balance in the Work in Process Inventory account for January and February 19xx.

January. The unit cost analysis schedule for January is shown in Exhibit 24-3. Total costs to be accounted for are $413,240. Of this amount, costs for materials are $154,375 and conversion costs are $258,865. When we divide these costs by the equivalent unit amounts (computed in Exhibit 24-1), we get costs per equivalent unit of $3.25 for materials ($154,375 ÷ 47,500) and $5.75 for conversion costs ($258,865 ÷ 45,020). Total unit cost for the period is $9.00. The per unit cost amounts are then used in the cost summary schedule to compute costs transferred to the Finished Goods Inventory account and the cost of the ending Work in Process Inventory account.

Danelid's cost summary schedule for January is shown in Exhibit 24-4. No units were in process at the beginning of January, so no costs are entered for beginning inventory. (Even though there was no beginning inventory for January, the headings are included so that the form can be used for any process costing situation.) Units transferred to the finished goods inventory in January were made up entirely of units started and completed, since there were no units in beginning inventory. These 41,300 units cost $9.00 each to produce (total cost per equivalent unit). So $371,700 must be transferred to the Finished Goods Inventory account. We debited $413,240 to the Work in Process Inventory account during January and then transferred $371,700 of that amount to the Finished Goods Inventory account. The difference of $41,540 remaining in the account is the ending Work in Process Inventory balance. This amount is verified in Exhibit 24-4. Using the ending inventory amounts from the schedule of equivalent production in Exhibit 24-1 and the costs per equivalent unit from the cost analysis schedule in Exhibit 24-3, we make the following computations:

Materials costs: 6,200 equivalent units × $3.25 per unit $20,150
Conversion costs: 3,720 equivalent units × $5.75 per unit   21,390
Ending Work in Process Inventory balance $41,540

The check of computations at the bottom of Exhibit 24-4 ensures that all the arithmetic is right. Total costs computed in Exhibit 24-3 have been accounted for.

Exhibit 24-4. Ending Inventory Computation: No Beginning Inventories		

Danelid Clothing, Inc.
Cost Summary Schedule
For the Month Ended January 31, 19xx

	Cost of Goods Transferred to Finished Goods Inventory	Cost of Ending Work in Process Inventory
Beginning inventory		
None	—	
Units started and completed*		
41,300 units × $9.00 per unit	$371,700	
Ending inventory*		
Materials costs: 6,200 units × $3.25		$ 20,150
Conversion costs: 3,720 units × $5.75		21,390
Totals	$371,700	$ 41,540
Check of computations		
Costs to Finished Goods Inventory		$371,700
Cost of ending Work in Process Inventory		41,540
Total costs to be accounted for (unit cost analysis schedule)		$413,240

*Note: Unit figures come from the schedule of equivalent production for January (Exhibit 24-1).

February. The cost analysis for February is a bit more difficult because units and costs in beginning Work in Process Inventory must be considered. February operating results are analyzed in Exhibits 24-5 and 24-6. Total costs to be accounted for in February are $551,530. Included in this amount is the beginning Work in Process Inventory balance of $41,540 (see Exhibit 24-4) plus current costs from February of $190,060 and $319,930 for materials and conversion costs, respectively. These costs are added to the materials and conversion costs carried over from January in the Work in Process Inventory account. The total costs to be accounted for are then divided by the equivalent unit figures computed in Exhibit 24-2. February's $8.90 cost per equivalent unit includes $3.30 per unit for materials and $5.60 for conversion costs.

The February cost analysis is completed by preparing the cost summary schedule (Exhibit 24-6). Costs transferred to the Finished Goods Inventory account total $522,430. This amount includes costs of $55,180

Exhibit 24-5. Unit Cost Determination: With Beginning Inventories

Danelid Clothing, Inc.
Unit Cost Analysis Schedule
For the Month Ended February 29, 19xx

	Total Costs				Equivalent Unit Costs	
	Costs from Beginning Inventory	Costs from Current Period	Total Costs to Be Accounted For	÷	Equivalent Units*	= Cost per Equivalent Unit
Materials costs	$20,150	$190,060	$210,210		63,700	$3.30
Conversion costs	21,390	319,930	341,320		60,950	5.60
Totals	$41,540	$509,990	$551,530			$8.90

Exhibit 24-6. Ending Inventory Computation: With Beginning Inventories

Danelid Clothing, Inc.
Cost Summary Schedule
For the Month Ended February 29, 19xx

	Cost of Goods Transferred to Finished Goods Inventory	Cost of Ending Work in Process Inventory
Beginning inventory* 6,200 units × $8.90 per unit	$ 55,180	
Units started and completed* 52,500 units × $8.90 per unit	467,250	
Ending inventory*		
Materials costs: 5,000 units × $3.30		$ 16,500
Conversion costs: 2,250 units × $5.60		12,600
Totals	$522,430	$ 29,100
Check of computations		
Costs to Finished Goods Inventory		$522,430
Costs to ending Work in Process Inventory		29,100
Total costs to be accounted for (unit cost analysis schedule)		$551,530

*Note: Unit figures come from the schedule of equivalent production for February (Exhibit 24-2).

for the 6,200 units in beginning inventory and $467,250 for the 52,500 units started and completed during February. The ending Work in Process Inventory balance of $29,100 is made up of $16,500 of materials costs and $12,600 of conversion costs. At the bottom of the cost summary schedule, we check to make sure that no arithmetic errors were made in our computations.

Journal Entry Analysis

OBJECTIVE 6
Make the journal entry(ies) needed to transfer costs of completed units out of the Work in Process Inventory account

Although schedules for (1) equivalent production, (2) unit cost analysis, and (3) cost summary have been emphasized, none of the schedules offers a direct way to transfer costs in the accounting records. All three schedules deal mostly with the Work in Process Inventory account. The goal of completing the process costing analysis is to compute the dollar totals for goods completed and transferred to finished goods inventory, and for partly completed products that stay in the Work in Process Inventory account. However, the three schedules alone do not cause costs to flow through accounts in the general ledger. They only give the information needed for journal entries. It is the journal entries that actually move costs from one account to another.

The final step in a process costing analysis, then, is a journal entry to transfer costs of completed products out of Work in Process Inventory. Remember that all of the entries analyzed in Chapter 23 are also necessary in a process costing system. Only one entry is highlighted here, however, because it is involved directly with the transfer of costs of completed goods. To transfer the costs of units completed, we debit Finished Goods Inventory (or the Work in Process Inventory of a subsequent department) and credit the Work in Process Inventory account of the department being analyzed. The amount of the cost transfer was calculated in the cost summary schedule.

In the example of Danelid Clothing, Inc. the following entries would be made at the end of each time period:

Jan. 31	Finished Goods Inventory	371,700	
	Work in Process Inventory		371,700
	To transfer cost of units		
	completed in January to		
	Finished Goods Inventory		
Feb. 29	Finished Goods Inventory	522,430	
	Work in Process Inventory		522,430
	To transfer cost of units		
	completed in February to		
	Finished Goods Inventory		

Once the entries are posted, the Work in Process Inventory account appears as follows:

Work in Process Inventory

Balance	—	Transferred to Finished	
Jan. materials costs	154,375	Goods in Jan.	371,700
Jan. conversion costs	258,865		
Balance 1/31/xx	**41,540**		
Feb. materials costs	190,060	Transferred to Finished	
Feb. conversion costs	319,930	Goods in Feb.	522,430
Balance 2/29/xx	**29,100***		

*This amount can be verified by comparing it with the data in the cost summary schedule in Exhibit 24-6. The $29,100 is made up of $16,500 of materials costs and $12,600 of conversion costs.

In the analysis of Danelid Clothing, Inc., we assumed that the company had only *one* production department, and the example centered on two consecutive monthly accounting periods. Because there was only one production department, only one Work in Process Inventory account was needed. The following example deals with *two* production departments in a series. The product passes from the first to the second department and then to the finished goods inventory. This production flow is similar to that illustrated in Figure 24-1.

When the production process requires two departments, the accounting system must maintain two separate Work in Process Inventory accounts, one for each department. This situation calls for more work, but the computations are the same. The key point is to treat *each* department and its related Work in Process Inventory account in a separate analysis. A three-schedule cost analysis must be prepared for *each* department. Departments should be analyzed in the order in which the products flow through them.

Illustrative Problem: Two Production Departments

Bryant Manufacturing Company produces a liquid chemical for converting salt water to fresh water. The production process involves the Mixing Department and the Cooling Department. Every unit produced must be processed by both the Mixing Department and the Cooling Department. Cooling is the final operation.

In the Mixing Department, a basic chemical powder, Material BP, is added to water, heated to 88° Celsius, and mixed for two hours. Assume that no evaporation occurs and that Material BP is added at the beginning of the process. Conversion costs are incurred uniformly throughout the process. Operating data for the Mixing Department for April 19xx are presented on the following page:

Beginning Work in Process Inventory
    Units 20% complete   1,450 liters
    Costs: Materials costs $ 13,050
                Conversion costs $ 1,760

Ending Work in Process Inventory
    All units 70% complete

April operations
    Units started   55,600 liters
    Costs: Cost of materials used $488,990
                Conversion costs $280,115
    Units completed and transferred to
    the Cooling Department   54,800 liters

Required

1. Using good form and an average costing approach, prepare (a) a schedule of equivalent production, (b) a unit cost analysis schedule, and (c) a cost summary schedule for the Mixing Department.
2. From information in the cost summary schedule, prepare the proper journal entry to transfer costs of completed units for April out of the Mixing Department.

Solution

1. Before doing the three schedules and preparing the journal entry, it is necessary to make a special analysis of the units (liters) worked on during April. To complete the schedule of equivalent production, we must first find the number of units started and completed and the number of units in ending work in process. These amounts were not provided, but they can easily be computed from the information we already know.

Units started and completed:
	Units completed and transferred (given)	54,800 liters
Less:	Units in beginning inventory (given)	1,450 liters
Equals:	Units started and completed	53,350 liters

Units in ending inventory:
	Units started during April (given)	55,600 liters
Less:	Units started and completed (above)	53,350 liters
Equals:	Units in ending inventory	2,250 liters

Now that we know the number of units started and completed and the number of units in ending work in process, we can prepare the three schedules in the cost analysis (presented on the following page).

2. The costs of completed units for April are now ready to be transferred from the Mixing Department to the Cooling Department. The required journal entry would be as follows:

Work in Process—Cooling Department	756,240	
Work in Process—Mixing Department		756,240
To transfer cost of units completed in		
April from Mixing Department to		
Cooling Department		

Bryant Manufacturing Company
Mixing Department—Process Cost Analysis
For the Month Ended April 30, 19xx

1a. Schedule of Equivalent Production

Units—Stage of Completion	Units to Be Accounted For	Equivalent Units Materials Costs	Equivalent Units Conversion Costs
Beginning inventory	1,450	1,450	1,450
Units started and completed in this period	53,350	53,350	53,350
Ending inventory—units started but not completed in this period (Materials—100% complete) (Conversion costs—70% complete)	2,250	2,250	1,575 (70% of 2,250)
Totals	57,050	57,050	56,375

1b. Unit Cost Analysis Schedule

	Total Costs Costs from Beginning Inventory	Costs from Current Period	Total Costs to Be Accounted For	÷	Equivalent Unit Costs Equivalent Units	=	Cost per Equivalent Unit
Materials costs	$13,050	$488,990	$502,040		57,050		$ 8.80
Conversion costs	1,760	280,115	281,875		56,375		5.00
Totals	$14,810	$769,105	$783,915				$13.80

1c. Cost Summary Schedule

	Cost of Goods Transferred to Cooling Department	Cost of Ending Work in Process Inventory
Beginning inventory 1,450 units × $13.80 per unit	$ 20,010	
Units started and completed 53,350 units × $13.80 per unit	736,230	
Ending inventory Materials: 2,250 units × $8.80 Conversion costs: 1,575 units × $5.00		$ 19,800 7,875
Totals	$756,240	$ 27,675
Check of computations: Costs to Cooling Department Costs in ending Work in Process Inventory		$756,240 27,675
Total costs to be accounted for (unit cost analysis schedule)		$783,915

Note that the $756,240 is being transferred from one Work in Process Inventory account to another. The $756,240 attached to the units transferred into the Cooling Department during April would be accounted for in the same way as materials used in the Mixing Department. All other procedures and schedules illustrated in the Mixing Department example would be used again for the Cooling Department. See the Special Review Problem at the end of this chapter for the accounting treatment of the Cooling Department (found on pages 1032–1034).

Cost-Based Pricing of Products

Product cost information is used not only for inventory pricing. Companies also depend on it for setting the selling price of a product. Setting a selling price is an art rather than a science. There is no magic formula that will pump out consistently valid prices for a company's products. One approach is to charge whatever the buying public will bear. Another is to use your competition's prices to help in setting your own prices. A third approach is to use product cost information. Most successful companies probably use a combination of these approaches. Cost-based pricing is a conservative, yet wise route to setting prices. First the product's manufacturing costs are computed. Then an amount is usually added in to cover the operating and selling costs of the business. Finally, a factor is added for profit.

The cost-based price, however, is just the starting point in selecting an effective selling price of a product. Knowing the competition and using your intuition are also important. Years of experience go into good price development. Remember, though, that the basic number on which to adjust and build is product cost. A cost-based price is the lifeline of a business.

Chapter Review

Review of Learning Objectives

1. **Explain the role of the Work in Process Inventory account(s) in a process cost accounting system.**
   The Work in Process Inventory account is the heart of the process cost accounting system. Each production department or operating unit has its own Work in Process Inventory account. All costs charged to that department flow into this inventory account. Special analysis, using three schedules, is needed at period end to determine the costs flowing out of the account. All special analyses in process cost accounting are related to costs in the Work in Process Inventory account.

2. **Describe product flow and cost flow through a process cost accounting system.**

Process costing is used to account for liquids or long, continuous production runs of identical products. Thus, products flow in a FIFO fashion (first in, first out). Once a product is started into production, it flows on to completion. Manufacturing costs are handled differently than in a job order costing system. Following the average costing approach, current costs of materials, direct labor, and factory overhead are added to costs in beginning inventory when computing unit costs. The unit costs are then assigned to completed units or to units in ending work in process.

3. **Compute equivalent production for situations with and without units in the beginning work in process inventory.**

The number of equivalent units is found with the aid of a schedule of equivalent production. Units worked on during the period are classified as being (a) in beginning inventory (started last period and completed this period), (b) started and completed this period, *or* (c) started this period and still in process at period end. Percentage of completion data are used to compute equivalent units separately for materials and conversion costs.

4. **Compute product unit cost for a specific time period (unit cost analysis schedule).**

Unit costs are found using a unit cost analysis schedule. Materials costs for units in beginning inventory and costs of the current period are added together. The same is done for conversion costs. Next, the total cost of materials is divided by the equivalent unit amount for materials. The same procedure is followed for conversion costs. Then unit cost for materials and unit cost for conversion costs are added to reach final unit cost.

5. **Prepare a cost summary schedule that assigns costs to units completed and transferred out of the department during the period, and find the ending Work in Process Inventory balance.**

The first part of the cost summary schedule helps compute costs assigned to units completed and transferred out during the period. This part is done in two steps: (a) Units in beginning inventory are assigned a full share of production costs. (b) Units started and completed during the current period are also assigned a full share of production costs. The total of these two calculations represents costs attached to units completed and transferred out during the period. The second part of the cost summary schedule assigns costs to units still in process at period end. Unit costs for materials and conversion costs are multiplied by their respective equivalent units. The total of these two dollar amounts represents the balance in the Work in Process Inventory account at the end of the period.

6. **Make the journal entry(ies) needed to transfer costs of completed units out of the Work in Process Inventory account.**

After completing the first part of the cost summary schedule (the part that assigns costs to units completed and transferred out during the period), a journal entry is prepared to transfer costs out of the Work in Process Inventory account. A credit is made to the account for the whole amount. The debit can be either to Finished Goods Inventory or to the Work in Process Inventory account of a subsequent department, depending on the network of production departments in the process.

Review of Concepts and Terminology

The following concepts and terms were introduced in this chapter:

(L.O. 3) **Average costing approach**:   A process costing method in which unit costs are computed based on the assumption that the items in beginning work in process inventory were started and completed during the current period.

(L.O. 3) **Conversion costs**:   The combined total of direct labor and factory overhead costs incurred by a production department.

(L.O. 5) **Cost summary schedule**:   A process costing schedule that facilitates the distribution of all production costs incurred and accumulated during the period among the units of output, either those completed and transferred out of the department or those units still in process at period end.

(L.O. 3) **Equivalent production or equivalent units**:   A measure of units produced in a period of time, expressed in terms of fully completed or equivalent whole units produced.

(L.O. 3) **Schedule of equivalent production**:   A process costing schedule in which the equivalent units for both materials costs and conversion costs are computed for the period.

(L.O. 4) **Unit cost analysis schedule**:   A process costing schedule in which (1) all costs charged to the Work in Process Inventory account of a particular department or production process are accumulated and added together to determine total costs to be accounted for and (2) costs per equivalent unit for materials costs and conversion costs for the period are computed.

Self-Test

Test your knowledge of the chapter by choosing the best answer for each item below and on the following page.

1. Which of the following industries is most likely to use a process costing system?
   a. Ship building company
   b. Oil refining company
   c. Made-to-order furniture company
   d. Bridge building company   *(L.O. 1)*

2. How many Work in Process Inventory accounts will a company employing a process costing system use in its product costing process?
   a. Only one
   b. Always three
   c. One for each production department
   d. Depends on the number of products produced   *(L.O. 1)*

3. If a department using a process costing system had 1,400 units in beginning WIP inventory 40 percent complete, started and completed 4,900 units, and had 1,200 units in ending WIP inventory 60 percent complete, what is the equivalent units for materials costs assuming materials are added at the beginning of the process?
   a. 7,500   c. 6,460
   b. 6,180   d. 6,820   *(L.O. 3)*

4. Conversion costs are
   a. all manufacturing costs.
   b. special product conversion costs.
   c. the total of direct labor and factory overhead costs.
   d. all period costs. *(L.O. 3)*

5. If a department using a process costing system had 1,600 units in beginning WIP inventory 50 percent complete, started and completed 6,900 units, and had 1,400 units in ending WIP inventory 80 percent complete, what is the equivalent units for conversion costs assuming materials are added at the beginning of the process?
   a. 9,900   c. 6,820
   b. 9,100   d. 9,620   *(L.O. 3)*

6. The Vlasho Company had the following information generated for March:

	Costs from Beginning Inventory	Costs from Current Period
Materials costs	$ 4,600	$ 41,480
Conversion costs	12,400	306,128

At the beginning of the period there were 1,000 units which were 40 percent complete as to conversion costs and 100 percent complete as to materials costs. During the current period, 8,600 units were started and completed. Ending inventory contained 640 units which were 80 percent complete as to conversion costs and 100 percent complete as to materials costs. The company uses the average costing approach to process costing. The equivalent units for materials costs were
   a. 10,240.   c. 9,840.
   b. 9,640.   d. 9,712.   *(L.O. 3)*

7. Assuming the same facts as in **6**, the equivalent units for conversion costs were
   a. 9,640.   c. 9,712.
   b. 10,112.   d. 10,240.   *(L.O. 3)*

8. Assuming the same facts as in **6**, the unit cost for the period was
   a. $37.10.   c. $35.55.
   b. $36.85.   d. $36.00.   *(L.O. 4)*

9. Assuming the same facts as in **6**, the total costs transferred to Finished Goods Inventory were
   a. $356,160.   c. $345,600.
   b. $353,760.   d. $341,280.   *(L.O. 5)*

10. Assuming the same facts as in **6**, the total costs assigned to ending work in process inventory were
    a. $19,008.   c. $23,744.
    b. $23,040.   d. $23,328.   *(L.O. 5)*

Answers to Self-Test are at the end of this chapter.

Special Review Problem
Costs Transferred In

(L.O. 3, 4, 5, 6) This problem reviews the three-schedule analysis used in process costing. It also introduces two new situations common in process costing.

1. **Costs transferred in.** Accounting for the second department's costs in a series of Work in Process Inventory accounts is very much like accounting for the first department's costs. The only difference is that instead of accounting for current materials costs, we are dealing with *costs transferred in* during the period. All procedures used to account for costs transferred in are exactly the same as those used for materials costs and units. *When accounting for costs and units transferred in, treat them as you would materials added at the beginning of the process.*

2. **Rounding of numerical answers.** Unlike the problems discussed so far in this chapter, most real-world unit costs do not work out to even-numbered dollars and cents. They must be rounded. Remember these three simple rules: (a) Round off all unit cost computations to three decimal places. (b) Round off cost summary data to the nearest dollar. (c) On the cost summary schedule, add or subtract any difference caused by rounding to or from the amount being transferred out of the department before the journal entry is prepared.

The purpose of this review problem is to illustrate the accounting approach for the second in a series of production departments and to show how to use cost rounding. We will continue with the example of the Bryant Manufacturing Company, concentrating this time on the Cooling Department. No new materials are added in this department; only conversion costs are added in the cooling process. Operating data for the Cooling Department for April 19xx are:

Beginning Work in Process Inventory	
Units (40% complete)	2,100 liters
Costs: Transferred In	$ 29,200
Conversion costs	$ 2,654
Ending Work in Process Inventory	
All units 60% complete	
April operations	
Units transferred in	54,800 liters
Costs: Transferred In	$756,240
Conversion costs	$172,130
Units completed and transferred	
to Finished Goods Inventory	54,450 liters

Required

1. Using good form, prepare (a) a schedule of equivalent production, (b) a unit cost analysis schedule, and (c) a cost summary schedule.
2. From the cost summary schedule, prepare the journal entry to transfer costs of completed units for April to Finished Goods Inventory account.

Answer to Special Review Problem

1. Before doing the three-schedule analysis on the facing page, we must first analyze the unit information on page 1034.

Bryant Manufacturing Company
Cooling Department
Process Cost Analysis
For the Month Ended April 30, 19xx

1a. Schedule of Equivalent Production

Units—Stage of Completion	Units to Be Accounted For	Transferred-in Costs	Conversion Costs
		Equivalent Units	
Beginning inventory—units completed in this period	2,100	2,100	2,100
Units started and completed in this period	52,350	52,350	52,350
Ending inventory—units started but not completed in this period	2,450		
(Transferred in—100% complete)		2,450	
(Conversion costs—60% complete)			1,470
Totals	56,900	56,900	55,920

1b. Unit Cost Analysis Schedule

	Costs from Beginning Inventory	Costs from Current Period	Total Costs to Be Accounted For	÷	Equivalent Units	=	Cost per Equivalent Unit
	Total Costs				Equivalent Unit Costs		
Transferred-in costs	$29,200	$755,240	$785,440		56,900		$13.804*
Conversion costs	2,654	172,130	174,784		55,920		3.126*
Totals	$31,854	$928,370	$960,224				$16.930*

1c. Cost Summary Schedule

	Cost of Goods Transferred to Finished Goods Inventory	Cost of Ending Work in Process Inventory
Beginning inventory		
2,100 units × $16.930 per unit	$ 35,553	
Units started and completed		
52,350 units × $16.930 per unit	886,286	
Ending inventory		
Transferred-in costs: 2,450 units × $13.804		$33,820[†]
Conversion costs: 1,470 units × $3.126		4,595[†]
Totals	$921,839	$38,415
Check of computations:		
Costs to Finished Goods Inventory	$921,839	
Costs in ending Work in Process Inventory	38,415	
Error due to rounding—subtract from costs transferred to Finished Goods Inventory	(30)	
Total costs to be accounted for (unit cost analysis schedule)	$960,224	

*Answer rounded to three decimal places
[†]Answer is affected by the use of rounded unit cost amounts

Units started and completed:

	Units completed and transferred (given)	54,450 liters
Less:	Units in beginning inventory (given)	2,100 liters
Equals:	Units started and completed	52,350 liters

Units in ending inventory:

	Units transferred in during April (given)	54,800 liters
Less:	Units started and completed (above)	52,350 liters
Equals:	Units in ending inventory	2,450 liters

With this unit information, we can prepare the three schedules on the previous page.

2. The costs of completed units for April are now ready to be transferred from the Cooling Department to the Finished Goods Inventory account. The proper journal entry is:

Finished Goods Inventory ($921,839 − $30)	921,809	
Work in Process—Cooling Department		921,809
To transfer cost of units completed in April to Finished Goods Inventory		

Chapter Assignments

Discussion Questions and Writing Assignments

1. What types of production are best suited to a process cost accounting system?
2. "In job order costing, *one* Work in Process Inventory account is used for all jobs. In process costing, *several* Work in Process Inventory accounts are used." Explain.
3. Define *equivalent production (equivalent units)*.
4. Why do actual unit data need to be changed to equivalent unit data for product costing purposes in a process costing system?
5. Define *conversion costs*. Why is this concept used in process costing computations?
6. What are the three schedules used in process costing analysis?
7. Why is it easier to compute equivalent units without units in beginning inventory than with?
8. What are the purposes of the unit cost analysis schedule?
9. What are the two important dollar amounts that come from the cost summary schedule? How do they relate to the year-end financial statements?
10. Describe how to check the accuracy of the results in the cost summary schedule.
11. What is the significance of the journal entry used to transfer costs of completed products out of the Work in Process Inventory account?
12. What is a "transferred-in" cost? Where does it come from? Why is it handled like materials added at the beginning of the process?

Classroom Exercises

Exercise 24-1.
Multiple Work in Process Inventory Accounts
(L.O. 1)

The Lake Irma Manufacturing Company has shifted from making highly specialized products to producing three mass-produced items. The factory has been redesigned so that each of the three products must be worked on in each of four work centers. These four work centers are positioned in such a way that the products can flow continuously from one process to the next. Only slight setup changes are necessary when shifting from one product to another.

Management has requested that their CPA, Jane Benedict, suggest changes in the accounting system to accommodate the change in production method. The CPA's first suggestion is to replace the old job order costing system with a process costing system, and to replace the existing Work in Process Inventory account with four Work in Process Inventory accounts, one account for each work center.

The company's president, Ronald Alva, is puzzled by the need for four Work in Process Inventory accounts. Prepare a response to the president.

Exercise 24-2.
Product Flow Diagram
(L.O. 2)

Lafite Paint Company uses a process costing system to analyze the costs incurred in making paint. Production of Quality Brand starts in the Blending Department, where materials SM and HA are added to a water base. The solution is heated to 70° Celsius and then transferred to the Mixing Department, where it is mixed for one hour. Then the paint goes to the Settling/Canning Department, where it is cooled and put into 4-liter cans. Direct labor and factory overhead charges are incurred uniformly throughout each part of the paint-making process.

In diagram form, show the product flow for Quality Brand paint.

Exercise 24-3.
Equivalent Units: No Beginning Inventories
(L.O. 3)

The Strefeler Stone Company produces slumpstone bricks. Though it has been in operation for only twelve months, the company already enjoys a good reputation for quality bricks. During its first year, materials for 580,500 bricks were put into production; 576,900 were completed and transferred to finished goods inventory. The remaining bricks were still in process at year end, 70 percent completed. In the company's process costing system, all materials are added at the beginning of the process. Conversion costs are incurred uniformly throughout the production process.

From this information, prepare a schedule of equivalent production for the year ending December 31, 19x1. Use the average costing approach.

Exercise 24-4.
Equivalent Units: Beginning Inventories
(L.O. 3)

Peggy Enterprises makes Sweetwater Shampoo for professional hair stylists. On January 1, 19x9, 9,200 liters of shampoo were in process, 80 percent complete as to conversion costs and 100 percent complete as to materials costs. During the year, 318,500 liters of materials were put into production. Data for work in process inventory on December 31, 19x9 were as follows: shampoo, 6,500 liters; stage of completion, 40 percent of conversion costs and 100 percent of materials content.

From this information, prepare a schedule of equivalent production for the year. Use the average costing approach.

Exercise 24-5.
Equivalent Units:
Beginning
Inventories
(L.O. 3)

The Lucas Company, a major producer of liquid vitamins, uses a process cost accounting system. During January, 19x0, 130,000 gallons of Material CIA and 40,000 gallons of Material CMA were put into production. Beginning work in process inventory was 55,000 gallons of product, 70 percent complete as to labor and overhead. Ending work in process inventory was made up of 36,000 gallons, 45 percent complete as to conversion costs. All materials are added at the beginning of the process.

From this information, prepare a schedule of equivalent production for January using the average costing approach.

Exercise 24-6.
Work in Process
Inventory
Accounts: Total
Unit Cost
(L.O. 4)

Scientists at Brooks Laboratories, Inc. have just perfected a liquid substance called D. K. Rid, which dissolves tooth decay without the use of a dentist's drill. The substance, which is generated from a complex process involving five departments, is very costly. Cost and equivalent unit data for the latest week are as follows (units are in ounces):

| | Materials Costs | | Conversion Costs | |
Dept.	Dollars	Equivalent Units	Dollars	Equivalent Units
A	$25,000	2,000	$34,113	2,055
B	23,423	1,985	26,130	2,010
C	48,204	2,060	20,972	2,140
D	—	—	22,086	2,045
E	—	—	15,171	1,945

From these data, compute (a) the unit cost for each department and (b) the total unit cost of producing an ounce of D. K. Rid. Round to two decimal places.

Exercise 24-7.
Unit Cost
Determination
(L.O. 4)

Guide Kitchenwares, Inc. manufactures heavy-duty cookware. Production has just been completed for July, 19x1. The Work in Process Inventory account showed the following costs at the beginning of July: materials, $31,700; conversion costs, $29,400. Cost of materials used in July was $242,150; conversion costs were $147,270. During the month, 15,190 units were started and completed. A schedule of equivalent production for July has already been prepared. It shows a total of 16,210 equivalent units as to conversion costs, and 16,450 equivalent units as to materials costs.

With this information, prepare a unit cost analysis schedule for July. Use the average costing approach. Round to three decimal places.

Exercise 24-8.
Cost Summary
Schedule
(L.O. 5)

The Svensson Danish Bakery produces the world-famous Kringle coffee bread. It uses a process cost system for internal record-keeping purposes. Production for August, 19x2 was as follows: (a) Beginning inventory, 450 units: costs attached from the preceding period were materials, $625; conversion costs, $385. (b) Units started and completed during the month totaled 14,200. (c) Ending inventory was as follows: materials, 420 units, 100 percent complete as to materials costs and 70 percent as to conversion costs.

(d) Unit costs per equivalent unit have been computed for August: materials costs, $1.40; conversion costs, $0.85.

Using the information given, compute the cost of goods transferred to the Finished Goods Inventory account, the cost remaining in the Work in Process Inventory account, and the total costs to be accounted for. Use the average costing approach. Round to the nearest dollar.

Exercise 24-9.
Cost Transfer:
Journal Entry
Required
(L.O. 3, 6)

The following cost summary schedule was prepared for the La Cava Paste Company for the year ended July 31, 19x9.

La Cava Paste Company
Cost Summary Schedule
For the Year Ended July 31, 19x9

	Cost of Goods Transferred to Finished Goods Inventory	Cost of Ending Work in Process Inventory
Beginning inventory 3,140 units at $4.60	$ 14,444	
Units started and completed 94,960 units at $4.60	436,816	
Ending inventory Materials: 4,200 units at $3 20		$13,440
Conversion costs: 2,100 units at $1.40		2,940
Totals	$451,260	$16,380

1. From the information given, prepare the journal entry for July 31, 19x9.
2. Draw up the company's schedule of equivalent production. Assume that materials are added at the beginning of the process.

Interpreting Accounting Information

Internal
Management
Information:
Tannet Tire
Corporation
(L.O. 4)

Tannet Tire Corporation makes several lines of automobile and truck tires. The company operates in a competitive marketplace, so it relies heavily on cost data from its process cost accounting system. It uses this information to set prices for its most competitive tires. The company's Blue Radial line has lost some of its market share during each of the past four years. Management believes price breaks allowed by the three competitors are the major reason for the decline in sales.

The company controller, Linda Sugarman, has been asked to review the product costing information that supports price decisions on the Blue Radial line. In preparing her report, she collected the data presented on the following page related to 19x1, the last full year of operations.

		Units	Dollars
Equivalent units:	Materials costs	90,540	
	Conversion costs	88,590	
Manufacturing costs:	Materials		$1,981,050
	Direct labor		770,410
	Factory overhead applied		1,694,902
Unit cost data:	Materials costs		23.50
	Conversion costs		27.00
Work in Process Inventory:			
Beginning (40% complete)		4,240	
Ending (50% complete)		3,900	

Units started and completed during 19x1 totaled 82,400. The costs attached to the Work in Process Inventory account at the beginning of the year were materials costs, $123,664, and conversion costs, $57,011. Sugarman found that little spoilage had occurred. The proper cost allowance for spoilage was included in the predetermined overhead rate of $2.20 per direct labor dollar. The direct labor cost, however, revealed that $189,270 was charged twice to the production account, the second time in error. So far in 19x2, the Blue Radial has been selling for $91 per tire. This price was based on the 19x1 unit data plus 50 percent to cover operating costs and 25 percent of the total unit cost for profit. During 19x2, the three competitors' prices for comparable tires have been about $85 per tire. In the company's process costing system, all materials are added at the beginning of the process, and conversion costs are incurred uniformly throughout.

Required

1. Point out how the cost-charging error is affecting the company.
2. Prepare a revised unit cost analysis schedule for 19x1. Use the average costing approach.
3. What should have been the minimum selling price per tire in 19x2?
4. Suggest ways for preventing such errors in the future.

Problem Set A

**Problem 24A-1.
Process Costing:
No Beginning
Inventories**
(L.O. 3, 4, 5, 6)

The Solinko Chewing Gum Company, which produces several flavors of bubble gum, began production of a new kumquat-flavored gum on June 1, 19x9. Two basic materials, gum base and kumquat-flavored sweetener, are blended at the beginning of the process. Direct labor and factory overhead costs are incurred uniformly throughout the blending process. During June, 135,000 kilograms of gum base and 270,000 kilograms of kumquat additive were used at costs of $162,000 and $81,000, respectively. Direct labor charges were $360,310, and factory overhead costs applied during June were $184,010. The ending work in process inventory was 21,600 kilograms. All materials have been added to these units, and 25 percent of the conversion costs have been assigned.

Required

1. Using proper form, prepare (a) a schedule of equivalent production, (b) a unit cost analysis schedule, and (c) a cost summary schedule for the Blending Department for June. Round unit costs to two decimal places.

2. From the cost summary schedule, prepare the journal entry to transfer costs of completed units for June from the Blending Department to the Forming and Packing Department.

Problem 24A-2.
Process Costing:
With Beginning
Inventories
(L.O. 3, 4, 5, 6)

O'Hara Food Products, Inc. makes high-vitamin, calorie-packed wafers used by professional sports teams to supply quick energy to players. The thin white wafers are produced in a continuous product flow. The company, which uses a process costing system based on the average costing approach, recently purchased several automated machines so that the wafers can be produced in a single department. Materials are all added at the beginning of the process. The cost for the machine operator's labor and production-related overhead are incurred uniformly throughout the process.

In February, 19x2, a total of 231,200 liters of materials were put into production at a cost of $294,780. Two liters of materials were used to produce one unit of output (one unit = 144 wafers). Labor costs for February were $60,530. Factory overhead was $181,590. Beginning Work in Process Inventory on February 1 was 14,000 units, 100 percent complete as to materials and 20 percent complete as to conversion costs. The total cost of these units was $55,000, with $48,660 assigned to the cost of materials. The ending Work in Process Inventory of 12,000 units was fully complete as to materials, but only 30 percent complete as to conversion costs.

Required

1. Using good form, and assuming an average costing approach and no loss due to spoilage, prepare (a) a schedule of equivalent production, (b) a unit cost analysis schedule, and (c) a cost summary schedule. Round unit costs to two decimal places.
2. From the cost summary schedule you prepared in 1 above, prepare a journal entry to transfer costs of completed units in February to the Finished Goods Inventory account.

Problem 24A-3.
Process Costing:
With Beginning
Inventories
(L.O. 3, 4, 5, 6)

Mohamad Bottling Company makes and sells several kinds of soft drinks. Materials (sugar syrup and artificial flavor) are added at the beginning of production in the Mixing Department. Direct labor and factory overhead costs are applied to products throughout the process. During August, 19x0, beginning inventory for the Citrus flavor was 2,400 gallons, 80 percent complete. Ending inventory was 3,600 gallons, 50 percent complete. Production data showed 240,000 gallons started during August. A total of 238,800 gallons was completed and transferred to the Bottling Department. Beginning inventory costs were $600 for materials and $576 for conversion costs. Current period costs were $45,456 for materials and $77,619 for conversion costs.

Required

1. Using good form and an average costing approach, prepare the following schedules for the Mixing Department for August: (a) a schedule of equivalent production, (b) a unit cost analysis schedule, and (c) a cost summary schedule.
2. From the cost summary schedule, prepare a journal entry to transfer the cost of completed units to the Bottling Department.

Problem 24A-4.
Process Costing:
One Process / Two
Time Periods
(L.O. 3, 4, 5, 6)

The Morlan Natural Products Company produces organic honey for sale to health food stores and restaurants. The company owns thousands of bee-hives. No materials other than the honey from the bees in the hives are used. The production operation is a simple one in which the impure honey is add-ed at the beginning of the process. A series of filterings follows, leading to a pure finished product. Costs of labor and factory overhead are incurred uni-formly throughout the filtering process. Production data for April and May, 19x1, are as follows:

	April	May
Beginning Work in Process Inventory		
Units (liters)	7,100	?
Costs: Materials	$ 19,600	?
Conversion costs	16,860	?
Production during the period		
Units started (liters)	288,000	310,000
Current period costs:		
Materials	$ 479,119	$ 520,030
Conversion costs	$1,052,565	$1,154,410
Ending Work in Process Inventory		
Units (liters)	12,400	16,900

April beginning inventory was 80 percent complete as to conversion costs, and ending inventory was 20 percent complete. Ending inventory for May was 30 percent complete as to conversion costs. Assume that there was no loss from spoilage or evaporation.

Required

1. Using good form and an average costing approach, prepare the following schedules for April: (a) a schedule of equivalent production, (b) a unit cost analysis schedule, and (c) a cost summary schedule.
2. From the cost summary schedule, prepare a journal entry to transfer costs of units completed in April to the Finished Goods Inventory account.
3. Repeat parts 1 and 2 for May.

Problem 24A-5.
Process Costing:
With Beginning
Inventories / Two
Departments
(L.O. 3, 4, 5, 6)

Canned fruits and vegetables are the main products made by Culley/Grove Foods, Inc. All basic materials are added at the beginning of the Mix-ing Department's process. When it has been mixed, the food goes to the Cooking Department. There it is heated to 100° Celsius and left to simmer for twenty minutes. When cooled, the mixture goes to the Canning Department for final processing. Throughout these operations, direct labor and factory overhead costs are incurred uniformly. No materials are added in the Cook-ing Department stage of production.

Cost data and other information for January were as follows:

Production Cost Data	Materials	Conversion Costs
Mixing Department		
Beginning inventory	$ 28,800	$ 5,056
Current period costs	$432,000	$182,400

(continued)

	Transferred-in Costs	Conversion Costs
Cooking Department		
Beginning inventory	$ 61,380	$ 13,320
Current period costs	?	$671,040
Work in Process Inventories		
Beginning inventories:		
Mixing Department (40% complete)	6,000 liters	
Cooking Department (20% complete)	9,000 liters	
Ending inventories:		
Mixing Department (60% complete)	8,000 liters	
Cooking Department (70% complete)	10,000 liters	

Unit Production Data	Mixing Department	Cooking Department
Units started during January	90,000 liters	88,000 liters
Units transferred out during January	88,000 liters	87,000 liters

Assume that no spoilage or evaporation loss took place during January. (Before completing this problem, refer to the Special Review Problem on pages 1032–1034.)

Required

1. Using proper form and an average costing approach, prepare for the Mixing Department for January: (a) a schedule of equivalent production, (b) a unit cost analysis schedule, and (c) a cost summary schedule.
2. From the cost summary schedule, prepare the journal entry needed to transfer costs of completed units for January from the Mixing Department to the Cooking Department.
3. Prepare the same schedules requested in part 1, this time for the Cooking Department.
4. Prepare the journal entry needed to transfer costs of completed units from the Cooking Department to the Canning Department.

Problem Set B

Problem 24B-1.
Process Costing:
No Beginning
Inventories
(L.O. 3, 4, 5, 6)

Winter Industries specializes in making Slik, a high-moisture, low-alkaline wax used to protect and preserve skis. Production of a new, improved brand of Slik began January 1, 19x2. For this new product, Materials A-14 and C-9 are introduced at the beginning of the production process, along with a wax base. During January, 320 pounds of A-14, 930 pounds of C-9, and 6,400 pounds of wax base were used at costs of $15,300, $29,070, and $2,295, respectively. Direct labor of $17,136 and factory overhead costs of $25,704 were incurred uniformly throughout the month. By January 31, 6,800 pounds of Slik had been completed and transferred to the finished goods inventory. Much of the month's production has already been shipped to customers. Since no spoilage occurred, the leftover materials remained in production, 40 percent complete on the average.

Required

1. Using proper form, prepare (a) a schedule of equivalent production, (b) a unit cost analysis schedule, and (c) a cost summary schedule for January. Round unit costs to two decimal places.

2. From the cost summary schedule, prepare the journal entry to transfer costs of completed units for January to Finished Goods Inventory.

Problem 24B-2.
Process Costing:
With Beginning
Inventories
(L.O. 3, 4, 5, 6)

Many of the products made by Baucum Plastics Company are standard replacement parts for telephones, requiring long production runs. One of the parts, a wire clip, is produced continuously. During April, 19x0, materials for 25,250 units of wire clips were put into production (1 unit contains 500 clips). Total cost of materials used during April was $2,273,000. Direct labor costs totaled $1,135,000, and factory overhead was applied to production using a rate of 180 percent of direct labor costs. The beginning work in process inventory contained 1,600 units, 100 percent complete as to materials costs and 60 percent complete as to conversion costs. Costs attached to the units in beginning inventory totaled $232,000, including $143,500 of materials costs. At month end there were 1,250 units in ending inventory; all materials had been added, and the units were 70 percent complete as to conversion costs.

Required

1. Using good form, and assuming an average costing approach and no loss due to spoilage, prepare (a) a schedule of equivalent production, (b) a unit cost analysis schedule, and (c) a cost summary schedule.
2. From the cost summary schedule, prepare a journal entry to transfer costs of units completed in April to the Finished Goods Inventory account.

Problem 24B-3.
Process Costing:
With Beginning
Inventories
(L.O. 3, 4, 5, 6)

Lasciandro Liquid Extracts Company produces a line of fruit extracts for use in producing homemade products such as wines, jams and jellies, pies, and meat sauces. Fruits are introduced into the production process in pounds; the product emerges in quarts (1 pound of input equals 1 quart of output). On June 1, 19x1, 4,250 units were in process. All materials had been added and the units were 70 percent complete as to conversion costs. Materials costs of $4,607 and conversion costs of $3,535 were attached to these units in beginning work in process inventory. During June, 61,300 pounds of fruit were added: apples, 23,500 pounds costing $20,915; grapes, 22,600 pounds costing $28,476; and bananas, 15,200 pounds costing $22,040. Direct labor for the month totaled $19,760, and overhead costs were applied at the rate of 160 percent of direct labor dollars. On June 30, 19x1, 3,400 units remained in process. All materials had been added, and 50 percent of conversion costs had been incurred.

Required

1. Using good form and an average costing approach, prepare the following schedules for June: (a) a schedule of equivalent production, (b) a unit cost analysis schedule, and (c) a cost summary schedule. Round unit costs to two decimal places.
2. From the cost summary schedule, prepare a journal entry to transfer costs of completed units to the Finished Goods Inventory account.

Problem 24B-4.
Process Costing:
One Process / Two
Time Periods
(L.O. 3, 4, 5, 6)

Ginnie Merkle Laboratories produces liquid detergents that leave no soap film. All elements are biodegradable. The production process has been automated, so that the product can now be produced in one operation instead of a series of heating, mixing, and cooling operations. All materials are added at the beginning of the process, and conversion costs are incurred uniformly throughout the process. Operating data for July and August, 19x9 are as follows:

	July	August
Beginning Work in Process Inventory		
Units (pounds)	2,300	?
Costs: Materials costs	$ 4,699	?
Conversion costs	$ 1,019	?
Production during the period		
Units started (pounds)	31,500	32,800
Current period costs:		
Materials costs	$64,253	$68,346
Conversion costs	$54,367	$54,774
Ending Work in Process Inventory		
Units (pounds)	3,050	3,600

Beginning Work in Process Inventory was 30 percent complete as to conversion costs. Point-of-completion information for ending work in process inventories was: July, 60 percent; August, 50 percent. Assume that loss from spoilage and evaporation was negligible.

Required

1. Using good form and an average costing approach, prepare the following schedules for July: (a) a schedule of equivalent production, (b) a unit cost analysis schedule, and (c) a cost summary schedule. Round unit costs to two decimal places.
2. From the cost summary schedule, prepare a journal entry to transfer costs of units completed in July to the Finished Goods Inventory account. Round cost summary amounts to three decimal places.
3. Repeat parts 1 and 2 for August.

Problem 24B-5.
Process Costing:
With Beginning
Inventories / Two
Departments
(L.O. 3, 4, 5, 6)

David Ganz Enterprises produces dozens of products for the housing construction industry. Its most successful product is called Sta-Soft Plaster, a mixture that is used to finish off wall surfaces after dry-wall sheets have been positioned. The product's unique quality is that it will not harden until it comes into contact with the dry-wall. Sta-Soft is produced using three processes, blending, conditioning, and canning. All materials are introduced at the beginning of the blending operation except for the can, which is added at the end in the canning process. Direct labor and factory overhead costs are applied to the products uniformly throughout each process. Production and cost information for September 19x1 follow.

Blending Department.
Beginning Work in Process Inventory contained 22,920 pounds of Sta-Soft, 60 percent complete as to conversion costs. Costs of $38,900 were assigned to these units, $28,600 of which was for materials. During September, 242,280 pounds of materials costing $302,900 were put into production. Direct labor for the month was $88,210, and an equal amount of factory overhead costs were charged to Work in Process. Ending Work in Process Inventory contained 32,480 pounds, 50 percent complete as to conversion costs.

Conditioning Department.
During September, 232,720 pounds of Sta-Soft were received from the Blending Department. Beginning Work in Process Inventory consisted of 10,500 pounds of Sta-Soft, costing $30,250 ($21,000 worth of Sta-Soft was

transferred-in costs). Direct labor costs incurred during September totaled $115,625, and factory overhead costs applied were $138,751. Ending Work in Process Inventory contained 8,900 pounds, 60 percent complete as to conversion costs. Assume no measurable loss due to spoilage or waste.

Required

1. Using proper form and an average costing approach, prepare the following schedules for the Blending Department for September: (a) a schedule of equivalent production, (b) a unit cost analysis schedule, and (c) a cost summary schedule. Round unit costs to two decimal places.
2. From the cost summary schedule, prepare the journal entry needed to transfer costs of completed units for September from the Blending Department to the Conditioning Department.
3. Prepare the same schedules requested in part 1, this time for the Conditioning Department. Round unit costs to two decimal places.
4. Prepare the journal entry needed to transfer costs of completed units from the Conditioning Department to the Canning Department.

Management Decision Case

CT&H Cola, Inc.
(L.O. 3, 4)

For the past four years, three companies have dominated the soft drink industry, holding a combined 85 percent of market share. CT&H Cola, Inc. ranks second nationally in soft drink sales; the company attained gross revenues last year of $27,450,000. Management is thinking about introducing a new low-calorie drink called Slimit Cola.

CT&H soft drinks are processed in a single department. All materials are added at the beginning of the process. Fluids are bottled at the end of the process in bottles costing one cent each. Direct labor and factory overhead costs are applied uniformly throughout the process.

Corporate controller Robert Buttery believes that costs for the new cola will be very much like those for the company's Cola Plus drink. Last year, he collected the following data on Cola Plus:

	Units	Costs
Work in Process Inventory		
January 1, 19x1*	6,420	
Materials costs		$ 5,140
Conversion costs		1,938
December 31, 19x1†	8,900	
Materials costs		7,120
Conversion costs		3,738
Units started during the year	459,380	
Costs for 19x1		
Liquid materials added		367,500
Direct labor		172,463
Factory overhead applied		103,477
Bottles		109,656

*50% complete   †70% complete   Note: Each unit is a twenty-four-bottle case

The company's variable operating and selling costs are $1.10 per unit. Fixed operating and selling costs are assigned to products at the rate of $.50 per unit. CT&H's two major competitors have already introduced a diet cola in the marketplace. Company A's product sells for $4.10 per unit, Company B's for $4.05. All costs are expected to increase by 10 percent from 19x1 to 19x2. The company tries to earn a profit of at least 15 percent on the unit cost.

Required

1. What factors should the company consider in setting a selling price for Slimit Cola?
2. Using the average costing approach, compute (a) the total production cost per unit and (b) the total cost per unit of Cola Plus for 19x1.
3. What is the expected total cost per unit of Slimit Cola for 19x2?
4. Recommend a unit selling price range for Slimit Cola for 19x2 and give the reason(s) for your choice.

Answers to Self-Test

1. b	3. a	5. d	7. b	9. c
2. c	4. c	6. a	8. d	10. a

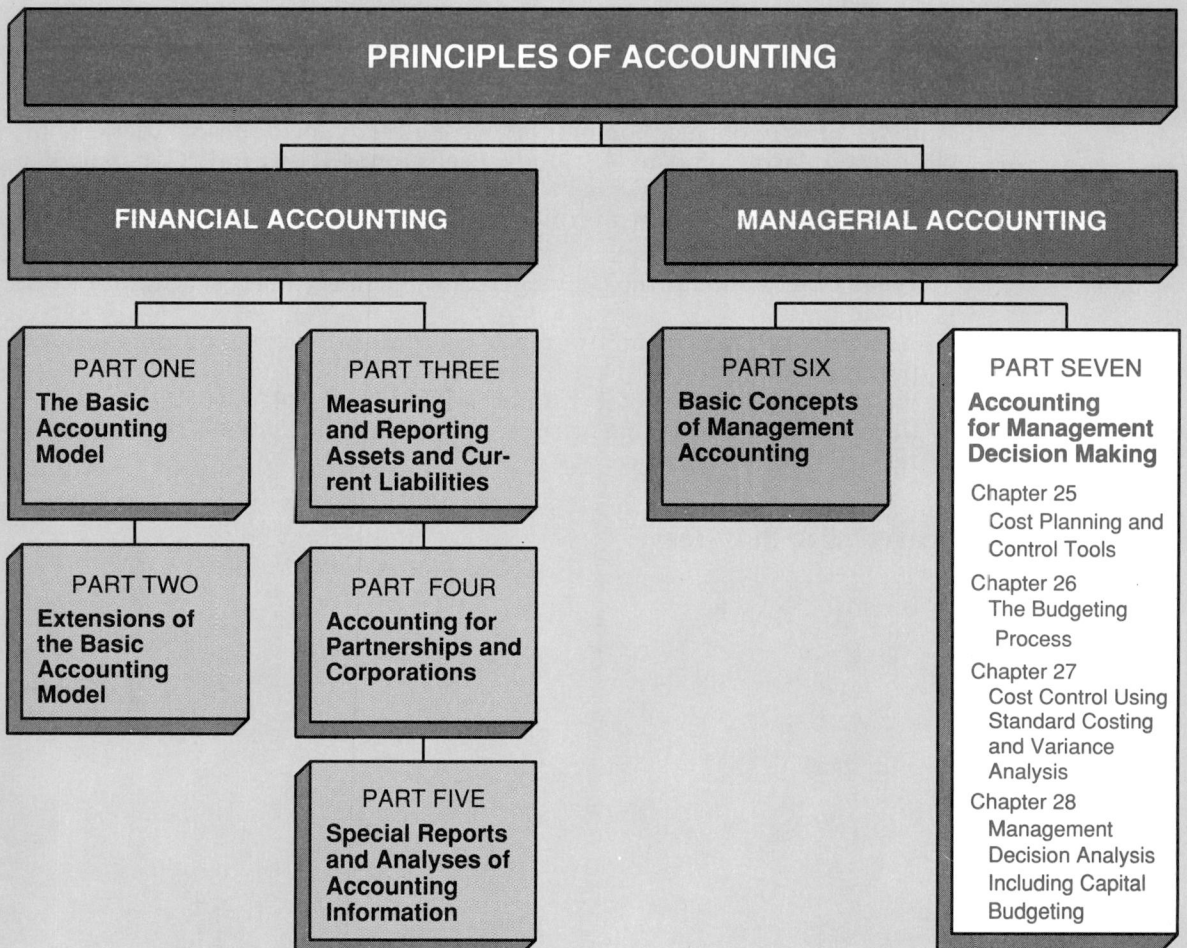

PRINCIPLES OF ACCOUNTING

FINANCIAL ACCOUNTING

PART ONE
The Basic Accounting Model

PART TWO
Extensions of the Basic Accounting Model

PART THREE
Measuring and Reporting Assets and Current Liabilities

PART FOUR
Accounting for Partnerships and Corporations

PART FIVE
Special Reports and Analyses of Accounting Information

MANAGERIAL ACCOUNTING

PART SIX
Basic Concepts of Management Accounting

PART SEVEN
Accounting for Management Decision Making

Chapter 25
Cost Planning and Control Tools

Chapter 26
The Budgeting Process

Chapter 27
Cost Control Using Standard Costing and Variance Analysis

Chapter 28
Management Decision Analysis Including Capital Budgeting

In Part Seven we analyze the final two aspects of the field of management accounting: management's need for (1) data used for planning and control of operations and (2) special reports and analyses used to support management decisions.

PART SEVEN

Accounting for Management Decision Making

Chapter 25 introduces cost planning and control, specifically focusing on cost behavior patterns, cost-volume-profit relationships, cost allocation, and responsibility accounting.

Chapter 26 uses the cost planning tools described in Chapter 25 to implement the planning function of the budgetary control process. Emphasis is placed on budgeting principles and preparation, including the cash budget.

Chapter 27 focuses on standard costing and concludes your study of the budgetary control process. Standard costing is analyzed by first looking at the nature, purpose, and development of standard costing information. Then variance analysis is introduced to aid in management's cost control of operations.

Chapter 28 deals with ways of developing and providing relevant information, including variable costing, contribution reporting, and incremental analysis. These approaches to information reporting are then applied to operating decisions involving capital expenditure analyses, make or buy alternatives, special product orders, and sales mix analyses.

CHAPTER 25

Cost Planning and Control Tools

Cost planning and control activities are vital to the ongoing life of any type of organization, whether it is a profit-oriented or a not-for-profit enterprise. Effective cost planning results in a strong and continuous flow of operations, and cost control leads to target attainment, whether the target is overall profit or completion of a project. An integrated cost planning and control system is referred to as a **budgetary control system**. To help achieve good cost planning and control, such a system relies on a set of management accounting techniques, including knowledge of cost behavior patterns, cost-volume-profit relationships, cost allocation procedures, and the use of responsibility accounting systems. The study of cost behavior and cost-volume-profit relationships centers on the ways costs react to changes in operating variables such as total units produced, total machine hours used, total sales, or total labor hours needed. Cost allocation techniques are used not only to assign incurred costs to products or services but also to plan future activities. Responsibility accounting focuses on a systematic internal information reporting system, based on the existing management structure or hierarchy. This chapter introduces these techniques and provides illustrations of their use. After studying this chapter, you should be able to meet the learning objectives listed on the left.

Cost Behavior

Before estimating a future cost or preparing a budget, a manager must know the basic behavior patterns of costs. Such knowledge is useful for analyzing past cost performance as well as predicting future costs. We can define **cost behavior** as the way costs respond to changes in activity or volume. To understand cost behavior, we must look at the basic characteristics and the accounting classifications of costs. Some costs are entirely variable in relation to volume or operating activity, whereas other costs remain fixed as volume changes. Within these two polar extremes are costs that exhibit characteristics of both variable and fixed costs. Complex cost behavior patterns must be separated into variable and fixed components before more sophisticated cost planning techniques can be applied.

The meaning of cost behavior depends on whether total costs are being analyzed or cost per unit is being computed. Variable costs vary *in total*; as activity or volume increases, total variable costs increase in direct proportion. But variable costs per unit remain constant as long as there are no price changes in goods and services consumed. Fixed costs, on the other hand, react in an opposite fashion. In total, fixed costs remain constant as volume changes. But on a per unit basis, fixed costs decrease as volume increases. The very fact that a fixed cost is constant in total means that the more that is produced, the less fixed cost is assigned per unit.

We will discuss these principles further as we examine variable and fixed costs in more detail. But it is important that you begin thinking about this phenomenon now. *Variable costs vary in total as volume changes, but are constant per unit. Fixed costs are fixed in total, but vary per unit as volume changes.*

Although we are focusing on cost behavior as it relates to production, you should realize that some costs are *not* measured that way. Sales commissions, for example, depend on the number of units *sold*, or total sales revenue, not on production-related measures. This distinction applies to nonmanufacturing industries as well. Service businesses experience much the same cost behavior patterns as manufacturing enterprises. As we discuss examples for a manufacturing company, remember that the same concept applies to a department store or a bank.

Variable and Fixed Costs

OBJECTIVE 1
Define and classify variable costs, semivariable costs, and fixed costs

Total costs that change in direct proportion to changes in productive output (or any other volume measure) are called **variable costs**. Consider the example of an auto maker. Each new car has four tires, and each tire costs $38. Thus the total tire cost is $152 for one automobile, $304 for two, $456 for three, $608 for four, $760 for five, $1,520 for ten, and $15,200 for one hundred. In manufacturing automobiles, total tire cost is a variable cost. On a per unit basis, however, the variable cost remains constant. In this case, tire cost per automobile is $152 ($38 × 4) whether one or one hundred cars are produced. True, the cost of tires varies depending on the number produced, and purchase discounts are available for purchases of large quantities. But once the purchase has been made, the cost per tire has been established.

In discussing variable costs, we have assumed that there is a linear relationship between cost and volume. Figure 25-1 shows this relationship. In this example, each unit of output requires $2.50 of labor cost. Total labor costs grow in direct proportion to the increase in units of output: for 2 units, total labor cost is $5; for 6 units, $15.

Not all variable costs behave in this way. Electricity rates, for instance, go down as the use of electricity goes up. But although electricity rates are variable in some ways, their cost pattern is more like that

Figure 25-1. A Common Cost Behavior Pattern: Variable Cost

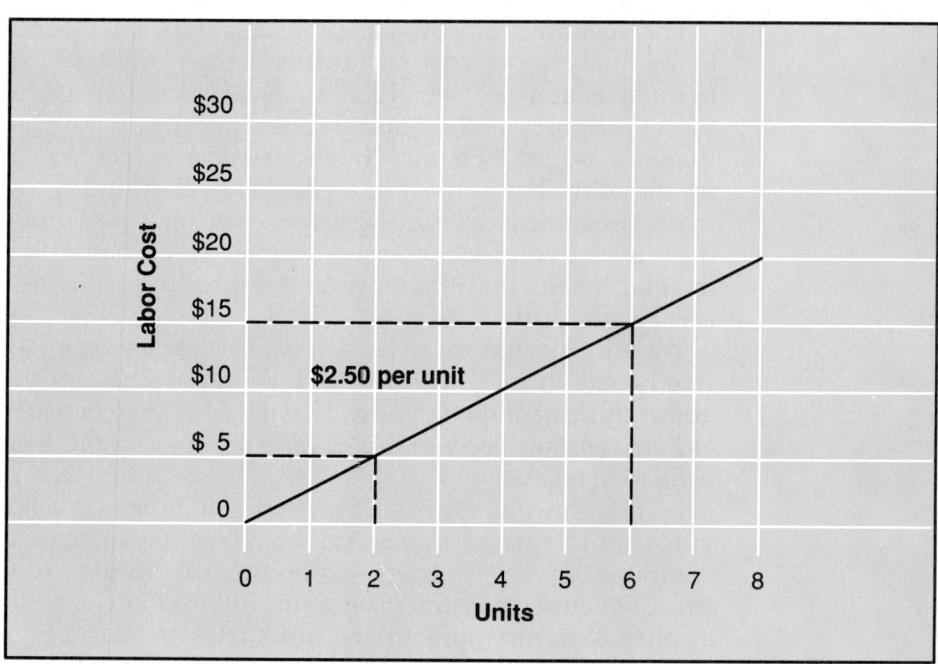

of semivariable costs, which are discussed in the next section. For now, we will assume that variable costs have a linear relationship to volume, as shown in Figure 25-1.

Fixed costs behave in an entirely different manner from variable costs. **Fixed costs** are total costs that remain constant within a relevant range of volume or activity. A **relevant range** is the range of activity within which actual operations are likely to occur. Annual straight-line depreciation of $200,000 and annual property taxes of $16,200 are examples of fixed costs. Reference to a particular time period is essential to the concept of a fixed cost, because according to economic theory, all costs tend to be variable in the long run. From the long-run viewpoint, a fixed cost can be increased or decreased within whatever time period is required to increase or decrease plant capacity, machinery, labor requirements, and other production factors associated with fixed costs. Thus a fixed cost is fixed only within a limited time period. For planning purposes, management usually uses a one-year time period, and fixed costs are expected to be fixed within that period.

Supervisory salaries are a good example of a fixed cost. Assume that a local manufacturing company needs one supervisor for an eight-hour work shift. Production can range from 0 to 500,000 units per month per shift. The supervisor's salary is $3,000 per month, and the relevant range is 0 to 500,000 units. The cost behavior analysis is as follows:

Units of Output	Total Supervisory Salaries per Month
100,000	$3,000
200,000	3,000
300,000	3,000
400,000	3,000
500,000	3,000
600,000	6,000

As noted, a maximum of 500,000 units can be produced per shift. So any output over 500,000 units calls for another work shift and another supervisor. On a per unit basis, fixed costs go down as volume goes up. In our example, supervisory costs per unit would change as follows:

Volume of Activity	Cost per Unit
100,000 units	$3,000/100,000 = $.0300
200,000 units	3,000/200,000 = .0150
300,000 units	3,000/300,000 = .0100
400,000 units	3,000/400,000 = .0075
500,000 units	3,000/500,000 = .0060
600,000 units	6,000/600,000 = .0100

The per unit cost *increased* at the 600,000-unit level because the volume was not within the relevant range, and another supervisor had to be hired.

A graphic view of this fixed overhead cost is shown in Figure 25-2. Fixed costs hold steady at $3,000 for any level of output within the relevant range, 500,000 units. But output over 500,000 units calls for another supervisor, so the cost level jumps to $6,000.

Semivariable and Mixed Costs

Some costs cannot be classified as either variable or fixed. A **semivariable cost** has both variable and fixed cost components. Part of the cost is fixed per time period, and part changes with the volume of output or usage. Telephone expense is an example. Monthly telephone charges are made up of a service charge plus extra charges for extra telephones and long-distance calls. The service charge and the cost of extra telephones are fixed costs. But the long-distance charges are variable, because they depend on the amount of use.

Mixed costs are also made up of variable and fixed costs. **Mixed costs** result when both variable costs and fixed costs are charged to the same general ledger account. The Repairs and Maintenance account is a good example of an account balance made up of mixed costs. Labor charges to this account may vary in proportion to the number of repairs done. However, only one repair and maintenance worker may be employed on a full-time basis (a fixed cost), with extra help hired only when needed

Figure 25-2. A Common Cost Behavior Pattern: Fixed Cost

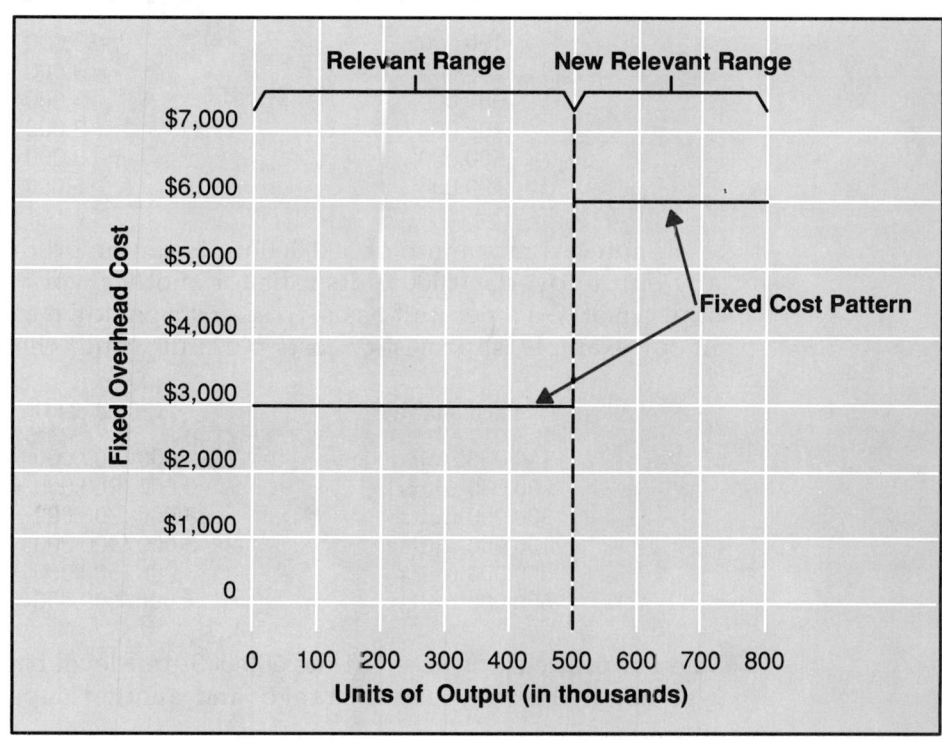

(a variable cost). Likewise, depreciation costs for repair and maintenance machinery are a fixed cost, but the cost of repair supplies varies with the amount of repair jobs worked on by the department.

For purposes of cost planning and control, semivariable and mixed costs must be divided into their respective variable and fixed cost parts. They can then be grouped with other variable and fixed costs for analysis. Several methods are available to differentiate variable costs from those that are fixed. The *high-low approach* is one. Assume the following monthly totals appeared in the Repairs and Maintenance account for the first six months of the year:

Month	Total Costs	Volume in Labor Hours
January	$3,728	1,200
February	4,016	1,400
March	4,304	1,600
April	3,872	1,300
May	3,440	1,000
June	3,584	1,100

In the high-low method the accountant identifies the high- and low-cost items, along with their respective volume levels, and notes the difference between them.

	Cost	**Activity Level**
High	$4,304	1,600 labor hours
Low	3,440	1,000 labor hours
Difference	$ 864	600 labor hours

You can see that as activity went up 600 labor hours, costs rose $864. Therefore, the variable rate is $864/600 labor hours, or $1.44 per labor hour.

To compute the amount of the fixed cost, multiply each activity level by $1.44 and subtract the amount from the total cost. Thus, at the 1,600 labor hour level, total variable costs equal 1,600 × $1.44, or $2,304. Since total cost minus variable cost equals fixed costs, fixed costs equal $4,304 – $2,304, or $2,000. The same procedure can be applied to each month's figures in order to break down the entire account balance into its variable and fixed components.

Operating Capacity: Definition and Cost Influence

Because variable costs increase or decrease in direct proportion to expected volume or output, it is important to know what a company's *operating capacity* is. **Operating capacity** is the upper limit of a company's productive output capability, given existing resources. There are several different measures of a company's operating capacity. **Theoretical** or **ideal capacity** is the maximum productive output a department or company could reach for a given period if all machinery and equipment were operated at optimum speed, without interruptions. Theoretical capacity is useful in thinking about maximum production levels. Although seemingly unrealistic, this concept is becoming more important with the advent of the Just-in-Time operating philosophy (see Appendix E). **Practical capacity** is theoretical capacity reduced by normal and expected work stoppages. Production may be interrupted by machine downtime for retooling, repair and maintenance, or employee work breaks. These normal interruptions and the resulting lower output should be considered when measuring capacity.

Most companies do not operate at either ideal or practical capacity. **Excess capacity**, which is extra machinery and equipment kept on hand on a standby basis, is included in both practical and ideal capacity. Such extra equipment may be used when regular equipment is being repaired. Or during a slow season, a company may use only part of its equipment. Or it may work just one or two shifts instead of around the clock. Because of these circumstances, managers often use a measure called normal capacity rather than ideal or practical capacity for planning. **Normal capacity** is the average annual level of operating capacity needed to meet expected sales demand. This demand figure is adjusted for seasonal changes and business and economic cycles. Therefore, normal capacity is a realistic measure of what is *likely* to be produced, rather than what *can* be produced, by an operating unit.

Cost-Volume-Profit Relationships

OBJECTIVE 2
Compute the breakeven point in units of output and in sales dollars

Cost behavior patterns underlie the relationships among costs, volume of output, and profit. These relationships are studied through **cost-volume-profit analysis** (or **C-V-P analysis**). Cost-volume-profit analysis is useful for predicting future operating results. A company may use C-V-P analysis as a planning tool when the sales volume is known and management needs to find out how much profit will result. Another way of planning is to begin with a target profit. Then, through C-V-P analysis, a company can decide the level of sales needed to reach that profit.

C-V-P analysis is also useful for cost control purposes. At the end of a period, a company analyzes sales volume and related actual costs to find actual profit. It measures performance by comparing actual costs with expected costs. These expected costs are computed by applying C-V-P analysis to the actual sales volume. The result is a performance report on which management can base the control of operations. (This process is explained further in Chapter 27.)

C-V-P Analysis: Breakeven Point and Profit Planning

Cost-volume-profit analysis is based on the relationships among operating costs, sales volume, sales revenue, and target net income. Before starting C-V-P analysis, we must first classify costs as either variable costs (VC) or fixed costs (FC). Sales (S) are computed by multiplying units sold by the selling price per unit. Target net income (NI) is decided by management. The usual formula for C-V-P analysis is

$$\text{Sales revenue} = \text{variable costs} + \text{fixed costs} + \text{net income}$$

Or, more simply,

$$S = VC + FC + NI$$

If we move the variable costs (VC) and fixed costs (FC) to the left of the equals sign and change their signs from positive to negative, the equation begins to look like the income statement:

$$S - VC - FC = NI$$

Breakeven Point. The **breakeven point** is that point where total revenue equals total costs incurred. Thus it is the point at which a company begins to earn a profit. When planning new ventures, you can quickly measure the likelihood of success by finding the project's breakeven point. If, for instance, breakeven is 50,000 units while the total market is only 25,000, the project should be promptly abandoned. When finding a company's or a product's breakeven point, only sales (S), variable costs (VC), and fixed costs (FC) are considered. There is no net income (NI) when a company breaks even. The goal is to find the level of activity at which sales revenue equals the sum of all variable and fixed costs. Breakeven data can be stated in either breakeven sales units or break-even sales dollars. The general equations for finding the breakeven point are as follows:

$$S = VC + FC \quad \text{or} \quad S - VC - FC = 0$$

An example will show how these equations can be used to find break-even units and dollars. Reed Products, Inc. makes wooden stands for portable television sets. Variable costs are $50 per unit, and fixed costs average $20,000 per year. Each wooden stand sells for $90. Given this information, we can compute the breakeven point for this product in both sales units and dollars. Here the breakeven point in sales units is represented by x:

$$S = VC + FC$$
$$\$90x = \$50x + \$20,000$$
$$\$40x = \$20,000$$
$$x = 500 \text{ units}$$

And the breakeven point in sales dollars is:

$$\$90/\text{unit} \times 500 \text{ units} = \$45,000$$

We can also make a rough estimate of the breakeven point using a graph. This method is less exact, but it does yield meaningful data. Figure 25-3 shows a breakeven analysis for Reed Products. This standard breakeven chart has five parts: (1) a horizontal axis in volume or units; (2) a vertical axis in dollars; (3) a horizontal line for the upper limit of fixed costs ($20,000); (4) a total cost line that begins at the point where the fixed cost line crosses the vertical axis and slopes upward to the right (the slope of the line depends on the variable costs per unit); and (5) a total revenue line that begins at the origin of the vertical and horizontal axes and slopes upward to the right (the slope depends on the selling price per unit). At the point where the total revenue line crosses the total cost line, revenues will equal total costs. The breakeven point, stated in either units or dollars of sales, can be found by extending lines from this point to the axes. As shown in Figure 25-3, Reed Products will break even when 500 television stands have been made and sold for $45,000 in sales.

Profit Planning. The breakeven process can be easily extended to include profit planning. Assume that Reed Products' president, Elaine Shirl, has set $10,000 profit as the goal for the year. How many television stands must Reed Products make and sell to reach the target profit? The answer is computed below (x = number of units).

$$S = VC + FC + NI$$
$$\$90x = \$50x + \$20,000 + \$10,000$$
$$\$40x = \$30,000$$
$$x = 750 \text{ units}$$

Figure 25-3. Graphic Breakeven Analysis: Reed Products, Inc.

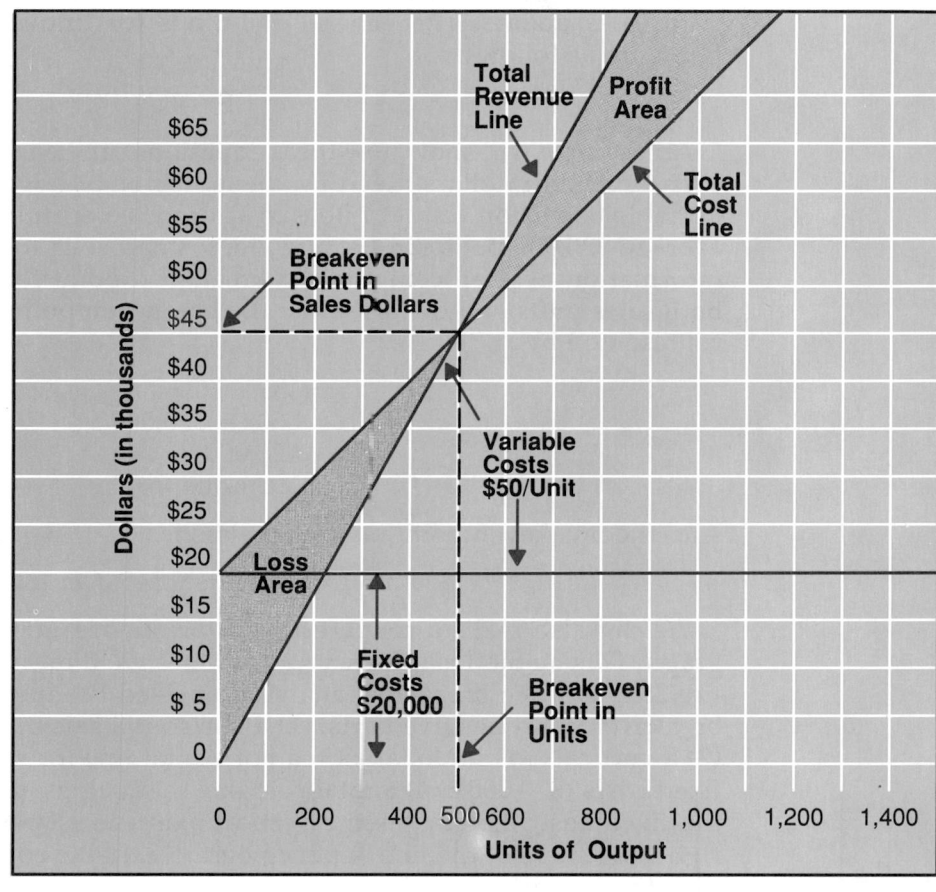

To check the accuracy of this answer, put all the known data into the equation for an income statement:

$$S - VC - FC = NI$$
$$(750 \text{ units} \times \$90) - (750 \times \$50) - (\$20,000) = \$10,000$$
$$\$67,500 - \$37,500 - \$20,000 = \$10,000$$

Contribution Margin Concept

OBJECTIVE 3
Use contribution margin analysis to estimate levels of sales that will produce planned profits

Our analysis of cost-volume-profit relationships would not be complete without a discussion of **contribution margin**, the excess of revenues over *all* variable costs related to a particular sales volume. Contribution margin represents the net contribution of a product, division, or company to paying off fixed costs and adding to profits. Net income for Reed Products, Inc., computed using the contribution approach, is shown as follows.

Symbols		Units Produced and Sold		
		250	500	750
S	Sales revenue ($90 per unit)	$ 22,500	$45,000	$67,500
VC	Less variable costs ($50 per unit)	12,500	25,000	37,500
CM	Contribution margin	$ 10,000	$20,000	$30,000
FC	Less fixed costs	20,000	20,000	20,000
NI	Net income (loss)	$(10,000)	—	$10,000

Adding contribution margin into C-V-P analysis changes the make-up of the equations as well as the format of the income statement. The equation now becomes

$$[S - VC = CM] - FC = NI$$

By definition contribution margin (CM) is what remains after variable costs are subtracted from total sales. So the breakeven point (BE) can be expressed as the point at which contribution margin (CM) minus total fixed costs (FC) equals zero. That is, breakeven occurs when CM – FC = 0. In terms of units of product, the breakeven point equation is changed as follows:

$$(CM/unit \times BE \text{ units}) - FC = 0$$

At this point we need to develop an equation that isolates the expression *breakeven units*. To achieve this goal, the equation can be rearranged as follows:

1. Move FC to the right side of the equation:

$$CM/unit \times BE \text{ units} = FC$$

2. Divide both sides of the equation by CM/unit:

$$\frac{CM/unit \times BE \text{ units}}{CM/unit} = \frac{FC}{CM/unit}$$

3. After canceling terms, the end result is

$$BE \text{ units} = \frac{FC}{CM/unit}$$

For profit planning, the equation can be adjusted to include target net income, as follows:

$$\text{Target unit sales} = \frac{FC + NI}{CM/unit}$$

Now we can insert the data given earlier for Reed Products:

$$\text{BE units} = \frac{\text{FC}}{\text{CM/unit}} = \frac{\$20,000}{\$90 - \$50} = \frac{\$20,000}{\$40} = 500 \text{ units}$$

$$\text{Target unit sales} = \frac{\text{FC} + \text{NI}}{\text{CM/unit}} = \frac{\$20,000 + \$10,000}{\$40} = \frac{\$30,000}{\$40} = 750 \text{ units}$$

Once mastered, the use of the contribution margin simplifies finding the breakeven point and planning for profits.

Assumptions Underlying C-V-P Analysis

Cost-volume-profit figures are useful only when certain conditions exist and certain assumptions hold true. If one or more of these assumptions or conditions are absent, the results of the analysis may be misleading. These assumptions and conditions are:

1. Behavior of variable and fixed costs can be measured accurately.
2. Costs and revenues bear close linear approximation. For example, if costs rise, revenues will rise proportionately.
3. Efficiency and productivity will hold steady within the relevant range of activity.
4. Cost and price variables will hold steady during the planning period.
5. The product sales mix will not change during the planning period.
6. Production and sales volume will be roughly equal.

Illustrative Problem:
Profit Planning—Contribution Margin Approach

Book production is a complex and costly process. Golner Publishing Company is taking a careful look at a new manuscript on cost management systems. Early estimates are that variable costs per book will be $20.40 and that total fixed costs will be $180,000. The company plans to market the book wholesale at $38.40 per copy.

Required

1. Using the contribution margin approach, compute how many copies of the book the company must sell to earn a profit of $36,000.
2. Using the same approach, and assuming that fixed costs are cut to $150,000, determine the number of copies that must be sold to earn a target profit of $57,000.
3. Given the original information, and assuming that 21,000 copies of the book can be sold, find the selling price that the company must set to earn a profit of $80,400.
4. The company's marketing director says that the most optimistic sales estimate for the book would be 36,000 copies. Assume that the highest possible price that the company can charge is $39.60 and that variable costs per unit cannot be reduced below $20.40. How much more can be spent on fixed advertising costs if the new target profit is $90,000?

Solution

1. Target units computed

$$\text{Unit sales} = (FC + NI) \div CM \text{ per unit}$$
$$= (\$180,000 + \$36,000) \div (\$38.40 - \$20.40)$$
$$= \$216,000 \div \$18$$
$$= 12,000 \text{ copies}$$

2. Units computed for higher profit and lower costs

$$\text{Unit sales} = (FC + NI) \div CM \text{ per unit}$$
$$= (\$150,000 + \$57,000) \div (\$38.40 - \$20.40)$$
$$= \$207,000 \div \$18$$
$$= 11,500 \text{ copies}$$

3. Selling price determined

$$\text{Unit sales} = (FC + NI) \div CM \text{ per unit}$$
$$21,000 = (\$180,000 + \$80,400) \div (x - \$20.40)$$

Multiplying both sides of the equation by $(x - \$20.40)$, we get

$$21,000 (x - \$20.40) = \$260,400$$
$$21,000x - \$428,400 = \$260,400$$
$$21,000x = \$688,800$$
$$x = \$32.80$$

4. Increased amount for advertising determined

$$\text{Unit sales} = (FC + NI) \div CM \text{ per unit}$$
$$36,000 = (x + \$90,000) \div (\$39.60 - \$20.40)$$
$$36,000 = (x + \$90,000) \div \$19.20$$

Multiplying both sides of the equation by $\$19.20$, we get

$$\$19.20 (36,000) = x + \$90,000$$
$$\$691,200 = x + \$90,000$$
$$x = \$691,200 - \$90,000$$
$$x = \$601,200$$

Total fixed costs allowed	$601,200
Less original fixed cost estimate	180,000
Additional dollars available for advertising	$421,200

Cost Allocation

Cost allocation, or assignment, is important to every part of management accounting, including the determination of unit costs for products and services. Some operating costs (direct costs) can be easily traced and assigned to products or services. But other costs (indirect costs) must be assigned using some form of allocation method. The need for cost allocation goes beyond just identifying product or service costs. Every report that a company accountant prepares requires some form of cost allocation. Depreciation expense on a building, for example, is often allocated to the departments housed in that building. Depreciation expense itself is originally established by allocating an investment's total cost to various time periods. Even the president's salary is allocated to the various divisions in a company.

In fact, without proper cost allocation techniques, management accountants could not do their work. Management accountants have three major tasks in preparing internal accounting documents: (1) They must find product or service unit costs. (2) They must work out cost budgets and cost controls for management. (3) They must prepare reports to aid and support management decisions. Each task requires proper cost allocation procedures.

Several terms are unique to the concept of cost allocation and should be discussed further. For instance, the terms *cost allocation* and *cost assignment* are often used interchangeably, although *cost allocation* is the more popular of the two. For our purposes, **cost allocation** is the process of assigning a specific cost to a specific cost objective.[1]

OBJECTIVE 4
State the role of cost objectives in the cost allocation process

A **cost objective** is the destination of an assigned or allocated cost.[2] If the purpose of a certain cost analysis is to evaluate the operating performance of a division or department, the cost objective would be that department or division. But if product costing is the reason for accumulating costs, a specific product, order, or an entire contract could be the cost objective. The important point to remember is that cost classification and cost allocation results differ, depending on the cost objective being analyzed.

A **cost center** is any organizational segment or area of activity for which there is a reason to accumulate costs. Examples of cost centers include the company as a whole, corporate divisions, specific operating plants, departments, and even specific machines or work areas. Once a cost center has been selected, methods can be worked out that will assign costs accurately to that cost center. No accounting report about a cost center can be prepared until all the proper cost allocation procedures have been carried out.

Finally, we need to expand the definitions of direct and indirect costs we have been using in connection with product costing. A **direct cost** is any cost that can be conveniently and economically traced to a *specific cost objective*. Direct materials costs and direct labor costs are normally thought of as direct costs. However, costs considered to be direct will

---

1. Cost Accounting Standard 402, promulgated by the Cost Accounting Standards Board in 1972, defined the term *allocate* as follows: "To assign an item of cost, or group of items of cost, to one or more cost objectives. This term includes both direct assignment of cost and the reassignment of a share from an indirect cost pool."

2. Cost Accounting Standard 402, promulgated by the Cost Accounting Standards Board in 1972, defined the term *cost objective* as follows: "A function, organizational subdivision contract or other work unit for which cost data are desired and for which provision is made to accumulate and measure the cost to processes, products, jobs, capitalized projects, etc."

vary with individual cost objectives. In general, the number of costs classified as direct increases with the size of the cost objective. If the cost objective is a large division of a company, then electricity, maintenance, and special tooling costs of the division may be classified as direct costs. An **indirect cost** is any cost that cannot be conveniently or economically traced to a specific cost objective. In an actual situation, any production cost not classified as a direct cost is an indirect cost.

Allocation of Manufacturing Costs

All manufacturing costs can be traced or allocated to a company's divisions, departments, or units of productive output. Direct costs, such as the cost of direct materials, can be assigned to specific products, departments, or jobs. Many manufacturing costs, however, are indirect costs that are incurred for the benefit of more than one product or department. These costs should be allocated to the departments and products that benefited from the cost. For example, electricity cost is incurred for the benefit of all departments or divisions of a company. The cost must be allocated to all the work done during a week or a month.

The cost allocation process is shown in Figure 25-4. All three cost elements are included: materials, labor, and factory overhead. Costs of lumber and the cabinet maker's wages are direct costs of the product. Examples of factory overhead costs include depreciation of the table saw, cleanup and janitorial services, and nails. All factory overhead costs are indirect costs of the product and must be assigned by means of an allocation method. In this example, the cost objective is the product. Various cost classifications and cost allocation methods are used, depending upon the specific cost objectives being analyzed.

Figure 25-4. Cabinet Making: Assigning Manufacturing Costs to the Product

To summarize, allocation of production costs calls for assigning direct and indirect manufacturing costs to specific cost objectives. A cost may be a direct cost to a large cost objective (a division) but an indirect cost to a smaller cost objective (a product). In each case, all manufacturing costs are assigned to the specific cost objective being analyzed as either direct or indirect costs.

The Role of Cost Assignment in Corporate Reporting

Accounting reports are prepared for all levels of management, from the president down to the department manager or supervisor. The president is responsible for all costs of the company. A department manager, on the other hand, is only responsible for the costs connected to that one department. Reports must be prepared for all cost centers, including the company as a whole, each division, and all departments within each division. The same costs shown in departmental reports will appear again in divisional and corporate reports, but perhaps in summary form. (This subject is expanded upon later in this chapter, when we discuss responsibility accounting.)

As the focus changes from one cost center or cost objective to another, so does the ease with which costs can be traced. Here is where cost allocation comes into the picture. As costs are reclassified and assigned to smaller cost centers or cost objectives, they become more difficult to trace. More costs are accounted for as indirect when the emphasis shifts from divisional to departmental reporting. When the cost objective is reduced to a single product, only direct materials and direct labor costs can be directly traced. All other costs are classified as indirect and must be assigned to the different products.

Table 25-1 shows how three manufacturing costs are traced differently as their cost objectives change. Direct materials costs can be traced directly to any level of cost objective shown. They are a direct cost at the divisional, departmental, and product levels. All 40,000 pounds of sugar were issued to Division A, so they can be traced directly to that division. Only half (20,000 pounds) was used by Department XZ, so only half can be traced directly to that department. At the product level, every unit of Product AB requires one-half pound of sugar. The cost of that one-half pound is a direct cost that can be traced to the product.

Depreciation of Factory Building G, which is used entirely by Division A, can be traced directly to Division A. For smaller cost objectives, though, it becomes an indirect cost. Building depreciation expense must be shared by the various cost centers in the building. Such costs must be allocated to departmental or product cost objectives using an allocation base such as space occupied.

Finally, depreciation costs of Machine 201 can be traced directly to either Division A or Department XZ. When Product AB is the cost objective, however, depreciation of machinery is considered an indirect manufacturing cost accounted for as a factory overhead cost. Factory overhead costs are accumulated and then allocated to the products produced in Department XZ, as we saw in previous chapters.

Table 25-1. Cost Classification and Traceability

Costs	Cost Objectives		
	Division A	Department XZ	Product AB
Direct Materials	*Direct cost:* 40,000 pounds of sugar were issued from inventory specifically for Division A.	*Direct cost:* 20,000 of the 40,000 pounds of sugar issued from inventory were used by Department XZ (can be directly traced).	*Direct cost:* Every unit of Product AB requires one-half pound of sugar.
Depreciation of Factory Building G	*Direct cost:* Factory Building G is used entirely by Division A. Therefore, all depreciation expenses from usage of Factory Building G can be directly traced to Division A.	*Indirect cost:* Department XZ is one of four departments in Factory Building G. Depreciation of Factory Building G is allocated to the four departments according to square footage used by each department.	*Indirect cost:* Depreciation of Factory Building G is an indirect product cost. It is allocated to individual products as part of factory overhead charges applied to products using machine hours as a base.
Depreciation of Machine 201	*Direct cost:* Machine 201 is located within Department XZ and is used exclusively by Division A (can be directly traced).	*Direct cost:* Machine 201 is used only by Department XZ. Therefore, its depreciation charges can be directly traced to Department XZ.	*Indirect cost:* Depreciation of Machine 201 cannot be directly traced to the individual products it produces. Depreciation charges are accounted for as part of factory overhead costs.

The principles of classifying and tracing costs we have discussed here play a part in the preparation of all internal accounting reports.

Assigning Costs of Supporting Service Functions

Every company and manufacturing process depends on the aid of many supporting service functions or departments. Although not directly involved in production activities, a **supporting service function** is an operating unit or department that is needed to support the activities of a company's production facilities. Examples include a repair and maintenance department, a production scheduling department, a central power department, an inspection department, and materials storage and handling.

Labor costs and various indirect operating costs are accumulated for each service function. The costs of these supporting departments are incurred for the purpose of producing a product, so they are product costs. They should be treated as indirect manufacturing costs and assigned to products through the Factory Overhead account. This type of cost allocation is done in two steps. First, the costs of the supporting service function are allocated to the departments or cost centers that benefited from the services. Then the assigned costs are included in the production department's Factory Overhead account and allocated to the end product.

Allocating factory overhead costs to products was discussed in Chapter 23. Here we will concentrate on assigning supporting service department costs to production departments. A service function must benefit other departments to justify its existence. It is on this concept of benefit that supporting service department costs are assigned to production departments. Benefit must be measured on some basis that shows how the service performed relates to the department that received the service.

Table 25-2 gives examples of bases used to allocate the costs of supporting service functions. Each should be used when there is a benefit relationship between the service function and the production departments. For example, each request for service may represent an equal

Table 25-2. Cost Allocation Bases for Assigning Costs of Supporting Service Functions	
Possible Allocation Basis	**When to Use**
1. Number of service requests	Used when each service takes the same amount of time, or when a record of service requests is maintained and no other basis is available
2. Labor hours	Used when labor hours are recorded for each service performed; a good basis when different services take different amounts of time
3. Kilowatt hours used	Used to distribute the costs of a central power department maintained by the company
4. Number of materials requisitions	Used to allocate costs of materials storage area requisitions

amount of benefit, or service, to the receiving department. In that case the number of service requests can be the basis. Or total benefit may be measured by the number of labor hours needed to complete the service. Then labor hours can be the basis. Similar relationships justify the use of kilowatt hours or the number of materials requisitions as the allocation basis. The following problem will help you understand the process of assigning supporting service department costs.

Illustrative Problem:
Assigning Service Department Costs

Haveard Metal Products Company has six production departments and three supporting service departments, including the Repairs and Maintenance (R & M) Department. Costs of the R & M Department are assigned to the six production departments on the basis of the number of service requests each department makes.

The production departments made the following numbers of service requests during February: 16 requests by the Cutting Department, 21 by the Extruding Department, 8 by the Shaping Department, 31 by the Threading Department, 24 by the Polishing Department, and 25 by the Finishing Department. Costs for the R & M Department that month were as follows:

Supplies and parts	
Small tools	$ 1,850
Lubricants and supplies	940
Replacement parts	2,100
Labor	
Repair and maintenance	3,910
Supervision	1,600
Depreciation	
Equipment	1,290
Machinery	1,620
Other operating costs	2,440
Total costs for February	$15,750

Required

1. Using the number of service requests, prepare a schedule allocating the R & M Department's operating costs for February to the six production departments.
2. Name and discuss another possible allocation basis for assigning the R & M Department's costs to the six production departments.

Solution

1. The goal of this part of the problem is to see what portion of February R & M costs should be assigned to each production department. The dollar amounts are found using a ratio of benefits received to total benefits rendered by the R & M Department. Using the number of service requests as the cost allocation basis, we can approach this problem in either of two ways:

a. Find the average cost per request and multiply it by each department's number of service requests:

$$\frac{\text{total cost}}{\text{total service requests}} = \frac{\$15,750}{125} = \$126 \text{ per request}$$

R & M Department cost allocation for February:

To Cutting Department (16 × $126)	$ 2,016
To Extruding Department (21 × $126)	2,646
To Shaping Department (8 × $126)	1,008
To Threading Department (31 × $126)	3,906
To Polishing Department (24 × $126)	3,024
To Finishing Department (25 × $126)	3,150
Total costs allocated	$15,750

b. Multiply the ratio of each department's requests to the total number of requests by the total costs to be allocated:

To Cutting Department (16/125) ($15,750)	$ 2,016
To Extruding Department (21/125) ($15,750)	2,646
To Shaping Department (8/125) ($15,750)	1,008
To Threading Department (31/125) ($15,750)	3,906
To Polishing Department (24/125) ($15,750)	3,024
To Finishing Department (25/125) ($15,750)	3,150
Total costs allocated	$15,750

The allocations are the same using method **b** as they were using method **a**, as they should be.

2. Labor hours used would be another possible allocation basis. Time records can be kept for each service call. Then costs can be allocated by finding the average R & M Department cost per labor hour. This cost would then be multiplied by the number of service labor hours used by each production department.

Accounting for Joint Production Costs

OBJECTIVE 6
Allocate common manufacturing costs to joint products

Joint or common costs represent a special case in cost allocation. A **joint cost** (or **common cost**) is a cost that relates to two or more products produced from a common input or raw material, and that can be assigned only by means of arbitrary cost allocation after the products become identifiable. Joint products cannot be identified as separate products during most of the production process. Only at a particular point in the joint manufacturing process, called the **split-off point**, do separate products evolve from a common processing unit. Joint products are often found in industries such as petroleum refining, wood processing, and meat packing. In all cases, more than one end product arises from a single input.

In the beef processing industry, the final cuts of meat (steaks, roasts, hamburger) do not appear until the end of the process. However, the cost of the steer, transportation costs, storage and hanging costs, and labor costs have been incurred in order to get the side of beef ready for final butchering. How do we assign these joint costs to specific cuts of beef?

Figure 25-5 shows a joint production situation and the accounting problem presented by joint costs. The $420,000 of joint costs can be assigned to Products AA and BB in several ways. We will outline the two most commonly used methods.

Physical Volume Method

One way to allocate joint production costs to specific products is called the **physical volume method**. This approach uses a measure of physical volume (units, pounds, liters, grams) as the basis for joint cost allocation. An example will show how the physical volume method applies to the problem in Figure 25-5. Assume that the Retlas Company makes two grades of paint from the same mixture of substances. During August, 75,000 liters of various ingredients were put into the production process. The final output for the month was 25,000 liters of Product AA and 50,000 liters of Product BB. Total joint production costs for August were $420,000: $210,000 for direct materials, $115,000 for direct labor, and $95,000 for factory overhead. The two products cannot be identified until the end of the production process. Product AA sells for $9 per liter and Product BB for $6 per liter. Taking total liters as the allocation basis, we apply a ratio of the physical volume of each product to total physical volume (see top of page 1068).

Figure 25-5. Joint Product Cost Allocation

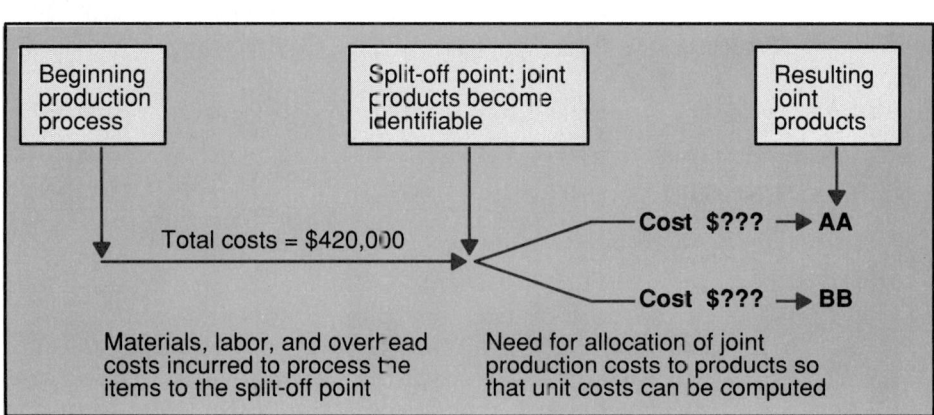

	Total Liters	Allocation Ratio	Joint Cost Allocation
Product AA	25,000	$\frac{25,000}{75,000}$ or $^1/_3$	$140,000 ($420,000 × $^1/_3$)
Product BB	50,000	$\frac{50,000}{75,000}$ or $^2/_3$	280,000 ($420,000 × $^2/_3$)
Totals	75,000		$420,000

Note that Product AA will generate $225,000 in revenues (25,000 liters at $9 per liter). Thus the net income for this product line will be $85,000. (We compute this by subtracting $140,000 of assigned joint costs from the total revenues of $225,000.) Product BB will sell for a total of $300,000 (50,000 liters at $6 per liter) and will show only a $20,000 profit ($300,000 minus $280,000 of assigned joint costs). The physical volume method is easy to use, but it often seriously distorts net income, because the physical volume of joint products may not be proportionate to each product's ability to generate revenue. In our example, Product BB's net income suffered because its high-volume content attracted two-thirds of the production costs, even though its selling price was much less than Product AA.

Relative Sales Value Method

Another way to allocate joint production costs depends on the relative sales value of the products. The relative sales value method allocates joint production costs to products in proportion to each one's revenue-producing ability (sales value). Extending the Retlas Company data, we can make the following analysis. (Costs are assigned to joint products on the basis of their relative sales value when they first become identifiable as specific products—that is, at the split-off point.)

	Liters Produced	×	Selling Price	=	Sales Value at Split-off	Allocation Ratio	Joint Cost Allocation
Product AA	25,000		$9.00		$225,000	$\frac{$225,000}{$525,000}$ or $^3/_7$	$180,000 ($420,000 × $^3/_7$)
Product BB	50,000		$6.00		300,000	$\frac{$300,000}{$525,000}$ or $^4/_7$	240,000 ($420,000 × $^4/_7$)
Totals	75,000				$525,000		$420,000

Product AA has a relative sales value of $225,000 at split-off; Product BB, $300,000. The resulting cost allocation ratios are 3/7 and 4/7, respectively. Applying these ratios to the total joint cost of $420,000, we assign $180,000 to Product AA and $240,000 to Product BB.

If we compare these results with those of the physical volume method, we see a wide difference in gross margin for the two product lines.

	Product AA		Product BB	
	Physical Volume Method	Relative Sales Value Method	Physical Volume Method	Relative Sales Value Method
Sales	$225,000	$225,000	$300,000	$300,000
Cost of goods sold	140,000	180,000	280,000	240,000
Gross margin	$ 85,000	$ 45,000	$ 20,000	$ 60,000
Gross margin as percent of sales	37.8%	20%	6.7%	20%

The major advantage of the relative sales value method is that it allocates joint costs according to a product's ability to absorb the cost. For this reason, gross margin percentages will always be equal at the split-off point, as the example shows. Under the relative sales value method, gross margin as a percentage of sales is 20% for both products.

As mentioned earlier, these approaches to assigning joint production costs are arbitrary. The reason for using them is that it is difficult to determine just how the end products (cost objectives) benefited from the incurrence of the cost. Both these approaches—the physical volume method and the relative sales value method—should be used only when it is impossible to tell how the cost benefited the cost objective.

Responsibility Accounting

OBJECTIVE 7
Describe a responsibility accounting system

Reporting operating costs invclves special report formats and reporting techniques. The goal of the statement of cost of goods manufactured is to translate manufacturing cost data into information that can be used for inventory valuation, profit measurement, and external reporting purposes. As seen in Chapter 22, all costs of materials, direct labor, and factory overhead are used to compute the cost of goods manufactured. However, management needs more than the data included in the statement of cost of goods manufactured. They also need information and costs on many day-to-day activities. Budget preparation, revenue and cost recording, cost control, and managerial performance evaluation all require a special system for collecting and reporting information.

Responsibility accounting meets these needs for extra information. A **responsibility accounting system** is an information reporting system that (1) classifies financial data according to defined areas of responsibility in an organization, and (2) reports the activities of managers by including only revenue and cost categories that a manager can control. Such a system personalizes accounting reports. Even though a company uses a responsibility accounting system, it still needs to collect normal cost and revenue data. It uses all the same recording practices, the same debit and credit entries, a general ledger, special journals, and a defined chart of accounts. However, responsibility accounting centers on the *reporting*—not the recording—of operating cost and revenue data. Once the financial data from daily operations have been recorded, specific costs and revenues can be reclassified and reported for specific areas of managerial responsibility.

Organizational Structure and Reporting

A responsibility accounting system includes several reporting centers, one for each area or level of managerial responsibility. Reports for each center include only those cost and revenue items that can be controlled by the manager of that center. If the manager cannot influence the amount of a certain cost or revenue item, that item is not included in the report. Because there is a report for each manager, and because lower-level managers report to higher-level managers, the same costs will appear in several reports. So lower-level operating data are included in reports to higher-level managers, but in summarized form.

A look at a corporate organization chart and a series of reports will show how a responsibility accounting system works. Figure 25-6 shows a typical management hierarchy, with three vice presidents under the corporate president. We have condensed the chart in the sales and finance areas in order to expand the manufacturing area. The production managers of Divisions A and B report to the vice president of manufacturing. Within Division B, the managers of the Stamping Department, Painting Department, and Assembly Department report to the division's production manager.

Exhibit 25-1 (page 1072) illustrates how operating reports are tailored to meet the individual needs of each level of management, focusing on the cost and revenue items over which each manager has control. Exhibit 25-1 shows how the responsibility reporting network is tied together. At the department level (bottom), the report gives a detailed listing of cost items under the control of the manager and compares expected (or budgeted) costs with actual costs to measure operating performance. The manager who receives the departmental report in Exhibit 25-1 should be particularly concerned with direct materials cost and maintenance salaries because they are so much over budget. The production manager of Division B is responsible for the three operating departments plus controllable division-wide costs. Note that the production manager's report (middle) includes only a summary of results from the Stamping Department, as well as from all other areas of responsibility. However, at the division level, the report does not present detailed cost items. Only departmental totals appear. The data are even more condensed in the vice president's report (top). Only corporate data and a summary of costs that can be controlled by the vice president are

Figure 25-6. Organization Chart Emphasizing the Manufacturing Area

included. Specific costs like the actual supplies cost at the department level are included in the vice president's report (in this case, in the $399,400 total for Division B), but like all costs reported at higher levels, they have lost their specific identity.

Cost and Revenue Controllability

Management aims for the lowest possible costs and the highest possible profits. To accomplish these goals, managers must know the origin of a cost or revenue item and be able to identify who is responsible for it. Responsibility accounting focuses on those costs that a manager can control.

Controllable costs are those costs that result from a manager's actions and decisions. If the manager can regulate or influence a cost or revenue item, the item is controllable at that level of operation. Managers who have the authority to acquire or supervise the use of a certain resource or service can control its cost.

Controllability is the key to a successful responsibility accounting system. By nature, it means that every cost incurred by a company can

Exhibit 25-1. Reporting Within a Responsibility Reporting System

Manufacturing: Vice President   **Monthly Report: November**

Amount Budgeted	Controllable Cost	Actual Amount	Over (Under) Budget
	Central production		
$ 281,400	scheduling	$ 298,100	$16,700
179,600	Office expenses	192,800	13,200
19,800	Operating expenses	26,200	6,400
	Divisions		
339,500	A	348,900	9,400
426,200	B	399,400	(26,800)
$1,246,500	Totals	$1,265,400	$18,900

Division B: Production Manager   **Monthly Report: November**

Amount Budgeted	Controllable Cost	Actual Amount	Over (Under) Budget
	Division expenses		
$101,800	Salaries	$ 96,600	$ (5,200)
39,600	Utilities	39,900	300
25,600	Insurance	21,650	(3,950)
	Departments		
46,600	Stamping	48,450	1,850
69,900	Painting	64,700	(5,200)
142,700	Assembly	128,100	(14,600)
$426,200	Totals	$399,400	$(26,800)

Stamping Department: Manager   **Monthly Report: November**

Amount Budgeted	Controllable Cost	Actual Amount	Over (Under) Budget
$22,500	Direct materials	$23,900	$1,400
14,900	Factory labor	15,200	300
2,600	Small tools	1,400	(1,200)
5,100	Maintenance salaries	6,000	900
1,000	Supplies	1,200	200
500	Other costs	750	250
$46,600	Totals	$48,450	$1,850

be traced to and controlled by at least one manager. Identifying controllable costs at lower management levels is often difficult. At these levels, managers seldom have full authority to acquire or supervise the use of resources and services. For this reason, managers themselves should help identify the costs for which they will be held accountable in their performance reviews. If cost and revenue items are truly controlled by the person responsible for the area in which they originate, then an efficient, meaningful reporting system can be designed for measuring operating performance and pinpointing trouble spots.

Chapter Review

Review of Learning Objectives

1. **Define and classify variable costs, semivariable costs, and fixed costs.**
   Variable costs are total costs that change in direct proportion to changes in productive output. Direct materials and direct labor are examples of variable costs. Semivariable costs act like both variable and fixed costs. That is, part of the cost is fixed and part changes with the volume of output. Examples are power costs and telephone charges. Total fixed costs remain constant within a relevant range of volume or activity. Examples of fixed costs include supervisory salaries and depreciation charges.

2. **Compute the breakeven point in units of output and in sales dollars.**
   The breakeven point is that point at which total revenue equals total costs incurred. The formula for the breakeven point is $S = VC + FC$ (sales equals variable costs plus fixed costs). In terms of contribution margin, the formula is

   $$\text{BE units} = \frac{FC}{CM/\text{unit}}$$

   Once the number of breakeven units is known, it can be multiplied by the product's selling price to get the breakeven point in sales dollars.

3. **Use contribution margin analysis to estimate levels of sales that will produce planned profits.**
   The addition of projected net income (NI) to the breakeven equation makes it possible to plan levels of operation that yield target profits. The formula in terms of contribution margin is

   $$\text{Target unit sales} = \frac{FC + NI}{CM/\text{unit}}$$

4. **State the role of cost objectives in the cost allocation process.**
   A cost objective is the destination of an assigned cost. The cost objective varies according to the focus of a particular report. It may range from an entire company or division to one particular product. Cost allocation is the process of assigning a specific cost to a specific cost objective. Cost objectives provide a target for the allocation process.

5. **Define a supporting service function and assign its costs to production departments.**

   A supporting service function is an operating unit or department that is needed to support the activities of the production facilities of the company. Examples include repairs and maintenance, production scheduling, and materials storage and handling departments. Costs incurred by supporting service departments must be accounted for as indirect manufacturing costs. They are allocated to production departments proportionally on a benefit basis. Several allocation bases exist to suit varying relationships between the service used and the production department receiving the service.

6. **Allocate common manufacturing costs to joint products.**

   Joint products evolve from a common processing unit. They cannot be identified as specific products until the split-off point in the process. All manufacturing costs incurred prior to the split-off point are shared by all the products. After the split-off point, costs are assigned to individual products by either the physical volume method or the relative sales value method.

7. **Describe a responsibility accounting system.**

   Responsibility accounting is an information reporting system that (1) classifies financial data according to defined areas of responsibility in an organization and (2) reports the activities of managers by including only those revenue and cost categories that a manager can control. A responsibility accounting system is made up of several personalized reports, one for each area of managerial responsibility.

Review of Concepts and Terminology

The following concepts and terms were introduced in this chapter:

(L.O. 2) **Breakeven point:**   The point at which total revenue equals total costs incurred.

(L.O. 1) **Budgetary control system:**   An integrated cost planning and control system.

(L.O. 3) **Contribution margin:**   The excess of revenues over all variable costs related to a particular sales volume.

(L.O. 7) **Controllable costs:**   Those costs that result from a manager's actions and decisions.

(L.O. 4) **Cost allocation:**   The process of assigning a specific cost to a specific cost objective.

(L.O. 1) **Cost behavior:**   The way costs respond to changes in activity or volume.

(L.O. 4) **Cost center:**   Any organizational segment or area of activity for which there is a reason to accumulate costs.

(L.O. 4) **Cost objective:**   The destination of an assigned or allocated cost.

(L.O. 2) **Cost-volume-profit analysis:** An analysis of the cost behavior patterns that underlie the relationships between cost, volume of output, and profit. (Also C-V-P analysis.)

(L.O. 4) **Direct cost:** Any cost that can be conveniently and economically traced to a specific cost objective.

(L.O. 1) **Excess capacity:** Extra machinery and equipment kept on hand on a stand-by basis.

(L.O. 1) **Fixed costs:** Costs that remain constant within a relevant range of volume or activity.

(L.O. 4) **Indirect cost:** Any cost that cannot be conveniently and economically traced to a specific cost objective.

(L.O. 6) **Joint cost:** A cost that relates to two or more products produced from a common input or raw material and that can be assigned only by means of arbitrary cost allocation after the products become identifiable. (Also common cost.)

(L.O. 1) **Mixed costs:** Costs that result when both variable and fixed costs are charged to the same general ledger account.

(L.O. 1) **Normal capacity:** The average annual level of operating capacity needed to meet expected sales demands.

(L.O. 1) **Operating capacity:** The upper limit of a company's productive output capability, given existing resources.

(L.O. 6) **Physical volume method:** An approach to the problem of allocating joint production costs to specific products that is based on or uses some measure of physical volume (units, pounds, liters, grams, etc.) as the basis for joint cost allocation.

(L.O. 1) **Practical capacity:** Theoretical capacity reduced by normal and expected work stoppages.

(L.O. 6) **Relative sales value method:** An approach to the problem of allocating joint production costs to specific products that is based on or uses the product's revenue-producing ability (sales value) as a basis for joint cost allocation.

(L.O. 1) **Relevant range:** The range of activity within which actual operations are likely to occur.

(L.O. 7) **Responsibility accounting system:** An information reporting system that (1) classifies financial data according to defined areas of responsibility in an organization and (2) reports the activities of managers by including only revenue and cost categories that a manager can control.

(L.O. 1) **Semivariable costs:** Costs that have both variable and fixed cost components.

(L.O. 6) **Split-off point:** A point in the joint product production process where joint products separate and become identifiable.

(L.O. 5) **Supporting service function:** An operating unit or department that is needed to support the activities of a company's production facilities.

(L.O. 1) **Theoretical capacity:** The maximum productive output a department or company could reach for a given period if all machinery and equipment

were operated at optimum speed without interruptions. (Also ideal capacity.)

(L.O. 1)   **Variable costs:** Total costs that change in direct proportion to changes in productive output (or any other volume measure).

Self-Test

Test your knowledge of the chapter by choosing the best answer for each item below.

1. The way that costs respond to changes in activity or volume is the definition of
   a. product costing.
   b. the breakeven point.
   c. cost behavior.
   d. cost flow.   *(L.O. 1)*

2. A cost that has both variable and fixed cost components is known as a
   a. direct cost.
   b. semivariable cost.
   c. indirect cost.
   d. product cost.   *(L.O. 1)*

3. The records of the Goldman Company revealed the data below:

Month	Cost	Activity
January	$ 8,978	1,920 machine hours
February	8,842	1,880 machine hours
March	10,066	2,240 machine hours

   Using the high-low method, the variable cost per machine hour during the quarter was
   a. $3.40.
   b. $4.68.
   c. $3.70.
   d. $4.49.   *(L.O. 1)*

4. Assuming the same facts as in 3, the monthly fixed costs during the quarter were
   a. $1,000.
   b. $1,890.
   c. $2,230.
   d. $2,450.   *(L.O. 1)*

5. The maximum productive output that an operating unit could reach for a given period if all machinery and equipment were operated at optimum speed without any interruptions is the definition of
   a. practical capacity.
   b. normal capacity.
   c. theoretical capacity.
   d. excess capacity.   *(L.O. 1)*

6. The process of assigning a specific cost to a specific cost objective is known as
   a. cost allocation.
   b. budgeting.
   c. process costing.
   d. controllable costing.   *(L.O. 4)*

7. Assigning a joint cost to products based on the product's ability to generate revenue is accomplished by using the
   a. split-off method.
   b. relative sales value method.
   c. process costing method.
   d. physical volume method. *(L.O. 6)*

8. Product DG's expected selling price per unit is $54, projected variable cost per unit is $30, and estimated fixed costs per month are $394,080. The breakeven point in unit sales per month is
   a. 16,240.   c. 16,420.
   b. 11,590.   d. 11,950.   *(L.O. 2)*

9. Assuming the same facts as in 8, the breakeven point in dollar sales per month is
   a. $645,300.   c. $625,860.
   b. $886,680.   d. $866,680.   *(L.O. 2)*

10. Assuming the same facts as in 8, how many units must be sold in order to earn a monthly profit of $13,920?
   a. 16,820   c. 12,530
   b. 12,170   d. 17,000   *(L.O. 2, 3)*

Answers to Self-Test are at the end of this chapter.

Review Problem
Breakeven/Profit Planning Analysis

(L.O. 2, 3) TK's Music City, Inc. is a major producer of large pipe organs. Model ERV is a double-manual organ with a large potential market. Data from 19x1 operations for Model ERV are summarized below.

Variable costs per unit	
Direct materials	$ 2,300
Direct labor	800
Factory overhead	600
Selling expense	500
Total fixed costs	
Factory overhead	195,000
Advertising	55,000
Administrative expense	68,000
Selling price per unit	9,500

Management is pondering alternative courses of action for 19x2. Each alternative should be treated as an independent action and not tied to the other alternatives.

Required

1. Compute the 19x1 breakeven point in units.
2. Calculate the amount of net income generated if 65 ERV models were sold in 19x1.
3. For 19x2:
   a. Calculate the number of units that must be sold to generate a $95,400 profit. Assume that costs and selling price remain constant.
   b. Calculate the net income if the company increases the number of units sold by 20 percent and cuts the selling price by $500 per unit.
   c. Determine the number of units that must be sold to break even if advertising is increased by $47,700.
   d. If variable costs are cut by 10 percent, find the number of units that must be sold to generate a profit of $125,000.

Answer to Review Problem

1. Breakeven point in units computed for 19x1:

Variable costs per unit	$ 4,200
Contribution margin per unit:	
$9,500 – $4,200	5,300
Total fixed costs	$318,000

$$\text{Breakeven point} = \frac{FC}{CM/unit} = \frac{\$318,000}{\$5.300} = \underline{60 \text{ units}}$$

2. Net income for 65 units calculated:

Units sold	65
Units required to break even	60
Units over breakeven	5

19x1 net income = $5,300 per unit × 5 = $26,500

Contribution margin equals sales minus all variable costs. CM/unit equals the amount of sales dollars remaining, after variable costs have been subtracted, to cover fixed costs and provide a profit for the company. If all fixed costs have been absorbed by the time breakeven is reached, the whole contribution margin of each unit sold in excess of breakeven represents profit.

3. a. Number of units calculated to generate a given profit:

$$\text{Unit sales} = \frac{FC + NI}{CM/unit}$$

$$= \frac{\$318,000 + \$95,400}{\$5,300} = \frac{\$413,400}{\$5,300} = \underline{78 \text{ units}}$$

3. b. Net income calculated under specified conditions:

$$\text{Units to be sold} = 65 \times 120\% = 78 \text{ units}$$
$$\text{New selling price} = \$9,000$$
$$\text{Contribution margin} = \$9,000 - \$4,200 = \$4,800$$
$$\text{BE units} = \frac{\$318,000}{\$4,800} = 66.25 \text{ units}$$

Units to be sold in excess of breakeven:

$$78 - 66.25 = 11.75 \text{ units}$$

Projected net income:

$$11.75 \text{ units} \times \$4,800 = \$56,400$$

3. c. Number of breakeven units calculated under specified conditions:

$$\text{BE units} = \frac{\$318,000 + \$47,700}{\$5,300}$$

$$= \frac{\$365,700}{\$5,300} = 69 \text{ units}$$

3. d. Number of units calculated to generate a given profit:

Variable cost per unit = $\$4,200 \times .9 = \$3,780$
Contribution margin per unit = $\$9,500 - \$3,780 = \$5,720$

$$\text{Unit sales} = \frac{\$318,000 + \$125,000}{\$5,720} = \frac{\$443,000}{\$5,720} = 77.45 \text{ units}$$

Chapter Assignments

Discussion Questions and Writing Assignments

1. What makes variable costs different from other costs?
2. "Fixed costs remain constant in total but decrease per unit as output increases." Explain this statement.
3. What is meant by the relevant range of activity?
4. Why is a telephone charge considered a semivariable cost?
5. What is the major difference between practical capacity and theoretical capacity?
6. Why does a company seldom operate at either theoretical or practical capacity?
7. What is normal capacity? Why is this expression of capacity more relevant and useful than either theoretical or practical capacity?
8. What is the relationship between cost-volume-profit analysis and the concept of cost behavior?
9. Define *breakeven point*. State why information on breakeven is useful to management.
10. Define *contribution margin*. How is this concept useful?
11. State the equation that determines target unit sales, using the elements of fixed costs, net income, and contribution margin.
12. What conditions must be met for cost-volume-profit computations to be accurate?
13. What is a cost objective, and what is its role in management accounting?
14. "As the size of the cost center or cost objective decreases, the ability to trace cost and revenue is limited." Explain this statement.
15. What is a supporting service department? Give examples.
16. What is a joint manufacturing cost?
17. Describe the physical volume method of allocating joint costs to products. List the advantages and disadvantages of the physical volume method.

18. Should joint costs be allocated to a product on the basis of the product's ability to generate revenue? Explain your answer.
19. How does a corporate organization chart help in designing a responsibility accounting system?
20. Define *controllable cost* and describe its role in a responsibility accounting system.

Classroom Exercises

Exercise 25-1.
Identification of
Variable and Fixed
Costs
(L.O. 1)

From the following list of costs of productive output, indicate which are usually considered variable costs and which fixed costs: (1) packing materials for stereo components, (2) real estate taxes, (3) gasoline for a delivery truck, (4) property insurance, (5) depreciation expense of buildings (straight-line method), (6) supplies, (7) indirect materials used, (8) bottles used in the sale of liquids, (9) license fees for company cars, (10) wiring used in radios, (11) machine helper's wages, (12) wood used in bookcases, (13) city operating license, (14) employer's share of social security payments, (15) machine operators' wages, (16) cost of required outside inspection of each unit produced. Could any of these costs be considered a semivariable cost? Explain.

Exercise 25-2.
Semivariable
Costs / High-Low
Method
(L.O. 1)

Herring Electronics Company manufactures major appliances. The company just had its most successful year because of increased interest in its refrigerator line. While preparing the budget for next year, Ms. Dora, the company's controller, came across the following data related to utility costs:

Month	Power Costs	Volume in Machine Hours
July	$60,000	6,000
August	53,000	5,000
September	49,500	4,500
October	46,000	4,000
November	42,500	3,500
December	39,000	3,000

Using the high-low method, determine (1) the variable power cost per machine hour, (2) the monthly fixed power cost, and (3) the total variable power costs and fixed power costs for the six-month period.

Exercise 25-3.
Breakeven
Analysis
(L.O. 2)

Mark Johnson Manufacturing Company makes head covers for golf clubs. The company expects to make a profit next year. It anticipates fixed manufacturing costs to be $126,500 and fixed general and administrative expenses to be $82,030 for the year. Variable manufacturing and selling costs per set of head covers will be $4.65 and $2.75, respectively. Each set will sell for $13.40.

1. Compute the breakeven point in sales units.
2. Compute the breakeven point in sales dollars.

3. If the selling price were increased to $14.00 per unit and fixed general and administrative expenses were cut by $33,465, what would the new break-even point be in units?
4. Prepare a graph to illustrate the breakeven point found in part 2.

Exercise 25-4.
Profit Planning
(L.O. 2, 3)

Short-term automobile rentals are the specialty of Sandelin Auto Loans, Inc. Average variable operating expenses have been $12.50 per day per automobile. The company owns 60 cars. Fixed operating costs for the next year are expected to be $145,500. Average daily rental revenue per automobile is expected to be $34.50. Management would like to earn $47,000 during the year.

1. Calculate the total number of daily rentals that the company must have during the year to earn the target profit.
2. On the basis of your answer to part 1, determine the number of days on the average that each automobile must be rented.
3. Find the total rental revenue for the year needed to earn the $47,000 profit.
4. What would the total rental revenue be if fixed operating costs could be lowered by $5,180 and target earnings increased to $70,000?

Exercise 25-5.
Contribution
Margin / Profit
Planning
(L.O. 3)

Starkville Systems, Ltd. makes undersea missiles for nuclear submarines. The management has just been offered a government contract that may result in a profit for the company. The contract purchase price is $130,000 per unit, but the number of units to be purchased has not yet been decided. The company's fixed costs are budgeted at $3,973,500, and the variable costs are $68,500 per unit.

1. Compute the number of units that the company should agree to make at the stated contract price in order to earn a target income of $1,500,000.
2. Using a lighter material, the variable unit cost can be reduced by $1,730, but total fixed overhead will increase by $27,500. How many units must be produced to make $1,500,000 in profit?
3. Using the figures in part 2, how many additional units need to be produced to increase profit by $1,264,600?

Exercise 25-6.
Cost Allocation
Basis
(L.O. 4)

A plan for cost assignment is vital to corporate reporting, product costing, and inventory valuation. Examples of costs and related cost objectives are presented below.

Cost	Cost Objective
Materials-handling costs	Product
Plant depreciation costs	Division
Repair and maintenance department costs	One of five production departments served
Corporate president's salary	Division

1. Which costs would be direct costs of the related cost objective? Which would be indirect costs?
2. For each indirect cost, choose a cost allocation basis that provides a logical relationship between the cost and the cost objective. Defend your answers.

**Exercise 25-7.
Cost Alloca-
tion —Direct
Versus Indirect**
(L.O. 4)

Classifying a cost as direct or indirect depends on the cost objective. Depreciation of a factory building is a direct cost when the plant is the cost objective, but when the cost objective is a product, depreciation cost is indirect.

For the following costs, indicate for each cost objective—division, department, or product—whether the cost would be indirect (I) or direct (D). Be
prepared to defend your answers.

Cost	Cost Objective		
	Division	Department	Product
Direct labor			
Departmental supplies			
Division head's salary			
President's salary			
Department manager's salary			
Direct materials			
Fire insurance on specific machine			
Property taxes, division plant			
Department repairs and maintenance			

**Exercise 25-8.
Service
Department Cost
Allocation**
(L.O. 5)

Delta Fundraising, Inc. has six departments that share the services of a single
central computer. Management has decided that the best basis for cost allocation is minutes of computer time used by each department. Usage per department for the first week in June was as follows: 6,200 minutes for
Department A; 8,400 minutes for Department B; 8,920 minutes for Department C; 4,160 minutes for Department D; 2,080 minutes for Department E;
10,240 minutes for Department F. The total for all departments was 40,000
minutes. The total cost of operating the computer during the month was
$28,056. Determine the computer expense to be assigned to each department
for the one-week period.

**Exercise 25-9.
Joint Cost
Allocation—
Physical Volume
Method**
(L.O. 6)

Hawaii's Mahalo Products Company produces molasses and refined sugar,
joint products that emerge from the juice extracted from sugar cane. The
company uses the physical volume method to assign common or joint costs
to the two products. Their allocation base is liters. During February, Mahalo
Products Company put 160,000 liters of sugar cane juice into production. The
final products from this input were 24,000 liters of molasses and 136,000
liters of refined sugar. The following joint product costs were incurred during February: $7,280 for materials; $18,480 for direct labor; and $23,060 for
factory overhead. Thus total joint costs amounted to $48,820. Assuming no
loss through evaporation, assign a portion of joint production costs to each
product.

Exercise 25-10.
Joint Cost
Allocation—
Relative Sales
Value Method
(L.O. 6)

In the processing of paper two distinct grades of wood pulp emerge from a common crushing and mixing process. O'Toole Paper Products, Inc. produced 88,000 liters of pulp during January. Direct materials used during the month cost the company $172,000. Labor and overhead costs for the month were $72,000 and $112,000, respectively. Output for the month was as the following table indicates:

Product	Quantity	Market Value at Split-off
Grade A pulp	56,000 liters	$7.00 per liter
Grade B pulp	32,000 liters	$5.25 per liter

Using the relative sales value method, allocate the common production costs to Grade A pulp and Grade B pulp.

Exercise 25-11.
Responsibility
Accounting /
Organizational
Structure
(L.O. 7)

The Gregor Shewman Company uses the following job titles:

Sales manager	Internal auditor
President	Supervisor, repairs and maintenance
Warehouse manager	Vice president, manufacturing
Cashier	Marketing manager
Controller	Engineering research manager
Production supervisor	Personnel manager
Vice president, sales	Treasurer
Purchasing agent	Vice president, administration

1. Design an organization chart for the company using the job titles listed above.
2. For each job title, list some possible costs for which the person holding the position would be responsible.

Interpreting Accounting Information

Internal
Management
Information:
Florida Produce
Company
(L.O. 7)

The Packing and Storage Department at Florida Produce Company is run by Shelley Guard. A responsibility accounting system was recently installed. A performance report is prepared monthly for each of the company's cost centers. Ms. Guard's performance report for May is shown on the next page. Top management sees that the overage of $3,345 is 8.06 percent over budget, far above the 4 percent tolerance that was agreed upon. Amounts allocated to the Packing and Storage Department were figured by means of appropriate allocation bases.

Required

1. Using the concept of controllable costs, identify the costs that should not be in Ms. Guard's performance report.
2. Recast the performance report using only those costs controllable by the department's supervisor.
3. How should Ms. Guard respond to top management?

Florida Produce Company
Performance Report
Packing and Storage Department
For the Month Ended May 31, 19x1

Amount Budgeted	Cost Item	Actual Amount	Over (Under) Budget
$ 4,500	Packing materials	$ 4,680	$ 180
2,800	Packing supplies	2,700	(100)
9,240	Wages, packing	9,110	(130)
6,680	Wages, storage	6,920	240
5,500	Salaries, packing and storage	5,690	190
1,600	Salaries, vice president's staff	3,100	1,500
1,840	Depreciation, packing machinery	1,820	(20)
3,200	Depreciation, storage warehouse	3,200	—
1,250	Depreciation, company-wide office building	2,500	1,250
870	Electric power, packing and storage	910	40
490	Electric power, main office	580	90
575	Heating, packing and storage	600	25
380	Heating, main office	440	60
780	Equipment rental, packing	750	(30)
410	Equipment rental, main office	470	60
290	Insurance, packing and storage	290	—
160	Insurance, total company	180	20
460	Equipment maintenance, packing and storage	440	(20)
220	Lift truck, packing and storage	200	(20)
250	Miscellaneous	260	10
$41,495	Totals	$44,840	$3,345

Problem Set A

Problem 25A-1.
Breakeven
Analysis
(L.O. 2, 3)

At the beginning of each year, the accounting department at Altman Lighting, Ltd. must find the point at which projected sales revenue will equal total budgeted variable and fixed costs. The company makes custom-made, low voltage outdoor lighting systems. Each system sells for an average of $435. Variable costs per unit are $210. Total fixed costs for the year are estimated to be $166,500.

Required

1. Compute the breakeven point in sales units.
2. Compute the breakeven point in sales dollars.
3. Find the new breakeven point in sales units if the fixed costs should go up by $10,125.
4. Using the original figures, compute the breakeven point in sales units if the selling price decreases to $425 per unit, fixed costs go up by $15,200, and variable costs decrease by $15 per unit.

Problem 25A-2.
Profit Planning—
Contribution
Margin Approach
(L.O. 3)

George Stevens is president of the UCF Plastics Division of Orlando Industries. Management is considering a new product line featuring a dashing medieval knight posed on a beautiful horse. Called Chargin' Knight, this product is expected to have worldwide market appeal and become the mascot for many high school and university athletic teams. Expected variable unit costs are as follows: direct materials, $18.50; direct labor, $4.25; production supplies, $1.10; selling costs, $2.80; other, $1.95. The following are annual fixed costs: depreciation, building and equipment, $36,000; advertising, $45,000; other, $11,400. Orlando Industries plans to sell the product for $55.00.

Required

1. Using the contribution margin approach, compute the number of products the company must sell to (a) break even and (b) earn a profit of $70,224.
2. Using the same data, compute the number of products that must be sold to earn a target profit of $139,520 if advertising costs rise by $40,000.
3. Assuming the original information and sales of 10,000 units, compute the new selling price that the company must use to make $131,600 profit.
4. According to the vice president of marketing, Wally Reiff, the most optimistic annual sales estimate for the product would be 15,000 items. How much more can be spent on fixed advertising costs if the highest possible selling price that the company can charge is $52.00, if the variable costs cannot be reduced, and if the target net income for 15,000 unit sales is $251,000?

Problem 25A-3.
Allocation
Process:
Cost-Base
Relationship
(L.O. 4)

Following are five costs for a typical manufacturing company. Each cost is allocated to a cost objective.

Cost	Cost Objective
1. Cost of corporate computer center	Production departments
2. Depreciation of division factory buildings	Production departments
3. Tool and die making costs (service department)	Production departments
4. Material storage costs	Products
5. Repair and maintenance department costs	Production departments

A number of allocation bases could be used to assign the costs listed in 1 through 5 above to their respective cost objectives. They include (a) machine hours, (b) direct labor hours, (c) direct labor dollars, (d) facility or service usage hours, (e) direct materials costs, (f) square footage, and (g) number of service requests.

Required

1. For each of the five types of costs, select the allocation base that best expresses the beneficial relationship between the cost and the cost objective. State the reasons for your answers.
2. What would be wrong with the idea of including all these costs in one overhead cost pool and allocating them to production departments on the basis of machine hours? What would be the advantage of taking such an approach?

Problem 25A-4.
Service
Department
Expense
Allocation
(L.O. 5)

Rockford Community Hospital has one respirator that is shared by the hospital's six departments. To ensure efficiency and to aid in future budgeting, each department's operating income or loss is figured separately each month. Before these calculations can be made, expenses that are considered common expenses must be allocated to each of the departments. Depreciation and maintenance expenses connected directly to the respirator are allocated to the departments according to hours of usage.

The costs for upkeep of the respirator for the month of June follow. Depreciation on the respirator was $1,400; on supplemental machinery, $340. Labor costs were $5,000 for the operators and $2,800 for maintenance. Materials costs were $5,200 for oxygen, $680 for small replacement parts, $1,050 for supplies, and $780 for other operating costs. Thus, total costs for June were $17,250. Respirator usage by department for June was as follows: 225.0 hours for the Oncology Department, 52.6 hours for the Orthopedic Department, 38.2 hours for the Nephrology Department, 113.8 hours for the Geriatric Department, 65.4 hours for the Pediatric Department, and 145.0 hours for the Maternity Department.

Required

1. Assign the respirator costs for June to each of the six departments according to hourly usage.
2. Identify other bases of allocation that could be used to assign costs in this case. Be prepared to discuss the advantages and disadvantages of each allocation basis.

Problem 25A-5.
Joint Cost
Allocation
(L.O. 6)

Three distinct grades of chocolate sauce are made by Tracey's Toppings, Inc. The ingredients for all three grades of chocolate sauce are first blended together. Then other ingredients are added to produce the three separate grades. The Extra-Rich blend sells for $8.20 per pound. The Quality blend sells for $6.60 per pound. And the Regular blend sells for $5.00 per pound. In July, 383,000 pounds of ingredients were put into production, with output as follows: 94,218 pounds of Extra-Rich blend, 153,966 pounds of Quality blend, and 134,816 pounds of Regular blend. Joint costs for the period were $401,200 for direct materials, $146,000 for direct labor, and $196,800 for factory overhead. Assume no beginning or ending inventories and no loss of input during production.

Required

1. Using the physical volume method, allocate the joint costs to the three different blends.
2. Using the relative sales value method, allocate the joint costs to the three blends.
3. Prepare a schedule that compares the gross profit at split-off point using the two methods of allocation. Compute gross margin both in total dollars and as a percentage of sales.
4. Additional processing costs could be incurred after split-off to add a special ingredient to the Extra-Rich blend. If the company spent $91,740 for this ingredient during the period, the selling price could be increased to $10.00 per pound. On these assumptions, how much profit could be earned from Extra-Rich blend sales? Should the company add the extra ingredient? **Hint:** Use the relative sales value method when referring to the allocated portion of joint processing costs.

Problem Set B

**Problem 25B-1.
Breakeven
Analysis
(L.O. 2, 3)**

Rosenberg & Kaminsky, a law firm in downtown Phoenix, is considering the development of a legal clinic for middle- and low-income residents of the city. Paraprofessional help would be employed, and an $18 per hour billing rate would be used. The paraprofessionals would be law students who will work for only $9 per hour. Other variable costs are anticipated to be $5.40 per hour and annual fixed costs are expected to total $27,000.

Required

1. Compute the breakeven point in billable hours.
2. Compute the breakeven point in total billings.
3. Find the new breakeven point in total billings if fixed costs should go up by $2,340.
4. Using the original figures, compute the breakeven point in total billings if the billing rate is decreased by $1 per hour, variable costs are decreased by $.40 per hour, and fixed costs go down by $3,600.

**Problem 25B-2.
Profit Planning—
Contribution
Margin Approach
(L.O. 3)**

Osburn Financial Corporation is a subsidiary of Henning Enterprises. Processing loan applications is the major task of the corporation. Last year, Ms. Nancy Barth, manager of the Loan Department, established a policy of charging a $250 fee for every loan application processed. Next year's variable costs have been projected to be as follows: loan consultant's wages, $15.50 per hour (a loan application takes 5 hours to process); supplies, $2.40 per application; other variable costs, $5.60 per application. Annual fixed costs include: depreciation of equipment, $8,500; building rental, $14,000; promotional costs, $12,500; other fixed costs, $8,099.

Required

1. Using the contribution margin approach, compute the number of loan applications that the company must process to (a) break even and (b) earn a profit of $14,476.
2. Continuing the same approach, compute the number of applications the company must process to earn a target profit of $20,000 if promotional costs increase by $5,662.
3. Assuming the original information and the processing of 500 applications, compute the loan application fee the company must charge if the target profit is $41,651.
4. Ms. Barth believes that 750 loan applications is the maximum number her staff can handle. How much more can be spent on promotional costs if the highest fee tolerable to the customer is $280, if variable costs cannot be reduced, and if the target net income for such an application load is $50,000?

**Problem 25B-3.
Allocation
Process—
Cost-Base
Relationship
(L.O. 4)**

Five costs incurred by a typical manufacturing company are shown on the following page. Each cost must be allocated to a cost objective. A number of allocation bases can be used to assign these costs to their respective cost objectives. They include (a) machine hours, (b) direct labor hours, (c) direct labor dollars, (d) engineering labor hours, (e) number of employees, (f) total labor hours, (g) number of units handled, (h) percentage of service costs, (i) number of service requests, (j) cost of materials, and (k) direct charges.

	Cost	Cost Objective
1.	Cost accounting department	Production departments
2.	Engineering (service) department	Products
3.	Materials handling function	Products
4.	Cafeteria (service) function	Production departments
5.	Production scheduling department	Production departments

Required

1. For each of the five costs, select the allocation base or bases that best express the beneficial relationship between the cost and the cost objective. State the reasons for your answers.
2. Some companies group all the costs listed above in one factory overhead cost pool and allocate them to products using just one allocation base, such as machine hours. What are the advantages and disadvantages of this approach?

Problem 25B-4.
Service
Department
Expense
Allocation
(L.O. 5)

Tenants at the Anders Tower Office Complex on Park Avenue in Winter Park, Florida, share certain supporting services. All operating costs are incurred centrally and allocated to the seven tenant businesses on the basis of usage. Word processing is one of the shared services. For August, the following costs were related to the word processing function: operator labor, 10 people at $1,500 monthly salary each; supplies, $920; equipment depreciation, $1,650; space rental, $2,500; utilities, $650; overhead charge, $2,380. Thus total allocable costs for August amounted to $23,100. Usage of the word processing service is recorded in hours, which is the basis for allocating the cost each month. During August, tenant usage was as follows: Braun Catering Service, 128 hours; Norman Realtors, Inc., 284 hours; Drown & Cobbs, Attorneys at Law, 422 hours; Bigson Inventory Service, 170 hours; Cuthill & Eddy, CPAs, 360 hours; University Sporting Goods, 126 hours; Pam's Hair Styling Supplies, 110 hours.

Required

1. Assign the costs of the word processing function for August to each of the seven tenant businesses on the basis of hours of usage.
2. List other bases of allocation that could have been used to assign costs in this case. Discuss the advantages and disadvantages of each.

Problem 25B-5.
Joint Cost
Allocation
(L.O. 6)

The processing of crude oil produces three joint products, gasoline, motor oil, and kerosene. Petropski Petroleum Products, Inc. is a Chicago-based processor. During April, the company used 1,950,000 gallons of crude oil at a cost of $.40 per gallon, paid $315,000 in direct labor wages, and applied $420,000 of factory overhead to the crude oil processing department. Production during the period yielded 950,000 gallons of gasoline, 350,000 gallons of motor oil, and 600,000 gallons of kerosene. Evaporation caused the loss of 50,000 gallons; the amount lost was normal, and its cost should be included in the costing of good units produced. Selling prices for the joint products are: $.80 per gallon of gasoline; $.95 per quart of motor oil; and $.50 per gallon of kerosene. Assume there were no beginning or ending work in process inventories, and that everything produced was sold during the period (Note: 4 quarts equal one gallon.)

Required

1. Using the physical volume method, allocate the joint costs to each of the three joint products.
2. Using the relative sales value method, allocate the joint costs to each of the three joint products.
3. Prepare a schedule that compares the gross profit at split-off point using the two methods of allocation. Compute gross margin both in total dollars and as a percentage of sales.
4. Gasoline could be processed beyond the split-off point to obtain a premium product. If the company incurred $148,500 of additional processing costs for gasoline in April, the selling price could be increased to $1.05 per gallon. Under these circumstances, how much additional profit would be earned from the sale of gasoline? Should the company process the gasoline beyond split-off? **Hint:** Use the relative sales value method when referring to the allocated portion of joint processing costs.

Management Decision Case

The Mississippi State Bank
(L.O. 5, 7)

Centennial Bancorp is the parent corporation for two state-wide banks, The Mississippi State Bank and The Alabama State Bank. The Mississippi State Bank is the responsibility of its president, Mr. Clyde Herring. Four senior vice presidents report to him; they coordinate the activities of Marketing, Operations, Commercial Loans, and Investments. (The Internal Audit Division reports directly to the Board of Directors.) Within the Operations area there are five departments, as follows:

Departments	Functions
Controller's Department	General ledger maintenance Assistant controller Special cost and revenue analyses
Data Processing Department	Programming Systems design Data entry Computer operators Systems maintenance
Customer Service Department	Tellers New account representatives Customer concerns
Bookkeeping Department	Customer statement preparation Telephone and wire dollar transfers Service and vault charges
Proof Department	Proving of bulk deposits Internal check clearinghouse

The Customer Service Department is considered the primary department in this division; the remaining four are supporting service departments.

According to the Controller's Department, fixed costs of the Operations area are shared by all five departments and should therefore be grouped together in a fixed overhead cost pool and allocated on the basis of total salary dollars. During 19x1, the entire Operations area expects to pay $1,300,000 in salaries. Costs projected to be charged to the fixed overhead cost pool include the following:

Depreciation, furniture and fixtures	$35,500
Telephone charges	$540/month plus an estimated $200/month for long-distance calls
Property tax	$19,240
Electricity expense	$920/month plus $.002 per kilowatt hour of usage*
Rent, buildings	$46,000
Insurance	$13,960
Gas heating	$940/month plus $.008 per cubic foot of gas consumption†
Equipment leasing expense	$175,000

*36,400,000 kilowatt hours are expected to be used
†2,640,000 cubic feet of gas are expected to be consumed

The Mississippi State Bank
Operations Area
Data Processing Department
Performance Report
For the Year Ended December 31, 19x1

Amount Budgeted	Cost Item	Actual Amount	Over (Under) Budget
$ 99,000	Salaries, programmers	$ 98,060	$ (940)
104,000	Salaries, system designers	103,080	(920)
129,000	Salaries, computer operators	129,820	820
72,000	Salary, manager	71,960	(40)
25,620	Salaries, bank administration	47,520	21,900
75,000	Equipment leasing	74,880	(120)
32,000	Computer supplies	30,420	(1,580)
70,000	Software purchases	70,480	480
7,000	Data storage diskettes	7,560	560
5,920	Depreciation, furniture and fixtures	6,120	200
100,500	Fixed overhead—Operations area	102,745	2,245
28,000	Back-up data file maintenance expense	26,540	(1,460)
12,000	Bank-wide overhead expense	14,500	2,500
3,000	Miscellaneous costs	2,980	(20)
$763,040	Totals	$786,665	$23,625

Required

1. Compute the fixed overhead cost rate for the Operations area for 19x1.
2. During 19x1, the Operations area departments will incur the following salary costs:

Controller's	$196,480
Data Processing	402,920
Customer Service	379,400
Bookkeeping	156,400
Proof	164,800

Determine the amount of fixed overhead costs that should be allocated to each department during the year.
3. Ms. Elaine Reed, manager of the Data Processing Department, received a performance report for the year ending December 31, 19x1, shown on the previous page. How good was Ms. Reed's performance? Criticize the performance report as part of your answer.

Answers to Self-Test

1. c	3. a	5. c	7. b	9. b
2. b	4. d	6. a	8. c	10. d

CHAPTER 26

The Budgeting Process

The budgetary control process includes cost planning and cost control. In this chapter the focus is on cost planning. We outline the principles of budgeting, which deal with long-term and short-term goals, human responsibilities, housekeeping, and follow-up. Using these principles along with a number of cost accounting tools explained earlier in the book, we describe the preparation of period budgets, the master budget, and the cash budget. After studying this chapter, you should be able to meet the learning objectives listed on the left.

What Is a Budget and What Does It Look Like?

Someone who has never worked with a budget may consider such a document a cure-all for the financial problems of an enterprise because almost everyone uses the word *budget* in this context. However, a budget is simply a plan, and specific management actions are needed to make it a reality. Recall discussions on television or in the newspapers regarding our federal budget. We have all heard about deficit spending by the U.S. government, and the cure for this deficit spending is to "balance the budget." This statement is misleading because the spending processes alone cannot be used to balance the budget. To reduce or reverse the current deficit, one must ensure that revenues are greater than expenditures. But there is only one way to balance the budget and that is by preparing a document so that the revenues equal expenditures.

A **budget** is a financial document created before anticipated transactions occur. It is often called a financial plan of action. The key to understanding the term budget is to realize that it is nothing more than a piece of paper on which financial data are printed. These data have been projected for a series of events that have yet to occur. It is a forecast of future financial transactions.

A budget can have an infinite number of shapes and forms. The structure depends on what is being budgeted, the size of the organization, the degree to which the budgeting process is integrated into the financial structure of the enterprise, and the preparer's background. Unlike the formal income statement or the balance sheet, a budget does not have a standard form that can be memorized. A budget can be as simple as the projected sales

OBJECTIVE 1
*Describe the
structure and
contents of a
budget*

and costs of a corner soft drink stand or as complicated as the financial projections of General Motors Corporation.

A budget should present information in an orderly manner so that its purpose is communicated to the user. Too much information clouds the meaning and accuracy of the data. Too little information may result in overspending because the reader did not understand the limits suggested by the document. A budget need not contain both revenue and expense components, nor does it have to be balanced. A materials purchase/usage budget, for example, contains only projected expenditures for raw materials and parts. A budget can also be made up *entirely* of nondollar data, such as hours, units of product, or number of services.

When preparing a budget, make sure you begin the document with a clearly stated title or heading and the time period under consideration. Label the budget's components, and list the unit and financial data in an orderly manner. The actual format of the budget is developed by the budget preparer. A company may have developed its own format for budgets used on a regular basis. But if a new product or service needs budget information to support its value to the company, the document need not follow other budget structures or formats. The only underlying concept that must be followed is that the information contained in the budget should be as accurate and as meaningful to the recipient as possible.

Exhibit 26-1 contains two simple budgets prepared for diverse purposes. Example 1 is the revenues and expenditures budget of the Boosters Club for the homecoming football game of the State University Knights. Example 2 contains projections of hotel occupancy for the Down Home Resort. Note that in Example 2, the budget contains no dollar information and is not balanced. These examples are for illustrative purposes only and should not be considered official guidelines for budget preparation.

Basic Principles of Budgeting

OBJECTIVE 2
*Identify the
five groups
of budgeting
principles, and
explain the
principles in each
group*

The preparation of an organization's budget is important to its success. First, it forces management to look ahead and plan in terms of both long-term and short-term goals and events. Second, it requires that the whole management team, from the lowest-level supervisor to the chairman of the board of directors, work together to make and carry out the yearly plans. Finally, by comparing the budget with actual results, it is possible to review performance at all levels of management. The principles of effective budgeting are summarized in Table 26-1. Each group of principles will be explained further to show how closely connected they are to the whole budgeting process.

Long-Range Goals Principles

Annual operating plans cannot be made unless those responsible for preparing the budget know the direction that top management expects

Exhibit 26-1. Examples of Budgets

Example 1

State University Knights
Boosters Club
Revenue and Expenditure Budget
Homecoming Activities—19x9

Budgeted Revenues		
Football Concession Sales	$22,500	
Homecoming Dance Tickets		
1,200 at $20	24,000	
Parking Fees	425	
Total Budgeted Revenues		$46,925
Budgeted Expenditures		
Dance Music Group	$ 8,500	
Hall Rental	2,000	
Refreshments	3,600	
Printing Costs	1,450	
Concession Purchases	12,200	
Clean-up Costs	4,720	
Miscellaneous	800	
Total Budgeted Expenditures		33,270
Excess of Revenues Over Expenditures		$13,655

Example 2

Down Home Resort
Room Occupancy Budget
For the Year Ending December 31, 19x7

	Projected Occupancy							
	Singles (50)		Doubles (80)		Mini Suites (10)		Luxury Suites (6)	
Month	Rooms	%	Rooms	%	Rooms	%	Rooms	%
January	20	40.0	30	37.5	2	20.0	1	16.7
February	24	48.0	36	45.0	3	30.0	1	16.7
March	28	56.0	42	52.5	4	40.0	2	33.3
April	32	64.0	50	62.5	5	50.0	2	33.3
May	44	88.0	60	75.0	6	60.0	2	33.3
June	46	92.0	74	92.5	7	70.0	3	50.0
July	50	100.0	78	97.5	9	90.0	4	66.7
August	50	100.0	80	100.0	10	100.0	5	83.3
September	48	96.0	78	97.5	10	100.0	6	100.0
October	34	68.0	60	75.0	8	80.0	5	83.3
November	30	60.0	46	57.5	2	20.0	3	50.0
December	34	68.0	50	62.5	4	40.0	4	66.7

Table 26-1. Principles of Effective Budgeting

Group A: Long-Range Goals Principles

1. Develop long-range goals for the enterprise.
2. Convert the long-range goals into statements about plans for product lines or services offered and associated profit plans in broad quantitative terms.

Group B: Short-Range Goals and Strategies Principles

3. Restate the long-range plan in terms of short-range plans for product lines or services available and a detailed profit plan.
4. Prepare a set of budget development plans and a specific timetable for the whole period.

Group C: Human Responsibilities and Interaction Principles

5. Identify the budget director and staff.
6. Identify all participants involved in the budget development process.
7. Practice participative budgeting.
8. Obtain the full support of top management and communicate this support to budget participants.
9. Practice full communications during the entire budgeting process.

Group D: Budget Housekeeping Principles

10. Practice realism in the preparation of budgets.
11. Require that all deadlines be met.
12. Use flexible application procedures.

Group E: Follow-Up Principles

13. Maintain a continuous budgeting process and monitor the budget throughout the period.
14. Develop a system of periodic performance reports that are linked to assigned responsibilities.
15. Review problem areas before further planning takes place.

for the organization. Long-range goals must be set by top management. Statements about the expected quality of products or services and about growth rates and percentage-of-market targets are among the long-range goals. Economic and industry forecasts, employee-management relationships, and the structure and role of management in leading the organization also bear on these goals.

It is necessary to name those responsible for achieving the long-term goals and to set actual targets and expected timetables. For example, assume that Kinlin Corporation has, as one of its long-term goals, the control of 15 percent of its product's market. At present the company holds only 4 percent of the market. The company's long-term goals may state that the vice president of marketing is to develop plans and strategies so that the company controls 10 percent of the market in five years and increases its share to 15 percent by the end of ten years.

Once all of the organization's goals have been developed, they should be compiled in a total long-range plan. This plan should state a broad range of targets and goals and give direction in trying to reach them. Specific statements about long-term goals, then, are the basis for preparing the annual budget.

Short-Range Goals and Strategies Principles

Using long-range goals, management prepares yearly operating plans and targets. The short-range plan or budget involves every part of the enterprise and is much more detailed than the long-range goals. First, the long-range goals must be restated in terms of what should be accomplished during the year. Decisions must be made about sales and profit targets by product or service line, personnel needs and expected changes, and plans for introducing new products or services. Budget statements must also cover materials and supplies needs; labor needs; forecasts of overhead costs such as electric power, property taxes, and insurance; and all capital expenditures such as new buildings, machinery, and equipment. These short-range targets and goals form the organization's operating budget for the year.

Once the short-range goals are set by management, the controller or budget director takes charge of preparing the budget. This person designs a complete set of budget development plans and a timetable with deadlines for all levels and parts of the year's operating plan. Specific people must be named to carry out each part of the budget's development and their responsibilities, targets, and deadlines clearly described.

The last step in the budget's development is to clearly communicate the plan to the participants. Each of the participants in the budgeting process has another job in the organization. The production supervisor, for instance, is most interested in what is happening on the production floor. Thinking about the next year's activities does not help to meet the current month's targets. It is the budget director's responsibility to organize all of the budget information, and a key part of that process is making sure each participant knows what he or she is expected to do and when.

Human Responsibilities and Interaction Principles

Budgeting success or failure is, in large part, determined by how well the human aspects are handled. From top management down through the organization, *all* appropriate people must take part actively and honestly. To get this kind of cooperation, each person must realize that he or she is important to the process.

Choosing a budget director (and staff, if necessary) is very important to an effective budgeting system. This person must be able to communicate well with the people both above and below in the organization's hierarchy. Top management gives the budget targets and organizational goals to the budget director. This person in turn assigns those targets and goals to managers at various levels. The managers then try to put into operation the goals and targets that have been assigned to them.

Problem areas found by the managers are communicated to the budget director, who analyzes and passes the information on to top management. The targets and goals are then reassessed, restructured, and passed back to the budget director, and the process begins all over again. The budget director acts as an information-gathering center and clearing house for the budgeting process.

All participants in the budget development process should be identified and told early of their responsibilities. The identification process begins with high-level managers. These people must then choose managers under their supervision who will actually prepare the data. At the lower levels, the organization's main activities take place, whether they are production, sales, health care, or education. From these managers, the information must flow through all the supervisory levels back to top management. Each one of these people plays a part in developing the budget and putting it to work. It is the budget director's job to coordinate all the different budgeting activities.

Participative budgeting means that all levels of personnel take part in the budgeting process in a meaningful, active way. If every manager has significant input into the goals and expectations of his or her unit, personal motivation enters the budgeting process. This sort of interaction and cooperation is the basis of participative budgeting.

Top management's role is also very important to the budgeting process. If targets and goals are simply dictated and sent down for implementation, participative budgeting is not being practiced. Such dictated targets are often hard to attain and do not motivate lower-level managers to try to reach them. Similarly, if top management lets the budget director handle everything, others are likely to feel that budgeting has a low priority and may not take it seriously. To have an effective budgeting program, top management must communicate its support and allow the managers to take part in a meaningful way. If this happens, the principle of practicing full communication has also been followed.

Budget Housekeeping Principles

In terms of "housekeeping," the budget process depends heavily on three things. First, a realistic approach must be taken by the participants. Second, all deadlines must be met. Third, the organization must use flexible application procedures.

Realism is a two-way street. Top management must first suggest realistic targets and goals. Then each manager must provide realistic information and not place departmental goals ahead of the goals of the whole organization. Inflated expenditure plans or deflated sales targets in one or two cases may make life easier for a manager's unit. However, they can cause the entire budget to be inaccurate and hard to use as a guide and control mechanism for the organization as a whole.

Budget preparation depends on the timely cooperation of many people. If one or two people ignore a deadline for submitting information, the budget will not be ready on time. Top management should communicate the importance of the timetable to all participants and should review timely budget data submission as part of each manager's performance evaluation.

Budgets are important guides to the actions of management. However, they should always be treated as "guides" and not as "absolute truths." Remember that budgets are prepared almost a year in advance of the actual operating cycle. During that time, unexpected changes may take place. A manager cannot simply ignore these changes just because they were not a part of the original budget. Instead, a means of dealing with revenue and expenditure changes should be worked out as part of budget implementation. A procedure for notifying the budget director of a change and receiving approval for it resolves the matter without disrupting performance.

Follow-Up Principles

Budget follow-up and data feedback are really part of the control aspect of budgetary control and will be explained further in Chapter 27. The follow-up principles play an important role in budgeting. Since we are dealing with projections and estimates as the budget is being developed, it is important that the budget be continuously checked and corrected. If a budget is in error, it makes more sense to correct the error than to work with an inaccurate guide.

Organizational or departmental expectations can also be unrealistic. Such problems are found when performance reports are used to compare actual results with budgeted or planned operating results. These reports are the backbone of the responsibility accounting system presented in Chapter 25. The budgeting cycle is complete when problems are identified in the performance evaluation of the last budgeting cycle and are analyzed and restructured to become targets or goals of the next budgeting cycle.

The Need for Budgetary Control

OBJECTIVE 3
Define the concept of budgetary control

Planning and control of costs and operations are the keys to good management. The process of (1) developing plans for a company's expected operations and (2) controlling operations to help carry out those plans is known as **budgetary control**. In Chapter 25, you studied cost behavior patterns and cost-volume-profit analysis, which are two of the tools used in developing a company's annual budget and profit goals. Profit planning is important to all successful profit-oriented companies as part of the budgeting program. In this chapter we will deal mainly with the planning element.

A business does not benefit from budgetary control by operating haphazardly. The company must first set quantitative goals, define the roles of individuals, and set intermediate operating targets. Short-term or one-year plans are generally formulated in a set of period budgets (also known as detailed operating budgets). A **period budget** is a forecast of a year's operating results for a segment or function of a company. It is a quantitative expression of planned activities. Period budgets are prepared by the whole management team. They require timely information and careful coordination. This process converts unit sales and production forecasts into revenue and cost estimates for each of the many operating segments of the company. Everyone involved in the budgeting process should take care to make these forecasts as accurate and realistic as possible.

Period budget preparation relies heavily on several management accounting tools already discussed. Knowledge of cost behavior patterns and the use of cost-volume-profit analyses help management project departmental or product-line revenue and cost amounts. Profit planning, in itself, is possible only after all cost behavior patterns have been identified. Responsibility accounting, with its network of managerial responsibilities and information flows, provides a blueprint for the structure of the budget-data gathering process. These tools, together with the concepts of cost allocation and cost accumulation, provide the foundation for preparing an organization's budget.

The Master Budget

OBJECTIVE 4
Identify the components of a master budget, and describe how they relate to each other

A **master budget** is a combined set of departmental or functional period budgets that have been consolidated into forecasted financial statements for the whole company. Each of the separate budgets gives the projected costs and revenues for that part of the company. When combined, these budgets show all anticipated transactions of the company for a future accounting period. With this information, the anticipated results of the company's operations can be put together with the beginning general ledger balances to prepare forecasted statements of the company's net income and financial position.

Three steps lead up to the completed master budget. (1) The period budgets are prepared. (2) The forecasted income statement is prepared. (3) The forecasted balance sheet is prepared. After describing each of these components and illustrating the types of period budgets, we will explain how the budgets are prepared.

Detailed Period Budgets

Period budgets are generally prepared for each departmental or functional cost and revenue producing segment of the company. These budgets consist of the following: (1) sales budget (in units and dollars), (2) selling expense budget, (3) production budget (in units), (4) materials purchase/usage budget (in units and dollars), (5) labor budget (in hours and dollars), (6) factory overhead budget, (7) general and administrative (G & A) expense budget, and (8) capital expenditures budget. Although these budgets are referred to by functional area, data are usually developed and transmitted to the budget director in departmental form and consolidated into the functional format described.

Sales Budget. The unit sales forecast is the starting point of the budgeting process and probably the most critical component. The sales target is developed by top management with input from the marketing and production areas. Since the entire cost portion of the budget is developed from this forecast, you can see how important it is to the master budget.

A **sales budget** is a detailed plan, expressed in both units and dollars, that identifies the expected product (or service) sales for a future period. A sales budget for the Erika Piano Company is shown in Exhibit 26-2. Sales information for all five piano models is stated in both units and dollar revenue amounts for the year under review. In addition, unit and dollar information for the current year is shown for comparison. Once the unit sales target has been agreed upon, all of the other period budgets can be prepared.

Exhibit 26-2. Sales Budget

Erika Piano Company
Sales Budget
For the Year Ending December 31, 19x3

Unit Forecast:

	Year Ended 12/31/x2		Year Ending 12/31/x3	
	Units	Selling Price	Units	Selling Price
Piano Models:				
Model J	70	$1,800	75	$1,840
Model O	40	1,940	50	1,990
Model N	65	2,025	60	2,125
Model E	100	3,400	120	3,600
Model S	58	3,900	50	4,200

Projected Total Revenue:

	Actual Results for Year Ended 12/31/x2	Percent of Total Sales	Budget for Year Ending 12/31/x3	Percent of Total Sales
Piano Models:				
Model J	$126,000	13.98%	$ 138,000	13.70%
Model O	77,600	8.61%	99,500	9.88%
Model N	131,625	14.60%	127,500	12.66%
Model E	340,000	37.72%	432,000	42.90%
Model S	226,200	25.09%	210,000	20.85%
Totals	$901,425	100.00%	$1,007,000	100.00%*

* Rounding error

Selling Expense Budget. The **selling expense budget** is a schedule developed from information on the sales budget and from the sales staff. It details all anticipated expenses related to the selling function of the business for a future period of time. Selling expenses may be variable, such as sales commissions and automobile expenses, or they may be fixed costs such as advertising expenses and supervisory salaries. The selling expense budget is the responsibility of the sales department and can be prepared as soon as the sales budget has been completed. The selling expense budget for the Erika Piano Company is shown in Exhibit 26-3. Two major cost categories are used: (1) Selling Commissions, and (2) Travel, Brochures, and Other Selling Support Materials. Every company will have its own approach to developing the selling expense budget, so understand that these cost categories are probably unique to the Erika Piano Company.

Exhibit 26-3. Selling Expense Budget

Erika Piano Company
Selling Expense Budget
For the Year Ending December 31, 19x3

	Sales Regions				
	Western Region	Southern Region	Midwestern Region	Eastern Region	Totals
Selling Commissions:					
Piano Models:					
Model J	$ 1,350	$ 1,890	$ 1,430	$ 1,890	$ 6,560
Model O	1,450	1,420	1,360	1,130	5,360
Model N	1,730	1,810	1,720	1,830	7,090
Model E	4,380	4,580	5,700	4,910	19,570
Model S	5,040	3,120	3,210	3,540	14,910
Totals	$13,950	$12,820	$13,420	$13,300	$53,490
Travel, Brochures, and Other **Selling Support Materials:**					
Piano Models:					
Model J	$ 730	$ 690	$ 710	$ 780	$ 2,910
Model O	860	790	870	890	3,410
Model N	710	740	670	760	2,880
Model E	1,100	1,120	1,200	1,240	4,660
Model S	1,300	1,350	1,320	1,250	5,220
Totals	$ 4,700	$ 4,690	$ 4,770	$ 4,920	$19,080
Total Selling Expense Budget	$18,650	$17,510	$18,190	$18,220	$72,570

Production Budget. Once the sales target in units has been established, the units needed from the production area (production budget) can be computed. The **production budget** is a detailed schedule that identifies the products or services that must be produced or provided to meet budgeted sales and inventory needs. Management must first determine if the finished goods inventory level should remain the same or be increased or decreased. The unit sales forecast along with the desired changes in finished goods inventory are then used to determine the unit production schedule. Exhibit 26-4 illustrates the production budget for the Erika Piano Company. In addition to quarterly and annual produc-

Exhibit 26-4. Production Budget

Erika Piano Company
Production Budget
For the Year Ending December 31, 19x3

Production Schedule:

	Year Ending 12/31/x3				
	First Quarter	Second Quarter	Third Quarter	Fourth Quarter	Totals
Piano Models:					
Model J	20	16	22	17	75
Model O	12	10	15	13	50
Model N	18	14	12	16	60
Model E	35	25	20	40	120
Model S	5	15	20	10	50
Totals	90	80	89	96	355

Detailed Production Schedule for First Quarter:

	January 19x3	February 19x3	March 19x3	Total Production for Quarter
Piano Models:				
Model J	6	9	5	20
Model O	4	6	2	12
Model N	9	5	4	18
Model E	15	8	12	35
Model S	2	2	1	5
Totals	36	30	24	90

tion schedules, a detailed view of the production schedules for the first three months of the budgeted year are shown. For illustrative purposes only, we assumed that there were no anticipated changes in inventory levels of the five piano models.

Materials Purchase/Usage Budget. The materials purchase and usage needs can be prepared as separate schedules or on the same document. We prefer to group these two categories in the same document. A **materials purchase/usage budget** is a detailed plan that identifies the number and timing of raw materials and parts to be purchased to meet production demands. (A merchandise purchasing budget is a similar document used by retail businesses.) Materials usage is determined by the production budget and the anticipated changes in materials inventory levels. This information will generate the units of materials to be purchased. Multiplying the number of units to be purchased by the estimated purchase prices for those materials will yield the materials purchase budget. An example of a materials purchase/usage budget is shown in the illustrative problem at the end of this section.

Labor Budget. The **labor budget** is a detailed schedule that identifies the labor needs for a future period and the labor costs associated with those needs. As with the materials purchase/usage budget, the forecasted labor hours and dollars can be structured in two separate schedules or in one comprehensive schedule. Labor hours can be determined as soon as the unit production budget has been set. Labor hours needed per unit are multiplied by the anticipated units of production to calculate the labor hour requirements for the budget period. These labor hours, when multiplied by the various hourly labor rates, yield the labor dollar budget. As shown for the Erika Piano Company in Exhibit 26-5, quarterly and annual data can be summarized in the labor budget. In addition, management of this company prefers to have all labor shown in its labor budget so the indirect labor costs are included here as well as in the factory overhead budget.

Factory Overhead Budget. The **factory overhead budget** is a detailed schedule of anticipated manufacturing costs, other than direct materials and direct labor costs, that must be incurred to meet the production expectations of a future period. The budget for factory overhead has two purposes: (1) to integrate the overhead cost budgets developed by production and service department managers; and (2) by accumulating this information, to compute factory overhead rates for the forthcoming accounting period.

The Erika Piano Company's factory overhead budget is illustrated in Exhibit 26-6. Again, it shows quarterly as well as annual forecasts of these factory overhead costs. Data from each of the three assembly operations, Sound System Assembly, Wood Cabinet Assembly, and Total Piano Assembly, were grouped together within the budget shown. A more detailed breakdown of this information may be needed to help control costs and can be supplied later.

Exhibit 26-5. Labor Budget

Erika Piano Company
Labor Budget
For the Year Ending December 31, 19x3

Direct Labor Hours and Rate Schedule:

	Sound System Assembly		Wood Cabinet Assembly		Total Piano Assembly	
	Hours per Unit	Rate	Hours per Unit	Rate	Hours per Unit	Rate
Piano Models:						
Model J	5.6	$10.30	5.8	$11.50	12.8	$12.40
Model O	6.2	10.30	6.0	11.50	13.6	12.40
Model N	6.6	10.30	6.2	11.50	14.4	12.40
Model E	8.2	10.30	7.4	11.50	22.4	12.40
Model S	9.4	10.30	9.2	11.50	28.6	12.40

Direct Labor Budget:

Year Ending 12/31/x3

	First Quarter	Second Quarter	Third Quarter	Fourth Quarter	Total Direct Labor Budget
Piano Models:*					
Model J	$ 5,662	$ 4,530	$ 6,228	$ 4,813	$ 21,233
Model O	3,618	3,015	4,522	3,919	15,074
Model N	5,721	4,450	3,814	5,085	19,070
Model E	15,656	11,183	8,946	17,893	53,678
Model S	2,786	8,359	11,145	5,573	27,863
Totals	$33,443	$31,537	$34,655	$37,283	$136,918
Budgeted Indirect Labor	15,240	16,220	16,180	17,260	64,900
Total Labor Budget	$48,683	$47,757	$50,835	$54,543	$201,818

*Amounts are rounded

General and Administrative Expense Budget. A **general and administrative (G & A) expense budget** is a detailed plan of operating expenses, other than those of the manufacturing and selling functions,
that are needed to support the overall operations of the business for a
future period of time. In preparing a master budget, general and admin-

Exhibit 26-6. Factory Overhead Budget

Erika Piano Company
Factory Overhead Budget
For the Year Ending December 31, 19x3

	First Quarter	Second Quarter	Third Quarter	Fourth Quarter	Totals
Factory Overhead Costs:					
Indirect Materials	$ 3,560	$ 3,850	$ 3,900	$ 4,000	$ 15,310
Indirect Labor	15,240	16,220	16,180	17,260	64,900
Assembly Supplies	1,700	1,750	1,800	1,850	7,100
Employee Benefits	19,474	19,102	20,334	21,817	80,727
Factory Supervision	15,000	15,000	15,000	15,000	60,000
Electricity Costs	1,980	2,100	2,150	2,200	8,430
Water Expense	870	900	920	950	3,640
Small Tools	1,200	1,200	1,200	1,200	4,800
Property Taxes	1,000	1,000	1,000	1,000	4,000
Insurance					
Fire	490	490	490	490	1,960
Liability	640	640	640	640	2,560
Depreciation, Machinery	3,100	3,100	3,100	3,100	12,400
Factory Rent	6,000	6,000	6,000	6,000	24,000
Repairs and Maintenance	2,800	2,900	3,000	3,000	11,700
Miscellaneous	500	500	500	500	2,000
Totals	$73,554	$74,752	$76,214	$79,007	$303,527

istrative expenses must be projected to provide information included in the cash budget. The G & A expense budget also serves as a means of controlling these costs. Most elements of this budget are fixed costs.

Capital Expenditures Budget. A **capital expenditures budget** is a detailed plan outlining the amount and timing of anticipated capital expenditures for a future period. Determining the capital facility needs and obtaining investment resources for such expenditures are very complex management accounting areas. Deciding what to buy or build and establishing the criteria for decisions regarding return on investment are topics covered briefly in Chapter 28 but are explored fully in an advanced management accounting course. For our purposes, information regarding capital facility investment decisions influence the cash budget as well as the interest expense on the forecasted income statement and the plant and equipment account balances on the forecasted balance sheet. Therefore, these decisions must be anticipated and integrated into the master budget.

Relationships Among the Period Budgets

The period budgets are closely related to each other. The sales unit forecast is the first step in the budgeting process. Following the sales unit forecast, the selling expense budget can be prepared. The production budget also depends on the sales forecast. Direct materials purchase/usage requirements are related to the production forecast. The production budget also leads to the labor and factory overhead budgets. In most cases, plans for general and administrative expenses and capital expenditures are made by top management. However, much of this information may be gathered at the departmental level and included in the period budgets. The key point to remember is that the whole budgeting process begins with the sales unit forecast. Figure 26-1 shows how the various period budgets set the stage for determining the effects of planned operations on the company's financial position.

Figure 26-1. Preparation of Master Budget

Forecasted Income Statement

Once the period budgets have been prepared, the controller or the budget director can begin to compile the information. He or she prepares a cost of goods sold forecast from data in the materials, labor, and factory overhead budgets. Revenue information is figured from the unit sales budget. Using the expected revenue and cost of goods sold data, and adding the information from the selling expense and general and administrative expense budgets, the controller can prepare the forecasted income statement. This step is also shown in Figure 26-1.

Financial Position Forecast

The last step in the master budget process is to prepare a financial position forecast or projected balance sheet for the company, assuming that planned activities actually take place. As Figure 26-1 shows, all budget data are used in this process. The controller prepares a cash flow forecast or cash budget from all planned transactions requiring cash inflow or expenditure. A more detailed explanation of cash budgeting follows later in this chapter. In preparing the forecasted statement of financial position, the budget director must know the projected cash balance and must have determined the net income and amount of capital expenditures. All of the expected transactions shown in the period budgets must be classified and charged to the different general ledger accounts. The projected financial statements are the end product of the budgeting process. At this point, management must decide whether to accept the proposed master budget, as well as the planned operating results, or ask the budget director to change the plans and do parts of the budget over again.

Budget Implementation

Budget implementation is the responsibility of the budget director. Two important things determine the success of this process. The first is proper communication of expectations and targets to all key persons in the company. All persons involved in the operations of the business must know what is expected of them and receive directions on how to reach their goals. Second, and equally important, is support and encouragement by top management. No matter how sophisticated the budgeting process, it will succeed only if middle- and lower-level managers can see that top management is truly interested in the final outcome and willing to reward people for meeting the budget goals.

Illustrative Problem: Budget Preparation

OBJECTIVE 5
Prepare a period budget

Period budget preparation and the make-up of the master budget vary from one company to another. Therefore, it is impossible to cover all procedures found in actual practice. The following illustrative problem will show one approach to preparing period budgets. However, by applying the tools of cost behavior, C-V-P analysis, and responsibility accounting to a particular case, one can prepare any kind of budget. There is also no standard format to use for budget preparation. Your only guidelines are that the budget be clear and understandable and communicate the information to the reader.

Ross Steelworks, Inc. manufactures cans from 4-by-8-foot sheets of steel of different thicknesses. The number of cans produced from each sheet of steel depends on the height and diameter of the cans. During 19x2, the company expects the following sales and unit changes in finished goods inventory:

Can Size	Unit Sales	Unit Change in Finished Goods Inventory
6″ × 3″	1,250,000	150,000 (increase)
8″ × 4″	710,000	8,000 (decrease)

Direct materials requirements for these two products are as follows:

Can Size	Sheet Steel Type	Average Usable Cans per Sheet	Average Usable Lids per Sheet
6″ × 3″	No. 16	90	500
8″ × 4″	No. 22	45	270

Usage is the same over a twelve-month period. On the first day of each operating quarter, 25 percent of the year's direct materials requirements will be purchased, starting January 1. Assume no changes in the balances of the Materials Inventory account and the Work in Process Inventory account.

Required

Prepare a materials purchase/usage budget for 19x2. Expected prices for the year are $21.00 per sheet for No. 16 type of steel and $23.40 for No. 22.

Solution

Before preparing the required budget, we must compute the total number of cans (including lids for tops and bottoms) to be produced per sheet of steel. The following relationships were supplied by the Engineering Department.

6″ × 3″ can: 450 cans (plus 900 lids) require 6.8 sheets of steel, so you can manufacture 66.176 cans and necessary lids per sheet of steel

8″ × 4″ can: 135 cans (plus 270 lids) require 4 sheets of steel, so you can manufacture 33.75 cans and necessary lids per sheet of steel

---

Ross Steelworks, Inc.
Materials Purchase/Usage Budget
For the Year Ending December 31, 19x2

Materials Usage Projections:

	Number of Cans
6″ × 3″ Can	
Expected Sales	1,250,000
Plus increase in inventory	150,000
Total to be produced	1,400,000

No. 16 sheets to be used:

$$\frac{\text{Units to be produced}}{\text{Cans per sheet}} = \frac{1,400,000 \text{ cans}}{66.176 \text{ cans/sheet}} = 21,155.71 \text{ or } 21,156 \text{ sheets}$$

	Number of Cans
8″ × 4″ Can	
Expected Sales	710,000
Less decrease in inventory	8,000
Total to be produced	702,000

No. 22 sheets to be used:

$$\frac{\text{Units to be produced}}{\text{Cans per sheet}} = \frac{702,000 \text{ cans}}{33.75 \text{ cans/sheet}} = 20,800 \text{ sheets}$$

Materials to be Purchased:

Sheet Steel Type	Unit Cost/Sheet	Sheets to Be Purchased Quarterly*	Total Quarterly Purchase Cost	Annual Cost of Purchases
No. 16	$21.00	5,289	$111,069	$444,276
No. 22	23.40	5,200	121,680	486,720
Total Purchases			$232,749	$930,996

* Purchases of one-fourth annual usage on January 1, April 1, July 1, October 1

Cash Budgeting

Cash flow is one of the most important aspects of a company's operating cycle. Within the master budget preparation, the cash budget is developed after all period budgets are final and the forecasted income

OBJECTIVE 6
*Describe the
purpose and
make-up of a
cash budget*

statement is complete. A **cash budget** (or **cash flow forecast**) is a projection of the cash receipts and cash payments for a future period of time. It sums up the cash flow results of planned transactions in all phases of a master budget. Generally, it shows the company's projected ending cash balance and the cash position for each month of the year. Thus, periods of high and low cash availability can be anticipated. Very large cash balances mean that funds may not have been used to earn the best possible rate of return. Low cash reserves may indicate that the company will not be able to pay current liabilities. To prevent either of these problems, careful cash planning is necessary.

The cash budget has two main parts—forecasted cash receipts and forecasted cash payments. Sales budgets, cash or credit sales data, and accounts receivable collection data are used to compute the expected cash receipts for the period. Other sources of cash such as the sale of stock, the sale of assets, or loans also enter into cash receipts planning.

Expected cash payments are taken from the different period budgets. The person preparing the cash budget must know how the direct materials, labor, and other goods and services are going to be purchased. That is, are they to be paid for with cash immediately or purchased on account with the cash payment delayed for a period of time? When dealing with accounts payable, it is important to know the company's payment policies. Besides the regular operating expenses, cash is also used for buying equipment and paying off loans and other long-term liabilities. All of this information must be available before an accurate cash budget can be prepared.

Purposes and Nature of Cash Budgeting

The cash budget serves two purposes. First, it shows the ending cash balance, which is needed to complete the projected balance sheet (see Figure 26-1). Second, it highlights periods of excess cash reserves or cash shortages. The first purpose focuses on the role of the cash budget in the master budget preparation cycle. The second purpose reflects its important use as a tool of cash management, which is important to any business. Without cash, a business cannot function. By comparing projected cash receipts and cash payments, the budget director can advise financial executives of the months when the company will need extra short-term financing because of cash shortages. Similarly, the budget director can point out times when excess cash will be available for short-term investments.

A cash budget combines information from several different period budgets. All elements of cash flow, both cash inflows (receipts) and cash outflows (payments) are brought together to show expected cash flows of the company. The cash budget of Neehon Shohkoo, Inc. is shown in Exhibit 26-7. To highlight the first quarter of the year, detailed cash inflows and outflows have been shown for January, February, and March. The remaining nine months of the year have been combined.

The cash budget shown in Exhibit 26-7 is closely related to the parts of the master budget shown in Figure 26-1. Since the master budget

Exhibit 26-7. Typical Cash Budget

Neehon Shohkoo, Inc.
Cash Budget
For the Year Ending December 31, 19x1

	January	February	March	April–December	Totals
Cash Receipts					
Sales—previous month (38%*)	$ 10,773	$ 7,182	$ 10,773	$ 14,364	$ 43,092
Sales—current month (60%*)	11,340	17,010	22,680	368,928	419,958
Total Receipts	$ 22,113	$24,192	$ 33,453	$383,292	$463,050
Cash Payments					
Direct Materials	$ 7,146	$ 7,146	$ 7,622	$ 72,434	$ 94,348
Operating Supplies	237	—	—	710	947
Direct Labor	3,700	3,850	4,220	34,940	46,710
Factory Overhead	3,440	3,480	3,750	32,580	43,250
Selling Expenses	8,585	10,000	11,420	109,870	139,875
General and Administrative					
Expenses	4,500	4,500	4,500	40,500	54,000
Capital Expenditures	4,200	—	7,920	14,780	26,900
Income Taxes	—	—	22,640	—	22,640
Interest Expense	6,000	—	—	8,920	14,920
Total Disbursements	$ 37,808	$28,976	$ 62,072	$314,734	$443,590
Cash Increase (Decrease)	$(15,695)	$ (4,784)	$ (28,619)	$ 68,558	$ 19,460
Beginning Cash Balance	36,275	20,580	15,796	(12,823)	36,275
Ending Cash Balance	$ 20,580	$15,796	$ (12,823)	$ 55,735	$ 55,735

* 2% of sales result in uncollectible accounts

summarizes the expected transactions for a future time period, it also includes expected cash transactions. To prepare the cash budget, then, one must analyze the master budget in terms of cash inflows and outflows. Table 26-2 focuses on the relationships between the master budget and the cash budget and explains how the cash budget for Neehon Shohkoo, Inc., shown in Exhibit 26-7, is created. For the next year, the company expects only cash receipts from sales. Note that 60 percent of all sales are for cash. Thirty-eight percent are credit sales collected in the following month. All of the necessary cash inflow information would come from the sales budget.

Information supporting cash payment forecasts comes from several different sources. Cash used to purchase direct materials and operating supplies is determined from the materials purchase/usage budget. Materials are generally purchased on account. Every company should have a policy about payment on account as part of its cash management. If

Table 26-2. Master Budget and Cash Budget Interrelationships

Elements of the Cash Budget	Sources of the Information
Cash Receipts	
Cash sales	Sales budget (cash sales)
Cash collections of previous sales	Sales budget (credit sales) plus collection record—percent collected in the first month, second month, etc.
Proceeds from sale of assets	Forecasted income statement
Loan proceeds	Previous month's information on cash budget
Cash Payments	
Direct materials	Materials purchase/usage budget
Operating supplies	Factory overhead budget and materials purchase/usage budget
Direct labor	Labor budget
Factory overhead	Factory overhead budget
Selling expenses	Selling expense budget
General and administrative expenses	General and administrative expense budget
Capital expenditures	Capital expenditure budget
Income taxes	Estimated from previous year's income statement and current year's projections
Interest expense	Forecasted income statement
Loan payments	Loan record

Note: Other sources of cash receipts and possible cash payments exist. The above analysis covers only the most common types of cash inflows and outflows.

the company's policy is to pay everything within the discount period, cash flow would take place in ten days, if the terms of the purchase were 2/10, n/30. If, however, the company wants to hold its cash for the maximum time, cash payments would not be made for thirty days. In most cases, labor cash flow, for obvious reasons, is delayed very little. Information from the labor budget is used to support the cash payments for both direct and indirect labor services. Cash payments for all factory overhead other than operating supplies and indirect labor are figured by using the factory overhead budget.

Cash requirements for selling expenses, general and administrative expenses, and capital expenditures are determined from their respective budgets. Again, the timing of the cash exchange is important. Selling expenses such as gasoline purchases and sales brochures may be made on credit, and the actual payment may be postponed for thirty days or more. The same may be true for large capital expenditures.

When preparing a cash budget, one must concentrate on the time of actual cash flow, not the time of the original transaction.

The final two cash payments shown in Exhibit 26-7 are for income taxes and interest expense. Corporations usually make quarterly tax payments that are applied against an estimate of the current year's tax liability. Any excess owed at year end is due on the fifteenth day of the third month following the close of the company's fiscal year. Interest expense payments may be made monthly, quarterly, semiannually, or annually, depending on the terms of the loan agreement.

Once the cash receipts and cash payments have been established, the cash increase or decrease for the period is computed. The resulting increase or decrease is added to the period's beginning cash balance to arrive at the projected cash balance at period end. In the case of Neehon Shohkoo, Inc., the first three months will put a heavy drain on cash reserves, but positive cash flow returns during the last nine months of the year. The company seems to have a favorable cash position for the year, except at the end of March. Depending on cash payment patterns, the company would want to plan on taking out a small loan to cover the cash shortage and protect itself in case a large payment becomes due unexpectedly. On the other hand, a $55,735 balance in cash at year end may be too much extra cash. Therefore, management may want to make plans for investing this money in short-term securities.

Illustrative Problem: Cash Budget Preparation

OBJECTIVE 7
Prepare a cash budget

Worrell Information Processing Company provides word-processing services for its clients. Worrell uses state-of-the-art equipment and employs five keyboard operators, who each average 120 hours of work a month. The following information was developed by the budget officer:

| | Actual—19x1 | | Forecast—19x2 | | |
	November	December	January	February	March
Client Billings (Sales)	$25,000	$35,000	$25,000	$20,000	$40,000
Selling Expenses	4,500	5,000	4,000	4,000	5,000
General and Administrative Expenses	7,500	8,000	8,000	7,000	7,500
Operating Supplies Purchased	2,500	3,500	2,500	2,500	4,000
Processing Overhead	3,200	3,500	3,000	2,500	3,500

The company has a bank loan of $12,000 at a 12 percent annual interest rate. Interest is paid monthly, and $2,000 of the principal of the loan is due on February 2, 19x2. No capital expenditures are anticipated for the first quarter of the coming year. Income taxes for calendar year 19x1 of $4,550 are due and payable on March 15, 19x2. The company's five employees earn $8.50 an hour, and all payroll-related labor benefit costs

are included in processing overhead. For the items included in the preceding chart, assume the following conditions:

Client Billings:	60% are cash sales that are collected during the cur- rent period 30% are collected in the first month following the sale 10% are collected in the second month following the sale
Operating Supplies:	Paid in the month purchased
Selling Expenses, General and Administrative Expenses, and Processing Overhead:	Paid in the month following the cost's incurrence

The beginning cash balance on January 1, 19x2 is expected to be
$13,840.

Required   Prepare a monthly cash budget for the Worrell Information Processing
Company for the three-month period ending March 31, 19x2.

Solution   The three-month cash budget for the Worrell Information Processing
Company is shown in Exhibit 26-8. Details supporting the individual
computations are shown below.

	January	February	March
Cash from Client Billings			
Current month = 60%	$15,000	$12,000	$24,000
Previous month = 30%	10,500	7,500	6,000
Month before last = 10%	2,500	3,500	2,500
	$28,000	$23,000	$32,500
Operating Supplies			
All paid in the month purchased	$ 2,500	$ 2,500	$ 4,000
Direct Labor			
5 employees × 120 hours/month × $8.50/hour	5,100	5,100	5,100
Processing Overhead			
Paid in the following month	3,500	3,000	2,500
Selling Expenses			
Paid in the following month	5,000	4,000	4,000
General and Administrative Expenses			
Paid in the following month	8,000	8,000	7,000
Interest Expense			
January and February = 1% of $12,000	120	120	
March = 1% of $10,000			100
Loan Payment	—	2,000	—
Income Tax Payment	—	—	4,550

Exhibit 26-8. Example of a Cash Budget

Worrell Information Processing Company
Monthly Cash Budget
For the Three-Month Period Ending March 31, 19x2

	January	February	March	Totals
Cash Receipts				
Client Billings	$28,000	$23,000	$32,500	$83,500
Cash Payments				
Operating Supplies	$ 2,500	$ 2,500	$ 4,000	$ 9,000
Direct Labor	5,100	5,100	5,100	15,300
Processing Overhead	3,500	3,000	2,500	9,000
Selling Expenses	5,000	4,000	4,000	13,000
General and Administrative				
Expenses	8,000	8,000	7,000	23,000
Interest Expense	120	120	100	340
Loan Payment	—	2,000	—	2,000
Income Tax Payment	—	—	4,550	4,550
Total Disbursements	$24,220	$24,720	$27,250	$76,190
Cash Increase (Decrease)	$ 3,780	$ (1,720)	$ 5,250	$ 7,310
Beginning Cash Balance	13,840	17,620	15,900	13,840
Ending Cash Balance	$17,620	$15,900	$21,150	$21,150

The ending cash balances of $17,620, $15,900, and $21,150 for January, February, and March, 19x2, respectively, appear to be comfortable but not too large for the company.

Chapter Review

Review of Learning Objectives

1. **Describe the structure and contents of a budget.**
   There is no standard form or structure for a budget. A budget's structure depends on what is being budgeted, the size of the organization preparing the budget, the degree to which the budgeting process is integrated into the financial structure of the enterprise, and the amount of training the budget preparer has. A budget should contain enough information in an orderly manner to communicate its purpose to the budget's reader or user. Too much information clouds the meaning and accuracy of the data. Too little information may result in overspending because the reader did not understand the spending limits suggested by the document.

2. **Identify the five groups of budgeting principles, and explain the principles in each group.**

The five groups of budgeting principles are (1) long-range goals principles, (2) short-range goals and strategies principles, (3) human responsibilities and interaction principles, (4) budget housekeeping principles, and (5) follow-up principles. Every organization needs to set long-range goals and convert them into plans for product line or service offerings. Short-range goals and strategies must be restated in terms of the annual product line or service offerings and associated profit plans. The budget development plans and timetable must also be set up. The human side includes identifying a budget director, staff, and participants. These people must be informed of their duties and responsibilities. It is essential to practice participative budgeting, obtain the full support of top management, and make sure of full and open communication among all participants. Being realistic, requiring that all deadlines be met, and using flexible application procedures are the housekeeping principles of budgeting. Finally, budget follow-up includes maintaining a continuous budgeting process and using a system of period reports to measure performance of the operating segments. Problems are identified for analysis and inclusion in the next period's planning activities.

3. **Define the concept of budgetary control.**

The budgetary control process consists of the cost planning function and the cost control function. Cost planning and control are key functions leading to effective management. Budgetary control is the total process of (1) developing plans for a company's expected operations and (2) controlling operations to help carry out those plans.

4. **Identify the components of a master budget, and describe how they relate to each other.**

A master budget is a combined set of departmental or functional period budgets that have been consolidated into forecasted financial statements for the whole company. First the detailed operating or period budgets are prepared. These are the sales budget, selling expense budget, production budget, materials purchase/usage budget, labor budget, factory overhead budget, general and administrative expenses budget, and capital expenditures budget. The selling expense budget and the production budget are computed from the sales budget data. Materials purchase/ usage, labor, and factory overhead budgets arise from the production budget. Materials purchases can be determined only after materials use is known. General and administrative expenses and proposed capital expenditures are determined by top management. Once these budgets have been prepared, a forecasted income statement, a forecasted cash flow statement (cash budget), and a forecasted balance sheet can be prepared.

5. **Prepare a period budget.**

A period budget, also known as an operating budget, is a forecast of a year's operating results for a segment of a company. It is a quantitative expression of planned activities. For examples of period budgets, see the exhibits and illustrative problems on pages 1099 through 1105. The period budgeting process converts unit sales and production forecasts into revenue and cost estimates for each of the many operating segments of the company.

6. **Describe the purpose and make-up of a cash budget.**

The cash budget's purposes are (1) to disclose the firm's projected ending cash balance and (2) to show the cash position for each month of the year so that periods of cash excesses or shortages can be anticipated. Cash management is critical to the success of an organization, and the cash budget is a major tool used in that process. The cash budget begins with the projection of all expected sources of cash (cash receipts). Next all expected cash disbursements or payments are found by analyzing all other period budgets within the master budget. The difference between these two totals is the cash increase or decrease anticipated for the period. This total combined with the period's beginning cash balance yields the ending cash balance.

7. **Prepare a cash budget.**

A cash budget or cash flow forecast is a projection of the cash receipts and payments for a future period of time. It summarizes the cash results of planned transactions in all parts of a master budget. For an example, see Exhibit 26-7.

Review of Concepts and Terminology

The following concepts and terms were introduced in this chapter:

(L.O. 1) **Budget:** A financial document created before anticipated transactions occur. (Also called a financial plan of action.)

(L.O. 3) **Budgetary control:** The process of (1) developing plans for a company's expected operations, and (2) controlling operations to help carry out those plans.

(L.O. 4) **Capital expenditure budget:** A detailed plan outlining the amount and timing of anticipated capital expenditures for a future period.

(L.O. 6) **Cash budget:** A projection of cash receipts and cash payments for a future period of time. (Also called a cash flow forecast.)

(L.O. 4) **Factory overhead budget:** A detailed schedule of anticipated manufacturing costs, other than direct materials and direct labor costs, that must be incurred to meet the production expectations of a future period.

(L.O. 4) **General and administrative (G & A) expense budget:** A detailed plan of operating expenses, other than those of the manufacturing and selling functions, that are needed to support the overall operations of the business for a future period of time.

(L.O. 4) **Labor budget:** A detailed schedule that identifies the labor needs for a future period and the labor costs associated with those needs.

(L.O. 4) **Master budget:** A combined set of departmental or functional period budgets that have been consolidated into forecasted financial statements for the entire company.

(L.O. 4) **Materials purchase/usage budget:** A detailed plan developed from information on the production budget and anticipated changes in the materials inventory level that identifies the number and timing of raw materials and parts to be purchased to meet production needs. (A merchandise purchasing budget is used by retail businesses.)

(L.O. 2) **Participative budgeting**: A managerial budget preparation process in which all levels of personnel take part creating budgets in a meaningful, active way.

(L.O. 3) **Period budget**: A forecast of a year's operating results for a particular segment or function of a company.

(L.O. 4) **Production budget**: A detailed schedule that identifies the products or services that must be produced or provided to meet budgeted sales and inventory needs.

(L.O. 4) **Sales budget**: A detailed plan, expressed in both units and dollars, that identifies the expected product (or service) sales for a future period.

(L.O. 4) **Selling expense budget**: A schedule developed from information on the sales budget and from the sales staff that details all anticipated expenses related to the selling function of the business for a future period of time.

Self-Test

Test your knowledge of the chapter by choosing the best answer for each question below.

1. A balanced federal budget is created when
   a. several expenditure categories are reduced.
   b. anticipated revenues equal anticipated expenditures.
   c. taxes are raised.
   d. taxes are raised and expenditures are reduced.   *(L.O. 1)*

2. Preparing a set of budget development plans and a specific timetable for the whole period is considered a
   a. long-range goals principle.
   b. budget housekeeping principle.
   c. human responsibilities and interaction principle.
   d. short-range goals and strategies principle.   *(L.O. 2)*

3. "Practice full communications during the entire budgeting process" is considered a
   a. long-range goals principle.
   b. budget housekeeping principle.
   c. human responsibilities and interaction principle.
   d. short-range goals and strategies principle.   *(L.O. 2)*

4. What period budget is considered the starting point in the budgeting process?
   a. Selling expense budget
   b. Sales budget
   c. Production budget
   d. Materials purchase/usage budget   *(L.O. 4)*

5. The amount of materials to be purchased can be estimated immediately after what period budget has been prepared?
   a. Selling expense budget
   b. Sales budget
   c. Production budget
   d. Materials purchase/usage budget   *(L.O. 4)*

6. A detailed schedule of anticipated manufacturing costs, other than direct materials and direct labor costs, that must be incurred to meet the production expectations of a future period is the definition of a
   a. factory overhead budget.
   b. master budget.
   c. capital expenditures budget.
   d. general and administrative expense budget. *(L.O. 4)*

7. The cash budget must be prepared before which of the following documents can be developed?
   a. Forecasted income statement
   b. Capital expenditures budget
   c. Sales budget
   d. Forecasted statement of financial position *(L.O. 4)*

8. The sales budget for the Greenmeadow Corporation indicates that 12,500 units of product ACQ and 33,100 units of product DAF are expected to be sold in October. Product ACQ sells for $22.40 while DAF's selling price is $32.00. Sales personnel receive a 6 percent commission on sales of ACQ and 8 percent on DAF sales. How much anticipated sales commissions are budgeted for the month?
   a. $84,736   c. $106,276
   b. $101,536   d. $92,436 *(L.O. 5)*

9. Assume that Bean Enterprises uses three gallons of material 1A, two gallons of material 3E, five gallons of material 6Q, and ten gallons of material 8H to make each twenty-gallon barrel of plant food. Expected costs per gallon are as follows: 1A, $2.40; 3E, $1.80; 6Q, $10.50; and 8H, $3.30. The production budget indicates that 12,400 barrels will be produced in April, 10,800 barrels in May, and 9,800 barrels in June. Materials are purchased one month ahead of production. What is the total dollar value of budgeted materials purchases in April?
   a. $549,040   c. $1,194,120
   b. $449,620   d. $1,040,040 *(L.O. 5)*

10. Bandy Company had sales on account of $134,000 in July, $226,000 in August, and $188,000 in September. Collection experience indicates that 60 percent of credit sales are collected in the month after the sale, 36 percent in the second month after the sale, and 4 percent are uncollectible. How much cash was received from sales on account in September?
    a. $183,840   c. $194,160
    b. $188,000   d. $226,000 *(L.O. 7)*

Answers to Self-Test are at the end of this chapter.

Review Problem
Forecasted Income Statement

(L.O. 5) Keith Bryant is president of Bryant Economic Forecasting Services, Inc. Last year's income statement for the company follows.

Bryant Economic Forecasting Services, Inc.
Income Statement
For the Year Ending December 31, 19x0

Revenues		
Consulting Fees	$246,500	
Special Forecasts	137,800	
Total Revenues		$384,300
Operating Expenses		
Economic Information Service Costs	$111,400	
Outside Economists' Fees	62,100	
Travel Costs	12,800	
Salaries		
Staff	60,000	
Executives	80,000	
Rent, Building	6,400	
Depreciation, Equipment	3,900	
Utilities	1,800	
Supplies	2,100	
Brochure Printing	3,500	
Computer Services	6,700	
Miscellaneous	900	
Total Operating Expenses		351,600
Income Before Taxes		$ 32,700
Federal Income Taxes (34%)		11,118
Net Income After Taxes		$ 21,582

During 19x1, the following changes are anticipated:

a. Consulting fees and special forecasts revenues are both expected to increase by 25 percent.

b. Economic information service costs are scheduled for a 30 percent increase in January, 19x1.

c. Outside economists' fees and travel costs will rise 20 percent.

d. All salaries will be increased by 15 percent.

e. Rent, depreciation, and utility expenses are expected to stay the same throughout next year.

f. Supplies costs will decrease by 10 percent.

g. Brochure printing costs will rise by 40 percent.

h. Computer services costs will double because of expanded services.

i. Miscellaneous expenses should total $1,000 in 19x1.

Required   Prepare the forecasted income statement for 19x1.

Answer to Review Problem

Bryant Economic Forecasting Services, Inc. Forecasted Income Statement For the Year Ending December 31, 19x1		
Revenues		
Consulting Fees ($246,500 × 1.25)	$308,125	
Special Forecasts ($137,800 × 1.25)	172,250	
Total Revenues		$480,375
Operating Expenses		
Economic Information Service Costs		
($111,400 × 1.3)	$144,820	
Outside Economists' Fees ($62,100 × 1.2)	74,520	
Travel Costs ($12,800 × 1.2)	15,360	
Salaries		
Staff ($60,000 × 1.15)	69,000	
Executives ($80,000 × 1.15)	92,000	
Rent, Building	6,400	
Depreciation, Equipment	3,900	
Utilities	1,800	
Supplies ($2,100 × 0.9)	1,890	
Brochure Printing ($3,500 × 1.4)	4,900	
Computer Services ($6,700 × 2)	13,400	
Miscellaneous	1,000	
Total Operating Expenses		428,990
Income Before Taxes		$ 51,385
Federal Income Taxes (34%)		17,471
Net Income After Taxes		$ 33,914

Chapter Assignments

Discussion Questions and Writing Assignments

1. What does a budget look like?
2. Name the three main phases of the budget preparation cycle.
3. Distinguish between long-term plans and yearly operating plans.
4. How does responsibility accounting help in period budget preparation?
5. What are the long-range goals principles of budgeting?
6. One of the budgeting principles listed was "Restate the long-range plan in terms of short-range plans for product lines or services available and a detailed profit plan." What is the purpose of this principle?
7. Why is it necessary to identify all participants in budget development?
8. Describe participative budgeting.

9. State the budget housekeeping principles.
10. Why use a continuous budgeting process?
11. What is the connection between periodic performance reports and responsibility accounting?
12. Describe the concept of budgetary control. Why is it important?
13. What is a period budget?
14. What is a master budget? What is its purpose?
15. Identify and discuss relationships among detailed operating budgets.
16. If someone asked you to describe the contents of a materials purchase/usage budget, how would you respond?
17. Does the labor budget contain projections of both direct labor and indirect labor costs?
18. Why is the preparation of a cash budget or forecasted cash flow statement so important to a company?
19. In the budget preparation cycle, what steps must precede the preparation of the cash budget?
20. How are sales and purchases on account handled when drawing up the cash budget?

Classroom Exercises

Exercise 26-1.
Budgeting
Principles
(L.O. 2)

Long-range goals principles and short-range goals and strategies principles are critical to a successful budgeting system. Assume that you work in the accounting department of a small wholesale warehousing business. The president has just returned from an industry association meeting where he attended a seminar on the values of a budgeting system. He wants to develop a budgeting system and has asked you to direct it.

State the points that you should communicate to the president about the initial development steps of the process. Concentrate on the two sets of principles mentioned above.

Exercise 26-2.
Budgetary Control
(L.O. 3)

You are a new employee of Sacks Laboratories, Inc. and have been assigned to the controller's department. This department employs 25 paraprofessionals (non-degreed people) who fill clerical positions. All are in need of supplemental knowledge in the budgetary control area.

The controller has asked you to team up with another accountant to prepare and present a four-hour seminar on budgetary control to these paraprofessional employees. Your particular assignment is to concentrate on the planning phase of budgetary control. Prepare an outline of the topics and ideas that you would cover in this seminar.

Exercise 26-3.
Master Budget
Components
(L.O. 4)

Snorek Prototype Research, Inc. is in its sixth year of operation. Known for "accomplishing the impossible," the corporation has grown from a moonlighting operation in an engineer's garage to a company employing 120 professionals and 15 staff employees. High-tech prototype design is Snorek's main product.

Two years ago, the financial vice president hired a controller who was instructed to install a complete budgeting system. To date, the budgeting system is composed of the following:

Sales revenue forecast
Cash budget
Capital expenditure budget

The financial vice president has called you (the company's independent CPA) for advice and ideas regarding a "complete" budgeting system.

Prepare a response to your client indicating what is needed to prepare an annual master budget.

**Exercise 26-4.
Production Budget
Preparation**
(L.O. 5)

The Stevens Specialty Door Company's forecast of garage door unit sales for 19x2 is as follows: January, 50,000; February, 40,000; March, 60,000; April, 70,000; May, 60,000; June, 50,000; July, 40,000; August, 50,000; September, 60,000; October, 70,000; November, 80,000; December, 60,000.

The forecast of unit sales for January 19x3 is 50,000. Beginning finished goods inventory on January 1, 19x2 contained 15,000 doors. Company policy states that minimum finished goods inventory is 15,000 units and that the maximum is one-half of the following month's sales. Maximum productive capacity is 65,000 units per month.

Using the information given above, prepare a monthly production budget stating the number of units to be produced. Note that the company wants a fairly constant productive output so a constant work force can be maintained. How many units will be in finished goods inventory on December 31, 19x2?

**Exercise 26-5.
Direct Materials
Purchases Budget
(Linked to
Exercise 26-4)**
(L.O. 5)

Refer to the data for the Stevens Specialty Door Company in Exercise 26-4. Prepare a materials purchases/usage budget for January, February, and March, 19x2, assuming the following breakdown of parts needed:

Hinges	4 sets/door	$11.00/set
Door panels	4 panels/door	$27.00/panel
Other hardware	1 lock/door	$31.00/lock
	1 handle/door	$22.50/handle
	2 roller tracks/door	$16.00/set of 2 roller racks
	8 rollers/door	$4.00/roller

All direct materials are purchased in the month before they are used in production.

**Exercise 26-6.
Factory Labor
Budget**
(L.O. 5)

Sterling Metals Company manufactures three products in a single plant with four departments: Cutting, Grinding, Polishing, and Packing. The company has estimated costs for products T, M, and B and is currently analyzing direct labor hour requirements for the budget year 19x3. The routing sequence and departmental data are presented on the following page.

Unit of Product	Estimated Hours per Unit				Total Estimated Direct Labor Hours/Unit
	Cut	Grind	Polish	Pack	
T	.8	1.1	.5	.3	2.7
M	1.2	—	2.9	.7	4.8
B	1.8	3.2	—	.5	5.5
Hourly labor rate	$12	$9	$7	$6	
Annual direct labor hour capacity	1,100,000	1,200,000	1,248,000	460,000	

The annual direct labor hour capacity for each department at Sterling Metals is based on a normal two-shift operation. Hours of labor in excess of capacity are provided by overtime labor at 150 percent of normal hourly rates. Budgeted unit production in 19x3 for the products is 210,000 of T, 360,000 of M, and 300,000 of B.

Prepare a direct labor budget for 19x3 showing annual and monthly costs. Assume that direct labor hour capacity is the same each month. Production should be close to constant each month.

Exercise 26-7.
Sales Budget
Preparation
(L.O. 5)

Sales for 19x2 for the Dockweiler Manufacturing Company are shown below. The data is presented in quarterly figures because management monitors its business activity in this manner.

Dockweiler Manufacturing Company
Actual Sales Revenue
For the Year Ended December 31, 19x2

Product Class	January– March	April– June	July– September	October– December	Annual Totals	Estimated 19x3 Percent Increases by Product Class
Marine Products	$ 42,500	$ 43,500	$ 46,200	$ 45,900	$ 178,100	10%
Mountain Products	36,900	32,600	34,100	37,200	140,800	5%
River Products	29,800	29,700	29,100	27,500	116,100	30%
Hiking Products	38,800	37,600	36,900	39,700	153,000	15%
Running Products	49,700	50,200	51,400	51,900	203,200	25%
Biking Products	65,400	65,900	66,600	67,300	265,200	20%
Totals	$263,100	$259,500	$264,300	$269,500	$1,056,400	

Prepare the 19x3 sales budget for the company. Show both quarterly and annual totals for each product class.

Exercise 26-8.
Factory Overhead
Budget
(L.O. 5)

Tom Brown is chief financial officer for Fullerton Corporation, a multinational company operating with three divisions. As part of the budgeting process, his staff is developing the factory overhead budget for 19x1. Data from the current year by division as well as projections for 19x1 have been received from each of the divisional controllers and are summarized below.

Fullerton Corporation
Factory Overhead Cost Summary Analysis
For the Year Ended December 31, 19x0

Cost Category	New Orleans Division		London Division		Mexico City Division		Corporate Totals
	19x0 Amount	Projected 19x1 Increase	19x0 Amount	Projected 19x1 Increase	19x0 Amount	Projected 19x1 Increase	
Indirect Materials	$ 76,900	10%	$ 85,900	12%	$ 96,400	10%	$ 259,200
Indirect Labor	82,100	8%	104,600	9%	112,400	6%	299,100
Factory Supervision	140,000	14%	180,000	13%	210,000	12%	530,000
Employee Benefits	65,120	20%	77,400	20%	23,600	20%	166,120
Insurance							
Casualty	3,240	5%	4,650	4%	6,940	5%	14,830
Flood	5,800	8%	6,800	5%	8,680	6%	21,280
Liability	4,120	10%	5,200	12%	6,340	15%	15,660
Taxes							
Property	16,480	4%	34,700	24%	49,700	30%	100,880
Other	2,400	10%	3,300	20%	8,640	20%	14,340
Depreciation, Machinery	78,400	2%	82,200	2%	42,100	2%	202,700
Depreciation, Buildings	62,000	4%	71,500	2%	39,600	8%	173,100
Repairs and Maintenance	24,600	4%	26,300	8%	6,800	6%	57,700
Supplies	13,200	2%	10,600	4%	3,600	8%	27,400
Special Tools	69,700	30%	45,600	25%	8,900	20%	124,200
Electricity	34,500	6%	29,800	10%	17,460	15%	81,760
Miscellaneous	2,360	5%	3,780	5%	2,200	5%	8,340
Totals	$680,920		$772,330		$643,360		$2,096,610

From the data given, prepare the 19x1 factory overhead budget for the corporation. Include divisional as well as total corporate amounts. Round to whole dollar amounts.

Exercise 26-9.
Cash Budget
Preparation—
Revenues
(L.O. 6, 7)

Storevik Car Care, Inc. is an automobile maintenance and repair organization with outlets throughout the midwestern United States. Ms. Stokes, budget director for the home office, is beginning to assemble next quarter's operating cash budget. Sales are projected as follows:

	On Account	Cash
October, 19x1	$652,000	$196,800
November, 19x1	590,000	214,000
December, 19x1	720,500	218,400

Storevik's past collection results for sales on account indicate the following pattern:

Month of sale	40%
1st month following sale	30%
2nd month following sale	28%
Uncollectible	2%

Sales on account during August and September were $446,000 and $395,000, respectively.

What are the purposes for preparing a cash budget? Compute the amount of cash to be collected from sales during each month of the last quarter.

**Exercise 26-10.
Cash Budget
Preparation—
Expenditures
(L.O. 7)**

Cabernet Corporation relies on its cash budget to predict periods of high or low cash. The company considers proper cash management to be a primary short-range strategy for achieving higher profits. All materials and supplies are purchased on account, with terms of either 2/10, n/30 or 2/30, n/60. Discounts are taken whenever possible, but payment is not made until the final day of the discount period. Purchases for the next quarter of 19x2 are expected to be as follows:

Date	Terms	Gross Amount	Date	Terms	Gross Amount
July 10	2/10, n/30	$ 7,400	Aug. 31	2/10, n/30	$5,800
16	2/30, n/60	9,200	Sept. 4	2/10, n/30	8,400
24	2/30, n/60	8,400	9	2/10, n/30	7,100
Aug. 6	2/10, n/30	7,200	18	2/10, n/30	6,500
12	2/30, n/60	11,400	20	2/10, n/30	9,400
18	2/30, n/60	12,500	24	2/30, n/60	8,300
30	2/10, n/30	13,600	29	2/10, n/30	3,900

Three purchases in June affected July cash flow: June 6, 2/30, n/60, $13,200; June 21, 2/30, n/60, $11,400; and June 24, 2/10, n/30, $5,400.

From the information given, compute total cash outflow for July, August, and September resulting from the purchases identified above.

Interpreting Accounting Information

**Internal
Management
Information:
Jessie Corporation
(L.O. 2, 4)**

Jessie Corporation is a manufacturing company with annual sales of $25,000,000. The controller, Mr. Hugo, appointed Ms. Shirley as budget director. She created the following budget formulation policy based on a calendar-year accounting period:

May 19x1   Meeting of corporate officers and budget director to discuss corporate plans for 19x2.

June 19x1   Meeting(s) of division managers, department heads, and budget director to communicate 19x2 corporate objectives. At this time, relevant background data are distributed to all managers and a time schedule is established for development of 19x2 budget data.

July 19x1   Managers and department heads continue to develop budget data. Complete 19x2 monthly sales forecasts by product line and receive final sales estimates from sales vice president.

Aug. 19x1   Complete 19x2 monthly production activity and anticipated inventory level plans. Division managers and department heads should communicate preliminary budget figures to budget director for coordination and distribution to other operating areas.

Sept. 19x1   Development of preliminary 19x2 master budget. Revised budget data from all functional areas to be received. Budget director will coordinate staff activities, integrating labor requirements, direct materials and supplies requirements, unit cost estimates, cash requirements, and profit estimates and prepare preliminary 19x2 master budget.

Oct. 19x1   Meeting with corporate officers to discuss preliminary 19x2 master budget; any corrections, additions, or deletions to be communicated to budget director by corporate officers; all authorized changes to be incorporated into the 19x2 master budget.

Nov. 19x1   Submit final draft of 19x2 master budget to corporate officers for approval. Publish approved budget and distribute to all corporate officers, division managers, and department heads.

Required

1. Comment on the proposed budget formulation policy.
2. What changes in the policy would you recommend?

Problem Set A

**Problem 26A-1.
Budget
Preparation
(L.O. 5)**

The main product of Revell Enterprises, Inc. is a multipurpose hammer that carries a lifetime guarantee. The steps in the manufacturing process have been combined by using modern, automated equipment. A list of cost and production information for the Revell hammer follows:

Direct materials
     Anodized steel: 2 kilograms per hammer at $1.80 per kilogram
     Leather strapping for handle: 0.5 square meter per hammer at $4.20 per square meter
     (Packing materials are returned to the manufacturer and thus are not included as part of cost of goods sold.)

Direct labor
     Forging operation: $12.50 per direct labor hour; 6 minutes per hammer
     Leather-wrapping operation: $11.00 per direct labor hour; 12 minutes per hammer

Factory overhead

Forging operation: rate equals 70% of department's direct labor dollars

Leather-wrapping operation: rate equals 50% of department's direct labor dollars

For the three months ended December 31, 19x2, management expects to produce 54,000 hammers in October, 52,000 hammers in November, and 50,000 hammers in December.

Required

1. For the three-month period ending December 31, 19x2, prepare monthly production cost information for the manufacture of the Revell hammer. In your budget analysis, show a detailed breakdown of all costs involved and the computation methods used.
2. Prepare a quarterly production cost budget for the hammer. Show monthly cost data and combined totals for the quarter for each cost category.

**Problem 26A-2.
General and
Administrative
Expense Budget
(L.O. 5)**

Rogne Metal Products, Inc. has four divisions and a centralized management structure. The home office is located in Spencer, Iowa. General and administrative expenses of the corporation for 19x2 and expected percentage increases for 19x3 are presented below.

Expense Categories	19x2 Expenses	Expected Increase in 19x3
Administrative Salaries	$145,000	20%
Facility Depreciation	47,000	10%
Operating Supplies	34,500	20%
Insurance and Taxes	16,000	10%
Computer Services	250,000	40%
Clerical Salaries	65,000	15%
Miscellaneous	22,500	10%
Totals	$380,000	

To determine divisional profitability, all general and administrative expenses except for computer services are allocated to divisions on a total labor dollar basis. Computer service costs are charged directly to divisions on the basis of percent of total usage charges. Computer charges and direct labor costs in 19x2 were as follows:

	Computer Charges	Direct Labor
Division A	$ 60,000	$125,000
Division B	54,000	100,000
Division C	46,000	150,000
Division D	40,000	200,000
Home Office	50,000	—
Total	$250,000	$575,000

Required

1. Prepare the general and administrative expense budget for Rogne Metal Products, Inc. for 19x3.
2. Prepare a schedule of budgeted computer service charges to each division and the home office, assuming that percentage of usage time and cost distribution in 19x3 will be the same as in 19x2.
3. Determine the amount of general and administrative expense to be allocated to each division in 19x3, assuming the same direct labor cost distribution percentages as in 19x2.

Problem 26A-3.
Master Budget
(L.O. 4, 5)

The Bank of Seminole County has asked the president of Naruse Laser Products, Inc. for a forecasted income statement and balance sheet for the quarter ending June 30, 19x1. These documents will be used to support the company's request for a loan. A quarterly master budget is prepared on a routine basis by the company so the president indicated that the requested documents would be forwarded to the bank.

To date (April 2), the following period budgets have been developed. Sales: April, $220,400, May, $164,220, June, $165,980; materials purchases for the period, $96,840; materials usage, $102,710; labor expenses, $71,460; factory overhead, $79,940; selling expenses for the quarter, $82,840; general and administrative expenses, $60,900; capital expenditures, $125,000 (to be spent on June 29); cost of goods manufactured, $252,880; and cost of goods sold, $251,700.

Balance sheet account balances at March 31, 19x1 were: Cash, $28,770; Accounts Receivable, $26,500; Materials Inventory, $23,910; Work in Process Inventory, $31,620; Finished Goods Inventory, $36,220; Prepaid Expenses, $7,200; Plant, Furniture, and Fixtures, $498,600; Accumulated Depreciation, Plant, Furniture, and Fixtures, $99,720; Patents, $90,600; Accounts Payable, $39,600; Notes Payable, $105,500; Common Stock, $250,000; and Retained Earnings, $207,158.

Monthly cash balances for the quarter are projected to be: April 30, $20,490; May 31, $5,610; June 30, $3,958. During the quarter, Accounts Receivable are supposed to increase by 30 percent, Patents will go up by $6,500, Prepaid Expenses will remain constant, Accounts Payable will go down by 10 percent, and the company will make a $5,000 payment on the Note Payable ($4,100 is principal reduction). The federal income tax rate is 34 percent and the second quarter's tax is paid in July. Depreciation for the quarter will be $6,420, which was already included in the factory overhead budget.

Required

1. Prepare a forecasted income statement for the quarter ending June 30, 19x1.
2. Prepare a forecasted statement of financial position as of June 30, 19x1.

Problem 26A-4.
Basic Cash Budget
(L.O. 7)

Produce World, Inc. is the creation of John Versackas, an immigrant from Lithuania. Mr. Versackas' dream was to develop the biggest produce store with the widest selection of fresh fruits and vegetables in the Northern Illinois area. In three short years, he accomplished his objective. Eighty percent of his business is conducted on credit with area retail enterprises, and 20 percent of the produce sold is to walk-in customers at his retail outlet on a cash only basis.

Collection experience has shown that 20 percent of all credit sales are collected during the month of sale, 50 percent is received in the month following the sale, and 29 percent are collected in the second month after the sale. One percent of the credit sales are uncollectible. Mr. Versackas has asked you to prepare a cash budget for the quarter ending September 30, 19x2.

Operating data for the period is as follows: Total sales in May were $132,000, and in June, $135,000. Anticipated sales include July, $139,000; August, $152,500; and September, $169,580. Purchases for the quarter are expected to be $77,400 in July; $97,850 in August; and $111,450 in September. All purchases are for cash.

Other projected costs for the quarter include salaries and wages: ($36,740 in July; $41,400 in August; and $46,600 in September), and monthly costs of $2,080 for heat, light and power; $750 for bank collection fees; $3,850 for rent; $2,240 for supplies; $3,410 for depreciation of equipment; $2,570 for equipment repairs; and $950 for miscellaneous expenses. The corporation's cash balance at June 30, 19x2 was $5,490.

Required

1. Prepare a cash budget by month for the quarter ending September 30, 19x2.
2. Should Produce World, Inc. anticipate taking out a loan during the quarter? How much should be borrowed? When? (Note: Management maintains a $5,000 minimum monthly cash balance policy.)

**Problem 26A-5.
Cash Budget
Preparation:
Comprehensive**
(L.O. 7)

Texas Mountain Ski Resort, Inc., located in the Texas panhandle, has been in business for twenty-two years. Although the skiing season is difficult to predict, the company operates under the assumption that all of its revenues will be generated during the first three months of the calendar year. Routine maintenance and repair work are done during the remaining nine-month period. The following projections for 19x1 were developed by Lou Vlasho, company budget director:

Cash Receipts

Lift tickets: January, 16,800 people @ $22; February, 17,400 people @ $23; March, 17,800 people @ $24
Food sales: January, $62,000; February, $56,000; March, $62,000
Skiing lessons: January, $158,000; February, $134,000; March, $158,000
Equipment sales and rental: January, $592,000; February, $496,000; March, $592,000
Liquor sales: January, $124,000; February, $92,000; March, $104,000

Cash Payments

Salaries:
 Ski area:
  Lift operators: 12 people @ $2,500 per month for January, February, March (first quarter)
  Instruction and equipment rental: 24 people @ $2,700 per month for first quarter
 Maintenance: $35,000 per month for first quarter, and a total of $96,000 for the rest of the year
 Customer service: Shuttle bus drivers, 10 people @ $1,400 per month for first quarter
 Medical: 8 people @ $6,400 per month for first quarter
 Food service: 24 people @ $1,800 per month for first quarter

Purchases:

Food: $30,000 per month for the first quarter

Ski equipment: Purchases of $340,000 in both January and February plus a $700,000 purchase anticipated in December 19x1

Liquors: $50,000 in each month of the first quarter

Tickets and supplies: $50,000 in January, $40,000 in February, and $80,000 in December 19x1

Advertising: $40,000 in January, $30,000 in February, and a total of $90,000 from April through the end of the year

Fire and liability insurance: January and June premium payments of $8,000

Medical facility costs: $15,000 per month during first quarter

Utilities: $5,000 per month for the first quarter and $1,000 per month for the rest of the year

Lift maintenance: $25,000 per month for the first quarter and $10,000 per month for the rest of the year

Property taxes: $180,000 due in June

Federal income taxes: 19x0 taxes of $364,000 due in March

The beginning cash balance for 19x1 is anticipated to be $10,000.

Required

1. Prepare a cash budget for Texas Mountain Ski Resort, Inc. for 19x1, using the following column headings:

Item	January	February	March	April–December	Total

Problem Set B

Problem 26B-1.
Divisional Budget
Preparation
(L.O. 5)

Lester Twichell is budget director for Villa Park Spectaculars, Inc., a multinational company based in California. Villa Park Spectaculars, Inc. organizes and coordinates art shows and auctions throughout the world. Budgeted and actual costs and expenses for 19x3 are compared in the following schedule.

Expense Item	19x3 Amounts Budget	Actual
Salary Expense, Staging	$ 230,000	$ 246,400
Salary Expense, Executive	190,000	223,600
Travel Costs	320,000	336,010
Auctioneer Services	270,000	224,910
Space Rental Costs	125,500	123,290
Printing Costs	86,000	91,250
Advertising Expense	74,500	91,640
Insurance, Merchandise	42,400	38,650
Insurance, Liability	32,000	33,550
Home Office Costs	114,600	109,940
Shipping Costs	52,500	56,280
Miscellaneous	12,500	12,914
Total Expenses	$1,550,000	$1,588,434
Net Receipts	$2,950,000	$3,184,600

For 19x4, the following fixed costs have been budgeted: executive salaries, $200,000; advertising expense, $95,000; merchandise insurance, $40,000; liability insurance, $34,000; total fixed costs, $369,000. Additional information follows:

a. Net receipts are expected to be $3,000,000 in 19x4.
b. Staging salaries will increase 50% over 19x3 actual figures.
c. Travel costs are expected to be 11% of net receipts.
d. Auctioneer services will be billed at 9.5% of net receipts.
e. Space rental costs will go up 20% from 19x3 budgeted amounts.
f. Printing costs are expected to be $95,000 in 19x4.
g. Home office costs are budgeted for $115,000 in 19x4.
h. Shipping costs are expected to rise 20% over 19x3 budgeted amounts.
i. Miscellaneous expenses for 19x4 will be budgeted at $14,000.

Required

1. Prepare the division's budget for 19x4. Assume that only services are being sold and that there is no cost of sales. (Net receipts equal gross margin.) Use a 34 percent federal income tax rate.
2. Should the budget director be worried about the trend of the company's operations? Be specific.

**Problem 26B-2.
Factory Overhead
Expense Budget
(L.O. 5)**

Stalcup Manufacturing Company has a home office and three operating divisions. The home office houses the top management personnel, including all accounting functions. The factory overhead costs incurred during 19x1 are summarized below.

Expense Categories	East Division	West Division	Central Division	Total	Expected Increase in 19x2
Indirect Labor	$ 32,500	$ 32,600	$ 38,200	$103,300	10%
Indirect Materials	12,800	13,200	14,000	40,000	20%
Supplies	11,900	12,900	12,000	36,800	10%
Utilities	14,200	15,400	11,100	40,700	10%
Computer Services	32,500	35,800	37,700	106,000	—
Insurance	11,400	12,500	13,600	37,500	10%
Repairs and Maintenance	13,600	14,000	15,400	43,000	20%
Miscellaneous	10,100	12,200	11,300	33,600	10%
Totals	$139,000	$148,600	$153,300	$440,900	

Expected percentage increases for 19x2 are shown for all categories except computer services. These services will increase by different amounts for each division: East Division, 25%; West Division, 30%; and Central Division, 40%. In 19x1, the home office was charged $55,000 for computer service costs. This amount is expected to rise by 25% in 19x2. During 19x2, the company will rent a new software package at an annual cost of $80,000.

Required

1. Find the total expected cost for computer services for 19x2 for the three divisions and the home office.
2. Assume that the new software package rental charge is allocated to computer service users on the basis of their normal computer use costs as a percentage of total computer service charges. Compute the allocation of the rental charges to the three divisions and the central office. (Use the 19x2 amounts computed in 1 above, and round to one percentage decimal place.)
3. Prepare the divisional factory overhead expense budget for Stalcup Manufacturing Company for 19x2.

Problem 26B-3.
Master Budget
(L.O. 4, 5)

Abramson Video Company, Inc. produces and markets two popular video games, "Grant Avenue" and "Thornton Adventures." The company's closing balance sheet account balances for 19x1 are as follows: Cash, $15,450; Accounts Receivable, $19,900; Materials Inventory, $18,510; Work in Process Inventory, $24,680; Finished Goods Inventory, $21,940; Prepaid Expenses, $3,420; Plant and Equipment, $262,800; Accumulated Depreciation, Plant and Equipment, $52,560; Other Assets, $9,480; Accounts Payable, $52,640; Mortgage Payable, $70,000; Common Stock, $90,000; Retained Earnings, $74,980.

Period budgets for the first quarter of 19x2 revealed the following: materials purchases, $58,100; materials usage, $60,240; labor expense, $42,880; factory overhead expense, $51,910; selling expenses, $35,820; general and administrative expenses, $60,230; capital expenditures, $0; ending cash balances by month: January, $34,610; February, $60,190; March, $96,240; cost of goods manufactured, $163,990; and cost of goods sold, $165,440.

Sales per month are projected to be $175,210 for January, $124,890 for February, and $122,860 for March. Accounts receivable balance will double during the quarter, and accounts payable will decrease by 25 percent. Mortgage payments for the quarter will total $6,000, of which $2,000 is interest expense. Prepaid expenses are expected to go up by $20,000, and other assets are projected to increase 50 percent over the budget period. Depreciation for plant and equipment (already included in the factory overhead budget) averages 10 percent of total Plant and Equipment per year. Federal income taxes are 34 percent of profits and are payable in April.

Required

1. Prepare a forecasted income statement for the quarter ending March 31, 19x2.
2. Prepare a forecasted statement of financial position as of March 31, 19x2.

Problem 26B-4.
Basic Cash Budget
(L.O. 7)

David Schuelke is president of Nature's Nurseries of Idaho, Inc. This corporation has four locations in the state of Idaho and has been in business for six years. Each retail outlet offers over 300 varieties of plants and trees to its customers. Millie Cooper, the controller, has been asked to prepare a cash budget for the Southern Division for the first quarter of 19x2.

Projected data supporting the budget are summarized as follows. Collection history for the accounts receivable has shown that 30 percent of all credit sales are collected in the month of sale, 60 percent in the month following the sale, and 8 percent in the second month following the sale. Two percent of the credit sales are uncollectible. Purchases are all paid for in the month following the purchase. As of December 31, 19x1, Nature's Nurseries had a cash balance of $3,875.

Sales (60 percent on credit):

November, 19x1	$ 90,000
December, 19x1	100,000
January, 19x2	50,000
February, 19x2	80,000
March, 19x2	40,000

Purchases:

December, 19x1	38,400
January, 19x2	59,350
February, 19x2	31,720
March, 19x2	42,400

Salaries and wages were $12,600 in January; $16,600 in February; and $10,600 in March. Monthly costs were: utilities, $2,110; collection fees, $850; rent, $2,650; equipment depreciation, $2,720; supplies, $1,240; small tools, $1,570; and miscellaneous, $950.

Required

1. Prepare a cash budget by month for the Southern Division for the first quarter of 19x2.
2. Should Nature's Nurseries of Idaho, Inc. anticipate taking out a loan during the quarter? How much should be borrowed? When? (Note: Management maintains a $3,000 minimum cash balance at each of its four locations.)

**Problem 26B-5.
Cash Budget
Preparation:
Comprehensive**
(L.O. 7)

Emerson's Wellness Centers, Inc. operates three fully equipped personal health facilities in St. Paul, Minnesota. In addition to the health facilities, the corporation maintains a complete medical center specializing in preventive medicine. Emphasis is placed on regular workouts and medical examinations. The following projections have been made for 19x2.

Cash Receipts: First Quarter, 19x2

Membership dues:
  Memberships: December, 19x1, 870; January, 19x2, 880; February, 910; March, 1,030
  Dues: $90 per month, payable on the 10th day (80 percent collected on time, 20 percent are collected one month late)
  Medical examinations: January, $35,610; February, $41,840; March, $45,610
  Special aerobics classes: January, $2,580; February, $3,410; March, $4,980
  Suntan sessions: January, $1,440; February, $1,720; March, $2,150
  High-protein food sales: January, $4,890; February, $5,130; March, $6,280

Cash Payments: First Quarter, 19x2

Salaries and wages:
  Corporate officers: $24,000/month
  Medical doctors: 2 @ $7,000/month
  Nurses: 3 @ $2,900/month
  Clerical staff: 2 @ $1,500/month
  Aerobics instructors: 3 @ $1,100/month
  Clinic staff: 6 @ $1,700/month
  Maintenance staff: 3 @ $900/month
  Health food servers: 3 @ $750/month
Purchases:
  Muscle-tone machines: January, $14,400; February, $13,800; March, $0
  Pool supplies: $520 per month
  Health food: January, $3,290; February, $3,460; March, $3,720
  Medical supplies: January, $10,400; February, $11,250; March, $12,640
  Medical clothing: January, $7,410; February, $3,900; March, $3,450
  Medical equipment: January, $11,200; February, $3,400; March, $5,900
  Advertising: January, $2,250; February, $1,190; March, $2,450
  Utilities expense: January, $5,450; February, $5,890; March, $6,090
Insurance:
  Fire: January, $3,470
  Liability: March, $3,980
Property taxes: $3,760 due in January
Federal income taxes: 19x1 taxes of $21,000 due in March, 19x2
Miscellaneous: January, $2,625; February, $2,800; March, $1,150

The beginning cash balance for 19x2 is anticipated to be $9,840.

Required   1. Prepare a cash budget for Emerson's Wellness Centers, Inc. for the first quarter of 19x2. Use the following headings:

Item	January	February	March	Total

Management Decision Case

P.C. Enterprises
(L.O. 2, 5)

During the past ten years, P.C. Enterprises has practiced participative budgeting all the way from the maintenance personnel to the president's staff. Gradually, however, the objectives of honesty and decisions made in the best interest of the company as a whole have given way to division-benefitting decisions and budgets biased in favor of divisional interests. Mr. George, corporate controller, has asked Ms. Vrana, budget director, to carefully analyze this year's divisional budgets before incorporating them into the company's master budget.

The Electronics Division was the first of the six divisions to submit its 19x2 budget request to the corporate office. Its summary income statement and accompanying notes are presented on the next page.

P.C. Enterprises
Electronics Division
Forecasted Income Statement
For the Years Ending December 31, 19x1 and 19x2

	Budget 12/31/x1	Budget 12/31/x2	Increase (Decrease)
Revenues			
Sales:			
Radios	$ 850,000	$ 910,000	$ 60,000
Appliances	680,000	740,000	60,000
Telephones	270,000	305,000	35,000
Miscellaneous	84,400	90,000	5,600
Total Revenues	$1,884,400	$2,045,000	$160,600
Less Cost of Goods Sold	750,960	717,500[1]	(33,460)
Gross Margin	$1,133,440	$1,327,500	$194,060
Operating Expenses			
Wages:			
Warehouse	$ 94,500	$ 102,250	$ 7,750
Purchasing	77,800	84,000	6,200
Delivery/Shipping	69,400	74,780	5,380
Maintenance	42,650	45,670	3,020
Salaries:			
Supervisory	60,000	92,250	32,250
Executive	130,000	164,000	34,000
Purchases, Supplies	17,400	20,500	3,100
Merchandise Moving Equipment:			
Maintenance	72,400	82,000	9,600
Depreciation	62,000	74,750[2]	12,750
Building Rent	96,000	102,500	6,500
Sales Commissions	188,440	204,500	16,060
Insurance:			
Fire	12,670	20,500	7,830
Liability	18,200	20,500	2,300
Utilities	14,100	15,375	1,275
Taxes:			
Property	16,600	18,450	1,850
Payroll	26,520	41,000	14,480
Miscellaneous	4,610	10,250	5,640
Total Operating Expenses	$1,003,290	$1,173,275	$169,985
Net Income Before Taxes	$ 130,150	$ 154,225	$ 24,075

1. Less expensive merchandise will be purchased in 19x2 to boost profits.
2. Depreciation is increased because of a need to buy additional equipment to handle increased sales.

Required   1. Recast the Electronics Division's Forecasted Income Statement into the following format (round percentages to two places):

	Budget—12/31/x1		Budget—12/31/x2	
Account	**Amount**	**Percent of Sales**	**Amount**	**Percent of Sales**

2. Actual results for 19x1 revealed the following information about revenues and cost of goods sold:

	Amount	**Percent of Sales**
Sales		
Radios	$ 780,000	43.94%
Appliances	640,000	36.06%
Telephones	280,000	15.77%
Miscellaneous	75,000	4.23%
Total Revenues	$1,775,000	100.00%
Less Cost of Goods Sold	763,425	43.01%
Gross Margin	$1,011,575	56.99%

On the basis of this information and your analysis in **1**, what should the budget director say to officials of the Electronics Division? Mention specific areas of the budget that need to be revised.

Answers to Self-Test

1. b	3. c	5. c	7. d	9. d
2. d	4. b	6. a	8. b	10. a

1. Describe the nature
   and purpose of stan-
   dard costs.
2. Identify the six ele-
   ments of a standard
   unit cost and describe
   the factors to consider
   in developing each
   element.
3. Compute a standard
   unit cost.
4. Prepare a flexible
   budget.
5. Describe the concept
   of management by
   exception.
6. Compute and evaluate
   direct materials, direct
   labor, and factory overhead variances.
7. Prepare journal entries
   to record transactions
   involving variances in
   a standard costing
   system.
8. Evaluate employee
   performance using
   variances.

CHAPTER 27

Cost Control Using Standard Costing and Variance Analysis

Standard cost accounting is one of the most useful concepts in the budgetary control process. Once developed, standard costs become excellent tools for use in the planning phase of an operation. For purposes of control, standard costs can be used to measure operating performance. Variance analysis helps to separate areas with operating problems from efficient departments or work areas, so managers can concentrate their attention where it is needed.

Cost variances are usually associated with performance evaluation in the manufacturing environment. But standard costing and variance analysis are equally important to profitability and operating efficiency in service-oriented businesses, as well as in the sale and distribution of manufactured products. Though materials variances are unique to manufacturing, labor and factory overhead variances may be computed for service enterprises as well as manufacturing companies.

In this chapter, we will first look at the nature and purpose of standard costs. We will discuss ways of developing standard costs and then show how they can be used. Finally, after an introduction to flexible budgeting, we will examine standard cost variance analysis in depth. After studying this chapter, you should be able to meet the learning objectives listed on the left.

Standard Cost Accounting

Standard cost accounting is a tool used by management for cost planning and cost control purposes. A standard cost system is not a full cost accounting system by itself. Instead, it is used along with an existing job order or process costing system. When a company uses standard costs, all costs affecting the inventory accounts and the Cost of Goods Sold account are stated in terms of standard or predetermined costs rather than actual costs incurred. Together with cost behavior relationships and the various cost-volume-profit analyses, the incorporation of standard costs into a cost accounting system provides the foundation for the budgetary control process. Standard costs are useful for (1) preparing budgets and forecasts, (2) evaluating the performance of workers and management, and (3) helping to decide on appropriate selling prices.

Our discussion will be divided into two parts. First we will look at the nature and purpose of standard costs—their make-up, how they are developed, their use in product costing, and their related journal entries. Then we will concentrate on their primary use, as a cost control tool.

Nature and Purpose of Standard Costs

OBJECTIVE 1
Describe the nature and purpose of standard costs

Standard costs are realistically predetermined costs for direct materials, direct labor, and factory overhead. They are usually expressed as cost per unit of finished product. Predetermined overhead costs, which we discussed in Chapter 23, are different from standard costs. Standard costing focuses on *total* unit cost, which includes all three manufacturing cost elements. And the computation of standard costs is more detailed than that of predetermined overhead cost.

Predetermined overhead costing and standard costing do share two very important elements. Both forecast the dollar amounts to be used in product costing, and both depend on expected costs for budgeted items. But that is where the similarity ends. Standard costs are based on engineering estimates, forecasted demand, worker input, time and motion studies, and type and quality of direct materials. Predetermined overhead rates depend on much simpler projections based on past costs. The predetermined overhead rate does provide some of the same data as the standard overhead rate, and standard costing is expensive to use. If a company cannot afford to add standard costing to its cost system, it should continue to use predetermined overhead rates.

Standard costing is a total cost concept. In a fully integrated standard cost system, all actual manufacturing cost data are replaced by standard (or predetermined) cost data. Accounts such as Direct Materials Inventory, Work in Process Inventory, Finished Goods Inventory, and Cost of Goods Sold are all stated in terms of standard costs. All debit and credit entries made to these accounts are made in terms of standard costs, not actual costs. All inventory balances are computed using standard unit costs. Separate records are kept of actual costs in order to compare the standard costs (what should have been spent) with the actual costs incurred. The comparison is usually made at the end of the accounting period, whether weekly, monthly, or quarterly. If large differences (variances) exist, the management accountant looks for the causes of the differences. This process, known as variance analysis, is one of the most effective cost control tools. We will discuss it later in this chapter.

In summary, standard costs are introduced into a cost accounting system for several reasons. They are useful in preparing operating budgets. They make it easier to pinpoint production costs that need to be controlled. They help in setting realistic prices. And they simplify cost accounting procedures for inventories and product costing. Although expensive to set up and maintain, a standard cost accounting system can save a company money by helping reduce waste and inefficiency.

Development of Standard Costs

OBJECTIVE 2
*Identify the six
elements of a
standard unit cost
and describe the
factors to consider
in developing each
element*

A standard unit cost has six parts: (1) direct materials price standard, (2) direct materials quantity standard, (3) direct labor time standard, (4) direct labor rate standard, (5) standard variable factory overhead rate, and (6) standard fixed factory overhead rate. To develop a standard unit cost, we must identify and analyze each of these items.

Standard Direct Materials Cost. The **standard direct materials cost** is found by multiplying the standard price for direct materials by the standard quantity for direct materials. If the price standard for a certain item is $2.75 and a specific job calls for eight of the items, the standard direct materials cost for that job is $22.00 (8 × $2.75).

The **direct materials price standard** is a careful estimate of the cost of a certain type of direct material in the next accounting period. Possible price increases, changes in available quantities, and new sources of supply must all be taken into account. Any of these factors could influence the price standard. A company's purchasing agent is responsible for developing price standards for all direct materials. The purchasing agent also follows through with actual purchases at the projected standard prices.

The standard quantity of direct materials is one of the most difficult standards to forecast. The **direct materials quantity standard** is an estimate of expected quantity usage. It is influenced by product engineering specifications, quality of direct materials, age and productivity of machinery, and the quality and experience of the workforce. Production managers are usually responsible for establishing and policing direct materials quantity standards. However, engineers, purchasing agents, and machine operators can provide input into the development of these standards.

Standard Direct Labor Cost. The **standard direct labor cost** for a product, task, or job order is figured by multiplying the standard hours of direct labor by the standard wage for direct labor. Let us assume that a product takes 1.5 standard direct labor hours to produce and that the standard labor rate is $8.40 per hour. Even if the person actually making the product is paid only $7.90 per hour, $12.60 ($8.40 × 1.5) of standard direct labor cost would be charged to the Work in Process Inventory account.

Current time and motion studies of workers and machines as well as past employee and machine performance are the basic input for a **direct labor time standard**. Such standards express the time it takes for each department, machine, or process to complete production on one unit or batch of output. In many cases, standard time per unit will be a small fraction of an hour. Meeting time standards is the department manager or supervisor's responsibility. These standards should be revised whenever a machine is replaced or the quality of the labor force changes.

Labor rates are either set by labor contract or defined by the company, so standard labor rates are fairly easy to develop. **Direct labor rate stan-**

dards are the hourly labor costs that are expected to prevail during the next accounting period for each function or job classification. Though rate ranges are established for each type of worker and rates vary within these ranges, an average standard rate is developed for each task. Problems in controlling costs arise when a highly paid worker performs a lower-level task. For instance, a machine operator making $9.25 per hour may actually perform the work of a set-up person earning $4.50 per hour. Here, the actual cost for the work will be at variance with the standard direct labor rate.

Standard Factory Overhead Cost. The standard factory overhead cost is an estimate of the variable and fixed factory overhead in the next accounting period. Variable and fixed overhead costs depend on standard rates computed in much the same way as the predetermined overhead rate discussed in Chapter 23. There are only two differences. First, the standard overhead rate is made up of two parts, one for variable costs and the other for fixed costs. Second, more time and effort are put into calculating the standard overhead rates.

The reason for computing the variable and fixed rates separately is that different application bases are generally required. The **standard variable overhead rate** is total budgeted variable factory overhead costs divided by an expression of capacity, usually the *expected* number of standard direct labor hours. (Other bases may be used if direct labor hours are not a good barometer of variable costs.) The formula is as follows:

$$\frac{\text{Standard variable}}{\text{overhead rate}} = \frac{\text{total budgeted variable overhead costs}}{\text{expected number of standard direct labor hours}}$$

The **standard fixed overhead rate** is total budgeted fixed factory overhead costs divided by an expression of capacity, usually normal capacity in terms of standard direct labor hours. The basis is expressed in the same terms (direct labor hours, machine hours, etc.) as that used to compute the variable overhead rate. The formula is:

$$\frac{\text{Standard fixed}}{\text{overhead rate}} = \frac{\text{total budgeted fixed overhead costs}}{\text{normal capacity in terms of standard direct labor hours}}$$

Using normal capacity as the application basis ensures that all fixed overhead costs have been applied to units produced by the time normal capacity is reached.

If actual output exceeds expectations and the number of standard hours allowed for good units produced is greater than normal, a favorable situation will exist. More fixed overhead will have been applied than was actually incurred. But if actual output does not meet expectations—that is, falls short of normal capacity—then not all of the expected fixed overhead cost will have been applied. This is an unfavorable condition. The difference (variance) between factory overhead cost incurred and factory overhead cost applied will be discussed later in the chapter.

Using Standards for Product Costing

Using standard costs does away with the need to figure unit costs from actual cost data every week or month, or for each batch produced. Once standards are developed for direct materials, direct labor, and factory overhead, a total standard unit cost can be computed at any time.

Standard cost elements can be used to find the following: (1) cost of purchased direct materials entered into Materials Inventory, (2) cost of goods requisitioned out of Materials Inventory and into Work in Process Inventory, (3) cost of direct labor charged to Work in Process Inventory, (4) cost of factory overhead applied to Work in Process Inventory, (5) cost of goods completed and transferred to Finished Goods Inventory, and (6) cost of units sold and charged to the Cost of Goods Sold account. In other words, all transactions (and related journal entries) affecting the three inventory accounts and Cost of Goods Sold will be expressed in terms of standard costs, no matter what the amount of actual costs incurred. An illustrative problem will show how the system works.

Illustrative Problem: Use of Standard Costs

OBJECTIVE 3
Compute a standard unit cost

Bush Industries, Inc. uses a standard cost accounting system in its Houston, Texas, division. Recently the company updated the standards for its line of automatic pencils to agree with current costs for the year 19x1. New standards include the following: Direct materials price standards are $9.20 per square foot for casing materials and $2.25 for each movement mechanism. Direct materials quantity standards are .125 square foot of casing materials per pencil and one movement mechanism per pencil. Direct labor time standards are .01 hour per pencil for the Stamping Department and .05 hour per pencil for the Assembly Department. Direct labor rate standards are $8.00 per hour for the Stamping Department and $10.20 per hour for the Assembly Department. Standard factory overhead rates are $12.00 per direct labor hour for the standard variable overhead rate and $9.00 per direct labor hour for the standard fixed overhead rate.

Required

Compute the standard manufacturing cost of one automatic pencil.

Solution

Standard cost of one pencil computed:

Direct materials costs	
Casing ($9.20/sq ft × .125 sq ft)	$1.15
One movement mechanism	2.25
Direct labor costs	
Stamping department (.01 hr/pencil × $8.00/hr)	0.08
Assembly department (.05 hr/pencil × $10.20/hr)	0.51
Factory overhead	
Variable overhead (.06 hr/pencil × $12.00/hr)	0.72
Fixed overhead (.06 hr/pencil × $9.00/hr)	0.54
Total standard cost of one pencil	$5.25

Journal Entry Analysis

Recording standard costs is much like recording actual cost data. The only major difference is that any amount for direct materials, direct labor, or factory overhead being entered into the Work in Process Inventory account is stated at standard cost. This means that the Work in Process Inventory account is stated entirely at standard cost. Any transfer of units to Finished Goods Inventory or to the Cost of Goods Sold account will automatically be stated at standard unit cost. When actual costs for direct materials, direct labor, and factory overhead differ from standard costs, the difference is recorded in a variance account. (We will discuss such accounts in the next section.) In the following journal entry analysis, we will assume that all costs incurred are stated at standard cost. Again, we use Bush Industries as an example.

Sample Transaction: Purchased 500 square feet of casing materials at standard cost.

Entry:	Materials Inventory	4,600	
	Accounts Payable		4,600
	To record purchase of 500 sq ft of casing material @ $9.20/sq ft		

Here it does not matter if the actual purchase price differs from the standard price. The standard cost only is entered into the Materials Inventory account. (See also the journal entry for purchases on page 1157.)

Sample Transaction: Requisitioned 60 square feet of casing material and 240 movement mechanisms into production.

Entry:	Work in Process Inventory	1,092	
	Materials Inventory		1,092
	To record requisition of 60 sq ft of casing material (@ $9.20/sq ft) and 240 movement mechanisms (@ $2.25 each) into production		

Sample Transaction: During the period, 600 pencils were completed and transferred to Finished Goods Inventory.

Entry:	Finished Goods Inventory	3,150	
	Work in Process Inventory		3,150
	To record the transfer of 600 completed units to finished goods inventory (600 pencils × $5.25/pencil)		

We have shown only a few examples of the journal entries used in recording standard cost information. The examples given later in this chapter are more realistic because they are joined with the analysis of variances. Our purpose here is just to show that when a standard cost accounting system is being used, standard costs, not actual costs, flow through the production and inventory accounts.

Cost Control Through Variance Analysis

Performance evaluation is an important part of cost control. Both in manufacturing and in selling and service functions, managers are constantly comparing what did happen (actual costs) with what was expected to happen (budgeted or standard costs). Our discussion will focus on the differences between (1) actual costs and budgeted costs and (2) actual costs and standard costs. The difference between an actual cost and a budgeted or standard cost is called a variance.

Evaluating Performance

Performance evaluation is an integral part of budgetary control. The process has several aspects, some involving company policy and others involving human factors. An effective budgetary control program includes policies or procedures for (1) preparing operational plans, (2) establishing responsibility for performance, (3) communicating operational plans to key personnel, (4) evaluating each area of responsibility, and (5) if variances exist, learning the causes and making needed corrections. Performance is often measured by comparing actual data with budgeted results or targets expressed in terms of standard costs.

Company targets and policies regarding performance evaluation are important, but by themselves will not produce effective control of operations. The human factor is the key to meeting corporate goals. People do the planning, people perform the manufacturing operations, and people evaluate or are evaluated.

Some basic guidelines regarding human relations must be part of any cost control system. First, those who are responsible for an operating area must have direct input into the goal-setting process. Incentive to perform is a key factor in meeting goals. If a manager believes that an operating target is unrealistic, or if plans are developed without the participation of department-level personnel, the manager will have little desire to reach those goals. Second, management must clearly communicate every goal or plan to all the people involved, spelling out each person's exact responsibilities. Failure to communicate is a common cause of inefficient operating performance. Finally, responsible individuals must receive feedback on their performance. Management should praise good performance rather than take it for granted. Silence does not imply good performance, but rather bad management. If performance has been poor or substandard, the responsible individual should have the chance to defend him- or herself. There may be a good reason for a variance from the standard that was set. Perhaps the cause was beyond the person's control. In any case, management should develop appropriate policies and follow sound behavioral guidelines when setting up a performance evaluation process.

Flexible Budgets

OBJECTIVE 4
Prepare a flexible budget

Budgets were emphasized in Chapter 26, which focused on the planning process. Why then, you might ask, should we introduce the concept of flexible budgets as part of cost control, rather than as a planning tool? We do so because the flexible budget (also called a variable budget) is primarily a cost control tool used in evaluating performance. A **flexible budget** is a summary of expected costs for a *range* of activity levels, geared to changes in the level of productive output. The budgets we discussed as part of the planning function were static, or fixed, budgets—budgets that describe just one level of expected sales and production activity. The master budget, including all the period budgets, is usually prepared for a single expected or normal level of output.

For budgeting or planning purposes, a set of static budgets based on a single level of output is good enough. They show the desired operating results and provide a target for use in developing monthly and weekly operating plans. However, such budgets often prove inadequate for judging operating results. Exhibit 27-1 presents data for Nichole Industries, Inc. Actual costs exceed budgeted costs by $14,300, or 7.2

Exhibit 27-1. Performance Analysis: Comparison of Actual and Budgeted Data

Nichole Industries, Inc.
Performance Report—Tuscawilla Division
For the Year Ended December 31, 19x1

Cost Item	Budget*	Actual†	Difference Under (Over) Budget
Direct materials	$ 42,000	$ 46,000	$ (4,000)
Direct labor	68,250	75,000	(6,750)
Factory overhead			
Variable			
Indirect materials	10,500	11,500	(1,000)
Indirect labor	14,000	15,250	(1,250)
Utilities	7,000	7,600	(600)
Other	8,750	9,750	(1,000)
Fixed			
Supervisory salaries	19,000	18,500	500
Depreciation	15,000	15,000	—
Utilities	4,500	4,500	—
Other	10,900	11,100	(200)
Totals	$199,900	$214,200	$(14,300)

*Budget based on expected productive output of 17,500 units
†Actual cost of producing 19,100 units

percent. Such an overrun would be considered significant by most managers. But was there really a cost overrun? As explained in the notes to Exhibit 27-1, the budgeted amounts are based on an expected output of 17,500 units, but actual output was 19,100 units.

Thus, the static budget for 17,500 units is of no use for judging performance. Before analyzing the performance of the Tuscawilla Division, we must change the budgeted data to reflect an output of 19,100 units. This is the role of a flexible budget—to provide forecasted data that can be adjusted automatically for changes in the level of output.

Exhibit 27-2 presents a flexible budget for Nichole Industries, Inc., with budgeted data for 15,000, 17,500, and 20,000 units of output. The important part of this illustration is the flexible budget formula shown

Exhibit 27-2. Flexible Budget Preparation

Nichole Industries, Inc.
Flexible Budget Analysis—Tuscawilla Division
For the Year Ended December 31, 19x1

| | Unit Levels of Activity | | | Variable Cost |
Cost Item	15,000	17,500	20,000	per Unit*
Direct materials	$ 36,000	$ 42,000	$ 48,000	$2.40
Direct labor	58,500	68,250	78,000	3.90
Variable factory overhead				
Indirect materials	9,000	10,500	12,000	.60
Indirect labor	12,000	14,000	16,000	.80
Utilities	6,000	7,000	8,000	.40
Other	7,500	8,750	10,000	.50
Total variable costs	$129,000	$150,500	$172,000	$8.60
Fixed factory overhead				
Supervisory salaries	$ 19,000	$ 19,000	$ 19,000	
Depreciation	15,000	15,000	15,000	
Utilities	4,500	4,500	4,500	
Other	10,900	10,900	10,900	
Total fixed costs	$ 49,400	$ 49,400	$ 49,400	
Total costs	$178,400	$199,900	$221,400	

Flexible budget formula:
(variable cost per unit × number of units produced) + budgeted fixed costs
= ($8.60 × units produced) + $49,400

Note: Activity expressed in units was used as the basis for this analysis. When units are used, direct material and direct labor costs are included in the analysis. Flexible budgets commonly are restricted to overhead costs. In such a situation, machine hours or direct labor hours are used in place of units produced.
* Computed by dividing the dollar amount in any column by the respective level of activity

at the bottom. The $8.60 variable cost per unit is computed in the upper right-hand column, and the $49,400 is found in the fixed cost section of the analysis. Using this formula, we can draw up a budget for the Tuscawilla Division at any level of output.

Exhibit 27-3 shows a performance report prepared using the flexible budget data in Exhibit 27-2. Unit variable cost amounts have been multiplied by 19,100 units to arrive at total budgeted figures. Fixed overhead information has been carried over from the flexible budget developed in Exhibit 27-2. As the new performance report shows, costs exceeded budgeted amounts during the year by only $540, or less than three-tenths of one percent.

Using the flexible budget concept, we find that the performance of the Tuscawilla Division is almost on target. Performance has now been measured and analyzed accurately.

Variance Determination

We can evaluate operating performance by comparing actual results with either budgeted data or standard cost data. Budgeted data tend to be less precise than standard cost data, so we will focus on performance evaluation using standard costs.

Exhibit 27-3. Performance Analysis Using Flexible Budget Data

Nichole Industries, Inc.
Performance Report—Tuscawilla Division
For the Year Ended December 31, 19x1

Cost Item (Variable Unit Cost)	Budget Based on 19,100 Units Produced	Actual Costs at 19,100- Unit Level	Differences Under (Over) Budget
Direct materials ($2.40)	$ 45,840	$ 46,000	$(160)
Direct labor ($3.90)	74,490	75,000	(510)
Factory overhead			
Variable			
Indirect materials ($.60)	11,460	11,500	(40)
Indirect labor ($.80)	15,280	15,250	30
Utilities ($.40)	7,640	7,600	40
Other ($.50)	9,550	9,750	(200)
Fixed			
Supervisory salaries	19,000	18,500	500
Depreciation	15,000	15,000	—
Utilities	4,500	4,500	—
Other	10,900	11,100	(200)
Totals	$213,660	$214,200	$(540)

OBJECTIVE 5
Describe the concept of management by exception

The first step in performance evaluation is to find out if a cost variance exists. Variance determination helps to locate areas of operating efficiency or inefficiency, so that corrective steps can be taken if needed. But the key to effective control of operations is not just finding the amount of the variance, but finding the *reason* for the variance. Once the cause is known, steps can be taken to correct the trouble spot.

Variance analysis is employed selectively. Many companies are so big that it is impossible to review all areas of operations in detail. Only the areas of unusually good or bad performance are examined, a practice called **management by exception**. Let's assume management decides that performance within ±4 percent of budget or target is acceptable. When reviewing performance reports, they will examine only those cost areas where differences exceed these limits. In Figure 27-1, only direct materials C and E are outside the 4 percent limit, so only their costs will be analyzed.

Variances can be computed for whole cost categories, such as total direct materials cost, or for each item in a category. The more refined and detailed the analysis, the more effective it is for cost control purposes. This chapter presents standard cost variance analysis in simplified terms. In practice, variance analyses are much more involved, taking into account all facets of the production and distribution functions.

Variance Analysis

Variance analysis, the process of computing the amount of and isolating the causes of differences between actual costs and standard costs, is

Figure 27-1. The Management by Exception Technique

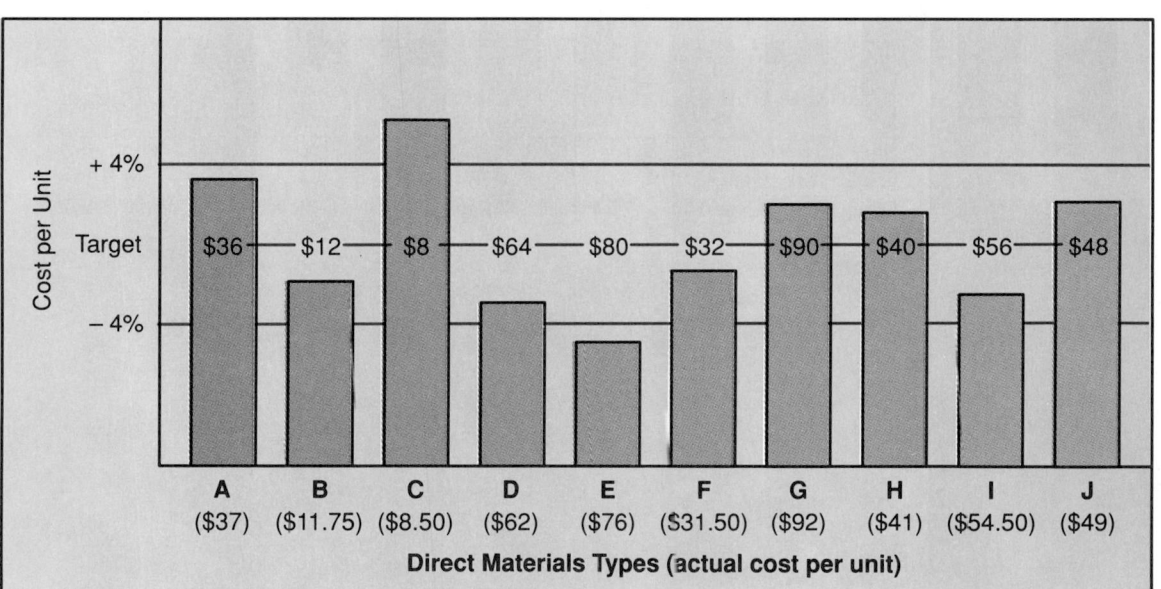

a cost control tool provided by standard cost accounting systems. The variances employed by analysts may be divided into three categories: direct materials variances direct labor variances, and factory overhead variances.

Direct Materials Variances. The total direct materials cost variance is the difference between the actual materials cost incurred and the standard cost of those items. Let us assume, for example, that Pearce Company makes leather chairs. Each chair should use 4 yards of leather (standard quantity), and the standard price of leather is $6.00 per yard. During August, 760 yards of leather costing $5.90 per yard were purchased and used to produce 180 chairs. The total direct materials cost variance is as follows:

Actual cost

$$\text{Actual quantity} \times \text{actual price} =$$
$$760 \text{ yd} \times \$5.90/\text{yd} = \$4,484$$

Less standard cost
$$\text{Standard quantity} \times \text{standard price} =$$
$$(180 \text{ chairs} \times 4 \text{ yd/chair}) \times \$6.00/\text{yd} =$$
$$720 \text{ yd} \times \$6.00/\text{yd} = \underline{4,320}$$

Total direct materials cost variance $\underline{\underline{\$ \quad 164 \text{ (U)}}}$

The *U* following the dollar amount indicates an unfavorable situation. (A favorable situation would be indicated by an *F*.)

The problem facing Pearce Company is that part of this variance is caused by price differences and part by direct materials usage. To find the area or people responsible for these variances, the total direct materials cost variance must be broken down into two parts: the direct materials price variance and the direct materials quantity variance. The direct materials price variance is the difference between the actual price and the standard price, multiplied by the actual quantity purchased. For the Pearce Company, the direct materials price variance would be computed as follows:

Actual price	$5.90
Less standard price	$\underline{6.00}$
Difference	$\underline{\underline{\$ \quad .10 \text{ (F)}}}$

$$\text{Price variance} = (\text{actual price} - \text{standard price}) \times \text{actual quantity}$$
$$= .10 \text{ (F)} \times 760 \text{ yards}$$
$$= \underline{\underline{\$76 \text{ (F)}}}$$

The direct materials quantity variance is the difference between the actual quantity used and the standard quantity that should have been used, multiplied by the standard price.

Actual quantity	760 yd
Less standard quantity (180 × 4 yd/chair)	720 yd
Difference	40 yd (U)

Quantity variance = (actual quantity − standard quantity) × standard price
= 40 yd (U) × $6/yd
= $240 (U)

As a check of these answers, the sum of the price variance and the quantity variance should equal the total direct materials cost variance as shown below:

Price variance	$ 76 (F)
Quantity variance	240 (U)
Total direct materials cost variance	$164 (U)

Sometimes cost relationships are easier to see when shown in diagram form. Figure 27-2 illustrates the cost variance analysis described above. Materials are purchased at actual cost but entered into the Materials Inventory account at standard price. Therefore, the materials price variance of $76(F) is determined before costs are entered into Materials Inventory. The materials quantity variance results from the use of more or less than the standard quantity of material in manufacturing the product. Spoilage and waste do occur, and some may be unavoidable and anticipated, when computing the standard quantity amount. A materials quantity variance occurs when standard quantity is not used. If more material than prescribed is used, as in the Pearce Company example, an unfavorable materials quantity variance results, here $240 (U). As shown, the standard quantity times the standard price is the amount entered into the Work in Process Inventory account.

Normally, the purchasing agent is responsible for price variances and the production department supervisors are accountable for quantity variances. In cases like this one, however, the cheaper materials may have been of such poor quality that higher scrap rates resulted. Each situation must be evaluated according to specific circumstances and not in terms of general guidelines.

Direct Labor Variances. The approach to finding variances in direct labor costs parallels the approach to finding direct materials variances. The **total direct labor cost variance** is the difference between the actual labor costs incurred and the standard labor cost for the good units produced. Expanding the Pearce Company example, we find that each chair requires 2.4 standard labor hours, and the standard labor rate is $8.50 per hour. During August, 450 direct labor hours were used to make 180 chairs at an average pay rate of $9.20 per hour. The total direct labor cost variance is computed as follows.

Figure 27-2. Materials Variance Analysis

Using Data from the Pearce Company Illustration:

Actual Materials Cost	Entered into Materials Inventory	Entered into Work in Process Inventory
Actual Quantity at Actual Price	Actual Quantity at Standard Price	Standard Quantity at Standard Price
760 yds. @ $5.90/yd $4,484	760 yds. @ $6.00/yd. $4,560	720 yds. @ $6.00/yd. $4,320

Price Variance	Quantity Variance
$76(F)	$240(U)

Total Materials Cost Variance

$164(U)

Actual cost

Actual hours × actual rate = 450 hr × $9.20/hr = $4,140

Less standard cost

Standard hours allowed × standard rate =

(180 chairs × 2.4 hr/chair) × $8.50/hr =

432 hr × $8.50/hr = 3,672

Total direct labor cost variance $ 468 (U)

Both the actual hours per chair and the actual labor rate varied from standard. For effective cost control, management must know how much of the total cost arose from differing labor rates and how much from varying labor hour usage. This information is found by computing the labor rate variance and the labor efficiency variance separately.

The **direct labor rate variance** is the difference between the actual labor rate and the standard labor rate, multiplied by the actual labor hours worked.

Actual rate	$9.20
Less standard rate	8.50
Difference	$ .70 (U)

$$\text{Rate variance} = (\text{actual rate} - \text{standard rate}) \times \text{actual hours}$$
$$= \$.70 \text{ (U)} \times 450 \text{ hr}$$
$$= \$315 \text{ (U)}$$

The **direct labor efficiency variance** is the difference between actual hours worked and standard hours allowed for the good units produced, multiplied by the standard labor rate.

Actual hours worked	450 hr
Less standard hours allowed (180 chairs × 2.4 hr/chair)	432 hr
Difference	18 hr (U)

$$\text{Efficiency variance} = (\text{actual hours} - \text{standard hours allowed}) \times \text{standard rate}$$
$$= 18 \text{ hr (U)} \times \$8.50/\text{hr}$$
$$= \$153 \text{ (U)}$$

The following check shows that the rate and the efficiency variances have been computed correctly.

Rate variance	$315 (U)
Efficiency variance	153 (U)
Total direct labor cost variance	$468 (U)

Labor rate variances are generally the responsibility of the personnel department. A rate variance often occurs when a person is hired at a rate higher or lower than expected or performs the duties of a higher- or lower-paid employee. Labor efficiency variances can be traced to departmental supervisors. As with direct materials variances, an unfavorable labor efficiency variance can occur if an inexperienced, lower-paid person is assigned to a task requiring greater skill. Management should judge each situation according to the circumstances.

Figure 27-3 summarizes the direct labor variance analysis. Unlike materials variances, the labor rate and efficiency variances are usually computed and recorded at the same time. This approach is used because labor is not stored in an inventory account before use, as are materials. The labor rate variance is the difference between wages paid to em-

Figure 27-3. Direct Labor Variance Analysis

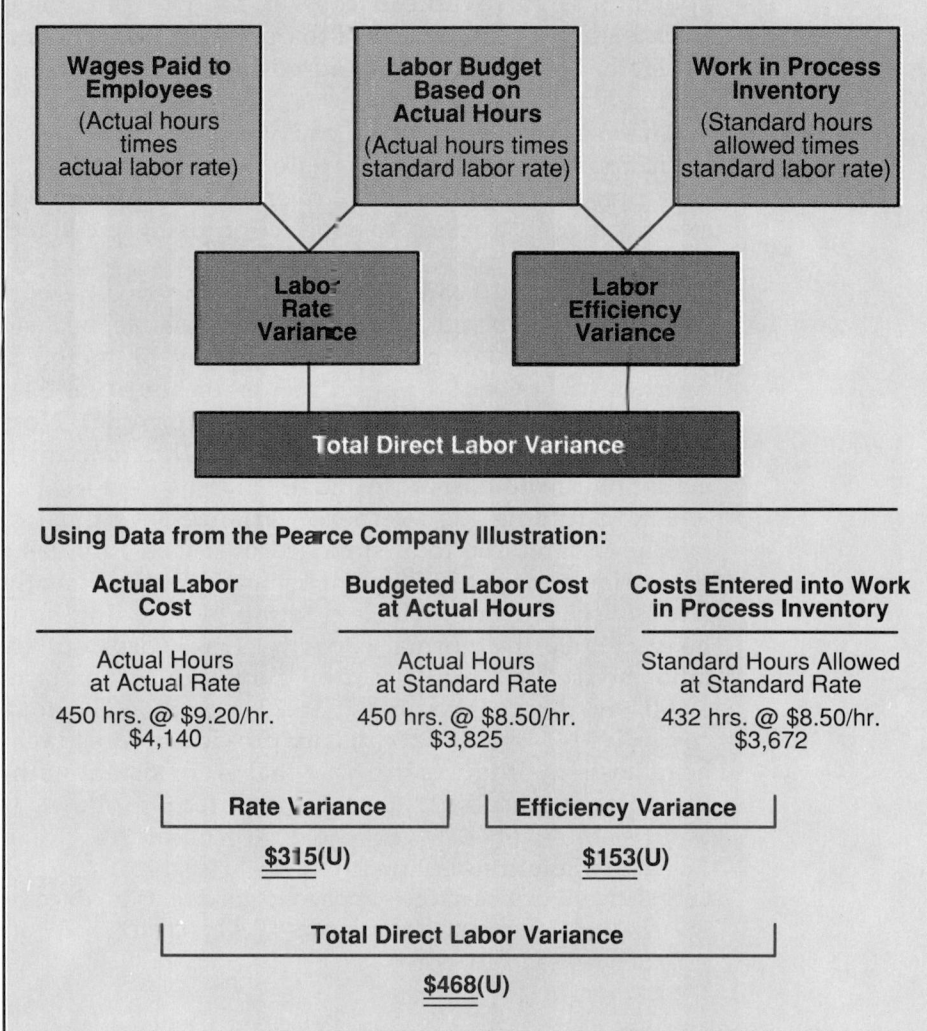

ployees (actual direct labor cost) and the budgeted wages based on actual hours (direct labor cost if standard direct labor rates were paid). The labor efficiency variance is the difference between the budgeted wages based on actual hours and the standard labor cost entered into the Work in Process Inventory account. Efficiency relates to the time taken to complete a task. Here, efficiency is measured as the difference between actual hours worked and standard hours allowed for the good units produced during the period. This difference is multiplied by the standard labor rate to compute the variance. Data from the Pearce Company were inserted into the lower portion of Figure 27-3 to illustrate this approach to labor variance analysis.

Factory Overhead Variances. Controlling overhead costs is more difficult than controlling direct materials and direct labor costs because responsibility for overhead costs is hard to pin down. But if variable overhead costs can be linked to operating departments, some control is possible. Most fixed overhead costs are not controlled by specific departmental managers.

Analyses of factory overhead variances vary in sophistication. The basic approach is to first compute the **total overhead variance**, which is the difference between actual overhead costs incurred and the standard overhead costs applied to production using the standard variable and fixed overhead rates. That amount is then divided into two parts: the controllable overhead variance and the overhead volume variance. Other, more involved approaches, are possible, but we will use this one.

In our example, the Pearce Company budgeted standard variable overhead costs of $5.75 per direct labor hour plus $1,300 of fixed overhead costs for August (flexible budget formula). Normal capacity was set at 400 direct labor hours per month. The company incurred $4,100 of actual overhead costs in August.

Before finding the overhead variances, we must calculate the total overhead rate. The total standard overhead rate has two parts. One is the variable rate of $5.75 per direct labor hour. The other is the standard fixed overhead rate, which is found by dividing budgeted fixed overhead ($1,300) by normal capacity. This works out to $3.25 per direct labor hour ($1,300 ÷ 400 hours). So the total standard overhead rate is $9.00 per direct labor hour ($5.75 + $3.25). The total fixed overhead costs divided by normal capacity provides a rate that assigns fixed overhead costs to products in a way that is consistent with expected output. The total overhead variance is computed as follows:

Actual overhead costs incurred	$4,100
Less standard overhead costs applied to good units produced	
$9.00/direct labor hour × (180 chairs × 2.4 hr/chair)	3,888
Total overhead variance	$ 212 (U)

This amount can be divided into two parts, the controllable overhead variance and the overhead volume variance. The **controllable overhead variance** is the difference between the actual overhead costs incurred and the factory overhead budgeted for the level of production reached. Thus the controllable variance for the Pearce Company for August would be as follows:

Actual overhead costs incurred		$4,100
Less budgeted factory overhead		
(flexible budget) for 180 chairs:		
Variable overhead cost (180 chairs		
× 2.4 hr/chair) × $5.75/direct labor hour	$2,484	
Budgeted fixed overhead cost	1,300	
Total budgeted factory overhead		3,784
Controllable overhead variance		$ 316 (U)

In this example, the controllable variance is unfavorable; the company spent more than it should have spent.

The **overhead volume variance** is the difference between the factory overhead budgeted for the level of production achieved and the overhead applied to production using the standard variable and fixed overhead rates. Continuing with the Pearce Company example, we have

Budgeted factory overhead (see page 1154)	$3,784
Less factory overhead applied	
(180 chairs × 2.4 hr/chair)	
× $9.00/direct labor hour	3,888
Overhead volume variance	$ 104 (F)

Checking the computations, we find that the two variances do equal the total overhead variance.

Controllable overhead variance	$316 (U)
Overhead volume variance	104 (F)
Total overhead variance	$212 (U)

Because the overhead volume variance gauges the use of existing facilities and capacity, a volume variance will occur if more or less capacity than normal is used. (The various operating capacities were discussed in Chapter 25.) In this example, 400 direct labor hours is considered normal use of facilities. Fixed overhead costs are applied on the basis of standard hours allowed. So in the example, overhead would be applied on the basis of 432 hours, even though the fixed overhead rate was computed using 400 hours (normal capacity). Thus more fixed costs would be applied to products than were budgeted. Because the products can absorb no more than actual costs incurred, this level of production would tend to lower unit cost. Thus when more than expected capacity is used, the result is a favorable overhead volume variance. When less than normal capacity is used, not all of the fixed overhead costs will be applied to units produced. It is then necessary to add the amount of underapplied fixed overhead to the cost of the good units produced, thereby increasing their unit cost. This condition is unfavorable.

Figure 27-4 sums up our discussion of overhead variance analysis. All procedures shown are exactly the same as those explained above. To figure the controllable variance, the accountant subtracts the budgeted overhead amount (using a flexible budget) for the level of output achieved from the actual overhead costs incurred. A positive result means an unfavorable variance, because actual costs were greater than budgeted costs. The controllable variance is favorable if the difference is negative. Subtracting total overhead applied from budgeted overhead at the level of output achieved yields the volume variance. As before, a positive result means an unfavorable variance, a negative result, a favorable variance. The data from the Pearce Company example are shown in the lower part of Figure 27-4. Carefully check the solution in the figure with that given earlier.

Figure 27-4. Overhead Variance Analysis

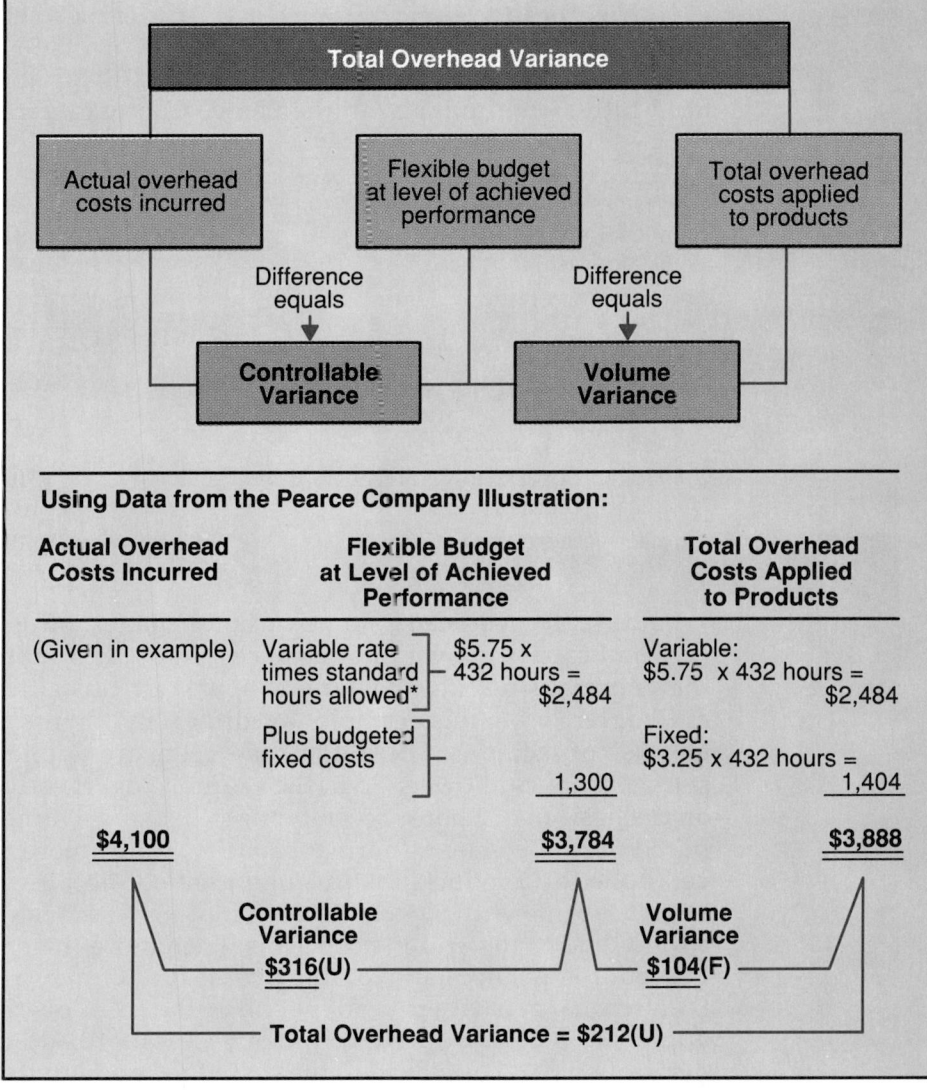

*Standard hours allowed (achieved performance level) is computed by multiplying good units produced times required standard time per unit. The computation is as follows:

180 chairs produced x 2.4 hours per chair = 432 standard hours allowed

Variances in the Accounting Records

Special journal entries are needed to record variances from standard costs.[1] The few simple rules stated at the top of the following page will make this recording process quite easy to remember:

1. It is possible to operate a standard cost system without recording the variances in the journals. Variances can be figured on work sheets, and actual costs can be run through the accounts. This approach is less costly than the standard cost approach, but it lacks the advantage of consistent pricing of products and inventories. It also complicates the recording of product cost flow.

OBJECTIVE 7
Prepare journal entries to record transactions involving variances in a standard costing system

1. As stated earlier, *all* inventory balances are recorded at standard cost.
2. Separate accounts are created for each type of variance.
3. *Unfavorable* variances are *debited* to their accounts; *favorable* variances are *credited*.

With these rules in mind, we will now record all the transactions of the Pearce Company described earlier.

Journal Entries for Direct Materials Transactions

a. Purchase:

Materials Inventory (760 yd @ $6/yd)	4,560	
Direct Materials Price Variance		76
Accounts Payable (actual cost)		4,484
To record purchase of direct materials on account and resulting variance		

There are two key points to this transaction. (1) The increase in Materials Inventory is recorded at the actual quantity purchased, but priced at standard cost. (2) Accounts Payable is stated at the actual cost (actual quantity purchased times actual price per unit) in order to record the proper liability.

b. Requisition:

Work in Process Inventory (720 yd @ $6/yd)	4,320	
Direct Materials Quantity Variance	240	
Materials Inventory (760 yd @ $6/yd)		4,560
To record requisition and usage of direct materials and resulting variance		

Note the important aspects of this entry. (1) Everything in the Work in Process Inventory is recorded at standard cost, which means standard quantity times standard price. (2) Actual quantity must come out of Materials Inventory at standard price, because it was recorded at standard price when it was entered. Remember that materials may be used in smaller quantities than purchased. In our example, the entire amount of the purchase was used during the period.

Journal Entry for Direct Labor Transactions

Work in Process Inventory (432 hr @ $8.50/hr)	3,672	
Direct Labor Rate Variance	315	
Direct Labor Efficiency Variance	153	
Factory Payroll (450 hr @ $9.20/hr)		4,140
To charge labor cost to Work in Process and to identify the resulting variances		

When recording labor costs, the same rules hold true as for the requisition of materials. (1) Work in Process Inventory is charged with standard labor cost—standard hours allowed times the standard labor rate. (2) Factory Payroll must be credited for the actual labor cost of the workers—actual hours worked times the actual labor rate earned. The variances, if computed properly, will balance out the difference between the two amounts.

Journal Entries for Application of Factory Overhead

Work in Process Inventory (432 direct labor hours @ $9/direct labor hour)	3,888	
Factory Overhead Applied		3,888
To apply factory overhead costs to Work in Process at standard cost		

Factory Overhead Applied	3,888	
Controllable Overhead Variance	316	
Overhead Volume Variance		104
Factory Overhead Control		4,100
To close out Factory Overhead Control and Applied accounts and record resulting variances		

Recording factory overhead variances differs in timing and technique from recording direct materials and direct labor variances. First, total factory overhead is charged to Work in Process Inventory at standard cost (direct labor hours allowed times the standard variable and fixed rates). The variances are identified later, when the Factory Overhead Applied and Factory Overhead Control accounts are closed out at period end.

Journal Entry for Transfer of Completed Units to Finished Goods Inventory

We now have $11,880 of standard costs recorded in the Work in Process Inventory account. Assuming that the 180 chairs have been completed, the following entry would be made:

Finished Goods Inventory (180 chairs @ $66/chair)	11,880	
Work in Process Inventory		11,880
To record transfer of completed units to Finished Goods Inventory		

The standard unit price of $66 was computed as follows:

Direct materials:	
4 yd @ $6/yd	$24.00
Direct labor:	
2.4 hr @ $8.50/hr	20.40
Factory overhead:	
2.4 hr @ $9/hr	21.60
Total standard unit cost	$66.00

All costs went into the Work in Process Inventory account at standard cost, so standard cost must be used when they are transferred out of the account.

Journal Entry to Transfer Cost of Units Sold to Cost of Goods Sold Account

Assume that the 180 chairs completed were sold on account for $169 per chair and shipped to a customer:

Accounts Receivable (180 chairs @ $169/chair)	30,420	
Sales		30,420
To record sale of 180 chairs		
Cost of Goods Sold	11,880	
Finished Goods Inventory		11,880
To record transfer of standard		
cost of units sold to Cost of Goods		
Sold account		

Journal Entry to Dispose of End-of-Period Variance Account Balances

The balances in the variance accounts at the end of the period are disposed of much as over- or underapplied overhead was earlier. Here we will continue to assume that all units worked on were completed and sold. If so, a period-end journal entry must be made to close all variances to Cost of Goods Sold:

Cost of Goods Sold	844	
Direct Materials Price Variance	76	
Overhead Volume Variance	104	
Direct Materials Quantity Variance		240
Direct Labor Rate Variance		315
Direct Labor Efficiency Variance		153
Controllable Overhead Variance		316
To close all variance account		
balances to Cost of Goods Sold		

If at period end balances still exist in Work in Process Inventory and Finished Goods Inventory, the net amount of the variances ($844 here) should be divided among Work in Process Inventory, Finished Goods Inventory, and Cost of Goods Sold, in proportion to their balances.

Performance Reports Using Standard Costs

OBJECTIVE 8
Evaluate employee performance using variances

Performance reports should be tailored to a manager's responsibilities. They should be clear and accurate, and should contain only those cost items that can be controlled by the manager receiving the report.

Exhibit 27-4 shows a performance report compiled using data that pertain only to the production department in the Pearce Company. The production supervisor is responsible for direct materials used (and the related direct materials quantity variance), for direct labor hours used (and the related direct labor efficiency variance), and for the costs included in the controllable overhead variance. Note that space has been left at the bottom for the manager to add the reasons for the variances. The report shown here is simpler than most. Normally such a report would show several items of direct materials, two or more direct labor classifications, and many overhead cost items.

Exhibit 27-4. Performance Report Using Variance Analysis

Pearce Company
Production Department Performance Report—Cost Variance Analysis
For the Month Ended August 31, 19x1

400 hours: Normal capacity (direct labor hours)
432 hours: Capacity performance level achieved (standard hours allowed)
180 chairs: Good units produced

Cost Analysis

	Cost		Variance	
	Budgeted	Actual	Amount	Type
Direct materials used (leather)	$ 4,320	$ 4,560	$240 (U)	Quantity variance
Direct labor usage	3,672	3,825	153 (U)	Efficiency variance
Factory overhead	3,784	4,100	316 (U)	Controllable overhead variance
Totals	$11,776	$12,485	$709 (U)	

Reasons for Variances

Direct materials quantity variance: (1) inferior quality-control inspection; (2) cheaper grade of direct materials
Direct labor efficiency variance: (1) inferior direct materials; (2) new, inexperienced employee
Controllable overhead variance: (1) excessive indirect labor usage; (2) changes in employee overtime; (3) unexpected price changes

Chapter Review

Review of Learning Objectives

1. **Describe the nature and purpose of standard costs.**

   Standard costs are realistically predetermined costs for direct materials, direct labor, and factory overhead. They are usually expressed as a cost per unit of finished product. Standard costs are introduced into a cost accounting system to help in the budgetary control process, as they are useful for evaluating performance and preparing operating budgets. They also help in identifying parts of the production process that require cost control measures, in establishing realistic prices, and in simplifying cost accounting procedures for inventories and product costing.

2. **Identify the six elements of a standard unit cost and describe the factors to consider in developing each element.**

   The six elements of a standard unit cost are (1) the direct materials price standard, (2) the direct materials quantity standard, (3) the direct labor time standard, (4) the direct labor rate standard, (5) the standard variable overhead rate, and (6) the standard fixed factory overhead rate. The direct materials price standard is found by carefully considering expected price increases, changes in available quantities, and possible new sources of supply. The direct materials quantity standard is an expression of forecasted or expected quantity usage. It is affected by product engineering specifications, quality of direct materials used, age and productivity of the machines being used, and the quality and experience of the machine operators and set-up people. The direct labor time standard is based on current time and motion studies of workers and machines and past employee and machine performance. Labor union contracts and company personnel policies influence direct labor rate standards. Standard variable and fixed factory overhead rates are found by dividing total budgeted or forecasted variable and fixed factory overhead costs by an appropriate application base, such as standard direct labor hours or normal capacity.

3. **Compute a standard unit cost.**

   A product's total standard unit cost is computed by adding together the following costs: (1) direct materials cost (equals direct materials price standard times direct materials quantity standard), (2) direct labor cost (equals direct labor time standard times direct labor rate standard), and (3) factory overhead cost (equals standard variable and standard fixed factory overhead rate times standard direct labor hours allowed per unit).

4. **Prepare a flexible budget.**

   A flexible budget is a summary of anticipated costs prepared for a range of activity levels geared to changes in the level of productive output. Variable and fixed costs are given for several levels of capacity or output, with each column showing the total expected cost at a different output level. Once prepared, the flexible budget is used to determine the flexible budget formula. This formula, which can be applied to any level of productive output, is a key tool in evaluating the performance of individuals as well as departments.

5. **Describe the concept of management by exception.**

   Management by exception is a performance evaluation technique in which significant variances from budgeted or planned operations are highlighted and analyzed. Variances within specific limits set by management are not analyzed. This technique is especially useful in companies that control a large number of cost centers or cost categories.

6. **Compute and evaluate direct materials, direct labor, and factory overhead variances.**

   Cost variances, or differences between actual and standard manufacturing costs, can be computed for direct materials, direct labor, and factory overhead. The direct materials price and quantity variances help explain differences between actual and standard direct materials costs. Direct labor cost differences are analyzed through the direct labor rate variance and the direct labor efficiency variance. The controllable overhead variance and the overhead volume variance help explain differences in overhead costs. Each variance results from specific causes, and these causes help pinpoint reasons for the differences between actual and standard costs.

7. **Prepare journal entries to record transactions involving variances in a standard costing system.**

Journal entries are used to integrate standard cost variance information into the accounting records. Unfavorable variances will create debit balances, and favorable variances will be credited. General ledger accounts are maintained for direct materials price variance, direct materials quantity variance, direct labor rate variance, direct labor efficiency variance, controllable overhead variance, and overhead volume variance. At the close of an accounting period, balances in these accounts are disposed of by either (1) closing them to Cost of Goods Sold, if the balances are small or most or all of the goods produced during the period were sold, or (2) dividing the net balance among Work in Process Inventory, Finished Goods Inventory, and Cost of Goods Sold, in proportion to their balances.

8. **Evaluate employee performance using variances.**

Introducing variances from standard costs into the performance report lends a degree of accuracy to the evaluation process. Variances tend to pinpoint efficient and inefficient operating areas better than comparisons between actual and static budget data. The keys to preparing a performance report based on standard costs and related variances are to (1) establish a responsibility accounting system and identify those responsible for each variance, (2) determine the causes for each variance, (3) establish a system of management by exception, and (4) develop a reporting format suited to the task.

Review of Concepts and Terminology

The following concepts and terms were introduced in this chapter:

(L.O. 6) **Controllable overhead variance:** The difference between actual overhead costs incurred and the factory overhead budgeted for the level of production reached.

(L.O. 6) **Direct labor efficiency variance:** The difference between actual hours worked and standard hours allowed for the good units produced, multiplied by the standard labor rate.

(L.O. 2) **Direct labor rate standards:** The hourly labor costs that are expected to prevail during the next accounting period for each function or job classification.

(L.O. 6) **Direct labor rate variance:** The difference between the actual labor rate and the standard labor rate, multiplied by the actual labor hours worked.

(L.O. 2) **Direct labor time standard:** The expected time that it takes each department, machine, or process to complete production on one unit or batch of output.

(L.O. 2) **Direct materials price standard:** A careful estimate of the cost of a certain type of direct material in the next accounting period.

(L.O. 6) **Direct materials price variance:** The difference between the actual price and the standard price, multiplied by the actual quantity purchased.

(L.O. 2) **Direct materials quantity standard:** An estimate of expected quantity usage that is influenced by product engineering specifications, quality of

direct materials, age and productivity of machinery, and the quality and experience of the work force.

(L.O. 6)   **Direct materials quantity variance:** The difference between the actual quantity used and the standard quantity that should have been used, multiplied by the standard price.

(L.O. 4)   **Flexible budget:** A summary of expected costs for a range of activity levels, geared to changes in the level of productive output.

(L.O. 5)   **Management by exception:** A management technique that locates and analyzes only the areas of unusually good or bad performance.

(L.O. 6)   **Overhead volume variance:** The difference between the factory overhead budgeted for the level of production achieved and the overhead applied to production using the standard variable and fixed overhead rates.

(L.O. 1)   **Standard costs:** Realistically predetermined costs for direct materials, direct labor, and factory overhead.

(L.O. 2)   **Standard direct labor cost:** The standard hours of direct labor multiplied by the standard wage for direct labor.

(L.O. 2)   **Standard direct materials cost:** The standard price for direct materials multiplied by the standard quantity for direct materials.

(L.O. 2)   **Standard factory overhead cost:** An estimate of the variable and fixed factory overhead in the next accounting period.

(L.O. 2)   **Standard fixed overhead rate:** Total budgeted fixed factory overhead costs divided by an expression of capacity, usually normal capacity in terms of standard direct labor hours.

(L.O. 2)   **Standard variable overhead rate:** Total budgeted variable factory overhead costs divided by an expression of capacity, usually the expected number of standard direct labor hours.

(L.O. 6)   **Total direct labor cost variance:** The difference between the actual labor costs incurred and the standard labor cost for the good units produced.

(L.O. 6)   **Total direct materials cost variance:** The difference between the actual materials cost incurred and the standard cost of those same items.

(L.O. 6)   **Total overhead variance:** The difference between actual overhead costs incurred and the standard overhead costs applied to production using the standard variable and fixed overhead rates.

(L.O. 6)   **Variance analysis:** The process of computing the amount of and isolating the causes of differences between actual costs and standard costs.

Self-Test

Test your knowledge of the chapter by choosing the best answer for each item below and on the following pages.

1. Realistically predetermined costs for direct materials, direct labor, and factory overhead are known as
   a. period costs.
   b. variable costs.
   c. predetermined rates.
   d. standard costs.   *(L.O. 1)*

2. Current time and motion studies of workers and machines as well as past employee and machine performance are the basic inputs for the
   a. direct labor rate standard.
   b. direct labor time standard.
   c. direct materials price standard.
   d. direct materials quantity standard.   *(L.O. 2)*

3. To compute the standard fixed overhead rate, the total budgeted fixed overhead costs are divided by the
   a. practical capacity.   c. normal capacity.
   b. excess capacity.   d. ideal capacity.   *(L.O. 2)*

4. Locating and analyzing the areas of unusually good or bad performance is called
   a. management by exception.   c. managerial emphasis.
   b. exceptional management.   d. standard costing.   *(L.O. 5)*

5. The Pappas Corporation uses a standard costing system in its ice cream division. The standard cost of producing a twenty-gallon can of ice cream is:

Materials (40 pounds @ $1.00/lb)	$40.00
Labor (2 hours @ $10/hr)	20.00
Factory overhead (2 hours @ $7/hr)	14.00
Total standard unit cost	$74.00

The current monthly flexible budget formula for factory overhead is

$4 per direct labor hour + $12,000

During August, the division produced 1,950 cans of ice cream compared to 2,000 cans at normal capacity. The actual costs per can were:

Materials (42 pounds @ $1.10/lb)	$46.20
Labor (2.2 hours @ $9.50/hr)	20.90
Factory overhead ($30,030/1,950 cans)	15.40
Total actual unit cost	$82.50

The total materials price variance for August is
   a. $8,190 (U).   c. $8,190 (F).
   b. $7,900 (F).   d. $7,900 (U).   *(L.O. 6)*

6. Assuming the same facts as in **5**, the total materials quantity variance for August is
   a. $4,290 (U).   c. $4,290 (F).
   b. $3,900 (F).   d. $3,900 (U).   *(L.O. 6)*

7. Assuming the same facts as in **5**, the total labor rate variance for August is
   a. $2,145 (U).   c. $2,145 (F).
   b. $2,350 (U).   d. $2,350 (F).   *(L.O. 6)*

8. Assuming the same facts as in **5**, the total labor efficiency variance for August is
   a. $3,600 (U).
   b. $3,900 (U).
   c. $3,600 (F).
   d. $3,900 (F).   *(L.O. 6)*

9. Assuming the same facts as in **5**, the total controllable overhead variance for August is
   a. $2,430 (F).
   b. $2,730 (F).
   c. $2,730 (U).
   d. $2,430 (U).   *(L.O. 6)*

10. Assuming the same facts as in **5**, the total overhead volume variance for August is
    a. $300 (U).
    b. $600 (F).
    c. $600 (U).
    d. $300 (F).   *(L.O. 6)*

Answers to Self-Test are at the end of this chapter.

Review Problem
Variance Analysis

(L.O. 2, 6) Clayton Manufacturing Company has a standard cost system and keeps all cost standards up to date. The company's main product is heating pipe, which is made in a single department. The standard variable costs for one unit of finished pipe are:

Direct materials (3 square meters @ $12.50/sq meter)	$37.50
Direct labor (1.2 hr @ $9.00/hr)	10.80
Variable overhead (1.2 hr @ $5.00/hr)	6.00
Standard variable cost per unit	$54.30

Normal capacity is 15,000 direct labor hours, and budgeted fixed overhead costs for the year were $54,000. During the year, 12,200 units were produced and sold. Related transactions and actual cost data for the year were as follows: Direct materials consisted of 37,500 square meters purchased and used; unit purchase cost was $12.40 per meter. Direct labor consisted of 15,250 direct labor hours worked at an average labor rate of $9.20 per hour. Actual factory overhead costs incurred for the period consisted of variable overhead costs of $73,200 and fixed overhead costs of $55,000.

Required Using the data given, compute the following:

1. Standard hours allowed.
2. Standard fixed overhead rate.
3. Direct materials price variance.
4. Direct materials quantity variance.
5. Direct labor rate variance.
6. Direct labor efficiency variance.
7. Controllable overhead variance.
8. Overhead volume variance.

Answer to Review Problem

1. Standard hours allowed = good units produced × standard direct labor hours per unit

    12,200 units × 1.2 direct labor hours/unit = 14,640 hr

2. Standard fixed overhead rate $= \dfrac{\text{budgeted fixed overhead cost}}{\text{normal capacity}}$

    $= \dfrac{\$54,000}{15,000 \text{ direct labor hours}}$

    = \$3.60 per direct labor hour

3. Direct materials price variance:

Price difference: Actual price paid	\$12.40 /meter
Less standard price	12.50 /meter
Difference	\$ .10 (F)

    Direct materials price variance = (actual price − standard price)
    × actual quantity
    = \$0.10 (F) × 37,500 square meters
    = \$3,750 (F)

4. Direct materials quantity variance:

Quantity difference: Actual quantity used	37,500 meters
Less standard quantity	
(12,200 units × 3 meters)	36,600 meters
Difference	900 (U)

    Direct materials quantity variance = (actual quantity − standard quantity) × standard price
    = 900 (U) × \$12.50/meter
    = \$11,250 (U)

5. Direct labor rate variance:

Rate difference: Actual labor rate	\$9.20 /hr
Less standard labor rate	9.00 /hr
Difference	\$ .20 (U)

$$\begin{aligned}
\text{Direct labor rate variance} &= (\text{actual rate} - \text{standard rate}) \times \text{actual hours} \\
&= \$.20 \text{ (U)} \times 15,250 \text{ hr} \\
&= \$3,050 \text{ (U)}
\end{aligned}$$

6. Direct labor efficiency variance:

Difference in hours:	Actual hours worked	15,250 hr
	Less standard hours allowed	14,640 hr
	Difference	610 (U)

$$\begin{aligned}
\text{Direct labor efficiency variance} &= (\text{actual hours} - \text{standard hours} \\
&\quad\ \text{allowed}) \times \text{standard rate} \\
&= 610 \text{ hr (U)} \times \$9.00/\text{hr} \\
&= \$5,490 \text{ (U)}
\end{aligned}$$

7. Controllable overhead variance:

Actual overhead incurred		$128,200
Less budgeted factory overhead for 14,640 hours:		
Variable overhead cost (14,640 hr × $5.00/direct labor hour)	$73,200	
Budgeted fixed factory overhead	54,000	
Total budgeted factory overhead		127,200
Controllable overhead variance		$ 1,000 (U)

8. Overhead volume variance:

Total budgeted factory overhead (see computation in part 7)		$127,200
Less factory overhead applied:		
Variable: 14,640 hr × $5.00/direct labor hour	$73,200	
Fixed: 14,640 hr × $3.60/direct labor hour	52,704	
Total factory overhead applied		125,904
Overhead volume variance		$ 1,296 (U)

Chapter Assignments

Discussion Questions and Writing Assignments

1. What is a standard cost?
2. What do predetermined overhead costing and standard costing have in common? How are they different?

3. "Standard costing is a total cost concept, in that standard unit costs are determined for direct materials, direct labor, and factory overhead." Explain this statement.
4. Name the six elements used to compute total standard unit cost.
5. What three factors could affect a direct materials price standard?
6. "Standard labor cost rests on degree of efficiency and union collective bargaining." Is this statement true? Defend your answer.
7. What general ledger accounts are affected by a standard cost system?
8. "Performance is evaluated or measured by comparing what did happen with what should have happened." What is meant by this statement? Relate your comments to the budgetary control process.
9. What is a variance?
10. In what ways can variances help management achieve effective control of operations?
11. What is a flexible budget? What is its purpose?
12. What are the two parts of the flexible budget formula? How are they related to each other?
13. What is the formula for computing a direct materials price variance?
14. How would you interpret an unfavorable direct materials price variance?
15. Distinguish between the controllable overhead variance and the overhead volume variance.
16. If standard hours allowed exceed normal hours, will the period's overhead volume variance be favorable, or will it be unfavorable? Explain your answer.
17. Can an unfavorable direct materials quantity variance be caused, at least in part, by a favorable direct materials price variance? Explain.
18. What are the three rules that underlie the recording of standard cost variances?

Classroom Exercises

Exercise 27-1.
Purpose of
Standard Costs
(L.O. 1)

Ron Bawmann is a senior accountant for a large public accounting firm, Swanson & Oliver, CPAs. One of his duties is to counsel and advise his clients regarding needed improvements or additions to their existing accounting system. His newest client, Augustana Industries of Rock Island, Illinois, is a manufacturer of rubber gaskets for automobile engines. These products are homogeneous and are produced in long production runs. The company currently uses a process cost accounting system, but has been experiencing both labor and materials inefficiencies. Total cost increases have far exceeded the labor rate and materials price increases.

Augustana's president, an engineer, has asked Mr. Bawmann for advice. He would like to know more about standard cost accounting systems and how they help in controlling costs.

Prepare a reply to the president.

Exercise 27-2.
Keeping Standards
Current
(L.O. 2)

NAA Paper Company recently installed a complete standard process cost accounting system. Sammy Samuelson, controller of the Washington, D.C., Division, is concerned about keeping cost standards on a current basis. He is thinking about establishing a maintenance program to help keep the standard costs current, and has asked Nat Naddio, assistant controller, to take charge of the project and to outline the system.

List the suggested policies, procedures, and people that Mr. Naddio should include in his analysis.

Exercise 27-3.
Standard Unit Cost
Computation
(L.O. 3)

Moustafa Aerodynamics, Inc. makes electronically equipped weather-detecting balloons for university meteorological departments. Recent na-tionwide inflation has caused the company management to order that stan-dard costs be recomputed. New direct materials price standards are $620.00 per set for electronic components and $13.40 per square meter for heavy-duty canvas. Direct materials quantity standards include one set of electronic components and 95 square meters of heavy-duty canvas per bal-loon. Direct labor time standards are 16 hours per balloon for the Electronics Department and 19 hours per balloon for the Assembly Department. Direct labor rate standards are $11.00 per hour for the Electronics Department and $9.50 per hour for the Assembly Department. Standard factory overhead rates are $16.00 per direct labor hour for the standard variable overhead rate and $10.00 per direct labor hour for the standard fixed overhead rate.

Using the production standards provided, compute the standard manufac-turing cost of one weather balloon.

Exercise 27-4.
Flexible Budget
Preparation
(L.O. 4)

Fixed overhead costs for the Karolinski Kostume Company for 19x2 are ex-pected to be as follows: depreciation, $72,000; supervisory salaries, $92,000; property taxes and insurance, $26,000; and other fixed overhead, $14,500. Total fixed overhead is thus expected to be $204,500. Variable costs per unit are expected to be as follows: direct materials, $16.50; direct labor, $8.50; op-erating supplies, $2.50; indirect labor, $4.00; and other variable overhead costs, $3.20.

Prepare a flexible budget for the following levels of production: 18,000 units, 20,000 units, and 22,000 units. What is the flexible budget formula for 19x2?

Exercise 27-5.
Management by
Exception
(L.O. 5)

Falcetta-Frank Instruments, Inc. produces scientific apparatus for food in-spection. During the past five years, the corporation has grown from sales of $2,800,000 to a current level of over $25,000,000. More than 500 types of mate-rials and the labor skills of more than 80 different specialists are used in the production process. The company's rapid growth has caused numerous vari-ances, which the controller's department has not had time to investigate. A standard cost accounting system was introduced two years ago, but it has proved impractical for analyzing the host of variances. The controller has been asked by the vice president of finance to develop an improved method of controlling costs.

1. Describe the concept of management by exception.
2. Discuss how the concept could prove useful to the controller of Falcetta-Frank Instruments, Inc.

Exercise 27-6.
Direct Materials
Price and Quantity
Variances
(L.O. 6)

The Marcos Elevator Company manufactures small hydroelectric elevators with a maximum capacity of ten passengers each. One of the direct materials used by the Production Department is heavy-duty carpeting for the floors of the elevators. The direct materials quantity standard used for the month ended April 30, 19x2 was 6 square yards per elevator. During April, the purchasing agent was able to purchase this carpeting at $11 per square yard; standard price for the period was $12. Ninety elevators were completed and sold during April, and the production department used 6.6 square yards of carpet per elevator.

Calculate Marcos Elevator Company's direct materials price and quantity variances for April 19x2.

Exercise 27-7.
Direct Labor Rate
and Efficiency
Variances
(L.O. 6)

Winter Park Foundry, Inc. manufactures castings used by other companies in the production of machinery. For the past two years, the largest selling product has been a casting for an eight-cylinder engine block. Standard direct labor hours per engine block are 1.8 hours. The labor contract requires that $17.00 per hour be paid to all direct labor employees. During June, 16,500 engine blocks were produced. Actual direct labor hours and cost for June were 29,900 hours and $523,250, respectively.

1. Compute the direct labor rate variance for the engine block product line during June.
2. Using the same data, compute the direct labor efficiency variance for the engine block product line during June. Check your answer, assuming that total direct labor variance is $18,350 (U).

Exercise 27-8.
Factory Overhead
Variances
(L.O. 6)

The Lowry Company produces handmade clamming pots that are sold to distributors throughout New England. The company incurred $11,100 of actual overhead costs in May. Budgeted standard overhead costs for May were $4 of variable overhead costs per direct labor hour plus $1,250 in fixed overhead costs. Normal capacity was set at 2,000 direct labor hours per month. In May, the company was able to produce 9,900 clamming pots. The time standard is 0.2 direct labor hours per clamming pot.

Compute the controllable overhead variance, the overhead volume variance, and the total overhead variance for May.

Exercise 27-9.
Standard Cost
Journal Entries
(L.O. 7)

Bush-Hunt Battery Company produces batteries for automobiles, motorcycles, and mopeds. Transactions for direct materials and direct labor for March were as follows:

1. Purchased 1,000 type A battery casings for $6.50 each, on account; standard cost, $7.00 per casing.
2. Purchased 5,000 type 10C lead battery plates for $2.40 each, on account; standard cost, $2.25 per plate.
3. Requisitioned 32 type A battery casings and 248 type 10C lead plates into production. Order no. 674 called for 30 batteries, each using a standard quantity of 8 plates per casing.
4. Direct labor costs for order no. 674 were as follows:

Department H
Actual labor	26 hr @ $10/hr
Standard labor	24 hr @ $11/hr

Department J
Actual labor	10 hr @ $13/hr
Standard labor	12 hr @ $14/hr

Prepare journal entries for the four transactions described above.

Exercise 27-10.
Evaluating
Performance
Through Variances
(L.O. 8)

Evaluating the operating performance of the Altman Health Club is the responsibility of its controller, Joe Dean. The following information was made available for March 19x1:

	Standard	Actual
Variable costs:		
Operating labor	$ 5,760	$ 7,350
Utility	1,440	1,680
Repairs and maintenance	2,880	3,570
Fixed costs:		
Depreciation, equipment	1,300	1,340
Rent expense	1,640	1,640
Other	852	930
Totals	$13,872	$16,510

Normal operating hours call for six operators, working 160 hours each per month. During March, seven operators worked an average of 150 hours each.

With this limited information, compute as many variances as possible for labor and overhead, and prepare a performance report for the month.

Interpreting Accounting Information

Internal
Management
Information: GINA
Realtors, Inc.
(L.O. 4, 6, 8)

Ms. Clayton, the managing partner of GINA Realtors, Inc., received the performance report shown on the next page. The report showed the company had experienced its biggest year in home resales since it began operating fifteen years ago. It indicates that although fees were over budget by $190,200, all cost categories were also over budget, cutting the increase in net income to only $1,847.

During 19x1, company sales personnel marketed 202 homes averaging $185,000 per unit. Budgeted data were based on 180 homes sold at an average market value of $190,000. Selling fees for all realty work are 6 percent of the selling price. Data supporting the budget figures were as follows:

Commissions:
  Salespersons: 25 percent of total fees
  Listing agents: 20 percent of total fees
  Listing companies: 25 percent of total fees
    (35 percent of homes sold by GINA Realtors
    were listed by another company)

Other variable expenses:
  Automobile expense, $200 per sale
  Advertising expense, $520 per sale
  Home repairs expense, $430 per sale
  Word processing expense, $225 per sale

General overhead:
  30 percent of total fees

GINA Realtors, Inc.
Performance Report
For the Year Ended December 31, 19x1

	Budget for the Year	Actual Fees and Costs	Variance Under (Over) Budget
Total Selling Fees	$2,052,000	$2,242,200	$(190,200)
Less Expenses			
Commissions			
Salespersons	$ 513,000	$ 560,550	$ (47,550)
Listing agents	410,400	448,440	(38,040)
Listing companies	179,550	196,193	(16,643)
Other variable expenses			
Automobile	36,000	39,560	(3,560)
Advertising	93,600	103,450	(9,850)
Home repairs	77,400	89,240	(11,840)
Word processing	40,500	44,310	(3,810)
General overhead expenses	615,600	672,660	(57,060)
Total expenses	$1,966,050	$2,154,403	$(188,353)
Net Income before Taxes	$ 85,950	$ 87,797	$ (1,847)

Required

1. Recast the performance report using a flexible budget based on the number of units sold.
2. Interpret the revised performance report for Ms. Clayton.

Problem Set A

Problem 27A-1.
Development of
Standards: Direct
Labor
(L.O. 2, 3)

Because of a planned change in labor structure, Rollins Salt Company must develop a new standard direct labor cost for its product. Standard direct labor costs per 1,000 pounds of salt in 19x1 were 2.5 hours in the Sodium Preparation Department, at $10.00 per hour; 1.6 hours in the Chloride Mixing Department, at $12.50 per hour; and 1.2 hours in the Cleaning and Packaging Department, at $8.50 per hour. Labor rates are expected to increase in 19x2 by 10 percent in the Sodium Preparation Department and 20 percent in the Chloride Mixing Department, and to decrease by 5 percent in the Cleaning and Packaging Department. New machinery in the Chloride Mixing

Department will lower the direct labor time standard by 20 percent per 1,000 pounds of salt. All other time standards are expected to remain the same.

Required

1. Compute the standard direct labor cost per 1,000 pounds of salt in 19x2.
2. Management has a plan to improve productive output in the Sodium Preparation Department by 20 percent. If such results are achieved in 19x2, determine (a) the effect on the direct labor time standard and (b) the resulting total standard direct labor cost per 1,000 pounds of salt. Round to three places.
3. Unskilled labor can be hired to staff all departments in 19x2, with the result that all labor rates paid in 19x1 would be cut by 30 percent in the new year. Such a change in labor skill would cause the direct labor time standards to increase by 50 percent over their 19x1 levels, based on skilled labor. Compute the standard direct labor cost per 1,000 pounds of salt if this change takes place.

**Problem 27A-2.
Developing and
Using Standard
Costs**
(L.O. 2, 3, 7)

The Otani Supply Company manufactures swimming pool equipment and accessories. To make umbrellas for poolside tables, waterproof canvas is first sent to the Cutting Department. In the Assembly Department, the canvas is stretched over the umbrella's ribs and attached to the center pole and opening mechanism. Then the umbrella is mounted on a heavy base before being packed for shipment.

The company uses a standard cost accounting system. Direct labor and factory overhead standards for each umbrella for 19x1 are as follows: Direct labor consists of .4 hour charged to the Cutting Department at $11.00 per hour and .6 hour charged to the Assembly Department at $12.50 per hour. Variable overhead is 120 percent, and fixed overhead 140 percent, of total direct labor dollars.

During 19x0 the company used the following direct materials standards: waterproof canvas was $4.60 per square yard for 6 square yards per umbrella; a unit consisting of pole, ribs, and opening mechanism was $20.50 per unit; and the umbrella base was $10.40 per unit.

Quantity standards are expected to remain the same during 19x1, but price changes are likely. The cost of waterproof canvas is expected to increase by 10 percent. The pole, ribs, and opening mechanism will be purchased from three vendors. Vendor A will provide 20 percent of the total supply at $21.00 per unit; vendor B, 50 percent at $20.80; and vendor C, 30 percent at $22.00. The cost of each umbrella base is expected to increase 25 percent.

Required

1. Compute the total standard direct materials cost per umbrella for 19x1.
2. Using your answer from part 1 and information from the problem, compute the standard manufacturing cost of one umbrella for 19x1.
3. Using your answers from parts 1 and 2, prepare journal entries for the following transactions in 19x1:

Jan. 20 Purchased 6,500 square yards of waterproof canvas at $5.10 per square yard, on account.
Feb. 1   Requisitioned 810 pole, rib, and opening mechanism assemblies into production to complete a job calling for 800 umbrellas.
Mar. 15 Transferred 600 completed umbrellas to finished goods inventory.

**Problem 27A-3.
Materials and
Labor Variances**
(L.O. 6)

The Connecticut Nut Packaging Company makes plastic walnut baskets for food wholesalers. Each basket is made of .9 grams of liquid plastic and .7 grams of an additive that includes color and hardening agents. The standard prices are $.060 per gram of liquid plastic and $.040 per gram of additive.

Three kinds of labor are required: molding, trimming, and packing. The labor time and rate standards per 1,000-basket batch are as follows: molding, .8 hour per batch at an hourly rate of $11; trimming, .6 hour per batch at an hourly rate of $9; packing, .2 hour per batch at $8 per hour.

During 19x1, the company produced 250,000 walnut baskets. Actual materials used were 224,000 grams of liquid plastic at a total cost of $14,560 and 176,500 grams of additive at a cost of $6,707. Direct labor included 190 hours for molding, at a total cost of $2,109; 150 hours for trimming, at $1,275; and 45 hours for packing, at $387.

Required

1. Compute the direct materials price and quantity variances for both the liquid plastic and the additive.
2. Compute the direct labor rate and efficiency variances for the molding, trimming, and packing processes.

**Problem 27A-4.
Direct Materials,
Direct Labor, and
Factory Overhead
Variances**
(L.O. 6)

Monroe Shoe Company has a Sandal Division that produces a line of all-vinyl thongs. Each pair of thongs calls for .4 meters of vinyl material that costs $2.00 per meter. Standard direct labor hours and cost per pair of thongs are .2 hour and $1.80 (.2 hour × $9.00 per hour), respectively. The division's current standard variable overhead rate is $1.40 per direct labor hour, and the standard fixed overhead rate is $.80 per direct labor hour.

In August, the Sandal Division manufactured and sold 60,000 pairs of thongs. During the month, 25,200 meters of vinyl materials were used up, at a total cost of $52,920. The total actual overhead costs for August were $24,200, of which $13,000 were variable. The total number of direct labor hours worked was 10,800, and factory payroll for direct labor for August was $95,040. Normal monthly capacity for the year has been set at 58,000 pairs of thongs. Budgeted fixed factory overhead for the period was $9,280.

Required

Compute (1) the direct materials price variance, (2) the direct materials quantity variance, (3) the direct labor rate variance, (4) the direct labor efficiency variance, (5) the controllable overhead variance, and (6) the overhead volume variance.

**Problem 27A-5.
Comprehensive:
Standard Cost
Journal Entry
Analysis**
(L.O. 3, 6, 7)

Plucinski Bottle Company makes wine bottles for many of the major wineries in California's Napa and Sonoma valleys, as well as for wineries in the grape-growing regions around Cupertino and Santa Cruz, California. Ken Fredonia, controller of the company, has installed the following cost, quantity, and time standards for 19x2:

Direct materials: 4 five-gallon pails of a special silicon dioxide and phosphorus pentoxide-based compound per one gross (144) of bottles; cost, $10.00 per pail.

Direct labor: Forming Department—.2 hour per gross at $12.80 per direct labor hour; Finishing/Polishing Department—.1 hour per gross at $9.40 per direct labor hour.

Factory overhead: variable—$3.20 per direct labor hour; fixed—$2.80 per direct labor hour.

All direct materials are added at the beginning of the bottle-forming process. Much of Plucinski Bottle Company's machinery is automated, and the compound is heated, mixed, and poured into molds in a very short time. Once cooled, the new bottles move via conveyor belt to the Finishing/Polishing Department. Again the process is highly automated. Machines scrape off excess material on the bottles and then polish all the outside and inside surfaces. After polishing, the bottles are fed into large cartons for shipping to customers.

During March 19x2, the following selected transactions took place:

March 2   Purchased 14,000 pails of compound at $9.80 per pail, on account.
3   Requisitioned 13,240 pails of compound into production for an order calling for 3,300 gross of wine bottles.
6   Requisitioned 11,200 pails of compound into production for an order of 2,900 gross of wine bottles.
12   Transferred 5,400 gross of bottles to finished goods inventory.
15   Requisitioned 9,240 pails of compound into production for an order calling for 2,300 gross of wine bottles.
16   For the two-week period ending March 14, actual labor costs included 1,660 direct labor hours in the Forming Department at $13.00 per hour and 810 direct labor hours in the Finishing/Polishing Department at $9.50 per hour. During the pay period, 8,200 gross of good bottles were produced.
16   Factory overhead was applied to units worked on during the previous two weeks.
18   Purchased 19,000 pails of compound at $10.25 per pail, on account.
20   Requisitioned 13,960 pails of compound into production for an order of 3,500 gross of wine bottles.
28   Transferred 9,600 gross of bottles to finished goods inventory.
30   For the two-week period ending March 28, actual labor costs included 1,420 direct labor hours in the Forming Department at $12.60 per hour and 750 direct labor hours in the Finishing/Polishing Department at $9.20 per hour. During the pay period, 7,300 gross of good bottles were produced.
30   Factory overhead was applied to units worked on during the two-week period.
31   During March, 9,800 gross of wine bottles were sold on account and shipped to customers. Selling price for these bottles was $76 per gross. Actual factory overhead for February was $14,500 of variable and $13,300 of fixed overhead. These amounts have been recorded in the Factory Overhead Control account. Budgeted fixed factory overhead for March was $12,600. Beginning inventory information included: Materials Inventory, $42,100; Work in Process Inventory, $30,064; Finished Goods Inventory, $146,772.

Required   1. Compute the standard cost per gross of wine bottles.
2. Prepare the entries necessary to record the above transactions (show calculations for each variance). For the direct labor entries, assume that

everything except the distribution of direct labor to Work in Process Inventory Control has already been recorded.
3. Analyze the factory overhead accounts and compute the controllable overhead and overhead volume variances. (Assume that actual overhead incurred has already been debited to the control account.)
4. Prepare the entry to dispose of the overhead accounts and record the overhead variances.
5. Close all variance account balances to the Cost of Goods Sold account.

Problem Set B

Problem 27B-1.
Development of
Standards: Direct
Materials
(L.O. 2, 3)

Brian & White, Ltd. assembles clock movements for grandfather clocks. Each movement has four components to assemble: the clock facing, the clock hands, the time movement, and the spring assembly. For the current year, 19x1, the company used the following standard costs: clock facing, $15.90; clock hands, $12.70; time movement, $56.10; and spring assembly, $42.50.

Prices and sources of materials are expected to change in 19x2. Sixty percent of the facings will be supplied by Company A at $16.50 each, and the remaining 40 percent will be purchased from Company B at $16.80 each. The hands are produced for Brian & White, Ltd. by Sawyers Hardware, Inc. and will cost $15.50 per set in 19x2. Time movements will be purchased from three Swiss sources: Company Q, 30 percent of total need at $58.50 per movement; Company R, 20 percent at $59.50; and Company S, 50 percent at $61.90. Spring assemblies will be purchased from a French company, and are expected to increase in cost by 20 percent.

Required

1. Determine the total standard materials cost per unit for 19x2.
2. If the company could guarantee the purchase of 2,500 sets of hands from Sawyers Hardware, Inc., the unit cost would be reduced by 20 percent. Find the resulting standard materials unit cost.
3. Substandard spring assemblies can be purchased at $45.50, but 15 percent of them will be unusable and cannot be returned. Compute the standard direct materials unit cost if the company follows this procedure, assuming the original facts of the case for the remaining data. The cost of the defective materials will be spread over good units produced.

Problem 27B-2.
Developing and
Using Standard
Costs
(L.O. 2, 3, 7)

Prefabricated, factory-built houses are the specialty of Young Homes, Inc. of Buffalo, New York. Although Young Homes produces many models, and customers can even special-order a home, 60 percent of the company's business comes from the sale of the El Dorado, a three-bedroom, 1,400 square foot home with an impressive front entrance. The six basic materials used to manufacture the entrance with their standard costs for 19x1 are as follows: wood framing materials, $1,720; deluxe front door, $380; door hardware, $160; exterior siding, $910; electrical materials, $480; and interior finishing materials, $1,140.

Three types of labor are used to build this section: carpenter, 20 hours at $14.00 per hour; door specialist, 4 hours at $16.00 per hour; and electrician, 8 hours at $18.00 per hour. In 19x1 the company used an overhead rate of 50 percent of direct labor dollars.

During 19x2, wood framing materials are expected to increase by 20 percent. The deluxe front door will need two suppliers: Supplier A will produce

40 percent of the company's need at $390 per door; Supplier B, 60 percent at $400 per door. Door hardware cost will increase by 10 percent; electrical materials cost, by 20 percent. Exterior siding cost should decrease by $10 per section. Interior finishing materials costs are expected to remain the same. Carpenter's wages will increase by $1 per hour, while door specialist's wages should remain the same. Electrician's wages will increase by 10 percent. Finally, the factory overhead rate will decrease to 40 percent of direct labor cost.

Required

1. Compute the total standard direct materials cost per front entrance for 19x1.
2. Using your answer to part 1 and other information from the problem, compute the 19x2 standard manufacturing cost for the El Dorado's front entrance.
3. From the information given, prepare journal entries for the following 19x2 transactions:

Jan. 6   Purchased 120 front doors from Supplier A for $45,120.
Jan. 14   Requisitioned 60 sets of hardware into production to complete a job calling for 56 entrance units.
Jan. 30   Transferred the 56 completed front entrances to finished goods inventory.

**Problem 27B-3.
Materials and
Labor Variances
(L.O. 6)**

Orange Coast Trophy Company produces a variety of athletic awards, most in the form of trophies or mounted replicas of athletes in action. Jacquelyn Landreth, president of the company, is in the process of developing a standard cost accounting system. Orange Coast produces six different standard sizes. The deluxe trophy stands three feet tall above the base. Materials standards include one pound of metal and 6 ounces of plastic supported by an 8-ounce wooden base. Standard prices for 19x2 were $3.25 per pound of metal, $.40 per ounce of plastic, and $.20 per ounce of wood.

Direct labor is used in both the Molding and Trimming/Finishing Departments. Deluxe trophies require labor standards of .2 hours of direct labor in the Molding Department and .4 hours in the Trimming/Finishing Department. Standard labor rates for deluxe trophies include $10.50 per hour in Molding and $12.00 per hour in Trimming/Finishing.

During January 19x2, 16,400 deluxe trophies were made. Actual production data were as follows:

Materials
Metal   16,840 lb @ $3.20/lb
Plastic   99,240 oz @ $.42/oz
Wood   131,480 oz @ $.25/oz

Labor
Molding   3,420 hr @ $10.60/hr
Trimming/Finishing   6,540 hr @ $12.10/hr

Required

1. Compute the direct materials price and quantity variances for metal, plastics, and wood.
2. Compute the direct labor rate and efficiency variances for the Molding and the Trimming/Finishing Departments.

Problem 27B-4.
Direct Materials,
Direct Labor, and
Factory Overhead
Variances
(L.O. 6)

During 19x1, Navas Laboratories, Inc. researched and perfected a cure for the common cold. Called Cold-Gone, the product comprises a series of five tablets and sells for $10.50 per package. Standard unit costs for this product were developed in late 19x1 for use in 19x2. Per package, the standard unit costs were: chemical ingredients, 6 ounces at $.40 per ounce; packaging, $1.20; direct labor, .4 hour at $14 per hour; standard variable factory overhead, $3.00 per direct labor hour; and standard fixed factory overhead, $5.00 per direct labor hour.

In the first quarter of 19x2, the peak season for colds, demand for the new product rose beyond even the wildest expectations of management. During these three months, the company produced and sold 4 million packages of Cold-Gone. The first week in April, 50,000 packages were produced using materials for 50,200 packages costing $60,240. Chemical use was 305,000 ounces costing $125,050. Direct labor was 20,120 direct labor hours at a total cost of $282,686. Total variable factory overhead was $61,100; total fixed factory overhead, $99,800. Budgeted fixed factory overhead for the period was $90,000.

Required

Compute (1) all direct materials price variances, (2) all direct materials quantity variances, (3) the direct labor rate variance, (4) the direct labor efficiency variance, (5) the controllable overhead variance, and (6) the overhead volume variance.

Problem 27B-5.
Comprehensive:
Standard Cost
Journal Entry
Analysis
(L.O. 3, 6, 7)

Scottsdale Lamp Company manufactures several lines of home and business lights and lighting systems. Mahogany table lamps are one of their most popular product lines. Since the wood is very difficult to work with, skilled wood carvers are employed. Deborah Shewman, controller, has developed the following cost, quantity, and time standards for one table lamp for the current year.

Materials: wood, 10 × 8 × 18-inch block of mahogany, $14.00; electrical fixture and cord, $5.50; shade and mounting, $9.20.

Direct labor: wood carvers, 6 hours at $14.50 per hour; assemblers and packers, 1.2 hours at $9.00 per hour.

Factory overhead: variable rate, $1.40 per direct labor hour; fixed rate, $2.10 per direct labor hour.

Mahogany table lamps sell for $250 each.

Selected transactions for August 19x1 are as follows:

Aug. 3 Purchased 800 blocks of mahogany for $11,280, on account.
      4 Requisitioned 70 blocks of wood into production for order 16, calling for 65 lamps.
      5 Purchased 500 electrical fixture kits for $2,700 and 600 lamp shades and mountings for $5,580, on account.
      7 Requisitioned 68 electrical fixture kits and 66 lamp shades and mountings into production for order 16.
     14 Semi-monthly payroll was paid, including the following wages for order 16: wood carvers, 400 hours, $5,760; assemblers and packers, 80 hours, $720. These labor efforts completed order 16.

Aug. 14 Factory overhead was applied to units worked on during the payroll period. (Assume order 16 represents the only units worked on during the pay period.)

16 Requisitioned 74 blocks of wood into production for order 26, calling for 70 lamps.

19 Requisitioned 78 electrical fixture kits and 75 lamp shades and mountings into production for order 26.

30 Labor for the previous half-month was paid. Labor costs associated with order 26 included: wood carvers, 434 hours, $6,293; assemblers and packers, 90 hours, $846.

30 Factory overhead was applied to the work performed during the last two weeks. (Assume order 26 represents the only units worked on during the pay period.)

30 Orders 16 and 26 were completed and transferred to Finished Goods Inventory.

31 Orders 16 and 26 were shipped to customers at the contracted price.

Beginning inventory information included: Materials Inventory Control, $15,400; Work in Process Inventory Control, $0; and Finished Goods Inventory Control, $9,102.

During August, actual factory overhead incurred for orders 16 and 26 was variable, $1,420, and fixed, $2,160. All actual overhead costs have already been recorded in the Factory Overhead Control account. Assume that budgeted fixed factory overhead was $2,697 for these two orders.

Required
1. Compute the standard cost for one mahogany table lamp.
2. Prepare the entries necessary to record the month's transactions (show calculations for each variance). For the direct labor entries, assume that everything has been recorded except the distribution of direct labor to Work in Process Inventory Control.*
3. Analyze the factory overhead accounts, and compute the controllable overhead and overhead volume variances.*
4. Prepare the entry to dispose of the overhead accounts and record the overhead variances.* (Assume that actual overhead incurred has already been debited to the control account.)
5. Close all variance account balances to the Cost of Goods Sold account.*

* Round answers to nearest dollar

Management Decision Case

Taube Aquatic Corporation
(L.O. 6, 8)

Taube Aquatic Corporation produces water sports gear including safety cushions, water skis, towing lines, goggles, and snorkeling equipment. Much of the operation involves the assembly of parts purchased from outside vendors. However, all rubber parts are produced by the company in the Shaping Department. Face masks and goggles are assembled in the Face Wear Department, using purchased clear plastic lenses and fastener devices. Rubber mask casings and head straps are transferred in from the Shaping Department. Anthony Zazzara is in charge of the Shaping Department, and Jo Ann Wolfe supervises the Face Wear Department.

At the end of April 19x2, the Accounting Department developed the following performance reports for the two departments:

Taube Aquatic Corporation
Shaping Department
Performance Report—Cost Variance Analysis
For the Month Ended April 30, 19x2

Supervisor: Anthony Zazzara

	Costs		Variance	
	Standard	Actual	Amount	Type
Direct materials used	$17,800	$18,000	$ 200 (U)	Quantity variance
Direct labor usage	9,640	10,120	860 (F)	Rate variance
			1,340 (U)	Efficiency variance
Factory overhead	6,400	7,390	990 (U)	Controllable variance
Totals	$33,840	$35,510	$1,670 (U)	

Taube Aquatic Corporation
Face Wear Department
Performance Report—Cost Variance Analysis
For the Month Ended April 30, 19x2

Supervisor: Jo Ann Wolfe

	Costs		Variance	
	Standard	Actual	Amount	Type
Direct materials used	$12,600	$16,450	$3,850 (U)	Quantity variance
Direct labor usage	8,200	11,580	20 (F)	Rate variance
			3,400 (U)	Efficiency variance
Factory overhead	5,460	7,220	1,760 (U)	Controllable variance
Totals	$26,260	$35,250	$8,990 (U)	

When asked to comment on his performance, Zazzara stated, "Compared with the Face Wear Department, my performance is very good. Most of the $1,670 (U) net variance arose because of two new, inexperienced workers, who increased the department's average labor hours. Since overhead is applied based on direct labor hours, an unfavorable controllable overhead variance was to be expected."

Ms. Wolfe was quite upset at Mr. Zazzara's comments. She said, "First of all, one of the variances is in error. The standard for direct labor usage should be $9,840 since 1,200 standard hours allowed were earned at an $8.20 standard labor rate. Also, the additional 200 standard hours allowed would cause the controllable overhead variance to decrease by $640, because of the

$3.20 per direct labor hour standard variable overhead rate." She continued, "Now let's focus on the large unfavorable quantity and efficiency variances. All my production problems can be traced to the poor quality of mask casings coming from the Shaping Department. Poor quality meant dozens of spoiled mask assemblies; my people had to work overtime to meet customer orders for the period. If we had had decent mask casings, we would have had an overall favorable performance for the period. Either the quality of the mask casings improves, or in the future I will ask to have them purchased from an outside vendor!"

Required

1. Recompute the variances and the performance report for the Face Wear Department, assuming that Ms. Wolfe is correct.
2. Which supervisor's performance should be further analyzed? Why?
3. If you were Vice President of Production, what steps would you take to correct the situation? Develop a plan of action.

Answers to Self-Test

1. d	3. c	5. a	7. c	9. d
2. b	4. a	6. d	8. b	10. a

LEARNING OBJECTIVES

1. Define and identify relevant decision information.
2. Describe the steps in the management decision cycle.
3. Calculate product costs, using variable costing procedures.
4. Prepare an income statement, using the contribution reporting format.
5. Develop decision data, using the incremental analysis technique.
6. Prepare decision alternative evaluations for (a) make or buy decisions, (b) special order decisions, and (c) sales mix analyses.
7. Evaluate capital expenditure proposals, using (a) the accounting rate of return method, (b) the payback method, and (c) the net present value method.
8. Analyze capital expenditure decision alternatives that incorporate the effects of income taxes.

CHAPTER 28

Management Decision Analysis Including Capital Budgeting

The fundamental tenet of management accounting is that the accountant supplies management with three basic types of information: (1) product costing data for pricing and inventory valuation; (2) cost analyses for operational planning and control; and (3) special analyses to support management decision making. Product costing techniques and planning and control procedures were studied in Chapters 22 through 27. Management decision making is the focus of this chapter.

Management often depends on accounting information to support its decision-making activities. Such information reveals important data about each alternative in a decision process. To evaluate alternatives, the accountant uses special decision models, analyses, and reporting techniques. In this chapter, we first focus on the concept of relevant information and then explore the decision cycle and specific analytical models. The short-term decision areas of make or buy, special order, and sales mix analysis are then examined. We conclude the chapter with an in-depth look at the capital expenditure decision process. The three primary capital expenditure evaluation methods, (1) accounting rate of return, (2) payback period, and (3) net present value, are discussed and illustrated. These methods are first analyzed using before-tax amounts; they are then reanalyzed, using after-tax amounts. These analyses show how income taxes affect capital expenditure decisions. After studying this chapter, you should be able to meet the learning objectives listed on the left.

Relevant Information for Management

The management decision process calls for comparing two or more possible solutions to a problem and deciding which one is best under the circumstances. Supplying relevant information to management for each alternative is the responsibility of the management accountant. Management should evaluate the possible solutions to a particular problem. To do so, they should not have to wade through pages and pages of data to find out how each alternative will affect business operations. Many of the

OBJECTIVE 1
Define and identify relevant decision information

facts may be the same for each alternative. For instance, total sales may not be affected by a cost-savings proposal. If there are three possible courses of action and total sales are the same in each case, the sales data would not influence the decision. The accountant often uses past data in preparing cost estimates of the decision alternatives. However, it is the estimated costs that are relevant to the decision, not the historical data. **Relevant decision information** is future cost, revenue, or resource usage data that will be different for the various alternatives being evaluated. A decision must be made on the basis of the alternatives available. So information that is alike for those alternatives or transactions that have already happened will not be helpful in picking the best alternative. Relevant information is limited to future data that differ among the possible alternatives.

Management Decision Cycle

OBJECTIVE 2
Describe the steps in the management decision cycle

The decision-making process is an unstructured area of responsibility. Many decisions are unique and do not lend themselves to strict rules, steps, or timetables. However, certain events accompany each kind of management decision analysis. Figure 28-1 shows the basic events that make up the management decision cycle. Following the discovery of a problem or resource need, the accountant should identify all possible courses of action that are open to management and that will solve the problem. Next, the accountant prepares a complete analysis for each action, showing its total cost, cost savings, or financial effects on business operations. Each type of decision calls for different information. When

Figure 28-1. The Management Decision Cycle

all the information has been gathered and organized in a meaningful way, management can select the best course of action. After the decision has been carried out, the accountant should prepare a post-decision audit analysis to provide feedback to management. If further action is needed, the decision cycle begins all over again. If not, this particular decision process has been completed.

Accounting Tools and Reports for Decision Analysis

Accountants usually supply the data for the management decision process. Certain accounting tools and reports are used for this purpose. Management expects decision information to be accurate, timely, refined, and readable. For these reasons, the accountant must be concerned not only with the information itself but also with the reporting form.

Variable costing and incremental analysis are the two most common decision tools used by the accountant. Each technique helps to identify information relevant to a particular decision. Each technique also provides the accountant with a special decision-reporting format.

Variable Costing

OBJECTIVE 3
Calculate product costs, using variable costing procedures

Variable costing (also called direct costing) is primarily an approach to product costing. Unlike absorption costing, which assigns all manufacturing costs to products, **variable costing** uses only the variable manufacturing costs for purposes of product costing and inventory valuation. Direct materials costs, direct labor costs, and variable factory overhead costs are the only cost elements used to figure product costs. Fixed factory overhead costs are considered costs of the current accounting period.

Support for variable costing stems from the fact that a company will have fixed operating costs whether it operates or not. For this reason, those who favor variable costing argue that such costs do not have a direct relationship to the product and should not be used to find the product unit cost. Fixed manufacturing costs are linked more closely with time than with productive output. Opponents of variable costing say that without the fixed manufacturing costs, production would stop. Therefore, such costs are an integral part of product costs.

Whatever side of this issue you are on, two points are certain. The first is that variable costing is useful for *internal* management decision purposes. The second is that neither the Internal Revenue Service nor the public accounting profession accepts variable costing for *external* reporting purposes. They reject it because fixed costs are not included in inventory and cost of goods sold. Therefore, this approach cannot be used for computing federal income taxes or for reporting the results of operations and financial position to stockholders and others outside the company. Nevertheless, variable costing remains a useful tool for the management accountant.

Product Costing. For product costing purposes, variable costing treats fixed manufacturing costs differently from production costs that vary with output. An often overlooked point is that fixed manufacturing costs are also left out of all inventories. For this reason, the value of inventories arrived at by means of variable costing is lower than the value of those computed by means of absorption costing.

An example will help to explain the differences between these two product costing approaches. Emma Industries, Inc. produces grills for outdoor cooking. During 19x2, the company put a new disposable grill into production. A summary of 19x2 cost and production data for the grill follows: direct materials costs, $82,260; direct labor, $43,415; variable factory overhead, $47,985; and fixed factory overhead, $41,130. There were 22,850 units completed and 21,000 units sold during 19x2. There were no beginning or ending work in process inventories.

Using this data, we can find the unit cost as well as the ending inventory and cost of goods sold amounts for 19x2 under a variable costing approach and under an absorption costing approach. This information is summarized in Exhibit 28-1.

Exhibit 28-1. Variable Costing Versus Absorption Costing

Emma Industries, Inc.
Unit Cost and Ending Inventory Values
For the Year Ended December 31, 19x2

	Variable Costing	Absorption Costing
Unit Cost		
Direct Materials ($82,260 ÷ 22,850 units)	$ 3.60	$ 3.60
Direct Labor ($43,415 ÷ 22,850 units)	1.90	1.90
Variable Factory Overhead		
($47,985 ÷ 22,850 units)	2.10	2.10
Fixed Factory Overhead		
($41,130 ÷ 22,850 units)	—	1.80
Total Unit Cost	$ 7.60	$ 9.40
Ending Finished Goods Inventory		
1,850 units at $7.60	$ 14,060	
1,850 units at $9.40		$ 17,390
Cost of Goods Sold for 19x2		
21,000 units at $7.60	$159,600	
21,000 units at $9.40		$197,400
Plus Fixed Factory Overhead	41,130	—
Costs Appearing on 19x2 Income Statement	$200,730	$197,400
Total Costs to be Accounted For	$214,790	$214,790

Unit production cost under variable costing is $7.60 per grill, whereas unit cost is $9.40 with absorption costing. Ending Finished Goods Inventory balances are not the same because of the $1.80 difference in unit cost. Because fewer costs remain in inventory at year end with variable costing amounts, it is logical that greater costs will appear on the income statement. As shown in Exhibit 28-1, $200,730 of current manufacturing costs are considered costs of the period, to be subtracted from revenue in the variable costing income statement. Only $197,400 is shown as Cost of Goods Sold when absorption costing is used. The difference of $3,330 (1,850 units in inventory × $1.80 fixed costs per unit) is shown as part of inventory under absorption costing.

OBJECTIVE 4
Prepare an income statement, using the contribution reporting format

Performance Analysis: The Income Statement. The use of variable costing leads to differences in financial reporting as well as differences in product costing. Combining the concepts of contribution margin and variable costing results in an entirely new form of income statement. This new form emphasizes cost variability and segment or product line contributions to income. Costs are no longer classified as either manufacturing or nonmanufacturing costs. Instead, attention is focused on separating variable costs from fixed costs.

Adding further to the Emma Industries example will help to explain this point. Assume the following additional information for 19x2: selling price per grill is $25.50; variable selling costs per grill are $3.20; fixed selling expenses are $51,340; and fixed administrative expenses are $79,810. Net income under both variable costing and absorption costing procedures is compared in Exhibit 28-2.

The contribution format is presented first. Note that the term *gross margin* is replaced by the term *contribution margin* and that only variable costs (including variable selling costs) are subtracted from sales to get the contribution margin. This is the amount that each segment or product line is contributing to the fixed costs and profits of the company. Net income calculated using the conventional statement is shown in the lower part of Exhibit 28-2. Note that net income is different under the two methods. This difference ($139,750 − $136,420 = $3,330) is the same amount noted earlier. It is the part of fixed manufacturing overhead cost that is inventoried when absorption costing is used.

Contribution Reporting and Decisions. Variable costing and the contribution approach to reporting are used a great deal in decision analysis. Their most common use is in deciding whether or not to continue a segment, division, or product line. Other uses are in the evaluation of new product lines and in sales mix studies. Decisions about the contribution of sales territories also use the contribution approach to income reporting. We will explain these uses later when we look at specific kinds of decisions.

Incremental Analysis

Incremental analysis, an approach often used in decision reporting, compares alternatives by looking only at information differences. Only

Exhibit 28-2. The Income Statement: Contribution Versus Conventional Formats		
Emma Industries, Inc.		
Disposable Grill Division		
Income Statement		
For the Year Ended December 31, 19x2		

Contribution Margin Format

Sales		$535,500
Variable Cost of Goods Manufactured	$173,660	
Less Ending Inventory	14,060*	
Variable Cost of Goods Sold	$159,600*	
Plus Variable Selling Costs		
(21,000 units at $3.20)	67,200	226,800
Contribution Margin		$308,700
Less Fixed Costs		
Fixed Manufacturing Costs	$ 41,130	
Fixed Selling Expenses	51,340	
Fixed Administrative Expenses	79,810	172,280
Net Income (before taxes)		$136,420

Conventional Format

Sales		$535,500
Cost of Goods Sold		
Cost of Goods Manufactured	$214,790*	
Less Ending Inventory	17,390*	
Cost of Goods Sold		197,400*
Gross Margin from Sales		$338,100
Selling Expenses		
Variable	$ 67,200	
Fixed	51,340	
Administrative Expenses	79,810	198,350
Net Income (before taxes)		$139,750

* Detailed computations are found in Exhibit 28-1

OBJECTIVE 5
Develop decision data, using the incremental analysis technique

relevant information, decision data that differ among alternatives, are of concern; and for decision purposes, only future data are included. By focusing on the differences among alternatives, incremental analysis helps highlight the important points. It makes the evaluation easier and reduces the time needed to choose the best course of action.

For example, assume that the Roush Company is trying to decide which one of two machines, M and S, to buy. Roush's management has been able to collect the following annual operating estimates on the two machines:

	Machine M	Machine S
Increase in revenue	$32,400	$39,600
Increase in annual operating costs		
Direct materials	5,600	5,600
Direct labor	8,400	12,200
Variable factory overhead	4,200	6,100
Fixed factory overhead		
(depreciation included)	10,000	10,000

The best method of comparing these two decision alternatives is to prepare an analysis that will show the amount of increase in the revenues and costs that are relevant to the decision. This analysis is shown below.

Roush Company Incremental Decision Analysis			
	Machine M	Machine S	Difference in Favor of Machine S
Increase in Revenues	$32,400	$39,600	$7,200
Less Increase in Annual Operating Costs			
Direct Materials	$ 5,600	$ 5,600	—
Direct Labor	8,400	12,200	$3,800
Variable Factory Overhead	4,200	6,100	1,900
Fixed Factory Overhead	10,000	10,000	—
Total Operating Costs	$28,200	$33,900	$5,700
Resulting Increase in Net Income	$ 4,200	$ 5,700	$1,500

If we assume that the purchase price and useful life of the two machines are the same, the analysis shows that Machine S will generate $1,500 more in net income than Machine M. Thus the decision would be to purchase Machine S.

Special Reports

Qualitative as well as quantitative data are useful in decision making. When only quantitative data are considered, most choices can be made by using either contribution reporting or incremental analysis. However, in some decisions there are many different alternatives, each of which is the best one in certain circumstances. One may be more profitable, but another may further diversify a company's product line. A third alternative may help prevent a huge layoff of personnel in some part of the country, thus bolstering the company's goodwill there. Even though many qualitative decision alternatives may be available, management must choose only one course of action. In such cases, the accountant must use imagination and prepare a special decision report for the given circumstances. There is no set structure for these special reports. They are created by skilled, experienced accountants to fit individual situations.

Operating Decisions of Management

Management depends on the accountant to supply relevant information for many kinds of decisions. To illustrate the accountant's role, we will focus on the relevant data analysis for make or buy decisions, special order decisions, and sales mix analyses.

Make or Buy Decisions

OBJECTIVE 6a
Prepare decision alternative evaluations for make or buy decisions

One common group of decision analyses involves product assembly operations. Management is continually faced with the decision as to whether to make or to buy some or all of the parts. The goal of the **make or buy decision** is to identify those cost and revenue elements relevant to this kind of decision. Below is the information to be considered:

To Make	To Buy
Need for expensive machinery	Purchase price of item
Other variable costs of making the item	Rent or net cash flow to be generated from vacated space in factory
Repair and maintenance expenses	Salvage value of machinery

To illustrate a make or buy decision, consider the case of the Eubanks Electronics Company. For five years, the firm has been purchasing small transistor casings from an outside supplier at a cost of $1.60 each. However, the supplier has just informed Eubanks Electronics Company that the price will be raised by 20 percent, effective immediately. The company has idle machinery that could be used to produce the casings. Also, management has determined that the costs of producing the casings would be $94 per 100 casings for direct materials, six minutes of labor per casing at $6 per direct labor hour, and variable factory overhead at $3 per direct labor hour. Fixed factory overhead would include $5,000 of depreciation per year and $7,000 of other fixed costs. Annual production and usage would be 30,000 casings. The space and machinery to be used would not be utilized if the part were purchased. Should Eubanks Electronics Company make or buy the casings?

From the information given, the company should make the casings. An incremental cost analysis of the two decision alternatives is presented in Exhibit 28-3. All costs connected with the decision are shown in the analysis. Because the machinery has already been bought and neither the machinery nor the required factory space has any other use, the

---

Exhibit 28-3. Incremental Analysis: Make or Buy Decision

Eubanks Electronics Company
Incremental Decision Analysis
Current Year—Annual Usage

	Make	Buy	Difference in Favor of Make
Raw Materials			
(30,000 ÷ 100 × $94)	$28,200	—	$(28,200)
Direct Labor			
(30,000 ÷ 10 × $6)	18,000	—	(18,000)
Variable Factory Overhead			
(30,000 ÷ 10 × $3)	9,000	—	(9,000)
Fixed Factory Overhead:			
Depreciation*	5,000	$ 5,000	—
Other*	7,000	7,000	—
To Purchase Completed Casings			
(30,000 × $1.92)	—	57,600	57,600
Totals	$55,200	$57,600	$ 2,400

*Irrelevant because these amounts are the same for both decision alternatives. Amounts have not been included in totals.

---

fixed factory overhead costs are the same for both alternatives. For this reason they are not relevant to the decision. The cost of making the needed casings (leaving out the fixed overhead costs) is $55,200. The cost of buying 30,000 casings will be $57,600 at the increased purchase price. It is clear, then, that $2,400 will be saved if the casings are made within the company.

Using incremental analysis is a useful approach to the make or buy decision. It allows the analyst to use all decision data available and quickly identify anything that is irrelevant to the final decision.

Special Product Orders

OBJECTIVE 6b
Prepare decision alternative evaluations for special order decisions

Management is often faced with **special order decisions** about whether to accept or reject unexpected special product orders. These orders are normally for large numbers of similar products to be sold at prices below those advertised. Because management would not have expected such orders, the orders would not have been included in any annual cost or sales estimates. Generally, these orders are one-time events and should not be included in estimates of subsequent years' operations. (Because standard products are sold to the public at stated prices, legal advice on federal price discrimination laws should be obtained before accepting special orders.)

To illustrate special order analysis, consider Huband Sporting Goods, Inc., which manufactures a complete line of sporting equipment. Earnest Enterprises operates a large chain of discount stores and has approached Huband Sporting Goods, Inc. with a special order. The order calls for 20,000 deluxe baseballs, to be shipped with bulk packaging of 500 baseballs per box. Earnest is willing to pay $2.80 per baseball.

The following data were developed by the Huband accounting department: annual expected production, 300,000 baseballs; current year's production, 310,000 baseballs; maximum production capacity, 350,000 baseballs. Additional data are presented below:

Unit cost data	
Direct materials	$ .90
Direct labor	.70
Factory overhead	
Variable	.40
Fixed ($90,000 ÷ 300,000)	.30
Packaging per unit	.25
Advertising ($60,000 ÷ 300,000)	.20
Other fixed selling and administrative	
costs ($105,000 ÷ 300,000)	.35
Total unit cost	$ 3.10
Unit selling price	$ 4.00
Total estimated bulk packaging costs	
(20,000 baseballs: 500 per box)	$2,500

Should Huband Sporting Goods, Inc. accept the Earnest offer?

A profitability analysis reveals that the special order from Earnest Enterprises should be accepted. Exhibit 28-4 contains a comparative analysis based on the contribution reporting format. Net income before taxes is computed for the Baseball Division for operations both with and without the Earnest order.

The only costs affected by the order are for direct materials, direct labor, variable factory overhead, and packaging. Materials, labor, and variable overhead costs are shown for sales of 310,000 and 330,000 baseballs, respectively. Sales data were computed using these same unit amounts. Packaging costs will increase, but only by the amount of the added bulk packaging costs. All other costs will remain the same in each case. The net result of accepting the special order is a $13,500 increase in contribution margin (and net income before taxes). This amount can be verified by the following computation:

$$\text{Net gain} = [(\text{unit selling price offered} - \text{unit variable mfg. costs}) \\ \times \text{units}] - \text{bulk pack costs} \\ = [(\$2.80 - \$2.00) \times 20,000] - \$2,500 \\ = \$16,000 - \$2,500 = \$13,500$$

Exhibit 28-4. Contribution Reporting: Special Product Order		
Huband Sporting Goods, Inc.	
Comparative Decision Analysis	
Special Product Order—Baseball Division	
	Without	**With**
	Earnest Order	**Earnest Order**
Sales	$1,240,000	$1,296,000
Less Variable Costs		
Direct Materials	$ 279,000	$ 297,000
Direct Labor	217,000	231,000
Variable Factory Overhead	124,000	132,000
Packaging Costs	77,500	80,000
Total Variable Costs	$ 697,500	$ 740,000
Contribution Margin	$ 542,500	$ 556,000
Less Fixed Costs		
Factory Overhead	$ 90,000	$ 90,000
Advertising	60,000	60,000
Selling and Administrative	105,000	105,000
Total Fixed Costs	$ 255,000	$ 255,000
Net Income before Taxes	$ 287,500	$ 301,000

For special order analysis, both the comparative contribution reporting approach and incremental analysis can be used. In the above case, we chose contribution reporting because of the misleading fixed cost data given in the problem. Contribution reporting highlights the effect of variable cost changes on contribution margin and net income.

Sales Mix Analysis

OBJECTIVE 6c
Prepare decision alternative evaluations for sales mix analyses

Profit analysis and maximization are possible only when the profitability of all product lines is known. The question is, Which product or products contribute the most to company profitability in relation to the amount of capital assets or other scarce resources needed to produce the item(s)? To answer this question, the accountant must measure the contribution margin of each product. The next step is to determine a set of ratios of contribution margin to the required capital equipment or other resources. Once this step is completed, management should request a marketing study to set the upper limits of demand on the most profitable products. If product profitability can be computed and market demand exists for these products, management should shift production to the more profitable products.

Many kinds of decisions can be related to the approach described here. **Sales mix analysis** involves determining the most profitable combination of product sales when a company produces more than one product or offers more than one service. Closely connected with sales mix analysis is the product line profitability study designed to discover which products are losing money for the company. The same decision approach is used, but the goal is to eliminate the unprofitable product line(s). Another decision area is that of corporate segment analysis. The contribution margin approach is again used, with the goal of isolating production costs to identify the unprofitable segment(s). If corrective action is not possible, management should eliminate the noncontributing segment(s). Even though not all of these decision areas will be discussed, it is important to remember that the same kind of analysis can be used for product line profitability studies and corporate segment analyses.

An example of this kind of analysis will aid understanding. The management of Christensen Enterprises is in the process of analyzing its sales mix. The company manufactures three products—C, S, and F—using the same production equipment for all three. The total productive capacity is being used. Below are the product line statistics:

	Product C	Product S	Product F
Current production and sales (units)	20,000	30,000	18,000
Machine hours per product	2	1	2.5
Selling price per unit	$24.00	$18.00	$32.00
Unit variable manufacturing costs	$12.50	$10.00	$18.75
Unit variable selling costs	$6.50	$5.00	$6.25

Should the company try to sell more of one product and less of another?

Because total productive capacity is being used, the only way to expand the production of one product is to reduce the production of another. The sales mix analysis of Christensen Enterprises is shown in Exhibit 28-5. Though contribution reporting is used here, contribution margin per product is not the important figure for a decision about shifts in sales mix. In the analysis, Product F has the highest contribution margin. However, all products use the same machinery and all machine hours are filled. So machine hours become the scarce resource.

The analysis in Exhibit 28-5 goes one step beyond the computation of contribution margin per unit. A sales mix decision such as this one should use two decision variables: contribution margin per unit and machine hours required per unit. For instance, Product C requires two machine hours to generate $5 of contribution margin. But Product S would generate $6 of contribution margin using the same two machine hours. For this reason, we have calculated contribution margin per machine hour. Based on this information, management can readily see that it should produce and sell as much of Product S as possible. Next, it should push Product F. If any productive capacity remains, it should produce product C

Exhibit 28-5. Contribution Reporting: Sales Mix Analysis			
Christensen Enterprises			
Sales Mix Analysis			
Contribution Reporting Format			
	Product C	Product S	Product F
Unit Sales Price	$24.00	$18.00	$32.00
Variable Costs			
Manufacturing	$12.50	$10.00	$18.75
Selling	6.50	5.00	6.25
Total Variable Costs	$19.00	$15.00	$25.00
Contribution Margin per Unit (A)	$ 5.00	$ 3.00	$ 7.00
Machine Hours Required per Unit (B)	2	1	2.5
Contribution Margin per Machine Hour (A ÷ B)	$ 2.50	$ 3.00	$ 2.80

The Capital Expenditure Decision

Among the most important kinds of decisions facing management are those about when and how much to spend on capital facilities for the company. These are called **capital expenditure decisions**. Included under this heading are decisions about installing new equipment, replacing old equipment, expanding the production area by adding to an existing building, buying or building a new factory, or acquiring another company. All of these decisions call for careful analysis by the accountant and generally involve comparing two or more alternatives.

Capital Budgeting: A Cooperative Venture

Capital budgeting is the process of identifying the need for a facility, analyzing different courses of action to meet that need, preparing the reports for management, choosing the best alternative, and rationing capital expenditure funds among the various projects. This process calls for input from people in every part of the business organization. Finance people are expected to supply a target cost of capital or desired rate of return for the decision analysis and an estimate of how much money can be spent on any one project. Without this kind of information, a decision cannot be reached. Marketing people identify areas of the business that need plant and facility expansion through their predictions of future sales trends. Management people at all levels help to identify facility needs and often prepare preliminary cost estimates of the desired facility. These same people then assist in carrying out capital expenditure decisions by trying to keep actual results within the estimates.

The accountant organizes the decision information into workable, readable form. Generally, he or she applies one or more evaluation methods to the information gathered for each alternative. The most common capital expenditure proposal evaluation methods are (1) the accounting rate of return method, (2) the payback method, and (3) the net present value method. Once these methods have been applied, management can make a choice based on the criteria used for the decision. The following discussion centers on the accountant's evaluation of each proposal using these methods and describes the final selection process.

Accounting Rate of Return Method

OBJECTIVE 7a
Evaluate capital expenditure proposals, using the accounting rate of return method

Among the methods used to measure the estimated performance of a capital investment, the accounting rate of return method is a crude but easy approach to understand and use. With this method, estimated useful performance of a capital investment is measured by two variables: estimated annual after-tax net income from the project and the average investment cost. The basic equation is as follows:

$$\text{Accounting rate of return} = \frac{\text{project's average annual after-tax net income}}{\text{average investment cost}}$$

To compute average annual after-tax net income, we use the revenue and expense data prepared for evaluating the project. Average investment cost in the proposed capital facility is figured as follows:[1]

$$\text{Average investment cost} = \frac{\text{total investment} + \text{salvage value}}{2}$$

For example, assume that the Erickson Company is interested in purchasing a new bottling machine. Only projects that promise to yield more than a 16 percent return are acceptable to management. Estimates for the proposal include an increase in revenues of $17,900 a year and operating cost increases of $8,500 a year (including depreciation). The cost of the machine is $51,000. Its salvage value is $3,000. The company's income tax rate is 34 percent. Should the company invest in the machine? To answer the question, compute the accounting rate of return as shown at the top of the next page.

---

1. The procedure of adding salvage value to the numerator may not seem logical. However, a fixed asset is never depreciated below its salvage value. Average investment is computed by determining the midpoint of the depreciable portion of the asset and adding back the salvage value. Another way of stating the above formula would be

$$\text{Average investment cost} = \frac{\text{total investment} - \text{salvage value}}{2} + \text{salvage value}$$

which reduces to the formula used above.

$$\text{Accounting rate of return } = \frac{(\$17,900 - \$8,500) \times .66}{(\$51,000 + \$3,000) \div 2}$$

$$= \frac{\$6,204}{\$27,000} = \underline{\underline{22.98\%}}$$

The projected rate of return is higher than the 16 percent minimum desired rate of return, so management should think seriously about making the investment.

Because the accounting rate of return method is easy to understand and apply, it is widely used. However, it is important to know its disadvantages. First, the use of averages tends to equalize all information, leading to errors in annual income and investment data. Second, the method is hard to use if estimated annual net incomes differ from year to year. Finally, the time value of money is not considered in the computations. Thus future and present dollars are treated as being equal.

Cash Flow and the Payback Method

OBJECTIVE 7b
Evaluate capital expenditure proposals, using the payback method

Instead of measuring the rate of return on investments, many managers would rather estimate the cash flow to be generated by a capital investment. In such cases, the goal is to determine the minimum length of time it may take to pay back the initial amount of the investment. If two investment alternatives are being studied, the better choice will be the investment that pays back its initial amount in the shorter time. This period of time is known as the payback period, and the evaluation approach is called the **payback method**.

We compute the payback period as follows:

$$\text{Payback period } = \frac{\text{cost of investment}}{\text{annual net cash inflow}}$$

To apply the payback method to the proposed capital investment of the Erickson Company discussed earlier, we need further information. We need to determine the net cash flow. To do so, find and eliminate the effects of all the noncash revenue and expense items included in the analysis of net income. In this case, assume that the only noncash item is machine depreciation. Calculate this amount from the asset life and the depreciation method. Suppose that the Erickson Company uses the straight-line depreciation approach and that the new bottling machine will have a ten-year estimated service life. Using this information and the facts given earlier, compute the payback period as shown below:

$$\text{Annual depreciation } = \frac{\text{cost} - \text{salvage value}}{\text{asset life}}$$

$$= \frac{(\$51,000 - \$3,000)}{10 \text{ years}}$$

$$= \underline{\underline{\$4,800 \text{ per year}}}$$

$$\text{Payback period} = \frac{\text{cost of machine}}{\text{cash revenue} - \text{cash expenses} - \text{taxes}}$$

$$= \frac{\$51,000}{\$17,900 - (\$8,500 - \$4,800) - \$3,196}$$

$$= \frac{\$51,000}{\$11,004}$$

$$= 4.635 \text{ years}$$

If the company's desired payback period is five years or less, this capital investment proposal would be approved.

The payback method has the advantage of being easy to compute and understand and, therefore, is widely used. However, this approach has a number of major disadvantages, which should not be overlooked. First, the method does not measure profitability. Second, the present value of cash flows from different periods is not recognized. Finally, emphasis is on the time it takes to get out of the investment rather than on the long-run return on the investment.

Net Present Value Method[2]

OBJECTIVE 7c
Evaluate capital expenditure proposals, using the net present value method

Today there are many opportunities to invest capital other than by purchasing fixed assets. As a result, management expects a competitive return from an asset during its useful life. Capital expenditure decision analysis calls for evaluating estimated capital outlays for several future time periods. Cash flows from different periods do not have the same values when measured in current dollars. For this reason, to treat all future income flows alike ignores the time value of money. Both the accounting rate of return and payback period evaluation methods have this disadvantage.

The concept of **discounted cash flow** helps to overcome the disadvantages of the accounting rate of return and payback methods in evaluating capital investment alternatives. By using the present value tables found in Appendix B, it is possible to discount future cash flows back to the present. This approach to capital investment analysis is called the **net present value method**. Multipliers used to find the present value of a future cash flow are found in the present value tables. Which multiplier to use is determined by the minimum desired rate of return and the life of the asset or length of time for which the amount is being discounted. Each element of cash inflow and cash outflow to be realized over the life of the asset is discounted back to the present. If the present value of all expected future net cash inflows is greater than the amount of the current investment, the expenditure meets the minimum desired rate of return, and the project should be carried out.

2. This section is based on the concept of present value. Appendixes A and B explain this concept and provide tables of multipliers for computations.

The net present value method is used in different ways, depending on whether annual cash flows are equal or unequal. If all annual cash flows (inflows less outflows) are equal, the discount factor to be used will come from Table B-4 in Appendix B. This table gives multipliers for the present value of $1 received at the end of *each period* for a given number of time periods. One computation will cover the cash flows of all time periods involved. If, however, expected cash inflows and outflows differ from one year to the next, each year's amount has to be discounted back to the present. Discount factors used in this kind of analysis are found in Table B-3 in Appendix B. Multipliers in Table B-3 are used to find the present value of $1 to be received (or paid out) at the end of a given number of time periods.

An example will help to show the difference in the present value analysis of expenditures with equal and unequal cash flows. Suppose that the Hoffman Metal Products Company is trying to decide which of two stamping machines to buy. The Red Machine has equal expected annual net cash inflows, and the Green Machine has unequal annual amounts. Information on the two machines follows:

	Red Machine	Green Machine
Purchase price: January 1, 19x1	$16,500	$16,500
Expected life	5 years	5 years
Estimated net cash inflows:		
19x1	$5,000	$6,000
19x2	$5,000	$5,500
19x3	$5,000	$5,000
19x4	$5,000	$4,500
19x5	$5,000	$4,000

The company's minimum desired rate of return is 16 percent. Which—if either—of the two alternatives should be chosen?

The evaluation process is shown in Exhibit 28-6. An analysis involving equal annual cash flows is easier to prepare. Present value of net cash inflows for the five-year period for the Red Machine is found by multiplying $5,000 by 3.274. The multiplier, 3.274, is found in Table B-4 in Appendix B by using the 16 percent minimum desired rate of return and the five-year life of the Red Machine. Present value of the total cash inflows from the Red Machine is $16,370. When we compare this figure with the $16,500 purchase price, the result is a *negative* net present value of $130.

Analysis of the Green Machine alternative gives a different result. As shown in Exhibit 28-6, unequal net cash inflows require more calculations. Multipliers for this part of the analysis are also found by using the 16 percent rate. But five different multipliers, one for each year of the life of the asset, must be used. Table B-3 in Appendix B applies here, because each annual amount must be individually discounted. For the Green Machine, the $16,851.50 present value of net cash inflows is more than the $16,500.00 purchase price of the machine. So there is a positive net present value of $351.50. A positive net present value figure means that the return on the asset exceeds the 16 percent minimum desired

Exhibit 28-6. Net Present Value Analysis: Equal Versus Unequal Cash Flows

Hoffman Metal Products Company
Capital Expenditure Analysis

Red Machine

Present value of cash inflows	$5,000 × 3.274 = $ 16,370.00
Less purchase price of machine	(16,500.00)
Negative net present value	$ (130.00)

Green Machine

Present value of cash inflows:

19x1 ($6,000 × .862)	$ 5,172.00
19x2 ($5,500 × .743)	4,086.50
19x3 ($5,000 × .641)	3,205.00
19x4 ($4,500 × .552)	2,484.00
19x5 ($4,000 × .476)	1,904.00
Total present value of cash inflows	$ 16,851.50
Less purchase price of machine	(16,500.00)
Positive net present value	$ 351.50

rate of return. A negative figure means that the rate of return is below the desired minimum. In the Hoffman Metal Products case, the right decision would be to purchase the Green Machine.

Incorporating the time value of money in the evaluation of capital expenditure proposals is the major advantage of the net present value method. This method also deals mainly with total cash flows from the investment over its useful life so the analysis includes total profitability. The major disadvantage of the net present value method is that many managers do not trust or understand the procedure. They prefer the payback or the accounting rate of return methods because the computations are easier.

Income Taxes and Business Decisions

Tax Effects on Capital Expenditure Decisions

OBJECTIVE 8
Analyze capital expenditure decision alternatives that incorporate the effects of income taxes

Income taxes are an important cost of doing business, and they often have a major impact on business decisions. The aim of capital budgeting evaluation techniques such as payback period and net present value is to measure and compare the relative benefits of proposed capital expenditures. These measurements focus on cash receipts and payments for a given project. For profit-oriented companies, income taxes are important in capital budgeting analyses because they affect the amount and timing of cash flows. For this reason, capital expenditure evaluation must take tax effects into account.

Corporate income tax rates range from 15 percent for low incomes to 34 percent on income over $335,000.

Taxable Income	Tax Rate
$0 to $50,000	15%
$50,000 to $75,000	$7,500 + 25% of amount over $50,000
$75,000 to $100,000	$13,750 + 34% of amount over $75,000
$100,000 to $335,000	$22,250 + 39% of amount over $100,000
Over $335,000	$113,900 + 34% of amount over $335,000

Because of different tax rates and changes from year to year, this text assumes a corporate tax rate of 34 percent. Suppose a project makes the contribution to annual net income as follows:

Cash revenues	$ 400,000
Cash expenses	(200,000)
Depreciation	(100,000)
Income before taxes	$ 100,000
Income taxes at 34%	(34,000)
Income after taxes	$ 66,000

Annual cash flow for this project can be determined by two procedures presented below:

Cash Flow—Receipts and Disbursements

Revenues (cash inflow)	$ 400,000
Cash expenses (outflow)	(200,000)
Income taxes (outflow)	(34,000)
Net cash inflow	$ 166,000

Cash Flow—Income Adjustment Procedure

Income after taxes	$ 66,000
Add: Noncash expenses (depreciation)	100,000
Less: Noncash revenues	—
Net cash inflow	$ 166,000

In both computations, the net cash inflow is $166,000, and the total effect of income taxes is to lower the net cash flow by $34,000.

Revenues and gains from the sale of equipment both increase taxable income and tax payments. When dealing with cash inflows, you must distinguish between a gain on the sale of an asset and the proceeds received from the sale. *Gains* are the amount received that is over and above the book value of the asset, whereas *proceeds* include the whole sales price and represent the cash inflow. Gains are not cash flow items, but they do raise tax payments. If equipment with a book value of $80,000 is sold for $180,000 in cash, the gain is $100,000. Assuming that this gain is taxable at the same rate of 34 percent,[3] we analyze the cash flow as follows:

Proceeds from sale		$180,000
Gain on sale	$100,000	
Capital gains tax rate	× .34	
Cash outflow (tax increase)		(34,000)
Net cash inflow		$146,000

As the cash inflows from the receipt of revenues and proceeds from the sale of assets are reduced because of income taxes, so too are the amounts of cash outflows. Expenses lower net income and result in cash outflows only to the extent that they exceed the related tax reductions. This generalization is true for both cash operating expenses, noncash expenses, and losses on the sale of fixed assets. The following examples show the cash flow effects of increases in cash and noncash expenses and losses on the sale of equipment:

Cash expenses:		
Increase in cash operating expenses	$100,000	
Less: tax reduction at 34%	(34,000)	
Net increase in cash outflow	$ 66,000	
Noncash expenses:		
Annual depreciation expense	$200,000	
Corporate tax rate	× .34	
Tax reduction = cash savings	$ 68,000	
Loss on the sale of an asset:		
Proceeds from sale		$150,000
Loss on sale	$100,000	
Corporate tax rate	× .34	
Reduction of taxes and cash outflow		34,000
Total cash inflow resulting from sale		$184,000

Depreciation expense is not a cash flow item itself, but it does provide a cash benefit equal to the amount of the reduction in taxes. Losses on the sale of fixed assets also are not cash flow items, but they provide a cash benefit by reducing the amount of taxes to be paid in cash. For illustrations of the above ideas, see the review problem for this chapter (page 1206).

Minimizing Taxes Through Planning

In operating a business, there are many ways to plan for keeping the tax liability as low as possible. One of the most important is the timing of business transactions. For example, a corporation that is nearing

---

3. Capital gains are currently taxable at the same rates as ordinary income.

$50,000 of taxable income for the year may want to put off an income-producing transaction until just after the end of the year to avoid the higher tax rate. Or it may speed up making certain expenditures for the same reason.

Another important way to reduce tax liability through operating decisions is by the timing of transactions involving depreciable business assets and land. For example, instead of selling an appreciated asset at the end of the year, management might sell an asset after year end in order to defer taxes.

It is always a good management strategy to try to take advantage of provisions of the tax law that allow preferential treatment. For example, the tax law has often been used to encourage investment in areas thought to be important for achieving national goals. Because these goals change over the years, the tax law has been used to promote everything from emergency war equipment to pollution control devices. Special credits are also allowed for certain spending that lowers unemployment or encourages the hiring of under-employed groups such as the handicapped. Therefore, business owners or managers should try to keep up with current tax laws so that they can maximize their return on investment.

Chapter Review

Review of Learning Objectives

1. **Define and identify relevant decision information.**
   Any future cost, revenue, or resource usage data used in decision analyses that will be different for the decision maker's alternative courses of action are considered relevant decision information. Recognition of relevant data comes from the development of a comparative analysis for each of the alternatives.

2. **Describe the steps in the management decision cycle.**
   The decision cycle begins with the discovery of a problem or resource need. Then, the various alternative courses of action to solve the problem or meet the need are identified. Next, a complete analysis to determine the effects of each alternative on business operations is prepared. With this supporting data, the decision maker chooses the best alternative. After the decision has been carried out, the accountant should do a post-audit to see if the problem was resolved or if other needs have arisen.

3. **Calculate product costs, using variable costing procedures.**
   Variable costing uses only variable manufacturing costs for product costing and inventory valuation. Direct materials costs, direct labor costs, and variable factory overhead costs are the only elements used to compute product costs. Fixed factory overhead costs are considered costs of the current period and are not included in inventories.

4. **Prepare an income statement, using the contribution reporting format.**
   Unlike the conventional form of income reporting, which depends on the absorption costing concept, the contribution form is based on variable costing procedures. Variable costs of goods sold and variable selling expenses are subtracted from sales to arrive at contribution margin. All fixed costs, including those from manufacturing, selling, and administration, are subtracted from contribution margin to determine net income (before taxes).

5. **Develop decision data, using the incremental analysis technique.**
   Incremental analysis is a form of decision reporting in which the various decision alternatives are identified and differences in information about them are examined. When all revenue and cost data are examined in this way, the data relevant to the decision are highlighted, since they are the ones where differences exist. Revenue and cost items that are the same under the various alternatives are not relevant to the decision.

6. **Prepare decision alternative evaluations for (a) make or buy decisions, (b) special order decisions, and (c) sales mix analyses.**
   Make or buy decision analysis helps management decide whether to buy a part used in product assembly or to make the part inside the company. This analysis centers on an incremental view of the costs of each alternative. Special order decisions have to do with unused capacity and finding the lowest acceptable selling price of a product. In most cases, fixed costs are irrelevant to the decision because they have been covered by regular operations. Contribution margin is a key factor. Sales mix analysis is used to learn the most profitable combination of product sales when a company makes more than one product using a common scarce resource. A similar approach can be used for decisions connected with identifying profitable sales territories or corporate segments. Comparative analyses using the contribution reporting format are important in all of these studies.

7. **Evaluate capital expenditure proposals, using (a) the accounting rate of return method, (b) the payback method, and (c) the net present value method.**
   When using the accounting rate of return method to evaluate two or more capital expenditure proposals, the alternative that yields the highest ratio of net income after taxes to average cost of investment is chosen. When using the payback method to evaluate a capital expenditure proposal, emphasis is placed on the shortest time period needed to recoup in cash the original amount of the investment. The net present value method depends on the time value of money. Present values of future cash flows are studied to see if they exceed the current cost of the capital expenditure being evaluated.

8. **Analyze capital expenditure decision alternatives that incorporate the effects of income taxes.**
   Income taxes affect the results of all capital expenditure analyses. Care must be taken to look at both sides of income tax effects. Revenues and gains on the sale of assets increase taxes. Increased expenditures, noncash expenditures, and losses from the sale of assets decrease taxes. Tax-related inflows result from capital losses, increased expenses, and noncash expenditures. Tax-related cash outflows arise when a company has capital gains from the sale of fixed assets or from increased sales revenue.

Review of Concepts and Terminology

The following concepts and terms were introduced in this chapter:

(L.O. 7a)   **Accounting rate of return method**: A capital investment evaluation method designed to measure estimated useful performance; it employs two variables: the project's average annual after-tax net income and the average cost of the investment.

(L.O. 7)   **Capital budgeting**: The process of identifying the need for a facility, analyzing different courses of action to meet that need, preparing the reports for management, choosing the best alternative, and rationing capital expenditure funds among the competing capital resource projects.

(L.O. 7)   **Capital expenditure decisions**: Management decisions about when and how much to spend on capital facilities for the company.

(L.O. 7c)   **Discounted cash flow**: The process of discounting future cash flows back to the present using an anticipated discount rate.

(L.O. 5)   **Incremental analysis**: An approach often used in decision reporting that compares alternatives by looking only at information differences.

(L.O. 6a)   **Make or buy decision**: A decision analysis that identifies those cost and revenue elements relevant to deciding whether to make or buy some or all parts used in product assembly operations.

(L.O. 7c)   **Net present value method**: A capital investment evaluation method based on future cash flows that are discounted back to their present value before being used to support a capital expenditure decision.

(L.O. 7b)   **Payback method**: A capital investment evaluation method based on the minimum length of time it will take to get back the initial investment.

(L.O. 1)   **Relevant decision information**: Future cost, revenue, or resource usage data that will differ for the various alternatives being evaluated.

(L.O. 6c)   **Sales mix analysis**: A special analysis prepared to determine the most profitable combination of product sales when a company produces more than one product or offers more than one service.

(L.O. 6b)   **Special order decisions**: A decision analysis designed to help management determine whether to accept or reject unexpected special product orders at prices below normal market prices.

(L.O. 3)   **Variable costing**: A costing method that uses only the variable manufacturing costs for product costing and inventory valuation purposes (as contrasted with absorption costing, which uses all product costs).

Self-Test

Test your knowledge of the chapter by choosing the best answer for each question below and on the following pages.

1. Which of the following is not a capital expenditure evaluation method?
   a. Make or buy method
   b. Payback method
   c. Accounting rate of return method
   d. Net present value method   *(L.O. 7)*

2. Future cost, revenue, or resource usage data that will differ for the various alternatives being evaluated is the definition of
   a. incremental information.
   b. variable costing information.
   c. relevant decision information.
   d. capital budgeting information.   *(L.O. 1)*

3. When using the variable costing approach for product costing, which of the following is true?
   a. Fixed manufacturing costs are inventoriable costs
   b. Only materials and labor costs are inventoriable costs
   c. Variable selling costs are inventoriable costs
   d. Variable manufacturing costs are inventoriable costs   *(L.O. 3)*

4. Finding unit contribution margin per scarce resource is part of the
   a. sales mix analysis.   c. capital expenditure analysis.
   b. special order analysis.   d. make or buy analysis.   *(L.O. 6)*

5. A capital investment evaluation method based on the minimum length of time it will take to get back the initial investment is known as the
   a. make or buy method.   c. accounting rate of return method.
   b. payback method.   d. net present value method. *(L.O. 6)*

6. The process of identifying the need for a facility, analyzing different courses of action to meet that need, preparing the reports for management, choosing the best alternative, and rationing capital expenditure funds among the competing capital resource projects is the definition of
   a. special order budgeting.   c. payback budgeting.
   b. capital budgeting.   d. sales mix budgeting.   *(L.O. 7)*

7. Four products, 1A, 3C, 5E, and 7G, are produced by the Roof Company. Machine hours is the company's scarce resource. Data on the four products in their respective order include: contribution margins—$4.50, $6.00, $12.00, and $9.00; use of labor hours—4 hrs., 6 hrs., 8 hrs., and 9 hrs.; and use of machine hours—2 hrs., 4 hrs., 12 hrs., and 5 hrs. From this limited information, which product should be pushed by the Roof Company?
   a. 1A   c. 5E
   b. 3C   d. 7G   *(L.O. 6)*

8. Morlan Enterprises is contemplating a major investment in a new flexible manufacturing system (FMS). Its minimum desired rate of return is 16 percent. The total investment is $2,500,000 with a 10 percent salvage value at the end of its eight year expected life. The company uses straight-line depreciation. The FMS should produce $1,400,000 of additional cash revenue annually. Annual cash operating costs are expected to be $600,000. The company is in the 34 percent tax bracket. Using the accounting rate of return method, what is the expected after-tax rate of return from the proposed FMS project?
   a. 38.4%   c. 24.9%
   b. 26.6%   d. 19.2%   *(L.O. 7)*

9. Assuming the same facts as in 8, and using the payback method, what is the expected after-tax payback period for the proposed FMS project?
   a. 3.625 years   c. 3.954 years
   b. 3.125 years   d. 4.009 years   *(L.O. 7)*

10. Assuming the same facts as in **8**, and using the net present value method, what is the expected after-tax net present value of the proposed FMS project?
   a. Positive net present value of $1,051,450
   b. Negative net present value of $12,455
   c. Positive net present value of $285,277
   d. Negative net present value of $62,235   *(L.O. 7)*

Answers to Self-Test are at the end of this chapter.

Review Problem
Tax Effects on a Capital Expenditure Decision

(L.O. 7, 8)   The Roland Construction Company specializes in the development of large shopping centers. The company is considering the purchase of a new earthmoving machine and has gathered the following information regarding the potential purchase:

Purchase price	$600,000
Salvage value	$100,000
Useful life	4 years
Effective tax rate*	34%
Depreciation method	Straight-line
Desired before-tax payback period	3 years
Desired after-tax payback period	4 years
Minimum before-tax rate of return	15%
Minimum after-tax rate of return	9%

The before-tax cash flow estimates are as follows:

Year	Revenues	Expenses	Net Cash Flow
1	$ 500,000	$260,000	$240,000
2	450,000	240,000	210,000
3	400,000	220,000	180,000
4	350,000	200,000	150,000
Totals	$1,700,000	$920,000	$780,000

Required

1. Using before-tax information, analyze the Roland Construction Company's investment in the new earthmoving machine. In your analysis use (a) the accounting rate of return method, (b) the payback method, and (c) the net present value method.
2. Repeat part **1** using after-tax information.
3. Summarize your findings from parts **1** and **2**.

---

* All company operations combined result in a 34 percent tax rate. Because of this, we did not use specific tax rates in the tax schedule for this analysis.

Answer to Review Problem

1. Before-tax calculations

The increase in net income is as follows:

Year	Before-tax Net Cash Flow	Depreciation	Income before Taxes
1	$240,000	$125,000	$115,000
2	210,000	125,000	85,000
3	180,000	125,000	55,000
4	150,000	125,000	25,000
Totals	$780,000	$500,000	$280,000

1a. (Before-tax) Accounting rate of return method:

$$\frac{\text{Accounting}}{\text{rate of return}} = \frac{\text{average annual net income}}{\text{average investment cost}}$$

$$= \frac{\$280,000 \div 4}{(\$600,000 + \$100,000) \div 2} = \frac{\$70,000}{\$350,000} = 20\%$$

1b. (Before-tax) Payback method:

Total cash investment		$600,000
Less cash flow recovery		
Year 1	$240,000	
Year 2	210,000	
Year 3 (5/6 of $180,000)	150,000	(600,000)
Unrecovered investment		—

Payback period: 2.833 (2 5/6) years or 2 years, 10 months

1c. (Before-tax) Net present value method (multipliers are from Table B-3):

Year	Net Cash Flow	Present Value Multiplier	Present Value
1	$240,000	.870	$208,800
2	210,000	.756	158,760
3	180,000	.658	118,440
4	150,000	.572	85,800
4	100,000 (salvage)	.572	57,200
Total present value			$629,000
Cost of original investment			(600,000)
Positive net present value			$ 29,000

2. After-tax calculations

The increase in net income after taxes is as follows:

Year	Before-Tax Net Cash Flow	Depreciation	Income Before Taxes	Taxes (34%)	Income After Taxes
1	$240,000	$125,000	$115,000	$39,100	$ 75,900
2	210,000	125,000	85,000	28,900	56,100
3	180,000	125,000	55,000	18,700	36,300
4	150,000	125,000	25,000	8,500	16,500
Totals	$780,000	$500,000	$280,000	$95,200	$184,800

The after-tax cash flow is as follows:

Year	Net Cash Flow Before Taxes	Taxes	Net Cash Flow After Taxes
1	$240,000	$39,100	$200,900
2	210,000	28,900	181,100
3	180,000	18,700	161,300
4	150,000	8,500	141,500
Totals	$780,000	$95,200	$684,800

2a. (After-tax) Accounting rate of return method:

$$\text{Accounting rate of return} = \frac{\text{average annual after-tax net income}}{\text{average investment cost}}$$

$$= \frac{\$184,800 \div 4}{(\$600,000 + \$100,000) \div 2} = \frac{\$46,200}{\$350,000} = 13.2\%$$

2b. (After-tax) Payback method:

Total cash investment		$600,000
Less cash flow recovery		
Year 1	$200,900	
Year 2	181,100	
Year 3	161,300	
Year 4 (.4007 × $141,500)	56,700	(600,000)
Unrecovered investment		—

Payback period: 3.4 years

2c. (After-tax) Net present value method (multipliers are from Table B-3):

Year	Net Cash Inflow after Taxes	Present Value Multiplier	Present Value
1	$200,900	.917	$ 184,225*
2	181,100	.842	152,486*
3	161,300	.772	124,524*
4	141,500	.708	100,182
4	100,000 (salvage)	.708	70,800
Total net present value			$ 632,217
Cost of original investment			(600,000)
Positive net present value			$ 32,217

*Rounded

3. Roland Construction Company: summary of decision analysis

	Before-Tax		After-Tax	
	Desired	Predicted	Desired	Predicted
Accounting rate of return	15%	20%	9%	13.2%
Payback period	3 yrs	2.833 yrs	4 yrs	3.4 yrs
Net present value	—	$29,000	—	$32,217

Based on the calculations for parts 1 and 2, the Roland Construction Company's proposed investment in the earthmoving machine meets all of the company's criteria for such investments. Given these results, the company should invest in the machine.

Chapter Assignments

Discussion Questions and Writing Assignments

1. What is meant by the term *relevant decision information*? What are the two important characteristics of such information?
2. Describe and discuss the five steps of the management decision cycle.
3. Describe the concept of variable costing. How does variable costing differ from absorption costing?
4. Is variable costing used for financial reporting purposes? Explain.
5. What is the connection between variable costing and the contribution approach to reporting?
6. What are the purposes of incremental analysis?
7. Discuss and illustrate some of the qualitative inputs of decision analysis.
8. How does one determine the data relevant to a make or buy decision?
9. Identify and discuss information that bears on special product orders.
10. What question must be answered in trying to maximize product line profitability? Give some examples of approaches to the solution of this question.

11. What is a capital expenditure? Give illustrations of different types of capital expenditure decisions. Define capital budgeting.
12. What is a crude but easy method for evaluating capital expenditures? List the advantages and disadvantages of this method.
13. What is the formula used for determining payback period? Is this decision measure accurate? Defend your answer.
14. "To treat all future income flows alike ignores the time value of money." Discuss this statement.
15. What is the objective of using the concept of discounted cash flows?
16. Why is it important to consider income taxes when evaluating a capital expenditure proposal?
17. Company Q has net cash inflow from operations for 19x2 of $42,000, non-cash expenditures of $8,000, and a sale of an asset that netted $36,000 in proceeds and involved a $10,000 capital gain. Using the 34 percent tax rate for normal income and for capital gains, compute the company's tax liability.

Classroom Exercises

Exercise 28-1.
Relevant Costs
and Revenues
(L.O. 1)

Old Dominion Enterprises manufactures various household metal products, such as window frames, light fixtures, and doorknobs. In 19x1 the company produced 10,000 special oblong doorknobs but sold only 1,000 doorknobs at $20.00 each. The remaining 9,000 units cannot be sold through Old Dominion's normal channels.

For inventory purposes, costs on December 31, 19x1 included the following data on unsold units:

Direct materials	$ 6.00
Direct labor	3.00
Variable factory overhead	1.00
Fixed factory overhead	4.00
Cost per knob	$14.00

The 9,000 oblong knobs can be sold to a scrap dealer in another state for $7.00 each. A license for doing business in this state will cost Old Dominion $400. Shipping expenses will average $0.10 per knob.

1. Identify the relevant costs and revenues for the scrap sale alternative.
2. Assume the oblong knobs can be reprocessed to produce round knobs, that normally have the same $14.00 unit cost components and sell for $16.00 each. Rework costs will be $9.00 per unit. Determine the most profitable alternative: (1) doing nothing, (2) reprocessing the knobs, or (3) selling them as scrap (assuming a market exists for the reworked knobs).

Exercise 28-2.
Relevant Data and
Incremental
Analysis
(L.O. 1, 5)

Mr. Richard, business manager for Bebee Industries, must select a new word processor for his secretary. Rental of Model A, which is like the model now being used, is $3,200 per year. Model B is a deluxe word processor that rents for $3,900 per year, but it will require a new desk for the secretary. The annual desk rental charge is $750. The secretary's salary of $1,200 per month will not change. If Model B is rented, $280 in training costs will be incurred. Model B has greater capacity and is expected to save $2,550 per year in part-time secretarial wages. Upkeep and operating costs will not differ between the two models.

1. Identify the relevant data in this problem.
2. Prepare an incremental analysis for the business manager to aid him in his decision.

Exercise 28-3.
Variable Costing:
Unit Cost
Computation
(L.O. 3)

Suny Corporation produces a full line of energy-tracking devices. These devices can detect and track all forms of thermochemical energy-emitting space vehicles.

The following cost data are provided: Direct materials cost $1,185,000 for two units. Direct labor for assembly is 4,590 hours per unit at $26.50 per hour. Variable factory overhead is $48.00 per direct labor hour, and fixed factory overhead is $2,796,000 per month (based on an average production of thirty units per month). This amount includes fixed packaging overhead. Packaging materials come to $127,200 for two units, and packaging labor per unit is 420 hours per unit at $18.50 per hour. The variable factory overhead rate for packaging is the same as for production. Advertising and marketing cost $196,750 per month, and other fixed selling and administrative costs are $287,680 per month.

1. From the cost data above, find the unit production cost, using both the variable costing and the absorption costing methods.
2. Assume that the current month's ending inventory is eight units. Compute the inventory valuation under both variable and absorption costing methods.

Exercise 28-4.
Income Statement:
Contribution
Reporting Format
(L.O. 4)

The income statement in the conventional reporting format for Brosi Products, Inc. for the year ended December 31, 19x0, appeared as shown below.

Brosi Products, Inc.
Income Statement
For the Year Ended December 31, 19x0

Sales		$296,400
Less Cost of Goods Sold		
Cost of Goods Available for Sale	$125,290	
Less Ending Inventory	12,540	112,750
Gross Margin from Sales		$183,650
Less Operating Expenses		
Selling Expenses		
Variable	$ 69,820	
Fixed	36,980	
Administrative Expenses	27,410	134,210
Net Income before Taxes		$ 49,440

Fixed manufacturing costs of $17,600 and $850 are included in Cost of Goods Available for Sale and Ending Inventory, respectively. Total fixed manufacturing costs for 19x0 were $16,540. There were no beginning or ending work in process inventories. All administrative expenses are considered to be fixed.

Using this information, prepare an income statement for Brosi Products, Inc. for the year ended December 31, 19x0, using the contribution reporting format.

Exercise 28-5.
Make or Buy
Decision
(L.O. 6a)

One of the parts for a radio assembly being produced by Mount Vernon Audio Systems, Inc. is being purchased at present for $225 per 100 parts. Management is studying the possibility of manufacturing these parts. Cost and production data are as follows:

Annual production (usage) is 70,000 units. Fixed costs (all of which remain unchanged whether the part is made or purchased) are $38,500. Variable costs are $.95 per unit for direct materials, $.55 per unit for direct labor, and $.60 per unit for manufacturing overhead.

Using incremental decision analysis, decide whether Mount Vernon Audio Systems, Inc. should manufacture the part or continue to purchase it from an outside vendor.

Exercise 28-6.
Special Order
Decision
(L.O. 6b)

Alvin, Cabot, & Hunter, Ltd. produces antique-looking lampshades. Management has just received a request for a special-design order and must decide whether or not to accept it. The special order calls for 9,000 shades to be shipped in a total of 300 bulk pack cartons. Shipping costs of $180 per carton will replace normal packing and shipping costs. The purchasing company is offering to pay $22 per shade plus packing and shipping expenses.

The following company data has been provided by the accounting department: Annual expected production is 350,000 shades, and the current year's production (before special order) is 360,000 shades. Maximum production capacity is 380,000 shades. Unit cost data include $9.20 for direct materials, $4.00 for direct labor, variable factory overhead of $6.80, and fixed factory overhead of $2.50 ($875,000 ÷ 350,000). Normal packaging and shipping costs per unit come to $1.50, and advertising is $.30 per unit ($105,000 ÷ 350,000). Other fixed administrative costs are $1.30 per unit ($455,000 ÷ 350,000). Total normal cost per unit is $25.60, with per unit selling price set at $38.00. Total estimated bulk packaging costs are $54,000 ($180 per carton × 300 cartons).

Determine whether this special order should be accepted.

Exercise 28-7.
Using the
Present Value
Tables
(L.O. 7c)

For each of the following situations, identify the correct multiplier to use from the tables presented in Appendix B. Then compute the appropriate present value.

a. Annual net cash inflow of $30,000 for five years, discounted at 16%.
b. An amount of $25,000 to be received at the end of ten years, discounted at 12%.
c. The amounts of $21,000 to be received at the end of two years and $15,000 to be received at the end of years four, five, and six, discounted at 10%.
d. Annual net cash inflow of $22,500 for twelve years, discounted at 14%.
e. The following five years of cash inflows, discounted at 10%.

Year 1	$25,000
Year 2	20,000
Year 3	30,000
Year 4	40,000
Year 5	50,000

f. The amount of $60,000 to be received at the beginning of the seventh year, discounted at 14%.

Exercise 28-8.
Capital
Expenditure
Decision:
Accounting Rate
of Return Method
(L.O. 7a)

Winter Haven Corporation manufactures metal hard hats for on-site construction workers. Recently, management has tried to raise productivity to meet the growing demand from the real estate industry. The company is now thinking about a new stamping machine. Management has decided that only capital expenditures that yield a 16 percent return before taxes will be accepted. The following projections for the proposal are given: the new machine will cost $325,000; revenue will increase $98,400 per year; the salvage value of the new machine will be $32,500; operating cost increases (including depreciation) will be $71,200.

Using the accounting rate of return method, decide whether the company should invest in the machine. (Show all computations to support your decision, and ignore income tax effects.)

Exercise 28-9.
Capital
Expenditure
Decision: Payback
Method
(L.O. 7b)

MJK Sounds, Inc., a manufacturer of stereo speakers, is thinking about adding a new injection molding machine. This machine can produce speaker parts that the company now buys from outsiders. The machine has an estimated life of fourteen years and will cost $415,000. Gross cash revenue from the machine will be about $397,500 per year, and related cash expenses should total $265,000. Taxes on income are estimated at $45,050 a year. The payback period as set by management should be five years or less.

On the basis of the data given, use the payback method to determine whether the company should invest in this new machine. Show your computations to support your answer.

Exercise 28-10.
Capital
Expenditure
Decision: Net
Present Value
Method
(L.O. 7c)

Steven Altman and Associates is thinking of buying an automatic extruding machine. This piece of equipment would have a useful life of six years, would cost $219,500, and would increase annual after-tax net cash inflows by $57,250. Assume that there is no salvage value at the end of six years. The company's minimum desired rate of return is 14 percent.

Using the net present value method, prepare an analysis to determine whether or not the company should purchase the machine.

Interpreting Accounting Information

Internal
Management
Information:
Coconino Federal
Bank
(L.O. 7c)

Automatic round-the-clock tellers are rapidly becoming a common element of the banking industry. Several companies have developed these computerized money machines and are bombarding bank managers with salespeople and advertising brochures. Coconino Federal Bank is planning to replace some old machines and has decided on the Sedona Machine. Ms. Pitt, the controller, has prepared the decision analysis shown on the next page. She has recommended the purchase of the machine based on the positive net present value shown in the analysis.

Coconino Federal Bank
Capital Expenditure Decision Analysis
Before-Tax Net Present Value Approach
March 2, 19x1

Year	Net Cash Inflow	Present Value Multipliers	Present Value
1	$ 55,000	.909	$ 49,995
2	80,000	.826	66,080
3	85,000	.751	63,835
4	90,000	.683	61,470
5	95,000	.621	58,995
5 (salvage)	35,000	.621	21,735
Total Present Value			$322,110
Initial Investment	$385,000		
Less Proceeds from the Sale of Existing Teller Machines	85,000		
Net Capital Investment			(300,000)
Net Present Value			$ 22,110

The Sedona Machine has an estimated life of five years and an expected salvage value of $35,000. Its purchase price would be $385,000. Two existing teller machines, each having a book value of $25,000, would be sold for a total of $85,000 to a neighboring bank. Annual operating cash inflow is expected to increase in the following manner:

Year 1	$55,000
Year 2	80,000
Year 3	85,000
Year 4	90,000
Year 5	95,000

The bank uses straight-line depreciation. Before-tax minimum desired rate of return is 16 percent, and a 10 percent rate is used for interpreting after-tax data. Assume a 34 percent tax rate for normal operating and capital gains items.

Required

1. Analyze the work of Ms. Pitt. What changes need to be made in her capital expenditure decision analysis?
2. What would be your recommendation to bank management about the Sedona Machine purchase?

Problem Set A

Problem 28A-1.
Variable Costing:
Contribution
Approach to
Income Statement
(L.O. 3, 4)

Roofing tile is the major product of the Lilja Corporation. The company had a particularly good year in 19x2, as is shown by the following operating data. It produced 92,600 cases (units) of tile and sold 88,400 cases. Direct materials used cost $384,290; direct labor was $208,350; variable factory overhead was $296,320; fixed factory overhead was $166,680; variable selling expenses were $132,600; fixed selling expenses were $152,048; and fixed administrative expenses were $96,450. Selling price was $18 per case. There were no partially completed jobs in process at the beginning or the end of the year. Finished goods inventory had been used up at the end of the previous year.

Required

1. Compute the unit cost and ending finished goods inventory value, using (a) variable costing procedures and (b) absorption costing procedures.
2. Prepare the year-end income statement for the Lilja Corporation, using (a) the contribution format based on variable costing data and (b) the conventional format based on absorption costing data.

Problem 28A-2.
Make or Buy
Decision
(L.O. 6a)

The Rock Springs Refrigerator Company purchases and installs defrost clocks in its products. The clocks cost $138 per case, and each case contains twelve clocks. The supplier recently gave advance notice that, effective in thirty days, the price will rise by 50 percent. The company has idle equipment that, with only a few changes, could be used to produce similar defrost clocks.

The following cost estimates have been prepared under the assumption that the company could make the product itself. Direct materials would cost $100.80 per twelve clocks. Direct labor required would be ten minutes per clock at a labor rate of $8.00 per hour. Variable factory overhead would be $4.60 per clock. Fixed factory overhead, which would be incurred under either decision alternative would be $32,420 a year for depreciation and $234,000 a year for other expenses. Production and usage are estimated at 75,000 clocks a year. (Assume that idle equipment cannot be used for any other purpose.)

Required

1. Prepare an incremental decision analysis to figure out whether the defrost clocks should be made within the company or purchased from the outside supplier at the higher rate.
2. Compute the unit cost to make one clock and to buy one clock.

Problem 28A-3.
Sales Mix Analysis
(L.O. 6c)

The vice president of finance for Winslow Machine Tool, Inc. is evaluating the profitability of the company's four product lines. During the current year, the company will operate at full machine-hour capacity. The following production data have been compiled:

Product	Current Year's Production (Units)	Total Machine Hours Used
24F	30,000	75,000
37N	50,000	100,000
29T	20,000	20,000
40U	90,000	45,000

Sales and operating cost data are as follows:

	Product 24F	Product 37N	Product 29T	Product 40U
Selling price per unit	$20.00	$25.00	$30.00	$35.00
Unit variable manufacturing cost	8.00	17.00	21.00	29.00
Unit fixed manufacturing cost	4.00	3.00	2.50	2.00
Unit variable selling cost	2.00	2.00	4.50	3.25
Unit fixed administrative cost	3.00	2.00	3.00	1.75

Required

1. Compute the machine hours needed to produce one unit of each product type.
2. Determine the contribution margin of each product type.
3. Which product line(s) should be pushed by the company's sales force? Why?

Problem 28A-4.
Capital
Expenditure
Decision: Net
Present Value
Method
(L.O. 7c, 8)

The management of Tempe Plastics has recently been looking at a proposal to purchase a new plastic injection-style molding machine. With the new machine, the company would not have to buy small plastic parts to use in production. The estimated life of the machine is fifteen years, and the purchase price including all set-up charges is $395,000. Salvage value is estimated to be $39,500. The net addition to the company's cash inflow due to the savings from making the parts is estimated to be $65,000 a year. Tempe Plastic's management has decided on a minimum desired before-tax rate of return of 14 percent.

Required

1. Using the net present value method to evaluate this capital expenditure, determine whether the company should purchase the machine. Support your answer.
2. If management had decided on a minimum desired before-tax rate of return of 16 percent, should the machine be purchased? Show all computations to support your answer.
3. Assuming straight-line depreciation, a 34 percent tax rate, and an after-tax minimum desired rate of return of 8 percent, should the company purchase the machine? Show your computations.

Problem 28A-5.
Capital
Expenditure
Decision:
Comprehensive
(L.O. 7, 8)

The Bagdad Manufacturing Company, based in Wikieup, Arizona, is one of the fastest-growing companies in its industry. According to Mr. Weaver, the company's production vice president, keeping up with technological changes is what makes the company successful.

Mr. Weaver feels that a machine introduced recently would fill an important need of the company. The machine has an expected useful life of four years, a purchase price of $225,000, and a salvage value of $22,500. The company controller's estimated operating results, using the new machine, are summarized on the next page. The company uses straight-line depreciation for all its machinery. Mr. Weaver uses a 12 percent minimum desired rate of return and a three-year payback period for capital expenditure evaluation purposes (before-tax decision guidelines).

Cash Flow Estimates

Year	Cash Revenues	Cash Expenses	Net Cash Inflow
1	$305,000	$250,000	$55,000
2	315,000	250,000	65,000
3	325,000	250,000	75,000
4	325,000	250,000	75,000

Required

1. Ignoring income taxes, analyze the purchase of the machine and decide if the company should purchase it. Use the following evaluation approaches in your analysis: (a) the accounting rate of return method, (b) the payback method, and (c) the net present value method.
2. Rework part 1, assuming a 34 percent tax rate, after-tax guidelines of an 8 percent minimum desired rate of return, and a 3.5-year payback period. Does the decision change when after-tax information is used?

Problem Set B

**Problem 28B-1.
Variable Costing:
Contribution
Approach to
Income Statement
(L.O. 3, 4)**

Interior designers often utilize the deluxe carpet products of Sierra Estrella Mills, Inc. The Maricopa Blend is the company's top product line. In March, 19x1, Sierra Estrella produced 187,500 square yards and sold 174,900 square yards of Maricopa Blend. Factory operating data for the year included: direct materials used of $1,209,375; direct labor of .50 direct labor hours per square yard at $14.50 per hour; variable factory overhead totaled $243,750; and fixed factory overhead was $346,875. Other expenses included: variable selling expenses, $166,155; fixed selling expenses, $148,665; and fixed general and administrative expenses, $231,500. Total sales revenue equaled $3,935,250. All production took place in March and there was no work in process at month end. Goods are usually shipped when completed but at the end of March, 12,600 square yards still await shipment.

Required

1. Compute the unit cost and ending finished goods inventory value, using (a) variable costing, and (b) absorption costing procedures.
2. Prepare the year-end income statement for Sierra Estrella Mills, Inc. using (a) the contribution format based on variable costing data, and (b) the conventional format based on absorption costing data.

**Problem 28B-2.
Make or Buy
Decision
(L.O. 6a)**

The Havasu Furniture Company of Prescott, Arizona is famous for its dining room furniture. One full department is engaged in the production of the Cottonwood line, an elegant but affordable dining room set. To date, the company has been manufacturing all pieces of the set, including the six chairs.

Management has just received word that a company in Blythe, California is willing to produce the chairs for Havasu Furniture Company at a total purchase price of $2,688,000 for the annual demand. Company records show that the following costs have been incurred in the production of the chairs: wood materials, $2,250 per 100 chairs; cloth materials, $850 per 100 chairs; direct labor, 1.2 hours per chair at $14.00 per hour; variable factory overhead, $7.00 per direct labor hour; fixed factory overhead, depreciation, $135,000 and other, $109,400. Fixed factory overhead would continue whether or not the chairs are produced. Assume that idle facilities cannot be used for any other purpose and that annual usage is 56,000 chairs.

Required

1. Prepare an incremental decision analysis to determine whether the chairs should be made by the company or purchased from the outside supplier in Blythe.
2. Compute the unit cost to make one chair and to buy one chair.

Problem 28B-3.
Special Order
Decision
(L.O. 6b)

On March 26, the San Luis Boat Division of Rio Colorado Industries received a special order request for 120, 10-foot aluminum fishing boats. Operating on a fiscal year ending May 31, the division already has orders that will allow them to produce at budget levels for the period. However, extra capacity exists to produce the 120 additional boats.

Terms of the special order call for a selling price of $625 per boat and the customer will pay all shipping costs. No sales personnel were involved in soliciting this order.

The 10-foot fishing boat has the following cost estimates: direct materials, aluminum, 2 4′ × 8′ sheets at $145 per sheet; direct labor, 14 hours at $14.50 per hour; variable factory overhead, $5.75 per direct labor hour; fixed factory overhead, $4.50 per direct labor hour; variable selling expenses, $46.50 per boat; variable shipping expenses, $57.50 per boat.

Required

1. Prepare an analysis for management of the San Luis Boat Division to use in deciding whether to accept or reject the special order. What decision should be made?
2. To make an $8,000 profit on this order, what would be the lowest possible price that the San Luis Boat Division could charge per boat?

Problem 28B-4.
Capital
Expenditure
Decision: Net
Present Value
Method
(L.O. 7c, 8)

The Twelfth of Leo is a famous restaurant in the New Orleans French Quarter. "Bouillabaisse Kathryn" is the house specialty. Management is currently considering the purchase of a machine that would prepare all the ingredients, mix them automatically, and cook the dish to the restaurant's specifications. The machine will function for an estimated twelve years, and the purchase price including installation is $246,000. Estimated salvage value is $24,600. This labor-saving device is expected to increase cash flows by an average of $42,000 per year during its life. For purposes of capital expenditure decisions, the restaurant uses a 12 percent minimum desired rate of return.

Required

1. Using the net present value method to evaluate this capital expenditure, determine whether the company should purchase the machine. Support your answer.
2. If management had decided on a minimum desired rate of return of 14 percent, should the machine be purchased? Show all computations to support your answer.
3. Assuming straight-line depreciation, a 34 percent tax rate, and an after-tax minimum desired rate of return of 7 percent, should the company purchase the machine? Show your computations.

**Problem 28B-5.
Capital
Expenditure
Decision:
Comprehensive
(L.O. 7, 8)**

Quality work and timely output are the benchmarks upon which Casa Grande Photo, Inc. was organized. Now a nationally franchised company, there are over 100 Casa Grande Photo outlets scattered throughout the eastern and midwestern states. Part of the franchise agreement promises a centralized photo developing process with overnight delivery to the outlets.

Because of the tremendous increase in demand for their photo processing, Mr. Whitehorse, the corporation's president, is considering the purchase of a new, deluxe processing machine. At a cost of $320,000, this machine will function for an estimated five years and should have a $32,000 salvage value at the end of that period. Mr. Whitehorse expects all capital expenditures to produce a 20 percent before-tax minimum rate of return and the investment should be recouped in three years or less. All fixed assets are depreciated using the straight-line method. The forecasted increase in operating results of the new machine are as follows:

Cash Flow Estimates

Year	Cash Revenues	Cash Expenses
1	$310,000	$210,000
2	325,000	220,000
3	340,000	230,000
4	300,000	210,000
5	260,000	180,000

Required

1. Ignoring income taxes, analyze the purchase of the machine and decide if the company should purchase it. Use the following evaluation approaches to your analysis: (a) the accounting rate of return method; (b) the payback method; and (c) the net present value method.
2. Rework part **1**, assuming a 34 percent tax rate, after-tax guidelines of a 10 percent minimum desired rate of return, and a four-year payback period. Does the decision change when after-tax information is used?

Management Decision Case

**McVan Hotel
Syndicate
(L.O. 7c, 8)**

The McVan Hotel Syndicate owns four resort hotels in southern Iowa and Missouri. Because their Hermann, Missouri operation (Hotel 3) has been booming over the past three years, management has decided to add a new wing to increase capacity by 20 percent. A construction firm has bid on the proposed new wing. The building would have a 20-year life, and the company uses straight-line depreciation. Deluxe accommodations are highlighted in this contractor's proposal. The new wing would cost $29,000,000 to construct, have a salvage value of $2,900,000, and is expected to generate the following cash flows:

Year	Increase in Cash Inflows from Room Rentals	Increase in Cash Operating Expenses
1–7 (each year)	$17,900,000	$12,800,000
8	20,000,000	14,600,000
9	22,100,000	15,900,000
10–20 (each year)	24,200,000	17,700,000

Capital investment projects must generate a 12 percent after-tax minimum desired rate of return to qualify for consideration. Assume a 34 percent tax rate.

Required

Evaluate the proposal from the contractor using net present value analysis, and make a recommendation to management.

Answers to Self-Test

1. a	3. d	5. b	7. a	9. d
2. c	4. a	6. b	8. c	10. c

1. *Distinguish simple from compound interest.*
2. *Use compound interest tables to compute the future value of a single invested sum at compound interest and an ordinary annuity.*
3. *Use compound interest tables to compute the present value of a single sum due in the future and an ordinary annuity.*
4. *Apply the concept of present value to simple accounting situations.*

APPENDIX A

The Time Value of Money

Interest is an important cost to the debtor and an important revenue to the creditor. Because interest is a cost associated with time, and "time is money," it is also an important consideration in any business decision. For example, an individual who holds $100 for one year without putting that $100 in a savings account has forgone the interest that could have been earned. Thus, there is a cost associated with holding this money equal to the interest that could have been earned. Similarly, a business person who accepts a noninterest-bearing note instead of cash for the sale of merchandise is not forgoing the interest that could have been earned on that money but is including the interest implicitly in the price of the merchandise. These examples illustrate the point that the timing of the receipt and payment of cash must be considered in making business decisions.

Simple Interest and Compound Interest

Interest is the cost associated with the use of money for a specific period of time. **Simple interest** is the interest cost for one or more periods, if we assume that the amount on which the interest is computed stays the same from period to period. **Compound interest** is the interest cost for two or more periods, if we assume that after each period the interest of that period is added to the amount on which interest is computed in future periods. In other words, compound interest is interest earned on a principal sum that is increased at the end of each period by the interest of that period.

Example: Simple Interest. Joe Sanchez accepts an 8 percent, $30,000 note due in ninety days. How much will he receive in total at that time? Remember the formula for calculating simple interest, which was presented in Chapter 9, on notes receivable:

$$\text{Interest} = \text{principal} \times \text{rate} \times \text{time}$$
$$\text{Interest} = \$30,000 \times 8/100 \times 90/360$$
$$\text{Interest} = \$600$$

The total that Sanchez will receive is computed as follows:

$$\text{Total} = \text{principal} + \text{interest}$$
$$\text{Total} = \$30,000 + \$600$$
$$\text{Total} = \$30,600$$

Example: Compound Interest. Ann Clary deposits $5,000 in a savings account that pays 6 percent interest. She expects to leave the principal and accumulated interest in the account for three years. How much will her account total at the end of three years? Assume

OBJECTIVE 1
Distinguish simple from compound interest

that the interest is paid at the end of the year and is added to the principal at that time and that this total in turn earns interest. The amount at the end of three years may be computed as follows:

(1) Year	(2) Principal Amount at Beginning of Year	(3) Annual Amount of Interest (col. 2 × .06)	(4) Accumulated Amount at End of Year (col. 2 + col. 3)
1	$5,000.00	$300.00	$5,300.00
2	5,300.00	318.00	5,618.00
3	5,618.00	337.08	5,955.08

At the end of three years, Clary will have $5,955.08 in her savings account. Note that the annual amount of interest increases each year by the interest rate times the interest of the previous year. For example, between year 1 and year 2, the interest increased by $18 ($318 − $300), which exactly equals .06 times $300.

Future Value of a Single Invested Sum at Compound Interest

OBJECTIVE 2
Use compound interest tables to compute the future value of a single invested sum at compound interest and an ordinary annuity

Another way to ask the question in the example of compound interest above is, What is the future value of a single sum ($5,000) at compound interest (6 percent) for three years? **Future value** is the amount that an investment will be worth at a future date if invested at compound interest. A business person often wants to know future value, but the method of computing the future value illustrated above is too time-consuming in practice. Imagine how tedious the calculation would be if the example were ten years instead of three. Fortunately, there are tables that make problems involving compound interest much simpler and quicker to solve. Table A-1, showing the future value of $1 after a given number of time periods, is an example. It is actually

Table A-1. Future Value of $1 after a Given Number of Time Periods

Periods	1%	2%	3%	4%	5%	6%	7%	8%	9%	10%	12%	14%	15%
1	1.010	1.020	1.030	1.040	1.050	1.060	1.070	1.080	1.090	1.100	1.120	1.140	1.150
2	1.020	1.040	1.061	1.082	1.103	1.124	1.145	1.166	1.188	1.210	1.254	1.300	1.323
3	1.030	1.061	1.093	1.125	1.158	1.191	1.225	1.260	1.295	1.331	1.405	1.482	1.521
4	1.041	1.082	1.126	1.170	1.216	1.262	1.311	1.360	1.412	1.464	1.574	1.689	1.749
5	1.051	1.104	1.159	1.217	1.276	1.338	1.403	1.469	1.539	1.611	1.762	1.925	2.011
6	1.062	1.126	1.194	1.265	1.340	1.419	1.501	1.587	1.677	1.772	1.974	2.195	2.313
7	1.072	1.149	1.230	1.316	1.407	1.504	1.606	1.714	1.828	1.949	2.211	2.502	2.660
8	1.083	1.172	1.267	1.369	1.477	1.594	1.718	1.851	1.993	2.144	2.476	2.853	3.059
9	1.094	1.195	1.305	1.423	1.551	1.689	1.838	1.999	2.172	2.358	2.773	3.252	3.518
10	1.105	1.219	1.344	1.480	1.629	1.791	1.967	2.159	2.367	2.594	3.106	3.707	4.046

Source: Excerpt from Table B-1 in Appendix B.

part of a larger table, B-1 in Appendix B. Suppose that we want to solve the problem of Clary's savings account above. We simply look down the 6 percent column in Table A-1 until we reach period 3 and find the factor 1.191. This factor when multiplied by $1 gives the future value of that $1 at compound interest of 6 percent for three periods (years in this case). Thus we solve the problem:

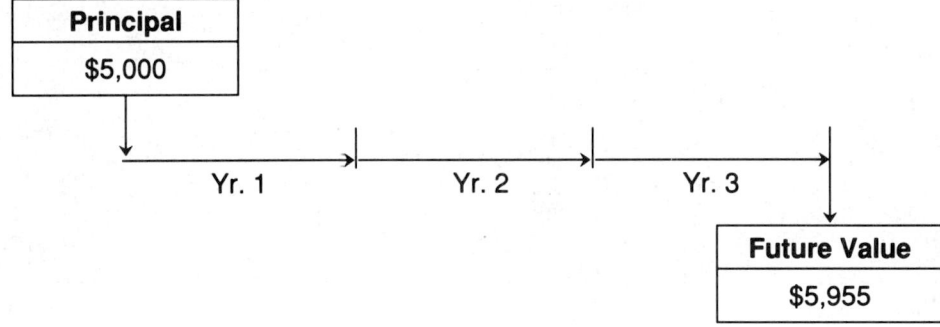

$$\text{Principal} \times \text{factor} = \text{future value}$$
$$\$5,000 \quad \times \; 1.191 \; = \quad \$5,955$$

Except for a rounding error of $.08, the answer is exactly the same as that calculated on the previous page.

Future Value of an Ordinary Annuity

Another common problem involves an **ordinary annuity,** which is a series of equal payments made at the end of equal intervals of time, with compound interest on these payments.

The following example shows how to find the future value of an ordinary annuity. Assume that Ben Katz deposits $200 at the end of each of the next three years in a savings account that pays 5 percent interest. How much money will he have in his account at the end of the three years? One way of computing the amount is shown in the following table:

(1) Year	(2) Beginning Balance	(3) Interest Earned (5% × col. 2)	(4) Periodic Payment	(5) Accumulated at End of Period (col. 2 + col. 3 + col. 4)
1	$ —	$ —	$200	$200.00
2	200.00	10.00	200	410.00
3	410.00	20.50	200	630.50

Katz would have $630.50 in his account at the end of three years, consisting of $600 in periodic payments and $30.50 in interest.

This calculation can also be simplified by using Table A-2. We look down the 5 percent column until we reach period 3 and find the factor 3.153. This factor when multiplied by $1 gives the future value of a series of three $1

Table A-2. Future Value of an Ordinary Annuity of $1 Paid in Each Period for a Given Number of Time Periods

Periods	1%	2%	3%	4%	5%	6%	7%	8%	9%	10%	12%	14%	15%
1	1.000	1.000	1.000	1.000	1.000	1.000	1.000	1.000	1.000	1.000	1.000	1.000	1.000
2	2.010	2.020	2.030	2.040	2.050	2.060	2.070	2.080	2.090	2.100	2.120	2.140	2.150
3	3.030	3.060	3.091	3.122	3.153	3.184	3.215	3.246	3.278	3.310	3.374	3.440	3.473
4	4.060	4.122	4.184	4.246	4.310	4.375	4.440	4.506	4.573	4.641	4.779	4.921	4.993
5	5.101	5.204	5.309	5.416	5.526	5.637	5.751	5.867	5.985	6.105	6.353	6.610	6.742
6	6.152	6.308	6.468	6.633	6.802	6.975	7.153	7.336	7.523	7.716	8.115	8.536	8.754
7	7.214	7.434	7.662	7.898	8.142	8.394	8.654	8.923	9.200	9.487	10.09	10.73	11.07
8	8.286	8.583	8.892	9.214	9.549	9.897	10.26	10.64	11.03	11.44	12.30	13.23	13.73
9	9.369	9.755	10.16	10.58	11.03	11.49	11.98	12.49	13.02	13.58	14.78	16.09	16.79
10	10.46	10.95	11.46	12.01	12.58	13.18	13.82	14.49	15.19	15.94	17.55	19.34	20.30

Source: Excerpt from Table B-2 in Appendix B.

payments (years in this case) at compound interest of 5 percent. Thus, we solve the problem:

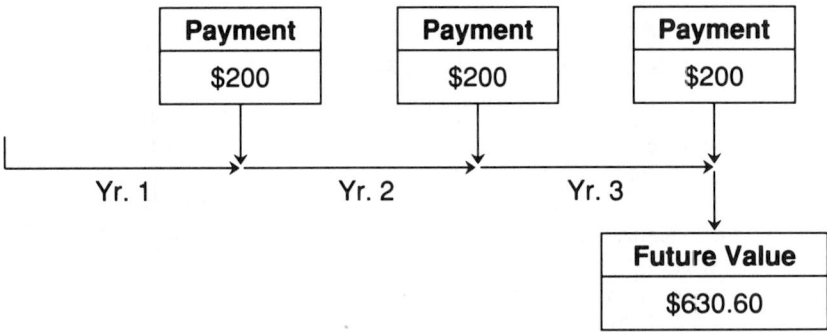

Periodic payment × factor = future value
$200   × 3.153 = $630.60

Except for a rounding error of $0.10, this result is the same as the one above.

Present Value

Suppose that you had the choice of receiving $100 today or one year from today. Intuitively, you would choose to receive the $100 today. Why? You know that if you have the $100 today, you can put it in a savings account to earn interest and will have more than $100 a year from today. Therefore, we can say that an amount to be received in the future (future value) is not worth as much today as an amount to be received today (present value) because of the cost associated with the passage of time. In fact, present value and future value are closely related. **Present value** is the amount that must be invested now at a given rate of interest to produce a given future value.

For example, assume that Sue Dapper needs $1,000 one year from now. How much should she invest today to achieve that goal if the interest rate is 5 percent? From earlier examples, the following equation may be established:

Present value × (1.0 + interest rate) = future value
Present value ×   1.05   = $1,000
Present value   = $1,000 ÷ 1.05
Present value   = $952.38

Thus, to achieve a future value of $1,000, a present value of $952.38 must be invested. Interest of 5 percent on $952.38 for one year equals $47.62, and these two amounts added together equal $1,000.

Present Value of a Single Sum Due in the Future

OBJECTIVE 3
Use compound interest tables to compute the present value of a single sum due in the future and an ordinary annuity

When more than one time period is involved, the calculation of present value is more complicated. Consider the following example. Don Riley wants to be sure of having $4,000 at the end of three years. How much must he invest today in a 5 percent savings account to achieve this goal? Adapting the above equation, we compute the present value of $4,000 at compound interest of 5 percent for three years in the future.

Year	Amount at End of Year	Divide by		Present Value at Beginning of Year
3	$4,000.00	÷	1.05 =	$3,809.52
2	3,809.52	÷	1.05 =	3,628.11
1	3,628.11	÷	1.05 =	3,455.34

Riley must invest a present value of $3,455.34 to achieve a future value of $4,000 in three years.

This calculation is again made much easier by using the appropriate table. In Table A-3, we look down the 5 percent column until we reach period 3 and find the factor 0.864. This factor when multiplied by $1 gives the present value of the $1 to be received three years from now at 5 percent interest. Thus we solve the problem:

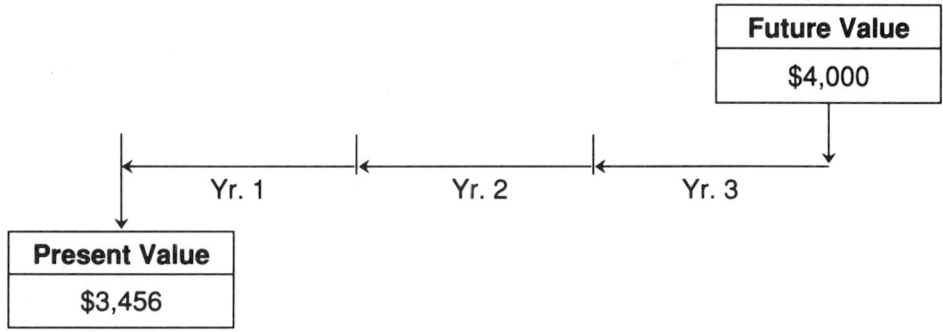

Future value × factor = present value
$4,000   × 0.864 = $3,456

Except for a rounding error of $0.66, this result is the same as the one above.

Table A-3. Present Value of $1 to Be Received at the End of a Given Number of Time Periods										
Periods	1%	2%	3%	4%	5%	6%	7%	8%	9%	10%
1	0.990	0.980	0.971	0.962	0.952	0.943	0.935	0.926	0.917	0.909
2	0.980	0.961	0.943	0.925	0.907	0.890	0.873	0.857	0.842	0.826
3	0.971	0.942	0.915	0.889	0.864	0.840	0.816	0.794	0.772	0.751
4	0.961	0.924	0.888	0.855	0.823	0.792	0.763	0.735	0.708	0.683
5	0.951	0.906	0.883	0.822	0.784	0.747	0.713	0.681	0.650	0.621
6	0.942	0.888	0.837	0.790	0.746	0.705	0.666	0.630	0.596	0.564
7	0.933	0.871	0.813	0.760	0.711	0.665	0.623	0.583	0.547	0.513
8	0.923	0.853	0.789	0.731	0.677	0.627	0.582	0.540	0.502	0.467
9	0.914	0.837	0.766	0.703	0.645	0.592	0.544	0.500	0.460	0.424
10	0.905	0.820	0.744	0.676	0.614	0.558	0.508	0.463	0.422	0.386

Source: Excerpt from Table B-3 in Appendix B.

Present Value of an Ordinary Annuity

It is often necessary to compute the present value of a series of receipts or payments. When we calculate the present value of equal amounts equally spaced over a period of time, we are computing the present value of an ordinary annuity.

For example, assume that Kathy Foster has sold a piece of property and is to receive $15,000 in three equal annual payments of $5,000, beginning one year from today. What is the present value of this sale, assuming a current interest rate of 5 percent? This present value may be computed by calculating a separate present value for each of the three payments (using Table A-3) and summing the results, as shown below.

Future Receipts (Annuity)			Present Value Factor at 5 Percent (from Table A-3)		Present Value
Year 1	Year 2	Year 3			
$5,000			×	0.952 =	$ 4,760
	$5,000		×	0.907 =	4,535
		$5,000	×	0.864 =	4,320
Total Present Value					$13,615

The present value of this sale is $13,615. Thus there is an implied interest cost (given the 5 percent rate) of $1,385 associated with the payment plan that allows the purchaser to pay in three installments.

We can make this calculation more easily by using Table A-4. We look down the 5 percent column until we reach period 3 and find factor 2.723. This factor when multiplied by $1 gives the present value of a series of three $1 payments (spaced one year apart) at compound interest of 5 percent. Thus we solve the problem:

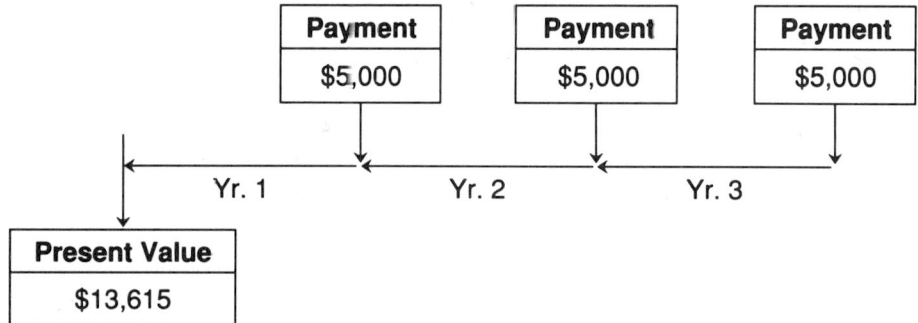

Periodic payment × factor = present value
$5,000 × 2.723 = $13,615

This result is the same as the one computed on the previous page.

Time Periods

In all the examples above and in most other cases, the compounding period is one year, and the interest rate is stated on an annual basis. However, in each of the four tables the left-hand column refers, not to years, but to periods. This wording is intended to accommodate compounding periods of

Periods	1%	2%	3%	4%	5%	6%	7%	8%	9%	10%
1	0.990	0.980	0.971	0.962	0.952	0.943	0.935	0.926	0.917	0.909
2	1.970	1.942	1.913	1.886	1.859	1.833	1.808	1.783	1.759	1.736
3	2.941	2.884	2.829	2.775	2.723	2.673	2.624	2.577	2.531	2.487
4	3.902	3.808	3.717	3.630	3.546	3.465	3.387	3.312	3.240	3.170
5	4.853	4.713	4.580	4.452	4.329	4.212	4.100	3.993	3.890	3.791
6	5.795	5.601	5.417	5.242	5.076	4.917	4.767	4.623	4.486	4.355
7	6.728	6.472	6.230	6.002	5.786	5.582	5.389	5.206	5.033	4.868
8	7.652	7.325	7.020	6.733	6.463	6.210	5.971	5.747	5.535	5.335
9	8.566	8.162	7.786	7.435	7.108	6.802	6.515	6.247	5.995	5.759
10	9.471	8.983	8.530	8.111	7.722	7.360	7.024	6.710	6.418	6.145

Table A-4. Present Value of an Ordinary Annuity of $1 Received Each Period for a Given Number of Time Periods

Source: Excerpt from Table B-4 in Appendix B.

less than one year. Savings accounts that record interest quarterly and bonds that pay interest semiannually are cases where the compounding period is less than one year. In order to use the tables in such cases, it is necessary to (1) divide the annual interest rate by the number of periods in the year, and (2) multiply the number of periods in one year by the number of years.

For example, assume that a $6,000 note is to be paid in two years and carries an annual interest rate of 8 percent. Compute the maturity (future) value of the note, assuming that the compounding period is semiannual. Before using the table, it is necessary to compute the interest rate that applies to each compounding period and the total number of compounding periods. First, the interest rate to use is 4 percent (8% annual rate ÷ 2 periods per year). Second, the total number of compounding periods is 4 (2 periods per year × 2 years). From Table A-1, therefore, the maturity value of the note may be computed as follows:

$$\text{Principal} \times \text{factor} = \text{future value}$$
$$\$6,000 \quad \times \ 1.170 \ = \quad \$7,020$$

The note will be worth $7,020 in two years.

This procedure for determining the interest rate and the number of periods when the compounding period is less than one year may be used with all the tables.

Applications of Present Value to Accounting

The concept of present value is widely applicable in the discipline of accounting. Here, the purpose is to demonstrate its usefulness in some simple applications. In-depth study of present value is deferred to more advanced courses.

Imputing Interest on Noninterest-Bearing Notes

OBJECTIVE 4
Apply the concept of present value to simple accounting situations

Clearly there is no such thing as an interest-free debt, regardless of whether the interest rate is explicitly stated. The Accounting Principles Board has declared that when a long-term note does not explicitly state an interest rate (or if the interest rate is unreasonably low), a rate based on the normal interest cost of the company in question should be assigned, or imputed.[1]

The following example applies the principle stated above. On January 1, 19x8, Gato purchases merchandise from Haines by issuing an $8,000 noninterest-bearing note due in two years. Gato can borrow money from the bank at 9 percent interest. Gato pays the note in full after two years.

Note that the $8,000 note represents partly a payment for merchandise and partly a payment of interest for two years. In recording the purchase and sale, it is necessary to use Table A-3 to determine the present value of the note. The calculation follows.

$$\text{Future payment} \times \text{present value factor (9\%, 2 years)} = \text{present value}$$
$$\$8,000 \qquad \times \qquad\qquad 0.842 \qquad\qquad = \qquad \$6,736$$

---

1. Accounting Principles Board, *Opinion No. 21*, "Interest on Receivables and Payables" (New York: American Institute of Certified Public Accountants, 1971), par. 13.

The imputed interest cost is $1,264 ($8,000 − $6,736) and is recorded as prepaid interest in Gato's records and as unearned interest in Haines' records. The entries necessary to record the purchase in the Gato records and the sale in the Haines records are shown below.

Gato Journal			Haines Journal		
Purchases	6,736		Notes Receivable	8,000	
Prepaid Interest	1,264		Unearned Interest		1,264
Notes Payable		8,000	Sales		6,736

On December 31, 19x8, the adjustments to recognize the interest expense and interest earned will be:

Gato Journal			Haines Journal		
Interest Expense	606.24		Unearned Interest	606.24	
Prepaid Interest		606.24	Interest Earned		606.24

The interest is calculated by multiplying the original purchase by the interest for one year ($6,736 × .09 = $606.24). When payment is made on December 31, 19x9, the following entries will be made in the respective journals:

Gato Journal			Haines Journal		
Interest Expense	657.76		Unearned Interest	657.76	
Notes Payable	8,000.00		Cash	8,000.00	
Prepaid Interest		657.76	Interest Earned		657.76
Cash		8,000.00	Notes Receivable		8,000.00

The interest entries represent the remaining interest to be expensed or realized ($1,264 − $606.24 = $657.76). This amount approximates (because of rounding errors in the table) the interest for one year on the purchases plus last year's interest [($6,736 + $606.24) × .09 = $660.80].

Valuing an Asset

An asset is recorded because it will provide future benefits to the company that owns it. This future benefit is the basis for the definition of an asset. Usually, the purchase price of the asset represents the present value of these future benefits. It is possible to evaluate a proposed purchase price of an asset by comparing that price with the present value of the asset to the company.

For example, Sam Hurst is thinking of buying a new labor-saving machine that will reduce his annual labor cost by $700 per year. The machine will last eight years. The interest rate that Hurst assumes for making managerial decisions is 10 percent. What is the maximum amount (present value) that Hurst should pay for the machine?

The present value of the machine to Hurst is equal to the present value of an ordinary annuity of $700 per year for eight years at compound interest of 10 percent. From Table A-4, we compute the value as follows:

$$\text{Periodic savings} \times \text{factor} = \text{present value}$$
$$\$700 \qquad \times 5.335 = \quad \$3,734.50$$

Hurst should not pay more than $3,734.50 for the new machine because this amount equals the present value of the benefits that will be received from owning the machine.

Other Accounting Applications

There are many other applications of present value in accounting. The uses of present value to value a bond and to record lease obligations were shown in Chapter 17. A few other applications are the recording of pension obligations; the determination of premium and discount on debt; accounting for the depreciation of property, plant, and equipment; analysis of the purchase price of a business; evaluation of capital expenditure decisions; and generally any problem where time is a factor.

Exercises

Tables B-1 to B-4 in Appendix B may be used to solve these exercises.

Exercise A-1.
Future Value
Calculations
(L.O. 2)

Naber receives a one-year note that carries a 12 percent annual interest rate on $1,500 for the sale of a used car.

Compute the maturity value under each of the following assumptions: (1) The interest is simple interest. (2) The interest is compounded semiannually. (3) The interest is compounded quarterly. (4) The interest is compounded monthly.

Exercise A-2.
Future Value
Calculations
(L.O. 2)

Find the future value of (1) a single payment of $10,000 at 7 percent for ten years, (2) ten annual payments of $1,000 at 7 percent, (3) a single payment of $3,000 at 9 percent for seven years, and (4) seven annual payments of $3,000 at 9 percent.

Exercise A-3.
Present Value
Calculations
(L.O. 3)

Find the present value of (1) a single payment of $12,000 at 6 percent for twelve years, (2) twelve annual payments of $1,000 at 6 percent, (3) a single payment of $2,500 at 9 percent for five years, and (4) five annual payments of $2,500 at 9 percent.

Exercise A-4.
Future Value
Calculations
(L.O. 2)

Assume that $20,000 is invested today. Compute the amount that would accumulate at the end of seven years when the interest is (1) 8 percent annual interest compounded annually, (2) 8 percent annual interest compounded semiannually, and (3) 8 percent annual interest compounded quarterly.

Exercise A-5.
Future Value
Calculations
(L.O. 2)

Calculate the accumulation of periodic payments of $500 made at the end of each of four years, assuming (1) 10 percent annual interest compounded annually, (2) 10 percent annual interest compounded semiannually, (3) 4 percent annual interest compounded annually, and (4) 16 percent annual interest compounded quarterly.

Exercise A-6.
Future Value
Applications
(L.O. 2)

a. Two parents have $10,000 to invest for their child's college tuition, which they estimate will cost $20,000 when the child enters college twelve years from now.

Calculate the approximate rate of annual interest that the investment must earn to reach the $20,000 goal in twelve years. (**Hint:** Make a calculation; then use Table B-1.)

b. Bill Roister is saving to purchase a summer home that will cost about $32,000. He has $20,000 now, on which he can earn 7 percent annual interest.

Calculate the approximate length of time he will have to wait to purchase the summer home. (**Hint:** Make a calculation; then use Table B-1.)

Exercise A-7.
Working
Backward from a
Future Value
(L.O. 2)

May Marquez has a debt of $45,000 due in four years. She wants to save money to pay it off by making annual deposits in an investment account that earns 8 percent annual interest.

Calculate the amount she must deposit each year to reach her goal. (**Hint:** Use Table B-2; then make a calculation.)

Exercise A-8.
Present Value of
a Lump-Sum
Contract
(L.O. 3)

A contract calls for a lump-sum payment of $30,000. Find the present value of the contract, assuming that (1) the payment is due in five years, and the current interest rate is 9 percent; (2) the payment is due in ten years, and the current interest rate is 9 percent; (3) the payment is due in five years, and the current interest rate is 5 percent; and (4) the payment is due in ten years, and the current interest rate is 5 percent.

Exercise A-9.
Present Value
of an Annuity
Contract
(L.O. 3)

A contract calls for annual payments of $600. Find the present value of the contract, assuming that (1) the number of payments is seven, and the current interest rate is 6 percent; (2) the number of payments is fourteen, and the current interest rate is 6 percent; (3) the number of payments is seven, and the current interest rate is 8 percent; and (4) the number of payments is fourteen, and the current interest rate is 8 percent.

Exercise A-10.
Noninterest-
Bearing Note
(L.O. 4)

On January 1, 19x8, Olson purchases a machine from Carter by signing a two-year, noninterest-bearing $16,000 note. Olson currently pays 12 percent interest to borrow money at the bank.

Prepare journal entries in Olson's and Carter's records to (1) record the purchase and the note, (2) adjust the accounts after one year, and (3) record payment of the note after two years (on December 31, 19x9).

Exercise A-11.
Valuing an Asset
for the Purpose
of Making a
Purchasing
Decision
(L.O. 4)

Kubo owns a service station and has the opportunity to purchase a car wash machine for $15,000. After carefully studying projected costs and revenues, Kubo estimates that the car wash will produce a net cash flow of $2,600 annually and will last for eight years. Kubo feels that an interest rate of 14 percent is adequate for his business.

Calculate the present value of the machine to Kubo. Does the purchase appear to be a correct business decision?

Exercise A-12.
Determining an
Advance Payment
(L.O. 2)

Ellen Saber is contemplating paying five years' rent in advance. Her annual rent is $4,800. Calculate the single sum that would have to be paid now for the advance rent, if we assume compound interest of 8 percent.

APPENDIX B

Future Value and Present Value Tables

Table B-1 provides the multipliers necessary to compute the future value of a *single* cash deposit made at the *beginning* of year 1. Three factors must be known before the future value can be computed: (1) time period in years, (2) stated annual rate of interest to be earned, and (3) dollar amount invested or deposited.

Example. Determine the future value of $5,000 deposited now that will earn 9 percent interest compounded annually for five years. From Table B-1, the necessary multiplier for five years at 9 percent is 1.539, and the answer is:

$$\$5,000(1.539) = \underline{\underline{\$7,695}}$$

Situations requiring the use of Table B-2 are similar to those requiring Table B-1 except that Table B-2 is used to compute the future value of a *series* of *equal* annual deposits.

Example. What will be the future value at the end of thirty years if $1,000 is deposited each year on January 1, beginning in one year, assuming 12 percent interest compounded annually? The required multiplier from Table B-2 is 241.3, and the answer is:

$$\$1,000(241.3) = \underline{\underline{\$241,300}}$$

Table B-3 is used to compute the value today of a *single* amount of cash to be received sometime in the future. To use Table B-3 you must first know: (1) time period in years until funds will be received, (2) annual rate of interest, and (3) dollar amount to be received at end of time period.

Example. What is the present value of $30,000 to be received twenty-five years from now, assuming a 14 percent interest rate? From Table B-3, the required multiplier is 0.038, and the answer is:

$$\$30,000(0.038) = \underline{\underline{\$1,140}}$$

Table B-1. Future Value of $1 After a Given Number of Time Periods

Periods	1%	2%	3%	4%	5%	6%	7%	8%	9%	10%	12%	14%	15%
1	1.010	1.020	1.030	1.040	1.050	1.060	1.070	1.080	1.090	1.100	1.120	1.140	1.150
2	1.020	1.040	1.061	1.082	1.103	1.124	1.145	1.166	1.188	1.210	1.254	1.300	1.323
3	1.030	1.061	1.093	1.125	1.158	1.191	1 225	1.260	1.295	1.331	1.405	1.482	1.521
4	1.041	1.082	1.126	1.170	1.216	1.262	1 311	1.360	1.412	1.464	1.574	1.689	1.749
5	1.051	1.104	1.159	1.217	1.276	1.338	1 403	1.469	1.539	1.611	1.762	1.925	2.011
6	1.062	1.126	1.194	1.265	1.340	1.419	1.501	1.587	1.677	1.772	1.974	2.195	2.313
7	1.072	1.149	1.230	1.316	1.407	1.504	1.606	1.714	1.828	1.949	2.211	2.502	2.660
8	1.083	1.172	1.267	1.369	1.477	1.594	1.718	1.851	1.993	2.144	2.476	2.853	3.059
9	1.094	1.195	1.305	1.423	1.551	1.689	1.838	1.999	2.172	2.358	2.773	3.252	3.518
10	1.105	1.219	1.344	1.480	1.629	1.791	1.967	2.159	2.367	2.594	3.106	3.707	4.046
11	1.116	1.243	1.384	1.539	1.710	1.898	2.105	2.332	2.580	2.853	3.479	4.226	4.652
12	1.127	1.268	1.426	1.601	1.796	2.012	2.252	2.518	2.813	3.138	3.896	4.818	5.350
13	1.138	1.294	1.469	1.665	1.886	2.133	2.410	2.720	3.066	3.452	4.363	5.492	6.153
14	1.149	1.319	1.513	1.732	1.980	2.261	2.579	2.937	3.342	3.798	4.887	6.261	7.076
15	1.161	1.346	1.558	1.801	2.079	2.397	2.759	3.172	3.642	4.177	5.474	7.138	8.137
16	1.173	1.373	1.605	1.873	2.183	2.540	2.952	3.426	3.970	4.595	6.130	8.137	9.358
17	1.184	1.400	1.653	1.948	2.292	2.693	3.159	3.700	4.328	5.054	6.866	9.276	10.76
18	1.196	1.428	1.702	2.026	2.407	2.854	3.380	3.996	4.717	5.560	7.690	10.58	12.38
19	1.208	1.457	1.754	2.107	2.527	3.026	3.517	4.316	5.142	6.116	8.613	12.06	14.23
20	1.220	1.486	1.806	2.191	2.653	3.207	3.370	4.661	5.604	6.728	9.646	13.74	16.37
21	1.232	1.516	1.860	2.279	2.786	3.400	4.141	5.034	6.109	7.400	10.80	15.67	18.82
22	1.245	1.546	1.916	2.370	2.925	3.604	4.430	5.437	6.659	8.140	12.10	17.86	21.64
23	1.257	1.577	1.974	2.465	3.072	3.820	4.741	5.871	7.258	8.954	13.55	20.36	24.89
24	1.270	1.608	2.033	2.563	3.225	4.049	5.072	6.341	7.911	9.850	15.18	23.21	28.63
25	1.282	1.641	2.094	2.666	3.386	4.292	5.427	6.848	8.623	10.83	17.00	26.46	32.92
26	1.295	1.673	2.157	2.772	3.556	4.549	5.807	7.396	9.399	11.92	19.04	30.17	37.86
27	1.308	1.707	2.221	2.883	3.733	4.822	6.214	7.988	10.25	13.11	21.32	34.39	43.54
28	1.321	1.741	2.288	2.999	3.920	5.112	6.649	8.627	11.17	14.42	23.88	39.20	50.07
29	1.335	1.776	2.357	3.119	4.116	5.418	7.114	9.317	12.17	15.86	26.75	44.69	57.58
30	1.348	1.811	2.427	3.243	4.322	5.743	7.612	10.06	13.27	17.45	29.96	50.95	66.21
40	1.489	2.208	3.262	4.801	7.040	10.29	14.97	21.72	31.41	45.26	93.05	188.9	267.9
50	1.645	2.692	4.384	7.107	11.47	18.42	29.46	46.90	74.36	117.4	289.0	700.2	1,084

Table B-2. Future Value of $1 Paid in Each Period for a Given Number of Time Periods

Periods	1%	2%	3%	4%	5%	6%	7%	8%	9%	10%	12%	14%	15%
1	1.000	1.000	1.000	1.000	1.000	1.000	1.000	1.000	1.000	1.000	1.000	1.000	1.000
2	2.010	2.020	2.030	2.040	2.050	2.060	2.070	2.080	2.090	2.100	2.120	2.140	2.150
3	3.030	3.060	3.091	3.122	3.153	3.184	3.215	3.246	3.278	3.310	3.374	3.440	3.473
4	4.060	4.122	4.184	4.246	4.310	4.375	4.440	4.506	4.573	4.641	4.779	4.921	4.993
5	5.101	5.204	5.309	5.416	5.526	5.637	5.751	5.867	5.985	6.105	6.353	6.610	6.742
6	6.152	6.308	6.468	6.633	6.802	6.975	7.153	7.336	7.523	7.716	8.115	8.536	8.754
7	7.214	7.434	7.662	7.898	8.142	8.394	8.654	8.923	9.200	9.487	10.09	10.73	11.07
8	8.286	8.583	8.892	9.214	9.549	9.897	10.26	10.64	11.03	11.44	12.30	13.23	13.73
9	9.369	9.755	10.16	10.58	11.03	11.49	11.98	12.49	13.02	13.58	14.78	16.09	16.79
10	10.46	10.95	11.46	12.01	12.58	13.18	13.82	14.49	15.19	15.94	17.55	19.34	20.30
11	11.57	12.17	12.81	13.49	14.21	14.97	15.78	16.65	17.56	18.53	20.65	23.04	24.35
12	12.68	13.41	14.19	15.03	15.92	16.87	17.89	18.98	20.14	21.38	24.13	27.27	29.00
13	13.81	14.68	15.62	16.63	17.71	18.88	20.14	21.50	22.95	24.52	28.03	32.09	34.35
14	14.95	15.97	17.09	18.29	19.60	21.02	22.55	24.21	26.02	27.98	32.39	37.58	40.50
15	16.10	17.29	18.60	20.02	21.58	23.28	25.13	27.15	29.36	31.77	37.28	43.84	47.58
16	17.26	18.64	20.16	21.82	23.66	25.67	27.89	30.32	33.00	35.95	42.75	50.98	55.72
17	18.43	20.01	21.76	23.70	25.84	28.21	30.84	33.75	36.97	40.54	48.88	59.12	65.08
18	19.61	21.41	23.41	25.65	28.13	30.91	34.00	37.45	41.30	45.60	55.75	68.39	75.84
19	20.81	22.84	25.12	27.67	30.54	33.76	37.38	41.45	46.02	51.16	63.44	78.97	88.21
20	22.02	24.30	26.87	29.78	33.07	36.79	41.00	45.76	51.16	57.28	72.05	91.02	102.4
21	23.24	25.78	28.68	31.97	35.72	39.99	44.87	50.42	56.76	64.00	81.70	104.8	118.8
22	24.47	27.30	30.54	34.25	38.51	43.39	49.01	55.46	62.87	71.40	92.50	120.4	137.6
23	25.72	28.85	32.45	36.62	41.43	47.00	53.44	60.89	69.53	79.54	104.6	138.3	159.3
24	26.97	30.42	34.43	39.08	44.50	50.82	58.18	66.76	76.79	88.50	118.2	158.7	184.2
25	28.24	32.03	36.46	41.65	47.73	54.86	63.25	73.11	84.70	98.35	133.3	181.9	212.8
26	29.53	33.67	38.55	44.31	51.11	59.15	68.68	79.95	93.32	109.2	150.3	208.3	245.7
27	30.82	35.34	40.71	47.08	54.67	63.71	74.48	87.35	102.7	121.1	169.4	238.5	283.6
28	32.13	37.05	42.93	49.97	58.40	68.53	80.70	95.34	113.0	134.2	190.7	272.9	327.1
29	33.45	38.79	45.22	52.97	62.32	73.64	87.35	104.0	124.1	148.6	214.6	312.1	377.2
30	34.78	40.57	47.58	56.08	66.44	79.06	94.46	113.3	136.3	164.5	241.3	356.8	434.7
40	48.89	60.40	75.40	95.03	120.8	154.8	199.6	259.1	337.9	442.6	767.1	1,342	1,779
50	64.46	84.58	112.8	152.7	209.3	290.3	406.5	573.8	815.1	1,164	2,400	4,995	7,218

Table B-3. Present Value of $1 to Be Received at the End of a Given Number of Time Periods

Periods	1%	2%	3%	4%	5%	6%	7%	8%	9%	10%	12%
1	0.990	0.980	0.971	0.962	0.952	0.943	0.935	0.926	0.917	0.909	0.893
2	0.980	0.961	0.943	0.925	0.907	0.890	0.873	0.857	0.842	0.826	0.797
3	0.971	0.942	0.915	0.889	0.864	0.840	0.816	0.794	0.772	0.751	0.712
4	0.961	0.924	0.888	0.855	0.823	0.792	0.763	0.735	0.708	0.683	0.636
5	0.951	0.906	0.883	0.822	0.784	0.747	0.713	0.681	0.650	0.621	0.567
6	0.942	0.888	0.837	0.790	0.746	0.705	0.666	0.630	0.596	0.564	0.507
7	0.933	0.871	0.813	0.760	0.711	0.665	0.623	0.583	0.547	0.513	0.452
8	0.923	0.853	0.789	0.731	0.677	0.627	0.582	0.540	0.502	0.467	0.404
9	0.914	0.837	0.766	0.703	0.645	0.592	0.544	0.500	0.460	0.424	0.361
10	0.905	0.820	0.744	0.676	0.614	0.558	0.508	0.463	0.422	0.386	0.322
11	0.896	0.804	0.722	0.650	0.585	0.527	0.475	0.429	0.388	0.350	0.287
12	0.887	0.788	0.701	0.625	0.557	0.497	0.444	0.397	0.356	0.319	0.257
13	0.879	0.773	0.681	0.601	0.530	0.469	0.415	0.368	0.326	0.290	0.229
14	0.870	0.758	0.661	0.577	0.505	0.442	0.388	0.340	0.299	0.263	0.205
15	0.861	0.743	0.642	0.555	0.481	0.417	0.362	0.315	0.275	0.239	0.183
16	0.853	0.728	0.623	0.534	0.458	0.394	0.339	0.292	0.252	0.218	0.163
17	0.844	0.714	0.605	0.513	0.436	0.371	0.317	0.270	0.231	0.198	0.146
18	0.836	0.700	0.587	0.494	0.416	0.350	0.296	0.250	0.212	0.180	0.130
19	0.828	0.686	0.570	0.475	0.396	0.331	0.277	0.232	0.194	0.164	0.116
20	0.820	0.673	0.554	0.456	0.377	0.312	0.258	0.215	0.178	0.149	0.104
21	0.811	0.660	0.538	0.439	0.359	0.294	0.242	0.199	0.164	0.135	0.093
22	0.803	0.647	0.522	0.422	0.342	0.278	0.226	0.184	0.150	0.123	0.083
23	0.795	0.634	0.507	0.406	0.326	0.262	0.211	0.170	0.138	0.112	0.074
24	0.788	0.622	0.492	0.390	0.310	0.247	0.197	0.158	0.126	0.102	0.066
25	0.780	0.610	0.478	0.375	0.295	0.233	0.184	0.146	0.116	0.092	0.059
26	0.772	0.598	0.464	0.361	0.281	0.220	0.172	0.135	0.106	0.084	0.053
27	0.764	0.586	0.450	0.347	0.268	0.207	0.161	0.125	0.098	0.076	0.047
28	0.757	0.574	0.437	0.333	0.255	0.196	0.150	0.116	0.090	0.069	0.042
29	0.749	0.563	0.424	0.321	0.243	0.185	0.141	0.107	0.082	0.063	0.037
30	0.742	0.552	0.412	0.308	0.231	0.174	0.131	0.099	0.075	0.057	0.033
40	0.672	0.453	0.307	0.208	0.142	0.097	0.067	0.046	0.032	0.022	0.011
50	0.608	0.372	0.228	0.141	0.087	0.054	0.034	0.021	0.013	0.009	0.003

Table B-3. (continued)

14%	15%	16%	18%	20%	25%	30%	35%	40%	45%	50%	Periods
0.877	0.870	0.862	0.847	0.833	0.800	0.769	0.741	0.714	0.690	0.667	1
0.769	0.756	0.743	0.718	0.694	0.640	0.592	0.549	0.510	0.476	0.444	2
0.675	0.658	0.641	0.609	0.579	0.512	0.455	0.406	0.364	0.328	0.296	3
0.592	0.572	0.552	0.516	0.482	0.410	0.350	0.301	0.260	0.226	0.198	4
0.519	0.497	0.476	0.437	0.402	0.328	0.269	0.223	0.186	0.156	0.132	5
0.456	0.432	0.410	0.370	0.335	0.262	0.207	0.165	0.133	0.108	0.088	6
0.400	0.376	0.354	0.314	0.279	0.210	0.159	0.122	0.095	0.074	0.059	7
0.351	0.327	0.305	0.266	0.233	0.168	0.123	0.091	0.068	0.051	0.039	8
0.308	0.284	0.263	0.225	0.194	0.134	0.094	0.067	0.048	0.035	0.026	9
0.270	0.247	0.227	0.191	0.162	0.107	0.073	0.050	0.035	0.024	0.017	10
0.237	0.215	0.195	0.162	0.135	0.086	0.056	0.037	0.025	0.017	0.012	11
0.208	0.187	0.168	0.137	0.112	0.069	0.043	0.027	0.018	0.012	0.008	12
0.182	0.163	0.145	0.116	0.093	0.055	0.033	0.020	0.013	0.008	0.005	13
0.160	0.141	0.125	0.099	0.078	0.044	0.025	0.015	0.009	0.006	0.003	14
0.140	0.123	0.108	0.084	0.065	0.035	0.020	0.011	0.006	0.004	0.002	15
0.123	0.107	0.093	0.071	0.054	0.028	0.015	0.008	0.005	0.003	0.002	16
0.108	0.093	0.080	0.060	0.045	0.023	0.012	0.006	0.003	0.002	0.001	17
0.095	0.081	0.069	0.051	0.038	0.018	0.009	0.005	0.002	0.001	0.001	18
0.083	0.070	0.060	0.043	0.031	0.014	0.007	0.003	0.002	0.001		19
0.073	0.061	0.051	0.037	0.026	0.012	0.005	0.002	0.001	0.001		20
0.064	0.053	0.044	0.031	0.022	0.009	0.004	0.002	0.001			21
0.056	0.046	0.038	0.026	0.018	0.007	0.003	0.001	0.001			22
0.049	0.040	0.033	0.022	0.015	0.006	0.002	0.001				23
0.043	0.035	0.028	0.019	0.013	0.005	0.002	0.001				24
0.038	0.030	0.024	0.016	0.010	0.004	0.001	0.001				25
0.033	0.026	0.021	0.014	0.009	0.003	0.001					26
0.029	0.023	0.018	0.011	0.007	0.002	0.001					27
0.026	0.020	0.016	0.010	0.006	0.002	0.001					28
0.022	0.017	0.014	0.008	0.005	0.002						29
0.020	0.015	0.012	0.007	0.004	0.001						30
0.005	0.004	0.003	0.001	0.001							40
0.001	0.001	0.001									50

Table B-4. Present Value of $1 Received Each Period for a Given Number of Time Periods

Periods	1%	2%	3%	4%	5%	6%	7%	8%	9%	10%	12%
1	0.990	0.980	0.971	0.962	0.952	0.943	0.935	0.926	0.917	0.909	0.893
2	1.970	1.942	1.913	1.886	1.859	1.833	1.808	1.783	1.759	1.736	1.690
3	2.941	2.884	2.829	2.775	2.723	2.673	2.624	2.577	2.531	2.487	2.402
4	3.902	3.808	3.717	3.630	3.546	3.465	3.387	3.312	3.240	3.170	3.037
5	4.853	4.713	4.580	4.452	4.329	4.212	4.100	3.993	3.890	3.791	3.605
6	5.795	5.601	5.417	5.242	5.076	4.917	4.767	4.623	4.486	4.355	4.111
7	6.728	6.472	6.230	6.002	5.786	5.582	5.389	5.206	5.033	4.868	4.564
8	7.652	7.325	7.020	6.733	6.463	6.210	5.971	5.747	5.535	5.335	4.968
9	8.566	8.162	7.786	7.435	7.108	6.802	6.515	6.247	5.995	5.759	5.328
10	9.471	8.983	8.530	8.111	7.722	7.360	7.024	6.710	6.418	6.145	5.650
11	10.368	9.787	9.253	8.760	8.306	7.887	7.499	7.139	6.805	6.495	5.938
12	11.255	10.575	9.954	9.385	8.863	8.384	7.943	7.536	7.161	6.814	6.194
13	12.134	11.348	10.635	9.986	9.394	8.853	8.358	7.904	7.487	7.103	6.424
14	13.004	12.106	11.296	10.563	9.899	9.295	8.745	8.244	7.786	7.367	6.628
15	13.865	12.849	11.938	11.118	10.380	9.712	9.108	8.559	8.061	7.606	6.811
16	14.718	13.578	12.561	11.652	10.838	10.106	9.447	8.851	8.313	7.824	6.974
17	15.562	14.292	13.166	12.166	11.274	10.477	9.763	9.122	8.544	8.022	7.120
18	16.398	14.992	13.754	12.659	11.690	10.828	10.059	9.372	8.756	8.201	7.250
19	17.226	15.678	14.324	13.134	12.085	11.158	10.336	9.604	8.950	8.365	7.366
20	18.046	16.351	14.878	13.590	12.462	11.470	10.594	9.818	9.129	8.514	7.469
21	18.857	17.011	15.415	14.029	12.821	11.764	10.836	10.017	9.292	8.649	7.562
22	19.660	17.658	15.937	14.451	13.163	12.042	11.061	10.201	9.442	8.772	7.645
23	20.456	18.292	16.444	14.857	13.489	12.303	11.272	10.371	9.580	8.883	7.718
24	21.243	18.914	16.936	15.247	13.799	12.550	11.469	10.529	9.707	8.985	7.784
25	22.023	19.523	17.413	15.622	14.094	12.783	11.654	10.675	9.823	9.077	7.843
26	22.795	20.121	17.877	15.983	14.375	13.003	11.826	10.810	9.929	9.161	7.896
27	23.560	20.707	18.327	16.330	14.643	13.211	11.987	10.935	10.027	9.237	7.943
28	24.316	21.281	18.764	16.663	14.898	13.406	12.137	11.051	10.116	9.307	7.984
29	25.066	21.844	19.189	16.984	15.141	13.591	12.278	11.158	10.198	9.370	8.022
30	25.808	22.396	19.600	17.292	15.373	13.765	12.409	11.258	10.274	9.427	8.055
40	32.835	27.355	23.115	19.793	17.159	15.046	13.332	11.925	10.757	9.779	8.244
50	39.196	31.424	25.730	21.482	18.256	15.762	13.801	12.234	10.962	9.915	8.305

Table B-4 is used to compute the present value of a *series* of *equal* annual cash flows:

Example. Arthur Howard won a contest on January 1, 1989, in which the prize was $30,000, payable in fifteen annual installments of $2,000 every December 31, beginning in 1989. Assuming a 9 percent interest rate, what is the present value of Mr. Howard's prize on January 1, 1989? From Table B-4, the required multiplier is 8.061, and the answer is:

$$\$2,000(8.061) = \$16,122$$

Table B-4 (continued)

14%	15%	16%	18%	20%	25%	30%	35%	40%	45%	50%	Periods
0.877	0.870	0.862	0.847	0.833	0.800	0.769	0.741	0.714	0.690	0.667	1
1.647	1.626	1.605	1.566	1.528	1.440	1.361	1.289	1.224	1.165	1.111	2
2.322	2.283	2.246	2.174	2.106	1.952	1.816	1.696	1.589	1.493	1.407	3
2.914	2.855	2.798	2.690	2.589	2.362	2.166	1.997	1.849	1.720	1.605	4
3.433	3.352	3.274	3.127	2.991	2.689	2.436	2.220	2.035	1.876	1.737	5
3.889	3.784	3.685	3.498	3.326	2.951	2.643	2.385	2.168	1.983	1.824	6
4.288	4.160	4.039	3.812	3.605	3.161	2.802	2.508	2.263	2.057	1.883	7
4.639	4.487	4.344	4.078	3.837	3.329	2.925	2.598	2.331	2.109	1.922	8
4.946	4.772	4.607	4.303	4.031	3.463	3.019	2.665	2.379	2.144	1.948	9
5.216	5.019	4.833	4.494	4.192	3.571	3.092	2.715	2.414	2.168	1.965	10
5.453	5.234	5.029	4.656	4.327	3.656	3.147	2.752	2.438	2.185	1.977	11
5.660	5.421	5.197	4.793	4.439	3.725	3.190	2.779	2.456	2.197	1.985	12
5.842	5.583	5.342	4.910	4.533	3.780	3.223	2.799	2.469	2.204	1.990	13
6.002	5.724	5.468	5.008	4.611	3.824	3.249	2.814	2.478	2.210	1.993	14
6.142	5.847	5.575	5.092	4.675	3.859	3.268	2.825	2.484	2.214	1.995	15
6.265	5.954	5.669	5.162	4.730	3.887	3.283	2.834	2.489	2.216	1.997	16
6.373	6.047	5.749	5.222	4.775	3.910	3.295	2.840	2.492	2.218	1.998	17
6.467	6.128	5.818	5.273	4.812	3.928	3.304	2.844	2.494	2.219	1.999	18
6.550	6.198	5.877	5.316	4.844	3.942	3.311	2.848	2.496	2.220	1.999	19
6.623	6.259	5.929	5.353	4.870	3.954	3.316	2.850	2.497	2.221	1.999	20
6.687	6.312	5.973	5.384	4.891	3.963	3.320	2.852	2.498	2.221	2.000	21
6.743	6.359	6.011	5.410	4.909	3.970	3.323	2.853	2.498	2.222	2.000	22
6.792	6.399	6.044	5.432	4.925	3.976	3.325	2.854	2.499	2.222	2.000	23
6.835	6.434	6.073	5.451	4.937	3.981	3.327	2.855	2.499	2.222	2.000	24
6.873	6.464	6.097	5.467	4.948	3.985	3.329	2.856	2.499	2.222	2.000	25
6.906	6.491	6.118	5.480	4.956	3.988	3.330	2.856	2.500	2.222	2.000	26
6.935	6.514	6.136	5.492	4.964	3.990	3.331	2.856	2.500	2.222	2.000	27
6.961	6.534	6.152	5.502	4.970	3.992	3.331	2.857	2.500	2.222	2.000	28
6.983	6.551	6.166	5.510	4.975	3.994	3.332	2.857	2.500	2.222	2.000	29
7.003	6.566	6.177	5.517	4.979	3.995	3.332	2.857	2.500	2.222	2.000	30
7.105	6.642	6.234	5.548	4.997	3.999	3.333	2.857	2.500	2.222	2.000	40
7.133	6.661	6.246	5.554	4.999	4.000	3.333	2.857	2.500	2.222	2.000	50

Table B-4 applies to *ordinary annuities*, in which the first cash flow occurs one time period beyond the date for which present value is to be computed. An *annuity due* is a series of equal cash flows for N time periods, but the first payment occurs immediately. The present value of the first payment equals the face value of the cash flow; Table B-4 then is used to measure the present value of N − 1 remaining cash flows.

Example. Determine the present value on January 1, 1989, of twenty lease payments; each payment of $10,000 is due on January 1, beginning in 1989. Assume an interest rate of 8 percent:

$$\text{Present value} = \text{immediate payment} + \begin{cases} \text{present value of 19} \\ \text{subsequent payments at 8\%} \end{cases}$$

$$= \$10,000 + [10,000(9.604)]$$
$$= \$106,040$$

LEARNING
OBJECTIVES

1. *Explain and differentiate some basic concepts related to income taxes and accounting.*
2. *Identify the major components used in determining the income tax liability of individuals.*

APPENDIX C

Overview of Income Taxes for Individuals

The United States Congress first passed a permanent income tax law in 1913, after the Sixteenth Amendment to the Constitution gave legality to such a tax. Its original goal was to provide revenue for the U.S. government, and today the income tax is still a major source of revenue. Of course, most states and many cities also have an income tax. Because these tax laws are in many cases much like those in the federal tax system, the discussion in this appendix is limited to the federal income tax. After studying this appendix, you should be able to meet the learning objectives listed on the left.

Although it is still an important purpose of the federal income tax laws to produce revenue, Congress has also used its taxing power as an instrument of economic policy. Among the economic goals proposed by Congress are a fairer distribution of income, stimulation of economic growth, full employment, encouragement of exploration for oil and minerals, control of inflation, and a variety of social changes.

All three branches of the federal government have a part in the federal income tax system. The Internal Revenue Service (IRS), which is an agency of the Treasury Department, administers the system. The income tax law is based on over fifty revenue acts and other related laws that have been passed by Congress since 1913. Also, the IRS issues regulations that interpret the law. It is the federal court system, however, that must uphold these important regulations and that has final authority for interpreting the law.

The income tax has had important effects on both individuals and businesses. In 1913, an individual who earned $30,000 paid only $300 or $400 in income taxes. Under the Tax Reform Act of 1986, an individual who earns the same amount may pay as much as $5,000 or more, and corporations may pay as much as one-third of their income in taxes. Clearly, the income tax is an important cost of doing business today.

Some Basic Concepts Related to Federal Income Taxes

To understand the nature of federal income taxes, it is important to distinguish between taxable income and accounting income, between tax planning and tax evasion, between cash basis and accrual basis, and among classifications of taxpayers.

Taxable Income and Accounting Income

OBJECTIVE 1
Explain and
differentiate some
basic concepts
related to income
taxes and
accounting

The government assesses income taxes on **taxable income,** which usually is gross income less various exemptions and deductions specified by the law and the IRS regulations. Taxable income is generally found by referring to information in the accounting records. However, it is very unlikely that taxable income and accounting income for an entity will be the same, because they have different purposes. The government levies income taxes to obtain revenue from taxpayers and to carry out economic policies totally unrelated to the measurement of economic income, which is the purpose of accounting.

Tax Planning and Tax Evasion

The arrangement of a taxpayer's affairs in such a way as to incur the smallest legal tax is called **tax planning.** For almost every business decision, alternative courses of action are available that will affect taxable income in different ways. For example, the taxpayer may lease or buy a truck, may use LIFO, FIFO, or average cost to account for inventories, or may time an expenditure to be accounted for in one accounting period or another. Once the taxpayer chooses and acts upon an alternative, however, the IRS will usually treat this alternative as the final one for income tax determination. Therefore, in tax planning it is important to consider tax-saving alternatives before putting decisions into effect.

It is the natural goal of any taxable entity to pay as small a tax as possible; both the tax law and the IRS hold that no entity should pay more than is legally required. The best way to accomplish this goal is by careful tax planning. It is, however, illegal to evade paying taxes by concealing actual tax liabilities. This is called **tax evasion.**

Cash Basis and Accrual Basis

In general, taxpayers may use either the cash basis or the accrual basis to arrive at their taxable income. Most individuals use the **cash basis**—the reporting of items of revenue and expense when they are received or paid—because it is the simplest method. Employers usually report their employees' income on a cash basis, and companies that pay dividends and interest on a cash basis must also report them in this way.

Professional and other service enterprises such as those of accountants, attorneys, physicians, travel agents, and insurance agents also typically use the cash basis in determining taxable income. One advantage of this method is that fees charged to clients or customers are not considered to be earned until payment is received. Thus it is possible to defer the taxes on these revenues until the tax year in which they are received. Similarly, expenses such as rent, utilities, and salaries are recorded when they are paid. Thus a business can work at tax planning by carefully timing its expenditures. Still, this method does not apply to expenditures for buildings and equipment used for business purposes. Such items are treated in accordance with the accelerated cost recovery system discussed in Chapter 12.

Businesses that engage in production or trading of inventories must use the **accrual basis** of accounting rather than the cash basis. In other words, they must report revenues from sales in the period in which they sold the goods, regardless of when they received the cash. And they must record purchases in the year of purchase rather than in the year of payment. They must follow the usual accounting for beginning and ending inventories in determining cost of goods sold. However, the tax laws do not require a strict accrual method in the accounting sense for manufacturing and merchandising concerns. Various modified cash and accrual bases are possible as long as they yield reasonable and consistent results from year to year.

Classifications of Taxpayers

The federal tax law recognizes four classes of taxpayers: individuals, corporations, estates, and trusts. Members of each class must file tax returns and pay taxes on taxable income. This appendix discusses only individuals. Taxation of corporations is covered in Chapter 17. Taxation of estates and trusts is left for a more advanced course.

Although they are business entities for accounting purposes, sole proprietorships and partnerships are not taxable entities. Instead, a proprietor must include the business income on an individual income tax return. Similarly, each partner in a business must include his or her share of the partnership income on an individual return. Each partnership, however, must file an information return showing the results of the partnership's operations and how each partner's share of the income was determined.

In contrast, corporations are taxable entities that must file tax returns and are taxed directly on their earnings. If, after paying its income tax, the corporation distributes some of its earnings to its stockholders, the stockholders must report the dividend income as part of their gross income. This rule has led to the claim that corporate income is subject to **double taxation**—once when it is earned by the company and once when it is paid to the owners of the company's stock.

Income Tax for Individuals

OBJECTIVE 2
Identify the major components used in determining the income tax liability of individuals

It is important to study income tax for individuals for several reasons. First, most persons who earn taxable income must file a tax return. Second, all persons who operate proprietorships or partnerships must report the income from their businesses on their individual tax returns. Third, many of the same tax terms are used for both individuals and corporations.

The Internal Revenue Code establishes the method of calculating taxable income for individuals. The starting place for figuring taxable income is finding gross income. The next step is to find the amount of adjusted gross income by subtracting deductions from gross income. Under this heading are the expenses of running a business or profession and certain other specified expenses. Then, from adjusted gross income one subtracts a second kind of deduction, called deductions from adjusted gross income, to arrive at taxable income. Under this second heading come (1) certain business and personal expenses and (2) allowances known as exemptions. These procedures can be outlined as follows:

Gross income	$xxx	
Less deductions from gross income	xxx	
Adjusted gross income		$xxx
Less deductions from adjusted gross income:		
a. Itemized or standard deductions	$xxx	
b. Exemptions	xxx	xxx
Taxable income		$xxx

Gross Income

The Internal Revenue Code defines **gross income** as income from all sources, less allowable exclusions. Under this heading are wages, salaries, bonuses, fees, tips, interest, dividends, pensions, and annuities. Rents, royalties, alimony, prizes, profits or shares of profits from business, and gains on sale of property or stocks are also included. Income from illegal sources also must be reported as gross income.

Deductions from Gross Income

The calculation of **adjusted gross income** is important to the individual because it serves as the basis for certain personal deductions in figuring taxable income. These **deductions from gross income** are meant to give people a fairer base than gross income. For example, some people may have a high gross income but may have had many business expenditures to gain that gross income. It is fair to let them deduct the amount spent in earning the gross income.

Deductions from Adjusted Gross Income

Deductions from adjusted gross income fall under two headings: (1) the standard deduction or itemized deductions, and (2) exemptions. The **standard deduction** is an amount allowed every taxpayer for personal and business expenses. The amounts allowable to taxpayers according to their filing statuses is shown in Table C-1. If the taxpayer's actual itemized allowable deductions exceed the standard deduction, the taxpayer may deduct the expenses as itemized deductions. Allowable itemized deductions for this purpose include medical and dental expenses, taxes, casualty losses, employee business expenses not reimbursed by employers, and other miscellaneous expenses such as union and professional dues, all subject to certain limitations.

Besides the standard deduction and itemized deductions, the taxpayer is allowed another kind of deduction, called an **exemption**. For each exemption, the taxpayer may deduct $1,900 ($1,950 in 1988, $2,000 in 1989) from adjusted gross income. A taxpayer is allowed one exemption for himself or herself, and one for each dependent. To qualify as a dependent, a person must be (1) closely related to the taxpayer or have lived in the taxpayer's house for the whole year, (2) must have received over half of his or her support during the year from the taxpayer, (3) must not file a joint return with his or her

Table C-1. Amounts Allowed as Standard Deductions

Filing Status	1987	1988	1989
Married filing jointly, and surviving spouses	$3,760	$5,000	$5,200*
Heads of households	2,540	4,400	4,550*
Single individuals	2,540	3,000	3,100*
Married individuals filing separately	1,880	2,500	2,600*

*These amounts will be adjusted by a cost of living adjustment for 1990 and years thereafter.

spouse, if married, (4) must have a limited amount of gross income, and (5) must be a U.S. citizen or a resident of the United States, Canada, or Mexico. If a husband and wife file a joint return, they may combine their exemptions. Elderly and blind taxpayers are no longer allowed additional exemptions for age or blindness, as they were before 1987, but they are allowed increased standard deductions.

Computing Tax Liability

In general, the income tax is a **progressive tax,** which means that the rate becomes larger as the amount of taxable income becomes larger. In other words, the higher a person's taxable income, the larger the proportion of it that goes to pay taxes.[1] Different rate schedules apply to single taxpayers, married taxpayers who file joint returns, married taxpayers who file separate returns, and single taxpayers who qualify as heads of households. Taxpayers can calculate their **tax liability** by referring to the tax rate schedules in Exhibit C-1.[2] By looking at these schedules, one can easily see the progressive nature of the tax. It is clear from Exhibit C-1 that the marginal tax rate (that is, the rate of taxation on each *additional* dollar of taxable income) used to go as high as 38.5 percent. Subject to further amendments of the Internal Revenue Code, the highest marginal rate in 1988 and following years will be 28 percent (33 percent, including surtax, for certain individuals).

Capital Gains and Losses

The income tax law accorded capital gains special treatment from 1922 through 1987. Beginning in 1988, the special treatment for net capital gains was eliminated. Nevertheless, certain limitations have been retained for taxpayers who suffer capital losses. Assets subject to these rules, called **capital assets,** usually include stocks, bonds, and other investment property. Under certain circumstances, business buildings, equipment, and land are included. Capital assets usually do not include trade receivables, inventories, and other properties created by the taxpayer, such as literary or artistic works.

One effective means of tax planning is to arrange transactions involving capital assets to reduce or defer taxes. If a taxpayer sells stock at a gain near the end of the year, the gain is taxable during that year. By waiting until just after the first day of the next year, a taxpayer can defer the tax on the gain for an entire year.

Net Capital Gain. Net capital gains were taxed at an optional, preferential rate of 28 percent in 1987. After 1987, net capital gains have been taxed at the same rate as other income of the taxpayer.

Net Capital Loss. Can a taxpayer reduce taxes by selling stock or other investments that have declined in value at a loss? In other words, can a

---

1. In contrast to a progressive tax rate, a **regressive tax** rate becomes less as one's income rises. An example of a regressive tax is the social security (FICA) tax, which is levied on incomes only up to a certain amount. A **proportional tax** is one in which the rate is the same percentage regardless of income. Examples are most sales taxes and the income taxes of some states, such as Illinois.
2. The Internal Revenue Service provides tax tables in which the tax liabilities for specific taxable incomes for taxpayers in each filing status are calculated for taxpayers' convenience.

Exhibit C-1. Tax Rates in 1987 and Following Years

Tax Rate Structure for 1987

For taxable years beginning in 1987, five-bracket rate schedules are provided, as shown in the table below.

	Taxable Income Brackets		
Tax Rate	Married, Filing Joint Returns	Heads of Household	Single Individuals
11 percent	0–$3,000	0–$2,500	0–$1,800
15 percent	$ 3,001–28,000	$ 2,501–23,000	$ 1,801–16,800
28 percent	28,001–45,000	23,001–38,000	16,801–27,000
35 percent	45,001–90,000	38,001–80,000	27,001–54,000
38.5 percent	Over $90,000	Over $80,000	Over $54,000

For married individuals filing separate returns, the taxable income bracket amounts for 1987 begin at one-half the amounts for joint returns. The bracket amounts for surviving spouses are the same as those for married individuals filing joint returns.

Tax Rate Structure in 1988 and Following Years

The tax rate structure for 1988 and following years consists of two brackets and tax rates—15 and 28 percent—beginning at zero taxable income.

Filing Status	Tax Rate	Brackets
Married Individuals Filing Jointly and Surviving Spouses	15%	0–$29,750
	28%	$29,751–$71,900*
Heads of Household	15%	0–$23,900
	28%	$23,901–$61,650*
Single Individuals	15%	0–$17,850
	28%	$17,851–$43,150*

For married individuals filing separate returns, the 28 percent bracket begins at $14,875, i.e., one-half the taxable income amount for joint returns. Note: For certain taxpayers, a 5 percent surcharge is applicable for dollar amounts above the 28% tax bracket, which would bring the maximum tax rate to 33 percent.

* Beginning in 1989, the taxable income amounts at which the 28 percent rate starts will be adjusted for inflation.

taxpayer deduct such losses from other income, such as salary income, and thereby reduce the tax on the other income? When a taxpayer's transactions involving capital assets for a year result in a *net* capital loss, the amount of the loss that may be deducted from other income is limited. Capital losses can be offset against capital gains. Other income, however, can only be reduced by a maximum of $3,000 in any one year. Any excess *net* capital loss over the $3,000 must be carried forward to be deducted in future years.

Credit Against the Tax Liability

Tax credits are subtractions from the computed tax liability and should not be confused with deductions that are subtracted from income to determine taxable income. Since tax credits reduce tax liability dollar for dollar, they are more beneficial to taxpayers than equal dollar amounts of deductions from gross income. Tax credits are allowed to the elderly, for dependent care expenses, for income taxes paid in foreign countries, and for jobs provided to members of certain groups.

Withholding and Estimated Tax

For most individuals the tax year ends on December 31, and their return is due three and one-half months later, on April 15. If they are wage earners or salaried employees, their employer is required to withhold an estimated income tax from their pay during the year and remit it to the Internal Revenue Service. The employer reports this withholding to the employee on form W-2 on or before January 31 for the preceding year (see Chapter 12 for a discussion of payroll procedures). Taxpayers who have income beyond a certain amount that is not subject to withholding must report a Declaration of Estimated Tax and pay an **estimated tax,** less any amount expected to be withheld, in four installments during the year. When taxpayers prepare their tax returns, they deduct the amount of estimated tax withheld and the amount paid in installments from the total tax liability to find the amount they must pay when they file the tax return.

Discussion Questions and Writing Assignments

1. What is the difference between tax planning and tax evasion?
2. What are the four classes of taxpayers?
3. J. Vickery's sole proprietorship had a net income of $37,500 during the taxable year During the same year, Vickery withdrew $24,000 from the business. What income must Vickery report on his individual tax return?
4. Which of the two methods of accounting, cash or accrual, is more commonly used by individual taxpayers?
5. Why is it sometimes claimed that corporate income is subject to double taxation?
6. If a friend of yours turned down the opportunity to earn an additional $500 of taxable income because it would put him or her in a higher tax bracket, would you consider this action rational? Why?

Exercise C-1

**Computation of
Tax Liability
(L.O. 2)**

From Exhibit C-1, figure the 1987 and 1988 income tax for each of the
following: (1) single individual with taxable income of $12,500, (2) single
individual with taxable income of $59,000, (3) married couple filing jointly
with taxable income of $11,250, (4) married couple filing jointly with taxable
income of $59,000. Assume that none of these taxpayers has deductions other
than the standard deduction or income tax credits to apply against the
amounts due. Round answers to nearest dollar.

1. Explain and differentiate some basic concepts related to governmental and not-for-profit accounting.
2. Describe the types of funds used in governmental accounting.
3. Explain the modified accrual basis of accounting used by state and local governments.
4. Describe the financial reporting system used in governmental accounting.
5. Provide a brief introduction to other types of not-for-profit accounting.

APPENDIX D

Overview of Governmental and Not-for-Profit Accounting

State and local governments and not-for-profit organizations account for a significant share of all spending in the American economy. Courses in accounting, however, have devoted relatively little time to discussing the accounting and reporting issues unique to these organizations. This appendix provides a brief introduction to accounting for several categories of governmental and not-for-profit groups. They include state and local governments, colleges and universities, hospitals, and voluntary health and welfare organizations. After studying this appendix, you should be able to meet the learning objectives listed on the left.

Governmental, Not-for-Profit, and Business Accounting

Businesses in the United States are organized to produce profits for their owners or shareholders. This fact requires that the accounting system provide shareholders, creditors, and other interested parties with information that will help them evaluate the firm's success in making a profit. The rules and practices of business accounting are referred to as generally accepted accounting principles (GAAP), which are established by the Financial Accounting Standards Board (FASB). Historically, governmental GAAP have been the responsibility of the National Council on Governmental Accounting (NCGA). In 1984 the Financial Accounting Foundation founded the Governmental Accounting Standards Board (GASB). The GASB has the power to establish accounting rules and practices for governmental units. Its responsibilities parallel those of the FASB in that it defines generally accepted accounting principles for governmental units. Standards set by the GASB do not apply to nongovernmental not-for-profit organizations like private universities and hospitals. Accounting practices for these nongovernmental not-for-profit organizations fall under the pronouncements of the FASB.

Financial Reporting Objectives of Governmental Units

State and local governments have different objectives from those of businesses, and thus they have traditionally had different GAAP.

OBJECTIVE 1
Explain and differentiate some basic concepts related to governmental and not-for-profit accounting

Government units chiefly provide services to citizens, with expenditures for these services limited to the amounts legally available. Governmental units need not be profitable in the business sense; however, they do need to limit their spending to the funds made available for specific purposes. For these reasons, the GASB has established the following financial reporting objectives for governmental units:

1. Financial reporting should assist in fulfilling government's duty to be publicly accountable and should enable users to assess that accountability.
2. Financial reporting should assist users in evaluating the operating results of the governmental entity for the year.
3. Financial reporting should assist users in assessing the level of services that can be provided by the entity and its ability to meet its obligations when due.[1]

The primary objective of governmental GAAP is, therefore, not profit measurement, but the assessment and accountability of the funds available for governmental activities. To help satisfy this objective, governmental GAAP have several unique accounting features, the most important of which are the use of funds to account for various activities and the use of modified accrual accounting. A **fund** is defined as a fiscal and accounting entity. **Modified accrual accounting** attempts to provide an accurate measure of increases and decreases in resources available (especially in cash) to fulfill governmental obligations.

The operations of state and local governments are recorded in a variety of funds, each of which is designated for a specific purpose. This means that each fund simultaneously shows (1) the financial position and results of operations during the period and (2) compliance with legal requirements of the state or local government. State and local governments rely on the following types of funds:

OBJECTIVE 2
Describe the types of funds used in governmental accounting

General fund To account for all financial resources not accounted for in any other fund. This fund accounts for most of the current operating activities of the governmental unit (administration, police, fire, health, and sanitation, for example).

Special revenue funds To account for revenues legally restricted to specific purposes.

Capital projects funds To account for the acquisition and construction of major capital projects.

Debt service fund To account for resources accumulated to pay the interest and principal of general obligation long-term debt.

Enterprise funds To account for activities that are financed and operated in a manner similar to private business activities. These funds are most appropriate for activities that charge the public for goods or services, such as municipal golf courses or utilities.

Internal service funds To account for the financing of goods or services provided by one department or agency of a governmental unit to other departments or agencies of governmental units.

---

1. *Concept Statement No. 1,* "Objectives of Financial Reporting" (Stamford, Conn.: Governmental Accounting Standards Board, 1987).

Trust and agency funds To account for assets held by a governmental unit acting as a trustee or agent for individuals, private organizations, or other funds.

The first four funds are called **governmental funds.** The enterprise and internal service funds are **proprietary funds.** Trust and agency funds are **fiduciary funds.** A political unit may properly have only one general fund. There is no limit, however on the number of other funds used. There is also no requirement that a state or local government have all of these funds; individual needs govern the type and number of funds used.

In addition to the above funds, state and local governments use two unique entities called **account groups** to record certain fixed assets and long-term liabilities.

General fixed assets account group To account for all long-term assets of a governmental unit except long-term assets related to specific proprietary or trust funds. This account group does not record depreciation.

General long-term debt group To account for all long-term liabilities of a governmental unit except for long-term liabilities related to specific proprietary or trust funds. This account group records the principal amounts of long-term debt as well as the amounts available in the debt service fund and the amounts to be provided in the future for the retirement of the debt.

Long-term assets and long-term liabilities related to proprietary and trust funds are accounted for in essentially the same manner as in business accounting.

Modified Accrual Accounting

OBJECTIVE 3
Explain the modified accrual basis of accounting used by state and local governments

Governmental funds, as well as certain types of trust funds, use the modified accrual method of accounting. Proprietary funds, as well as certain types of trust funds, use the familiar full accrual accounting common to business organizations. This section will concentrate on the less familiar modified accrual basis of accounting.

Modified accrual accounting has several features that distinguish it from accrual accounting used in business. The measurement and recognition of revenues and expenditures, the incorporation of the budget into the formal accounting system, and the use of encumbrances to account for purchase commitments will each be described briefly.

In governmental accounting, **revenues** are defined as increases in fund resources from sources other than interfund transactions or proceeds of long-term debt. They are recognized in the accounts when "measurable and available." In most cases these conditions are met when cash is received. **Expenditures** are defined as decreases in fund resources caused by transactions other than interfund transfers. These concepts of revenues and expenditures result in some unusual situations, as the following examples illustrate.

1. Assume that a city sells a used police car for $2,500 cash. This transaction would be recorded in the general fund as follows:

Cash	2,500	
Revenues		2,500
Sale of used police car		

2. When a city purchases a new police car for $12,000 cash, the transaction would be recorded in the general fund as follows:

Expenditures	12,000	
Cash		12,000
Purchase of new police car		

The transactions are recorded in this way because they satisfy the definitions of revenues and expenditures.

To further illustrate the contrast between governmental and business-type accrual accounting, we can examine the way in which a business would record the above transactions:

1. Assume that a firm sells a used car for $2,500 cash and that the car has a carrying value of $2,000 (cost of $7,500 less accumulated depreciation of $5,500):

Cash	2,500	
Accumulated Depreciation, Car	5,500	
Car		7,500
Gain on disposal		500
Sale of used car		

Unlike governmental accounting, accrual accounting recognizes revenues only to the extent that cash received exceeds carrying value.

2. If a firm purchases a new car for $12,000 cash, the transaction would be recorded as follows:

Car	12,000	
Cash		12,000
Purchase of new car		

The car would be shown as an asset on the firm's balance sheet. No expense would be recorded until depreciation is recognized in subsequent years. As discussed throughout this book, business accounting focuses on the matching of revenues and expenses to compute net income or loss for the period. Governmental accounting, in contrast, concentrates on inflows and outflows of fund resources.

Another unique feature of governmental accounting is the formal incorporation of the budget into the accounts of the particular fund. This approach is required for the general fund and the special revenue fund and is optional for the other governmental funds. The general fund, for example, would record its budget as follows:

Estimated Revenues	1,000,000	
Appropriations		950,000
Fund Balance		50,000
To record budget for fiscal year		

This example assumes that the governmental unit expects revenues to exceed legally mandated expenditures (or appropriations). The use of budgetary accounts enables the governmental unit to have a continuous check or control on whether actual revenues and expenditures correspond to original estimates. In addition, the various funds' financial statements will show both the budgeted and actual amounts of major revenue and expenditure categories. At the end of the accounting period, the budget entry would be reversed, since its control function is no longer needed. A new budget would then be recorded in the subsequent period to control revenues and expenditures in that period. Businesses also use budgets, but they do not integrate those budgets formally into the regular accounting system.

A third unique feature of governmental accounting is the use of **encumbrance accounting.** Since governments cannot legally spend more than the amounts appropriated for specific purposes, it is necessary to keep track of anticipated, as well as actual, expenditures. Whenever a significant lapse of time is expected between a commitment to spend and the actual expenditure, governmental GAAP require the use of encumbrance accounting.

For example, a city orders $10,000 of supplies on July 1, but does not expect to receive the supplies until September 1. The bill received on September 1 amounts to $10,200. The general fund would record this transaction as follows:

July 1	Encumbrances	10,000	
	Reserve for Encumbrances		10,000
	Order of supplies		
Sept. 1	Reserve for Encumbrances	10,000	
	Encumbrances		10,000
	Reverse encumbrance upon receipt of bill for supplies		
1	Expenditures	10,200	
	Cash (or Vouchers Payable)		10,200
	Payment for supplies		

The purpose of an encumbrance system is to ensure that the governmental unit does not exceed its spending authority. This is accomplished by recording not only actual expenditures but also anticipated expenditures under the current period's appropriations. In addition to normal expenditures, the Reserve for Encumbrances account represents that portion of the fund balance already committed to future expenditures. Regardless of the original estimated encumbrance amounts, on September 1, the encumbrance is eliminated by reversing the original entry of July 1, and expenditures is debited for the actual amount spent.

Financial Reporting System

OBJECTIVE 4
Describe the financial reporting system used in governmental accounting

The accounting system we have described is designed to produce periodic financial statements. The financial statements recommended by the NCGA in their Government Accounting Standard No. 1 include the following:

Combined balance sheet This statement is prepared for all fund types and account groups. Each fund type and account group lists major categories of assets, liabilities, and either fund balances or owners' equity accounts.

Combined statement of revenues, expenditures, and changes in fund balances—all governmental funds This statement is prepared for all governmental fund types. Since only governmental funds are reported in this statement, all revenues and expenditures would be measured according to the principles of modified accrual accounting.

Combined statement of revenues, expenditures, and changes in fund balances—budget and actual—general and special revenue funds This statement presents budget and actual amounts for general and special revenue fund types. The statement includes the budgetary data described earlier and directly compares actual revenues and expenditures to budgeted revenues and expenditures. It indicates, for each type of revenue and expenditure, the amount by which actual amounts differ from budgeted amounts.

Combined statement of revenues, expenses, and changes in retained earnings (or equity) This statement is prepared for all proprietary fund types. It is prepared on the full accrual basis and resembles the financial statements prepared by businesses.

Combined statement of changes in financial position This statement is prepared for all proprietary fund types.

Not-for-Profit Organizations

This section provides a very brief view of accounting for certain types of not-for-profit organizations. Colleges and universities, hospitals, and voluntary health and welfare organizations, among others, share characteristics of both government and business entities. Like governments, they are not intended to make a profit; however, they lack the taxing ability of a government. Because the lack of taxing ability requires that the revenues of not-for-profit organizations at least equal expenses over the long run, these organizations rely on accrual accounting for most of their activities. These organizations also use funds to account for different types of resources and activities. The use of funds is necessary because of the legal restrictions imposed on many of the resources available to these groups.

Colleges and Universities

Colleges and universities, with a few exceptions, use full accrual accounting. One exception is that depreciation need not be recorded on fixed assets, although the FASB has issued Statement No. 93 to eliminate this exception. Due to the controversial nature of the issue, FASB No. 93 is not scheduled to be implemented until 1990. Another is that revenues from restricted sources can be recognized only when expenditures are made for the purposes specified by the revenue source. Several types of funds are employed:

Unrestricted current fund Accounts for general operating activities.

Restricted current fund Accounts for funds available for a specific purpose, as designated by groups or individuals outside the school.

Loan funds Accounts for funds available for loans to students, faculty, and staff.

Endowment funds Accounts for gifts or bequests, the principal of which usually cannot be spent.

Annuity and life income funds Are similar to endowment funds, except that the donor receives some form of financial support from the school.

Plant funds Accounts for funds available for acquisition and replacement of plant assets, as well as retirement of debt. These funds also account for all plant assets of the school, except any that may be part of an endowment fund.

Agency funds Are similar to those used by state and local governments.

Financial statements used by colleges and universities include the following: (a) statement of current funds revenues, expenditures, and other changes; (b) combined balance sheet; and (c) statement of changes in fund balances.

Hospitals

Accounting for nonprofit hospitals closely resembles the accrual accounting methods used by businesses. Funds used include the following:

Unrestricted fund Accounts for the normal operating activities of the hospital. This is the only fund that records revenues and expenses. It accounts for all assets and liabilities not included in other funds, including plant assets and long-term debt.

Specific purpose fund To account for resources that are restricted by someone outside of the hospital for specific operating purposes.

Endowment funds Are similar to those used by colleges and universities. (Example: annuity and life income funds.)

Plant replacement and expansion fund Accounts for resources that are restricted by someone outside of the hospital for capital outlay purposes.

Nonprofit hospitals prepare a statement of revenues and expenses for the unrestricted fund, as well as a statement of cash flows. They also prepare balance sheets and statements of changes in fund balances for all funds.

An important aspect of hospital accounting is the classification of revenues and expenses. Revenues must be separated by *source*, including patient service and other operating and nonoperating revenues. Expenses must be classified by *function*, including nursing services, other professional services, administrative services, and so forth. Unlike other organizations described in this appendix, hospitals recognize depreciation on plant assets.

Voluntary Health and Welfare Organizations

Voluntary health and welfare organizations encompass a wide variety of groups, such as the Sierra Club, the American Cancer Society, and the National Rifle Association. Although accounting practices vary considerably, these organizations usually follow the full accrual basis of accounting. Their fund structure is as follows: current unrestricted fund; current restricted fund; land, building, and equipment fund; endowment funds; custodial (similar to agency) funds; and loan and annuity funds.

Three financial statements are prepared: (a) statement of support, revenue, and expenses, and changes in fund balances, (b) balance sheets, and (c) statement of functional expenses. These organizations must strictly classify revenues and expenses. Revenues must be separated into public support revenues, for which the donor expects nothing in return, and revenues from charges for goods and services. Expenses must be separated by *program* (those activities for which the organization has been established) and by *supporting services* (overhead). These classifications are useful in evaluating the relative efficiency of the groups' activities.

Table D-1. Overview of Governmental and Not-for-Profit Accounting			
	Type of Organization		
	Governmental Units	**Colleges and Universities**	**Hospitals**	**Voluntary Health and Welfare**
Funds and Account Groups	General	Unrestricted current	Unrestricted	Current unrestricted
	Special revenue	Restricted current	Specific purpose	Current restricted
	Capital projects	Plant	Plant replacement and expansion	Land, building, and equipment
	Debt service	Plant		
	Enterprise			
	Internal service			
	Trust and agency	Loan Endowment Annuity and life income Agency	Endowment Annuity and life income	Endowment
				Custodian
	General long-term assets	Plant		Land, building, and equipment
	General long-term debt			
Special Characteristics	1. Only one general fund	1. Revenues recognized in restricted funds only as specified expenditures made	1. Depreciation may be computed on a replacement cost basis	1. Revenues segregated between voluntary contributions and charges for goods or services
	2. Proprietary funds (enterprise, internal service) use full accrual accounting	2. Depreciation not recorded as an expense, but subject to change if FASB No. 93 is implemented	2. Only unrestricted fund shows revenues and expenses	2. Expenses segregated by program services and by supporting (overhead) services
	3. Number of funds used depends on needs and complexity of governmental unit			

(continued)

Table D-1 (continued)

	Type of Organization			
	Governmental Units	**Colleges and Universities**	**Hospitals**	**Voluntary Health and Welfare**
	Basis of Accounting			
	Modified Accrual	Accrual	Accrual	Accrual
Financial Statements	Combined balance sheet—all fund types and account groups	Combined balance sheet	Balance sheet	Balance sheet
	Combined statement of revenues, expenditures, and changes in fund balances—all governmental fund types	Statement of current funds revenues, expenditures, and other changes	Statement of revenues and expenses	Statement of support, revenues and expenses, and changes in fund balances
	Combined statement of revenues, expenditures, and changes in fund balances—budget and actual—general and special revenue fund types	Statement of changes in fund balances	Statement of changes in fund balances	Statement of functional expenses
	Combined statement of revenues, expenses, and changes in retained earnings—all proprietary fund types			
	Combined statement of changes in financial position—all proprietary fund types		Statement of cash flows	

Summary

Governmental and not-for-profit accounting, as we have seen, shares some of the characteristics of business accounting but has its own unique features. Primary among these is the use of funds to organize transactions. Table D-1 summarizes the types of funds used by various organizations and reviews some of the important details of their accounting systems.

Discussion Questions and Writing Assignments

1. How do the objectives of governmental accounting differ from the objectives of business accounting?
2. What is the purpose of a *fund,* as that term is used in governmental accounting?
3. Contrast the measurement of revenues and expenditures in governmental accounting with the measurement of revenues and expenses in business accounting.
4. What is a proprietary fund in governmental accounting? Why do such funds use accrual accounting?
5. What is the purpose of budgetary accounts in governmental accounting?
6. What are the major characteristics of modified accrual accounting as used in governmental accounting?
7. What are the purposes of recording encumbrances?
8. In what ways does accounting for colleges and universities resemble business accounting? How does it differ from business accounting?
9. Describe how revenues and expenses are classified in hospital accounting.
10. Describe and contrast the two types of revenues recognized in the accounts of voluntary health and welfare organizations.

Exercises

**Exercise D-1.
Basic Concepts
and Funds**
(L.O. 2, 3, 5)

Select the most appropriate answer for the following questions.

1. The fund that accounts for the day-to-day operating activities of a local government is the
   a. enterprise fund.
   b. general fund.
   c. operating fund.
   d. special revenue fund.
2. Accrual accounting is recommended for which of the following funds?
   a. Debt service fund
   b. General fund
   c. Internal service fund
   d. Capital projects fund
3. A debt service fund of a municipality is an example of what type of fund?
   a. Internal service fund
   b. Governmental fund
   c. Proprietary fund
   d. Fiduciary fund
4. What basis of accounting would a nonprofit hospital use?
   a. Cash basis for all funds
   b. Modified accrual basis for all funds
   c. Accrual basis for all funds
   d. Accrual basis for some funds and modified accrual basis for other funds
5. After the implementation of FASB No. 93, which of the following types of organizations will least likely record depreciation expense on property, plant, and equipment?
   a. State and local governments
   b. Colleges and universities
   c. Hospitals
   d. Businesses

**Exercise D-2.
Recording the
Budget in the
General Fund**
(L.O. 3)

The Village of Glencoe has adopted the following budget items for 19x4:

Estimated Revenues	$10,000,000
Appropriations	9,800,000

a. Prepare the journal entry to record the budget in the general fund for Glencoe on January 1, 19x4.
b. What entry, if any, would be required at the end of Glencoe's accounting year, December 31, 19x4?

Problem

**Problem D-1.
Journal Entries
for the General
Fund**
(L.O. 3)

The following transactions occurred in North Shore City during 19x1. Record the journal entries necessary to account for these transactions in North Shore's general fund.

19x1
Jan.   1   The budget was adopted. Estimated revenues are $4,000,000; appropriations are $4,100,000.
Feb. 11   Supplies with an estimated cost of $22,000 were ordered.
Mar.   1   Property taxes totaling $3,500,000 were levied. North Shore expects 2 percent of this amount to be uncollectible.
Apr. 10   The supplies ordered on February 11 were received. The actual bill for these supplies amounted to $21,750.
June   1   Property tax collections totaled $3,450,000. The rest were classified as delinquent.
Aug. 10   Equipment costing $11,300 was purchased for cash.
Dec. 31   Actual revenues for 19x1 totaled $4,050,000. Actual expenditures totaled $3,975,000.

APPENDIX E

The Just-in-Time Philosophy

During the past twenty-five years, the manufacturing environment has been significantly changing. The *computer* is now an integral part of the manufacturing process. This change evolved slowly as isolated machines were equipped with automated devices. Today, many companies are installing computer-integrated manufacturing (CIM) systems in their factories. A CIM system is a fully integrated computer setup in which everything connected with the manufacturing system is performed automatically.

During the time manufacturing here was being computerized, the Japanese business community began to develop a production philosophy known as just-in-time (JIT). Its premise was that too much waste was occurring, too many company resources were tied up in inventories, and wasted time and resources were causing higher production costs. By combining the ideas and technologies of computer-integrated manufacturing and just-in-time concepts, companies are able to improve product quality and cut operating costs by large margins.

The impact of automation and the JIT philosophy on management accounting has been significant. Inventory management has been completely revamped. Product costing has been restructured. Cost planning and control has new guidelines and techniques. Performance evaluation benchmarks have shifted. The entire field of management accounting is changing. The topics we covered in Chapters 22 to 28 are still relevant because a significant majority of companies use semiautomated or traditional production facilities. But more and more manufacturers are implementing automated and totally computer-integrated systems, and the JIT concept will eventually spill over into the service and merchandising industries as well.

This appendix introduces you to the concepts associated with just-in-time philosophy and computer-integrated manufacturing systems. Emphasis is on product costing and data recording in the new manufacturing environment. After studying this appendix, you should be able to meet the learning objectives listed on the left.

Computer-Integrated Manufacturing Systems

Computer-integrated manufacturing (CIM) is a production process in which all parts of the system are fully integrated through computer technology. Let us peek into our crystal ball for a moment to see

OBJECTIVE 1
*Describe a
·computer-
integrated
manufacturing
system*

how CIM systems affect productivity. Nichole Marie has just received an order for 1,500 pool cabana awnings from the Porter Hotel chain. The order is entered into the computer at 9:00 A.M. on Monday; the following sequence of events ensues:

Monday	10:00 A.M.	Order scheduled for production.
	10:10 A.M.	Supplier's computer is contacted by manufacturer's computer to order raw materials.
	12:30 P.M.	Supplier ships raw materials.
	2:45 P.M.	Raw materials arrive.
	3:10 P.M.	Machines are set up according to specifications and production begins.
	4:10 P.M.	Computer invoices for raw materials are electronically received.
	5:00 P.M.	All machines required for the job are programmed to run automatically throughout the night shift.
Tuesday	9:15 A.M.	Billings for raw materials are paid by electronic bank transfers.
	11:00 A.M.	Manufacturing and assembly of the 1,500 pool cabana awnings are completed.
	1:00 P.M.	Goods have been packaged and shipped.
	1:15 P.M.	Porter Hotels is computer-billed for the order.
	2:30 P.M.	Payment from Porter Hotels is received by electronic bank transfer.

Sound impossible? This scenario is far from impossible. Formerly, such an order took several weeks to fill; today, JIT work flow configurations are revolutionizing the business environment. Entire systems, including production, materials ordering, billing, payment, and accounting systems, are being reconfigured and linked by computers, eliminating 80 to 90 percent of the production time. Billing functions are performed automatically, and suppliers' computers can interact with manufacturers' computers to facilitate the materials ordering, billing, and payment processes. Verification procedures are also incorporated into the computer programs.

The Just-in-Time Philosophy Defined

The movement toward the just-in-time continuous work flow concept has been developing in Japan over the past decade. To improve productivity and gain footholds in several world markets, companies began to look for ways to streamline their manufacturing processes. *Eliminating waste* in raw materials, labor, space, production time, record keeping, and working capital areas was the key ingredient to the firms' success.

Two independent approaches to eliminating waste in manufacturing companies have emerged: automation and an operating philosophy called **just-in-time (JIT)**. Automation approaches the problem of waste from a physical angle. Repetitive, mechanical operations lend themselves to automated processes, and automation greatly reduces the waste of scrap materials and defective units. Automation also significantly reduces processing time. Computer numerically-controlled (CNC) machines and computer-assisted machinery (CAM) inject new life into the production process.

The just-in-time (JIT) approach to production prompted a total revamping of both manufacturing facilities and the events that trigger the production process. Just-in-time is an overall operating philosophy of management in which all resources, including materials, personnel, and facilities, are used in a just-in-time manner. JIT is based on the objective of continuous flow and requires that each part of the entire production process work in concert. JIT also changes the role of the direct labor worker and significantly reduces waste of labor, space, and production time. JIT production also cuts work-in-process and finished goods inventories by as much as 90 percent and has had a major impact in reducing the level of working capital tied up in inventories.

The most significant event during this period was the merging of these two manufacturing approaches. The synergism from the marriage of just-in-time and automation catapulted the Japanese manufacturing industry into world prominence. Waste was drastically reduced, product quality was enhanced and operations began to approach ideal capacity. Other manufacturers are now following the Japanese example. Over the next decade we will see continued movement toward this new manufacturing environment as more companies apply the JIT approach and install automated systems in order to compete in world markets.

Traditional Versus JIT Factory Layout

OBJECTIVE 2
Compare and contrast the traditional manufacturing system with the just-in-time approach to manufacturing

A critical change caused by applying the JIT philosophy focuses on the layout of machines and equipment on the factory floor. The key to an effective JIT environment is the elimination of all non-value added activities from the production and distribution processes. Breaking down the traditional manufacturing process, we find that the processing time of a product can be divided into five parts or time frames: actual processing (production) time, inspection time, move time, queue time, and storage time. A **non-value added activity** adds costs to the product but does not increase its market value. Traditional manufacturing and assembly operations have dozens of such activities incorporated into them. Of the five parts listed, the JIT environment tries to eliminate all but the actual production time because inspection time, move time, queue time, and storage time are activities that do not usually add value to the product.

The Traditional Manufacturing Environment

The most effective way to differentiate between the traditional and JIT environments is to analyze and compare product flow and plant layout. Figure E-1 illustrates a traditional plant layout. Fasteners such as screws, bolts, shoe nails, and specialty items are produced in this plant. Figure E-2 shows the operations needed to create a fastener. Raw materials arrive as coils of wire of various thicknesses. The wire is fed into a heading machine, which cuts the wire to length and forms the head. The headed blanks are then collected in large movable bins for temporary storage until transported to the next department. If the headed blank needs a slot (regular or Phillips head), it must be added. Then the products are again collected in movable bins. The next operation is threading the fastener, either by cutting away the excess

Figure E-1. Overview of Traditional Plant Layout

*Alternative routes

Figure E-2. Steps in the Production of a Fastener

metal or by rolling the headed blank between two dies to form the thread (similar to rolling a pencil between your hands).

At this point, the product looks like a screw or bolt, but additional operations are needed (see Figure E-1) before it can be considered a finished product:

1. The product must be washed, to remove excess oils and foreign materials.
2. Inspection is necessary to determine if the product meets customer specifications.
3. Heat treatment and plating may be performed.
4. Special packaging may be required.

The products in process are stored and moved in large bins from one operation to the next. Finally, they are transported to the finished goods inventory storage area to await sale and shipment.

Two important manufacturing support areas are also identified in Figure E-1. Product flow is designed so that production support services are located in the middle of the production process. The repair and maintenance, inventory management and control, production quality control, and production planning, scheduling, and routing functions are fairly self-explanatory. In addition, special tools and dies may be required to reshape the metal.

The lower part of Figure E-1 shows other common support services. The accounting, time and motion study, engineering, computer services, sales, personnel, and executive activity functions all support either the production or distribution of the company's products.

Can you identify any non-value added activities in the layout in Figure E-1? Several exist, but the most obvious are the raw materials and finished product storage areas and activities. The arrows represent product movements through the manufacturing process. The time taken to move the products between departments and the resulting queue time are also non-value added activities. Finally, the Inspection Department adds no value to the product, although it does contribute to the cost.

Many support functions are expensive to maintain and add cost to the product. When a company switches to a JIT environment, several of these functions are either reduced significantly or eliminated altogether.

The JIT Production Environment

The JIT production philosophy completely revamps the manufacturing plant layout, operating techniques, and role of personnel. Machinery and equipment are moved into layouts that comprise small, autonomous production lines called "cells" or "islands." Each manufacturing cell or island has a complete set of machines that can produce a product from start to finish. Former direct labor employees are now in charge of each production cell. Machine operators are expected to run several different types of machines, help set up for a production run, and identify and repair machinery needing maintenance. Incentives encourage workers to spot areas of inefficiency.

Figure E-3 depicts a hypothetical JIT plant layout. Instead of large departments containing dozens of similar machines (such as the Heading Department in Figure E-1), small operating units start and complete a product with minimal time, movement, and storage. To compare the traditional manufacturing layout with that required for a JIT production process, we converted the plant layout of our fastener company in Figure E-1 to satisfy the new JIT requirements.

In Subplant A (Figure E-3), raw materials are received on a timely basis and placed in the materials storage area adjacent to the header scheduled to fill that order. Each one of the six work cells may include header, slotter, threader, and cleaning machines. Each cell is designed to work on different sizes and types of fasteners. Instead of work-in-process inventory sitting in travel bins as it moves from one department to the next, wire is fed into the header automatically. The blank is moved via a conveyor to subsequent operations. If order specifications call for additional processing, such as heat-treating and/or plating, the computerized routing system will move the products to those locations. Packaging is the final phase; then the goods are shipped to the customer. The fastener order is completed in a matter of hours, as compared to the days necessary when the order was moved and queued for each operation.

Subplant B in Figure E-3 shows a flexible manufacturing system island or cell being used in a fastener manufacturing operation. A **flexible manufacturing system (FMS)** is an integrated set of computerized machines and systems designed to complete a series of operations automatically. An FMS often completes a product from beginning to end without the item being touched or moved by hand. Raw materials are fed in at one end of the FMS cell, and a finished product emerges at the other end.

Let us assume that Subplant B makes a special type of fastener called a "sems" screw. A locking washer is placed on the blank sems screw before the threading operation is performed. Once the threads are rolled on, the washer cannot be removed. The FMS island is used to produce all types and sizes of sems fasteners from start to finish. Each part of the FMS circular

Figure E-3. Overview of Plant Layout—JIT Format ▶

island represents a different operation, such as heading, slotting, lock washer fitting, threading, and pointing. All operations are computerized, and the manufacturing process is continuous. When the sems fasteners have been packaged, they are sent to the finished goods area to await shipment to the customer.

Several points are worth mentioning regarding the plant layouts in Figures E-1 and E-3. The support functions located in the front (lower part) of the drawings are similar, but the size of the Computer Center and the Engineering/Design Department has been enlarged in the JIT layout in Figure E-3. Production Scheduling, Production Quality Control, and Inventory Management in the JIT environment have been reduced in size and moved to the managerial office area. These functions now need to be closer to the computer area than to the production process. Supporting services such as the Tool and Die Center and Repairs and Maintenance Department should remain close to the manufacturing operation. Heat-treating facilities are very expensive and products are still batch-processed, so both subplant layouts share the same heat-treating furnaces. The remaining parts of the factory in Figure E-3 have been redesigned to satisfy the needs of the JIT production process.

JIT: Capital Intensive Versus Labor Intensive Manufacturing

Shifting the manufacturing process to a JIT approach increases the emphasis on the use of machine hours and reduces direct labor hour usage. The manufacturing process becomes capital intensive, with a heavy reliance on machinery. As the production process is automated, more capital is required. Of course, JIT practices can be followed without the process being completely computerized. Many companies have a partially computerized setup and use direct labor employees on independent computer numerically-controlled machines and other semiautomatic equipment. **Computer numerically-controlled machines (CNC)** are stand-alone pieces of computer-driven equipment, including operating machines, computer-assisted design technology, and robots. The closer a CIM environment is approached, the more automated the process becomes, and the wider the spread between machine hours and direct labor hours used in the production process. In business jargon, shifting to a JIT production process usually involves shifting from a labor intensive to a capital intensive process.

The characteristics of direct labor are changing as industry adopts more and more aspects of the JIT philosophy. In the new manufacturing environment, direct labor personnel no longer just "help shape" the product; workers are now responsible for many tasks that used to be indirect labor functions, including machine setup, machine maintenance, and product inspection. The new definition of a direct labor worker is a person who manages a JIT machine work cell. The indirect labor area has also changed: there is now heavy reliance on support labor to keep the manufacturing cells operating efficiently.

As the role of the direct labor employee changes, so do all of the management accounting procedures that depend on direct labor measures. This impact is significant. Direct labor has traditionally been the primary base for allocating factory overhead costs to products. Today, machine hours are replacing direct labor when overhead costs are assigned and product costs are established. Predetermined factory overhead rates used for pricing and budgeting can no longer use only direct labor as an application basis. Standard cost variance analysis must become more machine hour oriented to control manufacturing costs. Labor-related variances are no longer relevant. Labor measures used in short-run decision analysis and capital budgeting techniques must be replaced with more relevant forecasting techniques. As you can see, the management accounting discipline is affected in a major way by the adoption of JIT techniques.

After we discuss the elements of the JIT philosophy, we focus on the impact of capital intensive processes on product costing. We explore the various approaches to automating the manufacturing process, and identify and analyze "cost drivers," the new name for cost allocation bases. We introduce the Raw-in-Process Inventory account. Finally, direct versus indirect cost classification and process costing practices are revisited because of their unique role in the JIT environment.

Elements Supporting the JIT Philosophy

OBJECTIVE 3
Identify the elements supporting a JIT operating environment

Just-in-time is usually referred to as a philosophy upon which an approach to accomplishing a task is based. Ideas supporting JIT include (1) simple is better; (2) the emphasis is on quality and continuous improvement; (3) maintaining inventories wastes resources and often hides bad work; (4) any activity or function that does not add value to the product should be eliminated; (5) goods are produced only when needed; and (6) workers should be multiskilled and participate in improving efficiency and product quality. This philosophy is contained in the following elements of the JIT approach to production:

1. Maintain minimum inventory levels.
2. Develop pull-through production planning and scheduling procedures.
3. Purchase materials and produce products as needed in smaller lot sizes.
4. Perform simple, inexpensive machine setups.
5. Develop a multiskilled work force.
6. Create a flexible manufacturing system.
7. Maintain high levels of product quality.
8. Enforce a system of effective preventive facility maintenance.
9. Encourage continuous work environment improvement.[1]

Maintain Minimum Inventory Levels

The JIT philosophy centers on the objective of maintaining minimum inventory levels. Raw materials and parts are purchased and received only when needed. This approach is in contrast to purchasing parts, materials, and supplies far in advance, to be stored until the Production Department needs them. Cost savings result from reducing the space needed for inventory storage, the amount of material handling, and the amount of inventory obsolescence. There is also less need for inventory control facilities, personnel, and record keeping. The amount of work-in-process inventory sitting around the plant waiting to be processed is significantly reduced. The amount of working capital tied up in inventories is also reduced. Computerization of the production process was the key feature that enabled the JIT operating concept of minimum inventory levels to become a reality.

1. James B. Dilworth, *Production and Operations Management*, 3rd ed. (New York: Random House, 1986), pp. 354–360.

Develop Pull-Through
Production Planning and Scheduling Procedures

The term **pull-through production** means that a customer order triggers the purchase of materials and the scheduling of production for the required products. This approach is in sharp contrast to the *push-through* method, whereby products were manufactured and stored in anticipation of customer orders. The pull-through approach is a fundamental characteristic of the JIT production concept and requires purchasing materials and parts as needed.

Purchase Materials and Produce
Products as Needed in Smaller Lot Sizes

Using the pull-through approach means that the sizes of production runs will be influenced by the size of customer orders. Thus low inventory levels will be maintained, but machines will have to be set up more frequently, resulting in more work stoppages. Long production runs, previously thought to be more cost effective, are no longer the rule in a JIT environment; products are not manufactured to be inventoried.

Perform Simple, Inexpensive Machine Setups

One reason that traditional production processes relied on long production runs was to reduce the number of machine setups. Management felt that it was more practical to create large inventories rather than produce smaller lot sizes and cause frequent machine setups. This approach has been completely disproved during the past ten years. By placing machines in more efficient locations and scheduling similar products on common machine groupings, setup times can be minimized. In addition, more frequent setups provide experience for the workers. Suggestions for improvement from workers are encouraged, and ideas that result in reducing setup time are rewarded with bonuses.

Develop a Multiskilled Work Force

A key element of the JIT philosophy is that machines are grouped strategically into work centers and one worker may be required to operate several different types of machines simultaneously. Therefore, new operating skills must be learned. Many work centers are run by only one operator, who may, for example, have to participate in setting up machines and retooling.

Preventive maintenance of machines and equipment is an integral part of the JIT concept. Preventing machine breakdowns is considered more important and more cost effective than keeping the machine running continuously. Therefore, when machines are idle from a lack of work, the operator is expected to perform routine maintenance work on the equipment.

The multiskilled worker requirement has been very effective in the Japanese business environment. In the United States, labor union contracts often have a traditional focus on a single-skilled worker, which may cause problems as companies try to implement the JIT philosophy.

Create a Flexible Manufacturing System

In the traditional approach to factory layout, all similar machines are grouped together and functional departments or divisions are formed. Products needing work from several departments are routed through each department in proper sequence so that all the necessary operations are completed in order. This process can take several days or several weeks, depending on the size and complexity of the job.

A primary goal of the JIT production method is to cut the manufacturing time of processing a product from days to hours or from weeks to days. In many cases, time can be reduced more than 80 percent by rearranging the machinery into flexible work cells or islands that perform all required operations efficiently and continuously. These cells are developed to handle jobs of similar shapes and/or sizes of products. Minimum setup changes are required to move from one job to the next. The more flexible the work cell, the more effective the operation is in accomplishing the goals of the JIT philosophy.

Maintain High Levels of Product Quality

High-quality products are a by-product of the JIT production approach. High quality is also required for JIT to work well. One of the non-value added functions in the traditional manufacturing process is inspection. Instead of treating inspection as a separate function, JIT incorporates inspection into the continuous production operation. Machine operators are responsible for inspecting the products as they pass through the process. An operator who detects a product flaw, then determines what caused the problem. The operator may even help the engineer or quality control person find a way to correct the process.

Enforce a System of Effective Preventive Facility Maintenance

When a company's machinery is rearranged into flexible manufacturing units, each machine in the work cell or island becomes a critical, integral part of that cell. A machine breakdown causes the entire work cell to cease functioning. The product cannot be easily routed to another machine while the malfunctioning machine is repaired, so an effective preventive facility maintenance system is very important to the JIT environment. Machine operators are trained to perform minor repairs on machines as they detect problem areas. Machines are serviced regularly—much like an automobile—to help guarantee continued operation. The machine operator conducts routine maintenance during periods of machine downtime (caused by a lack of orders). Remember that in a JIT setting the work cell does not operate unless there is a customer order causing products to be pulled through the work cell. Machine operators take advantage of downtime to perform the maintenance procedures.

Encourage Continuous Work Environment Improvement

The JIT environment fosters loyalty of company personnel. Workers feel more a part of the team because they are so involved in the production process. Machine operators must have skills to run several different types of machines, be able to detect defective products, suggest measures to correct the problem, and maintain the machinery within their work cell. In addition, each worker is urged to make suggestions for improving the manufacturing and assembly processes. Some Japanese companies have received more than one million employee suggestions and have implemented a high percentage of these suggestions. Workers are rewarded for successful suggestions that improve the process. Such an environment is healthy for both the worker and the company.

The JIT approach to production is more than just lowering inventory levels or cutting production time. As described, JIT is a philosophy dedicated to creating a product of the highest quality in the most efficient manner. Every action by machine operators, setup people, repair and maintenance personnel, and company management must be dedicated to satisfying this objective. Every person involved in the production of the product must strive to perform at theoretical or ideal capacity.

Product Costing in a JIT Environment

OBJECTIVE 4
Analyze the impact of a change from a labor intensive to a capital intensive production process on product costing concepts and techniques

The JIT production environment has caused a reassessment of product costing techniques. For the first time in more than forty years, established product costing doctrines are being challenged as outdated and inaccurate. Cost allocation approaches are at the root of the problem. What happened to cause such a change? Why would product costing techniques that have been used for more than four decades all of a sudden become obsolete? There are two answers to this question: (1) The JIT philosophy has changed many of the relationships and cost patterns associated with the traditional approach; (2) automation has caused direct labor hours to be replaced by machine hours in the cost allocation process.[2]

JIT's Influence on Product Costing

Product costing changes caused by the JIT philosophy can be linked to the concept of the operating cell or island. JIT is a never-ending war against waste and the elimination of non-value added aspects of the production process; product costing techniques are influenced by JIT's obsession to eliminate these non-value added parts. Simplification is also an objective of JIT. To better understand the JIT approach to product costing, we need to refer to the time elements of the traditional production process:

Processing time   The actual amount of time that a product is being worked on

Inspection time   The time spent either looking for product flaws or reworking defective units

Moving time   The time spent moving the products from one operation or department to another

Queue time   The time the products spend waiting to be worked on once they arrive at the next operation

Storage time   The time the product is either in materials storage, work-in-process inventory or in finished goods inventory waiting to be sold and shipped.

---

2. The ideas in this section are from Robert D. McIlhattan, "How Cost Management Systems Can Support the JIT Philosophy," *Management Accounting* (September 1987), pp. 20–26.

These five time classifications are important to product costing under JIT. As Table E-1 shows, costs associated with actual processing time (product costs) are grouped as either materials costs or conversion costs and applied to products using the traditional process costing method. The costs associated with and traceable to the other four time classifications are not value-adding aspects of the production process and are either reduced or eliminated through cost control measures.

Accounting for product costs under JIT is not an overly complicated procedure. A product cost is classified as either a materials cost or a conversion cost. Product costs are traced to work cells. The process costing method (described in Chapter 24) is then used to determine product unit cost. (Process costing in a JIT environment is described and illustrated later in this appendix.)

Costs associated with the other time units in the production process are accumulated and classified as inspection costs, moving costs, waiting or queue costs, and storage costs. These costs undergo special analyses to determine which are or will be eliminated by the JIT production process. Inspection costs are partially eliminated by adopting a JIT approach; the costs associated with work cell inspection are traceable to that cell. Costs associated with moving the work-in-process from department to department are eliminated under a JIT setting. Waiting or queue costs should also be reduced or eliminated following JIT procedures.

Storage costs are reduced significantly. If the JIT production process operates in an optimal fashion, raw materials and parts arrive just in time to be used in the production and/or assembly work cells. There are minimal costs associated with storing work in process because goods flow continuously through the work cell. Finished products are packaged and shipped immediately to customers, so there should be only minimal finished goods inventory storage costs. Thus a large percentage of the old costs of storage are eliminated under JIT. Costs not eliminated can be treated as factory overhead costs and charged to work cells, becoming part of conversion costs.

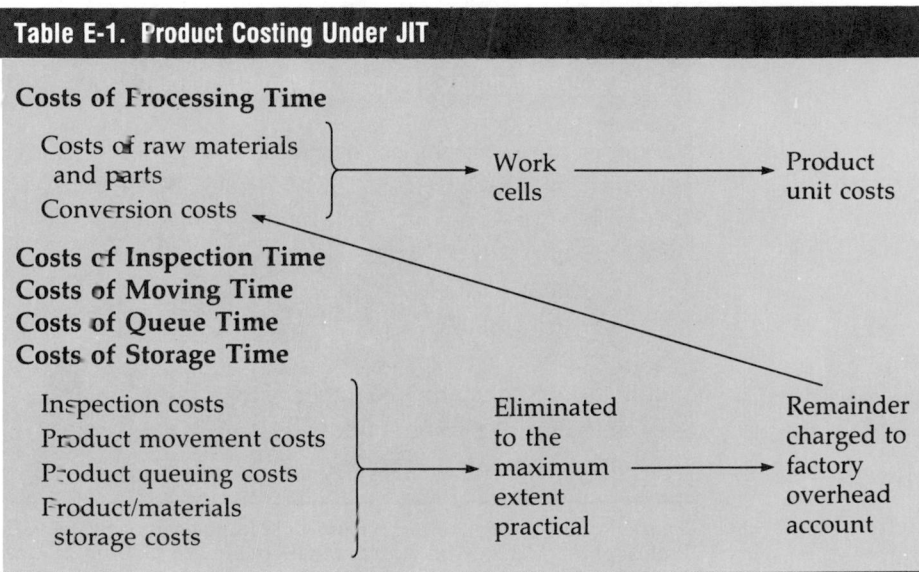

Table E-1. Product Costing Under JIT

Costs of Processing Time

Costs of raw materials and parts
Conversion costs ⎱ → Work cells ——→ Product unit costs

Costs of Inspection Time
Costs of Moving Time
Costs of Queue Time
Costs of Storage Time

Inspection costs
Product movement costs
Product queuing costs
Product/materials storage costs ⎱ → Eliminated to the maximum extent practical ——→ Remainder charged to factory overhead account

New Cost Drivers

OBJECTIVE 5
Define and give
examples of
"cost drivers"

The term "cost driver" is very important to managerial accounting in a JIT setting. A **cost driver** is any activity that causes costs to be incurred. In a traditional production operation, emphasis is on cost control. Cost allocation procedures are used to assign costs to cost objectives on a causal or beneficial basis. The managerial accountant looked for these relationships when cost allocation was necessary.

In a JIT setting, the objective is to eliminate all unnecessary costs rather than just reducing them through control procedures. But before you can eliminate a cost or account for it properly, you must know what caused the cost—you must know what "drives" the cost. Once the cost driver has been determined, the indirect costs it causes can be either (1) treated as a legitimate product cost and allocated as part of the conversion costs, or (2) eliminated by eliminating the need for the cost driver itself. Table E-2 lists various cost drivers. Let us take one cost driver and develop a list of costs that it causes.

Number of Engineering Change Orders

Possible costs caused by an engineering change order include:

Additional engineering time and labor cost
Utility and space costs associated with the extra work
Machine setup time caused by the change order
Product rework time in the work cell
Other conversion costs of cell

These costs and possibly others are reduced if the number of engineering change orders are reduced. By focusing on cost drivers and the costs associated with each driver, management can get to the root of operating inefficiencies and reduce overall product cost. These cost reductions make price reductions possible, which help increase sales and market share.

Table E-2. Examples of Potential Cost Drivers

Number of labor transactions
Number of material moves
Number of parts received in a month
Number of products
Number of schedule changes
Number of vendors
Number of units reworked
Number of engineering change orders
Number of direct labor employees
Number of new parts added

Source: Robert D. McIlhattan, "How Cost Management Systems Can Support the JIT Philosophy," *Management Accounting* (September 1987), p. 22. Used by permission of National Association of Accountants.

Standard Costs

A JIT environment enhances the role and use of standard costs. However, many of the common variances associated with a traditional standard costing system are no longer useful. But using standard costs for product costing and inventory valuation is very useful for JIT operations. Companies such as Harley-Davidson and IBM retained their standard cost system when they adopted the JIT approach. Emphasis may be on only two cost elements (materials and conversion costs), but the use of standard costs still makes product costing easier. Now companies need only concentrate on maintaining two standard costs, materials cost and conversion cost, so the procedures for reporting, calculating, and updating standard costs are also simplified.

Variances based on direct labor data are not as useful in a JIT environment. In addition, product quality requires high quality inputs and little scrap or rework, so materials price and quantity variances should be minimal. Computerized data processing enables management to use actual cost data to evaluate performance, thereby replacing many of the standard costing contributions to pricing decisions and cost allocation procedures.

Direct Versus Indirect Costs

OBJECTIVE 6
Describe how the JIT philosophy and CIM affect the classification of direct and indirect costs

Product costs in a traditional manufacturing system are heavily weighted by variable costs and especially by direct labor costs. Because direct labor is such a dominant force in the traditional system, most factory overhead costs are allocated to the products based on direct labor hours or dollars. Direct labor is either the main cost component or the primary cause of overhead cost incurrence—direct labor is the main cost driver.

The use of flexible manufacturing systems and automated production cells has changed the nature of product costs and offers alternative approaches to the application of costs to products flowing through each operation. Here we analyze two specific areas: (1) the elimination of work orders and (2) the merging of direct labor with factory overhead costs and accounting for only conversion costs.

In a traditional manufacturing system, the work order is a primary document. Labor time is accumulated as the order moves from one operation to the next. When the work order is completed, it is a record of all labor time required for that job. This labor time information makes it possible to determine the cost of direct labor and the application of factory overhead. By using JIT production cells and continuous production techniques, work orders are eliminated. Daily production schedules are maintained, and costs are assigned to the work completed during the day. Detailed reporting, such as completing documents like the work order, is not a part of the simplified JIT process.

In a JIT setting, costs have little correlation with direct labor time. Emphasis is on the time it takes to get a product through the entire process. Machine hours become more important than labor hours. Product velocity measures are used to apply conversion costs to products via process costing. In addition, theoretical capacity is used to establish conversion cost application rates. JIT means that the objective is no waste or downtime, but rather operating at theoretical capacity.

Sophisticated computer monitoring of the production cell allows many costs to be traced directly to the cells and the products being manufactured. As Table E-3 shows, several costs that used to be treated as indirect costs and applied to products using a labor base are now treated as direct costs of

Table E-3. Direct Versus Indirect Costs—Changes Caused by JIT		
Traditional Environment		JIT Environment
Direct	Direct labor	Direct
Indirect	Repairs and maintenance	Direct
Indirect	Materials handling	Direct
Indirect	Operating supplies	Direct
Indirect	Utility costs	Direct
Indirect	Supervision	Direct
Indirect	Depreciation	Direct
Indirect	Supporting service functions	Mostly direct
Indirect	Building occupancy	Indirect
Indirect	Insurance and taxes	Indirect

a work cell. The JIT approach centers on the concept that, if a cost cannot be traced directly to a work cell or product (caused by the actual shaping of the product), then it is suspect and should be analyzed to see if a non-value added function exists. If so, the cost should be eliminated.

Many of the costs in Table E-3 are directly traceable to the JIT production cell. If standard costs are used, products are costed using predetermined rates for materials and conversion costs. The JIT philosophy requires that each cell manufacture identical or similar products to minimize setup time. Therefore, materials and conversion costs should be near uniform per product per cell. Costs such as material handling, utilities, operating supplies, and supervision can be traced directly to work cells as they are incurred. Depreciation is charged based on units of output rather than according to time, so depreciation can also be charged directly to work cells based on the number of units produced. Building occupancy costs, property and casualty insurance premiums, and property taxes remain as indirect costs and must be allocated to the production cells for inclusion in the conversion cost category.

The IBM Approach

As described in McIlhattan's article referred to earlier, IBM's switch to the JIT production concept has been very successful. The company's experience has allowed more than 75 percent of the production support costs to become directly traceable to products (this figure was 25 percent before JIT was instituted). At IBM, costs are classified into three groups and associated with products:

1. Production floor expenses are charged directly to products as they flow through manufacturing cells.
2. Nonoccupancy-related support costs, such as cost accounting and data processing, are "billed" directly to the products utilizing their services. The billing rates are negotiated between support function managers and

product managers before services are rendered and are based on the amount of support given to a specific product.
3. Occupancy-related costs are still allocated to products.[3]

Direct charging of both production floor expenses and support costs provides product cost accuracy and increased knowledge about the importance of each cost to the manufacturing process.

The Raw-in-Process Inventory Account

OBJECTIVE 7
Record transactions involving the Raw-in-Process Inventory account

One of the most basic accounting changes caused by the JIT environment is the use of the **Raw-in-Process Inventory** account. This new inventory account replaces both the Materials Inventory and the Work-in-Process Inventory accounts. Because raw materials are ordered and received just in time for use, there is no need to debit them to a Materials Inventory account; they are debited directly to the Raw-in-Process Inventory account:

Raw-in-Process Inventory	50,000	
Accounts Payable		50,000
To record the purchase of raw materials		

In process costing situations, as goods were completed by one department and transferred to another department, the cumulative cost of the products had to be transferred from one work-in-process inventory account to another. This is also changed in the JIT environment. There is no need for numerous work-in-process inventory accounts because the products flow continuously through the flexible manufacturing cell. All conversion costs (direct labor and factory overhead costs) are debited to the single Raw-in-Process Inventory account. When the goods have been completed, the following entry is made:

Finished Goods Inventory	185,600	
Raw-in-Process Inventory		185,600
To record the transfer of completed products to Finished Goods Inventory		

If adjustments have to be made at the end of an accounting period because of over- or underapplied factory overhead, the debits or credits are made only to Raw-in-Process and Finished Goods Inventories. For example, assume that factory overhead was overapplied by $1,600 and that $100 should be taken back from goods in process and $500 from finished goods; the remaining $1,000 are in Cost of Goods Sold. The entry would be:

Factory Overhead Applied	1,600	
Raw-in-Process Inventory		100
Finished Goods Inventory		500
Cost of Goods Sold		1,000
To adjust for overapplied factory overhead		

3. Ibid., p. 24.

One last example helps clarify the Raw-in-Process Inventory account. Assume that $17,500 of raw materials were purchased and the accountant discovered that these goods were priced $1,500 over their standard cost. The following entry would be made to record the purchase:

Raw-in-Process Inventory	16,000	
Materials Price Variance	1,500	
Accounts Payable		17,500
To record the purchase of raw materials		
and the related price variance		

Using the Raw-in-Process Inventory account is an easy adjustment to make. Remember that this new account is used in every situation in which either Materials Inventory or Work-in-Process Inventory was used in the past.

JIT and Process Costing

OBJECTIVE 8
Use process
costing
procedures to
compute JIT
product costs

The process costing method can easily be adapted to compute product unit costs in a JIT manufacturing setting. Every manufacturing cost is classified as being either a materials or materials-related cost or a conversion cost. The following illustrative problem helps show how JIT product costs are developed, and ties together several sections of the appendix.

Illustrative Problem: JIT/Process Costing

The Metro Company produces steering wheels for all the major car producers in the United States. Three FMS cells are used in the process: one cell produces leather steering wheels, a second concentrates on plastic models, and a third makes special wood-grained wheels. The day-shift operator of each cell prepares the equipment so that all machines can run automatically during the two night shifts. Only indirect labor is needed during the night shifts.

During the week ended June 15, 19x9 the leather wheel JIT operating cell produced the following data:

Units:	
Beginning inventory	30
Units completed during week	4,600
Ending inventory (80 percent complete)	35
Hours worked:	
Direct labor— 40 hours	
Machine hours:	
Nine machines in cell	
FMS leather wheel cell ran	
110 hours during week	
Costs in beginning Raw-in-Process Inventory:	
Materials costs	$1,080
Conversion costs	265

Direct costs incurred for leather wheel cell:

Raw materials	$138,150
Direct labor (40 hours at $14 per hour)	560
Power costs	3,056
Cell machinery depreciation	2,420
Design costs	4,963
Indirect labor	11,970
Lubricants, supplies, and fasteners	7,242

Overhead rates used:
  Material handling overhead (included as part
    of materials cost in process costing analysis):
      20 percent of raw materials costs
  Factory overhead not traceable to cell:
    $37 per machine hour worked

Required

1. Compute the total materials costs and total conversion costs for the week.
2. Using good form and the average process costing approach, prepare
   a. Schedule of equivalent production
   b. Unit cost analysis schedule
   c. Cost summary schedule
3. From the cost summary schedule, prepare a journal entry to transfer costs of completed units to Finished Goods Inventory.

Solution

Before preparing the Cost of Production Report for the Metro Company, we will first categorize the costs of the period. Remember that two cost categories are used in a JIT system: materials cost and conversion costs. These same categories are also used in process costing.

1. Raw materials costs:

In beginning inventory	$ 1,080	
Used in production during the week	138,150	
Material handling overhead for the week:		
$138,150 × 20%	27,630	
Total materials costs	$166,860	

Conversion costs:

In beginning inventory		$ 265
Charged to FMS cell during period:		
Directly traceable costs:		
Direct labor (40 hours at $14 per hour)		560
Power costs		3,056
Cell machinery depreciation		2,420
Design costs		4,963
Indirect labor		11,970
Lubricants, supplies, and fasteners		7,242
Indirect factory overhead:		
110 machine hr × 9 machines × $37/machine hr		36,630
Total conversion costs		$ 67,106

2.

The Metro Company
Cost of Production Report
For the Week Ending June 15, 19x9

Schedule of Equivalent Production Completed

	Units to Be Accounted For	Equivalent Units	
Units—Stage of Completion		Materials Costs	Conversion Costs
Beginning inventory—units completed this period	30	30	30
Units started and completed this period	4,570	4,570	4,570
Ending inventory—units started but not completed	35		
(Materials—100% complete)		35	
(Conversion costs—80% complete)			28
Totals	4,635	4,635	4,628

Unit Cost Analysis Schedule Completed

	Total Cost Analysis			Equivalent Unit Costs	
	Costs from Beginning Inventory	Costs from Current Period	Total Costs to Be Accounted For	Divided by Equivalent Units	Cost Per Equivalent Unit
Materials costs	$1,080	$165,780	$166,860	4,635	$36.00
Conversion costs	265	66,841	67,106	4,628	14.50
Total	$1,345	$232,621	$233,966		$50.50

Cost Summary Schedule Completed

	Cost of Goods Transferred to Finished Goods Inventory	Cost of Ending Raw-in-Process Inventory
Beginning inventory		
30 units at $50.50 per unit	$ 1,515	
Units started and completed this period		
4,570 units at $50.50 per unit	230,785	
Ending inventory		
Materials:		
35 units at 100% at $36		$ 1,260
Conversion costs:		
35 units at 80% at $14.50		406
Totals	$232,300	$ 1,666
Computation check:		
Cost of goods transferred to Finished Goods Inventory		$232,300
Cost of ending Raw-in-Process Inventory		1,666
Error due to rounding		—
Total costs to be accounted for		$233,966

3. Journal entry prepared:

Finished Goods Inventory	232,300	
Raw-in-Process Inventory		232,300
To transfer cost of goods completed		
to Finished Goods Inventory		

Discussion Questions and Writing Assignments

1. What is a computer-integrated manufacturing system?
2. Describe the just-in-time philosophy.
3. What role did the elimination of waste play in the development of the JIT philosophy?
4. How does computer-integrated manufacturing assist the JIT philosophy?
5. Name and describe the five time frames included in the traditional manufacturing process.
6. What is a non-value added activity?
7. Contrast the traditional manufacturing layout and the JIT production layout.
8. What is a flexible manufacturing system cell?
9. How has the movement to automated manufacturing facilities affected the role of direct labor in management accounting?
10. Describe the pull-through production concept.
11. How has the role of the machine operator changed in the JIT computer-integrated manufacturing environment?
12. Explain the statement, "Preventive maintenance of machinery is critical to the operation of a flexible manufacturing system cell or island."
13. How has the inspection function changed in a JIT environment?
14. What is a cost driver? What is its role in product costing in a JIT setting?
15. Identify several costs that have changed from indirect to direct in a JIT environment.
16. Explain the meaning and use of the Raw-in-Process Inventory account.
17. Why is the process costing method useful for product costing in a flexible manufacturing system?

Exercises

**Exercise E-1.
Computer-
Integrated
Manufacturing—
Definition
(L.O. 1)**

Braden Plastics, Inc. has had trouble competing in world markets for the past five years. Every time the company attempts to reduce costs to maintain a price advantage, the quality of the products suffer. As the overall quality has decreased, so has the company's market share. Spruille Braden, founder and president of the company, has asked the production consulting firm of King & Bisgay to develop a strategic plan that would again make the company competitive and improve the quality of its products.

Lou Bisgay did the fieldwork for the consulting firm before preparing the company's plan. Bisgay spent two weeks at the company's facilities in New Jersey and obtained information from the plastics industry trade association regarding recent trends and changes in production. The latest manufacturing equipment was reviewed and compared to existing machinery. Product flow was observed. Inventory storage and management structure were studied. Customer complaints were analyzed.

King & Bisgay's recommerdations included the following statements:

Adopt the just-in-time production philosophy.

Purchase two flexible manufacturing systems to replace existing functional production lines.

Purchase enough computer support to enable your overall production setup to be linked in a computer-integrated manufacturing system.

Explain these three statements to Spruille Braden.

**Exercise E-2.
Old Versus New
Manufacturing
Environment
(L.O. 2)**

B. J. Cook Industries manufactures computer keyboard casings. The following machines and operations are involved in the production process:

Mixing machines	The Mixing Department has three machines that mix various chemicals to develop the raw material used in the molding operation.
Molding machines	The Molding Department uses six molding machines. Each machine can be set up to make any keyboard casing sold by the company.
Trimming machines	In the Trimming Department, casings removed from the molds are trimmed of all excess materials left by the molding operation. Six trimming machines are used.
Packing machines	Packing machines wrap and individually box each completed computer keyboard casing. Each of the two packing machines can keep pace with three trimming machines.

Products are moved from the mixing operation to the molding machines in large 200-gallon drums, and the drums usually sit one to three days before being used. Sometimes the mixture must be remixed before it is usable by the Molding Department. From molding to trimming, the casings are stacked on wooden skids and moved by small lift trucks. The same moving procedure is used from trimming to the packing operation. Total production time can range from two weeks to three months, depending on the urgency of the order. B. J. Cook is not happy with this rate of output. Suggest a plant layout for B. J. Cook that will transform her manufacturing operation into a JIT production operation without new equipment having to be purchased.

**Exercise E-3.
Elements
Supporting JIT
(L.O. 3)**

Barbara Wicks recently purchased Consolidated Metals Company from a family who owned the business for seventy-two years. During that time, Consolidated reached world prominence as a producer of high-quality stainless steel cutting tools. However, about ten years ago the company let the quality begin to slip because competition kept driving down the price. Today the company has only a small share of the market, with total revenues only 12 percent of what they were at their peak.

Wicks has been told that it will take a complete revamping of the production facility and the adoption of a just-in-time operating philosophy to turn the company around. However, she is a bit hesitant to make any drastic moves with only limited knowledge of the proposed operating environment. She has heard two supporting comments about this approach: (1) The emphasis is on quality and continuous improvement, and (2) simple is better.

You have been asked to prepare a summary of the elements supporting the JIT production philosophy. Include a brief description of each element as part of your analysis.

Exercise E-4.
Cost Driver
Determination
(L.O. 5)

Salesman Rick Vimmerstedt just stormed out of the office of controller Joe Umbriano. When asked what was wrong, Vimmerstedt stated that he had just been told to refuse any additional orders for goods that had to circumvent the existing three-week backlog period. Umbriano had just added $2,450 of additional scheduling costs to his recent order from Blaser Corp., and this charge turned a $2,200 profit into a $250 loss. Sales personnel earn commissions on the profitability of their orders.

Umbriano used the following analysis to back up his position regarding the Blaser order:

Costs associated with production schedule changes

Personnel overtime	$1,940
Extra computer time	1,260
Unanticipated supplies and utility costs	1,080
Communication with affected customers	620
Total costs of schedule changes	$4,900
50 percent traceable to Blaser order	$2,450

What is a cost driver? Does this case involve a cost driver? Should the cost of schedule changes be spread over all orders worked on or traced to specific orders? Do you agree with Umbriano's decision? Why or why not?

Exercise E-5.
Costs and Their
Cost Drivers
(L.O. 5)

The following cost items are from the trial balance of the Elmore Corporation in Huntsville, Alabama. Company accountants are in the process of establishing an overhead allocation system for factory-related costs. To help guarantee accuracy, several cost pools based on separate activities are desired. The company has a fully automated flexible manufacturing system in operation. Budget costs for the period were:

Repairs and Maintenance, Plant Building	$ 11,578
Engineering Department Salaries	22,190
Raw Materials	123,790
Depreciation, Tool and Die Department Equipment	7,270
Depreciation, Engineering Department Equipment	4,260
Marketing Expenses	21,320
Depreciation, Plant Building	8,150
Tool and Die Department Operating Supplies	1,274
Insurance and Taxes, Plant Building	3,520
Yard Maintenance, Plant Building	1,250
Electrical Costs, Tool and Die Department	2,310
Electrical Costs, Plant Building	3,520
Tool and Die Department Wages	19,740
Electrical Costs, Engineering Department	1,980

Divide these costs into separate activity cost pools. Recommend an allocation base for each pool that will distribute the costs fairly and equitably. Alternative allocation bases include direct labor hours, tool and die orders, engineering change orders, machine hours, engineering hours, tool and die labor hours, direct labor dollars, and square footage.

**Exercise E-6.
Raw-in-Process
Inventory
(L.O. 7)**

De Reyna Manufacturing Company installed a just-in-time/flexible manufacturing system in its Shovel Division, and the system has been operating at near capacity for about eight months. Transactions related to the JIT/FMS are recorded when incurred. The following transactions took place last week:

Sept. 5   Wooden handles for jobs 12A, 14N, and 13F were ordered and received, $3,670.
Sept. 6   Sheet metal costing $5,630 received from vendor B.
Sept. 7   Work begun on job 14N.
Sept. 8   Job 12A completed and shipped to the customer; total cost, $13,600. [Company uses a 40 percent markup to establish selling price.]

Using good journal entry form, record these transactions.

Problems

**Problem E-1.
Production Layout
Design
(L.O. 2)**

Bentley Automotive Products Company specializes in manufacturing chrome automobile parts, with front chrome grills being one of the company's most successful products. The following manufacturing operations and functions are part of the production of all types of automobile grills:

Assembly	Connecting devices are put on the completed grill.
Stamping	The grill shape is stamped out of a piece of sheet metal.
Plating	A chrome substance is adhered to a heat-treated product.
Receiving	The central receiving area receives sheet metal and assembly parts.
Welding	Connector pads are attached to a heat-treated product prior to plating.
Washing	Products are cleaned prior to being inspected for the first time.
Postassembly inspection	Products are inspected just prior to being packaged.
Raw materials storage	Sheet metal and assembly parts are stored prior to usage.
Drilling	Holes are drilled into the products before the connector pads can be welded.
Bending	Stamped grills are bent into shape.
Heat-treat	All products are heat-treated after passing the pre-assembly inspection point.
Sheet metal inspection	All sheet metal received is inspected.

Polishing	Plated grills are polished before being assembled.
Skid moving	All grills are moved on large wooden skids from operation to operation.
Shipping	Railroad cars are loaded for shipment to automobile-making companies.
Packing	Grills are packed in large wooden crates.
Preassembly inspection	All grills are inspected after the washing operation.

Required

1. Arrange these operations in the order they would be in a traditional manufacturing system.
2. Assume that a just-in-time approach is to be taken in redesigning this production process. Identify the:
   a. Operations or process elements that would be eliminated
   b. Operations that would be automated
   c. Possible operations that could be combined into operating cell(s)
3. Is this company a good candidate for the JIT/FMS environment? Defend your answer.

**Problem E-2.
Cost Allocation in
an Automated
Process
(L.O. 6)**

William Epps created Augusta Music Company fifteen years ago. The company specializes in speaker systems for home stereos. Two different types of speakers are produced in the Sound Department. The Casings Department makes the speaker casings. Speakers and casings are assembled in the Assembly Department. The Sound and Casings Departments are operated autonomously. The Sound Department utilizes a modern flexible manufacturing system and has very little direct labor expense. Casings, on the other hand, is still mostly a functional operation, with many direct labor employees.

The two types of speakers the Sound Department manufactures are identified as models X20 and Y16, respectively. The X20 is completely made by FMS equipment, whereas model Y16 requires some manual detailing after it has completed the full FMS cycle.

Following is a summary of plantwide overhead costs for the month of March:

Indirect support labor	$34,190
Machine repairs and maintenance	3,650
Materials delivery trucker wages	2,820
Depreciation, materials delivery trucks	1,120
Depreciation, building	2,640
Depreciation, machinery	5,370
Electrical power	2,490
Machinery supplies and lubricants	1,370
Engineering salaries	11,880
Depreciation, engineering equipment	1,450
Operating supplies, engineering	950
Fuel, raw materials delivery	310
Purchasing Department costs	2,260
Fire insurance, building	420
Property taxes, plant	550
Total	$71,470

The following information was also made available:

| | Sound Department | | | | |
	Model X20	Model Y16	Totals	Casings Department	Plantwide Totals
Direct labor hours	60	180	240	1,060	1,300
Machine hours	2,400	1,600	4,000	1,500	5,500
Engineering hours	30	120	150	300	450
Cost of raw materials used			$56,250	$28,125	$84,375
Floor square footage			7,500	15,000	22,500

Required

1. Allocate the plantwide overhead for the month to the Sound and Casings Departments, using direct labor hours as a base.
2. Using machine hours, cost of raw materials used, engineering hours, and floor square footage as cost drivers, separate the elements of the plantwide overhead cost pool into four different cost pools.
3. Using your answer to part 2 and the allocation bases mentioned, reallocate the plantwide overhead costs to the Sound and Casings Departments. Discuss the differences between the allocations of parts 1 and 3.
4. What are the advantages and disadvantages of this approach versus the allocation of plantwide overhead costs to cost or profit centers?
5. Assume the overhead cost allocated to the Sound Department was $25,600. Allocate the $25,600 to the two products manufactured by the Sound Department based on (a) direct labor hours and (b) machine hours. Which allocation approach is better? Why?

Problem E-3.
JIT and Process
Costing
(L.O. 7, 8)

The Forest Company is located in Durango, Colorado, and has been producing sink faucets for the past twelve years. The prices of the seven models of kitchen sink faucets range from $24 to $94. The Grand model is the highest-priced faucet, but its market share has been steadily declining during the past four years.

Bothered by the decline in market share, management recently purchased a JIT/FMS cell for the kitchen faucet line. Two day-shift operators are employed, and they prepare the equipment to run automatically during the two evening shifts. Only indirect support labor is needed during the night shifts. For the week ending July 30, 19x9, the Grand model was run, and the following data were generated:

Units:
  Beginning Raw-in-Process Inventory   45
  Units completed during week   6,295
  Ending Raw-in-Process Inventory (70 percent   50
    complete)
Hours worked:
  Direct labor—80 hours
  Machine hours:
    Fourteen machines in cell
  FMS cell ran 116 hours during week

Costs in beginning inventory:

Materials costs	$ 2,410
Conversion costs	765

Direct costs incurred by faucet JIT/FMS cell:

Raw materials	$157,458
Direct labor (80 hours at $16 per hour)	1,280
Electricity costs	6,056
JIT cell machinery depreciation	3,890
Engineering design costs	7,934
Indirect labor	12,000
Lubricants, supplies, and fasteners	8,110

Overhead rates used:
  Materials-handling overhead (included as part of raw
    materials cost in the process costing analysis):
      25 percent of raw materials costs
  Factory overhead not traceable to cell:
      $42 per machine hour worked

Required

1. Compute the total materials cost and total conversion cost for the week.
2. Using good form and the average process costing approach, prepare a
   a. Schedule of equivalent production
   b. Unit cost analysis schedule
   c. Cost summary schedule
3. From the cost summary schedule, prepare a journal entry to transfer costs of completed units to Finished Goods Inventory.
4. Do you think the $94 price is too high for the Grand model? Why?

GLOSSARY

Absorption costing: an approach to product costing in which all types of manufacturing costs are assigned to individual products. (23)

Accelerated cost recovery system (ACRS): a depreciation system requiring that a cost recovery allowance be computed on the unadjusted cost of the property being recovered. (12)

Accelerated methods: methods of depreciation that allocate relatively large amounts of the depreciable cost of the asset to earlier years and reduced amounts to later years. (12)

Account: the basic storage unit for data in accounting systems; there is a separate account for each asset, liability, component of owner's equity, revenue, and expense. (2)

Account balance: the difference in total dollars between the total debit footing and the total credit footing of an account. (2)

Accountant's report (or auditor's report): a report by an independent public accountant that accompanies the financial statements, communicating the nature of the audit (scope section) and the conclusion as to the fair presentation of the financial statements (opinion section). (8)

Accounting: an information system that measures, processes, and communicates financial information about an identifiable economic entity to permit users of the system to make informed judgments and decisions. (1)

Accounting cycle: all steps in the accounting process including analyzing and recording transactions, posting entries, adjusting and closing the accounts, and preparing financial statements; accounting system. (4, 6, 7)

Accounting equation: algebraic expression of financial position; assets = liabilities + owner's equity; also called the balance sheet equation. (1)

Accounting period issue: the difficulty of assigning revenues and expenses to short periods of time such as a months or years; net income must be regarded as tentative but useful; related to the periodicity assumption. (3)

Accounting rate of return method: a method used to measure the estimated performance of a capital investment that yields an accounting rate of return computed by dividing the project's average after-tax net income by the average cost of the investment over its estimated life. (28)

Accounting system, see Accounting cycle

Accounts receivable: short-term liquid assets that arise from sales on credit to customers at either the wholesale or the retail level. (9)

Accounts receivable aging method: a method of estimating uncollectible accounts expense based on the assumption that a predictable portion of accounts receivable will not be collected. (9)

Accrual: the recognition of an expense that has been incurred or a revenue that has arisen but has not yet been recorded. (3)

Accrual accounting: the attempt to record the financial effects on an enterprise of transactions and other events in the periods in which those transactions or events occur rather than only in the periods in which cash is received or paid by the enterprise. (3)

Accrual basis: the reporting of revenues from sales in the period in which they are sold, regardless of when the cash is received, and the reporting of expenses in the period of purchase, regardless of when payment is made. (Appendix C)

Accrued expenses: expenses that have been incurred but are not recognized in the accounts, necessitating an adjusting entry; unrecorded expenses; a liability account (3)

Accrued revenues: revenues for which the service has been performed or the goods have been delivered but that have not been recorded in the accounts; unrecorded revenue; an asset account. (3)

Accumulated depreciation: a contra asset account used to accumulate the total past depreciation of a specific long-lived asset. (3)

Activity accounting, see Responsibility accounting

Addition: an expenditure resulting from an expansion of an existing plant asset. (13)

Adjusted gross income: gross income minus deductions from gross income. (Appendix C)

Adjusted trial balance: a trial balance prepared after all adjusting entries have been posted to the accounts. (3)

Adjusting entries: entries made to apply accrual accounting to transactions that span more than one accounting period. (3)

Aging of accounts receivable: the process of listing each customer in accounts receivable according to the due date of the account. (9)

Allowance for uncollectible accounts: a contra account that serves to reduce accounts receivable to the amount that is expected to be collected in cash. (9)

American Institute of Certified Public Accountants (AICPA): the professional association of CPAs. (1)

Amortization: the periodic allocation of the cost of an intangible asset over its useful life. (12)

Annual report: a corporation's yearly report of the general-purpose external financial statements, sent as part of management's responsibility to report to the stockholders and other interested parties; also filed with the SEC. (8)

Articles of incorporation: a contract between the state and the incorporators forming the corporation. (1, 15)

Assets: probable future economic benefits obtained or controlled by a particular entity as a result of past transactions or events. (1)

Asset turnover: a ratio that measures how efficiently assets are used to produce sales; net sales divided by average total assets. (8, 19)

Attest function: the examination and testing of financial statements by a certified public accountant; also called auditing. (1)

Audit committee: in the organization of a corporation, a committee with several outside directors whose functions include engaging and monitoring the work of the external auditors. (15)

Auditing: the principal and most distinctive function of a certified public accountant; the process of examining and testing the financial statements of a company in order to render an independent professional opinion as to the fairness of their presentation; also called the attest function. (1)

Auditors: independent certified public accountants who check and test the accounting records and controls of a business as necessary to determine the quality of the financial statements of a business. (1)

Auditor's report, see Accountant's report

Audit trail: the sequence of written approval by key individuals reviewing and evaluating an expenditure in a voucher system. (7)

Authorized stock: the maximum number of shares a corporation may issue without changing its charter with the state. (15)

Average costing approach: a process costing method in which unit costs are computed based on the assumption that the items in beginning Work in Process Inventory were started and completed during the current period. (24)

Average-cost method: an inventory costing method which assumes that the cost of inventory is the average cost of all goods available for sale. (10)

Average days' sale uncollected: the length of the accounting period, usually 365 days, divided by the receivable turnover. Shows the speed at which receivables are turned over; literally, the number of days, on average, a company must wait to receive payment for credit sales. (19)

Balance: the difference in total dollars between the total debit footing and the total credit footing of an account; also called the account balance. (2)

Balance sheet: a financial statement that shows the assets, liabilities, and owner's equity at a specific point in time. (1)

Balance sheet equation, see Accounting equation (1)

Bank reconciliation: the process of accounting for the differences between the balance appearing on the bank statement and the balance of cash according to the depositor's records. (7)

Bank statement: a monthly statement of the transactions related to a particular bank account. (7)

Base year: the first year to be considered in any set of data. (19)

Batch processing: a type of computer system design in which separate computer jobs such as purchasing, inventory control, payroll, production scheduling, and so forth are processed in a logical order. (6)

Beginning inventory: merchandise on hand for sale to customers at the beginning of the accounting period. (5)

Beta (β): the measure of the market risk of an individual stock in relation to the average market risk of all stocks. (19)

Betterment: an expenditure resulting from an improvement to but not an enlargement of an existing plant asset. (13)

Bond: a security, usually long-term, representing money borrowed by a corporation from the investing public. (17)

Bond certificate: the evidence of a company's debt to the bondholder. (17)

Bond indenture: a supplementary agreement to a bond issue that defines the rights, privileges, and limitations of bondholders. (17)

Bonding: investigating an employee and insuring the company against any theft by that individual. (7)

Bond issue: the total number of bonds that are issued at one time. (17)

Bonus: in partnership accounting, an amount that accrues to the original partners when a new partner pays more to the partnership than the interest received or that accrues to the new partner when the amount paid to the partnership is less than the interest received. (14)

Bookkeeping: the means by which transactions are recorded and records are kept; a process of accounting. (1)

Book value: total assets of a company less total liabilities; owners' equity. (16)

Break-even point: that point in financial analysis at which total revenue equals total cost incurred and at which a company begins to generate a profit. (25)

Budget: a financial document created before anticipated transactions occur. (Also called a financial plan of action.) (26)

Budgetary control: the process of (1) developing plans for a company's expected operations and (2) controlling operations to help in carrying out those plans. (26)

Budgetary control system: an integrated cost planning and control system. (25)

Business transactions: economic events that affect the financial position of the business entity. (1)

Callable bonds: bonds that a corporation has the option of buying back and retiring at a given price, usually above face value, before maturity. (17)

Callable preferred stock: preferred stock that may be redeemed and retired by the corporation at its option. (15)

Capital assets: certain types of assets that qualify for special treatment when gains and losses result from transactions involving the assets. (Appendix C)

Capital budgeting: the combined process of identifying a facility's needs, analyzing alternative courses of action to satisfy those needs,

preparing the reports for management, selecting the best alternative, and rationing available capital expenditure funds among competing resource needs. (28)

Capital expenditure: an expenditure for the purchase or expansion of plant assets. (13)

Capital expenditure budget: a detailed plan outlining the amount and timing of anticipated capital expenditures for a future period. (26)

Capital expenditure decision: the decision to determine when and how much money to spend on capital facilities for the company. (28)

Capital lease: long-term lease in which the risk of ownership lies with the lessee, and whose terms resemble a purchase or sale. (17)

Carrying value: the unexpired portion of the cost of an asset; sometimes called book value. (3)

Cash: cash and cash equivalents. (18)

Cash basis of accounting: a basis of accounting under which revenues and expenses are accounted for on a cash received and cash paid basis. (3, 21, Appendix C)

Cash budget: a projection of cash receipts and cash payments for a future period of time. (Also called a cash flow forecast.) (26)

Cash disbursements journal, see **Cash payments journal** (6)

Cash equivalents: short-term (ninety days or less), highly liquid investments, including money market accounts, commercial paper, and U.S. Treasury bills. (18)

Cash flow forecast: a forecast or budget that shows the firm's projected ending cash balance and the cash position for each month of the year so that periods of high or low cash availability can be anticipated; also called a cash budget. (26)

Cash payments journal: a multicolumn special-purpose journal in which disbursements of cash are recorded. (Also called cash disbursements journal.) (6)

Cash receipts journal: a multicolumn special-purpose journal in which transactions involving receipts of cash are recorded. (6)

Cash short or over: an account debited for cash shortages and credited for overages that result from the handing of cash; can call management's attention to irregular activity. (7)

Certified internal auditor (CIA): professional certification for auditors who carry out their work from within a company. (1)

Certified management accountant (CMA): professional certification awarded to qualified management accountants by the Institute of Certified Management Accountants. (1)

Certified public accountant (CPA): public accountants who have met stringent licensing requirements as set by the individual states. (1)

Chart of accounts: a numbering scheme that assigns a unique number to each account to facilitate finding the account in the ledger; also the list of account numbers and titles. (2, 8)

Check: a written order to a bank to pay the amount specified from funds on deposit. (7)

Check authorization: a form prepared by the accounting department authorizing the payment of an invoice; supported by a purchase order, invoice, and receiving report. (7)

Check register: a special-purpose journal used in a voucher system to record each expenditure made by check. (7)

Classification: the process of assigning all the transactions in which a business engages to the appropriate accounts. (2)

Classified financial statements: financial statements divided into useful subcategories. (8)

Clearing entries, see Closing entries (4)

Closely held corporation: a corporation whose stock is owned by a few individuals and whose securities are not publicly traded. (20)

Closing entries: journal entries made at the end of the accounting period that set the stage for the next accounting period by clearing the temporary accounts of their balances. (4)

Combined balance sheet: the financial statement prepared for all fund types and account groups in governmental accounting. (Appendix D)

Combined statement of changes in financial position: the financial statement prepared for all proprietary fund types in governmental accounting. (Appendix D)

Combined statement of revenues, expenditures, and changes in fund balances—all governmental funds: the financial statement prepared for all fund types in governmental accounting; revenues and expenditures are measured according to the principles of modified accrual accounting. (Appendix D)

Combined statement of revenues, expenditures, and changes in fund balances—budget and actual—general and special revenue funds: the financial statement that presents budget and actual amounts for general and special revenue fund types in governmental accounting. (Appendix D)

Combined statement of revenues, expenses, and changes in retained earnings (or equity): the financial statement prepared for all propriety fund types in governmental accounting; prepared on the full accrual basis. (Appendix D)

Common cost, see Joint cost. (25)

Common-size statement: a statement in which all components of the statement are shown as a percentage of a total in the statement; results from applying vertical analysis. (19)

Common stock: the stock representing the most basic rights to ownership of a corporation. (15)

Common stock equivalents: convertible stocks or bonds whose conversion feature is an important part of determining the original issue price. (16)

Comparability: the qualitative characteristic of accounting information that presents information in such a way that the decision maker can recognize similarities, differences, and trends over time, and/or make comparisons with other companies. (8)

Comparative financial statements: financial statements in which data for two or more years are presented in adjacent columnar form. (8)

Compatibility principle: a principle of systems design that holds that the design of the system must be in harmony with organizational and human factors of a business. (6)

Compensating balance: a minimum account that a bank requires a company to keep in its bank account as part of a credit-granting arrangement. (9)

Complex capital structure: a capital structure with additional securities (convertible stocks and bonds) that can be converted into common stock. (16)

Compound entry: a journal entry that has more than one debit and/or credit entry. (2)

Compound interest: the interest cost for two or more periods, if one assumes that after each period, the interest of that period is added to the amount on which interest is computed in future periods. (Appendix A)

Comprehensive income: the change in equity (net assets) of an entity during a period from transactions and other events and circumstances from nonowner sources. It includes all changes in equity during a period except those changes resulting from investments by owners and distributions to withdrawals by owners. (8)

Computer: an electronic tool for the rapid collection, organization, and communication of large amounts of information. (1)

Computer-integrated manufacturing (CIM) a production process in which all parts of the system are fully integrated through computer technology. (Appendix E)

Computer numerically controlled machines (CNC): stand-alone pieces of computer-driven equipment used in manufacturing, including operating machines, computer-assisted design technology, and robots. (Appendix E)

Computer operator: the person who runs the computer. (6)

Condensed financial statement: a statement presenting only the major categories of a financial statement. (8)

Conglomerate: a company that operates in more than one industry; a diversified company. (19)

Conservatism: an accounting convention mandating that, in the face of two equally acceptable alternatives, accountants exercise caution and choose the procedure least likely to overstate assets or income. (8)

Consignment: goods placed on the premises of one company (the consignee) by the owner of the goods (the consignor) but not included in physical inventory because title to the goods remains with the owner until the goods are sold. (10)

Consistency: an accounting convention requiring that a particular accounting procedure, once adopted, will not be changed from period to period unless users are informed of the change. (8)

Consolidated financial statements: the combined financial statements of a parent company and its subsidiaries. (20)

Constant dollar accounting: the restatement of historical cost statements for general price level changes with the result that all amounts are stated in dollars of uniform general purchasing power. (21)

Contingent liability: a potential liability that can develop into a real liability if a possible subsequent event occurs. (9, 11)

Continuity issue: the difficulty associated with not knowing how long the business entity will last. (3)

Contra account: an account whose balance is subtracted from an associated account in the financial statements. (3)

Contributed or paid-in capital: that part of the owners' equity section of a corporation's balance sheet representing the investments made by the stockholders. (15)

Contribution margin: the excess of revenues over all variable costs related to a particular sales volume. (25)

Control: the process of seeing that plans are carried out; the ability of the investing company to determine the operating and financial policies of another company through ownership of more than 50 percent of its voting stock. (1, 20)

Control (of parent over subsidiary): in connection with long-term investments, the ability of the investing company to determine the operating and financial policies of the investee company. (20)

Control environment: the overall attitude, awareness, and actions of the owners and management of a business, as reflected in philosophy and operating style, organizational structure, methods of assigning authority and responsibility, and personnel policies and practices. (7)

Controllable costs: those costs that result from a particular manager's actions and decisions and over which he or she has full control. (25)

Controllable overhead variance: the difference between actual overhead costs incurred and factory overhead budgeted for the level of production achieved. (27)

Controlling (or control) account: an account in the general ledger that summarizes the total balance of a group of related accounts in a subsidiary ledger. (6, 23)

Control principle: a principle of systems design that holds an accounting system must provide all the features of internal control needed to safeguard assets and ensure the reliability of data. (6)

Control procedures: additional procedures and policies established by management to provide assurance that the objectives of internal control are achieved. (7)

Conversion costs: the combined total of direct labor and factory overhead costs incurred by a production department or other work center. (24)

Convertible bonds: bonds that may be exchanged for other securities of the corporation, usually common stock. (17)

Convertible preferred stock: preferred stock that may be exchanged at the option of the holder for common stock. (15)

Corporation: a body of persons granted a charter legally recognizing it as a separate entity having its own rights, privileges, and liabilities distinct from those of its owners. (1, 15)

Cost: exchange price associated with a business transaction at the point of recognition; original cost; historical cost. (2)

Cost allocation (assignment): the process of assigning a specific cost or pool of costs to a specific cost objective or objectives. (25)

Cost behavior: the way costs respond to changes in activity or volume. (25)

Cost-benefit principle: a principle of systems design that holds that the value or benefits from a system and its information output must be equal or greater than its cost. (6, 8)

Cost center: any organizational segment or area of activity for which there is a reason to accumulate costs. (25)

Cost driver: any activity in manufacturing that causes costs to be incurred. (Appendix E)

Cost flow: the association of costs with their assumed flow within the operations of a company. (10)

Cost method: a method of accounting for long-term investments when the investor owns less than 20 percent of the voting stock of the other company; the investor records the investment at cost and recognizes dividends as income when they are received. (20)

Cost objective: the destination of an assigned or allocated cost. (25)

Cost of equity capital: the rate of return to the investor that maintains the stock's value in the marketplace. (28)

Cost of goods manufactured: a term used in the statement of costs of goods manufactured that represents the total manufacturing costs attached to units of product completed during an accounting period. (22)

Cost of goods sold: the amount paid for goods that were sold during an accounting period. (5)

Cost principle: the principle of recording the cost of assets when they are acquired so that their "value" is held at that level until they are sold, expire, or are consumed; a principle of systems design that defines cost as the value of

an item at the time it was brought into or taken out of the business entity. (2, 6)

Cost summary schedule: a process costing schedule that facilitates the distribution of all production costs incurred and accumulated during the period among the units of output, either those completed and transferred out of the department or those units still in process at period end. (24)

Cost-volume-profit (C-V-P) analysis: an analysis based on the relationships among operating cost, sales volume and revenue, and target net income; used as a planning device to predict one factor when the other two factors are known. (25)

Coupon bonds: bonds whose owners are not registered with the issuing corporation but that bear interest coupons stating the amount of interest and the payment date. (17)

Credit: the right side of an account. (2)

Crossfooting: horizontal addition and subtraction of adjacent columns on the same row. (4)

Cumulative effect of an accounting change: the effect that a new accounting principle would have had on net income of prior periods if it had been used instead of the old principle. (16)

Cumulative preferred stock: preferred stock on which unpaid dividends accumulate over time and which must be satisfied in any given year before a dividend may be paid to common stockholders. (15)

Current assets: cash or other assets that are reasonably expected to be realized in cash, or sold, or consumed during a normal operating cycle of a business or within one year if the operating cycle is shorter than one year. (8)

Current liabilities: obligations due to be paid within the normal operating cycle of the business or within a year, whichever is longer. (8, 11)

Current ratio: a measure of liquidity; current assets divided by current liabilities; used as an indicator of a company's liquidity and short-term debt-paying ability. (8, 19)

Current value accounting: a method of accounting that recognizes the effects of specific price changes on the financial statements. (21)

C-V-P analysis: see **Cost-volume-profit analysis.** (25)

Data processing: the means by which the accounting system collects data, organizes them into useful forms, and issues the resulting information to users. (6)

Debenture bonds, see **Unsecured bonds** (17)

Debit: the left side of an account. (2)

Debt-to-equity ratio: a ratio that measures the relationship of assets provided by creditors to the amount provided by stockholders; total liabilities divided by owner's equity. Used to measure the relationship of debt financing to equity financing, or the extent to which a company is leveraged. (8, 19)

Declining-balance method: an accelerated method of depreciation. (12)

Deductions from gross income: certain personal deductions allowed in computing taxable income. (Appendix C)

Deferral: the postponement of the recognition of an expense already paid or of a revenue already received. (3)

Deferred income taxes: the difference between the Income Taxes Expense and the current Income Taxes Payable accounts. (16)

Deferred revenues: obligations for goods or services that the company must deliver in return for an advance payment from a customer. (See also **Unearned revenues**) (11)

Deficit: a debit balance in the Retained Earnings account. (16)

Definitely determinable liability: a liability that is determined by contract or statute and that can be measured precisely. (11)

Deflation: a downward change in the general price level. (21)

Depletion: the proportional allocation of the cost of a natural resource to the units removed; the exhaustion of a natural resource through mining, cutting, pumping, or otherwise using up the resource. (12)

Deposits in transit: deposits mailed or taken to the bank but not received by the bank in time to be recorded before preparation of the monthly statement. (7)

Deposit ticket: a document used to make a deposit in a bank. (7)

Depreciable cost: the cost of an asset less its residual value. (12)

Depreciation (depreciation expense): the periodic allocation of the cost of a tangible long-lived asset over its estimated useful life. (3, 12)

Direct costs: production costs that can be conveniently and economically traced to specific products or cost objective(s). (22, 25)

Direct costing, see **Variable costing.** (28)

Direct charge-off method: a method of accounting for uncollectible accounts by debiting expenses directly when bad debts are discovered instead of using the allowance method; a method that violates the matching rule but is required for federal income tax computations. (9)

Direct labor costs: all labor costs for specific work performed on products that can be conveniently and economically traced to end products. (22)

Direct labor efficiency variance: the difference between actual hours worked and standard hours allowed for the good units produced, multiplied by the standard labor rate. (27)

Direct labor rate standards: the hourly labor cost per function or job classification that is expected to exist during the next accounting period. (27)

Direct labor rate variance: the difference between the actual labor rate paid and the standard labor rate, multiplied by the actual hours worked. (27)

Direct labor time standard: an hourly expression of the time it takes for each department, machine, or process to complete production on one unit or one batch of output; based on current time and motion studies of workers and machines and past employee/machine performances. (27)

Direct materials: materials that become an integral part of the finished product and can be conveniently and economically traced to specific units of productive output. (22)

Direct materials price standard: a carefully derived estimate or projected amount of what a particular type of material will cost when purchased during the next accounting period. (27)

Direct materials price variance: the difference between the actual price paid for materials and the standard price, multiplied by the actual quantity purchased. (27)

Direct materials quantity standard: an estimate of the expected quantity usage that is influenced by product engineering specifications, quality of direct materials, age and productivity of the machinery, and the quality and experience of the workforce. (27)

Direct materials quantity variance: the difference between the actual quantity of materials used and the standard quantity that should have been used, multiplied by the standard price. (27)

Direct method: the procedure for converting the income statement from an accrual basis to a cash basis by adjusting each item in the income statement separately. (18)

Discontinued operations: segments of a business that are no longer part of the ongoing operations of the company. (16)

Discount: (verb) to take out the interest on a promissory note in advance; (noun) the amount by which the face value of a bond exceeds the issue price; for bonds issued when the market rate of interest is greater than the face interest rate. (9, 17)

Discounted cash flow: the process of discounting future cash flows back to the present using an anticipated discount rate. (28)

Dishonored note: a promissory note that the maker cannot or will not pay at the maturity date. (9)

Disposal value, see **Residual equity** (15)

Dissolution: a change in the original association of the partners in a partnership resulting from such events as the admission, withdrawal, or death of a partner. (14)

Diversified company, see **Conglomerate**

Dividend: a distribution of assets of a corporation to its stockholders. (15, 16)

Dividends in arrears: the accumulated unpaid dividends on cumulative preferred stock from prior years. (15)

Dividends yield: the current annual dividend divided by the current market price of a stock; used as a measure of the current return to an investor in a stock. (19)

Double-declining balance method: an accelerated method of depreciation, related to the declining-balance method, under which the fixed rate used in the method is double the straight-line rate; this rate is the maximum allowable for income tax purposes. (12)

Double-entry system: an accounting system in which each transaction must be recorded with at least one debit and one credit in such a way that the total dollar amount of debits and total dollar amount of credits equal each other. (2)

Double taxation: a term referring to the fact that earnings of a corporation are taxed twice, both as the net income of the corporation and as the dividends distributed to the stockholders. (15, Appendix C)

Duration of note: length of time in days between the making of a promissory note and its maturity date. (9)

Early extinguishment of debt: the purchase by a company of its own bonds on the open market in order to retire the debt at less than face value. (19)

Earnings per share (net earnings per common share or net income per share): item on corporate income statements that shows the net income earned on each share of common stock; net income divided by the weighted average number of common shares and common share equivalents outstanding; used as a measure of profitability and a means of comparison among stocks. (8, 16, 19)

Effective interest method: a method of amortizing bond discounts or premiums in which a constant interest rate, the effective rate (market rate) at the time the bonds were issued, is applied to the carrying value of the bonds at the beginning of each interest period. (17)

Effective rate: the interest rate used to amortize bond interest discounts and premiums under the effective interest rate method; equal to the market rate of interest at the time the bonds are issued (17)

Eliminations: adjustments that appear on consolidated work sheets to eliminate transactions between parent and subsidiary companies. (20)

Employee earnings record: a record of earnings and withholdings for a single employee. (11)

Encumbrance accounting: in governmental accounting, the recording of anticipated, as well as actual, expenditures under the current period's appropriations. (Appendix D)

Ending inventory: merchandise on hand for sale to customers at the end of the accounting period. (5)

Equity: the residual interest in the assets of an entity that remains after deducting its liabilities. (1)

Equity method: a method of accounting for long-term investments in which the investor records its share of the investee's periodic net income or loss as an increase or decrease in the Investment account. (20)

Equivalent production, see **Equivalent units** (24)

Equivalent units: a measure of productive output of units for a period of time, expressed in terms of fully completed or equivalent whole units produced; partially completed units are restated in terms of equivalent whole units; also called equivalent production. (24)

Estimated liability: a definite obligation of the firm, the exact amount of which cannot be determined until a later date. (11)

Estimated tax: an amount paid in advance by a taxpayer in anticipation of income not subject to withholding. (Appendix C)

Estimated useful life: the total number of service units expected from a long-term asset. (12)

Evaluation: the examination of the entire decision system with a view to improving it. (1)

Excess capacity: machinery and equipment purchased in excess of needs so that extra capacity is available on a standby basis during peak usage periods or when other machinery is down for repair. (25)

Exchange gains or losses: changes due to exchange rate fluctuations that are reported on the consolidated income statement. (21)

Exchange rate: the value of one currency in terms of another. (21)

Exchange transaction: when used in connection with the statement of changes in financial position, an exchange of a long-term asset for a long-term liability. (18)

Ex-dividend: a description of capital stock when the right to a dividend already declared on the stock remains with the person who sells the stock and does not transfer to the person who buys it. (15)

Exemption: a type of deduction from adjusted gross income based on personal characteristics and number of dependents. (Appendix C)

Expenditure: a payment or incurrence of an obligation to take a future payment for an asset or service rendered; in governmental accounting, decreases in fund resources caused by transactions other than interfund transfers. (13, Appendix D)

Expenses: decreases in owner's equity that result from operating the business; outflows or other using up of assets or incurrences of liabilities from delivering or producing goods, rendering services, or carrying out other activities that constitute the entity's ongoing major or central operations. (1, 2)

Extraordinary item: an event or transaction that is distinguished by its unusual nature and the infrequency of its occurrence. (16)

Extraordinary repairs: repairs that affect the estimated residual value or estimated useful life of an asset. (13)

Face interest rate: the rate of interest paid to bondholders based on the face value or principal of the bonds. (17)

Factory overhead budget: a detailed schedule of anticipated manufacturing costs, other than direct materials and direct labor costs, that must be incurred to meet the production expectations of a future period. (26)

Factory overhead costs: a varied collection of production-related costs that cannot be practically or conveniently traced to end products. (22)

Fiduciary funds: in governmental accounting, term applied to trust and agency funds. (Appendix D)

Financial accounting: accounting information that is communicated to those outside the organization for their use in evaluating the entity as well as being used internally. (1)

Financial Accounting Standards Board (FASB): body that has responsibility for developing and issuing rules on accounting practice; issues Statements of Financial Accounting Standards. (1)

Financial equities: common stock and other forms of ownership. (11)

Financial instruments: any contract that results in an asset in one entity's records and a liability in another entity's records. (11)

Financial liabilities: loans, mortgages, bonds, leases, and other forms of debt financing. (11)

Financial plan of action, see budget 26)

Financial position: the economic resources belonging to a company and the claims against those resources at a point in time. (1)

Financial statement analysis: the collective term used for the techniques that show significant relationships in financial statements and that facilitate comparisons from period to period and among companies. (19)

Financial statements: the primary means of communicating important accounting information to users of financial reports. (1)

Financing activities: business activities that involve obtaining or returning resources from or to owners and providing them with a return on their investment. (18)

Finished goods inventory: an inventory account unique to the manufacturing or production area, to which the costs assigned to all completed products are transferred. The balance at period-end represents all manufacturing costs assigned to goods completed but not sold as of that date. (22)

First-in, first-out (FIFO) method: an inventory costing method under which the cost of the first items purchased are assigned to the first items sold and the costs of the last items purchased are assigned to the items remaining in inventory. (10)

Fiscal year: any twelve-month accounting period used by an economic entity. (3)

Fixed assets: another name, no longer in wide use, for long-term nonmonetary assets. (12)

Fixed cost: a cost that remains constant in total within a relevant range of volume or activity. (25)

Fixed manufacturing costs: production-related costs that remain relatively constant in amount during the accounting period and vary little in relation to increases or decreases in production. (22)

Flexibility principle: a principle of systems design that holds that the accounting system should be sufficiently flexible to accommodate growth in the volume of transactions and organizational changes in the business. (6)

Flexible budget: a summary of expected costs for a range of different activity levels, geared to changes in the level of productive output. (27)

Flexible manufacturing system (FMS): an integrated set of computerized machines and systems designed to complete a series of operations automatically. (Appendix E)

FOB destination: term relating to transportation charges meaning that the supplier bears the transportation costs to the destination. (5)

FOB shipping point: term relating to transportation charges meaning that the buyer bears the transportation costs from the point of origin. (65)

Footing: (noun) a memorandum total of a column of numbers; (verb, to foot) to total a column of numbers. (2)

Franchise: the right to an exclusive territory or market. (13)

Fraudulent financial reporting: the intentional preparation of misleading financial statements. (8)

Freight in: transportation charges on merchandise purchased for resale; transportation in. (5)

Full-costing: a method of accounting for oil and gas development and exploration under which the costs associated with both successful and unsuccessful explorations are recorded as assets and depleted over the useful life of the producing resources. (13)

Full disclosure: an accounting convention requiring that financial statements and their accompanying footnotes contain all information relevant to the user's understanding of the situation. (8)

Fully diluted earnings per share: net income applicable to common stock divided by the sum of the weighted-average common stock and common stock equivalents and other potentially dilutive securities. See also **Earnings per common share**. (16)

Functional currency: currency of the country where the subsidiary carries on most of its business. (21)

Fund: a fiscal and accounting entity in governmental and not-for-profit accounting; shows the financial position and results of operations during a period and compliance with legal requirements of the state or local government. (Appendix D)

Funds: equivalent to working capital when used in connection with the statement of changes in financial position. (18)

Future value: the amount that an investment will be worth at a future date if invested at compound interest. (Appendix A)

General and administrative (G&A) expense budget: a detailed plan of operating expenses, other than those of the manufacturing and selling functions, that are needed to support the overall operations of the business for a future period of time. (26)

General fixed assets account group: entity used to account for all long-term assets of a governmental unit except long-term assets related to specific proprietary or trust funds; does not record depreciation. (Appendix D)

General fund: a fund in governmental accounting that accounts for all financial resources not accounted for in any other fund. (Appendix D)

General journal: the simplest and most flexible type of journal. (2)

General ledger: the book or file that contains all or groups of the company's accounts. (2)

General long-term debt group: entity used to account for all long-term liabilities of a governmental unit except for long-term liabilities related to specific proprietary or trust funds. (Appendix D)

Generally accepted accounting principles (GAAP): the conventions, rules, and procedures necessary to define accepted accounting practice at a particular time. (1)

General price level: a price level that reflects the price changes of a group of goods or services. (21)

General-purpose external financial statements: means by which the information accumulated and processed in the financial accounting system is periodically communicated to those persons, especially investors and creditors, who use it outside the enterprise. (8)

Going concern (continuity): the assumption that unless there is evidence to the contrary, the business will continue to operate for an indefinite period. (5)

Goods available for sale: the total goods during the year that could have been sold to customers; the beginning merchandise inventory plus net purchases. (5)

Goods flow: the actual, physical movement of inventory goods in the operations of a company. (10)

Goodwill (goodwill from consolidation): the excess of the cost of a group of assets (usually a business) over the market value of the business's assets individually; the amount paid for a subsidiary that exceeds the fair value of the subsidiary's assets less its liabilities. (13, 20)

Government Accounting Standards Board (GASB): board established in 1984 under the same governing body as FASB with responsibility for issuing accounting standards for state and local governments. (1)

Governmental funds: in governmental accounting, a term applied to the general fund, special revenue funds, capital projects funds, and the debt service fund. (Appendix D)

Gross income: income from all sources, less allowable exclusions. (Appendix C)

Gross margin from sales: the amount of revenues from sales, after deducting cost of goods sold, that is available for operating expenses. (5)

Gross method: system of recording purchases initially at the gross purchase price; does not allow for discounts lost, only discounts taken. (5, 15)

Gross payroll: a measure of the total wages or salary earned by an employee before any deductions are subtracted. This amount is also used to determine total manufacturing labor costs. (22)

Gross profit method: used to estimate the value of inventory; assumes that the ratio of gross margin for a business remains relatively stable from year to year. (10)

Gross sales: total sales for cash and on credit for a given accounting period. (5)

Group depreciation: the grouping of items of similar plant assets together for purposes of calculating depreciation. (12)

Hardware: all the equipment needed for the operation of a computer data processing system. (6)

Horizontal analysis: a technique for analyzing financial statements that involves the computation of dollar amount changes and percentage changes from year to year. (19)

Ideal capacity, see **Theoretical capacity.** (25)

Imprest system: a petty cash system in which a petty cash fund is established at a fixed amount of cash and is periodically reimbursed for the exact amount necessary to bring it back to the fixed amount. (7)

Income from operations: the excess of gross margin from sales over operating expenses. (8)

Income statement: a financial statement that summarizes the amount of revenues earned and expenses incurred by a business entity over a period of time. (1)

Income summary: a temporary account used during the closing process in which all revenues and expenses are summarized before the net income or loss is transferred to the capital account. (4)

Income tax allocation: an accounting method designed to accrue income tax expense on the basis of accounting income whenever there are differences in accounting and taxable income. (16)

Income taxes: an account that represents the expense for federal and state income tax on corporate income; this account appears only on income statements of corporations; also called income taxes expense or provision for income taxes. (8)

Incremental analysis: a decision analysis format that highlights only relevant decision information or the differences between costs and revenues under two or more alternative courses of action. (28)

Index number: in trend analysis, a number against which changes in related items over a period of time are measured; calculated by setting the base year equal to 100 percent and calculating other years in relation to the base year. (19)

Indirect costs: production costs that are not conveniently and economically traced to specific products or cost objectives and must be assigned using some kind of allocation method. (22, 25)

Indirect labor: labor costs for production-related activities that cannot be associated with, or are not conveniently and economically traceable to, end products and must be assigned by some allocation method. (22)

Indirect materials: less significant materials and other production supplies that cannot be conveniently or economically assigned to specific products and must be assigned by some allocation method. (22)

Indirect method: the procedure for converting the income statement from an accrual basis to a cash basis by adjusting net income for items that do not affect cash flows, including depreciation, amortization, depletion, gains, losses, and changes in current assets and current liabilities. (18)

Inflation: an upward change in the general price level. (21)

Installment accounts receivable: accounts receivable that are payable in a series of time payments. (9)

Intangible assets: long-term assets that have no physical substance but have a value based on rights or privileges accruing to the owner. (8, 12, 21)

Interest: the cost of borrowing money or the return for lending money, depending on whether one is the borrower or the lender. (9, Appendix A)

Interest coverage ratio: net income before taxes plus interest expense, divided by interest expense; used as a measure of the degree of protection creditors have from a default on interest payments. (19)

Interest earned: payment by a bank of interest earned on a company's average balance which is reported by the bank on the bank statement. (7)

Interim financial statements: financial statements prepared on a condensed basis for an accounting period of less than one year. (8, 19)

Internal control: the plan of organization and all of the policies and procedures adopted within a business to safeguard its assets, check the accuracy and reliability of its accounting data, promote operational efficiency, and encourage adherence to prescribed managerial policies. (7)

Internal control structure: a structure established to safeguard the assets of a business and provide reliable accounting records; consists of the control environment, the accounting system, and the control procedures. (7)

Internal Revenue Service (IRS): federal agency that interprets and enforces U.S. tax laws governing the assessment and collection of revenue for operating the government. (1)

Inventory cost: the price paid or consideration given to acquire an asset; includes invoice price less purchases discounts, freight or transportation in, and applicable insurance, taxes, and tariffs. (10)

Inventory turnover: the cost of goods sold divided by average inventory; used as a ratio to measure the relative size of inventory. (19)

Investing activities: business activities that include the acquiring and selling of long-term assets, the acquiring and selling of marketable securities other than cash equivalents, and the making and collecting of loans. (18)

Investments: assets, generally of a long-term nature, that are not used in the normal operation of a business and that management does not intend to convert to cash within the next year. (8)

Invoice: a form sent or delivered to the purchaser by the vendor (seller) giving the quantity and price as well as a description of goods delivered and the terms of payment. (7)

Issued stock: shares of stock sold or otherwise transferred to the stockholders. (15)

Item-by-item method: a method of applying the lower-of-cost-or-market rule to inventory pricing; cost and market are compared for each item in the inventory, with each item then valued at its lower price. (10)

Job card: a labor card supplementing the time card, on which each employee's time on a specific job is recorded; used to support an employee's daily time recorded on the time card and to assign labor costs to specific jobs or batches of products. (22)

Job order: a customer order for a specific number of specially designed, made-to-order products. (23)

Job order cost accounting system: a product costing system used by companies making one-of-a-kind or special-order products. (23)

Job order cost card: a document maintained for each job or work order in process, on which all costs of that job are recorded and accumulated as the job order is being worked on. These cards make up the subsidiary ledger of the Work in Process Inventory Control account. (23)

Joint cost: a cost that relates to two or more products produced from a common input or raw material and that can be assigned only by means of arbitrary cost allocation after the products become identifiable (also called a common cost). (25)

Journal: a chronological record of all transactions; place where transactions are first recorded. (2)

Journal entry: a separate entry in the journal that is used to record a single transaction. (2)

Journalizing: the process of recording transactions in a journal. (2)

Just-in-time (JIT): an overall operating philosophy of management in which all resources, including materials, personnel, and facilities, are used in a manner that preserves a continuous work flow, with each part of the entire production process working in concert. (Appendix E)

Labor budget: a detailed schedule that identifies the labor needs for a future period and the labor costs associated with those needs. (26)

Last-in, first-out (LIFO) method: an inventory costing method under which the costs of the last items purchased are assigned to the first items sold and the cost of the inventory is composed of the cost of items from the oldest purchases. (10)

Leasehold: a right to occupy land or buildings under a long-term rental contract. (13)

Leasehold improvement: an improvement to leased property that becomes the property of the lessor at the end of the lease. (13)

Ledger: a book or file of all of a company's accounts, arranged as in the chart of accounts. (2)

Ledger account form: a form of the account that has four columns, one for debit entries, one for credit entries, and two columns (debit and credit) for showing the balance of the account; used in the general ledger. (2)

Legal capital: the minimum amount that can be reported as contributed capital; usually equal to par value or stated value. (15)

Leverage: the use of debt financing; the amount of debt financing in relation to equity financing is measured by the debt-to-equity ratio (19)

Liabilities: probable future sacrifices of economic benefits arising from present obligations of a particular entity to transfer assets or provide services to other entitites in the future as a result of past transactions or events. (1, 11)

License: official or legal permission to do or own a specific thing. (13)

LIFO liquidation: the reduction of inventory below previous levels so that income is increased by the amount that current prices exceed the historical cost of the inventory under LIFO. (10)

Limited life: the characteristic of a partnership shown when certain events such as the admission, withdrawal, or death of a partner can terminate the partnership. (14)

Limited partnership: a partnership formed for a specific objective in which a general partner with unlimited liability operates the partnership business and the investors or limited partners generally have their liabilities limited to their investments in the partnership. (14)

Liquidating dividend: a dividend that exceeds retained earnings. (15)

Liquidation: the process of ending a business; entails selling assets, paying liabilities, and distributing any remaining assets to the partners. (14)

Liquidity: the position of having enough funds on hand to pay a company's bill when they are due and provide for unanticipated needs for cash. (8)

Long-term liabilities: debts of a business that fall due more than one year ahead, beyond the normal operating cycle, or are to be paid out of noncurrent assets. (8, 11)

Long-term nonmonetary assets: assets that (1) have a useful life of more than one year, (2) are acquired for use in the operation of the business, (3) are not intended for resale to customers; fixed assets. (10, 12)

Lower-of-cost-or-market (LCM) rule: a method of valuing inventory at an amount below cost if the replacement (market) value is less than cost. (10)

Major category method: a method of applying the lower-of-cost-or-market to inventory pricing; the total cost and total market for each category of items are compared, with each category then valued at its lower amount. (10)

Make-or-buy decision: a decision analysis that identifies those cost and revenue elements relevant to deciding whether to make or buy some or all parts used in product assembly operations. (28)

Management: the group of people in a business who have overall responsibility for operating the business and for achieving the company's goals. (1)

Management accounting: the aspect of accounting that consists of specific information gathering and reporting concepts and accounting procedures that, when applied to a company's financial and production data, will satisfy internal management's needs for product costing information, data used for planning and control of operations, and special reports and analyses used to support management's decisions. (1, 22)

Management advisory services: consulting services, offered by public accountants. (1)

Management by exception: a review process whereby management locates and analyzes only the areas of unusually good or bad performance. (27)

Management information system: the interconnected subsystems that provide the information necessary to operate a business. (1)

Manual data processing: a system of accounting in which each transaction is entered manually from a source document into the general journal (input device) and each debit and credit is posted manually to the correct ledger (processor and memory device) for the eventual preparation of financial statements (output device). (6)

Manufacturing cost flow: the flow of manufacturing costs (direct materials, direct labor, and factory overhead) from their incurrence through the Materials, Work in Process, and Finished Goods Inventory accounts to the Cost of Goods Sold account. (22)

Marginal tax rates: the tax rate that applies to the last increment of taxable income. (Appendix C)

Market: in inventory valuation, the current replacement cost of inventory. (10)

Marketable securities: investment in securities which are readily marketable; short-term investments. (9)

Market interest rate: the rate of interest paid in the market by bond investors for bonds of similar risk. (17)

Market risk: the volatility of the price of a stock in relation to the volatility of the prices of other stocks. (19)

Market value: the price investors are willing to pay for a share of stock on the open market. (16)

Master budget: an integrated set of departmental or functional period budgets that have been consolidated into forecasted financial statements for the entire company. (26)

Matching rule: the rule of accounting that revenues must be assigned to the accounting period in which the goods were sold or the services rendered, and expenses must be assigned to the accounting period in which they were used to produce revenue; the rule underlying accrual accounting. (3)

Materiality: an accounting convention that requires an item or event in a financial statement to be important to the decisions made by users of the financial statements. (8)

Materials inventory account: an inventory account made up of the balances of materials and supplies on hand at a given time. Also called the Stores, Raw Materials Inventory, or Materials Inventory Control account. (22)

Materials purchase/usage budget: a detailed plan developed from information on the production budget that identifies the number and timing of raw materials and parts to be purchased to meet production needs. (A merchandise purchasing budget is used by retail businesses.) (26)

Materials requirements planning (MRP): a computer-assisted planning process that anticipates raw materials needs, minimizes materials inventory levels, triggers materials purchase orders, and directs the movement of materials and products within the manufacturing process. (26, Appendix E)

Materials requisition: a document that must be completed and approved before raw materials are issued to production. This form is essential to the control of raw materials and contains such information as the types and quantities of raw materials and supplies needed and the supervisor's approval signature. (22)

Maturity date: the due date of a promissory note. (9)

Maturity value: the total proceeds of a promissory note including principal and interest at the maturity date. (9)

Merchandise inventory: goods on hand and available for sale to customers. (5, 10)

Minority interest: the amount appearing in the stockholders' equity section of a consolidated balance sheet representing the holdings of stockholders who own less than 50 percent of the voting stock of a subsidiary. (20)

Miscellaneous charges and credits: bank charges for services such as collection and payment of promissory notes, stopping payment on checks, and printing checks. (7)

Mixed cost: a cost category that results when more than one type of cost is charged to the same general ledger account. The Repairs and Maintenance account is an example of a mixed cost account. (25)

Modified accrual accounting: a government accounting system that attempts to provide an accurate measure of increases and decreases in resources available (especially in cash) to fulfill government obligations. (Appendix D)

Money measure: the recording of all business transactions in the form of money. (1)

Mortgage: a type of long-term debt secured by real property that is paid in equal monthly installments. (17)

Multinational corporations: corporations that do business or operate in more than one country (also, transnational corporations). (21)

Multistep form: a form of the income statement that arrives at net income in steps. (8)

Mutual agency: the authority of partners to act as agents of the partnership within the scope of normal operations of the business. (14)

Natural resources: long-term assets purchased for the physical substance that can be taken from them and used up, rather than for the value of their location. (12)

Net assets: the total of assets remaining after deducting liabilities; sometimes equated with owner's equity. (1)

Net income (loss): the net increase in owner's equity resulting from the profit seeking operations of a company; net income = revenue – expenses. (1)

Net income per share, see **Earnings per common share** (8, 16, 19)

Net loss: the net decrease in owner's equity that develops when expenses exceed revenues. (1)

Net method: recording purchases initially at the net price; allows a business to identify discounts lost, as well as discounts taken. (5)

Net of taxes: the effect of applicable taxes (usually income taxes) on an item when determining the overall effect of the item on the financial statements. (16)

Net payroll: the amount paid to the employee (cash or check) after all payroll deductions have been subtracted from gross wages. (22)

Net present-value method: a capital investment evaluation method based on future cash flows that are discounted back to their present value before being used to support a capital expenditure decision (also called present value method). (28)

Net purchases: under the periodic inventory method, gross purchases less purchases discounts, purchases returns and allowances, plus freight charges on the purchases. (5)

Net realizable value: the amount for which an asset can be sold. (21)

Net sales: gross proceeds from sales of merchandise less sales returns and allowances and sales discounts. (5)

Neutrality: carrying out generally accepted accounting principles as faithfully as possible, the main concern being relevance and reliability of the accounting information rather than the effect on a particular interest. (8)

Nominal accounts: temporary accounts showing the accumulation of revenue and expenses for an accounting period only; at the end of the accounting period, these account balances are transferred to owner's equity. (3)

Noncash investing and financing transactions: significant investing and financing transactions that do not involve an actual cash inflow or outflow but involve only long-term assets, long-term liabilities, or stockholders' equity, such as the exchange of a long-term asset for a long-term liability or the settlement of a debt by the issue of capital stock. (18)

Noncumulative preferred stock: preferred stock on which the dividend may lapse and does not have to be paid if not paid within a given year. (15)

No-par stock: capital stock that does not have a par value. (15)

Non-value added activity: a process that adds costs to a product but does not increase its market activity; eliminated from the production and distribution processes in the just-in-time approach to manufacturing. (Appendix D)

Normal balance: the balance one would expect an account to have; the usual balance of an account; also the side (debit or credit) that increases account. (2)

Normal capacity: the average annual level of operating capacity that is required to satisfy anticipated sales demand; adjusted to reflect seasonal business factors and operating cycles. (25)

Notes payable: collective term for promissory notes owed by the maker to other entities. (9)

Notes receivable: collective term for promissory notes held by the entity (payee) to whom payment is promised. (9)

Notes to the financial statements: a section of a corporate annual report that contains notes that aid the user in interpreting some of the items in the financial statements. (8)

Notice of protest: a sworn statement that a promissory note was presented to the maker for payment and the maker refused to pay. (9)

NSF (non sufficient funds) check: a check that is not paid when the depositor's bank presents it for payment to the maker's bank. (7)

Obsolescence: the process of becoming out of date; a contributor, together with physical deterioration, to the limited useful life of tangible assets. (12)

On-line processing: a type of computer systems design in which input devices and random-access storage files are tied directly to the computer, enabling transactions to be entered into the records as they occur and data to be retrieved as needed. (6)

Operating activities: business activities that include the cash effects of transactions and other events that enter into the determination of net income. (18)

Operating capacity: the upper limit of a company's productive output capability, given existing resources. (25)

Operating expenses: expenses other than cost of goods sold incurred in the operation of a business; especially general and administrative expenses. (5)

Operating lease: a short-term cancelable lease for which the risks of ownership lie with the lessor, and whose payments are recorded as a rent expense. (17)

Opinion section (of auditor's report): the portion of the report that tells the results of the accountant's audit of the financial statements. (8)

Ordinary annuity: a series of equal payments made at the end of equal intervals of time, with compound interest on these payments. (Appendix A)

Ordinary repairs: expenditures, usually of a recurring nature, that are necessary to maintain an asset in good operating condition. (21)

Organization costs: the costs of forming a corporation. (15)

Other assets: all of the assets owned by a company other than current assets and property, plant, and equipment. (8)

Other revenues and expenses: the section of a classified income statement that includes nonoperating revenues and expenses. (8)

Outstanding stock: the shares of a corporation's stock held by stockholders. (15)

Overhead volume variance: the difference between the factory overhead budgeted for the level of production achieved and the overhead applied to production using the standard variable and fixed overhead rates. (27)

Owner's equity: the claims by the owner against the assets of the business; assets – liabilities = owner's equity (also called residual equity). (1)

Owner's investments: assets that the owner puts into the business. (1)

Owner's withdrawals: assets that the owner takes out of the business. (1)

Paid-in capital, see **contributed capital** (15)

Parent company: a company that owns a controlling interest in another company. (20)

Participative budgeting: a managerial budget preparation process in which all levels of supervisory personnel take part in creating budgets in a meaningful, active way. (26)

Partner's equity: the owners' equity section of the balance sheet in a partnership. (14)

Partnership agreement: the contractual relationship between partners that identifies the details of the partnership; agreement should clarify such things as name of the business, duties of partners, partner investments, profit and loss ratios, and procedures for admission and withdrawal of partners. (14)

Partnership: an association of two or more persons to carry on as co-owners of a business for profit. (1, 14)

Par value: the amount printed on each share of stock, which must be recorded in the capital stock accounts; used in determining the legal capital of a corporation. (15)

Patent: an exclusive right granted by the federal government to make a particular product or use a specific process. (13)

Payback method: a method used to evaluate a capital expenditure proposal that focuses on the cash flow of the project and determines the payback period or the time required to recoup the original investment through cash flow from the item or project. (28)

Payroll register: a detailed listing of a firm's total payroll, prepared each payday. (11)

Pension fund: a fund established through contributions from an employer and sometimes employees that pays pension benefits to employees after retirement or on their disability or death. (17)

Pension plan: a contract between a company and its employees wherein the company agrees to pay benefits after retirement. (17)

Percentage of net sales method: a method of estimating uncollectible accounts expense based on the assumption that a certain percentage of total net sales will not be collectible. (9)

Period budget: a forecast of annual operating results from a segment or functional area of a company that represents a quantitative expression of planned activities. (26)

Period costs (expenses): expired costs of an accounting period that represent dollars attached to resources used or consumed during the period; any cost or expense item on an income statement. (22)

Periodic inventory method: a method of accounting for inventory under which the cost of goods sold is determined by deducting the ending inventory, which has been determined by a count of the physical inventory, from total of purchases plus beginning merchandise inventory. (5, 10, 22)

Periodicity: the recognition that the measurement of net income for any period less than the life of the business is necessarily tentative, but is still a useful estimate of the net income for that period. (3)

Permanent (real) accounts: balance sheet accounts; accounts whose balances can extend past the end of an accounting period. (3)

Perpetual inventory method: a method of accounting for inventory under which the sales and purchases of individual items of inventory are recorded continuously, therefore allowing cost of goods sold to be determined without taking a physical inventory. (5, 10, 22)

Petty cash fund: a system established by a company to make small payments of cash for minor purchases when it is inconvenient to pay with a check. (7)

Petty cash voucher: a form that supports each payment made out of a petty cash fund. (7)

Petty cash system, see **Imprest system** (7)

Physical deterioration: one of two major factors causing tangible assets to have a limited useful life. (see also **Obsolescence**) (12)

Physical inventory, see **Taking a physical inventory** (57)

Physical volume method: an approach to the problem of allocating joint production costs to specific products that is based on, or uses some measure of, physical volume (units, pounds, liters, grams, etc.) as the basis for joint cost allocation. (25)

Planning: the process of formulating a course of action. (1)

Portfolio: a group of loans or investments designed to average the return and risks of a creditor or investor. (19)

Post-closing trial balance: a trial balance prepared after all adjusting and closing entries have been posted: serves as a final check on the balance of the ledger. (4)

Posting: the process of transferring journal entry information from the journal to the ledger. (2)

Potentially dilutive securities: the potential to dilute earnings per share, as held by stock options and convertible preferred stocks or bonds. (16)

Practical capacity: theoretical capacity reduced by normal and anticipated work stoppages. (25)

Predetermined overhead rate: an overhead cost factor used to assign manufacturing (factory) overhead costs (all indirect manufacturing costs) to specific units, jobs, or cost objectives. (23)

Predictive value: usefulness of information to the decision maker in making a prediction, that is not in itself a prediction; a qualitative characteristic of accounting information. (8)

Preferred stock: a type of stock that has some preference over common stock, usually including dividends. (15)

Premium: the amount by which the issue price of a stock or bond exceeds the face value; for bonds issued when the market rate of interest is less than the face interest rate. (17)

Prepaid expenses: expenses paid in advance that do not expire during the current accounting period; an asset account. (3)

Present value: the amount that must be invested now at a given rate of interest to produce a given future value. (Appendix A)

Present value method, see Net present value method. (28)

Price/earnings (P/E) ratio: a ratio that measures the relationship of the current market price of a stock to the earnings per share: used as a measure of investor confidence in a company and as a means of comparison among stocks. (19)

Price index: a series of numbers, one for each period, that represents an average price for a group of goods and services, relative to the average price of the same group of goods and services at a beginning date. (21)

Primary earnings per share: net income applicable to common stock divided by the sum of the weighted-average common shares and common stock equivalents (See also Earnings per (common) share). (16)

Prior period adjustments: events or transactions that relate to an earlier accounting period but were not determinable in the earlier period. (16)

Proceeds from discounting: the amount received by the borrower when a promissory note is discounted; proceeds = maturity value – discount. (9)

Process cost system: a product costing system used by companies that produce a large number of similar products or have a continuous production flow where manufacturing costs are accumulated by department or process rather than by batches of product. (23)

Product cost: costs identified as being either direct materials, direct labor, or manufacturing overhead, traceable or assignable to products; they become part of a product's unit manufacturing cost and are in inventories at period end. (22)

Production method: a method of depreciation that bases the depreciation charge for a period of time solely on the amount of use of the asset during the period of time. (12)

Production budget: a detailed schedule that identifies the products or services that must be produced or provided to meet budgeted sales and inventory needs. (26)

Profit margin: a measure of profitability; the percentage of each sales dollar that results in net income; net income divided by sales. (8, 19)

Profit: imprecise term for the earnings of a business enterprise. (3)

Profitability: the ability of a business to earn enough income to attract and hold investment capital. (1, 8)

Program: the means by which a computer is instructed; consists of a sequence of instructions that, when carried out, will produce a desired result. (6)

Programmer: the person who writes the programs that instruct the computer based on the specifications of the systems analyst. (6)

Progressive tax: a tax based on a rate structure that increased the rate of tax as the amount of taxable income becomes larger. (Appendix C)

Promissory note: an unconditional promise to pay a definite sum of money on demand or at a future date. (9)

Property, plant, and equipment: tangible assets of a long-term nature used in the continuing operation of the business. (8)

Proprietary funds: in governmental accounting, a term applied to the enterprise and internal service funds. (Appendix D)

Protest fee: the charge made by a bank for preparing and mailing a notice of protest. (9)

Proxy: a legal document, signed by the stockholder, giving another party the authority to vote his or her shares. (15)

Public accounting: the field of accounting that offers services in auditing, taxes, and management advising to the public for a fee. (1)

Publicly held corporation: a corporation registered with the Securities and Exchange Commission; its securities are traded publicly. (20)

Purchase method: a method of accounting for parent company/subsidiary relationships in which similar accounts from separate statements are combined. (20)

Purchase order: a form used to communicate a company's raw materials and/or parts needs to a supplier; contains a description of the items needed, the quantities of each, and any other distinguishing features. Also a document prepared by the accounting department authorizing a supplier to ship specified goods or provide specified services. (7, 22)

Purchase requisition (request): a form, used to begin the raw materials purchasing function, that originates in the production department and identifies the items to be purchased, states the quantities required, and must be approved by a qualified manager or supervisor. (7, 22)

Purchases: an account used under the periodic inventory system in which the cost of all merchandise bought for resale is recorded. (5)

Purchases discounts: allowances made for prompt payment for merchandise purchased for resale; a contra purchases account. (5)

Purchases journal: a type of special-purpose journal in which is recorded credit purchases of merchandise (if it is a single-column journal) or credit purchases in general (if it is a multi-column journal). (6)

Purchases returns and allowances: account used to accumulate cash refunds and other allowances made by suppliers on merchandise originally purchased for resale; a contra purchases account. (5)

Purchasing power: the ability of a dollar at a point in time to purchase goods or services. (21)

Purchasing power gains and losses: gains and losses that occur as a result of holding monetary items during periods of inflation or deflation. (21)

Qualitative characteristics: criteria for judging the information accountants provide to decision makers; the primary criteria are relevance and reliability. (8)

Quick ratio: a ratio that measures the relationship of the more liquid current assets (cash, marketable securities, short-term investments, and receivables) to current liabilities; used as a measure of short-term liquidity. (19)

Ratio analysis: a technique for analyzing financial statements in which meaningful relationships are shown between components of financial statements. (19)

Raw-in-Process Inventory: under the Just-in-Time philosophy of manufacturing, an inventory account that replaces both the Materials Inventory and the Work in Process Inventory accounts. (Appendix E)

Real accounts: balance sheet accounts; accounts whose balances can extend past the end of an accounting period. (3)

Receivable turnover: the relationship of net sales to average accounts receivable. Used as a measure of the relative size of a company's accounts receivable and the success of its credit and collection policies; shows how many times, on the average, receivables were turned into cash during the period. (19)

Receiving report: a document prepared when ordered goods are received, the data of which are matched with the descriptions and quantities listed on the purchase order to verify that the goods ordered were actually received. (7, 22)

Recognition issue: determination of when a business transaction is to be recorded. (2)

Recognition point: the predetermined time at which a transaction is to be recorded; usually the point at which title passes. (2)

Registered bonds: bonds for which the name and address of the bond owners are recorded with the issuing company. (17)

Relative sales value method: an approach to the problem of allocating joint production costs to specific products that is based on or uses the product's revenue-producing ability (sales value) as the basis for joint cost allocation. (25)

Relevance: standard of quality requiring that accounting information bear directly on the economic outcome of a decision for which it is to be used; one of the primary qualitative characteristics of accounting information. (8)

Relevant decision information: future cost, revenue, or resource usage data used in decision analyses that differ among the decision's alternative courses of action. (28)

Relevant range: a range of productive activity that represents the potential volume levels within which actual operations are likely to occur. (25)

Reliability: standard of quality requiring that accounting information be faithful to the original data and that it be verifiable and neutral; one of the primary qualitative characteristics of accounting information. (8)

Replacement cost: an entry value that represents the cost to buy (or replace), in the normal course of business, new assets of approximately equivalent operating or productive capacity. (21)

Reporting currency: currency in which the consolidated financial statements involving foreign subsidiaries are presented. (21)

Representational faithfulness: the agreement of information with what it is supposed to represent. (8)

Residual equity: the common stock of a corporation. (15)

Responsibility accounting system: an accounting system that personalizes accounting reports by classifying and reporting cost and revenue information according to defined responsibility areas of specific managers or management positions; also called activity accounting or profitability accounting. (25)

Restatement: the stating of one currency in terms of another. (21)

Restriction on retained earnings: a restriction of retained earnings indicating that a portion of a company's assets is to be used for purposes other than paying dividends. (16)

Retail method: a method of estimating inventory in which inventory at retail value is reduced by the ratio of cost to retail price. (10)

Retained earnings: the account representing the stockholders' claim to the assets earned during profitable operations and reinvested in corporate operations; the accumulated earnings of a corporation from its inception less

any losses, dividends, or transfers to contributed capital. (8, 16)

Return on assets: a measure of profitability that shows how efficiently a company is using all its assets; net income divided by total assets. (8, 19)

Return on equity: a measure of profitability related to the amount earned by a business in relation to the owners' investment in the business; net income divided by owner's equity. (8, 19)

Revenue: a measure of the asset values received from customers during a specific period of time; equals the price of goods sold and services rendered during that time; in governmental accounting, increases in fund resources from sources other than interfund transactions or proceeds of long-term debt. (1, Appendix D)

Revenue expenditure: an expenditure for repairs, maintenance, or other services needed to maintain and operate plant and equipment; charged to expense because the benefits from the expenditure will be used up in the current period. (13)

Revenue recognition: the process of determining when a sale takes place; a technique of accrual accounting. (3)

Revenues from sales: revenues arising from sales of goods by the merchandising company. (5)

Reversing entries: optional general journal entries made on the first day of an accounting period that are the exact reverse of adjusting entries made in the previous period. (4)

Salaries: compensation to employees who are paid at a monthly or yearly rate. (11)

Sales budget: A detailed plan, expressed in both units and dollars, that identifies the expected product (or service) sales for a future period. (26)

Sales discounts: discounts given to customers for early payment for sales made on credit; a contra sales account. (5)

Sales journal: a type of special-purpose journal used to record credit sales. (6)

Sales mix analysis: an analysis to determine the most profitable combination of product sales when a company produces more than one product. (28)

Sales returns and allowances: account used to accumulate amounts of cash refunds granted to customers or other allowances related to prior sales; a contra sales revenue account. (5)

Salvage value, see **Residual equity** (15)

Schedule of equivalent production: a process costing schedule in which equivalent units for both materials costs and conversion costs are computed for the period. (24)

Scope section (of auditor's report): the portion of the auditor's report informing users that the examination was made in accordance with generally accepted auditing standards. (8)

Secured bonds: bonds that give the bondholders a pledge of certain assets of the company as a guarantee of repayment. (17)

Securities and Exchange Commission (SEC): an agency of the federal government that has the legal power to set and enforce accounting practices for firms reporting to it. (1)

Selling expense budget: a schedule developed from information on the sales budget and from the sales staff that details all anticipated expenses related to the selling function of the business for a future period of time. (26)

Semivariable cost: a cost that possesses both variable and fixed cost behavior characteristics, in that part of the cost is fixed and part varies with the volume of output. (25)

Separate entity: a concept in accounting that treats a business as distinct and separate from its creditors, customers, and owners. (1)

Serial bonds: a bond issue with several different maturity dates. (17)

Share of stock: a unit of ownership in a corporation. (15)

Short-term investments (marketable securities): temporary investments of excess cash, intended to be held only until needed to pay a current obligation. (9)

Short-term liquid assets: financial assets that arise from cash transactions, the investment of cash, and the extension of credit; these assets are not used in the productive functions of the enterprise. (9)

Signature card: a card signed by a depositor in exactly the same way he or she expects to sign checks; used as evidence in the opening of a bank account. (7)

Significant influence (of investor over investee company): ability of an investor to affect operating and financial policies of an investee company, even though the investor holds less than 50 percent of the voting stock of the investee. (20)

Simple capital structure: a capital structure with no other securities (either stocks or bonds) that can be converted into common stock. (16)

Simple interest: the interest cost for one or more periods, if one assumes that the amount on which the interest is computed stays the same from period to period. (Appendix A)

Software: comprises the programs, instructions, and routines that make possible the use of computer hardware. (6)

Sole proprietorship: a business owned by one person. (1)

Source documents: written evidence supporting and detailing transactions. (6)

Special-order decision: a decision analysis designed to help management determine whether to accept or reject unexpected special product orders at prices below normal market prices. (28)

Special-purpose journal: an input device in an accounting system used to record a single type of transaction. (6)

Specific identification method: a method of determining the cost of inventory by identifying the cost of each item. (10)

Specific price levels: the price changes of very closely related groups of items or services. (21)

Split-off point: the point in the manufacturing process where joint products separate and become identifiable. (25)

Standard costs: realistically predetermined costs for direct materials, direct labor, and factory overhead that are usually expressed as a cost per unit of finished product. (27)

Standard deduction: an amount allowed every taxpayer for personal and business expenses. (Appendix C)

Standard direct labor cost: a standard cost computed by multiplying the direct labor time standard by the direct labor rate standard. (27)

Standard direct materials cost: a standard cost computed by multiplying the direct materials price standard by the direct materials quantity standard. (27)

Standard factory overhead cost: a standard cost computed by multiplying the standard variable overhead rate and the standard fixed overhead rate by the appropriate application base. (27)

Standard fixed overhead rate: an overhead application rate computed by dividing the total budgeted variable overhead costs by the application base being used by the company. (27)

Standard variable overhead rate: total budgeted variable factory overhead costs divided by an expression of capacity, usually expected number of standard direct labor hours. (27)

Stated value: a value assigned by the board of directors of a corporation to no-par stock. (15)

Statement of cash flows: a financial statement that shows the inflows and outflows of cash from operating activities, investing activities, and financing activities over a period of time. (1, 18)

Statement of cost of goods manufactured: a formal statement summarizing the flow of all manufacturing costs incurred during a period; yields the dollar amount of costs of products completed and transferred to Finished Goods Inventory in that period. (22)

Statement of owner's equity: a financial statement that shows the changes in the owner's capital account over a period of time. (1)

Statement of retained earnings: a statement summarizing the changes in retained earnings during an accounting period. (16)

Statement of stockholders' equity: summary of changes in components of the stockholders' equity section of the balance sheet; also called a statement of changes in stockholders' equity. (16)

Stock certificate: a document issued to a stockholder in a corporation indicating the number of shares of stock owned by the stockholder. (15)

Stock dividend: a proportional distribution of shares of a corporation's stock to the corporation's stockholders. (16)

Stockholders' equity: the owners' equity section of a corporation's balance sheet representing the owners' claims to the business. (15)

Stock option plan: an agreement to issue stock to some or all employees according to terms set in the plan. (15)

Stock split: an increase in the number of outstanding shares of stock accompanied by a proportionate reduction in the par or stated value. (16)

Stock subscription: an issuance of stock where the investor agrees to pay for the stock on some future date or in installments at an agreed price. (15)

Straight-line method: a method of amortizing bond discount or premium in which amor-

tization of the discount or premium is equal for each interest period over the life of the bond. (12, 17)

Subsidiary: an investee company in which a controlling interest is owned by another company. (20)

Subsidiary ledger: a ledger separate from the general ledger; contains a group of related accounts, the total of whose balances equals the balance of a controlling account in the general ledger. (6)

Successful efforts accounting: a method of accounting for oil and gas development and exploration costs under which the costs of successful exploration are recorded as an asset and depleted over the useful life of the producing resources and the costs of unsuccessful explorations are written off as a loss. (13)

Summary of significant accounting policies: section of a corporate annual report that discloses which generally accepted accounting principles the company has followed in preparing the financial statements. (8)

Sum-of-the-years'-digits method: an accelerated method of depreciation. (12)

Supporting service function: an operating unit or department not directly involved production but needed for the overall operation of the company. (25)

System design: a phase of system installation whose purpose is to formulate the new system or make changes in the existing system. (6)

System implementation: a phase of system installation whose purpose is to put in operating order a new system or change in an existing system. (6)

System investigation: a phase of system installation whose purpose is to determine the needs of a new system or to evaluate an existing system. (6)

Systems analyst: the person who designs a computer data processing system on the basis of information needs. (6)

T account: a form of an account which has a physical resemblance to the letter T; used to analyze transactions. (2)

Taking a physical inventory: the act of making a physical count of all merchandise on hand at the end of an accounting period. (5)

Tangible assets: long-term assets that have physical substance. (12)

Taxable income: the amount on which income taxes are assessed; usually gross income less various exemptions and deductions specified by the law and the IRS regulations. (Appendix C)

Tax credits: deductions from the computed tax liability. (16, Appendix C)

Tax evasion: the illegal concealment of actual tax liabilities. (Appendix C)

Tax liability: the amount of tax that must be paid based on taxable income and the applicable tax table. (Appendix C)

Tax planning: the arrangement of a taxpayer's affairs in such a way as to incur the smallest legal tax. (Appendix C)

Tax services: services offered by public accountants in tax planning, compliance, and reporting. (1)

Temporary (nominal) accounts: accounts showing the accumulation of revenues and expenses for only one accounting period; at the end of the accounting period, these account balances are transferred to owner's equity. (3)

Term bonds: bonds of a bond issue that all mature at the same time. (17)

Theoretical capacity: the maximum productive output a department or a company could reach in a given period if all machinery and equipment were operated at optimum speed without any interruptions (also called ideal capacity). (25)

Time card: a basic time record of an employee on which either the supervisor or a time clock records the daily starting and finishing times of the person. (22)

Timeliness: the qualitative characteristic of accounting information that reaches the user in time to help in making a decision. (8)

Total direct labor cost variance: the difference between actual labor costs incurred and the standard labor cost for the good units produced. (27)

Total direct materials cost variance: the difference between the actual materials cost incurred and the standard cost of those same items. (27)

Total inventory method: a method of applying the lower-of-cost-or-market method to inventory pricing; the entire inventory is valued at both cost and market, and the lower price is used; not an acceptable method for federal income tax purposes.(10)

Total manufacturing costs: a term used in the statement of cost of goods manufactured that represents the total of direct materials used, direct labor, and manufacturing overhead costs incurred and charged to production during an accounting period. (22)

Total overhead variance: the difference between actual overhead costs incurred and the standard overhead costs applied to production using the standard variable and fixed overhead rates. (27)

Trade credit: credit to customers at either the wholesale or the retail level. (9)

Trade discounts: a price quoted below the catalogue or list price; a device to avoid frequent reprinting costs. (5)

Trademark: a registered symbol that gives the holder the right to use it to identify a product or service. (13)

Transportation in, see **Freight in** (5)

Treasury stock: capital stock of a company, either common or preferred, that has been issued and reacquired by the issuing company but has not been sold or retired. (16)

Trend analysis: the calculation of percentage changes for several successive years; a variation of horizontal analysis. (19)

Trial balance: a listing of accounts in the general ledger with their debit or credit balances in respective columns and a totaling of the columns; used to test the equality of debit and credit balances in the ledger. (2)

2/10, n/30: credit terms enabling the debtor to take a 2 percent discount if the invoice is paid within ten days after the invoice date; otherwise, the debtor must pay the full amount within thirty days. (5)

Uncollectible accounts: accounts receivable from customers who cannot or will not pay. (9)

Underapplied or overapplied overhead: the difference resulting when the amount of factory overhead costs applied to products during an accounting period is more or less than the actual amount of factory overhead costs incurred in that period. (23)

Understandability: the qualitative characteristic of accounting information that is presented in a form and in terms that its user can understand. (8)

Unearned revenues: revenues received in advance for which the goods paid for will not be delivered or the services paid for not performed during the current accounting period; a liability account. (3)

Unit cost: the amount of manufacturing costs incurred in the completion or production of one unit of product; usually computed by dividing total production costs for a job or period of time by the respective number of units produced. (23)

Unit cost analysis schedule: a process costing statement used to (1) accumulate all costs charged to the Work in Process Inventory account of each department or production process, and (2) compute cost per equivalent unit for materials and conversion costs. (24)

Unlimited liability: each partner has a personal liability for all debts of the partnership. (14)

Unrecorded (accrued) revenues: revenues for which the service has been performed or the goods have been delivered but which have not been recorded in the accounts; an asset account. (3)

Unsecured bonds: bonds issued on the general credit of a company; debenture bonds. (17)

Use of working capital: a transaction that results in a net decrease in working capital. (18)

Valuation issue: the process of assigning a value to all business transactions. (2)

Variable costs: total costs that change in direct proportion to changes in productive output (or any other volume measure). (25)

Variable costing: a costing method that uses only the variable manufacturing costs for product costing and inventory valuation purposes, as contrasted with absorption costing, which uses all product costs (also called direct costing). (28)

Variable manufacturing costs: types of manufacturing costs that increase or decrease in direct proportion to the number of units produced. (22)

Variance analysis: the process of computing the amount of, and isolating the causes of, differences between actual costs and standard costs. (27)

Verifiability: the qualitative characteristic of accounting information that can be confirmed or duplicated by independent parties using the same measurement techniques. (8)

Vertical analysis: the calculation of percentages to show the relationship of the component parts of a financial statement to the total in the statement. (19)

Voucher: a written authorization prepared for each expenditure in a voucher system. (7)

Voucher check: a check specifically designed for use in a voucher system; tells the payee the reason for issuing the check and includes remittance advice to the payee. (7)

Voucher register: the book of original entry in which vouchers are recorded after they have been properly approved. (7)

Voucher system: any system providing documentary evidence of, and written authorization for, business transactions; usually associated with expenditures. (7)

Wages: compensation for employees at an hourly rate or on a piecework basis. (11)

Wasting assets: another term for natural resources; long-term assets purchased for the physical substances that can be taken from the land and used up rather than for the value of their location. (13)

Working capital: the amount by which total current assets exceed total current liabilities. (8)

Working papers: documents prepared and used by the accountant that aid in organizing the accountant's work and provide evidence to support the basis of the financial statements. (4)

Work in process inventory: an inventory account unique to the manufacturing or production area to which all manufacturing costs incurred and assigned to products are charged. The balance at period-end represents all costs assigned to goods partially completed at that particular time. (22)

Work sheet: a type of working paper that is used as a preliminary step in and aid to the preparation of financial statements. (4)

Zero coupon bonds: bonds with no periodic interest payment, but simply a promise to pay a fixed amount at the maturity date. The only interest earned by the buyer or paid by the issuer is the discount on the issue date. (17)

INDEX

Accounting Format Guide

Joan Miller Advertising Agency
Income Statement
For the Month Ended January 31, 19xx

Revenues

Advertising Fees Earned	$4,400	
Art Fees Earned	400	
Total Revenues		$4,800

Expenses

Office Wages Expense	$1,380	
Utility Expense	100	
Telephone Expense	70	
Rent Expense	400	
Insurance Expense	40	
Art Supplies Expense	500	
Office Supplies Expense	200	
Depreciation Expense, Art Equipment	70	
Depreciation Expense, Office Equipment	50	
Total Expenses		2,810

Net Income $1,990

Joan Miller Advertising Agency
Statement of Owner's Equity
For the Month Ended January 31, 19xx

Joan Miller, Capital, January 1, 19xx		—
Add Investments by Joan Miller	$10,000	
Net Income	1,990	$11,990
Subtotal		$11,990
Less Withdrawals		1,400
Joan Miller, Capital, January 31, 19xx		$10,590

Commonly Used Formats